The Dictionary of Ant

The Dictionary of Anthropology

Edited by Thomas Barfield

First published 1997
Reprinted 1998, 1999, 2000, 2001

Blackwell Publishers Ltd
108 Cowley Road
Oxford OX4 1JF
UK

Blackwell Publishers Inc.
350 Main Street
Malden, Massachusetts 02148
USA

Library of Congress Cataloging-in-Publication Data

The dictionary of anthropology / edited by Thomas Barfield.
    p.   cm.
  Includes bibliographical references.
  ISBN 1-55786-282-6 (hbk). – ISBN 1-57718-057-7 (pbk.)
  1. Ethnology – Dictionaries. I. Barfield, Thomas.
  GN307.D485 1997
  306'03 – dc21

                         96-37337
                         CIP

British Library Cataloguing in Publication Data

A CIP catalogue record for this book is available from the British Library.

Commissioning Editor: John Davey
Desk Editor: Jason Pearce
Production Controller: Emma Gotch

Typeset in 9 on 10 pt Plantin
by Best-set Typesetter Ltd, Hong Kong
Printed in Great Britain by T.J. International Ltd, Padstow, Cornwall

This book is printed on acid-free paper.

Contents

Preface

Over the past century anthropology has developed from an obscure discipline associated primarily with the study of the exotic cultures into a comparative social science that has made fundamental contributions to the understanding of the world around us. It initiated the cross-cultural study of kinship and social organization, introduced the concept of cultural relativism into common parlance, and pioneered the use of participant-observation as a research tool. And anthropology's holistic and cross-cultural perspective has produced a treasure trove of data and theory, which have attracted researchers and general readers alike. How could it not? Its subjects are human beings, a topic of endless fascination for researchers and readers who are also human beings.

Yet for all the public interest in anthropology, the field has lacked a short accessible reference guide that provides clear and concise statements laying out the important issues, significant concepts, methodologies, and theories in anthropology along with a guide to the key literature on these topics. There are, of course, a plethora of textbooks (with a weakness for easily repeated generalizations) and an extensive professional review literature (aimed at a handful of like-minded specialists), but very little in between. *The Dictionary of Anthropology* aims to fill this gap.

The need for such a work is clear. As anthropology has grown and specialized it has become more and more difficult to assess the state of the field. In part this is because the number of professional anthropologists has grown so large, and the topics researched so diverse, that it is not possible to keep current with all, or even most, of the work in the field. Yet, in spite of this growth, anthropologists still think of themselves as members of a face-to-face community where traditions are best transmitted orally: if you need to know, ask someone. In fact anthropology has not been such a community for many generations, and wishing it were will not make it so again.

A deeper problem, common to many other social sciences as well, has been the growing tendency for professionals to write only for one another, frequently employing jargon-soaked theory. Debates within the field often appear abstruse or irrelevant, even when they focus on issues that are of wide interest and importance. This was not always the case. At the beginning of the twentieth century anthropologists felt an obligation to write not only for other specialists, but for an educated public as well. The books of Margaret Mead and Bronislaw Malinowski were known far beyond the confines of academic anthropology because, in addition to describing the ways of other cultures, they also dealt with issues of broad concern in their own.

Today, with public controversies about issues such as a "clash of civilizations," multiculturalism, gender, ethnicity, family structure, religious revitalizations, and the problems associated with economic change, anthropology again should be at the forefront. But anthropology is, like Sherlock Holmes's "dog that did not bark," a voice that is strangely absent from debates about what it purports to know best. A discipline that should have growled at (and perhaps bitten) the bearers of ideas and theories based on ethnocentric notions and narrow constructs of human potential instead wonders why it is ignored. While some anthropologists assume that ordinary readers cannot appreciate their ideas because they are too rich with detail or theoretically sophisticated, a simpler answer is that anthropologists have not really tried very hard to explain what they do and why it is important. One goal of this *Dictionary* is to make a start by providing an intelligent entry-point into the world of anthropology. If the field is now too diverse and contentious for a single voice to represent it, then perhaps the variety of entries here (authored by over 125 anthropologists) will provide examples of how much the field offers to those who know where to look.

Structure of the Dictionary

The use of the term "anthropology" varies by national tradition. In Britain it normally means social anthropology, while in the United States it also encompasses cultural anthropology, archaeology, biological anthropology, and linguistics. European usage varies even more. We have split the difference: the *Dictionary* focuses primarily on topics in cultural and social anthropology, but also includes related topics in archaeology, biological anthropology, and linguistics. The book cannot cover all aspects of the field in detail, however; it is, of course, first and foremost a dictionary of, and a guide to, the discipline of anthropology – concepts, theories, and approaches – rather than an encyclopedia, of which there are several substantial recent examples. That is why descriptive entries on specific cultures are absent per se. That said, anyone reading the *Dictionary* cannot fail, through the many examples given in the entries, to discover a great deal about the diversity and in some cases the unity of human nature and its manifestations in culture and society.

The focus is on what anthropology has contributed to social science, and not just the immediate concerns of the discipline. The 500-plus headwords include short definitions of terms regularly used by anthropologists, topical entries on significant anthropological concepts and theoretical approaches, and survey entries on some of the broader fields within the discipline. There are also a small number of biographies of prominent anthropologists designed to flesh out the topical entries. We gave priority to entries on deceased anthropologists who can no longer speak for themselves, but have also included some very widely cited living scholars.

We asked contributors to provide balanced coverage of their assigned topics, but no particular theoretical approach was privileged nor did we seek a set of like-minded souls. Indeed, some contributors disagreed with one another, often fiercely, on specific issues. In these cases, my task as editor was not to hide such disagreements, but to ensure their balanced presentation, if not in a single entry then at least in terms of cross-referencing other entries or providing citations of publications that take a different point of view. For this reason we have allowed generous space for references so that readers who wish to dig further will have the tools to do so. The integrated master bibliography contains almost 3,000 separate citations (including sub-titles since so many titles are opaque) and information about the original dates and places of publication for translated works.

The *Dictionary* does not, in the manner of the Académie française, attempt to establish or to set the limits to a canonical vocabulary. But the elements of a common language form the basis of the communal understanding that is vital in any kind of scientific or intellectual enterprise. The task that this book sets itself of explaining the language and the concepts of anthropology as they are currently used – without glossing over those areas where there is a disagreement on meaning – is by no means an unambitious venture in a subject characterized throughout its history as much by dissension as by agreement. Insofar as it succeeds, I hope that it will perform a valuable service not only for students of anthropology, but also for those students and scholars in our neighboring disciplines (of whom there are rumored to be a fair number) who wish to know more clearly what we are talking about, what kinds of understanding we are seeking, and what we can offer that will be of use to them.

Thomas Barfield
Executive Editor

How to Use the *Dictionary*

The *Dictionary* consists of more than 500 individual entries listed alphabetically by headword. Small capital letters in the text indicate cross-references to related entries. Such markers appear only once per entry – sometimes in a slightly different form from the actual headword (e.g. "SOCIOBIOLOGICAL" instead of "SOCIOBIOLOGY") to avoid clumsy linguistic contortions. Other useful but uncited cross-references appear at the end of the entry under "see also".

Bibliographic references appear in author–date format within the text (e.g., Malinowski 1922). Where two or more authors share a surname, enough of their first names is given to differentiate between them. Many entries also have a "Further Reading" section that lists suggested references not already cited. The integrated master bibliography at the end of the *Dictionary* contains the full citations of all references. The bibliography uses the first publication date (and for translated works the date of their first publication in English) as its standard, except for revised editions. For translated works we have also included the original-language title, place, and date of publication. This provides for consistency among the entries and preserves a chronological sense of the field's development, but more recent republications or paperback editions are also often widely available. Similarly, many anthologies republish older articles and are easier to find than old journals. For this reason we have tried to provide full names of authors where possible to facilitate searches of computer databases that would list such new editions.

Authors have signed their entries with initials, a master list of which appears on pages x–xiii along with authors' institutional affiliations.

Contributors

James M. Acheson (JA)
University of Maine

Nicholas J. Allen (NA)
Oxford University

Herbert Applebaum (HA)
Hartz Mountain Industries

William Arens (WA)
State University of New York, Stoney Brook

Robert Aunger (RA)
Northwestern University

William Badecker (WBad)
Johns Hopkins University

William Balée (WBal)
Tulane University

Thomas Barfield (TB)
Boston University

R. H. Barnes (RB)
Oxford University

William Beeman (WBe)
Brown University

Christopher Boehm (CBo)
University of Southern California

Candice Bradley (CBr)
Lawrence University

Peter J. Brown (PB)
Emory University

Andrew S. Buckser (AB)
Purdue University

Luigi Burzio (LB)
Johns Hopkins University

Michael Carrithers (MC)
Durham University

Tammy Castleforte (TC)
East–West Center, Hawaii

Steven Caton (SC)
New School for Social Research

E. M. Chilver (EC)
Queen Elizabeth House, Oxford

Bernard Comrie (BC)
University of Southern California

Lewis A. Coser (LC)
Cambridge, MA

Martin Daly (MD)
McMaster University

John Davis (JD)
Oxford University

Robbie E. Davis-Floyd (RDF)
University of Texas, Austin

Michael R. Dove (MRD)
East–West Center, Hawaii

Malcolm M. Dow (MMD)
Northwestern University

Paul Dresch (PD)
Oxford University

Robert C. Dunnell (RD)
University of Washington

Timothy Earle (TE)
Northwestern University

Elizabeth Edwards (EE)
Oxford University

T. M. S. Evens (TMSE)
University of North Carolina, Chapel Hill

Burt Feintuch (BF)
University of New Hampshire

R. Brian Ferguson (RBF)
Rutgers University–Newark

Michael M. J. Fischer (MF)
Massachusetts Institute of Technology

James Flanagan (JF)
University of Southern Mississippi

Thomas F. Glick (TG)
Boston University

Anne Grodzins Gold (AGG)
Syracuse University

Jack Goody (JG)
Cambridge University

Alma Gottlieb (AG)
University of Illinois, Urbana

Derek Gregory (DG)
University of British Columbia

Ellen Gruenbaum (EG)
California State University, San Bernadino

Matthew C. Gutmann (MG)
Brown University

Jane I. Guyer (JIG)
Northwestern University

Niloofar Haeri (NH)
Johns Hopkins University

Shahla Haeri (SH)
Boston University

Thomas D. Hall (TH)
DePauw University

W. Penn Handwerker (WPH)
University of Connecticut

Faye Harrison (FH)
University of Tennessee

Elvin Hatch (EH)
University of California, Santa Barbara

Dwight B. Heath (DH)
Brown University

Allan Hoben (AH)
Boston University

Michael Horowitz (MH)
State University of New York,
  Binghamton

Jun Hu (JH)
Emory University

Robert Hunt (RHun)
Brandeis University

Ronald Hutton (RHut)
University of Bristol

James Ito-Adler (JIA)
Florida International University

Jean Jackson (JJa)
Massachusetts Institute of Technology

William Jankowiak (WJ)
University of Nevada, Las Vegas

James Jones (JJo)
Harvard University

Glenn Jordan (GJ)
University of Glemorgan

Bruce Kapferer (BK)
James Cook University

David Kaplan (DK)
Brandeis University

Michael Kearney (MK)
University of California, Riverside

Charles Keyes (CK)
University of Washington

Arthur Kleinman (AK)
Harvard Medical School

Igor Kopytoff (IK)
University of Pennsylvania

Shepard Krech III (SK)
Brown University

Henrika Kuklick (HK)
University of Pennsylvania

Krishan Kumar (KK)
University of Virginia

Greg Laden (GL)
Harvard University

J. Stephen Lansing (JSL)
University of Michigan

Denise Lawrence (DL)
California State Polytechnic University

Richard Lee (RiL)
University of Toronto

Robert A. Le Vine (RAL)
Harvard University

Robert Levy (RoL)
Duke University and University of North
  Carolina

Marilyn M. Li (ML)
East–West Center, Hawaii

Charles Lindholm (CL)
Boston University

Tanya Luhrmann (TL)
University of California, San Diego

Carol MacCormack (CM)
Bryn Mawr College

Thomas McDade (TMc)
Emory University

T. MacDonald (TMac)
Harvard University

Alan Macfarlane (AM)
Cambridge University

Carla Makhlouf Obermeyer (CMO)
Harvard University

Joseph A. Marcus (JAM)
Harvard University

David Maybury-Lewis (DML)
Harvard University

Sally Engle Merry (SEM)
Wellesley College

Ellen Messer (EM)
Brown University

Peter Metcalf (PM)
University of Virginia

John Middleton (JM)
Yale University

Margaret Mills (MM)
University of Pennsylvania

Emilio F. Moran (EFM)
University of Arizona

Stephen O. Murray (SM)
San Francisco, CA

Laura Nader (LN)
University of California, Berkeley

Frederick J. Newmeyer (FN)
University of Washington

Charles Nuckolls (CN)
Emory University

Steven M. Parish (SP)
University of California, San Diego

David Parkin (DP)
Oxford University

Robert Parkin (RP)
Oxford University

Diane B. Paul (DBP)
University of Massachusetts, Boston

David W. Plath (DWP)
University of Illinois

Elizabeth Povinelli (EP)
University of Chicago

Colin Quigley (CQ)
University of California, Los Angeles

S. P. Reyna (SPR)
University of New Hampshire

Michael Rhum (MR)
Chicago, IL

Suzanne Romaine (SR)
Oxford University

William Roseberry (WR)
New School for Social Research

Abraham Rosman (AR)
Columbia University

Paula G. Rubel (PR)
Columbia University

Carl Ruck (CR)
Boston University

Candelario Saenz (CS)
Wellesley College

Fereydoun Safizadeh (FS)
Boston University

Stephen K. Sanderson (SS)
Indiana University of Pennsylvania

Alice Schlegel (ASc)
University of Arizona

David Schneider (DS)
University of California, San Diego

Eugenia Shanklin (ES)
Trenton State College

Warren Shapiro (WS)
Rutgers University

Parker Shipton (PS)
Boston University

Anna Simons (ASi)
University of California, Los Angeles

Raymond T. Smith (RS)
University of Chicago

Marc Sommers (MS)
Boston University

Leslie E. Sponsel (LS)
University of Hawaii

Ian Stevenson (ISt)
University of Virginia

Marcelo Suárez-Orozco (MSO)
Harvard University

Ida Susser (ISu)
Hunter College, City University of New
  York

Marlene Sway (MSw)
Los Angeles, CA

John Terrell (JT)
Field Museum of Natural History, Chicago

Kendra Hatfield Timajchy (KHT)
Emory University

Thomas R. Trautmann (TT)
University of Michigan

Joel Wallman (JW)
Harry Frank Guggenheim Foundation,
  New York City

D. Michael Warren (DW)
Iowa State University

Christopher Waterman (CW)
University of California, Los Angeles

Michael Watts (MWa)
University of California, Berkeley

Geoffrey M. White (GMW)
University of Hawaii

Gordon R. Willey (GRW)
Harvard University

John van Willigen (JvW)
University of Kentucky

Margo Wilson (MWi)
McMaster University

Peter Wyatt Wood (PW)
Boston University

Walter P. Zenner (WZ)
State University of New York, Albany

Arnold M. Zwicky (AZ)
Ohio State University

A

acculturation is the process of culture change set in motion by the meeting of two autonomous cultural systems, resulting in an increase of similarity of each to the other. It always involves a complex interaction with attendant social processes, the parameters of which were most carefully laid out in two important memoranda commissioned by the Social Science Research Council (Redfield et al. 1936; Broom et al. 1954). In such conjunctions the donor culture may not present the full range of its cultural elements, and the recipient culture's own value system may act to screen out or modify certain elements. Acculturation may also be sharply socially structured, as in the case of conquest or other situations of social or political inequality, which channel the flow of cultural elements. Acculturation subsumes a number of different processes including DIFFUSION, reactive ADAPTATION, various kinds of social and cultural reorganization subsequent to contact, and "deculturation" or cultural disintegration. The range of adjustments that results includes the retention of substantial cultural autonomy ("stabilized pluralism") or, more typically, the assimilation of a weaker by a stronger contacting group, and (though rarely) cultural fusion, whereby two cultures may exchange enough elements to produce a distinctive successor culture.

Inasmuch as acculturation involves the interaction of two or more distinct groups, social interaction among them strongly conditions the outcome. The extreme social pressure attendant upon conquest, for example, may prove effective in breaking down the mechanisms by which the conquered group has maintained its culture. In other cases, a high degree of enclosure may preserve a politically weak culture in spite of seemingly overwhelming odds. Furthermore, the lessening of culture distance (acculturation) may not be accompanied by a symmetrical lessening of social distance (assimilation) if, for whatever reason, one group refuses to validate the other's acculturation.   TG

adaptation refers to (1) changes in gene frequencies that confer reproductive advantage to a population in a particular environment, and (2) physiological and sociocultural changes that enhance individual fitness and well-being. The concept of adaptation is central to ECOLOGICAL ANTHROPOLOGY, although some scholars have emphasized evolutionary and genetic adaptation (a slow population-level process that involves random processes of natural selection) while others have seemed to privilege behavioral and historical processes. All agree that individual organisms, including human beings, respond to their environment.

Individuals can respond to changes in their environment through morphological and functional adjustments. These take three forms: regulatory, acclimatory, and developmental. Regulatory adjustments, which include a great deal of behavior, occur rapidly and reflect the physiological and behavioral flexibility of our species. Cultural practices of clothing and shelter often, but not always, reflect an effort to achieve an acceptable level of protection from the elements (i.e., adaptation). Acclimatory responses take longer to come into operation than regulatory ones because they require some change in organismic structure, such as muscle enlargement to meet demanding physical tasks or, in mountain regions, greater blood volume to carry more oxygen to the body's cells. Developmental responses, unlike these two other kinds, are not reversible and occur during the growth and development of an individual as a response to the severity of the prevalent environmental conditions. A child growing at very high altitude will develop larger lung volume and chest capacity to meet more effectively the low oxygen conditions (Moran 1979).

Explanations in anthropology have fluctuated over the years in the role they accord the concept of adaptation. Some seemed to imply a human incapacity to overcome environmental constraints (Glacken 1967), but modern evolutionary theory and genetics have put to rest simplistic notions of environmental determinism (R. Foley 1987). The functions and forms of organisms can be understood by careful scrutiny of the complex interaction processes of individuals in a landscape. In evolutionary theory the effect of environment on the genotype is indirect. Adaptive changes in all organisms, including our species, are mediated by the hereditary genetic material passed on from one generation to the next. Biological adaptation is seldom perfect and is opposed by many factors, including mutations and gene flow, evolutionary opportunity, physical limits, problems of allocation, and the ever-changing nature of environment (Ricklefs 1973). No matter how well adapted a population may be, new random mutations (and behavioral diversity) occur and are regularly introduced and diffused in a population, leading to change.

Adaptation is essentially a compromise. The results are rarely the "optimum" solution, but represent chance, competition, and opportunity. This is because environments are always changing, populations are always incorporating innovative behavioral, physiological, developmental, and genetic features, and their interactions are complex and largely unpredictable.

This interactive dimension of adaptation has gone one step further in recent years with the emergence of an emphasis on "historical ecology." This approach (see Crumley 1994) takes the view that human behavior is contingent and quite capable of overcoming "environmental limitations." Thus, a population confronted by poor soils may act to improve its economic situation through changes in labor allocation, technological skill, and political goals. It is being recognized that not only do humans adapt, or adjust, to what the environment presents to them, but that they make efforts to change the impact of the physical environment upon them. This is not just a recent capacity growing out of contemporary technological prowess; it has been there from the beginning of our species and can be observed in such agricultural techniques as terracing, ridging, and mulching (Moran 1990).   EFM
See also AGRICULTURE,   BIOLOGICAL ANTHROPOLOGY, SOCIOBIOLOGY
further reading Netting 1986; Rappaport 1967; Eric Smith & Winterhalder 1992; B. Turner et al. 1990

address terms   are those kinship terms used in addressing a person directly. A kinship system that differentiates various types of cousin might still use the generic term "cousin" as a single form of address for all of them. Thus, anthropologists often find that terms of address are distinct from REFERENCE TERMS.   MR

adolescence   is a stage of life between childhood and adulthood recognized in many, if not all, human cultures (Schlegel & Barry 1991). As a biological transition, adolescence is marked by the passage through puberty, associated with a growth spurt, the development of secondary sexual characteristics, and, most crucially, the development of reproductive capacity. As a social stage, adolescence demands the social reincorporation of biologically maturing individuals into the cultural life of their communities on altered terms. In some cultures a social adolescence may be initiated in advance of these biological events through life-cycle rites or systems of child marriage, but in all cultures puberty has important social repercussions. Distinguishing what is culturally determined about adolescence, and what is biologically determined, has been a long-standing issue in anthropology (M. Mead 1928).

The transformation of social status associated with the transformation of the body at puberty may involve a radical reorganization of an individual's self-understanding and social behavior. In some societies the break is sharp and dramatic, marked by changes in clothing and deportment and the assumption of new rights and responsibilities. In other societies changes are more gradual, with greater continuity between childhood and adolescence (and adolescence and adulthood). The experience, social roles, and socialization of adolescents may differ on the basis of gender, with males more often being organized into peer groups that are relatively detached from domestic life and females more fully integrated into domestic units. Sexual interests and the question of future roles become salient in adolescence; peer groups often assume an even greater role than before. The socially defined interval between childhood and adulthood may be relatively brief (two to four years) in societies where marriage, parenthood, and increased social responsibility are assumed soon after puberty and menarche, or relatively prolonged, as it is in industrial societies (Schlegel & Barry 1991). While the biology of adolescence may be a constant, changes in the historical conditions of cultural life can lead to changes in the social organization of adolescence that reshape what adolescence means and how it is experienced (Burbank 1988).   SP

further reading Condon 1987; S. S. Davis & Davis 1989; Moffatt 1989; Schlegel 1995

adoption "In almost all societies there are protectors and supporters of the young in addition to, or in place of, parents. So-called juridical parenthood, which embraces various forms of adoption, is . . . a not uncommon fact" (E. Parsons 1906: 112). The first observation is true; the second, because of its emphasis on parenthood as a legal relationship, is less universally so. Western societies conventionally make a clear legal distinction between fosterage (giving parental care to others) and adoption (the legal act of assuming parental responsibility for a minor born to other parents "as if" the child were one's own). However, in many societies such legalistic distinctions make little, if any, sense (J. Goody 1976: 66–85).

For example, a linguist's attempt to create a working definition of adoption free of cultural bias, at least for Oceanic societies, described adoption as any customary and optional procedure for taking as one's own a child of other parents (Carroll 1970: 3). But Carroll himself found difficulties in refining such a definition to fit all, or even most, ethnographic cases because it incorrectly assumes that the definitions of "child" or "parent" are cross-culturally consistent.

Adoption in Oceania is typically a transaction between close relatives and the adoption of strangers is uncommon – although native Maori families in New Zealand adopted European children in the nineteenth century (Else 1991: 179). It rarely involves formal legal proceedings, except in places like Hawaii and New Zealand, where there may be government and, increasingly, social pressures to conform to Western conventions. Giving a child to others for adoption in Oceania is usually considered a generous, loving act and is much more frequent than in the United States, for example, where only an estimated 2 percent of children are adopted. Americans who give a child to another are usually stigmatized. From this cross-cultural comparison Carroll (1970: 7) concluded:

The characteristics of adopters and adoptees, the motivations of adopters and the natural parents from whom they adopt, the social form of the process of adoption, and the cultural meaning of the act – all differ significantly between Eastern Oceania and the United States.

Despite such terminological and classificatory difficulties, studying how responsibilities for the welfare of children are or are not shared by individuals other than biological parents can shed light on other facets of life. In the United States today adoption is commonly discussed by those directly involved – including social workers, private agencies, and state welfare departments – using the metaphor of the "adoptive triangle" or "triad," that is, adoptees, adoptive parents, and "birth parents." Much of the focus is on improving the quality of individual psychological adjustment to the fact of adoption and on whether the "bonds" between individuals in the triad created by birth and adoption should all be socially recognized and celebrated (J. Strauss 1994). Much attention is given to the "rights" of the individuals involved.

Contrast this understanding of family and adoption with the New Zealand Maori perspective in which there is no sense of children as property (Else 1991). Maori children know many homes but one *whanau* (family). And "adopted" children usually know both birth parents and adoptive parents alike. Terms for adopters and adoptees are very warm and positive, and their relationship is an open one, "because of the need to transmit knowledge of kinship ties, descent lines and connections with the land" (Else 1991: 177).

This example illustrates that adoption as a category of meaning, like adoption as social practice, is problematic. Adoption belies what David Schneider has called "biologistic" ways of marking and defining human character, human nature, and human behavior (D. Schneider 1984: 175). Studying adoption, however, can be a way of exploring not only the nature of KINSHIP in different societies but also the meanings and implications of concepts such as identity, FAMILY, RACE, ETHNIC GROUP, and NATIONALISM (Terrell & Modell 1994).   JT
further reading J. Bates 1993; Brady 1976; R. Levy 1973; M. Marshall 1977; Modell 1994

advocacy anthropology *See* ECO-LOGICAL ANTHROPOLOGY, HUMAN RIGHTS

affines are consanguines of a spouse. In the modern Anglo-American kinship system affines are known as "in-laws." In a lineage system of regular marriage exchange, a relationship of **affinity** may exist between two lineages such that all consanguine members of the spouse's lineage may be deemed affines. These relationships of affinity are often of a systematic and enduring character, forming the basis of ongoing relations between kin groups or marriage classes.   MR
See also CONSANGUINITY
further reading Dumont 1983

agency or human agency is the capacity of human beings to affect their own life chances and those of others and to play a role in the formation of the social realities in which they participate. It is less a force of individual action than a dimension of the institutions and relations that human beings form such as social CLASS, hegemonizing ideologies, and bureaucracies that deprive them of agency.

Anthropologists who stress agency are prone to reject overly abstract structural and system models of cultural and social action that give little or no place to the way human beings make and participate in the realities that they construct. Many agency approaches are rooted in subject/object dichotomies and emphasize the primacy of subjectivist orientations and strategies. These include:

1. TRANSACTIONAL ANALYSIS, which reduces cultural and social processes to principles of individual interaction (Barth 1966; Kapferer 1976a)
2. Social constructionist and various symbolic approaches, often influenced by PHENOMENOLOGY (Husserl 1964; Schutz 1967), that describe the conceptions and ongoing process of social creation as objectifications of subjective experience
3. CULTURE AND PERSONALITY or psychoanalytic schools of anthropology such as the work of Victor TURNER, who combined psychoanalytic insights and phenomenological/existential perspectives in his SYMBOLIC ANTHROPOLOGY in opposition to STRUCTURALISM

Other perspectives on agency take a less subjectivist position and see individuals as already acting within historically formed structures and processes but through their action achieving new conjunctions and directions in the formations of social life. Both Sahlins (1985) and Bourdieu (1977, 1990) have developed variants on such a perspective. Recent work in anthropology appears to be breaking away from subject/object or self/other distinctions while giving greater focus to the diverse interpretations and socially inventive practices of individuals.   BK
further reading Goffman 1956

age systems   employ a series of formal fixed ranks (**age grades**) through which all individuals pass successively as members of distinct **age classes** or **age sets**. Although these terms tend to be used interchangeably in the anthropological literature, Bernardi (1985) pointed out that age grades (ranks) are conceptually quite distinct from the people (age groups, sets, or classes) who pass through them.

Although age is an important criterion in determining rank or status in all societies, formal age sets are not. They are found almost exclusively in patrilineal societies with acephalous political organizations and are used primarily to organize men. (Female age systems are either nonexistent or pale reflections of their male counterparts, because women tend to acquire their social rights and obligations individually through marriage and motherhood.) Age systems are found in sub-Saharan Africa, particularly East Africa where they take on their classic form, among Plains Indians in North America, and in Amazonia (F. Stewart 1977).

Age-class systems are distinctive because they are all-encompassing and also extend throughout the entire adult life cycle. Every rank has its prescribed areas of competence, rights, duties, and obligations, with each rank filling a distinct social role. Equally important, as each class moves through the system, it gives up one set of obligations to take on another as a group: no individual, however talented, can take on new responsibilities except as part of his whole age set, and no individual, however ill-suited to his new status, can be left behind. A classic example is found among the Masai of Kenya and Tanzania, where there are four major age sets, each about 15 years in duration. Boys between the ages of 15 and 20 are initiated through circumcision into the first set as warriors (*moran*), subdivided into junior and senior sections based on how recently they were initiated. Prohibited from marrying, warriors were stereotyped as carefree and irresponsible, focusing their attention on herding, raiding, warfare, and impressing young women and girls. They then graduate to the second grade of junior elder status, when they marry, establish households, and build

their wealth. The third grade is that of elder, when men (now old enough to have sons who are becoming warriors themselves) reach the peak of their power and influence. Promotion to the next stage of senior elder is a form of retirement where men relinquish their formal political power for key roles in ritual affairs.

In the absence of more formal organization age sets provide a transferable set of relationships that, as among the highly mobile Turkana of Kenya, created a ready-made structure for interaction: "Wherever a man goes in the course of nomadic movement or in travelling, he finds men who are his age-mates, comrades, and supporters. He also finds his seniors and juniors to whom he can easily adjust his attitude and behavior. He can never be socially isolated" (Gulliver 1958: 917). On a larger scale, warriors could be mobilized as a military force or a council of elders could be assembled to designate a spokesman to negotiate on behalf of the group. Age sets served as a framework for political action only where kinship groups were poorly developed, local residence groups were unstable, and there was no institutionalized leadership (Baxter & Almagor 1978).

Outside of the East African context, age systems often took on somewhat different and less encompassing forms, but they all commonly segregated the young men into separate groups where they could be socialized or pick up new skills. The most unusual example of this occurred among the Nyakyusa of southern Tanzania, who formed "age villages" where boys' groups became the basis of new communities that would last a lifetime (Monica Wilson 1951). Among the Plains Indian tribes there were age societies to which individuals bought memberships to learn songs and dances, and that also served as military or police forces (Hanson 1988). The Shavante of Brazil separated groups of young men into bachelor huts before reintegrating them back into society with great ceremony (Maybury-Lewis 1967).

Formal age systems are fragile as a means of organizing a society. The American examples are known mostly through historical accounts, not observation. In the presence of centralized political leadership they tend to disappear or are transformed. Perhaps the most dramatic example of this was the reorganization of warrior age sets into formal and permanent military regiments by nineteenth-century Nguni leaders in southern Africa, such as Shaka Zulu, who then used them to centralize power and conquer much of the region (Gluckman 1940a). Even strong kinship ties without formal leaderships, like the segmentary system of the Nuer (Evans-Pritchard 1940), can relegate age systems to the function of organizing men for ritual occasions such as funerals and little more.

TB

further reading Eisenstadt 1956; Gulliver 1968; Kertzer 1978

aggression Human aggression is behavior intended to harm others, although some researchers regard self-injurious behavior as essentially similar. While inflicting physical harm (pain and injury) is certainly included, some scholars argue that behavior intended to inflict psychological SUFFERING, a common goal of gossip and OSTRACISM, should be as well. In addition, there is debate over whether aggressive behavior can be defined without reference to its results, since this definition admits practices that, though malevolent in intent, are of dubious efficacy, such as SORCERY. The psychological literature on aggression commonly employs a conceptual distinction between instrumental aggression (deployed as a means to an end) and hostile aggression (harm inflicted as an end in itself). Of course, any particular instance of aggressive behavior may represent some degree of both.

Whether humans are aggressive "by nature" is a perennial preoccupation of intellectuals and lay thinkers alike. Since any behavior observable in a species must be a potential of its genetic endowment, the conclusion must be affirmative, if only in a trivial sense. However, this assertion is far from the broader claim that humans are congenitally inclined to be aggressive. The latter conception of human aggression, central to the semi-popular human–nature literature of the 1960s and 1970s termed "naked apery" by Pilbeam (1983), is associated most prominently with the ethologist

Konrad Lorenz. Lorenz's characterization of aggression as a genetically ordained compulsion triggered by external stimuli has been rejected by today's students of human aggression and ethologists as an example of how not to think about aggression, in any species. Related efforts to explain violent conflict between human groups in terms of aggressive proclivities of the individual are fundamentally wrongheaded.

More useful than grappling with this question is addressing variability within the species. What determines situational variability in aggressiveness in an average person? What accounts for consistent differences in aggression between persons? What explains cross-cultural differences in levels of aggression?

Situational variability

Most theoretical work on the situational determinants of aggression is concerned with hostile rather than instrumental aggression. Excepting Freud's and Lorenz's notions of aggression as an insistent drive requiring periodic satisfaction, the most influential modern account of human aggression is the venerable "frustration–aggression" hypothesis, in which hostile aggression results when a person's goals are blocked. This bold account has undergone a number of revisions since its development in the 1940s. One of the more compelling replaced frustration as the causal term with unpleasant states, both emotional and physical. Proponents of this model cite evidence ranging from the flash of anger one stubbing a toe feels toward anyone in the vicinity to a study reporting a strong correlation between daily temperature and violent crime rates in Houston (Berkowitz 1989).

The level of arousal of the autonomic nervous system plays a role in aggressive behavior. Because autonomic arousal is identical in quality regardless of the emotion that induces it, preexisting arousal from any cause can augment the emotional arousal produced by a current situation and intensify the resulting behavior. Thus, experimental work has shown that when one responds to a situation aggressively, the responses will be more intense if one comes to the situation with a residue of autonomic arousal from fear, anger, sexual excitation, or mere physical exertion (Zillmann 1983).

Individual differences

Although it is not a cause of aggressiveness, the single best predictor of level of aggressiveness in adults is their level of aggressiveness in childhood (see SOCIALIZATION). Aggressiveness, at least in the American and European populations in which it has been studied longitudinally, is a remarkably stable trait, and persistent differences appear at an early age. Aspects of the child's home environment, especially those related to parental discipline, are well correlated with levels of aggressiveness later in life. Harsh and erratic discipline are each "risk factors" for problem aggressiveness, but so too is lax discipline (Loeber & Stouthamer-Loeber 1987).

The few fairly convincing connections between aggressiveness and biological characteristics pertain to pathological aggression rather than that in the normal range of behavior. (And it is important to observe that, in any society, the great majority of aggressive acts, including both mild and violent forms, are carried out by "normal" people rather than those afflicted with psychopathy.) The most robust finding of this sort is that a deficit of the neurotransmitter serotonin is more common among people diagnosed as given to impulsive aggression. However, it is not clear that aggressiveness in particular rather than reduced impulse control in general is the outcome of this deficit (Insel et al. 1990).

It could be said that sex is the most powerful biological factor in individual differences in aggressiveness throughout the life cycle. Aggressiveness is one of the most consistently found male–female differences in ethnographic research, with males evincing greater aggressiveness at every stage of life, but especially at puberty and beyond. It is of course conceivable that it is not the more-or-less direct physical consequences of having the XY or XX genotype – sex – that account for this difference but rather what cultures make of them – gender. The great diversity among cultures in the magnitude of the male–female difference in aggressiveness testifies to the power of cultural inflection, if not determination, of this difference (see GENDER).

Cross-cultural variation

The gamut of acceptability of VIOLENCE ranges from cultures in which any expression of aggression is abhorrent to ones in which bellicosity is not only acceptable but positively enjoined. To this dimension must be added a second, independent, one, representing the proportion of aggression that is directed toward others within a community as opposed to those outside of it. However, the level of within-group aggression does not provide a straightforward indication of the extent of hostilities between groups: most of the conceivable combinations can be found in the ethnographic record.

Theoretical work on violent intergroup conflict typically invokes social organization and political dynamics as elements of explanation, while treatments of group-internal aggression more often look to early childhood socialization. A safe generalization from the literature in the latter tradition is that, while affectionate and moderately indulgent parenting will not guarantee gentle adults, harsh socialization of children almost certainly precludes this outcome. Young CHILDREN universally resort to aggression, among other sorts of behavior, to secure desired things or prosecute their grievances. In cultures notable for low levels of everyday aggression, however, this behavior is progressively curtailed in favor of prosocial modes, not through punitive suppression but through parental modeling and shaping. Adults in such groups evince a positive fear of the destructive potential of aggression, and this aversion is inculcated in children early on.

JW

See also ETHOLOGY, FEUDING, SOCIOBIOLOGY, WAR

further reading P. Brown & Schuster 1986; Groebel & Hinde 1989; Montagu 1978

aging is a biological process of entropy operating in individual organisms from conception until death. It is also a cultural process of self-embodiment and learning that operates in persons as actors in society's daily dramas. Both processes are locked in a dialectic of mutual constraint and influence. Aging is a multimodal process that cannot be explained by simple linear models (Hareven & Adams 1982).

In scholarly practice, as in popular thinking, aging is usually framed as a problem of *old* age, a curve of decline in the elderly. Textbooks used to define gerontology as the study of human decay. Chronology (years since birth) is commonly used as an index of aging even though it is a poor predictor of anyone's biological wellness or capacity to contribute to society. But age is so convenient a measure of worth that few state bureaucracies or large-scale organizations are able to resist employing it as a way to categorize and control people. Early empires in Asia and Europe were measuring subjects by age at least 2,000 years ago. In our era it has become as universal a mark of identification as GENDER.

The maximum possible age seems not to have changed since prehistoric times. Most estimates put it in the range 120–140 years, although there are disputed cases of much older Methuselahs past and present. Life expectancy, however, has nearly doubled – from around 40 to around 80 years – in INDUSTRIAL SOCIETIES and is rising in the rest of the world as well. Mass longevity has radically altered life trajectories for the modern self and has turned aging into a new frontier for humanity – and for anthropology (Kertzer & Keith 1984).

Old people, particularly in industrial societies today, are seen as a "problem category," barred from the labor force by age but at the same time denounced as a burden on their juniors. Ideologies of progress exacerbate this bias by claiming that this year's new model is superior to last year's, and that older versions of humanity might as well be trashed.

But if there is an increase with age in the *percentage* of persons needing health and welfare services, the majority enjoy good health and can look after their daily needs well into their eighties. The "aged society" of the future cannot be extrapolated directly from present conditions. In the twentieth century each cohort entering old age has been healthier, better schooled, and more accustomed to dealing with the bureaucratic tangles of life in a mass society than its predecessor (Silverman 1987). Every community must begin to manage the changing mix of age groups in the population just as it must try to manage the shifting diversity in the biome.

Earlier ethnographers often obtained much of their data from older persons: those with more experience of local life and more leisure to sit and instruct the outsider. However, old persons were not seen as a topic for inquiry, and ELDERS were mentioned mainly as occupants of the last stages of the LIFE CYCLE. Leo Simmons's (1945) book based on HRAF data was the only extended study of old people by an anthropologist until the 1960s.

Anthropological research on aging has come of age since then as a specialty with its own professional organization and journals. Many colleges offer instruction on aging in cross-cultural perspective. And a number of ethnographic books, films, and videos now foreground the life situations of older people in an array of social settings (Keith et al. 1994). This battery of evidence is helping to correct both the bias against the old in our era and the nostalgia that imagines a premodern era when family and tribal values "naturally" assured loving care for the elderly. Most societies before the Industrial Revolution made a distinction between hale and frail elders. Respect might be accorded to the former but the latter often received death-hastening treatment. With all its failings modern society may be doing more for its frail elderly than did any "traditional" community (Cowgill & Holmes 1972).

Issues of aging have moved anthropologists to collaborate with colleagues in many fields and subfields (Fry & Keith 1986). But the glaring weakness is that research on aging too often transmutes into a study of old people as if they were a newly discovered tribe. We preach that aging is a lifelong process, but in practice we examine only the latter arc of the curve.

DWP

further reading Amoss & Harrell 1981; Counts & Counts 1985; Myerhoff 1978; Sokolovsky 1990; Vesperi 1985

agnates are patrilateral kin, that is people who are related to an individual on the father's side.   MR
See also COGNATES, ENATES

agriculture is the deliberate growing and harvesting of plants, but the term is often extended to include the raising of animals. As a mode of livelihood over 10,000 years old, agriculture is practiced in every part of the world where plants will grow, even within cities. Agriculturalists are called "farmers," "cultivators," or "agrarians" fairly interchangeably, while those who are under the control of a state system that extracts rent are often labeled "PEASANTS," a term with varying and sometimes contradictory political overtones. Agriculture is commonly combined with other livelihoods such as foraging (see FORAGERS), FISHING, TRADE, or craft production, particularly as part of a seasonal cycle that includes periods of rest, migration, and role shifting. These complex relationships are often underestimated because farmers sometimes overstate their reliance on farming and understate exchanges with other peoples.

Typologies of agriculture (Ruthenberg 1980) variously focus on crops grown and their uses, sources of water, degree of mechanization (particularly for land preparation), regimes of fallow or rotation (if any), ways of organizing labor, intensities of capital investment, and degrees of centralization of authority, among other things. Many schemas distinguish HORTI-CULTURE, including SWIDDEN agriculture, from sedentary farming; rainfed from irrigated or flood-recession farming; cash crops from food crops; and pure agriculture from agropastoralism or agroforestry. In reality these types mix and merge in countless combinations. Where soils are poor in nutrients, plants may feed on other living and decaying plant matter (a common pattern in tropical rainforests and in green manuring systems) or on inflowing waterborne nutrients (as in many irrigated areas).

Agriculture always involves more, technically and culturally, than just planting and harvesting crops. It may include tasks as diverse as tool manufacture and repair, crop magic, flood and pest control, ritual coordination, and investment management. The more complex the technology, the greater the DIVISION OF LABOR. Land, labor, capital, and other factors of agricultural production are all subject to varied cultural definition and classification; there are many tongues to which these terms, and others such as "farm," do not neatly translate.

The social units of agricultural production coincide often, but not always, with families or HOUSEHOLDS (Netting 1993). Where so, capabilities for agricultural production can vary markedly by stage of the family DEVELOPMENTAL CYCLE (Chayanov 1966; J. Goody & Fortes 1958). They also vary over the individual and community life cycles. Almost all agriculturalists learn how to farm (and to herd, where they do) from kin and neighbors by play-practicing in childhood, by assisting their elders, and by absorbing oral history (J. Whiting & Child 1953). Agrarian people everywhere divide their labor roles by sex to a greater degree than survival would appear to require. Where kept separate, male and female tasks may yet remain highly interdependent: field clearing is usually a male task worldwide; planting, weeding, and harvesting may be done by one or both sexes, separately or together; domestic food processing tends to be female; bulk marketing tends to be male almost everywhere (C. Ember 1983).

From horticulture among sparse rural populations to irrigation among dense ones, technological change entails social and political adjustments too. IRRIGATION farming does not always require centralized or hierarchical polity, but flood control in threatened areas usually does. Rules and practices of LAND TENURE and water rights tend to vary and to change with population densities and competition for these resources (Grigg 1980). KINSHIP systems tend very roughly to coincide, geographically and historically, with particular ecosystems, subsistence strategies, and settlement densities, though the causes and generalities concerned remain much debated (Forde 1934; Steward 1955; L. A. White 1959a). Rules and practices of marriage payments such as BRIDEWEALTH and DOWRY, sometimes interpreted as compensations for labor among other things, tend, again very broadly, to coincide with particular kinds of agricultural or pastoral regimes (Boserup 1970; J. Goody & Tambiah 1973; J. Goody 1976).

Humans perceive their agriculture in symbolic and religious terms that structure beliefs about ultimate causes and effects (Rappaport 1979), including metaphors by which agriculture is likened to other processes in the body, society, or the cosmos (Croll & Parkin 1992). These understandings may underpin or justify people's rights and duties in relation to productive resources. But farming peoples defy simple generalization in their knowledge and belief, variously recognizing land and farming as sacred, profane, neither, or both. Most agrarian societies, including those that do not view farming as closely linked to religion, do celebrate growth or fruition through ritual or ceremony (Lanternari 1976).

Anthropological research has challenged some conventional agricultural-economic views that define rationality as just the maximization of yields and profits. Small-scale farmers commonly seek to reduce their risks by measures such as diversifying crops, planting drought-resistant varieties, and farming fragmented fields on varying soils (for instance along a catena from valley bottom to hilltop). They try to smooth the peaks and troughs in labor demands (by intercropping, mixing fast- and slow-maturing seed varieties, etc.). Poorer farmers needing to spread capital expenditures through the year sometimes find it expedient to borrow at high interest, or to sell low after harvests and buy high before the next. Farmers also engage in reciprocal and redistributive exchange of farm inputs and outputs for social, political, symbolic, religious, or aesthetic purposes as well as agronomic or economic ones. In some times and places, magico-religious sanctions, such as WITCHCRAFT accusations, inhibit agricultural innovation or visible enrichment (Favret-Saada 1980; Malinowski 1935). Ritual-political control over planting and harvesting may serve agronomic purposes, for instance in synchronizing activities to prevent pests roaming from field to field over a longer period (Lansing 1991). Such findings have led to revised theories of rationality, profit maximization, risk aversion, price response, technical efficiency, and modernization. Farmers' rationality can be subtle and complex; and it is not their only way of thinking.

Anthropologists like Paul Richards (1985) have also focused on indigenous forms of technological experimentation and innovation, qualifying developers' assumptions that science or progress spreads from a few centers. Sympathetic ethnography has often discerned subtle local rationales behind practices like slash-and-burn agriculture, intercropping, or scatter planting, once disparaged by Euro-American scientists; and by the 1970s, such studies had strongly influenced more progressive "farming systems research" in agronomy, economics, and other disciplines (Ruthenberg 1980). In a more critical vein, some anthropologists have identified in farming economy and technology the roots of rural class formation, dependency, and conflict (E. Wolf 1966; J. C. Scott 1976; Shanin 1990). Sometimes unheeded in policy circles, or solicited too late, anthropological recommendations have influenced, and sometimes rendered more appropriate to context, many practical interventions undertaken in the name of economic development.   PS

See also FOOD PRODUCTION, FOOD SYSTEMS, GREEN REVOLUTION, HUNGER, PASTORAL NOMADS

further reading Bennett 1976; *Culture and Agriculture* [periodical]; Netting 1986; Shipton 1990; Vayda 1969b

alcohol is the generic name for a number of chemical compounds, but the one most important to humankind is ethyl alcohol (or ethanol, C_2H_5OH), the active component of many popular beverages that have been variously used by most populations throughout history. It is psychoactive, meaning that it can affect both mood and behavior by changing the nature and function of neural connections in the brain. A natural product of fermentation, it is the common factor shared by beers, ales, home-brews by various names, wines and distilled spirits, often with elaborate preparation and various additives. Fermented drinks rarely exceed 12 percent alcohol and can be made from almost any fruit, berry, tuber, or grain; distilled spirits also have many bases, but can exceed 50 percent alcohol.

In many cultures people use fermented drinks as nutritious staples in their diet; while others enjoy them episodically as adjunct to sociability, pay for communal labor, relaxation, offerings to supernatural or ancestral spirits, and otherwise. Archaeological remains of both wine and beer appear in the Near East prehistorically; but distillation appears to have been monopolized by alchemists until about 1200 C.E. In moderation, drinking can be healthful, but because behavioral and physiological reactions are related to dose and rate, it can be harmful in excess. As with other mind-altering substances, attitudes range from veneration as a sacrament to scorn as an abomination. Historical and ethnographic accounts often show alcohol as integrally linked with the economy, religion, social organization, and other aspects of culture; similarly, such descriptions provide valuable case studies or natural experiments that qualify the ethnocentric presumptions that color much of the psychological and sociological literature (D. Heath 1987). Anthropology's major contributions have been the sociocultural perspective – showing how attitudes and values affect drinking and its outcomes more than simple physiology and pharmacology – and the demonstration that alcohol plays many roles, even where alcoholism is unknown.   DH
See also DRUGS
further reading D. Heath 1995; D. Heath & Cooper 1981

alliance systems are created by the regular exchange of spouses between lineages, clans, or other marriage classes. Lineages in such a relationship can be said to have a permanent affinal relationship (see AFFINES). An alliance system in which the exchange of marriage partners is associated with the ranking of lineages is called an "**asymmetrical alliance**." In these systems either the wife-giving lineage (hypogamous systems) or the wife-taking lineage (hypergamous systems) is of higher status. A body of work, ALLIANCE THEORY,

emphasizes the importance of these permanent exchange relationships in the maintenance of social relationships over the concern with DESCENT that has traditionally dominated kinship theory (Lévi-Strauss 1969a).   MR

alliance theory refers to societies whose constituent units have enduring ties of marriage with each other. Anthropologists have long studied societies divided into intermarrying halves (see DUAL ORGANIZATION). In the 1930s Dutch anthropologists working with J. P. B. de Josselin de Jong at Leiden analyzed various Indonesian systems that defined the kind of marriage that individuals should contract and could therefore build their institutions around (Wouden 1968).

Alliance theory was most fully developed by Claude LÉVI-STRAUSS in *The elementary structures of kinship* (1969a), a work in which he presented a general theory of KINSHIP and MARRIAGE. He argued that the prohibition of INCEST originally established humankind's passage from a state of nature to a state of culture. It forced proto–human beings to organize themselves in groups that exchanged spouses and firmly established the principle of exchange as the prime motive force in social life (see MAUSS). Lévi-Strauss suggested that early humans could marry out (but not risk marrying too far out) by marrying their CROSS-COUSINS. Unlike PARALLEL COUSINS, cross-cousins are close relatives but always outside one's own descent group, whether descent is traced in the male or the female line. There are three kinds of cross-cousin marriage. From a man's point of view they are: matrilateral (with the mother's brother's daughter (MBD)), patrilateral (with the father's sister's daughter (FZD)) and bilateral (with someone who is both MBD and FZD at the same time). Figure 1 shows what happens in societies that institutionalize these forms of marriage. If men marry their bilateral cross-cousins, this results in two lines of men that marry each other's sisters. If men marry their matrilateral cross-cousins, this results in a cyclical system, where group A gives women to be wives of B, B to C, and so on. If men marry their patrilateral cross-

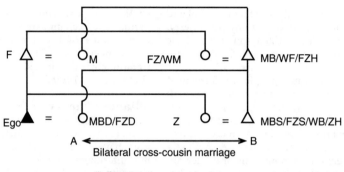

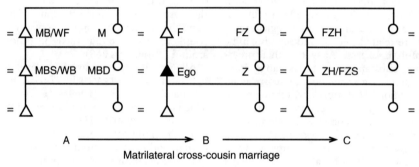

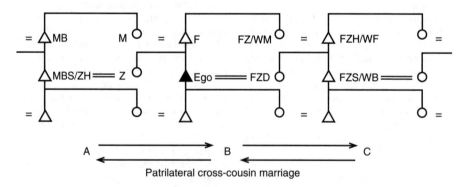

Figure 1 Alliance systems.

cousins, then women are passed from A to B to C but also from C to B to A. These are the *elementary structures* of kinship, which specify who must be married, as well as who may not. Lévi-Strauss suggested that human societies progressed from the re- stricted exchange of bilateral cross-cousin marriage to the generalized exchange of matrilateral cross-cousin marriage, occa- sionally passing through the intermediate form of patrilateral cross-cousin marriage. Eventually they transcended elementary structures and moved to *complex structures*, where marriage with certain kinds of relative is prohibited but anyone else is a possible spouse. Much of Lévi-Strauss's book was devoted to documenting this evolution by analyzing the societies of Aboriginal Australia, Indonesia, Asia, and the Americas. The societies of Europe and Africa, being complex structures, were left for a subsequent study that was never written.

How could such elementary structures work? For example, it is demographically impossible for every man in a matrilateral alliance system to marry his actual MBD. The society could arrange things so that some people marry their actual MBDs and others classificatory MBDs. Rodney Needham (1962) suggested that such arrangements are in fact regularly made in what he termed "prescriptive" alliance systems and that Lévi-Strauss's theory applied to such systems. Lévi-Strauss rejected this restrictive defense of his theory, insisting instead that his was a general theory about kinship systems and human social evolution. His elementary structures were models that did not correspond to actual marriage patterns but rather to the ideas governing those marriage patterns in the minds of the peoples who practiced them. These contentions have been strongly criticized (see especially Korn 1973). Lévi-Strauss drew conclusions about marriage systems from kinship terminologies, but the correlation between the two is not tight enough to permit such inference. Much of his supporting analysis must thus be rejected and his theory of social EVOLUTION with it. Nor do anthropologists now accept that kinship systems are essentially alliance systems.

Lévi-Strauss's book is still considered a brilliant treatise on the formal properties of alliance systems. Meanwhile other anthropologists, notably Edmund LEACH, have pointed out that those theories which stressed the role of descent in human affairs had been developed by Africanists and worked well in Africa. In other parts of the world, notably in Southeast Asia and Indonesia, societies built their institutions around marriage, leaving descent as a secondary principle. Hence alliance theory

had greater explanatory value in those areas of the world than DESCENT THEORY.

DML

further reading Dumont 1971a; Leach 1954; Maybury-Lewis 1971

altruism is action undertaken for the benefit of other individuals where the altruist incurs some cost or sacrifice. Some definitions also stress benevolent intent as the core concept, while others differentiate between altruism as a description of unique acts and altruism as a sustained moral stance governing principled decision making.

A substantial body of experimental research in social psychology has addressed the determinants of altruistic action in staged situations with opportunities for helpful interventions (D. Krebs 1987). The likelihood of helping is affected by various stable and transitory characteristics of what helpful interventions are possible, the attributes of the party in need, and the relative characteristics of the people involved. In general, however, this research has been restricted to stranger interactions, whereas most real-world cooperative and helpful behavior occurs among family members, friends, and acquaintances (Hames 1979; Essock-Vitale & McGuire 1985; D. Schneider & Cottrell 1975). The fact that altruistic acts toward strangers (heroic rescues, charitable works, and other philanthropic efforts) are so often deemed worthy of special recognition and honor bespeaks the fact that they are exceptional. In contrast, the lifelong one-way flow of resources from parents to children is only to be expected and is rarely honored.

Why altruistic inclinations and actions exist has been called the "central problem" of SOCIOBIOLOGY. This is because Darwin's theory of evolution by natural selection is a theory of the competitive ascendancy of traits that enable individuals to garner and retain a disproportionate share of reproductive resources. It would seem that selfish tendencies and types would generally outreproduce altruistic alternatives, driving the latter to extinction. In fact, many animals, like people, exhibit behavior that bestows benefits on others and cannot plausibly be dismissed as accidental. For example, many animals alert their neighbors when they spot a potentially dangerous predator in the vicinity by emitting a context-specific "alarm call." And many others, such as worker bees, expend a lifetime of nonreproductive service, helping other individuals to reproduce. One cannot, of course, attribute "intention" in these cases. These acts are not necessarily motivationally analogous to prototypical instances of human altruism, but they are certainly carried out "in order to" confer benefits on others in that they are adaptively organized to produce that end (Cronin 1991).

Two main solutions to the problem of how altruism could evolve have been proposed: nepotism and reciprocity. Each applies to certain cases.

(1) Much apparent altruism can be understood as "nepotism": animals are discriminative in how they bestow benefits on others and the beneficiaries are often kin. Since relatives are disproportionately likely to share the heritable basis underlying a rare or novel act of altruism, the altruistic tendency can be naturally selected (W. Hamilton 1964). By this "kin-selection" theory, altruism at the level of the organism may nevertheless represent "selfishness" at the level of the gene. A classic example is Sherman's (1977) study of alarm calling by ground squirrels: having detected a predator, a squirrel may or may not call, and the probability that a given squirrel will call increases the closer its genealogical relationship to the neighbors who might benefit. Thus, alarm calling is facultatively deployed exactly as expected on the hypothesis that its function is nepotistic.

A common fallacy (S. Washburn 1978) is to suppose that such nepotistic discrimination can be selectively favored only if the altruist's relatives and nonrelatives are genetically different at relevant loci. This is a fallacy because the issue is one of evolutionary stability, not genetic similarity. A population of indiscriminate altruists is vulnerable to invasion by an initially rare "nepotistic allele," but a population of nepotists cannot be invaded by a gene for indiscriminate altruism (Dawkins 1979). Thus, alleles engendering nepotistic phenotypes should routinely go to fixation and stay there.

(2) A second basis for the evolution of altruism is reciprocity (you scratch my back and I'll scratch yours). Trivers (1971) observed that the benefit enjoyed by the recipient of an altruistic act often exceeds the cost incurred by the donor. So if roles are likely to be reversed in a future interaction, it may be worth the while of both parties to enter into a relationship of mutual support. Vampire bats, for example, regurgitate blood to starving roost-mates who have failed to find a blood meal, and do so selectively for particular, known "exchange partners" who have performed complementary service (Wilkinson 1984). An impediment to the evolution of such reciprocity is the ever-present temptation to defect: to accept benefits but later refuse to give. Hence, reciprocal altruism is apparently confined to cases in which individualized social relationships endure and there is no great imbalance between the exchange partners in their frequency of being in need of help or able to provide it.

Game theorists have modeled reciprocal altruism as an iterated Prisoner's Dilemma in which two players are each tempted to defect in any single game, but will enjoy the best results if they can sustain cooperation. A dominant strategy in such a circumstance is "tit-for-tat"; cooperate as long as the other player does likewise but penalize each defection in kind, no more and no less (Axelrod & Hamilton 1981). The similarity of this simple strategy to the "eye-for-an-eye" ethos of balances of power and measured revenge FEUDING in nonstate societies suggests that the model may capture some of the considerations that shaped the psychology of cooperation and competition in human evolution (Daly & Wilson 1988b).   MD & MWi

further reading R. Alexander 1987; Axelrod 1984; Bernstein et al. 1994; Stacey & Koenig 1990

ambilineal descent   is the principle by which an individual may affiliate with a descent group through either their father or mother, but not both.   MR
See also DOUBLE DESCENT KINSHIP TERMS

ambilocal residence   is a postmarital residence rule requiring a newly-married couple to reside with the parents of either the bride or the groom, but not neolocally.
                                                     MR
See also NEOLOCAL RESIDENCE

ancestors   are people (and occasionally purely mythological creatures) from whom an individual or lineage is descended according to a system's reckoning of DESCENT. More narrowly, ancestors are those socially significant progenitors the memory of whom, as individuals or a group, has been preserved by individuals, a kin group, or a society.   MR

ancestor worship   refers to the performance of major rituals focused on ancestors. The phrase is now in disrepute because of its baggage of nineteenth-century ideas. In the schema of Herbert SPENCER (1876) and Edward Burnett TYLOR (1871), it constitutes a supposedly early EVOLUTIONARY STAGE of human ideas. They deduced that primitive peoples must first have experienced dreaming, and from that arrived at a notion of soul (see SPIRIT). The persistence of souls after death then made necessary the propitiation of ancestors. The logic may be easily reversed, however; there is no reason why an interpretation of dreaming could not be derived from a preexisting notion of spirit worlds. Moreover, in almost all their examples, the "worship" of ancestors is found in association with ritual directed to "higher" deities.

Nevertheless, it remains true that ancestors figure prominently in very many religious traditions, particularly outside the handful of world religions. It is reasonable then to speak generally of ancestor worship or ancestor cults provided that it is kept in mind that they comprise very diverse phenomena, with no unifying essence. For example, the service of Sir Ghost (the last deceased head of household) in the Manus islands, as described by Reo Fortune (1935), has precious little in common with the formal rituals of Taiwanese Chinese lineage halls, as described by Emily Ahern (1973).   PM
See also RELIGION, TOTEMISM

animals   There is considerable evidence that humans have thought long, carefully, and often anthropomorphically about animals: from the first cave-bear cult among the Neanderthals and the Upper Paleolithic cave paintings of 125,000–10,000 years ago; through religious emblems such as the Lion of Judah and the Lamb of God; to literature, whether classical (*Aesop's fables*), folk (*Br'er Rabbit*), or modern (Orwell's *Animal farm*), and postmodern film epics such as Disney's *Lion king*. In addition to the frequent pitting of animal strength against human (bullfights, rodeos) or the use of totemic animals as representatives of human groups (Chicago "Bulls" vs. Minnesota "Timberwolves" or Cameroon's "Lions" and Nkongsamba's "Eagles"), animals have been cast into many roles: as part of nature that includes humans (Native American religions); as part of nature that excludes humans or sets them apart (*Genesis* in the Old Testament); as representatives of nature that reflect, betray, deceive, or instruct humans (African folk tales); as innocent victims of a human nature that destroys their habitats and disregards their needs (environmental movements). One generalization seems inevitable: as humans go, so go their animals. Thus in today's Western societies, some pet owners buy fur coats for their dogs while others lobby for animal rights; acupuncture enthusiasts may search for acupuncture-practicing veterinarians and vegetarians may impose vegetarian diets on their carnivorous pets.

In anthropology, the earliest questions posed about animal–human interactions pertained to how and why animals were domesticated (Childe 1936; Sauer 1952) and how they were classified (Durkheim & Mauss 1963). Darwin's (1868) study of the mechanics of human (artificial) selection of domesticated animal and plant population characteristics might be considered a philosophical forerunner of early speculations about the mechanisms and motives for domestication as a single, perhaps unique, event; but current theories are based on recent archaeological finds suggesting that animals were domesticated in several places, at different times, perhaps for a variety of reasons (Hesse 1982).

In recent decades, anthropological studies of animals have taken two main directions: first, animals are viewed as functional items or sustenance in an ecological/systemic perspective (see CATTLE COMPLEX, PASTORAL NOMADS), and, second, animals are seen as meaningful items or symbols in a structuralist or symbolic perspective (Shanklin 1985). New technological developments, combined with interdisciplinary efforts, have allowed many ways of exploring the first area. An early researcher was Marvin HARRIS (1966), who took issue with the philosophical abstractions explaining the "sacred" cattle of India by demonstrating instead the ecosystemic rationale that underlay the ban on slaughter and allowed for extensive use and recycling of cattle byproducts. R. A. Rappaport (1967) carried out a similar analysis of the many uses of pigs in New Guinea, interweaving caloric studies with ritual functions. Later researchers explored other directions, some following the pioneering efforts of Fredrik Barth (1961, 1969a), who used ecological perspectives to evaluate the role of animals in ethnic identification (J. Burton 1981; Galaty 1982; Leeds & Vayda 1965). One promising new research thrust is the development of "ethnoveterinary" medicine, involving collaboration between veterinarians and anthropologists interested in disease categories, "ethnoetiology," and folk remedies. Another is the study of the physiological and psychological effects on humans of keeping pets.

In contrast, the study of the meanings and metaphorical significance assigned to animals still seems a developing field, since its major philosophical assumptions remain a source of debate and its wealth of available information is susceptible to various interpretations. A main point explored here is what part animals play in metaphor and symbolic classifications: how animals are classified in indigenous taxonomies (Ellen & Reason 1979; M. Douglas 1966; ETHNOZOOLOGY); how they are perceived and discussed (Lévi-Strauss 1963b; Bulmer 1963); and how they are used as metaphors for human social arrangements (Leach 1964). A heated debate on the philosophical predicates of indigenous taxonomic schemes began when Mary Douglas (1963, 1990b) published her explanation of the Lele attribution of sacredness to the pangolin (scaly anteater). This debate has broadened understandings of relations between people and animals at a number of levels, as well as stimulating research in many parts of the world and providing data on a dizzying variety of little-known animals, obscure classifiers, and esoteric classificatory principles.

There is a strong need for integration of the animals studies perspectives developed within both fields into new studies and for incorporation of different dimensions in a nondeterminist approach. To paraphrase another illuminating anthropological debate (Tambiah 1969) on this subject: animals are good to think and good to eat.

ES

See also CLASSIFICATION
further reading Ingold 1988a; E. Lawrence 1982

animism is generally the doctrine that some vital principle, or some kind of soul, produces the living phenomena of organized bodies and yet exists apart from those bodies. TYLOR (1871) defined animism as the belief in spiritual beings and as the basis of all religions. POLYTHEISM characterized the multiplicity of such spirits and preceded the progression from a belief in many such spirits to ideas of a High God or MONOTHEISM.

Animists believed that a human's spirit could leave its body, an idea brought about in early humans through, among other things, the experience of dreams in which different personified images would appear as if unrooted in any material thing. Tylor linked this concept or SPIRIT with that of soul. He saw evidence of their believed separability from material host objects in the almost universal appearance in vocabulary from languages throughout the world. Concepts of shadow (shade), wind, breath, and life presuppose each other and may be covered by the same or similar vernacular words, as among many Bantu-speaking and other peoples of Africa (Mbiti 1990). Tylor also attributed to early religion the belief that spirit and even soul inhered in ANIMALS, plants, and nonliving objects. This is not, however, to be confused with the no-

tion of fetishism, in which objects are imbued with magical powers that humans may invoke, which was regarded by one or two early scholars as the earliest kind of religion. Tylor's view of animism as the basis of religion was countered by Marrett (1909), who argued that such origins were to be found in an impersonal supernatural force, such as the MANA of Polynesia or *orenda* of the Iroquois, which were not derived from specific persons or natural phenomena, though they might be associated with them (B. Morris 1987: 93–107).   DP
See also RELIGION
further reading Endicott 1979; Fardon 1990; J. Fernandez 1982; Karim 1981

anthropology, cultural and social

Cultural and social anthropology are distinguishable if not entirely disjunct intellectual traditions. The use of the terms "cultural" and "social" to draw the distinction became common in the 1930s, but the divergence arose earlier, most directly from the differences between the studies advocated by Franz BOAS (1858–1942) in the United States from the 1890s, and the new directions anthropology had begun to take in England around that time at the initiative of R. R. Marrett (1866–1943), C. G. Seligman (1873–1940), W. H. R. RIVERS (1864–1922), and Alfred Haddon (1855–1940).

Today the two terms do not denote a precise division of approaches and for this reason some anthropologists have dispensed with the distinction (e.g., R. Barrett 1984: 2). For many others, however, the difference remains important, at least as a shorthand way of characterizing ethnographic styles. The rubric "cultural anthropology" is generally applied to ethnographic works that are holistic in spirit, oriented to the ways in which culture affects individual experience, or aim to provide a rounded view of the knowledge, customs, and institutions of a people. "Social anthropology" is a term applied to ethnographic works that attempt to isolate a particular system of social relations – such as those that comprise domestic life, economy, law, politics, or religion – give analytical priority to the organizational

bases of social life, and attend to cultural phenomena as somewhat secondary to the main issues of social scientific inquiry.

National and international influences

Cultural anthropology continues to be the dominant tradition in the United States; social anthropology in Britain and the Commonwealth. The two traditions do not, however, correspond precisely with this division. The British anthropologist Edward TYLOR (1832–1917) is more clearly a forerunner of cultural anthropology, and the American anthropologist Lewis Henry MORGAN (1818–81) become a central figure in British social anthropology. Other anthropologists – Bronislaw MALINOWSKI (1884–1942), for example – defy simple categorization.

Moreover, the genealogy of these traditions only partially reflects their national character. Social anthropology drew from nineteenth-century British theorists such as Henry Sumner MAINE (1822–88), William Robertson SMITH (1846–94), and J. F. McLennan (1827–81), but also from such important figures as J. J. Bachofen (1815–87), who was Swiss, Carl Starcke (1858–1926), who was Danish, Edward Westermarck (1862–1939), who was Finnish, Arnold van GENNEP (1873–1957), who was Dutch, and above all from Emile DURKHEIM (1858–1917) and other French ethnologists of the *Année sociologique* circle, including Marcel MAUSS (1872–1950) and Robert HERTZ (1882–1915). Cultural anthropology at the beginning of the century looked as much to the tradition of such German historical geographers as Karl Ritter (1779–1859) and Adolf Bastian (1826–1905) as it did to the contributions of Morgan, Henry Schoolcraft (1793–1864), and the fieldworkers associated with the Bureau of American Ethnology under the directorship of John Wesley Powell (1834–1902).

Nomenclature

Sir James George FRAZER (1854–1941) was appointed to the first (honorary) professorship of social anthropology in 1907 (at the University of Liverpool), and he defined the field in his 1908 inaugural lecture as the branch of sociology that deals with primitive peoples. Similar definitions continue to attract adherents, but since the

1920s, social anthropology has been more strongly associated with the contributions of A. R. RADCLIFFE-BROWN (1881–1955) than with those of Frazer. In 1923, Radcliffe-Brown distinguished between ethnology as "the attempt to reconstruct the history of culture" and social anthropology as "the study that seeks to formulate the general laws that underlie the phenomena of culture" (1958: 8, 25). He illustrated his idea of ethnology by citing the work of BOAS and Boas's students. Radcliffe-Brown's emphasis on typology and rigorous abstraction also entered into the connotation of "social anthropology," if not into the practice of all social anthropologists.

"Cultural anthropology" is a more diffuse term. Boas himself did not place his studies under this heading, referring to his approach simply as "anthropology." Some of his students, however, noted the lack of a term to distinguish investigations of culture per se from physical anthropology, and, to a lesser extent, from ARCHAEOLOGY and LINGUISTICS. These students, including Clark Wissler (1870–1947), Alfred KROEBER (1876–1960), Robert LOWIE (1883–1957), Paul Radin (1883–1959), and Edward SAPIR (1884–1939), were clear about the focus on "CULTURE," but did not settle on a single nomenclature until the late 1930s. Sapir (1916) early on referred to "cultural anthropology" in its current sense. But the term did not immediately stick. In his 1929 textbook, *Introduction to social anthropology*, Wissler, for example, defined his field as "social anthropology" because:

our concern will be with the social life of man, rather than with his anatomy, physiology, and psychology. Sometimes we speak of this social life as civilization, but in social anthropology, the term culture is preferred; and culture, when used in this technical sense, includes all the group activities, or conventionalized habits, of a tribe or a community. (pp. 11–12)

Paul Radin's (1932) textbook, *Social anthropology*, continued this usage. The term "cultural anthropology" appears to have gained prominence first from the title of Lowie's (1934) text, *An introduction to cultural anthropology*, in which he declared: "The general goal of anthropological study

is to understand the whole of culture in all periods and ages, and to see each humblest fragment in relation to that totality" (pp. 384–5). Lowie nonetheless remained rather circumspect about the term, acknowledging in 1936 that the discipline "has been variously ticketed 'culture history,' 'ethnography,' 'ethnology,' or 'cultural anthropology,'" (1960: 391). In any case, by the end of the 1930s, American anthropologists whose studies focused on culture and whose work was largely informed by Boas's teachings generally called themselves cultural anthropologists.

Divergences and critiques

The relationship between cultural and social anthropology has some interesting asymmetries. Following Radcliffe-Brown, social anthropologists have often characterized cultural anthropology as a different field of inquiry, but cultural anthropologists have usually depicted social anthropology as a specialization within cultural anthropology. Social anthropologists have tended to dismiss some of the chief preoccupations of cultural anthropologists, such as CULTURE AND PERSONALITY studies, as based on false premises. Cultural anthropologists, in turn, have depicted social anthropologists as hair-splitting adherents of an overly narrow doctrine.

The most explicit outbreak of this skepticism was the 1951 exchange in *The American Anthropologist* between George Peter Murdock (1897–1985) and Raymond FIRTH (1901–). British social anthropologists, in Murdock's view, "fractionate their descriptions and analyses of social systems." He charged that the British concentrated "exclusively on kinship and subjects directly related thereto, e.g. marriage, property, and government" and ignored "such major aspects of culture as technology, folklore, art, child training, and even language" (1951: 466–7). He observed that British anthropologists operated from a narrow ethnographic base, rarely venturing outside sub-Saharan Africa for field studies, and more rarely still testing their generalizations against the broader ethnographic record. Finally, Murdock lashed social anthropology for ignoring history and psychology.

Firth offered a rather nuanced reply. He agreed with Murdock that British social anthropology was "hardly distinguishable in scope" from theoretical sociology, but added that Murdock's expressions of surprise on that score – following 30 years in which Malinowski, Radcliffe-Brown, Max GLUCKMAN (1911–75), and E. E. EVANS-PRITCHARD (1902–73) had claimed nothing less – represented either "judicial ignorance or magical fright." In Firth's view, the study of culture and the analysis of structure are complementary, and British social anthropology had proven sufficiently capacious for both. Firth said that he and his colleagues in Britain viewed their work as part of an international science in which they saw useful contributions "in the best American work." British anthropologists who characterized cultural anthropology as failing to rise to an appropriate level of abstraction were "unnecessarily censorious." On the other hand, the "heuristic advantages" that cultural anthropology may derive from what Clyde Kluckhohn called "holistic, controlled impressionism" depend on "the personal perceptions of the student – aided often by earlier training in another discipline" (Firth 1951a: 477, 480, 483, 484).

Evans-Pritchard's (1964: 17) explanation of why American anthropology was dominated by a preoccupation with culture rather than society is more invidious:

The fractionized and disintegrated Indian societies on which their research has been concentrated lend themselves more easily to studies of culture than of social structure [and] the absence of a tradition of intensive fieldwork through the native languages and for long periods of time, such as we have in England, also tends towards studies of custom or culture rather than of social relations.

In fact, the salvage ethnography pursued by some cultural anthropologists such as Lowie did pay considerable attention to social structure, but the analyses did not reach the sophistication of such British social anthropologists as Meyer FORTES (1906–83) and Audrey RICHARDS (1899–1984).

Cultural anthropology since the 1960s has absorbed some of the analysis of kinship and political order developed within social anthropology but has tended to dismiss – sharply – the larger project of social anthropology on the grounds that it was founded on static structural–functional models, false assumptions about the nature of kinship, and illusions about social integration. George Stocking (1984: 181) characterized this attitude toward the social anthropology of Radcliffe-Brown and Malinowski as a historical gulf:

Indeed, there are many today (especially, perhaps, in the United States) for whom the real problem of historical understanding would seem now to be how so many intelligent anthropologists have been so long infected by such a sterile and/or derivative viewpoint.

Declarations from the exponents of one tradition that the other is moribund, obsolete, or senescent are, of course, good evidence that the distinction between traditions still matters.

Enduring issues

Perhaps the most important question for students of anthropology is whether the distinction is merely a matter of style or academic tradition (colored by national identity), or whether it points to a more substantive and philosophically important divergence. The argument for the latter is as follows. Cultural anthropology, in the Boasian tradition, aims to comprehend the entirety of human cultural life. Social anthropology focuses on the organizational bases of human societies. In practice, some cultural anthropologists also give analytical priority to social structure, and some social anthropologists, in pursuing analyses of social systems, comprehend a great deal of cultural life. Be that as it may, one approach is basically synthetic, the other analytic and inductive.

Social anthropology's roots in a particular tradition of social inquiry have helped to shape its characteristic questions. In both Radcliffe-Brown's (1958: 147–52) and Evans-Pritchard's (1962: 21–5) accounts of the intellectual origins of the discipline, the key figures are not Hobbes and Locke, who *speculated* about the fundamental conditions of society, but Montesquieu (1689–1755) and the thinkers of the Scottish Enlightenment, including Adam Ferguson (1723–1816) and Adam Smith (1723–90), who attempted to derive general principles of structural interrelations in societies from analysis of particular instances. Social anthropology drew from many other intellectual sources as well, but the connection to the moral philosophers and political economists of the eighteenth century best explains its distinct intellectual preoccupations: the effort to discover the nature of social units on all scales, up to SOCIETY itself, and the institutions through which social units internally differentiate, sustain themselves over time, reproduce, and, in general, effect the creation of social order.

Cultural anthropology, which has roots in German historicist philosophy and American pragmatism, has sought to explore the variety of human experience and examine that variety in relation to a range of historical, psychological, ecological, and other comparative frameworks. Cultural anthropology in the broadest sense is a continuation of the intellectual impulse of observant travelers and writers of natural histories since the Renaissance to describe the world as it appears to be. Boas was interested in developing reasonable hypotheses but not in proposing systematic theories. He was skeptical about the observer's ability to determine with any surety what facts might prove to be of eventual scientific importance, and he therefore cast his net as widely as possible. His supposition that observation is prior to theory has fallen into considerable disfavor in recent decades, even among the inheritors of the cultural anthropological tradition, but it accounts for most of the vigor of that tradition, which has combined close attention to ethnographic detail with open exploration of novel ideas. Cultural anthropologists after Boas often adopted theoretical programs that were in no particular way "Boasian," except for the assumption that the task is somehow to understand culture, and the theory must prove itself by that criterion.

Social anthropology, because it focuses on a large but conceptually unified set of questions and methods, has a cumulative character. As a science of society, it has proceeded on the view that all human societies have deep commonalities and that so-cietal differences can be understood on the basis of universal principles. Cultural anthropology, by contrast, proceeds by the relativist postulate that each culture must be understood *sui generis*. One consequence of this is that it is difficult for cultural anthropologists to build on one another's work other than by emulating one another's techniques. The eclecticism of cultural anthropology, however, has given it an advantage in drawing on developments in other disciplines and raising some important questions (particularly in psychology) that social anthropology has found difficult to reach.

The attempt to account for the existence of social order and the attempt to capture the diversity of human experience are separate but not opposed philosophical ends. Among contemporary anthropological works that attempt to bridge the traditions might be mentioned Raymond Kelly's *Constructing inequality*, which sets out to "describe and analyze all social inequalities" in a Papua New Guinean social system (1993: 4).

The distinction between social and cultural anthropology continues in contemporary anthropology, although it has lost some of the force and much of the clarity that it had at mid-century. The decline may in part be due to the influence of LÉVI-STRAUSS (1908–), who declared in 1949 that cultural and social anthropology were both parts of ethnology and were virtually indistinguishable (1963a: 2; see ETHNOGRAPHY AND ETHNOLOGY). Edmund LEACH (1910–89) observed that the influence of French structuralism on British and American anthropology did not reduce "the width of the Atlantic Ocean" (1982: 34). It was, however, among the complications that displaced Boas and Radcliffe-Brown as key points on the anthropological compass.

Additional complications introduced since mid-century include marxist and other historical materialist approaches, feminist theory, semiotics, radical historicism, and the related movements for reflexive and postmodernist ethnography. In some cases these developments have merged with the older traditions, but they have been posed in other instances as reformulations of the epistemology and purposes of anthropology as a whole. The tradition of cultural anthropology has proven more susceptible to this challenge, and indeed, even the term "cultural anthropology" has been partially appropriated by advocates of an approach that is avowedly antiscientific. The contemporary journal *Cultural Anthropology* (begun in 1986), for example, has only remote connections to the tradition of scientific inquiry founded by Boas.

Despite these strictures, social and cultural anthropology remain recognizably different orientations to the study of human phenomena, and most anthropological monographs continue to be situated in one or the other tradition. To the extent that comparative analysis of social systems and searching explorations of particular cultures continue to attract disciplined attention from individuals committed to standards of objectivity, social and cultural anthropology are likely to remain important and complementary components of the social sciences.   PW

further reading S. Barrett 1984; Boas 1931, 1938; Darnell 1974; M. Douglas 1980; R. Firth 1968; Fortes 1969; Hays 1958; Hinsley 1994; Kuklick 1991; A. Kuper 1977, 1983; I. Lewis 1976; Lienhardt 1964; Mair 1965; Mandelbaum 1968; M. Mead & Bunzel 1960; Penniman 1935; Stocking 1968, 1984, 1987; Trautmann 1987; Voget 1973

applied anthropology is the use of anthropology beyond the usual academic disciplinary concerns for research and teaching to solve practical problems by providing information, creating policy, or taking direct action. The process takes many forms but is always shaped by the practical problem at issue, the available disciplinary knowledge, and the role the anthropologist is expected to play. Since the mid-1970s the term "practicing anthropologist" has increasingly come to replace "applied anthropologist" for those in the field. Practicing anthropologists who apply their knowledge to particular domains (such as health, development or education) also are increasingly defining themselves more specifically (i.e., as "medical anthropologist," "development anthropologist," or "educational anthropologist").

The number of practicing anthropologists has increased significantly in the last 25 years. This trend has been disguised because the anthropologists often hold titles and play a variety of significant roles that do not explicitly highlight their disciplinary background. Such roles currently include those of policy researcher, evaluator, impact assessor, planner, research analyst, advocate, trainer, culture broker, program designer, administrator, and therapist, among many others, and the range is increasing.

Conventional wisdom often assumes that academic anthropology arose first and that it came to be applied. In fact, in many areas the relationship was opposite: applied anthropology was often the starting point of research financed because its sponsors stressed the potential of its practical benefits. Only later did more exclusively academic projects emerge and receive support. For example, the first departments of anthropology in Britain appear to have been touted as kinds of applied anthropology training programs for colonial administrators. The term "applied anthropology" itself was, in fact, first used in a 1906 article describing a program for training administrators at the University of Cambridge. In the United States, The American Bureau of American Ethnology was established in the nineteenth century as a matter of national policy. Its voluminous research on native Americans greatly exceeded that of any university program at the time. This trend continues today. Much foundational work in LEGAL ANTHROPOLOGY, MEDICAL ANTHROPOLOGY, URBAN ANTHROPOLOGY, DIET, and DEMOGRAPHY was first done for applied reasons. Many of the anthropologists who are now regarded as founders of new fields in academic anthropology were at the time they conducted this research regarded as not doing "real" anthropology.

Applied anthropology falls into two general categories: applied research and intervention. Much of the former is done for reasons of social policy, that is, to help inform the policy development process either in a specific or general sense, assess the impact of policy or policy decisions, or evaluate something done because of a policy. It is often conducted under the rubric of social impact assessment, evaluation, cultural resource assessment, or technology development research. Intervention practices most commonly focus on communities rather than individuals. They attempt to (1) identify community perceptions of need as an important part of the program-design process and (2) foster the development of empowered community organizations. Such intervention practices include action anthropology, research and development anthropology, advocacy anthropology, cultural brokerage, participatory action research, and social marketing. Although some anthropologists have served as policymakers, this is still rather rare.

Applied anthropologists make somewhat greater use of QUANTITATIVE METHODS, particularly formal surveys and statistical analysis, than do anthropologists in general, a practice recommended by the 1994 "Guidelines for training practicing and applied anthropologists" (endorsed by both the Society for Applied Anthropology and the National Association for the Practice of Anthropology). As a result, applied anthropologists have contributed a great deal to the development of both time-effective and participation-maximizing survey techniques, such as rapid assessment procedures, rapid reconnaissance surveys, and participatory action research (van Willigen & Finan 1990). Although the disciplinary origins of these very interesting practices are clouded, the contribution of anthropologists in these areas is very important.

Anthropologists have applied their knowledge and skills in such a wide variety of domains that it is very difficult to find an area of practical concern where they have not been active. The areas of most concentrated effort include AGRICULTURE, EDUCATION, health, and natural resources; other areas include AGING, environment, GENDER, housing, HUMAN RIGHTS, REFUGEE resettlement, and abuse of DRUGS and ALCOHOL. Historically, applied anthropologists have been pioneers in numerous areas of research, such as urban life, population, law, and nutrition. The entire subdiscipline of medical anthropology appears to have emerged from applied work in international health.

Applied anthropology crosses many more boundaries than academic research. Practitioners must know the domain of application within which they work, including such things as relevant legislation, important community or professional organizations, and opinion leaders. Although it is true that anthropologists "apply anthropology," to be effective they almost always need to incorporate data or methods from cognate fields such as agronomy, environmental studies, public health, and education. For this reason the training literature in the field frequently recommends contact with other, related disciplines. And because the work experience itself usually involves working in multidisciplinary settings with persons trained in other fields, as well as the members of the host community, anthropologists usually find themselves working closely with nonanthropologists. This is one reason why internships are so important: they provide an experience difficult to acquire in academic anthropology departments.

Anthropologists in the business of applying their knowledge have organizational needs that are different from academic anthropologists. The most interesting manifestation of these differences is the development of local practitioner organizations (LPOs) as an alternative to national and international associations of anthropologists that operate on learned-society models. The LPOs serve as arenas for networking for jobs and contracts, as a source of information about current developments in the discipline, and as a channel for communicating one's work. Organizationally these groups are somewhat unstable, but a number of them have functioned since the late 1970s. National organizations in applied anthropology often attempt to foster relationships with LPOs in order to link themselves to the authenticities they represent. One aspect of this is to offer more skills-acquisition workshops at their national meetings. The most important national/international organizations in this realm are the Society for Applied Anthropology and the National Association for the Practice of Anthropology. These organizations have provided channels for professional communication in the form of conferences, journals and newsletters, computer websites, and list servers. In the United States at least, applied anthropologists have taken a lead in the development of standards for ethical practice. The first ethics statement by anthropologists was produced by the Society for Applied Anthropology in response to the negative reactions of a community to a research project.

Applied anthropologists tend to publish less in the high-prestige disciplinary journals. Their written output is primarily in the form of "fugitive" or "gray" literature, consisting of limited-distribution technical reports. Many of the journal articles that they do publish are in nondisciplinary journals that deal with their domain of application. Journals that publish articles with an applied cast include *Practicing Anthropology*, the *Bulletin* series of the National Association for the Practice of Anthropology (NAPA) and the *High Plains Applied Anthropologist*. These have much improved the availability of written materials for training and development of better practice.   JvW

further reading E. Chambers 1985; van Willigen 1991, 1993

archaeology Defined as the study of humankind's ancient societies and cultures, archaeology is an appropriate part of the broader field of anthropology, which is the study of humankind both past and present. However, archaeology as a formal discipline is older than academic anthropology and has had a history of its own that we should consider.

The name itself, literally "the science of the old," came into use in Europe to describe studies of medieval legends as well as the monuments and works of art of classical antiquity that were rediscovered in Renaissance times. Thus, the term tended to be restricted to those ancient cultures or civilizations that had writing. This usage has continued in European academic circles, where the term "prehistory" is used to refer to those ancient cultures that had no written languages. In this way, Paleolithic, Mesolithic, Neolithic, and early metal-age cultures were subsumed under "prehistory," while those of Egypt, Mesopotamia, and Classical Greece and Rome, with their written texts, were considered to be in the realm of "archaeology." In the latter case, however, it is fair to say that the primary emphasis has been upon the study of the material remains, the buildings, monuments, and artifacts, rather than the written texts (G. Daniel 1950, 1962, 1967; Willey & Sabloff 1993).

Archaeology partakes of both the "humanistic" and "scientific" traditions of learning (Trigger 1989). In the European archaeological writings of the sixteenth century, the humanistic tradition was heavily the dominant one. This was followed, although by no means superseded, by the more rational philosophies of the Age of Enlightenment, as reflected in the writings of seventeenth-century antiquarians. For a while, the eighteenth-century Romantic movement brought a swing back in the other direction with such concepts as Rousseau's "noble savage." Then, the early half of the nineteenth century saw the emergence – in northern Europe, France, and Britain – of the scientific archaeology that we know today, an archaeology in which Darwinian evolutionary thought and a recognition of the Pleistocene presence of humans were fully acceptable. Nevertheless, a humanistic outlook, one tied to linguistics and history, remained strong, especially in the "text-aided" archaeologies of the ancient civilizations. Today, both traditions continue in archaeology as we pursue the analogies upon which archaeological interpretations are based.

Analogy is the operative principle of archaeology. That is, the past is understood through analogies drawn from the present. These may be living situations that are known from direct, present-day observation, or they may be living situations described in historical documents. The analogies may be divided into two classes: general and specific (Willey 1953a, 1977). Analogies of a general class are those taken from our general experiences and knowledge of life. As an example, an archaeologist digs an ancient camp site. The place is so identified by fire-hearths, by fragments of blackened cooking vessels found near such hearths, by animal bone refuse in or near the hearths, and, perhaps, by sharpened bits of stone the archaeologist recognizes as spear or projectile points that have been used to kill game or as knives used to skin the animals or cut up the meat. The archaeologist makes these identifications and assumptions by drawing upon a very general knowledge of the living world.

In general analogy, however, there are always interpretive risks. For the archaeologist must always project analogies from a familiar experienced present back into an alien past. That past, or an image of that past, is a creation made by selecting and fitting together ideas and concepts from a selection of present-day sources. Not surprisingly, what one archaeologist believes to be a ceremonial baton may be thought of by another as no more than a utilitarian back-scratcher. In general, it is almost axiomatic that the closer the archaeologist is confined to the basic activities of food procurement, shelter, and clothing, the "safer," or more nearly correct, the analogies will be. The farther the archaeologist moves in the direction of attempting to understand the social or mental life of the people who left the remains under study, the more open to doubt and the less secure the interpretations will be (C. Hawkes 1954).

With specific analogies, the archaeologist is on somewhat firmer ground in addressing more complex past human social and cultural behaviors. Thus, an archaeologist might set about trying to understand some of the functions of the Inca empire through comparing some of its features – its highways, road station, fortifications, warehouses – with those of the better-known Roman empire. There is no historical connection between the two; their backgrounds and setting are entirely different; but in this kind of specific analogy an assumption is made that a certain type of political system will produce similar behaviors on the part of the people who created and lived within it. To examine them in a comparative way should enable archaeologists to learn more about each, and espe-

cially the one (Inca) about which less is known through contemporaneous written sources. But in making an analogy of this kind, the archaeologist must still proceed with caution. Although the two empires shared an expansionistic military policy and formal ways of incorporating neighboring territories and peoples into their political realms and governing them, they undoubtedly also differed in the way they functioned.

Still more promising are specific analogies that are carried out within the same historical context. There are many examples of this in New World archaeology, where the descendants of the prehistoric Precolumbian peoples are still on the scene. In the Puebloan archaeology of the southwestern United States an extraordinary insight into ancient native religious practices is afforded by the obvious continuities that exist between the archaeologically known subterranean *kivas*, or ceremonial chambers, and the *kiva* ceremonialism that is still being practiced today by such living southwestern tribes as the Hopi or Zuñi. Similar continuities are expressed in everything from food preparation and house construction to religious rituals among the modern descendants of the Precolumbian Mayan Indians in highland Guatemala.

But even in these relatively "tight" historical contexts, there are interpretive risks in analogy, and it is unlikely that we can ever recreate an absolutely true and flawless image of the past. Thus, while highland Guatemalan corn-grinding implements, houses, and ritual altars of today may look exactly like those used by their ancestors of the Precolumbian past, the present-day attitudes and meanings surrounding these things may be significantly different from those of the past. Indeed, it would be surprising if all belief and behavior went entirely unchanged over such long periods of time.

In brief, there are no fool-proof formulae in analogical interpretation. The best the archaeologist can do is to proceed in a trial-and-error fashion, constructing analogical models, testing these insofar as he can against the data, and, in so doing, being constantly aware of new data. As an example, let us go back to the analogies between the Inca and Roman empires. Peruvianists might be interested in the question of how Inca imperial conquests influenced local regional ceramic traditions. They could study the pre-Incaic pottery development of a region that was later incorporated into the Inca empire – for instance, the Chimu pottery of the north coast of Peru. How did the Chimu potters respond to the conquest? Did they assimilate Incaic pottery vessel forms and decoration into their manufactures? If so, was such imitated Inca ware found largely in elite or upper-class contexts? And how abundant and widespread was Cuzco-made, imported Inca pottery? Was it confined to Inca-established military garrisons and government buildings?

By comparing the ceramic histories of ancient Britain or Spain in pre-Roman-through-Roman times, the Peruvianist interested in the Inca empire might find interesting parallels and differences; and because there is some contemporary documentation in the Roman case the reasons behind, and the processes of culture change involved in, these parallels and differences might be better understood. Clearly, no one can be a "world archaeologist," at least not on any serious research level. Top quality research is, by necessity, carried out in limited and specific geographical and cultural contexts. At the same time, it behoves the archaeologist to have broader comparative perspectives and to ask questions about the processes of culture growth and change. What, for example, were those involved in the shift from a foraging subsistence (see FORAGERS) to one of agricultural FOOD PRODUCTION? To what degree and in what ways does such a major economic change result in population increase and settlement concentration? What are the circumstances leading to such craft developments as pottery making or metallurgy? How do social inequality and political complexity arise? And how are these social and political conditions revealed in the archaeological record?

These are some of the big questions confronting an anthropologically oriented archaeology today, and in the last three decades this concern with the delineation

of process as a basic goal of archaeology has been referred to by some as the New Archaeology, or "Processual Archaeology." Its chief spokesman has been an Americanist, Lewis R. Binford (1962, 1965; Binford & Binford 1968; see also Clarke 1968; Moberg 1970); however, the goals and procedures of this New Archaeology were gradually emerging and coalescing as long ago as the 1940s. These included: (1) the re-introduction of cultural EVOLUTION into archaeology; (2) the application of SYSTEMS THEORY to cultural variability and its systemic organization; (3) an ecosystemic perspective that was concerned with the links between cultures and their environments (see ECOLOGICAL ANTHROPOLOGY); (4) an appreciation of regional settlement patterns and systems; (5) the statistical control of cultural variability and attention to sampling techniques that would permit generalizations and such variability; (6) a general "scientific" approach that stressed explicitness of assumptions, problem orientation, and structured research strategies; (7) hypothesis testing (particularly in the deductive-nomological form); (8) a positivist philosophical position; and (9) the use of the computer and a bevy of new scientific techniques and procedures in materials analyses provided by the natural and physical sciences. In sum, the innovations of the New Archaeology mark a definite trend toward the "scientific," as opposed to the "humanistic" tradition.

Like all archaeology, New or Processual Archaeology has proceeded by analogical reasoning; however, it has been argued that to rely too heavily upon specific historical analogies is to limit the abilities of archaeologists to see the past in processual terms (L. Binford 1967b, 1968). It is a primary tenet of the New Archaeology that general comparative analogies, carried out in systemic frames of reference, better enable archaeologists to understand process and, eventually, to formulate laws of culture change.

A classic and convincing example of general comparative analogy operating within a systemic frame of reference is that offered by Binford (1962) for the Old Copper Culture of the North American Great Lakes region. This culture dated to the Archaic Period (ca. second millennium B.C.E.) so that easy recourse to specific historical or ethnographic analogy was not possible. This was especially so because the most diagnostic feature of that culture – its hammered copper tools and other objects – were not present in any later cultures of the region, all of which were characterized by stone tools alone. Binford questioned the efficiency of the copper tools and pointed to the inordinate amount of time that would be needed to collect the surface copper nuggets needed to make them. He suggested that the copper artifacts, rather than being strictly utilitarian, were primarily status symbols in an egalitarian society. The rarity of the copper objects and the fact that they were almost always found as grave goods supported this assumption. They were symbols of individual prowess in hunting, fishing, and woodworking activities and were taken with the individual into his "afterlife." From a strictly technological standpoint, copper was apparently not prized highly enough for the culture to have developed mechanisms for retaining the metal within the sphere of the living and using it to refashion new tools.

Of course, much of the disagreement over the value of specific historical, as opposed to general, analogy derives from a different emphasis on the objectives of archaeology. If one favors a reconstruction of a specific past, with interpretations of specific architectural features or artifacts found in a southwestern Pueblo ruin, say, then such interpretations, of necessity, can only be derived from specific historic analogies. In contrast, if the goal is processual explanation – concerning the use of tool and artifact types within the context of a culture of a certain type, as · in the Old Copper Culture example – then a general comparative approach seems preferable, especially if there are no reasonable immediate sources from which to draw historical analogies.

Still, is the perspective of technical–ecological interaction to be gained through general comparative analogy sufficient to explain all that it is important to know about past cultures? It is this question that has led to a counter-movement to the New

Archaeology, one that has been dubbed "Post-processualism." This does not mean that its proponents believe that archaeology has gone beyond the need for an understanding of cultural process; rather, they believe that the ways the Processualists have set out to achieve it are too limited. Post-processualism embraces several lines of reasoning. One of these is the Contextual or Hermeneutic outlook (Hodder 1985, 1991b; Preucel 1991b), according to which archaeological remains are to be "read" and interpreted as "texts." This is in contrast to the Processual approach, which is grounded in a "timeless past," eschewing cultural history and seeking processual explanation through concepts of utility, control, and ADAPTATION. Such an outlook, the Post-processualists argue, is out of step with a world anthropology that is now concerned with gender, power, ideology, text, structure, and – above all – history. In their opinion, it is only through such a broadening of vision that archaeologists will be able to come to grips with process in culture change.

Another, but clearly related, line of argument in Post-processualism has been referred to as "Critical Archaeology" (Shanks & Tilley 1987; Leone 1982). It is primarily concerned with ideology, which the Critical Archaeologists see as a powerful social force with more than an epiphenomenal role in culture development and change. Not only does ideology mask socioeconomic and political divisions within a SOCIETY, it can also be creative: it directs and determines CULTURAL CHANGE so that to ignore it is to fail to explain process fully. A critique of GENDER bias has also been advanced by the Critical Archaeologists (Gero 1985; Wylie 1991). According to this view, by ignoring WOMEN and generalizing about societies and cultures from a male perspective alone, archaeologists are turning their backs on much of the record that will lead to processual understanding.

Is there a middle ground in archaeological theory between the sought-after objectivity of the New Archaeological Processualism and the attempts to introduce the more subjective points of view of the Post-processualists? It seems necessary to find one – or at least a concession on both sides for the necessity of studying the past in both ways. This dialectic between "science" and "humanism" has persisted throughout the history of archaeology. Certainly, much of the modern formal edifice of archaeology – systematic typologies, stratigraphic and seriational procedures, and attempts to translate material artifacts and other remains into human social behavior – pertains to the scientific tradition. At the same time, the humanistic tradition has kept alive the notion that cultural choice – human cultural choice and the ideologies in which it is embedded – have been important in guiding our destiny from remote times onward; and, as yet, there seems to be no easy way to formulate covering laws that will predict what these choices will be. Yet we need the humanistic, as well as the scientific, tradition within archaeology.

For archaeology is about *all* aspects of ancient human life. It is not just concerned with the relationships of people to the land on which they lived to each other; we also want to know what those people thought about it all and what moved them to do the things they did. With the archaeological task so defined, the job ahead is, obviously, an enormous and complex one. No individual archaeologist can hope to master all of the ancient past. By necessity, he or she must select and specialize; but we cannot afford to neglect any part of that past.

GRW

further reading Robert Adams 1966; L. Binford 1983a,b; Burger 1988; Gero & Conkey 1991; Hodder 1991a; Preucel 1991a; Renfrew 1984; Sharer & Ashmore 1993; Sharer & Grove 1989; Tax 1953b; D. Thomas 1989; Willey 1953b; Willey & Phillips 1958; D. Wilson 1988

architecture consists of the material dimensions of culture that humans construct to (1) provide shelter to protect themselves and their stores from the elements, (2) enclose activities within physically defined or bounded spaces, and (3) express the symbolic meanings and collective values of their particular society or culture.

Architecture is a cultural trait typically defined by relatively permanent, monumental constructions, often financed by elites and self-consciously designed and built by specialists, and associated with COMPLEX SOCIETIES. The terms "built form" and "built environment" are more inclusive, referring universally to all human-made shelters, including ephemeral and insubstantial ones. This usage avoids typological debate over qualifying the term "architecture" with concepts such as primitive, traditional, vernacular, and folk. Anthropologists most frequently study built forms that are dwellings, but also include temples, meeting houses, men's and women's houses, animal shelters, storage facilities, and funerary structures.

The anthropological study of built forms crosses many disciplines including architecture, ARCHAEOLOGY, FOLKLORE, and geography. Seminal work by architect Amos Rapoport (1969) dismisses environmental factors as determinants of built form and introduces an explanation through a concept of CULTURE. Built forms in his scheme are a tangible product that links a particular worldview to a set of values, an image or schema, a lifestyle, and activities that most immediately determine physical forms. Although architectural approaches draw broadly on cultural concepts, anthropologists have rarely investigated built forms in their own right; rather, they have used forms as evidence to support particular theoretical perspectives. Recent anthropological interest in architecture and the materiality of culture results from efforts to re-situate social theory spatially (as well as temporally) and to ask what relationships exist between humans and the forms they construct (D. Lawrence & Low 1990).

Early anthropological studies viewed built forms as an integral part of social life and a universal element of culture, but typically portrayed them as passive in ethnographic descriptions that provided setting or evidence for various theoretical approaches. Louis Henry MORGAN (1881) used house forms as evidence of domestic social organization, inferring from large collective spaces the presence of cooperative domestic groups. This approach assumes a degree of "fit" or congruence between social groups and their activities that are contained by built form. The size and composition of HOUSEHOLDS are directly expressed in dwelling form and, as family size and composition changes through the DEVELOPMENTAL CYCLE, pressure is placed on residents to modify the physical structure. Activity-area researchers argue that the spatial organization of patterned social behavior is conditioned by sociopolitical complexity and determines the type, size, and layout of segmented or partitioned spaces (Kent 1990). But domestic forms do more than accommodate and regulate: they also express family hierarchies, gender relations, and social status. Household reproductive strategies may seek to utilize domestic architectural forms to inculcate familial values through the internal organization of space and express family status through exterior decoration (Blanton 1994).

Built forms are symbolic expressions of social, political, psychological, and even cosmological principles. Houses, temples, and public spaces constitute the material embodiment of structural homologies, formal generative capacities, and metaphor. According to STRUCTURALISTS, architectural forms replicate the structures of social and symbolic systems, which are all grounded in analogous unconscious mental structures organized into binary oppositions (Hugh-Jones 1979). Such unconscious mental structures also find expression in the production of formal geometries that may take precedence over the accommodation of activity during building design and construction (Glassie 1975).

In its mnemonic capacity architecture contains both cues for behavior (Hillier & Hanson 1984) and acts as metaphor, a representation and explanation of a culture's essential MYTH and COSMOLOGY (Griaule 1954). Architectural forms are evocative because humans predicate space upon themselves and incorporate qualities of that space in constituting themselves that they then project into other arenas of action (J. Fernandez 1984). Spatially constituted meanings may be activated through RITUAL or may be experienced in everyday life as a form of theater (see PLACE).

Architectural forms have a profound impact on such individual and group behaviors as perception, privacy, and personal space. People who live in "carpentered worlds" with three-dimensional architectural forms are more likely to be deceived by optical illusions than those who live with round buildings (Segall et al. 1966). Privacy, as defined by the individual's (or group's) control over access to the self (I. Altman & Chemers 1980), is often mediated by architectural forms. The Mehinacu have flimsy dwellings that create tensions by permitting full knowledge of neighbors' activities, but that also drive people to seek periodic seclusion. As a result, the Mehinacu become masters of manipulating information, according to Gregor's (1977) dramaturgical analysis. Asserted to be a cultural universal, the definition of privacy emphasizing the individual has been questioned as a largely Western European concept; nevertheless, it has been successfully adapted in non-Western studies (Pellow 1993). Proxemic studies of personal spatial relations postulate a bubble of variable size depending on the culture to regulate both interpersonal interactions and relations with the built environment (E. Hall 1966). Notions of "crowding" imply that built forms may pathologically pressure behavior, but in fact tolerance levels and preferences for certain spatial arrangements vary greatly across cultures (Pader 1993).

Architectural forms have complex interactions with social, political, economic, and historical forces that link ideological and symbolic factors with the social production of the physical environment. Research on this topic comes largely from geographers, historians, and social theorists, who examine how built forms are not only produced, but act on human behavior to reproduce the very conditions that gave rise to them. In spatializing social theory, Giddens (1984) proposed the notion of structuration to describe the process by which individuals are continually socialized through everyday activities within a spatial context, the locale, to generate individual (microlevel) behaviors that on a larger (macro) level reproduce the structural conditions of society. Similarly, Bourdieu

(1977) postulated the concept of "habitus," the predispositions people collectively use to produce, among other things, the material-environmental conditions that, in turn, act as mnemonics that are activated through action to socialize children and adults into reproducing those very same conditions.

The cultural examination of contemporary and urban architectural forms and spaces necessarily incorporates historical dimensions, such as Foucault's conception of architecture as a political technology rising to full power in the modern era. Foucault argued that modern institutions join special knowledge and power to subjugate and segregate the individual (body) through enclosure and segmentation. In the panopticon prison form, hierarchical spatial ordering and control of the individual are achieved in a single architectural form that permits surveillance, regulates circulation, and isolates inmates. As such, architecture acts as an institution for maintaining the power of one group over another and functions as a mechanism for coding reciprocal relationships (Foucault 1977b). Examination of architectural schemes created by modernists in developing countries finds an emphasis on defamiliarizing, dehistoricizing, and totalizing visions employed by designers and planners to create new urban forms (Rabinow 1989).   DL

further reading Blier 1987; M. Cooper & Rodman 1992; J. Duncan 1981; J. Fernandez 1977; Holston 1989; A. King 1984; Lawrence 1989; S. Low & Chambers 1989; P. Oliver 1987; Rapoport 1982

art In the sense of aesthetic embellishment of objects, dwellings, or even the human body, art is to be found in every culture, small-scale as well as complex. Each has its own distinctive art style. Style in art refers to a consideration of the component elements of art and how those elements are put together. Franz BOAS, who studied the distinctive art style of the Northwest Coast, described style as the result of the interaction between the medium being worked, the tools, and the culturally defined movements employed in using those tools (1927). Style is a hierarchical concept. One can speak of the style of the individual artist, of a city like Florence, or of a single society. At a still more abstract level, the general features that delineate the art style of the Italian Renaissance or of an entire cultural area such as the Northwest Coast can be discerned.

The art historian Meyer Schapiro had an important influence on how anthropologists viewed the art of the people they studied. Style to Schapiro constituted a language, with its own internal structure and expressiveness (Schapiro 1953: 287). Several anthropologists have also noted the analogy between art and language. Forge talked about the rules of combination of elements in art as being equivalent to syntax in language (1970, 1973). He showed how in Abelam art, the painted faces of the initiators of boys, the woven masks that decorate yams used in ceremonies, and the faces of carved ancestral *nggwalndu* figures are all stylistically the same, communicating ritually based male creativity, which contrasts with biologically based female creativity.

LÉVI-STRAUSS employed a STRUCTURALIST approach to meaning in art, in which the meaning of an element or object is revealed when it is shown to be an element within a structure of relationships (1982). He demonstrated how the Salish *Swaihwe* mask and Kwakiutl *Xwexwe* mask are both characterized by protuberant, cylinder-shaped eyes and a lolling tongue while the Kwakiutl *Dzonokwa* mask has deep, sunken eyes or narrow slits and a round, pursed mouth. Lévi-Strauss argued that the Salish *Swaihwe* mask, associated with copper and wealth acquisition diffused to the neighboring Kwakiutl where, known as *Xwexwe*, it became associated with the red cod, in *opposition* to copper, the Kwakiutl symbol of wealth. The Kwakiutl *Dzonokwa* mask, though in art style a reversal of the *Xwexwe* mask, has the same semantic value as the Salish *Swaihwe*, giver of riches. These masks therefore form a transformation set, whose meanings can only be determined when they are examined in relationship to one another.

To LEACH, the function of art was to illustrate moral principles by transgressing society's boundaries. Art crosses ambiguous cultural boundaries and says "what may not be said" in real life, that which is taboo. Leach showed how in Michaelangelo's "Pietà", the dead Christ and his Virgin Mother, across whose knees he is lying, are portrayed as being the same age, and that this creates latent incestuous emotions (Leach 1973: 230–2).

Leach also argued that intrinsically ambiguous things are SACRED, and therefore are given exaggerated aesthetic treatment (1983: 256). Kwakiutl art also crosses tabooed boundaries (Rosman & Rubel 1990). Summer and winter respectively represent secular and sacred periods, and the art employed in the rituals held at these different seasons contrasts in style. At summer POTLATCHES, chiefs wear masks, carved in a secular art style, that represent descent from their mythological ancestors, the wolf, raven, bear, eagle, etc. This reflects the notion that ANIMALS and humans are interchangeable. Winter is a sacred time when the spirits come into the village. At the Winter Ceremonial, young people initiated into secret societies cross the boundary from the natural world into that of the tabooed supernatural world and become dangerous cannibal spirits. The art style of the masks worn by the participants is an exaggerated, distorted style, contrasting with the art style used in the masks worn during the secular summer potlatch rituals. Thus, the strongly curved beak of the eagle in the Eagle mask used in the secular potlatch becomes the greatly distorted beak of the "Crooked Beak of Heaven."

Levi-Strauss's essay *The savage mind* explores the human propensity to create systems of classification (1966). Art provides an entry into a culture's system of CLASSIFICATION. Boas described how Northwest Coast societies have a single category of all things they see as "living" – mosquitoes, whales, wolves, earthquakes, and humans – and how this is recognized in their art by portraying all members of this category with a face (1927). The living things within the category are distinguished from one another in the art by a set of distinctive features (the way that eyes, ears, noses, and mouths are portrayed), which are the essential characteristics of the animals from the point of view of the "natives". Human beings and animals constitute subcategories, with animal ears placed on the top of the head and human ears always on the side. The Northwest Coast conceptualization of the relationship between humans and animals bridges the gap between nature and culture, since animals can be transformed into humans and humans into animals in art, RITUAL, and MYTH.

Some have argued that the art of small-scale societies is the product of a communal tradition and that the artist remains anonymous in these societies, whereas our society exalts the creativity of the individual artist. This erroneous idea is a construct of Western society (S. Price 1989). Though artists had to operate within the constraints of a cultural art style in small-scale societies, the art produced was an individual creative interpretation.

How can ordinary human beings create objects that people believe to be supernatural and sacred? Davenport, who worked in the eastern Solomon Islands, argued that, "Even the cognitive processes of creativity of the artist are interpreted in a supernatural way. Ask an artist how he conceived of a particular sculpture, and he will answer that he dreamed of it . . . [through] stimulation from a deity" (1968: 422).

The carvers of masks for the Poro Society of the Gola and Vai peoples of West Africa think that the supernatural is involved in the production of a mask, and in public they deny the local human workmanship of the art object. Carvers are seen as marginal, yet the artist's vision is essential to the society that views him with suspicion and scorn (d'Azevedo 1973: 144). The carver himself experiences great elation on seeing the mask he has carved come to life when worn in a performance. The carver feels as though he had given birth to a child.   AR & PR

assimilation *See*   ACCULTURATION, ETHNIC GROUPS

association includes identification, interaction, and recognition of commonalities between persons, things, and ideas; or an organization based on such principles. Humans associate with other humans, and also with nonhuman and nonliving beings such as deities, spirits, and totemic emblems. Associations among humans overlap in complex ways, and most people belong to various kinds simultaneously.

Concepts of associations vary widely cross-culturally, but anthropological usage often focuses on three distinct types:

1. *group*: a finite set, often named, whose members sense common belonging and might recognize a single leader or organizer. Examples are households, clans, churches, councils, companies, leagues, clubs, federations, and nation-states
2. *network*: a series or web of interpersonal linkages, not necessarily bounded or named, such that each member might be directly linked only to as few as one or two others, without knowing or contacting other members beyond, or sharing any feeling of common membership (M. G. Smith 1974). Examples are chains of friends, of neighbors, of affinal kin, and of trading partners; or a web of acquaintances combining different such links
3. *category*: any set of persons (bounded or unbounded) with one or more features, interests, or purposes in common; examples include women, sharecroppers, stamp collectors, migrants, and male infant Brahmins

Groups, networks, and categories can merge and overlap, and the first and third terms are sometimes loosely interchanged.

Anthropologists who study SOCIAL ORGANIZATION variously sort associations further into types by employing additional criteria such as namedness, boundedness, voluntariness, degree of centralization, autonomy, communality of property, and formality of procedure. Associations may be single- or multipurposed, stratified or egalitarian. Singularly important is whether an association's members share a sense of common belonging. For full corporate status a group should have the following characteristics: identity, presumed perpetuity, closure and membership, autonomy within a given sphere, exclusive common

affairs, set procedures, and organization (M. G. Smith 1974: 94). Corporateness may also be extended to control over property, limitations on personal liabilities, and other things. In practice, however, few associations have all these features.

Associations described as "informal" are those with casual, fluid styles of management, and those beyond government registration, taxation, and control. In studies of economic and political development, "voluntary associations," including self-help groups, are often considered an important alternative, or complement, to state and commercial organizations (March & Taqqu 1985).

A few principles variously underlying associations in many societies include sex, age (including age set and age grade), descent, kinship (fictive or real), marital status, locality (of origin or residence), mode of livelihood or occupation, language, marital status, religion, class, caste, race, rank, and political affiliation. These principles are often combined (as in the Young Women's Christian Association); and one principle can mask another (as in the Muslim Murid Brotherhood, which is also an organization of Senegalese Wolof-speakers). Associations differ in formality and in real or intended duration; some groups, like many East African lineages, come to life only in particular social contexts, or for particular purposes. Ad hoc or short-term political associations include factions, cabals, coalitions, caucuses, committees, assemblies, forums, and rallies.

In one common form of CLASSIFICATION, a set of persons, things, or ideas may be identified by "family resemblances" such that each member of the class has most but not all the features that define the class as a whole, and such that any single feature is common to some but not all the members of the class. Anthropologists usually call this kind of classification "polythetic" (R. Needham 1975); biologists, "polytypic."

Associations are best known in relation to other associations, and anthropologists have paid much attention to the structures and processes of social divisions between them: the "relations of relations." Groups gain solidarity by opposition to other groups. Cross-cutting schisms in society can ironically help bind SOCIETY together by enabling persons divided in one way (e.g., by ETHNIC GROUP) to find commonality another way (e.g., by GENDER). Deepening one social division may thus reduce another.

Many theorists of social EVOLUTION and MODERNIZATION since Sir Henry MAINE (1861), including Lewis Henry MORGAN (1877), Emile DURKHEIM (1933), Ferdinand Tönnies (1957), and Talcott Parsons (1966), have perceived the gradual replacement of associations based on ascribed STATUS (e.g., descent groups) with others based more on contract or voluntary association (e.g., companies, territorial chiefdoms, states). The latter can even take over some functions of human biological reproduction, as Robertson (1991) showed. Not all anthropologists agree, however, that evolutionary shifts from KINSHIP to other forms of association are inevitable, irreversible, or desirable. It seems that all societies combine ascribed and achieved associations, or voluntary and involuntary ones; moreover, many associations themselves combine the principles internally.   PS
further reading Boissevain 1974; K. Cook & Whitmeyer 1992; M. Douglas 1986; Vincent 1990; S. Wright 1994; Wuthnow 1991

asymmetric alliance *See* ALLIANCE SYSTEMS

augury is the divination of future events from omens, portents, or chance occurrences. It has been reported from all periods of human history – from classical Greece to contemporary times – and from all parts of the world. The medium of augury is often natural phenomena, such as the flight of birds among the Dayak of Borneo (Metcalf 1976; Sandin 1980), the splitting of heated animal bones among the Naskapi in North America (Speck 1935; O. Moore 1957), and the response of chickens to poison among the Azande in Africa (Evans-Pritchard 1937). Analyses of augural systems have varied between psychological (D. Freeman 1960) and functional-ecological interpretations (Dove 1993b).   MRD & TC
See also MAGIC, WITCHCRAFT

avunculate is the institution where a mother's brother has primary authority over his sister's son, who is also his primary heir. It is usually found in MATRILINEAL lineage systems where the father stands in a formal relation of affinity rather than ascendance to his sons, that is, he is viewed more as the mother's husband than as the child's father. In such cases it is the mother's brother who wields the sort of male authority held by the father in other systems because he is the son's nearest male ascendant. The avunculate is often associated with AVUNCULOCAL RESIDENCE.
                                                    MR

avunculocal residence is a postmarital residence pattern in which the newly married couple take up residence with one of their uncles, usually the husband's mother's brother (VIRI-AVUNCULOCAL RESIDENCE). This is typically found in MATRILINEAL societies and is associated with the AVUNCULATE. This residence pattern permits the geographical concentration of male lineage-mates and preservation of male-controlled lineage wealth in a matrilineal system.   MR
further reading Malinowski 1929

B

---

band societies are small-scale, mobile foraging societies organized on the basis of kinship (see FORAGERS). In Julian STEWARD's (1955) cultural evolutionary scheme, band societies exhibited a primary level of social integration that was contrasted with TRIBES, CHIEFDOMS, and STATES. Band organization is closely associated with forms of hunting and gathering subsistence in which mobility and small groupings are optimal in terms of survival. In much of anthropological theory, bands are assumed to be the basic social unit of human history larger than the family prior to the invention of agriculture.

Recent foraging bands share a number of characteristics: they are small in scale, composed of units of 30–50 people; nomadic, moving three or more times per year; and based on communal LAND TENURE. Most, but not all, are politically EGALITARIAN SOCIETIES with an absence of formal leadership, and almost all have a religious focus based on SHAMANISTIC healing. On two other key aspects band societies display considerable variation: GENDER egalitarianism is strong in some groups (Bushmen, Pygmies) but weakly developed in others (Eskimo, Australian Aborigines), and band societies in general are not particularly peaceful. Although comparisons are difficult some have higher rates of HOMICIDE than American inner cities (Lee 1979).

Not all foraging peoples are organized on the basis of bands. Where resources permit larger and more permanent settlements, more complex foraging societies appear, leading to the useful distinction in the archeological literature between simple and complex hunter–gatherers (T. Price & Brown 1985). Band organization has provided a rich source of anthropological

theory, beginning in the nineteenth century with speculation by classical evolutionists on the origin of the family. Scholars as diverse as MORGAN (1877), TYLOR (1871), Engels (1902), and Freud (1930) saw the primeval horde as the "Ur" unit of society, a grouping that was variously seen to be violent, promiscuous, incestuous, or all three. Ethnographic study of twentieth-century band societies supported none of these lurid projections, finding monogamous marriage and stable kin relations at the core of virtually all bands. Steward (1936) offered a serviceable typology of bands, dividing them into patrilineal, composite, and family bands depending largely on the nature of subsistence. More recent critics of Steward have questioned whether the three types are not overly reified. In writing about the seasonal life of the Eskimo, Marcel MAUSS had observed that they divided their year into a larger group phase, "la vie publique" and a smaller group phase, "la vie privée" (Mauss & Beuchat 1979). In Mauss's view these alternating phases served critically important social functions, balancing the need for sociability and interaction with the need for quiet family life. Since almost all band societies display this aggregation/dispersion pattern, Steward's composite and family bands may be two phases/moments of the same underlying social dynamic.

Since the 1960s students of band societies have become more attentive to the dimension of history. Elman Service (1966) was among the first to argue that Steward's composite band may be a response of foraging peoples to the disruption and depopulation brought about by colonization. He postulated that the patrilocal band was the basic human unit. This seemed problematic since the flexibility of the "composite" band was much more responsive to ecological and demographic variation in all historical circumstances. With the rapid incorporation in recent decades of most band societies into larger polities and their domination by markets and states, issues of history and the politics of domination and resistance have become paramount in current research. Some "revisionists" have gone so far as to argue that band societies are themselves a product of the destruction of indigenous societies by the inroads made by merchant capital (Wilmsen 1989a). Others, acknowledging the abundant archaeological and historical evidence for the antiquity of bands, have concentrated on the ways that band societies have been able to creatively adapt to living as encapsulated minorities while preserving their identities and way of life (Leacock & Lee 1982).

RiL

See also EVOLUTION

barter is a simultaneous economic exchange where one type of good or service is exchanged directly for another type of good or service without the use, or even the concept, of MONEY. Barter is distinguished from GIFT EXCHANGE by the lack of debt in the relationship: the two partners are not expected to participate in another barter exchange with the same partners, although they may do so. It is distinguished from commodity exchange (or MARKET exchange) by its inability to establish a price since there can be no price without money. In barter there are no mediating goods used to conceptualize, or express, the values of the two types of goods or services exchanged so there would seem to be no socially expressed way to establish the value of items bartered.

The spatial distribution of barter seems to be universal, occurring in foraging societies as well as in the most monetarized and market-dominated cases. Yet systematic knowledge of barter is lacking, and it is fairly clear that the term is used in a variety of senses.

RHun

further reading Humphrey & Hugh-Jones 1992a

Benedict, Ruth Fulton (1887–1948) Ruth Fulton was born in 1887 and spent her early years in Norwich, New York. Her father, a doctor, died when she was 2, and the family subsequently moved to Buffalo. In 1905 she entered Vassar College, where she studied English literature. After graduating in 1909, she spent several years in social work and teaching before marrying Stanley Rossiter Benedict in 1914. She then began a series of studies on feminist authors, and completed a book on Mary Wollstonecraft. In 1919 she enrolled at the New School for Social Research, where she studied anthropology under Alexander Goldenweiser and Elsie Clews Parsons. She moved to the graduate program at Columbia in 1921, studying under Franz BOAS. She wrote a dissertation on "The concept of the guardian spirit in North America," and received her Ph.D. in 1923.

Benedict spent the next eight years at Columbia, subsisting on part-time and summer teaching positions. From 1925 she served as editor of the *Journal of American Folklore*. She also conducted fieldwork among several Southwestern tribes, notably the Zuni. In addition, Benedict was active as a poet, publishing extensively under the pseudonym Anne Singleton. Her marriage to Stanley Benedict ended, and she developed close friendships with Edward SAPIR and Margaret MEAD. In 1931 she was appointed assistant professor at Columbia, and she became full professor in 1948. During World War II, Benedict worked in the Office of War Information, writing cultural studies of allied and enemy nations. She was elected vice-president of the American Anthropological Association in 1939, and president in 1946. She died in 1948.

Benedict's research investigated the relationship between cultural systems and personality. She pioneered the "configurational approach," which saw cultures as integrated systems that tended to produce characteristic personalities. In *Patterns of culture* (1934a), she analyzed the production of personality among the Zuni, the Dobuans, and the Kwakiutl; she argued that each culture represented a distinct configuration, which emphasized or suppressed particular emotional tendencies among its members. The book, with its relativist approach and its strong antiracist message, became one of the most influential social scientific works of the twentieth century. Benedict's writing sought to demonstrate the profound influence of culture on individual psychology, and to foster more tolerant attitudes toward cultural variation and deviance.

Later, while working in the Office of War Information, Benedict developed a variety of methods for studying "culture at a distance." In addition to interviewing expatriates, she analyzed literature, drama, and other artifacts of the cultures to be investigated. The results were surprisingly insightful ethnographies of societies that were wholly inaccessible to traditional anthropological fieldwork. After preliminary studies of Romania, the Netherlands, Germany, and Thailand, Benedict focused on Japan. The result was *The chrysanthemum and the sword* (1946), a study of Japanese NATIONAL CHARACTER. Many details of this work have since come in for criticism, but its continued influence in both Japan and the United States testifies to Benedict's ability to achieve penetrating insights under very difficult conditions. It is also an excellent example of her use of anthropology as a means of promoting intercultural understanding and reconciliation.   AB
See also CONFIGURATIONISM, CULTURE AND PERSONALITY, EMOTIONS, HUMANISTIC ANTHROPOLOGY, NATION, RACE, RACISM
further reading Benedict 1935, 1940; Caffrey 1989; M. Mead 1959; Modell 1983

berdache is the "man–woman" or "woman–man" of the North American Indians. The berdache were individuals who identified with the GENDER opposite to the one normal to their anatomical sex and adopted the modes of dress, behavior, and livelihood of that gender. Berdache were most commonly anatomical males. The berdache status was found throughout the North American West and the Great Plains, but was almost completely unknown in the East. Berdache often had a high ritual status.   MR
See also HOMOSEXUALITY, SEX, WOMEN
further reading Callendar & Kochems 1987; Roscoe 1987

bifurcate collateral is a system of kin terminology in which collateral ascendants are distinguished from lineals and from each other. For instance, the father, father's brother, and mother's brother would all be called by different terms in a bifurcate collateral system.   MR
See also BIFURCATE MERGING

bifurcate merging is a system of kinship terminology in which ascendants on one parent's side are merged with lineals. For instance, the father's brother may be merged, or called by the same term, as the father, while the mother's brother is called by another term. Classic examples of bifurcate merging systems are OMAHA and CROW KINSHIP SYSTEMS (Murdock 1947).   MR
See also BIFURCATE COLLATERAL

bigamy   *See* POLYANDRY, POLYGYNY

bigman, big-man, big man   Derived from the Melanesian Pidgin words *bikpela* (big fellow) meaning "big, large, great, well known, famous" and *man* (man). In Papua New Guinea the phrase *ol bikpela man* may refer to adults, headmen of a village, important men, or men of influence and authority (Mihalic 1971). In anthropology, "bigman" is now both a technical word and a textbook cliché, especially among scholars interested in social EVOLUTION who see the Melanesian bigman not only as a sociopolitical archetype but also as the typological marker of a primitive stage in the course of human social evolution leading to the development of CHIEFDOMS and COMPLEX SOCIETIES (i.e., civilization).

As a typological marker, a bigman is said to be the leader of a small group whose position of influence is not hereditary but acquired: "A bigman achieves his status by being particularly good at the male activities of his culture, whether it be hunting or fighting or raising pigs or growing crops or a bit of all these" (Orme 1981: 140). According to some authorities, the main difference between a bigman and a chief is whether leadership authority is hereditary or acquired (A. Johnson & Earle 1987: 220). Some claim this difference is a crucial step in human social evolution, although

Earle (1987: 288) considered the truly defining differences between bigman societies and chiefdoms to be contrasts in their scale of sociopolitical integration, centrality of decision making, and socioeconomic stratification.

The popularity of "bigman" as sociological type is due largely to an influential essay by Marshall Sahlins (1963). Its characterization of polities and economies in the Pacific under the rubrics "bigman" and "chief" has been popular in academic and lay discourse on the Pacific Islanders even though – as Sahlins disarmingly acknowledged – anthropologists (and Pacific Islanders) know that bigmen and chiefs share much in common and both are found in each area (G. Marcus 1989: 180).

Sahlins portrayed the world of the Melanesian bigman not only as different from that of Polynesian chiefs but also as inherently unstable because it sets ceilings on political authority that limit the intensification of household production and its use to support wider political organization. He said that these fundamental defects of the Melanesian plan had been overcome in Polynesia (for reasons he leaves unspecified) and as a consequence, political life in Polynesia constitutes an evolutionary advance over Melanesian orders of interpersonal dominance in the human control of human affairs. Sahlins saw chiefly power in Polynesia as a more effective, more successful "means of societal collaboration on economic, political, indeed all cultural fronts" (1963: 300). Or, as John Liep summarized: "Stated bluntly, Sahlins's conception was of a movement from anarchy towards the state" (1991: 28).

While the distinctions between Melanesian bigmen and Polynesian chiefs seen by Sahlins have often been contested (see Terrell 1986: 195–240), some scholars add that resorting to such stereotypes shows how easily locally constructed practices, interests, and meanings of leadership in different societies (e.g., Lederman 1990, 1991) may be bowdlerized or sacrificed in comparative research. Others, notably Maurice Godelier (1986), have responded by proposing refinements in Sahlins's original typology. Godelier said that anthropologists should distinguish Melanesian

"great men" from "bigmen" depending on how (and why) men transact exchanges with one another (M. Strathern 1991). Others further propose that a more realistic way of talking about great men, bigmen, and chiefs is to plot the similarities and differences of the types of society in which these kinds of leaders are found on a triangular graph so that the combinations of abstract elements defining their distinctive features can be seen as merely three idealized polar extremes that, in pure form, "do not correspond to any existing empirical societies" (Liep 1991: 33, fig. 2.1). However, if typological characterization of human societies is fundamentally flawed, as some maintain, it is unclear what is gained by this legerdemain (Mosko 1991).

JT
See also EVOLUTION, POLITICAL ANTHROPOLOGY

further reading Godelier & Strathern 1991; D. Oliver 1955; Ongka 1979; A. Strathern 1971

bilateral kinship is the reckoning of an individual's (EGO's) kin relations through both the mother's (matrilateral) and father's (patrilateral) sides. Bilateral kinship serves as the basis for the formation of egocentric KINDREDS. "Bilateral" is sometimes used loosely as a synonym for "COGNATIC."   MR

bilocal residence *See* AMBILOCAL RESIDENCE

biological anthropology is the study of humans and closely related extant and extinct species in an evolutionary framework. It incorporates, or overlaps with, such fields as human paleontology, DEMOGRAPHY, ecology, reproductive ecology, forensics and paleopathology, primatology, SOCIOBIOLOGY, evolutionary psychology, and the study of genetic and physical variation and ADAPTATION. The distinctions among these subfields have been shaped by historical developments and are largely a matter of taxonomic focus, temporal framework, or interest in a particular physiological or behavioral system.

Evolutionary theory

Perhaps the most significant recent over-arching development has been the introduction of a more mature evolutionary theory drawn from the biological sciences as a guiding principle and methodological substrate for the field (Dawkins 1986). Evolutionary theory is a powerful generator of new ideas, but serves equally well to limit the interpretation of physical and behavioral observations. For example, earlier physical anthropologists accepted the distinction between RACES based on overt physical differences as a self-evident feature of humanity, collecting countless measurements to support speculative theories. By contrast, modern evolutionary theory has found no clear lines among human races, other than some interesting "clines" of geographical variation, and can demonstrate no evolutionary significance to any such differences. Modern biological anthropologists focus on variation at the level of individual genes, and the partial and modified expression of this variation on the level of individuals – differences that are most often invisible (Cavalli-Sforza et al. 1994).

Primatology

The field of primatology overlaps significantly with biological anthropology. Although the majority of mammals do not possess complex social systems, most primates, humans included, do. The emergent view among primatologists is that primates benefit from group living by the protection it provides from predation and possibly INFANTICIDE, but at the cost of increased competition for resources (Hausfater & Hrdy 1984). This competition, together with strategic behavior associated with mating, probably shapes much of primate social behavior (Fleagle 1988). Primates are typically limited to tropical or subtropical habitats, reproduce slowly, and exhibit a wide range of locomotory and dietary adaptations. The physical, dietary, and social adaptations of different species of primate seem to vary according to phylogenetic and ecological factors (R. Martin & Martin 1990). Thus, many key questions in primatology address the causal relationships between individual behavior, group structure, and these physical and behavioral adaptations in an ecological context.

The term "primatology" also encompasses research using primates on cognition, language, anatomy, physiological systems, conservation, and ontogeny (development).

All animals partition their energy for growth and reproduction into ontogenetic stages and divide their efforts among different categories of behavior (foraging, mating, etc.). Strategies of life history and allocation of time and energy are subject to natural selection, optimizing reproductive success. However, since each species is virtually guaranteed to be unique with respect to genetic heritage and ecology, the creative process of natural selection inevitably generates results that are also unique. For this reason, biological anthropologists infer general patterns at broad taxonomic levels, in order to eventually understand physiology and behavior at the finer scales, such as species or sex. Individual males and females are inclined to a limited number of competitive, reproductive, and nurturing strategies. Although the distribution and quality of food, habits of predators, and interspecies competitors further shape the behavioral repertoire, individual species may diverge from the expected pattern in significant ways. For example, where social primate males expend some effort (indirectly) in offspring care and protection, human males contribute significantly to the nurturing of offspring (Kinzey 1987). Were it not for an understanding of how behavioral strategies vary across the larger taxonomic and functional groups, human fatherhood (for all its variation across cultures) would not be recognized as the unusual feature that it is.

Humans are unique in their vast intelligence, but few researchers agree on what intelligence is, what it does, how it develops, or how it arose through evolution. Therefore, much primatological research has attempted to define "intelligence" and outline the features of cognition that are shared among humans and other primates, and those that are unique to humans. One important method is the study of brain function and evolution by focusing on differences in raw and relative brain size, relative size and distribution of brain structures, connectivity and organization of brain structures, and the measurement and characterization of cognitive abilities. Primates (particularly humans) have relatively large brains for their body mass compared with other mammals and display significant differences in their cortical features. Between major primate groups, such as prosimians, Old World and New World monkeys, and apes, there are fundamental differences. Cerebral structures that are associated with memory, planning, and sequencing of events are larger and apparently more important in anthropoid primates, including humans, than in the average mammal. In humans, some of these structures appear to be used for language. Thus, although the uniqueness of human language cannot be denied, it may involve capacities, or at least brain structures, that are widespread among primates.

Theories about brain evolution and function abound, and are often maintained despite little support from the available evidence. It is still widely asserted that human intelligence and brain size increased in association with upright posture and locomotion, which freed the hands for manipulation of tools, although this is contradicted by the evidence. The idea that the human brain is a primate brain with novel structures added to it has also been proposed but is not supported. The reorganization of the connections among brain structures to support language or other unique human cognitive abilities has been assumed or proposed but again is not supported. Large changes in the relative size of different brain structures is likely an important difference between human and other primate brains. This, together with the recruitment of existing structures and circuits for novel functions, probably accounts for language abilities and other cognitive features found in humans (Deacon 1997).

Biological anthropology has essentially reached the conclusion that LANGUAGE is fairly uniform in its expression and function (deep universal GRAMMAR) across all societies and cultures (see HISTORICAL LINGUISTICS). However, there is no agreement on the ontogeny of language or on the selective forces that likely shaped language evolution. Chomskian ideas of a full-

blown, de novo emergence of language contrast with the view that language was shaped by natural selection, and thus probably went through stages of varying function and details of ontogeny. Another contrast exists between those who feel that language is a complex adaptive system underlain by a complex genetic structure, and those who propose that the operation and functionality of language develop from nonspecific underlying genetic structures and are shaped largely by the ontogenetic adaptation of the brain to the body in which it grows and thus also the physical and sociocultural environment in which the body exists (Pinker 1994).

Paleoanthropology

Paleoanthropology, including the use of molecular genetics to generate phylogenetic schema, incorporates evidence from a wide range of fields, including paleontology, paleoclimatology, archaeology, the sciences that support dating techniques, isotopic analysis of remains to determine diet and climate, etc. The key interests in the field include:

1. the origin of primates and the phylogenetic relationships among the major primate taxa
2. the divergence, diversification, and convergence of primate adaptations among the major groups (especially Old World versus New World monkeys)
3. the phylogeny, ecology, and behavior of Miocene hominoids (a term that refers to apes in general)
4. the patterns of speciation and extinction and the behavioral ecology of the australopithecines and other closely related bipedal apes
5. changing adaptations in the hominids of the early and middle Pleistocene, especially early *Homo* species and *Homo erectus*, including behavioral changes inferred from material culture and the geographic spread of hominids across a wide range of habitats
6. the evolution of modern humans, which includes a remarkable loss of robustness (muscle mass and bone thickness) relative to earlier hominids
7. the morphologically nondramatic but still important changes in behavior of

Homo sapiens with the development of horticulture and husbandry, the invention of ceramic and metal technologies, village and urban settlement, and migration and urbanization.

Issues and controversies in human paleontology fall into two categories. One concerns the pattern of evolution at the large scale for any given time period, including how many species are represented by the fossil record and how they relate to each other. The other attempts the functional or ecological reconstruction of particular taxa, such as the nature of australopithecine locomotion or the differences between the foraging behaviors of Neanderthals and modern humans.

In the fray of discussion over which (as well as whose) fossil is oldest and which species of early hominid can claim patrimony over all others, it is easy to lose sight of some of the most important realizations that have emerged since the mid-1970s (Brace 1995). For example, owing to advances in molecular genetics and reinterpretations of the fossil record, the time frame of human evolution has been significantly shortened. With rare (but not insignificant) dissent, the age of the split between chimps and humans has been placed at between five and six million years ago, a revision downward by more than half the time previously estimated. The search for the "last common ancestor" (a term that has replaced the much-maligned "missing link") for both humans and the chimpanzee now draws on the increasingly rich fossil record in the much tighter time frame of the late Miocene, the Plio-Pleistocene, and the early Pleistocene, when there was a profusion of hominid forms. Even modest "lumpers" (those who try to include the largest number of variations within a group or species) must admit that several species of hominid existed at the same time in East, South, and Central Africa. This radiation of hominids is associated with two major adaptive shifts: the beginnings of bipedalism (though not necessarily humanlike in form or function) and the enlargement of teeth with the associated thickening of tooth enamel (suggesting major dietary shifts from the presumed,

but not yet discovered, last common ancestor). From this bushy radiation of hominid forms arose, for reasons unknown, a single species or very closely related set of species widely referred to as *Homo erectus*.

Human evolution

The large human brain is generally considered to be one of our most important adaptations, even if there is very little agreement on what it is actually used for. The consensus about the timing and pattern of brain size increase in the *Homo* lineage is that there were probably two or three shifts (separated by periods of stasis, or very gradual change) to a somewhat larger brain. Early hominid brain size (relative to body size) was not impressive by primate standards. Approximately modern relative human brain size was achieved only a half a million years ago or less, about 10 percent of the entire history of our lineage since the split from the other African apes. And if the general rule of brain–body mass relationships holds for gracile modern humans (and it may not), relative brain sizes of modern measure may be as recent as 100,000–200,000 years ago. Thus, the major patterns of evolutionary change for virtually all of hominid evolution are not related to impressively (and expensively) large brains.

The origin of physiologically modern *Homo sapiens* is a central, perhaps infamous, debate in paleoanthropology. One theory argues that modern humans emerged in a limited geographic area of Africa and spread to colonize the rest of the world. An alternative model proposes that *Homo sapiens* arose simultaneously in many regions across the Old World. Few debates in anthropology have inspired so much public misunderstanding of an evolutionary issue or created so many false analogies. Although several genetic models based on mitochondrial DNA, and similar models based on nuclear DNA, suggest that all of modern humanity is descended from either one or a few small populations extant some time during the last 200,000 years, there is no scientific evidence that a single human female ("Eve") represented that gender's contribution to our species' breeding population (nor was there a Y-chromosome "Adam"). More importantly, the existence of such a demographic bottleneck is not necessarily connected to those changes that differentiate premodern humans (archaic *Homo sapiens*) from anatomically modern humans, because such a bottleneck could have occurred before, during, or after such evolutionary events. The essential relevance of the bottleneck model is that the vast majority of the premodern fossils found throughout the Old World cannot be genetically ancestral to any living humans. Molecular (DNA) and fossil evidence suggest that Africa is the homeland of any such single limited population. In contrast, the multiregional hypothesis, largely based on inferred similarities between archaic fossils and later skeletal remains and living humans, suggests simultaneous evolution across a wide geographic range, including Asia and Europe as well as Africa (Cavalli-Sforza et al. 1995).

Once physiologically (skeletally) modern humans arrive on the scene, research in biological anthropology narrows its focus with respect to broad evolutionary patterns, but does not reduce in significance. What were the processes involved in the historical spread of humans across the globe (remembering that primates are generally confined to tropical and subtropical habitats)? Of the many innovations (e.g., horticulture, animal husbandry, metallurgy), demographic changes (inferred decrease in birth spacing, changes in morbidity and longevity, shifts in population density), and other behavioral changes (different systems of kinship, trade and exchange, group organization, etc.), which if any may have been prime forces in affecting the others; what was the impetus for these changes; and why did these changes occur when they did rather than earlier or later? Biological anthropology addresses many of these issues with the use of archaeological data as well as isotopic study of bones and other remains.

Human behavioral biology
Human behavioral biology is one of the most recently developed and most misunderstood aspects of biological anthropology. The term "SOCIOBIOLOGY" was coined by the biologist E. O. Wilson (1975) to refer to the genetic and other biological underpinnings of social behavior in animals in general, and of ants and humans in particular. In the 1970s anthropologists and other evolutionary theorists began to employ such theoretical constructs as inclusive fitness or kin selection theory, reciprocal ALTRUISM theory, and parent–offspring conflict theory in the study of both human and nonhuman primate populations. A guiding principle in human behavioral biology is that humans are subject to the same biological principles that apply to primates, mammals, and animals in general. Any human exceptions must be proved; they cannot be assumed. Similarly, evolutionary (neo-Darwinian) hypotheses about human behavior must be tested with the same analytic rigor as any other scientific hypotheses. Along these lines, several studies of data from human societies have demonstrated that substantial proportions of observed variation in reproductive success, MARRIAGE SYSTEMS, inheritance rules, KINSHIP systems, manipulation of sex ratio, and the patterns of VIOLENCE or HOMICIDE, can be explained using evolutionary principles.

Evolutionary medicine and psychology
Two very recent subfields of biological anthropology have received a great deal of attention in the scholarly journals and public media: evolutionary (or Darwinian) medicine and evolutionary psychology. The former examines the discordance between a reconstructed human evolutionary heritage (as FORAGERS) and industrialized or urbanized life and the resulting diseases of the mind and body (Eaton et al. 1988). The latter postulates the existence of cognitive modules designed by natural selection to do well at solving certain kinds of problem common to an evolutionary context as foragers living off the land in small-scale societies (J. Barkow et al. 1992). Both fields apply evolutionary theory to answer questions about human behavior or physiology in novel ways, at the same time extending the purview of biological anthropology, one hopes usefully, toward new horizons.

GL

further reading Aiello & Dean 1990; Betzig et al. 1988; Cheney & Seyfarth 1990; Devor 1992; R. Foley 1987; Goodall 1986; Isaac 1989; S. Jones et al.

1992; Keller & Lloyd 1992; Konner 1982; Lewin 1993; Savage-Rumbaugh & Lewin 1994; Smuts 1987; Tanner 1990; Tattersall 1995; Trinkaus & Shipman 1993; K. Weiss 1993

birth control *See* EUGENICS, REPRODUCTION

blood is a bodily substance that has acquired extraordinary cultural elaboration such that its meanings go well beyond those derived from serology. Blood is never "just blood"; it always has powerful associations embedded in a variety of well-developed cosmological schema that are, nonetheless, quite variable cross-culturally.

Where blood is seen as a potent fluid whose alienation is dreaded, one may find bloodsucking rumors flourishing, as in East and Central Africa during colonial times when Europeans were believed to be vampires and their victims Africans (Luise White 1993). COLONIALISM, one might say, was sucking the life-blood out of Africa. The loss of blood is symbolically problematic even when it is not medically dangerous. For example, among the Kaguru of Tanzania, if blood is shed during a dispute, the offenders are fined more than if no blood is spilled, even if the injury is minor (Beidelman 1963).

The metaphoric power of blood is also evident in its role in RELIGION and particularly SACRIFICE. Throughout Africa, for instance, domestic ANIMALS are sacrificed to deities and ancestors (Heusch 1985), and the blood is often drizzled over an altar (Zahan 1979). In other religious traditions, the literal sacrifice of blood has been replaced by offerings that symbolize blood (M. Douglas 1970a), such as the Christian Eucharist in which red wine ritually drunk by the communicant is said to be transformed by MAGIC into the blood of Jesus Christ (Feeley-Harnik 1981). Religious law is often quite strict about the treatment of blood and whether it is proper to consume it: both Jews and Muslims may eat meat only from animals killed and drained of blood, which is blessed by prayer as the animal is slaughtered (R. Cernea 1981).

What passes for blood is not always immediately obvious. For example, in many languages throughout Africa, the word for "semen" is actually the same as that for "blood" (Héritier 1982: 172). A somewhat similar conceptual system exists in Jamaica, where it is thought that both men and women have red and white blood, although only white blood – combined from both sexual partners – leads to conception (Sobo 1993). Elsewhere, including many societies in Melanesia (Knauft 1989), it is said that a fetus receives its blood from one parent only (more often the mother), with the rest of the body (especially the bones) coming exclusively from the other parent. In such ways sex and blood are intertwined as metaphorical sources for a philosophically based understanding of human society.

Blood and blood-related diseases are frequently subject to culturally specific notions about, for example, the value of a copious versus a scanty flow of blood during MENSTRUATION in Wales (Skultans 1988), the spoilage of a nursing mother's milk in Haiti (Farmer 1988), or the causes of high blood pressure among the Canadian Ojibwa (Garro 1988). In Japan, there is a well-developed classical ideology concerning the role of blood in regulating the body's four humors, which serves as the basis of cures for assorted illnesses (Picone 1989). The blood transmission of the HIV virus has made AIDS particularly susceptible to culturally variable elaboration (Farmer 1990; D. Feldmen 1990).

Popular ideas about blood in contemporary North America are as well developed as they are anywhere – although, because they are couched in an idiom of (folk) biology, it is often believed they are somehow more "real" than in other cultures, where they are presumed to be "symbolic." Yet what passes for common sense in one cultural setting may be anything but common elsewhere (C. Geertz 1983: 73–93). For example, the American fixation that only "blood" relationships – which essentially index biogenetic connections – are real, and hence permanent, means that, as David Schneider (1968: 24) put it, one can have an ex-husband but not an ex-mother. Consequently, ADOPTION is frequently resisted by infertile couples in favor of expensive technologies to create a fetus via scientific manipulation, including "surrogate motherhood" (Ragoné 1994), so that the child will have what is commonly accepted as a "blood" tie (M. Strathern 1992). In other societies where kinship ties are overtly recognized as social, such a fixation with a blood link would seem very symbolic indeed.

Ideas about the nature of blood can have more sinister consequences. In medieval Europe, Jews were persecuted by Christians, who accused them of murdering Christian children to use their blood in making *matzos* (Dundes 1991). The persistence of blood FEUDS in portions of Eastern Europe (Boehm 1984) has had devastating repercussions in recent years. Likewise, miscegenation laws formerly applied in a variety of countries, including South Africa, and many states in the United States. The rhetoric of "racial purity," aired continuously in Hitler's Germany, and demands for ethnic purity in the former Yugoslavia, all use blood as a key symbol, highlighting the potential danger of simplistic thinking about humans in terms of their "blood" ties.   AG

See also CLASSIFICATION, CONSANGUINITY, FICTIVE KINSHIP, INCEST TABOOS, KINSHIP, SYMBOLIC ANTHROPOLOGY

further reading Meigs 1984; V. Turner 1967

blood brotherhood is a bond or agreement of trust or cooperation between two or more people by a BLOOD PACT ritual involving physical acts such as rubbing wounds or consuming samples of each other's BLOOD (by itself or mixed into other food or drink). "Body-substance siblinghood" would be a more encompassing and accurate term because such bonds may involve females or mixed sexes in eastern and western central Africa (Tegnaeus 1952: 165, map) and the substance shared need not be blood. Reported in sources as early as Herodotus in the fifth century B.C.E. among the Scythians, blood brotherhood is common in, but not limited to, Africa and Arabia (see Tegnaeus 1952; Luise White 1994).

Shared-substance siblinghood does not usually mirror biological siblinghood precisely. Some who practice it deem blood-siblinghood a deeper bond, impos-

ing sterner mutual responsibilities, than biological siblinghood. Usually, blood-siblings refer to each other in terms of absolute equality – whereas biological siblings in many of the same societies do not (see Evans-Pritchard 1933: 398ff). Whereas shared-substance siblinghood seems most often to be a supplement for KINSHIP, in some settings it overlaps and reinforces this "real" kinship. Blood-siblinghood has sometimes carried with it prescriptions for or proscriptions against marriage with the blood-sibling's close kin, and there are many settings, in India for instance, where spouses themselves have exchanged blood.

Blood brotherhoods vary widely in their allowable choice of partners, their voluntary or compulsory nature, and whether the act binds only individuals or whole groups. Reasons for forming blood brotherhoods include peace making, gaining allies for WAR and FEUD, providing protection during travel, cementing trust for trading partnerships, and so on. The SACRIFICE of ANIMALS sometimes substitutes for the sharing of human body substances. Such surrogate substances are particularly prominant in Christian communion rituals, where bread and wine explicitly symbolize body and blood.   PS

See also FICTIVE KINSHIP

blood pacts or blood covenants are oaths taken by two or more individuals who swear mutual loyalty, usually on pain of death, after exchanging BLOOD with one another through cuts made on each of their bodies (Beattie 1958). In some areas the prevalence of HIV infection through blood transmission has, however, made some of these practices medically risky, often leading to a change in the ritual.

Although found around the world, some of the most detailed research by anthropologists has come from Africa. There, blood partners generally swear oaths or utter prayers to pledge mutual allegiance while making cuts; they might also lick each other's wounds (Paulme 1973). If one later violates the pact, it may be thought that the partner's blood will automatically take vengeance (Evans-Pritchard 1933). Similarly, when one dies, the blood partners may still be mystically joined (Beidelman 1963). Blood pacts were usually concluded between status equals (Evans-Pritchard 1933), although occasionally they were concluded between royals and commoners. Often, as with the Nyoro and the Kaguru, blood pacts were done with strangers in a distant land, as a means of gaining a permanent ally while traveling (Beidelman 1963). Among the Soninke of Niger, a man might offer to become a *griot*, or praise-singer, for another man – in effect, voluntarily enslaving himself – and this arrangement was concluded via a blood pact (Paulme 1973). In general, the pacts were usually concluded between two men, but occasionally they may have been made between a man and a woman, as among some married Azande couples (Evans-Pritchard 1933).   AG

Boas, Franz (1858–1942) was born to middle-class parents in the Westphalian town of Minden in 1858. His early studies focused on science and mathematics, and his doctorate from the University of Kiel was in the field of physics. After completing the doctorate in 1881, he took up a position in geography at the University of Berlin. In 1883–4, Boas undertook an expedition to Baffin Land, where he intended to demonstrate the effects of the Arctic environment on Eskimo culture. His experiences there, however, turned his interests toward the study of culture itself. In 1886 he mounted a purely ethnographic expedition to British Columbia, where he studied the natives of the Northwest Coast, and he soon became a leading figure in anthropology.

Boas did not return to Germany after the trip; he settled briefly in New York, where he married Marie Krackowizer and worked as an editor for *Science*. After a teaching position at Clark University from 1888 to 1892, Boas became Chief Assistant in anthropology at the World's Columbian Exposition in Chicago. His work helped make the Columbian a landmark in the history of American anthropology, and he served briefly afterward as Curator of Anthropology at the Field Museum. Finally, in 1895, Boas returned to New York to work at the American Museum of Natural History and at Columbia University. He became a pro-

fessor of anthropology at Columbia in 1899, and he remained there for the rest of his career.

During his tenure at Columbia, Boas achieved virtually every scientific recognition available, including membership in the National Academy of Sciences, the presidency of the American Anthropological Association, and the presidency of the American Association for the Advancement of Science. He also achieved considerable notoriety for his statements on political issues, some of which were perceived as unpatriotic during World War I, and for which he was briefly censured by the American Anthropological Association in 1917. He was a prodigious author and fieldworker, publishing six books and over 700 monographs and articles. He retired in 1936, but remained active as an anthropologist until the very moment of his death in 1942. He was survived by three children and two grandchildren, and at his death was widely regarded as the world's leading anthropologist.

Work

When Boas began his ethnography in 1883, anthropology had neither a solid base of data nor a scientific theoretical approach. Anthropologists relied on travelers' accounts, missionary reports, and popular stereotypes for their information about non-Western peoples. Out of these dubious materials, they constructed elaborate theories of evolution, racial types, and the primitive mind. With a missionary's zeal, Boas fought to replace such practices with reliable information and careful theorizing. To the extent that anthropology became a science in the early twentieth century, it was due to Boas's work.

Gathering the data for this science was one of his primary concerns. As a physical anthropologist, Boas developed systematic methods for measuring human growth, development, and physical change. As a linguist, he established the recording and analysis of indigenous languages as a central task of ethnography. As a cultural anthropologist, he carried out extensive field research on the Northwest Coast, and dispatched graduate students all over the Americas and the Pacific. He pursued these projects with a desperate intensity, anxious to record as much as possible about non-Western cultures before the spread of European COLONIALISM destroyed them. His efforts generated an unprecedented wealth of systematically gathered information, and set anthropology for the first time on a sound empirical foundation.

This new information, he argued, exposed the weakness of the grand theories of RACE, EVOLUTION, and CULTURE that dominated nineteenth-century anthropology. Boas regarded generalization as inherently dangerous; cultures were so complex, and the historical processes that generated them so convoluted, that broad schemes explaining the "laws" of culture were seldom possible. The diverse developmental histories of the cultures he studied, for example, discredited popular orthogenic theories of cultural evolution. Likewise, theories of GEOGRAPHIC DETERMINISM collapsed in the face of the tremendous variety of solutions that his subjects found for the challenges of their environments. The road to understanding human beings lay not in the lofty realms of grand theory, but through limited studies of specific problems, set in the contexts of the cultures in which they occurred.

This approach implied a radical autonomy for culture. Most earlier theory had reduced culture to an expression of some deeper force, such as racial character, instinct, intellectual struggle, or a sort of evolutionary manifest destiny. For Boas, culture was itself an actor, shaping the material and psychological world of those within it. While any particular culture could be explained as a result of a specific history, none was reducible to a simple antecedent cause, and each could be understood only on its own terms.

Legacy

Boas has never been identified with a particular theory, and he founded no "Boasian school" of anthropology. His legacy was rather in the approach he fostered, the data he gathered, and the students he taught. In these areas, his influence on the discipline was profound. Boas effectively demolished race and orthogenic evolution as paradigms for anthropological thought; he established the methods and standards for field research that continue to guide the discipline;

he established CULTURAL RELATIVISM as a governing viewpoint within anthropology. His students dominated American anthropology for more than half a century. They included Alfred KROEBER, Margaret MEAD, Ruth BENEDICT, Edward SAPIR, Melville HERSKOVITS, Robert LOWIE, A. Irving Hallowell, Ashley Montagu, Ruth Bunzel, Paul Radin, Leslie Spier, and many others. Boas also established the relevance of anthropology for the larger world, arguing that their knowledge of human culture gave anthropologists an ability and a duty to critique the cultures in which they lived. His own fiery attacks on RACISM and unthinking NATIONALISM paved the way for Margaret Mead and others to make anthropology among the most visible and progressive of the human sciences.

AB

See also ANTHROPOLOGY, CULTURAL AND SOCIAL, HISTORICAL PARTICULARISM, HISTORY AND ANTHROPOLOGY

further reading Boas 1911, 1940; Goldschmidt 1959; Stocking 1974

body *See* ADOLESCENCE, BODY DECORATION, DEATH, PURITY/POLLUTION, REINCARNATION, SPIRIT

body decoration   A rather special kind of ART involves the decoration of the human body. Among the peoples of the central highlands of New Guinea, this is the most important type of art, since these people do little carving, painting, or mask making. In these societies, the decorations people wear and the painting of the body at ritual performances and exchange ceremonies convey messages about social and religious values and also demonstrate relationships to clan ancestral spirits. The Melpa of the central highlands of Papua New Guinea use particular colors in body painting and certain combinations of colors in feathers, shells, and beads that convey abstract qualities like health and vitality (A. Strathern & Strathern 1971). The Wahgi, who live near the Melpa, also express their aesthetic impulses through the decoration and adornment of the human body. Feather adornments and painting of the face and body during dances carried out at the Wahgi pig festivals serve to communicate the strength and health of the clan hosting the festival, particularly their moral strength. Absence of sorcery accusations or of friction within the group affects the brightness and quality of their adornment and the success of their performance during the ceremony (O'Hanlon, 1989).

Body decoration also includes tattooing, which becomes a permanent part of the individual and his or her presentation of self. It is found in many societies. Tattooing among the Marquesans in the Pacific demonstrates Gell's argument that tattooing serves to mediate between social maturation, personhood, and social reproduction (Gell 1993). Male and female gang members in America have themselves tattooed with their gang's "crest" to indicate their membership.   PR&AR

body language *See* GESTURE, NONVERBAL COMMUNICATION

bridewealth or brideprice is the transfer of symbolically important wealth as part of MARRIAGE, where property passes from the groom's kin, not to the bride, but to the bride's kin as compensation for her. It is technically distinct from DOWRY, where property passes from the bride's kin (or others) to the bride herself or to the new couple. Terminology such as "brideprice" or "marriage payment" often causes confusion because it seems to imply a sale and a market principle, concepts inadequate by themselves for understanding the broader sets of issues in marriage. For example, bridewealth can serve to cement a union, legitimize offspring, redistribute or consolidate wealth, and otherwise validate changes in the social identities, rights, and duties of the various persons involved. Where bridewealth involves animals, its redistributive effect may also subtly help conserve grazing land or serve other, often unspoken, purposes.

In bridewealth's most usual form one or more of the groom's kin transfer to one or more of the bride's kin some set of objects, animate or inanimate; these may be accompanied or substituted by labor (brideservice). The groom's father is likely to be a main giver and the bride's father a main receiver; but other kin of either sex

and of different generations may also be direct or indirect givers or takers. Typically the goods or objects transferred are deemed as compensation for the transfer of the woman, her sexual and reproductive rights, her labor, or other aspects of her person, from one group to the other – whether the groups in question be families, lineages, clans, or perhaps "houses" or homesteads not strictly composed of kin. In many societies, the bridewealth received for a sister's marriage is used to enable her brother to bring a wife into the kin group. Providing bridewealth generally gives a husband's natal kin group some claim over, or at least formal links to, his wife's offspring. Sometimes "childwealth" is transacted separately in installments as children are born.

The general types, quantities, and qualities of property required for bridewealth payments are usually prescribed by convention, but the details can be subject to protracted bargaining or renegotiation. The method of delivery, such as the use of intermediaries or particular ritual objects, and the celebrations surrounding bridewealth transfers, may be elaborately prescribed. The main transfers of the woman from her natal to conjugal groups, and of animals, money, or other goods in return, may be complicated and partly offset by smaller gifts or exchanges (which might include grain, meat, cooked food, or tools) back and forth, sometimes in precisely specified sequence. In some societies bridewealth transfers are made only in gradual installments because the marriage is thought to gel only gradually too. Indeed the bridewealth process may not necessarily be completed within the lifetimes of the principals; it may be carried on by subsequent generations. The property exchanges also create debts and imbalances that constitute important social ties, and they may establish or reconfigure political alliances. Bridewealth is typically returnable in theory, if not always in practice, and giving or taking it back generally signifies DIVORCE and an abnegation of the intergroup ties that marriage constitutes.

Bridewealth is widespread in parts of Africa, the circum-Mediterranean region, the Near East, South Asia, East Asia, and elsewhere (J. Goody & Tambiah 1973: esp. ch. 1). It plays its most important roles in Eastern and Southern African savanna societies that farm and keep cattle or other large animals. Bridewealth is common among African societies with PATRILINEAL kingroup recruitment, but it occurs too among some MATRILINEAL, AMBILINEAL, and BILATERAL kinship systems – usually in lesser, even token, quantities. Many societies practicing bridewealth also allow POLYGYNY. Where patriliny, bridewealth, and polygyny all coincide, they seem logically and practically to reinforce each other, as Parkin (1979) and others have argued. In many societies with high bridewealth in cattle, VIRILOCALITY and the levirate are also practiced. High bridewealth tends to promote and maintain the authority of fathers over sons, and of elders over juniors more generally – a point to which French anthropologists such as Meillassoux (1981) have applied class analysis. In politically stratified societies, elites may use high bridewealth to bolster their own distinct position.

Heated anthropological debates have surrounded bridewealth, particularly in the British social anthropology of Africa. Many have argued over whether bridewealth may be understood as a payment, and whether bridewealth, and what HERSKOVITS (1926) called the East African CATTLE COMPLEX, are economically rational. But the economic is not the only, or even necessarily the most important, dimension involved. Bridewealth is simultaneously a symbolic, political, dramatic, ecological, and aesthetic action. Goods involved in bridewealth are not always substitutable with cash or other goods, though bridewealth commonly does include cash even where money is newly spread. Where cattle do not survive, for instance in tsetse-ridden coastal West Africa, cash and household goods tend to feature more prominently in bridewealth.

Anthropologists and others have offered various generalizations about the incidence of bridewealth in relation to agricultural technology and the sexual DIVISION OF LABOR (Boserup 1970; J. Goody 1976), and in relation to the demographic ratios of humans to cattle (A. Kuper 1982a). Bridewealth in Africa tends to coincide with an important role of WOMEN in AGRICULTURE, and high bridewealth seems often to coincide with a predominance of agriculture over herding. Bridewealth practices are so widespread and diverse, however, that further generalization is difficult.

Church missions in Africa have opposed bridewealth as sinful, and secular governments in Eurasia have attacked it as wasteful. Many young, urban-educated women and others have also resisted bridewealth, deeming that it reduces women to the status of chattels (Hirschon 1984). Where economic and other changes have inflated bridewealth demands to levels hard for many young men and their families to reach, the results include postponed marriage and unwed unions. Despite these challenges, bridewealth continues to adapt and endure in countless settings.   PS

further reading Jane Collier 1988; Comaroff 1980; Evans-Pritchard 1951; Gulliver 1955; Hakansson 1988; Hutchinson 1996

C

cannibalism The allegation that other people engage in cannibalism, the consumption of human flesh as food or for ritual purposes, is common in the literature on non-Western societies. The origin of this idea in Western culture extends back to the beginnings of recorded history. In the fifth century B.C.E. Herodotus, the father of history and ethnography, mentioned that neighbors of the Scythians, a people on the eastern fringe of Greek civilization were *Androphagi*, literally "man-eaters" (1987 [440 B.C.E.]: 4.18). The pre-Christian Irish, Scots, and others were also characterized in this way, rationalizing wars of conquest against them. The same accusation also often surfaced in accounts of European minority groups (Mason 1990). Thus, the early Christians were accused of this practice by the Romans. In the Middle Ages women thought to be engaged in WITCHCRAFT and devil worship were assumed to eat human flesh, as were the Jews, accusations used to justify waves of persecutions, pogroms, and the excesses of the Inquisition in Europe for centuries.

This pre-existing cannibal imagery subsequently provided a blueprint for descriptions of truly exotic peoples encountered by Europeans during their overseas expansion in the fifteenth century. In the ensuing centuries almost every group encountered was accused of this practice. (See Sanday 1986 for a contemporary example of this line of thought.) Those labeled cannibals have included the Caribs, from whom we get the popular word for the practice (Palencia-Roth 1993), the Aztecs, and sundry other natives of North and South America. In time, the label was also pinned on the peoples of Africa, the scattered populations of the Pacific, such as the Hawaiian Island-

ers, the Australian Aborigines, the Maori of New Zealand, and most recently the Highland peoples of New Guinea, contacted only in this century. Interestingly, Europeans too have frequently been thought to be cannibals by those they encountered. Thus the persistent questioning by the British as to whether or not the Hawaiians ate Captain Cook after his death at their hands led these natives to conclude that cannibalism must be the accepted mortuary practice of their visitors (Obeyesekere 1992).

All this points to a recognizable and continuing pattern: the belief in "others" as cannibals. However, the evidence for such a custom is usually based on cultural misunderstandings or second-hand accounts repeated often enough to become accepted dogma (Arens 1979). This is not to suggest that cannibalism has not occurred in other places and times including the prehistoric past (see T. White 1992). Occasionally people in every society resort to such extremes for survival purposes, as an expression of deviant behavior, or for some presumed medicinal benefit (Gordon-Grube 1988). However, such rare instances are condemned, rather than condoned, by society at large, so it is grossly misleading to suggest that any given society is, or was, "cannibalistic" in the usual broad sense of the word.   WA

capitalism is a mode of organizing economic life, a period or epoch in human history, and a particular kind of social and cultural order. Students of capitalism as a mode of organizing economic life generally attempt to place its development in the context of human history. By contrast, those theorists who take the development of capitalism as unproblematic often fail even to define the term. Neoclassical economists, for example, simply assume that the foundations of their analysis (the exchange of goods and services and the propensity of individuals to seek their maximum advantage in acts of exchange) are universals.

There is little argument that exchange and maximization are defining features of capitalist economic practice and relationship, and that the MARKET is the arena and relational network through which such impersonalized, maximizing exchanges take place. Theorists with a historical perspective, however, argue that such arenas and networks are not universal, and that for much of human history economic and social life has been organized and integrated by other means. The most influential proponent of this view in anthropological thought was Karl Polanyi (1944), who argued that the "self-regulating market" was but one, relatively recent mode of effecting economic integration, or the transfer and distribution of goods. The emergence of markets depended on the creation of what he called "fictional" commodities – land, labor, and capital. Earlier modes of economic integration depended upon noncommoditized transfers and different "principles" of organization – householding, reciprocity, and redistribution.

Though Polanyi was not himself an anthropologist, his work influenced several generations of anthropologists and stimulated a rich body of work concerned not with capitalism but with earlier and other modes of organizing economic life. Concepts like RECIPROCITY and REDISTRIBUTION served as central defining features in schemes of cultural and political evolution. His work was also the point of departure in the 1950s and 1960s for the acrimonious FORMALIST–SUBSTANTIVIST DEBATE about whether neoclassical economic theory could be applied universally (formalists) or not (substantivists).

Polanyi's work, in turn, rested upon older traditions of economic and social thought, especially that emerging in Germany in the late nineteenth and early twentieth centuries in the work of scholars like Karl Bucher, Werner Sombart, and Max WEBER (1927) and in the work of non-

Germans influenced by them, such as (to take two rather different examples) A. V. Chayanov (1966) in Russia and Thorstein Veblen (1898) in the United States. This work in turn entered into complex dialogue with the writing of Karl Marx. We can explore the relevant issues in more depth by examining the work of Marx, on one hand, and Weber, on another.

Although classical economists had proclaimed the universal importance of exchange (Adam Smith's "universal propensity to truck and barter") from the mid-eighteenth century, their economic theories actually began with processes and relations of production. Explanations of exchange value were grounded not in the vagaries of market, but in the process of production itself, especially the amount of labor time accumulated in particular goods. Marx also began with production but, in his classic *Capital* (1887), emphasized an analysis of the commodity (which he saw as the "economic cell form" of capitalist society) and the circulation of commodities because, he wrote, capitalist society presents itself as a vast array of commodities. Marx's analysis therefore began with the commodity form, the problem of value, and the circulation of commodities before turning to an analysis of processes, and relations, of commodity production, which occupied most of his attention.

Capitalism is a particular type of commodity economy, in Marx's view, because its commodity relations and exchanges have so permeated social and economic relations that even the human capacity to work itself (labor power) is commoditized. For labor power to be a commodity, laborers must be "free" to sell it. They cannot be subject to obligatory claims upon their persons or work from groups such as slave-owners, landlords, or a community's corvée labor demands (that is, the wage laborer is not a slave, serf, or peasant). Equally important they must no longer own or control the productive resources that would provide an independent means of subsistence: they must sell their labor in order to survive. The wage relation depends on this double freedom (from bondage but also from control), so that when a person works for wages, they are selling a

particular kind of commodity – their capacity to work.

Much of Marx's economic analysis, and especially his analysis of exploitation under capitalism, begins with this wage relation, and it serves as the basis for his distinction between capitalism and other economic forms. But, Marx wrote, nature does not present, on the one hand, a mass of laborers with no control over means of production or subsistence with nothing to sell but their labor power, and, on the other hand, a mass of capital in the hands of a minority ready to employ labor (or purchase labor power). Thus, labor power is a fictional commodity, as Polanyi was to claim nearly a century later – not in the sense that it is made up but in the sense that it is made, in a historical process.

Weber too pointed to free labor as a defining feature of capitalism, but he saw it as one of several such features. He placed primary emphasis on the emergence and dominance of rational accounting, including, famously, the growth of a rational "spirit." But this spirit, and the practice of rational accounting, depended upon the emergence of an institutional complex, including (1) the treatment of all means of production as "disposable property," (2) free markets, (3) rational technology, including mechanization, (4) calculable law, (5) free labor, and (6) the commercialization of economic life (Weber 1930).

"Freedom," "disposability," and "calculability" figure predominantly here, implying that labor, goods, and resources have been "freed" from interpersonal or communal claims and obligations. In such a system land, for example, is no longer considered a collective resource designed to provide a livelihood for all members of the collectivity by virtue of their membership in the group. Similarly goods are no longer separable into items that are shared within a group of kin or community and those that may be sold to outsiders. For rational accounting to be effective, all such goods and resources had to be treated as subject to account, calculable in terms of quantifiable measures of benefit and cost.

Indeed, when Weber wrote of the "spirit of capitalism," he did not refer to the spirit of enterprise, or the search for profits. He pointed out that such spirit and search have been common in many types of society, though generally permissible only in dealings with people who lay beyond some social and cultural boundary. While the search for advantage and profit was not acceptable within this closed circle of kin and community, it was acceptable and expected outside the circle. In Weber's view, what distinguished the capitalist spirit was the *taming* of that search for profits and the *dissolution* of the boundary between insiders and outsiders. That is, within the former circle, social claims to shareable goods and resources were dissolved, and the exchange of goods and resources was subject to a single, quantifiable form of accounting. Outside the former circle, the emphasis was no longer on the highest possible profit, or in other language the quick buck or easy killing, but on the long-term profitability of the enterprise. This required that exchanges be recursive and that costs (and profits) be calculable and predictable.

The "freeing" of land, labor, capital, and other goods and resources for this singular kind of accountability is the result of a complex social history, and theorists like Polanyi were referring to that history when they stressed the "fictional" nature of commodities like land or labor. Much anthropological work on capitalism has concentrated on the social and cultural processes, relations, and problems associated with the development of capitalism in formerly noncapitalist milieus, where community values are other than those that can be registered on a balance sheet. In the process of freeing of labor from land, of resources from the claims of community and kin, and the blurring of boundaries between those inside and those outside, the consequences of capitalist development for such communities are more than theoretical.   WR

See also ECONOMIC ANTHROPOLOGY, GIFT EXCHANGE, SOCIALISM, TRADE

further reading Dobb 1946; D. Harvey 1982; Marx 1964

cargo cults are MILLENARIAN MOVEMENTS whose religious beliefs focus on the acquisition of material goods ("cargo") by ritual means. Melanesia is the *locus classicus* of these cults, which began in the last quarter of the nineteenth century in the wake of colonial domination by the European powers. Beliefs centered on the new relative deprivation of the indigenes and offered ritual means of acquiring Western goods. This was often combined with a belief in the return of ANCESTORS and a coming end to racial domination and antagonism either by the effacement of racial differences or the disappearance of the Europeans.

MR

further reading Worsley 1968

cargo system   is a set of ranked ritual or ritual–civil offices found in peasant communities of Mesoamerica. The offices are linked to saints of the Roman Catholic Church. Each adult male seeks to serve in each of these offices during the course of his life. Prestige, which increases as one mounts the hierarchy, accrues to the holders of cargo, as does the often enormous expense imposed by the obligations of office. The cargo system thus serves as a leveling mechanism inhibiting the differential accumulation of wealth by households.

MR

further reading Frank Cancian 1965

carrying capacity   denotes the factors internal or external to a population that limit its growth within the capacity of the environment to sustain it without irreversible depletion of natural resources and environmental degradation.   LS

caste, caste societies   In a caste society groups of persons engaged in specific occupations or with specific characteristics are ranked hierarchically. These ranks are ostensibly based on the degree of pollution incurred by work at the caste specialty or by other group characteristics, and one's position in the caste scale may be regarded as a reward or punishment for spiritual attainments (see PURITY/POLLUTION).

India is the most famous (some say the only) caste society. There caste is broken into four great *varnas*: the "twice-born" Brahman priests, Kshatriya warriors, and Vaisiya merchants, and the "once-born" Sudra peasants. Beneath these and offi-cially excluded from the caste system are the Untouchables (Gandhi's *harijans*, or "children of God," now self-designated as *Dalits*, or "oppressed"), who fill the most polluting occupations.

Although the Brahmans are universally recognized as the least spiritually polluted caste, there is no absolute consensus as to who is on top or why. For instance, religious renunciants can make claims to special holiness either by showing extraordinary asceticism and purity, or by engaging in cannibalism and self-degradation or indulging in intoxication and excess (J. Parry 1982; Lynch 1990).

Furthermore, the Kshatriya, who traditionally served as rulers, established competing axes of valuation for themselves to counterbalance the Brahmans' claims to pre-eminence (Inden 1990; Heesterman 1985). In fact, Dirks (1987) argued that the Brahmanical portrait of caste was simply a wishful fantasy of priests in a colonial atmosphere that favored the disjuncture between kingly power and religious legitimacy.

Among ordinary people, however, the main competition between castes remains at a lower level of organization. All the *varnas* are divided into multitudinous *jatis*, or local, endogamous occupational groups, that constitute the varied labor force of the society. These *jatis* can and do contest their relative positions and attempt to rise in the ranks through what Srinivas (1962) famously called "Sanskritization': emulating the attributes of higher caste groups. Thus, an economically successful lower caste may take up less polluting occupations and habits and claim higher caste status. Whether these claims are accepted varies (F. Bailey 1957), but clearly slow upward (and downward) mobility in the caste rank of *jati* was far more likely prior to colonial censuses, which fixed caste positions immutably in written records.

Academic definitions of caste are also not solidified, and fall into two mutually exclusive positions. The first is structural-functional and views caste as a category or type, comparable in many respects to hierarchical organizations elsewhere. In this vein, Gerald Berreman wrote that "a caste system resembles a plural society whose discrete sections are all ranked vertically" (1968: 55). Indian caste therefore is analogous to social structures elsewhere in which rank is ascribed, such as American racial grading (Goethals 1961; Bujra 1971).

The second school understands Indian caste as a total symbolic world, unique, self-contained, and not comparable to other systems. Most of these theorists would agree with the classic definition by Bougle, who wrote that "the spirit of caste unites these three tendencies: repulsion, hierarchy and hereditary specialization" (1971: 9); controversies are primarily over which of these aspects is stressed.

Dumont, the best known of the symbolic school, based his interpretation of caste on the attributes of hierarchy and repulsion. In his book *Homo hierarchicus* (1970), he focused on the rigidity of caste positions at each end of the hierarchical spectrum (Brahmans and outcastes) and the radical opposition in Hindu thought between categories of power and categories of status. LEACH, on the other hand, gave first place to hereditary specialization; the diagnostic of the system, for him, was that "every caste, not merely the upper elite, has its special 'privileges'" (1960a: 7).

A somewhat different approach was taken by Marriott and Inden. They postulated an indigenous monism, grounded in the assumption that in a caste society "all living beings are differentiated into genera, or classes, each of which is thought to possess a defining substance" (1974: 983). These substances, according to the theory, are formed by various transactions, particularly exchanges of food. Marriott and Inden were then able to develop transactional flow charts that locate all different Indian groups within their paradigm.

A difficulty for interpretive theory is the place of non-Hindus within a caste system. For instance, Muslims, who make up approximately 12 percent of India's population, advocate the equality of all believers and deny the validity of notions of pollution (Lindholm 1986). The problem of accommodating such nonbelievers within caste society is not merely academic, as present-day sectarian battles chillingly testify.   CL

See also PLURAL SOCIETIES, RACE
further reading Berreman 1979; Beteille 1965; Klass 1980; Marglin 1985; Marriott 1990

cattle complex   was the term coined by Melville HERSKOVITS (1926) to describe a set of beliefs among pastoral societies in eastern and southern Africa where the prestige value associated with cattle ownership appeared to overshadow their economic value to the point of irrationality. The complex was characterized by three aspects:

1. cattle were valued as wealth for social rather than economic purposes and exchanged only in the context of social relations, such as marriage, where they made up the bulk of brideprice payments (see BRIDEWEALTH)
2. cattle were not slaughtered for meat except on special ceremonial occasions
3. owners displayed strong personal, even emotional, attachments to their cattle

By "complex" Herskovits meant a set of traits, and not a fixed mental tendency or obsession, but the term quickly took on this psychological meaning.

The irrationality of these traits was rejected by later researchers, who found that cattle raising provided the economic infrastructure for a cultural belief system that centered on cattle, not the reverse. They argued that valuing cattle was sensible where agriculture was undependable (Porter 1965; H. Schneider 1979) and that trade was more widespread than Herskovits believed (Galaty & Bonte 1991). In addition "ritual slaughter" proved to be a surprisingly regular source of food (H. Schneider 1957). The debate today has shifted from the "cattle complex" to the "complexity of cattle," as anthropologists have attempted to trace the multiple relationships that give cattle key symbolic, economic, religious, and social roles simultaneously.   TB
See also PASTORAL NOMADS

centralized systems are conduits within COMPLEX SOCIETIES organized around central nodes through which flow goods, materials, information, decisions, and power. The structure of the system permits some individuals or groups to exert a degree of power from their centralized position. Therefore, attempts to create central systems and to control them involve political competition. Centralized systems vary in their organizational scope, the institutionalization of their structure, and the extent of overlap between the different centralized systems.

Centrality is a critical political dimension to complex societies. When a centralized system channels the flow of goods and information through a central node, the control over central nodes translates directly into social power. Such centralized conduits exist in many forms in human societies. A simply concrete form is an irrigation canal and its associated HYDRAULIC SYSTEMS. Water is centrally diverted from a stream or spring, flows through a primary ditch, and is diverted by distributary ditches to the agricultural fields. The administration of an irrigation system represents the immediate and direct control of the subsistence production of participating farmers. Control over the flow of water is a tool used to mobilize labor and goods from farmers as "rent" for using the irrigation system.

The exchange of goods and materials through a social network can be more or less centralized. Redistribution is the institutionalized payment of goods and services into a center, as to CHIEFS who then allocate them according to their political strategies (K. Polanyi 1957). MARKETS centralize the transfer of goods through a hierarchy of central places (Carol Smith 1976; see CENTRAL PLACE THEORY). Political and religious hierarchies are institutions that involve central decision making, holding of knowledge, and owning of special objects and properties (Maquet 1961). Associated with central institutions of economy, society, politics, and religion are settlement hierarchies.

Within CAPITALISM, class ownership of the technology of production underlies the political system of domination (Marx & Engels 1888). Althusser (1971) argued that an ideological state apparatus, involving schools, churches, and the like, is a formal institution created by the ruling elite to develop and deliver a ruling-class ideology. The administration of schools and religious institutions controls instruction and ritual performance to present an ideology in which social STRATIFICATION is legitimized. The centralized systems of the STATE thus function to maintain (reproduce) systems of inequality. Political (CLASS) conflict attempts to control the centralized systems of economy and ideology that it supports through power differentials and domination by a ruling class. Barry Barnes (1988) argued that social power derives from the distribution of knowledge, and centralized control over knowledge supports a centralized political system. Lack of control over social knowledge, on the other hand, results in decentralized political systems.

One of the most intriguing elements in comparative studies of human society is the relationship between scale and hierarchy. The extension of the scale of political integration requires the development and restructuring of a central hierarchy of decision makers (G. Johnson 1982). The development of more complex institutions requires centralized financial systems through which goods are mobilized and allocated to support the activities of the ruling institutions and the fulfillment of their functions (D'Altroy & Earle 1985). Scale of an institution translates into the degree of centrality for the conduits of resource and information flows.

To understand the dynamic character of any society requires investigations of the overlap between different centralized systems. Among comparatively small-scale chiefdoms, a single generalized hierarchy of chiefs can handle the full range of economic, political, and religious affairs. Chiefs try to be comprehensive leaders, acting to direct centrally the activities of the polity (Earle 1978). With the development of more complex state systems, to solve problems of scale, centralized institutions become specialized and internally differentiated (H. Wright 1984). It is then possible to speak of different sources of power – economic, military, political, and religious – associated with the different centralized systems of the state. Power can then be multicentric and contested in different arenas (Mann 1986), and such systems can be called a heterarchy (Crumley 1987).   TE

further reading Glassman 1986; A. Johnson & Earle 1987; Lenski 1966, E. Wolf 1982

central place theory As formulated by German geographer Walter Christaller in 1933, central place theory proposes that settlements cluster around nodes called central places, each of which is functionally associated with a surrounding area. The places are organized, by size, in a "nested hierarchy," according to the goods and services that higher-order places supply to lower-order ones. The logic of the hierarchy is that people will travel farther to obtain more specialized goods and services. The major organizing principle of settlement patterns, therefore, is access to a MARKET. On a uniform plain, with no topographical features to distort the pattern, the hierarchy of places takes the form of interlocking hexagons, the ideal arrangement for minimizing travel distance. Christaller's hypothesis contains three influential notions. The first is that the major function of an urban settlement was to be the organizational center of a given region. The second is functional exclusivity: higher-order centers possess all the tertiary functions of the next-lower level, and more. The third concept is the notion of geometrical space: Christaller's hypotheses are tested in abstract, not metric, space, in order to compare spatial variations in different systems of economic interaction. Christaller's hypothesis has been extraordinarily successful in generating research on the spatial components of economic processes and hierarchies of settlement (B. Berry & Pred 1961). Empirical tests of the hypothesis suggest that settlement hierarchies, with cultural variations, conform in a general way to Christaller's construction, but that the behavioral assumptions regarding the distance that a person will travel for goods or services are so variable that actual spatial patterns rarely conform to the predictions of the theory.   TG

further reading L. King 1984; Müller-Wille 1978

charisma First brought into sociological parlance by Max WEBER, "charisma" was originally a theological term, indicating the miraculous "gift of grace" that verified the sacredness of Jesus to his disciples (Eisenstadt 1968; M. Weber 1968). Weber expanded this concept beyond Christian doctrine to describe all forms of authority that rest on the attribution of superhuman character to the leader by the follower. Thus he categorized as charismatic a variety of characters, including berserker warriors, political demagogues, pirates, incendiary revivalists, and messianic prophets. All, he claimed, were sociologically equivalent in the sense that their appeal was primarily personal, emotional, and compulsive. The vernacular understanding of charisma as a capacity for irrational attraction is therefore sociologically accurate.

Weber explicitly counterpoised charismatic authority with both rational-legal rule and the constraints of tradition. Followers obeyed not because it made sense to comply, nor because submission was customary, but because they intuitively recognized the charismatic's intrinsic right to command. Jesus's words "It is written . . . But I say unto you" express the core of charismatic authority according to Weber (Gerth & Mills 1946: 249). Therefore, charisma is marked by an absence of fixed rules, a denial of economic and bureaucratic organization, and an affirmation of creativity, emotional fervor, millenarian hope, and revolutionary idealism. For Weber, it is the fountain of social change; only through charismatic annunciations can old orders be overturned and new ones brought into the world. But it is also ephemeral, soon rationalized into more routine forms of authority by acolytes desirous of maintaining the new order for their own advantage.

Weber understood charismatic appeal as arising from the vivid emotional intensity of the charismatic figure. In this he followed Nietzsche, whose superman was superior precisely because of the force of his passions. However, where Nietzsche imagined his hero in solitude, for Weber charisma could exist only in relationships. Concepts of emotional contagion and somnambulistic trance that the French crowd psychologists Gustave Le Bon (1896) and Gabriel Tarde (1903) had borrowed from mesmerism (Darnton 1968) were appropriated by Weber, who argued that the highly charged charismatic performance inspires reciprocal exaltation in onlookers, and consequently excites both awe and enthusiasm. Charisma thus begins in frenzy, and the archetypal charismatic is the epileptoid SHAMAN (Gerth & Mills 1946: 246).

However, for Weber, SOCIOLOGY could properly concern itself only with the construction of meaning and reasonable motivations for action; the rapture of charisma, though tremendously important in its consequences, could not be studied. Rather, focus had to be on the manner in which the original ecstatic impulse was rationalized into a system of sacred symbols and institutions (Greenfeld 1985).

Anthropologists and sociologists have followed Weber's advice, and have generally taken the rationalized form of institutionalized charisma as their sole object of study. Clifford GEERTZ (1983: 123), for example, argued that charisma is defined simply as "the inherent sacredness of sovereign power" (see also Shils 1965). From within this framework, the frenzy of the shaman is envisioned as a search for coherence and significance, and all legitimate authority is charismatic. This approach "makes sense" in that it allows a fruitful concentration on the development and legitimation of culturally constituted meaning systems, but fails insofar as it ignores the experiential ambiguities and compulsions of charisma in its primal emotional form.

Psychologically inclined theorists, on the other hand, have concentrated on the character structure that lies beneath the charismatic's impassioned presentation of self, and on the underlying reasons why the crowd finds this presentation mesmerizing (Erikson 1970; Bion 1961). But if sociological theory tends to "normalize" charisma, psychoanalysis tends to "demonize" it, turning leaders and followers into neurotics and psychotics.

A more holistic model of charisma can be constructed from the work of social theorists who give credit to the heightened emo-tion and confusion that is normally a precursor to charismatic involvement. This state, usually precipitated by a crisis of cultural or personal identity, can be conducive to attraction to a posturing and vital leader whose superhuman appearance derives in part from his uncanny actor-like capacity to manifest culturally valued emotional states; the performance of the leader reflects and amplifies the desires of the followers, and stimulates fusion within the empowering charismatic movement (I. Lewis 1986; Lindholm 1990; Willner 1984).

The study of charisma therefore offers a potentially fertile field of investigation, linking culture, personal experience and individual psychology to collective commitment and the creative construction of new meaning systems.   CL

See also BIGMAN, CULTS

further reading Devereux 1955; Glassman & Swatos 1986; Kracke 1978; Lindholm 1988; Zablocki 1980

Chayanov slope describes the variations in the use of labor under two contrasting agricultural systems where labor is scarce in respect to land. A milestone in understanding labor use in such systems was Sahlin's popularization (1971, 1972) of the early-twentieth-century work of the Russian peasant economist A. V. Chayanov.

Chayanov (1966) maintained that the use of labor in land-rich and labor-scarce societies varies according to the demands placed upon it by the demographic structure of the household. HOUSEHOLDS with higher (and more onerous) ratios of consumers to producers will have higher rates of labor use, whereas households with lower (and less onerous) ratios will have lower rates. The use of labor in either type of household is determined by the same factor – the intersection of the curve of the marginal utility of labor and the curve of the marginal disutility of the labor itself. The higher the ratio of consumers to producers, the greater the utility of additional product and the lower the disutility of additional labor; whereas the lower the ratio of consumers to producers, the lower the utility of additional product and the greater the disutility of additional labor. Represented

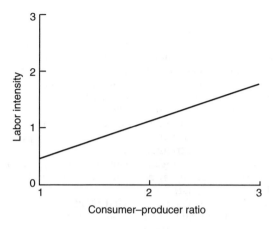

Figure 1   Chayanov slope for swidden cultivators in Borneo.

graphically, this relationship is termed the "Chayanov slope" (see figure 1).

Anthropologists have used (and abused) the Chayanov slope in analyzing all types of society, but its greatest explanatory power lies in the analysis of contemporary SWIDDEN-based communities (Dove 1984).   MRD&ML
See also AGRICULTURE
further reading Durrenberger 1984; Netting 1993

chief, chiefdom   Chiefs occupy offices of leadership within chiefdoms, emergent COMPLEX SOCIETIES that are regional polities (Carneiro 1981a). Common centralizing characteristics of chiefdoms include redistribution, warfare, and religious ideologies. Chiefdoms are an intermediate-level society, often seen as a stage in social evolution (Service 1962). (A closely related social type is RANKED SOCIETIES.) In contrast to the local-group level of EGALITARIAN SOCIETIES, chiefdoms organize several local groups or villages in a region with a composite population in the thousands or tens of thousands. Chiefdoms can be characterized as simple or complex in terms of the scale of integration and elaboration of institutionalization (Earle 1978). Chiefdoms represent a new level of integration, with institutions that incorporate the expanded size of the polity. Explanations of the evolution of chiefdoms have emphasized alternatively managerial and political causes (Earle 1987).

Within the chiefdom polity, the individuals occupying chiefly offices constitute a social segment and are ranked with respect to each other according to genealogies to create an institutionalized hierarchy of leadership. In simple chiefdoms, community leaders are the highest-ranked individuals of their community. In more complex chiefdoms, chiefs become a separate social segment set off from the commoner populace and designated by special dress and paraphernalia (Earle 1989). Genealogies become political tools, determining the pool of potential leaders, and often linking them to the gods.

Chiefs are leaders in economic, military, political, and religious affairs (Earle 1978). Chiefdoms differentiate a ruling institution, but this institution itself is not internally differentiated and specialized (see STATE). Ideally, a chief's powers combine and integrate within a single person all social power in society. The most basic source of power is economic, and Service (1962) has called chiefdoms "redistributional societies." As populations settled into economically diverse regions, regional chiefs were once thought to emerge to redistribute specialized products among different communities. Subsequent research has demonstrated that redistribution does not perform this function, but is instead a form of political economy (Earle 1977). By "owning" land, chiefs allocate use rights in subsistence plots in return for labor and goods given as "rent." The mobilized resources then support community labor and specialized activities under chiefly direction. Chiefs also attempt to control long-distance exchange (Junker 1990) and the manufacture of prestige goods by specialists who are attached to them. The prestige goods are distributed through the chiefly hierarchy as a means of political payment; the objects are symbolically charged and designate the superordinate status of their possessors.

To retain power, chiefs frequently resort to physical intimidation. They are often a warrior elite, and Carneiro (1981a) argued that chiefdoms are inherently militaristic. War is the means to expand chiefdoms through conquest and to coerce followers into compliance (see Haas 1982). Warfare as a source of power is inherently problematic, however; warriors are likely to turn treacherously on their former lord (Earle 1987). Some measure of control over warriors may be exercised through control over the production of weaponry, as with the bronze swords of northern European chiefdoms that were manufactured by specialists attached to the chiefs (Kristiansen 1987).

A closely linked source of power is the chiefly ideology. Originally, chiefdoms were seen as traditional, with their ranking religiously sanctioned (Fried 1967). Although chiefdoms are no longer viewed as theocratic polities, the ideological justification for chiefly rule is strongly emphasized. Chiefs maintain their institutionalized positions of leadership through a justifying ideology. They have special access to the gods or are thought to be gods themselves. The ruling ideology is materialized in objects with special esoteric knowledge (Helms 1979) and in burial and temple monuments creating the cultural landscape (DeMarrais et al. 1996). Ownership and control of the materialized ideology become a source of political power.

As a term "chiefdom" has been criticized because of its association with unilinear schemes of cultural evolution (Feinman & Neitzel 1984). It was common practice to take the best ethnographic case material to reconstruct indiscriminately historical and archaeological chiefdoms. Present work emphasizes the variation among chiefdoms that represent a plethora of historical developments and social forms (Kristiansen 1991). As a field for comparative analysis, the development of institutionalized leadership in regional polities is a challenging area of research.   TE

further reading Drennan & Uribe 1987; Earle 1991; Kirch 1984; Mann 1986–93

childbirth   is the work of women as they labor and bear down with their uterine muscles to push their babies from the private inner world of their wombs into the larger world of society and culture. Although childbirth is a universal fact of human physiology, where, how, with whom, and sometimes even when a woman gives birth can be culturally determined.

The upright stance necessary for bipedal locomotion made human birth more complicated than the births of other higher primates, whose quadrupedal locomotion allows a pelvis aligned for the direct descent of the fetal head, whereas the human infant must rotate as it descends through the pelvis (Trevathan 1987). Immediately after birth primate babies can climb onto their mothers' backs and cling; human infants, born earlier in their developmental cycle because of their larger brains, are relatively helpless at birth and require immediate nurturance. These factors may have encouraged the evolution of birth as a highly social process; in few societies do women give birth alone and unaided. Indeed it is reasonable to assume that midwifery must have evolved right along with human birth (Trevathan 1987). The presence of other women would have enhanced the success of the birth process as they acquired such skills as turning the baby *in utero*, assisting rotation of the head and shoulders at birth, or massaging the mother's uterus and administering herbs to stop postpartum bleeding.

The social nature and significance of birth ensure that this biological and intensely personal process carries a heavy cultural overlay. In all cultures birth is a

RITE OF PASSAGE (Gennep 1960) that embodies a culture's deepest beliefs, which are transmitted and reaffirmed during this critical transitional time. Birth practices point "as sharply as an arrowhead" to the core values of the culture, telling the observer a great deal about the way that culture views the world and women's place in it (Kitzinger 1978). For example, in the highly patriarchal Islamic society of Bangladesh, childbirth (like MENSTRUATION) is regarded as so polluting that a midwifery tradition never developed; women, assisted by female relatives, are expected to give birth on dirty linens, and infant mortality and puerperal infections are high (Blanchet 1984). Bariba women in Benin display core values of honor and courage through silent and stoic behavior during delivery (Sargent 1982, 1989). In Polynesia, where women's fertility is honored and celebrated (Ward 1989), pregnant women are pampered and nurtured, and skilled midwives readily available. The extreme emphasis on technology in the United States is mirrored in the birth practices there (E. Martin 1987; Davis-Floyd 1992). Laboring women are placed in hospitals and subjected to interventions such as electronic monitoring, artificial stimulation of labor, and high rates of surgery. The prestige of this Western high-tech approach has induced many developing countries to stamp out viable indigenous midwifery systems and import the Western model, although their hospitals are often underfunded, understaffed, and replete with expensive machines that few know how to use or repair (B. Jordan 1978/93; Sargent 1989). To counteract this unfortunate trend, the World Health Organization and UNICEF have been promoting traditional midwifery in developing countries through programs for "upgrading" skills. However, because the medically trained personnel in these programs value only the Western technomedical approach, they generally fail to take advantage of the knowledge and skills developed by community midwives within the context of their own cultural traditions. In the United States, such attitudes resulted in the near-complete elimination of midwifery by the 1960s; since then there has been a renaissance in mid-

wifery owing to the demands of many women for natural childbirth, coupled with scientific research into the dangers of interventionist hospital birth (Goer 1995) and the benefits of planned, midwife-attended births at home (Davis-Floyd 1992, 1997) or in freestanding birth centers (Rooks et al. 1989). Indeed, in the four countries in which infant perinatal mortality statistics are the lowest in the world – Japan, Holland, Sweden, and Denmark – over 70 percent of births are attended by midwives (M. Wagner 1994; Fiedler 1997).

Brigitte Jordan's (1978/93) comparative study of birthing systems in Holland, Sweden, the United States, and Mexico's Yucatan demonstrated wide variation in the definition, the locus, the attendants, and the artifacts of childbirth, and sparked general interest in the anthropology of birth. During the 1980s, this field expanded into the anthropology of REPRODUCTION (Browner & Sargent 1990; Ginsburg & Rapp 1991), which encompasses the cross-cultural study of all aspects of the reproductive process. Studies have most recently focused on the rapid development and spread of the new reproductive technologies (NRTs) such as *in vitro* fertilization, artifical insemination, surrogacy, and of diagnostic technologies such as amniocentesis and ultrasound, which make it possible for genetic defects to be diagnosed before birth, and for one child to have multiple biological parents (Ginsburg & Rapp 1995). Such technologies pose fascinating and disturbing ethical dilemmas that require radical rethinkings of KINSHIP, parental rights, women's rights to control of their bodies, and reproductive law (J. Edwards et al. 1993). In India, for example, the use of amniocentesis and selective abortion to ensure that the first child will be a boy is altering the male/female population ratio in some provinces (B. Miller 1987). Other important issues include the preservation of viable indigenous birthing systems (M. Wagner 1994) and the recent worldwide renaissance of midwifery (Kitzinger 1991).   RDF

further reading Davis-Floyd & Sargent 1997; Handwerker 1990; Laderman 1983; MacCormack 1982; Michaelson 1988; L. Whiteford & Poland 1989

children Anthropological studies of children examine: (1) the place of children in society, (2) cultural concepts of children, (3) child development and socialization in cultural context, and (4) child welfare and survival. These perspectives are not mutually exclusive: children are part of social and economic systems even as they experience processes of biological and psychological development and cultural education.

Margaret MEAD (1930) pioneered the ethnography of children and opened up inquiry into the role of culture in child development. Although keenly interested in cultural transmission, Mead did not see children only in terms of the adult world – as if they were passive subjects of the socialization process. She recognized that children often "live in a world of their own . . . based upon different premises from those of adult life" (1930: 81). She concluded that seemingly universal psychological processes were in some cases really culture-specific developments. While Mead's theories have been challenged, the issues she highlighted remain significant today and anthropologists continue to question universalistic models of child development. For example, theories of moral development based on observational data from Africa (C. Edwards 1987) and comparative studies of India and the United States (Shweder et al. 1987) challenge culture-specific assumptions that underlie psychological models of child development.

Not all researchers treat children as having a world of their own: much work takes the adult world as its point of departure and views children in terms of adult preoccupations with educating, controlling, and preparing them for adult life. Cultures differ, however, in how much explicit attention or training is thought to be necessary. Although certain parental goals are universal or nearly so (LeVine 1988), different cultures appear to have different concepts of the role of adults in shaping the process of child development: in some cultures children are regarded in ways that require massive intervention by adults, in others children are thought to develop with relatively little adult intervention (R. Levy

1973, 1978; Tobin et al. 1989). Both attitudes allow for complex socialization practices, but shape adult–child relationships in ways that may affect development.

Although it provides a necessary perspective, the adult world and its requirements do not offer the best basis for understanding children in all their dimensions. As any parent knows, children often do not passively accept adult demands, despite the very real ways children are socially and emotionally dependent on adults. When children are seen primarily in terms of their education for adult roles, they may be conceived as more passive than they are. Of course, children's relative lack of knowledge and lack of control over their lives cannot be ignored, but treating them only as passive recipients of adult knowledge does not give a complete picture of their lives or development. Child-centered research, by contrast, views children as dynamic agents who learn much of their culture informally and transmit what they learn to each other through talk and interaction (Bluebond-Langner 1978; Goodwin 1990).

Since they actively and collaboratively interpret the social world and the culture they encounter, children often resist the efforts of adults to socialize them, despite the general asymmetry of adult–child relationships (P. Miller & Hoogstra 1992). Children may register ambivalence or resistance in play, or in disturbed relationships with socializing figures (such as parents) or institutions (such as schools). Although parents, schools, and cultural media ranging from television and comic books to ritual and video games have critical roles in socialization and cultural transmission, it is important to recognize the ways children oppose socialization processes, reinterpret cultural knowledge, and generate values and understandings for themselves. Debra Skinner and Dorothy Holland (1996), for example, show how students in a rural Nepalese school developed understandings of caste, gender, and their futures that at once reflect, resist, and reinterpret the knowledge and values embodied in school lessons and community life.

ETHNOGRAPHY is a powerful method for understanding child development and can help integrate the study of culture and human development. Weisner (1996) argued that ethnography is central to the study of child development because it brings the cultural place where the child actually grows up into focus, showing how the cultural beliefs, meanings, and practices of a community, within its economic, ecological, and environmental context, affect development.

Most anthropologists share a commitment to studying children in "natural settings" that are not contrived for research purposes. It is the anthropologist who enters the child's world, and not vice versa. Any setting may be explored through ethnographic fieldwork: schools, playgrounds, homes, the streets of urban neighborhoods. Child-centered ethnography explores the full range of the social life of children, including child–child relationships such as those found in play or sibling groups as well as adult–child relationships (Goodwin 1990).

Ethnography reveals much about children's experience of cultural worlds. Hausa children may be concerned with purdah (Schildkrout 1978), while Hindu children must find ways to understand the concepts of purity and pollution associated with caste and gender in their communities. The ethnography of children sheds light not only on how children develop cultural abilities that build on processes of psychological development, but also how such processes of development are adapted to the cultural circumstances of life. Robert Levy (1973, 1978), for example, showed how Tahitian children develop "gentleness" in the cultural place in which they grow up. Children elsewhere are socialized for aggression, such as the children Belmonte (1979) observed growing up with violence in a poor neighborhood of Naples, Italy. In the United States, P. J. Miller and L. L. Sperry (1987) found that children in Baltimore learned to jusify anger and aggression in cultural terms. In such cases, social and emotional development occurs culturally: what develops reflects cultural values and experience, ways of life, and life circumstances.

In anthropology, theory for the study of children at first derived largely from Freud-

ian concepts of development. Researchers of the early CULTURE AND PERSONALITY school believed that specific child-training techniques had predictable effects on adult personality and could explain cultural differences in personality (Bock 1988). Later studies found surprisingly little evidence for the links between childhood experience and adult character postulated in this paradigm (see Shweder 1979, 1980; Bock 1988; Riesman 1983 for critiques). The question, however, of the place of culture in a child's development became firmly established as an important issue in theory and practice. In this tradition, Erik Erikson linked childhood and adult character in terms of historical and cultural experience for the Sioux of South Dakota and the Yurok of California. Erikson stressed the cultural context of child-care practices. He maintained that treating infants in a certain way does not necessarily cause adults to have specific characteristics – "as if you turned a few knobs in your child-training system . . . and fabricated . . . [adult] character" (1963: 137). Rather, he argued, it depends also on cultural factors. He pointed out that child-care practices are embedded in a cultural and economic synthesis, and insisted child care had a functional role in producing persons prepared for the way of life that synthesis represents, whether nomadic hunting and warring for the Sioux, or Yurok fishing. His approach brought sharply into focus the role of culture in development. Contemporary studies continue to stress the cultural and economic contexts of development, but today no single theory of development organizes research on children into a single paradigm.

In a changing world, as Erikson pointed out for the Sioux, what children learn from cultural traditions about who they are, and what they should become may prepare them for a way of life that no longer exists. This may lead to uncertainty and doubt. Where children must also cope with cultural differences between school and home, identity confusion may further disrupt processes of cultural transmission. How schools react to cultural differences remains an enduring policy problem. Some children may find that language and religious beliefs or cultural competencies learned at home are not recognized at school, or are actively devalued and even stigmatized. In a sensitive study of black and white working-class children, S. B. Heath (1983) showed how the ways these children learned to use language at home differed from the use of language valued in school.

One of anthropology's greatest contributions to understanding children has been its commitment to comparative CROSS-CULTURAL STUDIES. One of the most extensive was the Six Cultures Project directed by Beatrice Whiting and John Whiting of Harvard (Whiting & Whiting 1975; Whiting & Edwards 1988). Teams of researchers observed and coded the behavior of children in six cultures, documenting cultural differences and similarities, specifying behavior settings and relationships as crucial influences on children's behavior, and placing these behavior settings and relationships in social and economic context. However, the relative lack of interview data and THICK DESCRIPTION limits these studies to an "external" view that did not consider the cultural meaning of actions, particularly what the children themselves thought and felt. Following a general trend in anthropology toward interpretive and cognitive approaches, newer studies have focused on the meanings and experience neglected by strictly observational methods (J. Briggs 1992; Harkness 1992; Harkness et al. 1992; Parish 1994: ch. 5).

The ethnographic and comparative study of children has yielded a rich understanding of such crucial issues as the organization of social support systems (Weisner 1989), the role of sibling caretaking (Weisner & Gallimore 1977; Weisner 1982), the way familes adapt their routines and implicit models of "normal" development to children with developmental delays (Weisner et al. 1996), the cultural dimensions of school experience (Weisner & Garnier 1992), and cultural effects on learning (Weisner et al. 1988).

Cross-cultural studies remain controversial when they upset firmly held beliefs or challenge long-standing models of development. For example, Scheper-Hughes (1985, 1992) questioned the assumption that maternal bonding is universal in the light of her data on impoverished mothers and children in a Brazilian shantytown where people live in a state of life-threatening poverty. Here, in a kind of maternal triage, mothers apparently choose to let some children die by withholding resources they need to live. Not maternal bonding, but a state of detachment is supported by cultural imagery of a child who is not meant to live. While her position on maternal sentiment has been challenged (Nations & Rebhun 1988), her work is important because it focuses attention on the linkages between culture, human development, and political economy.

Other studies have also stressed the impact of demographic and economic conditions on children's lives. Family structure, the meaning of children, reproductive strategies, and parenting styles differ widely between rural agricultural societies and urban industrial societies (LeVine et al. 1988). The smaller families in low-fertility, low-child-mortality industrial societies stress psychological reciprocity and nurturing the child's psychological development, while the larger families of high-fertility, high-child-mortality agricultural communities inculcate obedience and affiliation. Economic and demographic conditions also help determine parental goals, influence adult preferences regarding family size and the gender of children, and shape the decisions adults make about investing resources (such as time, effort, money, care, and education) in children (LeVine 1988, 1990).

These patterns vary, of course, in detail from community to community in ways that reflect specific local conditions and cultural traditions, and not all of the content of folk models of children is related to reproductive and parental strategies and their contexts. Nonetheless, LeVine's (1988) analysis of parental goals suggests there is some important underlying structure to the apparent diversity of cultural beliefs and attitudes about children. But in rapidly changing societies, some adult expectations and concerns regarding children may reflect the past, not the present, and the cultural models of

child development that guide behavior may not fully reflect actual circumstances (Tobin et al. 1989). SP
See also ADOLESCENCE, PLAY, SOCIALIZATION
further reading J. Briggs 1970; Cook-Gumperz et al. 1986; Harkness & Super 1996; J. Henry & Henry 1944; Kakar 1981; Liederman et al. 1977; Middleton 1970; Riesman 1992; Scheper-Hughes 1987; Spiro 1958; Super & Harkness 1980

circumcision (literally, "cutting around") is most appropriately applied to male circumcision, the widespread cultural and religious practice of cutting off the foreskin of the penis, leaving the glans exposed. Muslims and Jews generally consider male circumcision a religious requirement, and it is celebrated, whether performed ritually – e.g., the Jewish bris (*Brith Milah*) on the eighth day after birth – or carried out later in childhood or upon religious conversion. Many North Americans and some Europeans and Africans who are neither Muslims nor Jews also circumcise boys, usually at birth, based on conformity to tradition. Many people believe it to be beneficial to health and hygiene, although US medical authorities generally oppose it as an unnecessary risk.

In some African and Aboriginal Australian cultures, male genital surgeries have been part of a rite of passage to manhood. Subincision – cutting underneath along the length of the penis, broadening the penis and commonly injuring the urethra – was sometimes performed in Australia, while superincision – cutting along the dorsal side of the prepuce – has been practiced in some Pacific Island cultures.

Female circumcision is a euphemistic but widely used term for several types of traditional female genital surgery. Most common in West, Saharan, and Northeast Africa, they have also been documented for some people in South Asia and the Americas (Toubia 1993: 5). In North America, one form was even imposed on mental patients in the early twentieth century as a treatment for masturbation. In cultures where the surgeries are performed generally, it is done either on very young girls (for example, ages 5–7 is common for Sudanese Arabs) or on adolescents as a rite of passage prior to marriage (as is the case for Maasai and Gikuyu in Kenya) (Davison 1989).

The least harmful form of female circumcision is the cutting away of the clitoral prepuce (hood), comparable to male circumcision, often accompanied by pricking or partial cutting away of the clitoris. When the clitoris itself is removed, the term "clitoridectomy" is used. "Excision" is often used to describe clitoridectomies and related surgeries that remove the clitoris and adjacent tissues of the prepuce and labia.

The most severe form of such surgeries is infibulation (or "pharaonic circumcision" in recognition of its supposed roots in ancient Nile Valley cultures). The clitoris, prepuce, labia minora (inner lips), and much of the labia majora (outer lips) are cut away and the opening is closed across the vaginal opening by joining the raw tissues from each side. After healing, scar tissue thus blocks the opening except for a single tiny hole, preserved by the insertion of a small object such as a straw during healing, through which urination and menstrual flow can pass. Intermediate forms which remove less tissue and only partially close the opening are also practiced (Abdalla 1982).

Health consequences can be quite severe. At the time of the surgeries, girls often suffer intense pain, bleeding, and sometimes shock, which may be followed by severe hemorrhage, septicemia, infections, and urine retention. When infibulation is practiced, scar tissue may later obstruct menstrual flow or make first intercourse extremely difficult, requiring cutting. Infibulation also obstructs normal childbirth, requiring a timely incision during delivery. Obstructed labor can result in vasico-vaginal fistulae, a serious complication in which tissue death results in openings between the vagina and other internal structures. Reinfibulation is usually done following the delivery. Psychological effects have also been noted (El Dareer 1982).

In recognition of the harmfulness of these surgeries, the label "female genital mutilations" (FGM) has come into common use.

Justifications for female circumcision vary by culture, and it is not associated with any single religious tradition. In Africa, for example, it has been performed by Muslims, Christians, Jews, and practitioners of other African religious traditions. Although most Muslims do not practice female circumcision and consider it against Islam, many Muslims in Northeast Africa believe the milder forms to be acceptable in Islam, based on interpretations of certain sayings attributed to the Prophet Mohammed. Since the traditions of the prophet are called "*sunna*," the less severe forms are often called "*sunna* circumcision" (Gruenbaum 1991).

Other cultural explanations for the practices include preservation of virginity (through reduced sexual desire and a barrier to penetration), beauty (conformity to a cultural aesthetic), cleanliness, purification (Arabic, "*tahur*"), gender identity (removing "male" parts), and ensuring male sexual pleasure.

Efforts in public health education to modify or eliminate the surgeries have gained momentum in recent years (Koso-Thomas 1987).   EG

further reading Hosken 1993; Paige & Paige 1981

clans are unilineal descent groups that unite a series of lineages descended from a theoretical common ancestor, the genealogical links to whom are often either not remembered or who may be purely mythological. Thus a clan's members may share a common name or ancestor, assume they are related, but not be able to trace the links among the component lineages. Clans are often exogamous, and localized clans can serve as territorial political units. A **matriclan** is a clan organized on matrilineal descent principles, a **patriclan** is organized on patrilineal principles. Alternatively the term is used to distinguish larger units from smaller ones where genealogical links are remembered and can be traced (technically creating a single, large lineage system), but where the higher-order lineages are functionally equivalent to clans.   MR

class   Social classes are major divisions of COMPLEX SOCIETIES, and the members of the various classes are possessed of differing amounts of wealth, power, and prestige derived from their respective positions in the DIVISION OF LABOR. Although "class" is one of the most powerful concepts available to students of large, complex societies, it is also one of the least uniform in its meaning and use.

The word gained currency along with the social transformations accompanying the growth of industrial CAPITALISM; its meaning is profoundly influenced by the work of Karl Marx, who formulated a developmental model setting out the emergent patterns of a simplified class structure as societies progressed toward a universal mode of social organization imposed by bourgeois capitalism as it spread to the whole world. Although Marx wrote little specifically on class, his general sequential scheme of epochs characterized by masters and slaves, lords and serfs, bourgeois and proletarians has been widely influential among anthropologists. Max WEBER accepted many of Marx's ideas about the global spread of MODERNIZATION, based on technological progress, but laid the groundwork for anthropology's contribution to the understanding of class through the recognition that societies are differentially "inserted" into the emerging WORLD SYSTEM, and also that the cultural, or ideological, dimension of class relations is more important than generally assumed, less easy to understand, and has a transformative capacity that complements, and often exceeds, that of technological change.

The approach to the study of class is dependent upon the most general theoretical assumptions of the investigator. Studies primarily concerned with the way in which societies cohere, and persist through time, generally treat classes as the outcome of the normal distribution of functional activities needed to ensure the operation of the social system. Such an approach is best considered under the heading of social STRATIFICATION. Where processes of change are the focus of theoretical attention, as in the writings of Marx, emergent classes are seen to arise as a result of changes in processes of production, thus introducing potential conflicts in the established political and status hierarchies. However, for such conflicts to become politically articulated requires the emergence of a consciousness of common interests and common destiny among the members of each class, a situation that opens up yet another dimension to the study of class.

Anthropologists influenced by Marx have generally laid primary stress upon social and cultural structures arising out of economic relations, or MODES OF PRODUCTION, and identified classes in terms of their position in those processes. Following an evolutionary sequence, classes emerge as modes of production become increasingly complex. Thus, considerable attention has been paid to peasants, landlords, and landless workers in preindustrial societies, and attempts have been made to identify the major characteristics of the way of life, or CULTURE, of each class as determined by its relationship to the means of production. A few anthropologists have attempted to apply Marx's concept of class directly to precapitalist societies (Terray 1975); but at their widest extension, studies of class formation within an emerging world system attempt to identify the sequences of development in the peripheral regions that correspond to those that took place as capitalism developed in the core areas of Europe and North America (E. Wolf 1982). Two excellent examples of anthropological studies that interpret local history, local social structure, and local cultures in terms of a single developing worldwide mode of production and class system, albeit with some accommodation of local conditions, are Gough (1981) on India and Vincent (1982) on East Africa.

An increasing volume of anthropological work deals with particular groups within industrialized or industrializing societies, frequently concentrating on the lower or working classes, or on the social and cultural characteristics that are supposedly produced by POVERTY. These studies often transform into descriptions of SUBCULTURES, conceived as either the localized emergence of particular modes of production, or as the coalescence of ethnic traditions with class adaptations. However,

some anthropologists have been sensitive to the class differences, and their cultural correlates, within racial or ethnic neighborhoods (Hannerz 1969). The methods of anthropological study, involving continuous, first-hand contact over a long period of time, have resulted in detailed analyses that complicate the more abstract theories of class structure and economic causation. At the local level it is usual to find class factions, intermediate strata, and indeterminate actors that do not fit easily into the more general class categories, but result in a rich tapestry of social action. The pioneering studies of W. Lloyd Warner (1941–59) and his associates, now unjustly neglected, attempted a comprehensive study of the social life of an American town, making class the central interpretive principle and paying close attention to the symbolic as well as the material dimensions of class relations. Although a few anthropologists may still regard beliefs, ritual, and similar customary practices as mere epiphenomena of economic and political relations, it is now more usual to accord culture and ideology a significant role in processes of social action. This opens up a significantly larger space for anthropological study of class and makes it complementary to macrosociological studies of large-scale objective structures (Bourdieu 1990).

The turmoil that has frequently followed the ending of COLONIALISM has presented new interpretive challenges to anthropologists, and stimulated many retrospective analyses of colonial societies in order to provide a baseline for contemporary studies. Class analyses have most often competed with models of PLURAL SOCIETIES. That is, the hierarchical order of colonial and postcolonial societies has been seen by pluralists to derive from the cultural, and often racial, characteristics of the various population elements incorporated into the colonial state with, of course, the representatives of the colonizing power occupying the dominant positions (L. Kuper & Smith 1969). Class analysis, by contrast, pays primary attention to the exploitative mode of production embodied in the colonial state and the class structure flowing from it. An integral part of that mode of production is a mode of ideological domination in which the differential evaluation of race and culture plays an important part. However, these overgeneralized models are gradually giving way to more fine-grained analyses of social process in which class domination and class conflict are inflected by a whole range of cultural and ideological factors (F. Cooper & Stoler 1989). The work of June Nash, beginning with her studies of Bolivian tin miners (1979), has been notable for its careful treatment of the relationship between the local cultural content of ideology and consciousness of class in its global, as well as local, manifestations.

Some of the most creative work in class analysis has been carried out under the general designation "cultural studies," originating in the work of the Centre for Contemporary Cultural Studies at the University of Birmingham from the late 1960s. Focusing particularly upon the convergence of class and racial oppression in Britain, and the varying modes of resistance to it, the publications of the Centre have had wide influence among anthropologists working in comparable situations ranging from the United States to South Africa, Latin America, and the Caribbean (see Lave et al. 1992 for a detailed review of the work of this group).   RS
further reading Lipset 1968; R. Smith 1984; B. Williams 1989; E. Wright 1985

classification is the conceptual arrangement of things. Anthropology examines the comparability of classifications cross-culturally. Research stresses cross-cultural comparisons of semantic domains, such as kinship, color, living things, race, disease, firewood, ceramics, automobiles, tools, and time.

Concern with classification originates with the field of kinship, founded by L. H. MORGAN (1818–81). Morgan (1871) proposed dividing kinship terminologies (or classifications) into two types: classificatory and descriptive. Classificatory terminologies, such as IROQUOIS KINSHIP SYSTEMS, merged lineal and collateral relatives under single terms, so that, for example, the term of reference for one's father's brother is "father" and that for mother's sister is "mother." Descriptive terminologies, by contrast, did not extend the meaning of lineal relatives to other collateral relatives, so that in English "mother" and "father" refer only to one's biological parents. A. L. KROEBER (1909), confused by Morgan's dichotomy, claimed that all kinship terminologies are really classificatory because some kin terms in all languages refer to more than one kintype (a genealogically defined individual). Even in English "uncle" denotes more than one kintype: father's brother, mother's brother, or husband of either mother's or father's sister. Kroeber suggested that kinship terminologies be compared from the perspective of distinctive attributes, such as whether sex, generation, collaterality, and lineality could be discerned as being definitive of the classification itself.

This proposal is often considered to be the cornerstone for COMPONENTIAL ANALYSIS, which sought to reduce kin terms in different languages to certain attributes that were meaningful to both the people who used them and to trained observers. It attempted to develop metalinguistic glosses for folk terms in semantic domains to facilitate accurate translation. In this sense, "uncle" in English could be translated most accurately as "collateral male of the first ascending generation (in relation to ego)." Componential analysis mainly focused on kinship classification, but it was closely related to studies on principles of classification of reality in other domains (D'Andrade 1995).

One of these domains concerned basic color terms – simple words referring only to given parts of the color spectrum such as "black," "white," and "red" in English. Long thought to be incommensurable across cultures, Berlin and Kay (1969) found that the more complex the culture, the more basic color terms in the lexicon. They also showed that basic color terms were essentially equivalent in meaning across a large sample of languages. They argued that basic color terms seemed to be encoded in the same sequence in diverse languages, such that languages containing a basic color term "red" always had basic color terms for "black" and "white." If two languages had the same number of basic color terms, one such term in one language was equivalent in meaning to another such term in the other. Native speakers of diverse languages tended to select the same focal type (or limited range of more than 300 Munsell color chips) for each basic color term. Berlin and Kay showed that the languages possessing a term for red, for example, tended to cluster around a highly specific part of the Munsell color chart for this term, which suggested a cross-culturally valid focal referent for "redness." The mutual translatability of basic color terms and the common sequence in which they are encoded seems to reflect a universal pattern in human classification of colors.

In related work on the classification of plants and ANIMALS (ethnobiology), Brent Berlin and his colleagues, building on the work of Harold Conklin, found that there were essentially only four or five ranks (or hierarchically nested categories) in diverse cultures (Berlin et al. 1973). Although many languages have no translatable label for "plant" or "animal" as understood in folk English, these were recognized as semantic domains because of words that allude nonpolysemously to plants or animals, such as terms equivalent to "fur," "feathers," "nectar," and "fibers." In other words, although the semantic domain of "plants" is unnamed (or covert) in many languages, it is nevertheless cognitively real, because of the vocabulary associated only with it. This covert category is called a "unique beginner" (somewhat akin to the kingdom in biological science). Hierarchically nested beneath it are three or four more ranks, in descending order of inclusiveness: life form, folk generic, folk specific, and folk varietal (absent in some languages). Life forms are major groupings within the unique beginner, such as "tree," "herb," and "vine" for plants, and "bird," "mammal," and "fish" for animals, in folk English. Folk generics are immediately subordinated to life forms, so that, the generic names "oak," "pine," and "maple" are kinds of tree. Folk specifics, as with scientific names, tend to be binomial, and are immediately subordinated to the rank of folk generic, so that "scrub oak" and "live oak" are kinds of oak. Finally folk

varietals, which are immediately subordinated to folk specifics, tend to be even more complex terms, such as black-and-tan German shepherd (vs. other kinds of German shepherd), itself a kind of "German shepherd" (folk specific), which is in turn a "dog" (folk generic), a "mammal" (life form), and an "animal" (unique beginner) in increasing magnitude of inclusiveness.

The evidence that the number of ranks (four or five) tends to be essentially the same across diverse cultures suggests another universal property of human classification. This suggestion is strengthened by the finding that the number of folk generic terms for plants or animals tends to cluster around 500 (Berlin 1992), which may indicate upper limits on memory in nonliterate cultures (Lévi-Strauss 1966).

In relation to scientific taxonomy, folk taxonomies may overdifferentiate or underdifferentiate living taxa. In a striking case of overdifferentiation, the Hanunóo of the Philippines use some 1,800 names for a scientifically recognized flora of only about 1,300 species (Conklin 1957). Cultures closely associated with the outdoors tend to display a much higher proportion of names for living things in their total vocabulary than languages associated with greater dependence on creature comforts (Berlin 1992). Moreover, languages associated with high technological complexity (such as US English) tend to exhibit more life form terms (as well as unique beginners) than do languages affiliated with societies intimately dependent on natural resources (C. Brown 1984). Similarities seem to outweigh differences overall among folk classifications themselves and between folk and scientific classifications. Both folk and scientific classifications of living things share criteria of ranking and morphology, despite differences in number of ranks, modes of naming the ranks, defining the ranks, naming the taxa themselves, the morphological aspects deemed important ('trees" are not a taxon in botany, but *Anacardiaceae*, which includes enormous cashew trees as well as herbaceous poison ivy, has certain distinctive features of flower and fruit morphology and is on that basis a taxon), and the range of geographical reference (folk classifications are restricted to locally occurring living things whereas scientific classifications are, in principle, generalizable). Even scientific taxonomy, dating from Aristotle, has roots in folk biology (Atran 1990).

In contrast to findings on the glossability of kin terms, mutual translatability of basic color terms, and common structuring of hierarchies of living things, Marvin HARRIS examined profound intracultural and intercultural differences in the classification of RACE. Whereas historically in the United States, one was either "black" or "white," Harris (1970) found in Brazil a total of 492 race-color terms from a sample of one hundred informants. Informants employed numerous terms in categorizing the race-color status of 72 standardized drawings representing different phenotypes. The race-color terms elicited for the cards did not indicate focal referents (such as prototypical "white" or "black" phenotypes), unlike Berlin's and Kay's study of basic color terms.

Folk Brazilian racial classification is clearly different from traditional US classification in that it names more possible race-color phenotypes. Although the use of race terms is independent of joint parentage in both the Brazilian and US cases, the principles behind that independence are quite different. In the United States, a caste system developed whereby one was either "black" or "white," and intermarriage was rare and often illegal. When it did occur, the offspring of such a union were automatically classified as "black," an example of hypodescent, whereby the racial classification of one parent is completely ignored in determining one's own racial classification. In Brazil full siblings are often classified into different "races," an impossibility in the US classification (Harris & Kottak 1963).

Races, as isolated breeding populations, are nonexistent. Harris and his colleagues pointed out that the Brazilian classification, however ambiguous, embraces a multitude of named phenotypes regardless of the classification of individuals' parents and is hence more accurate than the US, caste-based dichotomy of "black" and "white" (Harris 1970; Harris et al. 1993). The very confusion in assigning racial identity in Brazil, whether to oneself or to others, evinces a semantic chaos with the concept itself. Indeed the increase in the number of different ethnic groups in the United States and the demand by some that a "bi-racial" category be included in the national census, indicates that the notion of a simple fixed racial identity seems to be losing its grip.

The seeming incomparability of racial classifications in cross-cultural perspective suggests that the ethnoscientific goal of mutual translatability of cultural classifications is illusory here because race, as a semantic domain, never was universal, in contrast to kinship, basic color terms, and living things. Unlike some other semantic domains that figured in the cross-cultural study of classification of reality, that of race, as with the dichotomous classification in the United States, lacks empirical validity and cross-cultural regularity. Race is exclusively a folk construct, but relatives, colors, plants, and animals are everywhere real.   WBal

See also COGNITIVE ANTHROPOLOGY, DESCRIPTIVE KINSHIP SYSTEMS, ECOLOGICAL ANTHROPOLOGY, ETHNOBOTANY, ETHNOSCIENCE

further reading Rosch & Lloyd 1978; Tyler 1969

classificatory kinship systems

are kinship terminologies in which lineal and collateral kin are grouped under common terms. Mother and mother's sister, for instance, may be called by a single term "mother," as in HAWAIIAN KINSHIP SYSTEMS. These systems attracted early interest from scholars such as Louis Henry MORGAN (1871) who thought they might represent evidence for a postulated evolutionary stage of GROUP MARRIAGE. This hypothesis was based primarily on the false assumption that the use of common kin terms was evidence that "primitive" people could not initially distinguish their true fathers and mothers from other relatives. That celibate priests could be called "father," and monks and nuns "brother" and "sister," without confusion in many religions was apparently overlooked in this discussion.   MR

See also DESCRIPTIVE KINSHIP SYSTEMS

cognates are people related to individuals through consanguineal ties on either or both their mothers' or fathers' side. "Cognate" is sometimes used synonymously with "ENATE."   MR

cognatic descent encompasses all descendants of an ancestor traced by any combination of links through the mother's or father's line in any combination. The totality of cognatically related kin form a cognatic stock, from which groups or egocentric KINDREDS may be formed. Although cognatic descent cannot be used alone as the basis for forming DESCENT GROUPS, it is often used in combination with other recruitment criteria to form such groups. "Cognatic" is sometimes used as a synonym for "BILATERAL."   MR
See also AGNATES, ENATES

cognitive anthropology is the study of the relationship between mind and society. Traditionally, cognitive anthropology examines cultural knowledge in terms of its organization and application in everyday life, in activities such as classification and making inferences. Early in its development, in the 1950s, cognitive anthropology was synonymous with ETHNOSCIENCE or ethnosemantics. Studies focused on the structure of conceptual categories in folk CLASSIFICATION systems and the meanings encoded in these systems, in areas such as KINSHIP, ETHNOBOTANY, and color classification. The central unit of analysis was the shared conceptual category, a conjoined set of distinctive features.

More recent studies of classification systems have concentrated on the psychological reality of conceptual categories. If such categories are only conjunctions of features, then the members of a category should not vary in terms of their psychological salience. But they do. Take the category "bachelor," defined in traditional ethnoscience terms as the conjunction of three distinctive features: male, adult, and unmarried. Men are categorized according to whether or not they represent the conjunction of these features; there is no middle ground. This does not represent classification in real life, however, since

popes and priests are not normally viewed as bachelors. It is more likely that we apply categories like bachelor by matching potential instances to prototypes, which are stereotypical representations of concepts that serve as standards for evaluation (Rosch & Lloyd 1978). Since the prototypical bachelor is promiscuous, non-domestic, and also potentially marriageable, applying the category to popes and priests would strike most speakers of English as unnatural.

Research has shown that many categories are organized around prototypes, from kin terms to furniture (Lakoff 1987; Lakoff & Johnson 1980). Most of this work has been done by linguists, while cognitive anthropologists have focused on a related knowledge structure, the "schema," a term borrowed from the early work of F. C. Bartlett (1932) in social psychology. The difference between a prototype and schema is that while both are stereotypical, a prototype consists of a specified set of expectations, while a schema is an organized framework of relations that must be filled in with concrete detail. Schemas are highly generalized, culturally specific knowledge structures that help generate appropriate inferences. They fill in the gaps by supplying information that is usually taken for granted, thus enabling individuals to identify actions, events, and consequences based on only brief exposure to only partial information.

Consider these two sentences: *John went to a party. The next morning he woke up with a headache.* Many readers will assume that John's headache is related to the party since people often smoke and drink too much at parties and then wake up the next morning feeling hungover. Notice, however, that our causal explanation goes considerably beyond the information given. For all we know, John may have been run down by a bus on his way home or be suffering from food poisoning. Our chosen explanation is an inference produced from our organized cultural knowledge concerning what people do at parties. The arrangement of this knowledge is almost storylike; we seem to know what should happen next. Thus, by having access to this culturally constituted, storylike arrangement, we are able to make sense out of the ambiguous sentences above.

Cognitive anthropologists have found that much of everyday, applied social knowledge exists in such schematic arrangements, known also as cognitive models, scripts, or event scenarios. The range of these scripts is quite large. Notable anthropological studies have explored the well-organized scenario for entering and leaving a house among the Yakan in the Philippines (Frake 1980), scripts for adjudicating land-tenure decisions in the Trobriand Islands (Hutchins 1987), the common event scenario that governs the structure of American proverbs (G. White 1987), and how stereotypical emotion scenarios influence the social judgments and political decisions of Pacific Islanders (Lutz 1988).

Although the evidence that cultural knowledge structures are highly schematized is strong, studies by cognitive anthropologists generally avoid making encompassing ethnographic or psychological statements about whether some knowledge structures are universal, and (if they are) the extent to which they depend on universal cognitive processes. For such answers one must turn to the theorists who draw on research in artificial intelligence and cognitive psychology. They have proposed three basic models: information-processing models, cognitive-developmental models, and perception and experiential models.

(1) Information-processing models attempt to employ important general principles about the architecture of artificial intelligence systems and their implications for research in human cognition. Computer models provide a means of assessing the plausibility of particular proposals. Occasionally, such models have proved sufficiently well formulated to be subjects in experimental testing with human subjects. At present there is interest in parallel distributed processing (PDP) and connectionism, the idea that things that consistently occur together in an individual's experience become strongly associated in that person's mind (Bechtel & Abrahamsen 1991).

(2) Cognitive-developmental models compare cultures to find common developmental traits and themes. Most of this literature has focused on religious systems and ritual practices. E. Thomas Lawson and Robert McCauley (1990) borrowed the notion of "competence" from Chomsky to argue that participants in religious systems represent knowledge to generate definite intuitions about the "well-formedness" of religious phenomena. These intuitions are the basis of universal principles of religious ritual, specifically with regard to the relative centrality of specific ritual actions. Similarly, Boyer (1994) found that intuitions about religious phenomena spring from universal principles that act as tacit theories that are not in themselves intuitive and may require a "leap of faith". For example, the most widespread ontological assumption of religious systems postulates the existence of agencies such as SPIRITS whose physical properties are counterintuitive. Boyer hypothesized that because counterintuitive assumptions are the focus of more cognitive investment and more emotional effects than representations of other types, they are more likely to survive cycles of transmission.

(3) Perception and experiential models argue that shared perceptual processes and experiences in the environment shape cognitive forms cross-culturally, a view influenced by studies of human perception. Most notable in this category are the works of Lakoff (1987) and M. Johnson (1987), who argued for an "experiential realism" that is not prey to the conceptual trappings of subjectivism and objectivism. Lakoff and Johnson began with the premise that the movements of our bodies and their placement in space generate knowledge structures and modes of reasoning that are evident in linguistic usage. A central component of their argument is metaphor. Our thoughts, works, and even our actions are affected by networks of systematically structured metaphors, which reflect basic kinds of physiological experience. The difference between up and down, for example, is an essential aspect of human experience and is evident in English in the pervasiveness of expressions in which the words "up" and "down" metaphorically conceptualize moods, states, and emotional experiences. Other work has focused

on interconnections between perceptual experience and cognitive categories in Mayan deistic expressions (W. Hanks 1990), in Quechua sound-symbolic adverbs (J. Nuckolls 1996), and in Kilivila classificatory particles (Senft 1996).

At present, cognitive anthropology is influenced by recent work in cognitive science and linguistics and beset with problems with a long philosophical pedigree. Chief among these problems is motivation. Given that people have the models cognitive anthropologists ascribe to them, what makes such models compelling? Roy D'Andrade (1995) and Claudia Strauss (1992) have addressed this issue, redefining knowledge structures as goal-directed systems. The problem with this is that it tends to make us think in terms of discrete and isolable aims that are accessible to consciousness. Edwin Hutchins (1987) and Drew Westen (1992) have attempted to incorporate Freudian psychoanalysis in order to provide cognitive anthropology with a theory of deep motivation. Unfortunately, the ancient division of the field into the study of knowledge (cognition) and the study of motivation (psychoanalysis) makes a synthesis of the two difficult.

While the field acknowledges the explanatory theories of empirical cognitive psychology, it tends to avoid embracing them too closely for fear of reductionism. Some have argued against psychologism on the ground that it diverts attention from the political shaping of the contents of mind (Lutz 1992). Others disagree and advocate increased attention to experimental work in developmental cognitive psychology (Lawson & McCauley 1990). There is mounting concern about the very nature of cognition. Should we continue to regard it as a synonym for thinking, and define the anthropology of cognition as a field mainly concerned with knowledge? Issues like these make it difficult to imagine a strictly "cognitive" anthropology, and in the future, calls for its association with (or outright incorporation by) other disciplines, such as psychology and cognitive science, will probably increase.   CN

collaterals are kin, or lines of kin, not in a direct line of descent from an individual, such as siblings of parents or grandparents and their descendants (uncles, aunts, cousins).   MR

colonialism is the establishment and maintenance of rule, for an extended period of time, by a sovereign power over a subordinate and alien people that is separate from the ruling power. Colonialism is frequently associated with "colonization," namely, the physical settlement of people (settlers) from the imperial center in the colonial periphery (for example the ancient Greek colonies, or British settlers in the Kenyan White Highlands). Characteristic features of the colonial situation include political and legal domination over an alien society, relations of economic and political dependence, a reorientation of the colonial political economy toward imperial economic interests and needs, and institutionalized racial and cultural inequalities (Fanon 1963).

Colonialism is a variant of imperialism, the latter understood as unequal territorial relationships among states based on subordination and domination, associated with particular expressions of industrial capitalism such as financial monopolies and transnational capital flows. As a form of territorial expansion, colonialism is one expression of uneven development within a developing global capitalist system and of changing international divisions of labor (Barratt-Brown 1974).

In the modern period (since 1870), "colonialism" has been employed as a general description of the state of subjection of non-European societies as a result of specific forms of European, American, and Japanese imperial expansion, organization, and rule (Fieldhouse 1981). Colonialism, and anticolonial struggles, have been fundamental forces in the making of what, until recently, was termed the "Third World" and in the shaping of a distinctively modern global system (S. Hall 1996).

History
The age of colonialism began in the fifteenth century with the European expansion in Africa, Asia, and the New World. Spearheaded by Spain and Portugal, and subsequently by other Western European powers such as the Low Countries and

England, colonialism emerged in the wake of violent conquest and settlement after a period of extensive exploration. The most ambitious colonial project was established under Spanish auspices in the New World and involved complex forms of direct and indirect rule and administration, Spanish settlement through land and labor grants (the *encomienda* and the *repartimiento* system), and new forms of economic exploitation (plantations and haciendas, and labor-intensive intensive mining for bullion). This first phase of colonialism was driven in some ways by what Eric Wolf (1982) called "the search for bullion" and other forms of wealth (spices, ivory, and slaves), but the origins of European expansion are complex, rooted in growing European mercantile competition, religious and ideological impulses, and regional political developments associated with the crisis of European feudalism.

Colonialism was framed by limited technological capability (the colonies were often geographically distant from the imperial center and hence relatively autonomous) and by the social power and impulses of a particular mode of production (late feudalism). Although early colonialism is often seen as "mercantile" in nature, promoted by European states through merchant houses and chartered companies, its impact around the globe far exceeded the sphere of TRADE or exchange. For example, millions of people were forcibly taken from Africa to work in SLAVERY on plantations in the Caribbean and the US South while mining and ranching enterprises linked the New World into new circuits of international trade in mass commodities (Stavrianos 1981).

Colonialism as a moment of an emerging global system in the sixteenth century grew from the soil of European feudalism and lasted for three centuries. It was disrupted in the eighteenth century by the rapid advance of industrial CAPITALISM in England, France, and Germany and ushered in a second phase of colonialism, much shorter in duration and rooted in an expansionary world capitalism. The century between 1820 and World War I saw the growth of a modern colonial order backed by complete European hegemony over world trade, finance, and shipping and by new forms of political and military authority sustained by technology, applied science, and infomatics (the telegraph and so on).

Between 1870 and 1918, the colonial powers added an average of 240,000 square miles each year to their possessions; between 1875 and 1915 one-quarter of the globe's land surface was distributed or redistributed as colonies among half a dozen states (Hobsbawm 1987). Britain, France, and Germany increased their colonies by 4 million, 3.5 million, and 1 million square miles respectively; Belgium and Italy, and the USA and Japan each increased their holdings by roughly 1 million and 100,000 square miles respectively. This phase of "classical imperialism" was no longer cast in terms of *laissez-faire* and mercantilism but represented a new phase of capitalist development and of interimperial rivalry.

Modern colonialism

Modern colonialisms can be classified according to the timing and the manner in which alien territories were incorporated and subjugated, usually through violent conquest and plunder, into a WORLD SYSTEM. More precisely, variations in colonial experience arise from the specific combination of:

1. the form of capitalist political economy at specific moments in world time
2. distinctive forms of colonial state (understood as a cultural as much as a political project: Corrigan & Sayer 1985), and the interests they represented, such as the STATE
3. the diversity of precolonial societies upon which European domination was differentially imposed. Insofar as colonizer and colonized are geographically separated, all colonialisms must confront the critical questions of how the colonies are to be administered, financed, and made profitable (Crow & Thorpe et al. 1986)

Colonial states were central to the establishment of conditions under which revenue could be raised (i.e., taxation, customs), labor regimes (based on various forms of free or servile labor) instituted to promote commodity production, and political alliances sealed to maintain the fiction of local participation and yet ensure (an often fragile) imperial hegemony.

In its late-nineteenth- and early-twentieth-century guises colonialism assumed a variety of forms. One useful typology employs the coordinates of forms of commodity production, labor regime, and political rule (Hicks 1969). In the case of Africa there were three distinctive forms (Amin 1973):

1. settler colonies, such as Kenya and Mozambique, in which direct rule by a settler class was associated with plantation-based export-commodity production, including such products as cotton, tea, coffee, and sugar
2. trade or trading post economies, such as Nigeria and Senegal, that were characterized by indirect rule through local ruling classes (Native Authorities) who acted as colonial bureaucrats, and peasant-based production of export commodities, such as palm oil and peanuts
3. mine concessions in places like South Africa or Zaire, where transnational capital dominated the national economy and migrant labor was recruited, often by direct compulsion in the first instance, from spatially segregated "native reserves" for work in the mines that overdetermined the shape of the local political economy

Western education and missionary activity, introduced as a means of training lower-order civil servants and as the civilizing arm of the colonial state, had contradictory consequences. The first-generation anticolonial, nationalist leaders were often products of the civil service (clerks, teachers) and mission schools who continued their education beyond the limits set by their colonial teachers. In the period after 1945, the rise of anticolonial movements in the colonies, and the economic crises within an aging imperial system, both contributed to the rapid process of decolonization. The colonial system was found to be expensive by the imperial powers and increasingly ungovernable. Colonialism was politically and ideologically discredited by emergent nationalist movements, which were often actively supported by the Socialist bloc (see NATION).

Independence from colonial rule came quickly in the postwar period, though white settler colonies were especially resistant to any notion of indigenous rule. Independence was only achieved in such cases through organized insurrection, such as the Mau Mau in Kenya, or through a long guerrilla war of liberation, as in Mozambique. There is a general sense throughout much of the developing world that decolonization has not resulted in meaningful economic or political independence. The persistence of primary-export production and of dependent political elites linked to former colonial powers suggests that colonialism has been transformed into "perpetual neocolonialism" (Abdel-Fadil 1989).

Theoretical perspectives

Efforts to explain the origins and timing, and the character and consequences, of modern colonialism have produced a vast literature. Colonialism has been seen as a benign force of economic modernization and social advancement (the so-called *mission civilatrice*) ensuring law and order, private property and contract, basic infrastructure, and modern politicolegal institutions (Bauer 1976). It has also been posited within various traditions of marxism and neomarxism as an instrument of wholesale destruction, dependency, and systematic exploitation, producing "distorted" economies (see DEPENDENCY THEORY), sociopsychological disorientation, and massive poverty and neocolonial dependency (Rodney 1972; Baran 1957; A. Frank 1967). Some lines of neomarxist thinking have posited that colonial capitalism was "progressive," acting as a powerful engine of social change (B. Warren 1980); other marxist work has argued that colonialism was not progressive enough, provoking Kay's (1975) famous remark that what the Third World needed was *more* not less exploitation. Equally controversial research has posited a distinctive colonial MODE OF PRODUCTION (Alavi 1975). What is clear, however, is that the shift from informal "spheres of influence" to formal colonial rule in the nineteenth century was rooted in a new phase of capitalist transformation (sometimes called the "second" industrial revolution) in which intercapitalist rivalry and the growth of transnational forms of industrial and finance capital promoted a search for raw materials, new markets, and new investment opportunities.

Although anthropological research has in general not contributed to grand theories of colonialism, it has effectively focused on the particular cultural representations of non-European "Others," and the ideologies and practices (missionaries, travelers, scientists) associated with the colonial apparatuses that were part and parcel of the practices and experiences of local colonialisms of various sorts (Taussig 1987; Jean Comaroff & Comaroff 1992).

Anthropology and colonialism
The colonial experience involved complex and simultaneous patterns of resistance and adaptation to colonial rule, and it is to this terrain – the landscape of the consciousness and culture of the colonized and the colonizer – that anthropologists have contributed in important ways (Stoler 1995; B. Cohn 1987; Alonso 1995; Swedenburg 1995).

Anthropology is inseparable from the history and practices of colonialism in a double sense: on the one hand, anthropologists were frequently in the employ of the colonial state itself, and on the other, the science of RACE and of races was an integral part of the ways in which colonial powers represented themselves and non-European Others in the nineteenth- and twentieth-century modernist project (see also DEVELOPMENT, MODERNIZATION). It is with the tensions and contradictions within various colonial projects that much recent anthropological work has concerned itself.

There are several strands to this anthropological re-reading of colonialism. One part is to reclaim the lost voices – the silences and absences in the imperial record – of the struggles and resistances of subaltern groups such as peasants, low-caste workers, and prostitutes. Another is to recognize that the reclamation of such subalternity is to throw colonial hegemony into a different light, and to focus on the "tensions of empire" (F. Cooper & Stoler 1989) – the contradictions, disorder, and incompleteness of colonial rule – and the

dialectics of colonial consciousness. In this work colonialism as a monolithic process is refigured and replaced by a sensitivity to the local cultures as sites of struggle within historically specific global systems. And finally, and most ambitiously, some of this new reckoning of colonialism as an object of anthropological scrutiny reads colonialism as a transnational and transcultural global process that undercuts Eurocentric, nation-centered, imperial grand narratives (Said 1978). In this "postcolonial" view, the subjugated colonial Others were not simply the minor actors in a larger story of European domination but constituted what Stuart Hall (1996) called "the outer face of Western capitalist modernity" (see POSTCOLONIALISM).

Anthropologists have contributed to the sense of re-narrativizing the history of the West, of positing multiple histories and temporalities, and of recovering and reclaiming the displaced and decentered local histories and struggles rooted in local–global interrelationships (Escobar 1994; N. Thomas 1994; Gilsenan 1996; Stoler 1995; R. Young 1995).   MWa
further reading Brewer 1980; Etherington 1984; I. Wallerstein 1974

color terms   *See* CLASSIFICATION

commodities Aristotle, in his work *Politics* (bk. I, ch. X), was the first in a long line of thinkers to distinguish between what Karl Marx (1887, pt. I, ch. 1) would later call use value and exchange value of a particular commodity. Based on this distinction Marx divided economies into those based on production for use and those based on production for exchange.

In systems characterized by production for use, the members of society produce to meet the needs of themselves, their families, and the wider community. The pathway from production to consumption is not separated by a system of exchange such as buying and selling in the MARKET. The goods and services produced in such a system appear as use values. In precapitalist agrarian societies, like those Aristotle lived in and wrote about, the production of wealth was earmarked for luxury consumption, the maintenance of the political establishment, the construction of public monuments and religious structures, or simply conspicuous display.

In systems characterized by production for exchange, on the other hand, goods and services are produced for an impersonal market and therefore appear as commodities. Commodities have a special character, in this view, in that they embody both use values and exchange values. Use value inheres in the nature of an object and reflects its utility or the satisfaction we take in its direct consumption. By exchanging the good in the marketplace we are in effect transferring its usefulness to others in society and gaining the usefulness of some other good for which the exchange was made. In a market economy, said Marx, products take the social form of commodities, become commensurable one with another, and exchange at a rate determined by the social DIVISION OF LABOR. And in such an economy, if a product cannot be exchanged (that is, we cannot find a buyer for it), then according to Marx, it does not constitute use value to the society and the labor expended in its production is wasted.

Inspired by these kinds of distinction, anthropologists have often contrasted "commodity exchange" with "GIFT EXCHANGE." Gregory (1982), who has written extensively on these matters, characterized the difference in this way: commodity exchange is an exchange of alienable objects between persons who are in a state of reciprocal independence which establishes a quantitative relationship between the objects exchanged; gift exchange is an exchange of inalienable objects between persons who are in a state of reciprocal dependence that establishes a qualitative relationship between the persons involved in the exchange. Others, however, have suggested that these definitions make too sharp a distinction and that "gift exchange is much more like commodity exchange than [Gregory] is prepared to recognize" (Gell 1992b).   DK

See also ECONOMIC ANTHROPOLOGY, MARXIST ANTHROPOLOGY

further reading Humphrey & Hugh-Jones 1992b

communication is behavior resulting in the transfer of information among organisms, with the purpose of modifying the behavior of all participants involved in the process. Communication is basic to all life, and essential to living things whose lives are carried out in a social environment.

Anthropologists have long used complexity of communication abilities and practices as one measure of the differences between human beings and other life forms. Whereas many animals embody some form of information interchange in their primary behavioral repertoires, it has long been thought that only humans are capable of the complex form of communication known as LANGUAGE. The exclusiveness of this human ability has been called into question by experiments undertaken in recent years in communication with other animal species, notably chimpanzees and other great apes. However, it is reasonable to maintain that no other species has developed communication to the level of complexity seen in human life.

Theoretical models of communication Although the study of LINGUISTICS in some form dates back almost to the invention of WRITING SYSTEMS, theoretical models of communication as a general process, with language seen as only a particular instance, are fairly recent. The semiotician and linguist Ferdinand de Saussure and the pragmatic philosopher Charles Peirce provided the basis for much later work on the general structure of communication through their development of theories of the functions of signs.

The anthropologist Edward SAPIR provided one of the earliest general formulations of a behavioral approach to communication, writing that "every cultural pattern and every single act of social behavior involve communication in either an explicit or an implicit sense" (1931: 78). He also maintained that communication is fundamentally symbolic in nature, and is therefore dependent on the nature of the relationships and understandings that exist between individuals.

The German linguist Karl Bühler developed a field theory of language in his 1934 *Sprachtheorie*, which proved to be a sturdy model for mathematicians, linguists, and social scientists (Bühler 1990). Bühler saw language as consisting of four elements – speaker, hearer, sign, and object – and three functions: the expressive (coordinating sign and speaker), the appeal (coordinating sign and hearer), and the referential (correlating sign and object).

Claude Shannon and Warren Weaver of the Bell Telephone Laboratories collaborated in 1948 to develop a mathematical model of communication, which, though influential, eliminated any account of social and cultural factors from the communicative process. Shannon and Weaver's (1971) formulation contained six elements: a source, an encoder, a message, a channel, a decoder, and a receiver. These general elements could be realized in many different ways, but a common formulation would be to recognize the speaker as the source, the mind and vocal system as the encoder, a code system such as language or gesture as the message, sound waves in air or electronic signals as the channel, the auditory system and brain as the decoder, and the hearer as the receiver.

Shannon and Weaver also included in their model the concept of "noise" in the system. The mathematical description of noise later became known as "entropy" and was the subject of study in its own right. Information in this formulation is seen as the opposite of entropy. Both concepts are described in terms of probability. The less probable an event is within a system, the greater its information content. The more probable the event is, the smaller the information content, and the closer the event approaches entropy. The existence of a bounded system with evaluative parameters within which the probability of an event can be calculated is essential to this definition, otherwise an unexpected event will be seen as random in nature, and thus have little information content.

Roman Jakobson (1960), drawing on Bühler, developed a model for communication similar to that of Shannon and Weaver. This model is shown in figure 1. In the diagram each of what Jakobson called the "constitutive factors . . . in any act of verbal communication" is matched with a different "function" of language (indicated in italics). According to Jakobson, in each instance of verbal communication one or more of these functions will predominate. His particular interest in this article was to explain the *poetic* function of language, which he identifies as that function of language which operates to heighten the *message*.

Animal communication vs. human communication

Anthropologists have long identified linguistic communication as one of the principal elements – if not *the* principal element – distinguishing humans from other animal forms. In the 1950s and 1960s a number of researchers began to explore the continuity

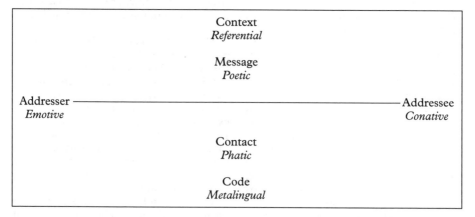

Figure 1 Design elements of communication (after Jakobson 1960).

Table 1   Thirteen design features of animal communication (after Hockett 1960)

Feature	Characteristics
1. Vocal auditory channel	Information is encoded vocally and decoded aurally
2. Broadcast transmission and directional reception	Information is transmitted through sound waves broadcast generally, but is received by hearing apparatus that is able to detect the direction of the source of sound
3. Rapid fading (transitoriness)	Information decays rapidly allowing for transmission of new information in sequential order
4. Interchangeability	Information that is encoded vocally is perceived as equivalent to information received aurally. Consequently, what is heard can be mimicked or repeated by the hearer
5. Total feedback	The information produced vocally by the originator of communication is also heard by that same originator, thus providing a feedback loop and self monitoring
6. Specialization	Different sound patterns are used for different communicative purposes. In humans, speech sounds are used primarily if not exclusively for communication
7. Semanticity	Sign phenomena are able to be understood as representations for referenced objects
8. Arbitrariness	There need be no intrinsic resemblance or connection between signs and the things for which they serve as reference
9. Discreteness	The continuum of sound is processed cognitively into discrete meaningful patterns
10. Displacement	Communication about object outside of the physical presence of the communicators or imaginary or speculative in nature is possible
11. Productivity	New and original communications can be created by communicators freely without their having experienced them previously
12. Traditional transmission	Communication structures and information conveyed through communication are transmitted and acquired as a result of social behavior rather than genetic capacity
13. Duality of patterning	Meaningful communication units are differentiated from each other in patterns of contrast. They simultaneously combine with each other in patterns of combination

of animal and human communication systems. Most work in this early period was speculative and programmatic, but nevertheless influential in setting research agendas.

Charles D. Hockett (1960) identified thirteen "Design-Features" of animal communication, some of which he saw as unique to human beings. These are summarized in table 1. Of the thirteen features, the last four – displacement, productivity, traditional transmission, and duality of patterning – were seen by later researchers as embodying exclusively human capacities.

They were therefore seen as constituting a test for the presence of *linguistic* abilities in other animal species.

Bühler's work and Jakobson's suggestive extension of it were also the basis for the study of animal communication. The semiotician Thomas Sebeok (1965) used their model but extended it by pointing out that visual and tactile channels are as important as auditory ones in the total spectrum of animal communicative behavior; thus the terms "source" and "destination" are more inclusive than "speaker" and "hearer."

Both Hockett's and Sebeok's work have been used in evaluating the linguistic capacity of chimpanzees and other great apes since the 1960s. The first of the so-called linguistic chimps was named Washoe, and was trained in American Sign Language by psychologists Allen and Beatrice Gardner at the University of Nevada in Reno. The scientific community immediately seized on Hockett's list of pattern variables as a way to evaluate how "human" Washoe's communications were. Linguists added further tests of Washoe's ability to exhibit syntactic capacity. The Gardners objected, pointing out that their experiment was designed merely to test the proposition of interspecies communication, not to measure Washoe's capacity for human language (R. Allen Gardner & Gardner 1969), but to no avail. Their research took on a life of its own as a number of researchers began to train and test a variety of nonhuman primates using standards designed to prove or disprove linguistic ability rather than communicative ability. The best of the primates developed some extraordinarily complex communication behaviors. Detractors claim that the behaviors are prompted by stimulus–response mechanisms and only appear to be communicative. These experiments though not conclusive, have nonetheless served to call into question the idea that linguistic communication serves as an absolute boundary between humans and animals.

The evolution of communication

Anthropologists have speculated that human communication may have evolved from gestural systems and verbal signals. Linguist Philip Lieberman suggested that true verbal linguistic communication only came about when the human vocal tract developed a particular shape as the result of full bipedalism that allowed for the production of a full range of vowels. He thus claimed that Neanderthal man did not have full linguistic ability, and that this may have led to his demise. Lieberman's theory has been questioned by a number of researchers who claim that the fossil record does not allow for the reconstruction of the vocal tract, since it consists of soft tissue (Lieberman, 1991).

In any case, gestures, cries, vocal tone and other nonverbal elements continue to play a crucial role in human communication. Edward Hall (1959) has pointed out the importance of interpersonal distance in communication – the study of which he labeled "proxemics.'

The ethnography of communication

Anthropology has tried to document the complexity of communication practices across cultures. One research agenda inspired by the Bühler/Jakobson model has been the "ethnography of speaking," later renamed the "ethnography of communication" by Dell Hymes and his students at the University of Pennsylvania. Hymes developed Jakobson's original list of constitutive elements and functions in several publications (1962, 1974). The most elaborate of these used the mnemonic "speaking" shown in figure 2.

Communication, poetics, and discourse structures

Anthropologists have in recent years turned to models of communication that take into account human creativity and the indeterminacy inherent in all communication operations. Friedrich (1986) pointed out that POETRY is a natural aspect of all human communication and is always open to multiple interpretation. Likewise studies of metaphoric structures in communication (J. Fernandez 1986; Lakoff & Johnson 1980) show how humans try to bridge impreciseness through imagery.

Increasingly, the study of actual DISCOURSE has become the preferred way to analyze human communication. This approach recognizes that the communication process is cooperative, involving a coordination and negotiation of behavior between two or more people. Discourse-centered approaches do not see communication as a set of isolated message transmissions from person to person. Rather, they view it as an emergent process, changing form and purpose continually as it proceeds (cf. Sherzer 1987). Discourse-centered approaches are likely to lead to much more complex models of communication in the future.   WBe

See also NONVERBAL COMMUNICATION, PRAGMATICS, SYMBOLIC ANTHROPOLOGY

S	Situation (setting, scene)
P	Participants (speaker or sender, addressor, hearer or receiver, addressee)
E	Ends (purposes – outcomes, purposes – goals)
A	Act sequence (message form, message content)
K	Key (tone, manner or spirit in which communication is carried out)
I	Instrumentalities (forms of speech, channels of speech)
N	Norms (norms of interaction, norms of interpretation)
G	Genres (culturally recognized types of communication)

Figure 2   Elements of communication (after Hymes 1974).

compadrazgo is a form of ritual kinship derived from Roman Catholic godparenthood found in Spain, Latin America, and the Philippines (Hart 1977). The godparent relationship creates permanent bonds of mutual obligation and affection between godparents and their godchildren and between the godparents and their godchildren's natural parents.

MR

comparative linguistics is the study of the relationships among genetically related languages. Genetically related languages, that is languages in the same language family, are those that descend from a common ancestor (or protolanguage); comparative linguistics is closely interrelated with HISTORICAL LINGUISTICS.

Comparative linguistics includes three main tasks: (1) establishing that two or more languages are genetically related; (2) in the case of three or more genetically related languages, establishing the subgrouping among the languages; and (3) reconstructing the common ancestor. Although these tasks present a logical order, in practice work is likely to be carried out simultaneously on all three.

Establishing that two or more languages are genetically related means finding properties common to them that are most plausibly explained in terms of inheritance from a common ancestor. Other possible explanations for common properties are universal features or tendencies, borrowing, and chance. Deciding among the four possibil-

ities, especially between common genetic origin and borrowing, is often difficult, with recent work suggesting that, given the appropriate circumstances, any feature can be borrowed (Thomason & Kaufman 1988). Nonetheless, there are different probabilities of different kinds of feature being borrowed. Thus, given that nouns are more readily borrowed than verbs, if two languages share a large number of verbs but few nouns, common genetic origin is more plausible than borrowing. A strong requirement on establishing common genetic origin, stemming from the Neogrammarian hypothesis of the regularity of sound change (see HISTORICAL LINGUISTICS), is that there must be systematic correspondences among the sounds of languages in items that descend from their common ancestor; thus, Germanic (including English) *f* corresponds regularly to Latin *p* in word-initial position (compare English *fish* and Latin *piscis*). However, regular correspondences can also characterize loanwords; thus, English /v/ corresponds regularly to /b/ in loans in Japanese. Thus, regular correspondence is not a sufficient criterion to establish common genetic origin over borrowing; while most linguists consider it a necessary condition, some linguists dispute even this.

To establish genetic relatedness, it is necessary to show that all major components – phonology, grammar, and basic vocabulary – of the languages go back to a common ancestor. Some languages thus do not belong to any language family, for instance pidgin and creole languages, which usually have their basic vocabulary from one source, but do not have a grammar derived from that source (Thomason & Kaufman 1988).

Subgrouping is carried out by determining which members of the language family share common innovations, again excluding innovations that are plausibly attributable to chance or to universal tendencies of historical change. Thus, if there are three languages *A*, *B*, and *C*, and *A* and *B* have both undergone a change that is not found in *C*, we may hypothesize that *A* and *B* form a subgroup as against *C*. Two main models have been proposed to represent subgrouping. The most widely used is the family tree (Schleicher 1967), which presents subgrouping as strictly hierarchical: the ancestor language splits into a number of languages, each of which may in turn split into a number of languages; but branches having once split cannot merge again. This model is an oversimplification in that languages do not always, or perhaps even typically, split in so clean a fashion, with no subsequent contact. The alternative, wave model represents a change as emanating from a center and spreading out, with the result that the speech of a particular area may share innovations with a number of different adjacent areas (Schmidt 1872).

Reconstructing the common ancestor of two or more languages involves the following procedures, which together constitute the comparative method in linguistics: (1) identifying those features that are common to all the languages, and reconstructing this feature back to the common ancestor; (2) for those features in which the languages differ, establishing the feature value that is more likely in the ancestor language. As an illustration of the second, consider that the oldest Greek distinguishes five vowel qualities (*a*, *e*, *o*, *i*, *u*), while Sanskrit distinguishes only three (*a*, *i*, *u*), where Sanskrit *a* corresponds to Greek *a*, *e*, and *o*. Given that there is no plausible phonetic environment that could have conditioned the split of Sanskrit *a* into three vowels, it is more plausible to assume that their common ancestor had (at least) five vowels as in Greek, with Sanskrit having merged *a*,

e, and *o* to *a*. Reconstruction can only be partial, since intervening changes may mean that the descendant languages do not present enough evidence to reconstruct some features.

Attempts to reconstruct the protoculture on the basis of the reconstruction of reconstructed vocabulary (linguistic paleontology) are fascinating but fraught with danger (Benveniste 1973). Although the presence or absence of reconstructed words for certain flaura and fauna may be indicative of the homeland of the proto–Indo-Europeans, one would not argue from the lack of a reconstructable word for "hand" that the proto–Indo-Europeans lacked hands.   BC

further reading Anttila 1989; Bynon 1977; Hock 1986; Jeffers & Lehiste 1979; W. Lehmann 1967; Mallory 1989; Meillet 1967; J. Nichols 1992; Pedersen 1931

comparative method involves the use of ethnographic data from many different kinds of society as a basis for constructing an evolutionary typology that is presumed to represent an actual historical sequence through which the different kinds of society moved. The nineteenth-century evolutionists depended heavily on this method for the construction of their evolutionary schemes, and were sharply criticized by the Boasian school of anthropology for doing so. More recent critics of evolutionism, such as Robert Nisbet, have perpetuated this criticism, claiming, as the Boasians did, that the comparative method involves too great an inferential leap to be justified. Use of the comparative method has been defended by, inter alia, Marvin HARRIS (1979), Robert Carneiro (1970), and Elman Service (1962). Harris noted that the method is subject to certain abuses, but that in principle it is sound. Moreover, he noted that the very same kind of method has been employed by evolutionary biologists and astronomers to order the data in their respective fields; why, therefore, should its use be prohibited in the social sciences? A realistic conclusion would appear to be that the comparative method is justified to the extent that evolutionary typologies constructed from ethnographic data correspond well to independently derived typologies that are themselves historical – that is, to typologies produced by archaeologists and historians. In fact, in the best contemporary evolutionary work, this is precisely the case. Although the rapid research advances made by archaeology in recent decades are rendering the comparative method less necessary than it once was, it is still an important methodological tool and will continue to be used.   SS

See also EVOLUTION, EVOLUTIONARY STAGES, HISTORICAL PARTICULARISM

further reading A. Johnson & Earle 1987 [a good example of a recent major evolutionary work that depends heavily on the comparative method and represents a collaboration between a cultural anthropologist and archaeologist]

complementary filiation is the process by which children in a unilineal descent system are attached to the parent who is not in their lineage and to that parent's kin. Thus, in a matrilineal system, complementary filiation involves the creation of bonds of affection and obligation between a child and its father and his kin; in a patrilineal system, to the mother's kin, particularly the mother's brother.   MR

complex society is a typological category for social EVOLUTION. Complex societies are large scale, differentiated, and show social STRATIFICATION. They are politically organized as large regional polities, CHIEFDOMS and STATE systems, ranging in population from the low thousands to the millions (A. Johnson & Earle 1987).

Complex society presumes its opposite – simple society – and this stark division immediately raises a fundamental anthropological question: why and how did complex society develop? We can imagine a time deep in human history when all societies were small scale and simple. From this rude, or paradisiacal, beginning develop divergent organizational forms – some extraordinarily complex and others much simpler. An evolutionary typology, although inherently problematic, lies at the foundation of comparative studies of human societies.

As a touchstone, simple societies can be characterized as small scale and segmental (modular). They are organized at the level of the FAMILY and the local group. Economically structured by a domestic MODE OF PRODUCTION (Sahlins 1972), the family unit is a microcosm of the social economy, encapsulating the fundamental division of labor by age and sex. Families are often organized into local groups, polities of a few hundred people, that occupy and defend a territory. An "egalitarian" farming community represents such a local group. The local group is organized according to elemental social divisions – family, kin, friends, sex, and age. Personal characteristics and capabilities guide further distinctions and differentiation: some become special hunters, basket makers, healers, or shamans. Statuses are created for the characteristics of individuals.

In many complex societies much continues unchanged from simple society, particularly within families and communities. Kinship, friendship, and an elemental division of labor organize most daily activities. But with the creation of the regional polities, new organizational layerings include institutions that control the specialized activities of governance, war, and religion. Associated with the new institutions are a proliferation of new statuses, each with rights and obligations within the regional polity. The actual characteristics of these institutions, the associated statuses, and their interrelationships are highly variable, but the institutions function to integrate the polity, and to establish and maintain social differentiation and inequalities (McGuire 1983). Degrees of centrality vary from central hierarchies to dispersed heterarchies (Crumley 1987).

Complex societies often have dual economies. The subsistence economy of a traditional complex society, as opposed to the modern nation-state, characteristically continues to emphasize the self-sufficient domestic unit and the local community. Economic specialization in the production of foods and crafts may be quite limited. Within the Inca empire, for example, the emphasis was on retaining household and community self-sufficiency without a market system (Murra 1980). But more commonly, the imposition of regional peace and the establishment of a political economy encourage the development of regional markets (Claessen & Skalnik 1978). Most households produce a specialty, but usually only on a part-time basis. For example, among the Aztecs, crafts and foods were exchanged within these markets between communities that specialized in ceramic manufacture, tomato farming, or the like (Brumfiel 1980).

The political economy was developed as a tributary mode of production (E. Wolf 1982) to finance the activities of the emergent regional institutions. The political economy could be organized in contrasting forms based on the units of accounting and payment (D'Altroy & Earle 1985). A system of staple finance, called redistribution, mobilizes foods and crafts from commoner producers for payment to those working for the new institutions. A system of wealth finance involves production and procurement of special goods, varying from prestige goods to primitive currencies, and their use in payment for political services. Associated with the new institutions and their operations are a proliferation of special activities and personnel: managers, administrators, accountants, warriors, craft specialists, ritual specialists, and a proliferation of minor service personnel. Statuses are determined by the organization of the new regional institutions and their local manifestations.

With increasing institutional differentiation comes increasing stratification. Placement within the new institutional structure determines differential rights within the social economy. Characteristically, land is held in an overlapping system of LAND TENURE such that use rights are allocated centrally, as seen for example in feudalism. The institutional control over land translates directly into control over the flow of wealth, whereby a small fraction of the society, the ruling elite, control a disproportionate part of the society's wealth. Individuals and groups compete for control of the institutions, their economic returns, and positions of dominance.

Human societies are infinitely variable. To understand this variation, anthropologists have devised many schemes for characterizing the degree of evolutionary complexity. Based on technological developments, MORGAN (1877) originally recognized a basic tripartite division into savagery, barbarism, and civilization; a modification of this scheme was adopted by Marx and Engels (Engels 1902). The most common schemes now used in anthropology are summarized in table 1.

From top to bottom, these schemes represent increasing complexity. As the scale of the polity increases, the internal differentiation of statuses and the extent of social stratification also increase. Divisions represent various structural transformations, most commonly associated with the devel-

Table 1   Some common anthropological typologies of social evolution

Childe (1936)	Service (1962) Johnson and Earle (1987)	Sahlins (1963) Earle (1978)	Fried (1967)
Hunter–gatherers	Band (family level)	Head man	Egalitarian society
Farmers	Tribe (local group)	Big man	Ranked society
Civilization	Chiefdom	Simple	
		Complex	Stratified society
	State	State	State

Source: Earle 1994.

opment of a new level of integration and its associated institutions. Reasons for the evolution of more complex societies are highly varied but combine an understanding of ecological, demographic, social, and political processes. Some processes are quite general and may be understood cross-culturally; others are highly particular and must be understood within their historical contexts.

A major question on the evolutionary typologies concerns whether the divisions between categories, such as simple and complex societies, is a sharp transformation or a gradual transition. Working from an implied marxist tradition, many have assumed that gradual (quantitative) change in underlying conditions involving the economy and population results in major organizational distortions (contradictions) that cause rapid (qualitative) structural transformations. So considerable attention was paid to the "origins" of the state or of chiefdoms. Spencer (1987) argued that the development of chiefdoms, as the first "complex society," involves a structural transformation. From this perspective, the evolution of human societies develops new levels of integration, in a stairlike fashion. The regional scale of interaction characteristic of complex society requires totally new institutional arrangements that makes such societies qualitatively distinct.

Others, such as Johnson and Earle (1987), have argued that social change is fundamentally continuous, a ramp model. Thus the spatial extent of the polity and the strength of its integration are inherently continuous variables. While a new institutional structure may be conceived at some point in time, its effect on the daily lives of the population may be slowly implemented, changing the new institution in a feedback process. Societal evolution can be modeled as a constant process of interaction between the levels of integration and the human actors involved.

Analytically a division between simple and complex societies may be drawn, but exactly where it is to be drawn is problematic. Drawing the line between BIGMAN and chiefly societies, for example, has brought controversy to Pacific anthropology because it shows a disrespect for the traditional political systems of Melanesia (B. Douglas 1979). It is important to recognize that the distinctions are in fact gradual and overlapping. Most now feel that typological classification is sterile and that stress must be placed instead on processes of change and transformation. Unilinear schemes in particular, running from simple to complex, are uniformly discouraged.

Research has shifted away from a search for the origin of complex society and toward understanding variation within broad categories, such as chiefdom and state systems. Most now assume that evolution is multilinear (Steward 1955) and reversible ("devolution"). Researchers investigate specific historical sequences (Drennan 1991). Recent reinterpretations of hunter–gatherer societies have emphasized emergent complexity with central leadership and ritual elaboration (D. Price & Brown 1985), and work on bigman political systems in Melanesia has emphasized their behavioral similarity to chiefdoms (Terrell 1986).

No simple dimension of variability exists against which anthropologists can measure complexity. Rather, a plethora of structural forms and behavioral patterns exist that can be analytically characterized as more or less complex along different dimensions. The challenge is to understand this variability. One dimension of variability is evidently scale of integration (G. Johnson 1982; Feinman and Neitzel 1984). As the size of a polity increases, the political structure and economic infrastructure of its organization must change. But solutions to the problems of integration and control can be highly variable and seem to depend on a series of ecological, economic, and historical conditions. Understanding the highly dynamic and changing nature of complex societies remains a major focus for anthropological research.   TE

See also CENTRALIZED SYSTEMS, RANKED
  SOCIETIES

further reading Childe 1936; R. Cohen & Service 1978; Fried 1967; Glassman 1986; Lenski 1966; Mann 1986–93; Service 1962; Leslie White 1959a

componential analysis is an analytic technique derived from LINGUISTICS. It is used by anthropologists in the SEMANTIC analysis of a relatively bounded set of words (lexicon) used in a particular culture to refer to items in specified domains of interest. It attempts to explain how native speakers apply the terms of a particular lexicon to individual items. This process includes correctly discriminating those items native speakers perceive as sufficiently similar to be categorized together under a single term, and those items that are so different that they require separate terms.

In linguistics, componential analysis is used for a number of tasks, including the definition of the PHONEMES of a given language. This is done by identifying a posited set of underlying components (i.e., features, attributes, dimensions, variables) whose combination differentiates each phoneme in the language from every other phoneme on at least one dimension. In the simplest case, with variables that each had only two values, two variables would produce 4 unique terms; three would yield 8 terms; four, 16 terms; five, 32; and so on.

In anthropology the exemplary domain of componential analysis is KINSHIP. For example, consider the four terms of reference for these CONSANGUINE relatives in English: aunt, uncle, niece, and nephew. Assuming that the definition of the domain of consanguine relatives is based on parent–child and sibling ties (i.e., mother, father, brother, sister), then a native speaker would properly refer to his/her mother's sisters and father's sisters as "aunts," and discriminate mother's brothers and father's brothers as "uncles." Brothers' daughters and sisters' daughters would be "nieces," and brothers' sons and sisters' sons would be "nephews." One possible set of underlying variables that would account for these kin terms from the lexicon might include generation $(+1,-1)$ and the sex of the relative (not the speaker) (M,F). The four terms could then be defined by the following combinations of the two components: aunt $(+1,F)$; uncle $(+1,M)$; nephew $(-1,M)$; and niece $(-1,F)$.

Componential analysis in anthropology was pioneered by the simultaneous but independent work of Ward H. Goodenough (1956) and Floyd G. Lounsbury (1956).

Widely debated in the 1960s (Goodenough 1964, 1967, 1970; Scheffler & Lounsbury 1971; Hammel 1965), it bore the brunt of heated criticism because there were often multiple ways of getting similar outcomes (Burling 1964; Spradley 1972a). Componential analysis was also instrumental in the emergence of the so-called NEW ETHNOGRAPHY and the wider field of ETHNOSCIENCE, and it laid the foundation for recent resarch in COGNITIVE ANTHROPOLOGY (D'Andrade 1995).   JIA

further reading Spradley 1980; Spradley & McCurdy 1972

composite or compound family   is a group of nuclear families linked by a common spouse, most commonly a husband in a polygynous marriage system.   MR
See also POLYGYNY

concubinage   is the state of being a minor wife; that is, a wife of lower jural status than a major or full wife. Polygynous state societies often recognize two or more ranks of wife who have differential rights and duties in relation to their husband and the rest of their household, as also do their offspring. The term is also used when referring to a woman cohabiting with a man to whom she is not married, a common-law wife.   MR

configurationism   Ruth BENEDICT made the notion of configurationism famous in her book *Patterns of culture* (1934a), when she portrayed cultures as analogous to human personalities; that is, each culture is understood as a coherent, complex, unique entity, bound together by highly patterned internal relationships producing multiple levels of significance.

These levels of significance could be interpreted by the anthropologist to produce a consistent and convincing portrait of the configuration and of the people within it. Even knowing only some aspects of the configuration would allow the prediction of others. CULTURE, then, could be known much as a person could be known, and each culture could be appreciated on its own grounds, as aesthetic and harmonious, or as discordant and neurotic.

Configurationism clearly reflected Benedict's training with Franz BOAS in the German tradition of aesthetic ethnography that was descended from Herder. But also influential was the holism of Gestalt psychology (W. Köhler 1929), the humanistic psychology of Harry Stack Sullivan (1964), and the romantic philosophy of Wilhelm Dilthey (1961).

Benedict's configurationist approach foundered on questions about her underlying assumption of coherence; nor was it clear exactly what aspects of the culture were essential, and which were purely secondary or ephemeral. Benedict also made use of literary–psychoanalytic models to give her configurations a skeleton, and these were not accepted as adequate by many anthropologists.

However, configurationism retains a strong hold on the anthropological imagination. For instance, Clifford GEERTZ (1973), like Benedict, emphasized the uniqueness and inner harmony of each cultural system, although he repudiated the psychological armature that was essential to Benedict's work. Outside anthropology, the cultural theorist Norbert Elias (1978) has had considerable success with an avowedly configurationist approach that unites psychoanalytic sophistication with the study of long-term historical processes in European culture.   CL

further reading Benedict 1946; C. Geertz 1983; M. Mead 1935

conflict resolution (or dispute settlement or dispute processing) is a field of study inspired by the shift in LEGAL ANTHROPOLOGY from the study of LAW to the study of disputing. Anthropologists examined the social processes through which conflicts were handled and began to view disputes as embedded in social relationships that directly affected the way litigants pursued and settled their grievances. For example, in his analysis of Barotse law, Max GLUCKMAN (1955a) argued that when disputing parties wished to preserve their relationships with each other, they were more willing to compromise and settle amicably. Such models therefore predicted that when social relationships among disputants were multiple and continuing, they would seek out conciliatory procedures of handling conflicts that produced compromise solutions; but when social relationships were few and fleeting, disputants would prefer more adjudicatory procedures that produced win–lose outcomes (Colson 1953). Laura Nader and her students (Nader & Todd 1978) expanded these models to examine how conflicts were handled in such diverse places as Turkish villages (Starr 1978) and highland New Guinea settlements (Koch 1978) by adopting the "trouble case" as the basic unit of analysis for studying conflict resolution (Llewellyn & Hoebel 1941).

Modes of handling disputes vary greatly but can be classified into a set of commonly used procedures (Gulliver 1963; Jane Collier 1973). Some are dyadic, such as negotiations involving only two parties, who construct their own rules and reach agreement through compromise. But many forms of conflict resolution are triadic and involve third parties. The role and power of such third parties depends on the structure of the resolution process. In mediation, a conciliatory process, the third party helps the two disputants reach a settlement but has no authority to impose one (Gulliver 1977). In arbitration, the disputants agree in advance to accept the decision of the third party as binding. In adjudication, the state authorizes a judge to render a binding decision without regard for the disputants' agreement. Procedures also differ according to type of outcome. Negotiation and mediation typically produce compromises while adjudication is more likely to result in zero-sum outcomes. Not all procedures are designed to resolve conflicts; some just reduce the potential consequence of a confrontation (Merry 1979). These include avoidance, in which one party simply breaks off relations with the other, or "lumping it," where one party becomes resigned to putting up with a difficult and irresolvable situation with no expectation of resolution (W. Felstiner 1974).

TIME and process are central to the analysis of conflict resolution. Disputes have trajectories, stages through which a conflict passes. Nader and Todd (1978: 14–15) analyzed three stages of a dispute: the grievance or preconflict stage, when a person feels unjustly treated, the conflict stage, when the aggrieved party confronts the other party, and the dispute stage, when the conflict escalates to a public confrontation involving a third party. Mather and Yngvesson (1981) showed how disputes are transformed over time as they pass through these stages and are defined in narrower or broader terms. Their work foregrounds the role of particular audiences and third parties, such as judges or court clerks, in transforming disputes (Yngvesson 1993).

The anthropological focus on disputes and disputing has an impact well beyond academia and was very influential in the early years of the alternative dispute-resolution movement (Sander 1976; *but see* Merry 1987). Proponents of alternative dispute resolution argued that consensual dispute settlement was more appropriate than adjudication in neighborhoods and community settings with ongoing social relationships. Yet considerable research suggests that urban neighborhoods in modern INDUSTRIAL SOCIETIES are rarely bound together by close-knit social relationships sufficient to foster the conciliatory forms of settlement envisaged by Gluckman (Merry & Milner 1993).

The relationship between compromise outcomes and ongoing relationships has been particularly criticized as too influenced by Durkheimian models of social cohesion: people involved in ongoing relations have often proved only too willing to sacrifice these relationships for control over scarce resources (Starr & Yngvesson 1975). Models of conflict resolution have also been attacked for their assumptions that actors make rational choices between alternatives rather than seeking justice or revenge (Merry & Silbey 1984; Merry 1990). Other critics contend that the dispute-processing paradigm has neglected the analysis of historical change and power relations (Starr & Collier 1989). If context is understood only in terms of social relationships, the analysis ignores the larger structural influences and historical forces, such as the expansion of CAPITALISM, that affect the very essence of what people dispute and why (Abel 1979).

In spite of these criticisms, anthropological concepts of conflict resolution have provided the foundation for an explosion of alternative dispute-resolution studies, processes and institutions in North America, Europe, and many other parts of the world since the 1980s. These have made conflict resolution a distinct discipline that extends well beyond anthropology with its own distinct literature and theories, advanced degrees, and scholarly associations.

SEM

See also FEUDING, PEACE, VIOLENCE, WAR
further reading Abel 1982; D. Black 1976; Hamnett 1977

consanguinity is the attribution of kinship relations by reason of biological relationship, commonly called "shared BLOOD." **Consanguines** are, therefore, kin linked by a common biological substance; that is, they are kin by birth, as opposed to AFFINES, who are related by marriage.

MR

conspicuous consumption is the public display of costly goods and use of costly services as a means of status display. Narrowly conceived, this phenomenon is specific to capitalist societies in which possessions define the person, and as such was coined by Veblen (1899) to describe the behavior of the US rich in the late nineteenth century. The term can be extended to other societies, however, in which the sumptuous display of goods, whose opulence in number or quality outweighs their utility, serves as a way of marking or claiming status.   MR
See also POTLATCH

contraception   *See* REPRODUCTION

cooking, cuisine   In all human societies the preparation of food includes the application of heat to raw products; that is, cooking. Cooking, understood as heating, is only one way of transforming the raw, but it remains the most important and is associated with the whole notion of the hearth (a defining unit in many early censuses) as the center of the house and the location of women's domestic activities. The hearth, with its permanent fire, is also the provider of warmth and so especially in northern climes becomes the focus of the HOUSEHOLD's social life. As such it attracts divinization in the form of the kitchen god of China, the fire gods of Indo-European mythology, or the even more general cults of the hearth and home that persist even in the secular societies of today.

In the nineteenth century anthropological interest in food centered upon TABOO, TOTEMISM, SACRIFICE, and communion, the religious aspects of the process of consumption. In the twentieth century functionalists continued these lines of inquiry and attempted to link such practices with the structure of social relations (the "sociological" dimension) and with the processes of production and reproduction, as in Audrey RICHARDS's study of *Land, labour and diet in Northern Rhodesia* (1939). More specifically concerned with cooking have been the structural analyses of LÉVI-STRAUSS (1963a), in which he saw the application of fire to transform food from the raw to the cooked state as marking the emergence of humanity, the culinary equivalent to the role of the incest taboo for sex. That interest led to an attempt to distinguish gustemes (in a binary fashion on the linguistic model), as in his contrast between English and French cuisines (Lévi-Strauss 1969b). The distribution of these features was then compared to those in homologous spheres in order to elicit "the unconscious attitudes" of the societies under consideration. He later shifted from binary distinctions to "the culinary triangle," based on the vowel triangle in linguistics (Lévi-Strauss 1965), which is continued in his analyses of South American mythology (Lévi-Strauss 1969–81). There the culinary triangle, with its apexes of raw, cooked, and rotten, is supplemented by a triangle of recipes, involving roasted, smoked, and boiled. Other writers (Lehrer 1974) have pursued this notion but on the basis of lexemes, units in a particular language, rather than analytic gustemes or even technemes.

Mary DOUGLAS used a form of cultural analysis to "decode a meal" (1971). She broke down its components but at the same time insisted that it should be set in the framework of other meals consumed; for "the meaning of a meal" is found by examining a series of repeated analogies, in a parallel manner to RADCLIFFE-BROWN's (1922) study of Andaman rituals. In the same vein the symbolic structure must be seen to fit with the pattern of social relations.

What tends to be omitted in these various approaches is any great stress on the internal (e.g. CLASS) differences in cooking practices, since the notion of culture tends to imply homogeneity. Nor is much made of changes arising from such internal conflicts, or the importation of new crops, new techniques, or new recipes from outside. Yet reflection on the world situation shows that such changes are not confined to advanced societies alone, though certainly the industrialization of food has speeded up the process, for example, in the production and use of sugar (Mintz 1985).

In some stratified societies different modes of life, based on access to resources of various kinds, mean that upper groups have different food from lower groups, where the hierarchical practices refer to the kinds of food used, the way they are prepared and served, and the way they are eaten (the whole sphere of "table manners").

State societies consisting of various estates are not necessarily marked by their own forms of cooking. In most African states there were few differences in the diets of the higher and lower groups. By and large, chiefly households had the same recipes as those in other strata, with the possible exception of more meat, more salt, and more of everything rather than more of different things. That situation is related to the fact that most households were dependent upon hoe agriculture, even those of merchants who engaged in trade and of the ruling estates who engaged in booty production, so that the economic differences were not great. Moreover, members of any one estate frequently married out, drawing their wives from other groups, leading to a homogenization of cooking practices among women. In general no major subcultures were formed and no differentiated cuisines emerged (J. Goody 1982).

Contrast this situation with that in the main societies in Europe and Asia, where upper groups developed more complex styles of cooking and had access to more complicated ingredients and recipes. These groups tended, as Marc Bloch (1967) pointed out, to marry in a circle, endogamously rather than exogamously, and hence to develop their own subcultures. In this they were supported by their much greater land-holdings under plough (or intensive) AGRICULTURE, where the harnessing of animal labor meant that one man could produce much more than another, enabling him to support a "higher" way of life. Since the prevailing DOWRY system encouraged a match of property and status, marriage tended to be within the group, among people of the same style of life.

Such differentiation was increased by the advent of writing, which helped specialist groups serving the upper strata, or indeed members of that strata itself, to collect and elaborate recipes in cookbooks that could then act as models for those aspiring to follow the same life-style. That was particularly the case with the arrival of print, when mass-produced editions opened up avenues of social mobility.

In certain societies of this type, the process reached a higher degree that gave rise not simply to a differentiated cooking but to *haute cuisine*. China is clearly one of those, and Michael Freeman (1977) has discussed the emergence of such a cuisine in terms of the wide availability of ingredients and recipes, a corps of adventurous eaters, the pleasure in cooking food, and the development of an advanced agriculture. Other places that produced such a cuisine were Hindu India, the Arab Middle East, and Renaissance Italy. To different extents, all developed restaurant cultures, which was critical to the emergence of the formalized regional cuisines of China.

Such elaborations of cuisine inevitably produced a backlash, not only on the part of the poor but also from ethical philosophers, who objected to waste, excess, differentiation, and POVERTY. At certain times and places such objections became dominant; both in Puritan England and in Communist China, severe restraints were placed on public banqueting.

One aspect of excess is the constant association of food with sex, a subject that has interested Crawley (1902), Lévi-Strauss, Khare (1976), and many other writers. Of China it has been said that the vocabularies of food and lust overlap. Not only at the symbolic but also at the domestic level the two are closely associated.   JG

corporate kin groups   are recognized social groups based on kinship that have control over common property or other rights, act as recognized legal entities, and have jural authority over their members.   MR

corroboree   is an Australian Aboriginal nocturnal dance festival.   MR

cosmology   entails both the overarching conceptions of the place of human beings in the general scheme of existence and the forces engaged in the constitution and generation of such a scheme. These forces relate to the ordering of supramundane beings and the overall cosmic processes that these beings represent and that have consequence for human experience. Cosmologies are usually explored in the context of religious beliefs and ritual practices but also apply to secular industrial and science/technologically driven realities. They infuse the routine activities and thoughts of all human beings.

Cosmological notions concerning the creative and degenerative forces affecting human existence in the universe are critical for comprehending the way human beings orient themselves within their environments. People form and attach significance to features connected with their social existence and physical environment. For example, Australian Aborigines invest all aspects of their lived environment, rituals, and social relations with meanings that are embedded in the mythological and ritual practices associated with primordial Dreamtime beings. Such Aboriginal cosmologies articulate a particular space–time vision that sees human beings as intimately bound together with cosmic processes from which they are generated and that they also play a key ritual role in generating.

Mary DOUGLAS, following the lead of DURKHEIM, has focused on the connections between types of cosmology and the organization of social and political groups. Thus, she suggests that societies with strong notions of political authority and sharply delineated boundaries between social groups are likely to have cosmologies that express powerful notions of destructive and transgressive EVIL force. SORCERY beliefs and practices are most prevalent in societies with high levels of STRATIFICATION, while WITCHCRAFT is a feature of more EGALITARIAN SOCIETIES (M. Douglas 1966, 1970a).

Critics argue that correlations between cosmology and types of society are difficult to establish: in Asia alone, many very different kinds of society embrace similar cosmological orientations. They also contend that cosmologies are not just representations of world orders but practices so ingrained that they affect the dynamics of social formation and have implications in the structuring of social practices. Bourdieu's (1977) analysis of the practices of the North African Kabyle is outstanding in this regard, demonstrating the role of cosmological assumptions in the creation and reproduction of the orderings of social space (e.g. the Kabyle house) and the temporal structure of the agricultural cycle (the Kabyle calendar).

Current anthropological study focuses on cosmologies as important forms of knowledge in themselves or as ways to understand the dynamics of social and political formations beyond the norms of commonsense, usually Western, rationalism. Griaule (1965) and Leenhardt (1979) are among the anthropological pioneers for the exploration of cosmologies as systems of knowledge, although the monumental work of LÉVI-STRAUSS in *Mythologiques* (1969–81) is the single greatest contribution. Lévi-Strauss opened the way to the great value of systematically analyzing MYTHS for understanding the knowledge of diverse peoples and in their own terms. Although Lévi-Strauss is criticized for constraining the cosmological thought embedded in myths to a Western binarism and Kantian transcendental logic, he, more than most anthropologists, freed other modes of cosmological thought from the tyranny of Western concepts and brought them into debate with Western philosophical and metaphysical understanding, which, of course, embed various cosmological orientations.

Approaches that regard cosmology as embedded in thought and practice challenged the view that it was a mere reflection of social processes. For example, Gluckman's (1965b) analysis of the Swazi royal *incwala* ritual had argued that its violent themes served a functional role in sustaining political order. But Beidelman rejected this approach as superficial, demonstrating that these conflicts were integral to specific Swazi cosmological themes underlying kingship in which chaotic and demonic forces played a vital role within an ordering power that was fundamentally ambiguous. Most recently a debate between Obeyesekere (1992) and Sahlins (1995) over the circumstances surrounding the death of Captain Cook in Hawaii hinged on the interpretation of cosmological dynamics within a social process. Obeyesekere challenged Sahlins's view that Cook was regarded as God by Hawaiians. But Sahlins retorted that Obeyesekere's argument was itself rooted in a Western rationalist notion of both deities and political processes, one that denied the role of Hawaiian cosmological notions in their own interpretation of historical events. Hawaiian thought and practice allowed for a continuity between divinities and human beings. Moreover, the cosmology of Hawaiian kingship had the potential to reconceive the presence of Cook in a manner most threatening to Hawaiian hierarchies.

The study of cosmology has strengthened anthropological self-criticism of its own cultural biases, including a too easy reliance on such familiar dichotomies as Sacred/Profane, Nature/Culture, Order/Disorder, Good/Evil, Material/Immaterial. Comparison with Hindu and Buddhist cosmologies (and those of numerous other societies) that do not express such disjunctions or radical oppositions reveal the Judeo-Christian cosmological foundations, as well as the historical/cultural basis, of anthropological concepts. Various scholars

(Blumenberg 1987; Dumont 1986b) have demonstrated remarkable continuities between many of the dominant concepts and paradigms of social science (including anthropology) and those philosophical/theological/scientific discourses emanating from within Judeo-Christian traditions. Sahlins (1996) contended that British structural-functionalism is a specific transformation of Western thought as a development within the Adamic theory of *Genesis*, which describes humankind as imperfect and the source of suffering (see STRUCTURALISM, FUNCTIONALISM). Thus, the structural functionalism extending from the work of Durkheim and MAUSS sublimates notions of an egotistical man generating suffering on the basis of the satisfaction of individual wants in the concept of "SOCIETY" as a superorganic entity.

In debates about the development of the modern world, it is repeatedly posited that in the emergence of the scientific attitude certain cosmological barriers to grasping the nature of existential realities were broken. Human beings were no longer the center of the scheme of things and their existence no longer had necessary meaning or rationale that was divinely ordained. However, this view assumes that modern science is not itself a type of cosmology. It also ignores the new understandings of the universe and forms of existence within it that are germinal in many cosmologies, even those that on the surface appear antiscientific. Moreover, the ways human beings grasp their realities are irreducibly human conceptions. The anthropological inquiry into cosmology concentrates on such a fact and its implications for the limitation as well as the expansion of knowledge.   BK

courtship   refers to the process whereby individuals acquire either a date or a spouse. The word "courtship" comes from the practice of courtly love in the medieval courts of Western Europe. In European and American dating, courtship and engagement denote varying degrees of commitment in the premarital social interaction of men and women (LeVay 1993). "The process of courtship may involve a great deal of time, energy and risk" (Frayser

1985: 24). Besides having to attract another through elaborate displays of behavior or artifacts of success or displays of physical beauty, suitors often have to deal with the aggression of competitors.

There are gender differences in courtship style and romantic expression that arise from cultural traditions as well as biopsychological factors. Evolutionary psychology asserts that the development of different love strategies is not always recognizable or readily understood. Men and women are typically attracted to different qualities in a potential lover or mate, which incline men to fall in love more quickly, and women to adopt a more cautious, deliberate tack (Symons 1979).

From this perspective, many of the characteristic "love acts" displayed during courtship are designed to enhance male and female attractiveness (Daly & Wilson 1978). For women these acts are geared toward measuring male ambition, industry, income, status, and generosity; whereas men are looking for evidence of female fertility, such as youth, health, sexual exclusivity, reproduction capability, and parental investment (Buss 1994).

The attitudinal differences of men and women may account, in part, for the phenomenon of instant attraction or "love at first sight." If erotic and romantic idealization for men is based on images of physical attraction, it would also account for men's ability to quickly shift between sexual fantasy and deep romantic affection. Customarily, women show more interest in assessing a man's social status or understanding his character. More so than physical attractiveness, this appears to be the critical criterion for female mate-selection and the formation of romantic fantasies. Since it takes much longer to evaluate character than it does physical beauty, women may be slower to become romantically involved or make a complete commitment (Jankowiak et al. 1992).

If physical appearance and social standing are valued, their very presence also increases apprehension and anxiety. The power of the love experience to distort judgment is a common cross-cultural fear. It can create imbalance, which leads men and women to think that they have been unfairly seduced or bewitched by each other. In cultures across the world, countless cautionary tales warn men and women of becoming stuck in a love that is excessive. Their clearest and most vivid manifestation lies in the near universality of tales that caution men and women to be wary of what is most desired in the opposite sex: for men, the allure of physical beauty; and for women, the power of social status.

It is when courtship is most intense and focused that love and sex, albeit separate EMOTIONS, are inextricably intertwined and intimately connected. The critical question then must be whether the twin emotions will be institutionalized inside or outside of MARRIAGE, or ignored and left to the individual to reinvent anew in each generation. In each pairing it is not the singular appearance, therefore, of ROMANTIC LOVE, monogamy, or individual choice, but the combination of all three occurrences *inside* the institution of marriage that is historically significant. What accounts for romantic love's emergence as the primary basis, as opposed to a possible consideration, for marriage?

Cultural anthropologists emphasize the structural impact of the transformation of the FAMILY from a unit of production to a unit of consumption, which, geographically speaking, reduced kinship ties while also providing youths with the economic and emotional resources to resist parental demands for self-sacrifice. Rapid social change also contributed to separating generations in terms of cultural values, which contributed to greater adolescent freedom (Goode 1959). In this situation, love becomes the basis of intergenerational discord. It also becomes a discourse of defiance whereby lovers circumvent the arrangements of the senior generations and choose their own marriage partners. Once marriage was redefined as an amorous union organized around personal choice, it entered the "visible or official culture." Under such circumstances love no longer had to be rediscovered anew in each generation. In the Western world, romantic love gradually, and in various intensities, became the language of gentility and social distinction (Jankowiak 1995).   WJ

See also SEX
further reading H. Fischer 1992; Jankowiak & Fischer 1992; Mellen 1981

cousins are the children of an individual's (Ego's) parent's siblings.
MR
See also CROSS-COUSINS, PARALLEL COUSINS

couvade is a ritual of giving birth undertaken by the father of a child while the mother is in labor. The father goes into seclusion, mimics some of the behaviors of CHILDBIRTH, and observes TABOOS.
MR

co-wife is a woman who shares a husband with one or more other women in a polygynous union.   MR

critical anthropology is (1) the epistemological and cultural critique perspectives that emerge from cross-cultural research, occasionally applied as full-blown practices to anthropologists' own societies; (2) anthropological work inspired by or participating in the general marxist tradition of social theory; (3) post-1960s anthropological work inspired by the FRANKFURT SCHOOL's "Critical Theory."

(1) Ethnographic descriptions of other societies have been pursued by anthropologists since the "Malinowskian revolution" of the 1920s, both to enlighten members of their own society about other ways of life and to challenge taken-for-granted cultural assumptions, thereby serving as a critique of the mass, liberal bourgeois societies produced by industrial capitalism. Anthropologists joined public debates about family (M. Mead 1928, 1930; Malinowski 1926, 1962), crime and punishment (Malinowski 1927), immigration policy (Boas 1928), and educational reform (Redfield 1947), based on their knowledge of comparative sociology and alternative ways of organizing society. Science was critiqued in terms of Azande WITCHCRAFT (Evans-Pritchard 1937), setting off a vigorous debate about the nature of rationality and both systems' protection against falsification. The analysis of CLASS and class con-

flict was formulated with insights into the cultural hegemonic processes of charter myths, symbolic condensation, ritual processes, small versus large-scale organizational forms, symbolic differentiation of interest and class groups, and self-presentation versus objective indices of social rank, inter alia (W. Lloyd Warner 1941–59; Gusfield 1963; R. Grimes 1976; Fischer 1980a). Numerous community studies contributed to the understanding of urban form, ethnic succession, matrifocal extended families, mutual aid mechanisms, and the dynamics of religious sect formation. Recently renewed efforts to pursue detailed ethnographic work in First World societies (Ginsberg 1989; Marcus 1992; Martin 1994; M. Strathern 1992; Traweek 1988) does not simply merge into SOCIOLOGY but retains the cultural, cross-cultural, transnational perspectives of anthropological critique as well as the signature functionalist methodological inquiry into the interconnections of differentiated social and cultural sites (see FUNCTIONALISM, POSTMODERNISM).

(2) The tradition of marxist or materialist-inspired anthropology in the United States, represented by such figures as Stanley Diamond, Eric Wolf, Sidney Mintz, and the early work of Marshall Sahlins (1960, 1968b, 1972), had older roots in the study of cultural ecology by Julian STEWARD and Leslie WHITE (see ECOLOGICAL ANTHROPOLOGY). In the post–World War II period, however, critical anthropology increasingly confronted questions of culture with power and political economy. It saw itself as an alternative to tendencies within anthropology to elide historical forces of CAPITALISM and COLONIALISM and make anthropology part of the hegemonic project of MODERNIZATION and DEVELOPMENT of the Third World during the 1950s and 1960s. The journals *Critique of Anthropology* and *Dialectical Anthropology* were associated with this initiative, as was the Department of Anthropology at Columbia University. Compared to marxist theorizing in England and France much of this move in anthropology was theoretically soft, reflecting the politics of the Cold War and the ideological animus against too explicit a marxist theory in the United States.

Therefore much of it went under the label of CULTURAL MATERIALISM, often devolving into studies that were more ecological than political-economic. Nonetheless, these orientations provided a route for anthropology to incorporate the rich work of underdevelopment theory (see WORLD-SYSTEM THEORY), STRUCTURAL MARXISM, British marxist historiography, and cultural studies (E. Thompson 1963; Aston & Philpin 1985; R. Williams 1958, 1975).

(3) In the 1960s, the student movement rediscovered the Critical Theory of the Frankfurt school, which become a major inspiration for critiques of mass societies, mass politics, and the control of bourgeois societies through diffuse hegemonic cultural mechanisms that could be applied to America and its national-security state, commoditization, and information-society global hegemonic reach. Popular culture was seen increasingly as a double-edged site where certain kinds of resistance could be formulated. Early British punk rock was an exemplary site in the ethnographic work of Birmingham Cultural Studies (Frith 1983; Hebdige 1979; P. Willis 1977) and was as easily coopted by the commodifying structures of the market and cultural economy. This revitalized sense of cultural critique in the 1980s and 1990s was further strengthened by inputs from French post–Algerian war and post-1968 thought (see POSTMODERNISM).

In anthropology, the Frankfurt school formed a background for anthropologists, allied historians, and cultural studies writers working in class-divided, market-dominated, and revolution-riven societies (M. Fischer 1980a, 1980b; Taussig 1980, 1987) as well as America (Lipsitz 1988, 1990; Frith 1983). Walter Benjamin (1994) was rediscovered as a critic who elaborated the oppositional side of modern culture that had resisted assimilation to existing modes of production and exchange. He provided an optimistic counterpoint to Adorno's pessimism about the (lack of) potential of modern technology to allow groups within society to express themselves and disseminate their subcultures and perspectives. Frankfurt-style questions were supplemented by the structural marxism of Althusser, which inquired into the structuring of ideological processes, and by Gramscian questions about the ways in which hegemonic cultural structures are formed. By the mid-1980s, these questions were being supplemented by formulations from the so-called postmodern group of writers in France (Foucault, Derrida, Lacan, Baudrillard). At issue increasingly were the ways in which the silicon chip or computer revolution of the 1970s was changing the nature of communication, and hence the possibilities of social organization. It brought pressure for increased flexibility of cultural forms, involving increased diffuseness yet pervasiveness of disciplinary control (Martin 1994), changing forms of the public sphere (the new anthropology-led journals *Late Editions* and *Public Culture*) and changing nexi between venture capital, government, and knowledge production (Rabinow 1996).

MF

cross-cousins are those whose parent is of the opposite sex to the linking parent of an individual (Ego). A MATRILINEAL cross-cousin is a mother's brother's child. A PATRILINEAL cross-cousin is a father's sister's child. In some systems both matrilateral and patrilateral cross-cousins are designated by a single term as "BILATERAL cross-cousins," in opposition to PARALLEL COUSINS. In systems that distinguish one or another type of cross-cousin, the cross-cousin often figures importantly in marriage rules, as in matrilateral cross-cousin marriage, where a man's wife should ideally be his mother's brother's daughter (MBD), although this tends to be category of individuals rather than a specific person.

MR

cross-cultural studies are comparisons between two or more societies, whether loosely constructed or rigorously systematic. More narrowly, **cross-cultural analysis** is a method that is "holocultural" – involving systematic comparison of ten or more societies worldwide. Systematic cross-cultural research is important in other disciplines, including psychology, political science, and demography, and each discipline has its own methods and research focus.

Herodotus (ca.485–425 B.C.E.) may be the earliest known cross-cultural researcher. His *History* compared and analyzed the many cultures that bordered the Greek world and excelled in ethnographic description but was prone to judge all non-Greeks as barbarians. In the nineteenth century cross-cultural comparison became used to rank societies by EVOLUTIONARY STAGES as part of a theory of social EVOLUTION, as in Lewis Henry MORGAN's *Ancient society* (1877). However, the societies compared were selected serendipitously rather than sampled, the data were anecdotal rather than systematically collected, and generalizations were not tested for statistical significance – defects not corrected when Friedrich Engels (1902) borrowed much of the data for his own, more widely known theories.

Edward B. TYLOR (1889) conducted the first true cross-cultural studies when he attempted to compare residence and descent to other societal characteristics. In response to this work, at a public meeting Francis Galton suggested that because Tylor's cases represented societies with shared histories, they were not independent cases and could not be compared as such. This argument, later known as "Galton's Problem," raised such a serious issue that systematic cross-cultural research largely disappeared for more than half a century, until the work of George P. Murdock (1949) revived it.

Systematic holocultural research gained new impetus when it began to focus on problems of methodology (D. Levinson & Malone 1980). Cross-cultural researchers were generally unconcerned with such issues until the 1930s, when Murdock introduced the use of a variety of basic sampling methods and statistical analyses. Since the 1970s researchers have used increasingly sophisticated statistical methods to control for Galton's Problem, regional variation, and group significance (M. Burton & White 1987; C. Ember & Levinson 1991; L. Freeman et al. 1989).

Cross-cultural analysts employ two kinds of sample: continuous-area samples and worldwide samples. The former use regionally comparative studies of societies that might be linguistically related, such as North American Indians (Driver 1961), and focus on the process of diffusion across a single world region. The latter seek to exclude societies that are linguistically or historically related by drawing on world-wide holocultural samples that can be shown to be independent of one another. Both kinds of research are valid.

Most cross-cultural research depends on extracting data from secondary sources that must be evaluated and coded for use. An important resource is the Human Relations Area Files, Inc. (HRAF). HRAF is a non-profit, international consortium of colleges, universities, and institutes that began in the 1930s, under the direction of Murdock, as the Cross-Cultural Survey. It became the Human Relations Area Files in 1949 and is housed on the Yale University campus in New Haven. The HRAF is an archive not a sample, dataset, or method. The files are a coded collection of ethnographic records on approximately 350 human societies worldwide. For each society, the HRAF microfiche files contain the entire texts of relevant ethnographic materials. In addition, the microfiche cards are organized by the codes of the *Outline of cultural materials* (OCM), allowing the researcher to quickly locate pages containing information on more than 700 different topics (Murdock et al. 1982). Thus, the HRAF is a resource facilitating the creation of cross-cultural codes and datasets. More than 300 institutions worldwide own partial or complete sets of the HRAF archive; computerization promises to make their use even more widespread.

Although it is much more expensive and difficult, a few researchers have managed to plan simultaneous comparative studies employing FIELDWORK in which a set of researchers focus on an agreed set of issues using the same or similar methods. One of the most notable was John Whiting and Beatrice Whiting's Six Culture Study, which examined similarities and difference in rearing CHILDREN (B. Whiting & Whiting 1975; B. Whiting & Edwards 1988). Even if the studies are not planned together, the data collected in separate projects using a single methodology may be compared by using a single, standardized

coding system, as in Allen Johnson's cross-cultural time-allocation studies (Johnson & Behrens 1989).   CBr

See also ETHNOGRAPHY AND ETHNOLOGY, QUALITATIVE METHODS, QUANTITATIVE METHODS

Crow kinship systems   produce a set of kin terms that, like the IROQUOIS, merges the mother's sister with the mother, the father's brother with the father, and parallel cousins with siblings (see figure 1). The Crow system is complicated by the fact that it also merges members of different generations, so that a woman's brother and her son are terminologically equivalent, as are mother's brother and one's own brother, while mother's brother's children share kin terms with brother's children. The Crow system is the exact inverse of OMAHA and is generally associated with MATRILINEAL DESCENT.   CL

cuisine   *See* COOKING

cults   are groups that follow an unorthodox religion, or are centered on a single person or principle, often associated with curing or salvation. However, the first thing that must be said about the term is that its sociological definition has been the matter of some considerable debate. Although in the popular mind the word "cult" often evokes images of crazed, messianic gunmen, the academic debate in the "cult and sect" literature usually focuses on organizational structure and the distance between the group and the mainstream religion. One of the classic definitions (G. Nelson 1969) underscores the stark simplicity of the organization: no bureaucracy, no priesthood, just the leader and a group of devoted followers. But many groups that are labeled as cults are of course far more complex than this definition suggests (David Bromley & Shupe 1981).

The sociological understanding of cults is grounded in a "relative deprivation" argument that explains recruitment to cults, sects, and other marginal groups as the consequence of relative economic, social, psychological, or other deprivation (Beckford 1975). Simple economic depri-

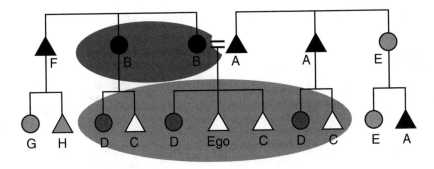

Figure 1 Crow kinship system.

vation, however, seems insufficient to account for the features of these groups, as do simple personality-disorder theories (J. Lofland 1969). More recent discussions of marginal religions, by Barker (1984) and Beckford (1975), have stressed a combination of risk-free problem solving, developing friendships within the group, and creative satisfaction as the factor that propels people toward the committed membership of such groups. As the discussions have advanced, the variety of cults and sects has multiplied worldwide, and particularly in the United States these new groups – formed around a self-styled prophet, or a utopian vision of a pre-Christian, preindustrial world – are now often referred to as "new religions."

Anthropologists, habitually nonchalant about their use of terms, rarely use "cult" to describe religious groups they have studied, even when such a term might readily be applied by virtue of its definition. Indeed, the point of most ethnographies on what could loosely be described as cults – such as Tsing's (1993) study of the Indonesian Dayaks, or Karen Brown's (1991) biography of a voodoo priestess – usually has little to do with the sociological formation of the group. Instead, the anthropologists who write about unorthodox, person- or principle-centered religions are more often concerned with two common characteristics: symbolic creativity and healing.

James Fernandez's work (1982) on a syncretic Cameroonian religion, Bwiti, is an important example of symbolic creativity. Crafted from Christianity and the indigenous spirituality, its leading characteristics are emotional intensity and symbolic inventiveness. Fernandez developed a theoretical apparatus around the role and nature of metaphor that embeds the emotional intensity in the "inchoate" and perpetually creative quality of metaphor. Similarly, in a study of nontraditional "neopagan" religion in the United States and England, Luhrmann (1989) argued that the participants' creative engagement with the symbolism was powerfully connected to the emotional vividness of the practice. They had not only chosen to enter these occult groups, but developed their own, partially idiosyncratic symbology.

Harriet Whitehead's (1987) study of the Scientology movement is a particularly interesting example of cults focused on healing. Seeking to understand what is often loosely called "symbolic efficacy" (the psychological process through which mere symbolic action has some therapeutic impact on the individual), Whitehead argued that the transformative mechanism of the ritual therapies involved a cognitive–affective "renunciation" of previous psychological orientations and a reformulation in the ritualistic symbolic language. (Her legal concerns about publishing the material indicate why research in nonmainstream American religions can be so fraught with difficulties.)

This is a process not confined to Scientology, of course; it is also found in most curing rituals around the world (including such practices as psychoanalysis). Most of the many anthropological studies of healing adopt some version of Jerome Frank's (1961) study of psychotherapy and its analogs: the cure is most effective when the patients believe that the ritual will help and are motivated to see that it does; when they organize their pain into a narrative in which they are emotionally engaged; and when the curer, who is validated by society, intervenes in the narrative to make it more adaptive and useful for the patients.

All this aside, it may be true that for most anthropologists, the word "cult" evokes the concept of the CARGO CULT, religious movements that occur in apparent response to invasion by or contact with the West. The movements are sometimes interpreted as attempts to reorganize socially as a means to more effective response. The word "cargo" is used because the religious movement sometimes focuses on the material goods – the planes, the guns, the trade goods – owned by nonindigenous people. The more generic terms for this phenomenon are "crisis cult" and "revitalization cult," and one of the classic examples is described in Anthony Wallace's (1970) study of such a cult among the Iroquois. At the end of the eighteenth century, the Iroquois of New York State had been defeated – they had supported the losing side in the American Revolution – had lost much of their land, and confronted social and economic disaster. A Seneca chief called Handsome Lake had a vision in which he was told that his people must stop their evil ways, stop drinking, quarreling and practicing witchcraft. Following this, over time, a new structure for Iroquois society was revealed to him. The Iroquois accepted a radically altered way of life as a result of their acceptance of religious truths. Wallace argued that the prophet experienced his visions as a consequence of personal crisis, and that it was the stressful social crisis of the society that persuaded the Iroquois to listen. Theodore Schwartz (1976a) challenged this perspective, arguing that in his study of Melanesian cargo cults there was no evidence for heightened stress among participants.   TL

cultural   advocacy *See*   HUMAN RIGHTS

cultural anthropology *See* ANTHROPOLOGY, CULTURAL AND SOCIAL

cultural change is both a process underway in all societies and a field of study in anthropology which has undergone complex development and several important transformations.

The cultural evolutionists of the late nineteenth century, such as Edward B. TYLOR (1881) and Lewis Henry MORGAN (1877), regarded non-Western cultures as relatively static (*see* EVOLUTION). For them societies could be ranked hierarchically on a single scale from the savage to the civilized, with the peoples at the bottom being less intelligent than those at the top. Therefore, on utilitarian grounds, the institutions of lower societies were less worthy, and non-Western peoples were seen as comparatively unreflective, their customs as tightly binding, and change as very slow. By contrast, civilized peoples were conceived of not only as more intelligent, but as less bound by the fetters of tradition and more amenable to progressive change. Combined with these notions was the view that there is an overall pattern to cultural change in which all societies are moving in the same direction, and that as a consequence, even the most savage societies will over time become more and more like the Western peoples who are at the top of the scale. The mechanism behind this development is the intellect: as savages apply their minds, they replicate the same, superior institutions that were invented by higher societies long ago.

The notion of a hierarchy of societies was widely criticized by anthropologists (most notably Franz BOAS) before the turn of this century, and it had been generally discredited by the 1920s. A variety of new ideas about cultural change then emerged in this context. Theories of DIFFUSION, according to which a key process in cultural change is cultural borrowing, or the diffusion of cultural traits (such as design motifs, folktales, and values) from one society to the next, became important in the first few decades of this century among North American anthropologists. An element of CULTURAL

RELATIVISM was inherent in the diffusion concept, because the borrowing of traits implied that the cultures or institutions of a society reflected not the level of the people's intelligence, but their position on the map. Even European cultures were now conceived of as unique concatenations of cultural traits, most of which had diffused from elsewhere, particularly the Middle East and Asia. The course of human history (and the overall direction of cultural change) became less a matter of progressive development and more a product of historical accident (see HISTORICAL PARTICULARISM).

A particular kind of cultural change that the American anthropologists were interested in was ACCULTURATION, by which was usually meant the changes that come about when Western and non-Western societies come into long-term contact, and especially the effects that dominant societies have had on indigenous peoples. In British anthropology, on the other hand, theorists of SOCIAL CHANGE looked at similar problems but from a different perspective.

Another important approach to cultural change in North American anthropology was that of cultural ecology, which was first articulated by Julian STEWARD (1955) and became very influential in the 1960s (Service 1971; see ECOLOGICAL ANTHROPOLOGY). Steward was critical of diffusionism, with its implication that change can be explained primarily as a product of historical accident, or the chance occurrences of contact among cultures. Rather, Steward sought to demonstrate that cultural change can be explained largely in terms of the progressive adaptation of a particular culture to its environment, with the result that the direction of change is predictable: given the subsistence base of a society, it should be possible, in principle, to predict how that society will change over time as a response to certain environmental conditions.

A strong alternative to cultural ecology soon emerged in cultural anthropology (Frake 1962b). The cultural ecologists tended to assume that all peoples will respond the same way under the same circumstances, and that such features as cultural values and beliefs do not play a significant role in influencing cultural change. The alternative view is that the environment is culturally mediated: people do not experience the world directly, but through cultural systems of thought, with the result that peoples with different conceptions of the world will respond to it in different ways. Thus, by this view, the cultural ecologists were mistaken when they failed to take cultural systems of thought into account in their analyses of cultural change.

In Britain a different approach to cultural change held sway from the 1920s through the 1950s. This was FUNCTIONALISM, which was associated with both RADCLIFFE-BROWN and MALINOWSKI. Functionalism took a conservative approach to change, since it assumed that societies and cultures are relatively well integrated and stable. By this view, if a culture undergoes change, then typically it is the result of outside influences. The functionalists were not oriented toward the study of change; their main interest was the functional interrelationships of cultural and social systems, not how they were transformed.

In the early 1970s the interest in cultural change took yet another important turn, a large majority of the work from that time has focused less on the problem of indigenous changes in culture – or on how "traditional" cultures came to be the way they are independently of the West – and more on understanding them in terms of the larger economic and political developments of the world. Particularly influential in this regard was WORLD-SYSTEM THEORY, which is associated with Immanuel Wallerstein (1974). Similarly, Eric Wolf (1982) and others have argued that the changes in local, indigenous cultures around the world are to be seen to a large extent in relation to several centuries of confrontation with and domination by Europeans. Consequently cultural change in non-Western societies is seen as an extension of the history of the West.

Not all anthropological research on cultural change today looks to world-systems theory for its inspiration, but nearly all of it is strongly influenced by the idea of the global society, or the view that a variety of transnational processes are critical for understanding cultural change among all peoples. The world is viewed as increasingly integrated economically, politically, socially, and culturally.   EH

further reading Lowie 1917

cultural ecology *See* ECOLOGICAL ANTHROPOLOGY

cultural materialism is a major theoretical approach in sociocultural anthropology that was named and largely developed by Marvin HARRIS (1968, 1979), although numerous other anthropologists (and even a few sociologists) have contributed to it. It represents a kind of theoretical synthesis of marxist historical materialism, ECOLOGICAL ANTHROPOLOGY, and social EVOLUTIONISM. It emerged in the period between the 1950s and the 1970s and in recent years, with the fragmentation of anthropology and the increasing growth of skepticism about the possibility of a scientific anthropology, has become less influential. However, it is still a major and important approach within anthropology.

Cultural materialism identifies three major components to all human societies, what Harris called the "universal pattern." All societies can be divided into infrastructures, structures, and superstructures. The infrastructure consists of those natural and cultural elements fundamental to human adaptation and survival. It has two subcomponents, the MODE OF PRODUCTION and the mode of reproduction. The mode of production includes technology, work patterns, features of the geographic or physical environment, and technoenvironmental relationships. It is basic to economic adaptation. The mode of reproduction consists of those things relating to the propagation of the species and is primarily demographic. It includes birth rates, death rates, size and density of population, rates of population growth, and technology relating to birth and population control. The structure consists of domestic and political economy. Domestic economy largely involves modes of family and kinship organization and gender and age roles. Political economy consists of patterns of class, caste, or other hierarchies, modes of

political organization, and warfare. Finally, the superstructure consists of shared cognitive and ideological patterns, as well as behavioral patterns that represent underlying patterns of thought and symbols. It includes such things as religion, science, art, music, dance, literature, sports, and rituals.

Cultural materialism has also depended on an important epistemological distinction between EMIC AND ETIC modes of analysis. Cultural materialists stress that both approaches are important to the conduct of anthropological research, but they consistly favor etic approaches in their own research endeavors.

Cultural materialism is best known for the way in which it links infrastructure, structure, and superstructure. In Harris's terms, these three sociocultural components are related through the Principle of Infrastructural Determinism. This principle asserts that the infrastructure provides the basic foundation of sociocultural life and is laid down first; it then exerts a strong determining influence on the formation of the structure, which in turns exerts a strong determining influence of its own on the formation of the superstructure. Harris stressed that the causal relationships between these components are probabilistic, and room is left for causal influence to operate in the reverse direction; that is, from superstructure to structure to infrastructure. However, it is assumed that causal influences flow in this reverse direction much less often and much less significantly. Harris has also formulated an argument as to why infrastructure should have the causal importance it does. In his view, infrastructure has causal priority because it involves those things that relate most fundamentally to human survival and physical well-being, aspects of life that humans must grapple with before they become concerned with matters relating to social organization and ideology.

Fundamental to cultural materialism is the notion that human individuals are cost–benefit calculators who choose courses of action that are rational from the standpoint of minimizing the expenditure of time and energy, maximizing health and physical well-being, transmitting wealth from one generation to the next, and a variety of other concerns. In his early work Harris's analyses were often carried out in a functionalist mode, but later (in approximately the mid-1970s) he shifted toward a more methodologically individualist position. Eschewing any notion of group selection, his mature work assumes that cultural patterns are large-scale aggregations of cultural selection operating at the level of individual cost and benefit. This makes cultural materialism highly analogous to Darwinian natural selection theory.

As a form of theoretical materialism, cultural materialism has drawn heavily on marxist historical materialism by dropping some of its assumptions and combining its materialist core with some of the leading notions in cultural ecology (i.e., the determining role of the physical environment) and social evolutionism (i.e., the cultural selection of adaptive sociocultural patterns). However, it is important to spell out the major differences between historical and cultural materialism. First, it is obvious that cultural materialism is a broader form of materialism, since it gives a degree of importance to the physical environment far beyond what Marx ever did. Moreover, cultural materialism's strong emphasis on demographic factors, especially the roles of population growth and population pressure, is totally at odds with historical materialism. Marx reacted very negatively to Malthus's notion that overpopulation was the primary cause of poverty, and marxists to this day are extremely reluctant to give population growth and population pressure an important causal role in social life. Indeed, they stress that rates of population growth are dependent rather than independent variables.

A second major difference between cultural and historical materialism concerns the placement of what Marx called the relations of production, or the forms of ownership of the productive forces. For Marx, these formed a fundamental part of the economic base. Harris, on the other hand, placed them within the political-economic component of the structure and argued that it is important to see how modes of economic ownership are shaped by the modes of production and reproduction.

However, it should be pointed out that Harris has not always been consistent in applying this formal theoretical argument to actual sociocultural cases. In his analyses of preindustrial and precapitalist societies, Harris generally has treated the form of economy as part of the structure; but in the analysis of modern capitalist societies, he has generally treated the relations of production (under the general heading of "economy") as among the leading causal determinants of the remaining sociocultural components. Thus, Harris comes closer to the original marxist position when he is engaged in studying the modern capitalist world.

Finally, Harris has been adamant in his rejection of the dialectical component of historical materialism. He has referred to Hegel as the "monkey on Marx and Engels's back," and asserted that dialectics is nothing but rarefied philosophical nonsense. For him, the main weakness of dialectics is the absence of any operational principle for specifying which particular social contradiction might be fundamental in any particular place and at any particular time. Since the notion of dialectics has no scientific validity, Harris recommends simply dropping it (see DIALECTICAL MATERIALISM).

As the person who named and largely created cultural materialism, Harris has unsuprisingly been the most vigorous proponent of its research application, and he has made more such applications than any other anthropologist. In a series of books Harris has attempted to explain a variety of cultural phenomena (Harris 1974, 1977, 1981, 1985). These include FOOD TABOOS and dietary practices (the Indian sacred cow, the Jewish and Muslim abominable pig, Aztec CANNIBALISM, and many others), primitive WARFARE, the great WITCH craze of late medieval Europe, the long-term evolution of human societies, the recent feminist movement in the Western world, the proliferation of religious CULTS and violent crime in the United States. Other anthropologists have also made important cultural-materialist research applications. For example, M. Kay Martin and Barbara Voorhies (1975) have developed a cultural-materialist interpretation of gen-

der roles, Mark Cohen (1977) has developed a cultural-materialist explanation of the origins of agriculture, and Robert Carneiro (1970) has developed a famous materialist theory of the origin of the state. (An excellent summary of the wide anthropological application of cultural-materialist principles is provided in Harris 1979: 77–114.)   SS
See also EVOLUTION, MATERIALISM
further reading E. Ross 1980

cultural   pluralism *See*   PLURAL SOCIETIES

cultural relativism expresses the idea that the beliefs and practices of others are best understood in the light of the particular cultures in which they are found. The idea is predicated on the degree to which human behavior is held to be culturally determined, a basic tenet of American cultural anthropology. This is often joined with the argument that because all extant cultures are viable adaptations and equally deserving of respect, they should not be subjected to invidious judgments of worth or value by outsiders. Alternatively, some argue that since all norms are specific to the culture in which they were formulated, there can be no universal standards of judgment.

Cultural relativism in American cultural anthropology is often attributed to the critique of social evolutionist perspectives by Franz BOAS and his students, especially Ruth BENEDICT, Margaret MEAD, and Melville HERSKOVITS. Boas criticized the use of EVOLUTIONARY STAGES as the basis for organizing museum displays, arguing that exhibits should display artifacts in the context of specific cultures.

Most societies are not relativist: they view their own ways as good, other people's as bad, inferior, or immoral – a form of ETHNOCENTRISM. However, the reverse is also possible, a syndrome Melford Spiro (1992b: 62–7) termed "inverted ethnocentrism," in which some anthropologists go well beyond relativism to assert that Western culture is globally inferior to Primitive or Third World cultures.

Cultural relativism as an approach can be contrasted with the search for human UNIVERSALS, the latter often grounded in claims based on such analytic perspectives as Freudian psychology, marxist political economy, Darwinian natural selection, or technoenvironmental determinism. Strong cultural relativists often see anthropology more as an art than a science and prefer to interpret symbolic meanings rather than explain social mechanisms. Clifford GEERTZ (1984b) has been an influential spokesman for this approach.

In the broader philosophical context, cultural relativism is sometimes merged with cognate forms of relativism (moral, ethical, cognitive, linguistic, historical, etc.) under the general rubric of Relativism, which is then seen in opposition to Rationalism, or occasionally, Fundamentalism (see M. Hollis & Lukes 1982). In treating the lively debates on cultural relativism in anthropology and philosophy, Spiro (1992b) discussed cultural relativism in relation to both cultural diversity and cultural determinism. Taking the existence of cultural variation as well documented, as do most anthropologists, he distinguished three types of cultural relativism – descriptive, normative, and epistemological – each with its attendant subtypes.

These detailed distinctions have not become conventional within the discipline. Most anthropologists remain content to distinguish the first-order methodological use of cultural relativism in anthropology from insensitive ethnocentric attempts to arrive at final ethical, moral, or scientific judgments.   JIA

culture The earliest anthropological use of "culture" was by E. B. TYLOR (1871), who defined it memorably as that "complex whole which includes knowledge, belief, art, morals, law, custom, and any other capabilities and habits acquired by man as a member of society." Tylor's formulation can still serve today to express anthropologists' views. First, culture comprises those human traits that are learned and learnable and are therefore passed on socially and mentally, rather than biologically. Second, culture is in some sense a "complex whole." Although hotly debated, the fundamental idea that all those "capabilities and habits" can and should be considered together is a powerful one. It means that vast areas of human life, spanning everything from techniques of food production to theories of the afterlife, have some coherence and a distinct logic that can be discovered by a single discipline.

It was Franz BOAS who championed the concept of culture, and with it the discipline of anthropology, to challenge the elaborate and influential late-nineteenth-century theories that attributed most human differences to RACE – that is, biological inheritance. Anchored in the new science of biology by evolutionary ideas, they suggested that some races, when compared to northern Europeans, were more primitive and therefore more animal-like in bodily form, mental ability, and moral development.

Boas (1911) broke the evidently seamless simplicity of this theory by showing that bodily form was not linked to language nor to any of the matters we associate with culture. In addition, he challenged the assumption that other "races" were less moral or less intelligent than northern Europeans. Whereas Tylor had spoken of "culture" in the singular, on the assumption that all societies possessed a more or less advanced version of the same heritage, Boas wrote of plural "cultures" that were different and could not be measured against some supposed single standard of advancement. Moreover, he argued that the complex forms and patterns in human life, when investigated through FIELD-WORK, were so various that they could not arise from a uniform process of social or cultural EVOLUTION, or from biological or geographical causes, but were fruits of complex local historical causes that escape simplification.

These ideas were later elaborated by his students, including Edward SAPIR, Alfred KROEBER, Margaret MEAD, and Ruth BENEDICT. They argued that although human beings everywhere possessed much the same biological heritage, human nature was so plastic that it could sustain kaleidoscopically different sets of values, institutions, and behaviors in different cultures. Margaret Mead, for example, spent a long career of fieldwork demonstrating how matters that might appear to be easily explained by human biology – the experience of ADOLESCENCE, patterns of SOCIALIZATION, SEX roles in society – vary so greatly that no simple natural scientific explanation could comprehend them. And Kroeber espoused the notion that culture is "superorganic," possessing a unique character within itself that goes beyond anything that could arise in the course of biological evolution.

Other Boasians devoted themselves to exploring the notion of culture within the bounds of anthropology. Benedict (1934a) argued that a culture was not simply a "planless hodgepodge" or an affair of "shreds and patches," as her older contemporary Robert LOWIE supposed. Rather, each culture "discarded elements which were incongruous, modified others to its purposes, and invented others that accorded with its taste" (p. 34). The result was a way of life arranged around a few aesthetic and intellectual principles that produced a unique *Weltanschauung*, a WORLDVIEW. These arguments contributed to setting an aspiration that is still very powerful today: the task of the anthropologist is not just to record a myriad of details about a people, but to demonstrate a deeper unity integrating different features of a culture. Running through her, and others', arguments were an aspiration to tolerance and a mutual informing and respect among societies.

It is difficult today to realize how important the ideas of Boas and his students were. At the end of World War II, US cultural anthropology set out upon an expansion that has made it by far the largest, and perhaps alongside French anthropology, the most generally influential national body of anthropology in the world. It was Boas and his students who set the agenda for that expansion, by establishing a faith and proposing a project. The faith lay in the force of culture, which distinguished human beings from animals and created an autonomous cultural and mental logic.

Leslie WHITE (1959c) asserted that, in some hypothetical beginning, "Between man and nature hung the veil of culture, and he could see nothing save through this medium . . . the meanings and values that lay beyond the senses." Over the next half-century the ceaseless efforts of biological scientists to comprehend the whole of human behavior in their schemes would only confirm anthropologists in this faith.

Contemporary anthropologists have approached culture in a variety of ways, all designed to realize the concept in a more full-bodied and cogent way that moves beyond the defensive assertion that culture is not single but unimaginably various and that it makes people different from animals.

One choice has been to treat culture as a system of symbols that includes language, art, religion, morals, and (in principle) anything else that appears organized in human social life. This has the effect of giving to culture some of the orderliness and concreteness that one observes, and can study systematically, in LANGUAGE. However, to treat culture as symbols stressed purely mental phenomena even more than Benedict had done and excluded the material and practical dimension of culture. And where the notion of symbolic system has been rigorously rather than loosely applied, as in COGNITIVE ANTHROPOLOGY, research has concentrated on only small domains of culture, such as the animal-CLASSIFICATION system of a people or even a single concept, such as marriage in America, and so the "complex whole" has quite disappeared.

An alternative to this focus on culture as symbol has been to take as an object of study those material dimensions undervalued by symbolic anthropologists, such as food production, crafts, and relationships to the physical environment. ECOLOGICAL ANTHROPOLOGY in particular has attempted to provide a new logic for underpinning cultural forms. The most famous (and least persuasive) example of this CULTURAL MATERIALISM is Marvin HARRIS's (1966) attempt to explain the worship of cattle in India by reference to the usefulness of cowdung to Indian farmers. A more plausible example is Roy Rappaport's (1967) painstaking attempt to explain the religion of a Papua New Guinea people by their ecology and mode of livelihood. Here the integration of culture is causal: the conditions of livelihood and the relations of production caused (in some sense) the other dimensions of culture, the religious life and worldview. But these explanations are characteristically thin when they attempt to cover religion and related matters, and so hardly count as perspectives on culture as a whole.

A third school of anthropologists accepted wholeheartedly Benedict's vision of culture as aesthetic choice and began to regard anthropology as the "translation of culture," as EVANS-PRITCHARD (1956) called it. On this view, wrote Clifford GEERTZ (1973: 5), "man is an animal suspended in webs of significance he himself has spun . . . I take culture to be those webs, and the analysis of it to be . . . not an experimental science in search of law but an interpretive one in search of meaning." The consequence was not only to place culture firmly beyond the bounds of natural science, but to set anthropology alongside such interpretive disciplines as literary criticism, which seek mainly to make the obscure clear and the unintelligible intelligible. But a sense of cultural unity is not very prominent in this enterprise, any more than it is in literary criticism, and Geertz could only manage to find as much integration in culture as in "an octopus, a rather badly integrated creature – what passes for a brain keeps it together, more or less, in one ungainly whole" (1984a: 19).

If anthropology were philosophy, then this failure to establish a satisfyingly general and robust view of culture's integration might be depressing. But the vast weight of effort in anthropology has fallen upon the doing of ETHNOGRAPHY, and here anthropologists now routinely demonstrate close connections, and underlying themes, that span different spheres of life within one culture or another, such as hierarchy in South Asia. The judgment here must be that the notion of culture is, in everyday practice if not in theory, a resounding and heroic success.

Despite the importance of culture to the discipline, anthropologists cannot realistically afford allegiance to the banner of culture alone, whether in theory or practice. Eric Wolf (1982) has shown that the idea of culture has often led anthropologists to a series of illusions: that cultures are homogeneous, that the world is divided into atomistic societies or "peoples," or that societies studied by anthropologists are traditional and unchanging. Yet societies are hardly autonomous; they exist in relations of commerce, of mutual dependence, and (above all) in relationships of dominance and subjection with others. Today more than half the world's people are multilingual, and this global changing and mingling is not recent (or postmodern) but dates right back to the period of the great European explorers and long before.

The irony is that the notion of culture was born partly as a response to the encounter of societies with each other on a world scale, and as a largely humane response that aimed to create a sound coinage of knowledge to support a traffic of tolerance and mutual understanding between people. Now only a modified notion of culture will do, one that challenges a notion that it is fixed, bounded, and unchanging. Human groups, however defined, are shifting and uncertain, and people belong to many competing categories, often involving power and subjugation. People work actively upon what they have received in order to respond to present circumstances, and in so acting, change their cultural inheritance. Finally, in recognizing that the social nature of the human species transcends the limits supposed by the idea of culture, we must also recognize that infants do bring something biological and innate into the world: an innate capacity for social relations. This capacity is set in motion by the acts of those around them, and then forms a scaffolding upon which, in the course of development, the "capabilities and habits" of culture can be acquired.   MC

See also ANTHROPOLOGY, CULTURAL AND SOCIAL

further reading Carrithers 1992

culture and personality was the name for a movement that related cultural anthropology to psychiatry and psychology from about 1928 to 1955. After 1960, this field became known as PSYCHOLOGICAL ANTHROPOLOGY, and in the academic psychology of the 1990s, cultural psychology.

The school and its aims

Culture and personality was a broad and unorganized movement that brought together anthropologists, psychiatrists, and psychologists who agreed on the mutual relevance of their disciplines but lacked a common theoretical position, an acknowledged leader, and an institutional base. Its founders were Margaret MEAD, Ruth BENEDICT, and Edward SAPIR, all students of Franz BOAS, whose influential concept of CULTURE had implied a psychological dimension they attempted to spell out and translate into research. They argued that culture played a role in individual psychological development (Mead) and in the emotional patterns typical of particular cultures (Benedict), and also that individuals of a particular society realized its culture in different ways (Sapir). They criticized psychological theories that posited UNIVERSALS for the human species without taking into account human variability as revealed by anthropological fieldwork in diverse cultures. At the same time, they were influenced by those psychological and psychiatric theories that emphasized social influences on the individual, such as the neo-Freudian formulations of Karen Horney and the interpersonal psychiatry of Harry Stack Sullivan. Although the movement had no formal organization, its anthropological founders were joined at seminars, conferences, and in publications by sociologists, psychologists, and psychoanalysts – including W. I. Thomas, John Dollard, Erik Erikson, Abram Kardiner, Henry A. Murray – and by a growing circle of anthropologists – Ralph Linton, A. Irving Hallowell, Gregory Bateson, Cora Du Bois, Clyde Kluckhohn, and John W. M. Whiting, to name but a few. The field of culture and personality studies was very active during the 1930s and in the postwar period 1945–50, as a new generation of anthropologists conducted studies among Native American peoples and in the Pacific.

Scholars of culture and personality were divided over many of the same issues that divided cultural anthropology as a whole: cultural relativism vs. universalism, materialism vs. idealism, scientific vs. humanist approaches. They also disagreed about issues specific to the field: the value of Freudian vs. other psychologies, collective-personality description vs. individual differences, the use of personality tests vs. life histories, comparative hypothesis testing vs. ethnographic case studies. Thus the study of culture and personality was not a school of thought with a single research program but a field of exploratory inquiry, and it remained provisional and experimental for almost thirty years.

Culture and personality was an American movement, and its exponents included some of the most prominent anthropologists of their time, but it was always regarded with skepticism by many American anthropologists. Given the heterogeneity of theoretical positions and exploratory research efforts in the field, it was never difficult to find examples of psychological reductionism, inadequate ethnography, or the pathologizing of other cultures, and these were used by critics to anathematize the field as a whole, particularly during the 1950s. By 1961, anthropologists remaining in the field distanced themselves from earlier work by renaming it "psychological anthropology". In fact, the 1950s had also seen the emergence of more mature empirical research, such as A. I. Hallowell's (1955) writings on the self, Beatrice Whiting's (1963) cross-cultural studies of SOCIALIZATION, and Spiro's (1957, 1958) monographs on ideology and childhood experience on an Israeli kibbutz, but these were not appreciated until later.

Culture and personality laid a basis for later theory and research not only in psychological anthropology but also in child development and medical anthropology. These contributions include cultural critiques of universal theories (particularly about child and adolescent development and mental disorder), the relationship between social structure and individual behavior, and the assessment of individual personality across cultures.

Critiques of universal theories

Members of the culture and personality school were suspicious of general theories of child and adolescent development, and they attempted to use ethnographic and behavioral data from diverse cultures to construct more accurate generalizations about human development. From Margaret Mead's (1928) *Coming of age in Samoa* to John W. M. Whiting's (1941) *Becoming a Kwoma* and *The Balinese character* by Gregory Bateson and Margaret Mead (1942), the early culture and personality research on child and adolescent development established the relevance and importance of anthropological data for the understanding of psychological development in humans. Although this work influenced child psychology during the period 1935–60, moving it toward a more cultural-relativist position, the rise of cognitive approaches in child development research after 1960 created the need for a new cultural critique, out of which the cultural psychology of the 1990s – involving anthropologists as well as psychologists – emerged.

Similarly, members of the school critiqued universal conceptions of mental disorder, particularly the boundary between normal and pathological behavior and personality. In "Anthropology and the abnormal," Ruth Benedict (1934b) proposed that definitions of normal and pathological behavior vary across cultures and thereby initiated the cultural approach to psychopathology that remains central to MEDICAL ANTHROPOLOGY. Although her extreme relativism is not consistent with all that is now known about major mental disorders, her recognition of cultural meanings as central to psychopathology provided a basis for cultural phenomenologies that emerged in medical anthropology later in the century.

Relationship of social structure and individual behavior

From the beginning of the culture and personality movement there was the conception of a functional relationship between the institutions of a society and the psychological make-up of its members, such that each side could affect the other, in maintaining a status quo and in a historical process of change. This was variously formulated by W. Thomas and Znaniecki (1918–20), R. Linton (1936), Kardiner (1939, 1945), J. Whiting and Child (1953), and Hallowell (1955). Alternative models, involving an interpenetration of culture and personality, were formulated by Benedict (1934a) and Spiro (1951), among others. These models are fundamental to any subsequent consideration of the ways in which institutions and cultural ideologies are related to psychological dispositions at the population level.

Innovative methodologies
Students of culture and personality gave a great deal of attention during the 1930s and 1940s to the development of methods that would provide investigative insight into the personalities of individuals in non-Western cultures. They pioneered attempts to assess individual personality in diverse cultures through the use of life histories, projective tests, and behavior observations. Although they did not solve this problem, their published findings, including book-length LIFE HISTORIES of particular individuals, provided the indispensable starting point for those who would subsequently approach this problem. RAL

culture area is a geographic region in which a common set of traits, often called a "culture complex" is found shared among a number of societies. The term was first used by champions of DIFFUSIONISM, who argued that such areas served as the source of innovations that were borrowed by neighboring groups. So-called core areas were the putative sources of these innovations and some anthropologists argued that their age could be inferred from the degree of spread (Kroeber 1939; Wissler 1926). A German variant of this idea was the *Kulturkreis*, or "culture circle," a complete set of traits that met all of a culture's needs and created a complex that defined a particular geographical area (W. Schmidt 1939). The culture-circle theorists also posited a very small number of original circles that both evolved and diffused over time, combining elements from two schools of explanation that were at odds with one another in the Anglo-American tradition.

Culture areas were generally defined by their food sources, such as the eight distinct New World areas identified by Wissler (1917), or by a complex of shared traits, such as the CATTLE COMPLEX in Africa (Herskovits 1926) or the horse complex among Plains Indians (Wissler 1923). Such research often involved comparing scores of traits and analyzing them statistically on the assumption that they could reveal links between cultures (H. Driver & Kroeber 1932).

Culture-area explanations fell out of favor with the demise of diffusionism and the rise of FUNCTIONALISM, although for years afterwards American anthropologists were often expected to be masters of such arcane lore as the distribution of eating utensils, genital mutilations, or round vs. square huts. Critics successfully argued that identifying traits was a poor way to understand CULTURE, and that INDEPENDENT INVENTION was as likely as borrowing because cultural adaptations to similar environments could bring about the same results. This latter view became the basis of Julian STEWARD's (1950, 1955) notion of a "cultural core," which inspired later students of ECOLOGICAL ANTHROPOLOGY to seek alternative explanations for the continuity of certain sets of cultural traits over large areas of the world. TB

culture of poverty was a term originally used by Oscar Lewis (1966) in his studies of poor communities in Mexico, Puerto Rico and New York City. Lewis argued that poverty was created by the political economy of CAPITALISM and reflected the uneven distribution of jobs and opportunities within Western societies. He saw poor people adapting to this situation of poverty through a "culture of poverty," which was then passed on from generation to generation. Lewis listed a number of traits that were incorporated in the culture of poverty. These included characteristics such as a present orientation and a failure to plan for the future, and a preponderance toward female-headed households. Lewis suggested that the culture was learned at a young age and that these traits then prevented the poor from seeking or succeeding in upward mobility.

Following Lewis, a number of social analysts and ethnographers used the culture of

poverty to explain the conditions of POV-
ERTY in the United States and elsewhere.
In a report for President Johnson's Commission on Poverty, Daniel Patrick
Moynihan, then a Harvard sociologist,
built on the idea of a culture of poverty to
explain the poverty of African-Americans.
His report focused specifically on the high
rates of female-headed households and argued that these were the cause for the
"tangle of pathology" in black families,
since children raised in such households
were likely to show behavioral problems,
fail to complete school, and repeat the
problems in the next generation (Rainwater
1967).

The idea of the culture of poverty itself,
as well as its applications in US government policy, have been severely criticized
in the anthropological literature (Leacock
1971). Four main points emerge from
these reviews. First, the concept assumes
a static view of culture. Traits are listed
and attributed to adaptation to poverty.
The continuous interaction between poor
people and employers, state institutions,
and commerce and the daily impact of
these interactions in maintaining poverty,
discrimination, and failure are not considered. No attention is paid to change over
time or historical periods, and the description of culture assumes a stereotypical and
reified form.

Second, despite the effort to conceptualize a CULTURE, Lewis's list of traits tends to
reflect negatives, such as a lack of plans for
the future or the lack of nuclear households. Culture as the creation of a people in
their attempts to work out a life, or culture
as something that may possibly incorporate
resistance to miserable conditions, is not
described or even considered. Thus, it
might be better to talk of the deprivations
of poverty rather than to suggest that "culture" is being described.

Third, children are supposedly socialized
into the culture of poverty at a young age
and then find themselves repeating the patterns of their parents. This assumes that
even should conditions improve for adults,
they will have learned adaptations to poverty and will not be able to take advantage
of the improved conditions. However, vol-

umes of data on upward mobility among
second-generation immigrant populations
as well as African-Americans belies this formulation. Many analysts have pointed out
that the unproven claim that, once learned,
behavioral adaptations to poverty cannot
be changed blames the victims for their
poverty.

Fourth, the concept of the culture of
poverty implied that poor people's values
and aspirations were different from those of
more affluent and successful members of
society. Data on the values of the poor did
not support this finding. In fact, contrary
to a "lack of future orientation," African-
Americans in the United States – one of the
quintessential groups to whom the culture
of poverty was thought to apply – valued
education more highly than the average
American. Thus, it appeared that there was
not a simple relationship between values
and poverty. People in poverty may adopt
or reject the values of the wider society
depending on historical conditions and a
multitude of other factors.

Despite this extensive criticism of the
concept of a culture of poverty, the ideas it
embodies are still repeated in writings on
social policy, education, health, and other
applied fields. In the anthropological literature, by contrast, the concept has not been
widely used since the 1970s. However,
questions about adaptation to poverty, socialization into poverty, and the differing
values of the poor remain. In the early
1980s the concept of "underclass" was introduced to describe and explain the persistence of extreme poverty in the United
States (W. Wilson 1987). Like the culture
of poverty, this concept involved a list of
behaviors attributed to the poor. These behaviors were seen as the problems that prevented poor people from benefiting from
the opportunities available in American society. Characteristics used frequently as
indices of underclass status included female-headed households, teenage pregnancies, and substance abuse.

Although some moderate exponents of
underclass theories placed their explanations of the SOCIAL ORGANIZATION of the
poor within the context of a changing
economy, the emphasis on measurement

and the policy applications focused on a static view of culture and socialization and was subject to the same criticisms that attended the culture of poverty of the 1960s. Like "the culture of poverty," many social analysts have discarded the term "underclass" in the face of critical review; however, the concept remains strong in the policy literature and popular writings.

ISu

See also URBAN ANTHROPOLOGY, URBANISM

further reading D. Jones & Susser 1993

D

dance is the creative use of the human body in time and space within culturally specific systems of movement structure and meaning. Anthropologists have focused on cross-cultural analysis of dance and its symbolic cognitive and affective nature, a feature distinguishing it from other species' dance-like behavior. Broadly viewed as the anthropology of human movement, dance research encompasses a general concept of structured movement systems and action signs as a form of COMMUNICATION (Hanna 1979; P. Spencer 1985; D. Williams 1991).

Early dance anthropology was strongly influenced by the German *kulturkreis* theory (see CULTURE AREAS), particularly through the work of Curt Sachs (1937). Although theoretically dated and dependent largely on second-hand descriptions, his work was notable for its ecumenical conception of dance and dance ETHNOLOGY. Alan Lomax, an American folklorist, brought a similar global comparative perspective but employed an "effort-shape" analysis of movement, such as dancers' use of a one- or two-unit torso, or one-, two-, or three-dimensional spatial patterns. Lomax and his colleagues measured the frequency of such movement features in a set of films and produced a movement "profile" for each culture they examined (Lomax 1976; Lomax et al. 1968). The film samples, however, were woefully uneven and inadequate. They did not cover any one culture in depth and efforts to correlate movement profiles with other traits though statistical CROSS-CULTURAL STUDIES were criticized as misguided and as confusing correlation with causation.

In Britain FUNCTIONALIST anthropologists focused on dance as a means to reinforce communal sentiments (Radcliffe-Brown 1922) or as an occasion for the release of social conflict and tension (Evans-Pritchard 1928). Identification and exemplification of the many possible functions of dance received extensive attention, and such functionalist explanations of dance as a social institution predominated in the literature well into the 1960s. In the United States Franz BOAS's daughter Franziska helped bring dance study and anthropology together in a series of seminars held in her New York dance studio in the 1940s. The published collection of seminar papers reflects the relatively few efforts at that time to apply current theory to dance in scattered cultures around the world (Franziska Boas 1944; G. Bateson & Mead 1952; Holt 1939).

The beginning of current anthropological work was marked by Gertrude Kurath's seminal article characterizing dance ethnology "not as a description of or reproduction of a particular kind of dance, but as an approach toward, and method of, eliciting the place of dance in human life" (1960: 250). Based on a combination of theories and methods characteristic of her own extensive research among Native American cultures and of those developed in European FOLKLORE, she approached MUSIC and dance in terms of structure and diffusion. Her work (Kurath 1986) inspired later researchers to more fully integrate dance as an anthropological subject, including studies on dance in Hawaii and among the Hopi (Kealiinohomoku 1976) and other wide-ranging cross-cultural studies (CORD 1974).

Other researchers have treated the study of dance from a LINGUISTIC or ETHNOSCIENTIFIC perspective. Kaeppler (1972) employed such an approach to uncovering dance structure, composed of such units as "kinemes" and "morphokines," through fieldwork in Tonga. Drid Williams (1991) has elaborated her own linguistic analogy for movement analysis, termed "semasiology," which emphasizes the identification of "action signs" as the analytical units, a perspective that has been applied to Plains Indian sign language (Farnell 1995a).

The most recent anthropological research uses dance as a window on larger theoretical issues (Giurchescu & Torp 1991). These have included studies on the gender of dance movement practice in northern Greece (Cowan 1990), the transformations of dance genres under the impact of tourism in the Philippines and Cuba (Ness 1994; Y. Daniel 1995), and movement analyzed through DISCOURSE THEORY in Brazil (J. Lewis 1992). Folklorists primarily concerned with traditional dance in North America and Europe have also found that it serves as an important site for configuring and representing ethnic, national, and other collective identities (Quigley 1993). Anthropological thinking has had a strong influence on dance history studies (Novack 1990), and history has become an important component of Kaeppler's (1993) work on Hawaiian dance. New avenues of description include PARTICIPANT-OBSERVATION, where anthropologists bring close attention to their own bodily experience of dance into their methodology (Sklar 1994). This in turn has informed some experimentation in both literary style and PHOTOGRAPHY. The emergence of CD-ROM technology seems particularly promising as a means to present movement ethnography. While such CDs have just begun to appear (Farnell 1995b), the ability to present sound, movement, and written analysis in a single integrated format promises to give the field a much wider audience.   CQ

See also ETHNOMUSICOLOGY

further reading Lange 1980; Royce 1977

Davis, Allison (1902–83) Allison Davis was an American anthropologist trained at Harvard, the London School of Economics, and Chicago, where in 1941 he received a Ph.D for his work on the political economy and violence of racial CASTE.

In the mid-1930s he was the leader of a research project that investigated caste and CLASS as intersecting principles of social organization in a Mississippi town situated in a historically significant cotton-producing region. The study was a southern extension of Lloyd Warner's "Yankee City" studies of a New England town in which social class was the key principle for allocating power and prestige. The southern study demonstrated that in the Mississippi a dual caste system served this function, with each caste being internally differentiated by class. *Deep South: a social anthropological study of caste and class* (Davis et al. 1941) was one of the earliest anthropological studies of both racial inequality and a US town. One of its principal contributions was its illumination of the political economy and social organization of RACE in the nexus of relations that characterized town and country interactions.

In later phases in his career, Davis's work focused on issues of personality development, childhood SOCIALIZATION, and the educational testing of intelligence, demonstrating the primacy of sociocultural environment over heredity. In this research he applied his interest in race and class to concerns within psychological and educational anthropology. In the earliest of his psychological studies, *Children of bondage* (Davis & Dollard 1940), he examined the effects of racial oppression on the psychic development of upper-, middle-, and lower-class African-American children. In a later work, *Father of the man: how your child gets his personality* (Davis & Havighurst 1947), he compared class-structured socialization patterns in black and white American families in Chicago, revealing that differences between classes were greater than those between racial groups and that early personality development was not irreversible.

Whereas his early work emphasized social structure, later research departed from conventional social anthropology by focusing more on culture as a psychological system and on classes as subcultures marked by distinctive lifeways learned during socialization. His research yielded important insights into the schooling of lower-class children, whose classways and social envi-

ronments and society's negative evaluations of them interfere with academic
achievement, which involves learning
middle-class culture. He also demonstrated
that IQ tests measure cultural training
and the competitive drive for middle-class
success rather than mental capacity.

Consistently interested in how unequal
status affects emotional and behavioral response, Davis (1960) studied adolescents
in family hierarchies, finding that middle-
class adolescents exhibit confusion and
hostility owing to the tension between
their restricted childhood status and their
emergent physiological adulthood. Davis
showed that although adolescents, particularly males, eventually grow up and assume
adult status in the family hierarchy, feminine status remains subordinate, reflecting
a life-long cultural attack on the female ego
in patriarchal family contexts. In his final
book (1983) he offered a psychosocial examination of the lives of four prominent
African-Americans (Frederick Douglas, W.
E. B. DuBois, Richard Wright, and Martin
Luther King, Jr.) who successfully con-
verted their anger and aggression into
constructive initiatives for effecting social
change.   FH
See also CULTURE AND PERSONALITY,
DRAKE
further reading Drake 1974; Harrison
1992

death, death rituals As a biological
phenomenon, human mortality is of concern in the fields of physical anthropology
and DEMOGRAPHY. But there is also a
cultural context, and one that has several
counterintuitive aspects. As such, it
presents striking material for archaeology and social and cultural
anthropology.

Perceptions of death
As an undoubted universal, frequently remarked upon by poets, one might assume
that death is everywhere understood in
the same way. But even who qualifies as
deceased is socially constructed. David
Sudnow (1967) showed that the chances of
being declared "dead on arrival" at a major
Los Angeles hospital were inversely correlated with the respectability of the
candidate's clothes. As medical innova-

tions make it possible to prolong vital signs,
it becomes courts of law that must decide
who is dead. Looking beyond Western
conceptions, W. H. R. RIVERS (1926)
remarked that the Polynesian term *mate*
("dead") might be applied to individuals
still walking around in the village. Owing to
particular ritual circumstances, they were
consigned to the world of the ancestors
rather than that of the living, and as such
they were neither fed nor addressed.

Moreover, what happens at death – what
death is – is understood differently in different cultures. It is often related to how life
is conceived, and ILLNESS treated. Where,
for example, Western medicine deals with
body as machine, and with death as its final
malfunction, in Borneo, life, illness, and
death have to do with relationships between body and soul (Metcalf 1982). As for
the individual's fate after death, conceptions vary as widely as can be imagined,
from no persistence at all, to afterlives short
or long, pleasant and unpleasant, or both in
turn, to a return to this world, to multiple
souls with different fates.

Emotional reactions to death
The undeniable power of death to unleash
the strongest emotions is often assumed
to be the well-spring of mortuary rituals
everywhere. But early in this century,
Emile DURKHEIM (1915) argued that psychic states can never account for cultural
practices, and his argument has been crucial in shaping modern social anthropology.
Psychoreductionism persists, however, especially in American anthropology, and the
issue remains controversial.

Durkheim's basic proposition in *The elementary forms of the religious life* is that we
do not invent RITUALS anew each time the
need arises, but instead make use of those
that our culture provides ready to hand.
These rites predate our individual existence
and have a history of their own, distinct
from personal experiences. The part of that
history that interested Durkheim is the effects that rituals have on social solidarity.
Significantly, he left funerals to his last
chapter. They posed a special problem for
him, in that death often releases passions
that seem only to cause further damage to a
group that has already suffered loss. He
quoted cases from the Australian Aborigi-

nes of appalling self-mutilation, committed in a frenzy of grief. But then he neatly turned the significance of this around by showing that the wounds inflicted are prescribed to people standing in specific kinship relations to the deceased. Even with such negative emotions, the norms of the group are still enacted.

As regards EMOTION, Durkheim reversed the commonsense proposition; if anything, it is the rites that create the appropriate emotion. We do not need, however, to assume that there is any positive relationship at all. All that is prescribed is appropriate behavior; we cannot know what emotions people actually experience. Moreover, the process of grieving, which is personal and idiosyncratic, has no necessary connection to funeral rituals at all.

The variety of death rituals

What finally makes a reductionist account untenable is the sheer variety of death rituals. The ethnographic record shows that they may be cursory (some foraging people simply abandon the location), or spread out over years and very costly. They may involve feasting or fasting, sobriety or drunken orgies. The corpse itself may be disposed of by burning or burial, or kept in the house, preserved by smoking or pickling; it may be left in a special house or exposed as carrion; it may be eaten, raw, cooked, or rotten, or dismembered and treated in a variety of these ways. How can a supposedly uniform human emotional reaction to death account for such diversity?

The meaning of death rituals

Instead of a universalistic explanation, the diversity of death rites calls for an exploration of particular cases, to discover how each relates to an encompassing social and cultural context. The value of ritual for the anthropologist is that it often makes manifest implicit cultural premises. The universal impact of death is such that mortuary rituals frequently give expression to the whole meaning of living and dying as they are experienced in diverse cultures.

Two figures are associated with the analysis of death rituals. Like Durkheim, Arnold van GENNEP, in a classic essay (1960), dealt with funerals last. Considered as RITES OF PASSAGE, they present a special problem, because the subject of the rites makes a transition into a condition that is unknown. Van Gennep began by pointing out that, surprisingly, rites of separation are few and simple, whereas transition achieves "a sort of autonomy." The model of rite of passage works best, in fact, not for the deceased but for the mourners. It is they who must repair the social fabric and move on. In his study of the funerals of the LoDagaa of West Africa, Jack Goody (1962) described how every role of the deceased person is carefully redistributed, even such informal ones as "friend" and "lover." In many places, issues of inheritance figure prominently in the activities of the funeral.

In contrast to van Gennep's wide-ranging essay, Robert HERTZ (1960a) focused exclusively on death rites – indeed on only one type, those involving secondary treatment of the corpse. Such rites are found worldwide, but the most celebrated cases come from Borneo, where corpses are brought back from the graveyard a year or more after death for a "great feast," prior to permanent entombment. Hertz worked out the meanings of these rites in terms of interrelationships between three dramatis personae: the souls of the dead, the living survivors, and the corpse. Two of these interrelationships turn on basically sociological features – the extinction of the social person, and the expression of the social order – and here Hertz's argument runs parallel to van Gennep's. It is the third side of Hertz's argument that is the most original. He showed that the soul of the deceased and the abandoned body are related metaphorically, and that this is the key to understanding the double format of the rites. As the body sinks into corruption, so the soul passes into a wretched state, rejected both by the living and the dead. When only dry bones are left, hard and imperishable, the deceased is ready to enter the company of the ancestors, and it is this that is celebrated in the "great feast." In the details of the rites, the metaphor is elaborated to provide a vision of the soul in this life and in the afterlife, and not only in transit between the two (Metcalf & Huntington 1991).

Political significance of death rituals

An aspect of death rituals that has received

considerable attention is their power to unite people, and so legitimize their leaders. A. M. Hocart (1954) went so far as to suggest that "the first kings must have been dead kings," that is to say, founding heroes who constituted the center of a national cult. The remains of former kings frequently constitute a source of charisma that each new incumbent tries to assume, and the control of death rites for a predecessor is a means to that end. In Thailand and Bali, for example, royal funerals are celebrated on a scale more grand than coronations. Such rites, however, are not simply tools of control in the hands of the status quo. They are often an arena of competition, and they may undermine aspiring leaders. As always, the role of ritual is a dynamic one.   PM

demographic transition is the period of change in a population's demographic profile from one characterized by high birth rates, high infant mortality, and short life expectancy to one characterized by low birth rates, low infant mortality, and long life expectancy. This transition, according to MODERNIZATION theory, accompanies the transition from a premodern to an industrial economy.   MR

demography is the study of the causes and consequences of population growth and decline. Demography's central concepts thus refer to numbers – population size, age structure, sex ratios, density, growth rate, and the rates of births, deaths, and movements that generate these characteristics. Consequently, demography relies heavily on numerical analyses and it requires distinctive methodological tools to capture its central concepts (Handwerker 1989a; N. Howell 1979; Hassan 1981).

Nonetheless, demographic analysis invokes most of the concepts that are used in any social and cultural analysis, and it bears on some of the most intriguing problems in the social sciences. Thus, demography intersects with the study of technological changes in the Paleolithic (B. Hayden 1981), the origins of AGRICULTURE (M. Cohen 1977; M. Cohen & Armelagos 1984), the rise of the STATE (Carneiro

1970), the origins and dissolution of feudalism (Brenner 1976), the growth of a world industrial economy (Deane 1965) and, consequently, the causes and consequences of "DEVELOPMENT" broadly conceived (Polgar 1972). The latter issues raise policy concerns of immense importance about whether or not the world is, or is soon to be, overpopulated, and on the policy corollary of how national and international resources should be allocated (Hern 1990). Thus, for anthropologists, demography's numerical concepts embody primary moral dimensions of human behavior and identify processes and structural relationships that profoundly influence the direction of social and cultural change.

For example, population collapse following the Black Death effectively destroyed the English manorial system (J. Bolton 1980; cf. Dumond 1965). Population growth creates conditions that can increase the efficiency of distribution (Handwerker 1980): the growth of a potential market makes agricultural intensification and specialization profitable (Netting 1993); light population densities in Africa unduly increase the costs of development (Amin 1972). Similarly, the high death rates and youthfulness that characterized all human populations until the last century imply a very different view of social relationships and different standards for viewing DEATH and the aged (Fourastie 1972). Infants may not be considered real people in societies in which 25–30 percent (or more) die before they reach their first birthday (Eng & Smith 1976; Milton Freeman 1971). Death and SUFFERING take on immense social significance where 50 percent of the people who were born during the same year die before they are 15 years old and 80 percent may die by their early 50s (Scheper-Hughes 1992). ELDERS may achieve respect merely because they have survived. The population aging that accompanies DEMOGRAPHIC TRANSITION to low birth and death rates induces an epidemiological transition in which chronic ILLNESS supplants acute, infectious DISEASE as the major social health problem (Omran 1971). The young may come to view their parents and other older people with less respect merely because there are so many of them (cf. Dorjahn 1989). Older populations grow slowly, and newcomers to the population – the young – may have fewer chances for upward economic and social mobility than their seniors. Conflicts arise in which seniors who continue to work may block opportunities for their juniors, or in which employment policy requires that active seniors retire before they wish to.

Anthropologists work with populations that vary enormously: individual FAMILIES or HOUSEHOLDS, bands of FORAGERS, ethnic units, the people who live within the confines of a village or a region, the citizens of a state, the employees of an organization, or all the people who live on our planet.

Irrespective of the scope of population studied, each birth, death, or movement constitutes a political event that may express, limit, create, or extend an individual's or an organization's power (Handwerker 1990; Hern 1971, 1975). To wit: some adolescent pregnancies empower girls who have no other effective way to improve their lives (Handwerker 1989b), while others occur as a consequence of sexual abuse (Handwerker 1993). Differential population growth – achieved by whatever combination of fertility, mortality, and MIGRATION – shifts the basis of political power (M. Ward 1986), may change profoundly the political complexion of a society (Borjas and Tienda 1987), and may either incite or suppress VIOLENCE between or within national borders (Chavez 1992; Hammel 1993). Patterns of population growth and decline thus both reflect and generate conflicting models of moral responsibility and constitute one of the most important driving forces of social change (Engelbrecht 1987; Thornton 1981). For anthropology, demography is therefore best understood as human population ecology sensitized to the moral and political dimensions of human lives.
WPH

See also BIOLOGICAL ANTHROPOLOGY
further reading Boserup 1965, 1981; Dumond 1975; Hammel & Howell 1987; Handwerker 1983, 1986a,b; Harris & Ross 1987a; Howell 1986; Scrimshaw 1978; Swedlund 1975

dependency theory explains slow or absent DEVELOPMENT in the Third World as a consequence of colonial, neocolonial, or postcolonial relations with capitalist states (see also COLONIALISM). Colonizing or metropolitan states exploit their colonial or satellite regions (or states) in a variety of ways that enhance their own development and accumulation of capital. The wealth extracted from satellites impedes local development and can even undo past development. Thus, lack of development – in contrast to the claims of MODERNIZATION theory – is not the result of local failure, but of deleterious external relations. This process is captured in Andre Gunder Frank's (1969) phrase, "the development of underdevelopment."

What development does occur in satellite regions is distorted by the dependency relationship – in both its internal and external aspects (Santos 1970). Metropolitan capitalists manipulate industrialization and modernization processes in order to increase their profits, often by undermining the satellite's autonomy. For instance, they may control supplies of sophisticated technology, or attempt to monopolize special skills or jobs. This is known as "dependent development" (P. Evans 1979). Dependency generally increases internal STRATIFICATION, as the limited benefits of dependent development are unevenly distributed within the region. This, in turn, often gives rise to social and political unrest.

Dependency theory has deep intellectual roots (Hendricks 1992). In Latin America, dependency theorists are known as *dependistas*. In English-speaking countries it has taken additional forms, which often entail trenchant criticism of foreign policy. Dependency theory is a direct intellectual ancestor of WORLD-SYSTEM THEORY (Chirot & Hall 1982).   TH
See also CLASS
further reading Chilcote 1984; So 1990

descent is the calculation of kin relations from earlier to later generations as a means of passing down social relationships. While often expressed in a biological idiom, it is widely used to refer to cultural succession of various kinds. An individual related to another by a relationship of descent is called a "**descendant**."   MR

descent groups are systems in which DESCENT figures as the primary criterion for membership; that is, systems in which the boundaries and recruitment principles of kin groups are defined primarily in terms of the common descent of their members. This may be traced in a number of ways:

(1) Unilineal descent systems trace descent through a single parental line, such as PATRILINEAL or MATRILINEAL descent. Individuals are members of only one lineage.

(2) Non-unilineal systems calculate descent indifferently through either the father's or mother's line, or both. Such systems include the BILATERAL, COGNATIC, and AMBILINEAL SYSTEMS. Depending on individual rules, individuals may be considered members of both parents' lineages, have a choice of either lineage, or establish relationships based on egocentric KINDREDS.

(3) DOUBLE DESCENT KINSHIP SYSTEMS trace descent through both the mother's and father's lines but keep the two clearly distinguished. Individuals in such a system would be members of their father's patrilineage and their mother's matrilineage.   MR

descent theory is an analysis of KINSHIP and SOCIAL ORGANIZATION that emphasizes the axial role of social relationships based on ties of CONSANGUINITY in societies whose political structure is largely formed by unilineal kin groups. In such societies the allocation of rights to group membership and property comes from a single parent (see MATRILINEAL DESCENT; PATRILINEAL DESCENT).

Descent theory, or "lineage theory," was largely the product of British social anthropology and its sustained engagement in the study and analysis of certain African societies. Its origins lie in EVANS-PRITCHARD's (1940) classic ethnographic monograph on the Nuer and Meyer FORTES's (1945) work on the Tallensi, as well as a series of studies on similar "stateless" societies in

Africa (Fortes & Evans-Pritchard 1940b). For several decades following World War II, British social anthropologists worked within the framework of this approach, while extending their analyses to societies beyond sub-Saharan Africa, such as China (Freedman 1958).

The strength of descent theory was in the presentation of a model that reconciled the organization of blood ties with the formation of social groups capable of forming a GOVERNMENT. The clearest model of this was the SEGMENTARY LINEAGE, where factions united and divided on the basis of genealogical ties. But the clean lines of unilineal descent were almost always clouded by the existence of KINDREDS that gave individuals close ties to people who were not members of their own lineage. The most often cited of these was the mother's brother in a patrilineal system. This led Fortes (1953, 1959a) to stress the distinction between relationships based on kinship and those based on descent and to introduce the concept of COMPLEMENTARY FILIATION, which bound nonagnates together. In his view kinship was personal, private, and domestic, whereas descent was public, political, and jural.

Descent theorists came under attack from many quarters. Proponents of ALLIANCE THEORY argued that marriage ties, not descent, were key to understanding social organization in many societies. Students of LÉVI-STRAUSS in France and elsewhere were particularly keen in their criticisms. Anthropologists in the United States, with their own parallel tradition of kinship studies, argued that the focus on unilineal systems was too limiting, particularly in its treatment of Oceanic societies (Murdock 1949; Davenport 1959). In COGNATIC or BILATERAL descent groups, which were by definition nonunilineal, membership could be gained through ties either to the mother or the father. Goodenough (1970) attacked the whole notion that descent was a clearly bounded concept. It could be used variously to mean how people reckon relationships (through father, mother, or both), as a defining principle for membership in social groups based on ancestry, or as a means of classifying whole societies based on their kinship patterns. It was both a part of kinship and yet apart from it.

As a result of these debates, descent theory as a cohesive explanatory scheme now holds few adherents and many have pronounced all or part of it intellectually moribund (A. Kuper 1982b; Schneider 1984). Yet because at base descent deals with parent–child and sibling relationships, the problematic keeps returning in new forms, particularly in understanding how descent organizes POWER in terms of gender and generation (Peletz 1995).

JIA

descriptive kinship systems are kinship terminologies based on the use of primary terms combined to indicate more distant kin. In such a system the single term "uncle" is expressed as "father's brother" or "mother's brother." Anthropologists often employ this method themselves in describing kinship relationships cross-culturally to avoid confusion.   MR
See also CLASSIFICATORY KINSHIP SYSTEMS

development refers to a process of change through which an increasing proportion of a nation's citizens are able to enjoy a higher material standard of living, healthier and longer lives, more education, and greater control and choice over how they live. Development is generally believed to rest on rising levels of labor productivity, which can be achieved through the application of science, technology, and more efficient forms of economic and managerial organization. Virtually all government leaders profess commitment to promoting development understood in this way. Leaders, policy makers, and academics disagree, however, about the relative importance of technical, economic, and political barriers to development and hence about priorities in achieving it.

Debates in anthropology have focused less on these broad goals but rather on the implications of a more restricted definition of development as the post–World War II effort by Western governments to contain communism, raise living standards, and foster mutually beneficial economic growth and trade through foreign-assistance programs. This effort (inspired by the success

of the Marshall Plan in rebuilding Europe), and the discourse associated with it, were grounded in the ethnocentric tenets of MODERNIZATION theory, which held that only by adopting "Western" beliefs and institutions could other societies hope to develop. Economists played a leading role in theorizing and implementing such a retricted notion of development, particularly in the United States through initiatives supported by presidents Truman and Eisenhower (1945–60). Though their models and prescriptions have varied in their mix of governmental action, markets, capital investment, management, and institution building, economists have not departed fundamentally from the assumptions of modernization theory.

Anthropologists have had an ambivalent relationship with government-sponsored development (Hoben 1982). In the 1950s anthropologists were employed to facilitate the diffusion of improved technology by overcoming resistance to change grounded in traditional values, institutions, and practices. Distinguished scholars, including Arensberg (1964), Goodenough (1963), M. Mead (1953b), and Spicer (1952), wrote guidelines for community development, and anthropologists were placed in many aid missions overseas. But, although anthropologists generally accepted the stated humanitarian goals of development, they came to dislike its ethnocentric bias and the way development assistance was used to promote American and Western political and commercial objectives.

During the 1960s anthropologists largely abandoned the field and in the United States virtually all anthropologists left the Agency for International Development (AID), which administered the largest development programs. There were several reasons for this. Economists' new "big push" and "trickle-down" theories of economic development emphasized investment in the urban industrial sector, infrastructure, and mechanized farming, rather than rural development. In such projects little need was seen for anthropologists and their positions were abolished by the Eisenhower administration in the 1950s. Anthropologists also became disenchanted with American foreign policy and angered by the involvement of anthropologists in counterinsurgency projects in Chile (I. Horowitz 1967), Thailand (Wakin 1992), and Vietnam (Hickey 1982). Finally, those anthropologists who had adopted theoretical perspectives from MARXIST ANTHROPOLOGY and DEPENDENCY THEORY began to argue that CAPITALISM and Western development initiatives were the cause, and not the cure, of underdevelopment.

Development strategies began to change during the 1970s with the failure of trickle-down economic policies. This led to a new policy emphasis on delivering development assistance directly to the rural poor, and by the end of the decade scores of anthropologists were working in AID and other major development agencies. Initially their involvement was limited to work on project design and evaluation in AGRICULTURE, rural development, and social-service delivery. Over time, as their contributions were recognized, they attained positions of greater influence, and they became involved in policy work and management. During the 1980s and 1990s anthropologists became instrumental in the articulation of new development initiatives focusing on the environment and sustainable development.

Anthropological contributions to development planning are more widely accepted and better institutionalized now than at any time in the past, though the future and direction of the development enterprise is uncertain in the post–Cold War world. Development anthropology is taught in a number of academic departments, largely in response to student interest, and there are a number of edited volumes summarizing its contributions (Derman & Whiteford 1985; Grillo & Rew 1985; Brokensha & Little 1988). Many academic anthropologists, however, still regard it as opportunistic and devoid of theoretical interest (Escobar 1991). The most significant exception to this is exemplified in the work of a number of scholars who have done research on the relationship between development discourse and hegemonic relationships in development (Hoben 1995; N. Long & Long 1992; J. Ferguson 1990).   AH

further reading M. Cernea 1991; Hobart 1993; M. Horowitz & Painter 1986

developmental cycle Cyclical change refers to regular, repetitive courses of growth, decline, and revival. The concept of a developmental cycle applies the biological metaphor of the life cycle to groups rather than individuals. Certain groups in all societies are thought of as permanent constituents (corporate groups); others are conceptualized as ephemeral. By definition, all ephemeral phenomena must follow some pathway of foundation, realization, and disappearance, and developmental cycle could be applied to any pathways that were predictable. In practice, the most important ephemeral unit to which developmental cycle refers is the DOMESTIC group. Domestic groups are founded (usually by marriage), they grow through the birth of children and the acquisition of other dependents, and they disperse through the marriage of the children and the death of the older generation. In all societies there is an expected pattern to this course of growth and decline, and the landmarks along the way are often ritually marked. This pattern differs from one society to another. A major theoretical innovation in British structural–functional anthropology, particularly in the work of Jack Goody and Meyer FORTES (1958), was to distinguish between the domestic domain of ephemeral groups and the politicojural domain of permanent groups, and to argue that the cycle of development of domestic groups was governed by the permanent structures (see FUNCTIONALISM, STRUCTURALISM). Variation in the pathway of domestic-group development from one society to another would be accounted for by differences in their encompassing structures.   JIG

deviance is the opposite of conformity to cultural norms. Deviance is a general category of non-normative behavior that includes crime, psychopathology, rebellion, or simple violation of social conventions. From the perspective of a community, individual actions are classifiable in terms of their degree of conformity to a prescriptive or proscriptive norm. An instance of nonconformity or deviance has a cultural meaning in terms of a collective code of conduct and a personal motive that accounts for its enactment by the individual. An action accurately coded as a social misdemeanor, crime, rebellion, or even a symptom of mental illness in one culture could be coded as conformity in another. Among the Yoruba of southwestern Nigeria, for example, a man is expected to greet his father and other respected elders and chiefs by prostrating himself so that his forehead touches the ground; failing to do so would be regarded as an intolerably deviant act of disrespect, motivated by a rebellious desire to insult or by a deranged mental state. One of the ethnographic tasks of the social anthropologist is to describe the contexts that distinguish acts of deviance from acts of conformity in a particular community and to reconstruct the social principles and cultural models that generate such judgments.

Crimes are deviant acts that violate the legal code of a particular community and for which there are legal remedies, such as punishment or compensation. The anthropology of LAW describes the definitions of crimes in particular cultures and the procedures through which cases are adjudicated and remedies applied in particular communities. In some East African cultures, for example, intergroup HOMICIDE is treated not as a punishable act of deviant behavior by an individual but as something more like a debt that can be compensated through payment by the group responsible for the killing, if compensation can be negotiated before retaliation takes place. Thus, although homicide is illegal, as in the West, the group contexts of the killing, the locus of responsibility, the legal remedies, and the place of negotiations differ greatly and need to be specified for an understanding of homicide as crime in an East African society.

Psychopathology is similarly variable in its behavioral boundaries, and it is the task of medical or psychiatric anthropology to describe these in different cultures. There is a danger, for example, that conformity to the norms of one culture will be misinterpreted as a symptom of mental illness in another. A Native American man behaving in an appropriately restrained way according to the interactive norms of Navajo culture may be mistakenly diagnosed as schizophrenic by Anglo-American psychiatrists. A Hopi woman who reports conversing with her dead husband, expectable in the Hopi context, may be thought to be hallucinating by an unsophisticated Anglo-American psychiatrist.

Rebellion is a form of deviance conspicuously antagonistic to authority or intended to overthrow a hierarchical status system. Apart from the military and political rebellions documented by historians, there are two kinds of culturally constituted pattern of rebellion described by social anthropologists. In one, custom dictates that on a particular day of the year, subordinates such as women or political subjects are licensed to insult or otherwise act disrespectfully in public to their superiors, returning to conformity thereafter; this is often interpreted as reinforcing rather than undermining the status quo. In the other, a deviant religious CULT or political movement may be formed that refuses to conform to a previously uniform orthodoxy; this can represent the onset of a broader social change in the norms themselves, but it may require several generations before the changes are evident. So rebellious acts can either support an existing order or result in its eventual overthrow, according to whether they are part of the predictable rhythm of community life or represent an unauthorized departure from it.

Although deviance is by definition the opposite of conformity, deviant behavior in general can be seen as organically related to the normative order. From a Durkheimian perspective, the occurrence of crime provides opportunities for its representation as an evil that is stigmatized and punished by the community, thus dramatizing the community's morality. From a Freudian perspective, visible deviance can represent the repressed and unconscious fantasies of conformists, permitting them to disavow their own dangerous impulses by attributing them to a stigmatized category of person, thus reinforcing their sense of moral rectitude. Deviance as a concept was associated with the structural–functional perspectives of A. R. RADCLIFFE-BROWN and

Talcott Parsons; it has been less used in anthropology than in sociology since the 1960s.   RAL
See also LEGAL ANTHROPOLOGY, PSYCHO-LOGICAL ANTHROPOLOGY

dialectical materialism   is a philosophy and method of history associated with Karl Marx that linked dialectical thought, especially that associated with Hegel, with a materialist perspective and emphasized the creative, transforming character of human labor (Marx 1903, 1963).

Central to dialectical thought is the perspective of the *totality*, often confused with simple holism. Although the perspective of totality is a vision of the whole, its emphasis is primarily *relational*. That is, rather than beginning with discrete, bounded objects and placing them in analytical relationships to each other, one begins with the relations themselves and understands objects (as "objects of relation" rather than "objects in relation") in terms of them. Second, dialectical thought emphasizes *process*, and the aim is not to produce a static analysis of relations and objects frozen in time but to see both relations and objects in formation and to grasp the directionality of that process, to understand the potentiality of relations and objects. Third, dialectical thought emphasizes *contradiction*, which must be understood in terms of the two previous emphases. The aim is to identify relations internal to a totality that pull in opposite directions, that contain within them coexisting mutually opposed possibilities (E. Thompson 1978).

Linked to a materialist analysis that centers on human labor, the method aims to explicate the characteristic forms and relations of labor socially and historically; that is, to examine the ensemble of forms and relations through which labor has been mobilized and appropriated over time, in terms of their internal relations and in terms of their historical relation to other such ensembles of forms and relations (Ollman 1971).   WR
See also MARXIST ANTHROPOLOGY

dialects   are varieties of a LANGUAGE. Traditionally, the term was applied to regional varieties (regional dialects), but nowadays it is also applied to varieties characteristic of particular social groups (social dialects).

The major problem in applying the term is drawing the dividing line between dialect and language. Linguists typically refer to two varieties as dialects if they are mutually intelligible and as distinct languages if they are not mutually intelligible, but this criterion is not foolproof. Mutual intelligibility is a question of degree, with 70 percent comprehension sometimes being taken as a convenient cutoff point. Mutual intelligibility is not always reciprocal: Spanish is more intelligible to speakers of Portuguese than vice versa. An insuperable problem is provided by dialect chains, where adjacent dialects are mutually intelligible, but the extremes are not; either all dialects in the chain are assigned to a single language, although some are mutually unintelligible, or more-or-less arbitrary divisions are proposed that assign adjacent, mutually intelligible varieties to different languages (as with the dialect chain stretching from northern France to southern Italy).

In common practice, languages are distinguished more on the basis of psychological and social (including political) factors, as when largely mutually intelligible Danish, Norwegian, and Swedish are considered distinct languages, or mutually unintelligible varieties like Mandarin and Cantonese are considered dialects of Chinese.

Outside linguistics, dialect is often used to refer specifically to a nonstandard or low-prestige variety of a language; structurally, however, a standard language is simply one dialect among many.   BC
further reading Chambers & Trudgill 1980; J. Grimes 1964

dialogic anthropology   *See* VOICE

diet   is the customary set of foods regularly prepared and consumed in a particular culture. More narrowly it describes the prescribed rules that restrict which foods may be prepared and eaten, in what manner and at what times, by particular categories of individuals or groups. All human societies use diet not only to support biological life, but to express social relationships and make statements fraught with cultural symbolism. For example, individual, household, or community differences in consumption patterns indicate social place within more inclusive social groups. Diet also provides evidence of social and cultural transformation, as localized human groups abandon tradition in favor of global dietary trends and associated life styles. All form part of the anthropological analysis of FOOD SYSTEMS or the complex linkages among FOOD PRODUCTION, distribution, and consumption and its consequences.

Early British social-anthropological studies of the economics and social organization of nonindustrialized societies subsisting mainly on local resources focused on how the search for, and preparation and consumption of, food provided the organizing structure for daily and seasonal activities, and how the symbolic and emotional values of foods, encoded in ritual contexts, mark social status, intervals in time, and culturally important environmental resources (A. Richards 1932, 1939). Subsequent ethnographies, especially in Africa, explicated food systems, and the ways in which social cooperation in the food quest and food sharing structure human social organization and culture, and continue to provide models for understanding food and culture (Huss-Ashmore & Katz 1989–90).

CULTURE AND PERSONALITY studies in American anthropology on "food habits" during the 1930s and 1940s explored how attitudes toward food developed early in life affected later kinship and gender relations, as well as the dynamics of dietary ACCULTURATION and its nutritional impacts (M. Mead 1964; C. Wilson 1973; NRC 1945). More recent studies have examined the EMOTIONS surrounding food, and the formation of indulgent or abstemious eating behaviors, eating disorders, and socioculturally desirable body weights and body images; the "fit" between sociocultural and scientific evaluations of diet-related health and disease. Obesity in adults and protein-energy malnutrition in children, it has been argued, are both biomedical "culture-bound" syndromes (Ritenbaugh 1982; Cassidy 1982). By the 1980s, however, food-habits literature had

atrophied and was replaced by work on the domestic economy and decision making (Sharman et al. 1991).

In the last 50 years, cultural-materialist, human-ecological, ideological–structural, and biocultural approaches that explore intracultural variation and dietary change have flourished, along with interests in international economic and human development (Messer 1984). Cultures and individuals select foods on the basis of sensory, cognitive, and symbolic dimensions. Tastes appear to be shaped by genetics, cultural experience, or both: all humans seem to like sweet, but only some are trained to enjoy the puckering of sours or the piquancy of chili pepper. People in cultures that value meat often claim that they remain "hungry" if it is not served, no matter how much vegetable matter they have ingested. By contrast people in vegetarian cultures that reject these flesh foods find satisfaction of their appetites with plants, and have festivities structurally similar to those that often accompany ritual animal slaughter and consumption.

Diets across the world have specific cultural, symbolic, and cognitive dimensions that include such binary oppositions as hot–cold, wet–dry, male–female, heavy–light, yin–yang, clean–poison, ripe–unripe, as well as flavor, sharpness, itchiness, and color. In particular cultures, these dimensions interrelate fauna, flora, medicine, health, ritual, and social relations. Indigenous American cultures honed food codes based on species, their "raw or cooked" state, and their manner of cooking (Lévi-Strauss 1969b, 1973, 1978). Hindu cultures appear to have developed the most elaborate rules for food classification and distribution: raw foods pass up, cooked foods down the caste hierarchy; eating food that someone else has touched is polluting; and FOOD TABOOS can reduce the quantity, variety, and frequency of eating many days of the year, especially for observant females (Khare 1976). In cultures that employ "humoral categories," the acceptance of new foods, especially infant or children's foods, may involve merging these categories with new notions of "nutritious" by the adopting community (Messer 1981). Flavor and cost, however, have much more impact on food selection than symbolic qualities that mostly affect food consumption by individuals experiencing physiological stress (illness, pregnancy), where food is medicine.

Diets are usually reported in terms of core (staple or superfoods), secondary-core, and peripheral foods, as they describe patterning in food items, recipes, meal formats, or meal cycles (Goode 1989). Typical cuisines may value segregation (as in Jewish dietary separation of milk and meat) or combinations (as in Italian meal formats of pasta and sauce) (see COOKING). Ethnic groups may also "mark" their new cultural setting with familiar traditional flavors and textures, and continue to eat customary foods particularly on ritual occasions.

People obtain food through food production, market exchange, foraging, or gifts (DeWalt 1983). An analysis of the dietary structure in rural settings provides an indicator of normal times vs. times of stress. It is generally measured by examining the ratio of grains or starches to leaf- or protein-based relishes and condiments. In times of HUNGER, people cut back on the number and contents of meals according to the availability of staple and other foods. In the past, disadvantaged individuals or communities increased their FORAGING during lean times as a way to survive, but that resource base has been shrinking around the world. Increasingly, such households rely on support from beyond the local community: remittances from migrant members to assist purchases of market sources of food, government relief programs, or some other social-security mechanism. The timing and patterning of ritual exchanges may also help equitably stretch and spread meager supplies.

Time allocation of the food providers and consumers is a factor in food selection in every culture. In INDUSTRIAL SOCIETIES both school and work schedules are transforming the "family meal" and the types of foods consumed commensally, and also contributing to the demand for "junk" snack foods of low nutritional value. Additional nutritional concerns include the impacts of urbanization, agricultural commercialization, and expansion of the international food trade, all of which have

caused a reduction in food self-sufficiency. Cash-cropping schemes in particular have been shown to worsen nutritional situations where the diversity and quantity of nutritious home-produced foods are reduced without a consequent increase in reliable income that would allow the household to sustain good nutrition throughout the year. Whether households and individuals are nutritionally better off when they diversify their diets through cash purchases or other sources depends on the extent to which purchased or other foods that replace home-produced items are adequate nutritional substitutes. Cash employment, as in the Brazilian production of sisal instead of food gardens, reduced incomes and household food availability for women and children (D. Gross & Underwood 1971). In addition, women's work can compete for time with food preparation.

The final message from dietary studies is to the consumer: eat responsibly to avoid the diseases of civilization that often accompany shifts to a modern diet and an underactive life style.   EM

further reading Arnott 1975; M. Douglas 1984; Farb & Armelagos 1980; J. Goody 1982; Jerome et al. 1980, Robson 1980

diffusion, diffusionism   is the transmission of elements from one culture to another. Such elements are transmitted by agents using identifiable media and are subject to different barrier or filter effects. It is one of the processes of ACCULTURATION but may lack the close contact between peoples that acculturation presupposes. Diffusionism refers to any learned hypothesis that posits an exogenous origin for most elements of a specific culture or cultural subset. An example is the proposition advanced by some nineteenth-century folklorists that most popular European story frames had been transmitted to Europe by Gypsies from India. The notion, however, that cultural evolutionists of the nineteenth century denied the significance of diffusion is not correct. Robert LOWIE in particular overemphasized the association of diffusion and historicism, independent invention, and evolutionism (Harris 1968: 173–6). The fallacy here is that evolutionists promoted independent invention not to defeat diffusionism but to demonstrate the PSYCHIC UNITY OF MANKIND.

Stimulus diffusion is a concept elaborated by A. L. KROEBER to describe the reinvention of an element transmitted across a social or cultural barrier to bring it into congruence with the values of the recipient culture. Popular diffusionism is the attribution, typically false or distorted, of certain cultural elements to foreign cultures, especially antecedent ones, such as the attribution by contemporary Europeans of anything old-looking to the Romans or Celts.

Recent diffusion research in anthropology, sociology, and geography has focused on the pattern of diffusion, producing convergent results. As far back as the end of the nineteenth century, Gabriel de Tarde (1903) noted that the rate at which innovations are adopted tends to follow an S-shaped curve. The curve is now conventionally divided into discrete phases associated with adopter categories (innovators, early adopters, early majority, late majority, and laggards), which have been used as ideal types to explain a range of behaviors with respect to innovation.

TG

further reading Rogers 1995

diglossia is a term in LINGUISTICS and SOCIOLINGUISTICS that characterizes societies in which two distinct varieties of the same LANGUAGE are used in different domains, generally one for written purposes and the other for oral interactions. The two varieties exhibit differences on every level of linguistic structure. Diglossia is to be distinguished from cases where a standard variety coexists with one or more regional and social DIALECTS, because in a diglossic setting, the superposed variety has to be learned formally by everyone, and no one in the community uses it as an ordinary medium of conversation. On the same basis, it is to be distinguished from societal bilingualism where (for some sectors of the population) the superposed language is their native language. Of particular interest to linguists is the impact of diglossia on language variation and change.

In his classic article, C. Ferguson (1959: 336) defined diglossia (from the French *diglossie*) as

a relatively stable language situation in which, in addition to the primary dialects of the language (which may include a standard or regional standards), there is a very divergent, highly codified (often grammatically more complex) superposed variety, the vehicle of a large and respected body of written literature, either of an earlier period or in another speech community, which is learned largely by formal education and is used for most written purposes but is not used by any sector of the community for ordinary conversation.

Using language situations from Egypt, Haiti, Greece, and German-speaking Switzerland, in every case he found that there are local terms for both varieties, which Ferguson labeled "High" and "Low."

"Diglossia" was first used in the 1880s to characterize the coexistence in Greece of the linguistic varieties Katharévousa ("puristic") and Dhimotiki ("common, colloquial") (Mackey 1993). Marçais (1930) was the first to apply the term to Arabic to describe the written Arabic and spoken Arabic that coexist in the Arab world. According to Marçais (p. 901), written Arabic is used in literary and scientific publications, in the press, judiciary system, private letters, and anything else that was written. Spoken Arabic, by contrast, is the language of conversation in all domains, whether "popular" or "cultivated."

Fishman extended the application to any sociolinguistic setting in which two or more languages, dialects, registers, or any "functionally differentiated language varieties of whatever kind" are employed (1972: 92) and argued that diglossia is the "societal normification" of bilingualism (1967: 37). Thus, diglossia has come to signify functional differentiation of language use regardless of the conditions under which the superposed variety is acquired. Such an extension of the term accounts in part for the tremendous outpouring of publications on the topic from 1960 to the present (A. Hudson 1992). Another recent bibliography on the subject (M. Fernández 1993) contains works in several languages on some 175 language situations around the world.

The use of Ferguson's typology as a "model of actual language use" that delineates the conditions under which one or both varieties may be employed in concrete verbal interactions has been criticized by scholars who found its dichotomous nature inadequate to explain their linguistic data (Caton 1991: 145). Students of Arabic, for example, have borrowed from creole studies the concept of a "continuum" (Rickford 1987) to allow for usages that mix Classical Arabic and nonclassical Arabic to various degrees. But factors influencing language use are far more complex than overarching norms of appropriateness prescribed ideologically and institutionally in any society. The merit of Ferguson's model resides in its focus on societal norms and the ways in which the superposed variety is acquired, because diglossia is not a property of languages, but of communities (C. Ferguson 1991).

However defined, diglossia has rarely been studied ethnographically and from the crucial angle of the nature of contact between the varieties. Different groups of speakers come into contact with the superposed variety in different ways and to various degrees: contact through other speakers, the mass media, bureaucracies, religion, formal education, and other ways. The claim that the varieties belong to the "same" language has been criticized on various grounds (see Valdman 1986 for Haiti), and "sameness" has not been explored from the point of view of speakers. Other central questions that have not received adequate attention are: (1) the impact of postcolonial educational systems on shaping, reproducing, or eliminating diglossia (Ibrahim 1983); (2) roles of class and gender (N. Haeri 1995); and (3) relationships between the often hegemonic dominance of the "High" language, identity, and nationalist ideologies (Gumperz & Wilson 1971; Fishman 1973; Altoma 1969; Grandguillaume 1983).   NH

See also ORAL CULTURES, POETRY, WRITING SYSTEMS

further reading Caton 1990; Chejne 1969; Messick 1993

disaster *See* NATURAL DISASTERS

discourse theory refers to several different analytic perspectives: (1) traditional SOCIOLINGUISTIC analysis of spoken language (Stubbs 1983); (2) recent work by more radical sociolinguists that explicitly focuses on questions of language and power (Fairclough 1989); (3) the dialogic discourse theory of Mikhail Bakhtin (Holquist 1990); and (4) critical interventions on discourse, "Truth", power, subjectivity, and the body by Michel Foucault (1980). Since the 1980s Bakhtinian and Foucauldian perspectives have become important in contemporary cultural anthropology, especially in the United States.

Contribution to a new cultural anthropology

With its emphasis on textuality, discourse, and the decentering of traditional ethnographic authority (Clifford 1983), new cultural anthropology is represented by:

1. anthologies such as Clifford & Marcus 1986; Bruner 1984; V. Turner & Bruner 1986; J. Fernandez 1991; Lavie et al. 1993; Benson 1993; Manganaro 1990; Brady 1991
2. book-length interventionist essays such as C. Geertz 1988; R. Rosaldo 1989; Taussig 1993; Visweswaran 1994
3. contributions to various anthropological and cultural studies journals, in particular, *Cultural Anthropology* (G. Marcus 1992)
4. an increasing number of experimental ethnographies, including Crapanzano 1985; J. Stewart 1989; Fabian 1990; Kondo 1990; Lavie 1990; Gottlieb & Graham 1993.

This body of work argues that, in addition to the long-standing concerns with FIELDWORK methods and theory, it is imperative that anthropologists reflect on our own textual productions. It pays attention to reflexivity, dialogue, and, sometimes, POWER. It encourages critical reflection on previous ethnographies, including "classic texts" (Karp & Maynard 1983), as well as on those texts, both "official" and popular, that anthropologists encounter "in the field," ranging from products of mass culture in contemporary Japan (John Russell 1991) to the graffiti of the Palestinian

Intifada (Peteet 1996). New cultural anthropology is critical of realist text-making strategies, positivist epistemologies, and functionalist ontologies. It challenges the commonsense view of language as a tool that simply reflects an already-given natural and social reality, communicating "immediacy of experience." If this commonsense view of language can be shown to be erroneous, then traditional notions of objectivity, value-free science, and the "transparent text" can no longer be sustained.

Bakhtinian discourse theory

In realist ethnography (G. Marcus 1986), like the realist novel, "the author" or narrator apparently occupies a position of unchallenged authority (Author-ity). The ethnographer/author has a privileged perspective, more comprehensive than those of any "informant" or reader. The realist ethnography is dominated by a single voice: that of the omniscient and omnipotent author. The author/ethnographer quotes other voices but these other voices do not converse with, challenge, or subvert that of the ethnographer.

Bakhtin (1981: 259–442) challenged this view. For Bakhtin, texts are always plural and – although some ethnographers inspired by Bakhtin forget this point – deeply embedded in relations of authority and power. Bakhtin argued that dialogic processes proliferate in even the most apparently monologic, realist text. Multiple voices compete for expression, as close analysis can reveal. As Clifford (1986: 15) explained, in traditional (realist) ethnographies, polyvocality was not eliminated but "restrained and orchestrated."

Bakhtin's dialogic perspective has impacted on a wide range of disciplines (Maranhao 1990). In cultural anthropology, it has encouraged reflexive perspectives on both fieldwork and ethnographic text making. Influenced by Bakhtin, Gadamer, and others, new cultural anthropologists seek to produce experimental ethnographic texts that explicitly foreground their polyphonic nature. Some are partially or wholly structured as dialogues, in which the ethnographer's voice is in conversation with or challenged by the voices of "the natives" (M. Jackson 1986; R. Price 1983; K. Dwyer 1982).

To argue that ethnographic production is dialogic is, in part, to undermine the power and authority of the anthropologist-as-author (W. Weiss 1990). Here, a Bakhtinian perspective echoes the poststructuralist impetus to "decenter" the Subject, including the Author (Foucault 1977a). New cultural anthropologists seek to decenter the ethnographer, including themselves – to challenge the ethnographer's authority to represent Others. They call attention to the ethnographer's rhetorical moves, seeking to show that they are not simply bits of neutral descriptive information but expressions of a will to power. Echoing Derrida (1976), who argued that philosophy is above all else a kind of writing with rhetorical moves and literary tropes, and Hayden White (1978), who made similar arguments for history, new cultural anthropologists maintain that "Literary processes – metaphor, figuration, narrative – affect the ways cultural phenomena are registered, from the first jotted 'observations' to the completed book, to the ways these configurations 'make sense' in determined acts of reading" (Clifford 1986: 4).

Foucauldian discourse theory

New cultural anthropology argues that all ethnographic texts (like all other texts) are produced in an *intertextual* situation (G. Jordan 1991). This is what Foucauldian discourse theory calls a "discursive field." Whereas traditional ethnography ignored or suppressed accounts from the field by nonanthropologists, the new cultural anthropologists seek to foreground them, even to begin their research or writing with them. The ethnographic account becomes one account among many competing accounts. In Foucauldian discourse theory the competing accounts are placed within a discursive field that is structured by power relations, highlighting the relationship between language and power. The view of ethnography-as-language (i.e., as modes of rhetoric and figuration) has been easier for the discipline to assimilate than the conception of ethnography-as-power.

In cultural anthropology, a Foucauldian perspective brings together the recent emphasis in cultural anthropology on language and textuality and a concern, derived from Foucault, with power, subjectivity, and the body (Foucault 1972, 1980, 1991). It endorses the emphasis in recent new cultural anthropology on ethnographic texts as narratives and discourse but places these in an historical and social context that highlights anthropology as an institutional practice concerned with power (Rabinow 1985). Such a perspective refuses to privilege texts over contexts and often raises larger political questions such as anthropology's relationship to COLONIALISM.

In anthropology Foucauldian discourse theory focuses on the ways in which ethnographies are constituted in, and constitutive of, larger relationships of power. The failure to ground analyses in historical, institutional, and social contexts leads to a failure to provide an understanding of how particular constructions of Others are contained and (re)produced. Most of the societies and social groups studied and portrayed by anthropologists are relatively subordinated in local or regional systems of power. The local literature on such groups is often part of a hegemonic discourse that contributes to their subjugation. Discourse theory pays attention to this dimension of the institutional role of anthropology in both reproducing and challenging power relations such as those under colonialism (D. Scott 1992) or underlying the Salman Rushdie affair (Asad 1990).

Analyzing accounts-as-discourse focuses one's attention on how knowledge and representations – constructions of "The Other" – are produced by and help to reproduce relationships of power in institutions and society. The classic example is Said (1978) on Orientalism. This discursive approach enabled Said to address "the enormously systematic discipline by which European culture was able to manage – and even produce – the Orient" (ibid: 3). It is precisely with such larger questions that Foucauldian discourse theory is concerned, including the issue of how anthropological discourse and practices produce our Others (see Fabian 1983).

Foucault's conception of discourse is closely allied to his view of power, disciplining, the body, and subjectivity. Some recent anthropological contributions take on board these Foucauldian ideas, looking at the body (T. Turner 1995), sectarian violence (A. Feldman 1991), academic institutions (Brenneis 1994), and RACISM (G. Jordan 1997), including the appropriation of Foucault's notion of the panoptican (M. Kaplan 1995; Devine 1995). A few, such as those among Native Americans (O'Nell 1994; Landsman & Ciborski 1992), also utilize, implicitly or explicitly, the concept of "reverse discourse," which is the Foucauldian version of counterhegemonic narratives. Meanwhile, some anthropologists (Sangren 1995) remain decidedly unimpressed by Foucauldian interventions.

GJ

See also CRITICAL ANTHROPOLOGY, LITERARY ANTHROPOLOGY, POSTMODERNISM

further reading R. Coward & Ellis 1977; Dant 1991; Dreyfus & Rabinow 1982; Eribon 1991; Foucault 1965, 1977b; Hoy 1986; G. Jordan & Weedon 1995; Macdonell 1986; Macey 1993; Rabinow 1991; Sarup 1988; Weedon 1996

disease refers to outward, "objective" clinical manifestations of abnormality of physical function or infection by a pathogen in an individual or host. It includes observable, organic, and pathological abnormalities in organs and organ systems, whether or not they are culturally recognized. The concept of disease is fundamental to biomedicine, and the official listing of disease categories, grouped by causal agents, is found in the *International classification of diseases*, currently in its ninth edition (the analogous reference for mental disorders is the *Diagnostic and statistical manual of mental disorders*, 4th edn). Disease is distinguished from ILLNESS, which refers to a person's perceptions and lived experience of being sick or "dis-eased" – a socially disvalued state that includes disease but is not limited to it. In recent years, the disease–illness distinction has been criticized because the process of separating biological "facts" from cultural constructions falsely suggests the superiority of the noncultural biomedical model (Hahn 1995).

From an anthropological perspective,

diseases have played a significant role in the evolution of both human biology and cultural systems. Infectious diseases, for example, represent challenges to survival and therefore act as agents of selection for biological or cultural adaptation. Livingstone's (1976) analysis of the history of the sickle-cell genetic trait in West Africa remains a classic example of this phenomenon. Here the introduction of SWIDDEN horticulture resulted in increased *P. falciparum* malaria, which, in turn, increased the frequency of the sickle-cell gene that gave resistance to that disease, in spite of the huge costs sickle-cell anemia otherwise exacts on the human body. A cultural-ecological approach to understanding disease emphasizes the fact that the environment and its health risks are largely created by culture (Inhorn & Brown 1997). Culture determines the social-epidemiological distribution of disease in two general ways. From a microsociological perspective, culture shapes individual behaviors (diet, exposure to contaminated water, sexual practices, etc.) that predispose people to certain diseases. From a macrosociological perspective, political-economic forces and cultural practices make people interact with their environment in ways that may affect health – either by exacerbating disease problems or protecting people from disease. The building of dams for the intensification of agricultural production, for example, can increase rates of schistosomiasis or malaria.

In epidemiology there is a distinction between *epidemic* diseases, which occur at greater than expected amounts, often in outbreaks linked by time or place, and *endemic* diseases, which occur at a more constant rate in a population. Epidemics are usually characterized by high mortality rates and socioeconomic disruptions, and have been very influential in history (McNeil 1976). Endemic diseases, often characterized by high morbidity, can be so commonplace in a population that they are considered normal rather than an illness. Infectious diseases caused by bacteria, viruses, fungi, unicellular parasites, and so on often trigger immunological responses in hosts so that individuals build up a repertoire of immunities to endemic (child-

hood) diseases. Infectious diseases can also be contrasted with *chronic* diseases (cardiovascular disease, hypertension, etc.); these are sometimes called the "diseases of civilization" because of their increased prevalence in wealthy populations. Chronic diseases have multifactorial causes, partly linked to diet and exercise patterns. Many anthropologists see the rise of chronic disease as a reflection of the discordance between ancient genes and modern lifestyles (Eaton et al. 1988).

Disease patterns change over historical time. Through a process of mutual adaptation of host and pathogen, an epidemic disease can become an endemic one within a single population. Armelagos and Dewey (1970) have identified three "epidemiological transitions" in human history. The first was a general decrease in health and increase in infectious-disease burden associated with the domestication of plants and animals (Neolithic Transition). The second was a decrease in infectious disease and an increase in chronic disease as a result of improved housing, sanitation, diet, and (to a lesser extent) medical care in Europe and the United States at the beginning of the twentieth century. The third epidemiological transition is the rise of antibiotic-resistant pathogens and the emergence of new diseases such as HIV/AIDS or Ebola viruses at the end of the century. These are not isolated phenomena. In 1992, the list of new diseases included 17 forms of bacterium, rickettsia, and chlamydia, 27 forms of virus, and 11 forms of protozoon, helminth, and fungus (Lederberg et al. 1992). In an ecological sense, these new diseases reflect evolutionary processes in which pathogens exploit new ecological niches created by environmental changes.   PB & KHT
See also AGRICULTURE, DEMOGRAPHY, DIET, ECOLOGICAL ANTHROPOLOGY

divination is the process of using RITUAL means to reveal things hidden to ordinary perception, such as information about future events, sources of illness, the identity of witches – indeed, anything that cannot be ascertained through profane methods of investigation. Divination occurs in all societies and takes a wide variety of forms, including ORACLES and AUGURY.

The purposes of divination vary according to the concerns of specific cultures. In many African cultures, for example, where WITCHCRAFT is an important factor in social relations, divination serves primarily to identify and forestall the activities of witches (Mair 1969: 76–101). An Azande who has suffered illness or misfortune may choose from a variety of oracles to divine his bewitcher; alternatively, he might hold a ceremony in which a visiting specialist publicly divines the culprit (Evans-Pritchard 1937). In hunting societies, divination may focus on where to find game or how to end a dry spell in hunting. In the American southwest, where access to water is both vital and difficult for farmers, the divination of water sources through dowsing has become particularly elaborate. In almost all societies, individuals use private divination to discover details about their own future: American girls, for example, have a variety of procedures for discovering whom they will marry and how many children they will have.

When divination seeks the source of misfortune, it generally provides a cure as well. This cure frequently involves redressing a ritual dereliction that has caused the problem. The Sisala of Ghana, for example, most frequently consult a diviner when they are ill. The diviner usually discovers that they have neglected one or another ritual duty, and that the offended ancestors are inflicting the illness as a punishment. By making a particular sacrifice, the patient can appease the gods and prevent further affliction. If witchcraft is responsible, the witch can be confronted and forced to halt his or her activities (Mendonsa 1989). In some cases, where festering interpersonal conflicts have poisoned the life of the group, the cure may require that these conflicts be brought into the open and settled (V. Turner 1961).

Many divination ceremonies center around augury, the interpretation of random occurrences. A ceremony creates a phenomenon over which human control seems impossible – the fall of a set of lots, for example, or the pattern of dealt cards,

or the condition of the entrails of an animal. Since human control is impossible, any patterns may be attributed to supernatural agencies. In Denmark, a Pentecostalist seeking guidance may reach into a jar full of slips of paper, each with a biblical verse printed on it. Since the seeker cannot distinguish the slips, the choice of a particular one is regarded as the work of God, and the verse on the slip as a divine message. By creating a random event, interpretive divination opens a space for the manifestation of supernatural signs.

Such signs are visible to all observers; in many cases, however, they can be properly interpreted only by ritual specialists, or diviners. Diviners have special training in the craft of divination, often acquired through a lengthy apprenticeship. More importantly, however, diviners usually have a special gift, a supernatural ability that enables them to see what others cannot. In many cases, they have a special ability to become possessed by spirits, who direct their actions. A Ndembu diviner, for example, is possessed during a divination ceremony by a shade; it is the shade speaking through the person who actually identifies the causes of illness. In other cases, such as dowsing or SHAMANISM, the diviner is himself invested with a special power.

Early anthropologists, like FRAZER and TYLOR, focused primarily on the intellectual dimensions of divination – why these ceremonies, so apparently fraudulent to the scientific eye, should seem real to primitives. Later writers have been more interested in the social and symbolic functions of divination. Victor TURNER (1968), for example, argued that witchcraft divinations among the Ndembu serve to reveal and heal social tensions and divisions. When considering candidates for witchcraft accusations, a diviner looks first to those who bear grudges against the victim. By bringing those grudges out into the open and prescribing remedies, the diviner provides an opportunity for the expression and resolution of local conflicts. Likewise, divination among the Sisala exposes social transgressions and forces the violators to acknowledge and atone for their misdeeds. By imposing a socially relevant cause on illness and misfortune, divination turns

them into tools for diagnosing and dealing with social problems. Similarly Omar Khayam Moore (1957) has suggested that hunting divination is also practically effective; by allowing random processes to determine a group's course of action, divination can provide a way out of stalled or unproductive patterns.   AB
See also RELIGION, RITUAL, SACRIFICE SYMBOLIC ANTHROPOLOGY
further reading Frazer 1890; Grindal 1983; Malinowski 1948

division of labor is the idea that the work of society is "divided" among its members. Although the concept is very old, it was fixed in the social science lexicon by Emile DURKHEIM's classic work *The division of labor in society* (1933). It implies that social life is a creation of human energy, and that in order to function it demands that people fulfill their part of the total work: in subsistence, maintenance of order, and contacting the gods. The nature of the tasks that constitute that total work, and the ways in which it is divided up and coordinated, make up the domain of enquiry of the division of labor.

The nineteenth-century theorists, including Marx as well as Durkheim, argued that certain aspects of the division of labor were universal and determined by human nature. The distribution and coordination of tasks by age and sex seemed self-evidently general: women cooked, took care of children and the sick, minded the internal comfort of the home; men dealt with making a living and ensuring security in the world outside the home. The younger generation were the workers and warriors; the older generation were the organizers and philosophers. What Durkheim saw as most interesting in the division of labor in society lay beyond all this. He argued that there were two basic types of division and coordination. Where technology was simple, the work of the units of society duplicated each other, the only genuine complementarities being in ritual life. This he called "mechanical solidarity," using the Australian Aboriginal section system as an example. Where technology was complex the units carried out different tasks, and were therefore profoundly dependent on

complementarities. This he called "organic solidarity," using modern industrial society as his example.

As the ethnographic record has become increasingly rich and varied, such simple categories and theories have been abandoned, without, however, the abandonment of the term "division of labor." For many years in the mid-twentieth century it became a simple descriptive term to apply to the customary definitions of who did what work. CROSS-CULTURAL STUDIES based on the Human Relations Area Files have attempted to correlate specific divisons of labor with other aspects of social life. These have found a few tasks that come close to being UNIVERSALS, such as men engaging in the HUNTING of large animals while women do routine COOKING; but even here there are many regional variations.

Two theoretical developments in the 1960s and 1970s revived analytic interest: neomarxism and feminism. Their main focus was not on the same division that had engaged the early theorists, namely, labor in society taken as a whole, but precisely on the dimensions they had relegated to human nature, namely, sex and generation. Neomarxist theorists such as Claude Meillassoux pointed out that there were labor relations that fulfilled all the criteria for permitting the appropriation of SURPLUS that was fundamental to marxist analysis: men and elders appropriated values created by the work of women and juniors. Feminists went further to argue two points. First, the idea of work itself, the assignment of tasks by GENDER, and their terms of complementarity, far from being natural, are rather a cultural construct. The very obviousness of the division of labor to participants is an indicator of the sophistication and pervasiveness of the cultural techniques of persuasion. Hence the now-accepted shift in terminology from the "sexual division of labor" to the "gender division of labor." Second, feminist theory attacked the conceptual frameworks that had misread gender as sex. This critique is best symbolized by Slocum's (1975) paper where she shows how anthropological attention in hunting and gathering societies had been almost entirely focused on Man the Hunter, whereas nutritional studies showed that much higher proportions of the diet were provided by Woman the Gatherer. Through a reanalysis of labor in gender terms new insights have been possible in the larger divison of labor in society as well as with respect to the domains relegated in the past to "the natural" (di Leonardo 1991b).

The current frontiers in understanding the division of labor are still driven primarily by GENDER studies. Most studies are now concerned with understanding change rather than describing and classifiying cultures and societies. The functional imagery of a "whole," divided up, hardly does justice to the current increase in workloads and the combinations of jobs amongst poorer workers and agriculturalists. Guyer (1988) suggested that for Africa's female farmers, their historical trajectory might be better summarized as "the multiplication of labor." Political-economic studies of the New World Order address the new international division of labor on a comparative scale, and again within anthropology much of this work focuses on gender: the employment conditions for both male and female factory workers and sex workers in the Third World (Nash & Fernandez-Kelly 1983).   JIG

See also FEMINIST ANTHROPOLOGY, MARXIST ANTHROPOLOGY

further reading M. Burton et al. 1977; Meillassoux 1981

divorce is the recognized termination of a marriage that releases both spouses from their marital rights and obligations. In some societies it is a defined legal process; in others it is informal and demands only social acceptance by the individuals and the communities in which they reside (J. Bernard 1970). For anthropologists, however, divorce is more complex and its attributes less precise because of the problems in assessing what constitutes a MARRIAGE. Forms of divorce are therefore closely related to the forms of marriage they dissolve.

Marriages in most societies involve BRIDEWEALTH or DOWRY payments. These include long- or short-term GIFT EXCHANGES, sometimes involving the transfer of land, cattle, or other valuable material objects between the intended spouses and their families (future affines). In such cases the implications of a marriage's dissolution, particularly where children are involved, are far-reaching. They involve not just the spouses but a much wider network of relatives who see their own invested resources threatened. Divorce here can lead to a breakdown of the extended family organization and threaten systems of sociopolitical alliances and ceremonial exchange. For this reason such marriage payment systems often provide a strong counterpressure to divorce.

Restrictions on divorce and approaches to marital-conflict resolution are culture specific, and legitimated by the prevailing cultural mores, religious precepts, and secular laws. Pressure to remain within marriage, however, is generally more directed at the wife, for the sake of either continuing the affinal relations and exchange, or the children. Nonetheless, all family systems have some kinds of escape mechanisms to permit individuals to survive the pressures of divorce (W. Goode 1956). Despite the changing attitude toward divorce in many contemporary INDUSTRIAL SOCIETIES, in many societies it is stigmatized and the institution is associated with moral ambivalence. Therefore, elaborate cultural means, social agencies, and legal institutions have evolved in societies to control, contain, and manage divorce.

Divorce is but one form of marital dissolution – albeit the prevalent one. Physical separation of the spouses, declaration of nullity, desertion, and abandonment are also considered, in some societies, as variations on the theme of divorce and dissolution of marriage. In many cultures, the distinctions between these categories are not quite clear, and in reality they may merge or overlap.

Conjugal separation is used in many societies in a quasi-legal sense as a means of recognizing the rights of the spouses to live apart without a final divorce settlement, restricting mostly their right to remarry. Annulment solves the problem of divorce by declaring that no valid marriage really existed to begin with. In some societies, such as the Hagen of New Guinea, the bridewealth that creates a marriage is usually delayed until the birth of children, and annulment of a marriage contract may be informal (M. Strathern 1972: 189). By contrast, among Christian Catholics and Calvinists, where marriage is perceived as a sacrament and its dissolution considered sacrilegious, annulment may be the only form of "divorce" possible, a small relief valve to the expectation that bad marriages should simply be endured. Annulment of a marriage is much rarer in those religious traditions, such as Judaism and Islam, where the possibility of marital incompatibility is anticipated and individuals (usually the husband) or other agencies are empowered to mediate the problems or dissolve the marriage (Qur'an 65: 1, 2: 226–37; Deuteronomy 24: 1). However in both of these cases the woman's power to initiate divorce against her husband's wishes are very restricted.

Other less-known, but nonetheless surviving, variations of divorce include expiration of a contract of temporary marriage in Iran (S. Haeri 1989) and "wife sale" in Britain (Menefee 1981). A contract of temporary marriage sets a mutually agreed time limit that dissolves the marriage contract automatically. Wife selling, associated with common-law marriage among the poor in nineteenth-century Britain, was "merely a public method of divorce by mutual consent" and served as a legal and valid form of divorce (Stone 1993: 19).

The question of why some marriages end in divorce, and the causes of marital strife in general, are subjects of sustained interest. CROSS-CULTURAL STUDIES – though not extensive – point to several "universals" that seem to traverse boundaries of traditional preindustrial societies and postindustrial secular states. Drawing on Darwin's (1871) theory of marriage for the sake of reproduction, Betzig (1989) enumerated nine causes for divorce, of which infidelity is primary, particularly that of the wife. Following a SOCIOBIOLOGICAL model she argued that this double standard is a product of the different reproductive strategies: "the injured wife has lost little, reproductively ... while the injured husband is likely to lose much more" in raising a child that is not his own (Betzig 1989: 661). Even where reproduction is not involved directly, adultery and infidelity remain strong underlying reasons for divorce.

Industrialization and urbanization have profoundly affected the organization of KINSHIP and FAMILY systems globally, changing the patterns of marriage and divorce, and consequently the moral values and cultural attitudes traditionally associated with these institutions. Worldwide, divorce has moved from the realm of religion into state legal codes. In the West, where divorce was once restricted by Christian moral codes and beliefs, it is no longer an anomaly or a flaw in the system, but an essential feature of it based on mutual consent and choice (O'Neill 1967: 7). At least in the eyes of law, it is no longer a sign of social pathology, family instability, and individual crisis, although many social critics still view it as such.

The shift of responsibility from the religious, communal, and social control in matters of marriage and divorce to individuals has been associated with a phenomenal rise in divorce rates cross-culturally. On the other hand, assumptions that marriages were more stable in preindustrial societies of Europe or preliterate societies have been challenged by cross-cultural studies that indicate divorce was "very common" among the latter (Murdock 1949), and a high mortality rate commonly resulted in early marital dissolution among the former (Segalen 1986: 151). The apparent marital stability in these societies was not a sign of marital bliss, but rather the product of sociocultural circumstances that compelled the individuals to endure it, particularly to preserve property rights.

SH

further reading R. Cohen 1971; Hutchinson 1990; Phillips 1988

domestic cycle The domestic group is the most important unit in society to which the idea of developmental cycle is applied. "Domestic" derives from Latin domus and refers to the home, a unit within which generations are continually born, grow to adulthood, and are replaced by their children. The smaller the social group, the more obvious the cyclical pattern linked to the human life cycle. Nuclear families contain only two generations: they are founded by a marriage, augmented by the birth of children, diminished by the marriage of those children, and disappear as social groups with the death of a spouse. Extended families follow more complex patterns, where married children stay in the unit until ultimate partition, often well after the death of the older generation. Larger kinship units do not usually show clear cyclical patterns of growth and decline, because their membership is continually replenished. In all societies there are culturally endorsed patterns of domestic-group growth and change that are supported by other institutions. People know how the cycle should be lived.

The main reason to take cognizance of the cyclical pattern of growth in the study of domestic groups is that field study describes the variety of groups at one point in time. We therefore need to be able to differentiate groups that are at differing stages of the cycle from groups that differ in size and composition because they exist under different conditions of status and wealth in society.   JIG

See also DEVELOPMENTAL CYCLE, SUCCESSION

double descent kinship systems trace DESCENT through both the mother's and father's lines but keep the two clearly distinguished. Individuals in such a system would be members of their father's patrilineage and their mother's matrilineage. The types of property, rights and responsibilities, or status transmitted in such systems typically differ, as do the purposes of each group. Real property, for instance, may be transmitted patrilineally while moveable property may be transmitted matrilineally (Ottenberg 1968).   MR

Douglas, Mary (1921–) Mary Douglas took her anthropology degree at Oxford in 1951. She studied with Max GLUCKMAN and Meyer FORTES, but was especially influenced by the neo-Durkheimianism of E. E. EVANS-

PRITCHARD and by Franz Steiner, who inspired her to study cultural anomalies. A renowned Africanist, she did fieldwork on the Lele of the Belgian Congo, focusing especially on patterns of marriage exchange (Douglas 1963). Mary Douglas taught at the University of London with Daryll FORDE and at Oxford before leaving England to become Avalon Professor of the Humanities at Northwestern University and resident scholar of the Russell Sage Foundation. Since her retirement in 1985 she has continued to publish prolifically.

One of the earliest British anthropologists to be influenced by LÉVI-STRAUSS, Douglas gained wide recognition in 1966 with the publication of *Purity and danger: an analysis of concepts of pollution and taboo.* Here she applied her own brand of structural analysis to what she famously called "matter out of place" (1966: 53) – that is, dirt. Ranging widely through ethnographic literature, she argued that dirt is a universal moral symbol marking the boundaries between social categories. She further argued that anxiety about pollution and loss of bodily control is most potent in societies where social categories are rigid. And, following Victor TURNER (see Douglas 1970c), she maintained that ambiguity and power are inextricably united (for a critique, see De Vos 1975).

Douglas expanded her structural model in her next book *Natural symbols* (1970a), claiming that cultures everywhere could be usefully compared along two rough dimensions: the degree to which internal social distinctions are elaborated and valorized (grid) and the strength of the division between insiders and outsiders (group). Various intensities of grid and group, she argued, would necessarily have different and predictable consequences; for instance, societies with strong group orientations would be obsessed with boundary maintenance and purity, and would develop central COSMOLOGIES and RITUALS of social control aimed at affirming group distinctiveness. Elsewhere (Douglas & Isherwood 1979), she utilized the same framework to generate cosmologies motivating economic behavior.

Douglas's paradigm of grid and group,

though sometimes derided as overly abstract, simplistic, and even tautological, has nonetheless been extraordinarily fertile. Of special interest has been her effort to imagine modern Western society as a peculiar type of social formation where egalitarian individualism (the repudiation of social distinctions) has paradoxically become a predominant social value. Douglas has pursued the ramifications of this paradox in a number of works, most famously and controversially in *Risk and culture* (1982 co-authored with Aaron Wildavsky), where she portrayed the American environmental protection movement as a paranoiac worldview characteristic of voluntary organizations that maintain internal solidarity and moral purity by demonizing their opponents (see Wuthnow 1984 for a discussion).

In her recent work, Mary Douglas has dealt with (among other things) the sociology of perception, Biblical exegesis, environmental regulation, religious revivalism, social justice, AIDS and contamination, the consumer society, the body as cultural artifact, the symbolism of food, and aesthetic taste. In her choice of subject matter, she has clearly prefigured many contemporary anthropological trends, but her approach has nonetheless remained resolutely and unfashionably sociological and structural, concerned above all with revealing and comparing the underlying premises and deep tensions of cultural and ethical systems. What is truly radical about her is that she applies the same diagnosis to "us" as to "them".   CL

further reading M. Douglas 1975, 1982, 1990a, 1993c, 1996; Spickard & Douglas 1989

dowry is property given by a family to its daughter upon marriage for the benefit of her new conjugal household, while **indirect dowry** is property that originates with the family of the groom and goes through the bride into their marriage. Both forms disburse property downward to related families, in contrast to BRIDEWEALTH, which disburses property laterally to unrelated families (see Schlegel & Eloul 1988). These forms of marriage transaction occur primarily in Eurasian societies (J. Goody &

Tambiah 1973) where there is substantial private property, such as land, money, and marketable herds.

Although dowry has been the ideal form in much of Eurasia, from ancient times (in Greece, Egypt, Babylonia, China) to the present, it has always been practiced primarily by elite (propertied) classes, with other forms practiced by lower classes. Thus, in a single heterogeneous nation like prerevolutionary China or present-day India there are castes or classes that practice dowry, indirect dowry, and even bridewealth.

There are two forms of indirect dowry. In one, the groom's family gives goods directly to the bride, which she then brings into the marriage. In the other, the groom's family gives goods to the bride's family, which in turn gives it or its equivalent (more or less) to the bride to take into her marriage. This latter form, technically bridewealth-plus marriage, has often been confused with bridewealth (Schlegel & Eloul 1987).

Indirect dowry as the preferred form appears to have been most concentrated among pastoral peoples in the Middle East and pre-Roman, Germanic Europe, although it was also practiced by nineteenth-century Kwakiutl. As an ancient Semitic form, it appeared in the Old Testament and was later encoded in the Qur'an as the *mahr*, the gift from the groom's family to the wife. It spread throughout the Islamic world along with Qur'anic law. Indirect dowry is a flexible form, since a society can institute it by adding some bridewealth to existing dowry, or some dowry to existing bridewealth, the latter occurring recently among the Digo in Africa (Parkin 1980).

Dowry serves the interest of the bride-giving family in two ways. First, it ensures that their daughter brings resources into the marriage. This is a form of insurance for her future, and it also means that she does not go into the marriage empty-handed. (It is probably no coincidence that dowry is found where female subsistence labor has little or no value.) Second, families can use their wealth to "buy" the kind of son-in-law they want. In peasant Europe, this seems to have been primarily men of equivalent social status. However, a loyal and clever client son-in-law, of a lower status but respectable, could be brought into a richer family to be supported through the daughter's dowry (and ultimate inheritance). The most publicized use of dowry, practiced in Europe from the Middle Ages to the early twentieth century, was the barter of a family's wealth for the connection to a higher-status groom (J. Goody 1983a). This last use of dowry, to "buy" a higher-status son-in-law, is also widely accepted in India among the dowry-giving castes. As a result, families with many daughters to dower could become impoverished. In Europe, the rich solved this problem by sending excess daughters to convents, where the "dowry" (or entrance fee) was much lower than a son-in-law would expect. In India, where all women should have a husband, families have tried to restrict the number of daughters they have.

Indirect dowry may provide some material recompense to the bride's family for the cost of rearing her, since in some cases, some of the goods given by the groom's family may be retained by the bride's family. However, the principal beneficiary of this form of marriage transaction seems to be the new conjugal couple.

In societies practicing dowry or indirect dowry, a family is tied to its daughter's husband and her conjugal family through property. The choice of a son-in-law is important to the well-being of the family, not just the daughter. This can account for the fact that a value on virginity is disproportionately found among societies with these practices. By contrast most societies practicing other forms of marriage transactions do not expect brides to be virgins. Secluding daughters, or forcing them into compliance with virginity rules, prevents a premarital pregnancy and an unwelcome claim on the girl and her property from an unsuitable would-be son-in-law (Schlegel 1991).   ASc

further reading John Comaroff 1980; Dickemann 1979; Harrell & Dickey 1985

Drake, St. Clair (1911–90)   St. Clair Drake (John Gibbs St. Clair Drake, Jr.), a

former professor at Roosevelt University and Stanford University, was an American social anthropologist specializing in race and power, Africa, and the African diaspora. Heartened by Boasian antiracism, his pursuit of a career in anthropology was a result of the influence and example of a former instructor, Allison DAVIS, under whose guidance he participated in the team research on southern US race relations that resulted in *Deep South: a social anthropological study of caste and class* (Davis et al. 1941).

In the aftermath of his fieldwork in Mississippi, Drake undertook graduate studies at the University of Chicago under the direction of Lloyd Warner, Robert REDFIELD, and Fred Eggan. While at Chicago, Drake participated in a federally sponsored Works Project Administration (WPA) effort, administered by Warner and sociologist Horace Cayton, on Chicago race relations and African-American community structure. That project was the first to involve anthropology in the investigation of a large metropolitan area in the United States. Its outcome was the publication of *Black metropolis: a study of Negro life in a northern city* (Drake & Cayton 1945). This study, like *Deep South*, was influenced by Warner's approach to urban and stratified societies as well as by W. E. B. DuBois's *The Philadelphia negro* (1899), one of the earliest ethnographic and sociological studies done in the urban United States. *Black metropolis* initiated discussion on several issues that later became key concerns in anthropology: the historical political economy of labor migration from agricultural to urban industrial settings; ethnic and racial competition and conflict in employment, housing, and politics; conditions stimulating or impeding social change; racial and class stratification; the presence of supralocal institutions in local community life; and the international nexus of class and racial subordination.

To satisfy his doctoral requirements, Drake did an ethnographic study of adaptation and resistance to British domination in Tiger Bay, a multiracial and multiethnic port community in Cardiff, Wales. As a result of his long-standing interests and his contact with anticolonial activists in Britain, he shifted his research focus to Africa. During an 11-year period in West Africa, he taught at and headed the University of Ghana's sociology department, developed cross-cultural training programs for the US Peace Corps, and conducted policy- and development-related research on the mass media, the impact of state-mandated relocation programs, and elite–chieftaincy conflicts.

In the mid-1960s he returned to the United States, and over the next three decades he directed his attention to race and social unrest, the history of blacks in anthropology, and the history of the African diaspora. In the two-volume *Black folk here and there: an essay in history and anthropology* (1987, 1990), he investigated the Old World African diaspora before the era of European colonial expansion. By marshaling evidence on the Nile River Valley, the Mediterranean, the Middle East, and northern European Christendom, he interrogated SLAVERY, skin-color prejudice, and RACISM as distinct sociohistorical phenomena that became inextricably entangled in the unprecedented racial slavery and white racism that developed in the New World context.

A recipient of many honors, Drake was a fellow of the Royal Anthropological Institute of Great Britain and Ireland and received the Bronislaw Malinowski Award from the Society for Applied Anthropology in 1990.   FH
See also URBAN ANTHROPOLOGY
further reading Drake 1955, 1960, 1980; F. Harrison 1988, 1992

Dravidian kinship systems organize kin-terms by distinguishing CROSS-COUSINS and other cross-relatives from PARALLEL COUSINS and other parallel relatives. Dravidian terminologies are often associated with cross-cousin marriage and two-section systems of exogamous MOIETIES. The Dravidian system is often classed with the IROQUOIS.   MR
further reading Trautmann 1981

drugs are pharmacological agents that alter cortical awareness, resulting in the modification of mental activity. There are three broad types of drug: (1) sedatives

used as narcotics, alcohol, barbiturates, and tranquilizers; (2) psychotropic substances that cause mood change, such as coca, marijuana, opium, morphine, and heroin; (3) hallucinogenic plants, such as peyote, and synthetic substances, such as LSD and psilocybinmescaline (Dobkin de Rios 1976: 7).

Drugs are highly valued as: (1) a medical agent in the treatment of pain and disease; (2) a "euphoric narcotic especially in activities requiring endurance or physical effort" (Schultes & Hoffman 1979: 86); (3) an inducement (or incentive) to attract laborers; (4) a basic ingredient in the preparation of love magic; (5) a presumed aphrodisiac; (6) a means to obtain "the maximum food value from a high starch diet" (Furst 1972: xvi); (7) an integral part of religious ceremony; (8) a way to an altered state of consciousness (Bourguignon 1973); (9) a temporary "time out" from ordinary life; (10) a means to develop and maintain social solidarity; (11) a critical factor in the expansion of trade within the emerging world economy (M. Marshall 1979); and (12) a cash crop (Wilbert 1987).

The desire for transcendental or religious experience may have been an important incentive in the domestication of some species of plants. Given the importance of tobacco (*Nicotiana*) in the American Indian cosmology, it "enjoyed a far wider geographical and cultural distribution than any other vegetal hallucinogen" (Wilbert 1987: 27), a fact that might have contributed to making it the oldest cultivated plant in the Americas. The value placed on the ecstatic experience may also have contributed to the cultivation and spread of hallucinogenic plants. La Barre (1938) suggested that SHAMANISM, a religion that used hallucinogenic plants to communicate with the supernatural world, was the primary catalyst for there being more hallucinogenic plants in the New World. From a botanical point of view it should have been the reverse (Furst 1976).

Throughout history, humans have sought an edge against labor drudgery. To this end, drug foods were employed as one way of overcoming fatigue. Labor-enhancing drugs (drugs used either by an individual or as part of an overall management strategy to increase work productivity) are thus not a European contribution to world culture (J. Cooper 1949); they existed well before the advent of mercantilism or market capitalism. The role of drug foods as a labor-enhancer may prove to be as important as religious orientation to understanding the reasons for the cultural use and geographical distribution of a specific plant species.

Before European contact, drugs were taken to enter the supernatural world or to enhance interpersonal relationships, rarely were they used to achieve a giddy escape or to engage in reflected solitude for its own sake. Native cultures were acutely aware that overindulgence in drug use could undermine the social order. Rules were needed. These rules contributed not only to defining social status and creating and nurturing social ties, but also to regulating access to the drug itself (Lebot et al. 1992). This is especially true in stratified societies. In Aztec and Inca societies only the religious specialist who had studied the art of religious interpretation was allowed to take mind-altering drugs. Here, drugs, regulated by customary restraints, served only to confirm the integrity of a culture's value system; they never led to questioning the prevalent social norms. After cultural contact, however, the newly introduced drugs were unrestricted. Without rules, people consumed drugs for personal pleasure, ignoring the possible negative, long-term social consequences.

Below is a brief overview of some of the more commonly used drugs found around the world:

(1) Cannabis or marijuana as it is popularly called in America is an Old World (10,000 B.C.E.) plant that quickly became one of the most prominent cultigens in the world (Emboden 1972b). In small or moderate doses, delta-9-tetrahydrocannabinol (THC), the plant's active ingredient, produces feelings of euphoria. In large doses, the drug can cause paranoia (Fackelmann 1993). It is the most popular illicit drug used in the United States.

(2) Coca, like marijuana, is a relatively mild stimulant or mood enhancer that is not a hallucinogen but a euphoriant. The sixteenth-century Spanish conquerors, seeking to increase production, encouraged its consumption among the laboring class. In this context coca serves as a medicine and a labor enhancer. Pure cocaine, which was first isolated in 1860, extracted from the coca leaf and then chemically refined, is more powerful (Furst 1972: xv). Cocaine, especially in the form of "crack," is the second most abused illicit drug in the United States.

(3) Opium, an addictive drug obtained from the juice of the seeds of the poppy plant, was used by the Sumerians, primarily for medical purposes, as far back as the third millennium B.C.E. It affects the central nervous system by reducing pain and lessening anxiety. The taking of opium and its refined derivatives morphine and heroin is viewed in Southeast Asia as a "habit rather than an illness" (Westermeyer 1982: 7).

(4) Peyote is used extensively among North and South American Indians as a means to make contact with the spirit world. In Mesoamerica it has been used for more than 2,000 years. In the United States there is a deep-seated ambivalence over the Native Americans' use of peyote as part of their religious ritual: some states approve of its use; others have declared it illegal under any circumstances.

(5) Datura is a widely employed hallucinogen that has played a major role among American Indian cultures. The Ecuadorian Jivaro use it to punish disobedient children in the belief that ancestral spirits carry out the reprimand. The ancient Chibcha of Colombia used it to induce a stupor in their wives and slaves so that they could easily be buried alive with their deceased husband or master (Schultes 1972).

(6) Kava (*Piper methysticum*) is a species whose natural range and area of cultivation is restricted to the tropical Pacific islands. It is the only cultivated plant of major regional economic importance. It is used primarily as a major muscle relaxant and as an anesthetic to treat toothache, a sore throat, or the pains common during pregnancy (Lebot et al. 1992: 100).

(7) Caffeine is an alkaloid found in tea and coffee that affects the brain, kidneys, heart, and respiratory system. Caffeine

drinkers often develop many of the same dependency traits commonly associated with drug addiction. It is an addicting drug with no known serious health risks. It is also the most popular and widespread labor enhancer used in the industrial world.

(8) ALCOHOL is made by the "natural process of fermentation and can be highly concentrated by the process of distillation" (Heath 1987: 99). It is the most widely used psychoactive drug in the world. MacAndrew and Edgerton (1969) insisted that the drunken comportment accompanying inebriation arises more from cultural attitudes than from biochemical and neuropharmacological factors.

There is a clear relationship between the quality of labor required to complete a task and a drug food's biochemical composition. For example, those drug foods (marijuana, hashish, opium, cocaine, nicotine, and alcohol) that increase or "stimulate" cortical alertness are preferred in a work context over drug foods capable of producing more intense and potent illusions (peyote, jimson weed, morning glory, and so forth).

There is also a strong relationship between subsistence, political complexity, and the relative frequency with which a drug is used as a labor inducer (i.e., drugs used to attract and compel people to work in return for the newly introduced drug food). Drugs have often been used as trade inducers in contact situations or under circumstances in which the balance of power between the expanding nation-state and the indigenous population is such that it is difficult to compel producers or workers to provide adequate quantities of trade goods or sustained labor activity. They were especially effective where the contactors were isolated traders operating beyond the frontiers of their own society; in contacts with mobile peoples exploiting difficult environments, such as FORAGERS or PASTORAL NOMADS; and, almost by definition, prior to effective establishment of imperial or colonial control over indigenous peoples and the territories they occupy. For example, historically trade in wine and later distilled alcohol has been characteristic of many frontier situations from ancient through modern times in the Old and New World. Similarly the Opium Wars between Britain and China were provoked in part by the British need to market a profitable drug to China to pay for its own massive import of tea, for which the Chinese originally demanded silver.

By contrast, after control has become institutionalized and the colonial power's infrastructure is fully developed, the rationale for using drug foods shifts from attracting laborers or goods to a concern for maximizing production as efficiently and as inexpensively as possible. This generally entails substantially more control over the population than arises when drug foods are simply used as an inducement to enter into some form of trade or labor exchange agreement. Indeed, the use of drug foods as labor enhancers generally presupposes some form of either direct or indirect political control over the population. In this way drug foods often serve as an alternative to military force and are generally selected because they are more efficient, more economical, or easier to sustain than force alone.

Some scholars have argued that this use of drug food was also closely tied to the rise of the industrial labor force in the West, as well as in colonial situations. The race to procure and produce such highly profitable products as sugar for rapid food energy (Mintz 1985), and caffeine-laden tea and coffee, chocolate, tobacco, or coca for mental energy (Braudel 1981: 227–65) revolutionized the habits of daily life in Europe and North America. And it is no accident that the licit drug trade in alcohol and tobacco constitutes an immense source of tax revenue for governments, while the illicit drug trade in refined cocaine and opium products generates equally huge sums of money for growers and smugglers.

WJ

See also ETHNOBOTANY
further reading Edward Anderson 1980; Harner 1973; Pan 1975; Plotkin 1993

dual organization refers to societies that are divided into halves or moieties. Individuals in such societies must belong to one or other moiety and the interactions between the moieties define the life of the society. Frequently, individuals must marry people from the other moiety, so that the society is organized in two intermarrying halves (see ALLIANCE SYSTEMS). This came to be thought of as the classic form of dual organization (Rivers 1924; Lévi-Strauss 1969a). Such systems were thought to be characteristic of remote, tribal peoples and regarded as primitive forms of society. More recently, anthropologists have concluded that intermarrying moieties are not the essence of dual organization, but merely one expression of it (Maybury-Lewis & Almagor 1989).

We now know that societies all over the world organize (or have organized) their social thought and social institutions in patterns of opposites, so this is a kind of system that human beings keep reinventing. In ancient Egypt the pharaohs were styled as rulers of Upper and Lower Egypt and as the embodiments of Horus and Seth, the gods whose hostility to each other was the symbol of conflict. The pharaoh thus mediated in his sacred person the contradictions of both the universe and the kingdom (Frankfort 1948). In ancient China the philosophers of the yin/yang school held that there was a necessary complementarity of opposites that made up the scheme of things and that human societies and human individuals should therefore do their best to attune themselves to this cosmic harmony (J. Needham 1956; B. Schwartz 1985). In pre-Conquest Peru the Inca empire was organized socially and spatially in terms of an opposition between the Upper and Lower moieties. It was linked to the cosmos by the Inca himself, who mediated in his own person the oppositions that made up the universe (Zuidema 1989).

Ancient empires could thus be organized in terms of dualistic theories of cosmos and society. We now know that societies organized according to such binary social theories are not invariably small or remote. Relatively large ones are found in Indonesia (J. Fox 1980) and parts of Africa (Maybury-Lewis & Almagor 1989). Smaller, tribal societies of this kind are found all over the world, among the native peoples of North and South America, in Africa, among the tribal peoples of India and Southeast Asia, in Indonesia and among the Australian Aborigines. Even

among tribal peoples, dual organization is not invariably a matter of intermarrying moieties or even of moieties at all. Some societies subscribe to dualistic cosmologies without organizing their institutions in the binary mode. Others organize themselves in terms of moieties that are not required to marry each other. Yet others may contain a number of different moiety systems. For example, individuals may belong by the rule of descent to moiety A and therefore be required to marry someone of moiety B. In another context, the same individuals may, by virtue of their age grade, be a member of moiety P and be required to interact on specific ceremonial occasions with members of moiety Q. In yet another context, the same individuals may, by virtue of the names they have been given, be a member of moiety X and required to interact with the people of moiety Y.

Dual organization is thus as much a matter of COSMOLOGY and social theory as it is of moieties or binary institutions. It is widespread because all human societies recognize and speculate upon certain polarities in human experience, such as life and death, male and female, night and day, and so on. These are highly charged antitheses over which people have brooded since time immemorial. Dualistic thinking insists that these antitheses need not tear the world apart, and humankind with it, because they are harmonized in the cosmic scheme of things. Conflict is similarly an unavoidable part of the human experience. Dualistic social institutions offer a solution to the problem of social order by balancing contending forces in perpetual equilibrium. Dual organization thus offers a reassurance of cosmic harmony, combined with social equilibrium, which explains why so many societies have found it attractive.

It is obviously not universal, though, and has been undermined by scientific thinking and the triumph of the secular over the sacred. In modern societies dualistic thinking has become the province of theologians and philosophers, but it is still found in the folk beliefs of people for whom the interaction of fundamental principles such as yin and yang remain the ideas by which they organize their lives. It is found at the systemic level only in societies that have succeeded in maintaining their traditional cultures in the face of MODERNIZATION.

DML

Durkheim, Émile (1858–1918)

Émile Durkheim, one of the few central figures in sociological theory, not only contributed seminal works to the field of sociology but also created a school of sociology that dominated French social sciences until World War II and had a major influence on, among others, British anthropology and American sociology. He was also the first French sociologist to enjoy a regular academic career crowned by a chair at the Sorbonne.

Durkheim was born at Epinal in the eastern French province of Lorraine on April 15, 1858. He was a son of a rabbi and descended from a long line of rabbis on both sides of his family. He was himself expected to follow the family tradition and assiduously studied Hebrew, the Old Testament, and the Talmud while at the same time pursuing the regular curriculum in secular schools. However, soon after his Jewish confirmation, he turned away from all personal religious involvement and became an agnostic. But throughout his scholarly career, and especially in the last third of it, religious phenomena were at the forefront of his concerns.

A brilliant student at his hometown's college, Durkheim was recommended to one of the great French high schools, the Lycée Louis-le-Grand in Paris and eventually, after two unsuccessful attempts to pass the rigorous entrance examinations, was admitted to the prestigious École Normale Supérieure, the traditional training ground for the intellectual elite of France.

In contradistinction to the career of his predecessors in French sociology, Auguste Comte and Henri de Saint-Simon, who attained only marginal positions in the scholarly world, Durkheim followed a regular and conventional academic career. He first taught philosophy in a number of provincial Lycées then moved to the provincial university of Bordeaux in 1887, where he taught both sociology and pedagogy. After nine years at Bordeaux, Durkheim was promoted to a full position in social science, the first such position in France. Finally, now a man of fully recognized stature in the academic world, he was called to the Sorbonne, first as a lecturer and then as Professor of the Science of Education, and finally to a newly created chair as Professor of the Science of Education and Sociology.

Still during the Bordeaux days, Durkheim founded the *l'Année sociologique*, a major scholarly journal devoted to the new sociological discipline and, more particularly, the Durkheimian vision of the subject. Together with Durkheim's major books and those of his disciples, *l'Année* spread the Durkheimian vision not only at home but also abroad. In addition, Durkheim, who was a major academic politician, succeeded in gaining appointments for a number of his young disciples in strategic positions in the heartland and the periphery of the academic world so that around the time of World War I Durkheimians had colonized much of the instructional system in the social sciences of the highly centralized French educational establishment. Passionately attached to the Third Republic, Durkheim and the Durkheimians were pillars of strength in the effort to combat the right-wing enemies of the Republic within the classroom and without, upholding Republican morality against the Church and its allies.

When it comes to Durkheim's intellectual ancestry, he was first of all a belated heir of the French Enlightenment. Rousseau and Montesquieu, about whom he wrote, and other Enlightenment thinkers stood very high on his intellectual agenda. The key nineteenth-century figure among his predecessors was Auguste Comte, to whom he always paid his respect even while often disagreeing with him. When it comes to intellectual influences from abroad, Herbert SPENCER and his evolutionary message deeply marked Durkheim's thought even when, most of the time, he threw critical arrows in his direction. Finally, a whole array of German social scientists, some of whom he had come to know during an extensive study tour of Germany – Wundt, Schaeffle, Tönnies, Gumplowicz, to mention just a few – found many echoes in the work of

Durkheim. Finally, one British scholar whose work Durkheim only encountered rather late in his career, William Robertson SMITH, author of *Lectures on the religion of the Semites* (1889), decisively influenced Durkheim's last major work, *The elementary forms of religious life* (1915).

The central insistence of Durkheim's work is that social behavior cannot be explained on psychological or biological levels. He offered a definitive critique of reductionist explanations of human behavior. Social phenomena are "social facts," and these are the subject matter of sociology. Their distinctive characteristics are not amenable to biological or psychological determinants and are external to individuals considered as biological entities. They endure over time while individuals die, and they have coercive power. A social fact can hence be defined as consisting "of manners of acting, thinking and feeling external to the individual which are invested with a coercive power by virtue of which they exercise control over him" (1938: 15). In later work Durkheim somewhat softened his rigid insistence on the externality of social facts by stressing that, although independent of individuals, they become effective only when internalized. Constraint is no longer a simple imposition of outside controls but rather a moral obligation to obey society's rules and injunctions.

Concern with group characteristics rather than individual behavior pervades all of Durkheim's work. *The division of labor in society* (1933) highlights the distinction between mechanical and organic society. In mechanical (relatively primitive) societies cohesion is achieved because of the minimization of individual differences; in organic (modern) societies differences resulting from a more advanced division of labor lead to complementary activities.

In *Suicide* (1951) Durkheim's concern was with rates of occurrence rather than incidence, and these differing rates are explained in terms of the different social milieu in which they occur. Social regulation, or lack of it, rather than individual motives, are the center of attention.

In *The elementary forms of religious life* (1915), dealing largely with data on Australian Aborigines and therefore of great interest to anthropologists, RELIGION is seen as a representation of the powers of society as a moral community that creates bonds of solidarity in ever-renewed rituals, festivities, and communal devotions. If religion has largely decayed as a binding force, what then can be its functional equivalent? Here Durkheim suggests, perhaps not too persuasively, that modern men and women now have to devote themselves to their society directly, where earlier they only recognized their dependence on society through the medium of religious representations and practices.   LC

See also DIVISION OF LABOR, FUNCTIONAL-
ISM, HERTZ, INCEST TABOOS, MAUSS,
SOCIOLOGY, SYMBOLIC ANTHROPOLOGY,
TOTEMISM

further reading Giddens 1979b

E

ecological anthropology Although the environmental sciences and environmentalism, including conservation, have roots extending back many centuries (Glacken 1967), they have crystallized mostly since the 1960s and their use in anthropology has been part of this historical process. Each of the subfields of anthropology has developed its own approach to human ecology: paleoecology in archaeology (Butzer 1982); primate ecology (Richard 1985), human adaptability or more narrowly physiological anthropology (Frisancho 1993), and human behavioral ecology (Eric Smith & Winterhalder 1992) in biological anthropology; cultural ecology and later systems ecology in cultural anthropology (Ellen 1982; Hardesty 1977; Netting 1986); and ethnoecology in linguistics (Berlin 1992). Here it must suffice to briefly review the most important developments in attempts by cultural anthropologists to understand human ecology and ADAPTATION since the pioneering work on cultural ecology of Julian STEWARD and others in the first half of this century.

Although continuities remain from the work of Steward (1955) and his cohorts and predecessors, many of the subsequent ecologically oriented cultural anthropologists have developed new approaches in response to perceived deficiencies in the work of their predecessors (Sponsel 1987). Among these are Andrew Vayda and Roy Rappaport (1968), who developed a systems approach to investigate the interplay of culture and ecology as human populations adapt to their ecosystem(s). They systematically applied concepts from biological ecology to human ecology, including population as the unit of analysis, ecosystem as the context, and adaptation as

the dynamic process of interaction between population and ecosystem. They first focused on an analysis of energy input and output in the technology and social organization of work to collect and produce food. All of this was set within the biological framework of limiting factors and CARRYING CAPACITY. Components of culture such as RELIGION and WARFARE were viewed as regulating mechanisms that helped to maintain a balance between the population and its resources. This theoretical framework was elegantly implemented by Rappaport (1967) in his fieldwork with the Tsembaga of New Guinea. He viewed their RITUAL and warfare as regulating the delicate balance between the human and pig populations to reduce competition between these two species. (Humans and pigs are surprisingly close in physiology, body and group size, and omnivorous diet). This "biologization" of the ecological approach in cultural anthropology led to the label "ecological anthropology" replacing Steward's label of "cultural ecology," although the two are sometimes used as synonyms (Bennett 1976, 1993).

Marvin HARRIS (1979) attempted to advance the ecological explanation as well as description of cultures by developing a more explicit and systematic scientific research strategy, which he called "CULTURAL MATERIALISM." In this strategy he assigned research priority and causal primacy to infrastructure over structure and superstructure because it is most fundamental for human survival and adaptation. Harris and his students have applied this research strategy to explain many puzzling customs and institutions. The classic case is the sacred cow of India. Harris (1985) argued that the cow is not sacred simply because of Hindu and other religious beliefs, but ultimately because the cow is indispensable to the agricultural economy in the environments of India, especially for plowing, fertilizer (dung), cooking fuel (dried dung), and milk (instead of meat).

The work of Rappaport, Harris, and others working along similar lines has been criticized on many points, but especially for confusing origins and functions (Moran 1990) and for assuming that almost anything that persists is adaptive (Edgerton 1992).

Whereas Harris concentrates on observable behavior because he is impressed with the discrepancy between what people say and do, ecologically oriented linguistic anthropologists have emphasized the investigation of native thought about environmental phenomena. Much of this work has concentrated on constructing hierarchical CLASSIFICATIONS of native terms referring to particular environmental domains such as soil types for farming or wild plants used for medicinal purposes. Ideally, ethnoecology encompasses local environmental knowledge, beliefs, values, and attitudes, and links environmental ideas with actions and their adaptive or maladaptive consequences. In practice, ethnoecology has often been confined simply to a native taxonomy of some environmental domain or a mere descriptive inventory of the names and uses of a subset of animal or plant species (Berlin 1992). However, some ethnoecologists, such as Harold Conklin (1957, 1980), have gone much further and published unusually detailed data, as exemplified by Conklin's research integrating the ethnoecology and cultural ecology of the agroecosystems of the Hanunoo and Ifugao in the Philippines.

Recently, a few anthropologists have started to transcend some of the limitations of the approaches previously discussed by adding a diachronic dimension in examining how both culture and environment mutually influence and change each other over time, an approach called "historical ecology" (Crumley 1994). Most notable is the work of William Balée (1994) on the Ka'apor in the Amazon of Brazil, who recognize 768 species of plants from seed to reproductive adult stages, the largest ethnobotanical repertoire reported for any

people in the Amazon. Moreover, Balée has applied historical ecology to integrate aspects of ethnoecology, cultural ecology, biological ecology, political ecology, and regional ecology in a processual framework. In this context he has analyzed the Ka'apor's response to adaptive constraints and opportunities in both their social and natural environments, including other indigenous societies, Afro-Americans, and European migrants who have each had an impact on their natural environment.

The anthropological approaches to human–environment interactions described above have been largely confined to basic research with very little attention paid to applied problems, let alone to action or advocacy work. However, beyond such symptoms of the environmental crisis as resource depletion, pollution, species extinction, tropical deforestation, and so on, there is an increasing recognition that such phenomena are often linked with various forms of VIOLENCE, including the abuse of HUMAN RIGHTS (Homer-Dixon et al. 1993; B. Johnston 1994). Thus, radical ecology, a conglomerate of diverse ecological approaches beyond anthropology, is beginning to influence anthropologists in combination with the profession's own applied and advocacy work (R. Wright 1988). Carolyn Merchant (1992: 1) provides the most concise description of radical ecology:

Radical ecology confronts the illusion that people are free to exploit nature and to move in society at the expense of others, with a new consciousness of our responsibilities to the rest of nature and to other humans. It seeks a new ethic of the nurture of nature and the nurture of people. It empowers people to make changes in the world consistent with a new social vision and a new ethic.

The exploitation and destruction of indigenous societies in FRONTIERS like the Amazon by STATES and their proxies link ecocide with ETHNOCIDE and even GENOCIDE. A specific case is the thousands of illegal gold miners who have caused brutal massacres, devastating epidemic diseases, mercury poisoning, and other grave problems through their invasion of the territory of the Yanomami nation in Brazil and Venezuela since the mid-1980s (Sponsel 1994;

Tierney 1995). Accordingly, there is an arena of mutual concern for ecological anthropology and advocacy including human rights (M. Miller 1993; Sponsel 1995).

One of the practical contributions of ecological anthropology has been to demonstrate the eco-logic or environmental rationale of aspects of the culture of indigenous societies that outsiders have otherwise evaluated negatively through their own ETHNOCENTRISM and RACISM (Bodley 1994). For example, traditional SWIDDEN (slash-and-burn) horticulture is sustainable as long as population density is low, it is used for subsistence, and there is plenty of forest for fallow, new GARDENS, and game habitat. Thus, although inhabited by indigenous societies for millennia, the Amazon as a whole was never endangered by deforestation until the Western-style economic DEVELOPMENT of recent decades. Moreover, traditional swiddening may actually enhance biodiversity by creating a mosaic of biotic communities in different stages of succession or development (Sponsel 1992). Environmentalists, conservationists, and others are increasingly recognizing the importance of local people and their knowledge, culture, and values in sustainable resource management and the conservation of biodiversity (Klee 1980; Sponsel et al. 1996).

Another component of radical ecology is ecofeminism, which views the male domination of women as linked with the human domination of nature. Accordingly, ecofeminists argue that to create a more ecologically sustainable society, male–female relations as well as human–environment relations must be changed. The role of women remains grossly neglected in ecological anthropology as well as in environmental development (Rodda 1991; Shiva 1989).

Finally, ecotheology, or spiritual ecology, has emerged as a transdisciplinary field in recent years, although this was foreshadowed by several superb ethnographic case studies, such as work on New Guinea (Rappaport 1979), organization of irrigation by temple priests in Bali (Lansing 1991), and forest use by native Americans in the sub-Arctic (R. Nelson 1983) and

Amazonia (Reichel-Dolmatoff 1971). It has developed out of a recognition that the deeper or ultimate cause of environmental and social disruption is a Western worldview and its associated values and attitudes, including materialism and consumerism, which when realized through behavior, have maladaptive consequences (Tucker & Grim 1994). This worldview is no longer confined to the geographic West; beginning with COLONIALISM it is a syndrome that has spread across the planet, along with industrialization, MODERNIZATION, and other forces of globalization, precipitating spiraling ecological and social disequilibrium (Bennett 1976; Dobson 1991).

RELIGION is viewed as another component for coping with the environmental crisis, since it is a cross-cultural universal (humans are spiritual animals), addresses elemental questions such as the place of humanity in nature, provides moral values such as reverence for life, and can be a powerful force that motivates individual believers emotionally as well as intellectually (Rockefeller & Elder 1992). Thus, the World Wildlife Fund sponsored a conference of leaders from the so-called great religions (Buddhism, Christianity, Hinduism, Islam, and Judaism) to extract from their doctrine the relevant ingredients for constructing a sustainable environmental ethic for the community of their believers. However, the discrepancy between religious ideals and actual behavior remains the greatest obstacle to using religion to promote a more sustainable society.

Contemporary ecological anthropology has the opportunity to make a considerable contribution to the environmental sciences and their application around the world. However, because most anthropologists have written primarily for one another, they have as yet had little influence on the wider public or government agencies (Milton 1993). The future challenge to ecological anthropologists is therefore to reach an audience beyond the profession itself and to see the communities that host their fieldwork as active collaborators in all phases of research (Sponsel 1995).

LS

See also ETHNOBOTANY, ETHNOSCIENCE, ETHNOZOOLOGY, FEMINIST ANTHROPOLOGY, FISHING, FOOD PRODUCTION, FORAGING, FUNCTIONALISM, GENDER, HUNTING, PASTORALISTS, SYSTEMS THEORY

further reading J. Anderson 1973; Bates & Plog 1991; B. Campbell 1985; Crosby 1972, 1986; Dobson 1991; J. Hughes 1983; McNeely & Pitt 1985; Merchant 1994; Moran 1979; Oldfield & Alcorn 1991; Orlove 1980; Shiva 1991; D. Spring & Spring 1974

economic anthropology focuses on two aspects of economics: (1) provisioning, which is the production and distribution of necessary and optional goods and services; and (2) the strategy of economizing, often put in terms of the FORMALIST–SUBSTANTIVIST DEBATE. Earlier anthropologists devoted almost all their time to the study of provisioning, but in the last half-century economizing has received substantially more attention.

Production

Production refers to the processes of acquiring resources and transforming them into useful objects and actions. The objects include food, shelter, and craft goods, as well as symbolic items ranging from totem poles to pyramids. Before 1940 anthropologists were expected to write a chapter on MATERIAL CULTURE, which at least gave us a partial inventory of the objects the culture contained.

FOOD PRODUCTION systems are often categorized into hunting and gathering (or foraging), horticulture, agriculture, and industry. The underlying dimension of this scale is probably energy input and energy output: both are low at the foraging end, and both are high at the industrial end (Leslie White 1943). Given the greater anthropological expertise with small-scale societies, this scale has more precision and validity at the low-energy end than at the high end.

FORAGERS utilize no domesticated species, and the dog is the only animal aid to production. While their technology is often said to be simple, it includes several additions to human muscle power, including fire, traps, spears, bows and arrows, spear

throwers, and poison. There is extensive use of bone, stone, plant fiber and wood for tools and objects. There are two views on the productivity of foraging. The ORIGINAL AFFLUENT SOCIETY view holds that stone-age economies produce substantially less than their potential although their technology is more than adequate to feed the population. Supporters note that foragers eat reasonably well (in terms of calories), work little, have a considerable amount of leisure time, and have few economic needs: hence affluence. Critics claim that the empirical measurements of work effort are too few and too brief to serve as a representative sample and note that the definition of WORK is crucial for the analysis of productivity. If one includes tool making and food preparation the work hours increase substantially. Although the evidence for it is meager, and the evidence against it is quite strong, most anthropologists (and others) have come to accept the original affluence position.

While all economies do some foraging (hunting wild animals, fishing, harvesting undomesticated plants), economies specializing in foraging have largely disappeared as the technology and food-stuffs of the industrial world have diffused everywhere. Eskimos still hunt and eat seal, but the killing is usually done with a rifle, and the seal meat will be eaten with vegetable foods bought at the store. HORTICULTURE, the cultivation of hundreds of species of domesticated plants along with some domesticated animals, is today much more widespread than foraging. Economies dependent upon horticulture, which are found mostly in the tropics, have higher population densities than foragers. Surplus food production is possible as one of the features of the domestic mode of production (see CHAYANOV SLOPE), but it is not realized. Our knowledge of the productivity of horticulture in every case includes the use of steel tools. Before metal tools became available, such societies were dependent upon stone tools for cutting wood, about which we have no productivity data. Thus the ability to gauge the capacity of stone-age technology is at best very weak.

There are many studies of AGRICUL-

TURE, which by and large has meant PEAS-ANT agriculture. Agriculture typically concentrates on growing a small number of domesticated crops, and relies on one, or just a few, for most of the calories. Agricultural systems are often characterized in a shorthand way by these key crops, particularly rice, wheat and maize. There is systematic and widespread use of domesticated animals, for traction, milk, dung, and meat. All peasants studied by anthropologists have at least iron technology. Agricultural systems produce considerable surplus, so the production of the peasant household is higher than its consumption.

Any economy that contains peasants also contains many other production sectors, including artisans specializing in leather, pottery, metal, glass, wood, and food products such as beer, wine, olive oil, and fish paste. There has been almost no investigation of the supply of raw materials, technology, energetics, organization of production, or productivity of these craft industries. A notable exception is Scott Cook's (1982) work on the stone-workers of Oaxaca, Mexico, who produce the grinding tools used for food preparation. Similarly although anthropologists now study many aspects of INDUSTRIAL SOCIETY, the economics of industrial production have received very little attention.

All of these economies employ both technology and the division of labor. Technology is often narrowly defined as the tools used, but more broadly it is the tools, plus processes, plus knowledge. For example, foragers have a simple technology and relatively few tools in their kit, and, compared with an industrial economy, they gain relatively little energy. But this materialist view overlooks the vast knowledge of animal behavior and plant characteristics, and probably knowledge of weather, that the average forager must command. Our knowledge of their knowledge is still in its infancy because we have concentrated only on the tools. In fact, given that humans have been foragers longer than they have been anything else, there should be no doubt that such small-scale societies have developed a considerable pool of knowledge and skill.

DIVISION OF LABOR refers to the number of specialists that an economy contains. Foraging and horticultural economies have a division of labor based only upon GENDER and AGE. Every person in a particular category is considered interchangeable, and the number of categories is small. With the invention of cities the division of labor grew very rapidly, as did the numbers of goods and processes. Presumably the full-time nature of a specialty is positively related to the growth of expertise and productivity. Technology is changing at the same time.

Distribution

Distribution is how goods (and services) are transferred from one person to another. Most of the effort in economic anthropology in the last 50 years has been on distribution rather than production. Very early on it was realized that "primitive" societies lacked MONEY, or at least our kind of money. How societies could distribute their goods without money was a key question. Implicated in the answer are questions of value and questions of property.

The work of economic historian Karl Polanyi dominated the scene for 30 years (K. Polanyi et al. 1957). Polanyi proposed that all economies were integrated by one of three major principles of distribution: RECIPROCITY, REDISTRIBUTION, and MARKET, although the remaining two were often present in subordinate roles. More recently the dominant scheme, drawing on MAUSS and Marx, has been GIFT commodity. Reciprocity and redistribution, and the gift, are forms of distribution that do not require the use of money.

All human societies have exchange institutions whereby goods and services are transferred from one local group to another (see TRADE). Even the smallest societies participate in these exchange networks. In larger-scale societies there are regular marketplaces where substantial amounts of exchange take place, exchanges associated with a high degree of division of labor and large numbers of goods and services. One major question is how these goods are distributed per capita. EGALITARIAN SOCIETIES, mostly foragers and horticulturalists, work hard to achieve roughly equal per capita access to resources and holdings of goods. Much larger-rank and stratified societies, on the other hand, are defined by their unequal per capita access to resources, unequal holdings of goods, and production systems based on agriculture or industry (see STRATIFICATION).

Topics

PROPERTY rights are implied by the transfer of goods from one person to another, but are one of the least well understood aspects of a society and economy. The transfer of a good from one person to another would seem to require either the concept of property or force. Yet most anthropological attention has been paid to transfers rather than the property aspects. Production may also be instrumental in creating property rights, in that there are natural resources (land, game, clay pits, etc.), tools, processes, and knowledge that can be, and in larger-scale economies usually are, the object of property rules.

SOCIAL STRUCTURE is a major concomitant of economic organization. Through the process of the division of labor societies create distinctive units of production, including work teams, households, men's houses, plantations, firms, and communities. There are also units of consumption (individuals, households, lineages, and communities). Property is held by a jural unit, which can be the individual, the household, a lineage, a village, or a polity. Thus the study of the economics of a society inevitably requires a clear description of some facets of the social structure.

Population has a curious history in economic anthropology. Anthropologists have long known that some economic features are associated with small populations with low population densities whereas others are associated with large populations and high densities. There is a strong correlation between population size and the basic form of production and the distribution of resources. Technology such as domesticated plants and animals, irrigation, and the wheel permits the emergence of much higher population levels than are possible in their absence. And some features of political structure are also correlated with the population size of the society: political office does not occur in the absence of unequal access to resources, which in turn

does not normally occur in the absence of intensive agriculture.

This has led to hotly debated questions over whether technology, social organization, or population is the driving force in the system. Population has been granted the status of driving force by such scholars as Boserup (1965), M. Cohen (1977), and HARRIS (1979), who see a rising population as the stimulus for changing technology, which in turn permits higher population levels. But if this is the case it does not explain why some societies, particularly foragers, underproduce and maintain long-term populations that stay well below carrying capacity (see ORIGINAL AFFLUENT SOCIETY).

DIFFUSION of culture traits has always been of interest to anthropologists. One presumes that there has been a noncoercive diffusion of traits over very large areas (at least continental in scale) for millennia. Copper, obsidian, and gems are routinely found thousands of kilometers from their sources at very early times. Some sort of exchange mechanism is almost certainly implied. Although the spread of physical objects is easier to document, ideas, tools, and knowledge of processes can spread in the same way. This model of diffusion based on noncoercive borrowing has more recently been replaced by the impact of forcible change wrought by CAPITALISM, COLONIALISM, and an accompanying WORLD-SYSTEM that has disrupted small-scale societies at least since the beginning of European expansion in 1400. As a result diffusion is now routinely seen as the impact of more powerful societies on less powerful ones, although a few scholars have objected that a penetration-subjugation model of the process is too simplistic, and that people in the smaller-scale societies exercise choice and creativity even in the face of powerful forces.   RHun

further reading Appaduarai 1986; Belshaw 1965; Bohannan 1963; C. Gregory 1982; Halperin 1994; Herskovits 1940; A. Johnson & Earle 1987; LeClair & Schneider 1968; Ortiz 1983; Plattner 1989; Sahlins 1972; Wallerstein 1974; E. Wolf 1982; *Research in Economic Anthropology* [a long-standing series of original journal articles in economic anthropology]

education is a general term for the social processes that facilitate learning in human communities. Education is universal among human societies and is as necessary for the continuity of social life as biological reproduction, economic subsistence, symbolic communication, and social regulation – all of which require that the young be educated for culturally appropriate participation. The terms "SOCIALIZATION," emphasizing preparation for *social* participation, and "ENCULTURATION," which stresses the *cultural* models to be acquired, are roughly equivalent to education in this broad sense. The human need for education is related to certain species characteristics:

1. neoteny, the extended dependence of offspring as they gradually become capable of participating in adult social life
2. the developmental flexibility of adaptive behavior, with codes for behavior that vary across human populations rather than being fixed for the species as a whole
3. the learning ability of humans, their facility in acquiring culture-specific codes for adaptive skills through a variety of learning processes

Human offspring are unique among animals in how much they need to learn to function as adults, but human communities are also unique in providing their offspring a culturally constructed environment of social interaction to facilitate that learning.

Educational patterns vary across cultures in institutional specialization, methods of facilitating learning, links to other institutions such as religion and the economy, and distribution within the population.

Institutional specialization

Schooling (education in a physical setting dedicated to that purpose, conducted by a teacher whose only role is to instruct) is a specialized institutional form that is not universal in human societies and did not involve the majority of CHILDREN even in the West until the late nineteenth century. In societies without schools, and for the non-schoolgoing members of societies with schools, all learning occurs at home and in other settings designed for purposes other than education, facilitated by experienced persons who transmit skills, knowledge, and models of virtue to the young in the contexts of economic, ritual, and recreational activities. In the many agricultural societies with domestically organized food and craft production, children participate in productive activities from an early age, gradually learning the more complex tasks from their older siblings as well as their parents. Where there was a specialized craft production system through which a child or adolescent was sent as an apprentice to a master craftsman, apprentices also learned through graduated participation in productive activities.

In the world of 1500 C.E., the urban civilizations of the Old World, including China, Japan, India, the Middle East, and Europe, had schools based on a master–apprenticeship model in which the primary goal was to acquire the literacy embodied in traditional religious texts from an acknowledged master, often at his home. These schools varied in many ways, but attendance was usually limited to a small proportion of the male population, which was also true of the schools of the pre-Conquest Aztec and Inca empires in the New World at the same time. In the twentieth-century Islamic world, including North and West Africa, Qur'anic schools have retained some of these traditional characteristics, such as memorizing the Qur'an, while incorporating features from Western schools (LeVine & White 1986).

The Western, or Euro-American, form of schooling, involving age-segregated classrooms in a school operated as a standardized unit of an educational bureaucracy, reached its modern form by the middle of the nineteenth century. Its worldwide expansion since then, and the dominance it has achieved as a model of education, have obscured the facts that it is not synonymous with schooling in general and that even in societies where individuals spend a major part of their lives in school, much of their education takes place elsewhere.

Methods of facilitating learning

Human societies organize the learning of children and other novices by teaching them, in school or other settings, and by providing opportunities to learn through guided participation in the practices of a community (Rogoff 1990). Societies with schools have an institutional investment in teaching as a means of transmitting socially important skills, knowledge, and models of personal conduct, but school instruction operates together with alternative forms of learning to support their acquisition. In the apprenticeship model of learning, novices begin through peripheral participation, such as performing routine, often menial, tasks while having observational access to the more complex tasks that are central to the productive process (Lave & Wenger 1991). For example, in Liberian tailors' workshops, the apprentices spend their time cutting pieces of cloth, but they are able at the same time to observe the mature practice of the master tailor who does the sewing (Lave 1990). This process, which can reduce the need for verbal instruction, contrasts with the typical sequence of learning in the classrooms of Western-type schools, where pupils are instructed to take one step at a time in a setting that often blocks visual access to the more mature practice of the older students. Yet in societies with Western-type schools, much of any individual's social learning, from first-language acquisition to job training, occurs through forms of apprenticeship practiced in homes, workplaces, and other non-school settings where skilled performances are called for.

Links to other institutions

Educational processes occur in all institutions, but where there are schools, they can be linked in various ways to other specialized institutions. In the premodern urban civilizations of the Old World, for example, schools were closely linked to the religious institutions – Christian, Hebrew, Islamic, Hindu, Buddhist and Confucian – whose texts were the focus of schooling. Religious functionaries were often the schoolmasters, and those pupils who advanced to the highest levels could become clerics, while those who dropped out after a few years became ordinary religious participants distinguished by a sacred experience in school. In Protestant Europe and North America, particularly among the Calvinists, the mass schooling of boys so they could read the Bible became widespread during the seventeenth century, and Jesuits established schools for the laity in Catholic countries. These church schools in much of Europe, and European colonies in the Americas, laid a basis for the mass secular schooling of the nineteenth century, much as the *terakoya* Buddhist schools did in Japan.

The links of schooling to economic institutions through educational qualifications for employment had precedents in the ancient Chinese practice of academic examinations for posts in the imperial bureaucracy and in the "learned professions" of medieval Europe. In Europe before the Industrial Revolution, those who had acquired skills of literacy and numeracy – including Jews, Presbyterians, and Franciscan monks – were able to make use of them in commercial activity. It was only in the second half of the nineteenth century, however, that schooling was defined as prerequisite for a wide variety of occupations. The economic rationale for schooling, as opposed to its moral and spiritual aims, has grown throughout the twentieth century.

Schools have been linked to military institutions, most notably when the Prussian defeat of the French in 1870–1 was widely attributed to the superior school attainment of the Prussian troops – a point not lost on the British and Japanese, who set about expanding their own schooling. At a more general level, there is the relationship of schooling to the national state, in which schools were increasingly defined as vehicles for building national loyalty as well as a more effective citizen army and worker corps. As NATIONALISM grew throughout the world during the late-nineteenth and twentieth centuries, so did policies for extending Western-type schooling to the entire population. (The United States is the only country in which universal schooling was achieved without a nationally organized educational system.)

Distribution

In societies without schools, all individuals

are educated through guided participation in the social institutions of a community; insofar as those institutions are differentiated – by CASTE, CLASS, or GENDER, for example – their education may be differentiated accordingly. Where there are schools, societies vary in the proportion of the population attending and in the distribution of school attendance by age, gender, social class, and other social categories. Virtually every program for national development since 1850 has included universal education, meaning the Western model of bureaucratically organized schooling. The Western-type school has become the symbol of hope for national and personal improvement on every continent, promoted by regimes otherwise diverse in governmental form and ideology. This consensus has not been matched by a uniformity in the actual distribution of school attendance; lags and gaps have developed across and within countries.

Western schooling at the primary level became legally compulsory and actually universal in Europe, North America, and Japan before 1900, and secondary education became virtually universal in those areas by 1950. The diffusion of the Western model of schooling to other parts of Asia, Africa, and Oceania began during the period of European COLONIALISM but was expanded to mass education only after 1945. Latin America had a long history of Catholic schooling during the colonial period and after, but there too mass education, particularly of women, was only achieved after 1945. Marxist revolutionary regimes in the Soviet Union (after 1917), China (after 1950), Cuba (after 1957), and other countries, gave high priority to universal schooling on the Western model, despite its bourgeois capitalist origins, and represent some of the largest and most thorough cases of mass education. This remarkable spread of Western schooling through the world between 1850 and 1980 reflects an increasingly global formula for nation building, involving the construction of bureaucratic organizations for the delivery of services (health, education, transportation, communication) to every region of a country in order to integrate social and economic participation at the national level and promote loyalty to the national state.

Since most countries continue to expand schooling for their citizens and to extend it to secondary and tertiary levels, and since poor countries have less capacity to do so than rich ones, the rich countries of the West and East Asia have retained their relative advantage in schoolgoing, while the poorer countries of Asia and Africa, despite expanding school enrollments substantially between 1960 and 1990, remain farthest behind in that respect. Women's school attendance has lagged behind that of men but increased enormously in the second half of the twentieth century. In many Latin American and African countries, for example, there are now no gender differences in primary school enrollment, though males may be more heavily represented at the higher levels. Among the major national populations of the world, only those of South Asia (India, Pakistan, and Bangladesh) have large proportions of children, especially girls, who never attend school.

In many countries that have invested heavily in schooling, schools are at the center of debates over social policy. They are credited with progress in health, economic production, and population control, and blamed for unemployment, social inequality, and declining quality. Changing the educational system (the schools) remains among the top priorities for national and international reformers seeking to improve the human condition.

Despite the global spread of Western schooling, schools – like other borrowed bureaucratic organizational forms – take on the norms and meanings of the cultures to which they have diffused. Thus the roles of teacher, pupil, and parent and their relations over schooling in a given community have been reinterpreted in local terms. The learning of children outside of school, in institutional settings defined by purposes other than education, is even more likely to vary across cultures.   RAL

See also ADOLESCENCE, AGE SYSTEMS, PLAY

egalitarian societies are those with "no sharp divisions of rank, status, and wealth" (Fortes & Evans-Pritchard 1940a:

5). In this negative sense, societies are egalitarian because they *lack* the characteristics associated with stratified, state-organized societies. They are the beginning point of a process of evolutionary differentiation, through competitive exclusion, whose inevitable end products are STATES. As the first and simplest form of society, egalitarian societies would seem to require little explanation, but much recent work is oriented to showing the error of this position.

Enlightenment political philosophers first took a keen interest in egalitarianism because their focus was on the presocial, and hence the establishment of SOCIETY. In *Leviathan* (1651), Thomas Hobbes hypothesized that the presocial condition of man (the state of nature) must have been one of equality because "the difference between man and man is not so considerable as that one man can claim to himself any benefit to which another may not pretend as well as he" (ch. 13, §1). But because people also displayed an innate and "perpetual and restless desire of power after power, that ceaseth only in death" (ch. 11, §2), an individual could only be secure within a society controlled by powerful rulers. For Hobbes the origin of inequality was contemporaneous with the origin of society itself. For the French political philosopher Jean-Jacques Rousseau inequality was, similarly, a product of society itself, albeit an unnecessary and undesirable one that derived from the establishment of private property. In *The social contract* (1791), he argued that man's egalitarian and altruistic nature was suppressed by the state and that humanity's pristine condition of equality could only be restored through social action. A concept of primitive egalitarianism is also the cornerstone of Karl Marx's nineteenth-century theorizing. Unlike in Hobbes and Rousseau, however, in both Marx's *Precapitalist economic formations* (1964) and Frederick Engels's *The origin of the family, private property, and the state* (1902), primitive egalitarianism was eminently social – an artifact of a SOCIAL ORGANIZATION built upon KINSHIP and DESCENT.

In *African political systems* (1940), a work that marks the beginning of modern PO-LITICAL ANTHROPOLOGY, Meyer FORTES and E. E. EVANS-PRITCHARD established the fundamental distinction between "centralized" and "uncentralized" societies. Political order in uncentralized societies is maintained by the balanced opposition of groups usually defined in terms of unilineal descent. These stateless societies provided anthropology with its first intensively described cases of "egalitarian societies." The "equality" described here was that between structural units, usually SEGMENTARY LINEAGES, that were conceptually equal irrespective of any power differentials that might exist in ethnographic fact. Fortes and Evans-Pritchard were more concerned with formal conceptual relations that the nuances of interpersonal relations; nevertheless, they established the ground upon which subsequent anthropological discussions of egalitarian societies would take place.

The anthropological focus on structural units rather than individuals has been defended as necessary because in a strict sense, a sense in which "every individual is of equal status and in which no one outranks anyone," there is not now and never has been a truly egalitarian society (Sahlins 1958: 1). All societies have minimal status differentiations based on AGE and GENDER. It is precisely how these status differentiations are distributed that is of consequence in discussing and maintaining a concept of "egalitarian society." But other scholars have taken issue with the easy acceptance of such inequalities as given. Maria Lepowsky (1993: 33) noted that "most influential anthropological constructions of political equality and inequality have implied, without fully analyzing, a universal principle of male dominance"; and Flanagan (1989: 253) commented that the "egalitarianism of egalitarian societies was an egalitarianism of men." The presumed precultural universal inferiority of WOMEN should be subject to an inquiry that would specify the ethnographic contexts and conditions under which such inferiority is manifest. Further, gender inequalities may themselves be part of a more inclusive gerontocratic system of inequality in which older men dominate younger men, and all men dominate women.

The term "egalitarian" has been applied to two very different kinds of social system, which we can label as "equal opportunity systems" and "equal outcome systems" (Flanagan 1988, 1989). The egalitarian ideologies of equal opportunity systems, as in American society, can be used to mask major inequalities in outcomes (wealth, status, power), treating them as mere artifacts of differential aptitudes and abilities. Equal outcome systems, such as age set systems, on the other hand, must employ structural constraints to overcome individual differences in aptitudes or abilities, and in the process, it has been argued, create structures that fail to reward individual initiative.

Recent anthropological approaches to egalitarianism have stressed the contextual nature of both hierarchy and equality. In *Constructing inequality*, the most comprehensive ethnographic treatment of hierarchy in recent years, Raymond Kelly (1993: 474–5) argued that where "socially differentiated categories, groups, or individuals are culturally evaluated as moral equivalents, the relationship between them can be described as an egalitarian relation." Similarly, Lin Poyer (1993) demonstrated the simultaneous maintenance and contextual manifestation of both hierarchy and egalitarianism on the South Pacific atoll of Sapwuahfik, and Robert Tonkinson (1988a,b) argued for a perspective that focuses on the contextual manifestation of hierarchy rather than on the characterization of a whole society as hierarchical or egalitarian.

In the face of the ethnographic reality of inequality and dominance symbolically created and maintained even in small-scale societies, how are we to usefully employ a concept of "egalitarian society?" One solution is to "refrain from characterizing systems as either hierarchical or egalitarian, because, whatever its attractiveness as a shorthand/indexical expression, the idea of egalitarian and inegalitarian societies may mask the very problem into which we wish to inquire" (Flanagan 1989: 262). What anthropologists confront in the field are egalitarian contexts, norms, values, strategies, etc., and their converse, as persons go about negotiating their social relationships.

The anthropologist's task is to create contextual or systemic definitions that simultaneously encompass both the hierarchical and egalitarian elements in any system and that demonstrate the complexity of so-called "simple egalitarian societies."

JF

See also BAND SOCIETIES, CHIEF, COMPLEX SOCIETY, EVOLUTIONARY STAGES, GOVERNMENT

further reading Beteille 1986; Jane Collier 1988; Dumont 1977; Flanagan & Rayner 1988; Joesphides 1985; Leacock 1978; A. Strathern 1982; M. Strathern 1987; Woodburn 1982

Ego is the term used in the anthropological charting of kinship to represent the arbitrarily designated individual who stands at the center of the system. Thus, **egocentric kinship** is that calculated from the point of view of such an individual. All kinship systems are egocentric to the extent that any given individual has a unique personal KINDRED. COGNATIC systems, owing to their frequent lack of corporate DESCENT GROUPS, however, are often more strongly characterized by egocentricity than are unilineal descent systems.   MR

elders are those who are older or higher in rank in a tribe, community, or other organization. Age is a physical characteristic easy to discern, and all societies rely on it when sorting and classifying humans. AGING does not automatically bring greater wisdom or achievement or more experience, but age is widely accepted as a handy index for such difficult-to-measure personal qualities. For this reason elders are commonly entitled to respect or deference, and many societies customarily have ceremonies to honor their elders. Modern states often transform these earlier practices into government-sponsored events, such as banquets for senior citizens.

In societies with extensive age sets or age grading (see AGE SYSTEMS), the elders occupy an advanced – but not always the last – stage in a LIFE-CYCLE sequence of stages with explicit rules for entry, exit, and promotion. In some communities and institutions (religious congregations in particular) "elder" is an office with well-delineated rights and duties to advise leaders, make policy, or even rule directly. Age is a necessary criterion for the office but seldom a sufficient one: ability also is taken into account.

One often hears that the traditional function of elders – to serve as a reservoir of knowledge for the community – has been rendered obsolete in INDUSTRIAL SOCIETIES by the relentless waves of new technology. This assumes that the newer always is better, but knowledgeable elders can be a renewable human resource of great value that is neglected only at a society's peril.

DWP

further reading Kertzer & Keith 1984; Sokolovsky 1990

elementary families consist of a husband, a wife, and their children.   MR

elementary kinship systems are those in which all members of the society are classified as kin and divided into marriageable and nonmarriageable categories (Lévi-Strauss 1969a).   MR
See also MOIETY SYSTEMS

emic and etic distinguish the understanding of cultural representations from the point of view of a native of the culture (emic) from the understanding of cultural representations from the point of view of an outside observer of the culture (etic). Kenneth Pike (1954) coined the terms by analogy with the linguistic terms "phonemic" and "phonetic."   MR
See   also   ETHNOSCIENCE,   NEW ETHNOGRAPHY
further reading Headland et al. 1990

emotions refer to processes of the human mind and body that exert a compelling influence on thought and social interaction. They are nearly always embedded in the social and interpersonal realities of everyday life, where they shape, and are shaped by, cultural understandings and social institutions. In this sense, emotions are also, in a fundamental way, about the social problems and predicaments of the person-in-society (Lutz & White 1986).

Because of their association with the "natural," emotions have until recently been an ambivalent subject of research for anthropologists. Often aligned with a precultural realm of nature, emotions have been set in opposition to culture, the legitimate domain of anthropological investigation. These nature–culture and emotion–reason dichotomies pervade popular and professional theories of emotion and continue to set the terms for a wide range of scientific research on emotion.

From the time of Darwin (1872) onward, theorists have tended to naturalize the reality of emotions as springing from innate physiological processes. However, emotions (and talk of emotions) also function as communicative SIGNS that work to create understandings and relationships between people. Anthropological investigations increasingly focus on this semiotic aspect of emotions as culturally and socially constructed realities. Approaches often differ in their view of emotion as either an "independent variable" that precedes its expression in cultural forms or a "dependent variable" that is itself determined in part by cultural concepts and discursive practices.

The evolution of anthropological approaches to emotion reflects broader trends in cultural theory: away from the assumption that basic emotions are a constant, a "given" of human experience, toward recognition that they are always, in some measure, culturally constructed.

Anthropologists have long noted variation in emotional life across cultures. Gregory Bateson (1936) and others developed the concept of "ethos" to refer to the distinctive ways emotions are patterned throughout an entire society. Similar to Ruth BENEDICT's (1934a) concept of "configurations" of culture, the idea of a societal ethos suggested that cultures selectively transform the raw materials of human nature. Using psychoanalytic distinctions of "primary" process and "secondary" process, CULTURE AND PERSONALITY theorists of the 1940s and 1950s tended to regard emotions as universal psychobiological processes underlying the expressive forms of collective culture (see PSYCHIC UNITY OF MANKIND).

Similar assumptions of a universal human nature generally also guide CROSS-CULTURAL STUDIES on emotions and emotional disorder in psychiatry. For example, the primary approach of modern psychiatry has been to develop standard diagnostic categories of major "affective disorders," such as depression and anxiety, capable of discriminating the biopsychological conditions that produce them. The focus of anthropological research, by contrast, has been to identify the culture-specific ways in which these types of emotional disorder are experienced and expressed across cultures (Kleinman & Good 1985). In addition, anthropologists have sought to call attention to the cultural and historical framework(s) in which psychiatric categories are themselves produced and applied.

A. I. Hallowell's (1955) call for attending to local or "ethno-" psychologies signaled an expanding interest in cultural concepts of emotion. Subsequent ethnographic accounts, such as those of Hildred Geertz (1959) in Java and Jean Briggs (1970) in the Arctic, have shown the complex ways that cultures conceptualize, express, and manage emotions. By examining ordinary emotion concepts and practices, these studies precipitated further questions about the basis for interpreting emotions across languages and cultures; specifically, to what extent can researchers presume a set of basic or core affects as a framework for comparison? (This is a particularly lively debate in the study of Pacific island cultures – Gerber 1985; Lutz 1988.)

An important set of cross-cultural studies by the psychologist Paul Ekman (1984) suggests that a small number of core affects, including anger, sadness, fear, surprise, disgust, and happiness, form a set of universal emotions coded in facial expressions everywhere. But the interpretation of these results, particularly concerning their use of English-language emotion terms as the basis for comparison, remains a point of disagreement. Linguistic analyses show that words such as "anger" are much more complex than simple labels for facial expressions. Not only do they signify complex cultural knowledge about the mind and social action (Lakoff & Kövecses 1987), emotion words and expressions also play

key roles in the interactional "negotiation" of interpersonal relations. One hypothesis, inspired by research on the universal meanings of color terms, is that it may be possible to find a universal kernel of meaning in basic emotion terms if they are represented as a *prototypical* core and an array of associated meanings (Gerber 1985).

As research on the local meanings of emotion in different languages and cultures has increased, the relationship between commonsense concepts of emotion and scientific theories has become problematic. Comparative studies suggest that English-language terms and concepts do not provide a neutral ground from which to interpret emotional experience across cultures (Wierzbicka 1986). Some of the most interesting work on emotions in anthropology is using cross-cultural research to critique English-based social science conceptualizations of emotion (Lutz 1988). The critique of psychological theories of emotion opens up a wide field of investigation for comparative research on the emotions in their social, cultural, and political contexts.   GMW

See also CONFIGURATIONISM, PSYCHOLOGICAL ANTHROPOLOGY

further reading L. Abu-Lughod 1986; Heider 1991; Hochschild 1983; Kitayama & Markus 1994; R. Levy 1973; M. Lewis & Haviland 1993; Lutz & Abu-Lughod 1990; M. Rosaldo 1980; Wikan 1993

enates   are matrilineal kin; that is, they are related to an individual on the mother's side.   MR

See also AGNATES, COGNATES

enculturation   is the process by which an individual acquires the mental representations (beliefs, knowledge, and so forth) and patterns of behavior required to function as a member of a culture. It can be seen as the counterpart, at the level of culture, of the process of SOCIALIZATION. Enculturation is largely seen, for native members of a culture, as taking place in childhood as part of the process of CHILD training and education. Initiation rites and other forms of training later in life can also be seen to have an enculturating function.   MR

endogamy is the rule or preference that individuals marry only within their particular kinship group, social group, or other defined category (locality, class, religion, etc.). For example, Indian castes are endogamous and marriage between castes is strictly forbidden. Endogamy also describes a statistical pattern of in-marriage even in the absence of an explicit rule.
    MR

See also EXOGAMY

environmental   determinism/ possibilism *See* STEWARD

epidemic is a rate of DISEASE that reaches unexpectedly high levels, affecting a large number of people in a relatively short time. Epidemic is a relative concept: a small absolute number of cases of a disease is considered an epidemic if the disease incidence is usually very low. In contrast, a disease (such as malaria) is considered *endemic* if it is continuously present in a population but at low or moderate levels, while *pandemic* refers to epidemics of worldwide proportions, such as influenza in 1918 or AIDS today.

The field of epidemiology was founded in an attempt to understand epidemics of infectious disease, particularly a series of severe cholera outbreaks in Europe at the beginning of the twentieth century. Descriptive epidemiology studies the distribution of disease in regard to time, place, and person. Analytic epidemiology uses this data to identify the causal agents and conditions of a disease outbreak. While the concept of epidemic has traditionally been used with respect to infectious disease, it has recently been expanded to include many chronic diseases, such as coronary heart disease, that are occurring at increasingly high rates.

Epidemic disease is relevant to anthropology because human behavior shapes both the causes and consequences of epidemics. Anthropologists interested in the causes of epidemics generally take an ecological approach; investigations of the consequences of epidemics may examine either demographic impact or the influences on social processes like stigma.

The dynamic interactions between human host, environment, and pathogen define the course of a disease. Therefore, a consideration of human behavior, culture, and ecology are critical to understanding the distribution and severity of disease. From an evolutionary perspective, infectious disease has been a primary agent of natural selection during the course of human evolution (Peter J. Brown et al. 1996). For example, Francis Black (1990) argued that genetic susceptibility prevented indigenous New World populations from mounting effective immune responses to Old World pathogens such as measles, leading to disproportionately high mortality rates in these populations.

The field of paleopathology has reconstructed patterns of disease transmission and distribution in prehistoric populations and suggests that the agricultural revolution may have created ecological conditions that foster epidemic disease. The transition from nomadism to sedentism associated with agriculture posed problems of waste disposal and exposure to disease-transmitting vermin; intensification of agricultural production can change the ecology and increase exposure to disease-transmitting insects. Susceptibility to infectious disease is synergistically related to food shortages and malnutrition. Moreover, the population growth associated with agricultural intensification provides a reservoir of human hosts that allow diseases to become epidemic (M. Cohen 1989).

In historiography, epidemics of bubonic plague have become prototypical examples of epidemic disease. The "Black Death" of the mid-fourteenth century killed more than one-quarter of the population of Europe and the Middle East. Diseases can be spread through trade or population movements. An epidemic, however, requires particular local ecological conditions. In the case of the bubonic plague, years of economic growth followed by famine and depression created crowded and squalid living conditions in urban centers, bringing human hosts in frequent contact with the rat-borne fleas that spread the disease.

McNeill (1976) has suggested that epidemics on a similar scale to the Black Death have regularly occurred during the expansion of empires. Culture contact, or the "confluence of disease pools," resulted in epidemics in populations without previous experience of, and immunities to, a pathogen. Epidemic diseases have shaped human history from prehistoric to contemporary times. Because they decimate and demoralize susceptible populations, they become tools of expansion for "civilized" societies, facilitating military conquest and subjugation.

Anthropologists are interested in the social consequences of epidemic disease. For example, Neel (1958) suggested that high mortality rates during epidemics are the result of social collapse – including a sense of helplessness, poor medical care, and insufficient nutritional intake. Thus, an epidemic in a tribal society may be more important than genetic or immunologic susceptibility. Just as important, epidemics exacerbate problems like xenophobia (the fear of strangers) and stigmatization; and such consequences add to the human suffering caused by epidemics. Whereas some social reactions to epidemics (e.g., isolation of the sick; rapid disposal of the dead) may be biologically adaptive, other social reactions (e.g., fleeing the epicenter of a disease outbreak) may worsen the spread of the disease.

Over the past 150 years, birth and death rates have dropped dramatically in most First World populations. This DEMO-GRAPHIC TRANSITION has been accompanied by an epidemiologic transition in the rates and causes of disease. The traditional agents of epidemic disease – plague, tuberculosis, smallpox, typhus – have given way to chronic "diseases of civilization" such as obesity, heart disease, and several cancers. Improving sanitary conditions, immunization programs, and antibiotics have helped control infectious disease and have allowed chronic diseases to become epidemic in longer-living populations. More recently, however, the emergence of AIDS, the resurgence of tuberculosis, and a wide variety of "emerging infections," many of which are antibiotic-resistant strains of previously controllable disease agents (Garrett 1994), remind us that epidemics of infectious disease are not a thing of the past. Because human behavior is essential to both the causes and consequences of epidemics, medical anthropologists can contribute to the understanding, control, and prevention of future epidemics.   PB & TMc

See also DEMOGRAPHY, MEDICAL ANTHROPOLOGY

Eskimo (or lineal) kinship systems

employ a kinship terminology in which members of the NUCLEAR FAMILY are distinguished by generation and gender, while kin outside the family are more broadly lumped together (see figure 1). The terms applied to members of the nuclear family are not extended to other categories of kin. Cousins, in particular, are not distinguished by type. The English-language

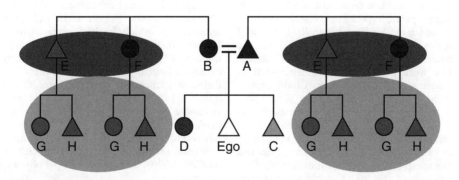

Figure 1   Eskimo kinship system.

system of kin terms is an Eskimo system. The Eskimo system is typically associated with COGNATIC descent.   MR

ethnic groups, ethnicity   were terms first used in anthropology to refer to a people presumed to belong to the same SOCIETY and who shared the same CULTURE and, especially, the same LANGUAGE – a culture and language that had, moreover, been transmitted unchanged from generation to generation. The terms began to be used in the period immediately after World War II as a substitute for older terms as "TRIBE" and (in British usage) "RACE." This usage is reflected, for example, in works such as *Ethnic groups of northern Southeast Asia* (Embree & Thomas 1950).

Even as the term "ethnic group" was introduced, the theoretical assumption that cultures or social structures are associated with clearly bounded discrete groups was facing a strong challenge. A few American anthropologists had begun to question this approach in the 1930s, when they began to reflect on the consequences of cultural contact between peoples and the ACCULTURATION of peoples from small-scale societies to the more powerful societies that had imposed themselves on them. A more sustained and persuasive questioning of the theory that divided the world into discrete societies with discrete cultures appeared with the publication of *Political systems of highland Burma* by E. R. LEACH (1954). Leach demonstrated that "in contexts such as we find in North Burma, the ordinary ethnographic conventions as to what constitutes *a* culture or *a* tribe are hopelessly inappropriate" (p. 281). Despite efforts a decade later by Raoul Naroll (1964) and others, attempts to refine and save the model of "culture-bearing units" failed. The work of Leach and others, such as Moerman (1965), together with the experience of anthropologists during World War II, and the observation of societies undergoing decolonization in the postwar period, had made such an effort a futile enterprise. In 1967 participants at an American Ethnological Society symposium on "the problem of the tribe," demonstrated conclusively that the older theory was inad-

equate for understanding the complex relationships between cultural expression, speech, and social and political organization (Helm 1968). Ethnic groups cannot be said to be sociocultural collectivities with   species-like   (i.e.,   "natural') characteristics.

Ethnicity subsequently came to assume a new meaning in anthropology with the publication of Fredrik Barth's (1969a) Introduction to *Ethnic groups and boundaries*, the most influential and widely cited anthropological essay on ethnicity. Barth began with a rejection of the idea that ethnic groups are definable by some total inventory of cultural traits that their members share. Rather, he argued,

when one traces the history of an ethnic group through time, one is *not* simultaneously, in the same sense, tracing the history of "a culture": the elements of the present culture of that ethnic group have not sprung from the particular set that constituted the group's culture at a previous time, whereas the group has a continual organizational existence with boundaries (criteria of membership) that have marked off a continuing unit.   (p. 38)

Barth proposed instead that the boundaries of an ethnic group are constituted through "self-ascription," whereby people choose to utilize a few cultural attributes, "often such features as dress, language, houseform, or general style of life," as the "overt signals or signs" of their distinctiveness (1969a: 14).

The question thus arises as to why people seek to draw boundaries that can be indicated by a small number of "overt signals or signs." Barth's own answer was still strongly influenced by the structural FUNCTIONALISM of the British anthropological approach in which he had been trained. Ethnic groups, he argued, "may provide important goods and services for each other, i.e., occupy reciprocal and therefore different niches but in close interdependence" (1969a: 19). Although this "ethnic DIVISION OF LABOR" approach has been useful in understanding some situations where cultural differences have been used to clothe economic interests (Bonacich & Modell 1980), it has proven wholly inadequate for understanding the ethnic confrontations, conflicts, and violence that have become so common in the late twentieth century (E. Wolf 1994).

The motivation to insist, even to the death, that certain cultural characteristics mark fundamental and perduring distinctions between peoples can be understood only by recognizing that there is some "primordial" quality to ethnic identity (C. Geertz 1963b). Ethnicity, in other words, entails an assumption that there is something essential or given in the distinctions between peoples. But one has to look beyond some set of cultural traits to find this primordial basis for ethnicity.

A number of theorists, beginning with Max WEBER (1968: 385), have posited that the roots of ethnic identity lie in a presumption of common or shared descent (Keyes 1976). Although a few social scientists, drawing on SOCIOBIOLOGICAL theory, have argued that recognition of shared descent is a direct manifestation of a genetic predisposition (Van den Berghe 1978, 1981), most have rejected this new version of racial theory. The more prevalent view is that the "given-ness" of shared descent is a product of distinctive forms of cultural practice (Keyes 1981; G. Bentley 1987).

The mechanism for establishing a shared descent among those who claim a common ethnic identity is not, as with kin groups, a genealogy that establishes links to a common ANCESTOR. Rather linkages to the apical ancestors or forebears of an ethnic group are established through narratives of origin, migration, and especially SUFFERING at the hands of others. These narratives are conveyed in stories told by parents, elders, and leaders through songs, folklore, ceremonies commemorating historical events, dramatic performances, artistic creations, and written ethnic histories. A compelling sense of identification with an ethnic group emerges from the interweaving of personal biography and public narrative (Obeyesekere 1975). Such an identity becomes part of what Bourdieu (1977) termed "habitus," that set of unreflected dispositions that orient people toward acting in the world.

While the drawing of ethnic distinctions is possible in any situation in which people living in proximity to each other follow different cultural practices (T. Schwartz

1975), ethnicity becomes particularly salient in social relations when the politics of everyday life accentuate the significance of certain cultural differences. The work of Bourdieu and Michel Foucault has led a number of anthropologists in recent years to focus attention on how the modern nation-state has proven to constitute an especially fruitful context for the expression of ethnicity. Whereas an earlier generation of anthropologists and other social scientists viewed the persistence of ethnic identities in the modern world as atavistic, students of ethnicity today recognize that, very much to the contrary, ethnicity has become a much more significant factor in social relations since the emergence of the nation-state (B. Williams 1989; Donald Cohen 1989).

Modern states or movements seeking to capture state power have sought to promote ("invent") dominant narratives about the cultural heritage and the destiny of those claimed to constitute a national community. Nationalist discourses have created an environment in which ethnicity has flourished. This has been especially true because national cultures have been promoted through the invasive and effective "technologies of power" that were not available to premodern states (B. Cohn & Dirks 1988). State-sponsored enterprises such as compulsory EDUCATION have been especially significant in the superimposition of national identities on local identities (Keyes 1991). In national narrative communicated through, and backed by, a state's technologies of power, the histories of some indigenous peoples have often been ignored, marginalized, or even specifically rejected. Migrants who come from states with different national narratives are also defined as outsiders. In the modern context, therefore, the term "ethnic group" has devolved and come to refer primarily to a minority whose cultural heritage is recognized as different from the majority's in a way that sets it apart from the dominant national culture.

In some societies, especially those in which ruling elites have drawn from the marxist–Leninist–Stalinist theory of "nationalities," states have instituted policies that have fixed ethnic differences and boundaries by law (Connor 1984). Others, most notably the United States, have also accorded legal status to ethnic differences through policies promoting affirmative action. State sponsorship of ethnic CLASSIFICATION has made peoples' assertions of their own formulations of ethnic identities more credible, but also more contentious, since such assertions have practical economic and political consequences. The result has been an intensification of ethnic discourse in the contest for power. In some cases, states have collapsed as ethnic groups have seceded to form their own "nations" or have warred with other ethnic groups over the drawing of new national boundaries. The former Yugoslavia, which has undergone violent dismemberment and genocidal "ethnic cleansing," has come to stand as a metaphor for ethnic conflict in the late twentieth century (Denich 1994).

The relationship between ethnic and national identities has become more complicated with the increased possibility of moving back and forth across state boundaries through travel and telecommunications. Early-twentieth-century sociologists developed a theory of ethnicity, based primarily on studies of migrants to the United States, that assumed ethnic groups would exist only during a transitional period while they were being assimilated into the dominant culture of their new homes, a process expected to be complete by the third generation. This theory presupposed that migrants and their descendants would continue to have few ties to their homelands and would lose contact with old kinsmen and friends. The migrants of the late twentieth century, however, are much more likely than those of the late nineteenth century to remain in close contact with the world from which they came. Telephones allow instant communication across the globe, cassette and videotapes of personal activities are easily produced and transmitted, and air travel, quite inexpensive by comparison with travel by ship earlier in the century, makes visits in both directions much more simple than in the past.

Assimilation is not a possibility for many migrants. Many countries deny the rights of certain types of immigrants to become citizens. Saudi Arabia and Kuwait, for example, have imported large numbers of Filipinos, Thai, Sinhalese, as well as Pakistanis and Palestinians, to work in their countries, but refuse to allow them to become citizens. In Germany, where ethnicity is defined "by blood," the children of Turkish immigrants who are born and brought up in Germany are granted only the status of "guest-workers" in the land of their birth, whereas citizenship is automatically granted to new arrivals from Central Asia who can prove German ancestry from centuries past.

Indigenous minorities living under one state have increasingly joined movements with those from many other states to seek international support for their right to have cultural or socioeconomic autonomy. Tourism has also led to the resituating of ethnicity in an international context. Not only have selected cultural practices been re-presented to tourists as manifestations of "authentic" ethnic cultures, but some forms of ethnic craft and artistic work have also been packaged as commodities for tourists and for international art and craft markets (Graburn 1976). The ethnicity that anthropologists began to explore when they finally discovered the modern state appears to be taking on yet another dimension as the boundaries of states become more porous and more problematic (Gupta & Ferguson 1992).   CK
See also NATION
further reading Francis 1976; De Vos & Romanucci-Ross 1975

ethnobotany   is the study of indigenous systems of knowledge about plants. It is a multi-disciplinary field in which botanists and anthropologists have played key roles. Historically the botanists' approach was utilitarian; they organized their data according to principles of scientific classification. By contrast, anthropologists took "the native's point of view and his rules and categories for organizing the universe" (R. Ford 1978: 39). Anthropological research has focused on the classification of plants; how people use plants as food, medicine, building material, etc.; and the symbolic importance of plants, particularly in religious beliefs.

CLASSIFICATION is a topic that has been key to anthropology from its inception and the classification of plants and animals is particularly significant because it is highly elaborated in almost all cultures. Early theorists viewed classification systems as a way of understanding "primitive" thought (Durkheim & Mauss 1963), but later researchers saw them as a means to explore human perception itself, laying the basis for COGNITIVE ANTHROPOLOGY. Key studies have included how plant color categories are distinguished (Conklin 1954b; Berlin & Kay 1969) and the existence of four or five hierarchically nested categories of plants across a range of diverse cultures (Berlin et al. 1973). Anthropologists have also found that scientific taxonomies of plants differ from folk taxonomies, both in the way they distinguish species and the criteria they take for granted (Berlin et al. 1966, 1968).

Seeking out new plants that can be used as food or medicine long predates their formal scientific study. The great transmigration of plants and animals that followed the discovery of the Americas by Europeans had an enormous impact on AGRICULTURE and FOOD SYSTEMS throughout the world. During the nineteenth century the systematic collection of such information developed into the field of economic botany. One criticism of the field was that it mindlessly collected and listed plants without a theoretical framework (W. Davis 1995). Anthropology's focus on the interaction between people and plants provided such a framework, which quickly took root among botanists as well. For example, Harold Conklin (1957, 1980) analyzed the whole agricultural and ecological systems of the Hanunoo and Ifugao in the Philippines in addition to his work on classification. Questions of how culture and environment mutually influence each other over time has also been the focus of research, as exemplified in William Ballée's (1994) exhaustive study of the Ka'apor in the Amazon of Brazil. The attempt to discover potentially useful drugs for curing disease, particularly in the tropical forests, has depended on tapping the knowledge of local curers, shamans, and other specialists. This requires long-term fieldwork, language skills, and collaboration across cultures. It has also recently led to the question of compensation for the communities and nations that provided the knowledge or plant materials that later became money-making "discoveries" for others (Toledo 1995).

The symbolic importance of plants in culture is rooted in what people believe about them, how they are used as a form of communication, and their role in religious belief and ritual. Particular plants are often believed to carry certain powers or spirits, particularly those used for medical purposes, and sacred trees or groves are common to many religions. Plants are so woven into human culture that they often form a field of communication, such as the display of flowers (J. Goody 1993). But by far the greatest amount of research in this area has been on DRUGS, psychoactive plants that alter an individual's perception of the world. These include a wide variety of mushrooms (Wasson 1968, 1980), peyote (La Barre 1938), cannabis (La Barre 1977), narcotic plants (Emboden 1972a), hallucinogens (Harner 1973; Schultes & Hofmann 1979) and many others (Furst 1972). A key debate concerns the relationship between drug experiences and religious beliefs (Reichel-Dolmatoff 1971).

TB

See also ETHNOSCIENCE, ETHNOZOOLOGY
further reading Berlin 1992; Bohrer 1986; Ford 1985; La Barre 1995; G. Martin 1995; Prance 1991

ethnocentrism   is the belief that one's own culture is superior to others, which is often accompanied by a tendency to make invidious comparisons. In a weaker form, ethnocentrism is the tendency to look at other cultures through the filter of one's own cultural presuppositions. This can lead to a failure to appreciate the different frames of reference within which members of other cultures operate. All cultures and people are to some degree ethnocentric. Anthropologists also refer to a "secondary ethnocentrism" in which an observer uncritically takes on the biases of an adopted culture as a lens to view behavior and beliefs elsewhere, a trait often found in religious converts and scholars of other cultures.

MR

ethnocide refers to the deliberate attempt to eradicate the culture or way of life of a people. Its extreme form involves GENOCIDE, the extermination of the people themselves. Ethnocide depends on the use of political power to force relatively powerless people to give up their CULTURE and is therefore characteristic of colonial or other situations where coercion can be applied. The Europeans who invaded the Americas after 1492 practiced systematic ethnocide against indigenous peoples, seeking over time to abolish their religions, communities, languages, and eventually their cultures. In the nineteenth century many independent nations of the Americas sought to abolish "Indian-ness" altogether, insisting that Indian peoples should give up being Indian and blend as individuals into the mainstream. Similar policies were followed in other parts of the world but have been strongly contested since the 1970s by the worldwide movement for indigenous rights.

Ethnocide can also be used against ethnic minorities, who are coerced into abandoning their languages and cultures by the prospect of facing discrimination if they do not. The term is sometimes used to refer to any process or policy that results in the disappearance of a people's culture. For example, the building of dams and other ecologically induced changes, and the introduction of new industries and job opportunities all potentially induce or force people to abandon their traditional ways. Such usage renders the concept of ethnocide almost meaningless, so it should preferably be reserved for instances where power is used systematically for deliberate cultural eradication.   DML

ethnographic analogy Analogy is a form of argument in which if two objects or events resemble one another in some features they are held to be likely to resemble each other in additional features. Analogical arguments are ampliative; that is, the conclusions contain more information than the premises. Consequently, conclusions do not follow necessarily from premises, and analogic arguments are suggestive not demonstrative. In ethnographic analogy, resemblances between an ethnographic and an archaeological object or event create the analogs; the ethnographic function or other archaeologically unobservable feature is taken to characterize the archaeological object or event.

Ethnographic analogy has little role in scientific archaeology, but it is the cornerstone of the reconstructive approach, the principal means by which the archaeological record is reconstructed. Early analogical arguments were haphazard. By the late 1950s, the role of analogy was recognized. Initial attempts at improvements focused on analog construction (R. Asher 1961): analogs were limited to cases where historical continuity between the prehistoric and historic cases was assumed or the two cases were drawn from cultures of similar developmental stage and ecological setting. Later it was argued that the "probability" (actually "plausibility", since there is no way to calculate probability) of inferred properties being true was enhanced if inferred properties were functionally related to initial resemblances. It was also argued that analogies should be "tested" (L. Binford 1967a). Analogical arguments cannot be tested, however. Today reconstructionists generally admit the unsatisfactory nature of ethnographic analogy, but persist in its use because no other methodological alternative seems to exist within reconstructionism (Wylie 1985).   RD

See also ARCHAEOLOGY, COMPARATIVE METHOD

further reading Dunnell 1978; R. Gould & Watson 1982

ethnographic present is the convention in anthropology of writing about a culture in the present tense regardless of its distance in time from the actual act of observation or historical existence. The practice was particularly common in early American anthropology, where authors were keen to describe the cultures of native American groups whose historical way of life had vanished before the time of observation and was being reconstructed from interviews and documents. More broadly, the use of the ethnographic present is tied to the notion that ethnographic description is an accurate representation of a culture at

a given moment in time and that the totality of these descriptions (of all cultures) forms a timeless ethnographic record.   TB
See also ETHNOGRAPHY AND ETHNOLOGY

ethnography and ethnology In contemporay usage, ethnology is the attempt to develop rigorous and scientifically grounded explanations of cultural phenomena by comparing and contrasting many human cultures. By contrast, ethnography is the systematic description of a single contemporary culture, often through ethnographic FIELDWORK. The two concepts are often combined in anthropological writings and they have a close and complex historical relationship.

The words "ethnography" and "ethnology" appear to have been introduced in the late eighteenth century. Hans Vermeulen (1995) cited the German historian and linguist August Ludwig Schlözer's *Allgemeine nordische Geschichte* (1771) as probably the first use of the term "Ethnographie," which Schlözer seemed to employ interchangeably with the term "Völkerkunde" to designate the descriptive and historical study of peoples and nations. Vermeulen noted Schlözer's involvement with the Imperial Russian Academy of Sciences and his residency in St. Petersburg in the 1760s, where he worked with G. F. Müller, J. E. Fischer, and other German scholars recruited by the Russian government to report on the peoples of the newly explored eastern territories.

Vermeulen traced the word "ethnology" (in the form "ethnologia") to the Slovak historian Adam Frantisek Kollár's *Historiae jurisque publici Regni Ungariae amoenitates* (1783: 80). Both words, as well as variant and vernacular forms (e.g. "ethnographisch," "Ethnograph," "Völkskunde") were rapidly assimilated by European scholars. Some of Schlözer's colleagues at the University of Göttingen, including the historian Johann Christoph Gatterer, adopted "Ethnographie" and "Völkerkunde," and these two terms were in broad use among German-speaking scholars by the 1790s. "Ethnology" was taken up in 1787 by the German historian Johann Ernst Fabri and, in the same year,

by the Swiss theologian Alexandre-César Chavannes, whose use of the word has often been cited as its origin.

Vermeulen's research on the origin and reception of these words stands as a major corrective to long-established views among English-speaking anthropologists that "ethnography" and "ethnology" – and the intellectual enterprises they name – were of much more recent origin (see, for example, Lowie 1937; Voget 1975). "Ethnographie" did not appear in French until 1820, and the *Oxford English dictionary*'s earliest citations of "ethnography" and "ethnology" date from 1834 and 1842, although a diligent search will certainly reveal earlier English usages. Vermeulen noted, for example, that Thomas Jefferson's instructions in 1802 to the Lewis and Clark expedition include a section titled "Ethnological information desired."

The discipline of anthropology has complex intellectual roots in the Enlightenment, the European discoveries of non-Western peoples, and the rise of the natural sciences. A specific – and until recently overlooked – debt to the German scholars who attempted to conceptualize the ethnic diversity of the Russian Empire's eastern frontier is strongly indicated by the origin of the key words that crystallized the need for systematic and comparative study of cultures.

Within the two-hundred-year history of the human sciences, however, the denotations of the words "ethnology" and "ethnography" have shifted several times. The English scholars who took these words up from the 1830s onwards seem to have de-emphasized the geographic and linguistic aspect of ethnological and ethnographic inquiry in favor of a study of racial origins. James Prichard's *Researches into the physical history of mankind* (1813) is the first prominent work in English to deal explicitly with ethnology. For Prichard, ethnology aimed "to trace the history of the tribes and races of men from the remotest periods which are within the reach of investigation, to discover their mutual relations, and to arrive at conclusions, either certain or probable, as to their affinity or diversity of origin" (1847: 231). Prichard's larger project was to establish through comparative study the unity of the human species. Although the technical meaning of "ethnology" soon moved beyond Prichard's definition, something of his larger project remained in the connotations of the word: ethnology implies a study of humanity that is particularly attentive to cultural commonalities.

Prichard's idea of ethnology as a reconstruction of racial history and human origins survived into the early twentieth century. But the word had already acquired a distinct new meaning by the 1860s, with the rise of evolutionists, who took the unity of mankind as already established and turned their attention to tracing the progressive development of human society. The Ethnological Society, founded in 1842 along Prichardian lines, had become closely associated with TYLOR, Lubbock, Huxley, and other theorists in this new mode. In opposition to their focus, James Hunt founded the anti-Darwinian Anthropological Society of London in 1862. Reviewing the divergence of these two organizations, Stocking (1987) noted that Hunt, who rejected what he denounced as Darwinian dogmatism and claimed to speak for "the science of the whole nature of man," in practice promoted a barren emphasis on racial classifications (see RACE). One result of this dispute was that "ethnology" was, at least temporarily, set in contrast to "anthropology" and gained legitimacy as the view of an emerging scientific establishment (Stocking 1987: 253).

"Anthropology," of course, eventually won out as the general name for the discipline, but anthropologists have continued to find it useful to have recourse to a term that points toward their scientific, theoretical, explanatory, developmental, and comparative ambitions. Robert LOWIE adopted the term "ethnology" in this sense in *Culture and ethnology* (1917), and again in *The history of ethnological theory* (1937), and it remains in similar use among anthropologists who are entirely innocent of the racist and evolutionist roots of the word.

"Ethnography" appears to have taken even longer to catch on in English. The *Oxford English dictionary* cites both the *Penny cyclopedia* (1834), "The term ethnography (nation-description) is sometimes used by German writers in the sense which we have given to anthropography," and Cardinal Wiseman (1836): "Nor is this confined merely to the members of the same ethnographic family." The "-graphic" suffix, however, appears to have channeled the word into a recognizably modern meaning. The *O.E.D.* also cites Theodore Ross (1852), "The ethnographic document called *El Auto de Figueroa* is one of the most curious records of the barbarism of the first *conquistadores*."

Even in these early examples, there is a duality in the idea of ethnography. On one hand, the word designates observations, ranging from isolated remarks to extended studies of nations, tribes, or peoples, by anyone who has recorded what he has seen or heard. The genre in this sense extends from Herodotus (and before him, a Greek tradition of writing about foreign nations) to Marco Polo, and to the reports of missionaries, soldiers, and travelers of all sorts. Furthermore, the people described in ethnographic reports might have their own accounts of foreigners.

On the other hand, ethnography also designated the aspiration to collect systematically, and according to rigorous procedures, facts about human languages, customs, arts, and achievements. Ethnography in this sense included the culling of material from documents and interviews with visitors returning from foreign lands and the redaction of this material into learned treatises. The scientific ethnographer was someone who staked a fairly large claim on erudition, breadth of learning, and capacious memory; thus ethnography gained a certain reputation as a field for pedants.

Ethnology and ethnography developed, of course, dialectically. As the antiquity of man became established in the mid-nineteenth century and anthropological inquiry began to focus on evolutionary questions, the need for better data became clear. In 1843, Prichard and two of his colleagues drew up a schedule of questions to guide observations of native peoples (Penniman 1935: 53). Lewis Henry MORGAN began sending his first kinship terminology questionnaires to missionaries and commercial agents in January 1859 (Trautmann 1987: 103). In 1874, the British Association for the Advancement of Science published its first edition of *Notes and queries on anthropology, for the use of travellers and residents in uncivilized lands.* These attempts to guide inquiry sometimes had richer returns than their authors anticipated, as recipients began to engage the larger problem of putting the answers into local context. The outstanding example is the ethnographic work of Lorimer Fison and A. W. Howitt in Australia, culminating in *Kamilaroi and Kurnai* (Fison 1880), which grew out of the missionary Fison's original correspondence with Morgan (see Stocking 1995: 17–34). By the last decades of the nineteenth century, there were several examples of a new kind of ethnographic book in which the hypothetical pronouncements of armchair theorists were tested against the author's own observations. Robert Henry Codrington's *The Melanesians* (1891) and Baldwin Spencer and Frank Gillen's *The native tribes of central Australia* (1899) exemplify this new, theoretically informed style of extended first-hand observation. Also during this period, the Bureau of American Ethnology began its publication of ethnographic monographs based on systematic fieldwork.

Writers in the middle decades of the nineteenth century varied widely in the degree to which they subjected sources, such as travelers' reports, to critical review or insisted that details be viewed in social context. Indeed, some writers ransacked disparate sources for facts to support a preconceived argument; but there is a more thoughtful winnowing of ethnographic data even in the works of Gustav Klemm (1802–67), Theodor Waits (1821–64), and Adolf Bastian (1826–1905) than may appear at first glance. The modern conceit that anthropology has only recently begun to grapple with the elusive nature of ethnographic facts is not supported by the record, although it is clear that contemporary skepticism about the possibility of accurate generalization and adequate representation runs deeper than it once did.

As early as 1850, Prichard's disciple Robert Latham complained about the sheer accumulation of facts that had to be considered in formulating ethnological arguments (Stocking 1987: 103). The expansion of ethnographic data remains, at least in principle, an unsolved problem for anthropology. Individual researchers may attempt to avoid it by narrowing their ethnographic focus or choosing specialized topics, but anthropology would seem to retain from its founding an obligation to consider propositions in light of the *whole* ethnographic record.

This problem was immensely compounded by the holistic ethnography that Boas enunciated, and by the ascension of ethnographic monographs by relatively well-informed observers, from W. H. R. Rivers's *The Todas* (1906) to the decisive breakthrough in 1922 of Radcliffe-Brown's *The Andaman Islanders* and Malinowski's *Argonauts of the western Pacific.* For most of the twentieth century, writing an ethnography has meant mastering in tremendous detail the particulars of a people in a certain time and place. Anything approaching a good understanding of the ethnographic record now requires close reading of hundreds of such books, as well as a reasonable command of the partial syntheses by Kroeber, Lévi-Strauss, and Murdock, among others.

With the admission of photography, film, sound recordings, and other archival media as ethnographic documents, ethnography has annexed another meaning: it has become not only that which describes culture (primarily through language), but that which presents culture (through artifacts, images, music, etc.).

The dedication of early anthropologists to mastering all of the data that bore on their theoretical formulations is rarely matched in contemporary anthropology, and this, too, colors the meaning of the word "ethnography." For Tylor, Morgan, or Frazer, ethnography comprised the totality of ethnographic facts comprehended by their theories. As intensive case-study ethnographies multiplied, many anthropologists transferred this idea of totality to the level of abstract ideal. Kroeber (1957: 196) wrote that an ethnography is "a brick that gets built – by others if not by the author – into a structure, namely, the record and understanding of all human culture through time and area, which makes it more than just another tribal ethnography." Contemporary anthropologists, however, are more likely to think of ethnographies as discrete works of varying degrees of familiarity, theoretical sophistication, and interest. Similarly, ethnology has become less a matter of advancing hypotheses that have been severely tested against the broader ethnographic record than of venturing formulations that seem consistent with the portions of the ethnographic record the researcher knows best.

Some anthropologists have proposed rhetorical or epistemological ways to escape the large and growing burden of the ethnographic record. Likening ethnography to literature emphasizes the author's creative sensibilities at the expense of the substance of his report and displaces questions about thoroughness and accuracy with questions about style (see LITERARY ANTHROPOLOGY). Attempts to historicize ethnographies by emphasizing their colonial or national contexts usually imply that the ethnography is better understood as documentary proof of political inequality than as a record of ethnologically pertinent observations (see COLONIALISM, POSTCOLONIALISM). Emphasis on the personal experiences of anthropologists turns attention away from actual ethnographic data. Other theorists castigate earlier generations of anthropologists for being insufficiently aware of how theory-laden their ethnographic facts were (see INTERPRETIVE ANTHROPOLOGY).

This is a formidable and broad-based attack on ethnography as a record of fact. One effect of the attack is to have produced a new, ironic meaning for the word "ethnography," to describe a self-consciously and radically subjective literary work that acknowledges the tradition of ethnography as description built on systematic and scientific inquiry only as a tissue of obsolete assumptions. It seems unlikely that anthropology will long be able to sustain both senses of the term.   PW
See also PARTICIPANT–OBSERVATION, QUALITATIVE METHODS

ethnohistory Both "ethnohistory" and the related term "ETHNOLOGY" have his-

torical connotations. The latter initially meant the study of man but, supplanted by "anthropology," came to denote historical analysis of society and custom. After 1900, consensus on what distinguished ethnology evaporated and as it was relegated to the study of material culture, dismissed as conjectural history, or made synonymous with an emergent social or cultural anthropology, ethnohistory appeared. In 1909, Clark Wissler spoke of combining "ethno historical" with archaeological evidence in order to reconstruct prehistoric cultures (Baerreis 1961). For Wissler, "ethno" meant an ethnic group like an American Indian tribe, and evidence was documentary and nonnative in origin.

Wissler's approach – the use of documents to speak about a small-scale society's past – ruled ethnohistory for decades. After mid-century it was reinforced by the institutionalization of ethnohistory and the participation of ethnohistorians in land claims cases. The former occurred in two ways: through the journal *Ethnohistory*, the focus of which in 1955 was on "the documentary history of the culture and movements of primitive peoples, with special emphasis on the American Indian"; and through a succession of academic organizations culminating, in 1966, in the American Society for Ethnohistory. Emphasis on documents was coupled with antipathy toward the historicity of oral traditions, which also had deep roots: Robert LOWIE long ago denigrated oral traditions as history because "we cannot know them to be true" (1915: 598). The journal *Ethnohistory*'s agenda remained Wissler's and its biases (against oral tradition) Lowie's. The emphasis on documentary evidence was also prominent in "applied" ethnohistory for land claims cases brought before the Indian Claims Commission during the 1950s, a legal context privileging documentary not oral sources (Krech 1991).

Defining ethnohistory
Ethnohistorians have been preoccupied with defining their field. Most past definitions have stressed the eclectic use of data obtained in the field, archive, and museum, and the combination of the skills of the historian and the anthropologist. It was assumed that history contributed a concern

for accuracy, anthropology an interest in generalization and culture theory. Ideally, methodological skills and intellectual forces fused in the ethnohistorian, who thereby wrote a fully balanced or "rounded" history of a particular society, which, perhaps, brought understanding of cultural change or persistence (Axtell 1981b; Ewers 1961; Lurie 1961; W. Washburn 1961). William C. Sturtevant offered one of the most influential and lasting definitions of ethnohistory: "(the study of) the history of the peoples normally studied by anthropologists" (1966: 6–7).

But anthropology (and history) have changed. At the time Sturtevant wrote, conventional anthropology focused mainly on remote, exotic people and presumed that explanation required theory, typology, and generalization; in contrast, conventional history dealt primarily with Western people and unique or particular events, and favored narrative over explicit generalization. Today, those conventions no longer hold. Not just theory has changed. Anthropologists are as likely to study Westerners as exotic people (who daily become less so), and historians increasingly work on history from below (B. Cohn 1987). But there is no consensus that both write ethnohistory.

Moreover, the "ethno-" in "ethnohistory" has become problematic because it excludes certain people. "Ethno-" betrays its classical roots: *ethnos* ("nation," in Greek) was applied to tribal people and barbarians. Today, it has not shaken its tribal or pagan referent: tribal groups have ethnohistory, "minority" groups may have it, but rarely do majority groups. In practice, ethnohistory has been exclusionary (Krech 1991).

A definition and name (anthropological history) for today

The dilemma has become more acute since 1980 because of the extraordinarily active play between anthropology and history. Why reserve a special name for the history of ethnic groups whose cultural distance from the typical historian is greatest, or for those in which anthropologists traditionally had stated vested interests? The solution may be to take the "ethno-" out of "ethnohistory" and use instead the label "anthropological history": *history* is being done, and the decision that an anthropological analysis is also historical (or vice versa) should be straightforward. As for a definition, anthropological history, at its heart, as with ethnohistory, is the combination of method and theory current in history and anthropology, and the focus on history or historiography in or of some ethnic group.

Types of anthropological history

The principal products of anthropological history (ethnohistory) have most often been called "historical ethnography," "specific history," and "folk history" or "ethno-ethnohistory." Historical ethnography is a timeless or synchronic reconstruction of a culture or society at some past time. Specific history is diachronic historical study of a specific society or ethnic group written either from the earliest to most recent moment in time (a "downstream" direction) or, using direct historical method, from the present to the past ("upstream"). Conceptualized "downstream" specific history is often a traditional narrative history of events in the past of a tribe or other ethnic group. "Folk history," which Raymond Fogelson (1989: 134) called "ethno-ethnohistory," amounts to historiography as conceptualized by people in a particular, usually nonliterate, society. This is "ethnohistory" cognate with other "ethno-" terms such as "ETHNOBOTANY" and "ETHNOSCIENCE."

Since 1980, the interest in ethno-ethnohistory or folk history has escalated. In addition to Fogelson, Richard Price (1983) has led the way with his analysis of the presentist, fragmented, guarded historical thought of the Saramaka. Others have recently investigated the historical thought of indigenous people – the culturally specific ways of "knowing" or "making history" – and have been concerned with presentist history, how to capture an "authentic" native voice in colonial texts, and related issues. Much of this work is reflexive: to decipher historical thought, one must appreciate how history and narrative are produced, the perspectival and contested nature of histories, and invented tradition (Bruner 1986; Dening 1988; Hobsbawm & Ranger 1983). Marshall

Sahlins's (1985) related work, which emphasizes conflicting interests in particular structures of conjunctures, and hypothesizes that cultural structure may be open or closed to history – each ordering the other – has influenced many for whom culture, ideationally conceptualized as symbolic system or text, or in some manner structured, holds center stage in historical analysis.

The specific history written as a "downstream" narrative is the most common form of anthropological history. Usually, it is driven by data not theory, relies on documents not oral testimony, assumes that a descriptive chronological narrative is awaiting "release" from the archives, and is sensitive to native culture not perspective. It offers a people's history not historiography. Some narratives soar as sensitive explorations of culture and motivations but consider theory as intrusive (Peires 1989); others are marked by strong narrative style, careful weighing of evidence, and unpretentious engagement with theory (Merrell 1989; Axtell 1985).

Other specific histories (and non-narrative forms of anthropological history) are driven by interest in the historical analysis of social and cultural processes linking societies in an interconnected political economy that is world-historical or world-systemic in scope (E. Wolf 1982). Their language reveals a collective preoccupation with ecology, DEMOGRAPHY, mercantilism, WORLD-SYSTEMS, political economy, COLONIALISM, modes and relations of production, commoditization, and the like (Netting 1981; R. White 1983; Cronon 1983). The analyses are materialist, positivist, and implicitly or explicitly comparative. Some pay more attention than others to agency and oppositions to colonial relationships; to how local CULTURE mediates or structures outside forces, or human AGENCY overrides systemic POWER. These anthropological historians are writing not histories of the West's impact on the non-West but histories *of* the non-West: indigenous people are put as active agents into histories they help make (Jean Comaroff 1985; Sahlins 1995).

The future

Ethnohistorians once helped bridge anthropology and history at a time when anthropology largely ignored history and history paid no attention to small-scale, indigenous societies. Although the label "ethnohistory" may today be suspect, its methodology is not. Renamed "anthropological history," the methodology involves, as it always has, the combination of method and theory current in history and anthropology, and the focus on history or historiography in or of some ethnic group. The degree to which anthropological historians engage theory and structure history as narrative remains a matter of disciplinary preference – anthropologists tend to remain comparative, explicit, and analytic, historians tend to consign theory to endnotes and still privilege narrative – but each year there are new exceptions. There is no reason to think that ethnohistory, as anthropological history, will not continue to flourish.

SK

See also HISTORY AND ANTHROPOLOGY

ethnology *See* ETHNOGRAPHY AND ETHNOLOGY

ethnomusicology is the anthropological study of MUSIC as a culture-specific phenomenon and a universal aspect of human social behavior (see Merriam 1964; Nettl 1983). Sometimes classified as the musicology of "non-Western" or "ethnic" music, contemporary ethnomusicology is in theoretical and methodological terms more accurately regarded as a specialized branch of cultural anthropology, broadly parallel to ETHNOBOTANY, ethnopoetics, or ethnosemantics.

The range of topics investigated by ethnomusicologists includes the acoustic properties of musical sound, cognitive and somatic processes involved in music making, the physical construction of instruments, the social status of musicians, relationships between musical style and identity, and the economic structure of the recording industry. In conceptual terms, ethnomusicology is unified around a set of fundamental questions: Are there shared cognitive structures that underlie the creation and perception of music in all societies? How is music related to identity, and to the emotions? What is the relationship between music and other forms of expression, such as language and dance? What are the relationships between musical patterns and social organization?

Throughout its history, ethnomusicology has been energized by a dialectical tension between relativism – the idea that music must in the first instance be understood in emic or "native" terms – and cross-cultural or inter-musical comparison. As early as the eighteenth century, Jean-Jacques Rousseau (1768) used examples of American Indian, Chinese, Persian, and Swiss songs to support his argument that the "great effects of sounds on the human heart" were based not upon the physical laws of acoustics – as was widely believed at the time – but rather upon music's role as a culture-specific "commemorative sign." A century later, the English linguist and physicist Alexander J. Ellis, who conducted pioneering research into the organization of non-Western pitch systems, concluded that "the Musical Scale is not one, not 'natural', nor even founded necessarily on the laws of the constitution of musical sound . . . but very diverse, very artificial, and very capricious" (Ellis 1885). Ellis provided empirical confirmation of Rousseau's argument that musical processes are in large degree determined by culture rather than the physics of sound.

These comparative insights into the differences among musical systems informed the work of the scholars who established comparative musicology (*vergleichende Musikwissenschaft*) as an academic discipline. Working at the Berlin Phonogram-Archiv (founded 1900), Erich von Hornbostel and his colleagues analyzed gramophone recordings collected by scholars, missionaries, and colonial administrators, and their publications focused mainly on the description of tonal systems, classification of musical instruments, and the implications of musical data for the study of cultural diffusion. It is interesting to note that the very technology that made detailed comparison possible – the gramophone, invented in 1877 – was also responsible for the separation of musical sound from the social and cultural grounds of its existence (this is still an important issue in ethnomusicology, especially in the study of

mass-mediated popular music and "field recordings"; see Keil & Feld 1994: 247–89).

The adoption of ethnographic FIELD-WORK as a preferred method – and the opportunity to observe music making in cultural context – led during the early twentieth century to a rethinking of older comparative approaches. In his work on Pueblo music, Benjamin Ives Gilman (1908) went so far as to question the cross-cultural validity of the European concept of musical "scales" (Ellingson 1992: 123–5). Other scholars broadened the focus of musical analysis to include parameters such as rhythm, tempo, timbre ("tone-color"), and song texts (Densmore 1918), while others developed musical analogs of the anthropological notion of CULTURE AREAS (Herzog 1936: H. Roberts 1936).

Since the Second World War many ethnomusicologists, critical of earlier modes of cross-cultural comparison, have focused on ethnographic research. Although some of these publications attempt to describe music cultures as whole systems (McAllester 1954; Merriam 1967; Seeger 1990; Nettl 1989), the general trend has been toward studies focused on specific theoretical problems, such as the role of music in healing practices (Roseman 1991; Friedson 1996), emic CLASSIFICATIONS of music and musicians (Ames & King 1971; Sakata 1983), the cultural role of instruments (Berliner 1978), the SOCIAL ORGA-NIZATION of musicians (Neuman 1980), interactions between music and LANGUAGE (Agawu 1995), and the relationship of musical aesthetics, values, and social power (Chernoff 1979; Feld 1982; Keil 1979). Expanding earlier definitions of the field as the study of "ethnic music," ethnomusicology today includes within its purview the study of popular music (Guilbault 1993; Manuel 1993; Walser 1993), the music of migrant populations (Turino 1992; Erlmann 1995), and the ethnography of classical music conservatories (Kingsbury 1988; Nettl 1995).

Despite this overall predominance of particularistic studies, comparison has remained an important goal for ethnomusicologists. The most influential comparative scheme of the last 30 years is Alan

Lomax's Cantometrics project (Lomax 1968), which draws conclusions about the relationship of song style, cultural values, and social organization from statistical correlations. Although the statistical procedures and theoretical assumptions underlying Cantometrics have been criticized, recent attempts to develop a comparative "sociomusicology" informed by SYMBOLIC ANTHROPOLOGY, cultural studies, and ECOLOGICAL ANTHROPOLOGY (Keil & Feld 1994) explicitly recognize Lomax's work as a source of inspiration.

One of the central methodological issues in contemporary ethnomusicology is the epistemological status of the researcher's own musical experience. Beginning in the late 1950s, Mantle Hood championed the first-hand study of music as an avenue to "bi-musicality" (competence in two or more musical systems). This idea had a great impact on ethnomusicology in the 1960s and 1970s and led to the introduction of university courses in "world music," often taught by visiting artists. Although it is clear that performance is not always a privileged means of accessing other people's subjective musical experience, recent work on the phenomenology of ethnomusicological research (T. Rice 1994) suggests that the means by which a researcher learns to perform and interpret music is itself a process worthy of analytic attention.

In recent years issues of musical ownership, the ethics of fieldwork, and the politics of ethnomusicological representation (including sound and video recordings as well as textual documents) have provided new foci for discussion and debate. Struggling to rethink their techniques and theories in an era characterized by massive shifts in the global circulation of music, ethnomusicologists maintain their long-standing dual fascination with the diversity and universality of human musical expression.   CW
See also DANCE

ethnopoetry   *See* POETRY

ethnopsychology   is the study of indigenous theories of psychological structure and dynamics. It is the direct and most recent descendant of ETHNOSCIENCE, and, like its predecessor, generally relies on detailed linguistic analysis of native categories to gain insight into "the way they think they think." But whereas ethnoscience formally sorted responses to specific questions about categories into abstract taxonomies, often far removed from daily life, practitioners of ethnopsychology concentrate their attention on natural DISCOURSE and NARRATIVE. Major influences include Lakoff and Johnson's (1980) work on the metaphors and metonyms used for conceptualizing emotion and Roy D'Andrade's (1985, 1987) efforts to develop culturally constructed "schemas" for the working of the mind.

Along with the technical inspirations offered by linguistics and cognitive anthropology, ethnopsychology is clearly in debt to the Boasian anthropology of Ruth BENEDICT and Margaret MEAD, as well as the INTERPRETIVE ANTHROPOLOGY whose main representative is Clifford GEERTZ. Also often mentioned is Robert Levy (1984), who was one of the first to elicit native categories of thought. But perhaps most cited as exemplary are A. I. Hallowell's extensive and detailed phenomenological accounts of the subjective worldview of the Salteaux (for a characteristic example, see Hallowell 1960a).

All studies of ethnopsychology rest on two premises. The first is that what investigators have painstakingly collected from native narratives and discourse are not simply fragmented bits of contradictory folk wisdom, but rather constitute a deep, coherent, and organized pattern that can be convincingly reconstructed by the fieldworker (Kirkpatrick & White 1985). The second is that the cultural models so reconstructed serve as "vital understandings" that guide, orient, and direct action, constructing and constraining ordinary knowledge and experience in a particular cultural world (Quinn & Holland 1987: 12).

True to the roots in interpretive anthropology, the ethnopsychologists' project also often assumes that each culture has its own unique and irreducible way of experiencing the world (though this addendum does not necessarily follow from the first premises of the discipline), and many authors argue as well that Western theories of the mind and emotion are no more valid and no less culturally constructed than those posited by any other indigenous psychology. This orientation can become a critique of a presumed Western egocentricism in the light of the supposedly sociocentric views held in other cultures.

For example, Catherine Lutz (1985, 1988) argued that the "sociocentric" people of Ifaluk in the South Pacific have their own specific mental–emotional indigenous psychology that differs radically from that of the West in several important ways. The Ifaluk are said to unite feeling and thought into one single construct, and to emphasize will and control, so that Ifaluk are able to consciously choose to completely hide (as opposed to unconsciously repress) socially disruptive expressions of anger and irritation. The Ifaluk are also said to experience and cognitively construct specific emotional–mental states such *fago*, which is a combination of compassion, nurturant love, and sadness. Most importantly, in contrast to the West, the Ifaluk experience feeling not as arising from spontaneous and personal internal impulse, but rather as a natural result of prototypical social situations and relationships. Thus, an Ifaluk woman says: "I *fago* you because you give me things . . . If I take care of you, give you things, and talk to you, I'll know you *fago* me" (Lutz 1988: 139).

Although Lutz's work, and that of other ethnopsychologists, has produced interesting results, it remains vulnerable to the criticism that the indigenous models of psychology are a construct of the elicitation procedures used by the researcher and, perhaps, of the ethnographer's own attempt to create coherence (Keesing 1987). Furthermore, even if a coherent cultural indigenous psychology exists, can it actually account for the full range of psychological reality? Perhaps, as Gerber argued, "the cultural conceptual system may not express all phenomenological aspects of complex inner events, or may even serve to mask them" (1985: 159). Thus, by privileging the local account of emotional–psychological structures, ethnopsychology may be closing the door to cross-cultural

comparison, while also assuming that people are completely conscious, and in control, of their own mental lives – an assumption deeply questionable in the light of the work of DURKHEIM and Freud. Finally, ethnopsychology, like ethnoscience, may have a tendency to be ahistorical and insensitive to the nuances of context and conflict, privileging description of an abstract model over process, agency, and interest (see A. Howard 1985). However, despite caveats, ethnopsychology has proven invaluable in revealing "the conceptual system (that) serves as a model for proper feeling, shaping an emotional basis for the development of morally valued action" (Gerber 1985: 159).   CL

further reading Caws 1974; Fogelson 1982; Heelas & Lock 1981; Randall 1976; M. Rosaldo 1984; E. Schieffelin 1976; Spiro 1984

ethnoscience is a set of ethnographic methodologies used to record the knowledge systems of a given community from an EMIC perspective. It first gained popularity among cognitive anthropologists in the early 1960s as a way of referring to the knowledge systems of a community as well as the methodologies for recording these systems (Werner & Schoepfle 1987). Werner (1972) referred to ethnoscience as the ethnography and ethnology of knowledge or descriptive epistemology. He differentiated ethnographic ethnoscience (cultural knowledge accessible through a language, such as CLASSIFICATION systems for cultural domains, like ethnoanatomy or ETHNOBOTANY) from ethnological ethnoscience (theoretical and comparative studies seeking to formulate universal laws of knowledge). Ethnoscience focuses on cultural knowledge as a means of explaining cultural behavior from an emic perspective. "Ethnoscience" has also been used interchangeably with the "NEW ETHNOGRAPHY," referring to a set of ethnographic methods (Sturtevant 1964: 123).

The roots of ethnoscience can be traced to anthropologists such as Franz BOAS, Bronislaw MALINOWSKI and Benjamin Whorf, who attempted to understand culture from the insider's perspective, and who explored the interrelationships among language, culture, and cognition (Ervin 1964; Voegelin & Voegelin 1966). Ethnoscience began to take shape when Ward Goodenough (1957: 167) defined CULTURE cognitively as systems of knowledge:

A society's culture consists of whatever it is one has to know or believe in order to operate in a manner acceptable to its members. Culture is not a material phenomenon; it does not consist of things, behavior, or emotions. It is rather an organization of these things. It is the form of things that people have in mind, their models for perceiving, relating, and otherwise interpreting them.

Ethnoscience was influenced by structural linguists such as Kenneth Pike (1954), who coined the terms emic and etic, which are used by ethnoscientists to refer to the insider's and outsider's perspectives on a culture, respectively. Noam Chomsky (1965) also influenced ethnoscience, with TRANSFORMATIONAL GRAMMAR. Chomsky hypothesized that the infinite variety of verbalizations (surface structure) was based on a finite number of transformational rules (deep structure) carried unconsciously by members of a speech community. As in transformational linguistics, anthropologists embarking upon ethnoscientific studies in the newly emerging subfield of COGNITIVE ANTHROPOLOGY sought to understand the cultural competence within a community that influenced actual cultural performance (Tyler 1969). Culture was viewed as a set of rules that a community used unconsciously to determine appropriate behavior (Frake 1962a; Hymes 1964a; Murray 1982).

Ethnoscientists worked through the local language to understand how phenomena were classified. A new lexicon emerged. "Cognitive maps" organized as "taxonomies," "paradigms," and "tree diagrams" were comprised of "lexemes" that could be distinguished semantically through COMPONENTIAL ANALYSIS of their "semantic attributes," "features," or "components" (Burling 1964, 1969; Goodenough 1967).

There have been three distinct phases during the several decades that ethnoscience has played a role in ethnographic studies. The first focused on the development of a set of methodologies and techniques that allowed the ethnographer to record from an emic perspective various domains of knowledge within a community. The number of these ethnographic ethnoscience studies is enormous and spans the spectrum of topics for which a community defines, categorizes, and classifies phenomena in the social world (such as DESCRIPTIVE KINSHIP SYSTEMS), the ideational world (such as aesthetic systems), and the natural world (such as botanical and zoological systems) (Frake 1962b; Spradley 1970, 1972b).

As the number of studies expanded, other scholars began to focus on ethnological ethnoscience, comparative analyses seeking to identify apparent universal cognitive traits, such as the range of types of semantic relationship expressed through a language (Casagrande & Hale 1967). The classic cross-cultural study of color classification systems (Berlin & Kay 1969) led to new insights into universal characteristics of color categories. Berlin (1992) discovered that many ethnobiological systems have striking similarities to Linnaean taxonomic systems.

The third phase, which has emerged since 1980, is the interest in the role of indigenous knowledge systems in facilitating sustainable approaches to development (Brokensha et al. 1980; D. Warren 1991). Emerging from development or applied anthropology, the term "indigenous knowledge" was used to differentiate community-based knowledge systems from their counterpart global systems (Mathias-Mundy & McCorkle 1989; D. Warren et al. 1989). The way in which Yoruba farmers categorize and classify soils in Nigeria, for example, may differ in important ways from the soil science taxonomy taught in agronomy courses (D. Warren 1991). This has important communications implications for development practitioners expected to work with community members in participatory approaches to development.   DW

further reading Berlin et al. 1974; D'Andrade 1995; Hunn 1977; D. Warren 1990; D. Warren et al. 1995

ethnozoology is the study of "folk" zoology, or the taxonomic categories societies recognize. Alfred R. Wallace (1853) long ago observed that local taxonomies were often more precise than those of the natural historians, but his hint has seldom been noted. In studying classifications, anthropologists have emphasized exploration of the predicates underlying CLASSIFICATION systems and – under the heading of TOTEMISM – the widespread presumption of a special relationship between humans and ANIMALS.

Unilinear evolutionists posited three stages of human evolution, beginning with a "totemic" stage in which humans believed themselves descended from animals; thus, totemism had its origins as both religion and social institution. DURKHEIM (1915) later suggested that the two were inextricably intertwined. Freud (1918), RIVERS (1914b), BOAS (1914), MALINOWSKI (1948), and RADCLIFFE-BROWN (1930) speculated about totemic impulses among "primitives" in more empirically or functionally oriented ways. Later, Claude LÉVI-STRAUSS (1963b) asserted that totemism was a universal human thought process.

Recent debates identify three thrusts of classification studies:

(1) *naturalist*: animals have salient features that group together "naturally" (e.g., fur or feathers). This is confounded by such a classification as "charcoal animals" in which bears, eagles, deer, and swans are classed together because all have dark "tips" or extremities (Lévi-Strauss 1966: 147).

(2) *idealist*: symbolic systems are based on universally intelligible (or logical) principles.

(3) *constructivist*: classifications have their origin in (human) efforts to organize experience, and society arises through/from the meanings assigned in that classificatory process; thus it is expected that patterns of classification will be culturally unique.

ES

See also STRUCTURALISM

further reading M. Douglas & Hull 1992; R. Willis 1990

ethology is the biological study of behavior and its explanations address the four whys of biology: mechanism, phylogeny, ontogeny, and function (Tinbergen 1963).

Although its origins can be traced to Darwin's *The expression of emotions in man and animals* (1872), and through early researchers such as Heinroth, Huxley, and Whitman in the first part of the twentieth century, ethology developed primarily in Europe in the 1930s in response to American behaviorism, which was the dominant perspective on the study of behavior at the time. In contrast to behaviorism, with its emphasis on elucidating mechanisms of learning and memory through tightly controlled laboratory studies, the European ethological tradition stressed the consideration of behavior in relation to the animal's natural context. Under the leadership of Tinbergen (1951), Lorenz (1952), von Frisch, and Thorpe (1956), the period directly following World War II witnessed the flowering of what has been called the age of classical ethology.

The first ethologists were broadly trained zoologists, and the influence of their background was evident from the outset. Burghardt (1973) distinguished five features of the "ethological attitude" toward the study of behavior: (1) the study of ecologically meaningful behavioral patterns, (2) the foundation in descriptive studies, (3) the comparison of many behaviors across multiple species, (4) the comparison of similar behaviors in closely related species, and (5) a disdain for the exclusive use of domesticated animals.

Ethology is distinguished from its sister discipline behavioral ecology (or SOCIOBIOLOGY) primarily by the source of its hypotheses. Ethology is fundamentally an inductive enterprise (Tinbergen 1963). Hypotheses regarding the function of a given behavior are derived from careful observation of an animal, usually in its naturalistic context. Behavioral ecology, on the other hand, takes a more deductive approach to the study of behavior, characterized by tests of specific predictions derived from the theory of natural selection and the use of formal models such as game theory (J. Krebs & Davies 1993). Given the broad definition of ethology, behavioral ecology can be thought of as the area of ethology specifically concerned with functional aspects of behavior (G. Barlow 1990).

Early on, ethology became associated with the study of instinct, a poorly defined term roughly meaning "genetically determined" behavior (Tinbergen 1951). This approach drew considerable criticism, particularly from North American comparative psychologists. For example, Lehrman (1953) charged that ethologists, by focusing on instinct, had inappropriately dichotomized innate and learned behavior. This criticism was fundamental to Tinbergen's (1963) addition of ontogeny to the existing research foci of mechanism, phylogeny, and function previously proposed by Huxley (1942). This led to the integration of comparative psychology and ethology by Hinde (1966), whose synthetic work developed the concept of ontogeny as the process by which behavioral phenotypes become expressed through the complex dialectic of genotype and environment. Hinde's work led to the realization that specific learning processes were themselves subject to natural selection (G. Barlow 1989), a dynamic that J. Gould and P. Marler (1987) described as "learning by instinct." This approach has been particularly productive in work on human LANGUAGE acquisition (Pinker 1991, 1994).

Ethology had tremendous influence in anthropology in the early field studies of nonhuman primates (Kummer 1971) and in later studies on foraging human groups (Lee & DeVore 1976; R. Bailey & DeVore 1989). Most current ethological fieldwork on humans is being undertaken explicitly within the context of behavioral ecology; that is, it focuses on functional aspects of behavior such as strategies for reproductive success (Borgerhoff Mulder 1990), finding food (K. Hawkes 1991), or both (Kaplan & Hill 1985). However, recent advances in comparative biology (Brooks & McLennan 1991) have encouraged researchers to integrate their studies of particular behaviors into broader theories about their origin and evolution (phylogeny), including the vocalization (Hauser 1993) and estrous cycles (Pagel 1994).

Ethology has sparked both wide interest and controversy, as documented in Thorpe's (1979) history of the field, and human ethology in particular has attracted surveys that reach out to a broader audience. These surveys include Eibl-Eibesfeldt's (1989) more classical approach to human ethology and J. Archer's (1992) work on the links between ethology and human development.   JJO

further reading Borgerhoff Mulder 1991; Hinde 1982; Eric Smith 1992; Eric Smith & Winterhalder 1992

etic   *See* EMIC AND ETIC

eugenics   is a highly contested and protean concept defined by Francis Galton (a cousin of Charles Darwin) as "the science of improving stock, which is by no means confined to questions of judicious mating, but which . . . takes cognisance of all influences that tend in however remote degree to give the more suitable races or strains of blood a better chance of prevailing speedily over the less suitable" (1883: 24). While today there is near-consensus that eugenics (derived from the Greek *eugenes*, "good in birth") is bad, like RACISM there is little agreement on what it means.

From studies of eminent British families, Galton had concluded that virtually all mental and moral traits were passed from parent to offspring – and that the worthiest individuals were producing the fewest children. To counter what he saw as a catastrophic trend, Galton proposed extending animal breeders' methods to his own species. Humans should take charge of their own evolution, with those highest in "civic worth" encouraged to have more children ("positive" eugenics) and the stupid and reckless discouraged from having any ("negative" eugenics).

Galton was not the first to suggest that matings be controlled in the interest of improving the human race. In Plato's Republic, which provided the inspiration for many later utopias, rulers decided who would bear how many children. But Galton's proposal was the first to prompt a social movement.

That movement took quite different forms in different countries (M. Adams 1990). Religion, scientific tradition, and degree of racial mixing affected whether the outlook of these movements was hopeful or harsh. In Catholic countries with Lamarckian views of heredity and a high degree of race mixing (such as France and Brazil), hereditary and environmental improvements were thought to go hand-in-hand (W. Schneider 1990; Stepan 1991). In Britain, the United States, Scandinavia, and Germany, however, eugenicists tended to disparage the value of environmental reform and to view the poor as irremediably unfit. In the United States and Germany, ethnic minorities were also added to this danger list.

However, even in the latter countries, eugenics movements were considerably more diverse than historians once assumed. Most eugenicists were politically conservative and socially pessimistic. But the movement also appealed to a wide range of reformers. Eugenicists were found on every side of arguments about the value of CAPITALISM, WAR, and especially WOMEN's ROLES. While conservatives employed eugenic arguments to justify restrictions on contraception, suffrage, and educational opportunities for women, social radicals employed other eugenic arguments to attack them. Some eugenicists asserted that war would strengthen the RACE while others denounced it, arguing that modern warfare sacrificed the healthiest and bravest men (Crook 1994). Although most eugenicists defended capitalism, radicals argued that only in a classless society would it be possible to separate innate genetic worth from environmental good fortune (D. Paul 1984). Policies advanced under the banner of eugenics ranged from propaganda, tax breaks, advocacy of birth control, and "free love" to segregation and sterilization of the "feebleminded," immigration restriction, and, at its most extreme, to the Nazi *Lebensborn* ("well-of-life") and extermination programs.

In the first few decades of the twentieth century eugenics enjoyed widespread support. By 1910, it was already one of the most frequently referenced topics in the *Reader's guide to periodical literature* (Reilly 1991: 18). The message that good breeding was everyone's business was relayed in college and even high-school textbooks, popular magazines, church services, and films.

Apart from the Catholic Church and Britain's Labour Party, there was little organized opposition before World War II, although objections were sometimes raised to specific policies. Leading geneticists such as Charles Davenport and Edward M. East, and physical anthropologists such as Earnest Hooton and Ales Hrdlicka, were enthusiastic supporters. Eugenics was endorsed by every member of the editorial board of the American journal *Genetics*, founded in 1916 (Ludmerer 1972: 34). In interwar Germany, where the science of human genetics was particularly advanced, support was near-universal (Harwood 1989). Even those who denounced one or another aspect of eugenics rarely rejected it wholesale. That the state had a legitimate interest in who reproduced was simply taken for granted. In the United States, no scholar is more (correctly) associated with skepticism toward eugenics than Franz BOAS. But even he thought it proper to "suppress those defective classes whose deficiencies can be proved by rigid methods to be due to hereditary causes, and to prevent unions that will unavoidably lead to the birth of disease stricken progeny" (1916: 478).

Ideas such as eugenics that once seemed simple common sense are today no longer considered respectable. That change is largely explained by the convergence of various social trends; in particular, the rise of the women's movement, the trend toward respect for individual rights, and the development of a broad jurisprudence of privacy and reproductive freedom (D. Paul 1992: 676–79). By the 1960s, the principle of reproductive autonomy was widely accepted – and "eugenics" transformed from a term of praise to one of derision. Yet the issues that were the focus of eugenics have changed, not disappeared. The question of whether prenatal tests represent a new eugenics is particularly charged. Those who favor the expansion of testing tend to argue that only coercive programs deserve to be labeled "eugenics"; but for many critics it encompasses policies that increase our ability to choose the kind of children we want (Duster 1990).   DBP

further reading Kevles 1985; J. Marks 1995; Mueller-Hill 1988; D. Paul 1995

Evans-Pritchard, E. E. (1902–73)

Edward Evans-Pritchard was born in Sussex, England, in 1902. From 1946 to 1970 he was Professor of Social Anthropology at Oxford, where he attracted at various times such major figures as Lienhardt, Beattie, Pocock, Dumont, Needham, Douglas, and Beidelman. He died in 1973. Apart from his numerous books (described below) and articles, many of which were drafts for chapters, he coedited with Meyer Fortes, with mixed results, a volume on *African political systems* (1940).

At Oxford in the 1960s Evans-Pritchard encouraged interest in MAUSS, Hubert, and HERTZ, promoting a style of analytic thought that remains important. His students displayed great interest in the philosophical side of DURKHEIM's work, very little in Durkheim's FUNCTIONALISM. Most adopted Evans-Pritchard's later position, in contrast to RADCLIFFE-BROWN, that anthropology's place is with the humanities, such as history, not with imitations of natural science, and that "theory" too often is a substitute for thought (Evans-Pritchard 1964). When STRUCTURALISM arrived, many found affinities with Evans-Pritchard's interests. Affinities may also be found with the philosopher of history R. G. Collingwood.

Evans-Pritchard attended MALINOW-SKI's seminars in the 1920s, but Malinowski and he very soon fell out. The debts he acknowledged were mainly to the *Année sociologique*, and to W. Robertson SMITH. In lectures, printed posthumously, he found particular merit in thinkers of the Scottish and French enlightenments (Evans-Pritchard 1981).

From 1926 to 1936 Evans-Pritchard worked in Sudan, primarily with the Azande, though also, for shorter periods, with the Anuak and famously the Nuer, where political conditions were appalling (D. Johnson 1982). He also taught in Cairo. At the outbreak of World War II he led Anuak troops against the Italians on the border of Abyssinia (Ethiopia). Later he was posted to Lebanon, later still to Libya. One characterization, reworked through the years, was that of traveler, raconteur, casual pistol-shot(!), and determined drinker; but he was intellectually and mor-

ally a complex person, and the complexities increased with age. Around him clustered many anecdotes.

From his Libyan experience he wrote *The Sanusi of Cyrenaica* (1949). As anthropology it fails: the Arab tribes of Libya are sketched on the model of the very different (southern Sudanese) Nuer and reduced, along with all local history, to a backdrop for the Sanusi family of Islamic scholars. As political manifesto the book worked. The fledgling United Nations sanctioned an independent Libya with the head of the Sanusi Order as king. Evans-Pritchard's advocacy had perhaps more effect than usually falls to anthropologists. His academic reputation, however, rests mainly on analyses of southern (non-Muslim) Sudan.

Faced with apparently "irrational" beliefs such as WITCHCRAFT, anthropologists offered two replies. First, it was useful (the functionalist answer). Second, it made intellectual sense. This second answer was Evans-Pritchard's. Stressing everyday practice, he argued that, given a few simple premises, the Azande's world of witchcraft was one in which sensible people acted with intellectual rigor. His arguments, decades later, attracted philosophers of science. Several key points are made in *Witchcraft, oracles and magic among the Azande* (1937: 5, 8):

> I have always asked myself "How?", rather than "Why?" ... My interpretations are [therefore] contained in the facts themselves, for I have described the facts in such a way that the interpretations emerge as part of the description. My aim has been to make a number of English terms stand for Zande notions and to use the same term only and always when the same notion is being discussed.

The weakness of the book, in retrospect, is its lack of historical awareness, for a hierarchy of knowledge, apparent in the use of oracles, belies the fact that colonial administration had broken the Zande polity.

The Nuer (1940), Evans-Pritchard's most widely read book, deals with pastoral groups that denied any settled leadership yet plainly formed a moral world. The book compromises two sections, one on ecology, one on the lineage and tribal system, linked by a chapter on time-reckoning. Some would read the last part of the book in terms of a balance of power. The more productive reading sees "opposition" as an abstract relation informing how the Nuer saw the world and their place within it. A relation of this kind may be "expressed" by events as different as feud and marriage. The analysis is explanatory, not predictive.

Nuer religion (1956) stands by itself but also develops the early work. The Nuer care for distinction and separation recurs in contexts as seemingly different as blood FEUD, territory, marriage, and the relation of spirit (*kwoth*) to creation. Collapse of distinctions threatens the moral order. The leopard-skin chief, or earth priest, who appeared in *The Nuer* as a mediator, appears here as the manager of such distinction, and his opposite, the Prophet, as the seeker after ideal union. Evans-Pritchard's own religious interests (in the 1940s he entered the Cathololic Church) color the book heavily, but Nuer statements are carefully left intact.

Consider his exposition, which takes up Levy-Bruhl (1926), of a Nuer statement that "Twins are birds." Twins in the Nuer view are extraordinary; the extraordinary is *kwoth*; *kwoth* is associated with the above; and birds, of the above, are *kwoth*'s children. The reader is even shown why twins were often named after particular types of bird. Each Nuer statement or action is carefully linked to others, while unsecured interpretation (too common now in anthropology) is minimized. There is no need for a mysterious "Nuer culture."

Kinship and marriage among the Nuer (1951) is a technical work, analyzing in effect what counts as "INCEST." Again the analysis is not predictive but explanatory, allowing one to follow Nuer arguments. These works have been reanalyzed many times. The careful style of exposition means one can disagree with Evans-Pritchard and arrive, from his own material, at views other than his own. Such openness remains the test of good ethnography.   PD

further reading Beidelman 1974a; J. Burton 1992; M. Douglas 1980

evil may first be defined as SUFFERING inflicted by one human on another, especially when the perpetrator enjoys causing harm. Such malice and destructiveness among fellow humans may be called moral evil, for such acts are morally judged. We also speak of the metaphysical evil of pestilence and plague, of poverty and famine, and of ignorance and disease, explaining it as harm brought about by nonhuman and sometimes nonliving forces. A third kind of evil is more descriptive and refers to sinister atmospheres and places inducing fear and characteristic of ghost novels of the Edgar Allan Poe kind.

Although we may distinguish analytically between moral, metaphysical, and descriptive evil, with most studies focused on the first two, anthropologists have generally used the term loosely and have approached it from different angles. For example, in his account of the Azande of Central Africa, EVANS-PRITCHARD (1937: 236–9) described WITCHCRAFT as their prototype of evil: certain animals may humorously be regarded as witches and yet admired as well as feared, such as the owl, whose nocturnal habits are associated with cunning and strangeness, or a species of wild cat that causes men's deaths if they see it, since it is associated with lesbianism and can have sex with a woman and produce kittens by her. A person who had cut his upper teeth first is witch-like in bringing bad luck but, being clumsy, does not actually kill like other witches.

The translation of evil through the concept of witchcraft thus covers a spectrum of senses from extreme fear, death, and destruction to lesser misfortunes. It may connote an agent's firm intention to harm, or may originate in an unintended human or nonhuman condition. Evil agents may be abhorrent, but they may also be admired for their cleverness and inspire humor. The clear-cut Western notion of moral evil, which is committed by a known person who must be judged and suffer the consequences of his or her intentional act, is implicit here. But it may be blurred, because in many non-Western societies people can be judged to have unconsciously committed witchcraft when they harbor enough hatred or envy that these EMOTIONS alone unleash a kind of psychic drive causing physical harm.

Such translation is only ever partial, since it is rare to find words in the language of another culture that reflect the English sense precisely. Certain basic ideas do, however, recur as generally sharing some meaning with the English term. Thus, in a number of African Bantu, Amazonian, and Asian languages, some terms translatable as "bad" or "evil" also have a sense of "physically rotten, misshapen, ugly, and dirty" (Parkin 1985: 6–9). Continuing with this metaphysical perspective on evil, Ricoeur (1967: 25–46) regarded it as a primordial kind of defilement or staining of something that was once clean and pure. It connotes a feeling of incompleteness and O'Flaherty (1976: 2) drew attention to a view attributed to Max WEBER (1963) that premature DEATH is perhaps the most evident form of incompleteness (see Parkin 1985: 7–8; Metcalf 1982: 254–7 on "bad deaths"; and Needham 1973 on physical imperfection as sinister). Given the premise in most monotheistic religions that a supreme God should be strong or benevolent enough to prohibit the occurrence of evil death, it is regarded as a paramount evil that needs to be explained. Such explanations are called "theodicies."

A second set of terms found in the languages of other cultures and connoting and roughly translatable as "evil," turn on a sense of excess or over-abundance. The very term "evil" derives from the Teutonic *ubiloz*, the etymology of which reveals a primary sense of "exceeding due measure" or "overstepping the limits." Many peoples in the world believe that too much knowledge is a very bad thing and may cause terrible destruction. This is reflected in the Biblical story where Adam's discovery through Eve of nakedness, sexuality, and mortality could both destroy them and yet allow them to reproduce themselves: the line between abundance and overabundance is, then, culturally a precarious one to maintain.

This suggests another associated sense of "evil," namely that of ambivalent power: a benign force can, through its misuse, cause evil. Middleton (1960) showed how, among the Lugbara of Uganda, a mystical power called *ole* cures and restores when used by acknowledged elders but is maleficent when illicitly used by juniors. Kiernan (1982) showed that ancestors may be seen as noxious, and thereby evil, when they punish affines, but as firm and caring, like parents, when they punish lineal descendants. The Lugbara further describe as bad those persons whose bitter emotions involuntarily harm others, but consider irredeemably evil those who deliberately hire magical specialists to kill good people, suggesting that the graded triad of concepts (good, bad, and evil) is found outside the West when human intentionality is called to account.

Hindu and Buddhist theodicy is not, however, easily understood in terms of current human intentionality. Since one's evil actions may derive from one's karma (itself the result of past deeds committed by transmigrating souls), evil effects can only be reduced by the person's good deeds in the present. Here, the distinction between moral (humanly intentional) and metaphysical evil is difficult to sustain (Obeyesekere 1968).

Similar conundrums exists with regard to questions of a God's omnipotence and benevolence. Some Islamic Sufi movements argue that, since God controls all actions and thoughts, then even evil is created by him. A skeptical, contrary view questions whether God is really so powerful and caring, if he allows evil on the earth. If such questions are more typical of monotheistic societies, then under POLYTHEISM, evil is more likely to be seen as caused by human neglect of ANCESTORS and SPIRITS, by cosmic order caused by transgressions of sexual rules or other prohibitions, or by capricious forces beyond human control.

DP

further reading Beidelman 1981; Boyd 1975; G. Evans 1982; Ling 1962; Nietzsche 1917; Nugent 1983; Taussig 1980; M. Weber 1958

evolution, evolutionism, social (and cultural)

The concept of social evolution is one of the most important in the history of the social sciences. In the nineteenth century the disciplines of sociology and anthropology were greatly devoted to studying the evolution of human societies from their earliest and simplest forms to the present day. Social evolution is today only one among many issues pursued by sociologists and anthropologists, but it remains an important concern nonetheless.

As used by most social evolutionists, "social evolution" refers to social changes that exhibit some sort of directionality or linear sequence. In addition, it is usually thought to involve transformations in the form or type of society or one of its subunits (qualitative change), and not just changes in degree or extent (quantitative change). Theories of social evolution are thus theories that concentrate on identifying and explaining directional sequences of qualitative social change. Many scholars have claimed that an evolutionary theory assumes some sort of teleological unfolding of potentialities that are latent in social life, but this is not so. Many evolutionary theories including most of the recent ones have not rested on this assumption. It has also frequently been assumed that evolutionary theories postulate a rigid sequence of stages through which all societies must move, and that evolutionary theories deny the possibility of regression, or even of long-term steady states, in social life. But these, too, are misconceptions. Most evolutionary theories propose flexible typologies that give to history a certain open-ended quality, and most likewise see social continuity and regression as important social phenomena that, like evolution, cry out for explanation.

Historical development of evolutionary theories

Evolutionary theories of human society emerged with full force in the second half of the nineteenth century. There were many evolutionary social scientists during this time, but space permits discussion of only the most important: Herbert SPENCER, Lewis Henry MORGAN, Edward Burnett TYLOR, and Karl Marx and Friedrich Engels.

Spencer (1876) formulated a general law of evolution that asserted a tendency for all societies to change from a state of incoherent homogeneity to a state of coherent heterogeneity – that is, a tendency for phenomena to undergo increasing differentiation. Spencer identified four evolutionary types of human society: simple, compound, doubly compound, and trebly compound. These ranged from primitive societies that were politically headless to complex civilizations. Spencer also developed another typology, the military–industrial typology. Military societies were characterized by the subordination of the individual to the social whole, whereas industrial societies are those in which individuals have much greater freedom. In general, Spencer saw an evolutionary movement from the former to the latter.

Morgan developed a different conception of social evolution, which was set forth in his *Ancient society* (1877). He traced out three major "ethnical periods" in human history, Savagery, Barbarism, and Civilization. These are essentially stages of technological development in which humans moved from primitive hunter–gatherers to societies based on complex agriculture and writing. Morgan also examined the evolution of government the family, and property. In his analysis of governmental institutions, to which he devoted great attention, he conceived of two main evolutionary plans of government: *societas* consists of relatively democratic and egalitarian societies that are organized around kinship relations; *civitas*, by contrast, is characterized by property and territory as the integrating principles of society. Social and economic inequalities are widespread, and the state has come into existence.

Tylor (1871) is famous for his use of "survivals" as a basis for demonstrating evolutionary sequences. These are aspects of culture that have been carried into stages of social evolution beyond the one in which they originated. For Tylor, they proved that contemporary stages of culture had evolved from earlier ones. Tylor's evolutionism, much more than Spencer's or Morgan's, concentrated on the evolution of the mental and ideational aspects of social life, especially on religion.

The thinking of Marx and Engels ran in a very different direction from that of Spencer, Morgan, and Tylor. Marx and Engels concentrated on the evolution of MODES OF PRODUCTION in world history. Modes of production were concatenations of forces of production (largely level of technological development) and relations of production (forms of ownership of the productive forces). In *The German ideology* Marx and Engels (1947) identified four basic evolutionary stages, each of which is associated with certain relations of production: primitive communism, slavery, feudalism, and capitalism. After Marx's death Engels developed his own, somewhat different, evolutionary ideas (Engels 1902). He developed two dialectical laws of change, which he referred to as the Law of the Transformation of Quantity into Quality and the Law of the Negation of the Negation. These laws point to the Hegelian notion of the "inner contradictions" of a phenomenon as the engine of its movement from one historical stage to another.

The "golden age" of social evolutionism had basically ended by the 1890s, and after that time a sharp reaction against evolutionary theories emerged. In anthropology this reaction was led by Franz BOAS and his students and disciples and lasted into the 1940s and 1950s. The Boasian school objected to evolutionary theories on four basic counts: the use of an illegitimate methodological device, the COMPARATIVE METHOD; the development of rigid schemes of unilinear evolution in which all societies were assumed to progress in lockstep fashion through the same set of stages; inadequate recognition of the process of DIFFUSION; and the illegitimate equation of evolution with progress (see Sanderson 1990). Nonetheless, by the 1930s the extreme HISTORICAL PARTICULARISM espoused by the Boasian school of anthropology began to be challenged, and an "evolutionary revival" was underway.

The first to lead this revival was the archaeologist V. Gordon Childe (1936, 1951). Emphasizing the broad technological changes characteristic of human prehistory, Childe identified two great technological revolutions that had occurred in several regions of the world. The Neolithic Revolution brought about the domestication of plants and animals. It gave humans the possibility of accumulating economic surpluses, and thus paved the way for the second revolution, which Childe called the "urban revolution." This involved the passage of human societies into a much more complex form character-ized by occupational specialization, cities, sharp class divisions, and the state. Beginning in the 1940s, Leslie WHITE (1943, 1959a) developed a version of social evolutionism similar to Childe's. White insisted that evolutionary theories did not try to explain specific sequences of historical change, but rather focused on the overall movement of human culture as a whole. He formulated a law to explain this general evolution of culture, which stated that culture evolved in proportion to the amount of energy harnessed per capita per year, or by an increase in the efficiency of putting this energy to work. In other words, technological change is the driving force of the evolution of culture. Julian STEWARD, the third important figure in the evolutionary revival, reacted against what he thought were the overly general and excessively simplified evolutionary conceptions of Childe and White, which he called "universal evolution." He proposed instead what he termed "multilinear evolution" (Steward 1955). Multilinear evolution concentrated less on the overall movement of history and more on the different lines along which social evolution moved. Steward granted that there were broad parallels in historical change, but he did not want these overstated. There were still many different lines along which evolution radiated, and these could not be ignored.

Since about 1960, there has been a new wave of important evolutionary work among American anthropologists, most of whom have been greatly influenced by the evolutionism of Childe and White. Marshall Sahlins (1958) wrote an important book on the evolution of social stratification that was inspired by the technological emphasis of Childe and White. He also contributed an important article (Sahlins 1960) that distinguished between general and specific evolution, the former being the overall movement of historical development, the latter the more specific radiation of culture and society along many lines. Elman Service (1962/71) and Robert Carneiro (1970) have also made important contributions to the study of political evolution. Service advanced the typology of "band–tribe–chiefdom–state" to characterize political evolution, a typology that has been widely employed in ethnographic and archaeological research. The evolution from one stage to another is a movement to more hierarchical and complexly integrated political systems. Service's theory is a kind of functionalist one in which new political forms are said to evolve because of their greater functional effectiveness. Carneiro, by contrast, presented a conflict theory to account for the evolution of chiefdoms and states. He saw population pressure and warfare as contributing to the development of more complex political systems in areas that are environmentally circumscribed. As population pressure and warfare increase, people have nowhere to go and ultimately become conquered and subordinated by other groups. As a result, political systems grow increasingly powerful and complex. Gerhard Lenski (1970), a sociologist by training, worked out a well-known theory of social evolution that was largely an extension and elaboration of the ideas of Childe and White. Lenski saw technological expansion as the prime mover of social evolution. As TECHNOLOGY expands, economies become more productive and economic surpluses emerge and expand. These technoeconomic changes ramify throughout social life and lead to major evolutionary transformations. One of Lenski's most important applications of this theory was to the evolution of social stratification.

Marvin HARRIS (1977, 1979) has presented a quite different conception of social evolution. Rather than viewing technology as evolution's driving force, he sees most people throughout history resisting technological change because of the greater costs in human time and energy it requires. What drives social evolution is the tendency of humans to suffer eventual depletions in their standard of living as the result of population pressure and environmental degradation. People must then work harder and longer and eventually advance their technology – that is, they must intensify their production – just to keep their standard of living from falling even lower. But these changes produce yet further (and even greater) depletions, and so the depletion–intensification–depletion process spirals ever forward and upward.

The current situation is a mixed one. In recent years there has been a substantial reaction against general theories of historical change, and many scholars now assume it is only possible to do limited kinds of theorizing about specific historical situations and trajectories. All of this has meant a sharp decline in confidence in any type of evolutionary theory. Indeed, some social scientists have been severely critical of evolutionism (see Sanderson 1990: ch. 9). Nonetheless, many social scientists remain committed to evolutionary analyses and extensive research on social evolution continues. This is especially true in anthropology and its subfield of ARCHAEOLOGY. Archaeology has long been evolutionary, and, although some archaeologists have turned against evolutionism, most probably remain within that camp.

Key issues and debates in the study of social evolution

Perhaps the central issue revolving around the concept of social evolution concerns the degree of directionality that is perceived to exist in human history. Traditional historians have long argued that historical events are unique occurrences that must be explained on their own terms. History reveals no general directional patterns, and therefore, from the historian's perspective, social evolutionists assume the existence of something that does not, in fact, exist. In recent years a number of anthropologists and historically minded sociologists have taken a similar view, and thus they too have become very skeptical of evolutionary theories.

The social evolutionist's response to this is basically to claim what Childe (1951) argued many years ago: if we ignore many details and focus on long periods of prehistory, a number of general directional patterns may be perceived. Contemporary evolutionists would note as the most important of these the Neolithic Revolution, which was associated with the emergence of settled village life based on agriculture and which occurred all over the world beginning around 10,000 years ago, and the rise of civilization and the state, which involved the creation of a radically new kind of society and which occurred all over the world beginning around 5,000 years ago.

Social evolutionists would also go on to argue that the claim made by many critics that evolutionary theories are always unilinear in nature is entirely unwarranted. The nineteenth-century evolutionists did hold a strongly (though not entirely) unilinear view of history, but most contemporary evolutionists give explicit recognition to historical diversity and divergence. As Sahlins did years ago, they acknowledge that social evolution reveals both general and specific outcomes. In Marvin Harris's (1968) terminology, they acknowledge "parallel," "convergent," and "divergent" evolution. Societies not only follow parallel paths, but also converge from different starting points and diverge from similar starting points.

The concept of ADAPTATION is another essential element of evolutionary theories. However, various theories have differed in terms of how they have conceived the unit of adaptation – that is, just what it is that does the adapting. This can be illustrated by way of a comparison of the evolutionary theories of Talcott Parsons (1966, 1971) and Marvin Harris. Parsons used the concept of adaptation in a thoroughly functionalist way. It is always an entire society (or one of its major subsystems) that is doing the adapting, and societies struggle to improve their level of adaptation. Social evolution is a process whereby societies undergo "adaptive ungrading," or an improvement in their level of functioning. In Harris's nonfunctionalist usage, on the other hand, it is individuals rather than entire social systems that do the adapting. Harris made the notion of adaptation a primarily heuristic one. He assumed that particular social arrangements arise from the efforts of individuals to satisfy their various needs and wants. The concept of adaptation is thus a starting point for social analysis, a basis for asking useful questions. Harris rejected Parsons's notion of "adaptive upgrading." New social arrangements are not necessarily adaptively superior to old ones. New arrangements represent responses to changed circumstances, and are adaptive only in terms of those particular circumstances (rather than in some more general or absolute way). (A much more extended treatment of the adaptation

concept is given in Sanderson 1990: 180–90.)

Like the concept of adaptation, the concept of progress has been seen as fundamental to evolutionism, and this has frequently been a basis for the rejection of evolutionism by its critics. It is claimed that evolutionary theories generally assume improvements in the human condition and in the effectiveness of societal functioning with social evolution. It must be admitted that this criticism has considerable merit. The nineteenth-century evolutionists are well known for their strong progressivist views, resting as they did on their highly ethnocentric beliefs. And, although progressivist notions have been toned down and highly qualified in many contemporary versions of evolutionism, they persist nonetheless. Childe and White saw in technological expansion an overall improvement in the quality of the human condition, and Lenski has perpetuated this idea. Sahlins argued that general evolution leads to an increase in "all-round adaptability," and Service saw the evolution of the state as marking a definite improvement in the political functioning of human societies. Parsons is an even stronger progressivist, believing that modern societies represent the culmination of the human achievement so far, and that the United States is the "new lead society of modernity." Progressivism has clearly been the norm throughout the history of social evolutionism.

Nonetheless, there is no inherent association between evolutionary and progressivist views. It is entirely possible to be an evolutionist while rejecting the notion that human history has been an onwards-and-upwards process. Once again it is the (antiprogressivist) evolutionism of Marvin Harris that clearly demonstrates this. The driving engine of social evolution is the spiral of ecological depletion and intensification of production. Humans evolve new modes of living primarily because they are compelled to do so by falling standards of living. But the record of social evolution shows that each new mode of production is associated with a lower rather than a higher standard of living. Early agriculturalists (horticulturalists) were worse off in some respects than the hunter–gatherers who preceded them, and agrarian peasants were worse off than horticulturalists. And even today, despite the affluence of industrial societies, most people are poor peasants or urban workers in the underdeveloped world. Social evolution represents a continuous struggle between humans and nature in which humans run faster and faster just to try to stay in the same place.

SS

further reading Sanderson 1995a,b

evolutionary stages The study of EVOLUTION has invariably involved the formulation of evolutionary stages. Perhaps the oldest typology of evolutionary stages is that of Savagery–Barbarism–Civilization. This was made famous by Lewis Henry MORGAN (1877), but it was also used by Edward Burnett TYLOR (1871, 1881) and, in fact, dates to the eighteenth century. Herbert SPENCER (1876) classified societies in terms of their levels of differentiation or complexity, and distinguished between simple, compound, doubly compound, and trebly compound societies. In the mid-nineteenth century Karl Marx and Friedrich Engels (1947) classified societies according to their modes of production, identifying four stages in the evolution of production: primitive communism, slavery, feudalism, and capitalism.

Recent evolutionary typologies include those of Gerhard Lenski, Elman Service, Morton Fried, and Eric Wolf. Lenski's typology (1970) rests on the level of development of subsistence technology and distinguishes hunting and gathering, simple horticultural, advanced horticultural, agrarian, and industrial societies in the course of evolutionary development. Service's typology (1962/71) involves the mode of sociopolitical organization, and is one of the most popular typologies in modern anthropology. Four stages of sociopolitical organization are identified: bands, tribes, chiefdoms, and states. The movement from one stage to another involves the development of increasingly formalized, specialized, and hierarchical political institutions. Fried's typology (1967) rests on the extent of social inequality and demarcates three types of society:

egalitarian, rank, and stratified. Eric Wolf (1982) employed a contemporary marxist typology that distinguishes three major evolutionary types of society based on the underlying mode of production: the kin-based mode, the tributary mode, and the capitalist mode.

SS

evulsion is the practice of pulling teeth (usually in front) for aesthetic reasons, most commonly found in sub-Saharan Africa.

MR

exchange *See* GIFT EXCHANGE, SOCIAL EXCHANGE, TRADE

exogamy is the rule or preference for individuals to marry only outside their particular social group or category, most commonly a kinship group. Exogamy rules are a necessary feature of any system of MARRIAGE EXCHANGE or alliance. Exogamy can also describe a statistical pattern of outmarriage even in the absence of an explicit rule.

There is some controversy surrounding the relationship of exogamy to the INCEST TABOO. LÉVI-STRAUSS has argued that the two are complementary expressions of the same requirement to engage in spouse exchange. Others, arguing that the two are not connected, have pointed out that they are of logically different types – the exogamy rule is a prescription while the incest taboo is a prohibition – and that the categories of kin prohibited by the incest taboo are frequently narrower than the categories of kin excluded as marriage partners under the rules of exogamy. The incest taboo, furthermore, concerns sexual relations and not marriage per se.

MR

exploitation in the most general, non-technical sense means "taking advantage of," "benefiting unfairly from," "using a person for one's aggrandizement," and so forth. But the term has a more specific, technical meaning derived from the writings of Karl Marx: exploitation occurs when a category or class of persons creates more economic value ("surplus value") than they receive back in the form of a customary level of maintenance. The above senses of "exploitation" have strong moral overtones. Hence, it has been said that exploitation is the recurrent and regular appropriation of economic goods from people who have a moral right to them. In an industrial capitalist society, for example, workers are said to create greater economic value than they receive back in wages (see CAPITALISM). This "surplus value" is appropriated by the capitalist entrepreneur in the form of profits. This argument, it should be noted, rests upon some version of the labor theory of value (that the economic value of a good reflects the socially necessary labor embodied in it). This construal of "exploitation" also implies that whatever organizational skills, knowledge, and innovative ideas the capitalist entrepreneur might bring to the productive process do not in any way contribute to the economic value of the goods produced. In capitalist economies, according to this view, exploitation is hidden by those arrangements concerning wages and prices freely negotiated in the market; whereas in precapitalist agrarian systems, where underlings are obligated to turn over their surplus production to some superior economic class, the exploitation is open and visible.

Critics (Dalton 1974, 1977) of the "exploitation" concept point out that the term is more an evaluative and ideological one than an analytic one. Even when employed analytically the concept raises certain questions usually left unanswered: for instance, when producers in agrarian societies are required to turn over their SURPLUS to some central political agency, what do they receive in return in the way of traditional governmental services such as the maintenance of law and order? Moreover, these critics say, is it not the case that citizens in all industrial societies (capitalist as well as socialist) make obligatory payments to some central government? Is this also exploitation? In fact, even in small-scale societies, such as the hunter–gatherer Bushmen, adult producers have to meet certain obligations to relatives, as when a new son-in-law may be expected to work for his wife's family for as long as eight to ten years. How noncoercive are such obligations?

It would seem, say the critics, that the only societies free of exploitation are those where the producers consume or control 100 percent of the fruits of their productive efforts. Are there any empirical examples of such societies?   DK
See also MARXIST ANTHROPOLOGY
further reading Derman & Levin 1977; Newcomer 1977

extended families   consist of a multigenerational series of NUCLEAR FAMILIES, most often living as a common domestic group. For example, a family consisting of parents and their married children is a *lineally* extended family. Upon the death of the parents, the family would become a *collaterally* extended family if the siblings stayed together. Extended families are often transitory, dissolving at the death of the parents when inheritance makes it possible to divide family property among the component households.   MR
See also DOMESTIC CYCLE, STEM FAMILIES

F

family To an earlier generation of anthropologists in Europe and America defining the word "family" evidently seemed straightforward. Melville HERSKOVITS (1948: 61) observed "There are not many ways in which the primary family can be constituted. One man may live with one woman, one man may have a number of wives, one woman may have a number of husbands." Similarly, George Peter Murdock began his book, *Social structure* (1949: 1), by declaring:

The family is a social group characterized by common residence, economic cooperation, and reproduction. It includes adults of both sexes, at least two of whom maintain a socially approved sexual relationship, and one or more children, own or adopted, of the sexually cohabiting adults.

Even the controversial French anthropologist Claude LÉVI-STRAUSS, who stressed that DESCRIPTIVE KINSHIP SYSTEMS are symbolic systems, accepted the family, more or less as thus defined, as a building block of social life (Lévi-Strauss 1963a: 48–9).

In contrast, today there is little consensus among anthropologists on the meaning of the word "family," and even less on how to generalize about family life around the world (Jane Collier et al. 1992).

Even Murdock had acknowledged that the term on its own was ambiguous. However, based on his survey of 250 "representative human societies" (see CROSS-CULTURAL STUDIES), he concluded (1949: 1–2) that the first and most basic type of human family organization was the NUCLEAR FAMILY comprising

a married man and woman with their offspring, although in individual cases one or more additional persons may reside with them . . . The nuclear family will be familiar to the reader as the type of family recognized to the exclusion of all others by our own society. Among the majority of the peoples of the earth, however, nuclear families are combined, like atoms in a molecule, into larger aggregates.

Such definitions come from an era when anthropologists championed anthropology as science, and anthropological definitions often had a legalistic tone. It seemed critical to establish that there were UNIVERSALS, categories of culture (including basic institutions such as the family) that could serve as invariant points of reference for description and comparison. As Clyde Kluckhohn (1953: 507) explained, "genuine comparison is possible only if nonculture-bound units have been isolated."

It has proved difficult, however, to take elementary biological facts such as the existence of two sexes, their roles in procreation, and the helplessness of human infants (Malinowski 1913; E. Parsons 1906) and weave them into convincing or interesting anthropological theories of family life. Perhaps biological, psychological, and sociosituational "givens" of human existence ought to serve as invariant points of reference on the basis of which cross-cultural comparison may proceed without begging questions that are themselves at issue. But the claim that the nuclear family is a building block of society comparable to the atom is belied today by the diversity of families even in America and Europe.

Ask, for example, how is a family different from a HOUSEHOLD? It might seem that the referent of "family" is kinship and the referent of the word "household" is common residence (Yanagisako 1979). Yet David Schneider (1968, 1984) argued from his study of American kinship that the conventional notions that blood is thicker than water and biology is the basis of family kinship are erroneous. It cannot be taken for granted that kinship is based on biology, that sexual reproduction creates social links between persons, that child bearing establishes consequential ties between mothers and children, and that genetic ties have invariant meanings or qualities apart from the social and cultural attributes attached to them.

Similarly, the idea that families and most households normally comprise adults of both sexes together with their offspring overlooks the current popularity of childless marriages, the existence of families built solely by ADOPTION or alternative insemination, the growing frequency of unmarried single parents and single-parent households in Western societies, and the increasing visibility of gay and lesbian same-sex unions that often include children and may be marked by sexual relationships between two or more adults who may or may not be residing in the same household. Our commonsense understanding of families is also insensitive to economic, social, and historical diversity. Are foster families included? What about stepchildren? What about incest (see INCEST TABOO)? Or households with servants, slaves, and concubines? Is there a place in the nuclear family for the dead, that is, family ANCESTORS?

The conventional maneuver around questions like these has been to argue that such diversities in the underpinnings and forms of family life are simply extensions of, or deviations from, the norm of the nuclear family. Thus foster families or gay and lesbian families may look like families, but they are fictive extensions or elaborations on the category "family."

It is not obvious what is achieved by such terminological legerdemain, especially when exceptions begin to overwhelm the alleged norm numerically. And if statistical tabulations are the goal, it might be preferable to use a strategy employed by the US Census Bureau: let the word "family" arbitrarily mean two or more persons, related by birth, marriage, or adoption, who reside in the same household. Unfortunately the strategy of categorizing highly variable data

using arbitrary pigeonholes easily leads to the impression that exceptions are not even logical extensions or empirical deviations from the norm but something different altogether. Here the social, emotional, and domestic arrangements of unconventional families not covered by the category "nuclear family" may get them labeled "non-families."

Unlike the Census Bureau, anthropologists are more disposed to adopt less arbitrary ways of abstracting and labeling the observable diversity of human life. Perhaps the easiest strategy is to use common sense: start off with your own cultural understanding of families merely as a point of departure rather than as an invariant point of reference. There is obvious danger, however, that by using common sense, it may be hard to recognize that things looking very similar to – or quite different from – what you are accustomed to seeing are not really as similar, or as different, as they appear to be. Focusing on the single-parent family, for example, as "almost like" the nuclear family except for a missing spouse can be misleading. For instance, the roles of resident or nonresident grandparents, siblings, and friends in such households may be analytically slighted.

Another approach is more a question than a strategy to get around the lack of cultural universals. Instead of thinking of the word "family" as a category that must be defined before it can be filled with data, why not focus instead on issues and research problems that should be of greater interest anyway? Domestic violence and child abuse happen in many families, traditional and untraditional. Both of these issues (and these two categories) are no more invariant points of reference (i.e., universal in their meaning and implications) than the word "family." But studying who does what to whom, when, how often, and so on may be a more reliable way of answering also the question why people do what they do. Said differently, we need to wonder under what circumstances "family" is a significant research issue, not just an empty category in need of being filled with worldly examples.   JT

further reading Bartholet 1993; Jane Collier & Yanagisako 1987; J. Goody

1983a; Harriss 1991; Hewlett 1991; A. Kuper 1988; Peristiany 1976; Rivers 1914a; Weston 1991

family types *See* ELEMENTARY, EXTENDED, JOINT, NUCLEAR

farming *See* AGRICULTURE

feminist anthropology takes as its major premise the idea that the study of women's roles, beliefs, and practices in society is critical to understanding both the particulars and potentials of human social life. Although feminist anthropology focuses on WOMEN and women's roles its goal is to provide a more complete understanding of human society. Most feminist anthropologists believe that the insights gathered in Western and non-Western contexts should be used to better the lives of people throughout the world.

Historically, anthropology, like other academic disciplines, was androcentric with a "deeply rooted male orientation" (Reiter 1975b: 12). Bronislaw MALINOWSKI, the founder of the contemporary anthropological method of PARTICIPANT-OBSERVATION, typified a variant of this bias when he quipped that "Anthropology is the study of man embracing woman" (Moore 1988: 1). But alongside a general demeaning of the agency of women and the importance of their social roles to the central meaning of human life, anthropologists were likely to present men's perspective as the general perspective of a social group.

For example, when anthropologists wished to study the ritual beliefs of an Australian Aboriginal group they would study the ritual practices of male Australian Aborigines in the mistaken belief that they were the most sociologically important practices. In short, men's roles were not only more centrally studied, but they were also presented as representative of the entire community's beliefs and experiences. Some of the earliest works in feminist anthropology countered this presumption by demonstrating the importance of women and their social and cultural roles to the anthropological endeavor. They studied women and women's roles in the EVOLUTION of human society, in the maintenance

and negotiation of KINSHIP and the FAMILY, and in the operation of global CAPITALISM. Feminist anthropologists posit that it is only by studying women and men across their various age groups that anthropology can truly consider itself a student of the cross-cultural variety of human social experience.

Feminist anthropology and the broader field of contemporary feminist studies arose in the late 1960s and early 1970s during what is commonly referred to as the "second wave of feminism." During these years, Western European and American women in the feminist liberation movement petitioned for their civil and economic rights. The academic, social, and political goals of the feminist liberation movement were developed alongside the black power, native American, and gay and lesbian liberation movements. All these social groups, with representatives in and outside the academy, argued that their social perspectives, experiences, and cultural practices were critical to a proper understanding and appreciation of modern society. The movements came to be known as "identity politics" and helped lead to the institutionalization of women's studies programs, ethnic studies programs, and queer studies programs and to the increase of women and minorities in various academic disciplines.

The analytic concepts sex-difference, gender, and sexuality are critical to the methods and theories utilized in feminist anthropology. The meaning and use of these three terms has changed over the last one hundred years and are currently undergoing significant revision. Generally, "sex-difference" is used to refer to the biological and anatomical differences that exist between males and females. Thus, whether ultimately referred to genetic, genital, hormonal, brain, or physiological differences, sex-difference was privileged over sex-similarities between women and men. This was not always the case even in Western history, where women and men were once believed to share one sex (Laqueur 1990). Throughout history, moreover, there have been "hermaphroditic" humans whose sex organs include components of both female and male physiology.

"GENDER" is commonly used to indicate the meanings and roles that a society assigns to sex-difference. Gender is what a society makes of the physical, anatomical, and developmental differences it recognizes. The concepts of masculine and feminine behavior – the type of demeanor, activities, and speech that "real men" and "real women" are expected or allowed to have – are gender constructs. They are cultural beliefs that organize social practice, not biological facts. Indeed, feminist anthropologists have shown that there are no universal gender roles for women or men. Thus, more than 50 years ago, Margaret MEAD (1935: 16, 18) could speculate that,

while every culture has in some way institutionalized the roles of men and women . . . the temperaments which we regard as native to one sex might be mere variations of human temperament, to which the members of either or both sexes may, with more or less success in the case of different individuals, be educated to approximate.

Recently, a number of poststructural feminists and gender theorists have argued that, in a similar manner to how it constructs gender, culture constructs sex (Butler 1990). In other words, all societies, these theorists argue, construct the body differently, selecting which anatomical differences will be construed as sex-differences and which will not. Moreover, sex is as available for cultural manipulation and alteration as gender, especially in technologically advanced nations. Much of this research has been inspired by, and conceptualized within, the study of sexuality.

"Sexuality" generally refers to how a society and individuals within it organize, act on, conceive of, and represent their erotic and reproductive acts (see SEX). Influenced by the emergence of modern psychoanalysis and psychology, anthropologists have studied both institutionalized and noninstitutionalized forms of heterosexuality and HOMOSEXUALITY. Harriet Whitehead (1981: 80) has, however, noted a parallel between the androcentrism of early anthropology and a contemporary "anthropological solecism that often appears in studies . . . interpreting the styles

of homosexuality that are fully institutionalized in the light of those that are not." Irrespective, anthropologists have now demonstrated that sex, gender, and sexuality are often closely linked concepts in other cultures and are often utilized for social control. For instance, a society may attempt to control the sexual practices of some age and gender groups but not others. Moreover, societies often represent the sexuality of men and women quite differently: the former as active, virile, and productive, and the latter as dangerous, polluting, or socially problematic. Societies also vary widely in how they think about, represent, and regulate the sexual practices of same-sex couples and cross-sex couples. In the West, same-sex partners suffer political and economic discrimination. But in many societies same-sex sexuality is accepted as a vital erotic practice, part of religious ceremonies, or part of the kinship and alliance systems. Influenced in part by the works of Michel Foucault, recent theorists of culture and sexuality have begun to question the applicability of Western notions of homosexuality and heterosexuality to non-Western cultures.

From its earliest days, feminist anthropology has included a wide variety of theoretical perspectives, geographical concerns, and methodological approaches. Feminist anthropology spans the classic four fields of anthropology: sociocultural, linguistic, physical and archaeological. For example, in sociocultural ANTHROPOLOGY feminist anthropologists have studied the social practices and experiences and the cultural representations and meanings of women in societies throughout the world. No subfield of sociocultural anthropology has been left untouched. Studies in kinship, marriage, and the family were revised once ethnographers began to understand women's roles in negotiating marriages for their daughters and sons, manipulating kinship ties for economic and political gain, and acting as sexual agents rather than passive objects of men's desire. Likewise the anthropological study of religion, political systems, and the economy was theoretically revised and ethnographically enriched after women's lives, histories, and perspectives were taken into account.

Feminist anthropologists have also considered the relationship between gender and LANGUAGE. Influenced by trends in LINGUISTICS and SOCIOLINGUISTS, they have studied both what special linguistic registers women may speak and how their speech varies from men's speech in their society. Thus, early works in feminism and linguistics were interested in why women's speech was cross-culturally seen as having less prestige than men's and why many languages were structured in a sexist manner; why, for example, in English one says "mankind" for "humankind," "he" to include "she," and so on. Later works have studied how women and men talk and cultural understandings of gendered ways of speaking. But whether interested in the structure of language, the use of language, or their interface, feminist anthropologists have sought to show how and why language and speech symbolically situate women in an inferior position vis-à-vis men.

In physical anthropology, feminist anthropology has studied a wide range of topics, including women's physiological reproduction and its relationship to social structure, the evolution of sex roles in the greater apes, and the use of nonhuman primate social and sexual behavior to understand prehistoric or contemporary human behavior (Hrdy 1981). The views of feminist anthropologists working within physical anthropology diverge sharply between those who believe that the biological differences between women and men do not significantly limit the social capacities of either for mothering, aggression and warfare, and labor and intellect, and those, influenced by trends in SOCIOBIOLOGY, who believe that there is an essential difference in women and men's physiology that makes each more or less suited for certain social roles.

Finally, feminist anthropology has greatly influenced method and theory in ARCHAEOLOGY and thus our understanding of human evolution and prehistoric and classical society. Feminist archaeologists have revised our understanding of what the archaeological record tells us and can tell us about women's roles in prehistory. A significant influence on archaeology, for instance, has been the feminist insight that

archaeologists often project gender onto archaeological materials rather than finding it there (Conkey & Williams 1991). For example, because it was generally believed that in most hunter–gatherer societies men hunted and women gathered, if an archaeologist found a stone point ("arrowhead") this showed that men hunted in the region. But the actual stone point cannot tell us who once hurled it.

Feminist anthropology has also been informed by, and contributed to, a range of theoretical approaches such as cultural studies, political economy, structuralism, and poststructuralism. Early works in feminist anthropology were concentrated on a broad range of political economic and structuralist questions. For example, one of the first edited volumes on feminist anthropology, *Toward an anthropology of women* (Reiter 1975a), was strongly informed by political economic and MARXIST ANTHROPOLOGY. Many of the contributors were concerned with women's roles in the family, the production and reproduction of their society, and their alternate styles of gender and sexuality. Other early influential edited volumes (Rosaldo & Lamphere 1974; MacCormack & Strathern 1980) demonstrated the cultural logic of gender in non-Western societies and the impact of this cultural logic on local social structure.

More recent work has focused on two broad areas: first, the relationship between cultural understandings of gender and sexuality and the distribution of power in a society and, second, the insights and conundrums that poststructural, postcolonial, and postmodern studies have brought to the wider field of feminist anthropology. Many feminist anthropologists now question the usefulness of the category "WOMEN." They are interested in how women of various social, ethnic, and sexual orientations have not only been oppressed and ignored by androcentric, patriarchal institutions but also oppress and ignore women from other classes, ethnicities, and sexual orientations.   EP

See also CLASS, ETHNIC GROUPS, POST-MODERNISM, STRUCTURALISM

further reading P. Caplan 1987; di Leonardo 1991b; S. Errington &

Atkinson 1990; Ortner & Whitehead 1981; Philips et al. 1987; Smuts 1985; M. Strathern 1987; Yanagisako & Collier 1987

fertility rites and cults Fertility rites may occur in calendric cycles, as RITES OF PASSAGE within the LIFE CYCLE, or as ad hoc rituals of affliction to deal with, for example, miscarriage or prolonged barrenness. Cults may focus specifically on fertility, but more commonly fertility rituals are embedded within larger-order religions or other social institutions.

Aboriginal people of Australia, the Amazon basin, and other areas have rituals of cyclical renewal. MENSTRUATION is often a key symbol relating health and fertility to a balance between "heat" and "cold," "dryness" and "wetness." Nature achieves such a balance by alternating between night and day, wet season and dry. Often women's menstrual cycles are defined as synchronically linked with the moon's periodic "death" and "rebirth." In some puberty rites men must learn to menstruate in a ritual and symbolic sense to safeguard the rhythm of renewal (Knight 1985). Diane Bell (1983) described Australian Aboriginal women's rituals of love, fertility, and health for the land and people that had a nurturing motif. They linked the "growing up" of people and land in a harmonious relationship that must be ritually maintained.

In Hindu areas of India and Muslim areas of Sudan, women's sexuality and fertility are both powerful and polluting. Their misuse may dishonor a family and therefore should be controlled toward proper ends by men. If a woman clearly orients her power toward the well-being of her husband and children she enjoys some self-esteem, but C. Thompson (1985) has suggested, based on her work in India, that this is an ideology encouraging women to participate in their own subordination. However, all cultures are heterogeneous, with competing dominant and subordinate ideologies. Women-centered cults, such as Zar in Sudan, give a more positive symbolic message about women's reproductive power as an alternative to formal jural rules that give control of women's sexuality to men. In the cognitive domain of jural rules, male con-

trol is symbolized in BLOOD marking the life-cycle stages of infibulation, defloration, or childbirth. Yet in Zar ceremonies the cult spirits, controlled by strong female leaders, are clearly acknowledged as the "owners" of women's blood in all its symbolic meanings (Constantinides 1985). Within female-focused religions throughout the world, women's control of their own fertility is sacralized or institutionalized (Sered 1994).

In Sierra Leone menstruation, pregnancy, birth, and nurturing are positively defined by Sande, a widespread women's religion. It ritually transforms girls into fertile wives, wives into mothers through childbirth, and mothers into ancestresses at death. Ancestresses generate nurturing goodness as wives and mothers do. Those separate rituals are metaphoric transformations of each other. Sande "owns" secret knowledge, technical skills, legitimate sanctioning power, and hierarchical organization. Unlike Zar, Sande is in the cultural mainstream and helps to undergird the relatively high social status of those West African women (MacCormack 1982). Where important ritual knowledge is controlled by women, puberty rites for girls are major ritual events.

In Papua New Guinea most ritual knowledge is in the male domain, and prolonged male puberty rites, sometimes including HOMOSEXUALITY, attempt to make boys into sexually mature men (Herdt 1982). Harriet Whitehead (1986) has contrasted those "rituals of manhood" found mostly in lowland areas with "rituals of clanhood" in the highlands. In the former, cult groups are more important in the politics of exchange transaction, and initiates are given semen by potential affines or ceremonial exchange partners so as not to violate INCEST TABOOS. In the latter, patrilineal kinship groups are more important and rites help boys shed their "female" identity through ritual bleeding to rid them of mother's womb blood. In a matrilineal Zambian example, Victor TURNER (1967) described the rich symbolism of fertility rituals that ultimately serve to remind people that CHILDREN belong to the matrilineage, and all people should honor clan obligations or risk fertility disorders.

Rituals to cure reproductive disorders use analogy by mirroring girls' puberty rites. The patient is like a novice, and is ritually "grown" into full womanhood.

Fertility is explicitly linked with political hierarchy in Swazi royal ritual, where the king is identified with the health and fertility of the nation. The yearly *incwala* ceremony unites the people with their king and brings fertility and new strength to crops, animals, and people (H. Kuper 1947). The ceremony ceases with the king's death, and is reborn with his mature successor. Mortuary rites often express the fertile power to recreate. The negative aspects of death may be symbolically expressed, then rituals transform them into positive images of a strong and ordered society. Maurice Bloch and Jonathan Parry (1982) suggested that where women are socially weak, associated with pollution and sorrow, they tend to be the chief mourners. Death can then be "overcome" by pure, collective transcendence, associated with men.

Modern European culture has largely subsumed that transcendence within a scientific worldview. Davis-Floyd (1992) described the operating room where birth takes place in American hospitals as the *sanctum sanctorum*, a sacred shrine in American culture. CHILDBIRTH is everywhere highly ritualized, and American hospital birth rituals express the deepest cultural beliefs about the rightness of cultural control over natural process, unworthiness of nature and the female body, the superiority of "male" science and technology, and the importance of institutions and machines. Women who do not believe in those rituals tend to leave hospital angry or depressed.   CM

See also   RELIGION,   REPRODUCTION,   WOMEN

festivals   *See* RITUAL

fetish is an object imbued with ritual potency, often surrounded with taboos and conferring material benefits upon its keeper.   MR

feudalism   *See* COLONIALISM, EVOLUTION

feuding is a culturally regularized homicidal activity (sometimes called "vendetta") that involves reciprocating application of measured VIOLENCE between rival groups. It occurs mainly in BAND and TRIBAL societies, which lack the centralized authority needed to stop lethal retaliation after HOMICIDES. Feuding differs from dueling because duels involve individuals, not groups; it differs from raiding because raids are aimed at obtaining resources; it differs from WAR because warfare involves large-scale battles. Feuding is far more bound by rules, and the revenge killings involve redemption of HONOR; they also make it manifest that aggrieved groups will not submit to further aggression. The name of the game is carefully measured retaliation, with careful keeping of score so that "blood money" can be paid eventually.

Feuding is not universal to all small-scale societies that lack centralized social control, but it is found on all continents, and, being game-like, it limits retaliation to one or a few homicides at a time. Basically the lower-scoring side goes on "offense" while the opposition remains on "defense," and when resolution becomes possible (both sides have to be willing) this is accomplished through material compensation from the higher-scoring group. Feuding occurs between bands, between clans within a tribe, between some PEASANT communities, and even between street gangs, but it is always prohibited within the same family or clan because the explicit purpose is to even the score between groups. Some experts (Black-Michaud 1975) treat single acts of vengeance that automatically end the chain of violence as different from feuds, which can persist for years or decades or centuries until pacified.

The first anthropological explanations of feuding looked to SOCIAL ORGANIZATION: as a self-organizing system, feuding was thought to have some important positive functions. EVANS-PRITCHARD's (1940) classic analysis of Nuer feuding in Africa suggests that with formal government absent, feuding institutions function as an implicit social sanctioning device: people usually avoid committing murder because this brings predictable retaliation. He suggested that violence (close to home) was actually being contained by feuding. Boehm (1984) has added an intentional component to such functional analyses, to suggest that in feuding societies people deliberately limit violence close to home by setting up rules that prevent all-out clan warfare from erupting, and that they knowingly maintain institutions of blood-money payment because they understand their functions. Thus, a violent institution can be seen as involving not only conflict resolution through aggressive "self-help," but also elements of deliberate social control. Material compensation, sometimes including marriages, as a means of pacifying feuds is widespread, and it also took place in medieval Europe. This cultural invention of paying money for BLOOD suggests that feuding systems everywhere are associated with similar aims: to limit and "manage" retaliatory violence that is all too predictable in the absence of centralized governmental control.

Social structure and residence rules are relevant to feuding, for matrilineal–matrilocal societies are less likely to exhibit it. A statistical CROSS-CULTURAL survey by Furer-Haimendorf et al. (1960) demonstrated that fraternal power groups (male-bonded clans that live in one place) exhibit higher levels of mutual violence than other types of group. This pattern was elaborated by Otterbein and Otterbein (1965), who used a similar approach to emphasize feuding's strong association with "fraternal interest groups" and lack of centralized control.

There are scholarly disagreements that stem from differences of definition. Black-Michaud, working with Middle Eastern societies in general, and E. Peters (1967), working with Bedouins and their coalitions, have argued that feuding is interminable because pacification efforts often break down and then feuds resurface because economic competition is involved. However, others have contended that the closer the conflict is to home, the more quickly and permanently the problem of retaliatory homicide is resolved by means of pacification. While Peters did show that Bedouin groups that compete for resources also feud, such a theory is difficult to generalize:

for example, among head-hunting Jivaro Indians in Ecuador feuding is endemic, yet there is no competition for scarce resources aside from manly status, which is always scarce for the losers.

Revenge killing is found among extant FORAGERS such as Bushmen, Eskimos, and Australian Aborigines, so it would appear that feuding goes back deep into prehistory, even though anthropologists remain unsure about war. Various "natural history" aspects of feuding have been explored by Chagnon (1988), who used excellent quantitative data on the Yanomamo to evaluate the individually adaptive effects of taking revenge, by Boehm, who related feuding to human and primate nature, and by Daly and Wilson (1988b), who discussed feuding in a variety of social and biological contexts.   CBo

See also EGALITARIAN SOCIETIES, LEGAL ANTHROPOLOGY, POLITICAL ANTHROPOLOGY

further reading Boehm 1989 [probes human nature through ambivalence about revenge killing]; Chagnon 1992 [detailed account of South American tribal warriors whose system of revenge involves only weak conflict resolution institutions]; Ferguson & Farragher 1988 [this bibliography has several dozen sources on feuding; see Section 12]; Hasluck 1954 [a fascinating and unusually well-defined oral feuding code from a Balkan tribal society]; Meggitt 1977 [a very detailed account of low-casualty intergroup violence in highland New Guinea, including "great fights"]; Turney-High 1949 [discusses the psychology of taking vengeance]

fictive kinship is the creative imprecision by which an idiom of relatedness is used to strengthen an image or feeling of identification between two or more persons or beings. In one form or another (blood brothers, soul sisters, mothers superior, etc.) fictive kinship occurs in every known society, often with deep and complex meanings.

Kinship fictions are associative (as in ADOPTION or sodality), dissociative (as in DIVORCE, denied paternity, or disinheritance), or transmutative (as in cases of grandparents and grandchildren who jokingly call each other spouses). Associative forms link humans with other humans, with other animate or inanimate beings (as in some forms of TOTEMISM – see Frazer 1890; Lévi-Strauss 1963b), or with spiritual entities. Children worldwide create kinship fictions by ROLE-PLAYING, and among young and old, most forms of fictive kinship project the image of the biologically closest kin ties onto other, more distant relationships.

Religious and secular communities, including communes, collectives, utopian settlements, and revolutionary movements, have used idioms of siblinghood and parenthood in many settings, sometimes expecting members to renounce prior kinship. Several of the world's major religions, most notably some Catholic and Protestant sects of Christianity, rely heavily on images of kinship that nonparticipants, at least, deem fictive, as in liturgies about God as a father, about marriage of nuns to Christ, and so on. Members of priesthoods and other holy orders commonly address and rank each other, and outsiders, with kin terms (e.g., White Fathers, Sisterhood of the Holy Cross). Adherents to many religious traditions seek to extend kinship idiom more universally, as in Christian "brotherly love." Jamaican and other Rastafarians who call themselves "Children of Jah," imply relatedness to divinity as well as each other. Ritual or ceremonial kinships known as coparenthood (*compadrazgo*) and godparenthood (*padrinazgo*) prevail together in Catholic societies with bilateral kinship in southern Europe, in Latin America (where they are nearly ubiquitous), in the Philippines, and elsewhere. Established during RITES OF PASSAGE, *compadrazgo* links ritual sponsors with parents of offspring undergoing the rituals such as baptism, communion, marriage, or school graduation, and (as *padrinazgo*) with those offspring themselves. It effectively extends and complements biological kindred, sometimes to create patron-client bonds or wider webs of human contacts with economic and political as well as symbolic and religious content (see G. Foster 1953 on Spain and Spanish America; Gudeman 1972 on Panama;

and Mintz & Wolf 1950, Nutini & Bell 1980–4 on Mexico; see also Blok 1974 on Sicily).

Fictive kinship is sometimes sealed by ritual or ceremony involving the sharing of bodily substances or other substances that symbolize them, as in BLOOD BROTHERHOOD (Tegnaeus 1952; Gennep 1960), once widespread in Africa and Arabia, or church communion (see also BLOOD PACTS). As with *compadrazgo*, some who practice blood-siblinghood appear to deem it a deeper bond, imposing sterner mutual responsibilities, than biological siblinghood.

Kinship imagery pervades political rhetoric, as in nationalist expressions like "motherland," "Uncle Sam," or "*ujamaa*" (Swahili, "familyhood," used in Tanzania) or factional ones like "Afrikaner Broederbond" (in South Africa) or "sisterhood is powerful." In commerce, companies of all sizes style themselves as families or pseudo-families (see Rohlen 1974 on a Japanese bank). In education, fraternities, sororities, and expressions like *alma mater* exemplify fictive kinship. Some organizations of fictive kin, for instance Muslim brotherhoods (Cruise O'Brien 1971), can serve religious, political, commercial, and educational purposes all at once.

What counts as real or fictive kinship is a matter of much debate both within and between societies. Surrogate motherhood and high-technology reproductive experiments blur the lines further. Some of the most creative and ramified inventions in kin idiom are found in some of the societies where biological families are most fragmented and perhaps most lacking in life altogether, suggesting a vacuum-filling function. Often the difference between being and resembling is not a sharp break, but a continuum. Fictive kinship can provide art, humor, or worldly gain. But it points to deep, and sometimes subtle, human needs. The ubiquity and variety of fictive kinship testify to the power of close kin and family over the human psyche, and of analogy and metaphor over the human imagination.

PS

See also CLASSIFICATORY KINSHIP SYSTEMS, KINSHIP, MARRIAGE

further reading Amadiume 1987; Evans-

Pritchard 1940; Freud 1918; Pitt-Rivers 1958

fieldnotes are literally those notes written by a researcher while in the field. However, while psychologists and sociologists (or ecologists, for that matter) write fieldnotes, it is anthropologists who have invested them with the most meaning (Jean Jackson 1990).

The anthropologist Roger Sanjek (1990b) distinguished four varieties: "scratchnotes" quickly written during an event; "fieldnotes proper," which are fully fleshed-out notes written later; "headnotes," which consist of memories and reflections that were never written down; and "filednotes," which are any of the above further processed after leaving the field. Unlike laboratory notebooks, there is no standard format for fieldnotes. The idiosyncrasies of the anthropologist, the field situation, the nature of the research, issues of confidentiality, and the enormous variety of people being studied mean that a fieldwork manual with rigid instructions about how to take fieldnotes will probably never be written.

Anthropologists differ about the ownership of fieldnotes (especially after the author's death) and their use by others (Obbo 1990). In some countries there have been attempts to provide legal status to such documents that clarifies the conditions under which the subjects (or sponsors) of the research have access to them (Greaves 1994). Although some anthropologists see their notes as repositories for future research, many others regard them as confidential because they contain a mix of personal information and data in raw form that could easily be misinterpreted or misused. And given the abundance of instances in which fieldnotes have been used for purposes far afield from the original intention – the most famous being the posthumous publication of Malinowski's field diary (1967) – this attitude will probably persist (Forge 1972; C. Geertz 1988). But interest in INTEPRETIVE ANTHROPOLOGY, critiques of overly positivist anthropology (G. Marcus & Fischer 1986; Clifford 1988), and the larger "ethnographies as text" discussions (G. Marcus & Cushman 1982; Clifford & Marcus 1986) have made writings of all types, and the production of scientific knowledge itself, subjects of investigation in their own right.   JJa

See also FIELDWORK, PARTICIPANT-OBSERVATION

further reading Sanjek 1990a

fieldwork is intense, long-term anthropological research conducted among a community of people. Archaeologists also do fieldwork, but not, for the most part, with living people. Sociologists carry out fieldwork as well (Hammersley & Atkinson 1995); however, this kind of research, also called "qualitative sociology," has never been the dominant paradigm in the discipline, whereas anthropologists have always been expected to go to the field at least for their initial dissertation research because "being there" is seen to result in superior work. Anthropological fieldwork differs in conceptualization, and for the most part in practice, from other kinds of field research because of its epistemology, history, and socialization practice. The stereotypical ethnographer is seen as doing PARTICI-PANT-OBSERVATION, but researchers also perform quantitative, survey, textual, demographic, and other types of analysis, depending on local conditions and the nature of the research project. Until recently the optimal choice was to seek out as exotic a locale for research as possible; choosing sites closer to home and writing library dissertations were viewed as inferior alternatives.

The question of just what anthropological fieldwork should consist of has occasioned a great deal of literature. The classic and often-revised field manual *Notes and queries* (BAAS 1874), which attempted to cover everything under the sun, was supplemented by a large number of new works that began to appear from the 1960s onwards (examples include Ellen 1984; Agar 1980; and Bernard 1988). There has been a more recent explosion of reflexive books on fieldwork, focusing on the experience itself as opposed to how to carry out the research. Earlier such works adopted such genres as thinly disguised fiction (E. Bowen 1954) and autobiography (Lévi-Strauss 1963c), in addition to more straightforward accounts of life in the field (Powdermaker 1966; Wax 1971; Maybury-Lewis 1965a). Among the more recent books, Rabinow's description of fieldwork in Morocco (1977) and Cesara's (1982) book provoked some controversy because of their candor about sexuality in the field. Beginning with women in the field (Golde 1970), GENDER has become a much-analyzed issue (T. Whitehead & Conaway 1986; Diane Bell et al. 1993) that includes feminist field research (H. Roberts 1981) and fieldwork by gays and lesbians (Leap & Lewin 1996). Finally, some writings have focused on ethical issues (Rynkiewich & Spradley 1976) and other specific issues including stress arising in fieldwork (F. Henry & Saberwal 1969).

Researchers carrying out traditional fieldwork are supposed to immerse themselves, taking in large amounts of vastly different kinds of data. This range and abundance of "raw" experience and observation helps put the more formally acquired information, gathered through structured interviews, for instance, into context. Supporters of traditional fieldwork also argue that a great deal of learning about people and CULTURE needs to occur through direct experience, as opposed to the distancing and objectivity of the scientific method. Learning through senses other than seeing and hearing – by smelling or imitating habitual body postures, for instance – should occur (Stoller 1989). Through using their senses anthropologists serve as data-gathering instruments and alterations in themselves become a way of knowing; or, as Susan Harding states, "the only certain evidence of the reality that preoccupies ethnographers, of shared unconscious knowledge, is experiential" (1987: 180).

Proponents of "total immersion" fieldwork argue that the members of the community being studied will be far more forthcoming with information, confidences, intimacies, permissions to attend rituals, and so on, if they see that the fieldworker is really trying to live the way they do, speak their language, and understand their lives in as many dimensions as possible. A second advantage derives from researchers' being ripped away from their familiar routines and unexamined assumptions. With such abrupt, at times violent, changes, it is argued, they are able to acquire new languages and habits more quickly and completely. The fact that fieldwork is often called a RITE OF PASSAGE signals not only the pre-dissertation anthropologist's passing through an important career stage, but also recalls analyses of the painful, disorienting practices in initiation rites that function to eradicate the initiate's taken-for-granted, comfortable, familiar habits and expectations. Such violent ritual practices have been said to achieve the tasks of inscribing a new social status and teaching new concepts and behaviors far more effectively than would happen if an initiate learned new knowledge with a minimum of affect and bodily participation. Anthropologists who discuss such phenomenological learning in the field include Jean Briggs (1970) on the Inuit and Michael Jackson (1989) on African systems of thought.

The long-term, intense, "experience-near" fieldwork is proposed and defended by its adherents as a way to achieve a profound, multidimensional knowledge not available to someone who visits a community for a few days or weeks. One is more likely to learn secret or esoteric knowledge this way, and the kinds of knowledge that the possessors do not have immediate access so must, therefore, be acquired using means other than direct interrogation. Bourdieu's (1977) notion of habitus (repetitive, unconscious, mundane practices) is pertinent here. Virtually all of anthropology's ancestral figures have contributed to the extensive debates in the social sciences over how to interpret a postulated meaning that is not readily available to the consciousness of the members of the community being studied. Examples are Marx's false consciousness, Gramsci's hegemony, and Bourdieu's *doxa* (unquestioningly accepted authoritative discourses and practices).

Most publications on fieldwork discuss the best mix of scientific (stressing objectivity and replicability) and experiential, empathic, intuitive approaches (stressing that fieldworkers must "get under the native's skin" and come close to "going native").

Anthropology's most revered fieldworker, MALINOWSKI, stated that "natural intercourse" is superior to information acquired from "a paid, and often bored, informant" (1922: 7). The lore about "going native," that quintessentially anthropological occupational hazard (albeit mostly apocryphal), illustrates the advantages and perils of fieldwork. Participating too much results in one's going native; participating too little turns one into a superficial, ethnocentric, survey-wielding, number-crunching social scientist with, some say, zero insight into the people being studied. Ultimately all fieldwork hinges on a rather dynamic and contradictory synthesis of insider and outsider. As an outsider, the fieldworker sees things, makes comparisons, and has experiences that insiders cannot see, make, or have. As an insider, the fieldworker learns what the behavior observed means to the people themselves. Anthropology offers an instructive history of master theories being applied to radically different cultures only to be discredited later as crudely ethnocentric (Tambiah 1984).

All variants of fieldwork have been thoroughly scrutinized and criticized since the mid-1970s. Hyper-positivist fieldwork methods are under fire from POSTMODERNISM and fieldwork in general has been faulted for overprivileging the knowledge gained "on location" because it results in fixing people in an unreal, arbitrary TIME (Fabian 1983) and in an equally unreal space – a mystified, never-neverland that exists only as an anthropological construct. Because anthropology finds it convenient to claim a unique understanding based on this methodology, so this argument goes, the result is an underprivileging of all of the non-contiguous information controlled by the people being studied and a systematic obscuring of how "unnative" many research subjects in fact are. Gupta called this "empiricist epistemology" (1995: 377), and Appadurai (1988b: 36) argued that the native becomes metonymically frozen in place. A heightened awareness has emerged that acknowledges that much of what anthropologists observe in a given locale has meaning only in connection with activities and meanings located elsewhere, both tem-

porally and spatially. Local communities are constructed by regional, national, and transnational forces; research situations like diasporas and refugee camps illustrate this especially well, as does work in creolized societies that draw on multiple cultural threads (Hannerz 1987). Hence, although as James Fernandez says, "being there" is mainly what anthropology is about (1985: 19), this "there," especially the consequences of its role in constituting anthropological professional identity, needs to be problematized. The unwarranted assumptions behind fieldwork understood as necessarily carried out in spatial and temporal confines become apparent as researchers grapple with such sources of data as newspapers, television, film, and other forms of public culture. Another source of critique is postcolonial studies, which deconstruct how a hegemonic Western social science such as anthropology fashions its particular alterity. In other words, "the field" is reified and assumptions are made about unity, cohesiveness, and so on, and this renders it problematic in terms of conceptualization and of its claims as a superior methodology. Current critiques of many analytic concepts reveal similar problems of reification in such terms as "CULTURE," the "STATE," and "SOCIETY" as well.

With an increase in debate about the how and why of anthropological research (as well as an increase in Third World countries that deny permission to anthropological researchers and a drying-up of funding for such projects), carrying out fieldwork in distant places has decreasing cachet. Some anthropologists have found traditional anthropological fieldwork so problematic that they advocate cultural history approaches.   JJa

further reading *manuals* – Crane & Angrosino 1992; Jongmans & Gutkind 1967 [annotated bibliography on anthropological fieldwork methods is extremely useful]; Kottak 1982; Spradley 1980; Spradley & McCurdy 1972 [for anthropology students]; *fieldwork accounts* – Freilich 1970; Kimball & Watson 1972; Spindler 1970

filiation is the process by which individuals are socially attached to their parents. It establishes both parent–child bonds and the associated legal rights based on this relationship.   MR

Firth, Sir Raymond William (1901–)

Raymond Firth was born in Auckland, New Zealand. He studied economics there before coming to England in 1924 to pursue a doctorate in that field. At the London School of Economics, however, he encountered Bronislaw MALINOWSKI and switched his focus to anthropology, although his interest in economics ran like a bright thread through all of his subsequent work. He wrote a doctoral dissertation on the Maori economic life in 1927. With the exception of a short time in Australia, he taught continually at the LSE for the rest of his career, succeeding to Malinowski's chair in 1944 and retiring in 1968. During this time Firth took a leading role in building anthropology at the LSE and helped train a distinguished cohort of students – including Edmund LEACH, who succeeded him. He was knighted in 1973.

Firth's ethnographic and theoretical interests are wide-ranging. It is hard to find a topic on which he did not write something. He published monographs on fieldwork conducted among the Maori of New Zealand (1929), the Tikopia of the Solomon Islands (1936, 1940, 1967, 1970), Malay fishermen (1946), and urban Londoners (1956c; Firth et al. 1970). His 1936 *We the Tikopia*, vast in scope (over 600 pages) and discursive in nature, quickly became a classic, but far more people cite the book today than read it. An example of FUNCTIONALISM, it showed how many aspects of life were interrelated but gave little attention to how and why. Firth himself recognized that this lack of structure was a problem and fell back on his interests in economics to provide one in his subsequent work.

Firth was one of the founders of ECONOMIC ANTHROPOLOGY. He was particularly interested in questions of individual choice, the structure of economic institutions, and the organization of economic affairs. Thus Firth's work on RELIGION, and SACRIFICE in particular, tended to focus on the practical aspects of belief

systems, explaining their functionality and rationality in economic terms. His view that cultural beliefs structured economic life had a strong influence on Karl Polanyi (see FORMALIST–SUBSTANTIVIST DEBATE).

A strong proponent of Malinowski's functionalism, Firth (1956a, 1957) attempted to provide it with a firmer theoretical framework that would account for SOCIAL CHANGE. His best-known works along these lines focused on SOCIAL ORGANIZATION, arguing that it needed to be distinguished from social structure (Firth 1951b, 1964). The latter constituted the rules of the game, the former how the actors actually behaved while playing the game. His restudy of the Tikopia after a NATURAL DISASTER was a particular object lesson in how much flexibility there was in seemingly fixed social structures (Firth 1959). He defended this approach in British social anthropology against attacks from American cultural anthropologists who felt it was too sociological (Firth 1951a; see also ANTHROPOLOGY, CULTURAL AND SOCIAL). After his retirement he played a significant role in bringing the two traditions into harmony through a series of visiting professorships in North America.   TB

fishing

fishing is the killing or capture by whatever means of all species of fish and shellfish. FORAGERS exploited many kinds of marine resources, and some of the largest concentrations of humans in the Paleolithic lived along the shores (Yesner 1980), making extensive use of shellfish, a predictable resource that could be taken by most members of such bands. They also commonly used fish weirs or permanent fish traps to catch fish migrating along shore (G. Bailey & Parkington 1988). Settlements occurred in protected areas from which small boats could be operated in relative safety, and these boats allowed access to a variety of ecozones (rivers, estuaries, and open ocean) where fish, sea mammals, and birds regularly came near land.

The primary contribution of modern maritime anthropology has been to document the ways in which people have adapted to the problems of earning a living from the sea. Fishing takes place in an uncertain, heterogeneous, and risky environment with the constant threat of storms, accidents, or equipment failure (Binkley 1991). Poggie and Pollnac (1988) showed that those exploiting the sea cope with irreducible risk through the use of RITUAL and MAGIC. Even locating one's position at sea is always a problem. Marine ecozones typically contain a very large number of species with different habits that require different capture techniques (Cove 1973); and unlike HUNTING on land, it is far more difficult to learn about and observe desirable species. Those exploiting the sea also have to contend with volatile MARKETS, unpredictable catches, and periodic stock failure.

A variety of institutions lower risk and uncertainty in many contemporary fishing societies (Acheson 1981). Crews are usually paid on a shares basis, enhancing motivation and ensuring that boat owners will not have to pay fixed wages when catches are poor. Flexible crew-recruitment processes permit captains to obtain skilled crew members who can cooperate under the stress of prolonged periods at sea. In most fishing societies, boat operators establish strong bilateral ties with fish buyers, which reduces risks for both parties (Acheson 1981), while other fishers have formed cooperatives to ensure markets, fair prices, access to credit, and information about markets. In addition, boat captains often form "fishing clusters" (Barth 1966) – networks that aid members in finding fish, assessing prices, and evaluating innovations.

Fishers have developed a number of competitive strategies. Skills and knowledge of the fishery are a prime asset that is generally kept secret (Andersen 1972). There is currently a lively debate concerning the "skipper effect" (i.e., the effect of fishing skill) and ideologies connected to it (Durrenberger & Pálsson 1986; Bjarnason & Thorlindsson 1993). Territoriality is common, which helps to conserve the resources in a particular area for the "owners" (Acheson 1981; Berkes 1989; Ruddle & Johannes 1985). Fishers also compete by seeking more effective innovations, and by

the strategy of combining occupations and switching fisheries over time.

Because boats are at sea for so long, special problems arise for crew members and their families. Boat crews must cope with crowding, long hours, lack of privacy, and separation from loved ones. The women must raise children, manage business affairs, and cope with household emergencies without male help much of the time (Nadel-Klein & Davis 1988). In virtually all societies, fishing families have a different status from people who earn their living on shore.

At present, many major marine fisheries are in a state of crisis (McGoodwin 1990). The most common explanation is that as "common property" or "open-access resources," fisheries are not under the stewardship of any private owner and are subjected to escalating overexploitation. An important contribution of maritime anthropology has been to show that traditional coastal communities are in fact capable of generating conservation rules (Berkes 1989; McCay & Acheson 1987; Pinkerton 1989). Here, depletion of fish stocks has only occurred as conservation rules have broken down under the pressure of the MODERNIZATION process (Johannes 1978). Attempts to regulate national and international fisheries on a scientific basis have been questioned recently because it appears that they are highly chaotic and that the fish stock recruitment models on which management is based are not adequate to the task (Estellie Smith 1990; J. Wilson et al. 1994). With the demise of so many natural fisheries, aquaculture is developing rapidly in many parts of the world.

JA

further reading Acheson 1988; F. Cohen 1986; Cole 1991; Faris 1968; R. Firth 1946; T. Gladwin 1970; Johannes 1981; Orbach 1977; Pálsson 1991; Prins 1965; Robben 1989; Courtland Smith 1979; Tunstall 1962; William Warner 1983

folklore consists of the cultural materials attributed to premodern, nonliterate, or peasant societies, circulated and preserved orally or in noninstitutional communicative channels, and traditional (i.e., handed down and dependent for authority primarily on persistence through time rather than tested pragmatic or logical content). The term was coined in 1846 by William John Thoms, a British antiquarian, to replace "popular antiquities" and was an English equivalent for the German *Volkskunde* in use since 1787. The term "folklore" has since been borrowed in numerous languages to designate either the body of such cultural materials, or the discipline dedicated to their documentation. In English "folkloristics" is used to designate the discipline, its methods; and theories, as opposed to the materials themselves.

Current everyday uses of the terms "folk" and "folklore" provoke two highly contrasting images: the traces of an idealized, aesthetically satisfying, and politically serene preindustrial past vs. the remains of an irrational, superstitious premodernism. Especially in eighteenth- and nineteenth-century Germany, but also in other settings, romantic nationalism, or other ethnic and linguistic (including postcolonial) nationalisms, have been prominent in conceptualizing and institutionalizing the field. Indeed the original development of the concept of *Volk* and *Volkskunde* may be read as in part a German-nationalist response to Napoleonic France's heritage of Enlightenment philosophy and imperial expansionism (Cocchiara 1981).

In tracing and attempting to institutionalize human commonalities based on language and common history (especially language-based ethnic or racial identity) such romantic nationalism offered a counterstatement to the eighteenth-century Enlightenment program of pragmatic and objective rationalism. For romantic nationalists the folk community became the repository of a vernacular language and an assumed body of shared indigenous knowledge or beliefs, often poetic, imaginative, or spiritual in content, generally communicated face-to-face by community members (and not mediated by print or generated by and across impersonal institutions).

These characteristics were taken positively as the psychological and ideological basis for an emerging national identity. Thus Johann Gottfried von Herder, in collecting and publishing German-language folksongs in the late eighteenth century, and the brothers Grimm, in their nineteenth-century collections of folktales (*Märchen*) and legends, pursued policies of selection intended to provide a cultural base for both a common national consciousness and the proper raising of children imbued with ethics and loyalty to a German nation-state, then not yet politically realized. In Europe until quite recently, a prominent line of folklore study has been regional, national, and international mapping. This historical–geographic school focused on taxonomic identification and worldwide comparison of forms of cultural expression characteristic of locales, regions, linguistic groups, or nations. Its work is exemplified by Antti Aarne's *The types of the folktale* (1928). Georges Dumézil's (1981) twentieth-century Indo-European comparative mythology shares with it strong nineteenth-century roots in comparative philology and historical linguistics, but is not considered a part of the historical–geographic folkloristics.

The development of folklore studies in nineteenth-century England counterpoised a premodern cultural base, barely surviving in rural communities, to a dehumanizing and demoralizing industrial urbanism, seen by some Victorian intellectuals as particularly destructive to working-class morality. Thus the theme of ethnic nationalism, although present in other UK folklore studies (especially in Ireland, Wales, and Scotland), was less prominent in England itself, where it was replaced by a nostalgic critique of industrialization and urbanization.

Folklore study in England took an intellectual position at odds with early-twentieth-century British FUNCTIONALISM, an anthropological theory that emphasized the synchronic study of social systems deemed both structurally coherent and "functional." Functionalists rejected the past-oriented, historically reconstructive study of threatened "cultural survivals," assuming that when such cultural materials lost utility in maintaining a community (physically, socially, or ideologically) they would naturally disappear. But if cultural properties were in use, then they were to be considered functional, and the researcher was to discover how they functioned. The theory implied an Enlightenment-inspired, modernist, utilitarian model of social change as adaptation, producing synchronic "snapshots" of communities. Folklore study, on the other hand, leaned toward a "salvage" investigation of cultural materials, often fragmentary and in danger of loss. Folklorists did not assume that such fragmentation implied inutility, especially given the aesthetic or ethical significance of their material, and held that change is more often the product of aggressively intrusive, destructive outside influences than indigenous adaptation. If functional anthropology took primacy under colonial regimes (customs being documented in order to integrate local communities into colonial legal and administrative structures), however, in the POSTCOLONIAL era folklore documentation has been fostered by new states promoting national self-identification (e.g., through the Irish Folklore Commission in Ireland or the Bangla Academy in Bangladesh).

While English (and American) folklore's model was not explicitly antipragmatic, one tendency in its adversarial relation to pragmatic modernism was a focus on aesthetic and expressive productions (especially verbal texts, but also ritual and customary or ritualized knowledge) rather than on material-cultural production. Insight into nonliterate modes of textual production was one important product of the aesthetic reexamination of texts deemed to be oral in origin, or found in oral performance in particular social contexts, as in the widely debated "oral-formulaic theory" of epic verse composition devcloped by Milman Parry and Albert Lord (Lord 1960; Finnegan 1977; J. Foley 1990). Very different lines of textual analysis also developed in the early to mid-twentieth century. STRUCTURALISM (Lévi-Strauss 1963a, 1969–81, 1995; Bremond 1973; Greimas 1983), Formalism (Propp 1958), and more recently, ethnopoetics (Hymes 1981; Tedlock 1983; see POETRY) have all furnished different approaches to meaning and form in verbal texts. A structuralist approach to material culture was explored by Glassie (1975).

Thus "folklore" and its field of reference vary with each national or communal history in which the development occurred, and tap diverse theoretical trends in linguistics and psychology, among other disciplines. Before the current, highly self-conscious era of intellectual historiography, many definitions of "folklore" resorted to lists of types of material. These included noninstitutionalized pre-Enlightenment attitudes, beliefs, and values, indigenous preindustrial technologies, and products and genres of verbal art, such as oral epic, folktale, legend, folk song, proverbs, riddles, and later folk sermons and personal-experience narratives. On the other hand homiletics as taught in seminaries, novels, or the first book of *Genesis* (as opposed to belief in fairies), were deemed nonfolkloric and excluded from study.

After some decades in which pragmatic issues were downplayed in American folklore studies in favor of verbal texts, the term "folklife" was introduced in the United States in the 1960s to emphasize not just verbal arts, ritual, and custom but a wider range of material-cultural production as well. In Europe, *Volkskunde* did not entail any marginalization of material-culture studies: a community's way of making bread or cloth was as centrally implicated as were folktales. American adoption of the term "folklife" under European influence (Dorson 1972) signaled a revival of interest in non-text-centered matters, and also a more systems-oriented, phenomenological approach to belief studies. The lists of forms or processes documented still varied with the interests of particular scholars, and debates continued about the "authenticity" of different cultural productions ("authenticity" being a key concept under scrutiny in folklorists' present assessments of their intellectual and ideological history).

Yet there were and are common aspects of the field across all its variations, such as the ever-almost-disappearing status of many objects of study. Of course, memory cultures are perpetually losing their oldest generation, who are their deepest repositories of information. But more than that, folklore was, and often is, perceived as the culture of marginal, embattled, or threatened communities, whole systems on the brink of obliteration. From its inception, the field had a fairly explicit commitment to cultural advocacy; not to study from a neutral position, but to preserve certain cultural materials in the face of the corrosive effects of "social change," "modernization" or "Westernization," "capitalism," "commoditization," "cultural imperialism," etc.

The appropriate forms of cultural advocacy have been debated. Preservationists have varied in their emphasis on the folk or the lore: whether the preservation of the knowledge is more important than (or possibly without) the protection of communities or populations. Similarly there are different sets of relationships among members of a cultural community who generate and perpetuate local knowledge and those who can socially or pragmatically deploy that knowledge. A conservative strain was led in the United States during the 1960s by Richard Dorson, head of Indiana University's Folklore Institute, constructing folklore (the discipline) as exclusively academic documentation and analysis, not social activism promoting cultural productions outside the academy, or protecting social groups directly. Dorson applied the term "fakelore" (1971) to cultural productions that quoted (or masqueraded as) locally based, vernacular, preindustrial forms, presented for a nonlocal, nonfluent, postindustrial, popular audience (e.g., the then vigorous Folksong Revival). Meanwhile, European scholarship, also taken up in the US, recognized processes as "folk" in the midst of postindustrial urban society (Bausinger 1990). This critique entailed eventual recognition that literacy or print culture does not necessarily exclude or marginalize oral processes, and furthermore that some writing practices should be counted "folk" – from graffiti to xerox lore and e-mail narratives, thus opening up the large topic of ethnographies of literacy (Finnegan 1988). Most recently, the recognition of "folk" processes in interactive electronic communications makes "face-to-face" no longer a criterion for folk group membership; hence folk groups and vernacular discourses on the Internet.

In the United States, the civil-rights movement and feminism pointed out processes of marginalization and cultural maintenance other than technological or rural-to-urban. American folkloristics, both academic and "applied" (in cultural advocacy), emphasized how folklore, as knowledge, values, beliefs, and practices, both derives from communities and functions to constitute them. Alan Dundes's (1966a) influential definition stipulated that "The term 'folk' can refer to *any group of people whatsoever* who share at least one common factor. It does not matter what the linking factor . . . a group for whatever reason will have some traditions that it calls its own." Thus "folk" groups and their shared "lore" exist at all levels of society: professional groups and gender- and age-graded groups (e.g., children of different ages: their shared lore in part constitutes their "age group" as we perceive it), historical cohorts (Holocaust survivors), voluntary associations, and local, ethnic, racial, and class enclaves. This shift questioned the salience, if not the objective existence, of analytic "genres" extrinsically defined, favoring attention on genres or categories of cultural production as perceived by practitioners. One aspect of this shift from artifacts to events and processes was to emphasize the self-aware, reflexive, and critical aspects of communicative acts. Documentation shifted from texts and objects to forms of social interaction, performance events and processes, sharings of "lore" (with an eye to their significance as internally interpreted by participants), and how such interactions create and maintain social groups, making people "insiders" and "outsiders." Although group consensus processes remain a central interest, issues of contest, difference, and multiple or ambiguous group membership are directly implicated. Cultural advocacy airs issues of group self-presentation in local folk festivals displaying ethnically or regionally derived cultural productions, in heritage museums and other sites. In the United States, the National Folk Festival showcases different regions and ethnic and professional groups annually on the Capitol Mall in Washington, DC (Regina Bendix 1988; Kirshenblatt-Gimblett 1988).

Most recently, the performance-studies emphasis (Baumann 1977; Bauman &

Briggs 1990), prominent in American folkloristics from the late 1960s through the 1980s, has shifted to examine how cultural formulations transcend individual moments of enactment: thus "traditional" as an index of the "authenticity" of a practice or a text is now studied as "traditionalizing," the process by which aspects of the past are evoked as significant and authoritative in the present, a topic of general relevance to historical studies. The idea of context has come to designate not some prior array of conditions under which a particular performance or communication occurred, but the ways in which participants in communicative events negotiate and thus create what they deem to be the relevant contexts and continuities, as aspects of the nature of the event itself. Beyond the cataloguing of texts as autonomous objects, "entextualization" receives new interest: how specific formulations (verbal, material, or "scripted" actions of ritual or custom) are transported and identifiable from one performance to another. The interest is now not just in taxonomic comparison, but in participants' awareness of taxonomic features as one aspect of the phenomenon of textuality, the persistence and mutability of cultural forms and their consensual meanings across time and different contexts of enactment. Issues of contest, marginalization, colonization, subversion, and representation figure prominently in current debates (C. Briggs & Shuman 1993; Radner 1993). The ambitious goal is an effective examination of meaning making in the interaction of individual creative agency with bodies of social or cultural expectation, forms of received knowledge, and authority.   MM

further reading Bauman 1992; Ben-Amos 1976; Briggs 1993; Handler & Linnekin 1984; S. Hollis et al. 1993; Limón & Young 1986; Paredes & Bauman 1972; Toelken 1979

folk–urban continuum is a model developed by Robert REDFIELD (1897–1958) to classify different types of community and historic process, which he illustrated with examples from the Yucatan peninsula of Mexico (Redfield 1941). At one end of the continuum was the "modern" city of Merida, while at the other was a small, "traditional" indigenous village. These two communities represented the most and the least developed types. In comparing them Redfield examined their respective TECHNOLOGY, SOCIAL ORGANIZATION, and WORLDVIEW (Miner 1952). Thus Merida was a modern city populated with many individuals who participated in national and international affairs, were relatively free to make social and economic decisions, and had modern worldviews. In contrast the "Indians" of the village lived from foraging (see FORAGERS) and SWIDDEN agriculture. They had a prescientific worldview and unlike the individual freedom and modernity of the urbanites, they were tightly incorporated into familial and community social relationships that restricted personal freedom. Intermediate between these polar extremes Redfield identified two other communities: a commercial rural "town" with close ties to the city, and the PEASANT community of Chan Kom, which had a mix of "traditional" and "modern" features but more closely resembled the village. Redfield saw historical change as occurring by the DIFFUSION of modern technology, social forms, and ideas outward from the city toward the folk end of the continuum in a gradual process of MODERNIZATION.

MK

food production began more than 10,000 years ago when broad-spectrum procurement was supplanted by the domestication and cultivation of edible plant and animal species in many parts of the world (Flannery 1973; Spielmann & Eder 1994). Since that time agricultural methods have ranged from extensive SWIDDEN cultivation, which allowed farmers to continue to forage, to intensive permanent cultivation in which farmers came to depend entirely on cultivated crops and domestic animals for subsistence. AGRICULTURE relying on IRRIGATION developed along rivers and streams, progressing from pot irrigation to canals and finally state-run complex HYDRAULIC SYSTEMS, creating competition for land, and demands for coordination of labor, water, and conflict negotiation. Differential production of livestock and plant crops is governed by access to land, available labor, political-economic conditions, and terms of exchange with specialist groups such as PASTORAL NOMADS.

Close linkages exist between water control and command over food and people. Anthropologists continue to argue over what stimulates technological innovation and agricultural intensification: population pressure or culture? Rejecting environmental determinist or possibilist views, Boserup (1965) argued that the process is largely cultural, and that population is more a stimulus than a drain. In fact, Wittfogel's (1957) hypothesis that states evolved in order to organize large hydraulic irrigation systems has not been widely confirmed; outside of Peru, nuclear zones of irrigated agricultural development show that population growth and centralization preceded the rise of complex irrigation systems; the key factor may be the possibility to exploit multiple forms of irrigation.

MODES OF PRODUCTION reliant on kinship and sexual division of labor, and governed by cultural rules dictating land tenure, labor-sharing, and particular planting materials for particular cropping conditions, are detailed in traditional ethnographies from all parts of the world. More focused, problem-oriented studies document how intergenerational fragmentation of plots, competing uses for land and labor, and restricted access by women to new technologies may undermine household food (production) security and the success of development programs meant to increase food and income (Shipton 1994). Attrition of traditional seed stocks may accompany the demise of traditional diversified, risk-averse planting strategies that emphasize food security rather than maximum possible yields of single crops. Political or market pressures for greater yields and income through monocropping or cash cropping in Africa have led to the abandonment of traditional drought-resistant sorghums and millets in favor of maize; and, worldwide, they have reduced literally hundreds of traditional rices to a few modern varieties. Communities may also lose traditional knowledge of practices that enabled them to cope with climatic and biological (weeds, insects, diseases)

stressors over the cultivation cycle. The pollutant load on the environment of chemical-pesticide-intensive agronomic methods also upsets local ecology and damages human health.

Further stressors on food production are population growth, changes in land-use patterns that reduce forageable areas, and famine-relief policies that keep people in fixed locations where they cannot support themselves in a bad year or season. The requisition of crops by local interests, the state, or insurgents, and social instability or warfare that interfere with agricultural and market processes, are additional elements spelling HUNGER for local populations or certain households (S. Whiteford & Ferguson 1991).

Key concerns for the future are the sustainability of energy- and chemical-intensive agricultural production, and its capacity to adapt to climate change and to the increasing food demand of burgeoning human populations (L. Brown & Kane 1994). APPLIED ANTHROPOLOGY has devoted considerable effort to understanding the conditions, or decision-making rules, under which peasant cultivators accept more modern methods and intensify production for market production (Barkin et al. 1990). However, the challenge of feeding all the people on earth in the next century must be addressed by added emphases on the potential contributions of indigenous knowledge and women, and on diets that rely less on resource-demanding livestock.   EM
See also DIET,   FOOD   SYSTEMS, TECHNOLOGY

food systems interrelate all aspects of food from procurement through consumption: the ecology of food production and marketing; food classification and social rules for food distribution; nutritional and health consequences of particular patterns of food use, especially patterns of food sharing; and also the political contexts of food production and consumption strategies (Messer 1984).

Food systems shape culturally constructed DIETS so that societies and individuals acquire the right quantities and combinations of foods to meet essential nutritional needs. These have been examined in a variety of different ways: ARCHAEOLOGY has traced population growth and the rise and fall of civilizations against transformations of food species, production and processing technologies, and water management (Flannery 1973). CULTURAL MATERIALISM has argued that food-related shifts in ecology can be traced to changes in political-economic power (Harris 1979; Harris and Ross 1987a). SYMBOLIC ANTHROPOLOGY has focused on the dietary dimensions of myth and folklore, ritual and social identity (L. Hanks 1972; Manderson 1986), and LINGUISTIC anthropology has collected and analyzed indigenous "ethnoclassifications" of food species, productive environments, nutrition and health, and "food codes" as social markers of class, caste, or ethnicity (Farb & Armelagos 1980; M. Douglas 1984). In MEDICAL ANTHROPOLOGY and nutritional anthropology, researchers have combined scientific and folkloric analysis to map changing diets and their health consequences. These interconnect food and nutrition at individual, household, community, national, and global levels (Quandt & Ritenbaugh 1986; Pelto et al. 1989).

Ethnographic studies

Ethnographic studies have advanced analyses of small-group "optimal foraging strategies," community agriculture and diet, and nutritional, political, and semiotic dimensions of complex diets in industrialized countries. Food-focused Pacific ethnologies, such as of the Tikopia (R. Firth 1936), the Dobu (Fortune 1932), and the Massim (Michael W. Young 1971), depict societies where kinship, gender, and superhuman relationships are all brokered in terms of food with prescriptions and proscriptions (taboos) on what, and with whom, one could eat.

Classic British FUNCTIONALIST ethnographies were usually community studies, set in the context of the greater colonial or national political economy. They focused particularly on the local ecosystem as managed by local agricultural customs and identified what factors reduce food production, household food availability, and individual nutrition. The best known is Audrey RICHARDS's (1939) study of politics, agriculture, and malnutrition among the Bemba of Northern Rhodesia (Zambia), which analyzes in detail the cropping system based on shifting millet cultivation, multi- and intercropping with seasonal foraging, the cultural rules for ranking staples (millet was preferred over maize because of its higher bulk and capacity to stave off hunger), and preferred ratios of porridge to relish. It also considers how food was rationed and food sharing shrank during seasons of dearth. It also describes nutritional (functional) consequences of these production and consumption shortfalls: cultivators were hungry and exhausted during planting season and so could not expand production. The British had drawn men away to work in the mines, leaving local communities with a shortage of labor, a deteriorating food situation, and a cycle of undernutrition.

Impacts of the larger political-economic and technological context on food systems have been addressed in historical and ethnographic accounts focusing on: the intercontinental diffusion, such as the "Colombian Exchange" of food crops (N. Foster & Cordell 1992); agricultural intensification or involution (C. Geertz 1963c); the cultural history of national diets (Chang 1977; Eugene N. Anderson 1988); and the human significance of particular cash crops, such as sugar (Mintz 1985). Anthropologists have also looked at political economy (Harris & Ross 1987b), energy flow (Rappaport 1967; R. Thomas 1973), tastes and symbolism (J. Goody 1982), and intrahousehold resource allocations (Sharman et al. 1991). Action-oriented studies look increasingly also at the terms under which households and communities are integrated into the larger state or global food economy, highlighting the failures of development policy, states, and food relief (Huss-Ashmore & Katz 1989–90).

The United Nations Research Institute for Social Development (UNRISD) has investigated the ecological, market, socioeconomic, sociocultural, and nutritional-health consequences of the Green Revolution seed–water–chemical technologies in Indonesia, India, Malaysia, Mexico,

Bolivia, Sri Lanka, and the Philippines (Hewitt de Alcantara 1994). These food-systems analyses depart from other Green Revolution studies, in that they examine simultaneously the impacts of the new technologies on the distribution of resources, the natural environment, and farmers in different social strata who may be rendered more vulnerable to international market fluctuations or political manipulations as a result of the changes in subsistence and cash cropping. Food-systems analyses go beyond other types of evaluative analyses, carried out principally by political economists, that focus on production or consumption, or both, but not all factors together. They trace the impacts of higher-level food policies on lower social levels or scales, and provide up-to-date critiques of both Western and communist-socialist regimes. Ideological differences notwithstanding, from a food-systems perspective, both seem to be more concerned with power than people's well-being (Barraclough 1991).

Biocultural studies of nutrition and foodways

Foodways are the ideas and behaviors that affect what people eat. These include culturally specific definitions of what does or does not constitute food, the ranking of desirable foods, their preparation and COOKING and how these together create a cuisine. They also encompass such fields of social interaction as distribution rules (including ritual exchange) and obligatory or prohibited commensalism. Rules that prescribe or proscribe specific foods often single out particular social categories (especially reproductive-aged women and younger children). Such rules sometimes pit local understandings of the nutritional consequences of particular diets against scientific ones.

Biocultural anthropologists have combined folkloric, technological, and nutritional analyses of human consumption patterns to focus on the evolution of human foodways (Ritenbaugh 1978). The key issues include the biological consequences of particular diets on individuals, populations, and the environment, and the impact of human biological characteristics on the cultural selection and processing of food.

Because food customs evolve through time, a key question is whether particular foodways are "adaptive," that is, whether they allow a human population to be better nourished or to maintain the same level of nutrition with less stress on environmental resources. Case studies focus on how a cultural group renders a particular plant, animal, or microbe nutritionally valuable in their diet. For example, Mediterranean herders who cannot digest milk use traditional food fermentation technology to turn milk into yogurt or curds, digestible matter that extends the nutritional life of milk. Western-hemisphere cultivators of maize alkali-treat the grain by soaking it in woodash or boiling it with limestone, so that it is easier to process and also more digestible and nutritious.

More problematic are the changing dietary and "adaptive" values of particular food species, flavors, or textures, especially sweets and fats. In nature, sweetness, in contrast to bitterness, usually characterizes pleasant and desirable foods that are not poisonous and are good sources of calories. From birth, humans seem to have an ingrained preference for sweet foods (which include breastmilk) that contribute to good nutrition (Messer 1986). But as refined sugar in large measure replaces more nutritious sugar calories, a biological and cultural taste preference for "safe," "adaptive," high-energy sweet foods can become a health hazard. Similarly, a taste for fat as a rich source of energy and carrier of fat-soluble vitamins had past adaptive value for foragers and others on more restricted diets. But fat overindulgence in wealthy INDUSTRIAL SOCIETIES contributes to obesity and cardiovascular illness. The more general demand for flesh foods, which are concentrated sources of quality nutrition, also reduces land and water available for plant food production, and grain resources available for direct human consumption.

The implications of the apparent biological ability of humans to survive on less than optimal quantities of food has been the subject of considerable debate (Messer 1989b). Eating less in childhood results in individuals with lowered growth, more sickness, and reduced activity over their lifetimes. But a willingness to eat less also may be reinforced culturally in harsh environments by a positive value on appetite control and slimness, reflected through principles of moderation in normal times and self-denial in designated periods of fasting. Hindu and Muslim populations in South and Southeast Asia, and Native American populations prior to dietary modernization, encouraged and celebrated the ability to fast periodically because it prepared individuals to withstand periodic food shortages and famine. Modern nutritional anthropologists question how rapidly such customs change; although adaptive to dearth at a population level, they may be harmful to individuals and unnecessary in modern contexts where food is not in such short supply.

Access to marketed foods and to nonagricultural employment income or relief are increasingly parts of even the most rural food systems. Such dietary diversification and delocalization, however, is not necessarily replicated in systems of FOOD PRODUCTION, which under modernization tend more toward single crops and are more vulnerable to crop failures. In addition, the demand by governments and growers for cash may increase the production of marketed crops, such as peanuts, over traditional grains and destroy traditional symbiosis between herders and farmers (Franke & Chasin 1980).

Food-distribution rules can create pathways through which the less entitled receive food in ordinary or more stressful times. However, foodflows may also be indicators of stress: as resources shrink, networks of hospitality also shrink and people tend to eat alone so that they will not have to share. The ultimate outcome of inadequate food and diet for individuals is malnutrition, illness, and death. Unbalanced diets, particularly micronutrient deficiencies, can also affect the health and social functioning of entire communities. Iodine deficiencies, historically endemic to many mountainous regions and communities, slow down sociocultural life and economic production (Greene 1977). Vitamin A deficiencies increase the burden of blindness for affected individuals and communities. Some micronutrient deficiencies characteristic of sparse

and monotonous local diets are being removed by greater market integration and delocalization of diets. But more reliance on market sources of food also increases the likelihood that adaptive dietary patterns will be abandoned in favor of relatively costly but less nutritious prestige items such as Coca Cola, or less nutritionally diverse diets based on preferred staples, as when polished rice replaces brown rice.

More reliance on MARKETS assumes, but cannot guarantee, a steady, reliable food supply and the ability to buy it. Access to markets for labor and products, in the context of cultural food preferences and social rules for food and labor sharing, greatly shape food strategies and household and community vulnerability to local climatic or political hazards. For example, political policies may limit refugees' market options and force such displaced populations to become entirely dependent on aid (Harrell-Bond 1986). In the modern world isolation from markets can be as food depriving as natural ecological factors.   EM

See also AGRICULTURE, FOOD TABOO, HUNGER

further reading Clark & Brandt 1984; Fitzgerald 1976; Rindos 1984; Robson 1980

food taboo   is the intentional avoidance of an otherwise comestible item because of its culturally alleged sacred or social character. Early anthropologists drew on FRAZER's (1910) association of TABOOS with clan TOTEM species and Freud's (1918) observation that both food and sexual avoidances shared the common characteristics of mysterious and sacred power, capacity for good or harm, and desirability and obtainablility. DURKHEIM (1915) and RADCLIFFE-BROWN (1939) interpreted the common avoidance of tabooed species or substances (such as BLOOD) by clan members as a social and psychological functional bond, uniting and setting them apart from other social groups. Commensalism formed the shared identity: "you are what you (don't) eat." LÉVI-STRAUSS (1963b) explored totem–taboo as social-structural principle: totemic species and food taboos are "good to think with," a principle also developed by Leach

(1964) and Tambiah (1969) – "animals are good to think and good to prohibit."

In *Purity and danger* (1966), Mary DOUGLAS argued that tabooed species tend to be phylogenetically or structurally anomalous, and are used to highlight the internal structure and boundaries of the animal kingdom and social world. Physical or behavioral traits of the tabooed species enable the society to distinguish between pure or complete vs. anomalous or dangerous categories that appear to cross and therefore threaten social or natural boundaries. The pangolin or the monitor lizard (a "reptile that flies") and the baboon (which was associated with "spirit" places and bears single young) came too close for comfort to the category "human" and were therefore objects of ritual cult and avoidance among the Lele in Africa. Similarly the Biblical exclusion of the pig was based on its anomalous characteristics: it lacked cloven hooves and did not chew the cud as permitted "clean" animals did. Other tabooed animals were also close to humans, such as dogs in modern Western society, or chickens for women in Chad (O'Laughlin 1974). An additional step for Douglas was to interpret shared cognitive categories and food taboos as boundary-maintaining mechanisms. Thus, avoidance of pork became a key symbol of Jewish survival, and defiance of those who would try to humiliate or subdue them by forcing them to eat pork. Yet in acculturating circumstances, forbidden foods become dangerously desirable for those experiencing or asserting freedom from the boundaries, bounds, or bonds of tradition, as where modern American Jews eat pork or shellfish, modern Muslims consume alcohol, and Hindus try goat or beef.

Juxtaposed to these functional, structural, and semiotic understandings are CULTURAL MATERIALIST frames of analysis, which have examined the nutritional-health or ecological consequences of food taboos in particular contexts. Special dietary restrictions most noticeably influence the nutritional intakes of reproductive-aged women during menarche, menstruation, pregnancy, the postpartum period, and lactation; and children prior to weaning and during their subadult years. Children in African societies may be denied eggs, while in Southeast Asian societies boys do not eat green leafy vegetables (Manderson 1981). In all cases, the ostensible purpose of taboos is to protect the fertility of women or proper maturation of children. Actual nutritional impact is influenced by whether the rules are harmful and depriving: are there alternative sources of the food energy, protein, or vitamins that are being denied? Health consequences also depend on how recognized or widespread such prohibitions are, because some taboos are only for particular seasons or circumscribed periods in the life cycle. They also depend on whether individuals follow the rules; not all individuals know or observe taboos, and some even take special ritual measures to thwart them, as where women in certain African settings join cults that allow them access to otherwise forbidden dairy products.

Food taboos have been studied especially among FORAGERS, who ordinarily know and consume hundreds of food species, but surround them with hundreds of taboos. In the Ituri forest of Zaire, Aunger (1994a,b) elicited more than 300 reasons for particular food avoidances: most common were appearance (homeopathic avoidance – not wanting to look like the item), place in myth or history, or perceived dirty, predatory, or humanlike characteristics. But many food restrictions were limited to a certain life stage; and there was abundant intracultural variation in knowledge. Food taboos were usually handed down from father to son, or from mother to daughter, and in practice individuals accidentally or intentionally often forgot to observe them. Nevertheless, food taboos may magnify effects of seasonal or other restrictions on nutrient intake. They may put women particularly at nutritional risk during critical periods in their reproductive cycles, and as a result, lower fertility, raise infant mortality, and decrease child survival (Laderman 1983). Taboos on feeding infants colostrum or other "bad milk" associated with a mother's new pregnancy or other illness may also jeopardize child survival (C. Wilson 1980). At a population level, food avoidances may have insignificant consequences, although practice may affect individual consumption, nutrition, and health (Messer 1981).

Alternatively, food taboos can be analyzed as beneficial for nutrition, health, or for ecology and sustainable livelihoods. Asian cultures that ban foods, particularly shellfish species that are classified as "itchy" or "poison," may be reducing intake of annoying or more damaging allergens. Taboos associated with salt consumption may be helping infants or others in hot dry climates maintain electrolyte balance. Improperly cooked pork may carry trichinosis. All are examples of the ways dietary taboos may protect individual or group health; although, as Douglas has opined, to treat dietary laws only as public health and medicine belittles their spiritual significance and social value. In modern secular society, characterized by global nutrition culture, salt, fat, and especially cholesterol have become "taboo" for health reasons, but symbolism is diminished.

Other cultural-materialist analyses interpret restrictions as unconscious mechanisms through which ritual manages the ecology and preserves human populations and the edible species on which they rely. HARRIS (1974) has also suggested that the Hebrew ban on pig was a cultural and ecological marker: pastoral or nomadic people could not keep pigs, a houseyard species. The Tikopian chief's ban on consumption of his produce and underripe specimens after a devastating cyclone is perhaps the finest example of the ecological, nutritional, and survival value of taboos, which also are central symbols in the social structure of Tikopian culture (R. Firth 1959).   EM
See also DIET, FOOD, PURITY/POLLUTION
further reading Farb & Armelagos 1980; Spielmann 1989

foragers, foraging Foragers are peoples who subsist on hunting, gathering, and fishing with no domesticated plants, and no domesticated animals except the dog. Sociopolitical organization varies: many foragers were organized into seminomadic bands of 25–50 people, but a significant number lived in ranked societies with the beginnings of centralized leadership. Before the beginnings of AGRICUL-

TURE, 10,000–15,000 years ago, foraging was the universal mode of human subsistence. Even 500 years ago, up to one-third of the habitable world was still occupied by hunters and gatherers. Today foraging persists as a way of life only in a handful of remote and sparsely populated areas. The last 30 years have seen the most precipitous decline; many peoples who were foraging even in the 1960s have been settled (some forcibly) and integrated into national polities and world markets.

Although many people continue to seek in the study of foragers insights into human history and human nature, it is necessary to proceed with great caution. Foragers are in no way missing links; their history is as long as the history of any other human group. And notions of forager isolation have been exaggerated. Some foragers in Asia and Africa have been in contact with nonforagers for fifteen hundred years. In the last three centuries tens of thousands of former foragers in the Americas, Asia, and Africa have been incorporated into the agrarian and industrial structures of their surrounding societies, usually at the bottom of the social scale. Nevertheless what is remarkable is that dozens of foraging peoples have resisted these pressures and have maintained their identity and way of life. Used prudently, the study of foragers can yield insights into the human condition in societies lacking state structures or complex technology (Clastres 1987).

Today foragers and former foragers persist in a number of world regions:

(1) North America: Before colonization about two-thirds of North America was occupied by hunters and gatherers, including most of what is now Canada and much of the United States west of the Mississippi. Viable contemporary foragers include the James Bay Cree, the subarctic Dene in western Canada and Alaska, and the Inuit (Eskimo) of the arctic littoral.

(2) South America: The southern third of the continent was occupied by foragers, including the Ona and Yaghan of Tierra del Fuego and the Toba of Argentina. Some of these became mounted hunters with the arrival of the horse, a process that paralleled the situation of the Plains Indians of North America. The numerous

peoples of the Amazon and Orinoco basins combined foraging with shifting horticulture, with a few peoples like the Cuiva of Venezuela, relying almost entirely on foraging.

(3) Africa: Africa is home to several well-known foraging peoples. The Pygmies, occupying the equatorial rain forest from Cameroon to Rwanda, divide their time between work for their farming neighbors and independent forest-dwelling. In the Kalahari Desert of Botswana and Namibia live the San peoples or Bushmen. While some, like the Ju/'hoansi and /Gwi, remained relatively autonomous into the postwar period, the majority have been reduced to serflike status in African villages or European farms. In East Africa the Hadza of Tanzania have remained independent, and the Okiek of Kenya have long-established trade relations with the Maasai.

(4) South and Southeast Asia: In this region of ancient civilizations a surprising number of foragers exist, occupying upland forested areas and providing forest products (honey, medicinal herbs, rattan) to the lowland markets. It is this economic niche presumably that has allowed the South Asian hunter–gatherers to persist to the present and remain viable. Examples include the Veddahs of Sri Lanka, the Nayaka of Kerala, the Birhor of Bihar, and the Chenchu of Assam. Most famous are the Andaman Islanders, some of whom remained isolated into the late nineteenth century and in one case well into the twentieth. "Orang-asli" is a cover term for the indigenous nonagricultural peoples of the Malay peninsula. Best known are the Semang, Semai, and Batek. Other groups are found in Thailand, Burma, Laos, and China's Yunnan province. On the island of Borneo live the Penan of Sarawak, firmly rooted in hunting and gathering until recent displacement by multinational logging interests. The Philippines have several pockets of foraging peoples, including the Agta of northeastern Luzon, famous for their women hunters. The "discovery" of the Tasaday of Mindanao in the 1970s caused a media sensation when they were touted as the "Lost Stone-Age Find of the Century." It now seems clear that claims

for their isolation and stone-age technology were greatly exaggerated.

(5) Russia: Over 40 of northern Russia's "small peoples" have traditionally followed a foraging way of life, combined in varying degrees with reindeer herding. Examples include the Khanty, Nenets, Evenki, Nganasan, Chukchi, and Itelmens. During the Soviet period the heavy industrialization of the north caused serious environmental degradation, which has adversely affected the survival of the small peoples.

(6) Australia: Prior to European colonization, Australia was entirely occupied by hunting and gathering peoples. Today the Aborigines are divided between the urbanized south and the rural north; in the latter a significant degree of foraging occurs. After centuries of racism, Australia has made a strong commitment to Aboriginal welfare and self-government, highlighted by the 1992 Supreme Court "Mabo" decision, which recognized the validity of Aboriginal land rights.

Once the exclusive human occupants of planet earth, the foraging peoples of today are now encapsulated minorities whose social conditions and life chances vary widely. While some occupy stable ecosystems under no immediate threat, many find themselves directly in the path of mining, logging, and agricultural megaprojects. A number of groups have gone to the courts, international organizations, and the world media to gain support in countering these threats to their survival (M. Miller 1993). The future of former foragers is now closely bound up with worldwide social movements for environmental justice and human rights.   RiL

See also BAND SOCIETIES, HUNTING

further reading Bettinger 1991; Bicchieri 1972; Burch 1994; Ingold et al. 1988; Kelley 1995; Lee & DeVore 1968

Forde, Daryll (1902–73)

Daryll Forde was one of the most important figures in British social anthropology, yet has rarely been given his full appreciation. He was in many ways a maverick, and his publications were relatively few. He was one of the few social anthropologists of his period who was not a member of

MALINOWSKI's famed seminar in the 1930s; and he never troubled to become the leader of a "school" of younger anthropologists. Yet those who were taught by him or worked with him consider him to be one of the few figures of historical importance in the discipline.

Cyril Daryll Forde was born in London in 1902, the son of a Church of England clergyman. He went to school in London and then to University College London to take his BA in Geography and his Ph.D in Prehistoric Archaeology. In later years he remained closely associated with the great archaeologist V. Gordon Childe, a leading academic marxist theoretician of the time. In 1928 he took the then unusual step of going to the University of California at Berkeley to work with A. L. KROEBER and Robert LOWIE, and carried out field research among the Yuma of California and the Hopi of Arizona. In 1930, at the early age of 28, he became Professor of Geography and Anthropology at the University College of Wales at Aberystwyth, where he continued archaeological excavation in Wales and initiated research in contemporary Welsh towns and villages. In 1935 he went to Nigeria to work among the Yako of the Cross River. After spending most of the World War II years as a researcher for the Foreign Office, in 1945 he became Professor of Anthropology at his old college, University College London, where he remained until his death in 1973. Against what was then the fashion in Britain, he retained his devotion to a single discipline comprising social, biological, archaeological, and linguistic anthropology, and trained many of the leading younger anthropologists of the 1950s and later.

In 1944 he also took over the nominal, part-time directorship of the then largely colonialist and semimoribund International African Institute, in London, and transformed it into the leading Modern-Africa research and publishing institution: he edited the journal *Africa* and published many volumes of ethnography and also the *Ethnographic survey of Africa, African abstracts* and other publications. He worked tirelessly at administering the Institute; was a thoughtful, detailed, and encouraging editor; and organized and obtained funding for the long series of successful seminars held in various African countries and on various subjects. These were chaired and attended by local researchers within Africa itself as well as academics from Europe; by doing this Forde built a new network of modern African scholars, not only in anthropology but also in economics, geography, history, religion, and aesthetics. Some recent attacks on Forde and the Institute as "colonialist" are quite unfounded: few if any did so much to break down the colonial intellectual boundaries between Africa and Europe.

His anthropological thinking is preserved more in the memories of those whom he knew and helped than in his own publications, which included many detailed accounts of aspects of Yako society and its culture (1941, 1958, 1964), the reports on Yuma and Hopi (1931), and many general papers on problems of research and development, in which he drew upon his wide knowledge of all fields of knowledge about Africa and his insistence on ethnography being both detailed and firmly based on ecological, economic, and demographic factors. He thought and wrote quickly and clearly, and abominated the masking of thought with jargon and pretentious recourse to "theory." His book *Habitat, economy and society* (1934) and his edited *African worlds* (1954) are both longstanding classics. A list of his publications is in *Man in Africa* (Douglas & Kaberry 1969). JM

formalist–substantivist debate is the dispute in ECONOMIC ANTHROPOLOGY between those scholars who argue that formal rules of neoclassical economic theory derived from the study of capitalist market societies can be used to explain the dynamics of premodern economies ("formalists") and those who argue that goods and services in the substantive economy are produced and distributed through specific cultural contexts ("substantivists"). Formalists contend that because all economies involve the rational pursuit of, access to, and use of, scarce resources by self-interested, maximizing social actors, formal economic rules can be used to explain them

(H. Schneider 1974). Substantivists, by contrast, contend that different forms of exchange have different sets of rules and expectations (Dalton 1961). Following Karl Polanyi the substantivists argue that there are three major forms of exchange: RECIPROCITY, REDISTRIBUTION, and MARKET exchange (K. Polanyi et al. 1957). By this view, the rational, maximizing strategizing that lies at the heart of neoclassical economics and formalist economic anthropology is characteristic only of market economies.   MR

Fortes, Meyer (1906–83) Meyer Fortes was born in Britstown, Cape Province, South Africa in 1906, to Russian Jewish immigrants. His early career was in psychology, in which he took a Ph.D. and helped pioneer the development of cross-cultural tests. His work with disadvantaged children in the East End of London in the late 1920s and early 1930s reinforced his appreciation of the collective dimension to human problems. This eventually led to an association with MALINOWSKI, under whom he switched over entirely to anthropology. Although a psychological undercurrent remained in all his work, henceforward he developed into one of the leading structural-functionalists (see FUNCTIONALISM). After fieldwork among the Tallensi of what is now Ghana in the mid-1930s, he obtained a lectureship in Oxford, only to see his career interrupted by World War II. After a brief period at the new West Africa Institute in Accra, he returned to Oxford as a Reader before going to Cambridge as William Wyse Professor, a position he retained until his retirement in 1973. He died in Cambridge in 1983.

Fortes contributed significantly to the anthropology of kinship, politics, religion, and the person, mostly using Tallensi material as the ethnographic basis for his theoretical discussions. In discussing kinship he made a distinction between the domestic and the politicojural domains (see 1949b, 1945, respectively; also 1953). The former revolved around the FAMILY, the unit of domestic production and reproduction, in which constraint was ultimately moral. Here, Fortes followed Malinowski in maintaining that psychological mechanisms of care and support – what Fortes variously called "the axiom of amity" and "the rule of prescriptive altruism" – were ultimately more significant than the jural rules and obligations that were operative in the politicojural domain. The latter was represented in the Tallensi case by the patrilineal *soog* or descent group. While the family was an institution that was basically temporary, dying with its members, the descent group was a perpetually existing corporation, which, by virtue of frequently acting as a unit in relation to other descent groups, could be seen as a "moral person."

Fortes also distinguished between descent and filiation, the former connecting several generations in one line (male or female) and thus necessarily being unilineal, the latter connecting children to their parents alone, and thus being bilateral (see Fortes 1953). From this, he developed the notion of COMPLEMENTARY FILIATION. He also stressed the vertical ties entailed by descent more than the horizontal ties between exogamous descent groups entailed by MARRIAGE, a view later characterized as "DESCENT THEORY" and opposed by proponents of "ALLIANCE THEORY" (Edmund LEACH, Louis Dumont, Rodney Needham, etc. after LÉVI-STRAUSS). For Fortes, DESCENT GROUPS were self-perpetuating and almost autonomous, whereas for alliance theorists they were interdependent because of their exogamy and consequent need for each others' women in marriage (see especially Leach 1957; Fortes 1959a; Leach 1960a; also Dumont 1971b: ch. 19).

Fortes's position in respect of descent also led to an interest in ANCESTORS as an object of worship, since they personified the descent group they initiated (1987: chs 3, 4). His interest in the person (1987: ch. 10) has to be linked to the family, at least initially, since this is the locus of upbringing and socialization. Yet here too the descent group is significant in the sense that membership of it, as much as marrying and producing children, is what makes one a moral person. Full personhood, however, depends on having a "good death," through having lived a full life, with heirs to leave behind one. Ancestor worship is at least partly a matter of removing or obviating the obstacles that one's ancestors might have placed in one's path. More generally, Fortes tried to move away from the Durkheimian view of the person as a largely passive responder to social dictates by adding to it a Malinowskian recognition of the legitimacy of self-awareness and reflexivity. Personhood was a matter not only of acquiring social knowledge but also of demonstrating it, in RITUAL in particular. However, for Fortes ritual also dealt with the unknown, reflecting Malinowski's view that ritual takes over where (technical) knowledge runs out.

As a functionalist, Fortes stressed the coherence of institutions in society, and his bias was firmly toward the synchronic, his idea of social dynamics being restricted to the notion of the LIFE CYCLE. He was less skeptical of general laws than his life-long friend and colleague EVANS-PRITCHARD and developed a view of kinship that went way beyond Malinowski's concentration on the nuclear family. In doing so – like Malinowski – he did not always resist the temptation to generalize from his main fieldwork area to the rest of humanity. Nonetheless, he consistently saw himself as a craftsman rather than a theoretician, always stressing the importance of ethnography. His reputation as a teacher stands high.   RP

further reading J. Barnes 1971; Fortes 1959b, 1969, 1970, 1978, 1983; Fortes & Evans-Pritchard 1940b; J. Goody 1983b; Schnepel 1991

Frankfurt school So called because of its location, the Frankfurt school offered a refuge for leftist intellectuals during the years prior to Hitler's takeover of Germany. It was the home of critical theory, a complex blend of sophisticated marxist thought, philosophy, psychoanalysis, literary speculation, and social research. Participants included the essayist Walter Benjamin, the psychoanalyst Erich Fromm, and the philosopher Herbert Marcuse. The present heir to the school is Jürgen Habermas, who has, however, moved far from the positions taken by the school's early leaders, Max Horkheimer and Theodor Adorno.

The major formative challenge to the Frankfurt school was the rise of Nazism, which obliged a rethinking of orthodox marxist doctrine. Frankfurt school scholars added cultural and psychological dimensions to the materialist model of society (Fromm 1941) and developed the F-scale, a still much-used psychological test for authoritarianism that links familial constellations with political attitudes (Adorno et al. 1950). Partly because of the results of this test, most members of the school relocated to New York, where they were instrumental in founding the New School for Social Research. Later work seriously scrutinized the paradoxes of mass culture and attempted to develop a liberating "negative dialectic" based on the self-subverting aesthetic of modern art and the liberating possibilities of the erotic (Marcuse 1968).

Because it argued against instrumental reason and positivism, the Frankfurt school is often seen as a precursor of romantic POSTMODERNISM; but these scholars believed strongly that rigorous intellectual work, a grasp of human contradiction, and strenuous cultural critique were the only possible avenues to human freedom.

CL

further reading H. Hughes 1975; Jay 1973; Wiggershaus 1994

Frazer, Sir James (1854–1941)
James George Frazer was born in Glasgow, Scotland, in 1854, son of a local pharmacist. He attended the city university from 1869 to 1874 and then Trinity College, Cambridge. After winning prizes at both, he was elected to a fellowship at Trinity in 1879, which was regularly renewed thereafter until it became a life tenure. In 1908 he accepted the first chair of social anthropology at Liverpool University, but missed Cambridge so badly that he returned there after only five months. After 1914 he lived for periods in London and Paris as well, before dying in his beloved Cambridge in 1941. He was knighted in 1914, and thereafter collected a string of honours that probably make him the most heavily decorated anthropologist to date.

Frazer is popularly known as the father of anthropology, but he began as a classicist and continued throughout his life to edit Greek and Latin texts and also works of eighteenth-century literary figures. His editions of Pausanias and Ovid are still highly regarded. His first publication was an essay in philosophy. His fame, however, derives from his writings on comparative RELI-GION, and in particular from the work collectively known as *The golden bough*, which was issued in three successive editions, growing from two to twelve volumes, between 1890 and 1915.

This represented the most celebrated application of a theory that had been popularized in the 1870s and 1880s by Sir Edward TYLOR in England and Wilhelm Mannhardt in Germany, and was itself inspired by the Darwinian thesis of EVOLUTION. It depended upon the belief that the minds of all humans worked in essentially the same way, but had developed at different rates, according to CULTURE and CLASS, along the same orderly and linear track. If this were true, then it was possible to treat the customs of tribal peoples and of European peasants alike as cultural fossils, representing earlier stages in the evolution of civilized societies, and by a comparative study of them to construct a general theory of religious development for the human race.

The golden bough was the most ambitious attempt to conduct such a study, bringing together data from all over the world and from all recorded time. It was made possible by Frazer's extraordinary industry and his gift for languages; he could read Greek, Latin, Hebrew, French, German, Spanish, Italian, and Dutch. What drove him, however, was a general suspicion and contempt for religion, and especially that based upon ritual and superstition. Having been brought up in a devout Scottish Presbyterian household, and become an agnostic at Glasgow University, he regarded Christianity as the most important adversary of all.

The central thesis of the first edition was that primitive religion had been based largely upon the veneration of the dying and returning spirit of vegetation, personified as a god and identified with human rulers who were killed after a set term or when their powers waned. In the second

edition he developed this into an open questioning of the basis of Christianity, and added the important thesis that human spiritual awareness evolved through three stages, of magic, religion, and science. In the third he called off the attack on the divinity of Christ, but enormously expanded his material for the other suggestions. The result was not merely an important theoretical structure but a vast compendium of human RITUAL practices, often lurid. Frazer intended it to reach the largest possible audience, writing in a deliberately vivid and accessible style, and briefing his publisher upon the cover engraving, front plate illustration, quality of paper, and type size and face to be employed.

He achieved his wish sensationally. The professional reception of *The golden bough* was at first enthusiastic, but then waned steadily as each edition appeared. This was the result of a collapse of faith in the methodology upon which Frazer depended, commencing in the 1900s and complete by the 1920s. Thereafter anthropology turned to studying social structure and function in primitive societies rather than assigning them places in an evolutionary structure. Historians of religion found his comparative deductions faulty.

At the same time, however, the popularity of *The golden bough* increased in directly inverse proportion to scholarly opinion. Frazer, like Freud, seemed to have uncovered the savagery that lay beneath the veneer of civilization, and he was hailed as a seer as the twentieth century dealt successive shocks to faith in that civilization. His striking images influenced the work of Eliot, Pound, Yeats, Edith Sitwell, Graves, Forster, D. H. Lawrence, and a host of lesser creative writers. In the 1980s they remained central to the film *Apocalypse now* and the American bestselling novel *The mists of Avalon*. The abridged edition of the *Bough*, issued in 1922, has never been out of print. It has become part of the Western popular consciousness.

In view of all this, it is heavily ironic that Frazer himself was a classic Oxbridge gnome. Painfully shy, he tried to avoid teaching, public lecturing, social life, and the reading of newspapers, and preferred to buy every book for his research in order to shut himself up completely to work. Work he did, for a minimum of thirteen hours a day, seven days a week, for fifty weeks each year. It is small wonder that after 1901 he had recurrent eye trouble, and went completely blind in 1931; after which he worked on with amanuenses. Despite his exotic interests, he himself never traveled further than Greece, and his general bewildered unworldliness was the subject of many humorous anecdotes. So was his rectitude; when a critic revealed that he had mistranslated a key phrase in Pliny, he reported this to the Council of Trinity College with the suggestion that it might reconsider a recent renewal of his fellowship. His isolation was much increased by his formidable wife, Lilly, a Frenchwoman whom he married in 1896. She set herself the task of ensuring that he was not troubled by other scholars, and this, and his disinclination to read critical reviews after 1901, greatly helped the petrification of his thinking.   RHut

further reading Ackerman 1987; Downie 1970; Fraser 1990a,b; Leach 1961c

frontier is a slippery concept fraught with multiple meanings. In the United States, it has a technical definition as any region with a population density of less than two persons per square mile. More generally, a frontier is a region or zone where two or more distinct cultures, societies, ethnic groups, or MODES OF PRODUCTION come into contact. Because frontier regions usually contain few resources that are readily exploitable by states, they are marked by low levels of state control. Often consisting of deep forests, deserts, grasslands, or mountains such regions are frequently considered marginal or wastelands by surrounding states.

The low level of state control makes frontiers attractive to outlaws and rebels, and offers refuge to nonconforming groups, both native and immigrant. Frontiers typically have highly variegated social and cultural populations. Armed conflict is not rare. Pressures for ACCULTURATION and assimilation are typically milder than in urban core areas, while resistance to change and state control can be quite strong.

In the United States, frontiers are associated with the work of Frederick Jackson Turner (G. Taylor 1972). Turner argued that frontier experience shaped American culture, promoting democracy, egalitarianism, and rugged individualism, while serving as a safety valve for urban pressures. Many students of Western history today reject Turner's thesis, noting that democracy was often absent, inequality abounded, and many people were highly dependent on others (Limerick et al. 1991). The harshest criticism, however, has been directed at the more or less implicit idea that the frontier was an empty wasteland. Obviously Native American Indian groups were there.

In Asia and the Middle East, frontiers are often associated with contact zones between "the steppe and the sown," that is, between nomadic pastoralists and sedentary farmers. Owen Lattimore (1962) has written extensively about these frontiers. His major points are that this frontier is one of both conflict and cooperation, where individuals sometimes change sides, even as the frontier persists. The differences are rooted in geographic conditions and the different modes of adaptation they support. Thomas Barfield (1989) modified and extended Lattimore's work. He demonstrated that both steppe confederations and the Chinese state have risen and fallen in tandem for millennia. He also noted that trading and raiding are alternative means to the same end, where violent raids constitute a form of extortion to gain more favorable terms of trade.

R. Ferguson and N. Whitehead (1992a) discussed a particular type of frontier, the contact zone between state societies and "tribal" societies (see TRIBE). They noted two general consequences of state–tribe interaction: (1) an increase in warfare between states and tribes; and (2) an increase in intertribal warfare. Both patterns are important to ETHNOHISTORY, since much early ETHNOGRAPHY was done in these zones. Thus, extreme caution must be used in interpreting the accounts of early observers.

Richard Slatta (1983) conceived of frontiers as membranes with asymmetrical permeability to individuals, cultural knowledge, practices, and material goods. Groups in contact along frontiers are able to be somewhat selective in those elements they take from each other. In southern South America, the frontier membrane was especially permeable to criminals and peasants avoiding conscription.

Finally, frontiers are zones where external forces shape local events (see COLONIALISM, WORLD-SYSTEM THEORY). These forces are modified by local conditions and the efforts of local actors. Local resistance to colonial efforts, often originating in frontier areas, can overtax state resources and contribute to unrest in the "home," colonizing country. The actions and interactions of frontier peoples often lead to ethnogenesis (formation of an ethnic group) or transformations of ethnicity (Chase-Dunn & Hall 1997; see ETHNIC GROUPS).

Most of these writers, save Turner, have pointed out that some frontier groups use and manipulate official state boundaries to their own advantage. For example, in the eighteenth and early nineteenth centuries Apache and Comanche bands raided deep into New Spain, while simultaneously maintaining peaceful relations in New Mexico. Later in the nineteenth century Apache bands used newly annexed US territory as a base to raid across the border into Mexico. More generally, when states attempt to monopolize trade, smuggling flourishes as a specialty for one or more frontier groups.

Many writers also note that frontiers are not permanent, but move. Indeed, Turner noted the "closing" of the American frontier in 1892 when the counties with less than two people per square mile no longer formed a clear line of westward expansion. However, according to the 1990 US census over 100 western counties retain such low population densities (D. Duncan 1993). Finally, a frontier may be a moving gradient of things other than human population. The crossing of the horse frontier, moving northeast from New Mexico, and the gun frontier, moving southeast from Quebec and New England, was the catalyst for the formation of Plains Bison hunting cultures among American Indians (Secoy 1953).

Frontiers are zones of mixture and change at some distance from state authority. They are the homes of many groups studied by cultural anthropologists. While frontier residents often try to maintain some degree of isolation, typically their lives are impacted by external social, political, and cultural forces. This is why the study of frontiers is at once fascinating and frustrating. TH
See also HISTORY AND ANTHROPOLOGY
further reading Baretta & Markoff 1978; R. Bartlett & McKay 1989; Dunaway 1996; Lamar & Thompson 1981; Slatta 1990

functionalism is (1) an ethnographic methodology distinctive of anthropology within the social sciences and humanities; (2) a historical school of anthropology also known as "British social anthropology"; (3) a school of sociology and social relations that attempted to integrate sociology, psychology, and anthropology; and (4) a "philosophy of the social sciences" within Anglo-American analytic philosophy. "Functionalism" is no longer a label much used by anthropologists; but this is in part because the legacies of functionalism are now everyday anthropological common sense.

Ethnographic approach
Functionalism asks how any particular institution or belief is interrelated with other institutions and to what extent it contributes to the persistence either of the sociocultural system as a whole or its parts. It is the sociological equivalent of the basic rule of ecology: that you cannot change only one thing. Functionalism emerged in the 1920s as a sharp methodological break with overly facile and decontextualized comparisons ("among the so-and-so's") manifested by much nineteenth-century evolutionary anthropology: museum displays organized as linear sequences of progress (sharply critiqued earlier by E. B. TYLOR (1889)); diffusionist maps of cultural traits or limited cultural complexes; or grand narratives illustrating the progress of reason, such as James FRAZER's *The golden bough* (1890).

Functionalism required a more sophisticated comparative method, interested in what institutions and beliefs meant to participants of a society, as well as social correlations and interconnections. Such correlations could not be established by studying single societies, but required comparison among societies, focusing, for example, on the relationship among matrilineal kinship systems, shifting cultivation, witchcraft, and high divorce rates. Functionalists liked to show how kinship or religion structured ostensibly economic institutions, how the ritual system stimulated economic production and organized politics, or how myths (previously dismissed as idle stories or speculations) served as charters that codified and regulated social relations.

This early functionalism of British social anthropology was informed by Durkheimian sociological theory, particularly the notion that the social was a level of organization *sui generis* that could not be reduced in any simple way to the motives and intentions of individuals. It exerted a moral force upon individuals through "collective representations" or the "conscience collective" (both socially structured internalized "conscience" and semiotically public cognitive "consciousness"). Functionalism thus sustained a productive tension between a commitment to context ("holism") and problem-oriented comparison. It also sustained a productive tension between focusing attention on the beliefs, motivations, and meanings of actors (out of which INTERPRETIVE ANTHROPOLOGY evolved) while simultaneously arguing that "social facts" could not be reduced to individual will, desire, or cognition (out of which STRUCTURALISM and "antihumanist" poststructuralism evolved).

Anthropology today continues its distinctive commitment to ethnographic THICK DESCRIPTION of interconnections among different institutional and discursive parts of society. This can be seen in new arenas of research by anthropologists of science (Traweek 1988, 1992; E. Martin 1994) who refuse to restrict themselves to the walls of the laboratory, the ethnomethodology of a procedure, a dispute, or genre of communication. A second feature of functionalism's legacy to anthropology is a continuing commitment to sociologically contextualized cross-cultural comparison, and refusal to allow the theoretical categories of North America and Europe to pass as unexamined universal parameters. Again, although the challenges of comparison in the late twentieth century are considerably different from what they were in the earlier part of the century (see POSTMODERNISM), this too remains a commonsense legacy of functionalism.

School of anthropology

"Functionalism" was the name adopted by Bronislaw MALINOWSKI, A. R. RADCLIFFE-BROWN, and their students. Also known as "British social anthropology," in its formative period this small group of anthropologists powerfully influenced the social sciences, the wider academy, and public-policy debates. Based on intensive studies of some 30 societies, it created a kind of canon for continual reanalysis and comparison.

Malinowski's ethnographies became new textual models with their realist style that unpacked the "native point of view" and involved the reader in an experience of "being there." Their authority rested on extended fieldwork and, more importantly, on the claims of methodological functionalism to unravel the structure of a society and culture better than had resident missionaries or colonial administrators. Their textual strategy represented the whole by the part through analysis of key institutions (Trobriand KULA, Azande WITCHCRAFT), emblematic cultural performances (Iatmul *naven*, Balinese cockfights), or privileged structures (kinship systems, ritual and belief complexes, political factions). The focus also included "the native point of view," which Malinowski presented through a tripartite strategy of TRANSLATION: supplying the transcript of the native text, providing a word-by-word translation and explication, and then producing a gloss in fluent English. By translating the exotic into the familiar, he attempted to show that other cultural formations had both a cognitive and social logic. His wide-ranging descriptions and native texts provided his ethnographies with much more material than he could analyze himself. Consequently his monographs on the Trobriand Islands (1922, 1927, 1935, 1948) have been among the most reanalyzed cultural and sociological accounts in anthropology, both by students in training and by scholars applying new theoretical approaches. Although some of Malinowski's theoretical formulations were naive (particularly his later theory of culture based on biological needs), he made enduring contributions in exchange theory, the analysis of MYTH as social charters, and the anthropological challenge to the universality of the Oedipus Complex. He was also a proponent of applying anthropology as practical knowledge for development and social reform and was entrepreneurially successful in raising funds for anthropological training on these grounds from the Rockefeller and Carnegie Foundations and the British Colonial Office. Functionalism's emphasis on indigenous incentive and motivational structures, legal systems, land tenure and agrarian systems, trade and exchange, social welfare and healing systems, fitted particularly well with Britain's colonial policy of indirect rule in which a relatively few officials were expected to oversee a vast empire by working through local economic and political structures.

Radcliffe-Brown was the other "father" of British social anthropology. Usually credited with being the more influential formulator of functionalist theory, he borrowed much from Durkheimian sociology and saw anthropology as a global, cross-cultural comparative sociology. He argued that social structure (composed of roles, jural obligations, and moral norms) was the key framework for comparative analysis (1952). With its attention to the tensions and conflicts between the purposes of individuals and the functions of social institutions, his notion of social structure bore traces of an older legacy of the language of morphology and pathology of organic systems (1957). His own fieldwork monograph on the Andaman Islands (1922) proved a textual struggle for him to complete, reflecting his early attempts to clarify his functional approach. It was never as influential as his teaching, in which he excelled, setting up important training programs in South Africa, Australia, and the United States (Chicago). His influence was particularly clear in functionalist studies

based on the comparative social-structural approach to kinship and politics (Radcliffe-Brown & Forde 1950; Fortes & Evans-Pritchard 1940b; Schneider & Gough 1961).

E. E. EVANS-PRITCHARD, a senior member of the second generation, is usually credited with providing the classic form of the ethnography in the Durkheimian, social-structure-based, mode. His series of monographs on the Nuer (1940, 1951, 1956) provided the second most popular canonical set for teaching students the arts of reanalysis. And his monograph on Azande witchcraft (1937) has proved a perennial favorite, in part for its comparative argument that shows how systems of argumentation protect themselves from falsification (science is the epistemological target here), and how technical-pragmatic explanations cannot resolve existential, moral, and social questions ("why me?").

Too often, sibling rivalries by American anthropologists have caricatured functionalism as a Panglossian theory that everything is ideally integrated or functional, arguing that functionalism could not deal with change or that it was only a handmaiden of COLONIALISM. This ignores the important contributions of the functionalist Manchester school, established by Max GLUCKMAN, which brought together the case-method presentation of conflicts from legal studies and Evans-Pritchard's Durkheimian concern with conflicts between individual interests and social forces. One of its major projects was an attempt to build up a mosaic regional analysis through a series of studies conducted in Northern Rhodesia (modern Zambia) through the Rhodes–Livingstone Institute (Gluckman & Colson 1951), one of the Social and Economic Research Institutes scattered across the British Empire that brought together agrarian and anthropological research. Motivated by his concern over the destruction of tribal economies caused by drawing male labor into the copper mines, its first director, Godfrey Wilson, proposed doing a study of labor in the mines. The colonial government rejected the proposal as subversive and barred him from the mines; it did not help that he was a communist (as was Gluckman). The government was concerned enough by the deterioration of tribal economies, however, to hire Audrey RICHARDS, who wrote a classic study of the Bemba (1939), who were among the leaders of strikes in the mines. Victor TURNER (1957, 1967, 1969) marked the high point of this style of functionalist monograph with his study of Ndembu ritual, where a case-method analysis of social dramas (taken from Arnold van GENNEP's model of ritual form) is embedded into a neo-Freudian framework. Turner's analyses of ritual process and the con-fusion (literally fusing together) of emotional and cognitive poles of meaning in ritually powerful symbols, for both individuals and their society, became an influential component of the Chicago school of symbolic anthropology in the 1970s.

Although this is not the place to cite all the key figures of functionalist British social anthropology – Abner Cohen, Elizabeth Colson, Mary Douglas, Raymond Firth, Meyer Fortes, Ernest Gellner, Jack and Esther Goody, Edmund Leach, Godfrey and Peter Lienhardt, Rodney Needham, S. F. Nadel, Emrys Peters, Julian Pitt-Rivers, Isaac Schapera, M. N. Srinivas, and Peter Worsley are some others – it is important to indicate at least through the above several, some of the range of concerns, methods, and political contexts in which functionalism evolved.

Structural-functionalism

At times Radcliffe-Brown's version of functionalism was tagged "structural-functionalism" because of his stress on social structure, but this name is more widely used for the sociological approach of the American sociologist Talcott Parsons (1937, 1951a, 1954) with its interdisciplinary vision combining anthropology, sociology, and psychology into a "layer cake," known as a quasi-cybernetic or SYSTEMS-THEORY analytic model. Psychological, social, and cultural systems, he suggested, can be analytically distinguished as different emergent levels of organization, each with its own logic of integration, but with feedback among the levels. Out of the Social Relations Department founded at Harvard on this idea came two key anthropologists of what would become the Chicago school of symbolic anthropology of

the 1960s and 1970s. Social systems, Clifford GEERTZ (1973) would later suggest, are causally integrated, whereas cultural systems are logicomeaningfully integrated, and psychological systems are psychodynamically integrated. Norms as statistical regularities, David Schneider (1968) would suggest, belong to the realm of the social system; norms as moral "ought statements" or as analytic principles underlying cultural conceptual forms belong to the cultural or symbolic system. Social organization and social structure were parts of the social system; values, norms, principles, symbols, and conceptual schemas were part of the cultural system.

Philosophical functionalism

Philosophers have examined the logical status of different variants of functional analysis (mathematical, organicist, teleological, cybernetic) and their relationship to causal and historical modes of explanation (Hempel 1959; Gardiner 1964). Methodologically, Aberle et al. (1950) pointed out that functionalism could not consist of specifying lists of human needs and the various functional equivalent institutions that could satisfy those needs because there was no way of delimiting either the definition of needs or the possible functional equivalents. Similarly Blake and Davis (1964) pointed out the circularity of deriving norms and values from behavioral regularities, while at the same time claiming that the latter structure the former. Ernest GELLNER (1959b, 1970), writing as anthropologist–philosopher, is perhaps the clearest in pointing out that functionalism for anthropology was primarily a methodological obligation to probe for interconnections, rather than a theory of society. In philosophically less rigorous forms, Malinowski's students attempted to show how functionalist methods had been applied to different substantive areas of ethnographic research (Firth 1956a, 1957). On the various efforts by Parsonians and other American sociologists to clarify structural-functionalism as a set of models and variables, see the surveys by M. Levy (1968) and Cancian (1968).   MF

Fürer-Haimendorf, Christoph von (1909–95) Christoph von Fürer-

Haimendorf was born in Vienna in 1909. Members of his family had served the Habsburg dynasty since the year 1273 and his father held a senior position in the Austrian civil service. He was trained in anthropology by Schebesta, Frobenius, and Heine Geldern at the University of Vienna from 1927. He received a D.Phil. in 1931 and, partly inspired by MALINOWSKI, went to Assam in 1936 for a year's fieldwork among the Nagas.

He returned to India in 1939 for further work but was interned as an enemy alien when the war broke out. He was confined to Hyderabad but was able to undertake a further three years of fieldwork among the Chenchus, Reddis, and Raj Gonds. He was also allowed to do fieldwork among the Apa Tanis and other peoples of the Arunachal Pradesh area of Assam. At the end of the war he became Adviser to the Nizam of Hyderabad and set up various educational and other welfare schemes for tribal peoples. In 1949 he was made Reader in, and then in 1951 Professor of, Anthropology at the School of Oriental and African Studies in London, where he developed the largest department of anthropology in Britain.

In 1953 he visited Nepal, thus adding a third area of competence to Assam and Hyderabad. In each area he studied the culture of between three and six societies. He published ten ethnographic monographs on his fieldwork, including *The Chenchus* (1943), *The Reddis of the Bison Hills* (1945), *The Raj Gonds of Adilabad* (1948), *The Sherpas of Nepal* (1964), *The Konyak Nagas* (1969) and *The Gonds of Andhra Pradesh* (1979). He also published several other volumes of essays and theoretical works, including *Morals and merit* (1967), which drew heavily on his fieldwork.

The published work is only the surface of his achievement. As well as his meticulous and detailed fieldnotes and diaries, he was the only anthropologist of the great interwar generation in Britain to realize the importance of visual documentation. His collection o2f black-and-white photographs extends to over ten thousand separate items, capturing memorably many aspects of tribal culture. They were accompanied by an equal number of color slides, documenting worlds which have since changed beyond recognition. He was also the most prolific of British ethnographic filmmakers, starting to film in the 1940s and shooting over one hundred hours of 16 mm film.

A number of traits help to explain his ability as an ethnographer. There was his curiosity; he was clearly immensely interested in people, in exploring, in wanting to know and understand and then to move on to a new encounter. There was his aesthetic ability and appreciation of beauty, which lay behind his photography and his delight in the graceful peoples with whom he worked. There was his photographic memory combined with selfdiscipline, which filled his notebooks and diaries with thousands of pages of vivid and insightful comment. There was his obvious sympathy for tribal peoples and their increasingly difficult position. There was his intelligence.

The immediate prizes in academic life go to those who engage in abstract theory. Although he put forward some exciting ideas, particularly on morality and religion in his Frazer Lecture on "The after life in Indian tribal religions" and his Henry Myers Lecture on "The sense of sin in cross-cultural perspective", his main interest was in understanding and describing how societies work. Good fieldwork requires a special form of intelligence, which he showed in large measure. His great ability to make friends and to manage human relationships, especially in difficult situations, won him the trust of both Europeans and his many non-European co-workers and colleagues. In all this he depended very heavily on his wife Betty, co-worker, organizer of his expeditions, inspiration, and herself a notable ethnographer.   AM

G

---

gardens or homegardens are an intense form of cropping that produces high yields on small permanent plots by employing a variety of crops throughout the year. Gardening is characterized by the use of hand tools, fencing, and close proximity to the home. Where land is in short supply it may be extended to the entire farming system (Netting 1993: 53). Gardens have traditionally played an important role in the agricultural systems of many less developed countries and they are today drawing the attention of scholars and planners interested in more diversified systems of cultivation, with lower inputs, and more focus on perennial species (J. Anderson 1986; Cleveland & Soleri 1987).

A notable example is the *pekarangan* "homegarden" of Central Java (Dove 1990; Stoler 1978), which averages 1,000 m^2 in area and contains about 50 individual trees representing a dozen different species (with 60 different species represented in all the homegardens in the village). These homegardens are more market oriented than commonly believed, and produce nuts, flowers, seeds, leaves, and saps of fruit trees such as the coconut for sale. This is such a major source of income for the poorer households that only the wealthier can afford to consume the greater part of the output of their homegardens. Productivity is so high that although the average homegarden covers only one-tenth of a hectare, it contributes 40 percent of the household's income, whereas the average rice field, covering more than two-tenths of a hectare, contributes just 35 percent.

Given their productivity and economic importance, the governmental (and, until recently, scholarly) neglect of the homegarden is curious. In fact, the complexity that is responsible for the homegardens' productivity also makes it more difficult for outsiders to exploit them, thus making them of less interest to the state. This income-sheltering effect is also supported by a cultural de-emphasis of homegardening in places where it is practiced, such as Java, where rice fields take precedence. MRD & ML

See also AGRICULTURE

Geertz, Clifford (1926–) Clifford Geertz is undoubtedly modern America's best-known, most quoted, and most intellectually influential cultural anthropologist. Head and founder of the hugely prestigious School of Social Sciences at Princeton's Institute of Advanced Studies, author and editor of many often-cited books and articles, winner of the National Book Critics Circle award and numerous other honors, and contributor to important scholarly journals, he has found an admiring audience in disciplines as diverse as history, literary theory, and philosophy. But within his own field his work has become ever more debated and controversial.

Geertz was born in San Francisco and attended Antioch College, where his early ambition to write fiction was set aside in favor of philosophy. In 1950, seeking something "more empirical," he entered graduate school in anthropology in the short-lived multidisciplinary Social Relations Department at Harvard. There he studied with Talcott Parsons, who was bringing the work Max WEBER and Emile DURKHEIM together into a new kind of systematic American sociology. Geertz found little to admire in Durkheim, and Parsons's own theories left him cold, but he took Weber to heart – especially the notion of *verstehen*, understanding the other's point of view.

In favoring a Weberian approach, Geertz opposed the FUNCTIONALIST paradigm dominating American anthropology in the 1950s. He argued that the task of anthropology was not the discovery of laws, patterns, and norms, but rather the interpretation of what he called the culturally specific "webs of significance" people both spin and are caught up in. These symbolic webs were taken by Geertz to be the essence of human social life. They legitimated power structures and channeled unruly human desires by offering believers a sense of purpose and agency within a world rendered orderly and meaningful. The way such understanding could be accomplished was through what Geertz famously called the "THICK DESCRIPTION" of another culture – that is, through writing dense and convincing ethnographic portraits.

Following his own prescription, Geertz has spent a very large amount of time doing FIELDWORK. His first research was two and a half years in eastern Java. From this period came a series of important books, including *The religion of Java* (1960), and *Agricultural involution* (1963c), which won acclaim not only among anthropologists but also among economists and development specialists. However, his approach to ETHNOGRAPHY was soon altered by his reading of Herder, Humboldt, and Dilthey during his stay at the Anthropology Department at the University of Chicago. Like Ruth BENEDICT, to whom he has often been compared, Geertz was inspired by the German romantics to increasingly emphasize an aesthetic appreciation of other cultures. His youthful ambition to be a writer of fictions could now be realized within the realm of anthropology; fictional artifice was recast as interpretation of the culturally formed symbolic worlds of others, which existed separately from, yet in dialectical relationship with, social action. For Geertz, the Weberian effort to establish a comparative sociology was now set aside; comparison, he argued, serves to show that societies are, in fact, incomparable – each is unique, and the anthropologist's job is to make his reader appreciate this uniqueness via authorial leaps of informed and artful imagi-

nation into the "webs of significance" inhabited by exotic others.

Concentrating on creating a new kind of anthropological writing, Geertz began to move beyond professional journals in hopes of reaching a wider audience. His prose now assumed a twisting syntactical structure replete with multiple clauses, lengthy lists, and erudite allusions to philosophy, literature, and popular culture. Two highly successful collections of essays, *The interpretation of cultures* (1973) and *Local knowledge* (1983), contained Geertz's best-known occasional pieces, and introduced the wider intellectual public to his romantic and writerly version of anthropology. His increasing fame coincided with his appointment in 1970 to Princeton's prestigious Institute of Advanced Studies.

Simultaneously, Geertz also undertook extensive new fieldwork, first in Bali, and then in Morocco. The latter culminated in his *Islam observed* (1968), which attempted to compare the distinctive practices and beliefs of Muslims in Indonesia and Morocco. Most influential, however, was his writing on Bali, which presented a striking portrait of the Balinese people as passionless aesthetic performers in a vast and timeless cultural play – a view much contested by other ethnographers, notably Unni Wikan (1993). The problems facing his increasingly aesthetic approach are best illustrated in what is possibly Geertz's most famous essay, "Deep play: notes on the Balinese cockfight" (1972), where he asserted that the cockfight is a moral text teaching the Balinese lessons about subjectivity and human action. This may be so, but the Balinese themselves are not consulted about this reading – it remains Geertz's own. Nor does he note that cockfights prevail in many very different cultures besides Bali. We are left, then, with evocative prose that tells us a great deal about the author's sensibility, but may tell us very little about Bali.

Perhaps in response to such critiques, Geertz has lately retreated toward an even more self-conscious concern with the role of the anthropological author in constructing and defining CULTURE. His award-winning book *Works and lives* (1988) is an analysis of several famous ethnographies as literary texts. However, even though Geertz, using his own considerable poetic talents, has painted the anthropologist, and especially himself, as an artist of culture, most practitioners still consider it their job to help their subjects to speak, not to speak for them.   CL

further reading Geertz 1963d, 1980, 1995; Geertz et al. 1979; Handler 1991; Munson 1986; Shankman 1984

Gellner, Ernest André (1925–95)

Ernest Gellner was a philosopher, historian of ideas, and sociologist of knowledge as well as a social anthropologist. Gellner was a Czech and a Jew, born in Paris and raised in Prague until he came to England in 1939. After serving in the Czech Armoured Brigade during World War II, he returned to Oxford and took his degree in Politics, Philosophy, and Economics. He joined the Sociology Department at the London School of Economics in 1949 and become Professor of Philosophy in 1962. He became William Wyse Professor of Social Anthropology at Cambridge in 1984 and from 1991 was the founding Director of the Center for the Study of Nationalism at the Central European University in Prague. He died in Prague a month short of his seventieth birthday.

Among philosophers Gellner was notorious for his rejection of the Oxford School of analytic philosophy. His first book *Words and things* (1959a) combined a philosophical analysis and a sociology of knowledge that placed the advocates of that school in a particular social and political and intellectual environment. This technique became one of Gellner's characteristic weapons in his critiques of hegemonic systems of thought – Islam, marxism, psychoanalysis, relativism, and hermeneutics – and was brilliantly deployed also in his accounts of things he approved of: the Enlightenment and social anthropology.

Gellner did his initial anthropological fieldwork among the Berbers of Morocco, published as *Saints of the Atlas* (1969), which focused on the SEGMENTARY LINEAGE SYSTEM of a people who had devised procedures and institutions to resist both absorption by and imitation of the Moroccan state. This Moroccan fieldwork led to three general works, both controversial and full of insight: *Muslim society* (1981) placed the religious and political lives of Muslims in a world-historical context and included the startling juxtaposition of Ibn Khaldun and David Hume; *Arabs and Berbers* (Gellner & Micaud 1973) and *Patrons and clients* (Gellner & Waterbury 1977) explored themes of ethnicity and political representation in Morocco and elsewhere in the Middle East.

From the early 1970s Gellner published work on Soviet anthropology, and began the studies that were to lead to the fieldwork in moscow in 1988. His polemics with Western marxists were based in his rejection of closed, illiberal systems. However he also appreciated the subtlety of academics in the Soviet Union and his edited volume *Soviet and Western anthropology* (1980) contains a fine exposition of Soviet work. For 15 years Gellner was the chief conduit between Soviet and Western anthropology, and was accepted as a severe but friendly critic in the USSR (Gellner 1988b). He was able to observe at first hand the transition from relatively modest efforts of early *perestroika* to an intellectually completely open society when the Soviet empire collapsed. He wrote various articles on this experience, modifying his earlier views (Khazanov 1992). Characteristically, the main outcome of this experience was not an academic study of the events of 1989, but his *Conditions of liberty* (1994), which reflects on discussions about the future within Russia, in the light of the history and ideology of Western democracies.

Gellner's (1983, 1994) contributions to the study of NATIONALISM were grounded in the history of European nation-states. They introduced a non-Western dimension often lacking in the work of political scientists, and contributed the insight (which he asserted was derived from Anthropology) that nationalism is the claim that each "culture" should be sovereign. Big nations are established by eliminating little cultures, as in France. Resistance to a state could be expressed as assertion that a local culture should be free from alien hegemony. Gellner argued most famously that the need to establish large states with homogeneous cultures was the consequence of the transition from closed, hierarchically stable agrarian societies, to open, socially mobile industrial ones; and in his later work he identified the shift with the Enlightenment – the Great Transition (Gellner 1988a). This was, he said, a period of economic and cognitive growth, establishing a scientific, technological, and rational mentality that was less comfortable but truer than anything that had preceded it, and superior. His combativeness in defense of this position was a consistent theme: he attacked "the hermeneutic plague," which, he said, had pursued him from philosophy to sociology and then to anthropology (Gellner 1975, 1992).

Gellner was sometimes mistaken for an austere and even forbidding person. But he was expansive and generous with his ideas and his time: he did not husband good arguments or ideas to present them in major tomes. Much of his best work began as reviews or review articles, later expanded into books; he was a tireless lecturer and participant in conferences, many of which he organized, and at which he presented new and original ideas that many eminent academics would have saved for more illustrious occasions. At Cambridge he equably supervised the theses of a number of graduates who have become notable scholars of the Middle East.   JD

further reading J. Davis 1991

gender refers to those culturally assigned behaviors and meanings, such as sex roles, attributed to the distinction all human societies make between male and female. For most scholars it is axiomatic that gendered behavior is shaped by historical forces and thus has nothing to do with biology (Ortner & Whitehead 1981; Rosaldo & Lamphere 1974; Sacks 1979; Sanday 1981a).

The anthropological study of gender has a feminized face. Although men have, on occasion, explored specific aspects of gender performance, its principal researchers and audience are women. Sanday and Goodenough (1990) remind us that women were the first to focus on the issue of gender inequality "from a cross-cultural perspective and to offer explanations that account for inequality in terms of cultural universals or of specific, historically constituted social formations." By challenging the "prevailing consensus about the nature of gender inequality and the theories that have dealt with it" (Sanday & Goodenough 1990: 15), female researchers provided a much-needed correction. The unintended consequence of having the predominance of investigators female has resulted, however, in the exclusive documentation and analysis of the problematic nature of one gender, while ignoring the other gender or portraying it as a caricature by omission.

Studies of gender range broadly and include work on the origins and persistence of certain forms of sex-linked behavior, the origins and meaning of sexual stratification, and the problematic nature of gender identity. The last focuses particularly on the formation of institutionalized "third gender" identities. No single theory accounts for all variation found in the ethnographic record (Quinn 1977), but three theories have commonly been used to explain the origins of cross-cultural patterns found in a culture's sexual division of labor:

(1) Strength theory holds that because males in any given society are larger on average than females, it is only natural that males should do the tasks that involve greater strength.

(2) Compatibility-with-child-care theory argues that women tend to perform activities that are most complementary with child-care roles, that is, ones easily interrupted and resumed, such as gathering wild plants, carrying water, cooking, and food preservation (Weisner & Gallimore 1977). Men, by contrast, are more likely to engage in activities that are sometimes dangerous, and often demand bursts of energy, such as HUNTING large land and sea animals, lumbering, clearing the land, long-distance TRADE, and WAR (Murdock & Provost 1973).

(3) Economy-of-effort theory argues that women's and men's tasks are divided in such a way that they maximize total production through gender specialization, and that the specific activities will be dependent on the economic structure of the society.

All of these theories have flaws. Economy of effort explains why there is division of labor, but begs the question of how the roles were divided up or came to be so fixed. Strength theory seems to account for men's propensity to do the heavy work, but cannot satisfactory explain why in some societies it is only males who also collect honey or make musical instruments. Neither the strength or compatibility-with-child-rearing theory can account for men's propensity to craft small light-weight musical instruments. (D. White et al. 1977 note that there is a relationship between working with the material in one context and using it in another context, and since men usually work with wood and bone, it is easier and thus more sensible for men to make the musical instruments.)

One of the most studied aspects of the gendered division of labor are the common cross-cultural relationships between the type of subsistence system and the degree of men's and women's labor efforts. Around the world men increase their labor input whenever intensive AGRICULTURE is practiced. In horticultural societies women's contribution is higher than it is in agricultural societies (Boserup 1970). This impacts on women's roles in two ways: (1) the production of these food crops usually entails longer food-preparation time and increases the number of women's household chores; and (2) women in such societies have more children, which means that much of their time is taken up with child care (C. Ember 1983).

A related, albeit separate, research focus explores the origins of sexual stratification or gender inequality. Because there is a lack of agreement on how to measure such concepts as autonomy, dominance, and relative social status, there are almost as many explanations of gender inequality as there are researchers. The discussion has centered on the degree of importance attributed to public as opposed to private performance and its relationship to power. Don Brown (1991), focusing entirely on public performance, noted that in every society men universally dominate the political arena. There are several reasons for this: (1) warfare is almost everywhere a male activity that enables males to become the focal point of decision making; (2) males are more involved in those activities, such as long distance trading, hunting, and fighting, that provide them with greater knowledge of the outside world; (3) women's more diligent involvement with child care often curtails their opportunities to develop the social ties and extrafamilial alliances necessary to develop and maintain political leadership (M. Ember & Ember 1971).

The relationship between child rearing and political leadership has been much debated. Lewellen (1992: 129–44) pointed out that whenever fecundity is not highly valued, women are often freer from the restraints of child bearing, which enables then to become more readily involved with community-wide decision making. This new found opportunity, however, is not without its cost. Schlegel (1972: 27, 298) wrote that "the promises of success and personal gratification [assured women] in one arena threaten to undermine those found in another arena" and went on to argue that the most important fact in determining women's status is not a culture's descent system but rather the organization of the domestic group.

Other theorists find fault with this emphasis on the domestic group. M. Ross's (1981) cross-cultural survey of women's social status found it varied less by the internal organization of the domestic group than it did by the presence or absence of fraternal organizations. He maintained that there is a correlation between patrilineal descent, patrilocal residence, and the subordination of women. Friedl (1975) has also insisted that women's relative social status is based more on the control of the distribution of goods than on the control of domestic production.

This has led some anthropologists to argue that male domination is a relatively recent occurrence in human history. They point particularly to societies of FORAGERS, which at least prior to Western contact, were for the most part sexually egalitarian (Leacock 1978). Friedl (1994) pointed out that the subordination of women appears to emerge as an aspect of state formation that results in the dismantling of kinship-based corporate groups, which inevitably results in the loss of women's status. On the other hand, M. Whyte's (1978) massive cross-cultural study of women's inequality did not find any single factor(s) that could account for women's relative social status in a given society or around the world. Thus the argument remains a difficult one.

Some researchers have turned away from the materialist theories discussed above in favor of more cultural-symbolic explanations. They attempt to explain the universality of male dominance through analyzing what is for them an underlying logic that negatively associates the female with nature and the male with culture, the more valued domain. Ortner (1974b) believed that it is this association (much more than pragmatic issues such as child care and inability to travel long distances, or a domestic organization) that accounts for the worldwide pattern in women's symbolic subordination. MacCormack and Strathern (1980) pointed out, however, that the nature–culture dichotomy is not all that universal. In some cultures the logic is reversed: men are to nature as women are to culture, and in others the folk ideologies are organized around entirely different sets of oppositions.

The origins of inequality, in gender as well as in other realms, may never be conclusively determined; and even if they were, they might be of little practical significance in understanding contemporary gender roles cross-culturally. The study of sexual stratification has therefore shifted away from origins toward a focus on understanding the rich complexities of family organization and decision making (Sanday & Goodenough 1990). This perspective investigates both the formal and the informal spheres of daily life and finds that women have counterbalancing, albeit often different, resources of power in which to counter men's expectations and demands (Lepowsky 1993; Schlegel 1990). The renewed interest in micropolitical processes coincides with Jane Collier and Sylvia Yanagisako's (1987) insistence that gender and KINSHIP are mutually constructed domains that need to be brought together into one analytic field.

Other anthropologists are less interested in the politics of inequality and domination than they are with documenting the presence of possible multiple gender configurations (Herdt 1994; W. Williams 1986). This research seeks to challenge the view that sex and gender are unchangeable, dichotomous units. If gender is simply a self-reference category, then people can define and redefine membership and participation in a given category over their life course (Munroe et al. 1969). Their research has found numerous cultures where people do not fit neatly into the conventional male–female gender categories. Perceived to be neither man nor woman, they are thought to possess the characteristics of both. In North America this alternative or "third" gender is referred to as "BERDACHE" or, most recently, the preferred Native American term "two-spirit" (S.-E. Jacobs 1983). In Oman, an Islamic society located on the Arabian peninsula, they are called "*xanith*" (Wikan 1977); in India, "*hijra*" (Nanda 1990); and, in Tahiti, "*mahu*" (R. Levy 1973).

There is no inclusive definition of the meaning of a "third sex" or "third gender." It is difficult therefore to determine if these folk CLASSIFICATIONS represent an alternative gender category or constitute nothing more than intersexed persons (hermaphrodites), cross-dressers (see TRANSVESTISM), or those who exhibit behavior deemed appropriate for the opposite sex (HOMOSEXUALS or transsexuals). The existence of folk categories beyond the two conventional genders does not in itself prove that the culture is organized around the notion of multiple gender categories. It could imply nothing more than tolerance of individuals who reject the more conventional gender categories. For example, American psychological studies have found that it is extremely difficult, especially after the age of 6 or 7, to remake or change one's gender identity. Since people who become a "third gender" do so at a later date, there should be some noticeable and long-lasting ambivalence toward adopting a new social identity. Since this question has not been systematically addressed, it is difficult to determine if some cultures have an authentic "third gender" or only a tolerated alternative life style organized around the rejection of a single-sex-role performance in favor of a male blend or a female blend of the culture's conventional gender traits. If the latter, it means there are two and only two gender categories, with everything else being defined in opposition to them (Schlegel 1972).

The most controversial trend in recent studies of gender is the application of SO-CIOBIOLOGICAL models that seek to identify innate behavioral differences that shape the style and form of sexual behavior (Cosmides & Tooby 1989; Draper & Harpending 1982). The biopsychological evidence comes from four sources: studies of cross-cultural uniformities, observations of infant behavior, comparisons with higher primates, and descriptions of physiological characteristics. It has been found that young boys are consistently more aggressive and competitive; whereas girls are more integrative (affectionate, willing to share, and cooperative) (Lewellen 1992). Research on infant behaviors reveals a similar pattern. The association of the male hormone testosterone with aggressiveness is well known (Maccoby & Jacklin 1974), but it would be incorrect to assume that males are always the aggressors and females always the victims. For example, Burbank (1994: 136) insisted that females often use aggression or anger to advance or protect their self-interest, citing a 1975 survey of 2,143 American families that found that "women directed nearly as much 'violence' against men as men directed against women." The greater gender bias in domestic violence is less who commits the violent act than the different motivations males and females have for engaging in it: male aggression is based more in fears of infidelity, whereas female aggression is motivated more out a concern with obtaining material support for themselves and their children.

The link between gender and SEX has focused anthropologists' attention on sex-linked differences found in men's and women's erotic aesthetics, most vividly manifested in the universality of mate-selection criteria and in different styles of sexual enticement and erotic avoidance (Symons 1979). Researchers have also sought to explore gender as a meaning sys-

tem that involves, depending upon context, invoking the appropriate gender-relevant and non-relevant traits (J. Williams & Best 1982). Jankowiak (1993) argued that the manipulation of gender identity is found, in its most salient form, in the sexual encounter (i.e., the context in which one strives consciously or unconsciously to present an image that the opposite sex finds most attractive). Outside of that context, men and women are more willing to engage in other types of behavior that may or may not be deemed sexually significant or even gender relevant. From this perspective gender performance involves the way men and women often assert, modify, or reject different aspects of their sexuality in order to convey gender and non-gender meanings. This line of research has been explored more by American psychologists interested in documenting the impact of social factors in the organization of perception than by anthropologists, who have turned their attention to investigating the interplay between biocultural factors as they are manifested in sexual and gender performance.   WJ

See also FEMINIST ANTHROPOLOGY, MASCULINITY

further reading Connell 1995; Gilmore 1990; Gregor 1985; Herdt 1984; Hewlett 1992; Murphy & Murphy 1974; Schlegel 1977

genealogies are the listings of kin by their descent relations, a "family tree." The keeping and recitation of genealogies often serve important social functions of legitimation and solidarity maintenance.   MR

generalized (or indirect) exchange is a system of MARRIAGE EXCHANGE in which the men of a group take wives from one group while giving wives to another, thereby linking all the groups of the society by means of a series of permanent affinal relations (Lévi-Strauss 1969a). In this system wife takers cannot also be wife givers to the same group.   MR

See also RESTRICTED EXCHANGE

generation In genealogical terms, a generation is the set of persons who stand at the same distance of lineal descent from a real or hypothetical common ancestor. **Generational kinship** is a system of kinship terminology that primarily classifies kin by generation.   MR

generative grammar   See GRAMMAR, TRANSFORMATIONAL GRAMMAR

genitor is the biological father of a child, as opposed to the socially recognized father (PATER). For example, in a society where the status of adopted children is jurally equivalent to that of natural children, the adoptive father has full social fatherhood of an adopted child, while the genitor relinquishes all rights over the child.   MR

Gennep, Arnold van (1873–1957) Arnold van Gennep was born in Ludwigsburg, Germany in 1873 and died in Épernay, France in 1957. He received his doctorate from the École des Hautes Études in Paris, where he combined the study of primitive religions, Egyptology, linguistics, Arabic, and Islamic culture. From this eclectic mix he came to focus on ETHNOGRAPHY AND ETHNOLOGY as his field of study before finally settling on French FOLKLORE, an area to which he devoted most of his life's work. He is considered one of the founders of modern folklore in France.

Van Gennep was an outstanding scholar but unsuccessful academic. His wide-ranging interests did not fit the molds of the time, and his blunt opinions often earned him as many enemies as admirers. For example, his open criticisms of DURKHEIM and his school closed off all university opportunities in France. Although he did briefly hold a chair in ethnography at the University of Neuchâtel in Switzerland (1912–15), he lost it when he was expelled from the country after complaining of pro-German violations of Swiss neutrality in World War I. He then became an independent scholar, supporting himself through his writings and by doing translations (he commanded 18 languages by his own count).

Van Gennep began his work on the topics of TOTEMISM and TABOOS, subjects that commanded much attention at the turn of the century for reasons that are today hard to fathom. Unlike other scholars who saw them as key to the origins of religion or kinship, van Gennep (1904, 1906, 1920) took the view that they were better understood as a form of CLASSIFICATION and that attempts to create great models of social EVOLUTION often depended on data that were suspect or misused. But his best-known anthropological work of this period was his classic *Les rites de passage* (1909). Using the COMPARATIVE METHOD he focused not on the diverse content of these rites but their common structures. He argued that all RITES OF PASSAGE had three phases: separation, transition, and incorporation. This seemingly simple model encompassed an enormous range of RITUALS and was well ahead of its time. Written when Sir James FRAZER's data-obsessed and ever-growing volumes of *The golden bough* brought him fame as the "father of anthropology," van Gennep's work was largely ignored. Instead he gravitated into folklore, which was then viewed as a completely different discipline, and became famous in France for his monumental nine-volume *Manuel de folklore de français contemporain* (1943–58). Its influence and success were in part the result of his belief that folklore studies were really just an extension of ethnography to rural Europe, an attitude many generations in advance of his contemporaries.

Van Gennep's influence has been very considerable in Anglo-American anthropology, particularly SYMBOLIC ANTHROPOLOGY. After laying dormant for many decades, the translation of *Rites* into English shortly after his death (Gennep 1960) brought him renewed fame and posthumous attention. Authors such as Victor TURNER and Mary DOUGLAS in particular have focused their work on his transition, or liminal, stage of the ritual process as key to understanding the power and danger inherent in such rites and why they have such staying power.   TB
further reading Belmont 1979

genocide is defined by the United Nations as "acts committed with intent to destroy, in whole or in part, a national, ethnical, racial or religious group as such."

But because this definition stresses intent, most critics find it inadequate and contend that "genocide" should refer to the destructive effect of the acts, rather than to the intent of the perpetrators. Another objection is that the UN definition would exclude certain obvious genocides, such as those committed in the Ukraine, Indonesia, and Cambodia, where regimes wiped out political opponents on a massive scale. The UN definition also blurs the qualitative enormity of genocide as a concept by including the *partial* destruction of a group. Some critics would prefer to label such acts "massacres" because of their more limited scope. By contrast a true genocide attempts, and sometimes succeeds, in the annihilation of a whole group. The difficulty of clearly defining "genocide" is compounded by the widespread political and metaphorical uses of the word. For example, when birth-control advocates, or even people who contract mixed marriages, are accused of "genocide," it reduces the concept to meaninglessness.

The systematic killing of Jews, Gypsies, and others carried out by Nazi Germany during World War II so horrified the world that the UN passed a unanimous resolution in its very first session making genocide a crime under international law and its punishment an international matter. However, this genocide convention was not signed at once by member states, and some states have still not signed. Because genocide is normally carried out by a state, whose representatives massacre a group of its citizens, its prevention or punishment normally requires international action (or action by a stronger power) against the genocidal regime. Since such remedies clash with the jealously defended principle of national sovereignty, regarded by states as the foundation of world order, they are loath to intervene lest such an action become a precedent that might be used by the international community to justify future intervention in their own internal policies.

This fear seems overdrawn, because, in fact, the world has been unable or unwilling to prevent the most notorious genocides of the twentieth century. During the world war of 1914–18 the Turkish government accused Armenians in Turkey of siding with the Russian enemy and massacred large numbers of them. In the Soviet Union of the 1930s Stalin's regime deliberately starved millions of Ukrainian peasants to death, accusing them of opposing collectivized agriculture and therefore being "enemies of the people." Hitler's Nazi regime systematically killed millions of Jews, Gypsies, and others. The Indonesian army slaughtered half a million people suspected of being communists in 1965–6. In the early 1970s the fighting in the Vietnamese War spread to Cambodia, where the United States backed the regime of Lon Nol. When Lon Nol was overthrown by the communist (Khmer Rouge) forces of Pol Pot, the latter massacred all those suspected of opposing them (about two million of Cambodia's then population of eight million). No systematic international attempt was made to prevent any of these genocides, and with one exception (see below) the only perpetrators who were ever punished were some Nazi leaders after World War II. They could be punished because they fell into the hands of the nations that had defeated them in the war.

Genocide is difficult to prevent and its perpetrators hard to bring to justice because the issue is invariably entangled with national and international politics. When East Pakistan (now Bangladesh) seceded from Pakistan in 1971, the Pakistani army massacred an estimated three million Bangladeshis before India came to their rescue. The issue was brought repeatedly before the UN, but it was powerless to act because the Soviet Union, allied to India, was supporting Bangladesh while the United States was "tilting" towards Pakistan. When Idi Amin of Uganda massacred his opponents, particularly the Acholi and Lango peoples in the early 1970s, the Organization of African Unity and the UN Commission on Human Rights both declined to intervene.

Only two people have been convicted of genocide since the Nazis. Macias, the dictator of Equatorial Guinea, was overthrown and condemned to death for numerous crimes, including (perhaps wrongly) genocide; Pol Pot of Cambodia was tried and

convicted in absentia of genocide after the overthrow of his regime (L. Kuper 1984a). But because Pol Pot and his Khmer Rouge were supported by China and the United States even after the genocide (since he opposed the North Vietnamese), he has continued to live in western Cambodia, under the protection of China and Thailand. The current inability of international organizations to prevent "ethnic cleansing" in the Balkans or large-scale ethnic massacres in Rwanda and Burundi underlines the conclusion that the prevention of genocide depends on revising the assumptions and practices of international relations between states.   DML
See also HUMAN RIGHTS, PLURAL SOCIETIES
further reading Charny 1988–94; Hoffman 1981; L. Kuper 1981, 1984b

gens (pl. gentes) is a now obsolete term for CLAN used primarily by Lewis Henry MORGAN (1877) and his followers.
                                                     MR

geographic determinism is the notion that geography determines both character and culture. The concept is an ancient one, found, for example, in the classical Greek division of the world into *klimata*, geometrically marked off zones that combined both geographic and character traits. This approach remained largely intact through the eigthteenth century, when European writers claimed that the supposedly noxious climate of the New World produced organic life inferior in size and vigor to its Old World counterparts, and that human emigrants to the Americas suffered a diminution of physical and mental powers. More recently, geographic determinism was cast in a SOCIAL DARWINIAN form by Friedrich Ratzel (1844–1904), who conceived of nations as organisms with territorial instincts and drives. He coined the term "*Lebensraum*" to describe the law by which states expand, driven either by population growth or by the exhaustion of their resource base. A later generation of German geopolitical theorists led by Karl Haushofer fashioned *Lebensraum* into a territorial imperative appropriated by Hitler. French geographers of the school founded by Paul Vidal de la

Blache (1845–1918) cultivated a more flexible form of geographic determinism (called "possibilism") through the concept of "*pays*," conceptualized as a natural microregion whose culture (*genre de vie*) was adapted to its environment and could be understood in terms of it. The rejection of geographic determinism played a signal role in the foundation of American anthropology because Franz BOAS, trained as a geographer, explicitly broke with the monocausal explanatory schemes advanced by the geographic leadership. As expressed as a "profession" by Boas's disciple, A. L. KROEBER (1915: 284), "Geography, or physical environment, is material made use of by civilization, not a factor shaping or explaining civilization."   TG

gesture consists of signs conveyed by the body. Although most communication takes place using verbal language, gesture is an essential form of nonverbal communication that is primarily visual and therefore largely produced by the visible parts of the body. Some researchers also include nonlinguistic sounds made by the vocal apparatus under the general term "gesture" (Armstrong et al. 1995).

Gesture is certainly one of the oldest communicative behavioral repertoires in the history of humanity. Students of primate behavior note that chimpanzees and other great apes have a fairly elaborate vocabulary of gesture. Philip Lieberman (1991) and others have speculated that the brain's capacity for verbal language evolved as an elaboration of the centers controlling manual dexterity. This makes the universal use of hand gesture as an accompaniment to speech seem to be a survival from a prelinguistic human state.

Human gestures differ from those of other animals in that they are polysemic – that is, they can be interpreted to have many different meanings depending on the communicative context in which they are produced. This was pointed out by pioneering researcher Ray Birdwhistell (1952, 1970), who called the study of human body movement "kinesics." Birdwhistell resisted the idea that "body language" could be deciphered in some absolute fashion. He pointed out that every body movement, like every word people utter, must be interpreted broadly, and in conjunction with every other element in communication. The richness of human communicative resources ensures that gesture will also have a rich set of meaning possibilities. Contemporary students of human gesture, such as Adam Kendon (1981), note that gesture can often be used as an additional, simultaneous channel of communication to indicate the mood or spirit in which verbal communication is to be understood. The actions of the body, hand, and face all serve to clarify the intent of speakers. Often humans display several kinds of gesture simultanously with verbal language.

Over the centuries deaf persons have elaborated gestures into a full-fledged linguistic system for all forms of face-to-face communication – including technical and artistic expression. There are many varieties of deaf "sign language," but most share certain structural similarities. All combine different hand shapes with distinctive movements in order to convey broad concepts. The semiotic system of these languages thus represents to some degree a pictographic communication system, like written Chinese. Gestural languages have also been used as a kind of pidgin communication for trade between people who do not share a mutually intelligible verbal language.   WBe
See also COMMUNICATION, LANGUAGE

gift exchange Whether or not Adam Smith (1776: Bk. 1, ch. 2) was correct in attributing a natural propensity to "truck, barter and exchange" to human beings, the fact of the matter is that exchange occurs in all societies. People exchange material things, they exchange services; people even exchange people, as in the marriage exchanges that take place in many societies.

Anthropologists have drawn distinctions between types of exchange that occur in human societies, based upon the degree of sociability involved in the exchange. At one pole are those exchanges wherein the relative economic value of the goods being exchanged is subordinated to the social relationship of the persons engaged in the exchange. The main purpose of such exchanges is to create or reaffirm a social bond between persons or groups. Anthropologists following Marcel MAUSS (1954) refer to such exchanges as "gift exchange". Mauss argued that a gift carries with it the personality of the giver, and that the basic function of gift exchange is to promote social solidarity. Gift exchange, he said, while giving the appearance of being "voluntary" and "spontaneous" is in actual fact "obligatory." This is as true of the reciprocal give-and-take of the Northwest Coast POTLATCH as it is of the exchange of gifts between friends and relatives on certain holidays or birthdays in modern societies. The universality of the exchange of gifts, he suggested, reflects a sense of obligation so pervasive in all cultures as to somehow be attributable to the nature of the human mind itself. The obligation he was referring to was the obligation to give as well as the obligation to reciprocate what one has received.

Although the main purpose of gift exchange is to forge or sustain a social relationship, this does not mean that the relative economic value of the gifts being exchanged is *totally* irrelevant. As some writers have recently pointed out (Humphrey & Hugh-Jones 1992a), there is probably a lot more economic calculation involved in gift exchange than Mauss was willing to recognize. This is as true of traditional societies as it is of industrial societies. If one were to exchange gifts with some friend or relative on some special occasion and these gifts were vastly different in quality or economic value, it is likely that some notice would be taken and some adjustment (down or up) made in the future. It is not the value of the gift, we say, but the thought that went into it – however, not entirely.

It is also noteworthy that gift exchange seems to perform its solidarity-creating function best when the exchange takes place between persons who are more or less equals. Between persons of markedly different statuses, gifts to inferiors look suspiciously like charity or noblesse oblige toward underlings; and gifts in the other direction can be construed as tribute or taxes, even though they may be phrased as gifts. The purpose of such exchanges is to reaffirm a hierarchical relationship rather than to cement a social relationship.

At the other end of the continuum are exchanges that contain a low degree of sociability and a high degree of impersonality. The social relationship of the persons engaged in the exchange is very much subordinated to the relative economic value of the goods being exchanged. The most obvious example is a person who makes a purchase in a department store from a salesman whom that person has never met before and is unlikely to meet again. This is an instance of what is usually referred to as "COMMODITY exchange."

Of course, there may be exchanges that incorporate some of the features of both gift and commodity exchange. Sometimes the social component of such a relationship can come into conflict with its economic component and cause problems. Hence one sometimes hears the admonition that one should not do business with close friends or relatives.

Although in most societies exchanges embody some elements of both gift exchange and commodity exchange, there are anthropologists who view these types as characteristic of two distinct types of economy. C. Gregory (1982), for instance, defined gift exchange as the exchange of inalienable objects between persons in a condition of reciprocal dependence thereby establishing a qualitative relationship between the persons involved that has little to do with the quantitative relationship between the objects exchanged (which is the essence of commodity exchange). Modern industrial societies, it is claimed, are dominated by commodity or commercial exchange; small-scale traditional societies are characterized by gift exchange.   DK

See also MARRIAGE SYSTEMS, MONEY

further reading Appaduarai 1986; Codere 1968; M. Douglas & Isherwood 1979; C. Gregory 1987; Leach & Leach 1983; J. Parry & Bloch 1989; Sahlins 1972 [see essays The spirit of the gift: pp. 149–83; On the sociology of primitive exchange: pp. 185–275]

glottochronology is a highly controversial method of calculating the time depth between two genetically related languages by computing the percentage of basic cognate vocabulary they share (Swadesh 1959, 1971). By "time depth" is meant the time separating the two languages from their common ancestor (see COMPARATIVE LINGUISTICS). By "cognate vocabulary" is meant words inherited from their common ancestor.

The method rests on two questionable assumptions. The first is that a set of universally valid, culture-independent basic vocabulary items can be identified. These include some personal pronouns, basic body parts, common natural objects, common activities, etc. But many items in Swadesh's 100-item wordlist are not culture independent (Teeter 1963). The second assumption is that the rate of replacement of such vocabulary items is constant across time. Swadesh's original assumption was that 20 percent would be replaced every thousand years, but this has been seriously questioned on empirical grounds (Ellergård 1959). The methodology also faces the practical problem of distinguishing between cognates and loans.

As originally formulated, glottochronology assumed that the genetic relationship of the languages and the cognacy of the vocabulary items had already been established. The use of glottochronology as an attempt to establish genetic relationships, by noting gross similarities between vocabulary items without first establishing cognacy, is an even more speculative use of the method.

Glottochronology is sometimes referred to as "lexicostatistics," although this term is also used in a broader sense to refer to the application of statistical methods in lexical, especially historical-lexical, investigations.   BC

further reading Embleton 1986; Gudschinsky 1956

Gluckman, Max (1911–75) Max Gluckman was born in Johannesburg, South Africa in 1911, of Russian-Jewish parents. He first encountered anthropology at the University of Witwatersrand through the teaching of Winifred Hoernl. After completing his doctorate at Oxford in 1936 on the southern Bantu and doing further fieldwork in Zululand, he joined the Rhodes–Livingstone Institute in what was then Northern Rhodesia in 1939, becoming its director in 1942. In 1947 he returned to Oxford as a lecturer, and in 1949 became the first Professor of Social Anthropology at the University of Manchester, from which he led what was later to become known as the "Manchester school." He died suddenly on a trip to Jerusalem in 1975, where he had gone as part of a new interest in Israel.

Almost throughout his career, Gluckman was concerned with problems of social control, social change, and apparent resistance to the former. Originally influenced by the equilibrium models of RADCLIFFE-BROWN, he soon sought to supplement these with a recognition of the importance of process and social dynamics and the possibilities for SOCIAL CHANGE that these opened up. The notion of rituals of rebellion was one of the most important elements in this view. This has often been characterized as the doctrine that such rituals contribute to social cohesion by allowing steam to be let off. In reality, however, Gluckman saw the problem more in terms of the maintenance of stability through overcoming or incorporating conflict than the use of instability in the service of its opposite (see Werbner 1984: 162; Kapferer 1987). Failure here could lead to social change, which Gluckman saw as more normal than stability, though as also reproducing, in a sense, the social system. This led him to distinguish change of this sort, which was the result of internal structural imperfections, from change coming from outside the system, through COLONIALISM, migration, etc. His work at the Rhodes–Livingstone Institute led him to an interest in these latter problems too. He went beyond the work of his predecessor Godfrey Wilson in recognizing that urban areas and the tribal areas from which urban migrants came were not simply versions of one another sociologically but different aspects of a common social system. This was equally true of the Whites and the Zulus, as he showed in his first major study (Gluckman 1940a).

As part of his interest in social control, Gluckman (1955a, 1963) also stressed the study of LAW and legal processes, showing how cultural norms influence the judgments of tribal courts. From this, he derived the notion of the "reasonable man" in any society, whose values were often a benchmark both in arriving at judicial decisions and in justifying them. Although thus distinguishing what he thought of as "custom" from law, and underestimating the extent to which "custom" could be manipulated and created (see Werbner 1984: 185), he nonetheless showed how the latter could not function without the former if stability through respect for legal decisions was to be maintained. He also developed the analytic notions of situational analysis (or the extended case study), an early example being his own study of a ceremony opening a bridge in White-controlled Zululand (Gluckman 1940b), and of intercalary roles, which explained the tensions that could arise between the politicojudicial role of the headman and his obligations to his own kin. In all these respects, he showed a concern for fixing precisely the position of the individual in society, prioritizing neither the former over the latter, as in pure psychology, nor vice versa, as in the Durkheimian tradition exemplified especially by his erstwhile teacher Radcliffe-Brown. Like his friend and colleague FORTES, he saw the psychology of the individual in collective terms, in a way that went far beyond MALINOWSKI's narrow FUNCTIONALISM.

As leader of the now defunct but historically important Manchester school, Gluckman developed a reputation as a charismatic if sometimes dismissive and authoritarian teacher, albeit one whose mind could change if left to its own devices. Those in the circle around him were united by the equal attention they gave to process as to structure, and by the concentration of research on south-central Africa, though there were notable exceptions here, including F. G. Bailey (on India) and R. Frankenburg (on British communities). Perhaps the most influential figure after Gluckman was Victor TURNER and his studies of RITUAL and PILGRIMAGE, though J. C. Mitchell (ethnic networks), J. A. Barnes (kinship, networks), Abner Cohen (ethnicity, politics), and Peter Worsley

(millenarianism) have also had significant impacts in their respective fields. The volume edited by Aronoff (1976b) contains a comprehensive bibliography of Gluckman's work.   RP
See also CONFLICT RESOLUTION, LEGAL ANTHROPOLOGY, POLITICAL ANTHRO-POLOGY, SYMBOLIC ANTHROPOLOGY
further reading Aronoff 1976a; Gluckman 1955b, 1965b; Handelman 1976

Goody, Jack (1919–) Throughout his career Jack Goody has been associated almost exclusively with the University of Cambridge, where he was FORTES's student and replaced him as William Wyse Professor in 1973. Like Fortes, he worked in Ghana, among the LoDagaa and other groups. He has made considerable contributions to the anthropology of KINSHIP, placing even more emphasis than his teacher on property as the basis of lineage structure and identity. Goody's lifelong interest in the transmission of property through inheritance and marriage payments can be seen in his first major published work, *Death, property and the ancestors* (1962), on the LoDagaa, a Dagara subgroup. This has led to further, more comparative work, encompassing at its widest, in *Production and reproduction* (1976), Africa and Eurasia. This work compares these two parts of the world, linking the difference between BRIDEWEALTH and DOWRY that characterizes them with a further difference in cultivation. Hoe cultivation in Africa cannot produce the surpluses of plow cultivation in Eurasia, which has allowed wealth to be accumulated more easily and made the control of land more important to ruling groups, as well as restricting both inheritance and marriage within them. This has led to different strategies of heirship (including widespread adoption in Eurasia, different attitudes to women, and different ways of consolidating the kingdom). In *The oriental, the ancient and the primitive* (1990), Goody focused in particular on dowry, arguing that conventional definitions obscure the fact that women may often control it in whole or in part, so that it may merge with the notion of matrilineal inheritance on

occasion, even in what are thought to be heavily patrilineal societies, such as India and China. A further book on this general theme, *The development of the family and marriage in Europe* (1983a), argues that the early Church managed to weaken the control of local kin groups over their members and encouraged greater control by individuals, especially over property, at the same time banning traditional strategies of heirship such as ADOPTION, CONCUBINAGE, and DIVORCE. This left the Church itself as the chief beneficiary of those who lacked natural heirs, a process further encouraged by a greater use of wills and the ban on clerical marriage.

Goody has pursued the comparison between Africa and Eurasia in relation to other topics, including especially food and flowers. In respect of the former, he noted that Africa is mainly a continent of subsistence AGRICULTURE with little variety beyond the basic DIET, whereas at least the upper classes in Eurasia enjoy a wide variety of food and dishes, and cooking becomes an art form (Goody 1982). Again, he related this to the difference in cultivation – more efficient plow cultivation has led to a greater variety of food crops – and the absence or presence of social STRATIFI-CATION, which has produced different cultural as well as social groups in Eurasia. A similar argument appears in *The culture of flowers* (1993), in which the lack of significance given to flowers in Africa compared to Eurasia is noted. In Eurasia flowers are often used in worship, and they may denote luxury and therefore wealth and status. Additionally cultivating and arranging them are seen as art forms.

Finally, there is Goody's work on literacy (several books, but especially *The domestication of the savage mind*, 1977; also 1986, 1987). Here, his basic argument is that in allowing knowledge to be stored, literacy enables texts to be both standardized and reflected upon, thus encouraging not only criticism and skepticism, but also the development of competing ideologies. In its turn, this process has aided transitions from magic to science, myth to history, and traditional rule to bureaucracy. This work in part reflects the influence of Sir James FRAZER, for whom Goody has always had a genuine if unfashionable affection (see also 1962, 1996).

Goody has proved an exceptionally prolific writer. His work is very wide-ranging in its scope, combining broad comparisons across half the globe with more narrowly focused ethnographic studies. It is explicitly not, however, grand theory, for Goody prefers the "middle-range theories" associated with the sociologist Merton (1949, ch. 2), in which generalizations can be based on a more manageable range of sources. In general, he treats anthropology as a cumulative science, in which results are assembled from which enduring theoretical perspectives can be developed. Often counted among the FUNCTIONALISTS, it is noticeable that he is not afraid to take account of material factors in discussing social organization, such as WRITING and agricultural techniques in FOOD PRODUCTION.   RP
See also COOKING, FOOD SYSTEMS, SUCCESSION, WRITING SYSTEMS
further reading J. Goody 1991

government is most broadly defined as a system of rules for maintaining social order. Such rules may be implicit or explicit, codified in writing or a matter of oral record only. Much of the debate in anthropology has focused on whether government requires visible institutions with power to implement its rules, or whether it can exist in societies where there are specific nodes of authority. In this debate one of the key problems has been the identification (and confusion) of government with the state.

Nineteenth-century theorists such as Sir Henry MAINE (1861) and Lewis Henry MORGAN (1877) had argued that simple societies with common property, where relations were status oriented and kin based, had evolved into more complex societies with private property where order was predicated on contractual ties and territorially based administration. In such schemes recognizable governmental institutions were a characteristic of "civilized" societies, while "primitive" societies lacked them.

British FUNCTIONALIST anthropologists such as Meyer FORTES and E. E. EVANS-PRITCHARD rejected the evolutionary schema of their predecessors but kept many of its categories. They were keen to sort out the dynamics of what they saw as two distinct types of African society: centralized and noncentralized. The first were characterized by "centralized authority, administrative machinery, and judicial institutions – in short, a government," and "cleavages of wealth, privilege, and status correspond[ed] to the distribution of power and authority." The second included "those societies which lack[ed] centralized authority, administrative machinery, and constituted judicial institutions – in short which lack[ed] government," and "there [were] no sharp divisions of rank, status, or wealth" (Fortes & Evans-Pritchard 1940a: 5).

This distinction did not mean that politics was lacking in noncentralized societies. Indeed, Fortes and Evans-Pritchard inspired a generation of fieldworkers to locate politics in societies that lacked government by their definition. In so doing, however, they also undermined their own typology and the rigor with which "government" could be defined. As more descriptions of political systems in acephalous societies accumulated, Fortes and Evans-Pritchard's yardstick for what comprised a government came to look increasingly like the trappings of a STATE, not government itself. Their own work on stateless societies among the Nuer and Tallensi suggested that people with no bureaucracy still managed to conduct their affairs and govern themselves quite effectively, and according to clear rules (Evans-Pritchard 1940; Fortes 1945). So, was it really government that such societies lacked, or simply the state?

Lucy Mair (1962: 16) argued that Fortes and Evans-Pritchard had indeed perpetuated a false dichotomy by neglecting a basic question: what does government do? Her answer was that

it protects members of the political community against lawlessness within and enemies without; and it takes decisions on behalf of the community in matters which concern them all, and in which they have to act together.

Accordingly, Mair rejected the notion that there could be any society without a government. Even the most "primitive" societies had government, if only of a minimal type that might result from the small size of the community, the paucity and impermanence of recognized leadership positions, or the inability of leaders to consistently and uniformly exert their authority. To make her case, Mair chose to single out the nomadic Nuer as a "supreme example" of a society possessing minimal government, despite the fact that Evans-Pritchard was their ethnographer and had declared that they lacked government. But using Evans-Pritchard's own data, Mair argued that because the Nuer share clear rules for redressing wrongs, and have recognizable leaders who achieve respect, even if they cannot command obedience, they do have a government (1962: 61–2).

A more subtle problem not addressed in these debates is the question of what rules apply to an individual and what constitutes legitimacy of governments, however defined. For example Edmund LEACH (1954) noted that in northern Burma the lowland Shan had a stratified society with fixed social roles, while the neighboring highland Kachin villages oscillated between hierarchical and egalitarian phases, each with different sets of rules. Who and what then comprised government for a Kachin (never mind "the" Kachin) depended on where in the system the individual happened to be at a particular moment in time. This, of course, raises a problem with which inhabitants of state systems are experientially familiar: despite the state's claims of singularity, most individuals are bound to other sets of rules (religious, cultural, ethnic, etc.) that govern behavior in ways that are often contradictory. In this way the anthropological debate about the nature of government has come full circle. Early anthropologists assumed that government in state systems was clear because it was institutionalized and so needed no explication, while societies without formal institutions demanded close inspection to see how they worked. Today anthropologists have realized that the formal institutions of government in state systems are hardly as fixed or clear as their predecessors assumed and demand the same level of attentive deconstruction that was once devoted to the Nuer.   ASi

See also LAW, LEGAL ANTHROPOLOGY, POLITICAL ANTHROPOLOGY

further reading Balandier 1970

grammar The grammar of a LANGUAGE or DIALECT or idiolect is (1) the set of generalizations about the way the sound and meaning of expressions in the variety are connected; (2) an encoding, in a metalanguage, of some portion of the grammar for that variety. The metalanguage can be some ordinary language, like English, supplemented by special technical terms (like *agent, state, verb, constituent, subject, person, obstruent,* and *mora*) or a formalism specially devised for the purpose. Descriptive linguists write grammars (in sense 2) as approximations to the grammar (in sense 1).

The grammar of a variety is naturally divisible into several parts, or components, each of which has an organization of its own: SEMANTICS (concerned with meaning), phonetics (concerned with the acoustic and articulatory properties of sounds, see PHONEMES), and at least three mediating components – PHONOLOGY (treating the way differences in sound are systematically used to signal differences in meaning), morphology (treating the part of the sound–meaning relationship that follows from the internal structure of words), and SYNTAX (treating the part of the sound–meaning relationship that follows from the way larger expressions – phrases, clauses, and sentences – are organized out of words).

The grammar of a variety is only one part of what its speakers know about it. In addition to the grammar, there are, at least, a lexicon (the set of words); a set of principles for the organization of discourse; a set of principles for effective language use; a set of associations between aspects of the grammar and the lexicon, on the one hand, and sociocontextual factors like generation, gender, social class, formality, and politeness, on the other hand; and all kinds of knowledge about how to construct special-purpose discourses (e.g., sonnets, newspaper headlines, recipes, knock-knock jokes).

Edward SAPIR (1921: 38) observed, "Unfortunately, or luckily, no language is tyranically consistent. All grammars leak." Certainly all grammars (in sense 2) do; there are so many details to the sound–meaning connection – even for just one speaker, even in a uniform style of speech, even on a single day of that speaker's life – that it would be as hopeless to suppose we could describe every relevant detail as it would be to suppose we could describe every relevant detail of an ecosystem. There is simply too much. Whether every grammar (in sense 1) leaks is not so clear; this is the question of whether there are inherent indeterminacies in the grammar of a variety – for instance, situations in which the grammar provides no fully acceptable expression, but only two (or more) somewhat unacceptable alternatives. Grammatical agreement is one area where it has been suggested that such indeterminacies are particularly likely to occur. Many English speakers find that there is no fully satisfactory way to select a form of the verb *be* to agree with the subject *either you or I*: not ?*either you or I are* or ?*either you or I am* or ?*either you or I is*.

These two senses of grammar must be distinguished from several other common uses of the word. First, there is a very widespread non-technical use of the word in which the grammar in question is for a socially privileged variety of a language (the variety used by an elite, or a standard variety prescribed by cultural authorities). For instance, varieties of English that have multiple negation (*I didn't see nobody*) are often characterized as having "no grammar," or at best "bad grammar," though in fact such varieties merely have a grammar (in sense 1) somewhat different from modern standard varieties of the language.

Second, linguists themselves sometimes limit the meaning of the word "grammar" (in either sense). Some choose to reserve the term for the components of a grammar that actually concern both sound and meaning (phonology, morphology, and syntax) and some for the components in which sound and meaning are actually linked (morphology and syntax), or to syntax alone, as the indispensable core of this linkage. There is even an older usage in which only inflectional morphology, the variation in the form of words to indicate syntactic relationships (like the choice between *am*, *is*, and *are* as present tense forms of the verb *be*), counts as grammar; this is the usage according to which languages like Chinese, which lack virtually any inflectional morphology, are sometimes said to be "without grammar."   AZ
further reading Lyons 1968

Green Revolution

Green Revolution refers to a major breakthrough in the application of genetic science to agricultural production during the 1960s, which first produced hybridized dwarf varieties of wheat and rice that were very responsive to high applications of fertilizer and produced yields two to three times higher than the varieties they replaced. It was this dramatic increase in yield per unit of land, and potential farm income, that made the new varieties truly revolutionary. The initial success of the high-yielding varieties led to the establishment of a worldwide network of agricultural research stations focused on regionally specific crops. Supported by international donors, this applied research seeks to improve farm productivity, alleviate world hunger, and increase farmer income through the development of new seeds and farming technologies.

Despite their clear successes in increasing crop yields, and despite some innovations in tillage, the early enthusiasm for the Green Revolution has been tempered by concerns for its frequently adverse social and environmental effects. Historically, farm production everywhere depended on human and animal labor, locally grown seeds, composting and manuring, crop rotation, intercropping, and fallowing to maintain soil fertility. In the twentieth century this pattern was broken by a new reliance on external inputs (machines for tillage and harvesting, fuel to run them, chemical fertilizers, pesticides and fungicides) that encouraged specialization through continuous monocrop farming without fallowing. Many critics have argued that the economies of scale required by such innovations, including dependence on oil products and wells for irrigation, have exacerbated social inequality and have marginalized, even bankrupted, smaller peasants and tenant holders who lack access to the state-subsidized credit. Critics also note that the high-yielding varieties' high need for irrigation water and chemical inputs jeopardizes the quality of the water table, threatens public health, and reduces the long-term productivity of the soil. The challenge to the Green Revolution today is to contribute to an agriculture that is both environmentally and socioeconomically sustainable.   MH

See also AGRICULTURE, FOOD PRODUCTION, TECHNOLOGY

further reading L. Brown 1970; K. Dahlberg 1979; Nicholson & Nicholson 1979

group marriage is a supposed form of primitive marriage hypothesized by early kinship theorists in which a group of men and women were jointly married and engaged in joint reproduction and raising of young. Lewis Henry MORGAN thought that CLASSIFICATORY KINSHIP SYSTEMS might be evidence of such a stage.   MR

gumsa and gumlao are the range of ideal-typical forms of social and political organization among the Kachin of highland Burma. The *gumlao* form is essentially egalitarian and acephalous, while the *gumsa* form is characterized by ranked lineages and hereditary chieftainship, mimicking in less stable form their lowland Shan neighbors who lived under a hierarchical system of hereditary princes. Edmund LEACH, who first described this system, characterized the *gumsa* system as "a kind of compromise between *gumlao* and Shan ideals" (1954: 9).   MR

H

hallucinogens *See* DRUGS

Harris, Marvin (1927–) Marvin
Harris is one of the most important anthropologists of the second half of the twentieth
century. His main contribution to anthropology is the development of a distinctive
theoretical approach, CULTURAL MATERI-
ALISM, which is a synthesis of marxist historical materialism, cultural ecology, and
social evolutionary theory. Harris was born
in Brooklyn, NY in 1927 and educated at
Columbia University, where he took his
Ph.D. in 1953. He then taught at Columbia until 1980, when he moved to the University of Florida as Graduate Research
Professor of Anthropology.

Harris has authored or edited nearly 20
books. His first major work, *Patterns of race
in the Americas* (1964), was based on his
own fieldwork in Brazil. It looked at the
development of different patterns of RACE
and ETHNIC relations in the US South,
highland Latin America (largely Mexico),
and the Latin American lowlands (largely
Brazil). Harris tried to explain, for example, the striking differences in the modes
of racial categorization in the US South
and Brazil. He also inquired into the question as to why the Spanish colonies in the
Americas made such limited use of SLA-
VERY while Portuguese America (Brazil)
employed it on a large scale.

In 1968 Harris published his most erudite work to date, *The rise of anthropological
theory*, 750-page history of anthropological
theory from 1750 to the present. In this
work, Harris laid out quite systematically
the basic principles of cultural materialism
and traced its origins. Other anthropological theories are discussed and assessed in
terms of their degree of departure from a
materialist perspective. The book garnered

both praise and criticism, the latter particularly intense from partisans for views that
Harris attacked.

Harris also wrote extensively for nonpro-
fessional audiences. He is best known for
Culture, people, nature (1997), a general anthropology textbook first published in 1971
that is now in its seventh edition and still
widely used. It provides an excellent introduction to cultural-materialist thinking by
extensively applying it to a wide range of
social and cultural phenomena. In 1974
Harris published *Cows, pigs, wars, and
witches: the riddles of culture*, based on a series of essays published regularly in *Natural
History Magazine*. The book attempted to
explain so-called cultural riddles, such as
the Hindu sanctification of the cow and
ban on eating it, or the Jewish and Muslim
abomination of the pig, by showing that
they were sensible ADAPTATIONS to the
practical conditions of life that people had
faced in different times and places. It was
quickly followed by *Cannibals and kings: the
origins of cultures* (1977), where Harris laid
out a theoretical model of social EVOLU-
TION and applied it to the last 10,000 years
of human prehistory and history. This
model made population growth, ecological
depletion, and technological change the
basic driving forces of history responsible
for the evolution not only of economic systems, but of all the major features of human
society. In 1985 Harris published *Good to
eat: riddles of food and culture*, one of his
most engaging works. This work was devoted to explaining FOOD TABOOS and DIET
patterns all over the world in terms of cultural materialist principles.

Harris developed the basic principles of
cultural materialism in the 1950s and
1960s, but it was in the 1970s and 1980s
that he wrote many of his most important

works applying this perspective to particular cultural phenomena. In 1979 Harris published *Cultural materialism: the struggle for a science of culture*, which laid out the basic principles of cultural materialism more extensively than Harris had done previously. The book also criticized, quite severely in most cases, the other major competing paradigms in anthropological theory. In a short book Harris (1981) later used cultural materialism to explain the most important changes in US society since the end of World War II; in another he attempted to explain population growth around the world and throughout history (Harris & Ross 1987a).

Harris's production has slowed in recent years, and he may have reached the end of his intellectual creativity. But even if he never writes another word, his intellectual production has been prodigious and enormously important. Modern anthropology is tremendously indebted to him, and his intellectual influence has been great.

SS

See also CLASSIFICATION, ECOLOGICAL ANTHROPOLOGY, ECONOMIC ANTHROPOLOGY, MATERIALISM

Hawaiian kinship systems

Hawaiian kinship systems classify kin terms primarily by generation relative to Ego, so that, for instance, all men of the father's generation are referred to by the same term as the father, and cousins are referred to as "brothers" and "sisters" (see figure 1). Hawaiian kinship terms are a variety of CLASSIFICATORY KINSHIP SYS-

TEM, often associated with AMBILINEAL DESCENT and AMBILOCAL RESIDENCE.

MR

head-hunting is the decapitation of enemies and the collection of their heads. It has been reported in the Americas, Asia, and Europe, but the motives given and the treatments of the severed heads vary. During interethnic warfare in the Balkans in the last century, men wore the heads of their enemies on their belts as proof of bravery (Durham 1923). The Ilongot of the Philippines left the heads of their victims at the scene of the killing, which they explained as relieving the "weight" of grief or insult (R. Rosaldo 1980: 140–2). In Papua New Guinea, the Marind Anim reportedly took heads in order to replenish their stock of personal names, whereas in Borneo newly obtained heads provided the focus of major festivals, which were said to revitalize whole communities. The Jivaro of Ecuador preserved only the scalp and facial tissues to produce the famous shrunken heads, whereas the ancient Scythians of the Black Sea region used the skullcap as a drinking cup (Herodotus 1987 [440 B.C.E.]: 4–65). The North American practice of scalping might be seen as a variant of head-hunting (Axtell 1981a).

The variety of beliefs and practices concerning head-hunting undermines universal explanations. The most prevalent theory posits a kind of alienable "soul-substance" concentrated in the head. The idea was first applied to the Toraja of

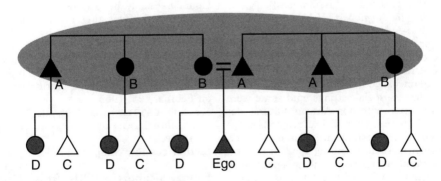

Figure 1 Hawaiian kinship system.

Sulawesi, who associate the possession of skulls with increased reproductive and agricultural fertility. But there is no such indigenous concept, and its quasi-physical nature is an expression of our ideas of causality rather than theirs (Needham 1983). Ecological explanations have attributed to head-hunting the function of spacing population density. The latest approaches have emphasized head-hunting as trivialized VIOLENCE akin to SACRIFICE, sought culturally specific interpretations, and taken into account the persistent fears of head-hunting that give it continued relevance in the modern world.   PM
See also WAR
further reading Hoskins 1996; R. Rosaldo 1980; Vayda 1969a

health See DISEASE, ILLNESS, MEDICAL ANTHROPOLOGY

Herskovits, Melville J. (1895–1963)

Herskovits was born in Bellefontein, Ohio on September 10, 1895. He received his doctorate under Franz BOAS at Columbia in 1923. He pioneered the study of African and Afroamerican culture and was the first professional Africanist in American academia. His doctoral thesis on "The cattle complex in East Africa" was related to his early work on African cultural areas, of which he described nine (Herskovits 1926). This preceded a field trip to Dahomey in 1931, where he developed the full range of his mature interests in religion, art and aesthetics, and anthropological economics. At the same time, he pursued parallel studies of African culture in the New World. This led to his famous book *The myth of the Negro past* (1941), which made African-American culture a recognized topic of anthropological research. Here he defined the range of ACCULTURATION of Africans in America: some elements were unchanged, others were reinterpreted within new social settings, and some were synthesized with non-African cultural elements (for example, African religious adaptation to Protestantism). Certain African elements, such as music, food tastes and preparation, religion, and magic had a higher rate of retention, whereas technology and economic life were generally submerged in a sharply different economic

world (although cooperative work habits were maintained). He related African polygyny to Caribbean plural marriage and identified the Yoruba connection of Afro-Catholic religion, such as Haitian voodoo. In his studies of pidgin DIALECTS, he found the persistence of African grammatical structures, used with English vocabulary. Much of his work in physical anthropology revolved around the genetics of miscegenation and cultural conditioning in the form of somatic-norm images, which associated prestige with skin color in African-American populations. His book on the economics of traditional societies, *The economic life of primitive peoples* (1940), was criticized for his avoidance of formal economic theory.

In ethnopsychology, Herskovits formulated the important distinction between SOCIALIZATION and ENCULTURATION. The latter he saw as comprising two successive phases, an unconscious level acquired during the childhood that lends stability to a culture and a conscious level that involves reconditioning and change. This interest led naturally to the role of EDUCATION in cultural dynamics.

Herskovits stressed the importance of acculturation as a process of CULTURAL CHANGE, criticizing the inadequacy of FUNCTIONALIST approaches developed in the study of stable, relatively isolated cultures in dealing with contact societies. Along with Robert REDFIELD and Ralph LINTON, Herskovits was an author of the influential "Memorandum for the study of acculturation" (Redfield et al. 1936) commissioned by the Social Science Research Council. Finally he played a key role in defining and advocating the doctrine of CULTURAL RELATIVISM, whereby conduct was to be evaluated in the light of the cultural context that generated it. He died in Evanston, Illinois, where he had been professor of African Studies at Northwestern, on February 25, 1963.   TG
See also CATTLE COMPLEX, ECONOMIC ANTHROPOLOGY, PSYCHOLOGICAL ANTHROPOLOGY
further reading Simpson 1973

Hertz, Robert (1881–1915)

Hertz was born in 1881 and educated at the École Normale Supérieure in Paris. Before World

War I, he briefly held a post at the École des Hautes Études. He was killed in 1915, in what Marcel MAUSS bitterly described as a "useless attack" on German machine-gun positions near Marcheville.

Robert Hertz is now principally remembered for just two long essays that exemplify the best of the *Année sociologique* school, that is, the students of Émile DURKHEIM who published in that journal. Less doctrinaire than his teacher, his ideas prefigured several developments in modern anthropology. Had he not been killed so young, he might have become a major figure in the field.

His essays were brought to the attention of English and American audiences through the translation project initiated at Oxford by E. E. EVANS-PRITCHARD. Rodney and Claudia Needham made the translations, which were published together under the title *Death and the right hand* (1960a,b). The volume was timely, helping to shape a renewed interest in symbolism in the 1960s.

The first essay, "A contribution to the study of the collective representation of death," was originally published in 1907 (Hertz 1960a). It focuses on one striking variety of DEATH rites, those involving secondary treatment of the corpse, but aims at general insights. After its translation, it was the sociological aspects of his argument that they were first developed, those concerning the status of the deceased and the scale of the rites. But in the long run, it was his analysis of the meaning of the rites in terms of perceptions of living and dying that proved most interesting.

The second essay concerns "The preeminence of the right hand," and originally appeared in 1909 (Hertz 1960b). Subtitled "A study in religious polarity," it relates the left–right dyad to others, and concludes, unsurprisingly, that they all derive from Durkheim's basic contrast of sacred–profane. The originality of the essay lies elsewhere, however. Hertz asked himself whether handedness is a biological or a cultural phenomenon, and concluded that it is both. If there is no basis in biology, why, across the whole world, is it almost invariably the right hand that is favored? But how can a slight physical predisposition explain the fantastic elaboration of dualistic sym-

bolism involving laterality, in some cases drawing in all living things, even the whole cosmos? Hertz's handling of the eternal nature–nurture problem is more useful than most of the materialist or idealist diatribes that have appeared in recent decades.

Hertz wrote other essays that are not widely known; studies of the cult of Saint Besse in an alpine village in 1913, and of stories told by French soldiers in the front in 1915. In these he showed an awareness of the necessity for first-hand fieldwork. Had he lived, French anthropologists might have begun field research a generation before they did. He planned a book-length study of sin and expiation in primitive societies, of which only the introduction was published, in 1922.   PM

further reading Hertz 1970

historical approach *See* HISTORY AND ANTHROPOLOGY

historical linguistics (or diachronic linguistics) is the study of how languages change over time, as all living languages do. The scientific study of LANGUAGE change developed in the nineteenth century and was initially most successful in its application to phonology. A major breakthrough was the recognition of systematic correspondences between Germanic consonants and those of other Indo-European languages by Jacob Grimm (1967). For instance, Germanic f (as in English *father*) usually corresponds to p in other Indo-European languages (e.g., Latin *pater*), establishing the operation of a sound change (or sound law) $p > f$ in the prehistory of the Germanic languages. The discovery in the 1870s that apparent exceptions to these correspondences could in fact be explained – for instance that p changed to v, rather than f, if noninitial and not immediately following the word accent (compare English *seven* and Sanskrit *saptá-*) – gave rise to the so-called Neogrammarian hypothesis, according to which sound change is always regular and can be stated in purely phonological terms (Osthoff & Brugmann 1967). Remaining apparent exceptions are often the result of borrowing from other DIALECTS or genetically related languages (dialect mixing), as when English *paternal*,

Table 1   The Great Vowel Shift: English long vowels before and after the shift.

Before		After		As in	
i:	u:	ay	aw	ride	mouth
e:	o:	i:	u:	meet	soon
E:	O:	e:	o:	meat	boat
a:		E:		mate	

a loan from Latin, fails to show the $p > f$ shift, or English *vixen* (in contrast to *fox*) unexpectedly shows *v* in initial position (the word is borrowed from dialects of southwestern England that regularly shift initial *f* to *v*). Another source of exceptions, recognized by the Neogrammarians, is analogy (Anttila 1977), whereby the formation of one word is influenced by that of another, as when the etymologically expected plural of *cow*, namely *kine*, was replaced by *cows*, by analogy with the more frequent plural pattern *dog–dogs*. Although few would today accept the Neogrammarian hypothesis without some qualifications (Wang 1977), the hypothesized regularity of sound change remains an important heuristic in historical and COMPARATIVE LINGUISTICS.

The development of structural linguistics in the first half of the twentieth century encouraged historical linguists to study not isolated changes, but the overall system within which such changes take place. For instance, in the fifteenth and sixteenth centuries all the long vowels in English underwent phonetic change, as shown in table 1. These changes fit into a general overall pattern: the tongue height of all vowels was raised, except that the originally high vowels, not being amenable to further raising, were diphthongized (the so-called Great Vowel Shift). The development of generative LINGUISTICS in the second half of the twentieth century has encouraged the search for even more abstract patterns underlying change (R. King 1969).

Although the importance of social factors in language change has long been recognized, for instance in facilitating the borrowing of vocabulary, it is especially in the second half of the twentieth century that their importance even in such traditional areas as historical phonology has come to the fore. In particular, a language at a given time is characterized by internal variation, and the interplay of these variants can be an important factor in language change. For instance, in the period immediately after the Great Vowel Shift, all three of *meet*, *meat*, and *mate* were pronounced differently (system I). Thereafter, the apparent development is that first *meat* and *mate* merged, pronounced much as present-day *mate* (system II), but that subsequently *meat* diverged from *mate* – in apparent violation of the Neogrammarian hypothesis – to be pronounced like *meet*, as in the contemporary standard language (system III). In fact, at the intermediate stage both systems II and III (and perhaps also system I) were coexistent, but system II was the prestige variety. Subsequently, the prestige values of systems II and III shifted, so that this is not strictly an instance of a sound change, but rather of a change in the social evaluation of variants (Weinreich et al. 1968).

In an important recent contribution to the social basis of language change, Thomason and Kaufman (1988) argued that what has traditionally been considered borrowing should be divided into two: (1) borrowing in the strict sense (when speakers of language X go on speaking X but adopt some features from language Y) and (2) language shift (when speakers of language X shift to language Y but carry over some features of language X). The outcomes of the two processes can be quite different: strict borrowing will tend in the first instance to graft only vocabulary onto language X, while language shift may graft phonological and syntactic features of X onto Y even in the absence of borrowed vocabulary.

No general theory of causes of linguistic change seems to be forthcoming; motivations can sometimes be given for individual changes, but they are rarely predictive explanations. Considerable progress has, however, been made in identifying plausible paths of change. In phonology, certain sound changes are much more likely than others, in part on the basis of articulatory and acoustic closeness of sounds. In grammar the phenomenon of grammaticalization plays a major role, whereby lexical items are reduced to affixes (as when Latin *lenta mente* "with a slow mind" gives Italian *lentamente* "slowly'), and affixes are reduced to morphophonemic alternations (as when older Germanic *mu:s*, plural *mu:si*, gives English *mouse*, plural *mice*) (Hopper & Traugott 1993). Another important grammatical principle is transparency (Lightfoot 1979), as when the *got* of *I got rhythm*, originally elliptical for *I have got rhythm*, is reanalyzed as a regular verb in nonstandard English, giving rise to the negative *I don't got (no) rhythm*. Historical semantics has a rich descriptive tradition, with classification of various kinds of meaning changes; and the recent upsurge of work on metaphor (Sweetser 1990) promises to provide new impetus.   BC

further reading Anttila 1989; Bynon 1977; Hock 1986; Jeffers & Lehiste 1979; Labov 1972, 1994; Lehmann 1967; H. Paul 1888; Pedersen 1931; Ullmann 1951, 1962

historical particularism is a school of thought associated with Franz BOAS that advocated an idiographic rather than a nomothetic approach to culture, arguing that every culture was unique and must be studied solely in terms of its uniqueness. Each culture had its own historical trajectory and could be understood only from the point of view of the particularities of that trajectory. There could be no "laws" of social organization and change, nor was it possible to formulate general theories of society or of historical development. Cultures intermingled and borrowed a great deal from each other, and every culture was, like a quilt, a thing of "shreds and patches." Boas and his followers were par-

ticularly critical of all evolutionary theories of human society, arguing that these had been formulated through reliance on an illegitimate methodological device, the COMPARATIVE METHOD. Under the Boasian influence, anthropologists turned their backs on evolutionary theories for more than 40 years, and EVOLUTION became a dirty word.

As a result of the Boasian domination of anthropology between about 1890 and 1930, it gave up scientific aspirations and saw itself instead as one of the humanities. The historical particularist outlook, but without the name, has always been the outlook of the great majority of historians. Although historical particularism retreated with the advance of neoevolutionary doctrines from the 1950s through the 1970s, it has (again, without the name) become popular once again among anthropologists, who stress "local knowledge" and the impossibility of general theories. Many sociologists have turned toward this perspective, especially in conjunction with an almost complete repudiation of evolutionary theories.   SS

further reading Boas 1940, Harris 1968

history and anthropology Through time, the relationship between history and anthropology has been both complex and paradoxical. From one standpoint, each developed largely without respect to the other. From another, anthropology has often been engaged in some sort of dialogue with history. It is helpful to distinguish between thought and discipline, and between a discipline's mainstream and periphery. Both anthropological and historical thought are ancient in the West, but history and anthropology took shape as formal disciplines in relatively recent times. Although historians have a deeper and more varied intellectual heritage on which to draw, they and anthropologists today identify some of the same classical, Renaissance, Enlightenment, and early-nineteenth-century thinkers as worthy forebears – for example, Herodotus, Montesquieu, Vico, Condorcet, Comte. By 1800, such overlap was ending and, following broad retreat in 1800–50, anthropology (also called ETHNOLOGY), which was newly forming as a discipline from a robust avocational heritage, and history, which was also undergoing professionalization, went largely separate ways. For a hundred years thereafter, the boundaries between the two disciplines remained sharp and at times virtually impermeable; the late twentieth century has brought rapprochement. However impermeable disciplinary boundaries may have been, historical thought has never been entirely absent from anthropology. If, in fact, history is conceptualized as what happened in the past (as well as the representation of the past in the present), then anthropology's aims must be characterized as historical when evolution, diffusion, social change, acculturation, ethnohistory, and history came to the fore as specific interests at particular times.

Evolution as universal history, 1860–1900

One of the most important of these times spanned virtually the entire second half of the nineteenth century, when anthropology, developing in the same intellectual climate that nurtured Darwin, was relentlessly evolutionary in design. From 1860 to 1885, major anthropological works were published – by Lewis Henry MORGAN, Henry MAINE, Edward B. TYLOR, John Ferguson McLennan, Jacob Bachofen and others – that collectively defined the era. Just as EVOLUTION was the rage in biology, so was it in the theory of anthropologists and related social philosophers like Herbert SPENCER. Disputes paled beside the shared belief that human beings go through a unilinear succession of stages in family organization, technology, religion, society, and so on. Through what they called COMPARATIVE METHOD, evolutionists tore institutions, customs, or artifacts from their contemporary cultural contexts and ordered them in evolutionary sequences. They projected synchronic data into diachronic sequences, a methodology that struck many historians as decidedly nonhistorical.

Diffusionist history, 1890–1925

In Germany in the 1890s, and later in Austria and England, DIFFUSION in space was proposed as an alternative historical explanation to unilinear evolution to account for the distribution of cultural elements. Like the evolutionists, the diffusionists had as their ultimate goal the discovery of laws governing historical change. Friedrich Ratzel, a cultural geographer, and his student Leo Frobenius were initially responsible for mapping geographical distributions of traits, grouping similar societies regionally (in *Kulturkreise*, CULTURE AREAS, or circles) on the basis of similar cultural features, and projecting time onto spatial patterns of inferred diffusion. Later adherents like Wilhelm Schmidt sought to construct a world history on the basis of diffusion of traits. When diffusionism spread to England in the 1920s, it took on an especially extravagant slant: G. Elliott Smith and W. J. Perry argued that Archaic Civilization was invented once, in ancient Egypt, whence its traits diffused throughout the world. Diffusionist theory was to attract more respectable adherents like W. H. R. RIVERS, but the absurd claims of the Egypto-centrists helped doom radical diffusionism as scientific or historical explanation. If it had not already, mainstream anthropology had turned its back on diffusionism (but not all diffusion) by the mid-1920s.

Historical particularism, 1900–35

The reaction to diffusionism simply intensified the criticism of all conjectural history that had started before 1900 when a sharp reaction to evolutionist theory had developed. Mainstream anthropology soon jettisoned evolutionist and diffusionist method and theory as indefensible. FIELDWORK became the preferred methodology as alternative explanations of culture hostile to history came to the fore. The first half of the twentieth century, and particularly the period after 1925, was remarkable for the antipathy shown by many influential anthropologists to history. Bronislaw MALINOWSKI, for example, the ethnographer and functionalist for whom CULTURE met human needs, was utterly indifferent to history. More influential and damning was A. R. RADCLIFFE-BROWN, who dominated social anthropological theory on several continents and put it bluntly in 1929 when he remarked that history "does not really explain anything at all" (1958: 40). He spoke for an entire generation of structural–functional social anthropologists, especially in Great Britain, that consigned historical process to ethnology, paid it little heed in their ethnographies, and proclaimed interest in the comparative study of institutions (see FUNCTIONALISM).

In America, Franz BOAS was opposed to history as practiced and written by the evolutionists and diffusionists. Boas had declared his opposition to the comparative method of the evolutionists in the mid-1890s; his influence in the swing away from evolutionist explanations was fundamental. Given his insistence that a historical account of a society's origins is not needed to understand behavior in that society, and given the opinion of major players like Boas's student A. L. KROEBER (1935: 558), who considered American cultural anthropology "anti-historical in tendency," it may come as a surprise to discover that Boas called his method "historical," that diffusion figured in that method, and that historians of anthropology regard this era in the United States as dominated by an "American historical school" (Eggan 1968: 130) or "American Historical Tradition" (Honigmann 1976: 192–231).

To explain these apparent contradictions we must understand that when Boas and others dismissed the history of the evolutionists or extreme diffusionists as conjectural and resulting from faulty methodology, they did not rule out diffusion or history as important at the level of a society. Through "historical method," Boas hoped to understand a specific society's particular history – without actually "doing" history as a historian might. Nevertheless, he thought of himself as a cultural historian. Antagonistic to independent invention as explanation of similar cultural traits, Boas thought that diffusion explained why similar cultural traits were found in different societies. But increasingly, "history" in Boas's method consisted mostly in insisting on full presentation of a society's local cultural-historical context. Without documentation and heavily dependent on inference, there was no way to determine precise historical sequences of events using this historical method. Boas's influence on his students varied greatly – hence the difficulty of using "school" for them – but their and the following

generation's widespread interest in local culture, the individual – and history – represents Boasian heritage. Their historical interests are shown especially in acculturation and ethnohistory.

During the period before diffusionism fell into total disrepute in anthropology, and when historical particularism captured the mainstream in American anthropology, most mainstream historians worked in their narrative tradition, were hostile to social scientific theory, and lacked interest in the history of indigenous people among whom anthropologists, to the exclusion of most other scholars, worked. In short, there was no significant contact between the two disciplines (Krech 1991).

Acculturation, social change, and ethnohistory as history, 1935–80

In the United States and Britain, the aversion to history among influential anthropological theorists peaked in the two decades from 1930 to 1950. There were exceptions on both sides of the Atlantic, notably E. E. EVANS-PRITCHARD and A. L. Kroeber. Few in-depth historical works came from Evans-Pritchard and Kroeber, but they did from others interested in three areas in which an anthropological concern for history was manifest: ACCULTURATION and ETHNOHISTORY in the United States, and SOCIAL CHANGE in Great Britain. In Britain, a relatively small number of social anthropologists interested in social change and history let time seep in; their work was not insignificant, but the analysis of society in British social anthropology, influenced strongly by Radcliffe-Brown's introduction of French sociology and STRUCTURALISM, remained overwhelmingly synchronic. The United States presented a different picture. For several decades, beginning in 1935, a significant number of American cultural anthropologists of the two generations following Boas wrote at length about acculturation and other processes of cultural change. Ethnohistory – a term initially used shortly after the turn of the century – first really came into its own in the 1940s and 1950s. It was distinguished by its insistence that the documentary record must provide an empirical base for chronology and analysis. Both acculturationists and ethnohistorians – the lines between the two often blurred – concretized Boas's interest in history in specific historical studies.

As for history's disciplinary mainstream, it largely neglected anthropology (as anthropology's structural–functional mainstream did history). But there were overlapping interests, especially in France, where Marc Bloch, Lucien Febvre, and other historians of the *Annales* school undertook comparative analysis that brought them far closer to then-current anthropological concerns than to many of their colleagues, for whom the description of political events or biography, framed by linear narrative, continued as the most important objectives of historical research (Krech 1991).

Anthropological history, 1980–95

Since 1980, conversation between the disciplines of history and anthropology has been intense, with ethnohistory's insistence on analysis grounded in documentary analysis providing the most direct methodological link with earlier historical interests in anthropology. Over three decades ago, Evans-Pritchard remarked that he would accept F. W. Maitland's dictum that "anthropology must choose between being history and being nothing" if he could add that "history must [also] choose between being social anthropology and being nothing" (1962: 190). Often prescient, Evans-Pritchard forecast one of the major trends in late-twentieth-century scholarship: the convergence of history and anthropology. The pace of dialogue between the disciplines has picked up notably in recent years, during which time sea changes in historiography have affected both disciplines. In anthropology, analyses incorporating history increase greatly in number each year. In history, various "new" histories have undermined the historicist political and biographical narratives dominating historiography. Today, anthropologists regularly use traditional historical materials and methods to make sense of the problems that interest them, and historians habitually employ traditional anthropological methodologies like ethnographic and informant work to make sense of theirs. The changes have been more pervasive in anthropology than history, although they have affected both disciplines, whose shared

pose today is predominantly humanistic, relativist, and contextual (Krech 1991).

SK

further reading G. Barraclough 1991; Butterfield 1973; Hallowell 1960b; Harris 1968; Hatch 1973; Herskovits 1965; Krieger 1989; Kuklick 1991; A. Kuper 1983; Lowie 1937; Stocking 1968; Stone 1977a; Trigger 1989; Voget 1975

holism   *See* FUNCTIONALISM

homicide   is the killing of a human being. As clear as this sounds, the definitional boundaries are tricky. The "cause" of a death is not necessarily singular, and accidental deaths vary in the extent to which someone can be deemed responsible, either causally or morally. Moreover, causes of death are open to rebuttable interpretation; consider accusations of homicide by SORCERY.

In practice, definitional criteria of homicide usually include hostile intent, or at least reckless disregard for probable harm to others. Hostile intent is a broader notion than lethal intent: the distinction between "murder" and "manslaughter" in Anglo-American law is largely, though not entirely, one of specific intent to kill, and this issue defines "degrees" of homicide in other legal codes, too. Several anthropologists have suggested that intent is ignored in "primitive" legal systems, but this claim has been thoroughly refuted (S. Moore 1978). Thus, homicides are deaths caused by interpersonal assaults or other acts directed against another person. (Collectively legitimized actions such as warfare and legal executions are excepted, however, and practice varies regarding whether killings by police officers in the line of duty are counted as homicides.) The scientific study of homicide has primarily been conducted by criminologists, but anthropologists, psychologists, psychiatrists, and epidemiologists have also done homicide research. Unfortunately, there has been little effort to synthesize insights from these diverse academic disciplines.

Homicide rates vary greatly between places and times. Governments derive statistics on criminal homicides from police and court records, and on causes of death including homicide from the records of coroners and medical examiners. The *United Nations Demographic Yearbook* reports cause-of-death data for some 80 nations. In 1985, countries with the highest per capita homicide rates included Guatemala, Venezuela, Brazil, and the United States, while England and Wales, Iceland, Greece, and Japan report some of the lowest rates (United Nations 1987). Within the United States, homicide rates vary greatly between states and cities. Some of the variation in aggregate homicide rates has been "explained," in the statistical sense, in terms of factors like city size, poverty, and income inequality (D. Archer & Gartner 1984).

The perpetration of homicides (other than INFANTICIDE) is universally male dominated. Males also outnumber females as victims, although not quite so universally. Cases involving unrelated men as victim and killer constitute the majority of homicides where rates are high, but where rates are lower it is mainly such cases that drop out, and where rates are lowest women may actually outnumber men as victims.

Homicide rates in nonstate societies without central authorities often greatly exceed even the highest rates in US cities (Knauft 1985), although the boundary between WAR and the private use of lethal VIOLENCE is often less clear in these cases. Variation in homicide rates between nonstate societies does not appear to be attributable to the same social and economic factors that account for variability between and within modern nation-states (Rosenfeld & Messner 1991).

Homicidal retaliation, especially in response to a prior homicide, is cross-culturally ubiquitous, and institutionalized FEUDING grades insensibly into chronic interlineage enmity and warfare (Daly & Wilson 1988b). Such blood-revenge feuds are apparently most common where strong legitimate central authority is lacking; and the mediation of such grievances through the specification of homicide compensation has been a major preoccupation of aspirant rulers and of early legal codes in all parts of the world. Cultural residua of feuding have been invoked to explain regional differences in homicidal violence within the

United States: Nisbett et al. (1995) convincingly linked high homicide rates in the southern states to a "culture of HONOR" that legitimates violent responses to insults, and traced this culture of honor to a pastoral tradition that differed from the settled crop agriculturalists' ethos that came to dominate northern conceptions of social propriety.

Distinguishing among victim–killer relationship categories is an essential (though often neglected) step toward explaining homicides and their variable incidence. The very existence of such words as "fratricide," "patricide," "regicide," "matricide," "filicide," and "uxoricide" suggests that these are psychologically meaningful categories of cases with different motives. Thus, factors affecting one sort of homicide risk differ from those affecting another, and may even have opposite effects. Increasing age is associated with diminishing risk that a woman will be killed by either her husband or a sexual assailant, for example, but with increasing risk that she will be killed by a robber (Margo Wilson et al. 1997). And although gross homicide rates vary greatly, consistency may be discerned at the level of relationship-specific risk patterns. Such factors as maternal youth and lack of male support are widely relevant to the risk of maternally perpetrated infanticide, for example. Daly & Wilson (1988a) developed a theory of interpersonal violence that takes into account the distinct sources of conflict characteristic of particular social relationships, and thus accounts for considerable variation in the relative rates and distinct demographic patterns of homicides in different victim–killer relationship categories.   MD & MWi

further   reading   Bohannan   1960; Chagnon 1988; Trillin 1984

homosexuality Homosexual behavior probably occurs everywhere, but defining persons by their sexual behavior or preference is not a universal domain of meaning for all peoples, and the modern northern European and American notion that everyone who engages in homosexual behavior is "a homosexual," a distinct "species" with unique features, is not universally credited.

R. Burton (1885–6) distinguished homosexual relations in which the older partner penetrates the younger one from relations in which a masculine partner penetrates a feminine person of the same sex. Both these age-stratified and gender-stratified homosexualities occur in diverse cultural areas with no obvious connection either to the size or the complexity of the societies in which they occur. An egalitarian/"gay" organization of homosexual relations has become increasingly prominent in industrialized, urban societies (D. Wolf 1979; Murray 1996).

All three of these are ideal types. Instances of each may occur simultaneously in a single locale. The typology seems to encompass the observed variance in societal schema of same-sex sexual relations for women as well as for men. There do not seem to be hundreds or even dozens of different organizing principles of homosexual relations in human societies. Moreover, one of these types tends to figure most prominently in "the dominant discourse" (and to predominate in explanation to aliens who ask about same-sex relations). For instance, age-graded homosexuality was the normative form in ancient Athenian discourse and was lexicalized with a term, "*kinaidos*," while gender-defined and comradely homosexuality were not. Similarly, the two-spirit/BERDACHE role among many indigenous North American peoples was lexicalized, while sexual relations between two warriors were not (Winkler 1990; Roscoe 1987).

In societies in which homosexuality is age defined, the norm is for men to "graduate" to insertor roles, ceasing altogether to play receptor, although not everyone in societies with age-defined structures of homosexuality "graduates" from the homosexual "phase." For example, in some sub-Saharan African societies an elite maintained "boy wives" who did women's work and provided sexual outlets to their "husbands." Later the boys, accustomed to exclusively receptive homosexuality, graduated to "husband" roles when they were older, and themselves took "boy wives" from a new generation (Evans-Pritchard 1970). In some Melanesian cultures, growing up male and a warrior requires several years of exclusively receptive homosexuality with physically mature males. The "ritualized" insemination is masculinizing for both participants; indeed it is a central part of a cult of masculinity (Herdt 1984; Herdt & Stoller 1990). In many contemporary Muslim societies, as in ancient Greece, adolescent "submission" to sex with one's elders does not necessarily foster lifelong effeminacy nor prevent later heterosexual relations (Murray & Roscoe 1996).

In gender-defined organizations of homosexuality, the sexually receptive partner is expected to enact some aspects of the feminine gender role: to behave, sound, or dress in ways appropriate to women in that society. The prototypical gender-defined role is the *pasivo* role widespread in the Mediterranean and Latin American culture areas. The *activo* male in homosexual copulation is an unmarked male, not officially regarded as "homosexual" (Carrier 1995). However, males in female roles and occupations retain some male prerogatives. They are also recurrently said to do "women's work" better than women (Roscoe 1991). In Afro-Brazilian cults some passive males exercise spiritual powers and claim the attendant prestige (Fry 1985). Important powers also attached to transvestite shamans along both sides of the North Pacific, and even down into Indochina (Murray 1992). Those playing the role were held in awe – an admittedly ambivalent emotion.

Whether a profession-defined organization exists, as distinct from the gender-defined one, is an open question. Debate centers on whether there is self-selection by those seeking a niche for either homosexual desire or (biologically based) inability to enact the male role, or sexual socialization produces roles such as shamans, dancing boys, transvestite singers, and prostitutes.

In recent times a "gay" organization of homosexuality has become prominent in cities worldwide. What is particular about this mode is a group consciousness of itself as distinct, with a separate subculture based on egalitarian sexual roles that accepts the possibility of exclusive (not bisexual) same-sex relations (Adam 1987).

For most cultures, data on homosexual behavior and societal reaction to it are so rare, recent, and incomplete that little can be said about changes. In Europe, Japan, and possibly China as well, a transformation from age to gender occurred during the late seventeenth century (Leupp 1996; Xiaomingxiong 1984 cited in Murray 1992: 141). During the 1960s and 1970s gender distinctions or "variance" moved from being normative to being stigmatized in urban North America (Murray 1996), and the "gay" model is increasingly prevalent in cities around the world (Allyn 1991).

The "native views" about gender-crossing and pederasty recorded by explorers, missionaries, travelers, and allegedly "objective" anthropologists similarly tend to be elite prescriptions that may have little do with statistical behavioral regularities, let alone the range of intracultural variation. Even what is the dominant normative/societal view of homosexuality is not mentioned in most ethnographies (e.g., for 114 of the 190 cultures surveyed by C. Ford and F. Beach [1951]). Where something about homosexuality has been noted, it usually concerns norms or descriptions of roles rather than how homosexuality is experienced by those involved in it. What Simon and Gagnon (1986) called "cultural scripts" for generating sexual meaning are adapted interactionally and intrapsychically in any and all cultures. Normative models may channel perception of others and conception of self, but they do not determine them and may not even be shared. What people do sexually, in contrast to what they say they do, is little known and not easily researched (R. Bolton 1992; Herdt & Stoller 1990).

SM

further reading D. Greenberg 1988; Herdt 1992; Kennedy & Davis 1993; R. Levy 1973; W. Williams 1986

honor is a form of respect accorded to people in recognition of their excellence or worth as persons. While an interest in honor is widespread among human societies, the cultural standards or frameworks that define it, and the degree of emphasis placed upon it, vary widely.

A large body of research has been done on the topic, especially among the peoples of the Mediterranean region. For example, among the Sarakatsan shepherd communities in the mountains of Greece, interpersonal relations are highly competitive, and conceptions of honor play a central role because an individual's honor is constantly threatened by insults or other forms of hostility (John Campbell 1964). For men the key to honor is manliness: the ability to protect the family's honor when it is threatened. For women, by contrast, the primary quality of honor is a sense of shame, especially sexual shame. A woman should find sexual activity loathsome and dress and deport herself to avoid the display of the physical attributes of her sex. She should be modest even in relations with her husband, remaining passive, for example, when having sexual relations with him. The honor of Sarakatsan men and women is closely linked: men's manliness protects the sexual honor of the women, while women's avoidance of shame protects the reputation of the men. Failure on either side puts the other at risk.

On a larger scale this pattern is seen among all the Bedouin tribes of the Near East and North Africa, who have an honor code that stresses principles of courage, generosity, honesty, and self-control, including control over the sexual appetites. In a study of a small group of recently sedentarized Bedouins in Egypt, Lila Abu-Lughod (1986) found that they stressed their blood relationship to the pastoral tribes of the desert, whom they regarded as more noble and as having a higher moral nature – and thus as being more honorable – than their peasant and urban neighbors. The Arab social historian Ibn Khaldun (1332–1408) noted a similar pattern in his own time; he argued that the Bedouin were not innately better people, but that desert life offered fewer opportunities for corruption and that codes of honor degenerated after a few generations of urban life (1967: 94).

Among the Trobriand Islanders, a Pacific island people, conceptions of honor take a radically different form (Malinowski 1922; A. Weiner 1976). Among Trobriand men, yam gardening is an important avenue for achievement: a respectable man is one who raises large quantities of healthy yams. Yet there is a twist here because a man raises yams not for his own household, but for other households, especially for his married sister. Meanwhile other people raise yams for him and his household. The yams are stored in each man's yam house, but this too is constructed by other people in his village. Thus an important mark of distinction for the Trobriand man is to have a very large yam house (built by someone else) filled with very healthy yams (grown by someone else) – these are visible marks of the respect in which he is held by others. While yams are not the only form of wealth among the Trobrianders, they serve as very prominent objects in the acquisition of wealth of all kinds, which is then used in GIFT EXCHANGES to create obligations. By giving away a basket of yams, say, the Trobriand man obligates the receiver to present a return gift in the future. The greater the number of people who are obligated to him in this way, the greater his honor. There are other important elements of the Trobriand system of honor, including the vigor of the lineage and the individual's success in KULA exchanges.

Max WEBER produced an important analysis of honor in COMPLEX SOCIETIES (Reinhard Bendix 1960: 85–7) as part of his distinction between class and status groups. He defined CLASS in terms of the unequal distribution of economic power and opportunity – different classes are distinguished on the basis of the comparative economic advantages they enjoy. By contrast, status groups are distinguished on the basis of differences in social honor or prestige: they consist of social strata whose members both have a consciousness of themselves and enjoy a similar status. Status groups are characterized by different styles of life, including distinctive clothing styles, manners, and so on, and the higher the status group the more exclusive its style of life. Thus life-style is a critical mark of honor. The correspondence between classes and status groups in a society may be close but is seldom perfect, as illustrated by the *nouveaux riches*, whose economic resources are often far greater than their social honor.   EH

further reading Hatch 1989, Peristiany 1966

horticulture is (1) a mode of subsistence AGRICULTURE that involves small-scale farming or GARDENING practiced with simple hand tools, such as the digging stick, and without the use of the plow or irrigation; (2) a strategy of economic development, such as growing vegetables for a market; and (3) the growing of plants and flowers for aesthetic purposes as a specialization or pastime.

Horticulture, in the first and main usage, was probably the earliest form of agriculture. It often employs shifting cultivation, including SWIDDEN (slash-and-burn) and other bush-fallow farming, techniques commonly found in the humid and semihumid tropics (Ruthenberg 1980). There horticulture remains ecologically sustainable if there is enough land to support long-term field rotations. Highly efficient per unit of output produced, it requires relatively little labor, capital, machinery, or chemicals.

Horticulturalists generally live in widely scattered communities at relatively low population densities, higher than FORAGERS but lower than more sedentary farmers (A. Johnson & Earle 1987; Boserup 1965). Horticulture is often mixed with other livelihood strategies, including gathering, hunting, fishing, animal rearing, and wage-labor migration.

The LAND-TENURE systems of horticulturalists are commonly misunderstood because they lay claim not only to land that is currently in use, but to much larger tracts that are in fallow. Claims to "abandoned" fields may atrophy only gradually. Such usufruct or conditional land rights have been increasingly threatened by the encroachments of ranchers, miners, road builders, and others who see it as unused. The resulting territorial confinement often leads to patterns of continuous cultivation or shortened fallows that permanently damage thin tropical soils through water erosion and hardpan (Meggers 1995). Anthropologists and others in HUMAN RIGHTS advocacy groups have sought to defend many horticultural peoples against such threats to their livelihoods and cultures.   PS

house forms   *See* ARCHITECTURE

households are economic units based on common residence. Membership comprises a family or domestic group that may also include hired laborers and domestic servants. While used descriptively in most ETHNOGRAPHY, the term is used analytically in the study of PEASANT or smallholder production.

"Household" derives from the English version of feudalism, where each "holding" (of land) was identified with a house and its inhabitants, which was geographically fixed and had some social permanence. It was a legal unit of ownership and political representation responsible for payment of goods and services as tax and tribute to a feudal lord. Based on a monogamous MARRIAGE SYSTEM, the head of the household was the formal representative of the unit to higher levels in the social hierarchy as well as its manager for day-to-day life.

Although most societies have domestic groups of some kind, only some have this particular institution, and the English term "household" translates poorly, even into French. This is because although all human populations have dwellings, many groups who share a roof do not evoke the qualities associated with "household." Societies with compounds that include too many people, PASTORAL NOMADS or HUNTER–GATHERERS may inhabit temporary structures or change their membership too rapidly. More critically, in many societies landholding units are not key politicojural organizations, and headship may be more religious or ritual than managerial with respect to work and consumption. This is particularly true among those polygynous societies where each wife has her own economic means and supports her own children. Ethnographers therefore often use the term loosely, if at all, and refer to coresident units by the people's own term for them.

Anthropologists have therefore struggled with the universal applicability of the household concept (Guyer 1981). The reasons to retain the term rather than throw it out as unworkably ethnocentric are twofold. First, it applies well to societies when it corresponds to units recognized by the people themselves, and in those cases it is useful for comparative purposes. Second, economists have developed formal economic models for the household that anthropologists are keen to test cross-culturally.

Netting (1993), for example, argued forcefully in a comprehensive survey and analysis that smallholder farmers living at high population densities and using intensive methods of permanent land use are universally organized into units that we would recognize as households, regardless of the larger social and political structure. The core of the unit is a family of two or three generations. Marriage may be polygynous, but with very small numbers of co-wives. Land, the most important means of production, is owned by this unit, whose members preserve and develop its value with an eye to passing it on to the next generation. Members act as a single unit of production and consumption, coordinating their work across a complex spectrum of techniques and tasks. These include annual cropping of land, preserving land quality through manuring, IRRIGATION, terracing, and fencing. Although such a definition would not include all peoples defined as peasants, it does include the rural peoples of much of China, Japan, Indonesia, India, historical Western Europe, parts of Central America, and pockets in Africa and the Philippines. Since this group comprises a large proportion of the human population, "household" is a useful concept even if it applies only to these cases.

Economists, interested in decisions about consumption and labor-market participation of household members, started developing models of the household in the 1960s based primarily on examples in the West (Becker 1981). Many were concerned entirely with how distributive divisions within households for labor and for goods and services might affect their overall patterns of economic demand and supply in the marketplace. In the interests of quantitative modeling Becker went so far as to assume that the household was like a small factory with capital goods, raw material, and labor, and of course a manager. At about the same time, the seminal work carried out in the 1920s and 1930s by Russian economist A. V. Chayanov (1966) was belatedly translated into English and attracted the attention of anthropologists because he focused on peasant producers and not the consumers of industrial society. Chayanov argued that peasant households did not value their resources by market prices, but by standards dictated by their level of living. In particular, the value of labor could not be calculated as a wage because the amount of work carried out relative to returns depended on how many other, nonworking household members the worker had to support. The ratio of workers to dependents changed over the developmental cycle of the group. The resilience of peasants was the result of their capacity to continually shift the value of their labor in response to conditions, working much harder and tolerating low returns for a day's work when more mouths had to be fed and then easing up when needs were more easily covered. Unlike industrial production units, peasant households aim to stay in "business" however bad the circumstances because they are based on families. In brief, according to Chayanov, a household's qualities as a production unit do follow a rationality that can be modeled, but it is not a factory (see CHAYANOV SLOPE).

It is worth pointing out that both theorists assumed or prescribed a larger structure of which such households were a part, neither of which was feudal. Becker was analyzing modern industrial CAPITALISM, and Chayanov was prescribing a mode of linking rural industries to peasant cooperatives in a SOCIALIST structure. Netting also made the point that the household need not be restricted to feudalism or indeed any particular polity. Household analysis can be applied in differently structured societies, but scholars still assume that the households they study are small parts of larger, COMPLEX SOCIETIES, usually with a hierarchical economic order.

Agricultural economists have applied the theories of both Becker and Chayanov in a variety of non-Western societies, testing them through quantitative analyses of survey data. Anthropologists have found these studies interesting but limited by their assumption that households are bounded units that deal with the external world primarily through the MARKET, and the as-

sumption that the household has a single utility function. The presupposition of all household decision theory is that there is a decision maker, the household head, who represents the values and allocatory preferences of all the members. However in most societies anthropologists find that households are not autonomous purchasers and owners with respect to their resource access, but are embedded in local communities with external institutions for production and distribution. These commonly include labor sharing, GIFT EXCHANGE, a share of the harvest and often expensive ritual obligations to pay for community functions like festivals. Anthropologists, therefore, never felt that the community level of analysis could be short-circuited. Economist Udry (1990) has begun to illustrate how this level might be represented within decision theory in ways that are convincing to economists as well as anthropologists.

The existence of internal differentiation within households has been argued strongly by feminists. They suggest that the outcome of household decisions results from the struggle between men and women to define the terms of economic involvement based on their different positions of power and roles in the labor process (D. Dwyer & Bruce 1988). Using a bargaining (or collective) model, they highlight the intrahousehold processes, as distinct from the unitary household model of Becker and Chayanov. Such models allow GENDER to be incorporated and permit an analysis of "endowments," the different assets and capacities that underlie a person's economic activity and social power within the household.

All these theoretical positions have proponents who are engaged in active debate. Anthropologists lean toward institutional and gender analyses on the one hand and the historical study of AGRICULTURE on the other, while their use of formal decision-making household models is limited.

JIG

humanistic anthropology has gained ground as a label in American anthropological parlance since at least the mid-1970s, when the Society for Humanistic Anthropology was founded. It would be a mistake to assume, however, that it refers to a unified vision of anthropology, for nowhere in the writings of self-proclaimed humanistic anthropologists is the large-scale schema laid out below reproduced in full. Different scholars identify with different aspects of the "schema" and it is important to bear in mind that anthropologists who do not call themselves humanists may still identify with one or more of its aspects. Whatever their differences, the heterogeneous strains of what is now called "humanistic anthropology" has been deeply influenced by the work of previous generations of American anthropologists, such as (but hardly limited to) Edward SAPIR and Ruth BENEDICT.

Partly as a result of the deep influence that the Italian idealist philosopher Benedetto Croce's *Aesthetics* (1909) had on his thinking, Edward Sapir (1917, 1934) stressed the importance of studying the creativity of individual human beings in responding to cultural and historical forces. This foregrounding of the creative individual was later echoed by a leading voice of humanistic anthropology who proclaimed in the first issue of the *Anthropology and Humanism Quarterly* that,

The central focus, as we see it, of humanistic anthropology is the individual human being ... [and] the individual's striving for freedom and creativity within the confines and opportunities of nature, culture, and society. (Fratto 1976)

Under a different rubric, the study of the individual (personality) in culture by means of the LIFE HISTORY method was pioneered by a series of famous book-length autobiographies of native Americans by Boasians such as Radin (1920), Neihardt (1932), and Simmons (1942), as well as shorter collected works (E. Parsons 1922). More recently this tradition of life history has been further developed in PSYCHOLOGICAL ANTHROPOLOGY by Crapanzano's (1977, 1980) work in Morocco and Mandelbaum's (1973) analysis of Gandhi. It has also been enriched through the notion of the autobiographical individual by Langness and Frank (1981)

and through the study of language and the individual (Friedrich 1979).

Though Edward Sapir was crucial in establishing American LINGUISTICS on a modern, scientific footing, he came to lament the compartmentalization and specialization among the various disciplines that had grown up around the scientific study of humankind (E. Sapir 1929a). Sapir's emphasis on a more "inclusive" or interdisciplinary view of CULTURE was shared by Ruth Benedict (1948: 585, 591) who proclaimed that,

To my mind the very nature of the problems posed and discussed in the humanities is closer, chapter by chapter, to those in anthropology than are the investigations carried on in most of the social sciences ... Long before I knew anything about anthropology, I had learned from Shakespearean criticism ... habits of mind which at length made me an anthropologist.

This point was remarkably prescient of the influence that humanistic scholarship, and especially literary criticism, would have on the development of theoretical anthropology in the 1970s, as exemplified most clearly perhaps in the work of Clifford GEERTZ (1973), who acknowledged his own debt to the literary critic Kenneth Burke (1966)

If Boasian anthropologists like Benedict were most famously known as "relativists," they nonetheless adhered to some vaguely conceived notion of "pan-human" traits or "basic humanity," often derived from nineteenth-century humanistic thought. Although Benedict argued that different societies possessed distinct patterns of values or "cultures," she nevertheless insisted that they "select" these values from the same arch of universal "human" experience (1934a).

Although it is important to realize that American anthropology's concern with humanism has a history, there are also discontinuities, and even conflicts, between the articulation of the issues by previous generations and today's humanists, resulting from profound changes in theories of knowledge and representation that have emerged since the 1960s. Various critiques of science have been launched (see Kuhn 1962; Feyerabend 1975; Sandra Harding 1991) that have undermined scientific certainties in an all-encompassing (or context-free) truth. The idea that scientific practice is embedded in social context (M. Polanyi 1969; Latour 1979, 1987) renders the perspective of the scientific observer necessarily partial and incomplete (Haraway 1988).

Anthropologists generally are more critical of the way an older generation, including the humanistically inclined ones, might have "objectified" the lives and experiences of the peoples they studied in the name of science (R. Rosaldo 1989). In reaction to their perceived excesses, some humanists eschew the quest for certainty and large-scale generalization altogether, becoming radical critics of science. An earlier generation would have hoped for the humanistic tradition to remain complementary rather than antagonistic to the scientific one. In place of the search for large-scale certainties, today's humanists might substitute an evocation of "lived experience" and "real persons" through narrative ethnography (Stoller 1989), in which, it is claimed, "others" can be heard to speak or have a voice through collaboration between anthropologists and their subjects in the construction of an ETHNOGRAPHY.

The emphasis on narrative ethnography was made possible in part by the realization that anthropological monographs are a literary creation or *fictio*, as C. Geertz observed (1973) and Clifford (1988) expounded further. This followed on from the important analysis of historical texts as rhetorical and poetic in form by H. White (1973), who in turn was deeply influenced by literary critic Kenneth Burke (1941). Thus, whereas Benedict and her colleagues, such as Margaret MEAD, employed poetic imagery as a literary device through which to communicate scientific knowledge more vividly, their practice might have stopped short of the proposition that the representation of anthropological knowledge takes the form of a NARRATIVE or poetic/rhetorical genre *tout court*. The status of the anthropological text is even more complicated these days by what C. Geertz (1983: 19–35) called the deliberate "blurring" of genres. A particularly innovative experiment in genre blurring took place in the 1970s, when

anthropologist Victor TURNER collaborated with theater director Richard Schechter to *perform* ethnographies on stage (Turner 1982; Turner & Bruner 1986). Consonant with this blurring of genres is the increasingly popular experiment in ethnography-cum-memoir such as Stoller and Olkes's (1987) apprenticeship with sorcerers or Ghosh's (1992) investigation of linked lives in medieval Egypt. Its relevance to anthropology should go beyond making anthropological writing more compelling, however, for when "reflexive" anthropologists such as Myerhoff (1978), Scholte (1978), and Rabinow (1977) bring the personal into the account of their fieldwork, they have an epistemological aim of showing *how* what is known about another culture is deeply influenced by the circumstances *in* which it is known, including of course the subject-position of the investigator (Favret-Saada 1980).

Humanistic anthropologists are themselves now subject to the most radical critiques coming out of the humanities today. For example, the notion that there are "transcendent humanistic" values, central to the articulation of any version of humanistic anthropology, comes under severe criticism from feminists, Foucauldians, and others. And an appeal to "radical empiricism" (M. Jackson 1989; Stoller 1989) comes close to being a "metaphysics of presence" that would be questioned by deconstructionists (Derrida 1976; Joan Scott 1993). SC

See also CRITICAL ANTHROPOLOGY, CUL-
    TURE AND PERSONALITY, LITERARY
    ANTHROPOLOGY

further reading C. Geertz 1988; E. Sapir 1949

Human Relations Area Files *See* CROSS-CULTURAL STUDIES

human rights   are those that any person naturally deserves, merely by virtue of being human, in order to survive, enjoy well-being, and gain fulfillment. Moreover, not only does every human being have a right or claim to these essential rights, they are simply right in the sense of morality and justice. Although there are many different kinds of rights, human rights are the most fundamental, universal, and inalienable, and governments are expected to advance and defend them (Donnelly 1989).

Ideas about universal rights for all people developed during the Enlightenment in Europe, were codified in international conventions following worldwide concern over Nazi GENOCIDE and other horrors of World War II, and have increasingly become a central concern in modern political theory and legal practice. There are substantial international conventions on human rights, such as the International Bill of Human Rights of the United Nations, which includes the Universal Declaration of Human Rights, the International Covenant of Political and Civil Rights, and the International Covenant of Economic, Social, and Cultural Rights. In general, these conventions encompass the following: the right to life and freedom from physical and psychological abuse including torture; freedom from arbitrary arrest and imprisonment, and accordingly, the right to a fair trial; freedom from slavery and genocide; the right to nationality; freedom of movement, including leaving and returning to one's own country, as well as the right to asylum in other countries from persecution in one's homeland; rights to privacy and the ownership of property; freedom of speech, religion, and assembly; the rights of peoples to self-determination, culture, religion, and language; and the right to adequate shelter, health care, and education (Edward Lawson 1991).

Anthropologists have usually remained on the periphery of human rights for several reasons: anthropology developed with COLONIALISM and the latter depended on the violation of human rights; human rights have been largely a governmental and legal matter; scientists are supposedly neutral to maintain objectivity; and since human rights are politically sensitive, involvement may endanger the personal safety of the anthropologist, informants, or host community as well as jeopardize future research in a foreign country. Nevertheless, since the time of Franz BOAS anthropologists have occasionally become involved in human rights, as in providing expert testimony in court cases on ancestral land and resource rights for indigenous societies. In recent decades the profession has given much more attention to human rights, as evidenced mainly by the growing literature on the subject (Downing & Kushner 1988; Messer 1993) and the emergence of advocacy anthropology (R. Wright 1988; Paine 1985) and corresponding organizations like Cultural Survival, International Work Group for Indigenous Affairs, and Survival International. Professional organizations such as the American Anthropological Association, Society for Applied Anthropology, and European Association of Social Anthropologists have all also established committees on human rights.

Anthropology has conceptual and practical relevance to human rights. Human rights are predicated on a theory of human nature, and anthropologists can contribute to this through their cross-species and cross-cultural comparisons (D. Brown 1991). Yet one of the greatest challenges to universal human rights is the concept of CULTURAL RELATIVISM, which Franz Boas and other anthropologists originated (Herskovits 1972) and others have criticized (Edgerton 1992; Hatch 1983). Some countries accused of violations of human rights have tried to hide behind cultural relativism and criticized their accusers of being Western moral imperialists. Every culture has its own ideas about morality, but these are usually not readily extended beyond its boundaries to other groups, let alone formulated as universals encompassing all of humankind. Anthropologists can help explore, understand, and mediate the cultural diversity of ideas about human rights (An-Naim 1992; K. Dwyer 1991), and they can attempt to reconcile the fundamental issues of universality vs. relativity (Renteln 1990).

At a practical level it must be acknowledged that violators of human rights often target individuals and groups based, at least in part, on their apparent biological, social, cultural, or linguistic differences. Anthropology can address this situation as the humanistic science that documents, interprets, and celebrates the biological and cultural unity and diversity of humankind. Moreover, during their FIELDWORK anthropologists often have a special opportunity to monitor and document human rights, although they must do so discretely because of potential dangers.

Traditionally, anthropology has concentrated on indigenous peoples and ethnic minorities. Frequently these societies are subjected to human rights abuses, and even ETHNOCIDE and genocide. They are usually the least powerful and vocal group within a country. Moreover, in the future their human rights may be abused increasingly since many are in the last FRONTIERS of the world, which are prime areas for land and resource exploitation because of growing levels of population and economic consumption (M. Miller 1993).   LS

See also ETHNIC GROUPS, ETHNOCEN-
TRISM, LAND TENURE, LEGAL ANTHRO-
POLOGY, NATIONALISM, PEACE, RACISM,
SOCIAL ORGANIZATION

further reading Afshari 1994; Amnesty International 1992; Bodley 1982; Mayer 1995; Milne 1986; Tibi 1994; W. Washburn 1987

hunger is the consumption of a DIET inadequate to sustain good health and normal activity, growth, and development. Subjectively, hunger encompasses both the desire and need for food as well as the discomfort, irritability, weakness, or lethargy caused by inadequate intakes. Objectively, hunger is measured in terms of the calories and nutrients necessary to sustain life and good health. Sociocultural anthropologists have analyzed hunger through the ecology and politics of FOOD SYSTEMS, including the functional consequences of malnutrition, such as impaired health. Biological anthropologists have examined human growth patterns, weight changes, and energy deficits connected to dietary and health practices. Since the mid-1970s the concerns of both subdisciplines have been combined in nutritional anthropology, which examines the biological consequences of particular foodways, and the cultural consequences of deficient or overly abundant intakes (Jerome et al. 1980; Messer 1984).

Hunger is caused by three distinct but interrelated phenomena: food shortage, food poverty, and food deprivation. There is currently no global food shortage because, since the early nineteenth century at least, the world food system has had technology sufficient to produce and distribute enough to feed all human inhabitants. Yet despite this overall capacity, an estimated three-quarters of a billion people still lack access to adequate nutrition at the end of the twentieth century because of unequal distribution or poor use of existing resources.

Food shortage

Food shortage, and in its extreme form, famine, can be caused by difficult climatic, political, or other socioeconomic conditions that affect a whole region or country. Food shortage is often linked simplistically to food production failures caused by such NATURAL DISASTERS as drought, cyclones, or crop plagues, but inadequate storage, heavy taxation, or export demands, as well as other market and political factors, can also reduce food supplies within a region. For example, famines often follow armed conflicts that reduce production, destroy supplies, and disrupt alternative lines of food relief. Most famines attributed to natural causes in Asia and Africa (as well as in nineteenth-century Ireland) are really entitlement failures, because food exists but the victims of starvation cannot afford it and lack the political power to secure disaster relief.

There is a regular sequence of responses to food shortages, whether they are seasonal or more prolonged and severe:

1. reducing intakes through rationing, eating fewer times per day, and consuming more roughage and less-palatable "emergency" foods
2. selling assets and diversifying sources of income, including migrant labor and servitude, which reduce the numbers of consumers
3. leaving an area to search for food elsewhere (Colson 1979)

Modern mechanisms to prevent or mitigate suffering from extreme supply failures include famine early-warning systems, food-for-work relief, and other global or national policies that tie relief to development activities (Torry 1988). Many of these processes have been analyzed by anthropologists "studying up" that is, studying the donors as well as the recipients of aid. For example, in response to the Ethiopian food crisis of 1983–5, ethnographers offered insights on how relief efforts might be more effective and interfere less with local coping mechanisms (de Waal 1989, 1990). Other studies were highly critical of relief and documented how food, especially in Ethiopia, was used as a tool of political coercion (Clay & Holcomb 1986).

As a profession, anthropology has attempted to apply its knowledge to the broader community with a series of task forces established by the American Anthropological Association. For example, the Task Force on African Famine, Hunger, and Food Systems provided information on the ecological and political roots of hunger in Africa, the impacts of development or relief policies on Africa's food problems, seasonal hunger, and the larger political-economic context (Huss-Ashmore & Katz 1989–90; Hansen & McMillan 1986). Another dealt with the hunger impacts of involuntary migration in Africa and elsewhere (Hansen & Oliver-Smith 1982). Such institutional structures aided the efforts of anthropologists, economists, and geographers to predict conditions of famine vulnerability and suggest ways to build on local coping mechanisms (Bohle et al. 1993; Drèze & Sen 1989). A separate ethnobiological literature also addresses famine foods (N. Turner & Davis 1993; Garine & Harrison 1988).

Food poverty
Food poverty occurs when people go hungry because they lack the resources to acquire food even when the regional food supply is sufficient. At this level, therefore, it is a HOUSEHOLD rather than societal problem. Case studies of food poverty from Latin America, Asia, and Africa demonstrate how inequitable LAND TENURE and low wages have caused household food insecurity in areas where food production should be abundant. Government policies that promote cash crops (including livestock) in preference to subsistence crops often reduce household food security and nutrition (Shipton 1990). In Africa such policies threaten traditional symbiotic exchanges between agriculturalists and pastoralists. In Asia, GREEN REVOLUTION

agricultural technologies that increased overall food supply also marginalized the poor, who could not afford the costly new seeds and fertilizers. Some anthropologists have even argued that greater food poverty is the inevitable consequence of the expansion of CAPITALISM (Harris & Ross 1987b).

Food deprivation
Food deprivation occurs at the individual level when food is distributed unequally within households that otherwise have access to adequate resources. It is usually a product of power differences or cultural restrictions on consumption that prevent individuals from getting an adequate share of calories, protein, and essential vitamins and minerals. It also occurs when people are ill and unable to benefit from the nutrients potentially available.

Food deprivation is a particular problem for so-called vulnerable groups: infants and young children, pregnant and lactating women, and others who are deprived because they are powerless or ill. Determinants of adequate food intake over the life cycle include constraints on breastfeeding (van Esterik 1989), appropriate weaning foods or customs, cultural dietary beliefs and practices that prevent male or female children from accessing adequate nutrition, and women's voluntary or involuntary self-deprivation where resources may be adequate. One key controversy is over whether mothers or alternative care givers intentionally deprive children or themselves of adequate nutrients, or are simply following local cultural nutritional wisdom. Deprivation of girl children, and of women throughout their lifetimes, is a special concern in South Asia, where lower ratios of surviving females relative to males suggest intrahousehold deprivation is not tightly linked to poverty, although poor girls and women suffer the most from gender discrimination (Das Gupta 1995). Additional sources of deprivation may be a cultural body image of slimness or a value of abstemiousness, which may prove adaptive for the population at large under conditions of dearth but subject some individuals to hunger and harm.

Food deprivation is also caused by the inability of the body to benefit fully from the nutrients that are potentially available because of ILLNESS that destroys appetite, prevents absorption through diarrhea, or otherwise raises demand for nutrients to fight infection. Illness of an adult worker at a critical point in the agricultural cycle, such as weeding or harvest, can jeopardize the harvest and earnings, and the nutrition of the entire household well beyond the short-term interruption. If whole communities are affected, as projected in the AIDS epidemic in Africa, it can create food shortages and produce a potential long-term regional hunger threat. These examples illustrate the synergisms among hunger, illness, and productivity, and also the wisdom of the UNICEF definition of nutrition as adequate food, health, and care.

The three levels of hunger described above are interrelated and create a problem of unmet HUMAN RIGHTS for individuals in each. Food deprivation of women farmers can set the stage for chronic food poverty and periodic shortage. A natural or social disaster that leads to food shortage can create situations of resource poverty that set the stage for chronic food poverty and individual deprivation. Alternatively, where MARKETS and food relief now penetrate what had been relatively isolated food systems, people may be exchanging periodic food shortages for chronic food poverty (Messer 1989b).   EM

further reading Downs et al. 1991; G. Harrison 1988; Newman 1990

hunter–gatherers *See* FORAGERS

hunting is the process of capturing and killing nondomesticated animals for subsistence, clothing, and other uses. It is a complex of behaviors demanding a variety of skills, such as programming (learning a variety of techniques), scanning (interpretation of visual signs), stalking, immobilization, killing, and retrieval (W. Laughlin 1968). It requires a variety of weaponry and tools, including projectiles, stabbing weapons, butchery implements, snares, deadfalls, blinds, and other fixed facilities, as well as tools for making weapons. Archaeologists have made the elaborate material culture related to hunting, especially

lithic analysis, a particular focus of research.

Hunting occurs widely in mammals, and predator–prey relationships are a major topic in behavioral biology. With the exception of chimpanzees, it is rare in higher primates. Nevertheless, because hunting has been so greatly elaborated in prehistoric and modern humans, it is often considered one of the primary innovations that set ancestral hominids on the path to becoming human. Researchers disagree on whether the adoption of hunting alone was the prime mover in hominization or just one of several innovations including gathering, sharing, extended infant care, and the capacity for speech (S. Washburn & Lancaster 1968; Lovejoy 1981), an issue raised particularly by feminists (F. Dahlberg 1981). What is not in question is that hunting was a central component of subsistence in proto- and early modern humans.

Types of hunting

Several forms of hunting method can be distinguished:

(1) Scavenging is the collection of animal carcasses that, although not strictly hunting, is viewed by some analysts as an intermediate step toward the proto-hominid adoption of hunting proper.

(2) Mobile hunting involves tracking, stalking, and wounding individual prey, followed by capture and killing. It is probably the most common hunting method.

(3) Group mobile hunting attempts to drive game toward a central point, such as a series of nets, a box canyon or precipice, where they can be captured or killed in large numbers. Notable examples include the famous buffalo jumps of western North America.

(4) Fixed hunting employs stationary hunters using blinds or hides who wait for prey to come to a waterhole or fly overhead. It is often combined with group mobile hunting where game is driven toward hidden hunters.

(5) Snare or deadfall hunting uses set and baited traps, often set along a route or line, that are periodically checked for prey.

(6) FISHING is a form of hunting in which land-based techniques are adapted

to river, lake, or maritime settings. It is usually considered a separate category of subsistence, but spear fishing in particular requires similar skills to mobile land hunting.

(7) Sea-mammal hunting of seals, otters, and whales from boats closely resembles mobile land hunting in technique except that harpoons must provide tethers to haul game to the boat or shore. It has been a major subsistence source in northern maritime settings.

Hunting and society

For most of human history hunting (and gathering) was the universal mode of hominid and later human subsistence. If one can speak of human nature, however defined, it was forged in our common heritage as hunter–gatherers. For example, hunting is highly GENDER linked, with over 90 percent of all hunting done by males. However the association of hunting with WAR and male aggression is far more complex, and arguments linking the two should be viewed with caution.

Today hunting peoples live only in a few isolated areas, but as recently as 1500 C.E. one-third of the habitable globe was occupied by nonagricultural people. Among contemporary FORAGERS hunting varied in its contribution to the DIET, from a low of 20 percent among some tropical foragers to upwards of 80 percent in the high Arctic Inuit.

Hunting continues to be an important source of subsistence among postforaging societies (and this category includes all of humanity). In parts of rural United States and Canada such as Newfoundland (P. Smith 1990) and North Carolina (S. Marks 1991) hunting may still provide 25 percent of a household's food supply. In early modern Europe hunting emerged as a key social indicator: a prestigious pastime among the very rich, who organized the fox hunts and grouse shoots; a subsistence activity for the very poor who had to rely on "poaching" to survive. In nonaboriginal contemporary North America, hunting has become a marker of machismo and male solidarity among working-class men from both cities and rural areas.

Philosophers and writers ranging from Robert Ardrey (1976) to Konrad Lorenz (1966) have reflected on the deeper meaning of hunting in the process of hominization, on how the violence inherent in the act of killing may be linked to the human propensity for interpersonal aggression and warfare. However when hunting peoples – the Cree, Bushmen, or Australian Aborigines – are interrogated on this subject, they regard hunting not as an act of VIOLENCE but as a highly instrumental act requiring cool emotions and careful preparations. They convey an attitude of reverence, not hostility, to their prey. This has led others to ruminate on the role of the sacred in hunting and its links to the ritual of SACRIFICE (W. Smith 1889; C. Martin 1978), a theme addressed by José Ortega y Gasset in his *Meditations on hunting* (1972).

RiL

hydraulic systems and societies A hydraulic system is a culturally distinctive package of techniques, institutions, and social practices whereby a society organizes and utilizes its water resources. Because of the physical characteristics of water flow, hydraulic systems are both integrative (requiring cooperation and organization) and conflict generating. For that reason they have been of particular interest to anthropologists, who have recognized that irrigation generates distinctive hydraulic solidarities to articulate the common interest of irrigators.

Therefore a number of theorists have characterized as "hydraulic societies" civilizations whose institutions appear to have been sharply structured by the development and management of hydraulic systems. First Hegel (1975: 158–9) proposed that early centers of civilization, embodied in independent states, arose in broad river valleys where the gradual accumulation of silt had made the soils fertile:

The river plains are the most fertile lands; agriculture becomes established there, and with it, the rights of communal existence are introduced. The fertile soil automatically brings about the transition to agriculture, and this in turn gives rise to understanding and foresight.

Hegel did not specify irrigation nor was he aware of the institutional specificity of irrigation agriculture. Then Karl Marx identified water control as a key factor in the development of what he called "Asiatic society," the element that was responsible for its differentiation from ancient, feudal, or capitalistic society. For Marx, control of water in arid lands was a requirement for the control of the means of production. Hegel's conclusion that river-basin agriculture stimulates the creation of "rights of communal existence" seemingly contradicts Marx's statement that the scale of broad river valleys was too large to generate voluntary associations. According to Hegel, alluvial agriculture provided the primary stimulus to the growth of high civilizations and created the communal solidarities that water management requires. Finally Karl A. Wittfogel (1957) systematized and extended Marx's hypothesis by observing that many irrigation-based societies of antiquity had developed similar political responses to water management, among which are despotic rule, the creation of "agro-managerial bureaucracies" whose core function is control of water, monumental building programs (including but not limited to hydraulic works), the use of mass labor corvées, the development of astronomical techniques sufficient to predict seasonal variation in water flow and the mathematics that such calculations, along with bureaucratic applications, required, and the emergence of priestly castes to guard such natural knowledge. At its most general level, Wittfogel proposed that who controls water, controls power, and that control of water requires a high degree of centralized authority. In the evolutionary scheme of Julian STEWARD (1955: 193–6) eras of "Regional Development and Florescence" include irrigation for all societies considered, such as Peru (intervalley irrigation), Meso-America (local irrigation, *chinampas*), Mesopotamia (large-scale irrigation), China (local well-and-ditch irrigation).

Wittfogel's thesis yielded a number of hypotheses (water-related tasks must be solved by mass labor; the scale of hydraulic works is related to general social organization; political leadership is identified with control of irrigation; the water-control regime is expressed in the dominant religion, etc.) that were then tested by anthropologists, archeologists, and historians in the 1960s and 1970s (see Gray 1963: 7–8). The consensus of this research is that hydraulic societies as defined by Wittfogel have indeed existed, but only within a very narrow range of parameters, namely in arid climates where irrigation is necessary and where, in addition, there are large rivers where seasonal flooding is a problem. Therefore, the hypothesis works for civilizations of ancient Egypt and the Fertile Crescent of Mesopotamia, the Indus Valley, China of the Yellow River and, with some adjustment, Aztec Mexico and Inca Peru. In semiarid environments, however, the institutional response is highly varied. Research in Balinese water-temples by Lansing (1991) shows that the coordination requirements of irrigation can produce a system that is centered administratively, not centralized politically, one which is independent of the state and partly in conflict with it (Valeri 1991).

Most anthropological comment has been on hydraulic systems in which IRRIGATION is the core component. But urban hydraulic systems present complexities of a somewhat different order, although clearly related to issues of centralization and control. Because water delivery and sewage systems are unseen by their users, bureaucratic control is virtually complete. As urban hydraulic infrastructures have become increasingly conceptualized as information systems (for purposes of their management) there have emerged in the late twentieth century urban "hydromanagerial" bureaucracies with distinctive arcane techniques, which, in the more circumscribed orbit of modern cities, display many of the characteristics of Wittfogel's agromanagerial bureaucracies.   TG
See also ORIENTAL DESPOTISM, STATE

hypergamy is the practice of women being married "up" in social status. In systems of MARRIAGE EXCHANGE, the practice designates wife-givers as lower in status than wife-takers. This can be as specific as the giving of women in tribute to political superiors or as vague as the general sense that it is more acceptable for women than men to marry above their station.

MR

See also ALLIANCE SYSTEMS, HYPOGAMY

hypogamy is the practice of women being married "down" in social status. In systems of MARRIAGE EXCHANGE, the practice designates wife-givers as higher in status than wife-takers. The cultural logic here is that women are given in marriage as gifts to dependents rather than as tribute to superiors. This is more likely to be found in asymmetrical ALLIANCE SYSTEMS and less likely to be found in state societies than HYPERGAMY. However, hypogamous marriages in which the man advances in social status, such as "marrying the boss's daughter," are common enough to have generated their own stereotypes.

MR

I

illness refers to a person's perceptions and lived experience of sickness or being "dis-eased" – that is, in a socially devalued state including but not limited to, DISEASE. In MEDICAL ANTHROPOLOGY the distinction between "disease" and "illness" has central importance. "Disease" refers only to outward, "objective" clinical manifestations of abnormality of physical function or infection by a pathogen in an individual or host. Thus disease is considered a biological phenomenon, while illness includes psychological and social dimensions as well. Within a population, the distributions of disease and illness do not completely overlap: there are people with diagnosable diseases, such as hypertension, who do not know or think of themselves as ill; correspondingly, a significant percentage of patients visiting physicians are ill but do not have an identifiable disease. In biomedicine, the illness of a patient with symptoms but no diagnosable disease can be referred to as "psychosomatic," referring to a psychological etiology. Although this term is infrequently used today, the negative implication was that the illness was not "real" since the patient's "abnormal" mind caused the abnormalities of the body. Patients, therefore, could be blamed as the cause of their own symptoms. The traditional biomedical logic subsumed under the concept of psychosomatic illness (and the disease–illness distinction) has been a central target of analysis in critical medical anthropology.

The distinction between disease and illness begs the question what is "health" – a concept that is notoriously difficult to define. According to the charter of the World Health Organization, health is not simply the absence of disease but a state of physical, social, and psychological well-being.

The conceptualization of health and illness, therefore, depends upon cultural constructions of "normality." When people define themselves as ill, it is in contrast to culturally allowable levels of symptoms or complaints. When people are defined by others as ill, the implied reference to "normality" can result in medicine being a mechanism of social control.

Medical anthropologists have shown that there is considerable cultural variation in the types and severity of symptoms considered salient and important for different social groups. Because they are biocultural creatures, people must filter the biological feedback from their bodies through culturally constructed filters of ethnophysiological and ethnomedical beliefs. Illness also has important symbolic dimensions, which Sontag (1990) described as cultural metaphors; and certain illnesses (e.g., tuberculosis, cancer, AIDS) can have powerful social meanings in particular social contexts. Although the symbolic dimensions of illness most often have negative valuations and result in social stigma and OSTRACISM (as with leprosy), in some contexts illness labels can have neutral or positive valuations and can be an attribute of personal identity.

From a sociological perspective, the perception of illness is a prerequisite for *illness behavior*, including the acceptance of the sick ROLE and the seeking of therapeutic intervention by a healer. People generally follow a patterned "hierarchy of resort" in seeking health care, moving to different, often more specialized, medical practitioners when previous efforts fail to cure and financial resources permit. Ethnographic descriptions of medical decision making and therapy-seeking behaviors comprise important aspects of the anthropological description of MEDICAL SYSTEMS. When an individual adopts the sick role, certain social responsibilities are temporarily suspended (like going to work) while other social expectations are enforced (like following the doctor's orders, attempting to get better, and gradually decreasing dependence on medical care).

From a cognitive perspective, the individuals make sense of their illness experience by using an *explanatory model* (EM) based on personal ideas of physiology and pathology that help in understanding why the illness occurred and make predictions of the illness's course (Kleinman 1980). In a clinical setting, the elicitation of a patient's EM by a healer can improve communication and, in some cases, the patient's adherence to a therapy plan. Anthropologists studying illness experience often use a qualitative method of collecting *illness narratives*, similar to a LIFE HISTORY of the illness. Analyses of multiple illness narratives from a group with a particular illness category can lead to a better understanding of the patient's point of view and improvements in health care. Since they are learned in a sociocultural context, EMs should not be considered as idiosyncratic to each patient. When EMs are shared by a group of people, they can be considered as *folk models of illness*. Illnesses that are not recognized within the categorization scheme of biomedicine are sometimes called "folk illnesses."

Susto, or soul loss, is a Latin American folk illness, which has been extensively studied in its ethnomedical, biomedical, and social psychological context by Rubel et al. (1984). Despite variations in the EMs of *susto* between people of Indian and "Mixed" descent, the illness is generally seen to result from the unintentional separation of the soul from the body after a frightening event. A variety of symptoms can be expressed, including listlessness, debility, loss of appetite, and trouble sleeping. The social-epidemiological distribution of the illness is higher in women than in men, in women with children than in the childless, and in people subjected to significant levels of social stress. Seven years after the original study comparing people who had suffered from *susto* with a control group matched for age, gender, and ethnicity, 17 percent of the *susto* sufferers had died, whereas there was no mortality in the control group. This proves that the biological consequences of a folk illness can be severe.

Medical anthropologists have long been interested in "exotic" psychiatric illnesses, also called "culture-bound syndromes" (CBS). As described by Simons and Hughes (1985) CBS include illnesses like *latah* (hyperstartling), *pibloktog* (Arctic hysteria), and *koro* (genital retraction syndrome). The central questions surrounding the CBS is whether psychiatric illnesses can be universal and cross-culturally recognizable, or only understood as particular cultural constructions from particular social contexts. The concept of CBS has been criticized as being based on a false nature – culture dichotomy for a phenomenon that is equally biological and cultural.

The entire distinction between disease and illness has been similarly criticized. Not only has disease been considered more "real" than the sickness and suffering originating from social or psychological processes, but according to some anthropologists, the distinction has led to a clinical neglect of the social dimensions of sickness because illness has become individualized and disease has become medicalized (Hahn 1995).

PB & KHT

See also ETHNOPSYCHOLOGY, SHAMANISM, SUFFERING

incest taboos concern the prohibition of sex and thus marriage between close kin and have continually perplexed social theorists. The problem has been addressed by all the major social scientists, including DURKHEIM (1963), MORGAN (1877), FRAZER (1910), TYLOR (1899), Freud (1918), LÉVI-STRAUSS (1969a), and even Karl Marx (see Engels 1902). A particular explanation was deemed necessary since the prohibition was assumed (erroneously as it turns out) to be both universal and consciously instituted by humans at some distant point in the past in order to achieve some beneficial psychological, social, or biological purpose.

These classic functionalist arguments,

focusing on the outcome of the practice, may be summarized as follows: first, incest avoidance has biological advantages since inbreeding exacerbates the rate of appearance of negative recessive genes in successive generations. Studies of rare inbred human populations bear out this argument. However, this genetic consequence, scientifically verified only in the nineteenth century, does not allow the conclusion that humans established the taboo to achieve this purpose. Second, sociological functionalist explanations focus initially on the advantages of eliminating sexual competition for mates within the nuclear family in order to achieve the procreation and socialization of the young in a relatively harmonious social setting. Third, the incest prohibition forces the members of each new generation to seek mates outside the family, creating in the process large cooperative networks based on marriage and extended kinship ties. From this perspective, the taboo results in society itself, in the form of social groups tied together by moral obligations. Although there is no denying that the incest taboo promotes these obvious social benefits to human society, such explanations are not complete. Specifically, they do not account for the origin of the taboo as opposed to its past and present functions. An explanation for the origin of the custom requires a different and broader theoretical perspective.

Such an approach was initially offered early in this century by Edward Westermarck (1891), who suggested that humans naturally avoid (rather than are prevented from) sex with family members. This line of reasoning assumes an evolutionary advantage of outbreeding and thus that humans emerged with an already-existing propensity to seek nonfamilial sexual partners. The argument proposes that close physical proximity from early childhood, rather than genetic proximity, inhibits sexual desire. As a result, individuals raised together (usually genetically related to each other, but even among those who are not) would seek different sexual partners at maturity. Conversely, since they are not repelled by their genes per se, siblings raised apart could find each other

attractive sexual partners. Despite some initial obvious objections, this "familiarity breeds sexual disinterest" argument has been revived and supported by circumstantial evidence on marriage customs.

First, there is A. Wolf and C. S. Huang's (1980) study of one form of traditional prearranged marriage (*sim pua*) in China and Taiwan, which involved the adoption into a household of an infant female who was raised along with a natural son. The expectation was that they would marry at a later date. Such marriages, when enforced (often with reticence on the part of now sexually mature children), resulted in a lower fertility rate and higher divorce rate than the arranged marriages of complete strangers – the more common arrangement. Second, Shepher's (1983) study of children originally from the same Israeli *kibbutz* documented an absence of marriages or even sexual liaisons (despite the fact that they were encouraged) among individuals raised together from early childhood. Third, McCabe's (1983) analysis of the Middle Eastern custom of marriage of paternal cousins – that is, the children of two brothers (normally raised in close physical proximity) – suggests that these unions are more likely to produce fewer children and culminate in divorce than other marriages, including those of other kinds of cousins raised further apart. Fourth, also in support of the Westermarck hypothesis, numerous studies of nonhuman primates describe a pattern of choosing a sexual partner from outside the natal group. Since all primate species exemplify this arrangement, it now considered to have been a social pattern of our last common primate ancestor, which existed some 20 million years ago (Maryanski & Turner 1992). Thus to suggest that humans emerged without such an outbreeding propensity, but rather invented it at some point in time for its advantages, is a highly convoluted approach to the problem. More elegant, in the sense of simpler, is to assume that *Homo sapiens* emerged with this propensity to outbreed and then created cultural rules, that is, incest prohibitions, to ensure this pattern for the sake of the functional advantages noted above.

However, if this natural aversion to inbreeding is indeed the case, then (1) why is the taboo universal and (2) why do humans need such a prohibition at all? The answer to the first question is straightforward: the taboo is not in fact universal. Some societies have no rule against incest, not because they have incest, but because they consider such behavior so repulsive that (in conformity with the Westermarck hypothesis) they need none. As to the second question, the taboo is required in many societies because humans – in contrast to other species – have a cultural capacity to overcome their biological inclinations. As a direct consequence of this intellectual ability, humans can consider and actually engage in behavior, such as incest, which may have deleterious biological, psychological, and social effects. Thus, it is in the interest of societies to ban this behavior for the sake of their own continued biological and social viability. And, unlike other species, humans also create categories of kin beyond the nuclear family, or raise genetic kin apart, thereby creating a need for a rule where it would otherwise be superfluous. In sum, it appears that the avoidance and/ or prohibition of incest is best understood as a feature of our species' complicated biosocial evolution.   WA

further reading Arens 1986; Robin Fox 1980

inclusive fitness *See* SOCIOBIOLOGY

independent invention is the autonomous invention in a culture of traits or technologies that are also found in other cultures. It is an alternate explanation to DIFFUSION, which posited that traits were borrowed from one culture by another, for the existence of cross-cultural regularities ranging from tattoos to pyramids.
MR
See also DIFFUSION, TECHNOLOGY, UNIVERSALS

indirect exchange *See* GENERALIZED (OR INDIRECT) EXCHANGE

industrial societies share a set of common elements based on their economic structure that, although there are no "typical" industrial societies, are similar cross-

culturally (Applebaum 1984b: 2). These include:

1. the mechanization of manufacturing and agriculture, along with a consequent dramatic increase in output of food, goods, and services
2. factory systems based on forms of energy more sophisticated than human and animal power, automatic and high-speed machinery, and continuous processes of production. Industrial factory production utilizes standardization of parts, repetitive and precise manufacturing cycles, and an intense subdivision of work tasks. In AGRICULTURE, increased productivity results from the use of farm machinery, chemical fertilizers, giant IRRIGATION systems, and scientific knowledge applied to soils, plants, and animals
3. an urban-based society with people moving from the countryside into the cities as the demand for factory and office labor increases and the need for farm labor decreases
4. developed TIME systems that permit the planning and coordination of future actions. Preindustrial societies do not carefully ration time but rather organize activities based on diurnal and seasonal rhythms. Industrial societies are preoccupied with time and watching the clock (Mumford 1934). Preindustrial societies have limited economic choices. Industrial societies permit wide ranges of choices and roles competing for a person's time. Time and the arrangement of persons and things in space is a way of locating human behavior and relating human acts to an objective environment (Richardson 1982). Some actions require synchronization of activities by a number of people at a particular time and place. Other activities require a sequence of actions, with one action starting after another has been completed (W. Moore 1963: 6–9; de Grazia 1962). Industrial societies' structuring of time through calendars and clocks permits exercise of foresight by individuals, organizations and nations

In terms of political and economic organization, industrial societies range from political democracies to authoritarian dictatorships, from capitalist economies to central command/socialist economies, and various combinations of capitalist, farmer, peasant, and governmental organization of socioeconomic life. The process of industrialization first begun in Western Europe and North America continues in Asia, South America, Africa, and the Middle East. Some industrial societies, such as Australia and South Africa, retain vestiges of preindustrial cultures within their borders. Industrializing societies, particularly in the formerly underdeveloped areas of the world, have become a major factor in international relations in the late twentieth century as the global economy has emerged to unbalance the former dominance of Western Europe, the United States, and Japan.

Since 1800, industrial societies have been buffeted by dramatic, and often painful, swings in the economic cycle. Periodic and regular economic and financial panics are part of industrial society and have laced it with a large measure of uncertainty. Economic cycles, along with rapidly occurring changes in technology, invention, population movements, and social structures, have bred a pervasive anxiety in industrial cultures. This uncertainty and anxiety find forms of expression ranging from art and culture to crime and psychosis and everything in between.

Communications and information are the lifeblood of an industrial society. The growing power and versatility of computers has changed the way individuals, companies, and governments do their business. Computers and communications are now part of information synthesis and decision making in industrial cultures. Communications and information are based on literacy and education, both of which are primary aspects of an industrial society, which functions according to science, technology, and shared knowledge. To cope with modern technology, industrial societies demand increasing literacy and educational levels. Some theorists believe that education is the key to the future of industrial society (Stonier 1989).

During the eighteenth and nineteenth centuries, industrial societies were capital accumulating and characterized by widespread scarcity. But as accumulation of capital advanced and reached enormous proportions in the twentieth century, industrial societies developed surpluses and affluent societies, with a consequent rise in consumerism and leisure. In the late twentieth century, industrial societies have become oriented toward massive outpourings of consumer goods and strong consumer demand in order to keep their economies healthy. Leisure and leisure industries have emerged as significant sectors in industrialized cultures (Coalter 1989). This has partially resulted from the fall in the average work week, which declined from 60 hours to 40 hours during the first half of the twentieth century in Europe and the United States. Rising living standards and rising life spans, which are characteristic of industrial societies, feed consumerism and leisure activities as more and more people are able to retire from work and are sustained through a combination of their own personal savings and government social security programs.

Industrial societies, especially in the twentieth century, have witnessed the rise of bureaucracies both in government and in private corporations. This has occurred simultaneously with the increase in the number of people available for white-collar and professional work (Gouldner 1954). Industrialized societies generally require no more than 25 percent of their population to produce their goods, with the balance of their work forces engaged in supplying services, management, and the gathering and storing of information.

In the past 50 years, a postindustrial thesis has emerged among theorists of industrial society (Daniel Bell 1973; Applebaum 1992b) in which it is argued that in the future industrial society will see a decreasing proportion of the population engaged in productive work, or work of any kind (Gorz 1985), and an increasing proportion engaged in leisure (Olszewska & Roberts 1989). Present and future industrial societies will be engaged in providing all kinds of services, from health care to recreation, from self-activated activities to educational and intellectual pursuits (Ginzberg & Vojt 1981: 48–9). However, these societies cannot ignore such continuing major problems as overcrowded cities, pollution, clogged roads and highways, crime, governmental and corporate corruption, oppression of HUMAN RIGHTS, unemployment, and wars.

There is no longer a strong demarcation between industrial and nonindustrial societies, since the global economy has brought all nations and societies into a single network. However, as the world economy grows at a rapid rate the gap between rich and poor societies has widened. The information and media revolution has brought all societies within the consciousness of citizens, with all societies, industrial and nonindustrial, seeking recognition and respect.   HA

See also CAPITALISM, SOCIALISM, TECH-
  NOLOGY, URBAN ANTHROPOLOGY, UR-
  BANISM, WORLD-SYSTEM THEORY

further   reading   Durkheim   1933;
Galbraith 1985; E. Thompson 1967; E. Wolf 1982

infanticide   is the killing of an infant, although the term is applied with different breadths in different disciplines. At its narrowest, in some legal contexts, it encompasses only maternally perpetrated killing of a human child at birth. At its broadest, in behavioral biology, the word has been used to encompass action, or inaction, by any creature leading to the death of a member of its own species at any stage before the victim's reproductive maturity (Parmigiani & vom Saal 1994).

In criminological studies, the term is usually limited to killings in the victim's first year of life, and may or may not be restricted to parentally perpetrated cases. In the United States "infanticide" is not a crime distinguished in law from other homicides, while in Canada and England it is. In the Canadian Criminal Code, for example, it is definitionally restricted to the killing of a newborn infant by the mother if "she is not fully recovered from the effects of giving birth to the child and by reason thereof or of the effect of lactation consequent on the birth of the child her mind is then disturbed" (S. 216).

Maternally perpetrated infanticide is not universally criminalized, however. In tradi-

tional, nonstate societies, it is widely considered an appropriate, perhaps even a prescribed, recourse in some circumstances. Daly and Wilson (1984) tabulated the circumstances in which infanticide was alleged to occur or to be legitimate in a standard, worldwide probability sample of 60 societies. They found that some such circumstances were noted in at least 39 of the 60 societies, and that most could be referred to one of three principal categories. Maternal incapacity to cope with the demands of child rearing accounted for half of all professed rationales for infanticides. Reasons included lack of paternal assistance, illness, famine, a still-nursing older sibling, or the birth of twins. The other major categories were poor phenotypic quality of the infant owing to deformity or illness, and inappropriate paternity. These three (and most of the other, rarer rationales, too) seem to reflect situations in which efforts to raise the baby are likely to fail, or to jeopardize the mother of prior children. In other words, they appear to represent "rational reproductive decisions," even when buttressed with superstitious justifications (as is often the case with infanticide of deformed children). The pragmatic element in these neonaticidal decisions is illustrated by Granzberg's (1973) analysis of the cross-cultural correlates of the practice of infanticide after the birth of twins: killing of both twins is extremely rare, and the routine killing of one is virtually confined to societies in which the burden of maternity is unrelieved by accessible female relatives or other social supports.

Female-selective infanticide has been the object of considerable study and debate, although it is by no means typical of societies in which infanticide may be common. Early discussions interpreted it (or infanticide generally) as a "strategy" on the part of entire populations or societies for "population regulation," but this idea has been discredited (Bates & Lees 1979). In complex, stratified societies, the practice is status-graded, with the upper classes eliminating daughters and concentrating investments in sons; there are both theoretical and empirical reasons to believe that this practice may be reversed in the lower strata (Cronk

1991), whose behavior is less well documented. Much more common than actual female-selective infanticide is some degree of preference for sons, perhaps especially where their role as warriors has been crucial.

Bugos and McCarthy's (1984) study of Ayoreo infanticide is the most detailed ethnographic report of its actual incidence and determinants in a traditional society. Ayoreo women sometimes disposed of several successive infants at birth, primarily in the context of a lack of reliable paternal support, but the likelihood of infanticide diminished with increasing maternal age, and even repeatedly infanticidal women later became devoted mothers under more auspicious circumstances. Maternal youth is a risk factor for infanticide in modern industrialized society, too (Daly & Wilson 1988a), and the decreased risk at the hands of older mothers has been interpreted as reflecting a life-span developmental change in women's valuation of their newborns as their capacity to produce additional future children shrinks.

In modern society, unwanted pregnancies are both circumvented by contraception and terminated by abortion. Moreover, there are often institutional supports for overburdened mothers, and those who cannot cope can relinquish children for ADOPTION. Not surprisingly, infanticide rates are low under these circumstances, and the infrequent cases are often attributed to pathologies such as "puerperal psychosis." It is noteworthy, however, that the same circumstances that are associated with infanticide in traditional societies are evident risk factors in the modern West, suggesting that even "psychotic" pathology may reflect a quantitative extreme of normal emotional response to desperate circumstances.   MWi & MD

further reading Dickemann 1979; Scheper-Hughes 1992

infibulation is a form of female CIR-CUMCISION, or genital mutilation, that involves the surgical removal of the vaginal labia, sometimes accompanied by the sewing shut of the vaginal opening. This procedure, found widely in northeastern Africa in a variety of societies, is often performed as part of the RITES OF PASSAGE for girls.   MR

informants are people who give information to an ethnographer. They are members of the culture or society being investigated, and were, until the mid-1960s, unselfconsciously referred to by the anthropologist as "native informants." Now, when "natives" may be high-energy physicists in a linear accelerator facility, this and similar words and phrases previously seen as quasi-technical and unproblematic are used ironically or within quotation marks. "Informant" is also used outside of anthropology (somewhat pejoratively) to refer to any insider who provides outsiders, such as law enforcement agencies, with information.

An informant consciously chooses to provide information; members of a culture who passively provide information just by being observed do not qualify. The transfer of information is usually through oral means, although informants may of course instruct in other ways, for instance, by drawing maps. Informants differ from interviewees in that the interaction is more long term, and, at times, far less structured. It is more a kind or relationship than a methodology per se. Often these relationships become intense and, if problems arise, a source of anguish for both parties (Rabinow 1977). Many ethnographies and reflexive accounts reveal the variety of interactions that can occur between informant and ethnographer (Casagrande 1960). These include teacher–student, elder–initiate, parent–child, therapist-analysand, employee-employer, and friend–friend. What is unusual, compared to other social sciences, is the degree of personal investment both parties have in the relationship and the often-shifting power relationship between anthropologist and informant depending on the specific context. Choosing good informants and maintaining the relationship properly has been the subject of a substantial amount of writing. As is the case for all aspects of traditional anthropological research, the moral and political aspects of this relationship have, especially recently, been closely examined (Sanjek 1993).   JJa

See also FIELDWORK, PARTICIPANT-OBSER-VATION

inheritance *See* SUCCESSION

intensification is (1) the increased application of some input or factor of production (such as water, labor, capital, or machines) to increase the yield of output per unit area; or (2) in SYMBOLIC ANTHROPOLOGY a kind of RITUAL (see RITES OF INTENSIFICATION). The former and more common usage contrasts with *ex*tensification: increasing yields by expanding the land area used while other factors are held constant. "Intensification" most often refers to AGRICULTURE, but the concept can also apply to FORAGERS, PASTORAL NOMADS or FISHING.

Population growth, human competition, and the spread of CAPITALISM are among the commonly cited stimuli for intensifying land or other resource use. In Thomas Malthus's (1789) classic formulation, a rising population tends to exhaust available resources and thus eventually holds itself in check. In Ester Boserup's (1965) contrasting argument, population growth stimulates innovation in farming techniques and thus raises production per unit of land (though not necessarily per unit of labor or capital), particularly through shortening fallow cycles and mechanizing. Both theories may hold true; indeed many populations grow, innovate, and yet exhaust available resources. Intensifying resource use can also stimulate population growth, in turn, by contributing to rising human fertility and child survival and by discouraging emigration.

Conventional schemas of social evolution depict foraging, pastoralism, and shifting and finally sedentary agriculture as steps of intensification that allow higher populations (A. Johnson & Earle 1987), but the ethnographic record contains countless combinations and many exceptions. IRRIGATION tends to raise land's carrying capacity dramatically, especially where inflowing water replenishes soil nutrients (see; in particular, Ruthenberg 1980 on the tropics and C. Geertz 1963c on Indonesia). Other measures, like multiple cropping, intercropping, terracing, manur-

ing or other fertilizing, and more careful tillage, weeding, and harvesting, are among common strategies of labor intensification that can raise yields per unit of land to high levels, often allowing small farms to outproduce large ones, as Robert Netting's (1986, 1993) West African, European, and worldwide comparisons show. Pastoralists' strategies for intensifying land use include altering herd structures through species mixtures and changing ratios of currently productive and unproductive animals.

Qualifying older theories of DIFFUSION and DEVELOPMENT, anthropologists, such as Paul Richards (1985) writing on the West African tropics, have documented much indigenous technological experimentation and innovation in societies once deemed traditional or peripheral. Some anthropologists also object to the economic idiom of "resources" and "intensification" as connoting culture-bound assumptions about human dominion, a teleology of human use or benefit, or a positive value on raised production or consumption.

PS

See also DEMOGRAPHY, FOOD PRODUC-TION, GREEN REVOLUTION

further reading Bennett 1976; Grigg 1980; B. Turner et al. 1993

interpretive anthropology simultaneously provides accounts of other cultural worlds from the inside and reflects on the epistemological groundings of such accounts. It is associated with the Chicago school of anthropology in the 1960s and 1970s, especially with the inflection given to SYMBOLIC ANTHROPOLOGY by Clifford GEERTZ. Interpretive anthropology was positioned against purely behaviorist, statistical, and formalist-linguistic approaches to human society because it insisted on the importance of the active negotiation of meaning, the decay and growth of symbols, and the richness of linguistic metaphoricity. The effort to unpack CULTURE as systems of meaning led to parallel interests in the processes of interpretation, and eventually, on the one hand, to a stress on differentiated competing discourses within a culture, hegemonic and counter-hegemonic processes, and critical anthropology, and on the other hand to a stress on ethnography as itself a process of interpretation (M. Fischer 1977).

The metaphor of cultures as texts, popularized by C. Geertz (1973), initially only meant that anthropologists read meanings in a culture as do native actors, and (in Ricoeur's 1981 influential version) that social actions leave traces that can be read like texts. Geertz's ethnography highlighted occasions when actors were at a loss to know how to construct a ritual, or when meanings needed to be renegotiated and established for particular interactions to be accomplished. Interpretive anthropology provided a devastating critique of COGNITIVE ANTHROPOLOGY's hopes for objective grids of meaning by showing that these grids were shot through with the analysts' own cultural categories and assumptions, thus vitiating the project. STRUCTURALISM was similarly, if less devastatingly, criticized as being too distant from the intentionality and experience of social actors. Interpretive anthropology in turn was itself criticized for seeing meaning wherever and however the analyst wished rather than having any objective method or criteria of evaluation.

One response to such criticism was to conceive of cross-cultural understanding, like any social understanding, as but an approximation, variably achieved through dialogue: a mutual correction of understanding by each party in conversation to a level of agreement adequate for any particular interaction. Geertz's own version of this argument for cross-cultural work was that ethnography is a translation between "experience-far" and "experience-near" languages. This relativist understanding of the distinction between EMIC AND ETIC categories avoids the need for, and denies the cogency of expecting, universally objective grids of meaning against which various cultural definitions might be measured. It focuses attention upon the ways in which meaning is established within communicative processes – both those processes that establish relatively stable meanings over time (such as Max WEBER's interest in legitimate forms of domination) and those that are fundamentally renegotiated in each interaction. Others took the idea of

dialogue in directions that empirically documented – from the sociolinguistic tape-recording to hermeneutical cultural accounting – how actors negotiate their understandings as well as how they interacted with cultural outsiders. At issue was not merely Max Weber's call for a *verstehendes Soziologie*, a sociology that gives a central role to actors' own understandings, but also the criterion of methodological individualism, the requirement that any sociological theory be able in principle to explain actions in terms of the intentions and purposes of individual actors. This criterion of acceptability was intended as a guard against essentializing Romantic group-mind characterizations of cultural beliefs and practices, so badly misused by the Nazis as well as ordinary racists, and does not necessarily contradict DURKHEIM's notions of the social or cultural as an emergent level of organization that cannot be simply reduced to individual intentions.

While the documentary and close analytic methods of sociolinguistics provided one direction in which the notion of dialogue was taken (Tedlock 1983), a second direction was the hermeneutics of cultural accounting. Hermeneutics in anthropology became a label for close reflection on the way natives decipher and decode their own complex cultural forms. In part this was seen as a fulfillment of Dilthey's insistence on a hermeneutical method for the social sciences that was as objective as the methods of the natural sciences while remaining focused on the meanings that allow actors to self-correct and change their actions (Makkreel 1975). It was also an extension of the Malinowskian interest in "the native point of view" and British social anthropology's concern with the ways in which social systems are organized to protect and reproduce their belief systems and structures of explanation. Like EVANS-PRITCHARD's (1937) classic analysis of Azande WITCHCRAFT, it concerned rules of inference, patterns of association, logics of implication, and culturally formulated critical apparatuses for aesthetic, cognitive, and moral judgment (R. Wagner 1972; R. Rosaldo 1980; Feld 1982; M. Fischer

1980a; M. Fischer & Abedi 1990). There was also an important interest in the psychodynamics of cultural logics without weakening the methodological obligation to pay close attention to local cultural interpretive procedures (V. Turner 1967; Crapanzano 1973; R. Levy 1973; M. Rosaldo 1980; Obeyesekere 1981, 1983).

A third direction was the use of "dialogue" as a metaphor for the complex exchanges between ethnographers and the cultures they study. Although at times this was reduced simplistically to a confessional mode of writing, as if the particular exchanges between anthropologists and their interlocutors were the object of interest, more useful are the efforts to turn the dialogue metaphor into an analysis of the circuits of representation, the communicative devices, the tropes and argumentative styles, and the cultural logics that are structured in institutionalized ways and carry differential weight or effect. For a time interest was generated in the resistances that local interpretations provide to hegemonic forces, but this dualistic simplification has now increasingly given way to a return to interest in the multiple, politically complex positions of interpretation that contend within the same social spaces of heterogeneous societies.

The mix of interests and kinds of ETHNOGRAPHY that interpretive anthropology generated – interest in the "native point of view," in the competing discourses within social fields, the ritualized ways in which hegemonic perspectives might be reinforced, in the negotiation of meaning and the changes in the constitution of culture that negotiation can sometimes effect, in the interpretive and dialogic processes both of social action and of ethnographic fieldwork and writing – constitute a transition between the discussions surrounding the ethnographies produced by FUNCTIONALISM and those surrounding the issues of POSTMODERNISM. Clifford Geertz (1995) himself is a rebel child of the various functionalisms of anthropology and Parsonian sociology, and father–teacher–defender to the ethnographers who are challenged by the postmodern. The philosophical issues raised, refined, and elaborated are perennial.   MF

Iroquois kinship systems classify kin terms so that the parallel collateral relatives, such as mother's sister and father's brother, are called by the same terms as the mother and father. Their children (Ego's parallel cousins) are called by the terms for siblings. In contrast, cross-collateral relatives such as mother's brother and father's sister, are called by distinctive terms, as are cross-cousins (see figure 1). Iroquois kinship is often associated with MATRILINEAL DESCENT.   MR

irrigation is the artificial watering of crops. It is a sociotechnical system that in-

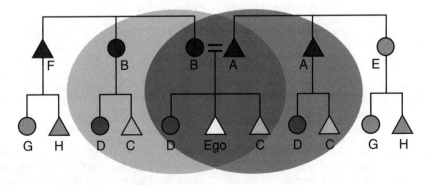

Figure 1 Iroquois kinship system.

tegrates physical or mechanical structures and allocation or distribution institutions organized according to priorities that represent the values of the irrigators. Inasmuch as all irrigation systems are designed, there are no reasonable criteria by which to label systems along some "primitive-to-advanced" axis. Irrigation systems that may appear to be rudimentary in terms of engineering or hardware may also display intricate and complex arrangements for water rights and distribution. Increase in physical scale may not require a more complex engineering design but may require a higher order of social design, inasmuch as longer canals or more complex networks of canals increase the prospective incidence of conflict. Communities of irrigators may therefore be conceived as distinctive design communities whose values are embodied in overall system design.

All irrigation systems require internal coordination to build the physical structures and keep them in running order; institutional arrangements for allocation; and some mechanism to control or resolve conflict. The three requirements are interrelated. Allocation procedures must be tailored to the physical contours of the system and designed to avoid conflict. But allocation procedures are the more socially significant because they encode communal values of the irrigators. Small irrigation communities will seek to enable a high degree of self-monitoring in order to maximize local control, and there is a high correlation between the frequency of operating-procedure decisions and level of control: the most frequently made decisions are resolved at the local level; infrequently made ones, higher up (R. Hunt & Hunt 1976). Routine maintenance is nearly always organized locally. Low-level conflict (characteristically embodied in the fine structure of a community) is also handled locally. It tends moreover to be functional by allowing minor infractions to be committed in a socially acceptable and personally neutral fashion. Certain structural kinds of conflict, like that between head-enders and tail-enders, are endemic, but irrigation communities appear to be remarkably successful in elaborating cultural mechanisms for containing such structural

sources of conflict to prevent the collapse of the system.

Although large-scale conflict may require the intervention of higher authorities, most irrigation communities have been successful in maintaining high degrees of local control. This is true in a wide variety of political systems cross-culturally and would appear to be a social-structural requirement for successful irrigation. Systematic exceptions to local control, as in the so-called ORIENTAL DESPOTISM seen in ancient centralized HYDRAULIC SOCIETIES, can be explained by the presence of specific hydraulic and hydrological variables. Wherever autonomous monitoring institutions are required, they typically embody consensual operating procedures. These procedures embody community values, such as equity, equality, justice, efficiency, and local control (Maass & Anderson 1978). Tribal irrigation communities will trade off economic efficiency to secure a higher degree of equality in consonance with communal norms. Because such institutions are both highly congruent with communal values and also embody in their design ways to limit allocation (by water rights, for example) to hydrologically feasible limits, they tend to be ultrastable, hardly changing over time unless physical circumstances so require. Operating procedures include internal switches that permit flexible adjustment to short- and long-term variation in water supply as well as other unforeseen social or environmental complications.

Allocation procedures typically manifest a high degree of complexity. For a variety of reasons, originally logical measurement units (for example, proportional units based on subdivisions of a 12- or 24-hour period) become so subdivided and recombined that the original logic is lost and irrigators no longer know how the value of their water right originated or what relation it has to those of others (Netting 1981). Distribution among canals presents the same analytic problem (Canfield 1973). Irrigation systems may also encode ritual practices (Lansing 1991) or kinship relationships (Fernea 1970) that further add to systemic complexity. Whatever form systemic complexity may take, it is highly functional because, to the extent that the rationale of the water-distribution system is not known to the irrigators, who must accept it as a given, water allocation is beyond argument and cannot be challenged. In this way, systemic complexity is a stabilizing feature in a such a conflict-prone activity (Pfaffenberger 1990).   TG

further reading E. Coward 1980; Glick 1970; William Mitchell et al. 1994

J, K

joint family *See* EXTENDED FAMILIES

kindreds are a bilateral collection of kin unified by a shared sense of KINSHIP or DESCENT. An egocentric kindred is the personal kindred of an individual (see EGO). Kindreds are not strictly speaking KIN GROUPS since they have neither a corporate character nor clear boundaries.   MR

kin groups are social groups whose boundaries and recruitment principles are defined primarily in terms of kinship relations as they are conceived in a particular society.   MR

kinship is the social organization of reproductive activity. In the nineteenth century, as Darwinian views replaced the explanatory powers of Scripture, it was thought that kinship (and the reproductive activity that underlay it) was of such a nature that it not only predated, but was functionally prerequisite to, other kinds of activity. So it was thought that political organization grew out of family and kinship organization, and economic institutions out of the economic activities of the reproducing unit and kin groups. And so on for other features of present-day social life.

And the nuclear or elementary FAMILY of a man and woman and their children was widely supposed to be the universal and crucial grouping, with critical functions in society. Since sexual activity was regarded as a strong motive on which enduring bonds of cooperation, protection, and parenthood could be formed and then maintained, and since these bonds were prerequisite to survival and successful socialization, the social regulation of reproductive activity was held to be integral. Hence the central place of the INCEST TA-BOO or prohibition. By forcing MARRIAGE with someone outside the nuclear family, two or more families could be allied through the bonds of kinship into a wider society. And the assumption was that ties of BLOOD or marriage (the tie of marriage was based on sex) were indeed the strongest, if not the only, bonds at first. And since a stable family was thought to be prerequisite to anything else, as well as to survival, the problem was to explain how the family got to be stable and why it remained that way. Indeed, the shift from the group of a man, a woman, and her children to the *socially defined* unit of husband, wife, and their children (the family) was held by many to be the crucial first step in sociocultural development.

Many of these views have persisted well into the present and although some see them as survivals, others see them as profound, almost sacred, truths.

Even during the period when evolutionary or developmental and later diffusionist questions dominated anthropology, social solidarity was implicitly or explicitly a central question, the answer to which was "kinship based on the social recognition of the biological facts of relatedness."

This formulation was made most clearly first in the anthropological literature by MORGAN and continued through RADCLIFFE-BROWN, Murdock, FORTES, and LÉVI-STRAUSS, and it rested on two assumptions. First, social kinship occurred when people themselves gave cultural recognition and cultural significance to the biological facts of their relatedness. That is, when the father's relationship to the child was recognized, then "fatherhood" as a social and cultural fact came into being. The child's relationship to the mother was held too obvious by birth to fail to achieve social recognition and value from earliest times. This assumption is only a special case of the more general one that CULTURE is built on the facts of nature. Such facts of nature become a social force when they are recognized or known; thus the genealogy, as a network of real biological ties, is the universe that is culturally partitioned to form a system of social categories and relations we call kinship. The invention of cultural CLASSIFICATION is almost if not entirely confined to giving names to the natural features as they are recognized for what they "actually are." This idea is obviously very close to the notion that culture is an adaptive system, adapted to the facts of nature and the environment in which humans live. That this assumption is inadequate can be seen from considering the nature of gods, ghosts, and ghouls whose reality is entirely cultural, lacking any real or natural base.

The second assumption on which social or cultural kinship was built by early thinkers, which continues to underlie contemporary thinking, is that these biological bonds have in fact considerable force. "Blood is thicker than water" is the saying among Westerners. That is, a biological link of consanguinity is a powerful bond of solidarity, mutual help, and reciprocity usually stronger than most other links; and people are biologically driven to obey the demands of these bonds. It is "natural" to do so, it is believed; it is a fact of "human nature," and their social or cultural recognition only formalizes this fact.

Another way to put this is that every society or sociocultural system must be integrated – both at the level of keeping the people together and at the level of keeping the sociocultural system together. The sociocultural construction of nature and the priority of the material, natural world in this scheme for explaining things is clear.

In one way, then, kinship has always been regarded as a system that provides for the solidarity, trust, and cooperation that are functionally prerequisite both to group living and to sociocultural life. What is contested is how much of this is purely cultural construction and how much, if any, is simply the facts of nature, including human

nature, merely celebrated by cultural recognition.

Particular societies, for various reasons, have then reduced the very large number of relations of affinity (by marriage) and consanguinity (by blood) by ignoring certain relations for social purposes and marking certain relations as socially and culturally significant. This is done by categorizing kinds of relation in two fundamental ways. First, certain distinctly different relations are classed together, for example, the children of parental siblings may be classed as "cousins" who are named (given kinship terms) and may have distinct, specialized roles to play (for example, the relationship between mother's brothers and sister's sons may be elaborated into the AVUNCULATE). Second, certain kinds of descent may be singled out for special recognition. For example, all those related by blood through men may be recognized as patrilineal relatives, those related through descent through women may be selected out as matrilineal relatives, while a selection of certain relatives whether through men or women, may form a nonunilineal descent category.

From category to group is thus an easy move and minimally consists in the presence of some special function like property holding or regulating marriage. Where *kinship* is, by definition, bilateral, the non-unilineal *descent* group is a subset of the network of bilaterally related kin. (The "kindred" is the group of bilaterally related kin socially and culturally recognized in a society by any Ego. "Kinship" and "kindred" should be analytically distinguished from "descent" and "descent group," which derive from ancestral figures.)

It is held that the easy development of kin groups out of the network of existing kin is what makes kinship so important in the development of society in earlier times and the basis of social cohesion, social solidarity, and survival then and in the present. Since the real biological bond of consanguinity is there anyway, its social recognition simply activates, marks, and makes effective the trust, cooperation, and solidarity necessary to social life.

Clearly, insofar as heterosexual intercourse has been (and usually still is) functionally prerequisite to reproduction, and stable relations prerequisite to survival and socialization, SEX and hence the GENDER distinctions that presumably depend on them have been integral to kinship and marriage. It has only recently become the case that the interdependence and solidarily of a couple do not necessarily depend on their being of two biologically different sexes or on sexual intercourse.

The sex–gender dichotomy (usually) integral to sexual reproduction is also elaborated throughout the whole sociocultural system and appears to be prerequisite even to differentiation within kinship itself.

Given the network of consanguineal and affinal kin with both gender and generational differentiation at least, and the possibility for ancestor-oriented or lineal- or descent-type differentiation as well, and with distinct roles and functions reserved to distinct kin or clusters of them, not only does a system of differentiated roles emerge, but there is also the possibility for distinct, differentiated groups to occur and even a whole, if not very large, fully functional and self-sustaining society.

The central features of the anthropological analytic scheme and presuppositions about kinship are remarkably similar to those of European culture (and its derivatives in North and South America, Australia, etc.). This is no accident, for so much social theory of the nineteenth and twentieth centuries seems to be little more than the systematic elaboration of the cultural presuppositions of those who formulate and use it.

In this connection, a good example is the very close association between the cultural conceptions of kinship and racism in contemporary Euro-American culture. Both postulate biological connectedness (in kinship "one flesh and blood") as of overriding significance, both treat common biology or "blood" as the source of common character ("all those Xs are that way"), and both emphasize their common biological character as the source of strong in-group solidarity and out-group hostility (that is, this "kind" against that "kind," "kind" being a variety of "kin").   DS

See also ADOPTION, ALLIANCE THEORY, ASSOCIATION, DESCENT THEORY, EVOLU-TION, HOUSEHOLDS, REPRODUCTION, SYMBOLIC ANTHROPOLOGY

further reading Fortes 1970; Robin Fox 1967; Goodenough 1970; Morgan 1871; Murdock 1949; D. Schneider 1968, 1984

kinship systems *See* DESCRIPTIVE KINSHIP SYSTEMS

kinship terminologies *See* KIN TERMS

kin terms   designate the various types of kin in a system and specify how they are to be addressed or referred to. The attempt to uncover the cultural logic behind the organization of these terms became one of anthropology's first great enterprises, the study of KINSHIP.   MR

See also ADDRESS TERMS, CLASSIFICATION, REFERENCE TERMS

Kroeber, Alfred L. (1876–1960)
Kroeber was born in Hoboken, New Jersey on June 11, 1876. He attended Columbia University both as an undergraduate and in graduate school, where he studied with Franz BOAS and received the university's first doctorate in anthropology, in 1901. He went to the University of California at Berkeley the same year and led the anthropology department there from 1909 until his retirement in 1946. A very prolific and broad-gauged scholar, Kroeber was mainly an ethnologist, although he also made contributions in linguistics, archaeology, and even physical anthropology. Thus some of his early papers were concerned with the archaeology of California and languages and ethnology of Amerindians, including the Yurok, Mohave, Arapaho, Bannock, and Shoshoni. These studies led to his monumental *Handbook of the Indians of California* (1925). He also studied the Zuñi, both archeologically and ethnographically, leading to his first extended works on kinship (1917b), although he had earlier attacked Lewis Henry MORGAN's kinship schemes in a famous article (1909). Morgan's approach was based on a distinction between CLASSIFICATORY and DESCRIPTIVE KINSHIP SYSTEMS of terminology. The former were associated with

unilinear descent groups and characterized most traditional societies; the latter reflected the transition from tribal to state-organized societies. Kroeber argued that all kinship terminologies were mixtures of the two modes, and there was no way to establish a causal relationship between either and specific social structures. Kroeber overreached and, in fact, Morgan's approach proved the more fruitful in the long run (M. Harris 1968: 321–4).

Kroeber, despite being a major theoretician of American cultural anthropology, was, in many public statements, resolutely antitheoretical, idiographic, and particularistic. He developed (1936) the notion of the CULTURE AREA and coined the concepts of "intensity" (how cultures build to their cultural level and maintain it) and "climax" (the most highly integrated center or focus of a culture area). Cultural intensification was measured statistically by compiling lists of cultural elements and plotting their distribution, and also evaluated subjectively by analyzing the styles of culturally sensitive institutions. Those elements that turned up most frequently he reckoned as older. He liked to work inductively, amassing data to see what patterns emerged (Kroeber 1939). In *Configurations of culture growth* (1944) he sought "common features" but concluded that the growth curves of different civilizations had no predictable similarities. Cultures, in his view, had to be inventoried and then classified according to something like a Linnaean scheme. He continued to be resolutely historicist, asserting that historical development always tended "toward the unique as historians have long ago learned to take for granted" and always denying that any laws analogous to scientific ones could be established for cultural processes. Along with his historicism went a brand of cultural relativism according to which each culture is unique and thus not amenable to cross-cultural explanation.

Nevertheless in his concept of the "superorganic" Kroeber developed something like the nomothetic approaches he professed to distrust and formulated a view of culture quite as reductionist as other reductionisms (structural, functional, etc.) that he opposed. He defined the superorganic as those aspects of culture that could not be explained in terms of individuals and therefore "above" the societies that support them. His original formulation (Kroeber 1917a) was a broadside against social evolutionists like Herbert SPENCER and Lester Ward, who portrayed society as an organism. Kroeber's inductive study of women's dress fashion, in which he charted changes over a 300-year period and discovered periodic oscillations in such features as skirt length, was designed to be a proof of superorganic action (Kroeber & Richardson 1940). At an explanatory level, the concept is very similar to the kind of culturological explanation later promoted by Leslie WHITE (although he criticized White for ignoring psychological explanation).

Kroeber stressed the great significance of unconscious processes in the development, maintenance, and change of human cultures. This view probably originated in his study of linguistic change and was extended to his studies of individual styles whose origins were nonrational and obscure. Specific changes in style have to do with more general value shifts or an alteration in the configuration of the entire culture. Individual elements of culture can be altered by such processes as imitation, diffusion, and reinvention – the processes of acculturation. But patterns or combinations of patterns are much more permanent and stable. Kroeber set the definition of CULTURE for American anthropology (Kroeber 1952) and assured through his intellectual leadership that the field would focus on culture rather than social structure (Kroeber & Parsons 1958). He died while vacationing in Paris, on October 5, 1960.

TG

further reading Steward 1973

kula **ring**   is a system of ritualized overseas exchange practiced in the area around the Trobriand Islands, east of New Guinea (Malinowski 1922). Shell necklaces (*soulava*) are exchanged for armshells (*mwali*) in a series of transactions that span many islands and many partners. These objects are held for a time and then later exchanged for others, with shell necklaces going in one direction, shell armbands in the other direction. The *kula* trade is strongly associated with the local prestige system and is accompanied by an extensive system of magic and mythology, as well as by barter trade (*gimwali*) of practical goods.   MR

further reading J. Leach & Leach 1983; Macintyre 1983

L

labor *See* WORK

land tenure refers to relationships between people and land, or to peoples' rights and duties toward each other with respect to land. The term itself has many varied meanings: matter underfoot, space marked on a map, a base of power, a resource to exploit, an aspect of divinity, or an anchor of social identity. Concepts of land and landholding seldom translate neatly between languages.

Land tenure is always more complex than simple distinctions between public or private PROPERTY would imply because mixtures of individual and group control of land are found everywhere. Rights over land may be divided into three kinds:

1. *use rights*: access for residence, passage, hunting, gathering, grazing, farming, collecting minerals, or building; rights of *disuse* may also be important
2. *transfer rights*: movement of ownership or possession through inheritance, gifting, lending, swapping, pledging, mortgaging, buying and selling, or other transfers
3. *administration rights*: the power or authority to allocate or withdraw land from use, to arbitrate disputes, to regulate transfers, to manage land for public use, to tax it or collect tributes from it, or to take over its possession by default or reversion

These rights are often divided among different units of aggregation (individuals, families, lineages, companies, villages, districts, states) that claim different combinations of rights in respect to any specific piece of land. Such "bundles of rights" may be ranked or nested in "hierarchies of estates" (Gluckman 1965a). But access to

land for one purpose does not automatically allow access to it for another. Land rights often come encumbered with responsibilities, such as to keep access routes clear or to maintain the land's fertility for future generations (Blaikie & Brookfield 1987).

Land tenure is tightly linked to kinship, rank, status, or acceptable social behavior in societies where social relations, not money, determine land rights (Meek 1946). It can also have a symbolic and religious component, particularly where graves, ancestors, or earth deities are involved, or where religious law is used to regulate inheritance. Euro-American concepts of resources, property, tenancy, domain, and title are far from universal and often distort other societies' notions of land tenure and its meanings (Goheen & Shipton 1992).

Concepts of land tenure are strongly rooted in a society's subsistence base and demography. More intensive land uses tend to squeeze out less intensive ones. For example, FORAGERS, who generally perceive land rights in terms of use, not ownership, have been gradually restricted worldwide to lands least usable for farming or herding, often in areas of extreme temperatures or precipitation that are not considered worth "owning." Claims by "aboriginal" peoples that their historic use rights constitute a form of recognizable land tenure have been the basis for legal battles in many countries (Wilmsen 1989b).

Similar disputes about land use arise between sedentary farmers and PASTORAL NOMADS, who graze their animals by moving though a series of pastures. Farmers often try, by law or force, to restrict herders' movements by arguing that the animals damage crops. More critically, farmers often plant crops in pasture land and then claim it as their own. Both tactics have brought about much ill-will and violence between such peoples worldwide. While sensitivity to the different perceptions of land rights can minimize such conflicts, ignorance is less the problem than competition to control valuable resources (L'Equipe écologie 1979).

Land tenure is a key issue in areas where a variety of people have intersettled. Distinctions between earlier and later settlers, conquered and conquerors, or aboriginal and immigrant often form the stuff of class or status hierarchy, whether mutually agreed or not. The perceived differences between hosts and guests, permanents and temporaries, or land patrons and land clients can be political and economic as well as symbolic. These perceived differences often widen as land becomes more scarce.

As a population grows denser, or land and its products commercialize, competition for land grows, in some cases provoking more frequent and intense litigation. Rules that were implicit become explicit; old rules are abandoned and new rules get elaborated; boundaries are redrawn, sharpened, or permanently marked (S. Moore 1978). Some nineteenth-century theorists hypothesized that it was such pressure that first created individual or private property itself (Engels 1902). Although this is generally true, there are exceptions: even under some market-oriented regimes, farmers, herders, and others have successfully devised methods of maintaining "managed commons" without reckless free-for-all exploitation (McCay & Acheson 1987). Socialist governments have also attempted to restrict private-property rights, albeit without much long-term success.

The optimal size for landholdings and the rules needed to maintain an ecological or economic system have been the subjects of much debate. Whereas modern agriculture has a bias toward large, compact holdings, in many situations fragmented holdings may help reduce farming risks (J. Bentley 1987). Access to a wide variety of land with multiple uses, and with overlapping rights over it, is characteristic of smallholders worldwide (Netting 1981, 1993). In other cases land tenure may be less important than access to some other input. In IRRIGATION systems, for example, rights to land are less critical than rights to water. Upstream positions in canal networks have obvious advantages over downstream ones, and these differences sometimes coincide with wealth or class as well as power (Hunt & Hunt 1976).

Urban land tenure has as yet been little studied by anthropologists, although it resembles rural tenure in that more than one principle or system may operate in the same time and place. Although officially titled properties and gang territories, for instance, may have little relation to each other legally, both can simultaneously structure city dwellers' access, rights, and responsibilities.

Attempts to modify existing land-tenure systems by law take two forms: (1) land reform that redistributes the holdings themselves; and (2) land-tenure reform that changes the rules or processes by which land rights are gained, held, or lost. Reasons used to justify such policies include increasing economic growth, redressing imbalances in equity, or increasing government control. Both kinds of reform are notoriously hard to accomplish, partly because land tenure is so intimately linked to other facets of society and culture (Bassett & Crummery 1993). Even avowedly egalitarian land reforms may worsen rather than improve the distribution of land if better positioned people or groups take advantage of early information or privileged contacts to gain the biggest and best holdings under the new regime (D. Lehmann 1974). Land nationalization programs, in particular, have historically provided easy cover for land grabs. Titling programs, even when intended to give women and men equal access to land, have sometimes instead concentrated rights into men's hands in practice. Prohibitions on sharecropping or other share contracting, often meant to curb human exploitation, can deprive the land-poor of a valued safety net, or of a chance to solidify more permanent land claims. Fencing or ranching schemes to sedentarize pastoralists, and villagization schemes to concentrate farmers around facilities like water works, schools, or clinics, have often done more ecological harm than good.

Land-tenure systems are often so complex that changes deemed by outside jurists and economic developers as necessary to ensure a "secure title" on a piece of land may in reality result in sets of rights that are less secure than those they are meant to replace. This is especially true if the changes tempt individuals to sell, mortgage, or gamble new land titles to the detriment of their dependents or of ancillary right holders. Attempting to replace one tenure system with another often merely entangles or superimposes the two, creating uncertainties manipulable by the wealthy, powerful, or clever (Downs & Reyna 1988; Shipton 1994). Involuntary resettlement is about the hardest of all "development" strategies to accomplish without causing social and economic hardship, if not also ecological damage (Hansen & Oliver-Smith 1982). The more abruptly it occurs, the greater its likely unintended consequences.   PS

further reading Biebuyck 1963; M. Cernea & Guggenheim 1993; Fortmann & Bruce 1988; Hoben 1973; E. Leach 1961a; S. Moore 1986a

language In its nonfigurative sense, "language" refers to the most frequent form of communication among human beings. It is unique to the human species; although other species, in particular chimpanzees, have made more progress in language acquisition than many linguists would have predicted.

Although language primarily uses the spoken medium, it can also be reduced to WRITING SYSTEMS, and other uses of the visual medium are also possible: the most striking instances of the latter are deaf sign languages (signs used as the primary means of communication and serving all the functions of a spoken language). Recent work on such sign languages has shown that they share the same levels of cognitive and structural complexity as spoken languages (Klima & Bellugi 1979). The term "language" is also used figuratively for other COMMUNICATION systems, such as "the language of music" or

"gesture language," but will not be so used here.

Various attempts have been made to provide a checklist of characteristics of language, one of the most widely cited being Hockett (1966). Although most individual criteria can also be found in other communication systems, their combination is unique to human language. Some of the most important of these features are noted below and supplemented by more recent suggestions.

Human language makes primary use of the vocal–auditory channel (but see above on sign languages). Indeed, evolutionary changes in the development of the vocal tract of *Homo sapiens sapiens* seem to have played a major role in the capacity for a system as rich as that of human language. In particular, the human vocal tract, unlike that of nonhuman primates (and even Neanderthal man), provides for rapid and fine control of a wide range of oral articulations (P. Lieberman 1984, 1991; Hawkins & Gell-Mann 1992), thus giving rise to the rich inventories of phonemes found in human language and serving to distinguish a large number of linguistic signs from one another.

Human language needs to be acquired on the basis of external stimuli, in contrast to the genetically transmitted communication systems of some other species, such as bee dancing. In the absence of external stimuli, as in the case of feral children, human CHILDREN do not acquire a language. More specifically, the acquisition of a human language involves the interaction of innate predispositions toward language and stimuli from the language spoken in the child's environment. Children acquire the language that is spoken around them, irrespective of whether or not this is the language of their biological parents; thus, there is no innate disposition for the acquisition of any particular language. Although certain features of certain languages are more difficult to acquire than others – for instance, children acquire the relatively transparent morphology of Turkish much earlier than the more opaque morphology of Serbo-Croatian (Slobin 1979) – in the absence of pathological conditions all children are capable of acquiring any language.

However, children acquire language much more rapidly than is plausible on the assumption that only general data-processing strategies are available, thus suggesting that they have a particular innate predisposition toward the acquisition of language.

The relation between form and meaning in human language is *conventional*. (Linguists usually, but perhaps unfortunately, use Ferdinand de Saussure's term "arbitrary" instead.) This means that there is no necessary relation between the form of a linguistics SIGN or MORPHEME and its meaning. Thus, the same concept is referred to as *bird* in English, *oiseau* in French, *ptica* in Russian, *tori* in Japanese, and so on. Exceptions, so-called onomatopoeia, are rare, and even here there is some degree of conventionalization: thus we find variation in the sound-imitative name of the bird called *cuckoo* in English, *Kuckuck* in German, and *kukushka* in Russian. In deaf sign languages too the relationship between a particular visual sign and its meaning is highly conventionalized.

A crucial characteristic of human language is that linguistic utterances are not directly tied to a particular stimulus. This distinguishes human language from most animal communication systems. For instance, bees dance only under the appropriate stimulus of having discovered a food source and needing to convey this information to other hive members, and birds emit danger cries only in the presence of a perceived danger. Human language can thus be used to discuss topics that are not present in the surroundings, and even to discuss hypotheticals, that is, to discuss what would happen if a certain situation were to obtain – this is one of the main foundations of scientific discourse.

A nontrivial characteristic of human language is its so-called double articulation (Martinet 1965). In spoken language, this refers to the fact that the meaningful elements of language (morphemes) are composed of meaningless elements (PHONEMES). Thus the English word *pig* is distinguished from *dig* by the initial phoneme (/p/ versus /d/); /p/ and /d/ have no meaning in themselves – the semantic distinction between *pig* and *dig* is not the same as that between *pen* and *den* – but serve to distinguish two meaningful elements from one another. In this way, a relatively restricted number of phonemes (around 40 in English) serves to distinguish a vast number of morphemes. The corresponding claim holds also of deaf sign languages, with a restricted number of hand shapes, orientations, and movements serving to differentiate a large number of morphemes.

Although not included in early checklists of features of human language such as Hockett's, SYNTAX, or rather the particular syntactic properties of human language, is another major characteristic. While languages differ considerably from one another in syntactic structure, certain features remain constant, most noticeably the relevance of hierarchical structure. An English sentence like *the good man saw the bad dog* is not just a sequence of seven words, rather these words are grouped into phrases: *the good man*, *saw*, and *the bad dog*; going further, *saw* and *the bad dog* can be grouped together as a single phrase consisting of these two phrases, to give the overall (simplified) structure [[the good man] [saw [the bad dog]]]. The phrase structure of a sentence is important not only to its semantics (thus, *good* must be related semantically to *man*, another constituent of the same phrase, rather than, say, to *dog*), but also to its relationships with closely related sentence types. For instance, in the passive equivalent of the sentence just given, *the bad dog was seen by the good man*, the phrases *the good man* and *the bad dog* remain intact, even though they show up in different positions in the sentence. The importance of hierarchical syntactic structure in the grammar of human language is referred to as "structure dependence." The emergence of syntax in child language at around age 2 marks a major step in language acquisition, one that is not matched by nonhuman primates acquiring language (P. Lieberman 1984, 1991).

It is customary to make a major division within language structure between GRAMMAR, the set of regularities that govern the structure of sentences, and lexicon, a repository of the conventional pairings of meaning and sound as linguistic signs. For instance, in the phrase *bad dog*, the lexicon will give the meanings of *bad* and *dog* and will also list any idiosyncratic properties (e.g. that *bad* has a comparative *worse* rather than **badder*), while the grammar will provide general rules showing how an adjective and a noun can be combined to give a noun phrase.

Although the above has emphasized the formal structure of human language, the fact should not be overlooked that some aspects of human language are more directly related to its function. For instance, some languages have distinct reflexive pronouns only in the third person (e.g. French *il se déteste* 'he detests himself' versus *il le déteste* 'he detests him', with a distinction between reflexive *se* and nonreflexive *le*, but in the first person *je me déteste* 'I detest myself' and *il me déteste* 'he detests me', with the same form *me* in both reflexive and nonreflexive interpretations). No language, however, is known to have the inverse system, that is, a distinct reflexive in the first person but not in the third person, although the two systems are of equal formal complexity. Functionally, however, the need to differentiate among potential referents is more acute in the third person than it is in the first person (there is normally only one speaker per utterance), which explains the greater richness of pronominal and other reference-tracking devices in the third person than in the other two persons. This suggests the possibility of close interaction between language structure (or linguistic competence) and language use (or linguistic performance).

The scientific study of language is called linguistics. It comprises a number of subdisciplines treating different aspects of language, including PHONOLOGY, morphology, SYNTAX, SEMANTICS, and PRAGMATICS. Relations between language and society are studied in SOCIOLINGUISTICS, those between language and cognition in PSYCHOLINGUISTICS. Linguistic studies concerned with the ways in which languages change over time fall under the domain of HISTORICAL LINGUISTICS.   BC

further reading Bloomfield 1933; Chomsky 1986; Fromkin & Rodman 1993; Jackendoff 1993; O'Grady & Dobrovolsky 1993; Pinker 1994; E. Sapir 1921; Saussure 1959

language classification The most traditional and common way of classifying languages is genetic (for the principles underlying genetic classification see COMPARATIVE LINGUISTICS). Table 1 (p. 278) lists the major language families (including some isolates, i.e., families with a single member) with representative languages. Not included are languages that lack a single genetic origin, such as pidgins and creoles. The classification is conservative; many linguists would group together some or all of Turkic, Mongolic, Tungusic, Korean, and Japanese as Altaic, and would recognize further large language families in the Americas, such as Hokan and Penutian. More radical and controversial proposals would group together all Papuan families as a single family (J. Greenberg 1971), and likewise all American Indian families other than Na-Dene as Amerind (J. Greenberg 1987), and many languages of Eurasia as Nostratic or Eurasiatic.

Languages can also be classified in terms of areally shared features, reflecting the results of contact among languages spoken in a particular geographic area, such as Meso-America (L. Campbell et al. 1986). Finally, languages can be classified typologically, in terms of shared structural features independent of genetic or geographical factors, as when Japanese and Haruai (a Papuan language) are grouped together as SOV (having subject–object–verb word order) (Comrie 1989).   BC

further reading B. Grimes 1992a,b; J. Grimes & Grimes 1993; Ruhlen 1987

langue and parole distinguish between language as a structured and unconscious system, existing independently of the individual speaker (*langue*) and the observable language of speech (*parole*). This distinction was first made by the French linguist Ferdinand de Saussure (1959) early in the twentieth century.   MR

law is the body of rules of conduct that a particular state or community recognizes as binding on its members or subjects. The great nineteenth-century theorists of social EVOLUTION emphasized the nature of law as a measure of civilization (Rouland 1994). Sir Henry MAINE (1861), for ex-

Table 1   Major language families and representative languages

Language family	Sample languages
Indo-European:	
Indo-Iranian	Sanskrit, Hindi-Urdu, Bengali, Sinhala, Persian
Armenian	
Balto-Slavic	Lithuanian, Russian, Polish, Czech, Serbo-Croatian
Albanian	
Greek	
Italic (including Romance)	Latin, French, Spanish, Portuguese, Italian, Rumanian
Celtic	Welsh, Irish
Germanic	English, Dutch, German, Norwegian, Swedish, Danish
Basque	
Northwest Caucasian	Circassian, Abkhaz
Northeast Caucasian	Chechen, Avar
Kartvelian (South Caucasian)	Georgian
Uralic	Hungarian, Finnish
Turkic	Turkish
Mongolic	Mongolian
Tungusic	Manchu
Korean	
Japanese	
Ket	
Yukaghir	
Gilyak (Nivkh)	
Chukotko-Kamchatkan	Chukchi
Dravidian	Tamil, Telugu
Burushaski	
Sino-Tibetan	Chinese (including Mandarin), Tibetan, Burmese
Miao-Yao (Hmong-Mien)	Hmong
Austroasiatic	Santali, Mon, Khmer, Vietnamese
Tai-Kadai	Thai
Andamanese	[indigenous languages of the Andaman Islands]
Austronesian	Malay-Indonesian, Javanese, Tagalog, Fijian, Tongan
Papuan language families	Enga, Chimbu
Australian	[all or most indigenous languages of Australia]
Afroasiatic:	
Semitic	Hebrew, Arabic, Amharic
Ancient Egyptian	
Berber	Kabyle, Tamasheq
Cushitic	Somali, Oromo
Omotic	[various languages of western Ethiopia and northern Kenya]
Chadic	Hausa
Nilo-Saharan	Kanuri, Luo, Maasai
Niger-Congo, including:	
Mande	Maninka, Mende
Atlantic	Fula, Wolof
Ijo	
Yoruba	
Bantu	Swahili, Xhosa, Zulu
Khoisan	Nama, !Kung
Eskimo-Aleut	Inuit, Aleut

Table 1   (cont.)

Language family	Sample languages
Na-Dene, including:	
Athabaskan	Navajo, Chipewyan
Other American Indian language families, including:	
Algonquian	Blackfoot, Cree
Iroquoian	Mohawk Seneca, Cherokee
Siouan	Crow, Dakota, Omaha
Salishan	Squamish, Shuswap
Uto-Aztecan	Shoshone, Hopi, Nahuatl
Oto-Manguean	Otomi, Mixtecan, Zapotecan
Mayan	Yucatecan, Tzeltal, Quiche
Chibchan	Cuna
Carib	Galibi
Arawakan	Arawak, Island Carib
Tucanoan	Tucano, Basarano
Tupi	Guarani
Gê Chavante	
Panoan	Cashinahua
Quechua	
Aymara	

ample, theorized that with the shift from kin-based to territorially based societies there was a parallel change in the law affecting persons from status to contract. Similarly in DURKHEIM's (1933) evolutionary schema, "primitive" societies held together by a MECHANICAL SOLIDARITY (the sameness of all constituent members) were characterized by repressive, punitive law that maintained cohesion, while complex societies organized by an ORGANIC SOLIDARITY (different and specialized members, but all interdependent) had restitutive law administered by specialized tribunals and functionaries. Although these theories proved empirically wrong, their tendency to link civilization with the form of law has affected subsequent debates within anthropology about how to define law and whether all societies have it.

During the early twentieth century, two major schools of thought developed on the definition of law. One defined law in terms of institutions that required socially authoritative mechanisms for enforcing rules through the imposition of SANCTIONS.

RADCLIFFE-BROWN pioneered this perspective, defining law as "social control through the systematic application of the force of politically organized society" (1933: 202). Under this definition, all societies have customs and sanctions, but not all societies have law. Hoebel defined law more broadly, but also within an institutional context, as "the legitimate use of physical coercion by a socially authorized agent" (1954: 26). Critics of this view of law have argued that it is based on Western conceptions (John Comaroff & Roberts 1981: 6–7).

A second school of thought, following MALINOWSKI (1926), defined law in functional terms, identifying it with a broad range of social processes that produced social conformity and order by pressure and by inducement. Reciprocity was a fundamental mechanism for maintaining social control. Under this definition, every society has law. Critics of this view have contended that defining law merely as social control is too broad and includes practices such as gossip, OSTRACISM, and nicknaming that are not lawlike (Redfield 1964; S. Moore 1970). This debate eventually became so sterile, however, that it was largely abandoned rather than conclusively resolved (Nader 1969).

From the 1970s anthropologists turned their attention from defining law and cataloguing rules to studying the processes by which conflicts are handled and resolutions achieved. This approach grew out of Llewelyn and Hoebel's (1941) earlier analysis of the three meanings of rule: as abstract principle, as actual behavior, and as principle abstracted from legal decisions in cases of hitch or trouble. Much of LEGAL ANTHROPOLOGY has adopted the third definition and turned to the study of processes rather than rules (Nader & Todd 1978; see also CONFLICT RESOLUTION). This can be seen particularly among those researchers who have advocated a processual paradigm, an approach that uses extended case studies and foregrounds the perspective of the litigants rather than that of the judges. Here the meaning and relevance of rules is negotiated in disputes, but although rules are negotiable, behavior is nevertheless rule-governed; rules create a normative repertoire that is central to the arguments and decisions in the dispute process (John Comaroff & Roberts 1981).

A more recent trend in the study of law has been the analysis of the conditions of legal pluralism, where two or more legal systems coexist in the same social field (S. Moore 1973; Merry 1988). Initially described in cases where a colonial power superimposed a European legal system on an existing indigenous system, legal pluralism is now understood as a fundamental characteristic of all legal systems. In advanced capitalist states as well as colonial and postcolonial states, multiple legal systems coexist, redefining and affecting the operation of one another while retaining distinctive normative codes and practices of judging and punishing (Macaulay 1986; S. Moore 1986a; Merry 1992).

Anthropologists have also explored the relationship between law and CULTURE, viewing law as constitutive of cultural practices and itself defined by culture (Rosen 1989; C. Geertz 1983). Consequently, analyzing the legal system of a society provides a way of understanding its fundamental value systems and normative orders. Law defines identities such as citizen and criminal and establishes rules for social ordering. The law also provides a rich vocabulary for describing and legitimating relationships of unequal power. At the same time, the language of law offers a fertile set of categories and avenues for forms of resistance. Law is now seen as fundamentally constitutive of social life. At the same time, what law is and does is the result of complex social processes that define, implement, circumscribe, and transform the texts of law into myriad everyday practices.   SEM

See also GOVERNMENT, POLITICAL ANTHROPOLOGY

further reading Jane Collier 1973; Gluckman 1955a; S. Moore 1986b; Pospisil 1971; Starr & Collier 1989

Leach, Edmund R. (1910–88)

Sir Edmund R. Leach was originally trained in mathematics and mechanical engineering at Cambridge. He became interested in anthropology while working in the early 1930s as an engineer in China and the Philippines. In the late 1930s Leach entered graduate school in social anthropology at the London School of Economics. Although strongly influenced by MALINOWSKI, he was molded more by Raymond FIRTH, who served as his academic mentor.

Leach's first field experience was with the Kurds in what is today Iraq. Just before the outbreak of World War II, he embarked on a field trip to upper Burma. In 1939–40 he spent nine months in the Kachin village of Hpalang, located east of Bhamo in northeastern Burma. In October 1940 he assumed active duty as an officer with the British Burmese army and was posted to Maymyo, just north of Mandalay. In Maymyo he completed a draft of a monograph on the Kachin but lost the typescript along with all his notes, photographs, and papers when the Japanese conquered Burma in 1942.

Leach worked for the remainder of the war to organize resistance against the Japanese among the hill peoples of upper Burma. He later observed that his experience with peoples throughout the Kachin Hills gave him an understanding of cultural and linguistic variation in the region he would not have had if his work had been restricted to a single village.

After the war, Leach returned to the LSE, where he wrote a dissertation based on library and archival research as well as his remembered experiences. After finishing his doctorate, he was introduced to French STRUCTURALISM as presented in Lévi-Strauss's 1949 publication of *Les structures élémentaires de la parenté* (Lévi-Strauss 1969a). Up to this point, Leach's theoretical orientation had been shaped by a materialism derived from his previous training as an engineer and his subsequent study of economic anthropology under Firth, and by the structural FUNCTIONAL-ISM of Malinowski. The addition of LÉVI-STRAUSS's structuralism was to give Leach's thought its distinctive cast.

In light of the new approach he had developed, Leach rethought his dissertation project. The result was *Political systems of highland Burma* (1954). Central to his argument in this book is the assumption that the language of myth and ritual entails "statement[s] about the social order" (p. 14). The anthropologist then seeks to interpret these statements in order to analyze the structures that underlie the social action one observes or learns about from historical sources. In a break with the dominant structural functionalism of the time, Leach cautioned that in making the move between the "poetic and ambiguous" language of MYTH and RITUAL to the "precise" and "technical" language of the anthropologist one should avoid imposing "a specious rigidity and symmetry" on "real life situations" (ibid.: 106). This warning notwithstanding, Leach adopted the view of Marcel MAUSS that underneath the "state of flux" that one encounters in real life there is a underlying "totality" and that "in order to describe this totality it is necessary to represent the system *as if* it were stable and coherent" (ibid.: 63). Thus, while emphasizing the importance of taking a long historical view, he still aligns himself with structural functionalism in a search for underlying continuities rather than for cultural contradictions and social

tensions that lead to fundamental shifts in the ways people think about the social order.

The lasting legacy of *Political systems of highland Burma* lies less in Leach's version of structural functionalism than in his successful challenge to what he termed "the ordinary ethnographic conventions as to what constitutes *a* culture or *a* tribe" (ibid.: 281). Leach demonstrated that the ethnonym "Kachin" points not to some homogenous cultural isolate but to peoples who speak diverse languages and follow different customs. These peoples possess a common political structure because they have adapted to the same upland environments and especially to the same political power in the lowlands. In his attention to how the Kachin must be understood not as a distinct society with a distinct culture but as the product of political relationships to other peoples, Leach foreshadowed subsequent anthropological interest in what came to be termed "ETHNICITY."

The politics of postcolonial Burma prevented Leach ever returning to undertake further fieldwork in that country. In the 1950s he undertook a new field project in Sri Lanka (then Ceylon) that resulted in a study that was economic rather than political in focus. Although *Pul Eliya: a village in Ceylon* (1961a) is an important work for those specializing on Sri Lanka, it has not had the theoretical impact of *Political systems of highland Burma*.

In subsequent years, Leach became an arm-chair anthropologist, devoting his attentions to the study of myth – especially the myths of the Christian tradition. Although Leach sought through these studies to develop a distinctive form of structuralism (see Leach 1976 for his most sustained statement of his structuralism), he himself grew skeptical of anthropological studies that were not based on FIELDWORK, what he had once called "the essential core of social anthropology" (Leach 1961b: 1). The model for fieldwork-based ETHNOG-RAPHY he bequeathed to anthropology remains his study of the "Kachin."   CK

legal anthropology Anthropological studies of law have been conducted within historical and cross-cultural frameworks and have contributed to the development of evolutionary, correlational, and ethnographic theories of social and cultural control. Among eighteenth-century European intellectuals the idea of LAW as universal was common. Nineteenth-century anthropologists, though armchair speculators, first began to document the differences between Western and non-Western law. In 1861, Sir Henry MAINE examined materials from Europe and India, arguing that changing relations in law (from status to contract) were the result of shifts from kinship-based societies to territorially organized societies. Later researchers, focusing on dominant modes of subsistence, argued that human societies could be scaled along a progressive sequence of legal systems from self-help to penal or compensatory sanctions. For example, Hobhouse (1906) correlated level of economy with types of law, while DURKHEIM (1933) associated sanctioning patterns with degrees of societal integration, repressive law in primitive societies being progressively replaced by restitutive law in civilized ones.

MALINOWSKI (1926) used direct ethnographic field observations to question widespread myths about law and order among preliterate peoples. He called attention to the important connection between social control and social relations, foreshadowing a generation of anthropological research on how order could be achieved in societies lacking central authority, codes, and constables. RADCLIFFE-BROWN (1933: 202) employed a more jurisprudential approach, making use of Roscoe Pound's definition of law as "social control through the systematic application of the force of politically organized society." By defining law in terms of organized legal sanctions, Radcliffe-Brown concluded that in some simpler societies there was no law.

Henceforth whether all societies had law became a hotly debated topic (Pospisil 1958). If law was defined in terms of politically organized authority, then not all societies had law. If law was defined as "most processes of social control," then all societies did have law, but social control became synonymous with law. Today most anthropologists do not seek to define law either so narrowly or universally. For purposes of analysis, they increasingly report data in the categories used by the people studied or in the analytic categories of the social scientist. Debate continues over whether Western jurisprudence is itself a folk or an analytic system.

Cultural diversity

In analyzing ethnographic diversity, anthropologists often characterized specific societies by their dominant legal procedures. Reports were punctuated with terms that encapsulated such idiosyncratic procedures: "Crossers" functioned as a double negotiating team among the Yurok of California (Kroeber 1925: 20–53); "go-betweens" mediated problems between families for a fee among the Ifugao of northern Luzon (Barton 1919); and Eskimos conducted "song duels" to bring serious disputes before a public jury (Hoebel 1954).

The discovery of such diversity led anthropologists to classify societies along several dimensions: economic, relational, procedural, and political. In the economic domain, distinctions were recognized between hunter–gatherers, nomads, horticulturists, agriculturists, and industrial societies. In the relational field, distinctions were recognized between simplex and multiplex relations and between continuing and noncontinuing relations. In the procedural domain, distinctions were based on the presence or absence of a third party and by the way unilateral behaviors were excluded. In the political realm, stateless societies were contrasted with states that had centralized authority. In these comparative studies, however, the discrete units themselves became problematic.

As the ethnographic detail improved, description became less a matter of contrast with Western notions and more one of understanding indigenous systems of social control in their specific context (Bohannan 1957), or of understanding the legal process as social and cultural control, whether internal or external to the peoples studied. Earlier broad generalizations correlating economic systems with social control mechanisms were challenged by the varieties of dispute-handling practices among similar subsistence strategies. For example, some hunting and gathering groups like the

!Kung San of the Kalahari Desert deal with disputes in a relatively peaceful way, whereas others like the Eskimos seem to regulate violence with violence (Gulliver 1979). Agricultural groups like the Shia Moslems of southern Lebanon have not developed third parties to handle village-wide problems while others like the Mexican Zapotec have developed courts (Nader 1965). Variations in dispute processing were found in agricultural societies such as those between the Jale of New Guinea, who quickly escalate to fighting, and the Zapotec of Mexico, who organize talk-directed settlement (Koch 1974; Nader 1990). The otherwise notable work of E. A. Hoebel (1954), which linked legal complexity to livelihood patterns, proved to be of limited use in explaining these differences.

The shift from analyzing systems of social control to systems of disputing, from positive inducement to handling norm violation after the fact, was a predictable result of specialization and narrowing of the subject matter. Whereas Malinowski (1926) had deliberately formulated a wide-angle framework for understanding law in society, Llewelyn and Hoebel shifted the focus to public forums. Llewelyn and Hoebel's work on the Cheyenne (1941) marked the beginning of many years of concentration on the "trouble case" approach. Using the case method, Max GLUCKMAN (1955a) developed a relational theory of decision making that argued if one could determine the nature of the social relationships between parties to a dispute, one could predict the procedure that would be employed in the decision-making process. His hypothesis was that the nature of relationships imposed restraints on the settlement process. The extended case method became central to ethnographic research on law and social control during the 1960s and served to highlight the activity of different mechanisms within the same society. Shame, ridicule, conflicting loyalties, fighting, in addition to negotiation, mediation, arbitration, and adjudication were accorded equal weight in field studies (Epstein 1974). Considerations of strategy pointed to the choices open to the parties involved. Analyses stylized by dominant patterns were re-placed with more elastic, more contextual models. Later the notion of power was linked to strategy and justice motive.

The ethnography of law

The theoretical work of Colson (1953), Barth (1966), F. Bailey (1957), and V. TURNER (1957) infused a partially static model with process modeling. But even before the shift to process appeared, an ethnography of law emerged that broadened the vision to include descriptions in which legal systems were not autonomous institutions independent and isolated from other institutions in society. It was a call for an ethnography-of-law approach to the study of the disputing process (Nader & Todd 1978). It attempted to describe and explain the processual models found within a society and to avoid caricaturing societies by using only the most salient or accessible means of disputing. The scope of work was delimited by the avenues chosen or developed by litigants themselves, not just the official legal procedure available to them. A user theory of law (Nader 1990) is thereby recognized by the cumulative directional patterns created by its users. As players in a dispute drama, the users are an interesting unit because the concept of strategy is added to third-party decision making. The interaction between the users, and their power relative to one another, become key factors in understanding how the law is made and how it is changed. In such a model the justice motive becomes central in incorporating the perspective of all the parties to a case, an invitation to use history and comparison as adjuncts to the ethnographic method.

Global systems and local law

Although the interest in particular societies may have been a justified response to earlier armchair theories, attention to societies as discrete units eventually provoked a reaction of its own. Anthropological theories had become more static, more correlational, and less concerned with change, even though anthropologists were often studying societies in a state of rapid change engendered by political, religious, and economic colonialism. Confronted by a shrinking world, and with the continuing diffusion of Western legal ideas to colonies and former colonies, anthropologists were forced to move beyond the study of particular societies and return to the examination of those larger patterns of structural change first noticed by earlier scholars such as Maine and Durkheim.

Process and power are indispensable critical variables in a world where disputants may become disempowered, especially in national and global situations where the social and physical distance between litigants is large and disputes are increasingly between strangers of unequal power. Law in face-to-faceless societies, characterized by unequal distribution of power, does not lend itself easily to the small-scale solutions for handling disputes in face-to-face communities. Such inequality often limits case action and anthropologists realized that power, as a concept central to disputing, could not be ignored. The conditions of state law, growing industrialization, and the separation of production from consumption have therefore had effects on dispute resolution as durable as the change from nomadic to agriculturally based societies.

Both historical materials and contemporary observation are useful in critically examining law as an agent of change (Starr & Collier 1989). Research on law and state power illustrates that law is not neutral; rather, it is often politically active, created by and for groups in power (J. Barnes 1961). The more attentive anthropologists become to settings where law or governmental social control reigns, in places where there are fully developed nation-states, the more anthropological studies center around law to the exclusion of other systems of social control. Although the traditional ethnographic studies of particular societies no longer provide a model in such circumstances, the ethnographic perspective may be creatively applied to a dynamic understanding of law in complex societies.

In the 1980s ethnographers developed ethnohistorical models of law that combined history and ethnography within the framework of power structures. An added introspective dimension, and the influence of WORLD-SYSTEM theorists, led to the examination of external forces, of macrostructures, on traditional microstructures

(Chanock 1985). Anthropologists have consistently underestimated the extent to which Western political and religious traditions have structured the social control aspects of law. Researchers now acknowledge and examine the ideological components of dispute processing.

Conclusion
The study of law as a process of control has advanced with the increasing use of law as control. Although law has been used as a means to power and mobility, to exert control over human and natural resources, anthropologists have still to examine functions of law not directly related to control. There are, in legal processes, elements that extend beyond the politics of power and control, that open windows into defining social relationships, that provide entertainment and dramas, that create new rights and remedies and institutions, and that define culture as property.   LN

further reading Greenhouse 1986; Merry 1990; S. Moore 1986a; Rose 1992

leopard-skin chief is a figure among the Nuer of the Sudan whose authority is at once political and religious, who has the authority to mediate disputes that might otherwise lead to blood feuds. The leopard-skin chief, also known as a leopard-skin priest, wears a leopard pelt as his badge of office (Greuel 1971). His role has been subject to debate, in part because of his seemingly anomalous position as a "leader" in a society portrayed by E. E. EVANS-PRITCHARD (1940) as largely acephalous.
                                           MR

levirate is a rule requiring or permitting a man to marry his deceased brother's wife or wives. This is often seen as a means in patrilineal systems for perpetuating the deceased's descent line in the case where he has died childless. The offspring of a levirate union are then socially defined offspring of the dead brother, and not of their GENITOR.   MR

Lévi-Strauss, Claude (1908–) Perhaps the most intellectually wide-ranging and theoretically daring anthropologist of the modern era, and the one who has had the most influence in philosophical and literary circles, Lévi-Strauss was born in Brussels in 1908 but grew up in Paris. He was a brilliant student with strong political convictions, writing his baccalaureate thesis on the philosophical implications of Marx before taking up a teaching post in the provinces.

Bored with his job, Lévi-Strauss was determined to reconcile his intellectual interests with his desire for adventure, and in 1935 he set off for São Paulo, Brazil to teach sociology at the newly formed University there. Without any formal training in anthropology, but inspired by his reading of American ethnographers, and especially by Robert LOWIE's *Primitive society*, he used his holidays to begin fieldwork with the Bororo and Caduveo tribes, and later conducted research with the Nambikwara – an experience wonderfully evoked in his memoir *Tristes tropiques* (1963c), which remains the best introduction to his elusive literary style – a seductive blend of erudition and intuition.

Lévi-Strauss returned to Paris in 1939 but soon was obliged to migrate to New York, where he taught afternoons in the New School, spent his mornings in the New York Public Library reading ethnographies, and mixed with a remarkable circle of French exiles and American academics in the evening. Especially influential was Roman Jakobson, who introduced Lévi-Strauss to the work of the Prague school of LINGUISTICS. It was with Jakobson's encouragement that he began work on the book that gained him his reputation, *The elementary structures of kinship* (1969a), which he completed in 1947 and presented as his doctoral thesis at the Sorbonne.

In this seminal piece of STRUCTURALISM, Lévi-Strauss argued that the logical implications of exchanges of "women, goods and words" could reveal "a principle of intelligibility behind an apparently chaotic jumble of arbitrary and irrational practices and beliefs" (Augé 1990: 86). Such a principle would predict transformations occurring when any element is changed, and coherently locate all observable social facts within the deduced systemic model. Lévi-Strauss (1963a) followed *Elementary structures* with demonstrations that patterns of exchange underlie such disparate cultural realms as spatial arrangement, economics, political hierarchy, totemism, art, and ritual. Comparisons were then undertaken to relate cross-cultural differences in exchange patterns to contrasts in social organization, mode of production, and ecology.

His publications won him wide recognition, and in 1959, sponsored by his close friend Merleau-Ponty, he was elected to the Collège de France as the first named chair in anthropology, and was voted into the Académie Française in 1973. He remained at the Collège throughout his career, directing a productive team of graduate students and beginning the journal *L'Homme* while simultaneously authoring a prodigious string of publications.

The appearance in France of *Totemism* (1963b) and *The savage mind* (1966) in 1962 marked a shift in his work away from kinship analysis and toward the study of religious representations and myth – an effort that would culminate in the massive four-volume *Mythologiques: introduction to a science of mythology* (1969–81). His work on MYTH had a great impact on non-anthropologists – especially in the literary world, where it was seen as heralding a new mode of textual analysis – though Lévi-Strauss did not necessarily approve of his literary disciples, any more than he approved of many of his would-be anthropological followers, whom he often scolded for misrepresenting his theories.

Opponents of structuralism soon recognized that a great problem of Lévi-Strauss's application of his brand of analysis to the study of myth was that the elements making up a unit of meaning lack the natural character of a PHONEME, and issue instead from the mind of the analyst. Lévi-Strauss tried to escape accusations of solipsism by arguing that all myth necessarily confronts some fundamental quandary within a particular social formation. Adversaries of the new method were not convinced. They deplored structuralism's apparent indifference to history and its restrictive model for consciousness. The validity Lévi-Strauss claimed for his analysis of myth was further undermined by alternative readings that seemed equally convincing – at least to structuralism's many enemies, who argued that the "science of myth" was actually an artifact of Lévi-Strauss's own creative imagination. And it certainly is true that Lévi-Strauss's work has always had a strong aesthetic element. After all, many of his closest friends were artists and he himself was the son of a painter, giving him perhaps a special ability not only to explicate artistic form (*The way of the masks* 1982) but also to incorporate into his writing artistic techniques of collage, abrupt juxtaposition (*The savage mind* 1966) and musical composition (*The raw and the cooked* 1969b).

However, whatever the aesthetic impact of his work, Lévi-Strauss always believed himself to be working toward a science that could link up mind and nature, using his own formidable generalizing capacity to reduce empirical differences and to reveal the commonalties that he thought must lie beneath the jumble of surface reality. It is ironic that Lévi-Strauss, who has wryly commented on his own "lack of imagination" (Lévi-Strauss & Eribon 1991: 22) and who wished to discover a universal theory of mind, has in fact at least partially inspired the modern turn toward subjectivity – a movement he deeply deplored.

In response to the new wave of interpretive anthropology, Lévi-Strauss retreated from making any global claims and distanced himself from the fray. Serene in his faith in the illusion of progress and the limits of human knowledge, he increasingly defined himself as an intellectual craftsman struggling to discover patterns in a recalcitrant world of dizzying uncertainty.　CL
further reading Barbossa de Almeida 1990; Charbonnier 1969; Hayes & Hayes 1970; Kurzweil 1980; LaPointe & LaPointe 1977; E. Leach 1970; Mehlman 1974; Pace 1983; Rosman & Rubel 1971

life cycle is the schedule of stages and roles a person should pass through in a normal human career and is culture's way of regulating human growth and change.

In the biological life cycle a new phase is signaled by changes in the individual organism. Body change may be one criterion for promotion to the next stage, but the chief measure is an actor's readiness to play new parts in society's dramas. Sexual maturity alone does not qualify a man for marriage in many societies, he must also have demonstrated his ability to support a HOUSEHOLD. Cultural schedules build on the person as social actor. As Jules Henry (1973) put it, people's social weight can be measured by their "capacity to be missed."

The term "life cycle" is extended loosely to other repetitive sequences in human affairs. Examples are the family life cycle or DEVELOPMENTAL CYCLE, the life cycle of fads, and the life cycle theories of the rise-and-fall of great civilizations. Such cycles may have no obvious connection with biological process, but visions of a "mature economy" or "senescent civilization" can be rhetorically seductive.

Cultural schedules help make social action more predictable by designating sequences of roles and rates of promotion through them as natural or desirable. For example, members of a society can readily judge when a person has contracted – by local standards – a "late marriage" or suffered an "early death." In actuality few people will realize a full career: some will not live long enough to pass through every stage; others will not be promoted at the right times or will prove unable to fill an expected role. But by providing a vision of normality the schedules dampen the turbulent waves of individuals moving through the system.

These timetables are a restraint on our conduct as persons but they also are a resource. They pressure us to move along "on time." When Japanese talk about the timing of marriage, for example, they may jokingly refer to women as "Christmas Cakes" and men as "New Year's Noodles": stale leftovers if not married by ages 25 and 31, respectively. But the schedules promise as well as threaten. They suggest that those who grow and mature correctly will be rewarded with a full cycle of human experience that culminates in wisdom and death at a ripe old age.

Cultural schedules differ in terms of defining the totality of the life cycle. For some it is only a shallow curve of change, for others a full circle that closes upon itself, and in others even an endless recycling of human substance in a continuing process of REINCARNATION. They also differ in how they define life. Most schedules recognize the person as a social entity from some time before birth until well after DEATH. Popular phrasing in the United States says that life runs "from cradle to grave." But some fetuses, cadavers, and dead owners of PROPERTY are social entities in the legal system of the United States. They may not be "full" persons, but they have particular rights enforceable by others or by the state. The moment when life ends or begins can become an issue disputed bitterly, as in current American battles over abortion and euthanasia.

Anthropologists have long made use of life-cycle schedules when portraying cultural systems for timing human events. Ethnographic reports routinely include a sketch of the ideal timetable and sometimes of its variants for males and females, elites and commoners. Deeper investigation and analysis, however, was usually limited to two topics, RITES OF PASSAGE (particularly in the works of Victor TURNER [1969] and Arnold van GENNEP [1960]) and SOCIALIZATION. For all their accomplishments both lines of inquiry have shared the people-processing bias inherent in definitions of the life cycle as a fabric of normative constraint.

By about 1970 anthropologists were shaking off this narrower approach to the currents of human life. Since then a new research frontier has opened up all across the biographical timelines of human existence (Plath 1987), and on this frontier anthropologists are joined by scholars from an array of social and medical sciences (Lock 1991). The term "life-course studies" is often applied to this arena of interest as a way of indicating that human growth, AGING, and health are fluid phenomena that cannot be explained adequately by any single linear sequence of stages (Hagestad 1990). Even a supposedly "simple" society has a number of timetables and they interact in contingent ways (A. Moore 1973; Roth 1963).

At the end of the twentieth century anthropology is setting aside its linear view of human ontogeny, in much the same way that, early in the century, it questioned its linear view of human phylogeny.

DWP

further reading Myerhoff 1978; Myerhoff & Simic 1978; Plath 1980

life expectancy *See* REPRODUCTION

life history is the biographical study of individual people. Edward SAPIR (1938) long ago noted that what anthropologists construct as CULTURE often fails to do justice to the experience of people who live cultural lives. The life history offers one way of relating actual people to culture, offering insight into the ways their lives are grounded in culture, and into the way in which culture is grounded in individual lives, experience, and agency. At their best, biographical and autobiographical accounts offer the insider's point of view at its most intimate and concrete.

A particular individual's life history may have little of "history" in it, in the sense that it records verifiable facts about what actually happened in a person's life. Nor should such testimony be accepted uncritically as revealing what people actually thought, felt, or did during their life careers. For however objective life accounts appear, memory and self-narrative invariably involve some degree of distortion and interpretation. Moreover, life stories always present a point of view and often incorporate aspects of fantasy or belief that cannot easily be corroborated. Indeed, in some cases, what individuals take as the central realities of their lives may seem impossible or unreal to the anthropologist. Crapanzano (1980) grappled with these issues in his portrait of Tuhami, a Moroccan tile-maker. Tuhami's narratives violate his interlocutor's sense of reality and consistency; the women he reports encountering may or may not be emanations of the demoness to whom he is married (Langness & Frank 1981).

Such reservations do not invalidate the significance of the life-history material – it may be highly illuminating when interpreted in ways sensitive to individuals and their cultural existence. Although a life history without corroboration cannot be accepted uncritically as a literal transcript of life events, it may reveal a personal world of meanings that can then be placed in cultural context.

What counts as personal history or the meaning of a life varies cross-culturally. So do the means of expressing life histories and personal meanings. Thus a researcher recording a life account must be sensitive to the way in which elements of culture such as symbols, concepts of the person, narrative styles, subsistence systems, political structures, gender roles, or the micropolitics of everyday life mediate and shape the way people experience, understand, and narrate their own lives (Keesing 1985). Life experience is shaped by an individual's place in a society, by the cultural vicissitudes of child development, by cultural definitions of self. And the way life experience becomes a life narrative is shaped by local conventions of narrative and communicative practices, by the encounter with an interlocutor, and by an individual's own agency, imagination, and verbal skills.

Recognizing the cultural aspects of life stories does not mean that the researcher need neglect more-or-less universal or transcultural aspects of lives. A life history always contains universal aspects common to all people, elements that are embedded in the culture of which they are a part, as well as the unique elements of the individual's own existence: a combination that has led to the enduring popularity of this form of narrative. Although biographical accounts vary in terms of which elements are stressed, life histories in anthropology often explore the social context of lives, as in James Freeman's (1979) life history of an Indian untouchable, or Blanca Muratorio's (1991) interweaving of life history with social history in her account of a Napo Runa elder of the Ecuadorian Amazon. Other studies focus more on the incorporation of cultural meaning into personal experience in ways that constitute lived worlds, as in Obeyesekere's (1981) psychobiographical interpretations of cases of spirit possession.   SP
See also HUMANISTIC ANTHROPOLOGY, PSYCHOLOGICAL ANTHROPOLOGY
further reading Radin 1926; Roy 1975; Shostak 1981; Watson & Watson-Franke 1985

liminality Humorously but accurately defined as the ambiguous state of being between states of being, the concept of liminality first came to anthropologists' attention through the work of the Dutch ethnographer and folklorist Arnold van GENNEP, a contemporary of DURKHEIM. Van Gennep's research led him to postulate a universal pattern within the ritual RITES OF PASSAGE marking the progress of an initiate from one status to another. This movement, van Gennep (1960) argued, is not abrupt, but requires a mediating period of "liminality."

Victor TURNER (1969, 1974) made great use of this concept in his research, contending that the liminal state was not simply a twilight moment in ritual transformations, but was also a period of special and dangerous power, which had to be constrained and channeled to protect the social order. Yet such moments were required both to complete the ritual process and to reinvigorate the culture itself.

Other, more structurally oriented anthropologists, such as Mary DOUGLAS (1966) and Edmund LEACH (1976), saw liminality as the mediating element between contrasting structural positions, associated with what Douglas called "matter out of place." Like Turner, these theorists too saw liminality as a source of dangerous power, and analyzed the ways in which various cultures conceptualized, controlled, or tolerated liminal situations.

One problem with liminality was deciding when a state was indeed liminal – the term, like the situation it described, tended to spread beyond definitional boundaries. But the ambiguity of ambiguity has its own advantages in social theory, and liminality remains a productive concept in anthropology.   CL
See also PURITY/POLLUTION, RITUAL, SYMBOLIC ANTHROPOLOGY

lineages are unilineal descent groups organized on the basis of common descent from a known ancestor. If that descent is traced in the male line it is called a "patrilineage"; if in the female line, a "matrilineage".   MR

lineal kinship system *See* ESKIMO KINSHIP SYSTEMS

linguistics and anthropology Anthropology and linguistics share a common intellectual origin in nineteenth-century scholarship. The impetus that prompted the earliest archaeologists to look for civilizational origins in Greece, early folklorists to look for the origins of culture in folktales and common memory, and the first armchair cultural anthropologist to look for the origins of human customs through comparison of groups of human beings also prompted the earliest linguistic inquiries.

There was considerable overlap in these processes. The "discovery" of Sanskrit by the British civil servant and intellectual Sir William Jones in the late eighteenth century set the stage for intensive work in comparative HISTORICAL LINGUISTICS that continues to the present day. Jacob Grimm was not only a pioneering folklorist, but the pivotal figure in nineteenth-century linguistics through his discovery of regularities in consonantal shifts between different branches of Indo-European languages over historical time. His formulation, called today "Grimm's Law," was not only the basis for modern linguistics, but also one of the formative concepts leading to twentieth-century STRUCTURALISM, particularly as elaborated in the work of Ferdinand de Saussure (1959), perhaps the most influential linguist of the twentieth century. The scholarly tradition that followed developments in historical linguistics in the Old World and Europe generally led to the development of formal linguistics as taught today in most university departments of linguistics.

American linguistic anthropology: early roots

Intellectual interest in Native American languages dates from the very earliest colonizing efforts in North America. Roger Williams, founder of Rhode Island, compiled a small dictionary of Narragansett. In the nineteenth century, this continuing

US governmental responsibility for tribal peoples led to the writing of a large number of studies by the Bureau of American Ethnology on tribal groups throughout the Americas, including many grammars, dictionaries, and compilations of folkloric material in original languages.

Linguistics was arguably introduced into the formal study of anthropology by Franz BOAS. Boas was interested in linguistics for a number of reasons. First, as a result of his early work in the Arctic, he made attempts to learn Inuit and found it an exceptionally subtle and complex language. Later this insight was incorporated into his antievolutionary theoretical perspective, HISTORICAL PARTICULARISM. He separated out the concepts of RACE, LANGUAGE, and CULTURE, maintaining that they were independent of each other. He maintained that any human was capable of learning any language, and assimilating any cultural tradition. Furthermore, different societies might have some aspects of their culture that were highly developed and others that were simple relative to other world societies. Thus the idea that a society might be "primitive" in all ways – linguistically, culturally, and biologically – because it was evolutionarily backward was rejected. Each society was seen by Boas to develop independently according to its own particular adaptive pattern to its physical and social environment. Language too was seen as reflective of this general adaptive pattern. Boas's views formed the basis for the doctrine of *linguistic relativism*, later elaborated upon by his students, whereby no human language can be seen as superior to any other in terms of its ability to meet human needs.

Boas's second reason for considering linguistics important for the study of anthropology had to do with his feeling that linguistic study was able to provide deep insight into the workings of the human mind without the need for judgments on the part of informants. By eliciting data from native speakers, a linguist could build a model for the functioning of language of which the speaker himself or herself was unaware. This avoided the "secondary rationalizations" that cultural anthropologists had to deal with in eliciting information from informants about politics, religion, economics, kinship, and other social institutions. As ephemeral and programmatic as these ideas concerning language were, they would set the agenda for anthropological linguistics for the balance of the century, since they were elaborated by Boas's students.

1920–50: Sapir, Whorf, and Malinowski

The most famous linguistic anthropologist to study with Boas was Edward SAPIR. Although Sapir did not concern himself exclusively with linguistic research, it constituted the bulk of his work, and remains the body of his anthropological research for which he is best known.

Sapir's interest in language was wide ranging. He was fascinated by both psychological and cultural aspects of language functioning. The newly emerging concept of the "PHONEME" was of special interest to him, and his seminal paper "The psychological reality of the phoneme" (1933) is an unsurpassed study showing that the phoneme is not just a theoretical fiction created by linguistic analysts, but represents a cognitive construct that is so strong that it leads individuals to assert the existence of sounds that are not present and deny the existence of sounds that are present. In another paper, "A study in phonetic symbolism" (1929b), he investigated the relationship between pure sounds and people's semantic associations with them. Taking nonsense syllables, Sapir was able to show that people associate high vowels with small sensory phenomena and low vowels with large phenomena. Only recently have acoustic phoneticians returned to this problem in investigating the psychoacoustic abilities of individuals to judge the length of the vocal tract of other speakers based solely on the sound of their voices.

Sapir also did pioneering work in language and GENDER, historical linguistics, PSYCHOLINGUISTICS, and in the study of a number of native American languages. However, he is best known for his contributions to what later became known as "the WHORFIAN HYPOTHESIS," also known as "the Sapir–Whorf hypothesis." Sapir maintained that language was "the symbolic guide to culture." In several seminal articles, the most important of which may be "The grammarian and his language" (1924), he developed the theme that language serves as a filter through which the world is constructed for purposes of communication.

This work was carried forward by Sapir's student Benjamin Lee Whorf (1956), who devoted much of his research to the study of Hopi. Whorf took Sapir's notion of language's interpenetration with culture to a much stronger formulation. Whorf's writings can be interpreted as concluding that language is deterministic of thought. Grammatical structures were seen not just as tools for describing the world, they were seen as templates for thought itself. To be sure, Whorf's views on this matter became stronger throughout his life, and are the most extreme in his posthumously published writings. The formulation of the Sapir–Whorf hypothesis was not undertaken by either Sapir or Whorf, but by one of Whorf's students, Harry Hoijer.

Aside from their views on language and thought, Sapir and Whorf were both exemplary representatives of the dominant activity in American anthropological linguistics during the period 1920–60: descriptive studies of Native American languages. This work focused largely on studies in phonology and morphology. Studies of syntactic structures and semantics were perfunctory.

During this same period in England a parallel interest in linguistics in anthropology was developed from an unexpected source: the well-known social anthropologist Bronislaw MALINOWSKI. Malinowski's work in the Trobriand Islands was becoming well known. In his study *Coral gardens and their magic* (1935), Malinowski included an extensive essay on language as an introduction to the second volume of the work. In this he addressed the problem of TRANSLATION, taking as his principal problem the issue of the translation of magical formulas. Magical formulas cannot really be translated, he maintained. They have no comprehensible semantic content. They do, however, accomplish cultural work within Trobriand society. They are therefore functionally situated. In order to "translate" such material, the ethnographer must provide a complete explanatory contextualization for the material. Otherwise it can make no sense. This functional theory of linguistics engendered a small, but active, British school of linguistic anthropology, whose principal exponents were the linguist J. R. Firth, and later Edwin Ardener.

1950–70: a period of transition
In the late 1950s and the 1960s a number of linguists and linguistically oriented cultural anthropologists collaborated on a linguistically based methodology called variously "ethnographic semantics," "the NEW ETHNOGRAPHY," and most commonly "ETHNOSCIENCE." Basing their work loosely on the Sapir–Whorf formulations, the most enthusiastic of these researchers maintained that if an ethnographic researcher could understand the logic of categorization used by people under ethnographic study, it would be possible to understand the cognitive processes underlying their cultural behavior (see CLASSIFICATION). The more extreme cognitive claims for ethnoscience were quickly called into question (Burling 1964), but the technique of ferreting out the logic of categorization proved useful for the understanding of specific domains of cultural activity. ETHNOBOTANY, ETHNOZOOLOGY, and the comparative study of color categorization (Berlin & Kay 1969) proved to be enduring lines of research.

An important collateral development growing out of structural-linguistic study was the elaboration of markedness theory by Joseph Greenberg (1966). Drawing from the phonological studies of the formal linguists of the Prague school of the 1930s, Greenberg showed that some categories of linguistic phenomena are more "marked" vis-à-vis other categories. The "unmarked" member of a pair is more general, and includes reference to a whole category of phenomenon as well as to a specific subcategory of that phenomenon. The "marked" member refers exclusively to a specific subcategory. Thus "cow" is unmarked vis-à-vis "bull," which is marked, because the former refers both to the general category of the animal and to the female, whereas

the latter refers only to the male member of the species. Greenberg showed that these distinctions pervade all formal grammatical systems, as well as other semantic domains, such as KINSHIP.

In 1957 Noam Chomsky published his revolutionary work *Syntactic structures*, and from this point onward linguistic anthropology began to diverge in its purpose and activity from linguistics as an academic discipline. Chomsky's theoretical orientation took linguists away from the descriptive study of phonology and morphology and focused activity on syntax as the central formal structure of language. Although it has been modified considerably since 1957, Chomsky's rule-based TRANSFORMATIONAL-GENERATIVE GRAMMAR has been the basic paradigm within which formal linguists have worked. Basing much of their work on the exploration of intuitive understanding of language structures, and often working only with English, formal linguists largely abandoned the practice of linguistic fieldwork. Ultimately, under Chomsky's direction, formal linguistics saw itself as a branch of cognitive science. The syntactic structures detected by linguists would, Chomsky believed, be shown to be direct emanations of the neural structures of the brain.

Anthropological linguists began during the same period to direct their work away from the study of formal linguistic structures and toward the study of language use in social and cultural context. Work in PHONOLOGY and morphology was largely directed toward the investigation of historical interconnections between language groups.

One important development was a growing interest in the investigation of language as a "uniquely human" phenomenon. Charles Hockett (1966) formulated a series of "pattern variables" to delineate the principal characteristics of human language (see COMMUNICATION). Hockett's list was widely adopted not only by anthropologists, but also by formal linguists and psychologists. In the 1970s it was used as a kind of checklist to measure the linguistic abilities of chimpanzees, who were being taught to communicate with humans using American Sign Language and other nonverbal techniques. Hockett's research also led him to speculate on the behavioral origins of human speech. This work was later carried forward by a small number of biological anthropologists, including Philip Lieberman (1984, 1991), and was supplemented by work among the animal psychologists looking at chimpanzee communication.

1970–85: sociolinguistics and the ethnography of communication

The period 1970–1990 saw anthropological linguistics concerned with the development of more sophisticated models for the interaction of language and social life. SOCIOLINGUISTICS, which had begun in the 1950s, was one important area of new activity embraced by anthropological linguistics. This later developed into a new activity called "the ethnography of communication" by Dell Hymes and John Gumperz, two of the pioneers in the field (see Hymes 1974).

Sociolinguistics came to be called by Hymes "socially realistic linguistics," since it dealt with language as it was found in the structures of social life. Much of sociolinguistics consists of seeing variation in the language forms of a particular community and showing how that variation correlates with, or is produced by, social and cultural divisions and dynamics in the community. These divisions can be based on gender, ETHNICITY, CLASS differences, or any other culturally salient division within the community. Variation can be a property of the language of a given social division (e.g., male vs. female speech, or the different vocabularies exhibited by different generations). It can also be produced by social processes that govern relations within and between divisions. Such factors as group solidarity in the face of external challenges, desire for prestige, and interdivisional conflict can manifest themselves in linguistic behavior that contributes to the variability seen within the community.

The ethnography of communication was first seen as a form of sociolinguistics, but it quickly took on a life of its own. Termed "socially constituted linguistics" by Hymes, the ethnography of communication deals with the ethnographic study of speech and language in its social and cultural setting.

In a manner reminiscent of Malinowski, language is viewed not just as a form, but also as a dynamic behavior. This "functional" linguistics shows what language does in social life. To this end, each society can be shown to have its own unique cultural pattern of language use that can be accounted for by looking at its interrelationship with other cultural institutions.

1985–present: discourse and expressive communication

It was not long before linguistic anthropologists began to realize that to study language in its full cultural context, it was necessary to study highly complex linguistic behaviors. These became known widely under the general rubric of "DISCOURSE." John Gumperz (1982), one of the pioneers in this area of study, pointed out that the careful scientific study of discourse would have been impossible if technology in the form of audio and video recorders had not been available when they were. Indeed, the study of discourse processes involves painstaking recording, transcription, and analysis of verbal interaction that would have been impossible in Sapir's day.

Discourse structures are seen to be highly patterned, with beginnings, endings, transitions, and episodic structures (see Goffman 1981; Silverstein & Urban 1996). They are, moreover, collaborative in their production. Therefore, it is impossible to study speakers apart from hearers in a linguistic event; all persons present are contributing participants, even if they remain silent. Additionally, it can be seen that all participants are not equal in every discourse event. Some participants are conventionally licensed to do more than others in their communicative roles. Discourse allows for the exercise of strategic behavior, so an adroit individual can seize an opportune moment in communication and advance an agenda. Here too, strategic silence may be as effective as strategic verbal behavior.

Within societies different social groups may have different discourse styles. These differences can impede communication between groups even when the individuals involved feel that they "speak the same language." Deborah Tannen (1984, 1990) has been successful in bringing to popular awareness the discourse differences seen between males and females in American society. Jane Hill has likewise investigated the differences in discourse structures in different bilingual Spanish–English communities in the American Southwest (Hill & Hill 1986).

Expressive communications in the form of POETRY, metaphor, and verbal art also constitute important elaborated communication genres in human life. Paul Friedrich (1986) has been a pioneer in the investigation of poetic structures in communicative behavior. Deriving his work in part from a direction suggested in a seminal paper by Roman Jakobson (1960), Friedrich concluded that the creation of poetic structures is a central feature of all linguistic behavior. The study of metaphor and symbols has been important in the study of ritual and religious life, but in this period anthropologists began to see the centrality of the creation of metaphor as a discourse process. Lakoff and Johnson's *Metaphors we live by* (1980) set the stage for other research in this area. James Fernandez's (1986) investigation of tropic structures throughout cultural life bridges the gap between linguistic anthropology and cultural anthropology.

Verbal art in the form of oration, narration, theatrical performance, and spectacle is perhaps the most directed and complex form of discourse for human beings (see Bauman & Briggs 1990; Beeman 1993). Richard Bauman (1977) has written extensively on the properties of verbal art and performative aspects of culture. One of the most interesting aspects of this area of human communication is its "emergent" quality. Of course all communication is to some extent emergent in that its shape and direction is continually modified by ongoing events and participants. However, performance is of special interest because it usually involves a fixed body of material that, despite its fixed character, is still modified by presentational conditions. In short, although it is possible to identify the roles of "performer" and "audience," all participants are in fact cocreators of the piece being performed. Their collaborative effort gives the final form to the work, the nature of which cannot be understood until it is completed. Consequently, every performance is a unique event. Since this is the case, the analysis of a given performance is of less interest than the analysis of the social and communicative processes that engender it.

Anthropology and linguistics in years to come

It seems certain that the mission of linguistic anthropology will remain the exploration of human communicative capacity in all of its forms and varieties. Although analysis of the formal properties of language will play a role in this work, it is not likely to have the central place in the work of linguistic anthropology that it does in linguistics. New technology will bring not only increasingly sophisticated investigative techniques for the study of language in human life, but also will provide for new forms of human communication. Some of these are already being studied by linguistic anthropologists. Computer-mediated communication in particular has taken many forms. Electronic mail (e-mail), direct "chat" via computer, and the use of electronic "bulletin boards" are only a few. Computer and satellite transmission of words and images over the planet has made it possible for people living at great distances to communicate regularly. Many thousands of such electronically constituted "speech communities" based on shared interests have already come into being. The rules for communication via these new channels are now being formulated by the communities that use them and should provide fertile ground for research in the future.   WBe

further reading Lutz & Abu-Lughod 1990

Linton, Ralph (1893–1953) Linton was born in Philadelphia on February 27, 1893. He attended graduate school at the University of Pennsylvania and Columbia, but received his Ph.D. from Harvard in 1925. He taught at the University of Wisconsin from 1928 to 1937, at Columbia (most of the time as chairman) from 1937 to 1946, and Yale from 1946 until his death. His dissertation subject was the material culture of the Marquesas Islands. In 1936 Linton published a general work titled *The study of man,* halfway between a textbook and a theorization of cultural anthropology. In it he described CULTURE as composed of a nested series of elements, traits, trait complexes, and activities. Each of these, in turn, has four qualities: form, meaning, use, and function. The scheme was particularly useful in analyzing the DIFFUSION of trait complexes from one culture to another. Form was easily identifiable, but the meaning of traits could change in a new cultural context, and their use and function modified. Linton was a major ACCULTURATION theorist, one of the team of authors who wrote the influential "Memorandum for the study of acculturation" (Redfield et al. 1936) commissioned by the Social Science Research Council. He noted that individual elements were more frequently borrowed than trait complexes, because less modification was required by the recipient culture. Borrowers typically adopt items whose utility they appreciate, without recognizing the trait complexes in which each is embedded. Tools are more readily comprehended and borrowed than are behavior patterns, which may require sustained contact to be understood and appreciated. The transfer of abstract ideas is even more constrained. Linton (1940) distinguished between the voluntary acceptance of innovations and the kind of "directed culture change" so characteristic of indigenous New World populations confronted with colonial rule by Europeans.

The other axis of Linton's research was the interaction of CULTURE AND PERSONALITY, the result of his participation in Abram Kardiner's seminars on anthropology and psychoanalysis held at the New York Psychoanalytic Institute between 1935 and 1938. The Seminar, with Linton as codirector, was transferred to Columbia as a regular course in 1940. On the basis of comparative data, Kardiner (1939) coined the notion of a "modal personality," which Linton described as a projective system, "that personality configuration which is shared by the bulk of a society's members as a result of early experience which they share in common" (A. Linton & Wagley 1971: 54). True to his methodology of trait complexes, Linton asserted that the

"modal personality for any society can be established directly and objectively by the study of the frequencies of various personality configurations among the society's members" (ibid.: 57). His ideas on the topic were refined in *The cultural background of personality* (1945), where he introduced the concept of "status personalities," responses that vary with social status and are superimposed on modal personality. This was a major departure from Kardiner's Freudian construction of the personality based on "primary" (that is, familial) relations. Linton died in New Haven on December 24, 1953.   TG

literacy   *See* WRITING SYSTEMS

literary anthropology is derived from studies in textual criticism, semiotics, psychoanalysis, hermeneutics, and the phenomenological philosophies of the 1960s and 1970s that championed a postmodern perspective and made literary anthropologists the patrons of POSTMODERNISM in anthropology in the late 1970s and 1980s. Although rarely self-identifying as a school, its major contributors have included James Clifford (1982), Vincent Crapanzano (1992), George Marcus and Michael Fischer (1986), Paul Rabinow (1988), and Renato Rosaldo (1989). The project is indebted to Victor TURNER (1982) and especially Clifford GEERTZ (1973, 1983); Geertz's opinions became something of its Vulgate.

A first canon of literary anthropology is that cultural analysis must proceed as if it were "penetrating" the "literary text," since a people's culture is like "an ensemble of texts" (Geertz 1973: 452, 448). Thus the goal of analysis is not to explain how social and cultural events operate, but to interpret what events – be they discourses, practices, or institutions – mean. CULTURE in such a perspective, in the famous metaphor of Geertz, is the "webs of significance," that is, the meanings, in which humans hang "suspended" (1973: 5). If hermeneutics is the interpretation of meaning, then a second canon of literary anthropology is that it should be cultural hermeneutics.

A third canon of those committed to such a hermeneutics is to perform a specific type of ETHNOGRAPHY, called by Geertz (1973: 10) "THICK DESCRIPTION," which involves analyzing practices in a manner that "is like trying to read (in the sense of 'construct a reading of') a manuscript." A "reading," that is, an interpretation, of practices involves TRANSLATION. This is the rendering of one group's meanings intelligible to other groups. In fact, ethnographers construct readings of readings. These include: (1) what natives think they mean, (2) what native informants think natives mean, (3) what ethnographers think the informants mean, and (4) what ethnographers think audiences want to know about what natives mean.

Two concerns have been raised about thick description. The first is that certain of its basic concepts, such as "meaning," "construct," and "translation," are unclearly defined. This makes the process of constructing an interpretation of meaning implausible, because the connotation of "meaning" and "construct" is garbled. A second problem, related to the first, is that literary anthropologists have neglected all consideration of problems of the validation of interpretation (Carrithers 1990; P. Roth 1989; Sangren 1988; Jonathan Spencer 1989). This means, as Geertz (1973: 20, 24) stated, that the ethnographers would be "guessing at meanings" and that "you either grasp an interpretation or you do not, see the point or you do not." The literary anthropologists' rejection of validation is not characteristic of all students of meaning. Eco (1990), Goodenough (1965a), Habermas (1971), Ricoeur (1971), Schutz (1967), and Max WEBER (1949b) have all sought to develop procedures for arriving at valid interpretations.

A final canon of many literary anthropologists is the rejection of science because it is an epistemological metanarrative – the modern story of the stories of how people know – and postmodern theory is based on "incredulity towards metanarratives" (Lyotard 1984: 4). Literary anthropology's critique, therefore, ultimately depends upon whether it provides credible reasons for rejecting science and whether its ethnography is a more rigorous epistemological tool than the science it proposes to replace.

The literary anthropologists' case against science is made in one of three ways: from their own arguments, those made by hermeneutical philosophers, or those made by relativist philosophers of science. At least one study (Reyna 1994) suggests that the literary anthropologists' own antiscience reasoning is unconvincing. For example, although hermeneuticists such as Hans Gadamer (1975) or Richard Rorty (1991) occasionally offer disparaging comments about certain aspects of science, they are generally neither especially knowledgeable about science nor particularly critical of it, typically averring that "there is nothing wrong with science" (Rorty 1991: 34). As for the relativists such as Paul Feyerabend (1975) and Thomas Kuhn (1962), they are both subject to criticism and, again, not especially antiscientific, because as Feyerabend puts it, "science can stand on its own two feet" (1975: viii).

Interpretations proposed in the absence of validation procedures are constructed without reason. Strictly speaking, such interpretations are arrived at through guessing, as Geertz said they should be. They are speculations of what the anthropologist says the informants say the natives say. Plainly spoken, they are gossip. So the literary anthropologists' interpretations seem to be their impressions of the Other's gossip. Any project which, like literary anthropology, proposes to replace science with gossip would seem to be of dubious merit.   SPR
See also PHENOMENOLOGY, SYMBOLIC ANTHROPOLOGY

longhouses are community dwellings consisting of a series of individual family apartments linked together to form a longhouse (or circular house). They have characterized tribal peoples all around the world (see figure 1). Such dwellings typically combine HOUSEHOLD and group spaces for both household and community functions. They facilitate the balancing of the economic, social, and political interests of the household with those of the group (Loeb & Broek 1947; D. Miles 1964). Longhouses have become increasingly scarce as nationalist governments have interpreted – often incorrectly – their func-

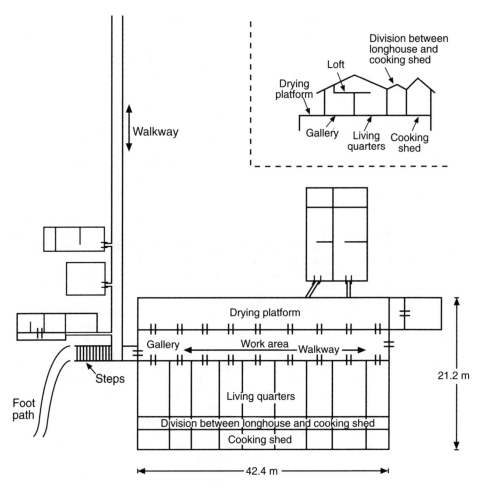

Figure 1 Floor plan of a typical longhouse.

tions as antithetical and superfluous to those of the state (Dove 1982).

MRD & TC

See also ARCHITECTURE

loosely structured kinship is a kinship system in which individual behavior is only loosely determined by the roles defined for given kinship statuses.   MR
further reading Embree & Evers 1969

Lowie, Robert H. (1883–1957)
Lowie was born to a middle-class Jewish family in Vienna in 1883 and emigrated with them to New York City when he was

10. He entered City College at 14 and graduated in 1901. After teaching for three years in the New York public schools, Lowie entered the graduate program in anthropology at Columbia University. He studied under Franz BOAS and Clark Wissler and wrote his dissertation on North American mythology. He received his Ph.D. in 1908. From 1907 to 1917, Lowie worked as a curator at the American Museum of Natural History, carrying out extensive field research among the Plains and Great Basin Indians of North America. After a lectureship at Columbia in 1920, he took a position as associate professor of

anthropology at the University of California at Berkeley. He married Luella Cole in 1933. He remained at Berkeley for the rest of his life, writing about Plains ethnography, social structure, and German national character. A quiet, courtly man with an uncanny memory for ethnographic detail, Lowie achieved a variety of academic distinctions, including the presidencies of the American Folklore Society (1916–17), the American Ethnological Society (1920–1), and the American Anthropological Association (1935–6). He published 14 books, 18 monographs, and hundreds of articles and reviews (Dundes 1966b). He died on September 21, 1957.

Lowie began his ethnographic research in 1906, with a field trip to the Northern Shoshone under the direction of Clark Wissler. Subsequent expeditions for the American Museum brought him to the Blackfoot, the Chipewyans, the Hidatsa, the Ute, the Paiute, and the Hopi; his most extensive and important fieldwork, however, was done among the Crow. This work covered issues of kinship, social organization, religion, and history and remains among the best and most comprehensive ethnographies in American anthropology (Lowie 1935). Through his fieldwork and teaching, Lowie was responsible for a large part of what is known about indigenous culture on the Plains (Lowie 1916, 1954b).

Lowie's theoretical influence was less constructive but still profound. Like Boas, Lowie was a rigorous empiricist who insisted (1917, 1934, 1937) that all theory be as economical as possible and be strongly supported by data. He held a particular disdain for the theories of cultural EVOLUTION developed by Louis Henry MORGAN and his followers: although Lowie acknowledged the possibility of convergent evolution, he argued that processes of DIFFUSION made any grand unilineal scheme untenable. His most influential work, *Primitive society* (1920), effectively demolished unilinealism with a bombardment of ethnographic examples. Lowie maintained a lifelong interest in psychology, and both *Primitive religion* (1924) and *Toward understanding Germany* (1954a) explored psychological themes. Even his psychology, however, was essentially behaviorist, with a persistent distrust of sweeping psychoanalytic models. While his critics accused him of being more destructive than constructive, Lowie was not antitheoretical; indeed, by holding the discipline to rigorous standards of argumentation and proof, Lowie helped create the conditions for the theoretical renaissance of the generation that followed him.   AB

further reading Du Bois 1960; Lowie 1959; R. Murphy 1972

M

---

magic describes supernatural actions done to achieve instrumental ends, such as acquiring love or money, punishing an enemy, or protecting a friend. It seems to rely on causal connections that a rational observer would describe as irrational; that is, it asserts causal connections that have no demonstrable existence in the natural world. One of the classic examples of magical systems is derived from EVANS-PRITCHARD's (1937) early study of the Azande, a Sudanese people who assumed that all deaths are ultimately caused by WITCHCRAFT. For example, when a man sitting under the granary was killed after it collapsed upon him, the Azande asserted that a witch had caused the death. When Evans-Pritchard pointed out that the granary's wooden structure was rotten and it was hardly surprising that it had collapsed, the Azande said he had missed the point. Any fool could see that the proximate cause of death was the rotten structure, but this begged a more important question: why did it collapse when this man, rather than any other, was seated beneath it? Witchcraft, the supernatural cursing of one man by another, was obviously the ultimate cause and the answer to why bad things happen to people according to the Azande. And this, they argued, was a much more satisfying explanation than claiming the universe was ruled by chance events.

The anthropological problem of magic is that anthropologists find similar practices in a wide variety of cultures, including their own, and yet anthropologists are usually unable to believe that these actions achieve their ends. The complex epistemological problems created by the Western-educated observer's willingness to call this behavior "irrational" has led to an exchange known as the "rationality debate." Mostly among philosophers, with some input from anthropologists, it takes the anthropological problem of magic (and usually Evans-Pritchard's monograph on the Azande) as its starting point and then develops an elaborate discussion of rationality, belief, cross-cultural understanding, and the problem of interpretation (Luhrmann 1989).

Within the anthropological literature, there are two standard approaches to the problem of magic. The first asserts that these practices are based on a theory of the world that happens to be false; the second that practitioners are not attempting to achieve some direct physical result but rather a psychological end. The debate is far from concluded; Horton (1993) argued in favor of the former approach, while Tambiah (1984) strongly defended the latter.

The classic proponent of the first approach, often labeled "intellectualist," was Sir James FRAZER, who argued that magic was characteristic of earlier stages of human culture and had as its primary end the need to ensure the continued fertility of the seasons, such as the return of spring after winter. Practitioners did not initially recognize the intellectual inadequacy of this theory of causation and when they eventually did so, RELIGION – with its attempt to propitiate supernatural beings – became the dominant mode of intellectual understanding, followed finally by science, which generates actions based on a theory of causation that approximates the world as it is. Frazer's analysis was embedded in expansive volumes and opulent prose in which he described a cluster of symbolic concepts – for example, that the king as a representation of fertile land must never fall ill or die

– that he framed through a rich historical and ethnographic trail (Frazer 1890).

The alternative approach argues, for example, that when the Dinka, a Sudanese people studied by Godfrey Lienhardt (1961), tie a knot in the grass to delay the passing of time, or the Trobriand Islanders of the Pacific sing songs to protect their gardens and to help them grow (Malinowski 1935), they are not victims of false beliefs. Using seagoing canoes as an example, MALINOWSKI (1948) forcefully argued that Trobrianders do not really believe that their recited chants make their canoes more sea-worthy and have no illusions that these chants can take the place of technical or "scientific" knowledge, as Frazer's theory seemed to imply. Indeed, they spent a great deal of time caulking and carving and engineering the most sea-worthy vehicle they could. They chanted, Malinowski explained, because they were anxious that, despite their efforts, the waves would overturn the canoes nevertheless, and the chanting relieved that anxiety and expressed their hopes. The core of this approach is that the magic is symbolic, in that it refers to something other than itself.

Some of these debates take on new meaning when the magical practitioners are sophisticated Westerners, because they believe in a theory of magic while having access to a "scientific" theory of nature. If magic is the result of ignorance of better models then it should not occur where these models are an ingrained part of the culture. Luhrmann (1989) described such a popular practice among contemporary "neopagans" in England and America who engage in magic for (at times) clearly instrumental ends. She argued that their actions must be understood as an unintended development of an interpretive approach in which expert knowledge and accumulated experience (often emotional) lead to rationalization. Such an interpretive development is characteristic of all specialists, not just magicians, which gives the system its reinforcement and power.

The study of conjuring magic is a subfield of the more general study of magic. Clearly, conjuring magic (the deliberate attempt to fool an audience that knows that it is being fooled) does not involve the same kind of intellectual problems as the study of magic as instrumental action. Nevertheless, conjuring magic can be understood as dependent upon the popular hope that there is such supernatural causation, and upon the human delight in illusion, and perhaps even a need for fantasy. An excellent example of that approach is Lee Siegel's (1991) study of conjuring magic in India, which not only explores illusion explicitly with theory but uses the text itself (in well demarcated sections) to play with the reader's capacity to suspend disbelief.

TL

See also DIVINATION, SORCERY
further reading Endicott 1970; Horton & Finnegan 1973; Middleton 1967; Skorupski 1976

Maine, Sir Henry James Sumner (1822–88) Maine was a distinguished lawyer, academic, and civil servant in mid-Victorian England. He held chairs in civil law at Cambridge and Oxford and was the legal member of the Council of India for seven years from 1862 and Master of Trinity Hall, Cambridge from 1877. But it is for his prolific writings and their influence on modern anthropology (of which, along with TYLOR and MORGAN, he is one of the founding fathers) that we best know him.

His central interest was to explain how modern civilization had emerged in certain "progressive" societies. His theory that political organization had originally been based on BLOOD (kinship) and later moved to territory, which is part of that famous transition from societies based on status to ones based on contract that he developed in *Ancient law* (1861), has provided a solid foundation for much work in POLITICAL ANTHROPOLOGY. His work on the difference between early communities and modern associations strongly influenced the contemporary work of Tönnies and DURKHEIM and later that of REDFIELD. His analysis of corporate institutions helped lay the foundation of modern studies of kinship as developed by FORTES and EVANS-PRITCHARD.

Maine showed the complexity of the "bundle of powers" in PROPERTY and the way in which these had been gradually separated into the institution of private, individual property. He outlined the importance of the development of notions of primogeniture and impartibility and the central device of wills. Supplemented by the work of F. W. Maitland, his characterization of the nature of property rights within feudalism is still valuable because he saw very clearly the mixing of political and economic power and the different layers of tenure in the feudal period.

His most famous work is on the development of the "individual" from the "group," that movement whereby status (family) is replaced by contract as the basis of modern nation-states. Although many other great Victorians, including SPENCER and Marx, were developing parallel ideas, his insight is unique.

There is much debate concerning his methodological importance and some criticism of his accuracy. Some believe that he introduced a new comparative and historical approach that laid the basis for the disciplines of anthropology and comparative jurisprudence. Others argue that his work was distorted by an evolutionary bias. In fact part of the tension in his writing results from the fact that he straddled the paradigm shift to evolutionism. He believed that stability was the norm and that the evolution of certain "progressive" societies was the exception. He was much more cautions in his generalizations than most of his critics realize. As Pollock wrote of him in the year of his death, "Maine can no more become obsolete through the industry and ingenuity of modern scholars than Montesquieu could be made obsolete by the legislation of Napoleon," for "At one master-stroke he forged a new and lasting bond between history and anthropology" (quoted in Grant Duff 1892: 48, 76).

AM

See also EVOLUTION, LEGAL ANTHROPOLOGY

further reading A. Diamond 1991; Feaver 1969

Malinowski, Bronislaw (1884–1942)

Malinowski was born in Krakow, Poland, in 1884. After taking his Ph.D. from the Jagiellonian University in 1908, he spent three semesters in Leipzig, working partly with the psychologist Wilhelm Wundt. He then moved to Britain, becoming a lecturer at the London School of Economics in 1913. At the outbreak of war in 1914 he found himself in Australia, where instead of internment as an enemy alien he was allowed to carry out fieldwork in the Trobriand Islands (off the north of New Guinea). He returned to England and resumed teaching at the LSE in 1920, becoming Reader in 1924 and Professor in 1927. Since he was in America at the outbreak of World War II, he took up a visiting professorship at Yale and carried out fieldwork in Mexico in 1940 and 1941. He died in New Haven in 1942.

Malinowski's most enduring legacy is his establishment of long-term FIELDWORK through the vernacular in a single community as the basic method of collecting data in anthropology. This was a reaction against the survey methods of W. H. R. RIVERS and his colleagues, which typically consisted of short-term visits to a number of different societies in order to compare them directly, working usually through interpreters. In abandoning Rivers's diachronic comparisons in favor of a synchronic approach, Malinowski – initially a survey anthropologist himself – was also led to develop a form of explanation based on function, to which was added an appreciation of individual motives – his well-known empiricism. These two aspects go together, in that fieldwork in a single village does not in itself allow comparisons between cultures to be made, as is necessary for any grand evolutionary theory, including Rivers's EVOLUTIONISM and DIFFUSIONISM. Equally, of course, it is difficult to derive any evolutionary theory directly from the study of a particular community in a society that lacks literacy and therefore historical records. Although Malinowski's antihistoricism was less uncompromising than A. R. RADCLIFFE-BROWN's, it nonetheless helped to lead anthropology to part company from history for a generation, and to become self-conscious of its use of it ever since. The narrow focus on one fieldwork area also influenced Malinowski's theorizing for the worse, in that he generalized too freely from Trobriand material to the rest of humanity.

That theory, FUNCTIONALISM, has lasted less well than the methodological shift to long-term fieldwork. With its partly individualist focus, it differed from Radcliffe-Brown's later version of functionalism, which was entirely sociological. Malinowski saw the basic function of culture and society as being the satisfaction of individual needs, both material (livelihood, shelter, clothing, etc.) and psychological (through magic, religion, myths, ritual, etc.). The psychological aspect was much stronger in his work than in that of many later anthropologists, including even his own students. It has a number of sources: the influence of Wundt, whose interest in psychology was largely its collective dimensions; the intellectualist explanations of Sir James FRAZER; and the example of the religious philosopher William James, who explained religion in functional terms that related to the satisfaction of human needs. One of its impacts on Malinowski was that his interest was not limited to social rules and norms but extended to individual responses to them and, more generally, to individual motives, an interest that started an intellectual lineage running via his successor as Professor at LSE, Raymond FIRTH, to Edmund LEACH and Fredrik Barth.

Malinowski's functionalism is best discussed in relation to the Trobriand ethnography with the aid of which it was developed. One theme here was the distinction between magic, religion, and science, which Malinowski broadly took over from Frazer (1890). In this view, science was empirical, rational knowledge, while magic was reasoning from false premises, though both had instrumental purpose. Malinowski detected both in Trobriand society, a derogation from Frazer's placing of them at opposite ends of a simple evolutionary sequence that linked but did not unify different societal types. This is connected with Malinowski's further observation that while some RITUALS, such as healing, were means to an end, others, such as the festival of *Milamala* (when ancestral spirits return briefly from Tuma, the next world), were not. Further, the

Trobrianders could give a clear reason for the former, but could only refer the latter to "custom." This also appears to be the distinction between MAGIC and RELIGION for Malinowski, though he also grouped them together as being miraculous, mythological, and linked with emotional stress. However, this was no picture of the Trobrianders being sunk in fear and awe for most of their lives. On the contrary, Malinowski regarded them as essentially practical and rational: it was only when reason, the empirical and scientific, could no longer provide an explanation that magic and religion were resorted to. Thus a Trobriander knew how to build a canoe technologically, but to cope with the emotional stress of going on a sea voyage into the unknown he needed magic and ritual. Similarly, inshore fishing was a purely technical matter of no great consequence, but open-sea fishing required magic. Religion, on the other hand, was essentially a response to the fear of annihilation through death (cf. *Milamala* above), while MYTH was important in providing a charter for present social norms and action, especially as regards the points of tension in society (e.g., the fact that the matrilineal rule of descent in Trobriand society meant that a man had to support his sister's children as much as his own).

Malinowski produced a similar psychological theory of needs in his treatment of kinship. Following Edward Westermarck (1891), one of his teachers at the LSE, he postulated the universal existence and primacy of the monogamous nuclear family, seeing it as the location of the satisfaction of human needs, such as food, shelter, and companionship. Further, he distinguished it from wider groupings, such as the clan, which he thought was never a domestic institution, a separation later articulated especially strongly by Meyer FORTES. The link between the two was provided by his theory of the "extension of sentiments," namely, that sentiments generated within the family were extended to more distant relationships within the clan. This theory reappears in respect of how terms for relatives are learned in infancy: the child learns to identify his relatives by starting from the nearest and proceeding to more remotely related ones, by an analogous process of extension from the nuclear family outwards – here, of knowledge as much as sentiment. Generally, however, Malinowski was derisive of what he called "kinship algebra"; this was part of his reaction to Rivers's approach to KINSHIP, which he felt was unduly reliant on the analysis of kinship terminologies as well as of clan systems. Instead, he postulated that kinship extensions were essentially metaphors, the real meaning being the primary one. The extensionist view was to bear fruit in the later American school of semantic analysis, led by Harold Scheffler and Floyd Lounsbury (1971).

Malinowski's own approach can also be criticized. In the first place, there are plenty of societies in which extended or joint families are the basic units, and in which POLYGYNY is significant if not general. Second, the "extension of sentiments" theory is a very dubious means of accounting for the genesis of social institutions, including kinship terminologies, and can be seen as mistaking effect for cause. Here, Malinowski parted company with the Durkheimian idea of social knowledge and institutions preexisting and surviving the individual: instead, he regarded them as the inevitable response to the basic needs of every individual born into the society. However, this stress on the individual also led to his interest in motivation, whether innate or acquired. His individual, unlike the Durkheimian automaton, was calculating, weighing the options available to him within his culture. He was thus led to make a distinction in fieldwork between thought or belief and action, and also between informants' statements and their actual actions, which often differed too. However, like Durkheim he sought to show how the various institutions in society are related, though the explanation was as much psychological as social.

Malinowski's main work consists of his Trobriand ethnography, published piecemeal as a series of separate studies, each treating a different theme. The first, *Argonauts of the western Pacific* (1922), dealt with exchange through the KULA cycle and considerably influenced Marcel MAUSS (1954) (see SOCIAL EXCHANGE). *The sexual life of savages* (1929) contains his views on the family, kinship, and marriage (see also Malinowski 1930), and *Coral gardens and their magic* (1935) treats of the relationship between technique and ritual in Trobriand gardening. Also important is the self-explanatory collection *Magic, science and religion* (1948). The early *The family among the Australian Aborigines* (1913) is an application of Westermarck's theories of the FAMILY to published sources on Australia, whereas the posthumously published collection *A scientific theory of culture* (1944) is more explicitly theoretical. Mention should also be made of Malinowski's personal diaries (1967) from the years he was in the field, which were published posthumously by his second wife without his authority. They give considerable insight into his state of mind in this period and are frequently shocking because of his unsympathetic attitude toward the people with whom he was living, which is quite at variance with his published writings.

Malinowski's influence was transmitted not only through his writings but also through his famous seminars at the LSE, which many of those who attended them likened to the performance of a charismatic visionary. His much-discussed relations with women were ultimately probably more significant for his lack of condescension toward them and encouragement of their own independent careers, including Lucy Mair and Audrey RICHARDS, than for his celebrated affairs. Despite the banality that many have found in much of his writing, his place as one of the founding fathers of the modern discipline of anthropology is secure.   RP

See also EVOLUTION

further reading R. Firth 1957; A. Kuper 1983, 1996; Paluch 1981; Michael W. Young 1979

mana is in certain religions, an impersonal supernatural force, thought to pervade the world and concentrate in divinities, sacred objects, and persons, and to be able to be transmitted or inherited. The term is of Polynesian origin but has been used in European languages since the mid-nineteenth century to indicate similar concepts found in many societies. Early

cultural evolutionists maintained that the concept of "*mana*" represented the earliest form of religious belief.   MR
See also RELIGION

market is an arena in which buyers (demand) and sellers (supply) come together for the purpose of engaging in exchange. The extent of the market may vary widely: from a specific locale to a region to a country to the entire globe.

There are significant differences between economies whose primary mode of allocation is a network of self-regulating markets and an economy of marketplaces. While anthropologists have written extensively about the latter (J. Alexander 1987; Beals 1975; Bohannan & Dalton 1962; S. Cook & Diskin 1976; Dewey 1962; C. Geertz 1979; Hodges 1988; Tax 1953), they have not contributed very much to our analytic understanding of the former, except by way of contrast with certain institutions in traditional societies. It is fair to say that most anthropologists who have discussed these matters have not looked with favor upon market exchange. As one anthropologist recently put it: "By and large, 'Maussian' gift institutions have had a favourable press in anthropology, and 'commodities' an unfavourable one. 'Gift–reciprocity–Good/market–exchange–Bad' is a simple, easy-to-memorize formula" (Gell 1992b: 142).

The economist Alfred Marshall (1890: I, 324–5) defined a market as a region or area located in time and space over which prices for the same good will converge toward uniformity independent of transport costs. Price differentials exhibited by separate local and regional markets provide an incentive for buyers, sellers, and the owners of resources to profit by moving from markets of low return to markets of higher return. As a consequence price differentials narrow and there is a widening of the arena over which a uniform price for the same good prevails. Markets formerly isolated from one another become better integrated. This process of integration is encouraged by certain critical developments: (1) improvements in transportation and the free flow of information across market boundaries; (2) most importantly, a loosening of the insti-

tutional restraints on both patterns of consumption (the abrogation of various forms of sumptuary restrictions) and the mobility of resources so that the "factors of production" can be combined in different ways and shifted from one employment to another according to the dictates of "economic rationality" rather than deployed according to custom or political concerns. With the forces of demand and supply given freer reign and a widening of the sphere of the market, the productive sector responds by a greater DIVISION OF LABOR and an increase in economic output (W. Rothenberg 1992).

Thus, in a market economy the various market arenas link up to form an integrated market network that is largely self-regulating in nature; that is, goods move into and out of the market in response to shifts in market prices rather than by directives from some central political agency. It is this network of markets that is the principal means by which goods and services are allocated in such an economy, including both consumer goods and the factors of production (land, labor, money). One of the ways in which the market performs its allocative function is by acting as an information-gathering and -dispensing mechanism: the market collates the preferences (reflected in purchases) of numerous buyers and sellers and expresses them in the form of a range of prices that for the same good will tend toward an "equilibrium price" said to "clear the market." Those market prices further act as signals to inform producers how much and what kinds of each good to produce, thereby allocating resources in best conformity with consumers' preferences.

The kinds of market most intensively investigated by anthropologists are marketplaces rather than the integrated, self-regulating market systems that characterize most modern industrial economies. When marketplaces do occur in modern societies, such as farmers' markets, they are clearly marginal and their allocative role in the overall economy is a minor one. Marketplaces as a prominent feature of the economic landscape are typically found in PEASANT societies or, historically, in agrarian states. They also tend to be located in pre- or nonindustrial urban centers, the reason being that traditionally the "peace of the marketplace" could best be secured in such centers. Marketplaces also are associated with economies – or rural enclaves – in which the HOUSEHOLD continues to function as a significant productive unit. When firms replace households as the primary productive units in the economy, they bypass the marketplace entirely and seek out what are emerging marketing networks as the place in which to transact their business. Finally, these marketplaces bring together buyers and sellers from different communities at certain times and places for the purpose of exchange; hence they have a periodic character and are sometimes referred to as "periodic" markets.

Marketplaces and the economists' markets have a number of features in common: buyers, sellers, prices, and fluctuations in demand and supply. At the same time, they tend to differ in a number of important respects. In marketplace systems various institutional restraints, together with what are often inefficiencies in transport and communication, act to discourage the mobility of resources. This is especially true of the factors of production, such as land and labor, which both historically and in contemporary peasant societies have been allocated mainly on the basis of custom and tradition, associated with the obligations of kin and community, rather than through the "impersonality" of the economic market. Hence, prices in the marketplace do not feed back into the rest of the system and serve as incentives and guides to productive activities in the same way as they do in market-organized societies. Equally noteworthy in this regard is the fact that prices for the same goods tend not to converge toward uniformity across several regional marketplaces that remain more or less separate from one another. In fact the goods produced are often so reflective of local skills and ecologies that is not clear what the "same good" means in this context. Under such conditions the marketplaces do not link up to form an integrated market system and their linkages tend to be partial and incomplete. In many "developing" countries, one finds a network of emerging markets that exist side by side

with the older pattern of regional marketplaces, which continue to serve the rural peasantry.   DK

further reading J. Alexander & Alexander 1991; Belshaw 1965; Dalton 1973; Dilley 1992; Plattner 1985; K. Polanyi et al. 1957; W. Skinner 1964–5; Carol Smith 1974

marriage is the socially recognized bonding of a man and woman, as these terms are culturally construed, typically for the purposes of legitimate reproduction, the establishment of a nuclear family, or the creation of a new household.   MR

marriage exchange is the system of reciprocal marriages that transfers spouses among kin groups or marriage classes. Often, if androcentrically, phrased as the "exchange of women," it is the basis for debate about ALLIANCE SYSTEMS.   MR
See also MARRIAGE SYSTEMS

marriage systems Things so simple and orderly as to deserve the name "marriage systems" exist only in the heads of certain anthropologists – especially those often called "alliance theorists." These scholars, though they overlap considerably with those dubbed "structural anthropologists," have in fact failed to appreciate the richness and complexity in the structuring of real-world behavior, have misinterpreted ethnographic data, have been oblivious to critics, and as a consequence have created what philosophers call "closed systems of thought." All of these charges have been sustained against LÉVI-STRAUSS (1969a), Dumont (1957), and others – primarily by Scheffler (1970, 1973), with some assistance from W. Shapiro (1982) and others. But because of its theoretical closure ALLIANCE THEORY has ignored the attacks and survived – though, with the general decline of KINSHIP studies from the preeminent position they once held, mostly in introductory and sometimes influential texts (e.g., Robin Fox 1967; Service 1971).

Alliance theory has employed an essentialist sense of marriage as a relationship between one male (or one collectivity of males) and another in which women figure only as "messages" or "prestations." It has thus (to say the least) not found favor among feminists. The same can be said of other assertive (and usually collective) male projects, like HUNTING, SACRIFICE, and men's CULTS. All this is to suggest that alliance theory is not a body of propositions about the external world but another set of androcentric fantasies in which the personhood of women is understated, ignored, or denied altogether. This is not to minimize them – such fantasies are a significant part of the ruling ideology of the "modern" world, and a still more important portion of that of "premodern" populations – but to call them what they are.

Behavior pertinent to real-world marriage is better approached by more humble labeling, like "arrangements" (Hiatt 1967, 1968) or – even better – "understandings," because this suggests more subtlety in life and hence a finer eye in anthropology. Thus comparativists have been arguing for decades about whether in all populations much the same understandings exist as we "moderns" associate with the word "marriage" (Leach 1961b; Rivière 1971; Krige 1974; J. Shapiro 1984). The chief grounds for controversy have been coresidence and GENDER identity. For example, members of a single caste-category in South India enact a ceremony in which a woman is linked to a man who has subsequent sexual and visitational rights in regard to her but who continues to reside in his natal abode (Gough 1959). The same pattern of "natolocal" residence has been reported elsewhere, as in parts of West Africa (Fortes 1949a). In East and South Africa couples bound in what we might be inclined to call "marriage" usually coreside, although sometimes both partners are female (Oboler 1980; O'Brien 1977). It would seem, however, that in these instances one of the partners assumes certain aspects of the "male" role – though obviously not that of genitor, for whom a surrogate is employed. These African "cases" are instructive not only as illustrative of some of the range of conjugal bonding accepted in human populations but also of the complexities involved in describing the life of a single population. For the "female husband" is locally recognized as such; she is therefore not simply a woman acting as a man but a partner to a union of a sort separable from most others. By contrast, the question as to whether the South Indian case is "really" marriage is a matter of definition and not an empirical issue (Goodenough 1970).

Although at first blush marriage in the Western world may appear quite different from all this, further consideration suggests otherwise. For we too have notions like "marital separation," which may – or may not – be a phase in the dissolution of a marriage (see DIVORCE). And especially in recent years we have experienced, if mostly vicariously, woman–woman marriages, presumably with considerably more erotic content than is the case in Africa (Weston 1994). These are further reminders of the complexity of marriage in a single population, and they proffer temporal perspectives: the construction (or deconstruction) of a marriage is more perceptively regarded not as an event but as a process; and the "institution" itself is not a Platonic essence but something subject to historical change. All of this, coupled with the African and South Indian data, should persuade us from drawing too sharp a line between "modern" and "premodern" marriage. Some of us may be comfortable with (say) woman–woman marriage and some of us may not be, but these "moral" judgments should not be made the basis of theories of social EVOLUTION – as they were in the progressivism of the nineteenth century (Morgan 1877) and are in more recent primitivist theory (Lee 1982; Service 1971). Real-world evolution is mostly divergent and favours a multiplicity of forms, not the metaphorical "unfolding" of an oversimple typology (Nisbet 1969).

In the same vein, the textbook (and alliance-theory) homily that marriage in modern society is a relationship between individuals, whereas in premodern populations it concerns "groups," besides preserving evolutionary typology, is overdrawn. Someone – usually her father – "gives a woman away" in most modern religious marriages. Parental consent is required for modern individuals to marry if they are below a certain age. And although it is possible in the modern world to maintain a marriage without acknowledging one's "in-laws" (or "affines," as anthropologists call them), most people seem to be under some pressure to maintain this sort of relationship.

By contrast, although marriage in premodern populations sometimes has implications for groups of the sort anthropologists have called "clans" and "lineages," this is by no means always the case. And even where such implications exist, the effective agents in arranging a marriage are not such groups but certain close kin of the bride and, less often, the groom: recent surveys of pertinent data for Aboriginal Australia (W. Shapiro 1979), Africa (J. Goody 1973; A. Kuper 1982a), and Melanesia (M. Strathern 1984) have made this plain. The age of potential spouses would appear to be a salient factor cross-culturally, affecting the degree to which people can control their own marital destinies: certainly this is the case in parts of the Northern Australia littoral, where females were traditionally assigned to males before their birth (Goodale 1971; A. Hamilton 1970) but where the age of marriage for both is nowadays mostly past puberty (Burbank 1988).

Similarly, the conceptions of "maleness" and "femaleness" that underlie marital economies may not be all that different between modern and premodern populations. To be sure, in the latter there is usually some sense of obligation on the husband's part to his wife's kin, as expressed by such established anthropological notions as "BRIDEWEALTH," "brideservice," and "exchange marriage." These notions should not be essentialized; rather, their ethnographic complexity needs to be realized. Thus Marilyn Strathern's (1984) survey of Melanesian exchange ideologies gives some idea of the diverse practical and conceptual structures in which such ideologies are embedded. Andrew Strathern (1980) has shown that, in two populations in Highland Papua New Guinea, bridewealth involves a variety of prestations made over a lengthy period, a minority moving from the wife's people to the husband's. And exchange marriage and brideservice are often combined.

Still, although there are occasional objectifications of maleness in marital understandings, and, more frequently, limitations on male AGENCY, there is no denying that it is usually the female partner who is objectified or, at least, whose agency is more drastically limited. Thus Jane Collier and Michelle Rosaldo (1981: 280), in their analysis of "brideservice societies," conclude that marriage in such populations is "a male achievement" (see also Jane Collier 1988; Kelly 1993). Notions of exchange marriage nearly always objectify the potential wives rather than the potential husbands, though – contra alliance theory – they often accord agency not only to males but to females in nonwifely capacities (W. Shapiro 1979). And although bridewealth, as noted, is sometimes countered by groomwealth, the prestations subsumable under the former rubric are probably always more substantial. (Eurasian DOWRY arrangements are in no sense construable as groomwealth: they are in fact prestations made to the bride herself, or to the newly married pair, by the bride's kin, with the intention of providing the couple with the economic basis of a life together – see J. Goody 1973; Tambiah 1973.)

There are two considerations that make the objectification of women more understandable. One has already been noted: the subadult age at which females usually marry, at least in their initial conjugal unions. By contrast, males at the same point in their conjugal lives are usually somewhat older, at least old enough to be reckoned semiadult by local standards. This in turn implies that they have, or promise to have, effected another sort (or sorts) of "male achievement," such as incorporation into male ritual hierarchy, the acquisition of skills in hunting or herding, or the beginnings of a "professional" career. The second consideration is that, even under bridewealth understandings, it is not the whole girl who is objectified but rather her reproductive capacities – so that, for example, payment is likely to be refunded if the girl is barren. By this reckoning, bridewealth is not unlike the modern notion that an individual may press suit for damage to a bodypart or insure that bodypart if it is deemed essential to their livelihood (H. Schneider 1968).

All this said, it remains remarkable that the attributes that marital bestowers generally require in a son-in-law – particularly the responsibility implied by the acceptance of male hierarchy and the ability, demonstrated or promised, to "provide for" – overlap substantially with those that, in "freer markets," impress potential wives themselves, and are fairly distinct from what the potential husbands tend to seek (Batten 1992). This suggests that there are some panhuman tendencies behind marriage arrangements. Although this may be an unpopular position to take in today's gender wars, it can no longer be seriously entertained that a "biological" perspective is necessarily politically reactionary (Degler 1990), or that it implies immutability and is incompatible with learning (Lehrman 1970), or that it disrespects the variety of "cultural constructions" (Borgerhoff Mulder 1987) and lacks predictive power (Buss 1989; A. Wolf 1993). All this being so, any theory of marriage that fails to incorporate a Darwinian perspective falls short of the mark of a general theory.   WS

further reading Hiatt 1965; F. Rose 1960; Scheffler 1977; W. Shapiro 1981; D. Turner 1974

marxist anthropology has a common basis in one or another aspect of Karl Marx's work, filtered through and shaped by the complex histories of marxist and anthropological thought. It encompasses a number of different anthropological projects and perspectives, but includes three major, often interrelated, analytic themes: MATERIALISM, social EVOLUTION, and CAPITALISM.

Materialism

The materialist perspective starts from and develops Marx's emphasis on the centrality of labor and the processes and social relations of production through which labor is mobilized, organized, and appropriated (Marx & Engels 1947). The central problem for this type of analysis is the relationship between the material base or economic structure, defined as a MODE OF PRODUCTION, and the social whole, especially the cultural and political "superstructure." This perspective is based on a model of society divided into structural layers, and the central problem is defined in terms of the relationship (of causality or determination) between layers, such that one of the layers (the economic basis, or mode of production) is seen to be superior to, the basis for, or the determinant of, the other (the juridical, political, ideological, or cultural superstructure). When the relationship is seen to be a straightforward one of base determining structure or superstructure, the approach can be considered mechanical.

An approach that tries to become more "dialectical" by suggesting that the causal arrows can flow both ways, from base to superstructure and from superstructure to base, does not necessarily solve the problem, however complex one's diagrams of the relationships and however many arrows and feedback loops one attempts to draw. A central problem here is the structural layercake itself, which may be useful as a metaphor and for some preliminary analytic purposes but cannot be taken as an adequate representation of any social whole or process. A related problem is its static conception of relations among levels or layers. If one can suggest that relations of determination are at work in social processes, they must be considered over time, and the material character of the superstructure (both as historical product and as historical force) needs to be recognized.

This does not invalidate a marxist or materialist approach to social and cultural processes. It does mean that the problem for materialist analysis is more complex than the structural layercake would suggest. Its resolution requires a rejection both of a reinvented holism in which everything is equally important in social and cultural relations and processes *and* a structural layercake that removes whole aspects of social and cultural relations from the realm of the material, making them immaterial ("superstructural") forms acted upon by more "basic" forms and processes. This perspective expands the conception of the material to include ideas, conceptions, and understandings, as well as the conception of determination, which becomes more social and historical.

Social evolution

A considerable body of marxist anthropological work applies Marx's concept of mode of production to processes of social evolution. Two modes of analysis have been especially important here: the first concentrates on the evolutionary questions themselves; the second on the relationship between infrastructure and superstructure in precapitalist societies.

Much of the debate on evolutionary questions limits itself to discussing those modes of production Marx mentioned in his more schematic statements, such as the primitive, ancient, Asiatic (in some versions), feudal, capitalist, and socialist modes. This work concentrates on an analysis of the fundamental relationships and dynamics of a particular mode of production, or on processes of transition from one mode to another. In both cases the proclaimed project may be one of *extending* marxist analysis to historical periods and processes that Marx himself did not take up. That is, while he suggested a succession of modes of production in human history, he did not himself devote much attention to the analysis of precapitalist societies or to the process of transition from one mode of production to another; nor did he speculate in detail on the constitution of postcapitalist societies. These studies tend to remain at an economic level, examining fundamental relations and antagonisms, including class relations, in terms of a range of modes of production.

A defect in this type of analysis, and evolutionary analyses in general, is its failure to make the distinction between what Raymond Williams (1977) labeled "epochal" and "historical" analysis. While epochal analysis aims at elucidating whole epochs of human history, historical analysis is concerned with the complex conjunction and relation of action, event, and structure in particular times and places. Williams noted that the two problems and processes require different concepts, methods, and referents. Simple reference to "epochal" structures and relations is, therefore, inadequate to resolve "historical" problems. Since concepts of modes of production that concentrate on "ancient," "feudal," or "capitalist" modes are by definition ep-

ochal concepts, their utility in historical analysis is limited – but not nil. The two modes of analysis exist in opposition *and* relation, in that "historical" processes always occur in "epochal" time and structure, and can be illuminated by placement within particular epochs, but "epochal" transitions always occur in historical times and places and therefore require reference to and understanding of events and relations not ordinarily included in "epochal" analysis. The conceptual and methodological problems confronting evolutionary and historical analysis are therefore complex, but the complexity can only be explored if the distinction between the two modes of analysis is recognized. Unfortunately, most evolutionary analyses follow exclusively epochal procedures and assumptions. Thus, ethnography – in terms of the opposition explored here, "history" in anthropological guise – becomes an adjunct of the analysis of epochal modes of production. Ethnographic cases become iconic exemplars of the particular epochal modes to which they are assigned.

The second approach also extends marxist analysis to precapitalist societies but it pays primary attention to the relationship between "infrastructure" and "superstructure" in precapitalist situations. Using a modes-of-production analysis it takes on classic anthropological themes such as RELIGION, KINSHIP, and SOCIAL ORGANIZATION (Meillassoux 1981; Terray 1972). Here the range of analyses and positions moves broadly from straightforwardly mechanical interpretations such as those encountered above (making social organization and religious belief simple functions or determined results of production processes and relations) to studies that explore the manner in which kin relations, or religious belief and practice, serve (in part, and in addition to other things they do) to organize and mobilize production processes themselves. Although such studies are susceptible to (and have often fallen into) FUNCTIONALIST renderings of economic, social, political, or religious structures or levels, they also tend to expand the notion of "the economic" and "production" in ways that are quite suggestive. These studies also tend to be more ethnographic and less content with the simple imposition of epochal labels.

Capitalism

A third area of marxist anthropology concerns studies of capitalist societies themselves and the expansion of capitalism in relation to precapitalist societies.

The examination of capitalist societies explores a wide range of ethnographic problems and issues – WORK and workplace relations, practices and ideologies in shops and factories, GENDER relations at home, in communities, and at shops and factories, community formation and ideologies, and political action, resistance, or quiescence. What ties the studies together are the facts that (1) they are conducted within capitalist societies; and (2) they find some aspect of Marx's analysis of capitalism (for example, his analysis of the commodity form, commodity circulation, and the "fetishism of commodities," or his analysis of the capital–labor relation) suggestive.

The study of the historical expansion of capitalism in relation to precapitalist societies is both historical and ethnographic. It may examine the consequences of the development of capitalism for noncapitalist groups and societies such as HORTICULTURALISTS and PEASANT villagers, or whole STATE systems or civilizations based on tributary forms of economic and political organization. These studies necessarily concern processes of COLONIALISM and imperialism, and they proceed at both processual and structural levels. Processually, studies are concerned with the problem of transition from noncapitalist toward capitalist social relations. Structurally, they examine complex structural mixes of capitalist and noncapitalist forms, relations, and classes, at particular moments within processes of transition, in particular societies (Rey 1973). During the 1970s and 1980s, these structural mixes were subjected to highly elaborate theoretical conceptualizations emphasizing the "articulation" of noncapitalist and capitalist modes of production (Kahn & Llobera 1981; E. Wolf 1982).

One area of tension in these studies has been the complex relationship between epochal and historical analysis, discussed above. Although studies of particular processes of transition, or of the introduction of capitalist forms and relations, would seem to require specific historical and ethnographic analysis, many students of these processes, especially those committed to the analysis of the articulation of modes of production, were content to remain at the level of epochal analysis, postulating certain structural relations between and among modes of production in a certain setting or during a certain period of transition.

Another area of tension concerns the relative weight of capitalist relations and structures, and of the West, within such processes of transition. Various groups of scholars stressed the overwhelming power of the West, and of capitalism. In some extreme cases, this involved an assumption that noncapitalist societies could be seen to be fully within the orbit of capitalist relations as soon as they were incorporated within circuits of world trade. In less extreme cases, the process of transition was seen to be unidirectional, leading inexorably toward capitalism. In response to these views, a number of scholars have stressed the local and cultural structuring of capitalist forms, relations, and processes. Here too one needs to recognize a range, from an extreme that would deny *any* transforming power to the capitalist West (thus reproducing, in a different register, a kind of epochal essentialism not unlike more mechanical marxist analyses) to studies that stress the importance of context and relation in any examination of historical processes. While positions in debates among students of these processes sometimes appear to be ethical and moral (for example, students emphasizing the power of capitalist relations and institutions have sometimes been accused of being ETHNOCENTRIC and adopting the "perspective of business"), the tensions can only be resolved by means of the sort of "historical" analysis envisioned by Williams.   WR

See also HISTORY AND ANTHROPOLOGY, STRUCTURAL MARXISM, WORLD–SYSTEM THEORY

further reading Donham 1990; Godelier 1977

masculinity is a concept that, like manhood, male identity, and men's roles, is variously understood as: (1) anything men think and do; (2) anything men think and do to be men; (3) anything some men think and do, in contrast to other, "less manly" men; and (4) whatever WOMEN are not, that is, whatever women do not think and do not do.

A central component of the discipline's study of men today involves debate over the definitions of masculinity in different contexts. Despite disagreements, one common theme implicit in many discussions of manhood concerns inequality, and whether and how GENDER inequality may characterize relations between women and men and between different men in diverse historical and cultural situations. Often linked to inequality are the concomitant issues of POWER, PATRIARCHY, and CULTURAL CHANGE.

Anthropology has long entailed men talking to men, of course, and thus the study of men is not inherently remarkable. Under different names and guises, ethnographers have provided insights into various practices associated with masculinity (see, for example, Malinowski 1927, 1929; Evans-Pritchard 1951, 1974; M. Mead 1935; O. Lewis 1961; Lévi-Strauss 1969a). But only in the 1980s did anthropologists systematically begin to explore men as engendered and engendering persons. What prompted the focused study of "second wave" feminism and FEMINIST ANTHROPOLOGY.

The study of masculinity in anthropology recognizes the importance of gender and sexuality as crucial avenues of research and a challenge to the continued marginalization of these topics in the discipline. Generally, studies of masculinity have rejected simplistic structuralist notions of binary man–woman dichotomies, a reflection of the theoretical impact of feminism on anthropological methods and conclusions. In their place ethnographies on manhood and male identities have focused on documenting both tremendous intercultural variation with respect to men's attitudes and behavior, and the intracultural diversity within specific populations, to show how the categories "men" and "gender" interconnect with CLASS, ETHNICITY, AGE, SEX, and other major social divisions (di Leonardo 1991a).

The study of men-as-men

Brandes's *Metaphors of masculinity* (1980) and Herdt's *Guardians of the flutes* (1981) represent two pioneering efforts by anthropologists in the study of men-as-men. By studying the folklore of Andalusia, Spain, Brandes detailed the psychological orientation toward women that was evident among men in various daily situations regardless of whether women were physically present. For his part, Herdt described how rites of fellatio were necessary for the social and physical maturation of men among the Sambia in New Guinea. These studies were followed shortly thereafter by Herzfeld's (1985) ethnography of the POETICS of manhood in Crete and Godelier's (1986) political economy of male domination among the New Guinea Baruya.

A variety of theoretical orientations and methodologies have been employed in the examination of men-as-men. Using a cultural-Marxist lens, R. Lancaster (1992) addressed the question of sexuality and eroticism between men as a defining feature of masculinity in Nicaragua (see also HOMOSEXUALITY). Examining activities like fathering, WORK, and ALCOHOL use, Gutmann (1996) showed how male identities get negotiated by both men and women in the very ambiguity of social life in Mexico. Other notable studies include Gilmore's (1990) functionalist compendium of the ubiquity, if not the universality, of masculine images in the world and Hewlett's (1991) quantitative behaviorial study of the Aka Pygmies.

The study of masculinity in anthropology has not generally succumbed to the me-tooism common in other disciplines, nor been much influenced by the New Men's Movement in the United States as reflected in works such as Bly's (1990) call for a return to a primal masculinity. However, a notable, if often unarticulated, current in much of this research has been its avoidance of feminist anthropology. Few studying men-as-men have seriously engaged with feminist theory. This has required for many an awkward silence about a body of theoretical and empirical work that is often very relevant to their own projects. Yet the study of masculinities has much to offer controversies regarding biological and social-constructionist explanations for male behavior; men's roles in the cultural reproduction of masculinity (and femininity); the relation of masculinity to NATIONALISM, VIOLENCE, and WAR; the existence of "third" genders and sexualities. In addition, the study of men-as-men can contribute to remnant discussions about the universal subordination of women and the search for ultimate causes of gender inequalities as well as about the place of women in the study of men (and of men in women's studies), to mention only a few areas of common interest.

Engendering men

Should masculinity be a "male only" concern? Ongoing debate is required concerning the role of women in the development and transformation of male identities, involving as this does men's emotional (as well as physical) relations with women. In a related manner, whereas numerous ethnographers have emphasized what they see as fundamental differences in RITES OF PASSAGE for men and women (more necessary for men than women since, some hold, men are "culturally made" while women are "naturally born'), others have questioned whether such mind–body and male–female distinctions might not reflect ethnographic bias more than the views of anthropological subjects of study (M. Strathern 1988).

There are many anthropological studies of men, but few studies of men-as-men. In the decades since the publication of the first explicitly feminist anthropological studies, anthropologists have become increasingly concerned with the development of studies of *gender* (in contrast to those of men *or* women) and sexuality. In these studies anthropologists have continued to ask whether gender differences necessarily imply inequalities and have begun to investigate how agency may contribute to changing gender relations in households and society as a whole. As salutary as this trend has been, however, there is a danger that by analytically separating men from women, students of masculinity may, by default,

write women out of such an ethnographic record both theoretically and empirically. This problem has increasingly induced anthropologists to critique notions of immutable categories of gender and sexuality, thereby heralding instead the advent of integrated, multigendered studies.

MG

material culture   encompasses all the physical objects produced by members of any particular CULTURE. These range from the purely utilitarian to the highly esoteric. Early anthropology focused on the collection of such artifacts as a way to place societies in schemes of EVOLUTIONARY STAGES, but this approach fell out of favor with the rise of FUNCTIONALISM. The study of material culture remains central to ARCHAEOLOGY because such artifacts provide the main body of data in that field.

TB

materialism   includes a variety of social theories that share certain critical assumptions: (1) that the existence of a real physical world sets constraints for, and has a significant impact on, human behavior; (2) that human behavior is part of nature and can be understood by using the kinds of method that the natural sciences employ in understanding nature. Materialists do not necessarily assume that material reality is "more real" than mental or subjective reality, but in the process of causal explanation they give priority to the objective material world over subjective reality or the world of the mind.

As a doctrine, materialism dates back to the Ionian philosophers of ancient Greece in the sixth century B.C.E. and the later Roman philosopher Lucretius. However, in the social sciences the grandfather of all materialist doctrines is that of the nineteenth-century social thinkers Karl Marx and Friedrich Engels, who developed the "Materialist Interpretation of History," now generally known as "historical materialism." Historical materialism divides all societies into base and superstructure. The base involves those elements essential to carrying out economic production, the "forces of production," which for Marx and Engels generally meant TECHNOLOGY, although they also included the human physical environment. When these were combined with the modes of ownership of the productive forces, known as the "relations of production," they created a distinct MODE OF PRODUCTION. Atop the mode of production sits the superstructure, consisting primarily of politics and ideology – but in the broadest sense, including all of the remaining institutions of society. Marx and Engels conceived the relationship between base and superstructure as one in which the former heavily determined the latter. We know that these scholars left room for a reciprocal influence of superstructure on base, but the extent to which this was possible has been the subject of much scholarly disagreement. Some interpreters have actually gone so far as to assert that Marx and Engels saw the relationship as fully reciprocal. However, this seems very dubious, because it would make a mockery of their self-identification as materialists.

In 1845–6 Marx and Engels (1947) used their concept of mode of production to periodize human history, identifying four main stages of historical development, which they called primitive communism, SLAVERY (or the ancient stage), feudalism, and CAPITALISM. They predicted that capitalism would eventually be superseded by a socialist mode of production.

The materialist doctrine of Marx and Engels has lived on in the thinking of modern Marxists and been modified by them. Numerous anthropologists have drawn on Marxist materialism. These include the archaeologist V. Gordon Childe (1936) and the cultural anthropologist Leslie WHITE (1943), both of whom have had a major impact on modern anthropology. Historical materialism has also had a major impact in anthropology through its incorporation into CULTURAL MATERIALISM, a theoretical approach developed by Marvin HARRIS (1979) and his followers.

There is actually another form of materialism, one that is usually not labeled as such, and this is the materialism of the body. The contemporary intellectual incarnation of this form of materialism is SOCIOBIOLOGY. Biological materialism starts with the reality of the human organism and examines how its characteristics have an impact on the formation of cultural practices.

Some social scientists believe that the economic materialism of Marx and Engels, the cultural materialism of Harris, and the biological materialism of the sociobiologists can and should be synthesized into a more grandiose "supermaterialism." This could well be a significant research agenda for the future.

Any discussion of materialism should make reference to its main oppositional doctrine, known usually as "idealism." Idealism in the social sciences assumes that the most important aspects of social reality, if not all of social reality itself, are emanations from the human mind. Society is a socially constructed set of agreements worked out by the human mind in different temporal and spatial settings. The modern grandfather of all idealists was Georg Wilhelm Friedrich Hegel (1770–1831), who saw society as a product of the Absolute Spirit. Idealist approaches have been highly influential in recent sociology and anthropology, and in fact have gained much ground in recent years. A quintessential idealist approach in anthropology is Claude LÉVI-STRAUSS's STRUCTURALISM, which has been revised and extended in the doctrines of poststructuralism and POSTMODERNISM.

SS

further reading M. Harris 1968 [organized around the opposition between materialism and idealism]

matriarchy is the dominance of women as a class over men and a system by which rights and duties to persons and things descend through the mother's line (Webster 1975: 142). Nineteenth-century social theorists developed the concept (also known as "Mother Right") to explain the evolution of civil society. These theorists, such as the Swiss historian and jurist Johann Jakob Bachofen (1967) and the German political economist Friedrich Engels (1902), argued that Mother Right was one of the earliest stages of human society: the rule and authority of the Mother and the ideals of nurturance and nonviolence were one of the first bases of social order. Matriarchy was seen to have been superseded by PATRIARCHY. Many cultural feminists, beginning in the 1970s, have appropriated the concept of matriarchal society as a model for transforming the patriarchal institutions of the Western world.

MATRILINEAL societies were initially thought to be matriarchal in nature. But anthropologists have shown that men may be economically and politically dominant in matrilineal societies and that women can have a high status in patrilineal societies. Moreover, the presence of matrilineality or patrilineality in a society does not correlate in any predictable way with the prevalence of the cultural ideals of nurturance or non-violence. Most anthropologists now believe that no solid evidence exists to show the existence of a stage of pure matriarchy.

EP

matrifocal kinship or social relations and structures are focused on the mother or on women more generally. The term is most commonly used in reference to the **matrifocal household**, which is structured around the mother and in which the father is absent or plays a relatively limited role (R. Smith 1973).   MR

matrilateral kin relations are those on the mother's side or through the mother. For instance, children of a mother's brother or sister are matrilateral cousins.

MR

matrilineal descent or inheritance passes from a mother to her children. In a matrilineal clan system, for instance, children belong to the clan of their mother and not that of their father.   MR

matrilineal dilemma is the conflict a father faces in a matrilineal descent system in which he is torn between his primary legal obligation to support and help his sister's children and his desire to help his own children, who are members of his wife's descent group: "I love my son but I gotta give my stuff to my lousy nephew."

MR

matrilocal residence *See* UXORI-LOCAL RESIDENCE.

Mauss, Marcel (1872–1950)

DURKHEIM's sister's son, Mauss left his Jewish family in the Vosges to study in Bordeaux with his uncle and in Paris with the Sanskritist Sylvain Lévi. He rapidly became one of Durkheim's closest collaborators in the production of the *Année sociologique*, and from 1901 lectured in religious studies at the École Pratique des Hautes Études. After World War I, in which he was decorated for bravery, he played a major role in continuing the efforts of Durkheim and his circle. He also lectured (from 1926) at the Institute of Ethnology, of which he was cofounder, and (from 1931) at the Collège de France. He retired at the start of World War II (Fournier 1994).

In contrast to his somewhat austere uncle, Mauss enjoyed company, the arts, and mountain walking, and he was also active in socialist committee work and journalism, criticizing Bolshevism and favouring the Cooperative Movement. He left many of his academic projects unfinished, including his thesis, and although he worked unselfishly to bring out the books of deceased colleagues, he never published a book of his own. However his notes for the lectures at the Institute were published by others (Mauss 1947), and his anthropological writings were collected posthumously (Mauss 1950, 1968–9). The texts translated into English represent less than half the corpus.

Mauss never undertook FIELDWORK or specialized in a region. Instead, publishing more than five hundred reviews, and remembering what he read, he accumulated remarkable, almost encyclopaedic erudition. He ranged with ease between the ancient Hebrew or Indo-European world (Sanskritic, Greco-Roman, Germanic) and contemporary ethnography (especially from Australia, insular Pacific, and native North America), often using original-language texts.

Though sometimes disagreeing with his uncle, Mauss remained at heart a Durkheimian – as aware of the statistical patterning of behaviour as of the ideological categories that underlie it, and more concerned with social cohesion than conflict, with world history than synchronic system, and with the collective than individual agency. Within "pure" theory his most discussed idea is that of the "total social fact" – those occasions that (in the limiting case) assemble the whole of society and mobilize all its institutions so as to present multiple aspects (sociostructural, jural, economic, aesthetic, religious, etc). But he distrusted high abstraction, always retaining a clear sense of social reality as lived.

In his first major essay in 1899 he interpreted philological material on SACRIFICE in terms of communication between man and god (H. Hubert & Mauss 1964). In 1903 he and Durkheim argued that in early totemic society the CLASSIFICATION of humans into units of social structure (such as clans) served as a template for the classification of the realms of nature, and that this form of ideological coherence has broken up in the course of world history (Durkheim & Mauss 1963; Allen 1994). In 1906 he contrasted the demographic dispersal of the Eskimo summer camps with the ritual "effervescence" characteristic of their communal winter settlements (Mauss & Beuchat 1979). His most famous text, published in 1925, is certainly *The gift* (Mauss 1954). Although gifts are ostensibly given spontaneously, in fact people are often acting under obligation, not only when giving, but also when receiving and returning. He envisaged three evolutionary stages of GIFT EXCHANGE. Under a system of total prestations, exchanges link clan with clan; in societies having POTLATCH or the like, exchanges are typically competitive or "agonistic"; and in the modern world, though older forms survive, it is the amoral MARKET that dominates. Mauss recommended that the individualism of the market be moderated by emphasis on the human propensity to give as well as to consume.

In later essays Mauss (1979) followed up Durkheim's *Suicide* by showing the physiological effectiveness of social imperatives to abandon life, and explored the cultural patterning of bodily posture and movement. His final masterpiece attempts for the category of the person, conceived of as a moral entity, what the 1903 *Primitive classification* essay had attempted for the cognitive category of class: the tribal "personage," incarnation of a specific mythical clan forebear, evolves into the contemporary person, bearer of universalistic human rights (see Carrithers et al. 1985).

Mauss's other pioneering texts cover magic, prayer, the relationship between sociology and psychology, joking relations, tribal segmentation, the nation, and much more (Mauss 1950, 1979). But Mauss's place in history is guaranteed not only by the quality of his major texts and by the numerous insights scattered throughout the oeuvre (many still awaiting exploitation), but also by his personal influence on scholars of the stature of Granet, LÉVI-STRAUSS, and Dumont. His work, though not always easy reading, retains the power to suggest and inspire.   NA

further reading Allen 1995; Dumont 1986a; Lévi-Strauss 1987; J. Parry 1986

Mead, Margaret (1901–78)

In the popular mind Margaret Mead is the best-known anthropologist of the twentieth century. Although she has had a less-lasting influence in academic anthropology, no one was her equal in relating conclusions drawn from research in distant and seemingly alien peoples to the concerns of her own society, particularly on issues such as ADOLESCENCE, GENDER, and SOCIALIZATION (particularly of CHILDREN).

Born in Philadelphia in 1901 into an academic family (her mother was a sociologist, her father a professor of finance), Mead became part of a second generation of Franz BOAS's students at Columbia, where she received her Ph.D. in 1929. She was particularly influenced by her somewhat more senior colleagues Ruth BENEDICT and Edward SAPIR, close friends with whom she founded the CULTURE AND PERSONALITY movement that attempted to relate cultural anthropology to psychiatry and psychology.

Mead was one of the first women in American anthropology to undertake intensive fieldwork overseas, beginning in the Pacific where she studied adolescent girls. Her book *Coming of age in Samoa* (1928) argues that the tribulations associated with adolescence in the United States were not found in Samoa, and that therefore they were a product of culture, not biology. Succeeding fieldwork in the late 1920s and the 1930s resulted in a number of academic monographs, but it was *Coming of age*, and other books like it, that gained her fame.

These included *Growing up in New Guinea* (1930), which focused on childhood socialization and the relationships among generations in a Manus village, *Sex and temperament in three primitive societies* (1935), which attempted to show the plasticity of gender roles for men and women, and *Male and female* (1949), a larger cross-cultural examination of gender.

These works had much in common: they were aimed at a popular audience as well as anthropologists, they took as their central theme a social problem of current concern in the United States, and they used cross-cultural data to draw parallels (by implication and directly) with specific aspects of American life that Mead wished to critique. They brought Mead considerable celebrity and have remained in print to this day. The major exception to Mead's emphasis on the popularly accessible studies from this period was a pioneering effort, conducted with Gregory Bateson, to document socialization in Bali by capturing social process, bodily expression, and spatial dynamics on film. This classic work (G. Bateson & Mead 1942) was much admired within anthropology (see PHOTOGRAPHY), but had little appeal to nonprofessionals.

By the beginning of World War II Mead had largely ceased her field research but had become active in a wide range of comparative projects. A strong supporter of the contention that childhood socialization had an impact on the formation of NATIONAL CHARACTER (Mead 1953a), she published a study of American culture from this perspective (Bateson & Mead 1942). She became involved in a large project, with Ruth Benedict, for studying "culture at a distance" where, for reasons of politics or extinction, cultures could not be studied directly (Mead 1953c). At this time Mead also participated actively in government-sponsored projects focusing on such international issues as DIET and DEVELOPMENT (Mead 1953b, 1964). Of particular interest is her work on the transformations that had occurred on Manus in New Guinea since her work there with Rio Fortune a quarter-century earlier (Mead 1956).

Throughout her career Mead was associated with the Museum of Natural History in New York. This base had provided the flexibility needed for her wide-ranging work, but as an institution it was far from supportive, only grudgingly promoting her to rank of curator after 40 years of service, and then only near her retirement. By the end of her life she was something of an anthropological icon, large staff in hand, testifying before Congress or lecturing large groups on how to improve the relations between generations. She published an autobiography in 1972, *Blackberry winter*, that mingled themes from her professional and personal life. She died in New York in 1978.

For most anthropologists, death brings an end to a scholarly career, but one of Mead's most important debates took place posthumously when Derek Freeman published *Samoa: the making of an anthropological myth* (1983). Freeman accused Mead of being tricked by her informants and being misled about Samoan culture, a dual deception in his view because he argued that Mead was determined to find evidence that would support Boas's premise that human nature was determined by culture and not biology. Freeman's Samoa, by contrast, was marked by violence and competition, where sexuality was far from open and free. This led to a series of debates and books on the controversy that swirled over issues of the conduct of FIELDWORK, the validity of the data and theoretical arguments, the history of anthropology, and large doses of ad hominem charges and countercharges (L. Holmes 1987; Orans 1996). Even with the handicap of being unable to respond personally with her staff, Mead's 50-year-old work emerged bruised but standing, and brought renewed attention to the themes she had spent a lifetime developing.

TB

further reading *American Anthropologist* 82 (1980): 261–373 [collection of articles "In memoriam: Margaret Mead 1901–1978"]; M. Bateson 1984; Gordan 1976; Handler 1990; J. Howard 1984

mechanical solidarity refers to the form of social solidarity found in small-scale societies where the strength of the collective conscience is high and individuals (as social persons) can be seen more or less as mechanical reproductions of each other. Coined by Emile DURKHEIM (1933), mechanical solidarity is associated with a very simple DIVISION OF LABOR.

MR

See also ORGANIC SOLIDARITY

medical anthropology studies human health problems and healing systems in their broad social and cultural contexts. Medical anthropologists engage in both basic research into health and healing systems and applied research aimed at the improvement of therapeutic care in clinical settings or community public health programs in prevention and disease control. Drawing from biological and social sciences, as well as clinical sciences, medical anthropologists have contributed significantly to the understanding and improvement of human health and health services worldwide. As a result, the growth of the subdiscipline in recent years – as reflected in publications and meetings, training programs, and influence outside of anthropology – has been remarkable.

Medical anthropology is not characterized by a single theoretical paradigm. For example, ethnographic description and analysis of religion and healing systems are as old as anthropology itself, while new approaches like critical medical anthropology are the product of more recent intellectual trends. This has sometimes led to intense debates within the field such as those between clinically applied medical anthropologists (interested in making cultural knowledge useful to the aims of medical practitioners) and critical medical anthropologists (interested in the phenomenology and political economy of biomedicine). But, even though the scope of intellectual inquiry is very diverse, it is possible to identify five basic approaches: biomedical, ethnomedical, ecological, critical, and applied. These approaches share three fundamental premises:

1. illness and healing are fundamental to the human experience and are best understood holistically in the contexts of human biology and cultural diversity
2. disease represents an aspect of the environment that is both influenced by human behavior and requires biocultural adaptations
3. the cultural aspects of health systems have important pragmatic consequences for the acceptability, effectiveness, and improvement of health care, particularly in multicultural societies

Ethnomedical approaches

All societies have MEDICAL SYSTEMS that provide a theory of disease etiology, methods for the diagnosis of illness, and prescription and practice of curative therapies. The initial development of medical anthropology derived from anthropological interest in different illness beliefs and healing practices (Rubel & Hass 1996). The earliest ethnomedical research was confined to the study of non-Western societies and exotic cultures and was generally subsumed under the comparative study of RELIGION. Ideas about sickness and therapeutic rituals were analyzed as a window on underlying cosmological beliefs and cultural values. As the intimate relationship between the concepts of illness and the social organization were recognized, ethnomedicine became a common focus of ethnographic research. Fabrega (1975: 969) defined this approach as "the study of how members of different cultures think about disease and organize themselves toward medical treatment and the social organization of treatment itself." Typical ethnomedical studies focus on the CLASSIFICATION and cultural meaning of ILLNESS (both somatic and mental), the health-seeking behaviors of people suffering from illness, and the theories, training, and practices of healers. Nichter (1992: x) described twelve areas of current ethnomedical work, including the "study of the afflicted body as a space where competing ideologies are contested and emergent ideologies are developed through medico-religious practices and institutions which guide the production of knowledge."

Ethnomedical research has had practical implications. The concept of explanatory models of illness, used in clinically applied anthropology, brings attention to the individual interpretation of the causation, course, and treatment of illness episodes. Ethnomedical understandings (e.g., the hot/cold theory of illness in Hispanic people, or the "high-blood"/"hypertension" distinction in African Americans) are significant for understanding how cultural beliefs influence health behaviors (P. Brown et al. 1994).

Biomedical approaches

Although not always recognized as such, much of the research in BIOLOGICAL ANTHROPOLOGY using the standard epistemology of science and focusing on human biology and the health consequences of different stresses is part of medical anthropology (F. Johnston & Low 1984). For example, it has long been recognized that DISEASE has acted as an important agent of natural selection in genetic and cultural EVOLUTION. Biomedical anthropologists have used immunological studies to trace EPIDEMICS. Biological anthropologists have examined human physiological adaptations to a wide variety of stresses, including high elevation, cold temperatures, nutritional deprivation, and infectious disease. Laboratory-based scientific methods (such as the biochemical analyses of ethnopharmacological compounds) are used to analyze the biochemical and physiological functioning of ethnomedical practices. This type of analysis played a role in the discovery of a Hepatitis vaccine (Blumberg 1982).

Ecological approaches

The ecological approach in medical anthropology focuses on how human cultural and behavioral patterns shape the complex interactions of the pathogen, the environment, and the human host, and produce both infectious and noninfectious disease states (Inhorn & Brown 1997). In recent years, ecological studies of health and illness have looked beyond local socioeconomic factors that influence disease rates to emphasize the larger political economic forces that constrain the behavior choices of populations. Both ECOLOGICAL ANTHROPOLOGY and political ecology examine how cultural, physical, and political-economic environments shape the distribution of disease morbidity and mortality. Disease patterns described with epidemiological methods (in regard to time, place, and person) often reflect cultural practices associated with diet, activity patterns, sexuality, and so forth. In addition,

culturally defined group practices such as the introduction of IRRIGATION agriculture can transform the disease ecological balance in favor of a pathogen like malaria or shistosomiasis, and in turn damage health. Ecological analyses in medical anthropology also reveal many cases where cultural changes improve health for some groups.

Critical approaches

Critical medical anthropology (CMA) is a label applied to two distinct intellectual movements that influenced the field during the 1980s and 1990s. One emphasized the marxist approaches to understanding how macrosociological political-economic forces influence health and structure health-care systems. The second movement is more epistemological, it questions the intellectual underpinnings of contemporary biomedical theory and practice. This approach has been influenced by postmodern thinkers like Foucault who emphasize the social-constructionist nature of reality and the social power inherent in hegemonic institutions like "Biomedicine." What these movements have in common is the demand for a fundamental rethinking of the premises and purposes of medical anthropology.

The political-economic orientation of CMA views health issues in the light of the larger political and economic forces that pattern human relationships, shape social behavior, and condition collective experience (Merrill Singer 1989). Macrolevel processes such as world CAPITALISM are seen as the dominant forces that shape clinical practice and influence the distribution of disease. Medicine is perceived not only as a set of procedures and treatments, but also as a particular set of social relationships and an ideology that legitimates them. Recognition of the centrality of the political-economic dimensions of both sickness and healing, as well as the unequal social relationships between healers and patients is the hallmark of this approach.

The second branch of CMA challenges the epistemology and universality of assumptions underlying the theory and practice of Western medicine, which were conventionally exempt from cultural analysis in medical anthropology. This approach has been responsible for the label "bio-medicine." Medical anthropologists like Lock and Scheper-Hughes (1996) advocate the deconstruction of how mind and body are conceptualized as a way to gain insight into how health care is planned and delivered in Western societies. The separation of mind and body in biomedical science is so pervasive that there is a need for more precise vocabulary for the interactions of mind, body, and society.

Applied approaches

Interest in the applied aspects of medical anthropology has been present since the initiation of the discipline. There are two branches of applied work, clinical and public health. Clinically applied medical anthropology is best known for its use of explanatory models to explore conceptual differences between physicians' and patients' perceptions of disease and illness. Clinically applied anthropologists work in biomedical settings with health practitioners and the delivery of health care services; they are also involved in the training of future professionals. Without a single theoretical proposition, it can be interpreted as anthropological theory and methods devoted to the topics of health, illness, and health care. Clinical medical anthropological research has a very wide range, including microlevel studies of health-care choices, illness beliefs, and life-course events like CHILDBIRTH or menopause; the examination of cultural influences on health-seeking behavior, disease distributions, the experience of illness (e.g., pain), and interactions of healers and patient (i.e., compliance); and macrolevel research on health-care systems and their political and economic contexts (Chrisman & Johnson 1996). Some clinically applied medical anthropologists are employed within hospitals and clinics as cultural mediators and interpreters.

Applied medical anthropology research in public health has gained importance in recent decades (Coreil & Mull 1990). More medical anthropologists are working in international health projects, particularly because of the programmatic emphasis on primary health care and interventions in nutrition and oral rehydration therapy that require community participation. Anthro-pologists have worked on all aspects of such projects, including problem identification and analysis, intervention, and evaluation of specific health problems.

PB, KHT, & JH

See also CRITICAL ANTHROPOLOGY, DIET, DRUGS, ETHNOBOTANY, ETHNOPSYCHOLOGY, ROLE, SUFFERING, TRANCE

medical systems comprised of both cognitive and behavioral components are found in all cultures and are studied as part of MEDICAL ANTHROPOLOGY.

The cognitive component of a medical system centers upon theories of etiology, or causation, of ILLNESS and usually involves a taxonomy of DISEASE categories grouped by causal agent. The study of cultural knowledge about illness and its linkages to differential diagnosis and curative actions is called ethnomedicine. The behavioral components of medical systems concern the social interactions of healers and their patients in a cultural and economic context. The social mechanisms through which healers are trained, the division of labor among healers, and the organization of the institutions through which medical services are delivered to a population are all important parts of medical systems.

In technologically simple societies like bands and tribes that employ SHAMANS as principal healers, the medical system is integrated into, and often indistinguishable from, the local RELIGION. By contrast, in technologically COMPLEX SOCIETIES, the primary medical system is more likely to be secular and characterized by simultaneous existence of multiple medical systems or traditions – a situation called medical pluralism.

In a cultural sense, a medical system is an organized set of ideas referring to a particular healing tradition (e.g., Chinese, ayurvedic, homeopathic, and biomedical). Medical anthropologists use the term "biomedicine" to refer to the tradition of scientific, biologically oriented methods of diagnosis and cure. Biomedicine is a relatively recent tradition that is technologically sophisticated and often extremely successful in curing. Historically known as allopathic medicine, the knowledge and technology of biomedicine has grown extremely fast, and with it the prestige and professionalization of biomedical practitioners. The scientific medical system is international, cosmopolitan, dominant, and hegemonic. It is not, however, culture free. The cultural and epistemological assumptions of biomedicine have been studied by medical anthropologists (Rhodes 1996), as have the significant and fascinating national and regional differences in the practice of biomedicine, especially between European countries and the United States. Documented differences include the interpretation of schizophrenia or what constitutes low blood-pressure, as well as the rates and styles of surgery practiced (Payer 1988).

In a behavioral sense, a medical system can be seen as an analog to the socioeconomic order. One or more medical traditions are used to produce and distribute medical services and outcomes in a particular community or region (A. Young 1983). Medical practitioners must be trained, patients must seek out their services, healing behaviors must be performed in particular fashions, and healers must be compensated for their work. Sociopolitical policies and philosophies vary between contemporary nation-states and this undoubtedly influences the practice of medicine and access to medical care.

When viewed as a cultural system, biomedicine becomes one ethnomedicine among many others, that is, rooted in cultural presuppositions and values, associated with rules of conduct, and embedded in a larger context (Hahn 1995). There is little doubt that the *belief* of patient and family in the healer and the power of the medicine plays a fundamental role in the process of healing. All medical systems manipulate symbols to invoke and enhance belief; in this regard, all medical systems involve symbolic healing processes (sometimes labeled as placebo effect).

Medical anthropologists have attempted to typologize medical systems cross-culturally. George Foster (1976), for example, distinguished between "personalistic" and "naturalistic" medical systems based on the predominant theory of disease causation. In personalistic systems, illness results from

individual situations resulting from SORCERY or retribution by spirits. In naturalistic systems, illness is the result of some imbalance in normal physiological processes, as in a humoral system, when the surfeit or excess of a bodily fluid causes disease symptoms.

A medical system can be understood as a social system consisting of organizational roles in institutional structures embedded within a larger social system. The two most important roles are the healer and the patient. As healers, shamans are usually independent and idiosyncratic; typically they use trance to communicate with the spirit world to arrive at a diagnosis. In more complex societies medical roles are usually specialized. Biomedical systems are characterized by high levels of specialization and a hierarchy of prestige between specialties. The sociopolitical processes of professionalization have been studied by medical anthropologists. Last (1996) identified three levels of profession: (1) conventional biomedical professions privileged by every contemporary state; (2) professions of alternative medicine (e.g. homeopathy, ayurveda, acupuncture, and chiropractic), which are often recognized by governments and maintain a formal system of therapy taught at special colleges; and (3) the emerging processes of the professionalization of traditional medicine by amalgamating a diverse group of local practitioners for obtaining government recognition, which has been occurring in Third World nations. The relationships between the diverse professions in a medically pluralistic society is important, but it is the health-seeking behavior of patients (the hierarchy of curative resort) that drives the overall medical system. The professionalization and utilization of traditional medical practitioners is an important topic because of the serious health-personnel shortages faced by many nations.

The patient's ROLE in the medical system involves the sick role, a concept developed by Talcott Parsons (1951b). A person taking the sick role is temporarily exempt from normative behavior and is instead expected to enact certain patient roles: to obey the doctor, gradually decrease dependence on the doctor's care, and get well, thereby resuming normative roles and behavior.

PB & KHT

See also CLASSIFICATION, ETHNOBOTANY, ETHNOPSYCHOLOGY, ETHNOSCIENCE

men   *See* MASCULINITY

menstruation is a bodily event that occurs in girls and women of childbearing age around the world. Although this may seem to make it an invariable biological process undeserving of anthropological scrutiny, in fact the period carries distinctive meanings: cross-culturally one finds positive, negative, neutral, and ambivalent views of menstrual blood or menstruating women.

TABOOS signal an assumption that menstrual BLOOD is special and contains unique powers. Whether these powers are denigrated or valued depends on local ideas and power structures circumscribing GENDER relations. For example, the Beng of Côte d'Ivoire see menstrual blood as a symbol of fertility, and their political structure mandates participation of men and women at every level. A taboo prohibiting menstruating Beng women from working in their fields is not indicative of female oppression but rather a sign of an effort to segregate human fertility from both the natural fertility of the forest and fields and the supernatural fertility of the spirits (Gottlieb 1988b).

Elsewhere, when several menstruating women collectively occupy a discrete space (sometimes termed "menstrual huts") they may see this as a welcome break from their normal labor and even a time for pleasant sociability with other menstruating women. On the other hand, menstrual segregation for ten days each month among Jews traditionally signaled a general image of menstruating women as polluted and even EVIL, until the ritual *mikvah* bath purified them (R. Cernea 1981: 62–3) – though recently, some American Jewish women have contested this view (Kaufman 1991). Among the Kel Ewey Tuareg of Niger, the existence of menstrual taboos serves to highlight sociological principles, such as CLASS distinctions between elites

and peasants, rather than gender ideologies per se (Rasmussen 1991).

Other societies reveal structural ambivalence concerning both menstruation and women as a group through the presence of menstrual taboos (M. Douglas 1966). For example, Yurok women of California traditionally segregated themselves for ten days each month during the paramenstruum. While at least some Yurok *men* seem to have viewed women's menses as a source of symbolic pollution, there is evidence that *women* emphasized renewing their spiritual powers by bathing in purifying rivers (Buckley 1988). Similarly, some Taiwanese women view their periods as a means of maintaining good health rather than the source of pollution that Taiwanese men stress (Furth & Ch'en 1992). Among the Siberian Khanty, menstrual taboos index a combination of men's denigration of women as polluting, and their acknowledgment that women gain power, especially in the spiritual and ritual domains, as they age (Balzer 1981).

Menstrual blood is different from venous blood not only biologically (it is incapable of clotting) but also culturally: it is frequently seen as uniquely potent and endowed with mystical properties. Thus it must be disposed of privately – others are frequently forbidden to see or touch it (hence the common taboo against menstrual sex). However, precisely because it is considered powerful, menstrual blood may be used for certain purposes, from WITCHCRAFT to love potions. For example, menstruation is celebrated in elaborate coming-of-age rituals for girls by the Asante of Ghana, and male Asante priests traditionally protected themselves against witchcraft with special brooms dipped in menstrual blood, although the Asante as a whole deem menstrual blood so dangerous that menstruating women who violated certain taboos were reputed to have been killed in precolonial times (Buckley & Gottlieb 1988a).

Although the above examples all point to elaborate cultural repertoires concerning menstruation, such is not universally the case. For example, the Rungus of Borneo have no taboos concerning menstruation, which is virtually a nonissue for both sexes (L. Appell 1988). And the psychological symptoms of premenstrual syndrome (PMS), now so prevalent in Western societies (E. Martin 1987), are not replicated in women living in at least some nonindustrial settings (Gottlieb 1988a). At the same time, some women in industrialized nations are now inventing their own menstrual rituals to celebrate the menstrual cycle and resist the increasingly hegemonic frame of PMS (Owen 1993).

The biology and psychology of menstruation are also variable cross-culturally. For instance, where little or no effort is made to limit pregnancy, women menstruate rarely, with frequent and long-term breastfeeding suppressing the menstrual cycle for up to several years postpartum (see REPRODUCTION). The length of the menstrual cycle itself can also attenuate the frequency of the period. For example, among the Gainj of New Guinea, the median cycle length is 36 days (P. Johnson et al. 1987). Additionally, in non-Western and preindustrial settings, menarche has occurred far later than it does in contemporary Western countries, thus shortening the duration of the entire cycle (Laslett 1973). Finally, when women live together in close quarters or experience the same exposure to light, the overall timing of the menstrual cycle may be keyed to the lunar cycle (M. McClintock 1971). A tendency for women to menstruate at either the new moon or the full moon may be encoded culturally in rituals (Lamp 1988) and myths (Knight 1991).

In sum, there is considerable variability cross-culturally both in the actual biology of menstruation and in the ways that the menstrual period is seen and treated. Menstruation is less a biological given than a cultural event that creates vastly different experiences for individual women.

AG

See also ADOLESCENCE, FERTILITY RITES AND CULTS, GENDER, PURITY/POLLUTION, RITES OF PASSAGE

further reading C. Bailey 1993; Brumberg 1993; Delaney et al. 1993; Golub 1983; Lupton 1993; McKeever 1984; Sobo 1992

mestizo is a person of mixed RACE in the former Spanish colonies of the Americas, usually of mixed indigenous and Spanish ancestry.

MR

middleman minorities are ethnic groups recruited to a country by those in power to fill a gap in the economic or labor structure. The term describes the economic and social position these groups occupy in society. Middleman minorities originate in immigration rather than conquest (Bonacich & Modell 1980: 15). In early anthropology and sociology such groups were referred to as "pariahs" and "guest peoples" (M. Weber 1952: 3) or "strangers" (Simmel 1950: 402). Historic examples of this phenomenon include the Jews and Gypsies in Europe; the Chinese throughout southeast Asia; the Chinese and Japanese in the United States; the Indians, Pakistanis, and Lebanese in Africa; and the Armenians in the Ottoman Empire. As diverse as these groups are, they share similar histories.

The societal dynamic that produces middleman minorities begins when the elites of a particular country lure them to settle with promises of economic opportunity and tolerance. The middleman groups are motivated to accept the risks involved in establishing themselves in an unfamiliar setting because of the difficulties they face in their own homelands or diasporic communities. Factors pushing them toward this decision include war, military occupation, famine, or the inability to earn a livelihood.

Middleman groups often view their relocation as temporary, but over time they become perpetual minorities in these host countries (Siu 1952). Never absorbed into the indigenous population, they live as nations within nations, with their own distinct culture and social organization (Sway 1975). Welcome at first for the skills and goods and services they offer, middlemen always eventually come to be viewed with antipathy by the masses and elites alike. Careful analysis reveals a linear progression of difficulties for them, or what Georg Simmel (1950: 402) referred to as "dangerous possibilities," including special and excessive taxes, discriminatory laws to thwart the groups' expansion or success, nationalization of businesses, stripping of property and wealth, forced emigration, containment, and lastly, in some cases, GENOCIDE. But these problems do not arise overnight; rather, they tend to evolve over a number of years, taking anywhere from two generations to centuries depending on the specific historical context.

Such dangerous antipathy begins to build toward middlemen when segments in the indigenous population covet their niche or believe they can't successfully compete with them. Middleman groups are vulnerable because their political and social isolation is fostered by the ruling class, who routinely use them as a buffer against the masses or as a scapegoat during times of crisis. Other institutions, such as the Church, guilds, unions, and political parties also find the middlemen convenient scapegoats. If it behooves those in power, official action is taken to dislodge the middlemen from their niche, often under the cloak of nationalism. A slogan like "Jew Free" before, during, and after World War II in Germany, Austria, and Poland illustrates the point. "Uganda for Ugandans" and "Africans First" were slogans aimed at the Indians and Pakistanis during Idi Amin's reign in the 1970s.

Characteristically, when a middleman minority's initial role has been played out, the middlemen usually develop other niches for themselves in the host economy rather than depart, persisting beyond the status gap for which they were originally recruited (Bonacich 1973). For example, in the late nineteenth century, after their work on the railroads was finished, the Chinese in the United States established themselves in laundry and restaurant businesses. Similarly, Japanese laborers who were brought to the United States to harvest California crops later established businesses in truck farming, fishing, and canning in the early decades of this century. However, frequently the only real contact middleman minorities have with the indigenous population is through business dealings. Though they may do well financially as a group, their MONEY is regarded as "weak money" because they rarely have the political clout

to protect themselves in times of trouble. They always have citizenship problems (Sway 1988). Ultimately, the middleman group is removed from the economic scene. Internal piracy is a benchmark of the process.

The question of whether, after finding a new niche, middleman minorities can establish themselves as a permanent fixture within a mixed society is hotly debated. Anthropologists writing on assimilation stress the possibility of acceptance or accommodation (Zenner 1988), whereas others (see D. Levinson 1994) argue that it is only a matter of time before the historical pattern of exclusion repeats itself and those groups fortunate enough to escape the final step of genocide must relocate to another society and begin again.   MSw

See also ETHNIC GROUPS, NATION

further reading Oxfeld 1993; Rao 1987; Seagrave 1995; Talai 1989; Zenner 1991

migration   is of two types: (1) the regular seasonal movement of residence from one place to another within a set territory, common among FORAGERS and PASTORAL NOMADS; and (2) the action of moving from one country or locality to settle in another, also called "emigration." It is the latter that has had greatest historical significance and attracted the most attention from anthropologists concerned with how migration is related to economics, politics, culture, and demography.

The current distribution of peoples around the world is the result in great part of previous migrations. Among the most notable prehistoric migrations were the first human movements of foragers out of Africa to Eurasia and from there to the Pacific islands, Australia, and North and South America. Anthropologists have examined blood types and other genetic markers and have used linguistic and archaeological methods to reconstruct these movements. The development of AGRICULTURE some 10,000 years ago made possible large settled populations, which often migrated because of conflict and environmental pressures. Ancient civilizations were often involved in wars that caused the displacement and enslavement of peoples. The rise of nomadic pastoralists in Eurasia and Africa made possible movement of large populations and through their predations on agrarian communities, the forced movements of the latter.

A different type of migration was associated with modern industrialization and urbanization. In the eighteenth and nineteenth centuries in Western Europe, growth of factory production in cities created demand for urban labor, which attracted rural people. These migrants were often PEASANTS pushed out of rural areas by labor-saving farm equipment. In some areas, particularly Britain, peasants were also forced from land to free it for the production of sheep to provide wool for the mills of the industrial revolution and for cattle to provide meat for urban populations.

Two of the largest migrations in world history – movements of millions of people to the Americas – also occurred in the nineteenth century. Previously, the largest movements to the New World were to Latin America and the Caribbean, including large numbers of enslaved Africans. Very high rates of migration to North America were produced first in the 1840s and 1850s by the potato blight and subsequent famine in Ireland and later by political upheaval in Germany. The second wave, from 1880 to 1910, was from Eastern and Southern Europe and was driven by economic difficulties in those lands and the demand for labor in a rapidly industrializing United States. This migration became the focus for one of the most important ethnographic studies of migration (W. Thomas & Znaniecki, 1918–20). In Europe a genocidal type of population movement took place during World War II with the forced relocation of some six million Jews, most of whom were murdered by Nazis. Another three million members of other ethnic minorities were also deported to labor camps, where most were worked and starved to death.

After World War II anthropologists become more involved in migration studies but their work was associated with rural–urban migrations, often inside a single country, rather than with the larger transnational types noted above. In particular field anthropologists who were working in rural-peasant and other types of "traditional" community in the 1950s and early 1960s became aware of large-scale migration from these communities into cities, and they (like the people they studied) also moved their research to these urban settings, advancing URBAN ANTHROPOLOGY (O. Lewis 1952). In general such research was grounded in the concept of MODERNIZATION, which predicted that migration, by increasing contact between "traditional" rural communities and the modernity of the cities, would promote the social and economic development of the former and also improve the standard of living of the migrants. But in the 1960s and 1970s urban ethnographic research among migrants from rural areas was instead documenting the proliferation of shantytowns and other types of low-income ghetto, which revealed that rural to urban migration was often associated with growing urban POVERTY (Lomnitz 1977). Also, numerous studies of return migration back to rural homes revealed that urban migration often had no positive economic or social impact on the "sending" communities (Kearney 1986). This awareness of the common failure of rural to urban migration to promote modernization caused some anthropologists to turn to other theoretical perspectives, such as dependency theory and articulation theory.

Modernization theory assumed that migrants would facilitate the diffusion of the modern cultural, social, and technological traits of the city back to the countryside and that these in turn would cause rural areas to develop. Dependency theory, by contrast, proposed that net economic value flowed from the countryside to the city and thus promoted the de-development of peripheral areas. It claimed that because capitalist relations of production were predominant in underdeveloped areas, rural to urban migration was one of many means by which economic surplus and human capital were drained from the countryside to the urban centers of Third World countries (Chilcote 1981). Rejecting both these views, articulation theory argued that noncapitalist modes of production were often preserved and even brought into being by integration with CAPITALISM, among other ways by migration between these two polar types (Meillassoux 1981).

International migration has become the focus of much political debate that often clouds its underlying dynamics. To a great extent transnational migrants are attracted by employment possibilities in industries desirous of cheap workers and thus offset the tendency for firms in developed nations to "run away" to lesser developed nations in search of cheap labor. In Europe research has focused on "guest workers" in Northern Europe from "sending" nations of the Mediterranean basin. In the United States anthropologists have looked at migrants coming from the Caribbean basin (Sutton & Chaney 1992), Mexico (Chavez 1992), and elsewhere. Similar migration patterns are found in Africa and Latin America. Contemporary research on rural-urban migration examines how migrants are incorporated economically, socially, and culturally. But whereas the previous research took place during a period of general economic expansion in the "receiving" areas, especially Western Europe and the United States, the economies of these areas were not so robust in the 1980s and 1990s. Antimigrant sentiment is now widespread in "receiving" countries and research on immigration in these areas has thus included related issues of ethnic conflict and identity formation (Mandel 1989).

Migration is most often associated with great suffering and misery, and nowhere is this more apparent than in the case of REFUGEES, who are a special category of migrants forced to move because of some combination of poverty, population growth, war, persecution, famine, and/or natural disaster (Malkki 1992). The United Nations estimates that 100 million people currently live outside of the country in which they were born; 30 million poor people move annually from rural to urban areas. The magnitude of these figures causes some experts to speak of a new era of human migration that will demand that anthropology give the topic a more central focus than it has in the past.   MK

further reading Castles & Miller 1993; Eades 1987; Malkki 1995a; Piore 1979

millenarian movements are characterized by declarations of the end of one age or form of life and the arrival or dawning of another. Many religious movements have their beginnings or revival in millenarianism. For example, the history of Christianity in Europe, and indeed much of European political history, may be seen as expressing a succession of millenarian waves and reactions to them. Norman Cohn (1970) described the numerous religious millenarian movements through the Middle Ages, which peaked in the Protestant Reformation. Many of them were motivated in the predictions of Joachim of Fiore, who calculated the start of an age when social inequalities would be abolished and the have-nots would inherit the wealth of the earth. Fiore's influence was far-reaching, evident in English Puritanism and Oliver Cromwell's New Model Army. Cohn argued that many secular political ideologies and movements in Europe continue to exhibit features of religious millenarianism. These include various anarchist and marxist political movements. Some contemporary forms of NATIONALISM, especially those that grew as resistance to the conditions of imperial and colonial expansion and domination, have millenarian aspects.

The social and political foundations of religious millenarianism are associated with modes of alienation, social and economic deprivation or political oppression. These have been broadly described on a global scale for colonialized peoples in Lanternari's (1963) classic survey. Among the best-recorded millenarian movements are the CARGO CULTS of Melanesia and the Pacific and the Ghost Dance and Peyote cults among North American Indians (La Barre 1970). The latter have been described as a response to COLONIALISM, with major explanations concentrating on the movements as reflecting the psychological consequences of, and expressing attempts to overcome, social and economic deprivation. The Ghost Dance is an important example of a religio-political resistance movement that drew much of its force from transformations within Indian cosmological and religious ideas. Similar dynamics can be identified in Melanesia and the Pacific, though the British anthropological structural–functional tradition reduces them to psychological and relative deprivation theories. One significance of Melanesian cargo cults – so-called because they prophesy the massive influx of wealth from overseas – is their non-peripheral character, for many millenarian movements appear to be most prevalent among socially and economically marginalized groups. Melanesian cargo cults are major, continuing and recurrent, religio-political movements involved in contemporary social and economic transformations in the region. There is evidence of cargo cult activity at the very start of European penetration. They seem to go through various phases ranging from acceptance to resistance. On the surface the Vailala movement in the Purari Delta of New Guinea during the 1920s appeared to colonial administrators to express an alarming destructive rejection of indigenous culture. On closer inspection it is seen to have manifested processes of social and political reorganization and strong indications of resistance to colonial rule (F. Williams 1976; Worsley 1968). The form and process of cargo movements are shaped by the particular cosmological and exchange basis of many Melanesian societies (see Burridge 1960, 1969). The cults demonstrate the force of indigenous cultural factors in the formations of change and provide considerable insight into the dynamics of cultural and cosmological invention.

Overall the impetus for millenarianism appears to be radical social, economic, and technologically based marginalization or shifts in the organization of experience. But ideological factors should not be excluded. Certain religious ideologies, such as Christianity, have doctrinal features that may encourage routine millenarian processes. In this sense the presence of Christian missionizing may be conceived as one motivating factor. The marked sectarianism of Christianity, especially manifest in colonialized territories or in socially and economically depressed regions, expresses strong millenarian elements. Millenarian movements are created and embraced by populations in an effort to imaginatively recenter themselves in the dynamics of their realities and to reestablish control over life circumstances. A rationalist tendency in much anthropology has often described millenarianism as an example of the irratio-

nal propensities in human activity, especially religious action. But it may be more fruitful to see the often fantastic cultural formings of millenarian movements as examples of the imaginative capacity of human beings, which is always engaged in some way or another in the processes whereby they reshape their realities.

BK

See also RELIGION, SOCIAL CHANGE

further reading Adas 1979; N. Cohn 1970; Eliade 1978; D. Martin 1990; Marty 1986

mode of production   is composed of *forces of production*, which can be defined as the array of tools, techniques, materials, and objects used in the labor process, or the objects that mediate the relations between humans and nature in production, and *relations of production*, which can be defined as the relations of property and distribution by means of which labor is mobilized and the objects of labor appropriated. It is a central concept in Marxist analysis and has also been used in a range of anthropological studies (Godelier 1977; Terray 1972; E. Wolf 1982).

Together, Marx understood the forces and relations of production to constitute the economic structure of society, and he placed forces and relations of production in dynamic relationship to each other, a relationship generally based on complementarity or correspondence. That is, relations of production can be seen to correspond to, or be appropriate for, a particular array or level of the development of productive forces, serving to organize production for a period. But forces and relations also develop according to differential dynamics and can enter into contradiction so that the complementarity or correspondence can be broken, creating a situation of economic and social crisis (Marx & Engels 1947).

To understand Marx's usage, one must first recognize the importance he placed on *labor* as a distinctively human activity and as a range of material activities and processes that serve to distinguish and define humans historically. Labor is a creative activity in which humans interact with nature, using a historically accumulated body of knowledge, techniques, and technology in

order to produce something useful within a particular, historically derived mode of life. It is also a social activity in that it is undertaken within a particular ensemble of social relations through which knowledge and techniques are communicated and TECHNOLOGY acquired, WORK is organized, and the products of labor are shared, appropriated, or consumed. Labor is an active, conscious process through which both the laborer and the object of labor are transformed. Even where the goal of labor is subsistence, or the reproduction of previously existing conditions, the process of labor is both destructive and creative: objects are worked on and made into something else. Thus people work within particular conditions and with particular objects, but their work necessarily changes those conditions and objects, and the relation of humans to them.   WR
See also MARXIST ANTHROPOLOGY, STRUCTURAL MARXISM

modernization is a process of economic, social, and cultural development that is expected to lead to a level of organization and production, along with belief systems, similar to those already achieved by INDUSTRIAL SOCIETIES, primarily based on examples from the West. Consistent with a general Western idea of progress according to which human knowledge and rationality increasingly triumph over ignorance and adversity and improve the conditions of human life, it was generally assumed that modernization was inevitable and global. But as former colonial societies in Asia, Africa, the Pacific, and the Caribbean became independent nations following World War II, much concern was expressed over how, or even if, this modernization process would occur. This concern was also directed at Latin America, which was similarly regarded as "underdeveloped."

Central to ideas about modernization is the assumption that underdeveloped nations are lagging behind the developed ones and that they will eventually catch up, but that such development entails industrialization and replacement of "traditional" SOCIAL ORGANIZATION, WORLDVIEW, CULTURE AND PERSONALITY, and so on by

their modern counterparts. All the social sciences participated in the study of modernization, with many overlapping interests in the relationships between modernization and family organization, education, mass media, religion, personality, and population growth, among other issues. Economists defined development mainly in terms of increased production per capita and the creation of economic surplus that could be invested in modern technology to break out of the static low productivity of traditional economies. They also assumed that increased consumption was a necessary component of this process that would drive production and attain self-sustaining growth. Sociologists examined the impact of formal education and mass media on traditional society, and political scientists looked at the formation of bureaucracies and the institutions of modern nation-states, and the modernizing influence of rationality and national bourgeoisie. Among sociologists Talcott Parsons (1964) saw modernization as the fulfillment of "evolutionary universals" such as the separation of occupational roles from domestic ones and legal principles from religion.

For anthropologists modernization theory was a return of earlier concepts of social EVOLUTIONISM and global DIFFUSIONISM, although applied not to the past but to the present and future. For anthropologists the primary issue was the one of CULTURE: replacing "traditional" with the "modern" version (G. Foster 1962). Boasian anthropology had previously conceived of cultures as consisting of complex assortments of distinct material and nonmaterial cultural traits and had examined cultural change in non-Western societies as the "acceptance" and "rejection" of different traits as a result of the receiving society's "cultural pattern" (Benedict 1934a) or "configuration" (Kroeber 1944). This diffusionist concept of cultural change was first systematically applied to the study of modernization by Robert Redfield in his FOLK–URBAN CONTINUUM model. The inevitable spread of modernity was impeded, however, by societies and cultures that resisted incorporating the modern traits. The identification and reduction of such barriers became one of the main concerns of APPLIED ANTHROPOLOGY, which grew rapidly in association with modernization theory.

In the 1960s dependency theory arose as a critique of modernization theory (Chilcote 1981) and inverted its assumption about the diffusion of the cultural and social traits of modernity from developed to traditional societies. Instead of focusing on cultural and social traits, dependency theorists emphasized the unequal power relations that existed between modern and traditional societies, epitomized in COLONIALISM, which enriched the colonial powers by a transfer of wealth from the colonies to the colonial powers, thus bringing about the "de-development" of the former. Thus, rather than being a result of historic lag, Third World poverty and backwardness had been created by the incorporation of "peripheral" areas into a system of world capitalism that enriched some regions – the "metropoles" – while also de-developing societies in the periphery. Proponents of dependency theory shared the basic assumptions of progress held by modernizationists, but they maintained that modernization in de-developed nations could only be completed in postcapitalist societies.

Since the 1970s much of the optimism about the inevitability of modernization has been offset by increasing poverty associated with constant population growth that exceeds the capacity of poor nations to produce and to distribute basic necessities and to improve the quality of life. Within this global context the social-evolutionary optimism of modernization theory has been dampened, and applied anthropologists now, instead of speaking broadly of "development," have become more concerned with "basic needs," and "sustainable development" in recognition of the fact that much of Africa, South America, and Asia is not developing as had been foreseen in the optimistic heyday of modernization theory in the 1950s and 1960s. On the other hand, the recent rapid economic growth in parts of East Asia and the restructuring of the former Soviet Union and its client states have given the theory new life, especially among economists. Anthropologists have become less involved in this debate than in the past because more recent views of history and social differentiation have rejected the dualist assumptions upon which modernization theory was based, that is, of firm distinctions between rural and urban society or between tradition and modernity.   MK

See also MARKET, POVERTY, TRADITION, WORLD–SYSTEM THEORY

further reading Esteva 1992; J. Ferguson 1990; Geertz 1963a

moiety systems divide a society into two social categories determined by DESCENT, each consisting of half that society's CLANS. The two moieties often play complementary roles in rituals. Moieties can also serve as the basis for a system of exogamous direct marriage exchange in which the men of one moiety marry the women of the other, and vice versa.   MR

further reading Maybury-Lewis & Almagor 1989

money in its strictest sense is a kind of material object that is useful only or mainly for exchange purposes and can circulate indefinitely among persons who use it without necessarily losing its value. The range of what constitutes money is enormous: gold and silver in Eurasia, iron rods in West Africa, large rocks in Yapp, shells in Polynesia, glass beads in India, cocoa beans in Meso-America, to name but a few. Many peoples use more than one form. Paper and electronic money expand the concept further. But money's classically defined economic functions – as a store and index of wealth, a medium of exchange, a means of payment, a standard of value, and a unit of account – all have limits, even in industrial and financial centers.

Money's oft-admired attributes, like countability, portability, divisibility, homogeneity (or uniformity), recognizability, and substitutability (money for other things and money for other money), have all led sociologists and some anthropologists to treat its use as a sign of increasing rationality of society (Simmel 1978; M. Weber 1968). Many evolutionary schemata suggest that money's useful functions are so great they must displace other forms of exchange over time. But true money also has other, less desirable attributes: material uselessness, volatility, and contestability. Money's divisibility, concealability, and wide exchangeability can tempt reckless spending. Policy changes and political conditions can reduce currency's functions through abolitions and devaluations that reduce its utility as a store of wealth over time (Guyer 1995). Inflation can render money worthless or make it less easily portable and countable. Border controls can reduce both its exchangeability and its movability. And money itself, when printed on paper, is susceptible to physical risks such as fire, flooding, and insects (all real hazards in some tropical settings). Thus, for any particular holder, liquid wealth can evaporate.

Although most modern languages have indigenous or borrowed terms corresponding to the English word "money," their meanings, conceptual boundaries, and connotations vary greatly. Central anthropological concerns in studying money have been the rationales behind its use and limitations, and the moral implications of its spread.

Money is a double-edged tool, and the topic has tended to polarize social theorists. Humans can use money to support DIVISION OF LABOR, and thus to increase production and productivity, as Adam Smith (1776) and countless other students of economy and society have shown. But they can also use it to exploit, subjugate, and impoverish other people, as Aristotle (350 B.C.E.), Marx (1887) and marxists, dependency theorists, and some latter-day political economists have made clear. Anthropologists have borrowed from and revised theories of political philosophers, economists, and sociologists (Ortiz 1983; Gudeman 1986).

People perceive in money both quantitative and qualitative values. Money's value is based on trust – in particular people or in broader social process – and social or political instability can destroy this trust. Quantitatively, money's officially mandated value and unofficial market value have often differed markedly, giving rise to illegal currency exchange and trade that are hard

for governmental or other authorities to control. Even where strong national currencies prevail, people constantly invent and use multiple forms of money, some with very restricted uses and circulation (for instance coupons, tokens, vouchers, food stamps, gambling chips, bond certificates, "IOUs," trade beads, gift certificates, company scrip, electronic money). These devices can restrict the things for which money can be exchanged, the times and places for exchange, or the persons eligible to participate.

The qualitative values of money and quasi-money may be symbolic, psychological, or aesthetic in nature. Money is made with symbols, and it is a versatile symbol itself. It can be conceived as lifeless and inert or as alive and growing; as having no inherent moral meaning (J. Parry & Bloch 1989) or as being loaded with its own symbolic valence of moral and other kinds (Simmel 1978). It is variously portrayed as a cause or an effect of social transformations. To some anthropologists money payment is a kind of ritual, but one that may have minimal cultural content of its own (Crump 1981: ch. 1). "Money" is the synecdochic handle *par excellence*, being made to stand for ideas like trade, price haggling, profit, individualism, liberty, exploitation, impersonality, temporal shortsightedness, or the reduction of quality to quantity that denies variation and uniqueness. Many variants of money have status or CLASS implications and are used in making or breaking human dependencies. Variously portrayed in classic philosophies as facilitating exchange, embodying the social contract, corroding social bonds, tempting souls, or driving apart social classes, money is often attributed with powers that really belong instead to the people doing its hoarding or exchanging.

Peoples who deem themselves fully monetized or capitalist turn out less so on deeper examination. For example, money does not inexorably replace BARTER, as some evolutionary schemata would have it; instead these disappear and reappear over time and place, often changing forms as they do (Humphrey & Hugh-Jones 1992a). No society fully condones the free exchange of money for everything by everyone, but nor is any society fully successful in enforcing all its sale or exchange prohibitions. Among the things most often kept apart from cash, or bought and sold only covertly, in most societies are land (particularly inherited or collective land); the human body and its fluids; objects associated with spirits or divinity; and religious, political, and educational offices and titles. Exchange prohibitions apply not only to particular objects, but also to particular relationships in societies, for instance parent–child, teacher–student, or monk–monk bonds.

Following the lead of Raymond FIRTH among Tikopia of the Pacific, ethnographers in many settings have described spheres of exchange, that is, culturally defined categories of things readily exchangeable for other things in the same categories, but not exchangeable, without moral opprobrium, for things in other categories. Societies often limit money's exchangeability and substitutability by "earmarking" its source. Among the Luo of Kenya "bitter money" derived from activities deemed as betrayals (e.g., selling inherited land) may not be used to finance bridewealth payments (Shipton 1989). Such limitations imbue money with moral and normative valence, attempting to keep sacred, long-term, or intimately familial relationships uncorrupted by gains from socially disapproved activities (Parry & Bloch 1989; Zelizer 1994). However, such money is often deemed convertible from moral impurity to purity. This may be a straightforward and open transaction, such as the historic exchange of coins by the biblical temple money changers, but more often it takes the form of laundering money through serial exchanges, religious charities, philanthropic foundations, or special rituals that erase or disguise its origin.

Money used to earn money is perhaps the most contentious cross-cultural category. Many financial terms in English, for instance "capital," "income," and "investment," fail to translate into all tongues or carry very different moral connotations in cultures where money-making activities are viewed with suspicion or disapprobation. Most of the world's great religions, including Catholicism, Hinduism, and Islam,

have wrestled with the question of whether lending money and taking interest is permitted to believers. A common solution historically has been to let such work be done by MIDDLEMAN MINORITIES; another has been to disguise such transactions in a terminology that avoids the word "interest." Terminological differences like these can indicate deeper differences in cultural concepts about the roles of finance and economy in social life.   PS
See also ECONOMIC ANTHROPOLOGY, TRADE
further reading R. Firth & Yamey 1964; Neale 1976; K. Polanyi 1944; Sahlins 1972

monogamy is the social rule restricting individuals to a single spouse at any given time.   MR
See also DIVORCE, MARRIAGE, POLYANDRY, POLYGYNY

monotheism Certain religions insist that there is only one God and that other spiritual beings are either figments of the human imagination or, if they exist, may be fallen, former god-like entities. The three so-called Semitic religions, namely, Judaism, Christianity, and Islam, claim to be monotheistic. Nevertheless, a belief in Satan, a being possessing only negative attributes harmful to mortals, may confer on the religion a dualistic theodicy, according to which God's omnipotence and benevolence stand opposed to Satan's evil powers.

Preprophetic Judaism most closely approached a monist position by reducing the significance of evil as a force opposed to God. Christianity rejected this view and developed an intermediary semidualist theodicy, according to which God's unity and goodness remain while Satan is allowed considerable opportunity to foster evil (Jeffrey Russell 1977). Fundamentalist Islam attempts to deny the belief in and power of Satan and his manifestations, while many local forms of Islam accommodate pre-Islamic beliefs in a variety of noxious demons or spirits and so tend toward a mild dualism. Some Islamic Sufi movements claim that, since God is responsible for all things, it follows that even the agents of EVIL, whether Satan or demons, are themselves expressly created by and indeed are part of God (Bousfield 1985).

The fullest expressions of dualistic theodicies within formal monotheism are those of the eastern Manichaean and Zoroastrian variety, which assert that good and evil, expressed as God and Satan, coexist as two eternal cosmic principles, the struggle between which is not preordained (M. Weber 1963). The Christian Cathars of southwest France provide a familiar example of a religion that is monotheistic in the sense of worshipping only one God but accepts that the goodness emanating from this one God is constantly threatened by Satan's evil forces.

It was assumed by evolutionist scholars of religion that monotheism developed after and out of POLYTHEISM (many gods and spirits). Schmidt (1912) argued against this, claiming that High Gods were evident among many technologically nonadvanced peoples and that this "primitive monotheism" in fact developed polytheistic features later.

The distinction between monotheism and polytheism especially shows its definitional limitations with respect to Hinduism and Buddhism. It is sometimes better to use the definition "immanent divinity." Hinduism is based on a divine hierarchy of an immanent God and various regional and local gods. Buddhism follows the example of the Buddha, an enlightened mortal, and so technically has no conception of a High God (Southwold 1978). It shares with Hinduism a nondualistic, immanent conception of divinity in which the doctrine of *karma* is central (B. Morris 1987: 77).

Whenever the term "monotheism" is applied, there are likely to be found alongside a High God, or as part of immanent divinity, a number of lesser or associated deities, rendering the term of dubious value for local-level anthropological study.

DP

See also RELIGION

further reading Gilsenan 1973; MacGaffey 1983; Obeyesekere 1981; Pocock 1973; Southwold 1983

Morgan, Lewis Henry (1818–81)

L. H. Morgan was a central figure in the formation of anthropology as a specialized discipline in the latter half of the nineteenth century. He is notable primarily for three things: his ethnography of the Iroquois; his worldwide comparative study of kinship systems, through which he largely created kinship as a field of study; and as a leading practitioner of the kind of social evolutionism that was dominant in the Victorian period. These are the respective subjects of his three major books: *League of the Hodé-no-sau-nee, or Iroquois* (1851), *Systems of consanguinity and affinity of the human family* (1871), and *Ancient society* (1877).

Morgan grew up in the village of Aurora in western New York State. After graduating from Union College, Schenectady, he read law and was admitted to the bar in 1842. He moved to Rochester in 1844, where he made a modest fortune representing railroad and iron-mining interests investing in Michigan; he was able to retire in the 1860s and devote himself wholly to his anthropological research.

Morgan's first book, on the Iroquois, grew out of a secret society he and his friends formed in Aurora called the Grand Order of the Iroquois (GOI). The GOI patterned itself upon the Iroquois League, which was a confederacy uniting the five nations of the Iroquois (Mohawk, Oneida, Onondaga, Cayuga, Seneca; a sixth, Tuscarora, was added later). As constitutionalist for the GOI Morgan made researches into the Iroquois League, including fieldwork assisted by Ely S. Parker, a Seneca. This became the basis of his book. At bottom, he found that the Iroquois League rested upon kinship relations in the form of matrilineal clans; that the eight clans (Wolf, Bear, etc.) were found in each of the Iroquois nations; and that the 50 chiefships that made up the deliberating body of the League were owned by particular matrilineal clan segments, so that they passed not from father to son but from mother's brother to sister's son. Furthermore, the Iroquois LONGHOUSE brought members of a clan segment together into a single household. These matters of Iroquois sociopolitical structure, plus his study of Iroquois material culture based on items he commissioned and collected for the state Cabinet of Natural History, form the substance of *League of the Ho-dé-no-sau-nee, or Iroquois*, which remains the best single book on Iroquois culture.

Morgan came to hypothesize that the Iroquois pattern of social organization would be found among all Indian groups and would prove their common origin. But when he tested his ideas out on the Ojibwa of Michigan's Upper Peninsula he found that they had clans but were decidedly patrilineal, not matrilineal. There was another feature of Iroquois kinship, however, that he also found among the Ojibwa: CLASSIFICATORY KINSHIP. Thus among the Iroquois the father's brother was called "father," and the mother's sister was called "mother." Finding the same pattern in Ojibwa, which falls in a different language family, Morgan concluded that he had come across a method of demonstrating historical relationships among American Indian groups beyond the powers of linguistics to do so.

Using this "new instrument for ethnology" to give scientific proof of the unity and Asiatic origin of the American Indians was the object of a big book on KINSHIP, the *Systems of consanguinity*. In a series of field trips to the west during the period 1859–62 he amassed information making up a table of kinship terms for over 200 genealogical positions for 80 Indian groups. He extended the comparison to other parts of the world by sending his printed questionnaire to missionaries, scholars, and US consuls in many places. In the book he showed that the "classificatory" pattern of kinship is not only common among American Indians but is found among Tamils and other groups of India and, more generally, of Asia and Oceania, and that it is different from the "descriptive" pattern of Europe and the Middle East – thus proving unity and Asiatic origin of the Indians. Although Morgan's proof is no longer considered valid, he identified the major types of kinship system and devised methods to describe and analyze kinship systems that remain widely in use today.

The third book, *Ancient society*, is Morgan's summing up of the results of his anthropological research and thought on the broadest canvas of time and space. It is a work of high Victorian social EVOLUTIONISM that traces the progress of the human family from savagery through barbarism to civilization, in respect of technology, political organization, kinship, and ideas of property. Like comparable works of his British contemporaries it is the story of progress on a grand scale; as a class these works are responses to the dramatic backward lengthening of human history with the discovery, at Brixham Cave and other sites, of human remains with the bones of extinct animals (Trautmann 1992).

Morgan's book was closely read by Karl Marx, whose notes (Marx 1972) show that he was interested in the most technical aspects of Morgan's kinship work; after Marx's death Friedrich Engels wrote up the marxist reading of Morgan's social evolutionism (Engels 1902). Morgan's book was attractive to Marx because it held out the promise of a scientific history and seemed to prove that bourgeois norms of property and family had been preceded by the "communism in living" exemplified by the Iroquois longhouse. And the proof had come from someone who was not a socialist but a Presbyterian and a Republican, and so was disinterested. In this way Morgan became authoritative in the anthropology of countries with marxist regimes.

In the anthropology of the West, social evolutionism fell from favor with succeeding generations, especially in the United States, where Franz BOAS redirected anthropology away from the deep past and toward issues of diffusion and function. Morgan's *Ancient society*, therefore, is largely interesting today as an example of the thinking of his time. On the other hand his Iroquois ethnography has never been bettered. And his most technical and difficult work, *Systems of consanguinity*, has been recognized as his masterpiece. It has had a profound influence on anthropology, especially in the work of such luminaries of the field as W. H. R. RIVERS, A. R. RADCLIFFE-BROWN and Claude LÉVISTRAUSS (see Fortes 1969; Trautmann 1987; Godelier 1995).   TT

further reading Resek 1960; Tooker 1983, 1992; Trautmann 1984; Trautmann & Kabelac 1994; Leslie White 1959b

morphemes are the basic word-forming units, such as prefixes, stems, and suffixes. They are defined by their consistency of sound and meaning across words. Partial inconsistencies, as in *i[n]-formal/i[l]-licit* [informal/illicit], *n[ey]ture/n[æ]tur-al* [nature/natural], where the bracketed portions differ in each pair, are attributed to the rules of PHONOLOGY, which adapt sound structure to context. Contextual variants of a single underlying morpheme are called "allomorphs."   LB
further reading A. Spencer 1991

murder   *See* HOMICIDE

museum   anthropology Bringing back artifacts from "exotic" places has a very long tradition in Western countries. The conjunction in the High Renaissance of the Age of Exploration and the development of humanist scholarship culminated in an explosion of curiosity about the new worlds that had been discovered as well as the collection of a wide range of objects. These became the basis for collections in the *Kunst* and *Wunderkammern* ("cabinets of curiosities") set up by kings, princes, archbishops and others (Pomian 1990: 36). In the late eighteenth century, such private cabinets of curiosities became public museums. In 1753, Sir Hans Sloane's collection was purchased by the British government from his executors and formed the nucleus for the British Museum. The museum of Sir Ashton Lever was moved to London in 1774, becoming the Leverian Museum, and that of William Bullock was moved from Liverpool to London in 1809.

As the activities of exploration became more organized toward the end of the eighteenth century, there was an explosion of collecting of both artificial and natural curiosities. Malaspina's great voyage of exploration from 1789 to 1794 took him along the entire west coast of North America as far north as Yakutat Bay in Alaska. His mission was to collect information about, and specimens of, minerals, animals, and plant life – "objects pertaining to anthropology and ethnography". The ethnographic objects he collected are presently in the Museo de America in Madrid.

The most famous voyages of exploration of this period were those of Captain James Cook. Though given no specific instructions to collect artifacts, he and his crew did collect many objects. Of these, more than 2,000 pieces can be found in various museums throughout the world (Kaeppler 1978). A number of the artifacts given to the British Museum were exhibited in the Otaheti Room. On Vancouver's voyage of 1792 to the Northwest Coast and the Pacific, Archibald Menzies, appointed as botanist, was given specific instructions to investigate "native customs" and to make a collection of ethnographic specimens. The purpose of the collecting was set forth as educational so that museums would be able to demonstrate the different crafts of mankind. The collection was given to the British Museum in 1796 (J. King 1981: 11).

When the discipline of anthropology began in the nineteenth century, an important component was the appropriation and collection of ethnographic objects. The Western colonial context formed the setting within which objects from the far-flung colonies were brought back to the mother country to be exhibited (Clifford 1988). The cultural meanings of the objects for the producers were of little interest to nineteenth- and even twentieth-century collectors. Though the museums of the time frequently served to motivate the collecting of objects, the collectors themselves might be traders, plantation owners, missionaries, or government officials.

Museums "are the self-appointed keepers of other peoples' material and self-appointed interpreters of others' histories" (Ames 1992: 140). Museum exhibits have always reflected the cultural assumptions of the people who made them, the curators and exhibitors. They have also articulated messages about national identity and the relationship of the nation to those "Others", their location in the evolutionary scale, and their difference from us (Karp and Lavine 1991). They became the "Primitives," and we the "Civilized." The location of these exhibits in natural history museums placed the "Others" with nature rather than with culture.

In addition, such exhibits made manifest the history of Western imperialism and defended the rightness of colonialism and the economic and cultural appropriation that characterized it (Pomian 1990). The exhibits of the nineteenth century reflected the West's power to classify and define "Others" in order to justify power and control over these "Others." However, ideas about national identity and the relationship between the nation and the rest of the world have changed over time and this has been reflected in changes in the way museums convey knowledge as well as in the knowledge being conveyed.

The artifacts of Others are now also to be found in art museums. Though Picasso and Vlaminck recognized the aesthetic qualities of African and Oceanic art at the beginning of the twentieth century, ritual artifacts were not welcomed into art museums until after World War II. At the Primitivism exhibit at the Museum of Modern Art in New York City, ethnographic objects from many parts of the world were used to illustrate the theme of Primitivism, which equates the temporally distant art in our history to the spatially distant art of the "exotic" Other (W. Rubin 1984). This latest transformation in meaning for the artifacts of Others fully recognizes their aesthetic qualities, moving them back from nature to culture.

Museums as "self-appointed keepers of other people's objects" are being challenged. Many of the descendants of those who made and used the ethnographic objects now to be found in museums around the world are demanding the cultural repatriation of those objects, from the Greeks who seek the frieze from the Parthenon in the British Museum, collected by Lord Elgin, to the Zuni who sought (and ultimately received back) their War Gods from the Smithsonian Museum. Cultural repatriation is an important issue in the museum world today, since it is clear that legislation, like the Native American Repatriation Act, supporting the return of cultural property, constitutes a threat to artifact collections and in turn to the very existence of the museum itself.

PR & AR

music is meaningfully patterned sound that is analytically distinguishable from LANGUAGE, though the two are closely interrelated. Cross-cultural research supports Aristotle's observation that "it is not easy to determine the nature of music." Ubiquitous yet highly culture-specific, music is used to enculturate children, mark important life-cycle stages, heal illness, communicate with the supernatural, organize subsistence activities, uphold (or criticize) political power, and provide sensual pleasure and intellectual stimulation. Even where music is disseminated via the mass media and regarded primarily as a form of entertainment, it nonetheless retains considerable efficacy as an expression of individual and communal identity.

The ancient Greek term *mousike*, which subsumed poetry, mathematics, acoustics, and ethics, suggests an etymological precedent for the inclusive and flexible definitions of music adopted by anthropologists. Although all societies have aural expressions that are broadly analogous to the English term "music," the precise sonic forms involved, and the concepts, values, and techniques underlying their production, vary quite widely. Therefore the cross-cultural study of music must focus as much on the interpretation of musical sounds and the social context of music making, as on the surface properties of the sounds themselves. Contrary to the oft-repeated claim that music is a kind of "universal language," the meaning of music has as much to do with the listener's prior experience and expectations as with the qualities of the sounds themselves. Performances by an African trumpet orchestra, a Chinese opera company, a military band, or an avant-garde chamber music ensemble may be interpreted as sonic chaos by listeners unfamiliar with the generative principles underlying the music, and a military march that evokes nationalistic pride in one listener may hold sexual significance for another. In some cultures, the concept of music may also include phenomena that produce no acoustic image at all, such as musical memories, dreams, visions, and other forms of internalized aural experience.

Musical sound may be analyzed into components such as pitch (the human experience of frequency), rhythm (patterns of temporal organization), texture (the cumulative interaction of individual parts or voices), and timbre (the quality of sound). The sound materials used to construct music, and the procedures by which they are combined, vary widely. In some traditions, melodies (sequences of pitches forming a coherent shape) are composed of only three or four distinct pitches, while others make use of seven or more pitches, augmented by complex "microtonal" variations (intervals smaller than the half-step of the Western tempered scale). Although almost all music relies upon patterns of repetition and variation, the specific forms involved range from strict repetition of a short melodic phrase to the elaborate (and quite diverse) theme-and-variation procedures of "classical" music in Eurasia. But reliance on repetition is not correlated with musical "simplicity": in many sub-Saharan African musical traditions, multiple repeated parts are staggered in time to create polyphonic textures of great complexity.

The role of the musician differs widely from society to society. In hierarchical systems the right to perform certain forms of music may be restricted to members of specific lineages, guilds, or castes, and the training of musicians is often highly specialized. By contrast, such relatively egalitarian peoples as the Bambuti of the Central African rain forests (Turnbull & Chapman 1992), the Kaluli of New Guinea (Feld 1982), and the Suyá of Amazonian Brazil (Seeger 1990) expect that any socially competent adult ought to be able to perform music.

Music's ability to establish special realms of experience, set apart from the mundane rhythms of everyday life, provides skilled performers with a unique (and often ambivalently regarded) source of power. If music typically lacks the denotative specificity of speech, it also draws potency from its ability to exceed, and sometimes even to challenge, the rhetorical truth-claims of language. When music and language are combined – as in song or instrumental genres that incorporate surrogate speech patterns – powerful and semantically complex forms of COMMUNICATION result.

Although anthropological studies of music have typically focused on music making in cultural context, it should be noted that music is itself often a context for other forms of symbolic communication and enactment. The ethnographic literature provides many examples of the ability of musicians to establish metacommunicative frameworks within which individuals have license to behave in extraordinary ways. The radiant properties of musical sound can be used to occupy, texture, and domesticate social space, or to intensify and focus the experience of ritual participants. Physically ephemeral, invisible, yet potent in its emotional and cognitive effects, music assumes many forms and serves many ends.

CW

See also ETHNOMUSICOLOGY

further reading Blacking 1973; Keil & Feld 1994; Merriam 1964

myth is commonly used as a term for purely fictitious narrative that often involves supernatural persons, actions, or events, but it also embodies popular ideas about the natural world and historical events in a given culture. Indeed it implies that the group telling the myth believes it is true. Myth (*muthos*) is ancient Greek for "story," or more accurately what we would call "history," for history itself is also Greek and was at first merely an uncritical assembling of the various accounts told about events. And mythology (or *muthologia*) was originally just the telling of stories: eventually, it insinuated that the stories were fantastic or implausible, unless they had a distorted or hidden meaning; but it was not until the late period of Latin that *mythologia* became, as it is today, primarily the compilation, interpretation, and study of such stories, now no longer just of the classical Greco-Roman tradition, but from cultures throughout the world.

The oldest stories predated the advent of writing and comprised an oral history, passed on from teller to teller, generation after generation, sometimes for millennia, carefully preserved as a sacred heritage of cultural identity through various mnemonic techniques: embellishment of generic situations and formulaic phrases, reinforced by musical cadence, rhythm, dance, and in some cultures, pictorial or emblematic prompts. What purported to be a verbatim transmission, inevitably, in the absence of a written record, was a continually evolving version of the stories, changing to keep pace with the newer concerns of the audience, and to assimilate events of more recent occurrence: so that the oral tradition actually may incorporate elements of language and historical events of differing antiquity, and offers an archaeological record of a people's sense of roots and cultural identity, its religious, psychological, and social evolution. Such stories have stood the test of time, sloughing off aspects of marginal interest and replacing them with a better match for the deeper, less-conscious anxieties of the listener.

These imperceptibly evolving stories were accepted as factually true and had a profound influence on how the culture structured and interpreted the experiential environment. What to outsiders might seem implausible was often validated by actual events, at least to the extent that the myth offered a way of experiencing them. The process of oral transmission, moreover, demanded that the listeners participated in the communal occasion of the teller's recall of the stories, so that they, the teller, and the tale formed one entity, an unjudgmental renewal of cultural identity, with no opportunity for criticism or rejection of details.

The invention of WRITING, which at first was simply a bureaucratic tool for the keeping of records, allowed the stories to be transcribed, taken down from dictation by individual tellers, thus fixing the version and putting a stop to the evolutionary process. The text served, however, more as an aid for remembering the already known, but now codified tale, still for public performance, rather than as something to be read anew, in silent and solitary contemplation. In the Western world, the art of reading lagged several centuries behind that of merely writing as a memory prompt in the Hellenic tradition. During this period, which corresponds to the Classical Age of Greece, new versions of the stories were created by individual authors for performances, either as the result of an exegesis of the older tellings or through the infusion of contemporary perspectives, which sometimes entail the first indications of doubt about the absolute veracity of the tradition. As the authors and their audience, which increasingly became one of readers, began to pick and choose, or juxtapose versions and judge, the myth gets out of step with reality and displays aspects of falsity.

The myths, however, were not rejected outright, for they comprised the cultural identity, enshrined in art of the Classical Age and before, a heritage that was ever more precious as the Greeks spread among other, polyglot peoples and were eventually subsumed in a world controlled by the growing power of Rome. Their dominance in the arts meant that other cultures would largely have to espouse the Hellenic myths in order to rank in the world of educated sophistication.

After the loss of confidence in its factual validity, myth has an afterlife as a product of cultural pride. New meanings are discovered in the old stories to justify their continued perpetuation, meanings that in some sense are actually there because of the universal aspects that are the result of its mode of evolution from preliterate, oral traditions. The universality of myth makes it always in some way still true.

Contacts between cultures have led to comparisons of different mythic traditions. Sometimes the initial contact was played out as a reciprocal investigation of each other's myths in an attempt to counter divergent views of religion or reality. As always, the oral accounts become fixed when taken down in writing; and the versions chosen belie the prejudices of the compiler and the uses to which the compilation will be put. Similarly, the common occurrences between cultures can be used to justify different theoretical explanations: such as instinctual patterns of thought (or archetypes), commonalty of personal psychological development, or structural elements of language or society. Since most of such cultural interaction was occasioned by European colonial expansion and its concomitant missionary proselytizing, the bias of classical myth is often manifest as a basis for expanding our knowledge to the myths of other peoples.

A number of other terms are sometimes substituted for "myth," particularly in the modern era, to downgrade its supposed validity, while still maintaining it within the heritage of a broadening cultural identity. Such terms categorize by subject matter. Examples are: "saga" (historical traditions, eventually in prose and generally implying Nordic origins), "legend" (historical story, originally a saint's life), "fairy tale" (simple cautionary tales for children, including fairies, ogres, magicians, witches, and the like, similar to those collected from oral tradi-tions by the brothers Grimm), "fable" (story generally in which animals act like people), and "FOLKLORE" (beliefs and customs that persist unreflexively among a people as oral traditions). Apart from their particularized subject matter and the emphatic distancing of credibility, these terms do not differ from the more general term of "myth."   CR

See also ORAL   CULTURES,   POETRY, STRUCTURALISM

further reading Joseph Campbell 1949; Freud 1913; Jung et al. 1964; Kirk 1970; Leach 1967; Lévi-Strauss 1963a; Ruck et al. 1994; S. Thompson 1932–6

N

narrative is the sequential report of two or more events in a way that asserts their shared significance or causal relationship. Narrative has both verbal and nonverbal discourse forms. For example, DANCE or mime can be narrative, while RITUAL, whether spoken or unspoken, can memorialize or replicate a sequence of events with the capacity to transform or reaffirm power inherent in a social system. The historian Hayden White has argued that all narratives are "intimately related to, if not a function of, the impulse to moralize reality" (W. J. T. Mitchell 1981: 14). White's argument underscores the importance of signification in narrative, regardless of its claimed truth value or seriousness (or lack thereof). A narrative may be perceived as incoherent or inconsequential because an outsider does not understand its appropriate significance, or because of the incompetence or insignificance of the report or rendition.

Making an outsider audience see the significance of events in an alien social setting is one task of ethnographic description, much of it carried out by various forms of narration, explicit or implicit. Observations and interviews in field settings address both sequences of events and their interpretation. Fashions of ethnographic representation have shifted in the last several decades from a preference for generalized descriptions, in which personal testimony about particular events was edited into statements of general social principles and their operations, toward a more confessional or anecdotal style in which events either witnessed by or reported to the researcher are narrated either in the researcher's words or in some edited version of the witness's words and presented in combination with interpretive discussions of various kinds.

Narrative theory in literature has informed anthropologists' recognition of the rhetorical power of narrative performance to "package" and render plausible a narrator's particular version of an event or situation.

MM

further reading Bruner 1984; Clifford & Marcus 1986; Gennette 1980; Kermode 1979; G. Marcus & Fischer 1986; Prince 1987; V. Turner & Bruner 1986

natal group is the social group, usually the kin group, into which an individual is born. MR

nation, nationalism The nation is an imagined community that often commands intense loyalty. Yet it also is always problematic, both because it is an artificial creation and because the state in which one lives may not be the nation with which one identifies.

Anthropologists discovered the "nation" as a subject of inquiry during World War II, when a number of American anthropologists turned their gaze away from small-scale societies to those that comprised citizenries of independent states (see Kroeber 1948: 226–8). The impetus came when several anthropologists were asked to help make sense of the motivations of those from enemy states. The method of studying the culture of such nations "at a distance" was deployed most effectively by Ruth BENEDICT in *The chrysanthemum and the sword* (1946) in which she sought to depict the salient features of Japanese "national character."

The NATIONAL CHARACTER approach that emerged from this wartime enterprise posited that the citizenry of a sovereign political state shared a social tradition (M. Mead 1953a: 642). Although Benedict, MEAD, and other proponents of the national character approach were well aware that cultural patterns could change, they assumed that because cultures were holistic and were properties of societies, national cultures could be distinguished from one another without difficulty. This then made it possible for them to argue that SOCIALIZATION by those sharing a national culture leads to the development of a common "intrapsychic structure" among their CHILDREN.

The national character approach proved a dead end in anthropological thought because by the end of the 1960s the basic assumptions on which it was based had been shown to be fundamentally flawed. One challenge was posed by those who focused on the absence of "national integration" in newly independent postcolonial states. In these "new states" the citizenry were typically divided rather than united by culture. Clifford GEERTZ's 1963 essay, "The integrative revolution: primordial sentiments and civil politics in the new states," opened a new inquiry in anthropology by directing attention to the problematic character of nations and national cultures. Even as Geertz embraced a MODERNIZATION theory that envisioned the ultimate success of nation-building enterprises, his analysis of the tension between "primordial" sentiments rooted in premodern differences in language, religion, and cultural heritage that divided peoples in the new states and "civil" sentiments instilled in a citizenry by the governments of successful modern states demonstrated that new states were far from being the realizations of deeply rooted national aspirations that both their leaders and many analysts had assumed them to be.

That nations are constructed rather than liberated became a major preoccupation of social science theory in the 1980s (Gellner 1983; Anthony Smith 1986; Richard Fox 1990). Every modern state with its well-defined and internationally recognized territorial boundaries encompasses peoples with diverse cultural characteristics. Nationalist programs seek to inculcate in most of the citizenry of a state an "imagining" of a national community (B. Anderson 1983/1991; Alonso 1988) and a "remembering" of a common past (Brow &

Swedenberg 1990; Fujitani 1993) that transcends their cultural heterogeneity. Such imagining and remembering typically entails an emotive appeal to remember the common BLOOD shed in the gaining of national independence or waging of patriotic WARS and the common dead whose sacrifice must not be forgotten (see Keyes et al. 1994: 6–9).

Anthropologists have been particularly influenced by how the construction of national communities has been effected through the conscious "invention" of national traditions (Hobsbawm & Ranger 1983) and through the deployment by states of "technologies of power" such as censuses, compulsory education, and official calendars (B. Cohn & Dirks 1988; R. Foster 1991: 244–8). If successful, such invention becomes "naturalized" or "primordialized," so that national symbols deployed in songs, flags, monuments, celebrations, and so on elicit deep and strongly held feelings of identification among the citizenry.

Although many national imaginaries have become hegemonic, they are everywhere contested (Handler 1988). The national vision promoted by a ruling elite with access to powerful instruments can embody within itself the seeds of its own questioning. Every national imaginary entails hierarchical distinctions among the citizenry of a state. Those whose cultural identities are marginal to the new national culture are relegated to ethnic or racial "minority" status (B. Williams 1989). If the basis of state power becomes problematic, minorities may seek to realize their own "national" aspirations. Anthropological studies have shown, for example, how the dissolution into constituent "nations" of a Yugoslavia defined as a multinational state in marxist terms was all but preordained when the Communist Party lost its legitimacy as the sole and undivided holder of state power (see Allock 1989; Denich 1994; R. Hayden 1995).

Anthropologists have given considerable attention to the VIOLENCE associated with promotion of and challenges to national visions such as in Sri Lanka (Kapferer 1988) or Venezuela (Coronil & Skurski 1991). Although national identities are most easily contested in weak multiethnic states (K. Warren 1993), they have no monopoly on the process. Even in countries like Japan or Thailand, which have been seen by outsiders as culturally homogeneous and have modern state structures that evolved out of premodern ones, debates over the "essence" of national identity are intense, even if nonviolent (Befu 1993; Keyes 1996).

National imaginaries are also questioned, often as much by action as in word, by those who live between states and between nations. Many migrants today, in contrast to the past, neither assimilate fully to the national culture of their new homes nor remain rooted in the national culture of their country of origin. Rather, as recent anthropological research has shown, their identities are often flexible or ambiguous (A. Ong 1993; Gupta & Ferguson 1992).

CK

See also ETHNIC GROUPS, MIDDLEMAN MINORITIES, POLITICAL ANTHROPOLOGY, RACE, STATE

national character is a concept developed by the American CULTURE AND PERSONALITY school to characterize the basic personality structure or psychological pattern of the citizens of contemporary nation-states.

Based on what Anthony Wallace (1961) termed "cultural deductive methods," one variety of national-character studies inferred the personality structures of the individual members of the society from broad ethnographic data using psychological models – often, but not exclusively, psychoanalytic. This approach attributed cultural values or themes to common shared experiences during infancy or early childhood. A second method, which Wallace labeled "organizational," attempted to characterize the personalities of a defined population in statistical terms based on the frequency distributions of various traits. It relied on psychologically oriented inquiries such as LIFE HISTORIES, ethnographic observations, and the results of projective tests to define the modal personality of a national group.

National-character studies became prominent with American involvement in World War II and remained so through the 1950s. Ruth BENEDICT's (1946) landmark study of Japan and Margaret MEAD's (1942) analysis of American culture were the best known of these works. Much of this effort was based on wartime attempts to study cultures at a distance (Mead 1953c).

National-character studies were severely criticized because of their eclectic use of ethnographic data, their tendency to stereotype very large populations, and the difficulty of applying psychological models of individual behavior to whole societies. Their origin as part of a wartime effort to "know the enemy" was also later stigmatized. Although the explicit research paradigm was abandoned and rejected, many of the issues and topics remain the focus of anthropological inquiry under new labels and rubrics and have flourished in sister disciplines such as social psychology (Inkeles & Levinson 1996), cultural analysis (Sollers 1986), and to a lesser degree in sociology (Daniel Bell 1968). JIA

nativistic movements was a term coined by Ralph LINTON (1943) in an article of the same name. Linton sought to generate a series of ideal types for understanding cultural and religious movements that emerged in situations of "cultural contact." Linton defined nativistic movements as "any conscious, organized attempt on the part of a society's members to revive or perpetuate selected aspects of its culture." Linton thus distinguished between societies in which cultures were reproduced through practices that were unconscious (or, in later terms, embedded in TRADITION) from those in which they emerged through self-conscious efforts (what more recently has been termed "invention"). In the latter case people seek to identify and valorize selected elements of culture as "symbols of the society's existence as a unique entity." "Nativistic movements" so defined foreshadow ideas about ETHNICITY.

Although Linton focused on movements that emerged among people who had been subjugated or dominated by Europeans, such as the Ghost Dance religion of Plains Indians at the end of the nineteenth century, he also suggested that another type of nativistic movement could be found among dominant peoples who constituted minorities in the societies they control or who otherwise felt culturally threatened. However, it would take nearly a half century before much attention was given to the cultural politics of dominant as well as marginalized peoples.

The concept of nativistic movements has given way to other terms for discussing cultural movements emerging in situations of intense and politically charged cultural contact – "millennialism" (a term that Linton himself recognized as related; see MILLENARIAN MOVEMENTS), "fundamentalism," "ethnicity," and "the politics of CULTURE." Linton's article stands, nonetheless, as a seminal piece in the development of anthropological reflection on how people seek consciously to perpetuate, revitalize, or invent their cultural heritage.

CK

See also NATION, RELIGION

natural disasters are sudden or great misfortunes, mishaps, or calamities triggered by forces such as floods, winds, drought or fire that are often perceived as "acts of God." Anthropologists initially studied natural disasters for what they revealed about local social systems (R. Firth 1959) and, subsequently, for what they revealed about how such systems adapted to calamity. Today, disasters are studied for what they reveal not about local communities but about the wider social systems that envelop them. It now is argued that differences between disastrous events and normal ones are not objectively given but subjectively constructed. This is based, in part, on evidence that the incidence and magnitude of disasters have increased in recent history owing to changes not in environment but in society.

Disasters have worsened because the world's poor have become more vulnerable by living in more marginal environments. This is the product not of nature, but of underdevelopment (Hewitt 1983; Wisner 1993). Calamitous losses of life caused by living in such environments are more properly termed "social" or "political" disasters (O'Keefe et al. 1976). The attribution of disastrous events to society as opposed to nature is a political question. This is illustrated by the public discourse that attends the storms and floods that periodically hit the coastal populations of some less developed countries (Dove & Khan 1995). Whereas national government and media tend to attribute these losses to nature, external observers may attribute them to a social order that systematically puts its poorest citizens at risk.   MRD & TC

See also EVIL, SUFFERING

neolocal residence is a postmarital residence rule permitting or requiring the newly married couple to establish a new household independent of their parents or other relatives.   MR

neuroanthropology occupies the intersection of anthropology and neuroscience and focuses on three major areas of research: (1) human and primate brain evolution, (2) modern human neuroanatomical variation, and (3) cross-cultural cognitive neuropsychology.

Brain evolution

Paleoneurology seeks to elucidate human brain origins from fossilized cranial evidence derived from latex and naturally mineralized "endocasts" that reveal brain size, shape, and surface morphology. Hominid brain size more than tripled over a span of 4 million years and this expansion (most of it cortical) is correlated with evolving cognitive and linguistic capabilities (Deacon 1992) and archaeological evidence of increasing behavioral complexity (Gowlett 1992). Preserved vascular channels demonstrate changes that accompanied or (more arguably) triggered neural adaptations (Falk 1990). Temporal changes in exocranial morphology (e.g., basicranial angle) have also been used to make inferences about the development of the vocal tract and its coevolving central language circuitry (P. Lieberman 1984).

Comparative neurobiology examines brain structure and function in contemporary animal species to deduce information about evolutionary process from homology (functional and topographic similarity of structures due to conserved genetic information). One major approach uses modern neuroanatomical tract-tracing techniques to reveal neural circuits, which can be neurophysiologically investigated in living primates (Steklis & Raleigh 1979). Alternatively, allometric studies use regression analysis to examine relative-brain-size expansion (Jerison 1973), a process that can be extended to the comparison of the internal components of the brain (Stephan et al. 1988). Comparative studies have often focused on structures allegedly unique to human brains, including neocortical and hemispheric specializations (Broca's and Wernicke's language areas, multimodal association areas such as the inferior parietal lobule), and even limbic, basal ganglia, and brainstem regions.

Evolutionary neuroanthropologists are divided between those who emphasize changes in particular local areas as critical and those who emphasize overall brain size, concomitant interconnectivity, and generalized cognitive capacity ("intelligence"). Researchers in both camps, however, have become increasingly dissatisfied with both "accretive" scala-naturae schemes (Deacon 1990a) and neurobiologically naive "prime-mover" scenarios (Landau 1991). In response they have attempted to investigate neuro-ontogenetic mechanisms underlying brain evolution by using more direct approaches (Deacon 1990b; Finlay & Darlington 1995).

Human neuroanatomical variation

Neuroscientific research has undergone a major shift in the past fifty years. Today research on GENDER and sexual orientation is flourishing (LeVay 1993; Finn 1996; Kimura 1996) while the neuroanatomical study of RACE has all but vanished. This was emphatically not the case in the early twentieth century, when extensive catalogs of racial differences in cortical convolutedness were published as purported proof of a biological basis for justifying racial classification. These interpretations were discredited by modern BIOLOGICAL ANTHROPOLOGY in two ways. First researchers realized that fissurization was a trivial mechanical function of the expanding cortical area, functionally equivalent to the headbumps that inspired the discredited nineteenth-century "science" of phrenology. Second, a more rigorous sampling of

populations demonstrated that the range of variation found within any single "racial" group (in neural as well as other traits) far exceeded the average difference between different groups. The recent development of more sophisticated morphometric tools has, however, spurred renewed interest in interpopulational differences (Klekamp et al. 1994). Whether such studies will simply recapitulate the racist abuses of the past or make a real contribution to understanding relationships among human populations remains to be seen (Shipman 1994; J. Marks 1995; S. Gould 1996).

Cross-cultural cognition

The contention that CULTURE is a uniquely *human* domain (Holloway 1992) implies that brain substrates for symbolic language are *the* critical objects of neuroanthropological inquiry. Challenges from linguistic relativism, in the form of the WHORFIAN HYPOTHESIS, and STRUCTURALISM, for example, provoked a spirited series of exchanges on whether cultures differ in cognitive style because of differential emphasis on right- versus left-brain specializations (J. Paredes & Hepburn 1976). Clinical neurolinguists have indeed mapped out significant differences in aphasic syndromes among speakers of different languages, while the "biogenetic structuralists" (C. Laughlin & D'Aquili 1974; D'Aquili et al. 1979) have explored ritual TRANCE and other manifestations of altered consciousness in ethnographic context.

Neuroanthropology still lies at the margins of anthropology, resisted by positivists on the grounds that its hypotheses are not easily tested and by more culturally oriented anthropologists who reject it as just a new form of biological determinism. If neurobiological hardware could be ignored in favor of an emphasis on cultural software – with which, after all, all humans are programmable (see PSYCHIC UNITY OF MANKIND) – why not leave brains to neurobiologists? In truth, the Cartesian fallacy that mind and brain are dissociable has been a paralyzing intellectual legacy for all behavioral sciences; the academic marginalization of neuroanthropology has been just one casualty.   JAM

further reading Deacon 1997; C.

Laughlin et al. 1990; Lumsden & Wilson 1981; Springer & Deutsch 1993; TenHouten 1991

new ethnography   is an EMIC approach to the description of a culture that focuses on the body of knowledge and the culture-bound rules that define and influence appropriate behavior for a speech community. The term dates to the early 1960s when a group of cognitive anthropologists, including Conklin (1964), Frake (1964), and Sturtevant (1964), began to assert along with Goodenough (1967: 1203) that "To describe the content of such a body of knowledge is to describe a community's culture," and proposed questions such as "What does a person need to have learned if he is to understand events in a strange community as its members understand them and if he is to conduct himself in ways that they accept as conforming to their expectations of one another?"

Attempting to bring linguistic rigor into the description of cultures, the New Ethnography was influenced first by structural linguists such as Kenneth Pike (1954) and then by the notion of TRANSFORMATIONAL GRAMMAR developed by Noam Chomsky (1965). Based on an emic perspective focused on explication of the culture-bound rules that account "for the behavior of a people by describing the socially acquired and shared knowledge, or culture, that enables members of the society to behave in ways deemed appropriate by their fellows" (Frake 1964: 132), the New Ethnography was expected to represent "its host culture with fidelity . . . good enough that the natives are able to recognize in it familiar features of their own culture" (Werner & Schoepfle 1987: 24). This would allow the ethnographer "to break through Euro-American ethnocentrism and try to see other cultures as natives see them" (ibid.: 61).

Defining culture cognitively as knowledge systems, the New Ethnographers developed a set of methods known as ETH-NOSCIENCE that allowed them to record topical domains within a culture such as ETHNOBOTANY and ethnoentomology. The ultimate aim was to describe explicitly methods and question frames so the ethno-graphic description could be replicated by others. The discovery of "rules of culturally appropriate behavior" (Frake 1964: 132) would provide economy in the description as well as predictability and productivity. The ethnographer was required to specify what one needs to know to make events maximally probable, describing as "equivalence acts" what a member of a community did under what conditions.

Although the New Ethnography was criticized by behaviorally oriented anthropologists as not being "new" and for not adequately addressing variability and complexity within cultural knowledge (Harris 1968: 568–604), the basic principles and methods of the New Ethnography of the 1960s are now regarded as standard features of contemporary ethnography (Keesing 1972; Manning & Fabrega 1976).

DW

nomadic pastoralists   *See* PASTORAL NOMADS

non-unilineal descent   *See* DESCENT

nonverbal communication   Most human COMMUNICATION is vocal in nature. However, anthropologists have long understood that much communication takes place using nonverbal behavioral mechanisms. These range from gesture and "body language" to the use of interpersonal space, the employment of signs and symbols, and the use of time structures.

Nonverbal behavior has been seen to have many sequential and functional relationships to verbal behavior. It can "repeat, augment, illustrate, accent or contradict the words; it can anticipate, coincide with, substitute for or follow the verbal behavior; and it can be unrelated to the verbal behavior" (Ekman & Friesen 1981: 61). In all of these situations humans have learned to interpret nonverbal signals in conventional ways. However, just as words must be taken in context to be properly understood, so must nonverbal behavior be interpreted in the whole context of any given communication (Birdwhistell 1952, 1970).

Perhaps the most important form of nonverbal communication is facial expression. Human beings are capable of interpreting an exceptionally large number of variations in facial configuration. This form of non-verbal behavior may also be one of the oldest forms of communication in evolutionary terms. Based on research on present-day groups of primates, such common facial movements as smiles or eyebrow raises may have been postures of hostility for prehistoric hominids. Facial expression is one of the most important sources of information about affect for human beings today.

Movements of hands or other body parts in clearly interpretable patterns are likewise important forms of nonverbal communication. These are generally classified as GESTURES. Birdwhistell called the study of body movement "kinesics." Many gestures "stand alone" for members of a particular society. Gestures of insult, of invitation, of summoning or dismissal, and of commentary appear to be universal for human society.

Edward T. Hall pioneered the study of body distance (*proxemics*) and time usage (*chronomics*) as forms of nonverbal communication. According to Hall (1959, 1966) there are important cultural differences in body distance for different social purposes. In American society, for example, normal social conversation takes place at about 18 inches distance between participants. In Egyptian society normal social distance may be as close as 6 inches. Americans who are unaware of this difference may find themselves uncomfortable in an Egyptian social conversation. Likewise Hall points out that different conceptions of TIME are communicative. These include the scheduling of daily routines such as meal and meeting times and ideas of punctuality. In some societies lack of punctuality conveys an insult, whereas in others rigid use of time creates discomfort.

Ekman and Friesen (1981) have developed a typology of nonverbal behavior following the work of Efron (1941). Their categories are:

1. emblems: nonverbal acts that have a direct dictionary translation well known by members of a particular culture
2. illustrators: body movement that accompanies speech and can either reinforce the words being said or show a contradictory, ironic, or other attitudinal posture toward the verbal message
3. affect displays: primarily facial expressions conveying emotional states or attitudes
4. regulators: acts that maintain and regulate the back-and-forth nature of speaking and listening, usually taking place during the course of face-to-face interaction
5. adaptors: often unconsciously performed body movements that help persons to feel more comfortable in social interaction, to deal with tension, or to accommodate themselves to the presence of others. Hall's proxemic and chronomic dimensions of nonverbal behavior fall under this category.

WBe

See also DANCE, LANGUAGE
further reading Kendon 1977, 1981; Key 1975

norms   *See* DEVIANCE, LAW, SANCTIONS

nuclear families   consist of a husband, wife and their children.   MR
See also FAMILY

O

Omaha kinship systems produce a set of kin terms that, like the IROQUOIS, merges the mother's sister with the mother, the father's brother with the father, and parallel cousins with siblings (see figure 1). The Omaha system, in addition, merges members of different generations on the mother's side, so that, for instance, mother's brother and mother's brother's son are indicated by the same term. The Omaha system is generally associated with PATRILINEAL DESCENT.   MR
See also CROW KINSHIP SYSTEMS

oracles are any devices or procedures, often supernatural, used to receive communications about the unknown. The form and function of oracles in a particular culture depends on the nature and purposes of WITCHCRAFT practiced there. In some the oracle is a human being; in others, a set of RITUAL practices.

In ancient times oracles, each associated with a particular deity, were scattered about the Hellenic world, where with the aid of elaborate rituals and a specialized priesthood, petitioners could receive communications about the future from the gods (Frazer 1890). Similar types of oracle, who go into a TRANCE state, are still widely used by Tibetans (Samuel 1993). Among the Azande of Zambia, who attribute virtually all misfortune to witchcraft, oracles determine whether witchcraft is likely to plague a planned project and identify the witches responsible for particular problems (Evans-Pritchard 1937). Their oracles are essentially random processes designed to produce positive or negative answers to specific questions, a form of AUGURY. In the termite oracle, for example, two sticks are inserted into a termite mound, left for a day, and the answer is obtained by observing which stick was eaten first. Azande oracles vary in their cost and efficacy; the termite oracle is easy and costs nothing, but its results are less reliable than the complex and expensive poison oracle that must be used to confront the discovered witch and to initiate vengeance procedures in cases of death (Mair 1969: 76–101).   AB
See also MAGIC, RELIGION, SHAMANISM

oral cultures Historically, anthropologists have seen themselves as studying oral cultures where people are thought to be unfamiliar with, or at the very least not primarily dependent upon, writing and literacy. For this reason RADCLIFFE-BROWN (1952: 3) argued that anthropologists could never really study the history of "primitive" peoples because they lacked written records.

This view of the primary orality of societies traditionally studied by anthropologists is controversial. First, even if it correctly defined the mission of anthropology in the past, the majority of anthropological studies now take place in societies where at least some people, sometimes most, are literate. Second, if WRITING is taken in its narrowest sense of linear, acoustic notation, then it is the case that of the thousands of languages that have been spoken in the course of human history, most have never been written. However, in the contemporary world it would be difficult to imagine a group so isolated that it has not been in contact with media that in one way or another are print based or ultimately dependent upon the institution of literacy, such as radio, telephone and television, and increasingly, computers. If writing is defined more broadly as any system of recording, then, as Jacques Derrida (1976) has pointed out in his critique of the

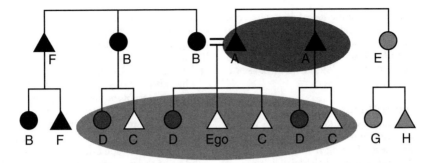

Figure 1   Omaha kinship system.

texts of anthropologists such as Claude LÉVI-STRAUSS, no group – even an "oral" society – is without it.

The importance of orality along with literacy as a continuum of expression and possibly of thought was first clearly understood in classics, particularly by Milman Parry (1971), who theorized the formulaic performance of Homeric texts. More recently, in a polemical and vastly influential book, Marshall McLuhan (1962) argued that it was not just literacy, but print technology that revolutionized the way human beings thought and societies organized themselves and created a "global village." The work of Jack GOODY (1968, 1977) in anthropology has entertained a more modest, but more carefully tested, hypothesis – namely, that the use of writing produces significant differences in psychological and social structures in societies when literacy is acquired.   SC

See also ETHNOGRAPHY AND ETHNOLOGY, FOLKLORE, POETRY

further reading Clanchy 1979; J. Goody 1987; Havelock 1986; W. Ong 1982; Street 1984

organic solidarity   refers to the form of social solidarity found in complex societies where the strength of the collective conscience is low and individuals (as social persons) are bound together by the complementarity of their economic functions. Coined by Emile DURKHEIM (1933), the term is associated with a highly differentiated DIVISION OF LABOR.

MR

See also MECHANICAL SOLIDARITY

oriental despotism   refers to the political organization of Karl Marx's "Asiatic" MODE OF PRODUCTION, as refined by Karl Wittfogel, especially for the cases of ancient Egypt, Mesopotamia, India, China, and the Andean and Mexican zones of America. Both authors stressed the hydraulic nature of these societies, which required the authoritarian control of labor.

Under primitive technological conditions farmers must "work in cooperation" with each other "and subordinate themselves to a directing authority" (Wittfogel 1957: 18). Inasmuch as the ancient civilizations considered were susceptible to annual inundations, the same community that "resorts to preparatory labor to safeguard the reproductive use of water may also have to resort to protective labor to safeguard its crops from periodic and successive inundations" (ibid. 24). The assignment of all adult males to communal work teams was standard in all these societies: corvée labor was used both to dig irrigation canals and for maintenance, as in annual cleanings. The organization of work in larger political entities required organized political or bureaucratic entities; thus it came to be that these early states were ruled by "agromanagerial bureaucracies." Effective governmental control involved, first, the political and fiscal superiority of the directing agency and, second, the means for conveying commands and commanders to the subcenters of control.

Thus all these societies developed long highways, navigation canals, and postal services to support and carry out their power (ibid. 54–5).   TG
See also HYDRAULIC SYSTEMS AND SOCIETIES, IRRIGATION, STATE

original affluent society The life of hunter–gatherers (FORAGERS) was viewed by early anthropologists as one of unremitting harshness. Toiling from dawn to dusk just to survive with little leisure time in which to engage in culture building they seemed to fit the dark picture of early man painted by Thomas Hobbes (1651: XIII):

In such condition there is no place for industry, because the fruit thereof is uncertain: and consequently no culture of the earth; no navigation, nor use of the commodities that may be imported by sea; no commodious building; no instruments of moving and removing such things as require much force; no knowledge of the face of the earth; no account of time; no arts; no letters; no society; and which is worst of all, continual fear, and danger of violent death; and the life of man, solitary, poor, nasty, brutish, and short.

This picture changed dramatically in 1968 with the volume *Man the hunter* (Lee & DeVore 1968) from which hunter–gatherers emerged as the "original affluent society" – the label was Marshall Sahlins's (1968a). An affluent society, Sahlins noted, is one in which a people's wants are easily satisfied. Unlike the economies of modern industrial societies, where wants expand indefinitely and means are limited, thereby condemning their members to a perpetual condition of scarcity, hunter–gathering societies are characterized by limited ends and modest but adequate means. Paradoxically, Sahlins went on to aver, this Zen strategy enables a people to enjoy "material plenty" with what can objectively be considered a low standard of living.

Sahlins (1972: 1–33) extended his original comments in an expanded essay using quantitative data drawn mainly from the Bushmen of the Kalahari and Australian Aboriginal societies. In these societies, he observed, people are able to meet their subsistence needs by working roughly 15–20 hours per week in work that is not terribly taxing. They also spend a great deal of time lounging about and sleeping. Hence, he concluded, contrary to what is usually thought, with the development of culture the amount of work per capita increases and the amount of leisure decreases.

The affluent society soon became as popular a stereotype in anthropology as its opposite had been, a staple of introductory anthropology texts. But critical questions have been raised by various specialists on hunter–gatherer societies concerning the validity of the empirical data employed by Sahlins and others. For example, Richard Lee – a proponent of the "affluent society" thesis on whom Sahlins drew for time-allocation data on the Bushmen – indicated, in a later publication (1984: 53), that when time spent on making and repairing tools and in housework is added to the time spent out of camp in subsistence work, !Kung Bushmen males work 44.5 hours per week and females 40.1 hours per week.

Questions can also be raised about whether concepts like "affluence," "work," and "leisure" mean the same thing in the context of hunter–gatherer societies as they do in industrial societies. Critics of the "affluent society" thesis have pointed out that data on such vital matters as infant mortality, the prevalence of disease, nutritional stress, and life expectancy strongly suggest the inappropriateness of the term "affluence." It may be that the "original affluent society" thesis is as much a commentary on modern industrial societies with their "infinite wants" as it is a description of hunter–gatherer societies. And that may be its lasting appeal.   DK
See also POVERTY
further reading Bird-David 1992

ostracism refers to a wide range of SANCTIONS, from informally refusing to recognize the presence of certain individuals to banishment in which individuals are excluded from a group of which they were formerly members. The term comes from the Greek word for a potsherd (*ostrakon*), which was used by Athenian voters in determining whether or not an individual should be exiled.

Human beings often informally but deliberately avoid others with whom they have quarreled, even when they must pass by them on a daily basis. Neighbors and kin may do this for a long time. Individuals who are fired from their jobs may during the transition period find that fellow workers will ignore them. Formal ostracism is the result of a collective decision, such as labor unions cutting off contact with strikebreakers. English school children will boycott a classmate who offends the group, a practice referred to as "sending to Coventry" (Opie & Opie 1959).

Religious communities and organizations have used excommunication to enforce obedience to their rules. Among American Mennonites and Amish, and in the Roman Catholic Church before 1200 C.E., this included *shunning*, which required that other members of the community refrain from ordinary social interaction with the person being shunned. This included doing business, eating together, and even the maintenance of marital relations for husbands and wives (Hostetler 1993: 85–7, 345–9). Rabbinic Judaism employed a similar technique (Jacob Katz 1993: 84–6). The severe cases of excommunication implied a kind of social death, and the ritual accompanying a severe decree included extinguishing candles to underline this condition.

In contemporary times, banishment has remained a sanction commonly used by both small communities and large states. The predominantly Catholic Chiapas Maya community of San Juan Chamula has attempted to prevent conversions by expelling Protestants (Gossen 1989). Czarist Russia and the former Soviet Union long used expulsion from the country and internal exile to Siberia as punishments. Ostracism in both its informal and formal configurations remains a powerful sanction in human societies.   WZ

P

parallel cousins are those whose parent is of the same sex as the linking parent of an individual (EGO). These would include a mother's sister's child or a father's brother's child.   MR
See also CROSS-COUSINS

pariah groups *See* MIDDLEMAN MINORITIES

parole *See* LANGUE AND PAROLE

participant-observation is long-term, intense interaction with members of a community during which the researcher plunges into their activities as completely as possible, for example, by attending rituals, "hanging out," or washing clothes at the river with other women. It is considered to be the hallmark of traditional anthropological field research. Advantages of participant-observation are numerous. (1) It is virtually the only way to conduct ethnographic research with people who do not speak a written language. (2) The researcher is "there" all the time, and consequently sees what happens when people are preparing for events or mopping up afterwards, behaving according to the rules or breaking them. (3) Immersion in community life results in the fieldworker becoming less intrusive, less of a stranger, and thus in increased trust and tolerance on the part of members of the community. (4) Being on their turf, the researcher can more easily discern the peoples' customary, unexamined habits and perspectives than if they were in a setting less familiar to them. (5) Behavior is observed first hand rather than elicited from peoples' accounts of what happened. (6) Being there and speaking the language vastly increases the chances of comprehending the meaning of what is happening from the peoples' point of view.

The disadvantages of participant-observation include: (1) the investment of a huge amount of time, some of which is not spent very efficiently. (2) People may resent what they see as snoopy, sneaky behavior by inquisitive anthropologists. (3) Participant-observation is sometimes difficult to explain to people (and university committees interested in informed-consent guidelines). (4) The presence of the anthropologist, at times strongly felt, affects the behavior being investigated. (5) It is virtually impossible to adequately demonstrate to readers of ethnographic reports why one's conclusions, if based on participant-observation, should be accepted beyond the assertion that "since I was there, my perceptions are accurate." This is why participant-observation is not, properly speaking, a methodology (although some speak of it as such: see Spradley 1980) and why researchers always utilize additional structured or semi-structured techniques such as censuses, genealogies, projective tests, or structured interviews with a carefully drawn sample.

Participant-observation is, ultimately, an oxymoron (see Herzfeld 1987; Favret-Saada 1990), since insofar as one is engaged in an activity one is not observing it. A great deal of reflexive anthropological literature discusses this tension. Ideally, ethnographers play a sort of double role: by carefully monitoring a constantly changing situation, they judiciously shift back and forth between participation and observation.   JJa
See also FIELDWORK, INFORMANTS, QUALITATIVE METHODS

pastoral nomads or nomadic pastoralists live in societies in which the husbandry of grazing animals is viewed as an ideal way of making a living and the regular movement of all or part of the society is considered a normal and natural part of life. Although the terms "nomad" and "pastoralist" are generally used interchangeably, they are analytically distinct: the former referring to movement and the latter to a type of subsistence. Not all pastoralists are nomadic (dairy farmers and cattle ranchers), nor are all nomads pastoralists (hunter–gatherers, Gypsies, migrant farm workers).

The variety of animals raised by nomadic pastoralists is surprisingly small: six widely distributed species (sheep, goats, cattle, horses, donkeys, and camels) and three with restricted distribution (yaks at high altitudes in Asia, reindeer at northern sub-Arctic latitudes, and llamas and other cameloid species in highland South America). Dogs are also often kept for protection.

Pastoral nomadism is commonly found where climatic conditions produce seasonal pastures that cannot support sustained agriculture. Organized around mobile households rather than individuals, it involves everyone – men, women and children – in the various aspects of production. This distinguishes nomadic pastoralists from European shepherds or American cowboys, who are recruited from the larger sedentary society to which they regularly return. Since people cannot eat grass, exploiting grazing animals effectively taps an otherwise unusable energy source. Using tents or huts to facilitate migration, they rotate their animals among extensive but seasonal pastures. Migration cycles vary in time and length depending on local conditions: few moves when pastures and water are dependable, many more when they are not. Nomadic pastoralists never "wander," however; they know where they are going and why.

Comparative surveys have questioned whether pastoral nomadism should be considered a unitary phenomenon (Dyson-Hudson & Dyson-Hudson 1981). Although they share such structural similarities as TRIBAL ORGANIZATION and a strong bias toward patrilineal kinship and residence, they form seven distinct pastoral zones, each with its distinctive cultural identity and set of research problems:

(1) In the high-latitude sub-Arctic nomadic pastoralism is the most sophisticated variation in a wide continuum of reindeer exploitation that ranges from their intensive use for milking and traction among the Lapps of Scandinavia, to raising the animals for meat alone, to simple hunting (Ingold 1980).

(2) In the Eurasian steppe horse raising is culturally preeminent, but herds also include sheep, goats, cattle, and Bactrian camels. Historically, groups such as the Scythians, Turks, Mongols, Kazaks, and Kirghiz were famous for their horse riding and archery, military talents used to found large empires that often terrorized their neighbors, under leaders like Genghiz Khan and Attila the Hun (Barfield 1989).

(3) In mountain and plateau areas of southwest Asia sheep and goat pastoralism predominates, while horses, camels, and donkeys are used for transport. Groups such as the Bakhtiari, Qashqa'i, Basseri, Lurs, and Pashtuns have a symbiotic relationship with neighboring towns and villages as pastoral specialists, trading meat animals, wool, milk products, and hides for grain and manufactured goods (Barth 1961).

(4) In the Saharan and Arabian deserts the Bedouins specialize in raising the dromedary camel for food and transport. Historically, they supplemented their income by selling protection to oasis farmers, providing camels for the caravan trade, and receiving subsidies for military support (W. Lancaster 1981).

(5) In the sub-Saharan savanna cattle are highly valued by groups such as the Nuer, Dinka, Masai, and Turkana (labeled a CATTLE COMPLEX by anthropologists). Sheep and goats also play a major role in subsistence, as does seasonal agriculture. Using huts instead of portable tents, they use only donkeys for transport (Gulliver 1955).

(6) In the Asian high-altitude plateau the yak makes pastoralism viable. Herds also include yak/cattle hybrids, high altitude varieties of sheep, cashmere goats, and a few horses. Tibetan pastoralists trade wool, skins, salt, and milk products to val-

ley villagers for barley, which is a mainstay of their diet (Goldstein & Beall 1989).

(7) In the high mountains of the Andes in South America llama-raising communities are integrated into alpine farming villages. This was the only area of indigenous large-animal domestication in the New World (Browman 1974); sheep, goats, horses, and cattle became widespread only after their introduction during the period of Spanish conquest.

Recent ethnographic work has largely discredited the notion of the "pure nomad" who subsists entirely on pastoral products, free of entanglements with the sedentary world. Historically, nomadic pastoralists have always been tied economically and politically to their sedentary neighbors – links without which they could not easily survive or prosper (Khazanov 1984). This is more true today as remaining groups have moved away from subsistence pastoralism to forms of cash ranching that tie them closely to market economies (Galaty & Salzman 1981).   TB

further reading Barfield 1993; Bulliet 1977; P. Carmichael 1991; Humphrey 1983; Monod 1975

pater   is the socially recognized father of a child, as opposed to the biological father. For example, in modern society the husband of a woman who conceives a child by artificial insemination is regarded as the child's father (pater) although he is not the child's biological father (GENITOR).
    MR

patriarchy   is the dominance of men as a class over women and also a system by which rights and duties to persons and things descend through the father's line. Nineteenth-century social theorists developed the concept of patriarchy (also known as "Father Right") in contrast to MATRIARCHY and in order to explain the evolution of civil society. The German political economist Friedrich Engels (1902), for instance, situated the "overthrow" of matriarchy by patriarchy in the "Greek heroic age." The social evolutionary frameworks in which the concepts of patriarchy and matriarchy were developed are no longer generally accepted.

Patriarchy is now used to describe a situation in which men have primary control of the most prestigious social, political-economic, and cultural institutions in their society. Patriarchy is sometimes associated with PATRILINEAL societies, but anthropologists and sociologists have shown that patrilineality is not a necessary condition for male dominance. Social theorists now believe that so-called patriarchal societies are actually cross-cut by other social identities; so, for instance, women of the dominant race, class, and religion tend to have more status and power than men of the nondominant race, class, and religion.
    EP

See also FEMINIST ANTHROPOLOGY, GENDER, MASCULINITY

further reading B. Fox 1988; R. Rosaldo 1993

patrilineal descent or inheritance passes from a father to his children. In a patrilineal clan system, for instance, children belong to the clan of their father and not their mother.   MR

patrilocal residence is postmarital residence with the husband's family or kin. It has largely been replaced by the term "VIRILOCAL RESIDENCE."   MR

peace and nonviolence Many people view peace as simply the absence of WAR and VIOLENCE. This approach is often correlated with the idea that human nature is inherently aggressive. In contrast, those who follow the positive concept of peace define it as the dynamic process that leads ideally to the relative conditions of the absence of direct and indirect violence plus the presence of freedom, equality, economic and social justice, cooperation, and harmony. (Direct violence includes war, while indirect violence includes structural violence, such as ethnocentrism, racism, and sexism.) This approach is often correlated with the idea that human nature is inherently cooperative and empathetic.

The first view, associated with the political philosopher Thomas Hobbes (1651), sees peace preserved only by the threat of retaliatory violence through government policies and the military, and nonviolence as just a narrow political strategy. Social scientists who take this position believe that nonviolence and peace may be ultimately achievable, but mainly through the reduction of AGGRESSION after research has accumulated sufficient knowledge to develop techniques to control it. Their investigations tend to focus mostly on violent conflict, and especially war at the national, international, and global levels.

The second view sees peace as a relative condition, involving dynamic processes that are life-enhancing; that is, they promote the survival, welfare, development, and creativity of individuals within a society, so that they may realize more of their physical, sociocultural, mental, and spiritual potential in constructive ways. Ultimately peace involves at least five mutually interdependent levels: individual, social, national, international, and global. Within the social sciences, anthropologists and sociologists usually concentrate on the social level, whereas psychologists emphasize the individual level, and political scientists the national, international, and global levels. Accordingly, peace studies is ideally a transdisciplinary field of research, education, and action that attempts to treat all levels and aspects of nonviolence, peace, violence, war, and related phenomena.

The positive concept recognizes that nonviolence/peace and violence/war each have their own attributes, and neither is merely the absence or opposite of the other. Those who follow the positive concept are more likely to directly study the phenomena of nonviolence and peace. Their assumption is that it is insufficient to study only violence and war; nonviolence and peace are also significant phenomena which require documentation, analysis, interpretation, and explanation. Also they assert that not only do violence and war need to be reduced and eventually eliminated, but that nonviolence and peace need to be further developed. Not surprisingly, their moral stance is that violence and war are not the best means to the ends of creating a more nonviolent and peaceful world! Furthermore, they view an exclusive focus on violence and war as not only incomplete and too narrow, but as a distraction from many of the underlying problems and is-

sues of peace, which encompass economic and social justice, and more broadly, inequities within and between societies (Barnaby 1988).

Although the terms "negative" and "positive" peace are both valuative, the distinction remains valid and useful. Allegiance to the negative concept of peace certainly has farreaching and serious consequences. There have been relatively few studies directly focused on nonviolence and peace, compared to the enormous volume on warfare and other forms of aggression (Ferguson & Farragher 1988). Thus, a survey of the contents of the *Journal of Peace Research* from 1964 to 1980 revealed that out of approximately 400 articles, research communications, and the like, only a single one was devoted to the empirical study of peaceful societies in order to try to understand their attributes and conditions (Wiberg 1981: 113).

According to Fabbro (1978), nonviolent and peaceful societies are characterized by small and open communities with face-to-face interpersonal interactions, EGALITARIAN SOCIETIES, generalized reciprocity, social control and decision making through group consensus, and nonviolent values and enculturation. They lack intergroup violence or FEUDING, internal (civil) or external warfare, threats from external enemy groups or nations, social STRATIFICATION and other forms of structural violence such as SORCERY or WITCHCRAFT, full-time political leaders or centralized authority, and police and military organizations.

Beyond Fabbro's pioneering article, only a few other studies have directly explored the anthropology of nonviolence and peace (S. Howell & Willis 1989; Montagu 1978; Sponsel & Gregor 1994). Yet a recent annotated bibliography documents some 50 examples of relatively nonviolent and peaceful societies (Bonta 1993). The positive concept of peace has the potential to open up a whole new world of exciting possibilities for research, teaching, and action by those anthropologists who are receptive and committed to the ideals of nonviolence and peace.   LS

See also CONFLICT RESOLUTION, ETHNOCENTRISM, HOMICIDE, HUMAN RIGHTS, LAW

further reading Dentan 1968; Kohn 1990; Laszlo & Yoo 1986; Waal 1989

peasants are small-scale agricultural producers organized into households that rely on family labor in a subsistence-oriented economy that is nevertheless a part of a larger state system that extracts various forms of rent from the communities it controls.

In peasant communities HOUSEHOLDS are the basic units of production and of consumption. Such households depend overwhelmingly on members of the household, both adults and children, to provide the labor needed to run a peasant farm and participate in a variety of reciprocal labor arrangements during peak labor periods. Peasants try to avoid hiring regular outside laborers except during periods of planting or harvesting, when they serve to supplement the labor provided by household members. Characteristically, outside helpers are often treated as if they were members of the household, particularly in the case of servants or adopted children (Chayanyov 1966).

Peasant households have a subsistence orientation aimed at the reproduction of the household. They attempt to provide most of the goods they need for household reproduction without recourse to markets – both the inputs necessary for agricultural production (seed, tools, etc.) and outputs (food, clothing, etc.). Of course, because such self-sufficiency at a household level is virtually impossible in most situations, peasants more often simply try to minimize the importance of market transactions in acquiring the goods and labor they need for agricultural production or consumption by employing a range of noncommoditized forms of exchange and acquisition. These include activating wider kin and community networks, creating webs of reciprocity, obligation, alliance, or debt, among other strategies. To the extent that peasants must resort to MARKETS, their *orientation* to exchanges is guided by a subsi2stence or reproduction logic: they sell in order to buy, and they buy in order to consume.

Peasant households are willing to adopt a wide range of strategies to secure household reproduction. Household members often pursue a variety of productive and reproductive tasks in addition to agricultural plots and livestock. These may include engaging in fishing or forestry, craft production, cooking food for sale in markets, or taking in laundry, sewing, weaving, or other outside work that can be done in the house. Such "supplementary" activities can take on more importance, both in terms of labor time and household income, than agriculture itself. In addition, household members may seek jobs outside the household, on a regular or seasonal basis. Those who do so may continue to live in the house or move to other areas on a seasonal or "permanent" basis. Here too "supplementary" labor outside the house may take on more importance than labor on the household farm, especially in terms of income, as the family farm farms the family out, so to speak.

Peasant households do not exist in isolation but in relation to others, both to other peasant households who may form a relatively loose or tight community, and to superordinates who press claims – for labor, goods, rent, taxes, and so on – on peasants. One way of describing these relations with superordinates is to say that peasants always pursue their livelihoods within wider systems of economic, political, and social relationships that include markets, outside labor, governments, religious institutions, landlords and other groups that extend well beyond the everyday social horizons of peasant villages.

Anthropologists have consistently stressed this relational character of peasant livelihood. In a classic statement, Alfred KROEBER (1923) defined peasants as "part" societies and "part" cultures. Robert REDFIELD, in one statement, emphasized the importance of the city in relation to peasant communities, and in another emphasized the importance of the "great tradition" of civilizations in relation to the "little tradition" of peasants (Redfield 1956). Eric Wolf (1966) took Redfield's reference to cities and suggested that the critical distinguishing feature was the importance of STATE systems that could press and enforce a range of claims upon peasant labor and income, a range that he classified as "rent."

In any particular historical or ethnographic situation, peasants fit more or less well into the key criteria of household centrality, emphasis on household labor, subsistence or reproduction orientation, and integration into markets and wider systems. Indeed, it would be rare to find *any* peasant household that fits *all* of these criteria. Each of the criteria points to social relations that are subject to complex historical processes and power dynamics. They are not simple givens but point to a range of possible social forms and strategies, of relations based upon and producing inequalities, and so on.

The utility of the definition is not typological but analytic. Each of the features points toward areas of peasant life that have received detailed ethnographic and historical attention. The centrality of the household has attracted studies of household formation, of gendered and generational inequalities and power dynamics within houses, and of household and family ideologies. The importance of household labor has served as a starting point for studies of household decision making, especially in relation to the developmental cycle of the household and the changing work and consumption requirements in houses as children are born, grow up, move out, press for their inheritance, and so on. The reproduction orientation has served as central assumption in studies that examine peasantries as a human type distinct from other types, but it can also serve to elucidate a variety of pressures placed upon peasants, as individuals and in households, as they engage in a range of strategies and enter into a variety of social and economic relationships in order to get a living. And the emphasis on wider relations has served as starting point for economic, political, and cultural studies of the effects of wider systems such as feudalism or capitalism on peasantries, or of the effects of peasant strata on the development of the wider systems. WR

further reading Gudeman & Rivera 1990; Redfield 1953; Shanin 1987; E. Wolf 1969

personality *See* CULTURE AND PERSONALITY

phenomenology is a philosophical movement, the principal aim of which is to describe phenomena in their most radical form, as they stand before they get defined by supposition. By "phenomena" is meant things as they appear to us.

Its beginnings are associated with the work of Edmund Husserl (1964, 1970) in the period just before World War I. Husserl regarded phenomenology as a method of description rather than of analytic or empirical research. It is nonempirical in that the truth of phenomenological descriptions is not thought to depend on sense data or empirical observation. Nor, however, are the descriptions thought to be true anatically, that is by definition, as in, say, a formal system of logic or mathematics.

According to Husserl, the trouble with the inductive sciences (what he called empiricism, psychologism, and behaviorism) is that their presuppositions go unexamined. These sciences all continue to presuppose the world they profess to explain. Though they are blind to this fact, they presume rather than discover the world in terms of naturalism: the view that all that is real is objectively real, so that even the psychical must be understood – if it is to be understood at all – in terms of the physical.

What is meant to guarantee the truth of phenomenological descriptions is the systematic suspension of all such presuppositions. When the latter are put aside, then by definition one is left with an unobstructed view of the essential forms – in a word, "phenomena." The intention is to reduce phenomena in the sense of restoring them to their most basic – which is to say, their transcendental or noncontingent – forms. Put another way, the phenomenologist aims to set off phenomena in brackets, shunting aside all but their ultimate limits. Hence the procedure is known as the phenomenological "reduction" or "bracketing."

It is difficult to overestimate the radicalness of this procedure, for what gets set aside is existence as it is taken for granted. How is it possible to hold in abeyance something so presumptive as one's everyday grasp of reality, what Husserl called the "natural attitude"? Here Husserl proposed a technique of imaginative variation, whereby the properties of a thing are systematically thrown into question, until such point as one arrives at the limits without which the thing can no longer appear at all.

The first and most important phenomenon illuminated by the epoche pertains to consciousness itself: that, far from being a subjective, interior realm opposed to the exterior substance of the objective world, consciousness is a field of experience, structured around a subject–object bipolarity. Husserl spoke of this essential structure of consciousness as "intentionality," by which he meant that the appearing object and attending subject are what they are only in virtue of each other. In other words, directly contrary to Cartesian dualism, and despite the usual acceptance of "intentionality," consciousness appears as neither subjective nor objective but as an experiential dynamic through which these two principles of ontology originate.

Husserlian phenomenology came under strong criticism because of its theoretically untenable goal of a wholly presuppositionless understanding. Correlatively, it came to grief in respect of the question of how the phenomena themselves were constituted. In response to this question of origin, Husserl posited a transcendental ego, thus falling back into a blatant idealism and subjectivism. As a reaction to these problems, the three most famous students of Husserl's phenomenology, Heidegger (1962), Sartre (1956), and Merleau-Ponty (1962), shifted the emphasis of this philosophy, each in his own highly distinctive way, from transcendental essence to worldly existence, or from pure form to embodied practice. Husserl's own concept of the "life-world" (Lebenswelt), the world in which we always already find ourselves, is consistent with this shift.

Phenomenology has not been a strong attraction in modern professional anthropology. In part, of course, this lack of influence may be explained by the fact that, whereas phenomenology extols nonempiricist understanding, modern anthropology has arisen as a committedly empiricist science. Still, the failure of an-

thropology to pay much attention to phenomenology is curious, in view of the fact that there are well-defined pockets of phenomenological scholarship in both psychology and sociology (phenomenological psychology (Berger & Luckmann 1966) and ethnomethodology (Garfinkel 1967), respectively).

There is a tendency in current anthropology to use the term "phenomenology" loosely to refer to any kind of interpretive or symbolic anthropology. Perhaps the most notable mention of phenomenology by an anthropologist, though, is in Tristes tropiques (1963c), where LÉVI-STRAUSS rejected it for reasons of its subjectivism. Ironically, despite their subjectlessness, Lévi-Strauss's "structures" have something substantial about them of the phenomenologist's "essences."

In fact, when it is considered from the perspective of its intrinsic pursuits, by contrast to its self-identification as positive science, sociocultural anthropology in general exhibits a profound resemblance to phenomenology. Notwithstanding the emphasis on empirical fieldwork, the most diacritical mark of anthropological research is the proscription on ethnocentrism. Plainly, that proscription, a constitutive disciplinary admonishment to suspend one's cultural presuppositions, is a form of the phenomenological reduction or bracketing. Only, instead of proceeding simply intellectually, by means of thought experiments, anthropological bracketing proceeds practically, by means of the disruption of meaning brought about naturally through the direct confrontation with other cultures.

What anthropology seeks to find through its special kind of bracketing (ethnography) has something fundamentally in common with the phenomenologist's idea of phenomena. Whatever anthropology's current attitude to evolutionism and universalism, and regardless of anthropology's characteristic sociological and culturological contextualization of its findings, the "primitives" anthropology pursues always remain in a sense human essences. The relevant sense has nothing to do with what is rudimentary and backward; it is, rather, a matter of what is first and fundamental, a limit that does not chronologically precede but rather continues to occur (Leenhardt 1975; Agamben 1993). "Primitives" of this kind – from ceremonial and kinship to reason and myth – are sought after by anthropologists as what always makes human beings human, even if it is no longer thought that such phenomena can be captured in the absolute terms of ontological naturalism.

The strong, ready identity between anthropology and phenomenology is manifest in the relatively few anthropological monographs in which a genuine phenomenological approach predominates. In this regard, Godfrey Lienhardt's *Divinity and experience* (1961) and Maurice Leenhardt's *Do kamo* (1979) are, though decidedly different from each other in ethnographic style, exemplary. It is difficult to say exactly where these two scholars absorbed phenomenology. Lienhardt was informed by his mentor EVANS-PRITCHARD, whose celebrated conversion to an historical approach over FUNCTIONALISM was, arguably, more a matter of antiscientism than anything else, and who had been influenced by R. G. Collingwood's somewhat Hegelian philosophy; it is certain that Maurice Leenhardt was exposed to Heidegger's thought (Clifford 1982). Both scholars were also informed by the work of Lucien Levy-Bruhl, whose paralogical notion of "participation" is, as over and against "causation," intrinsically phenomenological (Leenhardt 1975; Cazeneuve 1972). Finally, it is worth speculating that in their approach to the study of primitive RELIGION, both men were influenced by religious studies proper, where phenomenology has been an important strain of thought (Otto 1923; Leeuw 1938).

At any rate, both *Divinity and experience* and *Do kamo* seek to understand the religion of the Dinka and the Canaque respectively, by bracketing, quite radically, the natural attitude of Western thought in favor of a nondualist and experiential consciousness of the world. And, whereas Lienhardt's rich phenomenological exercise is curtailed by his adherence to a tropological interpretation, his French namesake's study describes the Canaque's nondualistic world as a perfectly earnest apprehension, and – exhibiting just how

radical phenomenology can be – gives to that prescientific world a genuine credibility.

Whatever the status of phenomenology or anthropology as a set of theoretical doctrines, each discipline stands peculiarly as a critical way of thinking that advances in application to itself: each proceeds purposefully by suspending its own presuppositions. Thus both are uniquely revolutionary, and for this crucial reason the identity between them runs deep.

TMSE

further reading   Binswanger 1963; Bruzina 1970; Lyotard 1991; Natanson 1973; Schutz 1962–6, 1967; Spiegelberg 1960; Zaner 1977

philosophical anthropology is a branch of philosophy concerned to show that, owing to his preponderantly underdetermined nature, man is that animal who must, in large part, determine himself. Although its roots are diffuse and its boundaries fuzzy, in its modern form philosophical anthropology got its beginnings in the 1920s and was especially prevalent in German philosophy. It has ties with existentialism, phenomenology, and Dilthey's "philosophy of life" (in which consciousness is understood in terms of lived or immediate experience). In its development it has drawn on a number of outstanding thinkers, including Kierkegaard, Nietzsche, Pascal, Herder, Goethe, Kant, Hegel, Feuerbach, and von Humboldt. Recent prominent scholars who may be associated with philosophical anthropology include Max Scheler, Adolf Portmann, Helmuth Plessner, Arnold Gehlen, F. J. J. Buytendijk, Medard Boss, Ludwig Binswanger, Erwin Straus, and Michael Landmann.

What distinguishes philosophical anthropology is its ontological focus on man as the mediator of his own nature. According to Herder, in whose ideas philosophical anthropology is rooted, in man instinct is replaced by freedom; the deficit of specific determinations becomes a condition for the emergence of reason, understanding, and reflection. "No longer an infallible machine in the hands of nature, [man] becomes a purpose unto himself." In effect, a qualitative leap is postulated by philosophical anthropology: "in man something is not simply added to the animal . . . [rather] he is fundamentally based on a completely different principle of organization . . . he is the only one who has an open world" (quoted in Landmann 1982).

The critical problem of philosophical anthropology is, then, how man's creaturely limitations lead to their own transcendence. As a result, an outstanding element of philosophical anthropology concerns itself with the meaningful, rather than simply physical, character of human biology. For example, in his study of upright posture, Erwin Straus (1966) argued that man's moral capacity is tied to this posture, not causally, but immanently. Again for example, according to Plessner (1970) man's position in the world may be distinguished as "eccentric," since, unlike the other animals, man always stands to some significant degree outside his own center – which is to say, outside his given nature. In light of this distinction, Plessner interpreted both laughter and crying as singularly human responses to situations in which man's (mediatory) capacity for eccentricity is stultified. As these examples suggest, one outstanding preoccupation of philosophical anthropology is the study of the dynamic of human creativity by virtue of which body and mind may be regarded as both different from and identical to each other.

Clearly, philosophical anthropology runs contrary to Cartesian dualism. Its focus is on, rather than an absolute divide between mind and body, the manner in which man's body is implicitly mindful. As this manner is irreducible to the positive reality of the physical world, it exhibits, in Pascal's terms, a *logique du coeur*, a logic above and beyond logic as such. Where this transcendental focus differs from traditional philosophical metaphysics is in its central concern for man in his own particular being, existentially bound up with the world.

Regarded from the perspective of his capacity to make meaning, man lends himself to interpretation rather than explanation. Therefore, consistent with the romantic re-action to Enlightenment thought, philosophical anthropology is inclined to question the ascendancy of science. It may take advantage of scientific research, but patently rejects the hegemony of scientific knowledge. From a strictly logical point of view, the relationship between mind and body ultimately presents an aporia, an existential opening that calls forth creative engagement of the world. Therefore, for philosophical anthropology, man is always pictured as logically indeterminate, and thus at bottom unfathomable in scientific terms.

In its existentialist emphasis on man as a creature that must make his own destiny, rather than as an object of science, philosophical anthropology is inclined to make man's self-understandings – his various anthropologies – the focus of study. For example, in his rich psychological study of a case of severe anorexia, Binswanger (1958) argued that the tragic life of the patient can be adequately understood only in terms of her inner life history, an autobiographical account of the meanings she made of herself through self-fashioning, existential choices. Relative to the study of CULTURE and SOCIETY, this approach makes common cause with modern professional anthropology, understanding human beings in terms of their various cultural self-images: humans are seen as shaping themselves in terms of what they happen to see themselves to be by nature (Landmann 1974).

Given its scientific aspirations, notwithstanding its strong turn towards hermeneutics, modern professional anthropology has been inclined to keep its distance from philosophical questions. By contrast, philosophical anthropology centers definitively on the philosophical and basically non-empirical question of man's ontological nature. Compared to modern professional anthropology, philosophical anthropology may seem speculative and lacking in methodological distinction. In relation to the former's defining holistic ambitions, however, there is much to be learned from the nondualism of the latter.

TMSE

further reading Boss 1965; Buytendijk

1968; Gehlen 1980; Landmann 1979; Portmann 1990

phonemes are the basic units of sound structure in the underlying inventory of a specific language. For instance, the aspirated and unaspirated *p* of *[pʰ]in* (pin) and *s[p]in* (spin) constitute distinct sounds but not distinct phonemes (in English). Rather, they appear to be contextual variants, or "allophones," of a single underlying phoneme /p/. Independent phonemic status is established by occurrence in identical environments, as for [*p*]/[*b*] in *cu[p]* versus *cu[b]*, a "minimal pair."   LB
See also PHONOLOGY

phonology is the branch of LINGUISTICS concerned with the organization of sound in natural languages. Contemporary theory postulates phonological representations such as that in figure 1, relative to the English word *victim*. Such representations aim to express the temporal organization of articulatory activity. The "segments" in figure 1 are shorthand notation for bundles of contemporaneous articulatory gestures

represented by the "distinctive features." Segments are mapped into a "CV [consonant–vowel] template" defining the basic time frame, in which consonants and vowels (the two major classes of segments) alternate. Mapping need not be one-to-one: long or "geminate" segments such as the [t] of Italian *vittima* are single segments mapped onto two temporal units (CC). Each cycle of CV alternation constitutes a "syllable," whose internal subconstituents are the *onset* and the *rime* (o/r). Syllables are in turn organized into accentual units or "(metrical) feet," with the stress/accent falling on the rightmost or (as in case of "victim") leftmost syllable of the foot, by language-specific choice.

A central problem in phonology is the apparent manipulation of sound structure in word formation. The English plural morpheme, for instance, takes on the different forms [s], [z], [iz] in *cats*, *dogs*, *churches*, respectively. A standard approach postulates two different levels of representation mediated by context-sensitive rules, allowing for a single plural morpheme /s/ at an "underlying" level, from which the dif-

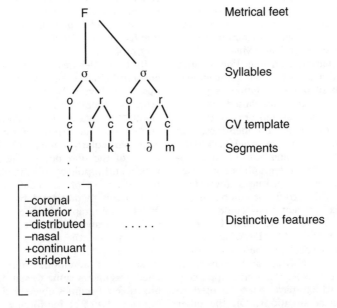

Figure 1 Phonological representations relative to English word *rictim*.

ferent noted "allomorphs" would result at a "derived/phonetic" level.   LB
See also MORPHEMES, PHONEMES

photography   has featured significantly as a research tool within anthropology since the emergence of the discipline in the nineteenth century and it can be argued that the two have an intertwined history, since photography authenticated and reified anthropological observation (Pinney 1992). Photography has a double agenda in the late twentieth century, first as a research tool and method and second as the focus of critical study of the photographic product itself in terms of representation.

In the production of ethnographic data, photography has conventionally been used as an inventory or survey tool. However, distinction must be made between incidental or ancillary use of the camera as a visual notebook and rigorously structured visual inquiry where both the subject matter and its interrogation, recording, and analysis are conceived in terms of visual communication. Photography is so used over a wide range of subjects, from the processes of MATERIAL CULTURE to behaviors that do not express themselves verbally or materially such as social process, body expression (kinesics), and spatial dynamics (proxemics). The most famous example is perhaps G. Bateson and M. MEAD's (1942) work on socialization in Bali. Photography is also used extensively in anthropology as the focus of photoelicitation or photointerview in studies as varied as continuity of material culture traditions, community histories, and identities, and ETHNO-HISTORY. It can yield rich data, INFORMANTS describing not only the concrete content of a photograph but articulating their projected attitudes toward it, investing it with significant emotional and psychological content that would not be articulated in other ways (John Collier & Collier 1986: 99–132). Drawing on the methods of psychology there are various methods for qualifying and quantifying such data, such as the Thematic Apperception Test, which have been adapted to anthropological situations. On the other hand, such use of photographs should also include consideration of culturally specific

roles of visual inscription and its relation to memory, the significance of the photograph itself as a cultural object, and ultimately the cultural components of visual perception itself.

While the production of hard ethnographic data remains a central role for photography, a second, strongly reflexive agenda has emerged. The crisis of representation that has permeated all aspects of anthropological text has suggested new perspectives on photography. No longer can photographs be seen as unproblematic transcriptions of a cultural truth, even at its simplest level. Despite the appearance of objectivity that photographic technology presents, its use must always be viewed as culturally grounded, a specific cultural response in a specific situation. Thus both what is considered relevant subject matter to be recorded by the camera and the contexts of its interpretation have changed radically over time. This is the basic tenet of much detailed deconstructionist analysis of the historical photographic legacy of colonial anthropology (Banta & Hinsley 1986; Geary 1988; Edwards 1992). Although much attention of this kind has centered on historical material, such analysis can be applied equally to modern material and its diverse uses in academic monographs, museum exhibitions, or community projects.

In these debates both anthropological and photographic theory have drawn variously but powerfully on MARXIST ANTHROPOLOGY, literary theory, psychoanalysis, SEMIOTICS, and POSTCOLONIAL theories of POWER relations (those of Foucault have been particularly influential). The significance of the ontology of the photograph within anthropology and the ultimately arbitrary nature of its signifiers have been part of this theoretical debate: the way in which photography fragments both space and time, transposing the content to different contexts where it assumes different meanings, perhaps transcending its original meaning and intention. From this, it is argued, fragments come to stand for wholes, the subject becomes objectified, perpetuating stereotypes or reinforcing the ETHNOGRAPHIC PRESENT (Barthes 1977; Tagg 1988).

This theoretical debate has had a profound effect on the way anthropologists use photography, not only in their own FIELDWORK (where the intrusive nature of the medium has long been recognized) and the development of reflexive models for producing primary data (Caldarola 1987; Piette 1993), but also within a broader frame of the politics of representation, where the ethical implications of contested photographic meaning must be addressed (L. Gross et al. 1988). If the POSTMODERN wave has decentered the certainties of photographic realism, creating sometimes methodological and representational paralysis, it has equally extended the boundaries of photographic possibility within anthropology, ranging from projects of self-representation (Penny Taylor 1988) to the interface with contemporary visual-arts practice (Banks & Morphy 1997).

Although ethnographic description, based firmly on ethnographic knowledge and addressing specifically anthropological problems, remains the primary function of photography for most anthropologists, a reflexive view of its cultural entanglements has become equally important.   EE

See also ART, COLONIALISM, ETHNOGRAPHY AND ETHNOLOGY, VISUAL ANTHROPOLOGY

further reading Barthes 1981 [a wonderful poetic]; B. Nichols 1981; Pinney 1989 [useful theoretical summary of nature of photography in contrast to film]; Scherer 1990; Sontag 1977; Worth 1981

phratries are three or more sets of CLANS related by common descent or other kinship alliances. The term is rarely used today.   MR

See also MOIETY SYSTEMS

physical anthropology   See BIOLOGICAL ANTHROPOLOGY

pilgrimage is the practice of journeying to physical sites on earth where special spiritual or sacred power is understood to be especially accessible. With ancient roots in many religious traditions of the world, pilgrimage – facilitated by ever-improving transportation – still remains a meaningful and popular contemporary ritual practice.

Every pilgrimage involves a goal or goals and the effort necessary to reach them. Pilgrims' destinations are usually sacred centers or regions, possessing complex mythologies and histories, such as the cities of Jerusalem and Mecca (F. Peters 1986). They are often sites of established religious institutions attended by organized ritual experts, such as the sacred Hindu city of Ayodhya (Veer 1988). Pilgrims' experiences on the road may involve spiritual quests and personal transformations in addition to more mundane hardships and pleasures, as described in Gold's (1988) study of villagers' journeys in India. While most studies of pilgrimage focus either on center or journey, Alan Morinis (1992: 9) commented that the "complementarity of structure and experience is one of the main contributions the study of pilgrimage stands to make to contemporary anthropological theory."

Although every pilgrimage is embedded in particular historical and cultural contexts, the comparative study of pilgrimage has attracted anthropologists and religionists in part because of perceptible commonalities existing even among widely divergent traditions. Movement is critical to pilgrimage, for what is important is not just visiting a sacred place but getting away from home. Thus in every case, pilgrimage is a break with mundane routines and familiar places. It consequently entails immersion in special time and space and intensified participation in ritual actions. Although some pilgrims travel alone, most go in groups, temporarily forging new collectivities and identities (E. Daniel 1984: 233–87).

Because pilgrimage always demands an out-of-the-ordinary effort, scholars have focused particular attention on pilgrims' motivations (Morinis 1992: 10–14). Important among these is a devotional complex that includes seeking blessings and making offerings – or more generally, interchange between people and divinity (Nolan & Nolan 1989). Often pilgrims wish to beseech, please, thank, or simply see and absorb the felt presence of a god, saint, or power. But aimlessness, a spiritual good in itself, may also lie at the heart of wandering.

In some religions pilgrimage is distinguished by its obligatory nature as a journey that is scripturally enjoined and specific in time and place – such as the Islamic *hajj* to Mecca, which was initiated by the religion's founding prophet, Mohammed (F. Peters 1994). Yet this obligation is also qualified by circumstances, and devotional motivations are also relevant for Muslim pilgrims. Other pilgrimage centers originate in places where miracles and visions occurred, and recur, such as a series of pilgrimage sites in northeastern Brazil (Slater 1986). Still others are closely tied to landscapes endowed with special natural beauty, made meaningful through cultural traditions, as in China (Naquin & Yu 1992), Japan (Reader 1987, 1988), and the Andes of South America (Sallnow 1987). Shrines grow up around tombs and relics of deceased holy persons who are understood as mediators of spiritual powers (Faure 1992). In several religions, pilgrimage is closely associated with care for and dealings with SPIRITS of deceased kin and with preparations for the pilgrims' own death – often likened to a journey (V. Turner 1979: 121–42). Such pilgrimages may explicitly effect purification from sins whether through external acts like penance and bathing or through internal vows (Parry 1994).

Among anthropological theories of pilgrimage, Victor TURNER's ideas remain influential, if contested, today. Turner's interest in pilgrimage developed out of his earlier work on RITUAL. Taking off from Arnold van GENNEP's comparative study of RITES OF PASSAGE, with their three stages of separation, liminality, and reaggregation, Victor Turner (1969: 94–130) focused on LIMINALITY, finding there a dissolution of social structure's hierarchies and boundaries, and a fruitful experience of camaraderie that he called "communitas." In several important articles (1974: 166–230; 1979) and a coauthored monograph (Turner & Turner 1978), he dealt with pilgrimage as a voluntary experience of prolonged liminality – which he eventually labeled "liminoid." Whether pilgrimages universally dissolve ordinary social hierarchies and foster a sense of communitas is debatable – and many have persuasively argued against attributing any universal applicability to Turner's nonetheless germinal ideas. Eade and Sallnow (1991: 5), for example, attempted to rethink pilgrimage studies within POSTMODERN social science, insisting that any pilgrimage presents "*a realm of competing discourses*" [original italics], neither supporting nor subverting established social order.

Today with anthropological interest heightened in secular arenas of public culture, new directions in pilgrimage studies include tourism, such as a trip to Graceland (Elvis Presley's home and burial site) or to a national park (E. Cohen 1992; Rinschede & Bhardwaj 1990). However, students of religion continue to attend to powerful ironies inherent in the paradoxical concept of sacred place – expressed in Solomon's question when he built his Temple in Jerusalem (*1 Kings* 8:27): "But will God indeed dwell on the earth? Behold, the heaven and heaven of heavens cannot contain Thee; how much less this house that I have built?" (cited in F. Peters 1986: 7). This enigma remains at the core of many pilgrims' journeys.   AGG

See also RELIGION, SYMBOLIC ANTHROPOLOGY

further reading Bhardwaj et al. 1994; D. Carmichael et al. 1994; Crumrine & Morinis 1991; Myerhoff 1974; Sax 1991

place is a space made meaningful by human occupation or appropriation and is a cultural concept fundamental to describing human beings' relations with their environment.

As a physical setting, place includes geographic location, econiche, or site of habitual occupation, a concept used principally by ethnographers to situate descriptions of peoples they study. As a theoretical concept place has been historically devalued or ignored in the social sciences, especially in the social and cultural anthropology, which has tended to define "CULTURE" in terms of intangibles such as sets of traits or collective mentalities without a specific location. Geographers, by contrast, have focused on place and its essential moral qualities but have often confused it with community. In the historic context of the Cold War, for example, both were seen as requisite preliminary steps to the development of modern societies (Agnew 1989). Recently, anthropologists have begun to resituate theory and rediscover the role of space and place in human society (see ARCHITECTURE).

Place as a geographic locale invested with moral value was a sociospatial concept employed by Louis Wirth and the Chicago school of sociologists. They proposed an urban ecology of the American city consisting in the morality of a spatial order identified by the specific habitual or sequential association of class and ethnic groupings with physically or conceptually bounded locales. Perin's (1977) analysis of codified land-use-planning or "zoning" practices revealed principles of social organization in American cities that accorded differential rights and privileges to people who own their own homes as opposed to renters. Australian Aborigines also invest their local environment with moral significance, which can be evocative of both historical sentiments associated with remembered events and transhistorical, timeless meanings created by and for the Dreamtime (Myers 1986).

How and why individuals and groups invest sentiment and emotional meanings in spaces, and how places evoke feelings that express a sense of identity, and people's bonds with spaces are key issues in research on place attachment. Drawing initially on PHENOMENOLOGICAL studies such as Bachelard (1964), these approaches explore how meanings develop and change over the course of the life cycle or historical time, or how meanings are invested in different ways through collective or community rituals or personal uses (I. Altman & Low 1992). Different places, such as MARKETS and plazas, can evoke totally different behaviors and feelings (Richardson 1982).

From the perspective of political economy, place is produced as a cultural construct and setting for action through collective activity over time. Places are not isolated but embedded in networks of relations created through historical and colonial contacts and through continuing pressure of world capitalist markets (S. Low 1993). As commodities, places are produced by design and planning specialists and consumed according to market forces (Zukin 1991). Although the global economy integrates spatially dispersed economic activities, its forces are responsible for reorganizing the social and spatial structures of "global" cities that act as centers of control in this economy, such as New York, London, and Tokyo (Sassen 1991).

As a cultural representation, place incorporates and transcends the actual physical site because it is invested with power through discourse: people use actual sites to represent themselves but characteristics of the sites also become part of their identities (Rodman 1992). Place acquires power when the figurative way of talking about a place becomes a part of the experience of that place; when place is conflated with way of life; or when the representation of place is contested. Place also acquires transcendent power through the invention of a site-specific tradition and its commodification (Dorst 1989). As a representation it also acts as a hidden concept in the anthropological construction of the native as revealed in the critique of anthropology (Appadurai 1988a). The "voice" of the anthropologist creates an authoritative representation of the native as the "other." Place names used by anthropologists to identify the location of groups in ethnographies are based on tacit notions of a cultural adaptation to an ecological niche; but these characterizations freeze the image of the native and imply their physical immobility and confinement to the periphery or margins. Actual mobility of these peoples through contemporary migration makes presumptions of "authenticity" of place-based culture impossible to sustain.

DL

See also PILGRIMAGE

further reading J. Duncan & Ley 1993; Gupta & Ferguson 1992; Pred 1984; Relph 1976; Soja 1989

play Whether viewed as an expressive symbolic activity, as a mechanism of socialization, or as a form of communication, play has perplexed and fascinated the anthropologists who have endeavored to understand its nature and its place in cultural life. (Schwartzman 1978 provided an excellent review of this literature.) Gregory

Bateson's influential theory of play treats it as a paradoxical form of communication in which actions taken as play do not mean what they would otherwise mean (1972: 177–93). He stressed the role of metacommunciation in play: a metacommunication being any statement or action that defines the nature of a statement, an interaction, or a relationship, thereby making possible actions and interactions that could not otherwise occur. According to Bateson, the metacommunication "This is play" (signalled in some fashion) is necessary to distinguish play from nonplay (e.g., a mock fight from a real fight, the playful pretense of anger from a real show of anger) by declaring that what would otherwise count as a certain kind of act means something else – as play. The process of metacommunication establishes the cognitive frame for play, allowing meanings to be detached from reality and mobilized in the imagination (see Vygotsky 1978: ch. 7). Establishing the play frame makes possible the creative nonreality of play in which ordinary actions and objects are subject to playful transformations (a rock into a car, a toy into a person, self into something else) in ways that may help individuals explore culture and self, learn about society and social roles, express feelings, and reorganize thought processes (Schwartzman 1978; Kelly-Byrne 1989).   SP
See also CHILDREN,   EDUCATION, SOCIALIZATION

plural marriage   *See* POLYGAMY

plural societies   are those that contain multiple ethnic populations within a shared economy and centralized political order dominated by one of the groups. The concept differs significantly from the widely used concept of "political pluralism," in which there is an accepted division of decision-making power across a society's range and variety of interest groups and institutions in competition with each other.

Drawing on research in India and Burma under COLONIALISM, J. S. Furnivall (1939, 1948) initially restricted the definition of plural societies to those multiracial, colonial societies created by the political expansion of Europe in the tropics. Based on historical research in Africa (Gann 1958), the Caribbean (De Waal Malefijt 1963; M. Smith 1965), and the Americas (Murra 1975), later researchers progressively expanded the concept well beyond these specific criteria. Though differing in many ways, at present most scholars share Van Den Berge's (1973: 961) definition of plural societies as those in which "several distinct social and/or cultural groups coexist within the boundaries of a single polity and share a common economic system that makes them interdependent, yet they maintain to a greater or lesser degree autonomy and discrete institutional structures in other spheres of social life."

Anthropological interest in plural societies has coincided with the discipline's turn away from an earlier focus on single cultures, which often appeared to exist in isolation. Although all contemporary societies are heterogeneous to some degree, it has been argued that plural societies are analytically distinct from other forms of heterogeneity. As M. G. Smith (1960) declared in a seminal article, plural societies are characterized by significant cultural differences and a coexistence of incompatible institutional systems, unlike those societies that have difference but still share common forms of kinship, education, religion, property and economy, recreation, or other sodalities. In particular, plural societies, regardless of other differences, are characterized by incorporation of disparate groups into a political system in which one group, a numerical minority, dominates.

Although initial models tended to take cultural distinctions between groups within plural societies as the basis of their analysis, current research gives analytic priority to the relationships among groups within a political arena, particularly the dominance by one group. Because ethnic hegemony is now acknowledged as the critical feature, many societies that are socially or culturally heterogeneous but do not manifest a structural asymmetry of ethnic power are not considered plural societies.

The emphasis on dominance led others to focus more on the coercion necessary to maintain structural positions. Some anthropologists stress that coercion alone is equivalent to the result of conquest in that it can be difficult to sustain and expensive to maintain. Unity can thus can be short lived without some other bond. Returning in part to Furnivall's initial criteria, researchers such as Van Den Berge (1973: 961) stress that "political coercion and economic interdependence (often of an exploitative nature) are necessary, sufficient and mutually reinforming bases of social integration in plural societies." Leo Kuper (1974), for example, included CLASS stratification as a form of plural society. The earlier emphasis on the "incompatibility" of member's cultures as an essential aspect of plural societies led some to ask how incompatibility is defined and who defines it. In brief, following Van Den Berge, a society is now considered plural when: (1) there is segmentation into functionally similar corporate groups whose members frequently though not always belong to different cultural groups and; (2) there is a social structure that is divided into analogous duplicatory, parallel, noncomplementary, but distinguishable sets of institutions.

Because of these complexities recent research has shifted away from defining a "plural society" as a formally distinct ideal type. To focus analytically on distinctive features reduces plural societies to the same sort of static or closed systems that the term first worked to expunge from anthropological research. Consequently many now begin with the notion that pluralism, to a greater or lesser extent, exists in all societies. Understood thus the unit of analyis shifts away from defining characteristics toward the particular society that manifests pluralism. Emphasis then rests on the manner, extent, and functioning of pluralism within societies rather than on identifying and defining plural societies.

The study of plural societies thus parallels the study of the ETHNIC GROUPS that make up these societies. Interest has shifted more toward the processes of pluralism and away from concern with static distinctive features of a "plural society" or an "ethnic group" toward the dynamic relationships through which the differences are manifested and the internal boundaries that are either maintained or manipulated.

TMac

See also CASTE, MIDDLEMAN MINORITIES, STATUS, STRATIFICATION

further reading Braude & Lewis 1982; Despres 1975; L. Kuper & Smith 1969; Maybury-Lewis 1984

poetry,   poetics,   ethnopoetics

Poetry is a genre of verbal art, and poetics is the aesthetic study of verbal art. As Roman Jakobson (1960: 350) put it, "Poetics deals primarily with the question, *What makes a verbal message a work of art?*" (original italics). In recent years, the term "ethnopoetics" has been coined (J. Rothenberg & Rothenberg 1983) (by analogy with "ETHNOBOTANY," "ETHNOMUSICOLOGY," or "ETHNOHISTORY") for a field that asks (to paraphrase Jakobson) what makes a verbal message a work of art in a particular cultural tradition.

Until the 1970s, poetics was left either to literary critics, who were concerned almost exclusively with Western, printed literature, or to anthropologists, who encountered oral and performative traditions outside of the industrialized West but treated them as a "datum" for inquiry into areas of culture such as religion and kinship, and hardly ever as an area of inquiry in and of itself. If Western, print-oriented scholars, including anthropologists, have had difficulty grasping the subtleties and complexities of performed verbal art, they have had even greater difficulty taking seriously the latter's centrality to everyday cultural thought and practice. Meeker (1979), in a pioneering work on Arabian poetry, challenged these perceptions by arguing that Bedouin poems expressed the core problems of their society: the uncertain nature of political relationships and the centrality of struggle between armed, mounted men that would seem to leave no recourse except to violence. It is now apparent from a number of studies that oral poetry, and poetics in general, are at the center of cultural debates in many different societies about personal identity (Caton 1985), gender roles (L. Abu-Lughod 1986), national identity (Lavie 1990), and politics (Bowen 1991).

The relative neglect of ethnopoetics began to change with the influence, for one, of FOLKLORE upon students of culture.

Folklorists had been rediscovering the "Parry–Lord hypothesis" regarding the oral-performative composition of the Homeric epics (M. Parry 1971; Lord 1960), launching what was to become an intense interest in the nature and significance of oral poetry globally (Finnegan 1977) and in the idea of verbal art as performance (Bauman 1977). The theoretical significance of the latter emphasis is that it is particularly in oral performances that cultural processes can be observed in which meaning and form are constituted (Caton 1990; Bauman & Briggs 1990).

Another important influence on the development of ethnopoetics was the ethnography of communication, which came to prominence in the 1960s (Hymes 1974). Ethnopoetics emerged and quickly established itself at the forefront of this subdiscipline with work such as Hymes's (1981) study of Native American literature of Northwest Coast and recent work in this vein by Sherzer (1990) on the Kuna of Panama. Dennis Tedlock's critical interventions encapsulated an important argument against what he called (after Derrida) the "logocentric" bias of LINGUISTICS in translation and transcription as exemplified, or so he claimed, in the work of Hymes and other ethnographers of communication (Tedlock 1983). He called for a new way of understanding and rendering oral art forms based upon a "dialogical" or Bakhtinian model of discourse (Bakhtin 1981). Of course, these approaches need not be mutually exclusive and they have both stimulated lively interest in problems of representing sound and meaning in cultural context.

Finally, poets, particularly in the United States over the past few decades, have stimulated ethnopoetics by researching other literary traditions as well as borrowing from them to create their own distinctive works, as is evident, for example, in the poetry of Olson, Snyder, and Baraka. Conversely, anthropologists have started to read their own poetry in public academic settings as a way of representing ethnography in new modes, thereby challenging the boundary between academic and artistic discourses, as happened in a session organized by Stanley Diamond at the annual meeting of the American Anthropological Association in December 1982. Related, then, to ethnopoetics but arising as a distinctive practice is what is sometimes called "anthropological poetics," which has more to do with the role of poetics and even poetry in informing anthropological theory and representational practice (Brady 1991), or with serving as a vehicle for the communication of ethnography (S. Diamond 1986), than it has with the study of "native" systems of poetics per se. It may well happen in the not too distant future that these strands will be interwoven into a more general field simply called "anthropology and poetics."   SC

See also COMMUNICATION

further reading Richard Brown 1977; J. Fernandez 1986; Friedrich 1986; J. Weiner 1991

political anthropology devotes itself to the study of law, order, conflict, governance, and power. Its origins are grounded in concepts drawn from such nineteenth-century theorists of social evolution as Sir Henry MAINE (1861), who distinguished societies organized by status and by contract in LAW, and Lewis Henry MORGAN's (1877) distinction between kinship and territory as the basis for the organization of GOVERNMENT. In addition it owes much to the discussions about the relationships between moral order and SOCIAL ORGANIZATION found in the writings of Emile DURKHEIM (1933), Max WEBER (1968), and Karl Marx (1887). More recent infusions of theory have come from social scientists such as Michel Foucault (1977b), Pierre Bourdieu (1977), and Anthony Giddens (1984), who focus on the structure of POWER in society.

Political anthropology today is the product of two different legacies. The first, primarily associated with cultural anthropology in the United States, remained focused on the comparative and historical questions of how and why political systems evolved. The second, associated with British social anthropology, was more interested in how politics worked in different societies and the roles of individuals.

The rise of the state has long been of theoretical interest to anthropologists intrigued by the evolution of societal forms. For decades evolution-minded anthropologists, along with archeologists, have busily classified societies into categories such as BANDS, TRIBES, CHIEFDOMS, and STATES, and then debated the merits of one another's typologies (Fried 1967; Service 1975). Conflict is often accorded a central if not catalytic role in virtually all these schemas. Yet though WAR has traditionally been studied as a means to an evolutionary end (Otterbein 1970), it has only recently been studied as an institution in and of itself (Turney-High 1949; R. Ferguson 1995; Otterbein 1994). This new focus on VIOLENCE in the contemporary world has made this branch of political anthropology much more salient than in the past. For example, although the FEUD (as a form of containable conflict) was one of the first political institutions to be studied, only recently have the uncontainable effects (and not just the causes) of organized violence in their various ethnic, political, sectarian, religious, and economic manifestations become subjects of research by anthropologists (Nordstrom & Martin 1992), along with possible solutions such as mediation and CONFLICT RESOLUTION.

The second, and perhaps more influential, branch of political anthropology has its origins in the experience of anthropological FIELDWORK and the very practical concerns associated with locating order in non-Western societies. This was the explicit aim of the founding work in the field, *African political systems* (Fortes & Evans-Pritchard 1940b). Based on a set of descriptions and analyses of centralized and decentralized systems of governance in Africa, societies were divided into two types: "primitive states" that possessed government institutions and "stateless societies" that did not. This work, and examples of detailed fieldwork on political systems such as EVANS-PRITCHARD's (1940) among the Nuer and FORTES's (1945) among the Tallensi, inspired a generation of fieldworkers to concentrate on the varied ways in which political order might be embedded in KINSHIP relations, RITUAL practices, AGE SYSTEMS, and other order-keeping institutions that did not require separate institutions of government. Such a focus was of clear con-

cern to colonial administrators anxious to understand how to govern and control "subject" peoples, and the role anthropologists may have played in aiding COLONIALISM has been the subject of considerable debate in recent decades (Asad 1973; Kuklik 1991). It is clear, however, that the results of such work, particularly in Africa, pushed anthropology in a number of new directions.

One such area was the question of conflict and conflict resolution which became the focus of the so-called Manchester school. Pioneered by the work of Max GLUCKMAN and his students, it encouraged anthropologists to study social mechanisms for coping with intersocietal tension and change. Gluckman, trained in both law and anthropology, also contributed heavily to the development of LEGAL ANTHROPOLOGY, which has always been closely linked with political anthropology because of a shared interest in conflict mediation and the maintenance of social order. Confronting anticolonial stirrings but still-firm color lines after World War II, Manchester school anthropologists experimented with new methodologies, including situational analyses (Velsen 1967) and network analysis (J. Mitchell 1969), to explain how seemingly apolitical events and organizations could in fact be laced with political meaning. Other scholars found that politics were embedded in all aspects of social life, including RITUAL. For instance, Victor TURNER (1957) described how village-level political crises were ritually solved by Ndembu in Zambia, and Abner Cohen (1969) unraveled ritual's political role in the development of Hausa ethnicity in a Yorubaland town in Nigeria.

Political anthropology, however, was not confined to Africa or the Manchester school. Edmund LEACH (1954) examined the connection between ritual, identity, and ethnicity among the Kachin of Burma in terms of an oscillating political system that regularly shifted between ranked and egalitarian forms of social organization (GUMSA AND GUMLAO). Leach's suggestions about the role of individual AGENCY in politics were followed up by F. G. Bailey (1960) in India and Fredrik Barth (1959a) among the Swat Pathans to explore the aggregate effects of political maneuvering.

During the 1960s and 1970s, the role of bigman networks, patron–client relations, peasantries, and elites became a focus of research. Borrowing from game theory, political anthropologists continued to analyze contests over status, prestige, and power in a wide range of arenas. In the 1980s developments in political economy and WORLD-SYSTEM THEORY introduced new comparative possibilities for analyzing political transformations and CLASS relations in truly global terms (E. Wolf 1982; Mintz 1985).

In addition to developing large-scale models to explain political systems, anthropologists have also focused more narrowly on understanding the strategies individuals and societies use to resist penetration by such external forces as capitalism, centralized state authority, and hegemonic authority. In seeking to explain how groups of all kinds resist, but also at times collude with, authority or the state, political anthropologists have utilized both top-down and bottom-up approaches to understanding power. Increasingly, this research has shifted from well-bounded and static units such as territorial states or formal political institutions to such political categories of people as refugees and to political and economic processes created by development projects and multinational corporations.

If earlier political anthropologists dealt with individual cases that were most often foreign and remote, current research strives to be both comparative and inclusive by using non-Western variants to probe Western practices of long-standing interest to political scientists such as SUCCESSION to high office (J. Goody 1966). For example, David Kertzer (1988) dissected political rites in Italy, the United States, and the Soviet Union, along with the Aztec, Bunyoro, and Swazi. This is exactly in keeping with the earliest aims of political anthropology. It has given the field a renewed vitality to go beyond questions of governmental institutions and the ability to cope with new issues of order, disorder, and projections of power that will shape the parameters of research in the future.

ASi

further reading Balandier 1970; Lewellen 1992; Vincent 1990

pollution   *See* PURITY/POLLUTION

polyandry   is a form of plural marriage allowing a woman to have more than one husband at a time, or conversely for men to share a single wife. It almost always takes the form of **fraternal polyandry** in which a group of brothers share a wife.   MR
See also POLYGYNY
further reading Levine 1983

polygamy   is the institution of plural marriage that permits individuals to have more than one spouse. It encompasses both POLYANDRY and POLYGYNY.   MR

polygyny   is a form of plural marriage allowing a man to have more than one wife at one time.   MR
See also POLYANDRY

polytheism   is the worship or recognition of many gods or spirits in a religious universe. The nineteenth century saw the rise of two main evolutionary ideas that lay behind definitions of polytheism (H. Spencer 1876; Tylor 1871). First, it was proposed that prehistoric peoples eventually came to distinguish between the material body and the soul or spirit, so fostering beliefs in a plurality of SPIRITS. Not only people, but also animals, plants, and inanimate objects might be credited with souls (see ANIMISM). Second, worship of the souls of ANCESTORS was put forward as the origin of RELIGION, with the further belief that such ancestral ghosts were sometimes manifested in totems. For DURKHEIM (1915), TOTEMISM, involving a plethora of collective and individual or personal totemic spirits, was at the origin of all religions. Opinion differed as to whether polytheism preceded MONOTHEISM, with most evolutionists, such as TYLOR and SPENCER, contending that it did.

A question arises as to whether all religions are in reality always to some degree polytheistic. There are two responses to this. First, although a High God or principal deity may well characterize a religion, which may therefore be defined as monotheistic, there may be well be a belief in the coexistence of demons, Satan, and impersonal as well as personified manifestations of EVIL. These are clearly not benign entities in the normal sense conveyed by the term "god," but they clearly are spiritual beings and so, in Tylor's definition, part of the basis of religious belief.

Second, it is often the case that a High God surmounts a hierarchy of lesser deities or godlike beings. In Christianity, God may communicate his will to mortals through spirits called "angels" (not all of whom are benevolent), who constitute a celestial hierarchy, with archangels occupying the eighth rank. A comparable situation exists within the other so-called Semitic religions of Judaism and Islam, despite an awareness of the danger of deities (and Satan) competing with God, which may provoke denunciation of the worship of other gods and idols.

Among many Muslims today, this denunciation of polytheism is at the basis of a radical fundamentalist Islam, which urges people to desist from venerating dead saints (and even the Prophet himself) in lavish rituals, and from seeking mystical supplication from spirits or *jinns*, despite the fact that some of these are mentioned, sometimes approvingly, in the Qur'an.

Hinduism, particularly as it is practiced locally, contains a divine hierarchy, from God as pervasive and unembodied, to deities that are embodied widely, such as Shiva, Parvati and Vishnu, to various regional gods, to local deities that protect villagers from evil gods, and finally to local deities that protect villagers from evil demons. Local forms of Buddhism involve the worship of and sacrifice to local deities, who have the power to cure and bring good fortune to mortal.

It is a short step from supplication to local deities to what is known as spirit possession, mediumship, and SHAMANISM, in which persons are much more likely to be in direct contact with local or lesser deities than with a High God. Spirit possession is the involuntary seizure of a person's mind and body by a spirit that enters him or her. Spirit mediums are involuntarily possessed by spirits that talk through the medium and can divine causes of misfortune, read the

future or facilitate communication with the dead. Shamans are specialists who actually control at will their own possessory spirits in order to provide these services (I. Lewis 1971; Riches 1994). Such instances can also be covered by the term "polytheism," with a dominant god or gods often much less significant in the everyday lives of worshipers.

Finally, a number of religions, perhaps most to some degree, have a notion of immanent and sometimes transcendent divinity. EVANS-PRITCHARD (1956) described God among the Nuer of Sudan as existing both in a transcendental exalted state and as refractions located as spirits or in various features of the natural environment. It is almost inevitable that immanent divinities will be reflected in this way. Polytheism may, then, be a shorthand term used to refer to a variety of conceptions of divinity within or unrelated to a hierarchy of spiritual beings.   DP

further reading Ahern 1981; Babb 1975; Firth 1940; James 1979; Lienhardt 1961; Tambiah 1970

population   *See* DEMOGRAPHIC TRANSITION, DEMOGRAPHY

possession   *See* TRANCE

postcolonialism   is a critical, interdisciplinary tradition that explores the impact of colonial power on the cultures of colonizing and colonized peoples in the past, and the reproduction of colonial relations, representations, and practices in the present.

Postcolonialism had its origins in the humanities, especially in literary and cultural studies, where it received its most decisive impetus from Edward Said's (1978) seminal critique of Orientalism. This text depended on a tense conjunction of humanism and antihumanism to expose the forms through which European and North American representations of "the Orient" had been produced and circulated, but the subsequent development of postcolonialism has been much more critical of Western humanism and has involved a much closer engagement with poststructuralism, especially the work of

Derrida, Foucault, and Lacan (R. Young 1990). In doing so, Said's original agenda has been radically revised: colonial discourses have been shown to be more ambivalent and contradictory than Said allowed; their analysis has been extended from his own base in "high" culture to popular culture, travel writing, and colonial governmentality; the formation of colonial subjectivities has been linked more explicitly to the unconscious and the play of desire; the binary distinctions between colonizer and colonized have been called into question more sharply through a recognition of mimicry, hybridity, and transculturation; and the agency of colonized peoples and their strategies of resistance have been explored in much greater depth than Said originally entertained (see Bhabha 1994; N. Thomas 1994; D. Scott 1995).

Although many of these inquiries have been concerned with the cultures of COLONIALISM, they also have important implications for the present. These are both historical and geographic. First, one of the major contact zones between postcolonialism and anthropology has been historical anthropology, particularly through the attempt of the Subaltern Studies project to decolonize Indian history in order to illuminate the predicaments of contemporary Indian politics (Chakrabarty 1992; Prakash 1994; Sivaramakrishnan 1995). Yet the general attempt to chart the cultural displacements of colonialism into the ("postcolonial") present has threatened to destabilize the term itself. Anne McClintock (1992) argued that postcolonialism is haunted by the very figure it seeks to displace, as it continues to privilege Europe as the central subject of "History" by reorienting the world around the single and abstracted axis of the colonial–postcolonial; but S. Hall (1996) suggested that the postcolonial is more productively seen as marking an uneven and serialized process of decolonization that calls into question the binary form in which the colonial encounter has conventionally been represented. Second, postcolonialism and anthropology meet on the terrain of globalization, a field where the local and the global interpenetrate in new and unsettling geographies (Appadurai 1996), where new and compound identities, mobilities, and marginalities are under construction (Yeager 1996), and where "difference is encountered in the adjoining neighborhood [and] the familiar turns up at the ends of the earth" (Clifford 1988: 14).

It is thus hardly surprising that postcolonial critiques intersect with the so-called crisis of representation in the human sciences, including reflection on the poetics of anthropological inquiry and the politics of location of intellectuals (Visweswaran 1994; John 1996). This has also produced some of the sharpest criticism of postcolonialism. Dirlik (1994) claimed that postcolonialism is a culturalism that is complicit with the new global regimes of capital accumulation: that its roots in poststructuralism make it incapable of theorizing the structures of contemporary capitalism, that its focus on the constitution of postcolonial subjectivity excludes "an account of the world outside of the subject," and that it is little more than a covert projection of the subjectivities of Third World intellectuals within the Western academy. Although it is true that postcolonialism has often been oddly distanced from previous and parallel work in political economy, it would be a mistake to treat its emphasis on culture as superficial; and some of the most exacting contributions to the postcolonial critique trade on a principled deployment of cultural studies and political economy (see Watts 1996).

DG

See also CRITICAL ANTHROPOLOGY, HISTORY AND ANTHROPOLOGY

further reading J. Jacobs 1996; Prakash 1995; P. Williams & Chrisman 1994; R. Young 1996

postmodern, postmodernism In anthropology postmodernism is (1) the study of social and cultural forms of the late twentieth century resulting from the intensification, radicalization, or transformation of the processes of modernity; (2) and therefore also renewed attention to the epistemological groundings of ethnographic authority and the relationship between form and content in ethnographic writing.

In contrast to the general theories of modernity, which have to do with the dynamics of class society and industrial processes (Marx), bureaucratic, psychological, and cultural rationalization (Weber), repression and redirection of psychic energy from gendered and familial conflicts (Freud), abstraction of signs and tokens of exchange (Saussure, Simmel, Veblen), and the complexification of the conscience collective with the division of labor (Durkheim), general theories of the postmodern era stress the processes and effects of the "third industrial revolution" (electronic media, silicon chip, molecular biology), as well as of decolonization and massive demographic shifts. These are transnational or global processes that thoroughly rework all local cultures. Some theorists stress the intensification of flexible capital accumulation, compression of space and time, and growth of multinational organizational forms (Harvey 1989a; Jameson 1991). Others stress the massive demographic shifts resulting from decolonization and ideological warfare that are challenging the homogenizing efforts of nation-states into more heterogeneous cultural formations (Lyotard 1984; and theorists of multiculturalism in the United States). Others stress the information-technology revolution that not only brings diverse parts of the world into daily contact, but constitutes an intensification of postliterate, more mathematical and graphic, styles of generating, monitoring, and absorbing knowledge: simulations and modelling replace direct experiential modes of knowing, a process with deep roots in the modernist experimental sciences (Poster 1990; Baudrillard 1994). Others stress the production of ecological hazards and risks by industrial capitalism, which necessitates a new political dynamic and cultural logic. These in turn lead to systemic contradictions and pressures for reversal of centralizing control, and toward increased democratic participation by diverse agents in the complex division of knowledge and labor in what, during modernity, were nonpoliticized areas of business decision making and private entrepreneurship; that is, toward a new "reflexive modernization" that emerges out of the contradictions of industrial society in parallel fashion to the ways CAPITALISM emerged out of the contradictions of feudal society (Beck 1992, 1995; Giddens 1990, 1991; Lash & Urry 1994).

These conditions of the late twentieth century challenge anthropology to provide ethnographic accounts in new ways both substantively and formally. Anthropology in the 1920s through 1950s had promised to provide a truly comparative study of cultures and societies. Using the COMPARATIVE METHOD anthropologists could juxtapose social arrangements and cultural conceptions in different societies, and then use them to critique as well the categories of analysis often derived from Western assumptions. Studies of small-scale societies were not an exercise in exoticism, but an effort to learn about social processes in settings small enough for one person to understand. These processes could then be extended to understanding similar ones in Europe and America. (W. Lloyd Warner 1937 was exemplary, working first with Australian Aboriginal society, then in Newburyport, Massachussetts [Warner 1941–59]; but Margaret MEAD's 1928, 1942 work and that of many others could also be cited.) By the 1980s, however, a stocktaking of anthropology (Marcus & Fischer 1986) argued that though these goals were still alive, more sophisticated methods were required to achieve them including:

1. to "repatriate" anthropology by producing as rich and wide-ranging ethnographic work on the central institutions of First World societies as had been done abroad, not restricting work at home to ethnic, exotic, or marginal "others", and without becoming subordinated as applied anthropologists to more dominant professions such as physicians in heath services or economists in development work
2. to write for multiple and diverse audiences with different sets of demands

and intellectual frameworks, including growing numbers among the populations being studied, by employing richer dialogic approaches, a different conception of TRANSLATION, and a more discursive understanding of power and circuits of representation. Having readers among the populations under study increases requirements to demonstrate competence and knowledge of the range of disagreements within cultural formations, and to write in a way that gains assent or intelligent critique from the groups under study. Among the tactics for achieving such double- or multi-addressed and -voiced textuality is to take more seriously the notion of ethnography as a collaborative and dialogic enterprise. "Dia-logue" in this sense is not a two-person conversation, but, in the Greek etymological sense, the display of cross-arguments and the social grounds that provide them with efficacy, authority, or utility. Translation, moreover, in a world where cultures are less and less bounded isolates, can no longer be only a matter of negotiating across languages and cultures; often far more important is the negotiation of difference within sharply class-divided and civil-war-riven societies, and among the increasing heterogeneities that transnational labor and refugee migration creates (viz. Lyotard's 1988 "*differend*"s; M. Fischer 1984)

3. to rework the comparative method itself to be able to deal with a globalizing world where not only do local settings require analysis of negotiations between localizing and transnational processes, but multisited ethnographies are needed to understand the geographically dispersed, technologically mediated processes at work

4. to foreground ethnographically the grounds for the pervasive feelings that social change has outrun the traditional categories of social theory formulated at the beginning of the twentieth century, and of actors in major institutions of society that they are living in worlds for which their training did not prepare them; and thereby to provide the empirical data for creating theorical frameworks more relevant to the new social and knowledge conditions emerging at the turn of the twenty-first century

Such concerns can be seen in the emergence of new topics and fieldwork sites in anthropology including:

1. the social and cultural study of science and technology and the ways in which the contemporary revolutions in electronics, communications, and biology rework both conceptual categories and social formations (Emily Martin 1994; Rabinow 1996; Marcus 1995)

2. media and information technologies, including computers, film and television, cassettes and popular music, and the changes in perceptual and communicative public spheres these help create (Fischer 1984, 1995; Ginsburg 1991; Turkle 1995; T. Turner 1991; and the journal *Visual Anthropology Review*)

3. the reconstruction of society in the wake of violence and traumatic upheaval (Werbner 1991; Tambiah 1992; Marcus 1993) and through the processes of corporate business worlds in the new political economy (G. Marcus & Hall 1992; J. Stacey 1990)

As fieldwork topics, sites, contexts, and readerships of anthropology have changed so too have styles of ethnographic writing. No longer is it credible, if it ever was, for a single author to pose as an omniscient source on complex cultural settings, nor to pose those settings as distanced exotic forms without direct interaction with the author's own society, time, and place (Fabian 1983). Epistemological credibility requires a greater level of precision, as do generational experiences out of which different sorts of appreciation for cultural difference arise. Whereas for the nineteenth century, cultural difference could still be seen in categories of exoticism and evolutionary development of social forms, by the late twentieth century television and intense interaction make cultural differences both more familiar and subjects of politicized negotiation. The generational experience for (especially German) social theorists and anthropologists between the two world wars was one of concern for the defense of civil society against the rationalizing of bureaucratic states, mass market forces, and fascist mass-political parties, and for a social order based on an expanding economy organized in the case of colonies by a bureaucracy that could operate with minimal need for force. By contrast, the generational experience of the post-1960s generations (particularly in France and the United States) has to do with a coming to terms with decolonization, deterritorialization, and the interpenetration of languages and cultural perspectives that do not have any immediate consensual translation. The leading theorists among the so-called French postmodern theorists (Derrida, Lyotard, Foucault, Cixous) all had formative experiences in North Africa and were shaped by the struggle over Algerian independence and the subsequent North African immigrations to France. Similarly, if more diffusely, the United States since the 1965 change in immigration laws has been experiencing a significant change in ethnic and demographic composition leading to a debate about "multiculturalism." Britain too has been transformed by Caribbean and South Asian diasporas. Much of the most powerful creative writing in England is a "decolonizing" of the English language and fusion musics, such as *bhangra*, are reworking popular culture. This parallels the interest in French postmodern thought in bi-lingual writing and music (Arabic-Berber-French; *rai* music; translation, genealogical, and etymological discursive issues), and in American multicultural initiatives by the resolute bilingualism of much Chicano and Hispanic writing. "Deterritorialization" refers not just to this bi- and multicultural set of migrations and interpenetrations, but also to the way in which the media allows cultural processes to operate across national borders (and hypertextual computerized forms allow rapid breaches and intermixtures of traditional boundaries of writing and data sets), and to ecological, disease, and financial processes that likewise do not respect traditional political, national, or local boundaries.

Grounded then in technological, scientific, and social processes of deterritorialization (and reconfiguration),

postmodern conditions support new writing styles to facilitate describing and modeling these processes. *Writing culture: the poetics and politics of ethnography* (Clifford & Marcus 1986) and *Anthropology as cultural critique: an experimental moment in the human sciences* (Marcus & Fischer 1986) are often pointed to as markers of heightened interest in ethnographic writing. The latter revived the idea that anthropological writing from the beginning was experimental and directed toward critiques of complex societies and the contemporary world (e.g., G. Bateson 1936; Malinowski 1922); the former positioned anthropology as gaining new critical reach by working across disciplinary boundaries with historians and literary critics. Among the writing techniques that have been taken up by ethnographic experimental writing in recent years in order to achieve greater epistemological precision through reflexivity and critique by cultural juxtaposition have been:

1. dialogic and collaborative formats: paying attention to the positionality of the writer, reader, and subjects of ethnographies (Lavie 1990; Sarris 1993); paying attention to writing and narrating that is intended to be therapeutic rather than pedagogic (Crapanzano 1980; Maranhao 1990; Tyler 1987); paying attention to the difference between translation and competitive discursive power relations that block out other points of view (David W. Cohen 1994; Fischer and Abedi 1990); juxtaposing fields of argumentative debate with other fields of debate that may be similar on some dimensions but are sociologically quite different, e.g., feminist and Buddhist notions of personhood (Klein 1994); paying attention to the linguistic forms of dialogue including the limitations of literalism (K. Dwyer 1982), pragmatics and sociolinguistic contexts of conversation (Tedlock 1983), interior dialogues that are linguistically marked in public discourse (Crapanzano 1992)

2. conceptual experimentation with metaphors that come from multiple sources but act as cultural switching stations in

popular imagination, e.g., "flexible bodies" as referring both to immunology and to political economy (Emily Martin 1994), mimetic powers of language (copying, reenactment, or repetition, each time with a slight difference, deceit, or substitution, thereby having the potential to upset normal institutional power) embedded in the quite different logics and power nexi of discourse circuits constructed by bureaucracies, markets, illness, fantasy, neurological signaling, and terror regimes (Taussig 1992, 1993); also recognition of ways in which cultural analyses can gain power by playing off commitments to several discourses (positive science, democratic socialism, feminism) that interrupt each other (Haraway 1991; compare H. White 1973 on historical experimental writing)

3. reworking of interview/*entretien* formats, as well as reworking of traditional ethnographic synecdochic frames (key institutions, emblematic cultural performances, life history, ritual process [Marcus & Fischer 1986])

4. using cultural forms as epistemological guides and comparative forms (Feld 1982; Layoun 1990; Lipsitz 1990; M. Mills 1991)

These and many other experiments contribute to a growing sophistication and reinvention of older styles of ethnographic description. Often glossed under the label "reflexivity," epistemological sophistication is trivialized if made to mean merely the confessional self-location of the writer, or if dismissed as pure relativism, as if increasing precision were a block rather than an aid to knowledge. At issue, moreover, is not merely descriptive precision for its own sake but the empirical grounds for understanding the late-twentieth-century social processes that press toward "reflexive modernization," that is, an increased pluralism of decision making required by a technological and social complexity that renders many forms of centralized decision making and norm enforcement increasingly self-destructive or simply ineffective. One technosociological icon of this emergent reality is the Internet, which began as a military requirement for a system of communication that could survive nuclear attack (that is, that would have no center vulnerable to disabling the whole system) but which has evolved into a civilian communications regime that opens information flow around all government efforts to enforce boundaries.   MF

See also CRITICAL ANTHROPOLOGY, INTERPRETIVE ANTHROPOLOGY, LITERARY ANTHROPOLOGY

potlatch is a Nootka Indian word for "gift" that describes a competitive GIFT EXCHANGE in which contenders for social rank organize elaborate feasts that include large distributions of possessions, and sometimes their destruction, in order to enhance the givers' prestige. Rivals were expected to respond by even more elaborate ceremonies or face humiliation.

Although found in many parts of the world, the indigenous peoples of the northwest coast of North America brought the potlatch to prominence in anthropology and gave it its name. Franz BOAS, who observed the ritual among the Kwakiutl in the 1890s, sought to describe it in detail, but he did not attempt to explain it (Rohner 1969). Later anthropologists, challenged by the contention that potlatches were wasteful and irrational, have produced a series of studies to show that they are neither, focusing on its historical development (Codere 1950), place in social structure (Rosman & Rubel 1971), political order (Drucker & Heizer 1967), ecological significance (Piddocke 1967), and symbolic meaning (Kan 1989).

                    TB

See also BIGMAN, SOCIAL EXCHANGE

poverty has been most effectively viewed as relative deprivation based on inequality. As such it is a culturally defined and contested concept that only applies in STATE societies with uneven distribution of resources and divisions between producers and nonproducers. Thus poverty cannot be measured by any absolute standard of material wealth. For example, although the Bushmen/San of the Kalahari lived as FORAGERS, had few possessions, and were seasonally deprived of food and water, anthropologists have not regarded this as poverty. In fact, debates have focused more on whether such foraging groups were "ORIGINAL AFFLUENT SOCIETIES" because of their apparently low ratio of work to leisure time.

In state societies, PEASANT producers who own land and houses can be poor because of their relationship to the cash economy, accumulated debts, lack of adequate nutrition for their household, lack of leisure time, and inability to provide funds for their children's future. Such poverty is created in the context of the inequalities of the state. The actual deprivation in terms of food, housing, and leisure time can only be measured according to the cultural expectations in each society over time.

In contemporary CAPITALIST societies, poverty is often defined and described through legislation that assigns supplementary assistance to poor households. Under such conditions, poverty becomes a highly contested terrain. What constitutes acceptable housing conditions and basic consumer necessities and medical needs are constantly renegotiated in the political struggle over the shifting inequalities upon which such societies are based (Susser 1982). Some anthropologists, most notably Oscar Lewis (1966), argued that this structural situation produced a distinct CULTURE OF POVERTY, which was then passed on from generation to generation, a position that did not hold up well when examined closely (Leacock 1971).

URBAN ANTHROPOLOGY has taken a keen interest worldwide in those sections of modern cities inhabited by the poor. Those described by anthropologists include squatter settlements (Peattie 1983), ethnic ghettos (Kwong 1996), low-CASTE communities (Lynch 1969), areas of high unemployment (Pappas 1989), outlying suburbs or townships (Pendleton 1996), and homeless communities (Susser 1993). In each case the areas may look different and the experience of poverty, the availability of housing, consumption goods, leisure time, educational opportunity, household structure, and health vary considerably. In the United States a poor family frequently may own a television, buy numerous con-

sumption goods, and even have a car. In other parts of the world, a poor family may not have access to electricity, water, or other resources common among the poor of Western industrial societies.

In spite of different manifestations of poverty in the current global economy, higher infant mortality rates and shortened life expectancy in relation to the rest of society characterize such populations uniformly. Although the forms of deprivation may be different and the DISEASES people suffer from vary, the overall effect of poverty, as defined in terms of inequality, has clear consequences on the health of populations.

Thus although poverty is a cultural construct that varies historically and across different societies, it defines people's life opportunities. Poverty is a product of the way in which inequality is constructed in different political and cultural contexts.

ISu

See also CLASS, COOKING, HUNGER, STRATIFICATION, SUFFERING

further reading De Soto 1992; Higgins 1983; Leeds 1994; Peattie 1968

power Major anthropological descriptions of the dynamics and institutions of power have until recently had a markedly Western bias. Thus, other systems of power often have been described as alternatives or variations of those found in Western industrial contexts. Major issues informing the direction of research appear to have been influenced by the problem of order, as first laid out by Thomas Hobbes (1651) in his discussion of the need for the state. Undoubtedly, the centrality of this question for early anthropologists related to the imperial dominance of the West and the development of anthropology in such a context. An early and important focus of anthropological inquiry concerned so-called "stateless societies." EVANS-PRITCHARD's classic study of the Nuer (1940) became the model for such investigation and demonstrated that the forces located in KINSHIP and other social processes obviated any necessary need for the state in the promotion of order. Evans-Pritchard implied that state forms are a potential, given certain historical conditions such as invasion or colonial conquest, of non-state systems. He showed this clearly in his *The Sanusi of Cyrenaica* (1949), a study that is of significance to later anthropological studies of power such as those of Bourdieu (1977). Pierre Clastres (1987) took important issue with the Western state-bias of many anthropological approaches to political processes as expressed specifically in the study of non-state systems and its implication that state systems are the "higher" political form. He argued that many non-Western systems of power are expressly oriented against the development of centralized political structures or the amassing of power by particular persons and, furthermore, that they recognize the socially destructive force of state forms. Many would argue that Clastres did not escape his own charge. But his work does mark an attempt to break away from Western assumptions in the study of power and is an illustration of the interest of many anthropologists to discover in non-Western systems real alternatives to the dilemmas surrounding centralized state systems that first Hobbes and then a succession of later Western political theorists have raised.

Most anthropological descriptions of political systems and power processes work with Western models (usually derived from the big three – DURKHEIM, WEBER, Marx). Anthropological research has increasingly stressed the different cultural conceptions of power that obtain. Dumont (1970), writing of Hindu India, has argued that power based in such hierarchical institutions as kingship and caste is conditioned within encompassing religious and ritual principles. Tambiah (1976), for Thailand and Sri Lanka, and Clifford GEERTZ (1980), for Bali, have argued that centralized state notions of power conceived from within a Western historical viewpoint are inappropriate. Tambiah and Geertz both argue that there is an ideology of powerful cosmic centers but this belies more fragmented systems of power. Power as might is more in the hands of local lords, who are legitimated through the pomp and splendor of the cosmic rites of the kings who occupy the centers. The continual cycles of rebellion that are a feature of such states are driven in their particular ideological and structural dynamic. Power is something that is conceived as coming from the periphery or from outside, which is a point that Hocart made for India early this century. It is interesting that other anthropologists have argued for similar processes, for example, in Africa and in the Pacific. All these approaches challenge Western political-economic perspectives, which nonetheless remain vital in the work of many ethnographers.

There is broad theoretical debate in anthropology concerning, on the one hand, the virtues of exchange, interactionist, or transactionalist perspectives – which tend to have an individualist and small-group dynamic focus – and, on the other hand, the virtues of those approaches that explore different institutional formations of power. This is not to discount some degree of overlap. Regardless of whether the orientation is interactionist or institutional there is a common tendency to search for the rudiments and development of power in the imbalances of exchange and the control and distribution of material resources. This is best illustrated in the now classic studies by Fredrik Barth (1959a) of the dynamics of power alliances among the Swat Pathans, and Edmund LEACH's (1954) examination of the shift between non-centralized egalitarian and state-oriented hierarchical political institutions among the Kachin of Highland Burma.

Both Barth and Leach were concerned to develop approaches that gave primacy to the processes of power in social institutional formation and in the construction of value. Their orientations had considerable influence during the 1960s and 1970s, and this influence continues. More recent perspectives that have achieved more attention are those of Marshall Sahlins and most especially Pierre Bourdieu. Sahlins (1985), largely in his Hawaiian and Fijian work, has addressed questions of the cultural forces engaged in the interplay and transformation of distinctly constituted cultural formations of power. These later interests had an earlier manifestation in Sahlins's (1961) classic essay on Nuer lineage organization, which he argued gave the Nuer expansionist advantage over other peoples in the region. Sahlins in his particular modifications of structuralist and marxist approaches has relevance for an understanding of the cultural constructions of power and how these influence practical action.

Bourdieu (1977) expresses a more pragmatic strategic individualist position on power than does Sahlins but, none the less, manifests the strong influences of marxism, Weberian process, and STRUCTURALISM. In many ways Bourdieu's approach to power represents an innovative synthesis of otherwise opposed modernist theories. This synthesis is congruent with some poststructuralist or POSTMODERN directions.

Bourdieu's concepts of symbolic power and VIOLENCE have been particularly influential. Through these concepts Bourdieu has explored the controlling and destructive sources of power that are located in institutional practices that may seem benign, progressive, or in some sense disconnected from, for example, central apparatuses of state power. Bourdieu has examined the "hidden" practices of power that are situated in activities that do not appear to be overtly concerned with control and domination yet have this effect (hence the distinction between symbolic power and that power exercised by the agents of formally powerful positions). There is a similarity in the objectives of Bourdieu and those of such poststructuralists as Foucault.

Foucault had marked impact on recent anthropological approaches to power – more so, perhaps, than other deconstructionist figures such as Derrida and Deleuze. Foucault's (1973, 1965, 1977b) major empirical works on medical discourses and forms of human incarceration and surveillance have been among the most influential. This is so in anthropological discussions of such sites of power discourse as gender and ethnic identity, nationalism, colonial practices, and so forth (Foucault 1980). Foucault revealed the constitutive and restructuring dynamics of power in a variety of discourses or practices that do not appear to be formally part of the institutions of government. Thus, Foucault demonstrated the discourses of medicine and crime control both as paralleling the discourses surrounding the formation of contemporary political systems and as becoming integral to their dynamics of control. The influence of scholars like Foucault has led to a stronger realization among anthropologists of their own enterprise as potentially a discourse of powerful domination – to be discovered even in the apparently innocent fascination of anthropologists with the exotic and certainly, as many marxist anthropologists had already asserted, in the application of self-interest or maximization theories of power akin to those of market CAPITALISM.

There is a great diversity of approaches to power available to anthropologists, and their ethnographic work provides support for many of them. However, the most valuable contribution by anthropologists to comprehending power in its manifold aspects is in their ethnographic descriptions regardless of the particular theory individual anthropologists may favor. Their studies have revealed the great variability of formations of power – their cultural shape, especially – and the practices that underpin them. As yet, no grand totalizing theory of power has been found to be generally applicable to the diverse systems and practices of power that anthropologists have recorded.   BK

See also GOVERNMENT, LEGAL ANTHRO-
    POLOGY, POLITICAL ANTHROPOLOGY,
    STRATIFICATION

practice theory has come to be largely associated with the work of Pierre Bourdieu (1977, 1990), though there are certain precursors. It has always been recognized that behavior differs from rules, norms, and so on, basically because people do not always observe the latter. This recognition is at its weakest in the work of DURKHEIM and his followers in anthropology, such as RADCLIFFE-BROWN, for whom social rules and rule-bound institutions produced both individual conformity to society's dictates and social equilibrium. For them, the problematic was not the individual's strategic responses to social rules – as it was already for MALINOWSKI – but how he or she is incorporated into society. In this view, departure from rules is deviance, not strategy.

One early reaction to this position came from LEACH. His initial view of the significance of action departed only slightly from Durkheim's in its recognition of actors' manipulation of social rules (Leach 1954), but he later argued "that jural rules and statistical norms should be treated as separate frames of reference [and] that the former should always be considered secondary to the latter" (1961a: 9). Here Leach was building on the work of Raymond FIRTH (1964), a student and successor of Malinowski, who distinguished social organization (the level of jural rules and social system) from social structure (the outcome of the application of those rules in practice). Leach was followed by some of his own students, especially Fredrik Barth (1969a), whose early work was more concerned with the behavior of individuals in crossing ethnic boundaries than with the description of what he saw as ephemeral and unstable cultures. Barth also became a proponent of TRANSACTIONAL ANALYSIS (1966; cf. Kapferer 1976a; F. Bailey 1969), to which can be added others' work on social networks (J. Barnes 1954; Bott 1957), all of which is concerned with the links people form with one another in practice, almost regardless of their expressed social rules and values. In America, Clifford GEERTZ (1973) advocated a similar switch to practice – which for him largely meant symbolic action – as an alternative to what he saw as LÉVI-STRAUSS's over-abstract STRUCTURALISM.

For Bourdieu, the general weakness of such models is their failure adequately to relate the two levels of jural rules, norms, ideals, and values on the one hand, and of practice, action, behavior, and statistics on the other (one exception is A. Good's 1981 account of affinal alliance in south India). By "relate" is basically meant to account for the two levels in terms of one another, rather than prioritizing either. Essentially, Bourdieu's argument is that many of those who have been reacting to Durkheim, Radcliffe-Brown, and Lévi-Strauss have overcorrected their faults and effectively become reliant on behavior alone. Bourdieu admits that ethnographers tend to objectify and privilege rules, norms, ideals, and values over what he calls "strategies of action," especially in basing their accounts mostly on indigenous statements about the ideal. However, he also argues that a balance is required: although strategies involve a certain degree of improvisation, they too relate to goals and interests that are no less socially constructed than rules, etc. Methodologically too, observation and statistical analysis are not enough, since they are just as subject to what Bourdieu calls the "synoptic illusion" as the abstraction of rules and values.

Bourdieu's theory relies on two particular notions that he himself has introduced and made his own on the basis of his early fieldwork in Algeria and the Béarn (France). One is "doxa," those aspects of the society's norms and values that are not discussed or challenged because they are deeply rooted through socialization and taken for granted (compare that with orthodoxy, ideology that is explicitly regarded as correct or standard, and heterodoxy, equally explicit deviations from it). The other notion is "habitus," normative aspects of behavior, collective habits, or "dispositions," which are also acquired through socialization but are produced unreflectively rather than totally unconsciously. Bourdieu regards practice as being based on the dispositions inherent in habitus and as taking the form of strategic improvisations – goals and interests pursued as strategies – against a background of doxa that ultimately limits them. These strategies are pursued in particular "social fields," social contexts shaped by the interests of individuals and their competition (over resources, status, etc., all of which Bourdieu objectifies as various forms of capital, whether economic, social, cultural, or symbolic).

It is this combination of habitus and doxa that links ideal and practice. Since both are unreflective, Bourdieu distances himself from any version of rational choice theory; at the same time the socialization that both involve rules out his theory entailing any form of behaviorism. Nonetheless, the theory has been dismissed as just another functionalist tautology, one that takes institutions for granted and only describes the processes it deals with rather than explaining either. The notion of habitus has also been criticized for having to be inferred from the practices it allegedly gives rise to, as well as for depriving social actors of the ability to challenge the social order (see Jenkins 1992).

Although innovatory within anthropology, Bourdieu's theory of practice has one major parallel in contemporary sociology in Giddens's (1976) theory of structuration, which aims to link structure and agency. The work of the earlier symbolic interactionists (especially Goffman 1956) is an acknowledged influence from the same direction.   RP

further reading Jenkins 1982; Ortner 1984

pragmatics is the study of meaning that arises from a SIGN's use in context. It is derived from the American pragmatist philosopher C. S. Peirce's (1931–58: vol. 2) famous trichotomy of signs (icon, index, and symbol), and has become enormously influential in anthropology and many other disciplines. Especially important is his notion of the index, a category of sign that is said to be "coexistential" with the thing it represents – smoke signaling fire, an exit sign next to a doorway, or a chime struck at the passing of the hour, for example. In other words, an index critically depends on a context of use for its meaning.

Pragmatic analysis was pioneered in structural linguistics by Emile Benveniste (1956) and Roman Jakobson (1957). Benveniste showed how the meaning of many linguistic forms, once thought to be purely semantic (that is, independent of their context of use; see SEMANTICS), could not be understood without reference to the speech situation. Take, for example, the category of pronouns. The first person pronoun "I" cannot be defined apart from its reference to the particular person speaking in a context of situation, just as the pronoun "you" cannot be adequately understood apart from its reference to a particular person being addressed in that situation. By contrast, all third person pronouns, such as "he," "she," and "they," can refer to persons outside the context of speaking and still be understood. Tense, demonstrative pronouns, and adverbials have also been the subject of pragmatic

analysis. Jakobson (1957) imported the term "shifter" for such linguistic signs; that is, their meaning "shifts" according to the context. He also used Peirce's "index" to capture the fact that certain linguistic signs have to be coexistential with the context of speaking if they are to be properly understood. Benveniste's and Jakobson's landmark studies more or less initiated what in grammatical analysis came to be known as "deixis." Work along this line has been carried out by anthropologists for languages such as Mayan (W. Hanks 1990) and Vietnamese (Luong 1990).

In their analysis of shifters and linguistic indices, Benveniste and Jakobson were mainly concerned with the referential function of language (see SEMANTICS). In anthropology, one of the earliest and most important figures to extend the study of meaning beyond pure reference was Bronislaw MALINOWSKI. In a seminal essay, he argued that it was vital to analyze the use of linguistic signs in the "context of situation," as opposed to the context of other words or discourse, which was the traditional preserve of philologists and linguists (Malinowski 1923). Besides reference, he delineated the conative function (the use of language to address a hearer in the context of situation), the emotive function (the use of language to express an attitude or emotion on the part the speaker), and, most important of all for Malinowski, the phatic function (the use of language to create and sustain a social relationship). Malinowski's formulation – without its behaviorist slant – was further developed by Jakobson (1960), who added the poetic and metalingual functions to the universal scheme. Like Malinowksi, he argued that linguistics had unduly confined itself to the study of linguistic structure in its referential function without considering the ways in which language can be differently structured to achieve other communicative purposes (what has sometimes been called a "structural–functional" approach).

In another major turn in anthropological pragmatics, Michael Silverstein (1976) extended Jakobson's use of linguistic indices to nonreferential functions of language (marking the gender and social-status relations of the communicants), claiming that

it was in such sign-uses that much, perhaps most, of cultural meaning was *constituted*. Critical in his formulation of the index is the notion that it not only presupposes aspects of the context of situation, but also can be creative or performative (Austin 1962). A relatively simple example is that of titles of address, which can help constitute a formal and deferential relationship between speaker and hearer or one of equality. It is through the notion of the "presupposing, creative" index that pragmatics can show how cultural forms and meanings are constituted. It is thus central to all debates about culture as a discursively constructed phenomenon, as can be seen in Dominguez's (1989) analysis of the construction of an Israeli identity.   SC
further reading Roger Brown & Gillman 1960; J. Firth 1957; S. Levinson 1983; C. Morris 1938

prayer is understood to mean direct address to a supernatural agency, requesting some kind of boon. It is often asserted that prayer is central to all religions, but this does not take into account the innumerable traditions outside the handful of world religions. Many of these lack prayer, although they may have other forms of ritual language, such as recounting the deeds of ancestors.

Where it is found, prayer varies widely in form. We are familiar with prayer as humble entreaty, but supernatural agencies are also invoked casually, or cajoled, even threatened. All kinds of phonological or metrical features may serve to mark prayer off as a particular speech genre. Prayer may require such skill that it is restricted to specialists and grand occasions, or it may be simple enough to be utilized widely.

For the student of comparative RELIGION, prayer is interesting because it is both part of the rite and a reflection on the circumstances of the rite. Frequently it contains formulaic or repetitive phrases but also sections explaining what is going on and why.

Prayer is often mentioned in accounts of RITUAL, but ethnographic studies have been rare. Gladys Reichard (1944) described Navaho prayer from a psycho-logical viewpoint. Peter Metcalf (1989) showed how speakers in different ritual contexts created their own personal styles by drawing on a repertoire of formal devices characteristic of Berawan prayer.
                                        PM
See also ORAL CULTURES, POETRY, SACRIFICE

preferential marriage systems are, according to ALLIANCE THEORY, those in which marriage rules are expressed as preferences rather than requirements or prescriptions.   MR
See also PRESCRIPTIVE MARRIAGE SYSTEMS

prescriptive marriage systems are, according to ALLIANCE THEORY, those in which marriage rules are obligatory rather than optional or simply preferred.
                                        MR
See also PREFERENTIAL MARRIAGE SYSTEMS

primogeniture is the inheritance rule prescribing that the eldest child (sometimes eldest male) receive either the whole or the greater portion of his or her parents' legacy.
                                        MR
See also SUCCESSION

property For most anthropologists, property involves (1) some jural entity that has (2) rights and (3) duties over (4) some object (of property) against (5) other jural entities (Hallowell 1943). The jural entities can be of many different types, including individuals, lineages, households, communities, nations, and corporations. The rights can be subdivided into use rights (cultivation, operation of tools or animals, consumption, hunting and fishing, and transit) and transfer rights (giving, selling, lending, and devolving). The duties include maintenance, preservation, paying taxes, and providing labor services. Virtually any good, service, or action can be included among the "objects" that are subject to property rules. Land, trees on the land, pasture grass on the land, annual crops on the land, water, roads, minerals, gems, clay pits, tools, buildings, clothing, weapons, pots, walking sticks, and a vast array of what are usually called services (curing, divination, songs, singing songs, dances, repairing objects, performing ritual) can all be subject to property rules.

There is no consensus on the origins of property. The implications for different forms of property on the rest of social life are vigorously contested. Because the analysis of property has been dominated by legal scholars, our ideas about property are firmly located in a jural domain. The usual focus is on a set of rules about how to peacefully acquire, use, and transfer away rights to "objects." However, there is one other major means of acquiring possession of such objects: force (war or theft). Although found universally, it is rarely the subject of analysis.

Property would seem to be confined to societies of *Homo sapiens*. (Territoriality in many species is not thought to be property – since presumably the jural domain is lacking among wolves, lions, and red-winged blackbirds.) If that is the case, then property is a human invention. Property in land has presumably evolved from territoriality. "Sweat equity" is a nearly universal folk principle of property. If a jural unit has put work into creating something, the "ownership" of that something is attached to those who did the work. Property rules over intangibles (songs, dances, ideas, spells, incantations, knowledge of disease and curing, etc.) are considered secondary to rules about objects, although the alternative view might be worth exploration.

In private property an individual (a jural person) is the owner, and a MARKET system of transfer is usually implied. In state property the STATE "owns" most of the means of production (land, factories, farms, tools, raw materials, processes), and use rights are assigned by the state. Transfer of ownership is not possible, and transfer of use rights is usually not done with market mechanisms. In communal property some small jural unit, such as a peasant community or a lineage, owns the "object," and is responsible for managing it. Ownership rights are not supposed to be transferable, and use rights are usually allocated only to members of the community.

"Common property" is widely used to refer to resources that are owned by no one (*res nullius*), such as fish in the open ocean or unclaimed forest. But the concept is often applied ambiguously to a property regime where the jural entity is a corporate group that has clear rights and duties over some objects (often pasture, forest, or irrigation systems), manages the use of the resource internally, and defends its right to exclude nonmembers from having access (*res communes*). The "tragedy of the commons" (overuse by maximizing individuals) is quite likely to occur with true commons, *res nullius*, but is thought to be unlikely with common property, *res communes*.

Anthropologists have several purportedly general rules about the correlations of property rules with other aspects of society and economy. Exchange would not seem to be conceivable without some sort of property rules. STRATIFICATION is built upon excluding some individuals from important resources, and many analysts see property rules as key to that exclusion. An economy dominated by the market principle would seem to demand individuals or very small groups as jural entities having rights to those objects transacted in the market. Marx and Engels (1888) and their followers have built a model of capitalism that is fundamentally based on private property in the means of production. Alienation and exploitation flow from the facts of private property. The New Institutional Economists (North 1981, Williamson, and their followers) have tried to explain property rules as a consequence of the need for efficiency in economic life. The "privatization" move of the late twentieth century is also based on convictions about the economic efficiency of "private" property compared with other forms of property. Others view these generalizations as predictions based upon ideology, rather than empirical findings of systematic comparative and historical research.

RHun

See also CAPITALISM, COMPLEX SOCIETIES, INDUSTRIAL SOCIETIES, SOCIALISM, TRADE

further reading G. Appell 1983; Fortmann & Bruce 1988; Herskovits 1940; Hoebel 1954; Lowie 1920; Netting 1982; North & Thomas 1977; Pryor 1973

psychic unity of mankind is the doctrine that all humans share a common underlying psychological structure, irrespective of RACE or CULTURE. In its modern form, it has its origin in E. B. TYLOR's project to find the basis of cultural EVOLUTION in the intellectual operations of humans at various cultural levels, which the researcher recovers by thought experiments. The doctrine of psychic unity in one form or another, however, is an underlying presupposition of social and cultural anthropology generally.   MR
further reading Levy-Bruhl 1926

psycholinguistics deals with a wide variety of issues relating to how language is acquired, represented, and processed by humans.

Language-acquisition research attempts to explain every normal child's capacity to acquire the rich array of language-specific knowledge that underlies adult competence. Some aspects of language acquisition represent the learning of idiosyncratic facts about words, phrases, and so on in a particular language; while other aspects embody the extraction of rule-like generalizations over these expressions. Although it is commonly assumed that parents mold the child's language learning by example and counter-example, research suggests that this is largely false. It is true that parents offer a positive model of the target language, but the model they provide is incomplete, and they rarely offer correction in terms of properties such as syntactic structure. How then can we explain the fact that during a critical developmental period children immersed in a particular language will converge on a common solution to the language-learning problem, despite the impoverished nature of the data provided to them? Although most contemporary linguistic theories posit an innate body of principles (often dubbed "universal grammar") to account for this ability, it remains to be determined what types of linguistic experience are sufficient to trigger the various components of the acquisition process (MacWhinney 1987; Wanner & Gleitman 1982).

Many experimental studies of acquisition focus on evaluating competing accounts of

disparities between child and adult patterns of comprehension (or production) of language. Children exhibit a remarkable uniformity in the kinds of production and comprehension errors they make at various developmental stages, and these errors reflect the nature of the process by which the language learner converges with the adult system. For example, do differences in the way children and adults interpret pronouns in particular contexts represent discontinuities between the developing and mature grammatical system? Or do such differences arise from early mistakes in recognizing the lexical categories that pronouns belong to, or even from nonlinguistic differences between the immature and adult cognitive systems?

Broadly speaking, language-comprehension research addresses such issues as what types of information are engaged in the course of interpreting sentences; how this information is represented; and how and when various information sources interact (G. Altman 1990). In the arena of language production, the process of transforming an intended message into phonetic form is approached in terms of identifying the mental representations that emerge in this mapping (including varieties of intermediate lexical, syntactic, and phonological representations), and how these representational types affect one another in the course of the transformation (Levelt 1989).

One example of such representational issues is how the processor deals with the morphology of familiar words. Does lexical production and comprehension normally involve only the retrieval of stored processing units, or does the language processor also compose new items out of more basic parts? This question may have more than one answer depending on the processing level or the type of lexical morphology under scrutiny. For example, the production (or recognition) of lexical forms such as *walk* and *ran* involves whole-word-based retrieval procedures, whereas the processing of regularly inflected words like *walked* and *running* implicates procedures that compose these words from (or decompose them into, in the case of comprehension) their morphological constituents. By the same token, however, the mental representations for *walked* and *ran* may be similarly composite (i.e., **walk** + [past tense] and **run** + [past tense]) at a processing level that pertains to the morphosyntactic properties of an utterance. A full psycholinguistic account of the mental apparatus underlying language comprehension and production must elaborate how these representational/processing distinctions apply to varieties of inflected, derived, and compound words at particular processing levels (Marslen-Wilson 1989).

Another prominent topic in current psycholinguistic research is the role that grammatical knowledge plays in language comprehension (Carlson & Tanenhaus 1989). Although there are few who would deny that the formal principles governing linguistic well-formedness are utilized when identifying the intended meaning of an utterance, it is nevertheless an open question as to how various aspects of this knowledge interact with other sources of information in the interpretive process (such as real-world knowledge or principles of discourse structure). Numerous findings indicate that, instead of maintaining multiple analyses of ambiguous sequences of speech or text, one immediately selects a favored reading. Some researchers have argued that the language processor initially structures linguistic input according to parsing preferences that are based on the structural properties of the possible analyses. For example, the analysis of newly encountered text that posits the fewest syntactic constituents will initially be preferred over competing analyses. This bias for the simplest syntactic structure was originally hypothesized to account for two elements: (1) the interpretive preferences that readers show when presented with structurally ambiguous sentences out of context (such as choosing the instrumental interpretation of the ambiguous prepositional phrase in *The man saw the thief with the telescope*), and (2) the processing difficulties encountered when one initially pursues the wrong syntactic analysis of a sentence such as the "garden path" phenomenon experienced with sentences like *The horse raced past the barn fell*. More recent accounts of such biases have invoked

preferences for the more frequent of alternative construction types that are compatible with the lexical items in an utterance, preferences based on the interaction of discourse principles and real-world knowledge, and combinations of all these factors (Clifton & Frazier 1994).

WBad

further reading Gernsbacher 1994

psychological anthropology approaches the comparative study of human experience, behavior, facts, and artifacts from a dual sociocultural and psychological – most often psychodynamic – perspective. It emerged in the early twentieth century as an attempt to understand our common humanity, led by such figures as Franz BOAS and his students – Edward SAPIR, Ruth BENEDICT, Margaret MEAD, Melville HERSKOVITS. Psychological anthropology displays an arc of theoretical approaches ranging from scientific positivism, which embraces objectivity and the scientific method, through various hermeneutic humanisms that emphasize the role of subjectivity in fieldwork and writing (Suárez-Orozco 1994).

Psychological anthropology has made one of its enduring tasks to cultivate the theoretical space where the individual emerges as an active agent in the cultural realm. Historically, psychological anthropologists have been critical of approaches to the human condition that privilege one level of analysis (such as the cultural) at the expense of others (such as the psychological). Sapir, for example, rejected Alfred KROEBER's (1917a) cultural overdeterminism as espoused in his "superorganic" model of CULTURE. Sapir (1917) argued that anthropology could not "escape the ultimate necessity of testing out its analysis of patterns called 'social' or 'cultural' in terms of individual realities," and that "we cannot thoroughly understand the dynamics of culture, of society, of history, without sooner or later taking account of the actual relationships of human beings."

Anthropology and psychoanalysis
Some early modern anthropologists became intrigued by many aspects of psychoanalytic theory, just recently developed by

Sigmund Freud, that could be applied to the study of culture. Similarly Freud, as well as most of the early Freudians, became interested in the relationships between psyche and culture (see, e.g., Freud & Oppenheim 1958; Money-Kyrle 1930; Reik 1931). In a series of works, most notably his controversial *Totem and taboo* (1918), Freud addressed the question of the nature and origin of culture, under the influence of W. Robertson SMITH (1889), Atkinson (1903), and Darwin (1871), as well as Lamarckian biology (Suárez-Orozco 1994).

MALINOWSKI's criticism of Freudian theory was a key encounter between psychoanalysis and anthropology. According to Freud, the Oedipus complex (when the boy falls in love with the mother and wants to get rid of the father) was a central psychological event and a universal, species-specific, feature of human nature. Examining this psychoanalytic model in light of comparative data from non-Western settings, specifically the Trobriand Islands, Malinowski (1929) argued that the classic Oedipal complex was not universal. The matrilineal Trobriand Islanders trace descent through women, so the child "belongs" to the mother's group and inherits property from the mother's brother, who also serves as disciplinarian and authority figure. By contrast, the Trobriand father is a generally benevolent, indulgent figure in the child's life. Thus, Malinowski argued, no traditional Oedipal complex developed in Trobriand society. Trobriand boys did not have hostile fantasies toward their fathers, nor did Malinowski find any evidence in their expressive life of sexual fantasies about their mothers. Rather, he contended that Trobriand boys felt hostility toward the *mother's brother* and had sexual fantasies about their *sisters*.

Freudians such Geza Roheim (1950) rejected Malinowski's interpretations. Ernest Jones (1925) contended that the Trobriand Islanders' belief that there was no connection between sexual activity and procreation was both a standard Oedipal denial of paternal sexuality and an example of unconscious hostility toward the father. This was similar, Freudians maintained, to the denial of paternal input in the curious motif

of the immaculate (virginal) conception of the Indo-European folk heroes (Rank 1914). More recently, in a detailed re-examination of Malinowski's Trobriand materials, Melford Spiro (1982, 1992a) concluded that a particularly marked Oedipus complex is indeed present.

Childhood and culture

Issues of SOCIALIZATION, CHILDREN, and CULTURE have been an enduring area of scholarship in psychological anthropology. Both European psychoanalysis and American behaviorist psychology have viewed early-age socialization as critical for understanding various aspects of functioning, including adult functioning, in society. Studies of socialization therefore became a common, key focus in psychological anthropology and other disciplines – although they used distinct terminologies, such as "impulse control" (psychoanalysis), "role training" (sociology), and "ENCULTURATION" (anthropology) (LeVine 1982: 61–8).

An example of this cross-disciplinary co-operation was the work of Abram Kardiner, a psychoanalytic psychiatrist who worked with anthropologists such as Ralph LINTON, Cora Du Bois, and Ruth Bunzel to apply psychoanalytic theory to CROSS-CULTURAL STUDIES in an attempt to reconcile the basic tenets of psychoanalytic theory with the anthropological idea of CULTURAL RELATIVISM (Benedict 1934a). Kardiner based his arguments on the central psychoanalytic idea that the infantile experience profoundly shapes adult personality structure and function. Yet as the ethnographic record made increasingly clear, early infantile experiences varied significantly from culture to culture. Kardiner reasoned that if the standard psychoanalytic model of "childhood determinism" was correct, then different childrearing practices should produce corresponding variations in adult personality structure. In *The individual and his society* (1939), Kardiner introduced an additional set of concepts relating early socialization experiences, later personality functioning, and the "projective systems of the culture" by arguing that each culture has a set of "primary institutions" that essentially represent modes of infantile caring. For example, "among primary institutions are family organization, in-group formation, basic disciplines, feeding, weaning, institutionalized care or neglect of children, anal training and sexual taboos including aim, object or both, subsistence techniques, etc." (Kardiner 1939: 471). These "primary institutions" mold the basic personality structure of the group. In turn, Kardiner claimed, the basic personality structure shapes the "secondary institutions" of a culture, including its FOLKLORE, RELIGION, RITUALS, and TABOO system.

Although Kardiner's ideas were influential, a number of scholars pointed out some weaknesses in this CULTURE AND PERSONALITY model (Barnouw 1985: 110–27), including a somewhat facile causality between "primary institutions" and "secondary institutions." It is of course arbitrary to select an institution of culture and assign it a primary and more influential causal role over all other institutions. Other important work in this line of research includes the contributions of Beatrice and John Whiting (1975; J. Whiting & Child 1953) and Robert A. LeVine (1982).

Current trends

Some POSTMODERN critics have complained that psychological anthropologists produce accounts of other cultures through the lens of a Western psychiatric gaze, often psychologizing social problems. Gananath Obeyesekere, for example, has recently argued that psychological anthropologists have tended to analyze "symbolic forms on the model or analogy of psychopathology" and, furthermore, have used a "pathological model of culture" (1990: xvii). In doing so, Obeyesekere claimed, Kardiner and some of his followers have privileged the "regressive" (or pathological) rather than the "progressive" (or transformative) potential of cultural formations such as rituals that, according to Kardiner's model, symbolically "repeat" some typically traumatic but culturally normative childhood experience. An example of this distinction can be seen by comparing Melford Spiro's classic study of Ifaluk religion with Obeyesekere's studies of ritual in Sri Lanka.

Spiro claimed that Ifaluk "aggressive" rituals represented a "symbolic expression of the hostility which, though repressed, was originally aroused by the frustrating

parents" (1978: 341–2). Following Kardiner's theoretical model, he approached these rituals as "acting out" a culturally normative infantile trauma. Although some temporary mastery might be gained through ritual, there was also a "compulsive" (pathological) quality to such performances. By contrast, Obeyesekere (1981) interpreted ritual performances of Sri Lankan ecstatic priestesses as transformational in a "progressive" sense because they enabled participants to move beyond "fixations," indeed to heal early traumas. Here the priestesses transformed "symptom [pathos] into symbol [health]" and, through the active manipulation of religious symbols, they overcame earlier traumas to achieve "a radical transformation of [their] being" (1990: 25).

The relationship between psychological anthropology and "mainstream" cultural anthropology has been ambivalent from the very beginning of the field. Paradoxically, in the 1990s perhaps more than ever before, cultural anthropology as a whole seems to be consumed with preoccupations that have been in the research agenda of psychological anthropologists for two generations. This may be seen in the interest in studying "self" and "personhood" in culture, "emotion" (or "sentiment"), "poetics," "cultural construction" (of gender, ethnicity, age, etc.), and the problem of subjectivity and reflexivity in fieldwork and in writing. These are a few examples of how anthropologists in general and psychological anthropologists in particular remain deeply concerned with psychosocial phenomena as they pursue their specialized topics of research.   MSO

See also EMOTIONS, ETHNOPSYCHOLOGY

further reading Bock 1988; Bourguignon 1979; D'Andrade & Strauss 1992; Devereux 1978; De Vos 1992; De Vos & Suárez-Orozco 1990; Hallowell 1955; Holland & Quinn 1987; Hsu 1961; La Barre 1980; R. Paul 1989; T. Schwartz et al. 1992; Shweder 1991; Stein 1987; Stigler et al. 1990; Suárez-Orozco 1989

purdah is the institution of the seclusion of women, particularly as practiced by high-caste Hindus in India. Although of

Hindu origin, the term is frequently used to indicate practice in some Islamic societies of isolating women in the home.   MR

purity/pollution Purity, in its contrasts to concepts of impurity and pollution (the flowing of impurity across boundaries to affect a relatively pure individual), extends powerful ideas and emotions about cleanliness rooted in anxieties about the integrity of the body for purposes of social organization and definition. Although purity and pollution ideas are said to be universal and to share many common features, the extent, usage, obsessiveness, and shape of these ordering constructions vary greatly from group to group (Ortner 1974a).

Concepts of purity and pollution are elaborated from peoples' sense of their body's (or self's) vulnerability to "dirt" as it (1) affects the body's surface through touch by a polluting person or object or (2) enters the body via oral ingestion of some polluting substance.

Surface pollution is intimately related to the feared responses (fantasized or actual) by others who may see, smell, or otherwise perceive such "dirt." It is felt to affect an individual's public presentation, social acceptability, and social value, and is thus associated with such socially constructed moral ideas as shame, embarrassment, and the protection of "face." Such ideas of status-ordering dirtiness as physically *real* often lead to the manipulation of the actual physical conditions of life so that "polluting people" are "objectively" dirty. This was the case among traditional "untouchables" in South Asia (R. Levy 1990).

Internal pollution has it roots in the fear of oral ingestion of polluted materials, including those that are transferred from the surface of the body into the mouth. Internal pollution is related more to the constitution of the body (and the "body self") than to its public appearance, and affects core private aspects of individuals' identities and self-esteem. Ideas about the pollution of the "body self" are often extended to such morally significant aspects of the self as "mind," "spirit," and "character" through metaphorical bridges to such putative sources of pollution as sin, moral error, the behavior of ancestors or contemporary family members, genes, and the like.

The primary reaction to "impurity" is disgust, the emotion specifically related to "dirty" ingested materials. Mary Douglas defined "dirt" as "matter out of place," material that violates (or is ambiguously on the border between) cultural categories. She argued that we should "treat all pollution behavior as the reaction to any event likely to confuse or contradict cherished categories" (1968: 340). But not all out-of-place material is dirty in the sense implied by pollution and disgust: ground glass in food is a *dangerous* contaminant, but not a disgusting one. Disgusting materials seem limited to organic "things that might conceivably be eaten" and that entail a forbidden *temptation* that has to be resisted by such semibiological and reflex-like reactions as disgust, retching, and rejection. TABOOS on making close contact with and, above all, touching "impure people" may similarly operate in opposition to temptations to embrace, to include socially forbidden people within one's affectional/erotic sphere. Strong social taboos serve to counter strong potential temptations to antistructural and potentially subversive pleasures: *communitas*, equality, and unrestrained desire.

Culturally elaborated concepts of pollution, and thus how to maintain purity, not only separate one from people who are both tempting and forbidden, but also serve to keep separate from the body materials that once constituted it. These materials include finger nails, saliva, mucus, feces, urine, and menstrual blood, which must be routinely separated and distanced from the body to delinate its boundaries. In the process of separation they become polluting not only for others but for the source individuals who might reintroduce them onto or into themselves. Thus, once "saliva" is expelled from the mouth it becomes disgusting "spit," the body's boundaries and conceptual clarity having become protectively clarified in the transition.

Another sort of oral pollutant is defined by FOOD TABOOS, categories of theoretically edible foods – palatable, in fact, to other groups (they take their social force from this fact) – that are "irrationally," "culturally," and, often, "supernaturally" forbidden to a particular group. They thus provide an arbitrary marker of in-group membership – "we are the people who do not eat X." As Mary Douglas (1966) argued in her analysis of Biblically tabooed foods (the "abominations" of *Leviticus* and *Deuteronomy*), the selection of forbidden items often appears motivated by blurred categories of CLASSIFICATION and suggests at least some cognitive bases for these culturally specific choices.

Whatever the personal intellectual, emotional, and experiential bases for purity and pollution ideas, these ideas provide powerful social markers, rules, and motivations that determine with or from whom one can legitimately eat, accept food, marry, have sex, and associate (rules that vary by context). In short they contribute greatly to moral ordering. Pollution ideas erect both *absolute* exclusionary boundaries (pure versus impure) and *relative* rankings of degrees and classes of purity (more or less pure). Such relative ranking affects social relations in quantitatively differentiated ways for whole groups, as in South Asian CASTE systems, or *differentially* affects the different types of social relations individuals have with one another – association, eating, sexual contact, marriage, entrance into some sacred arena, etc. The ordering of purity/impurity is integral to various hierarchies such as caste (Dumont 1970).

A cross-culturally pervasive use of the idea of impurity is in relation to MENSTRUATION, and thus to the impurity of women in relation to men. This obsession, making use of of feelings about detached BLOOD and CHILDBIRTH, is closely related to widespread ideas and feelings about the problematic and subsidiary status of sexually mature women, and to male anxieties related to them.

Ideas of impurity are related to POWER in systems where those who live in intimate association with impurity are believed capable of transcending purity's orderly categories, dangers, and taboos. In South Asia these individuals include holy men and certain classes of deity (notably the "creator goddess"), who are believed to have special powers for creation or destruction, as opposed to power for the *maintenance* of the relatively *static* social order associated with structures of purity and pollution. A pure person like a priest has high social status but is vulnerable, having to protect his purity through external social defenses, whereas the polluting individuals – often women, or people of very low or marginal status, witches, sorcerers, or holy men – are powerful directly in themselves and can stand against social forces. Those deities, such as are found in South Asian Tantrism, whose sacred power is associated with the ability to transcend impurity, are often sensed as "profane" or "satanic" in the Western tradition.

Purity is very frequently associated with religious ideas and amalgamated with ideas of the "sacred," particularly "sacred arenas" and "sacred states." These arenas and states require clearly demarcated and protected boundaries within which some "supernatural" combination of power and purity operates. They are subject to contamination by impure people or objects that can degrade their power and sacredness. To contaminate the sacred – or a person, place, or object of purer status in general – is very risky, and those responsible for the contamination are often severely punished for such sins or transgressions (R. Levy 1990: 375–97).

Some impurity is taken to be preventable and avoidable by careful adherence to elaborated systems of rules and taboos. Some is correctable through various purifying techniques, often administered by expert professionals. Because the idea of "dirt" figures so prominently in concepts of pollution, purity can be restored by cleaning the body's surface by physical or magical/metaphorical means, or prevented by cleaning the objects that will come into contact with bodily surfaces (particularly the mouth). Internal pollution is purged using powerful substances or various sorts of "abstinence" that clean the interior of the body. Metaphorically more distant impurities may be purged by other means, such as penance. Some personal impurity is not considered eradicable; it is thought to be a permanent quality of some class of individuals. This idea is potentially related to ideas of fixed "biological essence," and thus RACISM.   RoL

See also RELIGION, SYMBOLIC ANTHROPOLOGY

Q

qualitative methods are procedures for the analysis of raw data that consist of words or pictures rather than numbers. These raw data can be pre-existent, as in historical documents, or created by the research process, as through interviews. In qualitative research, data-collection and analysis methods are not standardized but unique, often with a variety of methods being used in an iterative fashion that fits the peculiarities of the research problem. Informal methods include PARTICIPANT-OBSERVATION and open-ended interviewing (H. Bernard 1994). Formal data-collection methodologies include structured interviewing, such as protocol analysis (Ericsson & Simon 1980) and categorization tasks like pile sorts (Weller & Romney 1990). Other formal approaches include:

1. textual analysis (Werner & Schoepfle 1987), including content analysis (R. Weber 1990), which is quantitative in the sense of counting words but qualitative in the sense of focusing on a single document
2. conceptual graphs, which take two main forms, depending on whether the nodes are mental or physical, and include directed graphs or a set of objects or properties linked by postulated causal relationships of various types. Psychological uses include semantic networks such as "cultural models" (D'Andrade 1990; Holland & Quinn 1987), the "activity record" (Werner & Schoepfle 1987), and ethnoscientific folk CLASSIFICATIONS (Weller & Romney 1990). The physical interpretation of nodes occurs primarily in the field of social network analysis, where nodes are generalized actors including individuals,

groups, organizations, and states, or events such as coattendance by actors (Wasserman & Faust 1994)
3. inferential models, which are either rule based, such as decision-trees (C. Gladwin 1989) and computer-based expert systems (Benfer et al. 1993), or logic based, such as Ragin's (1987) Boolean algebraic methods. In addition, Behrens (1990) combined the latter with computer randomization methods to yield probability values associated with observed logical combinations of variables

Historically, qualitative methods have been conceived as "interpretive" and quantitative methods as "analytic." Qualitative research in social science began with travelogues by explorers using the classic methods of participant-observation in anthropology and the informal interview in sociology. The general focus was on problems of data collection, entry into the field, interviewing techniques, ethnographic methods, and the like, while analytic considerations generally remained of secondary interest at best. Recent texts have emphasized the necessity of developing more explicit and more reliable methods for the analysis of qualitative data.

The difference between formal qualitative and quantitative approaches can be seen in their different analytic "orientations." Although the goal of quantitative research is almost always (at least implicitly) to explain cases, it is still fair to say that, analytically, most standard quantitative methods aggregate over cases. Interest generally focuses on isolating the most important themes that characterize similar cases. For example, standard statistical methods, such as regression, determine how much a given change in a particular independent variable affects the outcome, or dependent variable. Qualitative methods, on the other hand, are interested in the structural relationships between factors within cases. They are not necessarily interested in the ability to generalize beyond the individual case: understanding individual cases is argued to have intrinsic worth. As M. Miles & A. Huberman (1994) noted, although there are cross-case qualitative methods (Ragin 1987) and "qualitative comparative analysis" or "grounded theory" (A. Strauss & Corbin 1990), these typically remain limited to rather small numbers of cases, and interest focuses on understanding the necessary configurations of causal factors.

While it has long been assumed that numbers can lie, since the POSTMODERN-IST revolution of the 1980s it has also been recognized that words and pictures can be faked or misinterpreted as well (Manganaro 1990; Sanjek 1990a; van Maanen 1988). There is thus reason for reliability analysis and validation in any kind of research, but these problems have been neglected in qualitative research. Too often the data used to construct a theory are the same data used to test it (A. Strauss 1987). But it seems likely that randomization and resampling methods will become more commonly employed to deal with the degrees-of-freedom problem of classical statistical inferences that arise in qualitative research based on few cases and many variables.

Computers are playing an increasingly significant role in qualitative analysis. In addition to the expansion of software for randomization and resampling methods, substantial developments in software for the analysis of visual data are anticipated. Pattern recognition in visual data is an active field in artificial intelligence (Hildreth & Ullman 1989), and the techniques can be readily applied to any visual data. Although the analysis of pictorial data is still quite underdeveloped in the social sciences (but see Ball & Smith 1992; Harper 1989), new developments are constantly being made by creative statisticians and social science practitioners (as well as computer programmers), making what were once do-

mains considered unquantifiable amenable to such methods. Such inroads were made in earlier decades with the development of a variety of scaling methods, such as multidimensional scaling (MDS), correspondence analysis, and optimal scaling. For example, a number of sociologists have recently produced logical or empirical methods for the comparison of narratives – an area traditionally very far removed from quantitative science (Abell 1987; Abbott 1992; Heise 1991). The basic strategy for any of these formal methods of narrative analysis is to (1) determine a typology for events within a narrative; (2) determine how particular sequences of such events are structured (i.e., find a grammar to describe patterns in individual event histories); and (3) develop a framework within which different structures can be compared (i.e., determine the generality or breadth to which particular structures are applicable). Once the basic types of sequence structure are identified, the causes linking pairs of events in these structures can be inferred from independent databases. These comparative approaches allow the units of analysis to follow multiple causal pathways under specific circumstances, thus making them case specific or historical (Abbott 1988). Thus, the border between qualitative and quantitative methods can be expected to continue to shift.

RA & MMD

further reading Denzin & Lincoln 1994; C. Gladwin 1989; Weller & Romney 1988; Wolcott 1994

quantitative methods are procedures applied to numerical data. Although the measurements can be taken on any set of subjects (including observations, diary entries, historical documents, survey questions, and photographs), they must all be translated into numerical form prior to analysis. Each particular type of measurement is generally referred to as a "variable" or "variate," and the individuals or objects as "units" or "subjects." If only a single measurement is made on each unit then the data are said to be "univariate," otherwise they are "multivariate". In most empirical research, a number of variables are usually measured simultaneously on each unit.

The numerical values assigned to any variable can be either on a qualitative scale (categorical, ordinal) or a quantitative scale (interval, ratio).

Formal quantitative methods have been in use for more than a hundred years in anthropology. Harold Driver (1953) provided an account of the growing use of statistical methods in anthropology during the first half of this century and more recent applications and developments are discussed in the *Journal of Quantitative Anthropology* (see particularly Read 1989 for archaeology, K. Weiss 1989 for biological anthropology, and Romney 1989 for social and cultural anthropology). For the most part, the quantitative methods in common use in anthropology today have been imported from other disciplines: multiple regression and various extensions from econometrics; factor analysis and multidimensional scaling from psychology; categorical multivariate analysis from sociology and statistics; and so on.

1. Introductory statistical/quantitative methods

Bernard (1988) provided a nontechnical discussion of many topics that are usually prerequisites for the application of any quantitative method, including sampling, levels of measurement of variables, methods of data collection, and construction of scales and indices. Also included in the book are elementary discussions of several statistical methods. David Thomas (1986) gives an elementary introduction to classical statistical methods, such as bivariate correlation and regression, *t*-tests, analysis of variance, and nonparametric methods, such as chi-square, gamma, and tau-b, with applications to a wide variety of anthropological problems.

2. Multiple regression and extensions

The multiple regression model is the workhorse of applied statistical modeling in contemporary social science. The regression model attempts to explain as much of the variance as possible in a continuous dependent variable Y using a linear combination of k independent X variables, $b_1X_1 + b_2X_2 + \ldots + b_kX_k$. The X variables are either continuous or dummy variables, or products of both (interaction effects). Dummy variables take only 1 or 0 as values, and are used to indicate the presence (1) or absence (0) of traits of interest. The magnitude and statistical significance of the individual regression coefficients (the b's) are of major interest, since a statistically significant regression coefficient is usually taken as indicating support for the theory that suggests the corresponding variable as a partial explanation for variance in Y. It is also usually of interest to examine the proportion of variance in Y explained by all of the X variables simultaneously such as the R^2 statistic. Aunger (1994a) provides a recent example of the use of regression in cultural anthropology to examine food avoidances.

Over the past couple of decades a number of important extensions of the single-equation regression model to multi-equation structural equation models have been applied in anthropology. Path analysis involves writing out a set of regression equations where dependent variables in earlier equations may be treated as independent variables in later equations. This corresponds to one-way causal effects flowing from temporally prior to later variables in a theoretical system. Subject to various constraints, such recursive multiequation models are readily estimated equation by equation using the usual regression estimation procedures. Anthropologists have used these methods to examine such problems as DIVISION OF LABOR (J. Goody & Buckley 1980) and MODERNIZATION in rural Africa (Hadden & DeWalt 1974).

In some cases, the assumption that all causal effects are unidirectional is unrealistic and reciprocal effects between some variables must be included in the structural equations. In such cases, nonrecursive systems that allow reciprocal feedback among at least two dependent variables can be specified. An example of such a nonrecursive model is the use of cross-cultural data to investigate the relationship between craft specialization and agricultural practices (Dow 1985).

An important assumption underlying the regression model is that the observations must be statistically independent of one another, otherwise the regression coefficient estimates will be either inefficient or biased or both (Galton's problem). If the form of interdependence among units can be measured, a network autocorrelation regression model can be specified and estimated that yields efficient and unbiased estimates. Dow (1984) provided an empirical example and references to advanced topics, and Hodder and Orton (1976) discussed applications to archaeological topics.

If the dependent variable is not a continuous variable, the usual regression procedures yield inconsistent estimates. The logistic regression model is appropriate if the dependent variable is a single 0,1 variable. This method has been used to examine error in question responses in interview data (Aunger 1994b) and herd composition among pastoralists (Kuznar 1991). If the dependent variable is a multicategory variable (e.g. employment status) coded as a set of 0,1 dummy variables, then the probit analysis model is applicable.

3. Other multivariate models
Many multivariate statistical methods are straightforward extensions of univariate procedures to corresponding methods involving multiple dependent and independent variables. Canonical correlation analysis attempts to find a linear combination of one set of continuous variables that best correlates with a linear combination of a second set of continuous variables. If one of the variable sets (considered as a dependent set) is composed of 0,1 dummy variables that code for group membership, then discriminant analysis attempts to find one or more linear combinations of a set of independent continuous variables that best allocate individuals to their corresponding groups. Lydia Gans and Corinne Wood (1985) have applied this method to discriminate among groups of women who hold differing notions about ideal family size. If the set of dummy variables is considered as the independent (or treatment) variables, multivariate analysis of variance tests the hypothesis of equality of vectors of mean values for the continuous variables for each group. Allen Johnson and Clifford Behrens (1989) have used this multivariate

model to study time-allocation data on a sample of societies.

4. Categorical multivariate analysis
When all of the variables in a model are categorical the frequency data can be represented in a cross-classification or contingency table, where in general each combination of categories is observed more than once. Log-linear models allow the analysis of the effects of individual variables and combinations of variables on the logs of the frequencies in the cells of a multidimensional table. Although they bear some similarities to linear models, log-linear models do not distinguish a dependent variable. Rather, interpretation of the output from a log-linear model focuses on main effects of individual variables and the significance of two-or-more-way interactions among variables. (With only two categorical variables, this is just the usual chi-square test.) Log-linear modeling also allows certain restrictions to be placed on one or more cells, such as omitting impossible combinations of cells (e.g., males with ovarian cancer), which provides great flexibility in model testing. Anthropological questions addressed with these methods have included the relationships between agricultural techniques, female labor, and polygyny (M. Burton & Reitz 1981) and endogamy (D. Strauss & Romney 1982). Dow (1989) examined the use of chi-square inference procedures for models when the sample units are not independent of one another. If a dependent variable can be identified from theory, then log-linear modeling may be employed as a convenient means of fitting an equivalent logit model when all of the independent variables are categorical. If one or more variables are measured at the ordinal level, Clogg and Shihadeh (1994) and Agresti (1984) presented an analogous suite of multivariate categorical ordinal models that take advantage of the additional ranking information. A geometrically (as opposed to algebraically) based discussion of multivariate categorical data analysis was given by Van de Geer (1993).

5. Data representation: scaling and clustering
The multivariate methods discussed in the

previous sections have associated inference procedures that permit the testing of hypotheses about patterns or structures in the data of a priori interest. Other multivariate methods are geared toward the exploration and description of the underlying structure of a multivariate data set.

The main idea behind principal components analysis (PCA) is to reexpress a set of correlated variables as a much smaller set of uncorrelated variables that are linear combinations of the original variables. The first of the new variables, or first principal component, is essentially a scale, or dimension, along which the N units are maximally spread out (i.e., have maximum variance). Additional components also have maximum variance given that they are orthogonal to all preceding components. Plotting the N objects or units in Euclidean space using the first two or three component scores as coordinates may reveal interesting structural features of the data. Dunteman (1989) offers a relatively nontechnical discussion with examples.

Multidimensional scaling (MDS) is a related (set of) method(s) for finding a space of low dimensionality in which to plot sample units to reveal possible underlying structures in the data. Differences in these two methods of data reduction and representation lie primarily in (1) the input data (PCA requires the usual N-sample-units $\times$ p-variables matrix, whereas MDS requires an $N \times N$ matrix of "proximity" (similarity or dissimilarity) scores between each sample unit) and (2) the role of variables (in PCA the relevant variables and their measurement scales are known, but in MDS only pairwise "proximities" between units, or variables, are required and the relevant underlying scales must be inferred from the axes of the resultant spatial diagrams).

Nonmetric MDS can also produce two- and three-dimensional diagrams in Euclidean space, even when the proximities between units are rank ordered. Kruskal and Wish (1978) provided a nontechnical introduction to MDS, while anthropological applications were given by Romney (1980) and Magana et al. (1995). Correspondence analysis (CA) (also known as "dual scaling" or "optimal scaling") simultaneously plots units (rows) and variables

(columns) of a data matrix in the same low-dimensional space. Factor analysis (FA) is nowadays a little-used method to find a set of underlying "factors" that account for the intercorrelations within a set of variables. Weller and Romney (1990) discussed three scaling procedures (PCA, MDS, CA) and provided worked examples.

Cluster analysis comprises a very large number of techniques that attempt to lump a set of objects into natural groupings or classes within which objects are maximally similar to one another and between which they are maximally dissimilar. Based on a square matrix of pairwise similarity or dissimilarity scores among units, clustering algorithms generally yield some form of tree-diagram (dendrogram) that suggests how the units "clump" together into classes. Clustering methods have been widely applied in archaeology. Weller & Bucholtz (1986) pointed out some of the difficulties with one of the most widely used clustering algorithms.

6. Combinatorial assignment methods

Most of the multivariate methods mentioned in the previous section attempt to locate and describe underlying structure in a square unit $\times$ unit proximity matrix. The quadratic assignment paradigm (QAP) is a very general strategy for assessing whether or not a structure of a priori interest is present in the data by comparing two or more square proximity matrices. If, for example, the structure of a priori interest is formulated as one proximity matrix, then a simple element-wise correlation between it and the original empirical data matrix gives an index of "fit" between them. Significance testing involves randomly permuting the rows and simultaneously the columns of the data matrix and computing the correlation (or other measure of fit) at each randomization. The proportion of these correlations as large (small) or larger (smaller) than the initial correlation is taken as an approximate probability level of the test. This testing strategy has been applied to problems in animal behaviour (Dow & de Waal 1989), kinship (Nakao & Romney 1984), gene frequencies (Smouse & Wood 1987), subsistence and population patterns (Gorenflo & Gale 1986), among others. The basic text is L.

Hubert (1987). Extension of the two-matrix model to multiple regression of matrices is given by Smouse et al. (1986).

7. Other quantitative methods

The cultural consensus model generates estimates of the differential knowledge, or cultural competencies, among a set of informants concerning specific cultural domains (such as the identification of contagious and noncontagious diseases, or appropriate uses of corporal punishment) based on their responses to a list of true–false, multiple choice, or rank-order survey questions about the domain. If there is a sufficiently high degree of consensus, the model differentiates the "experts" or specialists from the nonspecialists. In addition, the model provides a probablity of being correct for each alternative to each question, which in effect provides an answer key to the questionnaire for which "correct" answers are not initially known by the ethnographer. This model was disussed in some detail by Romney et al. (1986; see 1987 for the extensions and applications).

Linear programming attempts to optimize an outcome such as mixed animal herd size that is subject to constraints such as available forage for each type of animal. Reidhead (1979) reviewed the early uses of linear programming in archaeology, and Kuznar (1991) both reviewed current work and provided an example using more general nonlinear approaches.

The contributions of anthropologists to methods of social network analysis through the early 1970s were reviewed by J. C. Mitchell (1974). Jeffrey Johnson (1994) provided a recent assessment of methodological contributions by cultural anthropologists. Sade & Dow (1994) discussed applications to primate networks. Wasserman & Faust (1994) gave a comprehensive guide to recent network methods.

8. Software

Software for classical univariate and multivariate statistical methods mentioned above is available in the usual commercial statistical packages, such as SPSS/PC+, BMDP, and SYSTAT. Scaling, clustering, QAP, MDS, and CA software is available in ANTHROPAC 4.0 (Borgatti 1993). UCINET IV (Borgatti et al. 1992) is a suite of network analysis programs.

MMD

See also CROSS-CULTURAL STUDIES, QUALITATIVE METHODS

further reading *Multiple regression models* – W. Berry 1993 [details underlying assumptions]; Judge et al. 1985 [advanced text]; Lewis-Beck 1980 [nontechnical introduction]; Montgomery & Peck 1992 [intermediate level]; Weisberg 1985 [intermediate level]; *Path analysis* – H. Asher 1983 [nontechnical introduction]; *Nonrecursive models* – W. Berry 1984 [nontechnical introduction]; Bollen 1989 [comprehensive discussion]; Hanushek & Jackson 1977 [intermediate and advanced discussion]; *Multivariate methods* – Krzanowski & Marriott 1994 [advanced discussion]; Manly 1986 [introductory text]; Rencher 1995 [advanced discussion]; *Log-linear, logit, and probit models* – Agresti 1990 [comprehensive discussion]; Bishop et al. 1975 [comprehensive discussion]; DeMaris 1992 [introduction]; Fienberg 1980 [intermediate text]; Liao 1994 [introduction]; *Scaling and clustering* – Aldrich & Nelson 1984 [introduction]; A. Gordon 1987 [excellent, comprehensive review of hierarchical clustering methods], 1981 [nontechnical discussion]; Greenacre 1984 [advanced discussion of CA]; Maddala 1983 [advanced discussion]; Menard 1995 [introduction]; Shepard et al. 1972

R

race is as much a symbol of social difference and politicoeconomic inequality as it is a taxonomic concept for classifying human populations on the basis of biophysical and morphological differences. An invidious distinction in social STRATIFICATION, race is a historically specific social and sometimes legal classification applied to populations presumed to share common physical and biological traits or, in the absence of anatomical and physiognomic homogeneity, to those assumed to share at least in part a socially and politically salient ancestry. Race is an ideologically charged cluster of contradictory and contested meanings as well as a socially constructed material reality of hierarchical relations.

As an intensely contested concept, race has provoked heated debate among biological and sociocultural anthropologists over valid approaches to understanding biological variation and social differences. During the first half of this century, Franz BOAS and many of his students and associates (e.g., Ruth BENEDICT, Melville HERSKOVITS, Margaret MEAD, and Gene Weltfish) led a campaign against biological determinism and the conceptual conflation of race, LANGUAGE, and CULTURE. Although it did not treat race as a sociocultural construct for interpreting human variation, Boasian anthropology cleared the ground for later critical formulations and theorizing. Since 1960, the concept has declined in anthropology because of its operational ambiguity, arbitrariness, artificiality, and erroneous and harmful assumptions concerning biological and social differences. According to the American Association of Physical Anthropologists' proposed update to the 1966 UNESCO document on biological aspects of race, all human beings, no populations of which are genetically homogeneous, share a common descent and belong to the same species. Most physical differences are shaped by nutrition, lifeways, and other environmental factors, and those differences with a genetic base vary only in the mean frequency with which those traits are represented across geographic populations. Indeed, geneticists assert that genetic variation within populations is greater than that among/across different populations.

While of indeterminate status as biological entities, human populations are always socially and culturally defined units. When "races" are discerned, they are demarcated in historically specific sociopolitical contexts (G. Marshall 1993: 117). Hence, whether based on scientific observations and classifications or folk perceptions and sensibilities, race is always a socially constructed taxonomic concept for classifying human populations in terms of socially salient physical or biological differences. It is noteworthy that intergroup phenotypic variability is not a necessary prerequisite for the construction of racial differences, but presumed biological traits and the untranscendable sociocultural characteristics that supposedly accompany them are. For instance, at points in the history of Great Britain and the United States, the Irish (as colonial subjects and as immigrants, respectively) were subjected to racialization. In another instance, some Americans classified as "black" are physically indistinguishable from "whites." Despite the ideological focus on physical and/or presumed biological differences and the appearance of objectivity, race is a symbol for nonbiological differences – for the tensions from sociocultural differences and politicoeconomic inequality (Howard and

McKim 1983: 259; Lutz and Collins 1993: 155).

Over the past three centuries race has been variously conceptualized and explained in terms of zoological concepts such as distinct polygenetically derived species, discrete and mutually exclusive types, geographically isolated subspecies, and cross-cutting gradients of populations or clines; elastic folk concepts such as lineage and common descent; sociopolitical concepts like minority, subnation, and nation; and administrative and legal criteria for defining the social boundaries of racial groups (Banton 1983). Particularistic folk classifications that highlighted stereotypical physical traits were not nonexistent in the record of precolonial societies (see Howard & McKim 1983: 259; Drake 1987). However, with the rise and consolidation of the modern WORLD-SYSTEM and the accompanying colonial conquest and domination of diverse non-Western peoples, some of whose very humanity was initially questioned, the salience, scope, and invidiousness of classification systems highlighting physical differences grew and changed qualitatively, becoming taxonomies of "race."

Beginning with Linnaeus in the eighteenth century, universal categories were formally formulated, and race became the focus of politically charged scientific and pseudo-scientific inquiry. Later, in the nineteenth century, discourses drawing upon Spencerian and Darwinist perspectives, advances in medical science, and statistics legitimated folk idioms about human differences. A systematically elaborated, biologically determinist ideology of race naturalized the virtually global institutionalization of a racial hierarchy in which Western Europeans occupied the highest-ranking position and Sub-Saharan Africans, presumed not to have developed civilization, the lowest (Pandian 1985: 81). In light of the far-reaching impact of the transatlantic traffic in enslaved Africans, the "black Other" came to be a central symbol against which the West defined and distinguished itself as a paragon of superior intelligence, sociocultural and moral characteristics, economic progress, and power (Pandian 1985: 84). Given the pro-found ideological and social transformations that gave rise to the Enlightenment and later to the industrial and democratic revolutions in the imperial centers, the enslavement of massive numbers of Africans posed a serious dilemma for adherents of a social philosophy emphasizing the achievement of progress and equality through education and knowledge. The relegation of Africans to perpetual servitude was only justifiable if black Otherness was defined as belong-ing outside the PSYCHIC UNITY OF MANKIND by virtue of unbridgeable natural differences.

Global categories of race facilitated the dehumanizing exploitation of large-scale, continent-wide populations in the historical development of world capitalism. As Eric Wolf noted, designations of race underscore the idea that certain targeted populations "were made to labor in servitude to support a new class of overlords" (1982: 380). Historically, phenotypic and characterological attributes rather than cultural ascriptions (see ETHNIC GROUPS) have been imposed on subjugated populations in contexts where the domination of peasant societies has been at issue. According to S. Greenberg, in the colonial contexts of Africa, Asia, and the Americas, race lines were similarly identified with land alienation, unfree labor, and state power, which constituted the major elements of a racial order (1980: 31). Basch et al. (1994: 38) pointed out that in addition to economic forces, the political processes engendering the rise of nation-states have also contributed to race making. International capitalist development stimulated not only capital accumulation but also the formation of nation-states in the core and colonies in the periphery. In that context, the wedded notions of nation and race were elaborated in the ideological construction of colonizers' national identities in opposition to their racially different colonial subjects.

All race-based societies have race classifications that are hierarchical and legally defined, associate races with stereotyped behaviors, and accept at least in theory that racial characteristics are unalterable and inherent. The United States and South Africa share the distinction of having "developed and institutionalized the concept [of race] to a degree more extreme than" in other societies, while the English in North America invented the most rigid and exclusionist race ideology (Smedley 1993: 9, 16). Nonetheless, as Omi and Winant (1986) indicated, even racial formation in the United States has historically been marked by instability, with sociopolitical struggles engendering shifts in racial meanings and categories.

In diverse racial orders the principal criteria for race categorization are ancestry, appearance, and sociocultural status, which vary in salience across sociocultural boundaries (Banton 1983). In the United States, ancestry is the most definitive basis for assigning racial status in a mode of bipolar classification and discontinuous ranking that has racialized descendants of Europeans and Africans according to a rule of hypodescent that defines anyone of any degree of known African descent "black" and claims "whites" to be racially pure. Consequently, the phenotypic range among American blacks spans the complete black–white continuum. Many of these persons would be assigned to separate racial categories in racial orders where appearance (e.g., Brazil) and sociocultural status (e.g., Mexico and Central America) operate as more salient markers in systems of continuous ranking.

Race is an unstable complex of social meanings that constitutes a worldview, a sociopolitical phenomenon that is not unitary but a synthesis of multiple ideological elements, some of which may permeate the realm of meanings usually attributed to ethnicity. Indeed, under certain conditions, presumed biological differences may be recast as bridgeable cultural differences, and previously presumed ethnic differences may be socially redefined in terms of essential racial distinctions. In the history of the United States the Irish, Italians, and Jews have managed to move from racialized to ethnicized social locations, achieving considerable social mobility and privilege as white ethnics vis-à-vis the more enduring racial minorities such as blacks, Puerto Ricans, and Native Americans. Some analysts suggest that contemporary "model minorities" such as Japanese Americans are in the process of shifting from racial to ethnic status in the interlocking hierarchies of race, ethnicity, and class. The fact that ethnic status may be vulnerable to latent racialization is evidenced in the case of the repressive campaign of "ethnic cleansing" in the former nation-state of Yugoslavia.

As a site for contesting RACISM and constructing oppositional and potentially subversive racial meanings, the politicization of race can provide an important impetus for group identity formation and empowerment. Racial identities are always embedded in a complex nexus of relations in which race intersects with such factors as ethnicity, class, gender, and sexuality.

Beyond earlier research in physical anthropology, race has received little theoretical primacy. It has often been conceptually subordinated to, or subsumed within, such categories as CASTE (see Allison DAVIS), ethnicity, class, and nation (Omi & Winant 1986). Current theoretical trends emphasize race's role as a fundamental axis of social organization and power that cannot be relegated to epiphenomenal status.

While race may have no validity as a biological concept, as a social phenomenon it continues to be a potent force in social stratification. The fact that racial inequality persists despite the deconstruction of the race concept attests to the pervasive structural power of racism.   FH

further reading Alland 1971; Berreman 1972; Frankenberg 1993; S. Gregory & Sanjek 1994; Sandra Harding 1993; L. Lieberman 1968; Livingstone 1962; Montagu 1942; Shanklin 1994; Stocking 1968

racism has been variously defined in terms of prejudice, belief, ideology, doctrine, theory, worldview, emotional conviction, unconscious fantasy, material relations, everyday practices, differential power, and institutionalized subjugation and exploitation. A largely neglected topic within anthropology, evidence indicates that racism is a historically specific and historically changing social phenomenon with cognitive, emotional, and material dimensions that penetrate economic, political, and sociocultural domains.

Anthropologists have always exhibited interest in RACE, and during the World War

II era in particular some Boasians devoted attention to the "natural history of racism" (Benedict 1940). However, following the debates that attenuated the biological race concept, a widely adopted "no-race" posture neglected to probe and interrogate the sociocultural conditions and relations of power that make socially constructed race salient and invidious. Following Montagu's (1942) lead, anthropologists shifted their attention to ethnicity and ETHNIC GROUPS, defined on the basis of cultural criteria. Consequently, populations customarily and, in some cases, legally designated as "races" were subsumed within the category of "ethnic group" without delineating their distinctive experiences and social locations within stratified societies where ethnicity interacts with and intersects race as well as class and gender. The no-race trend inadvertently erased the problem of racism from the core of anthropological inquiry. However, anthropology has recently experienced a resurgence of interest in both race and racism (Frankenberg 1993; S. Gregory & Sanjek 1994; Smedley 1993).

In Shanklin's (1994) discussion of the importance of "dealing with racism" (even without a viable notion of race), she surveyed definitions that appear in texts and indicated that most anthropologists, following Marger (1985: 106), underscore that racism

is the belief that humans are subdivided into distinct hereditary groups that are innately different in their social behavior and mental capacities and that can therefore be ranked as superior or inferior. The presumed superiority of some groups and inferiority of others is subsequently used to legitimate the unequal distribution of the society's resources, specifically various forms of wealth, prestige and power.

As such "racism is a special kind of prejudice, directed against those who are thought to possess biologically or socially inherent characteristics that set them apart" (Shanklin 1994: 16). Shanklin acknowledged that racism can also be viewed as practices of discrimination and domination. In this respect she is consistent with Omi and Winant (1986: 145), who viewed racism as "those social practices which (explicitly or implicitly) attribute merits or allocate values to members of racially categorized groups solely because of their 'race'."

Frankenberg (1993: 70) went further, incorporating prejudice and beliefs in her characterization of racism as "not only an ideology or political orientation . . . but also . . . a system of material relationships with a set of ideas linked to and embedded in those material relations." Wetherell and Potter (1993) posited a view of racism as whatever actions, whether intended or not, perpetuate and reinforce an oppressive structure of uneven power relations. In other words, racism can be the unintended outcome of everyday discourses and behaviors despite the absence of race-centered prejudice, and even actions intended to be antiracist may unwittingly have racializing rather than deracializing effects (Dominguez 1994). On the other hand, prejudice can exist without being openly expressed "if the sociocultural situation provides no reward for doing so or actually provides punishments for those who discriminate against another race" (Drake 1987: 33).

St. Clair DRAKE (1987) examined the multiple forms that racism assumes and the various concepts of racism that have emerged over time. As a concept, "racism" has multiple referents: an underlying cognitive or psychological orientation, attitudes, discrimination, differential power, and policies embedded in a system of control and domination. Analysts concerned with organizational and structural power often focus on "institutional racism," which exists when rules, regulations, and norms are "set up in such a way that they automatically operate to the disadvantage of some racial group" despite the absence of deliberate intent (Drake 1987: 34). Such a configuration may survive the demise of "dominative racism," which obtains "when manifest social-political institutions [exist] to support racism and racist behavior" (ibid.).

As a systematic nexus of meanings, relations, and practices, racism arose in the historically specific context of Western European colonial expansion and world capitalist development. The New World colonial enterprise provided settings in which SLAVERY, race-centered ideas, and skin-color (or phenotype) prejudice converged for the first time in human history, giving rise to racial stratification marked by the systemic ideology and structured domination of white supremacy, which became the most global form of racism (Drake 1987). Observing the legacy of the colonial past in the present, G. Köhler (1978) claimed that the international distribution of wealth, power, and life expectancy represents a "global apartheid" inflicting structural violence (e.g., food shortages, environmental degradation, and economic crisis) on the majority of the world's peoples.   FH

Radcliffe-Brown, A. R. (1881–1955)

Alfred Reginald Radcliffe-Brown was born in Birmingham, England, on 17 January 1881, and raised by his penniless mother after his father died. He won a scholarship in Moral Sciences at Trinity College, Cambridge, which included studying psychology under W. H. R. RIVERS, who had become interested in anthropology as the result of participating in the Torres Straits Expedition of 1898. When Radcliffe-Brown graduated he received various grants that enabled him to carry out research in the Andaman Islands from 1906 to 1908. He returned to present his preliminary findings and was awarded a fellowship. At this time he was known as Anarchy Brown because he was an acknowledged anarchist, though he later abandoned that creed for socialism. He began giving lectures in London on general ETHNOLOGY and in Cambridge on French sociology, influencing especially classicists like Jane Harrison.

In 1910 he went to northern Australia to carry out fieldwork of a survey kind. After returning to England, he came back to Australia, but the outbreak of war upset his plans and he became involved in education as a means of support, becoming Director of Education in the Kingdom of Tonga from 1916 to 1919. He caught influenza and went to join his brother in South Africa to recuperate, finding a post as ethnologist at the Transvaal Museum. Toward the end of 1920, on the initiative of A. C. Haddon, with whom he had worked at Cambridge, the University of Cape Town instituted a

Chair of Social Anthropology to which Radcliffe-Brown was appointed. There he contributed to both theoretical and applied anthropology, but his name really became known for *The Andaman Islanders: a study in social anthropology* (1922), which attempted to apply Durkheimian concepts to first-hand field material. His subsequent fame led Sydney University to appoint him in 1926 to a new Chair in Social Anthropology, established with the provision of ample research funds by the Rockefeller Foundation. These funds enabled him to encourage students to work in Australia and the Pacific, leading to the founding of the journal *Oceania* and to his classic monograph *The social organization of Australian tribes* (1930–31), a magnificent attempt at the synthesis and exploration of complex material. As in Cape Town, he engaged in the discussion of practical problems concerning the Aborigines and others. In 1930 the Depression began to bite in Australia and funding was uncertain, so Radcliffe-Brown accepted a Chair at Chicago. He stopped in Britain on the way, where he met EVANS-PRITCHARD, FORTES, and many other young anthropologists.

His influence in Chicago is amply demonstrated by *The social anthropology of North American tribes* (1937) edited by Fred Eggan, which includes work by his students. He became an important influence in American anthropology.

In 1937 he was invited to occupy the first Chair of Social Anthropology at Oxford. There he joined Evans-Pritchard, attracted Fortes, and became the nominal leader of a structuralist school that saw itself as opposed to certain aspects of Malinowski's FUNCTIONALISM. MALINOWSKI left for the United States in 1938 and Radcliffe-Brown became the senior figure in British Anthropology. But World War II reduced the scale of possible activity and he left for two years (1942–4) to teach in São Paulo, Brazil. Two years later he retired from the Oxford Chair, but subsequently taught at the University of Alexandria (1947–9). After spending some time in Manchester, he returned to South Africa to teach at Rhodes University (1951–4), coming back to England in poor health and dying in October 1955.

Radcliffe-Brown had a great influence on anthropologists in South Africa, Australia, the United States, and Great Britain, owing in part to the clarity of his thought and expression and to his undoubted skills as a teacher. His general approach owed much to the Durkheim school but also to the tradition of comparative sociology that looked back to SPENCER and to historical jurists such as MAINE and Vinogradoff. Spencer was particularly significant for his study of ritual institutions, in which he set himself apart from the approaches of FRAZER and TYLOR as well as Malinowski. He was interested primarily in the examination of ritual ideas in different social contexts and more widely in the contribution they made to the maintenance of social order. He set aside both the conjectural historical and the intellectualist approaches as dealing in unknowables, concentrating instead upon a very specific structural-functional framework.

His anarchist and philosophical past may have encouraged an interest in stateless societies and in the principle of distributive justice. But more important was the debt to jurisprudence and to some earlier anthropology, apparent in his articles on primitive LAW, SANCTIONS, and the jural (as distinct from the emotional and interpersonal) aspects of KINSHIP, which is most adequately seen in the brilliant and comprehensive introduction to *African systems of kinship and marriage* (Radcliffe-Brown & Forde 1950). In these articles he adumbrated his general principles of the unity of siblings and the unity of the lineage, which he saw as lying behind such disparate practices (see MARRIAGE SYSTEMS) as ghost-marriage, woman-to-woman unions, modes of descent and inheritance, preferential and forbidden marriages, and the FEUD. Although some of his attempts to elicit general trends have been criticized as "mere tautologies," he did succeed in "making sense" of many aspects of kinship systems that others had simply dismissed as primitive customs. He showed their place in SOCIETY and in the structure of KIN GROUPS. Where he concentrated on elements of order, it was a deliberate methodological choice, a conscious limitation with the aim of building up a comparative SOCIOLOGY.   JG

further reading R. Firth 1956b; Fortes 1955; J. Goody 1995; A. Kuper 1973

ramage is an internally stratified grouping of lineages. It is a term found primarily in works on Polynesian societies (R. Firth 1936; Sahlins 1958) and not widely used elsewhere.   MR

ranked societies In the evolutionary typology of Morton Fried (1967), a ranked society is of intermediate complexity – equated with BIGMAN systems and simple CHIEFDOMS in other schemes (Earle 1994). The political organization of ranked societies is one of graded statuses without sharp separations into social strata. Only a limited number of positions of valued status exist, however, and "not all those of sufficient talent to occupy such statuses actually achieve them" (Fried 1967: 109). Local polities have traditional ritual and political leaders who coordinate community activities involving everything from ceremonies to the construction of irrigation systems.

Fried's scheme recognizes a structural transformation in the nature of political and economic relationships: ranked societies, as a complex form of tribal organization, are structured by traditional principles, especially of kinship (Friedman & Rowlands 1977; Kristiansen 1984). Fried believed that positions of leadership did *not* confer differential access to economic resources and a resulting power differential. Rather, the evolution of stratified societies was the great transformation, as leaders seized economic advantage from their political position. This fundamental change underlay the rapid evolution of state society.

Fried's scheme has been criticized by those who see all leadership in human society as carrying some degree of differential access to critical economic resources. In this view, the evolution of complex political systems involves a gradual, quantitative increase in power and a corresponding institutionalization of leadership (A. Johnson & Earle 1987). Fried, in contrast, stressed qualitative (structural) change, fundamental to classical marxist theory.   TE
See also COMPLEX SOCIETIES, STATE, TRIBE

further reading Earle 1987; Feinman & Neitzel 1984; Service 1962

reciprocity   is a principle for organizing an economy in which exchanges are between those who are (more or less) equals and tend strongly to balance out in the long run, where both parties are free to withdraw from the exchange pattern, and where MONEY and price are not involved. All economies have exchanges based on the principle of reciprocity, but some economies have nothing else, particularly societies without social STRATIFICATION, MONEY, and prices. The term itself is associated with Karl Polanyi (1957), who drew heavily on MALINOWSKI's work in the Trobriand Islands. Polanyi saw reciprocity as one of the three principles organizing economies – the others being REDISTRIBUTION and MARKET.

Most economies that use redistribution or market principles for organizing the economy also contain substantial numbers of transactions made on the principle of reciprocity. For example, Christmas gifts are one of the major economic motors for retail sales in the United States. GIFT economies have been the major focus for recent research on reciprocity.

"Reciprocity" is also used in anthropology to define a set of exchange relationships among individuals and groups, proposed by Marshall Sahlins (1972): generalized reciprocity, balanced reciprocity, and negative reciprocity. Generalized reciprocity is the altruistic pole, a form of sharing in which accounts are not kept. You give something but expect (and usually get) nothing in return, at least immediately. Examples include parents housing and feeding children or paying for their education. Negative reciprocity is its evil twin; something is taken from you with no expectation of return, as when a thief steals your car. Balanced reciprocity is where the transfers are equal. However, it is not clear why the altruistic and theft extremes are to be called "exchange," since no reciprocal transfer is involved.   RHun

Redfield, Robert (1897–1958)   Robert Redfield was born in Chicago in 1897. He was closely associated with the University of Chicago: he took all of his education there, served on the faculty as professor and later dean, and was the son-in-law of the great Chicago urban sociologist Robert Park. He is best known for his studies of PEASANTS and his attempts to encourage multidisciplinary studies of living civilizations.

He trained originally as a lawyer, but a summer trip to Mexico turned Redfield's interest to anthropology. He completed a dissertation on the Mexican peasant village of Tepoztlán in Yucatan in 1928 (Redfield 1930), one of the first such studies in the field. He then went on to do a series of comparative projects in Yucatan that exemplified what he called the FOLK–URBAN CONTINUUM (Redfield 1934, 1941). Unlike other anthropologists at the time, Redfield recognized the importance of history and attempted to deal with questions of SOCIAL CHANGE, particularly in a restudy of the village Chan Kom a generation after his first fieldwork there (Redfield 1950).

Redfield's work in the Yucatan became the center of debate when Oscar Lewis (1951) restudied Tepoztlán and presented a very different picture from Redfield's. This led to the realization that the selection and presentation of ethnographic facts was not a neutral process but was influenced in part by the personality and theoretical interests of the investigator. Rather than seeing this as a defect, Redfield (1955) argued that such restudies (by different investigators and across time) should be done often.

Redfield's greatest influence, particularly outside of anthropology, derived from his broad theoretical writings on preliterate tribes, peasantries, and civilizations. In some ways his position was antiprogressive because he was concerned with what was lost with increasing social complexity. Redfield (1953) took an almost Rousseauvian view of primitive societies as reservoirs of social solidarity and close community that were doomed to suffer social disintegration and a decline of common values as they urbanized. However, far from ignoring COMPLEX SOCIETIES, Redfield was determined to examine the impact of world civilizations on local com-

munities. During the 1950s he organized and ran a large, multidisciplinary project to develop ways to understand and describe living civilizations across the world. He posited a tension between the "great traditions" embodied by the urban and complex ways of life associated with these civilizations and the "little traditions" of local knowledge underlying ways of life, often in peasant communities (Redfield 1956). It was his hope that anthropology would take the study of large civilizations as seriously as it had primitive societies and facilitate mutual understanding across cultures. He died in Chicago in 1958.   TB
further reading Murra 1976

redistribution is a principle for organizing an economy in which assets are collected by a centralized leadership and then redistributed to some or all of those units that produced or provided the assets in the first instance. Redistribution requires a formal political organization (which implies at least ranking). This political center can call forth raw food, prepared food, craft items, luxury items, tools and weapons, labor, and military service from the subordinate units (dependent political centers, communities, clans). This serves as a form of economic accumulation that can be transformed at the center by turning the raw materials collected into luxury goods for itself, support groups that serve the center, such as military, religious, or craft specialists, or be returned when needed to the general society as a form of insurance against disaster or famine. The term itself is associated with Karl Polanyi (1957) (see also RECIPROCITY, MARKET).

In a redistributive economy the center establishes its dominance over subordinate units by enforcing its demands for revenue on them. This revenue provides the income that provisions the political center and supports a hierarchy. While the center always profits, subordinate units often benefit through subsequent distributions that compensate for spatial and temporal patchiness in the production system. Certain economies are dominated by the principle of redistribution. On a small scale, CHIEFDOMS are principal examples. On a large scale, the command economies of the twentieth century (principally the former Soviet Union, its satellites, the People's Republic of China, and Cuba) have used redistribution from the center to organize all aspects of their economies. Although this type of redistribution is associated with SOCIALISM, every economy with a political center manifests the principle of redistribution. The market economies of the "First World" use it intensively. Assets are collected by taxation, often transformed in government labs and military factories, and then in part consumed by the center, and in part redistributed to citizens as goods (streets), income (transfer payments), and services (sewers, police, fire, airport control towers).   RHun

reference terms are those KIN TERMS used in referring to a person. These are often distinct from those used to address the person directly (see ADDRESS TERMS). For example, a kinship system may have a variety of reference terms to differentiate among different types of cousins that are not used when addressing a cousin directly.
                    MR

reflexive anthropology See INTERPRETIVE ANTHROPOLOGY

refugees are displaced people who have fled their homes to seek safety in another country. Originally defined by the United Nations as exiles who fear persecution if repatriated to their homelands, the term now encompasses much broader groups, including forced migrants, displaced persons, and asylum seekers. Displaced people who remain within their country of residence, and who therefore are not technically refugees, often share many of the same characteristics. One of the central problems is defining refugee identity, particularly since communities of refugees take a wide variety of physical forms, including urban neighborhoods, spontaneously settled villages, networks of individuals, and refugee camps.

Societies engulfed by upheaval have long challenged anthropological inquiry, if only because FUNCTIONALIST anthropology had assumed that their normal state was one of self-correcting equilibrium. Those societies that came unglued rarely became anthropological subjects, even retrospectively. Despite this bias some anthropologists could not help but notice that the twentieth century was hardly an era of graceful equilibrium anywhere in the world. Instead of considering them aberrations, anthropologists began to argue that conflicts and social disruptions across the world could be used as a means for understanding social behavior (S. Keller 1975). Extreme social change was all too often a central component of human experience, and thus deserved to be an important subject of study.

The resulting field of anthropological inquiry on refugees and their related groups is remarkably varied. Initial studies focused not on refugees themselves, but on the related problem of internal resettlement of communities by state authorities. For example, Elizabeth Colson's (1971) examination of the Tonga of colonial Northern Rhodesia was an impassioned description of the painful disruptions that their relocation caused. More recently a significant and growing body of work has concentrated on refugees living in camps, especially in Southeast Asia (L. Long 1993) and Africa (Harrell-Bond 1986; Christensen 1985). Whereas the study of refugees living outside camps began years ago (Hansen 1979; A. Spring 1979), the shift of refugees to urban areas is a more recent field of study (Heldenbrand 1996; Sommers 1993). Anthropologists have also made highly significant contributions toward understanding the historical and political disruptions that produce refugees, such as the 1994 Rwandan genocide (Prunier 1995).

Issues related to identity concerns form a central theme in the anthropological literature on refugees. Descriptions of the reconstruction of cultural identity have ranged from empowerment (Malkki 1995a) to marginalization (D. Edwards 1986). Often anthropologists reveal how ethnic or national identification takes new forms for people living in exile either in neighboring nations, such as the Burundians in Tanzania (Sommers 1995), or in regions far distant from their homelands, such as southeast Asians in the United States

(Muecke 1987; Tapp 1988) or Africans in Canada (Sorenson 1990, 1991).

Although the field of refugee studies has been criticized for its perceived theoretical weaknesses (Malkki 1995b), this is not for lack of diversity. Approaches have ranged from those in which theory takes precedence, often grounded in the work of French theorists such as Pierre Bourdieu (E. Daniel & Knudsen 1995) and Michel Foucault (Malkki 1995a), to those that emphasize the pragmatics of applied research and the strengths of anthropological methods (Camino & Krulfeld 1994; de Waal 1989; Van Arsdale 1993). Refugees, after all, constitute not only a varied field of anthropological inquiry, but a field of active anthropological activity, as well.

MS

further reading The American Anthropological Association's Committee on Refugee Issues (CORI) publishes a continuing series of papers on refugee concerns: DeVoe 1992; Hopkins & Donnelly 1993; Rynearson & Phillips 1996; Zaharlick & MacDonald 1994

reincarnation   describes the belief that a soul or mind separates itself from the physical body at death and later becomes associated with a new physical body in a gestating embryo or fetus. This belief is extremely widespread throughout the world. Indeed, Schopenhauer (1889) defined Europe as that part of the world in which the inhabitants do not believe in reincarnation. This is still broadly true: reincarnation beliefs are held by the Hindu and Buddhist inhabitants of South Asia, many cultures in East Asia, many African groups (especially those of West Africa), and are an essential component of the traditional religions of native North Americans. Although not a part of orthodox (Sunni) Islam, the belief is widely held among Shiite Moslems, such as the Druses of Lebanon and Syria and the Alevis of Turkey. Similarly, although not part of modern Christianity, surveys have nevertheless shown that perhaps as many as 25 percent of the inhabitants of Europe and North America – most of them formally Christians – also believe in reincarnation.

The details of what is believed about the

circumstances and processes of reincarnation vary widely. Hindus believe that a soul reincarnates more or less intact in a new physical body, as do Mahayanist Buddhists such as the Tibetans, who seek out the new incarnations to fill their previous religious office (such as the position of the Dalai Lama). By contrast, Theravadist Buddhists do not believe that any entity moves from one physical body to another, but that the dying personality initiates a new personality (in a new physical body) and influences it, just as the flame from one candle lights another. Theravadist Buddhists thus think the word "rebirth" expresses their concept better than "reincarnation."

The beliefs also differ regarding the interval between death and reincarnation. Both the Jains of India and the Druses of Lebanon believe that a soul cannot exist without connections to a physical body. For the Jains, a new connection occurs at the moment of the conception of the next physical body; for the Druses, however, the connection occurs at the moment of the next body's birth. Most Hindus and Buddhists believe in a variable interval between death and reincarnation. Other differences in the belief occur regarding the possibility of sex change from one life to another. The Buddhists of Burma and Thailand regard this as not only possible, but commonplace. In contrast, the Druses of Lebanon and the coastal tribes of northwestern North America consider sex change from one life to another impossible. Still another difference concerns whether or not reincarnation may occur between humans and animals. This is an important part of the Hindu and Buddhist religions, but is absent from most other beliefs in reincarnation.

A particularly important variation in reincarnation beliefs concerns the attributed connections between conduct in one life and its consequences in another. Obeyesekere (1968) has made a useful distinction between "primitive" and "ethicized" types of belief in reincarnation. In the primitive belief, moral values have no link to reincarnation; examples occur among the Trobriand Islanders and the Igbo of Nigeria. In the ethicized belief conduct in one life has an important causative

influence on the circumstances of a later life or lives. This division is helpful so far as it goes, but it is a mistake to conclude that ethicization of the belief in reincarnation inevitably leads to a doctrine such as that of "karma," as held by Hindus and Buddhists. Karma supposes an effect on a later life from actions in a previous one. The Druses have an ethicized belief in reincarnation, but they believe that accounts of one's conduct in all lives are kept and summed at the Day of Judgment; at that time appropriate rewards and punishments are distributed, but not before.

Still other important differences occur in the relative values attached by different peoples to terrestrial lives and the presumed discarnate existences between these lives. Parrinder (1956) pointed out that the Hindu and Buddhist religions are life-negating because they hold that life is fraught with inevitable suffering, the only escape from which lies in ceasing to be reborn – "getting off the wheel of rebirth," as the Buddhists say. The Igbo belief, on the contrary, is life-affirming. Igbos believe that a terrestrial life is desirable and the intermediate state between lives an uncongenial limbo. They want to be reborn.

Claims to remember previous lives have come down to us from early times, but have only recently received systematic investigation. The important correlations between such claims and the belief in reincarnation have begun to receive attention from anthropologists (Stevenson 1975–83).

ISt

further reading A. Mills & Slobodin 1994; Stevenson 1985, 1987

religion The anthropological approach to religion has two predominant traditions: the intellectualist and the symbolist, each of which may be further subdivided. Following TYLOR (1871), who argued that early religion arose from people's beliefs in SPIRITS of godlike beings (see ANIMISM), the first is called "intellectualist" because religion is seen as a system of explanation. People, it was claimed, invoked beliefs in spirits or gods in order to explain natural events and phenomena in the world about them. The symbolist approach, derived from DURKHEIM (1915), sees religion as making symbolic statements about the social order, not as explaining nature. Beliefs, RITUALS, or MYTHS may reinforce ideas about authority but are not peoples' attempts to explain why authority is there in the first place. Hence, for the symbolists, religion does not attempt to solve intellectual or empirical problems.

Tylor's intellectualist definition grew out of his theory of cultural EVOLUTION and the development of human reason. He saw MAGIC, science, and religion as manifestations of the human intellect and, though different from one another, as likely to coexist in all human cultures. Magic was a form of mistaken science. Whereas scientific assumption could be shown to be true or false through empirical tests, magic tried to solve problems through associations of ideas that simply seemed to fit with each other: he gave as an example the Greek view that the yellow of a gold ring could draw out the yellow of jaundice and so cure it. Magic and science were, however, similar to each other in seeking causal connections in an ordered nature, and differed from religion with its belief in spiritual beings, rather than an impersonal power, as having an effect on the world. FRAZER (1890) broadly followed Tylor's distinction between magic, religion, and science but saw them, in this order, as making up an evolutionary continuum. Much later, LÉVI-STRAUSS (1966, 1969b, 1973, 1978) was to revert in part to Tylor's insight and to demonstrate through detailed analyses of myths, ART, and custom, that magic, science, and religion were indeed to be regarded together as premised on the inherent human capacity for logical classification.

Durkheim's major study *The elementary forms of the religious life* (1915) did not concern itself with the truth or falsity of religious beliefs, but instead insisted that the many religions throughout the world and history were based on a human need and so could not be regarded as illusory. He found inadequate Tylor's definition of religion as belief in godlike entities and argued that a broader concept was required, namely that of the SACRED. All things classified by humans were either sacred or profane. The critical feature of the sacred was that it united worshipers in a single moral community.

Religion, therefore, had its basis in a social group, not individual psyches. The sacred had continuing rather than occasional effects on such groups because it derived from an early form of social differentiation, namely that of exogamous CLANS, each of which was symbolized by a specific animal or plant totem. These objects were not intrinsically sacred but drew their sacredness by virtue of a special ongoing relationship with what they symbolized.

In analyzing the religion among Australian Aborigines, which he called "TOTEMISM," Durkheim described the ways in which each clan constituted a CULT group concerned to preserve the sacredness of its totems, which in turn symbolized the well-being and continuity of the totemic group. In worshiping the totems, members of the group were in effect celebrating their own existence and continuity and giving concrete expression to it. Since the major totemic groups were also exogamous clans, the sacred distinctiveness of each was further reinforced by intermarriage between them, a view earlier developed in detail by W. Robertson SMITH (1889) in his study of Semitic societies in ancient Arabia.

Durkheim argued that totems symbolized not just the physical world of flora and fauna but, more importantly, the very society of which worshipers were members. Since the totemic principle, in some form or other, inhered in all religions, this meant that, in worshiping God, people worshiped society. In symbolizing divinity, the totem also symbolized society, and therefore, according to Durkheim, divinity and society were the same.

Although Durkheim has come to be known for his symbolist approach to the study of religion, there is also much in his work that lends itself to an intellectualist interpretation. He argued, for instance, that religion makes scientific thinking possible by allowing for the evolution of classificatory logic out of humanity's conceptual organization of the relationships between totemic plants, animals, and social groups. Horton and Finnegan (1973), in particular, drew attention to the fact that Durkheim was not only a symbolist interested in the way religion represented society but also, and perhaps mainly, an intellectualist in his contention that the route to science was by way of religion. Nevertheless, a broad distinction has persisted until recently in anthropology between the two approaches. Horton is thus opposed to those symbolists such as Beattie (1970), M. DOUGLAS (1970a), and V. TURNER (1968 and other studies) who held to that aspect of Durkheim's theory that religious expression and social organization tend to reinforce each other, a view that in its earlier renderings came to be called "FUNCTIONALISM," especially through RADCLIFFE-BROWN (1952).

Analyzing an example of traditional African thought among the Kalabari of Nigeria, Horton (1967, 1968) invoked Tylor in arguing that their religious worldview was a kind of theorizing about nature very much like Western scientific theory. The Kalabari wish to seek the unity behind the apparent diversity of nature, doing so through a conceptual schema based on a limited number of entities, including ancestors, cultural heroes, and water spirits, as causative agents. Just as scientists confine their search for order through such entities as atoms and molecules, so the Kalabari use categories drawn from their COSMOLOGY to impose and so explain the order in nature and the world around them. Again, Kalabari thinking relates cause and effect sequentially (as does science), such as the explanation of sickness through a rupture in social relations caused by envy, hatred, and hence WITCHCRAFT and spirit activity.

However, although both are theorizing activities, Horton did not argue that African religious systems *are* science. Comparing his findings to those of EVANS-PRITCHARD (1937) on witchcraft among the Azande of Sudan, Horton noted that these traditional modes of thought are self-sealed explanatory systems, regarded as sacred and so closed to outside theories. In response, other scholars have argued both that modern, Western scientific paradigms are more self-sealed than he allowed and that traditional theories do in fact accommodate externally derived ideas. It is an area of debate that continues to have relevance and links issues of religion and philosophy with those of rationality, especially in the context of modern technological developments occurring throughout the world (Overing 1985; Quarles van Ufford & Schoffeleers 1988).

Durkheim's argument that the social determines the religious is best seen in Mary Douglas's most famous studies, *Natural symbols* (1970a), where she argued that the structure of a society, whether it is an open or closed one, is reflected in and, in turn, reinforced by its members' use of their bodies and their understanding of authority. Where a society's cosmology emphasizes strict rules and is highly coherent, its individual members will tend to respect and venerate authority and to engage in bodily restraint: individuals here subordinate themselves to religious beliefs. The Tallensi of Ghana, studied by Fortes (1945), are a classic example of such a society. By contrast, the Mbuti forest foragers of Zaire (Turnbull 1965) are made up of groups whose membership is flexible and rules of conduct fluid, so that individuals are under much less constraint, a looseness that is reflected in a more benign religious cosmology. Douglas elaborated on this basic contrast and so identified a range of symbolic relationships between society and religion.

Discussion of the importance of symbolism in anthropological studies of religion raises the question of what the boundaries of a religious system are. Presumably not all symbols or rituals in society are religious rather than secular (S. Moore & Myerhoff 1977). How far should we go beyond Tylor's minimal definition of religion as belief in godlike beings? Durkheim had in fact questioned this definition in remarking that the Buddha was a mortal and not a god, yet Buddhism could hardly be excluded from the list of the world's great religions.

In the most exhaustive attempt so far, Southwold (1978), himself a student of Buddhism, attempted a "polythetic" definition of religion. He argued that we could not expect all religions to share the same cluster of attributes, but that we could expect there to be a number of overlapping resemblances between them. Thus, Buddhism might not be founded on a belief in a god, but there is clearly a concern with the distinction between the sacred and the profane and with priests, mythology, scriptures, the possibilities of otherworldly existence, ritual practices, precepts held on the basis of an empirically undemonstrable faith, and an ethical code and supernatural sanctions on breaches of the code. These, or some of these, tend to be found in the other world religions, such as Judaism, Christianity, Islam (the three so-called Semitic religions), Hinduism, and also in Taoism and Shintoism, and even Confucianism, which many would argue has to be regarded as more a philosophical than religious system, since it lacks a concept of the transcendentally mystical.

Southwold's point was precisely that there could be no one definition of religion and that we should recognize the multiplicity of these overlapping attributes as making up a general family of resemblances in human thought and practice. With the partial exception of Christianity since the Enlightenment, a sharp boundary is rarely made between a religion and a philosophy, or philosophy and ideology, but this is a problem not of the phenomena under discussion but of our own terms of reference. What may reasonably be claimed is that all peoples, everywhere and throughout all time, have been prepared to act, sometimes often and sometimes only occasionally, according to beliefs that are culturally prescribed and regarded as motivated by forces that may be impersonal or personified but are beyond those held by ordinary mortals. In the end this is not so different from Tylor's original definition of religion as belief in godlike entities, but it recognizes the plethora of variant possibilities such beliefs and the entities may take, together with their attendant practices and consequences.

Anthropology had for a long time followed the convention of making a distinction between the world religions and others supposedly not so globally comprehensive. A related but not isomorphic distinction is that between religions premised on a belief in a High God, perhaps the only permitted spiritual being, and POLYTHEISM (many gods), sometimes expressed as a pantheon

or assembly of gods, not necessarily hierarchically arranged. These distinctions are of limited usefulness. In what sense are the Semitic religions more globally comprehensive than, say, Hinduism and Buddhism? Each caters broadly for major areas of the world, but with significant minorities everywhere; similarly, since Taoism is practiced by vast numbers of people in China (Feuchtwang 1992), can it not be regarded as numerically if not geographically of equal significance? More importantly, we find influences of different religions on each other as a result of conquest and contact, making demarcation more a feature of the claims of a religion's priesthood than of worshipers' belief and practice.

As regards religions defined as based on a central belief in a High God, both Buddhism, for the reasons already given, and Hinduism, with its hierarchy of major and minor gods and of lowly spirits, cannot be covered by such a rigid criterion. Given the role of Satan in the Semitic religions, especially in those Manichaean or dualistic versions that cast the Devil's EVIL as a force of potentially equal strength to that of God's goodness, we have to ask whether Satan is not really another deity, albeit of a negative kind, and whether these religions are not really duo-theistic rather than simply examples of MONOTHEISM.

A more useful, though still shaky, distinction is between those religions that acknowledge dependence on written texts or scriptures that are held to be important and, in some cases, final arbiters of moral authority, and those that do not rely on written texts. Sacred texts presuppose a clergy able to read and interpret them and so set up a hierarchy of priests and worshipers who may sometimes only have access to their god(s) through such priests. Religious fundamentalists (L. Caplan 1987) argue that worshipers have strayed from a "true" understanding of the texts, which must therefore be followed strictly in order to restore people to their religion.

Those religions that do not have written texts, sometimes called "animistic," "pantheistic," and "polytheistic" and most commonly found in Africa (Parkin 1991), Amazonia (J. Kaplan 1975), Papua New Guinea (Gell 1975), Aboriginal Australia

(Berndt 1974), and parts of Malaysia (S. Howell 1984), may nevertheless have beliefs in a High God, though he or she tends to be of limited significance and is sometimes refracted as an immanent divine force in lesser spirits and objects of the environment, as among the Nuer of Sudan (Evans-Pritchard 1956). Priestly hierarchies are not absent in such nontextual religions, but less formal relations may obtain between priest and worshiper, who may also pray directly to ancestors or speak and negotiate with spirits through a medium or SHAMAN. Such distinctions between textual and nontextual, and world and local, religions are shaky because, throughout the world, it is the interpenetration of the two that is the lived experience of most people, as Kapferer (1983) showed in an account of the interrelationship between demons and Buddhism in Sri Lanka. In all religions, too, SACRIFICE and offerings to godlike entities or spirits (even in Buddhism the *nat* spirits receive offerings) are a feature, sometimes taking more the form of PRAYERS and homage than the preferment of goods and immolation of animals.

The place of sacrifice in religion is a recurring anthropological theme, from W. Robertson Smith (1889) to Heusch (1985), as is that of spirit possession and the manifestation of evil through witchcraft, and sorcery. The idea that these are properly to be regarded as religious phenomena arises from the anthropological method of cross-cultural comparison (see COMPARATIVE METHOD and CROSS-CULTURAL STUDIES), which goes behind conventional Western categories of understanding, including the distinctions made between textually based world religions and orally communicated local ones, or between the natural and supernatural. It seeks similarities between phenomena that might at first seem different. Looked at from a local-level viewpoint, such apparently distinct activities as sacrifice, witchcraft, ANCESTOR WORSHIP, DIVINATION, the consultation of ORACLES, and the veneration of and possession by demons make up the cosmologies according to which people in society try to explain and perhaps understand their sufferings and hopes.

Commonly there are rituals, as well as prayer and the consultation of oracles, enabling them to do this. The rituals may be appeals or tributes directed at specific deities or carried out at seasons of the year as demanded by, say, the agricultural cycle. They may take the form of RITES OF PASSAGE (Gennep 1960) marking the transition from childhood to adulthood and thence seniority, or of cleansing and healing rituals purging a community or an individual who has sinned or broken a moral rule and suffers the consequences.

These religious phenomena may in this way explain the world to participants and provide them with the means to cope with it, and to that extent seem to support the intellectualists' approach to the study of religion. But such pragmatism in religion is by no means incompatible with the symbolist view. The particular forms that rituals take, the structure of relationships between participants, and the organization of godlike entities in relation to humans and their beliefs may still be shaped by and in turn shape the distribution of power, wealth, and authority in society, and in this way also stand as symbols for each other. The explanatory and the socially symbolic are together most evident in religious MILLENARIAN MOVEMENTS, when a myth-dream explains a possible utopia or return to a golden age as attainable through certain symbolic acts, including those aimed at destroying or imitating despised or envied rulers (Burridge 1969).   DP

further reading J. Davis 1982; Evans-Pritchard 1965; Horton & Finnegan 1973; I. Lewis 1971; B. Morris 1987; R. Needham 1972; Skorupski 1976; M. Weber 1963

remote sensing employs a large number of technologies, from air photographs to satellite images, to map patterns from a distance that may be less than obvious on the ground. Anthropologists, and archaeologists in particular, have used air photos since the 1940s. Even today they provide a valuable kind of information intermediate in resolution between satellite data and ground-level surveys. They have also increased in usefulness because they can be digitized and incorporated into Geographic

Information Systems (GIS) data sets that can extend our capacity to deal with changes in landscape and settlement patterns.

Satellite remote sensing has been dominated until recently by geographers and geologists because of their early involvement in aerial photo interpretation and its cartographic applications. Ecologically oriented anthropologists and archaeologists have begun to acquire the technical skills to work with this kind of data and to pose new questions. Biological anthropologists working with primate species have also discovered the uses of these techniques to study habitats of species in a noninvasive way.

Satellite platforms have been collecting data of the entire earth since 1972, when Landsat I was launched by the United States. The resolution of these satellites improved over the next 20 years, so that SPOT, a French earth-observing satellite, now provides views with 10–30 meter resolution. However, in work with complex vegetation, Landsat satellites with lower resolution but greater bandwidth provide more useful data (Moran et al. 1994). For studying settlement patterns and other nonvegetative structures SPOT may be superior.

Satellite remote sensing is an ideal approach to hypothesis testing. Because the Landsat satellites collect data for any given spot on the earth every 16 days (for Landsat 4 and 5), it is possible to use a time-series of satellite images for a given area to test the duration of a subsistence practice and its effects on the surrounding area, to relate the size of area deforested to rates of forest regrowth, to examine the boundaries of settlements and their growth or decline, to evaluate plant communities such as pastures or tropical forests, and to answer other questions that are time- or space-dependent.

One of the important contributions of remote sensing is to give anthropologists a tool to extend their studies beyond the single community to the larger regional landscape within which people exist. Traditional ground-level surveys are too costly and time-consuming to address many questions of change – particularly when those changes may be occurring rapidly, as with deforestation. And few investigators have the resources to collect detailed land-use data beyond a single community or measure a large number of environmental variables. Within the last decade, nonanthropologists have been able to apply satellite-data analysis to monitor shifting cultivation, land-use patterns, deforestation, settlement patterns, and a host of other variables. Of contemporary importance may be the use of satellite data in conjunction with cultural information to delineate the territories of native peoples under pressure from developmentalist forces (Wilkie 1987, 1994). Balancing the needs of traditional populations with the protection of biodiversity requires techniques to establish the boundaries of reserves – a goal for which these techniques almost seem designed.

One of the hardest things for ecological and agriculturally oriented anthropologists is to carry out a detailed site characterization of a study region. Use of satellite images before field studies permits examination of the range of vegetation classes, soil classes, and water courses present in the area. This visual examination can be statistically analyzed using clustering techniques available in imaging software programs to develop preliminary classifications of vegetation classes that seem to be present. Representatives of each class can be marked on the image for sampling on the ground and used to verify the preciseness of the classification – which can be modified on the spot as needed. This is a far more efficient way to organize one's plant collecting than one based on other criteria (Moran et al. 1994; Brondizio et al. 1994).

Remotely acquired digital data have become an indispensable tool in environmental assessment and resource management. The feasibility of using this technology for ecological and agrarian studies has been demonstrated in other fields, and anthropologists have begun to incorporate these tools into their research (Guyer & Lambin 1993). Remote sensing is particularly valuable for work in regions where transportation and access are difficult, maps are of poor scale, and comprehensive surveys are limited in scope. Expertise in remote sensing is increasingly necessary to participate actively in interdisciplinary research on global environmental change. EFM

further reading Behrens 1994; Conant 1990

reproduction encompasses biological events occurring throughout the life cycle (of women primarily), including menarche, mating, pregnancy, CHILDBIRTH, and menopause, as well as the social construction of these events and the ideas and behaviors surrounding fertility, birth, and parenting in various cultures.

Studies of reproduction have traditionally been carried out within the two subfields of BIOLOGICAL ANTHROPOLOGY and sociocultural anthropology. The physiological and hormonal correlates of reproductive life events have been investigated through field studies of pre-industrial societies, primarily though not exclusively among hunting and gathering societies (Konner and Shostak 1987). Variations in reproductive endocrinology have been examined in relation to dietary, environmental, and behavioral factors, and the regulation of fertility has been analyzed from the perspective of MATERIALISM and population ecology. The biosocial study of reproduction has also used the concepts and methods of SOCIOBIOLOGY or evolutionary biology to study such topics as male and female mating strategies, parental investment in offspring, variations in sex ratios, the frequency of INFANTICIDE, and mother–infant bonding in primate and human societies (Betzig et al. 1988).

The norms and behaviors related to reproduction have long been a concern of cultural anthropology. Starting with the classic studies of MALINOWSKI and MEAD, research has documented tremendous variability in the definition of sexuality, in the permissibility of sexual behavior outside of socially recognized unions, and in beliefs regarding the connections between sexual behavior and reproduction (Vance 1991). There has also been a long-standing preoccupation with the subject of MENSTRUATION, in part because of its association with TABOOS and rituals, and numerous studies have revealed the ambivalence surrounding

menstrual blood as symbolic both of women's pollution and of the power attached to their reproductive potential (Buckley and Gottlieb 1988b). The bonds between parents and offspring have also been extensively investigated, and cross-cultural comparisons have shown the universality of MARRIAGE as a socially recognized union and the diversity of forms that it takes, in particular regarding the number of partners who may be involved and their respective roles, the relevant kinship units thus delineated, and the degree of involvement of fathers in parenting (including the possible separation of the roles of PATER and GENITOR). Studies of traditional societies have also reported varying degrees of control over reproductive processes and the existence of a wide assortment of methods to regulate births, ranging from ritual "closings," amulets, and magical practices, to lactation, abstinence, coitus interruptus, and other methods of contraception, to abortion and infanticide. The beliefs and practices surrounding pregnancy, birth, and breastfeeding have received a great deal of attention, and numerous studies have pointed out the appropriateness of some traditional practices for birth outcomes and child survival, and the problems that result from uncritically adopting Western technologies (B. Jordan 1978). Lastly, research on the end of the reproductive years has documented considerable variability in the symptoms that women experience at this time in their life cycle and has explored the association between the symptomatology of menopause and the social context in which this life transition takes place (Lock 1993b).

A concern with the determinants of human fertility has brought anthropological studies of reproduction into contact with a number of other disciplines, most notably DEMOGRAPHY. The gradual rapprochement between anthropology and demography began in the 1950s with joint discussions of the links between culture and fertility. It evolved episodically through efforts to provide a critique of "natural" fertility – the notion that deliberate fertility control is absent in some societies – and of the theory of the DEMOGRAPHIC TRANSITION, which seeks to explain fertility and mortality decline (Handwerker 1986b). There have been several attempts to foster multidisciplinary work that would combine the quantitative power of statistical analyses with the micro-level insights of ethnographic fieldwork. Recently, anthropologists have challenged the paradigm of MODERNIZATION that underlies many demographic analyses, drawn attention to the complexity of reproductive decision-making, and examined fertility and family planning in their social, economic, political, and historical contexts (Greenhalgh 1995; Kertzer and Fricke 1997).

Several developments have contributed to reframing anthropological research on reproduction within the broader context of GENDER studies and political economy (Ginsburg and Rapp 1991). Although the marxist intellectual tradition in sociology and anthropology, which conceives of production and reproduction as related aspects of the unequal distribution of resources in society, played a role in this process of reformulation, the major influence on studies of reproduction has been the growth of feminist studies. FEMINIST ANTHROPOLOGISTS have challenged the centrality of motherhood as the defining characteristic of womanhood, asserted the political dimension of reproductive behavior, and raised questions about the control over women's bodies. They have also taken a critical view of the scientific discourses about women's bodies and reproductive functions (E. Martin 1987) and of the medical management of contraception, pregnancy, childbirth, and infant feeding (Michaelson 1988; Davis-Floyd 1992). With the increasing medicalization of these life events, the issues of control and agency become especially acute, because the new reproductive technologies (including birth control, abortion, obstetrical care, and the treatment of infertility) are associated both with potential improvements in women's well-being and with more pervasive systems of surveillance of reproductive behavior (Sargent and Brettell 1996).

Another important development in the anthropology of reproduction has been the diffusion to various parts of the world of modern methods of fertility regulation and of public health strategies aimed at child survival, in parallel with the expansion of state and international policies linking socioeconomic development to the limitation of births. As a result, it has become increasingly clear that individuals' reproductive experiences are often defined by global forces, and that this dependency has brought about greater choices regarding fertility, but has also under certain circumstances been associated with negligence regarding women's health and abuses of individual rights (Ginsburg and Rapp 1995). In the past few years, reproductive rights have emerged as one of the themes that have been explored through comparative research and debated on the international scene (Makhlouf Obermeyer 1995). All these developments have converged to define reproduction as a contested domain of intellectual debates and activism, and as a central topic for anthropological inquiry.   CMO

residence rules   govern where a newly married couple will reside. These rules are usually grouped as MATRILOCAL, PATRILOCAL, UXORILOCAL, VIRILOCAL, AVUNCULOCAL, and NEOLOCAL.   MR

restricted (or direct) exchange   is a system of MARRIAGE EXCHANGE in which a society is divided into a pair, or sets of pairs, of marriage classes such that each pair reciprocally gives wives to the other (Lévi-Strauss 1969a). Wife-givers are also wife-takers in this system.   MR
See also GENERALIZED EXCHANGE, MOIETY SYSTEMS

revitalization   movements   *See* MILLENARIAN MOVEMENTS

Richards, Audrey I. (1899–1984) Audrey Richards, born in 1899 in India, was a daughter of a legal member of the Viceroy's council who returned to England in 1911 to an Oxford chair in international law. She went to Newnham College, Cambridge University, where she completed degree studies in Natural Sciences in 1922. Various jobs, including relief work in Germany, followed. In 1927 she enrolled as a graduate student at the London School of Economics, attending MALINOWSKI's seminars. Her thesis starts: "Nutrition as a biological process is more fundamental than sex." Written before she had seen a live African, and dealing with the Southern Bantu, it was revised after her first field trip to the Bemba of Zambia (then Northern Rhodesia), and published (Richards 1932) with an introduction by Malinowski, who described it as "the first collection of facts on food and eating." It also dealt comparatively with child-rearing notions and anticipated later studies of the gendered DIVISION OF LABOR.

She returned for 19 months to the Bemba in 1933–4 and on her return to the School, as lecturer, was a member of a joint working group of nutritionists and anthropologists set up by the International African Institute (Richards & Widdowson 1936). The main Bemba ethnography (Richards 1939) was described by her as an elaboration of her thesis designed to show how "the biological facts of appetite and diet are shaped by the particular system of human relationships and traditional activities." It raised other novel issues such as notions of TIME in relation to labor organization and adaptive responses to severe ecological constraints (Ellen 1982), as well as being an exemplar of Malinowskian field methodology, marked by a reflexivity ahead of its time.

In 1938 she migrated to the University of the Witwatersrand in South Africa. At the outbreak of war the Native Reserve where she had started work was barred to her. She returned to England to be recruited to the Social Services Department of the Colonial Office and to serve on committees concerned with postwar research plans, as she continued to do after her return, as reader, to the School. She gave up her readership in 1950 to undertake the direction of the new East African Institute of Social Research at Makerere College, Kampala, Uganda. By then, as can be seen from her contribution to the symposium *African kinship and marriage* (1950), she had moved, like others, away from the pure FUNCTION-ALISM of the 1920s to embrace the analysis of political and jural constraints on the domestic domain and to abstract them as "structure," in the sense in which her friend FORTES had employed the term.

The East African Institute became a regional center involving not only its Anglo-American and Ugandan staff but other researchers in East Africa. Its output was less in the nature of "practical research" (a commission for UNESCO apart) than in comparative studies of the effects and reception in African polities of modernizing colonial policies (Richards 1954, 1960), side by side with thorough ethnographic coverage. Its associates produced their own monographs besides contributing to combined studies and conferences. In 1956 Audrey Richards left the Institute for Cambridge. In the same year *Chisungu*, her long-delayed study of a Bemba girl's initiation, was published, perhaps now the most read of her works. It analyzes the meanings of initiation in terms of Bemba preoccupations with fire, blood, and sex. At Cambridge she directed its center for African Studies, became Smuts Reader in Anthropology, and returned to her old college. Here, much sought after for special lectures and to review noteworthy books (e.g., Richards 1967) she completed, in various collaborations, work she had initiated in East Africa. After her retirement she not only continued to publish (Luhrmann 1992) but turned her interests in methodology to an experimental study of the village in which she lived. She died in 1984, leaving her fieldnotes and papers to the London School of Economics.   SC
further reading La Fontaine 1972; M. Strathern 1981

rites of intensification are communal rites that function to intensify the social sentiments of a groups' members and the solidarity of the group.   MR
See also RITES OF PASSAGE

rites of passage First analyzed by Arnold van GENNEP (1960), who gave them their name, rites of passage are the ways in which human beings indicate transformation from one social status to the next, or the passage of calendrical time. Thus, rites of passage include irregular private ceremonies commemorating personal milestones such as birth, maturity, marriage, and death. They also include regular communal celebrations signaling the cycle of the seasons, such as Christmas, Easter, and so on. Of course, these categories are not mutually exclusive. For instance, seasonally linked ceremonies may mark the passage of an entire group from one age grade to another (see AGE SYSTEMS).

Beneath the specific content of any particular rite of passage van Gennep saw three stages: (1) separation, (2) a transitional state of LIMINALITY, and (3) incorporation. Typical symbols of separation include breaking, tearing, cutting, shaving, stripping away, followed by a liminal period of isolation and magical instruction, and concluding with symbolic tying back into the community. Thus van Gennep interpreted circumcision ceremonies as having nothing to do with sexuality, and everything to do with the social need to symbolically cut the child away from his past.

The concept of rites of passage has been criticized for being too broad (crossing any doorway can be construed as a rite of passage), and for vagueness (is a funeral primarily a rite of separation, transition, or incorporation?). But because of its astonishing applicability, the notion of rites of passage remains powerful, especially in the work of symbolically oriented writers such as Victor TURNER (1967, 1969), Edmund LEACH (1976), and Mary DOUGLAS (1966).   CL
further reading Peacock 1968; A. Richards 1956

ritual refers narrowly to prescribed, formal acts that take place in the context of religious worship – a Christian mass, for example, or a sacrifice to the spirits of ancestors. In this sense, favored by many early anthropologists, ritual is opposed to theology as practice is to theory. More commonly, however, anthropologists use "ritual" to denote any activity with a high degree of formality and a nonutilitarian purpose. This usage includes not only clearly religious activities, but also such events as festivals, parades, initiations, games, and greetings. In its broadest sense, ritual may refer not to any particular kind of event but to the expressive aspect of all human activity. To the extent that it conveys messages about the social and cultural

status of individuals, any human action has a ritual dimension. In this sense, even such mundane acts as planting fields and processing foods share a ritual aspect with sacrifice and the mass (Leach 1954).

Ritual provides anthropologists with one of their richest sources of information about cultures. In many cases, ritual explains and dramatizes a culture's mythology; in a Christmas pageant, for example, actors reenact in great detail the central story of their religion. Even where such explicit dramatization is absent, ritual contains a wealth of symbolic information about the participants' social and cultural worlds. The process of a Balinese cockfight tells not only about such social groupings but also about Balinese notions of time, of good and evil, and of life and death (C. Geertz 1973). Accordingly, the observation and analysis of ritual have been a primary concern of anthropology throughout its history.

Types of ritual
Anthropologists have developed a number of classifications of rituals, distinguishing between such phenomena as annual rituals, life-cycle rituals, civil ceremonies, rituals of rebellion, and many others. One category that encompasses many of these ideas is that of rituals of transition, often referred to as "RITES OF PASSAGE." Rites of passage occur when people cross boundaries of space, of time, or of social status. The transition from child to adult, for example, usually involves an initiation ritual; transitions into marriage, into death, and into membership of a group are occasions for ceremony in almost all societies. Likewise, most societies celebrate the passage from one year to another and from one season to another. Even crossing a national border may be an occasion for an elaborate display of uniforms, passports, and ritual paraphernalia.

Since rites of passage occur at the boundaries of cultural categories, they provide a valuable key to a society's social and temporal classifications. Even more, they may provide an insight into the basic workings of the human mind. As Arnold van GENNEP (1960) and Victor TURNER have shown, rites of passage exhibit a striking uniformity of structure within and across cultures. They tend to be divided into three distinct stages, known as separation (from the old status), liminality (neither one nor the other), and aggregation (into the new status). Each of these stages has definite characteristics: in the liminal phase, for example, rituals often involve role reversals, chaotic activity, and the leveling of status distinctions (Turner 1968; Leach 1961b: 1–10). These cross-cultural similarities suggest that there is a universal pattern to human CLASSIFICATION and symbolism.

Another important class of rituals are healing ceremonies. All cultures have some ritual means for curing ILLNESS; these means range from individual magical spells to exorcism ceremonies to the ministrations of a faith healer. In most cases, such rituals ascribe a spiritual cause to a physical problem, and they solve it by exorcizing or appeasing the spirit or witch responsible. Since these rituals connect the individual body to the social and spiritual world, they contain a wealth of information about a culture's views of the person and the universe. In addition, since they often work, healing ceremonies pose an intriguing problem for MEDICAL ANTHROPOLOGY and PSYCHOLOGICAL ANTHROPOLOGY. They demonstrate an intimate connection between mind and body, one relevant not only to anthropological theory, but also to medical practice.

Functions of ritual

Much of the anthropological study of ritual has dealt with its function, the extent to which ritual sustains and reproduces the social order. DURKHEIM (1915) saw in ritual the very fount of society; it was by coming together with others in ritual that primitive man experienced his membership in society and felt the "collective effervescence" that sustained community solidarity. Durkheim also recognized, as did MALINOWSKI, RADCLIFFE-BROWN, and other functionalists, that ritual provides a dramatic statement of the mythological charter of a society. In ritual, people often act out their MYTHS about the origin of SOCIETY, and in doing so they concretely avow the legitimacy of the established order of things. Even where rituals do not explicitly invoke myths, their structure tends to reflect and reinforce social distinctions.

The seating plan of a state dinner, for example, makes clear the hierarchical positions of the people in attendance. In both its content and its form, ritual tends to display and legitimate social structure.

Rituals are particularly important at moments of transition, when the social structure is at its weakest. Any social transition creates a chain reaction in a system of relationships; if a girl is suddenly changed into a woman, or a man into a king, the status of all those connected with her or him suddenly changes as well. Rites of passage dramatize these changes, allowing actors to settle into new roles and new relationships. They often also include a didactic element, instructing the changed person in the tasks and responsibilities of the new position. In many puberty rites, boys and girls learn the practical and magical wisdom they will need to function as adult men and women (Turner 1969).

Ritual also functions on a psychological level. It provides a coherent framework for the disorienting aspects of human life, such as illness, danger, and life changes (Malinowski 1948). It gives people a sense of control over disturbing and threatening events; an exorcism may not actually drive out any spirits, but it can drive out the sense of helplessness and despair associated with an illness. In addition, rituals provide an outlet for expressing emotion. Funeral ceremonies, for example, often provide standardized opportunities to express the grief and guilt suffered by mourners (Goldschmidt 1973). In some cases, rituals allow people to express feelings that would ordinarily pose a threat to the social order. Thus, the boisterous sexuality and role reversal of the carnival in Europe may channel disruptive and rebellious emotions into a safely bounded area.

This is not to say that rituals are always functional. Since rituals make statements about the social order, they constitute an important forum for those who wish to change the social order. In ritual, poor and oppressed groups can symbolically express their dissatisfaction with the system as it stands. They may do so covertly, by symbolically presenting their own understandings of themselves and the society (Jean Comaroff 1985), or explicitly, using ritual as a springboard for launching reforms or rebellions (Dirks 1994). As anthropology focuses increasingly on issues of power and cultural change, the essential conservatism of ritual is coming into doubt.   AB

See also DEATH, DIVINATION, LIMINALITY, ORACLES, MAGIC, RELIGION, SYMBOLIC ANTHROPOLOGY

further reading Eliade 1959; Firth 1940; Huntington & Metcalf 1979; La Fontaine 1985

Rivers, W. H. R. (1864–1922)

Rivers is claimed as an intellectual forebear in both anthropology and psychology. Trained as a physician, he brought to his work in both disciplines the medical professional's expectation that presented symptoms of any sort could not be understood without identification of the history of their emergence. His first anthropological experience was as a participant in the famous Cambridge Anthropological Expedition to Torres Straits of 1898 (Haddon 1901–35), which significantly affected subsequent British anthropological theory and method. The Expedition's stance that theoretical generalization should rest on personal experience of field research became standard in the discipline, and with the aid of Rivers's "Genealogical Method" (contrived for the expedition) anthropologists were able to document and elaborate the argument that institutionalized kinship notions were the constituents of social structure (Rivers 1914a). Permitting anthropologists to distinguish between the biological relationships that joined individuals in any given population and the CLASSIFICATORY KINSHIP patterns that governed routinized expectations about individuals' rights and duties, the genealogical method was a powerful tool for subsequent anthropologists. But the expedition was also notable because it brought Rivers's considerable expertise as an experimental psychologist to bear on anthropological issues. The psychological tests he imported from European laboratories to administer to the islanders demonstrated the association between environmental adaptation and behavioral variation; they showed that whatever differences obtained between the islanders and Englishmen in

diverse aptitudes and sensory skills were products of learning rather than biological endowments, indicating that culture was not a function of RACE – contrary to the conventional wisdom that had previously explained behavioral variation among Europeans and so-called primitives. (Tests similar to the expedition's would later be used by another of its members, Charles Myers, in creating the new field of industrial psychology after World War I.)

Rivers's subsequent work was consistent with the notions he developed on the expedition, although it has not always seemed so to anthropologists. He applied the model of the relationship between situational stimulation and the selective expression of individual potential in the psychiatric work he did during World War I, treating victims of the functional psychological disorder then termed "shell shock" (the term coined by Charles Myers, who also served as a military psychiatrist during the War, as did two other members of the expedition, C. G. Seligman and William McDougall). It was the fame he gained as a shell-shock psychiatrist that was Rivers's greatest, and he become Britain's leading advocate of Freudian therapy – although Rivers argued that Freud had overemphasized the importance of sexual urges in human motivation, suggesting that the instinct of self-preservation was the most important of human drives. His war work brought Rivers into association with prominent British cultural figures (Siegfried Sassoon, Robert Graves, Arnold Bennett, and Bertrand Russell among them) and led him to embrace a public role; at the time of his death, he was standing as a Labour candidate for Parliament. Then, at the end of his life, he also declared himself in sympathy with the DIFFUSIONIST anthropology of G. Elliot Smith and his student W. J. Perry (Rivers 1926). The association seems puzzling today, but the historical approach to explanation of phenomena that Rivers had learned as a physician informed the diffusionist approach, although the details of its explication made it vulnerable to justifiable attack by anthropologists in the 1920s.

Rivers and his colleagues on the Torres Straits Expedition – especially its organizer,

A. C. Haddon, and Seligman – assumed prominent roles in organized anthropology in Britain at the turn of the century, engendering a line of professional descendants. But Rivers's professional progeny were equally important in psychology. Through his student Myers his ideas had considerable influence in applied psychology, and through his student F. C. Bartlett his lineage in academic psychology was arguably the dominant one in Britain through the 1960s. In his capacity as an anthropologist he taught A. R. RADCLIFFE-BROWN, and he was (informally) a mentor to Bronislaw MALINOWSKI as well. Thus, he may be seen as a progenitor of the FUNCTIONALIST school of anthropology. Not only did he stand as mentor to the two men who articulated functionalist principles, but he also provided anticipatory formulations of these principles, most notably in his contributions to the 1912 edition of the handbook *Notes and queries on anthropology*, which Malinowski used as a guide in his field research.   HK

further reading Kuklick 1991; Slobodin 1978

role, role-playing A role is a part or function taken or assumed by any person or structure in a society. Role-playing calls attention to how the self is presented to others or to what people who interact expect of each other.

Appropriately, "role" originally referred to the parts played by dramatic actors and was borrowed by social scientists to describe the parts people play in everyday life. Roles are rooted in an individual's status, which is often fixed and assigned (at least for specific contexts). The number of such roles an individual fills on a daily basis, let alone a lifetime, may be quite large. When individuals adopt and put into effect the rights and duties that constitute their status, they are performing a role (R. Linton 1936; see also T. Parsons 1951a).

Role theory began with the publication of George Herbert Mead's influential book *Mind, self, and society* (1934). His emphasis was on overt role-playing and the researchable relationship between role expectations and role performances, particularly socially reflexive behaviors and the problem of

maintaining order in a changing social organization. Labeled "social" or "symbolic interactionism," it has three basic premises: (1) human beings act toward things on the basis of the meanings that the things have for them; (2) these meanings are handled in, and modified through, an interpretive process used by people in dealing with the things they encounter; and (3) parties to such interaction must necessarily take each other's roles into account, becoming simultaneously actors and audiences.

Interactionism stresses the microanalysis of informal encounters, in gatherings on the street, businesses, or courtrooms. An important early work in this tradition was *The presentation of self in everyday life* (1956) by the sociologist Erving Goffman, who used the language of dramatic performance to analyze the way people present themselves through roles in order to control both their own images and the overall themes of the interaction. For Goffman role was an achievement within specific social interactions and, since role performance could fail, its enactment required constant monitoring and negotiation. "Life may not be much of a gamble," he wrote, "but interaction is" (ibid. 243).

Representative studies of social role-playing and interaction include those by Glaser and Strauss (1964, 1971) on the interactions of hospital personnel, Goffman (1961) on the moral career of the mental patient, L. Lofland (1973) on the interaction of strangers, and T. Parsons (1951b) on illness and the role of the physician. One of the best recent studies is Kapferer's (1983) role-performance analysis of Sinhalese demon exorcisms in southern Sri Lanka.

Roles are important sources of tension and psychological stress. In a classic study S. Lieberman (1956) showed that factory workers who received either promotions or demotions experienced attitude changes and stress upon assuming their new positions, the product of shifting role expectations. When the original roles were restored, the levels of stress were reduced. This theory of role conflict and psychosocial stress was developed in detail by sociologist Robert K. Merton and enshrined in his *Sociological ambivalence*

(1976), which argued that conflict stems from the social situations in which incompatible attitudes or values are simultaneously expected by one person in the course of one relationship. Applying this idea to the study of physicians, Merton (1982) found they experienced considerable ambivalence because their ideal role demanded that they avoid becoming callous while still remaining emotionally detached in their attitudes toward patients (see also C. Nuckolls 1993).

Like Merton, anthropologist Victor TURNER examined social roles in conflict, because "conflict seems to bring fundamental aspects of society, normally overlaid by the customs and habits of daily intercourse, into frightening prominence" (1974: 35). Conflict manifested itself in public episodes of tension that erupted into "social dramas" that had a "processual form" of four main phases: breach, crisis, redressive action, and reintegration. Norms for the performance of roles are brought into high relief by being broken, and in trying to fix them, social group reveal aspects of functioning. Turner developed this analysis of role performance extensively in a series of studies (1957, 1967, 1968, 1975), focusing primarily on life crisis and divinatory rituals among the Ndembu of Zambia.   CN

romantic love   In Western folk culture, romantic love is portrayed as a mysterious attraction to an adored other person; life without the beloved is felt not to be worth living, while being close is an ultimate value in itself. Unlike the love of the Medieval courtier (Boase 1977), which emphasized the inferiority of the lover and the chastity of the beloved, romantic love in the modern West is conceived of as equalizing and sexual. It therefore cannot include the love of a mother for a child, or the love of God, nor can it be for a thing or a cause.

Rather, romantic love is understood as characteristic of ADOLESCENCE and as the precursor to MARRIAGE. It must occur spontaneously, and the intrusion of planning is almost as great a sin against love as selfishness. In love the attraction of the lovers is thought to oppose all social con-

straints, so that lovers are capable of obliterating boundaries of age, class, and race in their passion (although in fact, most lovers are far more alike than different).

When love occurs between two people, the couple is supposed to achieve a state of happiness extolled and sought after throughout contemporary Western culture. In truth, it is not too much to say that falling in love, rather than participation in RELIGION, is the locus for the experience of transcendence for most persons in modern Western society.

Yet romantic love has been little studied anthropologically or cross-culturally, and for many the final word was Linton's derisive dismissal of romantic love as a product of American media-induced self-delusion (R. Linton 1936: 95). Exceptions include W. Goode's early article (1959), where he placed cultures in a continuum according to their attitude toward romantic entanglement and the means by which desire is controlled and channeled. Later, Coppinger and Rosenblatt (1968), among others, sought, with ambiguous results, to make cross-cultural statistical correlations between love marriage and residence patterns.

More influential have been the attempts by Stone (1977b) and other historians to correlate the appearance of romantic love in the West with the atomization accompanying the rise of capitalism. Macfarlane (1986), on the other hand, argued that a culture of romantic love in England preceded, and contributed to, the rise of capitalism, not vice versa.

Elsewhere, Endelman (1989), taking a psychoanalytic perspective, asserted that romantic love cannot exist in "primitive" societies because of a supposed absence of intense bonding between mother and child. In contrast, Jankowiak and Fischer (1992) made claims for the cross-cultural universality of "falling in love," citing the love poetry and concern for sexual attractiveness that exist in various premodern cultures. Romantic love here is seen as sexual idealization, and is connected to a universal biological urge enticing lovers (especially men) to greater commitment to their mates and their offspring.

The biological approach has considerable appeal, but it must be noted as well that in cross-cultural terms romantic enchantment often stands opposed to marriage and child bearing, which is a political, not an emotional, relationship. Furthermore, romantic love in many other cultures is explicitly portrayed as nonsexual, as in the bond between the courtier and his lady love, or in the Victorian contrast between virginal pure love and illicit sexuality. Finally, a type of romantic love certainly flourished in ancient Greece, but was between men.

Another, more interpretive perspective is taken by those, such as the philosopher Robert Solomon (1981), who understand love as an act of imagination reflecting individualistic and self-actualizing values characteristic of Western society. Here love is seen as an example of what Michelle Rosaldo called "embodied cognition," that is, as a culturally specific symbol system felt in the body (1984: 138).

Lindholm (1988) took a more comparativist approach, arguing that romantic love is best understood as a form of intense idealization of a particular other person (GENDER is a secondary factor) roughly equivalent to other forms of idealization, such as CHARISMA, where one finds similar expressions of self-less ecstasy coupled with suicidal despair. Like charisma, romantic love is limited in time, and tends toward rationalization. In this definition sexual desire, equality between the lovers, a transformation of love into marriage, and the association between love and adolescence are taken to be secondary factors.

Romantic love, then, is one of the most complex and compelling of human emotional states. Anthropological understanding of this powerful experience is in its infancy. Treading a line between poetry and science, anthropology needs to consider both the subjective reality of romantic states, as revealed in discourse and behavior, and the ambiguous relationship between personal love and cultural obligation.   CL

further reading L. Abu-Lughod 1990;
Alberoni 1983; Gaylin & Person 1988;
Mukhopadhyay 1979; Pope 1980; I.
Singer 1984–7

S

sacred   denotes a class of objects, events, and beings that a culture defines as different from those of ordinary reality. As an adjective, "sacred" refers to a quality of difference, of being separate from, and more important than, the profane world. In many cases, it implies a link to an unseen or supernatural order of existence. A church or a priest may be sacred because of their association with a deity; a rock or a tree may be sacred because of an association with SPIRITS, ANCESTORS, or magical forces. Sacred objects are commonly central to both religious and secular rituals. In some cultures, though by no means all, sacred things are regarded with a special reverence, awe, and fear (Eliade 1959).

The sacred has been an important topic in the anthropology of RELIGION. Emile DURKHEIM (1915) argued that sacred objects are symbols of the social system. By representing the society, the sacred provides a tangible focus for the expression and inculcation of feelings of dependence on the group. The demarcation of this sacred realm, he said, is the root of all religion. Max WEBER (1946) correlated conceptions of the sacred with different types of religion. Whereas "primitive" religions see the sacred as permeating the world around them, the world religions concentrate the sacred in a few objects, deities, and persons. More recently, symbolic anthropologists have focused on the meanings of sacred symbols. Clifford GEERTZ (1973), for example, argued that sacred symbols contain complex messages about society and values that serve to make a culture's definition of the world seem both real and right.   AB

See also MAGIC, RITUAL, SYMBOLIC AN-
   THROPOLOGY, TABOO
further reading Gennep 1960

sacrifice   generally refers to the killing of animals or the destruction of goods in a religious context. There are many problems of definition, however. In their classic essay *Sacrifice* (1964), which provides the starting point for most recent anthropological discussions, Henri Hubert and Marcel MAUSS initially included "any oblation, even of vegetable matter" but soon began to speak of the sacrificial "victim" (1964: 12–13). The narrower sense is sometimes specified with the phrase "BLOOD sacrifice." When goods are involved, it is common to speak of "offerings," and it is not always clear how offering and sacrifice are distinguished. Moreover, sacrifice does not always involve physical destruction; in the Christian tradition it is familiar to speak of sacrifice in the sense of personal dedication or self-denial.

Since definitions are an attempt to isolate the essence of the practice, each implies a theory of sacrifice. Invariably, however, there are many cases that will not fit the theory, and this finding supports Luc de Heusch's (1985: 23) argument that we would do better to renounce any "formal universal sacrificial schema." Instead, the character of sacrifice should be examined in indigenous terms, and comparisons made between ethnographic cases without prejudgment.

Nevertheless, in a century of speculation, several aspects have been emphasized that are indeed prominent in the ethnographic record. These include:

Communication: Hubert and Mauss, following their teacher DURKHEIM, placed emphasis on the distinction between profane and sacred domains, with sacrifice providing a mode of communication between the two. The sacrificer (the person or persons sponsoring the rite) and the victim are all in different ways drawn into the sacred realm, so that they take on, for a time, the nature of gods. In its language of transitions back and forth, often spatially conceived, the essay by Hubert and Mauss prefigured the notion of RITE OF PASSAGE developed some years later by Arnold van GENNEP. Its utility is lessened, however, by its constant use of ethnocentric terminology taken directly from the Judeo-Christian tradition, such as "communion," "votive," and "piacular."

Substitution: Claude LÉVI-STRAUSS also saw sacrifice as connecting humans and deities. The connection is not made by movement between domains, however, but by a series of species linked together by the substitutability of one for another. His account is characteristically abstract; it occurs at the end of an extended discussion of TOTEMISM, compared with which Lévi-Strauss (1966: 223–8) seems to have found sacrifice inferior, even "false." Nevertheless, he pointed to a feature that is indeed widely characteristic of sacrifice. In the classic Nuer case described by E. E. EVANS-PRITCHARD (1956), an ox is the most prestigious victim, but a goat may be substituted for it without loss of ritual efficacy, and for the goat a hen, for the hen an egg, and in the last resort a common cucumber, which is cut with a spear as if it were an ox. In some series, the most weighty sacrifice of all is a human one – so that ritual regicide and headhunting may be brought into the schema – or even the sacrificers themselves, as in the Christian notion of self-sacrifice.

Commensality: Almost invariably, it is domestic ANIMALS that are sacrificed, and the meat they provide is seldom allowed to go to waste. Since the beasts have already been presented to deities, it is as if humans share a meal with them. This is the aspect developed by William Robertson SMITH (1889), who saw commensality as the mark of bonds between members of the community, and sacrifice as their extension into the supernatural world. This is the usual sense in which the term "communion" is used in anthropology.

Catharsis: Girard (1977) argued that the key feature of sacrifice is its VIOLENCE; by shedding blood, a community externalizes animosities between its members. Girard drew on Freudian theory, but is not supported by the ethnographic data. People who keep domestic animals generally regard the butchering of them as a routine matter hardly arousing any passion at all, let alone a catharsis.

Gift: Perhaps the oldest theory of sacrifice sees it as prestation. As Edward Burnett TYLOR remarked, "sacrifice is a gift made to a deity as if he were a man" (1871, 2: 340). As the Nuer case illustrates, the more valuable the gift to the giver, the more important the sacrifice. Moreover, the PRAYERS accompanying sacrifice often emphasize the act of giving. The same language, however, often acknowledges that the deities are the source of all life and wealth, and so underlines the unequal nature of the exchange. Nor does the gift theory explain why in most cases only a narrow range of animals or objects are judged suitable as sacrifices.

In particular ethnographic cases, any of these aspects may find representation, or a combination of them, or new ones not yet enshrined in theory. Consequently, the debate concerning the nature of sacrifice remains lively.   PM

See   also   RELIGION,   SYMBOLIC ANTHROPOLOGY

sanctions   are responses to actions that violate the social norms of a group. These reactions can be either positive (approving) or negative (disapproving). Taken together, social sanctions function to maintain social order and social control by rewarding conformity and punishing DEVIANCE, reintegrating a society after a breach. Whether delivered by individuals or by a group, sanctions are based on a collective normative order and reflect a shared sense of morality and wrong-doing. Legal sanctions are only one of many kinds of sanctions, which also include social pressure and self-help strategies (such as vengeance).

This understanding has its foundation in RADCLIFFE-BROWN's classic definition of a sanction as a social reaction by a society, or a good portion of its members, to varieties of behavior that are thereby approved or disapproved (1934: 205). His analysis of social sanctions focused on group rather than individual reactions and assumed that societies had a consensus about norms. For Radcliffe-Brown the function of such social sanctions was to restore social order through a collective reaction to misbehavior, thus reintegrating the community and restoring balance and harmony.

Theorists, particularly those working on URBANISM as a way of life (Wirth 1938), distinguish between formal sanctions (imposed by the state) and informal sanctions (imposed by members of a community). Formal sanctions are used most often in urban settings and include arrest and imprisonment; in rural areas informal sanctions are more prevalent and include gossip, nicknaming, practical jokes, and OSTRACISM.   SEM

See also DISPUTE RESOLUTION, LAW, LEGAL ANTHROPOLOGY, POLITICAL ANTHROPOLOGY

further reading Epstein 1968

Sapir, Edward (1884–1939)

Edward Sapir was one of the most outstanding students to emerge from Franz BOAS's program in anthropology at Columbia. He is most noted for his pioneering work in LINGUISTICS (particularly on North American Indian languages) and PSYCHOLOGICAL ANTHROPOLOGY. His interests in the arts and aesthetics laid the foundations for HUMANISTIC ANTHROPOLOGY.

Sapir was born in Prussia in 1884 into a Lithuanian Jewish family that soon emigrated to the United States. Living in New York as a child, he excelled in school and entered Columbia University, where he studied Germanic and Indo-European philology, the heart of linguistics at the turn of the century. However he quickly came under the influence of Franz Boas and took his graduate degree in anthropology. He did extensive fieldwork in the Indian languages of California and the Northwest Coast of North America and received his doctorate in 1909 at the age of 25.

Sapir was regarded as the leading figure in linguistic anthropology at the time because of natural ability, extensive fieldwork, and his formal training in classical linguistics (the last a rarity at the time).

Most of this research was carried on under the sponsorship of museums, which often expected scholars to add to their collections by acquiring odds and ends of material culture or whole sets of ethnographic information. Sapir's intense focus on linguistics often put him at odds with such sponsors and he appears to have suffered fools less than gladly.

His first major academic appointment was as Chief Ethnologist for the Geographical Survey of Canada in Ottawa in 1910, where he served until 1925. Here he pioneered work on Indian languages and developed a theory of classification of all North American Indian languages that divided them into six basic stocks (Sapir 1990–91). He also attempted to integrate history and ethnological theory (Sapir 1916).

Of greatest influence during his Canadian period, however, was the publication of a general book on linguistics, *Language* (1921). The work brought him international recognition and foreshadowed many of the advances in linguistic theory made explicit by others in later decades. (The book remains in print and influential to this day.) The introduction of the Boasian tradition to Canada by Sapir has led many to credit him as the founder of modern anthropology in Canada, a reputation tarnished (in Canadian eyes) by his leaving for Chicago in 1925, never to return.

At the University of Chicago (1925–31), and then at Yale (1931–9), Sapir shifted his research focus from linguistics to psychology. He had always had a large range of interests, but it was not until he moved out of a museum position and into an academic department that they could be developed. Along with close friends Ruth BENEDICT and Margaret MEAD, he is considered one of the founders of the CULTURE AND PERSONALITY school, which attempted to explore the psychological dimension of the Boasian concept of CULTURE and translate it into research projects. In his case these plans were largely unfulfilled: a planned book on culture and psychology was never completed and his proposed institute for cultural psychiatry never came into being. But his ideas, published mostly as articles (Sapir 1949), still had a great impact, particularly on the many students who attended his lectures (Sapir 1994).

By drawing on linguistics Sapir was able to raise many important questions, such as the relation between language and culture. Perhaps the most famous is the WHORFIAN HYPOTHESIS (also called the Sapir–Whorf hypothesis). It contended that highly habituated forms of language structured thought so that the "real world is to a large extent unconsciously built up on language habits of the group" (Sapir 1929a). Although cross-cultural research largely rejected this hypothesis (at least in its strict form), it entered popular culture as a firmly fixed notion.

Sapir died in 1939, but the influence of his work remains strong. His push to professionalize linguistics not only ensured its role in anthropology but laid the foundations for the emergence of linguistics as an independent discipline that would be concerned with all the world's languages. Sapir's insistence on the importance of studying people's creativity in responding to cultural and historical forces became the foundation for humanistic anthropology in the mid-1970s. His own interest in the arts, and poetry in particular, inspired a number of later anthropologists to break down the boundaries between the humanities and social sciences.   TB
See also COMMUNICATION, GRAMMAR, HISTORICAL LINGUISTICS, LANGUAGE, LIFE HISTORY
further reading Darnell 1990; Koerner 1984

science *See* TECHNOLOGY

section systems are a form of MARRIAGE EXCHANGE, classically associated with the Aboriginal people of Australia, in which a society is divided into a number of marriage classes, or sections, amongst which wives circulate such that each group is wife-giver to one group and wife-taker from another.   MR
See also ALLIANCE THEORY

sedentary societies *See* AGRICULTURE, EVOLUTION, INTENSIFICATION, PASTORAL NOMADS

segmentary lineage system is a model that uses the principles of unilineal DESCENT to explain the homeostatic functioning of acephalous or non-centrally organized societies. In anthropology the best-known such model is found in E. E. EVANS-PRITCHARD's *The Nuer* (1940), but as far back as 1873 A. Hanoteau and A. Letourneux described the Berbers of the Kabyle as possessing a system of interlocking alliances that produced, they believed, a balanced social structure that was leaderless, simple, and democratic. Emile DURKHEIM (1933) used their data as well as W. Robertson SMITH's (1885) historical recreation of early Arabic social organization as the basis for his famous theory of the replicative "mechanical" structure of primitive societies.

Evans-Pritchard's theory, however, was more complex than those of his precursors. Where they had only seen balanced opposition at one genealogical level, Evans-Pritchard said that Nuer social organization was built on a system of patrilineal descent that placed each individual in an internally balanced pyramidal structure made up of ever more incorporative levels of segmentation and opposition. Thus, the Nuer are described as segmented in a descending series of groups branching out from the most inclusive "tribal" level through primary, secondary, and tertiary or minimal lineages. The members of segments at each level are said to descend from groups of brothers, so that primary segments are descended from the sons of the apical ancestor, secondary segments from the sons of each of the apical ancestor's sons, and so on down to the minimal level. In principle, at each level of segmentation allies and enemies are automatically given by their relative genealogical position. Or as a Middle Eastern proverb puts it: "I against my brothers; my brothers and I against my (patrilateral) cousins; my cousins, my brothers, and I against the world." Social control in this system was said to be guaranteed by the system of *complementary opposition*, which in cases of social conflict was described as providing a uniquely effective deterrent to socially destructive VIOLENCE, because any individuals in conflict would find immediate support from the entirety of the lineage groups on both sides of the branching point in their segmentary lineages. The two groups would balance each other out and make mediation of the conflict a logical necessity.

The paradigmatic outline of the segmentary lineage system was made by Marshall Sahlins (1961). Aside from the principle of complementary organization and the need for internal mediation of disputes, he noted that segmentary systems replicate genealogical distance on the ground as physical distance between related groups and that membership in lineage units establishes rights to land and co-responsibility in feuds. Sahlins also posited the principle of segmentary sociability, whereby violence becomes more honorable in proportion to segmentary distance, and he drew attention to the relative nature of lineages, which coalesce only when aroused by opposition. As he wrote, "The lineage segment cannot stand alone, but can only stand 'against'" (1961: 333). Finally, he argued that segmentary systems would tend to expand at the expense of less well organized leaderless societies, which did not have the structural capacity to unite against their opponents.

By the second decade after the publication of *The Nuer*, the segmentary model had gained great currency and was being applied throughout Africa as well as elsewhere – especially in the Middle East. However, there were also major criticisms, which pointed to: (1) the lack of fit between the neat organization of descent groups as defined in theory and the often chaotic reality on the ground; (2) the absence of any practical corporate functions such as control over resources, marriage, religious cult, and defense among many of entities said to be lineage groups or clans; and (3) the disturbing way in which lineage affiliation in many tribal societies seemed to be optative and based on practical economic and political considerations rather than ascribed at birth as required by the theory. (See, e.g., E. Peters 1967; A. Kuper 1982b; Munson 1989.) Even Evans-Pritchard himself drew away from his earlier formulation and recast segmentary structure as an ideological or hermeneutic rather than a homeostatic or mechanical model (1950).

None the less, the segmentary lineage organization continues to have its defenders, who argue that it makes sense to use it with caution, as an indigenous conceptual framework that serves, along with other factors, to structure local relationships and rivalries (see, e.g., Gellner 1969; Salzman 1978; Dresch 1986).   CS

further reading Barth 1959b; Fortes 1949b, 1953; Middleton & Tait 1958; Montagne 1930

semantics is employed in philosophy, linguistics, and anthropology to denote the study of meaning in general (Lyons 1977). However, as a result of the increasing prominence of the field of PRAGMATICS in recent decades, the term has acquired a more restricted use. Today it may be said to be the study of referential meaning, such as the use of language to describe or inform, as opposed to other purposive uses (functions) of language, such as to express emotion or to have an effect on an interlocutor.

By far the most work done on the study of meaning has traditionally been limited to reference, on the assumption that this function is the most important for understanding human cognition and behavior (although this would be challenged by the pragmatists). Semanticists also claim the most important or interesting study of referential meaning to be maximally context-free, where context is defined as the immediate situation in which a speaker and a hearer are attempting to communicate with each other in order to be understood. For instance, an informative sentence such as "Gene is 34 years old" can be uttered in a wide variety of contexts, where the speaker and hearer (among other things) will differ, but the referential meaning will remain constant.

COMPONENTIAL ANALYSIS is perhaps the most famous semantic method and theory developed in anthropology, specifically for the study of the (referential) meaning of kinship terms. It originated in seminal articles by Lounsbury (1956) and Goodenough (1956) and was then taken over by linguists and applied to the study of lexical domains outside of kinship. Basically, the aim of this analysis was to elicit from informants a class of denotata (identified in terms of a "universal" genealogical grid) that corresponded to a particular kinship term, and then, from that class, to factor out a set of "components" or "distinctive semantic features" crucial for distinguishing that class of denotata from every other possible class in the local system of kinship. The kinship term would then be defined in terms of semantic (invariant, distinctive) features. This is not the place to review the method in depth or the criticisms of its assumptions (Bolinger 1963; D. Schneider 1984). Nevertheless, as a result of these criticisms componential analysis has considerably waned in influence in recent years.

It is perhaps also safe to conclude that semantic analysis has been eclipsed in importance by pragmatics, thanks especially to the critiques of Silverstein (1976) and others. There have been suggestions in philosophy that semantics is not even defensible in principle (Putnam 1975: 139–52), though these attacks have not been sustained or persuasive enough to eliminate it as a field of study altogether.   SC

further reading Dixon 1971; Jerrold Katz & Fodor 1963; Lakoff 1971; Weinreich 1972

semiotics was used to denote the general study of SIGNS by the philosopher John Locke in the seventeenth century. However, modern semiotics, also called "semiology," was established in the twentieth century by the Swiss linguist Ferdinand de Saussure and the American pragmatic philosopher Charles Sanders Peirce.

Saussure (1959) expressed the relationship between the sign and its object as the relationship between the "signifier" and the "signified." He identified all linguistic phenomena as sign phenomena, and thus established methods for the study of language as the basis for the study of nonlinguistic sign systems. Saussure's theory of signs posited that all speakers of the same language possess a body of shared understanding about the relationship between linguistic signs and their objects, which allows them to communicate. He termed this body of understanding "langue." Individual variations in language use were termed "parole." Langue and parole together constituted "langage" (language).

Peirce was a philosopher of logic who explored the relationship between object, signifier, and the process whereby the relationship between the two is understood, which he termed the "interpretant." He codified this as three levels of relationship, Firstness, Secondness, and Thirdness. Firstness refers to the intrinsic nature of objects. Secondness encompasses the relationship between object and its signifier, and Thirdness between object, signifier, and interpretant (Peirce 1931–58). Concatenation of these relationships produces a highly complex taxonomy of signs in Peirce's writings, but a simplified schema using the terms "icon," "index," and "symbol" gained widespread acceptance and was popularized by Peirce's contemporaries, including Charles Morris (1938).

An icon resembles the thing it represents (a picture of a tree), thus expressing a relationship of Firstness. An index bears an intrinsic relationship to the thing it represents (a weathervane indicating wind direction), thus representing a relationship of Secondness. A symbol is related to the object it stands for by virtue of a convention or agreement (the word "tree" representing a tree by convention among speakers of English), thus representing a relationship of Thirdness. The process of convention or agreement that underlies the construction of symbols is the interpretant and is the result of cultural processes.

Anthropologist Leslie WHITE (1940, 1949) called human beings "symboling animals," and other researchers have claimed that the ability to use signs, or semeiosis, is a basic, and perhaps unique, human capacity. Particular attention has been devoted to the human use of symbols, since these require the culturally dependent interpretant in order to be viable. Recent communication experiments with chimpanzees and other great apes have called into question the uniqueness of humans in using symbols. It is claimed that some of these primates have learned to use noniconic tokens to communicate with humans. Others have learned the rudiments of American Sign Language (Ameslan), the principal language used by the deaf in North America. One chimpanzee, Kanzi, does not speak but has learned to recognize human speech (Savage-Rumbaugh 1986). Current opinion is divided on the question of whether these primates are truly using language or are merely rehearsing stimulus-response training (Wallman 1992).

Whether the capacity to use signs is uniquely human or not, it is certain that humans have enormously elaborate repertoires of sign phenomena incorporated into their culture. The study of language alone is an enormously complex undertaking. Semioticians, such as Umberto Eco (1976), have applied the study of semiotics in virtually every area of human endeavor. An important aspect of the study of signs is the realization, dating from Saussure, that most signs do not exist in isolation but are organized in systems characterized by "oppositions" – the set of cognitive contrasts that differentiate each sign from all the other signs in the system. Thus any given sign is understood more by what it is not than by what it is. The totality of contrasts constitutes a "structure," and the study of any cultural institution (such as kinship) or product (such as a myth) based on the discovery and analysis of structure is called "STRUCTURALISM." The study of semiotics has thus been inextricably linked with this method of analysis (see T. Hawkes 1977), particularly as embodied in the structural analyses of Claude LÉVI-STRAUSS.

Since World War II, semiotics has had a strong influence on literary theory and psychiatry, owing in part to the enormous role of symbols in human psychology, literature, and art. A fusion of literary and psychiatric theory has been a particularly strong intellectual movement in France, and this movement in turn has been influential throughout the world. Among the most influential theorists have been Roland Barthes, Jacques Derrida, Michel Foucault, Julia Kristeva, and Jacques Lacan.

WBe

See also COMMUNICATION, POETRY, PRAGMATICS, SYMBOLIC ANTHROPOLOGY
further reading Sebeok et al. 1964

sex The anthropological study of sexual behavior focuses on the interaction between the biological, psychological, and cultural factors that foster erotic arousal, sexual attraction, and proper sexual behavior around the world (D. Davis & Whitten 1987).

At the turn of the twentieth century research on sexual behavior in non-Western societies was often patchy, highly impressionistic, and simply erroneous. By the 1950s anthropological studies of sexuality relied on CROSS-CULTURAL surveys and in-depth ethnographies to explore sexual behavior. Their methodology produced a number of often highly mechanical accounts of premarital sexual practices, erotic games, and extramarital affairs (C. Ford & Beach 1951). Some of the more interesting findings are: (1) in most societies men are more interested in having a quick orgasm than they are in extensive foreplay; (2) sexual modesty is a panhuman concern; (3) every culture implicitly recognizes and understands the erotic combustibility of sharing food between the sexes; (4) male impotence is associated with cultures that are severely sexuality restrictive; (5) in many societies premarital sex is tolerated provided the girl does not become pregnant; (6) kissing is less common than the manual and oral manipulation of the genitals; (7) sexual morality in every "society is directly related to the extent to which sexual and reproductive relations overlap" (Frayser 1985: 380); (8) rape is more common in cultures with a high degree of interpersonal violence and sexual segregation (Sanday 1981b); (9) "anthropologists have rarely studied the degree to which aging affects sexuality" (D. Davis & Whitten 1987: 76); and (10) actual sexual behavior seldom conforms to conventions of public morality.

Cross-cultural research's strength – finding general patterns – is also its limitation. By focusing on the normative or general pattern and ignoring the implicit exceptions, the full meaning of sexual behavior in a specific culture was overlooked. Anthropologists have sought to correct this methodological bias by producing several highly focused ethnographic case studies exploring how notions of sexuality serve as a primary means for organizing ordinary life (Crocker 1990).

Recently, evolutionary psychologists and anthropologists have sought to understand the forces that account for the universality of sex differences in the pursuit of erotic and romantic satisfaction (Symons 1979). They found that women, for the most part, are more interested in assessing male ambition, industry, income, status, and generosity; whereas men look for evidence of female fertility such as youth and health, sexual exclusivity, reproductive capability, and parental investment. These sex differences account for the "basic asymmetry found in the sexual encounter which gives a woman, especially before marriage, leverage to make considerable demands on a male" (LeVay 1993: 13). In effect, from biology can flow a very rudimentary, yet emotionally charged, kind of sexual display.

Humans' overriding interest in, and fascination with, sex accentuates the problem of how to regulate and control sexuality. Cultures seek to curb the potentially disruptive powers of sexual desire by integration into the institution of marriage or family life. All sexual practices function therefore within some kind of moral system (Davenport 1971).

There is a certain amount of extramarital sex present in every society, with married women (but not married men) having the lower incidence of extramarital sexual relations in all societies. In general, extramarital sexual relations are the "most strictly prohibited type of sexual relationships" (Frayser 1985: 209). PEASANT societies have the strictest codes regulating premarital and marital sexual conduct, and BAND SOCIETIES are the most open in their emphasis on sexual enjoyment.

Cultural attitudes toward sexual behavior range from a deep apprehension (or sex-negative orientation) to an open, naturalistic approach (or sex-positive orientation). Sex-positive communities tend to be small-scale communities where "sexuality is free from the engagements of arranged marriage, centralized religion, property rights, and political control" (Gregor 1985: 5). Whatever their level of social complexity or official position vis-à-vis erotic satisfaction, most cultures are strikingly ambivalent about sexuality and its place in daily life (Broude 1975).

No culture is ever completely successful, or satisfied, with its synthesis or reconciliation of love and sex, though every culture is compelled to attempt one. Whether in the technological metropolis or the tribal forest, in the industrial city or the agricultural village, there is tension between sexual mores and proscriptions regarding the proper context for either sexual acts or romantic displays of love. Ambivalence abounds in the Amazonian tribe of the Mehinaku, where sexual enjoyment is a matter of open discussion but declarations, public or private, of love are ridiculed; while the Fulbe of Nigeria, for example, encourage the pursuit of sexual variety and are thus continuously surprised whenever someone prefers an emotionally and sexually exclusive relationship. Among the Taita of Kenya, men and women do not eat their meals together – a common means of making and keeping the masculine and feminine polarities clear and sharp. It is also a way to lessen romantic entanglements (Jankowiak 1995).

The ambiguities that often arise from men and women seeking sexual satisfaction and emotional intimacy are most vividly found in the two prevalent discourse patterns that surround passionate expression. The Polynesian pattern is organized around savoring erotic sensuality through sexual banter and accentuates sexual imagery in ordinary speech. As with any form of speech, the use of sexual imagery has numerous connotations: good-natured joking, real sexual desire, a secret emotional attachment, or an ambivalence about the opposite sex. Significantly, cultures that favor the Polynesian pattern disapprove of public expressions of love and displays of emotional intimacy, behaviors that are considered to be private matters between individuals. In contrast, the American pattern is organized around the notion of idealized ROMANTIC LOVE, which approves and glorifies public displays of affection in speech and behavior, as long as such displays are not overtly sexual. Although romantic metaphors are the preferred language of courtship, it is understood that the metaphors may range in meaning and implications from pure lust to unrequited affection. In looking back over the historical record, it is painfully obvious that early ethnographers and explorers ignored or misunderstood the numerous forms of affiliation that can exist inside and outside the sexual encounter.

Early researchers were even less observant about HOMOSEXUALITY as a sex-orientation and a life style. Anthropologists have begun to study homosexuality (erotic preference for someone of the same sex) as both a biological and cultural phenomenon. The study has been limited, however, by methodological and theoretical problems that have resulted in focusing more on male and less on female homosexual behavior (Gregersen 1983: 81). Moreover, the "factors responsible for determining a person's sex-orientation are still largely unknown" (LeVay 1993: 129).

There are numerous forms of cross-gender behavior, such as the "manly hearted" woman, cross-dressing BER-DACHE, and gender identity disorders (transsexualism) found around the world (Whitam 1987). The relative frequency in which cross-gender behavior occurs around the world raises intriguing questions about the interplay between, on one hand, the biopsychological factors that affect the perception of stimuli and, on the other, the culturally patterned attitudes that structure the framework for social action.

To date, cultural anthropologists' study of sexual behavior has been more particularistic than comparative in its focus. Regional and topical studies are still rare (D. Davis & Whitten 1987).   WJ

further reading Buss 1994; Gregersen 1994; Herdt 1994; Opler 1965

shaman, shamanism The word "shaman" is derived from the Siberian Tungus word "saman", which means "to know in an ecstatic manner" (Shirokogoroff 1935). As a "technician of the sacred" (to use Mircea Eliade's famous phrase), the shaman is the charismatic figure par excellence, personally incarnating the spirits and inspiring the awe and worship of the congregation. As Weston La Barre (1970: 108) wrote, "the real difference between shaman and priest is who and where the god is, inside or out." Under-

stood in its widest sense as the embodiment of divinity, shamanism may well be the paradigmatic archaic RELIGION.

There remain, however, controversies over the exact way to categorize shamans. Is shamanistic ecstasy distinguishable from possession by a spirit, as occurs in Voodoo rituals? Does shamanism require a magical voyage to the spirit world? Must a shaman be aware of what occurs in the trance? Need a shaman have a tutelary spirit? Nevertheless, the heart of shamanism remains the public enactment of ecstatic TRANCE.

Typically, those who become shamans do not choose their occupation willingly; rather, they are "called" by SPIRITS who lead the initiate into realms of intense, and often terrifying, sensations of personal suffering, powerful emotion, and the disintegration of identity. The ferocity of the initiatory phase varies individually and cross-culturally, but very often the spirits are said to rend initiates, eviscerating them or breaking them into bits.

During the initiatory stage, threatened by visions of disintegration, initiates often appear to be seriously mentally disturbed. Afterwards, the shaman may continue to act strangely, and the relative sanity of shamans has been a matter for anthropological debate (see Winkelman 1986 for a general discussion).

Whatever the actual mental state of the shamans, their "oddness" is normally highly stereotyped. It often involves TRANSVESTISM, which graphically symbolizes the practitioner's "borderline" status – althougth it does not necessarily imply homosexuality, any more than a habitually abstracted expression implies insanity (Czaplicka 1914: 243–55).

Furthermore, in every culture where shamanism occurs, the people themselves clearly distinguish between the authentic shaman's mental state and insanity. Generally speaking, insanity (often culturally defined as spirit possession) is understood to be the precursor of the shamanic gift; however, unlike the madman, the shaman learns to tame the possessing spirits and to enter and leave a dissociated state at will (Noll 1983). The shaman is therefore a curiously divided figure, who is both caught up in, and yet outside of, the trance; a self-conscious actor, as well as the enraptured participant. The degree to which the whole performance is a fraud then becomes a matter of dispute. But despite the use of trickery to increase the awe of the audience, there is fair degree of agreement that the "best" shamans do indeed enter an altered state of consciousness while shamanizing.

Becoming a shaman, then, is a movement from an initiatory phase of identity disintegration, through painful self-reconstruction, and on to rebirth as a transformed practitioner able to control and reveal the potent spirits that fragment other, weaker, souls (see I. Lewis 1971 for this formulation). The powers the shaman acquires through his control over the fragmenting spirits often include an ability to read minds and to see at a distance, the power of x-ray vision, and magical capacities to heal (and cause) illness, to predict the future, and to travel out of the body, becoming one with a spirit familiar in the animal world. The epic battle to attain these powers forms the basis for the shamanic séance, which LÉVI-STRAUSS (1963a: ix) characterized as a kind of "abreaction" that dramatically recapitulates the shaman's original initiatory experience of disintegration and reintegration. Having made a mythic journey to the world of spirits and demonstrated powers of transfiguration and transcendence of death, the shaman then triumphantly returns with magical healing powers (see Grim 1983 for representative accounts). All of this occurs within a highly theatrical collective context in which "the audience consists at the same time of actors and participants" (Shirokogoroff 1935: 33).

Although the great religions of Asia and the Americas may have their roots in shamanic trance (Chang 1983), it is nonetheless the case that public expression of shamanic possession is less acceptable as society becomes more complex and more intolerant of potentially disruptive altered states of consciousness (Bourguignon 1968; Lindholm 1990). Under these circumstances, shamanism is marginalized, female shamans become more prevalent (Ohnuki-Tierney 1980), and the local

shamanic practitioner is often condemned as a WITCH. On the other hand, for the downtrodden, the witch–shaman may appear as a messianic prophet who serves as the inspiration for rebellion (I. Lewis 1971). Thus shamanism may have a crucial political, as well as spiritual, relevance.

CL

See also CHARISMA, DIVINATION, ETHNO-BOTANY, MEDICAL SYSTEMS

further reading Balzer 1990; Bogoras 1904; Devereux 1963; Dioszegi & Hoppal 1978; Erdsman 1967; Harner 1980; I. Lewis 1986; W. Park 1938; L. Peters 1982

sibs are CLANS or a group of clans. This term is now obsolete.   MR

sign In its simplest sense, a sign is anything that is understood to represent something to somebody. A sign can only be understood to *be* a sign when it is in a relationship to the thing it represents. Therefore the nature of the sign is determined by that relationship rather than by any essential quality the sign itself may possess. Furthermore, the relationship between a sign and its object is not intrinsic but is constructed by an external evaluator.

Signs are capable of being perceived. Concrete objects, odors, tactile sensations, written and spoken words, sounds, drawings, and gestures are a few of the many things that can serve as signs. Things represented by signs, by contrast, are without limit in their nature. They can also be quite concrete, like a rock or tree, or highly abstract, like an emotion, a mathematical theorem, or a musical phrase. In this way signs are an exceptionally important tool in human interaction, for they allow actors to concretize and convey personal experiences of the world, mental abstractions, and information about emotions and other inner states to others.

Human LANGUAGE is the most complex system of signs in existence, although humans use many extralinguistic signs as well. The Swiss linguist Ferdinand de Saussure (1959) and the American pragmatic philosopher Charles Sanders Peirce (1931–58) are generally acknowledged to be the founders of the modern study of signs, called "SEMIOTICS" (or "semiology").

WBe

See also COMMUNICATION, SYMBOLIC ANTHROPOLOGY

sister exchange is a form of MARRIAGE EXCHANGE in which two men, or members of two different kin groups, exchange actual or classificatory sisters as wives.

MR

See also ALLIANCE THEORY, RESTRICTED EXCHANGE

slavery is the product of the capture or purchase of human beings who, along with their descendants, are put to some use or sold or bartered to others. If we take such practices as the core of slavery, then it is not surprising that it should have been so widespread among human societies, though with an enormous range of variations around this simple core.

The most prevalent Western image of slavery derives from the particular and unusual systems of slavery that existed until recently in the New World and included the ownership of human beings as property to be used, bought, and sold, the primary use of slaves as uncompensated labor, and the placement of slaves in the lowest social stratum. Here, slavery was an economic institution where the idea that slaves lacked "freedom" was a key issue in defining their condition.

While some anthropologists have adopted this image as the basis for a universal definition of slavery (Nieboer 1910; Meillassoux 1991; J. Watson 1980), others (B. Siegel 1945; Miers & Kopytoff 1977) have argued that cultural variations render any such definition problematic. In Western thought, slavery is the antithesis of civic freedom. The free citizen is one who is not owned by another, who cannot be sold, who labors for others only by choice and for compensation, and who enjoys basic civic rights. The slave is none of this. Yet outside of the West, these seemingly fixed elements, and the configuration itself, fade away. Even "freedom" becomes a slippery concept, for what is considered normal individual autonomy varies greatly between societies. In other cultures the meaning of

"ownership" depends on the specific culturally defined rights that the "owner" holds in an object or a person. Indeed in many small-scale societies, such rights were traditionally vested not in individuals but in kin groups, which owned all their members and had the right to dispose of them by homicide or sale. Similarly, notions of free and unfree labor were ambiguous in societies where markets for compensated labor did not exist and the kin group normally owned its members' labor and its fruits. Finally, there is not necessarily a fixed relationship between social stratification and slavery: slavery may exist in the absence of social stratification or may not be a factor in it.

All this does not mean that slavery as understood by Westerners is purely a recent New World phenomenon. Many societies (ancient and medieval Europe, the ancient and Islamic Middle East, South and Southeast Asia) had similar institutions. But these also had features not found in prototypical Western slavery. Whereas in the New World slavery was bound up with distinct differences in appearance ("RACE"), in most societies slaves came from within the society or from nearby regions and they differed little in appearance, or (often) in culture, from their masters. Whereas the use of slaves was almost exclusively economic in the New World, in most other societies and historic periods slaves were also used as social and political resources, as wives, kinsmen, warriors, or bureaucrats. In some cases, such as Ottoman Turkey and Mameluk Egypt, a powerful self-perpetuating palace guard consisting of slaves sometimes controlled the regime. At these extremes, the very use of the term "slavery" becomes questionable and even absurd.

In brief, the theoretical issue is this: the fact that someone acquires complete control over a person says very little about how that person is used. Enslavement is an open-ended process that can involve quite different social trajectories. The notion of the slave as property holds well enough at the initial stage of the process, when a person is withdrawn from his or her social position (within or outside the society), deprived of social identity, and placed under the full control of the master. The person is socially dehumanized and depersonalized, undergoing what Patterson (1982) called "social death." But if put to a new social use (rather than being immediately disposed of by human sacrifice or resale), he or she must be repersonalized, given a new social identity, and inserted into a new social niche. This repersonalization may be minimal, as in much of New World slavery, or it may be socially dense, as in most African societies. The slave's trajectory in the host society depends on the social, political, and economic possibilities inherent in the structure of the society. The use of acquired persons as labor is but one of many possibilities, and by no means the simplest one. A nomadic hunting–gathering society would find it hard to use acquired persons as a labor force, for such use presupposes an economy in which labor can produce a usable surplus and a social system in which social controls over forced laborers can be effective.

The more socially and economically complex a society, the wider and more varied the possibilities of using human beings. In political and economic middle-range societies (and these constitute the largest portion of the anthropological sample), various kinds of kin group have usually been the fundamental social units. The competitive power of a kin group lay in its size, which could be increased by using acquired strangers as quasi kinsmen by ADOPTION. Here, the slave's potential trajectory led to assimilation. In more complex societies in the Middle East and Africa, the range of uses was much wider: in addition to being wives and relatives, slaves became retainers, dependents, trading agents, warriors, bureaucrats, and high functionaries, as well as household servants and laborers on farms and in mines. The fact that some slaves occupied powerful positions contradicts the assumption that slaves necessarily constituted a bottom stratum or class.

While social complexity offers many possibilities, it does not determine how slaves are actually used. For example, in the very complex antebellum American South slaves were overwhelming confined to the narrowest of uses: as laborers. The reasons for this included both the cultural attitudes about the very different origins of slaves and masters, and the slave-based economic specialization of the South as a producer of cotton in a large international system. This takes us back to the point made at the beginning – that the common Western (and especially American) image of slavery derives largely from a very unusual variant of it, one that is not easily transposed to most other societies.   IK

further reading Kopytoff 1982; Landtman 1938; J. Miller 1993; Winks 1972

Smith, W. Robertson (1846–94)

William Robertson Smith was born in Aberdeenshire, Scotland, in 1846. Educated at Aberdeen and Edinburgh, he was Professor of Hebrew and Old Testament Exegesis at Aberdeen, coedited the ninth edition of the *Encyclopedia Britannica*, and succeeded W. Wright as Thomas Adams Professor of Arabic at Cambridge. In his twenties he also published on philosophy and mathematics.

The son of a Free Church minister, he was expelled from his Aberdeen post by the "Wee Frees" for promoting modern forms of Bible criticism (Smith 1878). His influence on French anthropologists such as MAUSS and DURKHEIM and on British anthropology was vast.

Smith contended that, in ancient RELIGION, practice was prior to doctrine, and ritual to myth. His pursuit of tacit assumptions that inform practice is intensely modern. Also, "The circle into which a man was born was not simply a human society . . . for the social body was made up not of men only, but of gods and men" (1889: 30–1). This, with the work of Fustel de Coulanges, pioneered a sociological approach to cult and ritual. Smith's analysis of Arabian kinship was warped by the evolutionary doctrine of his friend John McLennan. Nonetheless, *Kinship and marriage in early Arabia* (1885) is the basis for important later views of "segmentation," and more generally for analyses of the self-definition of groups. Smith visited the Arab World more than once and wrote encyclopedia entries on a wide range of Arab topics as well as on Hebrew scripture. His scholarship and originality make him worth reading still.

His "communion" theory of SACRIFICE is not applicable everywhere. His views of TOTEMISM and MATRIARCHY were of their time, as was his view of moral progress from collective to individual religiosity. But his contention that everyone belongs, simply by upbringing, to a "natural society" marks the real beginning of social anthropology.   PD
further reading Beidelman 1974b; Dresch 1987; W. Smith 1882, 1912

social anthropology *See* ANTHROPOLOGY, CULTURAL AND SOCIAL

social change Most descriptions and theories of culture and society attempt to account for the dynamics and effects of change. However, for some time the consideration of change tended to be an afterthought – often the final chapter of an ethnography – rather than the central concern it is becoming today. Among the more important reasons for this were an anthropological focus on small-scale, non-industrial, "traditional" societies, and the nature of dominant analytic paradigms of FUNCTIONALISM, structural-functionalism, and STRUCTURALISM, and their stress on system coherence, institutional integration, and relative inattention to historical forces. Various cultural ECOLOGICAL, cultural EVOLUTIONIST, and CULTURAL MATERIALIST perspectives gave greater place to questions of change. A growing stress on historical forces, especially among those influenced by Marx and WEBER, has given issues of change a more central position and is sustained in POSTMODERN and deconstructionist perspectives.

Many anthropologists would assert that the circumstances of social and political life are constantly changing and new cultural meanings continually being invented. Max GLUCKMAN, a structural-functionalist anthropologist influenced by marxist and other historical approaches, claimed that change was the routine and less difficult to understand than the capacity of some cultural and social systems to maintain particular institutional arrangements over relatively long periods of time. Gluckman distinguished repetitive change or change *within* a system from revolutionary changes or change *of* a system. In the former circumstance the dynamics of the system tended to reproduce the same institutional arrangement; in the latter change was marked by a total reformation of the cultural and social order. There is some similarity here with LEACH's (1954) discussion of political change in Highland Burma. Both scholars focused on the role of internal conflicts and contradictions in promoting change. Gluckman and others in "the Manchester School" were critical of other functionalist approaches that described change as marked by social disorganization and social breakdown or as progressive ADAPTATION and ACCULTURATION (usually to dominant cultural and social forces). Their constructions of disorganization arose from the conflation of different systems: for example, interpreting forms of city life in the terms of conceptions of relatively isolated village communities (Malinowski 1945; Redfield 1955). Such approaches were often unidirectional, failing to see that distinct structurings of social action could coexist. Functionalists and others confused situational shifts in the styles of action with long-term historical changes in the forms of social institution. Furthermore, as many ethnographers have now shown, modes of SOCIAL ORGANIZATION and customary activity are not inimical to innovative economic and technological circumstances and may give them particular force, as Dore (1967) and C. GEERTZ (1963d) described for Japan and Indonesia respectively.

Social change and the concept of social transformation are occasionally used interchangeably. The notion of transformation generally indicates a reorganization in overall cultural or structural arrangements which while distinct, nonetheless maintain significant connection or continuity with neighboring or prior forms. LÉVI-STRAUSS (1969–81) examined diverse Amerindian myths and social forms as transformed variations on each other. Such structuralist perspectives have been ahistorical and were not engaged with understanding historical changes. However, Sahlins (1985) adapted a structuralist approach to understanding historical changes in Hawaii whereby he demonstrated the implication of archaic cultural and social institutions in the change into, and invention of, modern Hawaiian cultural and social capitalist forms. Anthropologists usually understand the forces of change as coming from outside. Sahlins indicated that this is also part of the understanding of ancient Hawaiians. But he demonstrated a perspective that highlights the social and cultural forces internal to a society as driving significant transformations in political and economic institutions.

Various approaches in MARXIST AN-THROPOLOGY (materialist, structuralist) are among the more important in understanding social change. They are particularly sensitive to the dynamics of change arising from industrial and technological developments. Recent years have seen them criticized for their economism, over-reliance on such concepts as MODE OF PRO-DUCTION, and their views of necessary and progressive advancement of social and political forms. Some anthropologists have shown that the Western industrial bias of marxist approaches in particular may reduce the applicability of marxist theories to cultural and social forms that have arisen in entirely distinct historical circumstances.

There is a shift in anthropology away from, on the one hand, over-systematized perspectives and grand theories of social changes and, on the other hand, universal and unidirectional theories of social change. Ideas that the Western direction will be the experience of all are now strongly resisted. Western forms are themselves undergoing radical changes with the impact of new technologies and reorientations in bureaucratic, corporative, and state structures. The unevenness of social change is being stressed, as is the fact that it takes multiple historical and cultural courses. Approaches to globalization emphasize the fact that communities, no matter how small or isolated, are part of broader worldwide economic and political changes that do not have a singular course or a homogenizing effect. New and different forms are continually emergent.

BK

See also MODERNIZATION
further reading Banton 1966; D. Miller 1995

social control   *See* GOVERNMENT, LAW, SOCIAL ORGANIZATION

Social Darwinism   refers both to the formal theories of SOCIAL CHANGE elaborated by early twentieth-century theorists such as Lester Ward or William Graham Sumner, and to folk models appropriated from different positivist sources, few of which are Darwinian in the strict sense (Bellomy 1984). The term can be applied more generally to any social theory that stresses the necessity of competition for social progress. The fact that such constructions stress competition rather than selection has led some historians to redefine Social Darwinism as social "Spencerism," after Herbert SPENCER, who coined the term "struggle for existence." Because all social theory at that time had to be at least nominally "Darwinian" to have credibility, pre-Darwinian notions of sociocultural EVOLUTION in anthropology were merged with Spencer's progressivism in the evolutionary schemes of such early anthropologists as Henry MAINE, John Lubbock, Lewis Henry MORGAN, and E. B. TYLOR (Burrow 1966). As a political ideology, Social Darwinism opposed virtually all governmental controls on social or economic processes, arguing that they interfered with the "natural" law of competition. Such extreme views, associated with Spencer, were opposed by staunch Darwinians like T. H. Huxley and by Darwin himself. (Darwin's view of social evolution is that such qualities as sympathy and self-preservation stressed by natural-man theorists of the eighteenth century had evolved by natural selection in the course of competition between groups of primitive people.) In the United States, Social Darwinism was associated with the ideology of industrialists like John D. Rockefeller and Andrew Carnegie, who viewed success in business as proof that competition leads inevitably to progress (Hofstadter 1955). In England, there was also a politically liberal version of Social Darwinism, which held that the origins of humankind should be investigated

scientifically and that Darwinism provided analogies to social behavior with which to attack privilege (G. Jones 1980).   TG
See also EUGENICS

social evolution, social evolutionism *See* EVOLUTION

social exchange examines the patterns of exchange of goods, services, and people to plot and delineate relationships, particularly among groups. Beginning with the work of Marcel MAUSS, the concept of exchange has proved extremely fruitful in anthropology, although there has always been a real problem of distinguishing GIFT EXCHANGE from economic transactions. Indeed, it is evident that in very many ethnographic cases the two cannot be separated. Even in Western, industrial countries, the epitome of market economies, there is an overlap: gifts and sending gifts are big business, while many firms send their valued customers at least a Christmas Card (J. Davis 1972).

One of the main themes of Mauss's famous work *The gift* (1954) is this very embeddedness of the symbolic, moral, legal, and economic aspects of exchange in one another. He attributed this especially to nonmodern and non-Western societies: modern training and INDUSTRIAL SOCIETIES, by contrast, tend to separate these aspects, especially in distinguishing giving from buying and selling. Mauss also regarded giving as a matter of relations between groups rather than individuals, though the latter might always represent the former. Giving also involved surface disinterestedness, masking a triple underlying obligation: to give, to receive, and to return (often with increment), all three being necessary to maintain the relationship, which may be permanent. From Maori material, he took the notion of *hau* (or the "spirit of the gift") as compelling a return, in that the gift contains something of the individual who has given it.

Mauss also discussed MALINOWSKI's (1922) material on the *KULA* of the Trobriands and adjacent groups of islands. In this dual cycle of exchanges, chiefs send red shell necklaces in a clockwise direction and white shell armbands in an anticlockwise direction. The chiefs gain prestige from their control of these items, which are made valuable through their ritual introduction into the cycles of exchange. However, the *kula* does not actually have the embeddedness that Mauss advocated: it is just one of very many categories of exchange recognized by the culture, some of which are purely economic, although it does also oil the wheels of economic exchange.

There are other indications that Mauss's model does not always fit facts on the ground. Ethnography from many stratified societies indicates that reciprocity is not only not required but positively disallowed: in India, for example, one acquires merit by giving to superiors, but provided no return at all is received from them. But this applies to fairly immediate return (direct exchange). In Mauss's defense, it can be said that religious merit is itself a return, though with a considerable delay and not coming identifiably from the recipient of the gift made earlier. There is also a problem here with the acceptance of gifts. Gifts invariably carry the sins of the giver, which the recipient must digest, either through ritual action or by passing them on again with increment – otherwise, the recipient risks losing the excellence that rendered him or her a worthy recipient in the first place (Raheja 1988).

Nonetheless, Mauss fully recognized the intangible in exchange, in the form of political, military, or economic support, prestige, care, and also hostility and warfare. (Others have added words and discourse.) Finally, cycles of even direct exchange can actually be extraordinarily long. The care of aged parents can be seen as a return (and an expected one) for one's own nurture and upbringing, while even tangible exchanges can take place over generations, even lifetimes, particularly systems of continuous MARRIAGE EXCHANGE.

Women are an even more prominent medium of exchange between groups. This development of Mauss's work is above all associated with the work of LÉVI-STRAUSS (1969a), and in that form it has entered the structuralist corpus (see ALLIANCE SYSTEMS, STRUCTURALISM). Another major development is TRANSACTIONAL ANALYSIS

(Marriott 1976), which approaches exchange from the point of view of behavior rather than seeing it as a set of ideas and norms, often arriving at the structure of society by plotting the direction and frequency of exchanges between individuals or groups. In this respect it can be seen as a special case of network analysis, which plots contacts between groups and individuals in a more general sense.

RP

further reading Cheater 1989; J. Davis 1992; Parry & Bloch 1989

socialism is (1) a mode of organizing production, (2) an epoch in economic history, and (3) a label for a wide and diverse array of ideologies. As ideology, socialist thought has accompanied the development of CAPITALISM, providing a focus for critical perspectives and movements against the capitalist system itself, or for diverse social and political experiments aimed at ameliorating the most damaging consequences of capitalist development and inequality. In practice, though not always in theory, both anticapitalist and ameliorative socialisms have concentrated on the action and institutions of the STATE. For ameliorative socialisms, this has involved state regulation of markets and the creation of a range of institutions and programs to support and supplement incomes, provide services to families and individuals, and so on.

For both ameliorative socialists and their critics, the critical distinguishing feature of socialism is state regulation of the MARKET because, if free markets are a defining feature of capitalism, then *any* state involvement in markets can be taken as socialist. But there are two difficulties with this view. First, theorists such as Karl Polanyi (1944) argued that states had been involved in the creation and regulation of markets throughout the history of capitalism and that truly "self-regulating markets" were relatively short-lived and ephemeral phenomena even during the nineteenth century. Second, from a marxist perspective, the critical aspect of socialism is state control of *production*, not state regulation of the market.

Marx focused largely on an analysis of capitalism and said little about socialism

(which he saw as a transitional period toward communism), so it was later generations of marxist theorists and political parties that developed a detailed and practical socialist theory and program. Thus the *theory* of socialism that emerged in the twentieth century was intimately linked with the experience of "actually existing" statist regimes controlled by self-proclaimed marxist and socialist parties in a world still dominated by capitalist production relations (Verdery 1991). The continuing importance of capitalism in the world economy both structured the statist economies themselves and undercut any evolutionist view of socialism as an epoch of economic history.

In a classic statement, Lenin (1926) claimed that the principal contradiction of capitalism was that while production itself became increasingly collective, the appropriation of production remained private. That is, as the scale of production became ever larger and more complexly organized, it still remained in the hands of individual capitalists or corporations. Lenin proposed to resolve this contradiction by having the state control production, as well as the social or collective relations of appropriation. This required that a political movement capture the state in the name of the collectivity, specifically the working class. However, this argument produces a conceptual slippage between the "social" and the "collective" and identifies the state as the agent and instrument of the social. But the state itself is a historical product and agent with "interests." It is associated with the institutional history and structure of the state apparatus, and with "clients" who staff or depend upon it, its resources, income, and power. These problems were especially important given the setting and history of the statist, socialist regimes that actually emerged between 1917 and 1989.

Marx himself was skeptical of the progressive role of the state in any postcapitalist society, complaining that "one does not get a flea-hop nearer to the problem by a thousandfold combination of the word people with the word state" (Marx 1933). For him, the state itself, as it had emerged in capitalist societies, would be abolished and exist only during a "transition period" between capitalism and communism as "the revolutionary dictatorship of the proletariat." But this in itself was no solution, as was to become clear in subsequent developments. For Marx, unlike Lenin, believed that capitalism's contradiction did not lie in the relationship between social production and private appropriation per se, but in the value form itself, in an economy organized around the production of commodities in which even labor power itself could be seen as a commodity. In the context of a commodity economy based on free wage labor, the state's organization and appropriation of production does not resolve anything: it simply replaces one owner with another. In practice, twentieth-century socialist regimes attempted to resolve this problem by creating economies based on the production, circulation, and distribution of use values via state mechanisms of appropriation and distribution, while maintaining the practical alienation of working people from means of production. By one, albeit superficial, reading, this could imply the union of collective production with collective appropriation, but in more direct language it represented social production and state appropriation.

There remains, nonetheless, the importance of socialist thought as a focus for critical perspectives on the development and practice of capitalism itself. As ideal, socialism's sharpest and most perceptive theorists have developed their ideas by means of a critique of the dynamics and fundamental relations of capitalism. The demise of a particular form of statist regime, and of the uncritical and justificatory theories that supported it, could clear the intellectual and political ground for new, creative work.   WR
further reading Konrad & Szelenyi 1979; Verdery 1996

socialization   has been defined as the "intergenerational transmission of culture" (T. Williams 1972) and as "the way individuals become members of a society, embodying in their own experience, and acting out in their learned behavior, a part of the culture of that society" (T. Schwartz 1976b: ix). From the time of Margaret MEAD's pioneering research on CHILDREN

and ADOLESCENCE it has been a continual topic of research and theory in anthropology. Margaret Mead (1963) herself distinguished between enculturation, the process of learning a particular culture, and socialization, which she defined as the demands made on human beings by human societies everywhere. Today the term commonly embraces both concepts.

Culture is normally transmitted from generation to generation by adults to children, and from those expert in a particular cultural domain to novices. But this notion of a direct cultural transmission may be misleading if it assumes that learning is essentially a passive process without active involvement by the learner. Recent studies have stressed that such active processes of meaning making are indispensable in acquiring culture (J. Briggs 1992).

Encounters that lead individuals to embody a specific culture in their own experience, and thereby make it possible for them to be integrated into the flow of social life, may be of various kinds. People encounter culture in the form of significant others (parents, teachers, heroes) who embody culture and with whom they come to identify, or they may encounter culture in the form of rituals into which images of self and life are incorporated, celebrated, and made experientially real (such as major life-crisis rituals of puberty, marriage, childbearing, and death) (Parish 1994). As every foreign-language student knows, to learn and use a language demands engagement with the culture that produced it: and children learn culture as they learn language (P. Miller & Hoogstra 1992; B. Schieffelin & Ochs 1986a). In the stories they tell themselves and each other about the world and the nature of their lives, society, and selves, people create and transmit cultural constructs (P. Miller & Moore 1989; P. Miller et al. 1990). As a result, redundancy about key meanings and values may be built into what for the cultural actor is life and reality (and what for anthropologists are cultural forms of life acquired through socialization) (R. Levy 1973, 1978). People may encounter such key cultural constructs in multiple contexts. Although each context helps actors to learn to organize their behavior and conceptualize themselves in specific cultural ways, it also modulates and shapes, reinforces and qualifies, specific actions and behaviors by transforming their meanings or premises. In terms of connecting self and self-image to social life, what cultural meaning systems choose to mute – and when and how – may be as significant as what they choose to emphasize (R. Levy 1984).

Socialization is not confined to the formal institutions of EDUCATION and social control in a society. Rather, socialization proceeds through multiple channels, informal as well as formal – and these may contradict each other. Thus, socialization does not always proceed in a "top-down" manner (although parents and teachers may define the process in this way), but can occur "from the bottom up," through and within peer groups (P. Willis 1977). Adult values imposed on children and youth who are exposed to alternative value systems may provoke conflict. In some societies this conflict is controlled through age sets, such as among the Masai of East Africa, where rebellious young men (*moran*) are grouped together and expected to act through a stage of irresponsibility until their age set is promoted into adulthood (see AGE SYSTEMS). In other societies adult pressures to conform may lead to alienation from such socialization institutions as schools and family, and to the formation of unsanctioned peer groups that cultivate values in opposition to the adult world. Street-gang membership is a classic example of this process in which alienation from school and family acts as a prelude to gang membership and subsequent "street socialization" (Vigil 1988).

Much recent research in socialization has examined such small-scale processes as the use of narratives and language in adult–child interactions. Although this has produced many insights into socialization, these small-scale socialization processes need to be fixed within larger historical, economic, and political contexts. Since the immediate cultural contexts of socialization always have ties to a wider world, Watson-Gegeo (1992) has argued that uniting these micro- and macroperspectives is essential for a full understanding of socialization processes.

LANGUAGE socialization has been among the most active areas of socialization research in recent years. Research in this field has examined not just processes of language acquisition in childhood, but also the many ways in which language contributes to processes of learning culture and shaping actors for participation in social life (B. Schieffelin & Ochs 1986b). Other topics of contemporary interest include the socialization of EMOTION (Lutz 1988; P. Miller & Sperry 1987) and moral socialization (Shweder et al. 1987; Parish 1994; Much & Shweder 1978; Shweder & Much 1986).   SP

further reading D'Andrade & Strauss 1992; De Vos 1973; P. Mayer 1970; Riesman 1992; Stigler et al. 1990

social networks *See* URBANISM

social organization Broadly speaking, the study of social organization is research on the bonds that link individuals in social groups. In simple societies these connections include descent, sex, age, religion, economic exchange, and marriage alliance; in stratified societies, occupation, ethnic group, race, and class are included as well. Although all these elements are theoretically implicated in the study of social organization, in practice anthropologists have focused primarily on the role of kinship terminology, lineage and clan structure, postmarital residence, and cross-cousin marriage in the construction of social ties.

Anthropological fascination with the relationship between kinship structure and social organization began with Lewis Henry MORGAN's impressive analysis of kinship terminologies from over a hundred societies, accumulated in part through questionnaires sent to traders, missionaries, and consular officials in Asia, Australia, Africa, and Oceania and in part by his own field investigation among Native American groups. From this data, Morgan identified a number of patterns of kinship terminology. Morgan believed these terminological systems represented the survivals of prehistoric marriage practices that generated the social organizations of the societies where they were found. In his great work *Ancient society* Morgan used his kinship material to elaborate an evolutionary scheme of nine stages, building from lower savagery, through barbarism, and ending in civilization. According to this scheme, the simplest "HAWAIIAN" terminology resulted from an early practice of primitive promiscuity, while "IROQUOIS" terminology represented a survival from an early period in which groups of brothers married groups of sisters (Morgan 1877). Our own "ESKIMO" terminology coincides with Western incest prohibitions and marriage patterns.

Morgan's pioneering work was hugely influential, especially in England, where Edward B. TYLOR drew attention to the practice of what he named "cross-cousin marriage" in organizing small-scale societies (Tylor 1865). Elsewhere, John Ferguson McLennan coined the term "EXOGAMY" and speculated on its possible relation to wife-capture and polyandry (McLennan 1896), while Sir Henry MAINE argued that the earliest societies were patriarchal (1883) and, like Morgan, claimed that primitive social organization was based exclusively on kinship relations.

Problems with this perspective soon emerged. For instance, W. H. R. RIVERS of Cambridge began extensive field studies attempting to show that forms of primitive marriage were the direct functional cause of kinship terminologies. In the Pentecost Islands he discovered kinship systems that merged older sister with mother's mother. Rivers decided that this meant that women there had once practiced marriage with their mother's father. However, corroboration of this theory was not forthcoming. Instead, it seemed that the merging of kin terms for older sister and mother's mother was most likely the result of their membership in the same matriclan. Morgan's earlier speculations about the relationship between kinship terminology and marriage patterns proved to be equally problematic.

In the United States, the Boasians Alfred KROEBER and Robert LOWIE generally avoided the British anthropologists' obsession with kinship terminologies. Kroeber shocked Rivers and his students by declaring that there was no necessary relationship between kin terms and social practices

(Kroeber 1909), while Lowie argued that Morgan had wrongly conflated succession, inheritance, and ascription – all of which could vary independently in matrilineal and patrilineal societies. Lowie also noted that religious groups, economic ties, and such non-kinship-based institutions as clubs, sodalities, and age-set organizations could vie with kinship as important factors in primitive social organization (Lowie 1920).

Difficulties with connecting terminology and structure led to the emergence of DESCENT THEORY in the early 1940s. E. E. EVANS-PRITCHARD and Meyer FORTES were the central figures in this movement through their study of the Nuer (Evans-Pritchard 1940) and the Tallensi (Fortes 1949b) and through their joint introduction to *African political systems* (Fortes and Evans-Pritchard 1940a). Also influential was A. R. RADCLIFFE-BROWN's introduction to *African systems of kinship and marriage* (Radcliffe-Brown and Forde 1950). The major focus here was on the workings of SEGMENTARY LINEAGE SYSTEMS that were thought to result from the working of the intrinsic principles of unilineal descent. However, this theory also was harshly criticized for failing to account for actual social complexity and for overemphasizing descent as the most important organizational factor among supposedly unilineal societies.

In 1949 two works of major importance in the study of social organization were published: G. P. Murdock's *Social structure* and Claude LÉVI-STRAUSS's *Elementary structures of kinship*. Murdock's massive work, based on a statistical cross-tabulation analysis of kinship material from his World Ethnographic Atlas, concluded that postmarital residence exerted the greatest effect on the generation of kinship terminologies (Murdock 1949). This result appeared to undermine the basic premise of DESCENT THEORY, i.e., that lineages were the most important determinants of kin terms and related social practices. However, Murdock's study was soon attacked for its problematic use of statistics and for the purported inaccuracy of some of the ethnographic data used in the sample.

Meanwhile, in his equally monumental

study, Lévi-Strauss proposed a solution to the problem posed by Tylor in 1878 concerning the significance of exogamy and cross-cousin marriage. In his analysis of Australian, Melanesian, and Southeast Asian societies Lévi-Strauss was concerned not with descent but with patterns of marriage exchange. Utilizing highly schematized (and idealized) diagrams Lévi-Strauss demonstrated that prescribed patrilateral cross-cousin marriage (father's-sister's-daughter marriage) produced symmetric alliances, in which lineage groups exchanging women both gave and received women in alternating generations. The practice of matrilateral cross-cousin marriage (mother's-brother's-daughter marriage), although it seemed to be only the inverse of the patrilateral practice, surprisingly resulted in a completely different system called asymmetric alliance, where groups exchanging women consistently received women from one group while giving women to another, different group generation after generation (Lévi-Strauss 1969a). This approach, called ALLIANCE THEORY, was said to explain the actual social organization of groups practicing the contrasting types of prescribed cross-cousin marriage. Furthermore, Lévi-Strauss suggested that his method might be expanded through mathematical analysis to decipher the nonprescriptive complex marriage structures associated with CROW and OMAHA terminologies, and even the marriage systems of modern Western societies.

However, alliance theory foundered, like descent theory, on the problem of defining the basic units involved and on the question of whether or not the forms of exchanges of women being described really took place. For instance, Rodney Needham asserted that matrilateral cross-cousin marriage was always preferential rather than prescriptive, and was statistically insignificant and in consequence incapable of affecting social organization (Needham 1963). In defense of alliance theory, David Maybury-Lewis argued that marriage exchange systems were prescriptive "at the level of the model" even though they might be preferential at the level of individuals in social groups (Maybury-Lewis 1965b).

A 1971 article on social organization in the *Biennial Review of Anthropology* predicted that alliance theory, in tandem with innovations in information theory and game theory, would lead to a revolution in the study of social organization. COMPONENTIAL ANALYSIS of the formal relationships among kin terms in a way analogous to the phonetic grids utilized by linguists was said to be the key to understanding social organization (Selby 1971). However, despite these brave words, 1971 was the last year in which the *Biennial Review* covered the field of social organization as such. In fact, within a few years the articles and debates on kinship theory that had filled the pages of anthropological journals were no more.

Despite its intellectual appeal and capacity to generate abstract conceptual generalities, the study of social organization, as traditionally defined by the analysis of kinship terminology and the development of descent and alliance theory, collapsed because it did not take into sufficient account the individual as a social agent. Neither did it consider the important effects of the broad ecological, economic, and religious/symbolic factors that motivate social action. Nor could practitioners agree on the definitions of the major social groups at issue, be they clans, sibs, lineages, descent groups, segmentary lineage systems, or units of marital exchange. And, as Lowie had noted, the emphasis on kinship led theorists to mistakenly downplay the role of clubs, sodalities, and other non-kinship associations in tribal societies.

Meanwhile, other approaches to social organization, which could be described as materialist, marxist, or ecological, proved to be more successful and lasting, though they never quite entered the mainstream of anthropological theory. These methods were primarily associated with Julian STEWARD, who, for example, was able to reliably predict the incidence of polyandry among the Great Basin Shoshone as a function of carrying capacity (Steward 1938). Later, in tandem with Robert Murphy, Steward was able to show by controlled comparison the role of the organization of work in motivating changes from matrilineal and patrilineal societies to neolocal non-lineage-based social organizations among the Canadian Algonquin and the Amazonian Mundurucu (R. Murphy and Steward 1955). In a similar vein, Morton Fried (1967) and Elman Service (1971) demonstrated the relationship between food-production technology, trade, ecological constraints, and the social organization of groups ranging from hunter–gatherers to chiefdoms and states.

Elsewhere, seminal publications by Fredrick Barth (1966), David Schneider (1965), Victor TURNER (1967), Sally Falk Moore (1986a), and Ivan Karp and Kent Maynard (1983) all pointed out the difficulties of reconciling idealized unilineal kinship structures with social practice and suggested a processual approach wherein terminological systems and lineages might be considered as idealizations that individuals manipulated for their own advantage in situations of social conflict. Kinship systems, clans, and lineage groups, in these dialectical analyses, were generated through practice but simultaneously structured practice and gave it meaning for social actors.   CS

further reading Bourdieu 1977; R. Firth 1964; Giddens 1979b; Lowie 1935; Morgan 1871; R. Murphy 1967; Scheffler 1966

social structure *See* SOCIAL ORGANIZATION

society   refers to the totality of social relations among men and women in their various statuses and roles within a given geographical area or among humankind at large. In European medieval social and political theory, the polity, the STATE, and society were not clearly distinguished. The differentiation of state from society emerged only in the sixteenth and seventeenth centuries, most clearly in the work of Hobbes and the utilitarian thinkers. Among modern thinkers, Hegel, and after him Marx, sharply separated the domains of the state and of (civil) society.

In the utilitarian tradition, Adam Smith (1776) clearly distinguished the state from society, concentrating in the main on societal phenomena. The latter were conceived of by him as the world of exchange dominated by MARKET relations. Ever since Smith, economists have concentrated on exchange and market relations, leaving the analysis of states and the polity largely to political scientists. Sociologists, on the other hand, ever since Auguste Comte, have devoted themselves mainly to societal data outside exchange and market relations.

For Hegel the state dominated society and inspired (or ought to inspire) veneration, whereas (civil) society lacked the dignity of the state. Marx, by contrast, concentrated his analytic attention on society and its roots in the sphere of production. To him, struggles among CLASSES built upon the world of production were basic determinants of human EVOLUTION, whereas state developments were only epiphenomena. Hence, though through different pathways, marxists and Comtean writers agree on the primacy of societal phenomena.

We owe to Ferdinand Tönnies (1855–1936), one of the founding fathers of German sociology, the distinction between *Gemeinschaft* and *Gesellschaft* that ever since his days has informed much sociological thought. In a book entitled *Community and society* (1957), which is nowadays perhaps more quoted than actually read, Tönnies compared medieval and postmedieval village communities with modern social structures based largely on market transactions and self-interested exchange relations as first conceptualized in the work of Thomas Hobbes (to whom Tönnies devoted a separate volume). In communities (*Gemeinschaft*), Toennies argued, the *We* had primacy over the *I*. Strong bonds of solidarity linked members to each other. In market- and exchange-based urban societies (*Gesellschaft*), on the other hand, the enhancement of the powers of the individual destroyed communal bonds and led to destructive competitiveness.

Tönnies did not wish to contrast specific historical formations, except as illustrations, but intended instead to delineate two contrasting existential formations that could be found in a variety of settings. He also argued that these were ideal types, whereas concrete historical realities often revealed mixed formations. *Gemeinschaft* predominates in the village community and in the family, in neighborhoods and guilds. *Gesellschaft*, on the other hand, characterizes urban relations, market exchanges and modern governmental structures.

Tönnies was often misunderstood to be a reactionary thinker who hated the modern world and wished to return to idyllic premodern days. This was emphatically not the case. He looked to the future rather than to the past. Having socialist sympathies, he argued that modern trade unions and other social movements provided inklings of a future in which community bonds would again prevail over *Gesellschaft* individualism and self-centered relationships. In the modern world, various types of yearning for new forms of community can be found on both wings of the ideological spectrum, among the nationalist right as well as the socialist left.

Until recently, anthropologists and sociologists used distinct terms to denote human collectivities: anthropologists used the term "CULTURE," sociologists referred to "society." This led to a good deal of confusion and misunderstanding, which the two deans of these respective disciplines at the time, A. L. KROEBER and Talcott Parsons, sought to resolve in a short but seminal paper (Kroeber & Parsons 1958), summarized below.

Sociologists tend to conceive of cultural phenomena as an outgrowth of developments within societies. They are hence seen as derivative. Anthropologists, on the other hand, give determinative primacy to a set of phenomena they denote by the term "culture." To them, societal phenomena are merely parts of culture. To Kroeber and Parsons neither of these terms had methodological primacy *a priori*. Separating cultural from societal aspects does not classify concrete and empirically discrete sets of data, but merely abstracts or selects two analytically distinct sets of phenomena. It serves no purpose to wish to decide which is more "important," "correct," or "fundamental."

For a considerable time in the history of the two disciplines both terms were frequently used more or less interchangeably. This did not do much harm as long as the differentiation between the two disciplines was operational rather than conceptual. Anthropologists tended to confine their studies to nonliterate societies, whereas sociologists tended to study literate ones. But when subject matters between the disciplines tended to overlap, it became imperative to clarify the uses of these terms more precisely. Kroeber and Parsons suggested that the concept of "culture" be confined to the contents and patterns of values, ideas, and other symbolically meaningful factors, whereas "society" should be used to designate the relational systems of interaction between individuals and collectivities.

Suggesting the analytic independence between culture and society is of course not to say that the two are unrelated. They evidently are so related. Provided that the analytic distinction between the two is maintained, it then becomes feasible to decide which of them in a given investigation deserves primary attention. The Kroeber–Parsons conceptualization seems eminently sensible and avoids unnecessary terminological quarrels. Indeed it has been so successful that there has been much more dispute in anthropology about how to define culture itself than in debating the distinction between society and culture.   LC
See also SOCIOLOGY

sociobiology has been defined as "the systematic study of the biological basis of all social behavior" (E. Wilson 1975: 4). The word was popularized by Edward O. Wilson, the eminent evolutionary biologist, Pulitzer-prize winner and conservationist, whose published tome of that name provided an extensive review of social phenomena in the animal kingdom in relation to current theories of population biology, genetics, and evolution.

Wilson's definition would seem to encompass diverse approaches to the study of social behavior, from ecological analyses to neuroscience. Indeed, since "biology" is the study of life in all its aspects, and since only living things are social in any interesting sense, "sociobiology" could be said to encompass all studies of social phenomena. In practice, however, the term has been applied mainly to an explicitly neo-Darwinian approach that crystallized in the 1960s under the influence of W. D.

Hamilton (1964) and G. C. Williams (1966) and has since come to dominate the study of nonhuman social behavior (although "sociobiology" has been largely supplanted in animal behavior studies by "behavioral ecology," which encompasses solitary as well as social behavior).

The hallmark of this approach is explanation of species-characteristic attributes in terms of Darwinian selection and adaptive function or "design" (Dawkins 1986). Researchers ask why the attributes of organisms take the particular forms that they do and not others, and seek answers in terms of the adaptive fit between the attributes and their hypothesized functions. Analytic approaches include optimality analyses (Maynard Smith 1978), systematic patterns of association among attributes across species (P. Harvey & Pagel 1991), and theoretical models of the specific workings of the natural selective process (Charnov 1982).

Like anatomists and physiologists, whose research is guided by their interpretations of the forms and functions of the constituent parts of organisms as devices "for" respiration, vision, circulation of the blood, and so forth (Mayr 1983), sociobiologists are "adaptationists." The details of such social phenomena as mating preferences, seasonal variations in aggressive inclinations, situationally contingent gregariousness, discriminative parental solicitude, etc., are assumed to have functional significance that can be elucidated by appropriate hypothesis testing. Natural selection designs adaptations as solutions to particular adaptive problems that have been sufficiently persistent across generations, both in their essential forms and in their significance. These evolved solutions are necessarily a product of the environmental features that were statistical predictors, on average, of the fitness consequences of alternative courses of action in the past. Functionally integrated systems of many evolved mechanisms may then be said to comprise a "strategy."

When a "reproductive strategy" is imputed to a plant that flowers in response to day length or sprouts in response to a threshold soil temperature, the metaphor is unlikely to be misunderstood. But with animals, the strategy metaphor is sometimes misleading, as one may slip unwittingly from claims about what the organism is "designed" to achieve into claims about what it is "trying" to achieve. The purposive functionality of adaptations invites an uncritical equation between "goals" and "adaptive functions." The seemingly uncontroversial proposition that sexual motivation has evolved to promote reproduction, for example, is sometimes taken to imply that reproduction itself is an objective pursued with strategic flexibility; a "prediction" is then that contraception will be eschewed unless it can be used as a means of allocating reproductive efforts to increase the numbers or improve the circumstances of one's young. By similar logic, voluntary childlessness and vasectomy have been deemed evidence against the "evolutionary hypothesis." But selection can only have designed the evolved mechanisms of information processing, decision making, motivation, and emotion to be effectively reproductive, on average, in the "environments of evolutionary adaptedness" in which the history of selection took place. It is perfectly conceivable that the techno-medical innovations of modern contraception have left people pursuing objectives that no longer contribute to their fitness.

By and large, the sociobiological paradigm is shared by self-termed "evolutionary anthropologists" and "evolutionary psychologists." All are primarily concerned with characterizing the species-typical behavioral "nature" that is shared by all normal individuals and generates behavioral variation as contingent responses, both immediate and enduring (developmental), to social and other environmental variation. Although it is often mistakenly supposed that hypotheses about evolved adaptations imply the existence of heritable genetic variation, just the opposite is true. A substantial amount of heritable variation is *prima facie* (though by no means conclusive) evidence that the attribute under consideration is not an adaptation, since selection tends to eliminate departures from optimal designs. Thus, the fact that human eye color is both highly variable and highly heritable (in some populations) provides a strong hint that iris color is irrelevant to visual function, for that is what would permit heritable variation to persist. Although the process of evolutionary adaptation over the course of generations as a result of natural selection indeed requires heritable variation, selection tends to "use up" heritable variation, leaving the genetic underpinnings of major adaptations (virtually) invariant.

A premise of sociobiology is that the psychological mechanisms and processes that evaluate social information and generate social behavior can be understood evolutionarily in much the same way as functional aspects of anatomy and physiology are understood. Just as the secondary sexual characteristics used by male birds in courtship displays evolve by selection, for example, so too does the form of the display behavior and the contingent determination of when it will be deployed, and so too do the females' mate-choice-preference criteria (Andersson 1994). Presociobiological animal behaviorists such as Lorenz (1941) had likewise assumed that the forms and causal controls of behavior evolve according to the same principles that govern morphological evolution, but they had not combined this insight with explicit analysis of the natural selection process.

Behavioral ecology and sociobiology began to flourish only after the fallacy of naive group-level adaptationism or "greater goodism" (Cronin 1991) was dispelled. Many biologists had blithely imagined that natural selection equips animals with the shared purpose of "the reproduction of the species." G. Williams (1966) demolished this fallacy, showing that because Darwinian selection is predominantly a process of differential reproductive success of alternative "designs" within species, the adaptive attributes produced by selection function primarily to outreproduce rivals; whether the good of the species is thereby advanced is irrelevant.

The other main conceptual development leading to the flowering of sociobiology and behavioral ecology was W. Hamilton's (1964) development of "inclusive fitness" (or "kin selection") theory. Classical Darwinism construed the "fitness" that selection tends to maximize as personal reproduction, but Hamilton noted that selection will favor any phenotype that effectively promotes the replicative success of copies of "its" genes, regardless of whether they reside in descendants or in other relatives. Thus, for example, the social behaviors of sterile worker bees can be favorably selected if they promote the reproduction of a queen closely related to the workers. Hamilton's analysis transformed evolutionists' conception of animals and plants from that of evolved "reproductive strategists" to one of evolved "nepotistic strategists" (see ALTRUISM). This development opened the way to theories of cooperation and conflict (R. Alexander 1974; Trivers 1971), and to a more gene-centered perspective in which some phenotypic manifestations serve the fitness interests of no organism at all but only of sets of genes (Haig 1993).

Darwin (1871) distinguished between "natural selection," which favors those improved phenotypic designs that enhance survival and the efficient transformation of resources into growth and reproduction, and "sexual selection" which is a matter of differential access to mates. Sexual selection may be further partitioned into selection for attributes promoting success in intrasexual competition (such weaponry as antlers) and selection for attributes attractive to the opposite sex, a topic that was neglected for a century but is now a major focus of sociobiological theory and research. Intrasexual competition is not necessarily overtly observable, commonly taking the form of "sperm competition" in the female reproductive tract, and mate choice may be similarly covert (R. Baker & Bellis 1995; Birkhead & Møller 1992). Wide use of DNA fingerprinting has recently revealed that animal mating systems are often rather different from what has been inferred from behavioral observation alone, stimulating new efforts to understand these systems as the products of natural and sexual selection and of the resolutions of conflicts among potential mates and rivals (Davies 1992). The issue of how the threats imposed by disease organisms selectively shape social behavior has also been addressed primarily in the context of sexual selection (Møller 1994).

Anthropology has led the social sciences in the application of sociobiological ideas to the study of human behavior (Betzig et al. 1988; D. Brown 1991; Chagnon & Irons 1979; Eric Smith & Winterhalder 1992). Some prominent anthropologists, such as Sahlins (1976b), have protested that culture has emancipated human behavior from evolutionary adaptationist analysis, but societal differences in social practices and institutions are not arbitrary, and much of the sociobiologically inspired research in anthropology explicitly addresses the sources of cultural variations. Statistical associations exist among marriage practices, modes of kinship reckoning, subsistence ecology, inheritance, incest rules, childhood socialization practices, and so forth. These associations have been increasingly successfully elucidated and predicted by evolution-minded anthropologists (Flinn & Low 1986; Gaulin & Schlegel 1980; B. Low 1989; Thornhill 1991).   MWi & MD

further reading J. Barkow et al. 1992; J. Krebs & Davies 1993; Trivers 1985

sociolinguistics is a term that was coined in the 1950s to try to bring together the perspectives of linguists and sociologists to bear on issues concerning the place of language in society, and to address, in particular, the social context of linguistic diversity. Educational and social policies played a role in turning linguists' attention to some of these questions, as did dissatisfaction with prevailing models of LINGUISTICS, which since the late 1950s has been conceived of as a largely formal enterprise increasingly divorced from the study of languages as they are actually used in everyday life. Although it is still a young field of research, sociolinguistics gathered momentum in the 1960s and 1970s and continues to do so.

Sociolinguistics has close connections with the social sciences, in particular, sociology, anthropology, social psychology, and education. It encompasses the study of multilingualism, social dialects, conversational interaction, attitudes to LANGUAGE, language change, and much more. It is impossible to put all the different approaches

to the topic into neat pigeonholes, each of which is distinct in terms of methodology, goals, and so on. There is considerable overlap, so that, for instance, although dialectologists too have studied speech varieties and language change, they have generally employed quite different methods of data collection and concentrated on rural rather than urban speech.

Different authors writing about what has now become a very broad field have divided it up in various ways. Some distinguish between theoretical and applied sociolinguistics. The former is concerned with formal models and methods for analyzing the structure of speech communities and speech varieties, and providing a general account of communicative competence. Applied sociolinguistics deals with the social and political implications of fundamental inequalities in language use in various areas of public life, such as schools and courts. A glance at the two-volume work *Sociolinguistics: an international handbook of the science of language and society* (Ammon & Dittmar 1987–8), which contains entries for nearly 200 topics, gives an indication of the multifaceted nature of the field.

More often, however, the field is subdivided into two broad headings: macro- and microsociolinguistics, with the macro domain sometimes also referred to as the "sociology of language." Macrosociolinguistics takes society as its starting point and deals with language as a pivotal factor in the organization of communities. Microsociolinguistics begins with language and treats social forces as essential factors influencing the structure of languages.

Fundamental notions such as "language" and "dialect" are primarily social, not linguistic, constructs, because they depend on society in crucial ways. Max Weinreich's oft-quoted dictum, "a language is a dialect with an army and a navy" attests to the importance of political power and the sovereignty of a nation-state in the recognition of a variety as a language rather than a dialect. Situations in which there is widespread agreement as to what constitutes a language arise through the interaction of social, political, psychological, and historical factors, and are not the result of any inherent properties of the varieties concerned.

Because languages are brought into being by acts of political and social power on the part of the speakers, linguistic differences enact and transmit inequalities in power and status. Languages and language varieties are always in competition, and at times in conflict. Choice of a particular language in multilingual societies is symbolic of various social and political divisions. While the media often suggest otherwise, conflicts involving language are not really about language, but about fundamental inequalities between groups who happen to speak different languages. In all these cases language is a symbol of a much larger struggle for the recognition of minority rights.

The notions of "speech community" and "communicative competence" are fundamental to understanding the ways in which social groups organize their linguistic repertoires. A speech community is a group of people who do not necessarily share the same language but share a set of norms and rules for the use of language. The boundaries between speech communities are therefore essentially social rather than linguistic. Sociolinguists use the term "communicative competence" to refer to a speaker's underlying knowledge of the rules of grammar (understood in the widest sense to include phonology, grammar, lexicon, and semantics) and the rules for their use in socially appropriate circumstances. This socially based concept is intended to replace the dichotomy between competence and performance central to mainstream linguistics.   SR

further reading J. Holmes 1992; R. Hudson 1980; Romaine 1994; Trudgill 1983; Wardhaugh 1992

sociology was coined by Auguste Comte in the nineteenth century to describe the study of SOCIETIES. Comte was one of many nineteenth-century thinkers who promoted the study of human social organizations in an attempt to make sense of the massive changes occurring in Europe and spreading to the rest of the world. Toward the end of the century, anthropology and sociology began to separate. A somewhat cynical, yet insightful, distinction holds that while sociocultural anthropology is the handmaiden of COLONIALISM, sociology writes the handbook of social reform.

More formally, sociology studies social structures and processes in modern, developed societies, whereas anthropology focuses on non-Western, and typically nonstate, societies, such as TRIBES and BAND SOCIETIES. This constitutes a division of labor in terms of EVOLUTIONARY STAGES: anthropologists study nonstate societies; sociologists study states. Yet, because of common origins and shared "ancestors" – DURKHEIM, WEBER, and Polanyi to name but a few – anthropology and sociology are often combined in the same academic department in the United States. Ideally, the two fields are complementary, but it is not uncommon for these departments to resemble a fission-prone MOIETY SYSTEM.

What sets sociology, and to a large extent sociocultural anthropology, apart from the other social sciences is the focus on entire societies and their subdivisions, not on individuals. This is not to say that individuals do not matter, but the object of study is that which persists despite turnover of personnel.

The major subjects of sociological study are: STRATIFICATION, or inequality, whether it be based on CLASS and occupation (economic characteristics), RACE, ETHNIC GROUP, or GENDER (status characteristics), or increasingly today the intersection of all of these; social mobility, both in terms of how individuals are sorted through various strata, and how strata themselves are constructed and reproduced; formal organization, or bureaucracies of all types; institutions, including the FAMILY, EDUCATION, RELIGION, occupations, prisons, and courts; social power in its myriad manifestations; social deviance, which encompasses casual violation of informal customs through felonious criminal activity; urban social structures; and collective action, which typically runs the gamut from crowds to organized revolutions.

Rural sociology, the study of agricultural communities, primarily in modern industrial states but also in the Third World, is often organized as a separate academic field from sociology. This is an area that may be of interest to cultural anthropologists since it overlaps considerably with the study of PEASANTS.

Beginning early in the twentieth century and accelerating considerably after World War II, American sociology became increasing empirical and quantitative, at times nearly obsessed with becoming a formal science. In recent decades this obsession has abated considerably. Still, sophisticated statistical techniques remain a major part of the methodological armamentarium of contemporary sociologists. Sociology also has a tradition of participant-observation. The study of global interactions (see WORLD-SYSTEM THEORY), comparative study of states, and historical sociology have burgeoned in the latter part of this century. Thus, sociology overlaps considerably with anthropology and blurs into political science, economics, history, and to a lesser extent social geography.

TH

See also ANTHROPOLOGY, CULTURAL AND SOCIAL DEVELOPMENT, HISTORY AND ANTHROPOLOGY

further reading Berger 1963; Borgatta & Borgatta 1992; Collins 1992; Shils 1985; Smelser 1988

sodalities are voluntary social groups organized by their members on the basis of a shared interest.   MR

song *See* MUSIC

sorcery is the term established early in British social anthropology to distinguish magical practices with actual practitioners from those with magical practitioners whose existence was only putative, who were more often referred to as "witches." Those who articulated their intent to work MAGIC, and who had training and implements, were called "sorcerers" or sometimes "witch doctors." The term "sorcery" however shares with "WITCHCRAFT" the malevolent association with harm rather than healing or protection. But, as in war,

few practitioners admit to being aggressors; instead, they assert that they only act in self-defense or to protect others by "unwitching" victims or taking revenge for an earlier attack (Favret-Saada 1980).

One of the best-known ethnographies of sorcery is Stoller and Olkes's (1987) *In sorcery's shadow*, where the text deliberately resists the denial of magical power. Stoller became apprenticed to a Songhay sorcerer in Niger and learned how to sing appropriate chants and use the appropriate magical items. Rather dramatically, he discovered to his shock that the magic seemed to work. By challenging standard approaches to the study of magic and the supernatural, the book identified itself as POSTMODERN and unusual by its willingness to experience another belief system as potentially valid. This has been a long-standing problem, and not just for anthropology.   TL

further reading Evans-Pritchard 1937; Fortune 1932; Lieban 1967

sororate is (1) the practice of providing a sister of a deceased wife to her widower as a replacement spouse by her kin group; (2) the practice of permitting the husband of a woman unable to bear children to marry her sister and designate at least some of the children of that union the children of his first wife.   MR

soul *See* SPIRIT

speech acts are forms of language behavior that accomplish social action. The term was derived by the language philosopher John Austin in his now classic work *How to do things with words* (1962). Austin was intrigued by forms of LANGUAGE that are not subject to truth or falsity criteria, because utterances of them are themselves recognizable and unfalsifiable acts. A common example is that of a preacher who in uttering "I now pronounce you man and wife" is in fact accomplishing the marriage of two people. Speech acts meet "felicity" tests rather than truth tests. The preacher's pronouncement is not felicitous (that is, it does not function correctly) if the two people do not intend to be married, or if one of them is already married, or if the preacher is not ordained. Promises, oaths, and assertions are other examples of speech acts. Austin's work in speech act theory was elaborated on by John Searle (1969). It was incorporated into Dell Hymes's (1974) scheme for the "ethnography of communication," and has recently become an important component of the growing field of performance theory.   WBe

See also COMMUNICATION, SOCIO-LINGUISTICS

Spencer, Herbert (1820–1903)

Herbert Spencer was the best-known British social and political thinker of his time and one of the most influential figures in European social thought. This is surprising to an age that has largely forgotten him. But it was Spencer who was largely responsible for developing the concept that dominated nineteenth-century sociology and anthropology: EVOLUTION. Though linked (often misleadingly) to Darwin, it was by Spencer that the concept was given its most elaborate form; and when, at the end of the nineteenth century, a reaction to evolutionism set in, it was Spencer who was mainly singled out for attack.

Spencer was trained as a railway engineer but soon abandoned that to devote himself to writing. Throughout his life his work carried the stamp of the self-taught thinker, at once his strength and his weakness. Like his older contemporary Auguste Comte, whom he admired and to some extent sought to emulate, he set himself the task of covering all the fields of human knowledge, from physics to ethics. Like Comte, he felt the task only possible if he could discover an overall unifying principle. Sometime in the 1840s Spencer decided that this principle was evolution. First enunciated in an essay of 1852, "The development hypothesis," evolution became the guiding thread of a whole "system of synthetic philosophy" that he expounded in a succession of major works stretching over half a century: *The principles of psychology* (1855), *First principles* (1862), *The principles of biology* (1864–7), *The principles of sociology* (1876), and *The principles of ethics* (1892–3). In between came a stream of essays on such subjects as population, progress, parliamentary reform, manners, morals, the philosophy of style, the physiology of laughter,

and the function of music – many of which were collected together by him as *Essays: scientific, political and speculative* (1858–74). Although these too tended to take evolution as the axiomatic principle, they mostly managed to evade its restrictive and rigid embrace and – although as much ignored today as his larger works – they contain some of Spencer's most imaginative and interesting ideas.

What did Spencer mean by evolution? Unlike Darwin, who was mostly concerned with its motor or mechanism – natural selection of random variations – Spencer was mainly interested in its direction: hence the famous formula that the law of all things, inanimate as much as animate, is the movement from simple to complex, or from "homogeneity to heterogeneity." Adopted to some extent by Emile DURKHEIM as the evolution of society from "mechanical" to "organic" solidarity, it was later reworked by sociologists such as Talcott Parsons, to emerge in the more familiar form of the process of differentiation. What this means is that from a condition in which things are more or less alike, interchangeable, and self-sufficient, we move to a condition in which there is a high degree of individualization, variety, and mutual interdependence and integration of parts.

All this Spencer derived from the fundamental postulate of "the instability of the homogeneous." Nothing remains in its pristine or primitive state; change is the principle of the universe, but not random, directionless change. There is increasing order, increasing complexity, increasing adaptedness of form (or structure) to function. Later in his life Spencer was to be tormented by the newly discovered principle of entropy, which suggested not increasing order and complexity but increasing disorder and relentless homogenization as the universal principle. But for most of the time Spencer was an optimist. As a Lamarckian, he believed that the adaptive characteristics acquired by one generation could be passed on to the next. There was therefore a general tendency toward perfect equilibrium as structures came to be more and more efficiently and harmoniously adapted to their environment. Hence his belief that, as he put it in an essay of 1857, progress is "not an accident, but a necessity."

If, in the event, Spencer's evolutionary progressivism proved unpalatable to a later generation (though there have always been adherents), there was another aspect of the theory that appeared more serviceable. For Spencer, all life-forms, the individual or organic and the social or "superorganic," exhibited the same features. He was constantly drawing analogies between (individual) organisms and societies, and searching for homologous structures and functions – for instance, trade and transportation are likened to the circulation of the blood, and the nervous system to the administrative machinery of the state. Here was the basic pattern of structural-functionalism, in which structures are explained by the particular contribution they make to the maintenance of the system as a whole (see FUNCTIONALISM, STRUCTURAL-ISM). It was perfectly possible for later sociologists and anthropologists, such as RADCLIFFE-BROWN and MALINOWSKI, to discard Spencer's evolutionism while retaining central features of his functionalism. Spencer has as good a claim as any to be considered the father of functionalism in sociology and anthropology.

"Who reads Herbert Spencer?," asked Talcott Parsons rhetorically at the opening of *The structure of social action* (1937). Parsons himself for one, it would seem, since he was one of the major twentieth-century exponents not just of structural-functionalism but also of social evolutionism. But it is true that, unlike say DURKHEIM or WEBER, Spencer is now largely a historical figure. This should not lead us to forget his major contribution to sociology and anthropology. When the excesses of his SOCIAL DARWINISM – which should really be called "Social Spencerism," as it was Spencer who coined the phrase "the survival of the fittest" and applied the concept most systematically to social life – are forgotten, there remains one of the most ambitious attempts to chart the progress of society and to understand the development of social institutions over time. Much in his *Principles of sociology* and the elaborate ethnographic material collected in the *Descriptive sociology* (1873),

which others continued after his death, can still be studied with profit. Spencer was the one true sociologist contributed by Britain in the nineteenth century to the emerging disciplines of sociology and anthropology. It is a measure of his success that so much of his thinking has been absorbed by these disciplines, even though many practitioners remain unconscious of its source.

KK

further reading Andreski 1971; Burrow 1966; Peel 1971; Rumney 1934; Sanderson 1990; J. Turner 1985

spirit is an odd-job word in comparative RELIGION. Even leaving aside such expressions as the "spirit of capitalism," or "the spirit of resistance," it has no precise or general definition. Instead it is best used to refer to some indigenous category of supernatural agencies, differing from case to case. For example, E. E. EVANS-PRITCHARD (1956) used "spirit" as a gloss for the Nuer word *kwoth*, a subtle concept of the divine that is at once unitary and diverse, like, in his striking analogy, the sun refracted through raindrops. His description is culture-specific, rather than imposing a Western category.

By contrast, in his account of Ngaju notions of the godhead, Hans Scharer (1963) used the word loosely to cover a heterogeneous collection of lesser supernatural agencies. It is not clear that "spirit" glosses any Ngaju category, and since it is implied that spirits represent a "lower" level of belief, an ethnocentric assumption is smuggled in. In this, Scharer followed EVOLUTIONARY-STAGE models like those of Herbert SPENCER (1876).

"Spirit" is often used in contrast to "soul," thought of as an immaterial component of living humans, usually persisting after DEATH. Ancestors, however, are frequently described as spirits (see ANCESTOR WORSHIP).

"Spirit possession" implies an altered state of consciousness attributed to the influence of some external agency, such as occurs in TRANCE and SHAMANISM.

PM

state, state systems States are regional polities, dynamically expanding through conquest. Within the polity, diverse hierarchies of offices are associated with specialized institutions that are financed by a political economy. They are characterized by social STRATIFICATION and constitute the governing political and administrative institutions that characterize COMPLEX SOCIETIES. States are typologically the most complex types of human society (Service 1962; Fried 1967). A basic division is often posited between states and traditionally organized, stateless societies (see CENTRALIZED SYSTEMS and CHIEF).

States organize an extensive population in the hundreds of thousands or millions (Johnson & Earle 1987), often representing many ethnic groups with separate historical traditions, economies, religions, and cultures. To integrate such a diverse populace requires elaborate and specialized institutions of governance and domination. General categories of state institution include administrative bureaucracies, legal systems, and military and religious organizations. Such institutions represent different sources of power – economic, political, military, and ideological. The degree of elaboration and the interrelationships between the various institutions differ considerably from state to state. The "state," as a category of social EVOLUTION, is internally highly variable in terms of scale of integration (from the city state to the empire), type of integration ("administrative" vs. "theater" state [C. Geertz 1980]), the nature of control ("territorial" vs. "hegemonic" [Hassig 1985]), and the basis of finance ("staple" vs. "wealth" [D'Altroy & Earle 1985]), among other characteristics.

ORIENTAL DESPOTISM, as conceived by Wittfogel (1957), was based on a strong centralized system: the state developed large IRRIGATION systems from which it extended control to other institutions of power. Alternatively, the different sources of power can be institutionally separated, and the different institutions (military vs. religious, for example) can vie for control. Mann (1986–93) captured a highly dynamic vision of the state as internally divided, competitive, and always threatening to dissolve. The development of the state does not necessarily result in increased overall centralization.

To finance the activities and personnel of state institutions requires a political economy (Earle & D'Altroy 1989). Staple finance mobilizes foods and other goods that are stored in state warehouses and used directly to support state personnel. Wealth finance, by contrast, uses valuables or currencies, characteristically produced and collected under state supervision, to pay state personnel. The use of wealth as a means of payment requires the development of MARKETS to convert the MONEY into usable products. Different forms of finance create differences in the strength and integration of state institutions (D'Altroy & Earle 1985).

Social stratification characterizes state societies. A ruling segment or CLASS retains differential access to "the basic resources that sustain life" (Fried 1967: 186). State societies are divided into classes with different economic and political interests (Marx & Engels 1888), and state institutions are developed to reproduce the social system of domination. Although this may be the dream of the ruling segment, life in complex society is more precarious. Brumfiel and Fox (1994) described the intense competition among elites for control over ruling institutions.

A focus of anthropological research has been to explain the "origin" of state society or "civilization" (Flannery 1972; H. Wright 1978). Theories have emphasized either the central management or the coercive power of states (Service 1975). Managerial theories outline how problems of survival require central management that supposedly only the state can provide, such as irrigation systems in the desert. Sanders (1956) argued that community specialization within ecologically diverse regions must have resulted in an integrated economy and market system; the peace of the market, then necessary for the regional economy, was thereafter guaranteed by the state. Carneiro (1970) described how competitive warfare required central organization for success; states, with more effective militaries, expanded at the expense of more simply organized societies. Underlying these adapationalist theories is either the advance of a new organizational form, like irrigation, or the creation of new problems with a growing population.

Coercive political theories emphasize two dynamics. First, states, and the extensive political integration that they represent, are fashioned through military conquest and suppression. Second, according to marxists, states function to perpetuate and extend domination by the ruling class (Haas 1982; Webb 1975). Control of weaponry is critical in this regard (J. Goody 1971). Marxist theories within anthropology have looked at the internal dynamics of social structure (Friedman & Rowlands 1977) and ideology (Althusser 1971).

TE

status Like "kinship," "marriage," and "ritual," the term "status" has become an essential concept in anthropological analysis, but has a variety of meanings. The most generally recognized meaning is to indicate a position in a social structure, with the closely related term "ROLE" referring to the expected behavior of any person occupying that position. This usage derives from the legal concept of status or standing, denoting an array of rights and duties attaching to a particular position. But once adopted by social scientists, the concept acquired more complex meanings. Other usages are more closely linked to its lay meaning of esteem, reputation, HONOR, or social rank, but again social scientists, in shaping the concept for their own analytic purposes, have added many layers of meaning. For example, Max WEBER decomposed the marxist concept of CLASS into class, status, and party (political power) and in the process fashioned a powerful concept focused upon the way in which social groups relate to each other (M. Weber 1968).

In the nineteenth century Sir Henry MAINE (1861) drew a contrast between status and contract that reflected the evolutionist assumption that societies progress from an original state in which all social relations derive from the family to one where social relations are increasingly based on contracts entered into freely among individuals. By the 1930s structural-functional theory, derived largely from the work of Emile DURKHEIM,

was dominant in Britain and the British Commonwealth and was beginning to make headway in the United States (see FUNCTIONALISM). The concept of "social structure," as a system of integrated social relations functioning to maintain the continuity and stability of the system itself, was well established, and although leading scholars, such as RADCLIFFE-BROWN, used "social status" interchangeably with terms such as "social person" and "social usage," the concept was increasingly used to refer to the articulated array of social positions making up the social structure. Ralph LINTON (1936) made an important contribution by formalizing the use of the term, defining statuses as polar positions in patterns of reciprocal behavior between individuals or groups of individuals, and role as the dynamic aspect of status – the acting out of the patterned expectations attributed to that position. Henceforth these two concepts were widely adopted by sociologists as well as anthropologists and were fundamental to the analysis of social structure. Linton's further distinction between "ascribed status" and "achieved status" also became standard; ascribed statuses are those assigned to individuals without reference to their innate differences or abilities, whereas achieved statuses are filled on the basis of competition and individual effort since they require special abilities. This contrast had many useful applications but, like Maine's proposed movement from status to contract, it contained an implicit evolutionary element and reflected the ideological assumptions that suffused much structural-functional theory.

These uses of the term "status" became subject to the general critique of structural-functional theory, which began with the allegation that they were too rigid and incapable of fully comprehending processes of change (shortcomings that were less inherent in the theory than in the particular ways in which it was used). In order to circumvent these perceived limitations Raymond FIRTH proposed the concept of "SOCIAL ORGANIZATION," focused on the elements of choice involved in social behavior. These elements were neglected in the over-formalized concepts of status, role, and social structure itself, which implied a passive acting out of socially prescribed activities (R. Firth 1951b). TRANSACTIONAL ANALYSIS went even further, arguing that social behavior is based less on *a priori* rules, embedded in statuses and roles, than upon the maximizing calculations of rational actors (Kapferer 1976b). With the more general decline in the conception of societies as organically integrated entities, the terms "status" and "role" have lost much of the refined meaning that they derived from structural-functional theory.

The Weberian conception of status is potentially the most valuable for contemporary anthropology. Believing that Marx's conception of class needed to be refined in order to grasp the complexity of the different bases of hierarchy and rank in modern societies, Weber reserved the term "class" for those who share common life-chances in relation to the MARKET (that is, their ability to secure income through disposition of goods and services). Groups of people sharing a common class situation do not necessarily share a consciousness of that situation, and indeed Weber proposed that "status" be defined as the positive or negative estimation of honor or prestige attributed to persons or groups. While common class situation may well give rise to common status, it need not do so and frequently does not; or at least the two elements may vary in empirically specific ways. Since status inheres in groups that exhibit common styles of life and have a consciousness of common interests and common destiny relative to other status groups, it is clear that they do not necessarily constitute an agreed-upon hierarchy in a functionally integrated totality, and are, in fact, usually engaged in struggle with other status groups for dominance or relative prestige.

Weber's concepts of "class situation" and "status situation" offer a much more realistic way of looking at structures of inequality than the notion of a socially agreed hierarchy of positions reflected in socially mandated rules for behavior, since they clearly recognize the potential disjunction between hierarchies of power, wealth, and prestige. In this way one sees that social mobility is not the rising and falling of socially disembodied individuals, but rather a process in which individuals must negotiate a transition from one combination of class and status situations to another. Style of life is the crucial element in the self-characterization of groups, and style of life, with its embodiment of social capital, is particularly appropriate for examination by anthropological field research. However, it is important to recognize that styles of life (sometimes called "subcultures") are both in competition with each other and, to a large extent, defined in relation to each other as distinctions of taste are drawn. The major error of some types of PLURAL-SOCIETY theory is to treat the constituent status groups of a social order as if they were totally discrete except for their relative positions in the political hierarchy. The work of Pierre Bourdieu (1984) draws explicitly upon Max Weber's model in constructing a monumental ethnography of French styles of life, an ethnography that makes clear the importance of these distinctions of taste and the way in which they define status boundaries.

Weber regarded the persistence of status groups in modern complex societies as one of their most fundamental features, thus rejecting the idea that they belong to an earlier evolutionary stage. In modern societies groups based on kinship, race, religion, or other characteristics believed to be "primordial," are joined by others that are the very products of the apparently rational legal and bureaucratic processes of modern society. Among the most important of these are the products of modern educational institutions that claim the right to distribute certificates, degrees, and diplomas, thus controlling the admission of individuals to the charmed circles of the "educated." It is not difficult to see the relevance of this for the United States, for Europe, and even more so for developing countries. As important is the process that has been called "the invention of TRADITION" (Hobsbawm & Ranger 1983), by which status groups – including nation-states – that have been created through processes of change, assert traditional, or primordial, legitimacy for their claims to honor, prestige and power (see NATION). The apparent upsurge of ethnicity in the modern world can be understood as a manifestation of this process, so that ETHNIC GROUPS are a special case of status groups (di Leonardo 1984; Alonso 1994).

RS

further reading Eisenstadt 1990; Goodenough 1965b; P. Willis 1977 [an influential study of the formation of status groups in a British working class community]

stem families are NUCLEAR FAMILIES with the addition of one or more relatives who do not form a separate nuclear family on their own. The most common form consists of a married couple, their children, and an elderly parent. It is generally a stage in the DOMESTIC CYCLE rather than a permanent form.

MR

See also EXTENDED FAMILIES, HOUSEHOLDS

Steward, Julian (1902–72) Julian Steward attended a preparatory school in the Owens Valley of California that included instruction in natural history. There he first experienced the desert environment and indigenous people, the Paiute and Shoshoni. As an undergraduate he studied zoology and geology at Cornell University. From 1925 to 1931 he was a graduate student in anthropology at the University of California in Berkeley with the Boasians Alfred KROEBER and Robert LOWIE. There he was also influenced by geographers Carl Sauer and Daryll FORDE, the latter as a visiting professor. At Berkeley Steward spent much of his early fieldwork compiling culture trait lists. He became saturated and eventually disillusioned with the HISTORICAL PARTICULARISM and CULTURE AREA approaches of his anthropology professors. His interests turned to the environmental influences on CULTURE and cultural EVOLUTION, something of a heresy for Boasians.

Steward's materialist orientation likely stems from a combination of factors, including his preparatory school experience, undergraduate studies, early fieldwork in the 1930s in ARCHAEOLOGY in the harsh environments of the southwest and Great Basin and Plateau, ethnographic field experience with the Shoshoni (whose culture appears to have focused on survival), and

the Dust Bowl and the Great Depression. Through his FIELDWORK he cultivated cultural ecology which eventually became a means to the end of his theory of multilinear evolution (Steward 1938). Ultimately Steward was always interested in the scientific and materialist explanation of culture, including causality; that is, discovering laws of regularities in the patterns, functions, and processes of cultural diversity. This penchant for theorizing and generalizing also set Steward apart from the Boasians. In short, Steward was a rebel, an inclination that actually started in his youth, when he turned away from the Christian Science religion of his parents to pursue instead natural causes through scientific explanations.

These considerations help explain why Steward became the single most important anthropologist in the development of cultural ecology from the 1930s into the 1960s. In his field research, publications, and teaching, Steward persistently developed a theoretical and methodological framework for studying CULTURAL CHANGE as adaptation in which environmental influences were especially important. Unfortunately, Steward did not develop his theory and method in a single, readily accessible publication. Rather, his theory and method have to be extracted from numerous sources, including two edited books of diverse essays (Steward 1955, 1977).

It is important to clearly distinguish two different levels at which Steward operated – the ethnographic sphere, in which a particular culture was described through intensive fieldwork in the Boasian tradition, and the ethnological sphere, in which a small number of cultures were compared for the purposes of generalization and explanation. Cultural ecology has continued to strongly influence anthropological research on human–environment interactions, while multilinear evolution has been pursued to a much lesser extent (Carneiro 1990; Kirch 1984). However, Steward is seldom adequately acknowledged by researchers studying cultural ecology or multilinear evolution.

Rather than arguing on the basis of available literature that either the environment rigidly determines culture (environmental determinism) or the environment allows some degree of latitude for alternative cultural responses (environmental possibilism), Steward avoided prejudgement and advocacy, allowing for influences in either direction (environment to culture and culture to environment). He subjected this relationship to direct empirical investigation through fieldwork on particular cultures in their habitat. Through ethnographic fieldwork with the Shoshoni and Paiute, Steward (1955) specified three successive but interrelated steps in the investigation of the cultural ecology of a particular society: (1) the natural resources and the technology used to extract and process them; (2) the social organization of work for these subsistence and economic activities; and (3) the influence of these two phenomena on other aspects of culture, including social, political, and religious institutions. In this manner Steward developed an ecological framework for describing and to some degree explaining a particular culture. This framework focused on the specific behavior involved in the technology and work of extracting natural resources for survival. Thus Steward's approach has proven most applicable to societies with economies focused on subsistence; that is, FORAGERS or hunter–gatherers, SWIDDEN horticulturalists, FISHERS, and PASTORAL NOMADS.

Steward, however, was not satisfied with this particular level of research. Ultimately he was more interested in the comparative level in order to discover the underlying causes and laws of cultural phenomena. He was especially concerned with employing empirical data from research in cultural ecology to compare a small sample of cultures in order to formulate generalizations about limited parallels in patterns, functions, and processes. He called this "multilinear evolution," as distinct from the unilinear evolution of Edward TYLOR and Lewis Henry MORGAN in the late nineteenth century, or the universal evolution of his contemporary Leslie WHITE (Carneiro 1973). Steward's methodological approach to multilinear evolution was to select for detailed comparison a small number of particular cultures that were in

similar environments (e.g., types of desert or forest) and at the same level of sociocultural integration (FAMILY, BAND, TRIBE, CHIEFDOM, or STATE), but widely separated geographically. The great spatial distance between the cultures chosen for the sample was supposed to eliminate the possibility of cultural similarities arising from DIFFUSION, thus controlling for the historical factor that had been so prominent in the anthropology of the Boasians. Accordingly, similarities in the sample of cultures that Steward selected would have to be the result of parallel adaptations, that is, similar responses to similar environmental conditions. In this way Steward attempted to go beyond ethnographic description to the scientific and materialist explanation of cultural similarities and differences (Sponsel 1987).

The principal criticisms of Steward's approach are that his theoretical concepts were not very clear and useful; that his method was mostly intuitive; that he was a FUNCTIONALIST; and that he focused rather narrowly on subsistence economy to the neglect of many other important factors, such as population dynamics, natural hazards, political institutions, and religion (see J. Anderson 1973; Orlove 1980; Vayda & Rappaport 1968). However, assessed in historical context, Steward's contributions were and remain significant.

Steward's influence endures to this day through his students as well as his publications. He taught at the University of Michigan (1928–30), where he started instruction in anthropology, and subsequently at Utah (1930–2), Berkeley (1933–4), Columbia (1946–52), and finally Illinois (1952–72). Among his students were William Alkire, Stanley Diamond, Clifford Evans, Morton Fried, Ernestine Friedl, Robert Manners, Sidney Mintz, Robert Murphy, Elman Service, and Eric Wolf, all prominent anthropologists (R. Murphy 1991). In 1964 Steward's colleagues and former students contributed essays to a book published in his honor (Shimkin 1964), and in 1969 graduate students at the University of Illinois honored him by establishing the *Journal of the Steward Anthropological Society*.

Finally, beyond his work on cultural

ecology and multilinear evolution, Steward had several other outstanding accomplishments. While working at the Bureau of American Ethnology of the Smithsonian Institution, Steward edited the monumental multi-volume *Handbook of South American Indians* (Steward 1946–59) and coauthored its summary synthesis (Steward & Faron 1959). These remain unsurpassed and indispensable background for anyone interested in that continent, and they have had considerable influence on ecological research by anthropologists in the Amazon (Sponsel 1986, 1995). As Director of the Institute for Social Anthropology at the Smithsonian Institution, Steward encouraged and funded extensive research on the peasantry of Latin America (1956). Steward was also a pioneer in area studies, team research (1950), and the modernization of traditional societies (1967), and he wrote a biography of his former teacher Alfred Kroeber (1973). In these and other respects Steward contributed substantially in an enduring way to the foundations of modern anthropology.   LS
See also ADAPTATION, CULTURAL MATERI-
    ALISM, ECOLOGICAL ANTHROPOLOGY,
    SOCIAL ORGANIZATION, TECHNOLOGY

stratification   "Social stratification" is the most general term used to describe the hierarchical division of a SOCIETY whereby its members are ranked according to their relative power, wealth, or prestige. Although it is often used as a generic term applicable to all RANKED SOCIETIES, including CASTE SOCIETIES and those based on social CLASS, "stratification" is more generally used when the theoretical focus is upon individual action, so that the overall patterns of social stratification are regarded as the outcome of individuals' efforts to achieve social mobility. Stratification theorists can thus compare societies according to the nature and extent of vertical mobility within them, and can arrange them along a scale from the supposed rigidities of caste to the hypothetically completely open societies of the modern world – a scale that inevitably turns into an evolutionary sequence leading to MODERNIZATION. (See Dumont 1970, App. A, for criticism of at-

tempts to include caste in a general theory of stratification.)

The concept of stratification is particularly appropriate to structural-functional analyses of complex societies, where the theory assumes a mode of social integration around the common values of achievement and individual responsibility for social STATUS. The resulting hierarchy is then assumed to represent the distribution of individual talents, responsibilities, and appropriate rewards. This model of perfect individual social mobility then becomes the benchmark against which other societies are measured, a procedure adopted by sociologists employing sophisticated statistical techniques. Lloyd Fallers (1963) pointed out that the reason for the sociological concern with stratification is the prominent role played by questions of equality in the history of Europe and North America over the past 250 years or so. He went on to warn, however, that the concepts and methods used for studying these matters in the West might not be appropriate for understanding the equally intense concern with equality displayed by non-Western societies in the wave of independence movements that swept over previously subject peoples after World War II. Nonetheless, he, along with many other anthropologists at that time, accepted the broad assumptions of modernization theory, seeking only to understand "the interaction between the forces of generic modernity . . . and the traditional societies and cultures upon which, and within which, modernity works" (Fallers 1963: 160). Although anthropologists preferred to concentrate upon aspects of social and cultural change that were not quantified in the style of sociological stratification analysis, most shared the general theoretical orientation toward modernity and modernization – a fact that made possible the collaboration among social scientists from different disciplines in the production of such works as *Old societies and new states: the quest for modernity in Asia and Africa* edited by Clifford GEERTZ (1963a).

The United States was usually depicted as the epitome of an egalitarian society in which unlimited social mobility was possible, and therefore a model of modernity. Indeed, S. M. Lipset depicted it as *The first new nation* in an explicit attempt to show other excolonies how revolutionary values can legitimate political institutions. His view of the way in which the values of equality and achievement have produced exemplary national institutions and national character was quite tendentious. Only in an epilogue did he mention the fact that "American egalitarianism is, of course, for white men only" (1963: 379).

Even a cursory examination of any empirical case, including the United States of America, reveals structural barriers to perfect mobility. There are no societies in which rank and rewards are anywhere nearly perfectly matched to talents and achievement. Anthropologists working in the United States soon developed subsidiary theories to account for these apparent flaws in the system of equal opportunity. One approach was to study SUBCULTURES, which were regarded as the residues of the culture of immigrant groups not yet fully absorbed into the mainstream of American society and not fully sharing its values and way of life. Some segments of the population appeared to lack either the will or the potential to move up from the lowest rungs of the occupational ladder or escape from POVERTY. One explanation was that persistent poverty produces a CULTURE OF POVERTY through which individuals are socialized into behaviours that militate against occupational achievement and social mobility (Lewis 1966). This strategy has persisted into the present, with urban poverty populations being characterized as a disorganized "underclass," culturally incapable of functioning in mainstream society (Jencks & Peterson 1991).

The interest in comparative social stratification waned with the gradual demise of the theoretical assumptions on which it rested – modernization theory and structural-functionalism. Fallers (1973: 3) himself felt obliged to write that "I have . . . come to the conclusion that the phenomenon does not exist, or at any rate that 'social stratification' is a poor name for it." Developments in the "new nations" have rarely followed the path of a smooth transition from tradition to modernity, and even less from hierarchy to egalitarianism, so that anthropologists now find themselves much more concerned with concepts such as ETHNICITY, GENOCIDE, and POSTMODERNISM than they would have predicted 30 years ago.   RS

further reading John Jackson 1968 [esp. essays by Allardt, Eisenstadt, and Shils]; Plotnicov & Tuden 1970

structural-functionalism *See* FUNCTIONALISM

structuralism is a method, an aesthetic–analytic style, and a philosophical temper, articulated most fully by the anthropologist Claude LÉVI-STRAUSS, but of importance as part of a larger movement within the modernisms of the twentieth century: formalisms in music (serialism), drama (Becket, Artaud), the novel (Roussel, Perec), and so-called antihumanist philosophy and literary criticism (Bathes, Foucault, Lacan, Derrida), which have provided the terrain of so-called poststructuralism.

As a method, structuralism in its Lévi-Straussian (and anthropological) form derives most directly from the structural linguistics of Ferdinand de Saussure (1959) and Roman Jakobson (1956, 1978, 1987), the Durkheimian sociology of Marcel MAUSS, and information theory, but also, Lévi-Strauss noted, from deep structures in geology, marxism, and psychoanalysis. Saussure argued that units of meaning in language ("langue") are constituted as a system of differences, each unit being given its value by its distinctiveness from other units of the system. This is most easily illustrated by the phonemic system (see PHONOLOGY), but also by difference in SEMANTICS (e.g., French *mouton* versus English differentiation between *sheep* and *mutton*). GRAMMAR and structural LINGUISTIC forms at all levels are not conscious, yet they are systemic: speakers can recognize correct and incorrect forms without being able to articulate the rules. So too, Lévi-Strauss argued, the anthropologist needs a systematic method to uncover the underlying structure of cultural forms, which are equally systematic. This method relies on a binary mode of description through distinctive features and redundancy, as is most completely developed in information theory. Its force lies on the unconscious level, or more accurately on the level of social facts in the Durkheimian sense. Folk explanations of these forms are illusory because people do not have a conscious grasp of their structure.

Lévi-Strauss (1963a, 1969a) applied his structural method first to ELEMENTARY KINSHIP SYSTEMS (prescriptive systems of marriage in which categories of relationship foreclose who is marriageable and who is not), mainly in Australia, south and southeast Asia, and some PREFERENTIAL MARRIAGE SYSTEMS, arguing that the structural rules of these marriage exchange systems have implications for regional integration of small-scale societies. After elaborating on Marcel Mauss's sociological investigations of exchange theory, which involved a complete reworking of nineteenth-century theories of TOTEMISM (Lévi-Strauss 1963b), and a brilliant reconsideration of classificatory logic (including the theory of proper names as cultural sets, the CASTE system, and a challenge to Sartre and "humanist" history), Lévi-Strauss (1969b, 1973, 1978, 1981) turned to the analysis of some eight hundred South American and North American myths. These tour-de-force analyses, conceived of as a formal harmonic system like a symphony, organized a wealth of detailed ecological, historical, sociological, and semiotic information.

At minimum Lévi-Strauss suggested that the structuralist method is a way to reconstruct the conceptual systems of depopulated and fragmented cultures. Quite stunning is the systemic, almost predictive, nature of many of his analyses, such as those of the masks of the Northwest Coast Indians (Lévi-Strauss 1982) and of the historical relations of neighboring Plains Indians derived from the ways in which neighbors inverted each other's myths, and the ways in which ecological and geographic information is encoded (Lévi-Strauss 1963a: xii). More broadly, the structuralist analyses of myths – pioneered also by the folklorist Vladimir Propp

(1958) and the Indo-Europeanist Georges Dumézil (1970a,b, 1988) – forever changed the way social scientists think about MYTHS: no longer is it credible to identify a god or mythic figure as a personification of a single idea or natural phenomenon; to establish the meaning of any figure within a myth or of a mythic plot one needs to consider the multiple variants of the myth, thereby gaining access to the logic and potentials of the underlying mythic structure. Perhaps the most impressive application of the structuralist method was to Greek classical studies (Vernant 1980, 1982, 1983; Vidal-Naquet 1986; Detienne 1978; Friedrich 1978), but various extensions have also been made to South Asian kinship and social organization (Yalman 1967), dual societies in Amazonia (Maybury-Lewis 1979), Central American mythology (E. Hunt 1977), and modern America and Hawaii (Sahlins 1976a, 1985).

On a more philosophical level, Lévi-Strauss became the key figure in France to challenge the existentialist projects of the early post-war decades presided over by Jean-Paul Sartre, arguing that phenomena such as language and culture cannot be easily changed by the heroic will and consciousness of individuals or political groups. This debate over the nature of history (Lévi-Strauss 1966, 1981) also provided the grounds for the emergence first of STRUCTURAL MARXISM (see CRITICAL ANTHROPOLOGY) and then of the generation of so-called poststructuralists (see POSTMODERNISM). Although poststructuralists challenge the sometimes mechanical binarism of structuralism as information-theory-based logic, on a philosophical level they continue at least that part of Lévi-Strauss's project that looked to the systematicities that operate against or despite the will of the individual. As more than one commentator has noted, there are two sides to the Lévi-Straussian coin: one is scientific, interested in applying the latest techniques in set theory, chemistry, etc. to unpacking other modes of thought; the other side is a mood of atonement for cultures destroyed by colonialism and modern civilization by way of creating a new talmud, a collection of fragments from the past together with a critical apparatus that can revivify those fragments as tools for speculative thought.

Although structuralism itself has fallen out of fashion among many anthropologists, other allied initiatives stemming from the information-theory revolution of the 1950s continue apace, in "artifical life" computer simulations in theoretical biology, for instance, and the contemporary investigations of "complexity" and "emergence," which rework the intuitions of Durkheimean sociological theory about emergent levels of organization. One research arena in which these computer and biological theories reapproach anthropology is in the investigation of social and cultural forms mediated by electronic and computer media. Examples include the effects of hyperreality and simulations, and parasitic switching mechanisms between different levels of biological, informational, organizational, and cultural forms (Serres 1982; Latour 1979; Deleuze & Guattari 1977). Others examine the relationships between psychological states of dissociation, multiple personality, and computer-mediated environments and therapeutic programs (Glass 1993; Turkle 1984, 1995). All these arenas belong to what Lévi-Strauss called "hot" (or change-valuing) societies; work on the "cold" (or change-denying) societies to which he devoted most of his own work remains deeply indebted to structuralist analyses even when they are not the only methods used.

MF

structural marxism is an intellectual linkage of French STRUCTURALISM with marxist theory that was especially important from the 1960s to the 1980s. While one important line of work, initiated by Maurice Godelier, approached anthropology through an engagement with the themes and perspectives of Claude LÉVI-STRAUSS, many others began with the highly elaborated marxist structuralism of Louis Althusser, applying his conceptual repertoire to the study of precapitalist societies (Althusser & Balibar 1970).

Central to this thought were the twin concepts of mode of production and social formation, and the linked idea of articula-tion. In general terms, a central problem for analysis was the specification of the relationship between the MODE OF PRODUCTION and the rest of the social whole, but the precise statement of the problem, and its underlying concepts, varied. Common to all such statements was the view that mode of production was an abstract concept that had no existence in reality and could only be apprehended in thought. The social formation, on the other hand, while also a concept, was the concept of a particular society (e.g., the French or English social formation). The capitalist or feudal mode of production might be common to, say, the French or English social formations, but their concrete forms and appearances will be different because of the different articulated combinations that occur in each.

Exploration of these different articulated combinations was directed at distinct problems such as the relationship between the "infrastructure" and the "superstructure." While this relationship was conceived as one of articulation, there were important differences between those who conceived of the mode of production as limited strictly to the infrastructure and those who defined it more broadly. The former looked only at the forces and relations of production while the latter included an array of superstructural "levels" and "instances" appropriate to a particular set of forces and relations of production. In both cases, the relationship between levels was conceived as one of relative autonomy, and one of the perceived advances of structural marxist thought was its rejection of mechanical models of determination even while retaining the emphasis on infrastructure (or base) and superstructure.

Among French anthropologists, Maurice Godelier (1973), Emmanuel Terray (1972), and Claude Meillassoux (1981) were important early figures in pursuing the first line of work and were especially interested in exploring the problem of kinship and religion in relation to production relations in precapitalist societies. Despite important disagreements, one common feature in their work was the claim that in precapitalist societies the economy is not an autonomous sphere and that various apparently superstructural elements (especially KINSHIP) organize production relations and serve to mobilize and appropriate labor. Debates concentrated on the proper conception of "infrastructure" and "superstructure" in such a situation. Their work was translated, and their themes picked up, especially in British social anthropology in the 1960s and 1970s, where the structural analysis of kinship in relation to other structural domains already had a long history.

Another line of work concentrated on the relationship, again conceived as one of articulation, among various modes of production within a particular social formation. Here some of the most important work was aimed at understanding processes of development under COLONIALISM and CAPITALISM in terms of their changing structural connections and configurations. Of special interest here were the relationships between the capitalist mode of production and a variety of noncapitalist modes. Among French anthropologists, early contributors to this line of work included Pierre-Phillipe Rey (1973) and Claude Meillassoux (1991), but the method of analysis was widely extended, partly due to the concurrent rise of studies of DEVELOPMENT and underdevelopment. The analysis of articulating modes of production, especially capitalist and noncapitalist modes, provided a language for analyzing the structural and historical complexities of capitalist development in colonial and postcolonial situations (E. Wolf 1982).

Seen across these lines of work, "articulation" was a complex concept designed to understand connection, relative autonomy, and process. In the history of marxist thought, structural marxism represented an important advance as an attempt to escape mechanical models of determination and simplistic stage theories of social EVOLUTION, dealing more seriously with the complexities of modern history. Yet one of the difficulties with the resolutions they offered was their resolutely structural understanding of connection, autonomy, and process. Thus their conception of the relationship between kinship and production in "lineage-based" societies never left the social

anthropological terrain they had inherited, leading one group of formerly sympathetic anthropologists to complain that they had been captured by FUNCTIONALIST anthropology rather than transforming it.

With regard to the second line of work, two problems emerged. On one hand, many analyses became embroiled in "naming" controversies concerning the nature of modes of production in a particular situation (capitalist? feudal? colonial? petty commodity?), so that the analysis of modes of production became an end in itself rather than a means to another end – the economic and political analysis of complex relations and processes of development and underdevelopment (Roseberry 1989). On the other hand, many analyses of sectoral unevenness and inequality in underdevelopment reverted to a kind of functionalism, understanding the existence of a particular noncapitalist sector, or the presence of particular groups of people, in terms of the presumed needs of the capitalist sector or mode.   WR

See also MARXIST ANTHROPOLOGY

further reading M. Bloch 1975; Foster-Carter 1978; Kahn & Llobera 1981; E. Thompson 1978

subcultures are groups with distinct cultural characteristics or patterns of life within larger societies to which they belong or are associated. Classic examples include ETHNIC GROUPS, MIDDLEMAN MINORITIES, CHILDREN, or CLASS.   MR

subincision is the slitting of the underside of the penis. This operation is performed as part of male puberty rites among some Australian Aboriginal groups.

MR

substantivist *See* FORMALIST–SUBSTANTIVIST DEBATE

succession It is useful to follow W. H. R. RIVERS (1914a) in distinguishing between the inheritance of property, succession to office, and rules of descent (which define eligibility to kin groups). Each system of transmission takes a different form because of what is being transmitted, eventually between the generations. There are clearly a number of ways of transferring property, but inheritance is what Commons (1924) called "an authorized transaction." The handing-over of property is not necessarily a matter of transferring objects but of rights in objects (or in people). A distinction is often made between ancestral and self-acquired property, with the latter being less circumscribed by obligation. In many societies another distinction exists between immovables (such as land, often the basic productive resource, and real property) and movables (chattels), especially since movables are divisible whereas immovables may have to be kept intact to maintain the resident family (J. Goody 1962, 1966).

PROPERTY may be handed down agnatically to children or in a uterine mode to the children of sisters. In both cases it may first go laterally to "brothers" before dropping a generation. This is the case for many preliterate societies, where the wider clan is important. In contemporary Europe property generally goes directly to the children in a lineal fashion, within the restricted conjugal family. However the first recipient is usually the surviving spouse, more often the widow as she tends to be younger and to live longer.

Ruth BENEDICT (1936) remarked that in simple societies the most important economic rights were transmitted between consanguineal kin to the exclusion of spouses. The contrast is with the legal codes of the major Eurasian societies, by which the widow inherited a portion at her husband's death. Or rather, she acquired rights to certain parts of the conjugal estate that had been established at marriage and that she and her kin had in fact helped to set up by endowments. Conjugal inheritance is closely linked to the dowry proper (parental transfers to daughters), since both involve the transmission of property across sex lines (J. Goody & Tambiah 1973). Indeed inheritance at death has to be seen as part of the wider process of the devolution of rights from the senior generation, an important variable in which is not only to whom property goes, but when, whether *mortis causa* (on account of death) or *inter vivos* (between the living), usually at marriage.

Property, often of different types, is always vested in both males and females in a manner linked to the sexual DIVISION OF LABOR. Hence it must be transmitted by both sexes, a process that can take several forms:

1. homogeneous or monosexual transmission: the transfer of property between members of the same sex, which is very frequent in Africa and connected with the organization of clans and lineages
2. diverging transmission: the transfer of rights to members of both sexes, as in the DOWRY systems of Eurasia
3. cross-sexual transmission, which is rare

Each of these methods of passing property *between* persons of the same or different sex may also take place *through* persons of different sex. In the usual terminology, inheritance may be either "PATRILINEAL" or "MATRILINEAL." But as those terms are generally used for membership of unilineal descent groups, it seems preferable to use "agnatic" and "uterine" to describe the transmission of property. To put it another way, the property of both males and females can be transferred *directly* to the children or *indirectly* to the children of siblings of opposite sex (for example, the sister's child in the case of a man). Different sexes may transmit rights by different means and for different types of property.

Although it is often important to make an analytic separation between the transmission of property and eligibility to membership of a descent group, the two may be related. Thus in a patrilineal clan, property will tend to be transmitted agnatically, ensuring a continuing connection between a social group and a fixed body of resources such as land. Indeed land is often restricted to the male sex because of the division of labor and subject to homogeneous transmission to prevent it being dispersed. However, although women may normally be excluded from the basic productive resources, in Eurasian societies they may be entitled to inherit them in the absence of brothers. The situation of the "heiress" is connected with a number of features of marriage, such as in-marriage to cousins (again to prevent dispersal), or in other cases, with the ability to attract a male to live with them (uxorilocally of filialocally) when residence is otherwise determined by the husband. That situation lies at the basis of "the woman's property complex" (J. Goody 1990).

Within the sibling group, inheritance may privilege one sex or individual. Males are often privileged because of the division of labor. One among them is often privileged when it comes to succession to office and with that may go the bulk of the estate (unigeniture). That is usually the first son (primogeniture) with landed estates, but with ordinary holdings the younger son may be privileged because he is the one required to stay at home with aging parents (ultimogeniture). However, among the Basques it is the eldest child irrespective of sex who takes over the house. In some other cases complete equality may be required (as under the Napoleonic code) and it has been proposed that in Europe this method stimulates the local landmarket (Habbakuk 1955). However neither complete unigeniture nor complete equality are likely be practical. Younger sons and daughters are endowed even under primogeniture; and in egalitarian systems some children are bound to be favored, depending upon their continuing obligations.

JG

further reading J. Goody et al. 1976; Habbakuk 1950

Sudanese kinship systems employ a large number of primary kin terms, such that most socially significant categories of kin are distinctively named (see figure 1). The Sudanese kinship system is typically associated with patrilineal social organization among PASTORAL NOMADS in northeast Africa.

MR

suffering is the central concern of the great RELIGIONS and also was a founding concern of the social sciences (Bowker 1970). In its narrower guise of illness experiences and disability narratives, suffering has been a, perhaps *the*, central focus of MEDICAL ANTHROPOLOGY (Kleinman 1980; B. Good 1994). Pain, with its ramifications in language, media imagery, bodily experience, and their political uses, is the most widely studied form of suffering (M.J. Good 1992). However, suffering also encompasses a much wider field of research and theoretical concerns that includes such collective experiences as the traumatic consequences of political (or domestic) VIOLENCE, forced uprooting, and the grinding adversity of routinized misery in settings of extreme POVERTY, to name just a few. This broader inquiry into suffering is found throughout anthropological writings because anthropologists have come to appreciate that, though the causes may be quite different, the forms (or modes) of suffering are often alike across very different kinds of experience. In this way, suffering has confronted anthropologists with a social reality that, though constructed in vastly different ways, cannot be reduced by cultural essentialism (any more than by biological essentialism) merely to construction. "The world calls for words," wrote the postmodern philosopher Stanley Cavell (1994: 116), and suffering is one of the ways that the world calls for responses

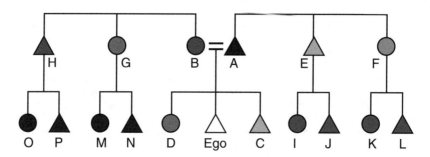

Figure 1 Sudanese kinship system.

and engagement, insisting upon the salience of existential conditions as the grounds for construction and the workings of power (Kleinman 1995).

Anthropological research on suffering includes a strong orientation toward the PHENOMENOLOGY of the experiences in particular social and historical contexts, but it has also come increasingly to incorporate a focus on the interaction of collective experience, political economy, and semiotics (M. Jackson 1996). Thus, Margaret Lock (1993a) showed that menopause, a common form of adversity in later life for women in North America (though not as common as biomedical practitioners and the hormone replacement industry assume), is not a major source of suffering for Japanese women. By contrast, Paul Farmer (1992, 1994) demonstrated how the structural violence of extreme poverty among Haitian peasants underlies both AIDS and tuberculosis as the deep grounds of human misery. Similarly Nancy Scheper-Hughes (1992) illustrated how an entire moral world can be remade by the grinding effect of extreme poverty on many aspects of social life, creating worlds of pain. Pierre Bourdieu and his colleagues (1993) offered a social theory of the destructive effects of social power on groups, including in disintegrating communities in America and France documented by such ethnographers of violence as Loic Wacquant (1993) and Phillipe Bourgois (1995).

Closely connected to these developments is the emergence of a genre of narrative studies that give voice to individual tales of misery (Kleinman 1992; S. Mattingly & Garro 1994; Murphy 1987). What is particularly anthropological about these works is that rather than sponsor a biographical or autobiographical analysis of a person, they deepen our understanding of the interpenetration of subjectivity and collective practices, agency and intersubjective connections. Studies of family and community responses to suffering increasingly turn away from depiction of "modal" or ideal-typical patterns to reveal the contradictions and contestations that grow out of social differences. Libbet Crandon-Malamud (1991) showed, for example, that use of ethnomedical and biomedical health services in the Bolivian Andes was more strongly influenced by choices about ethnic identity than by the experience of complaints. Veena Das (1995) explored works of fiction to get at what the social imaginary represents about the body, language, and imagery of suffering. She also demonstrated how class, communal, and gender differences inflect both the experience and consequences of suffering.

Studies of suffering have explored the moral requirements of the anthropologist's own engagement with others in pain. Here a debate has opened between those who call for an explicit ethnography of testimony and those who call for a return to an objectivist approach. Most ethnographers probably fall between these extremes. Many lobby for greater involvement with policies and programs; some campaign for experiential engagement as a model of moral practice. Although many have noted a curious resistance in the languages of philosophy and political theory to suffering as an object of inquiry, this is not the case with contemporary anthropology. Indeed it could be said that anthropology has been so absorbed with the traumatic consequences of political violence, economic restructuring, forced uprooting, community breakdown, structural deprivation, the failures of social development, and the global appropriations of suffering for commercial purposes, that it is as if suffering *were* its subject matter.   AK

See also EMOTIONS, PSYCHOLOGICAL ANTHROPOLOGY

further reading Csordas 1994; Desjarlais 1992; Hahn 1995; Janzen 1978; Kleinman et al. 1995

supernatural *See* MAGIC, SORCERY, WITCHCRAFT

surplus in its most general sense refers to a society's productive output beyond its customary subsistence level. The concept is often used by anthropologists as an enabling device to help explain cultural development or socioeconomic change (see EVOLUTION). The argument goes something like this: a society, given the constraints of its environmental and technological means, produces a material surplus (that is, the increase in net output beyond its customary level of production). If some group, such as religious, political, or military leaders, manages to commandeer this surplus (or part of it) to underwrite its own activities, this will induce specialization and a greater DIVISION OF LABOR in the economic sphere and create a more complex political organization.

Critics (Pearson 1957; Dalton 1960, 1963) point out that since it is difficult to determine what a customary subsistence level is, it is hard (perhaps impossible) to determine what a surplus beyond that customary level might be. Because all societies are capable of producing a surplus, the critical question is how surpluses are called forth and institutionalized in different times and places. This difficulty has been belittled by defenders of the surplus concept on the grounds that determining the necessary level of maintenance is indeed quite feasible and has cross-cultural applicability (Harris 1959). Therefore it is possible to assess with some degree of accuracy whether or not a society produces a surplus and the size of that surplus. In any case, it is argued, higher levels of productive output are clearly correlated with more complex forms of economic and sociopolitical organization (see COMPLEX SOCIETIES). Critics of the surplus concept countered that, although there is indeed a correlation between higher levels of productivity and more complex forms of sociopolitical organization, this does not explain what institutional mechanisms or processes called forth such higher levels of productivity. Populations do not always produce up to the limits of their environmental and technological opportunities.

The nub of the argument is clear but not easy to resolve: surplus theorists see the sequence of causation going in one direction (material surpluses arise and then lead to sociopolitical change); critics argue that the reverse is just as plausible (changes in sociopolitical organization bring forth an increase in output and a redeployment of its uses).   DK

See also CLASS, ECONOMIC ANTHROPOLOGY, STRATIFICATION

further reading Orans 1968

suttee (sati) is the practice of self-immolation on a husband's funeral pyre by Hindu wives.   MR

swidden agriculture is the scholarly term for "shifting cultivation" or "slash-and-burn." It is derived from the Old English "swithen" (from the Old Norse term "sviona"), meaning to singe (Pine 1995: 81–2). The role of fire is central to this system of cultivation: burning of cleared vegetation creates a temporary niche for cultigens by eliminating competing plants, and it sustains these cultigens by converting the extant biomass to nutrient-rich ash. After these nutrients are exhausted, the field is permitted to return to fallow under forest cover and the farmers "shift" to another plot in the forest to begin the cycle again. It is the fields, rather than the farmers, that are shifted in this system; there are few, if any, "nomadic" swidden cultivators (Padoch 1982). After a field has been fallowed, nutrient levels can usually be restored to the point that cultivation is again possible, provided the fallow period exceeds the cultivation period in length, which is one of the defining characteristics of swidden agriculture (Conklin 1957).

Swidden cultivation has been the subject of widespread myths, one of which is that such agriculturalists own and work their land communally. In fact, in swidden systems land is owned by individual HOUSEHOLDS: rights to given sections of land typically are created when a household clears the primary forest for planting. Land often is worked by reciprocal work groups: the labor given by one household to another in such arrangements is reciprocated on a strict day-for-day basis. Another myth is that swidden economies are cut off from the rest of the world. In reality, swidden agriculturalists, in addition to planting subsistence food crops, typically plant market-oriented cash crops such as pepper, coffee, coconuts, tobacco, and rubber (Pelzer 1978). As a result, swidden farmers often are more integrated into the world economy than many of the participants in more intensive forms of agriculture.

Theoretical study of swidden agriculture has focused on its ecological sustainability and whether this is based on "mimicry" of natural forest ecology (Beckerman 1983; C. Geertz 1963c); its ability to support (as opposed to undermine) the conditions of its own reproduction; its economic vitality and its place in complex, "composite" economic systems (Dove 1993a); and its relationship to, and ability to support, state formations (Friedman 1975). Perhaps of greater importance, swidden systems provided the setting for many of the key ethnographic studies that led to the development of ethnoecological and ETHNOSCIENTIFIC approaches (Conklin 1954a; Frake 1962b) and the subfield of ECOLOGICAL ANTHROPOLOGY.   MRD & ML

See also AGRICULTURE

further reading Condominas 1977; Dove 1985; D. Freeman 1970; Joseph Spencer 1966

symbolic anthropology takes as its basic tenets the ideas that indigenous meanings are the goal of research and that these meanings, though not explicit, may be discovered in the symbolism of such things as MYTH and RITUAL. It is a term that marks both an intellectual movement of the 1970s and 1980s and an anthropological method.

The interpretation of symbolism per se is nothing new, of course. Presumably, it is as old as literature. Moreover, it was the stock in trade of the first generation of anthropologists, in the late nineteenth century. For example, Edward Burnett TYLOR (1871) based a reconstruction of the stages of human mental EVOLUTION on what was then known about "primitive religions," that is any other than a handful of world religions. By contemporary standards, however, Tylor's interpretations are naive and ethnocentric. They are naive because, in the rationalist mode of his time, Tylor began with the assumption that all the complex rites of primitive religions are a result simply of faulty logic: wrong answers to questions about real phenomena. Tylor's program is often characterized as "intellectualist" in a derogatory sense, but J. W. Burrow caught it better: "the sociology of error" (1966: 7–9). Tylor's interpretations are ethnocentric because he saw no need to delve into other cultures; on the contrary, he assumed that he could see di-

rectly into the mind of "primitive man," so that his approach is also called "empathic," again in a derogatory sense.

In the middle decades of this century, interest in symbolism retreated as FUNCTIONALISM advanced. The new paradigm emphasized sociological topics, such as kinship and politics, at the expense of religion. Moreover, the old symbolic studies were tarnished by their association with nineteenth-century evolutionism, which functionalism condemned. British functionalists like A. R. RADCLIFFE-BROWN saw themselves as building a new science of SOCIETY, and they distrusted, with good reason, the manner in which Tylor and his contemporaries had dwelt on the bizarre and the sensational. A concern with symbolism survived only where FUNCTIONALISM failed to gain the ascendancy, notably in the American CULTURE AND PERSONALITY school, which included several members with psychiatric training. But their predisposition toward the universalizing theories of Freud obstructed culturally specific interpretation and tended to perpetuate the ethnocentrism of the evolutionists.

In one important respect, however, functionalism prepared the way for symbolic anthropology by its insistence on holism. Where nineteenth-century anthropologists had made customs seem odd by tearing them out of their proper cultural contexts, functionalism sought to make sense of them by putting them back. It escaped ETHNOCENTRISM by expecting institutions to be intelligible only as parts of whole social systems, and symbolic anthropology does the same with regard to ritual and belief.

Consequently, there was no major break between functionalism and symbolic anthropology. Moreover, interest in religion had never completely disappeared; Max GLUCKMAN wrote interestingly about ritual while remaining the archfunctionalist, for instance in his study of Swazi royal rites (1954). A re-study by T. O. B. Beidelman (1966) demonstrates nicely how a symbolic approach might differ from a functionalist one.

In bridging the two approaches, the most important figure was Gluckman's student Victor TURNER. Turner began his research among the Ndembu of northwestern Zambia with issues of SOCIAL ORGANIZATION, which he found intractable because of the instability of Ndembu villages. By degrees, he realized that the true continuity of Ndembu life lay in its rituals and the ideas and values they expressed. To arrive at these ideas, he devised or adapted methods of interpretation that are best described in the essay "Symbols in Ndembu ritual," which was first published in a collection (Gluckman 1964) and later as a chapter in Turner's most widely read book *The forest of symbols* (1967). Turner listed three sources of relevant information: "(1) external form and observable characteristics; (2) interpretations offered by specialists and laymen: (3) significant contexts largely worked out by the anthropologist" (1967: 20). In arriving at his interpretations, Turner moved constantly between these sources, checking one against another. The key point is that an interpretation arrived at with one source of data gains conviction when it provides insight elsewhere; it was an inductive process that genuinely sought Ndembu meanings, and in that lies its power and appeal.

At the same time, Turner's mode of operation re-admits comparativism under heading (3), where the "significant contexts" may include similar rites performed in other cultures, perhaps on the other side of the world. This is not, however, a reversion to universal symbolism, because any imported interpretation must be confirmed by the precise details of what happens in these particular rites by whatever indigenous exegesis is forthcoming, and by other rituals and myths belonging to the culture under study. In effect, a knowledge of ritual worldwide provides a store of ready hypotheses that will be confirmed or discarded according to how they fit with the culture under study. Meanwhile, each new ethnographic case investigated contributes to the accumulation of knowledge about just how widespread items of symbolism are, and this accumulation is the major substantive contribution of symbolic anthropology to the discipline as a whole.

For example, few anthropologists are unaware of the pervasiveness of symbolism of left and right. A collection edited by

Rodney Needham (1973) underlines it, while also showing variation in how it is applied from one case to another. Particularly interesting are those cases where our expectation of the primacy of right over left is overturned. Needham's volume includes a translation of the classic article on polarity written in 1909 by Robert HERTZ, and this reminds us that the agenda of symbolic anthropology was already worked out in large part by the students of Emile DURKHEIM in the early decades of this century. Had World War I not intervened, they might well have carried it through to field research.

When Turner began his work with Ndembu ritual, the relationship between comparativism and ethnography in symbolic studies, between the universal and the particular, was not clear. Turner felt obliged to defend himself against an attack made by Monica Wilson on an anthropological literature "bespattered with symbolic guessing" (in Turner 1967: 26). What Wilson had in mind was Freudian interpretations imposed on people whose interpersonal relations were entirely different from those that Freud knew. Instead, Wilson wanted ethnographers to stick to what the participants themselves said were the meanings of their rituals, and this was the sticking point, because Turner by no means intended to be restricted in this way. In his famous step-by-step unfolding of the symbolism of the *mudyi* tree, which the Ndembu describe as the "flag," Turner went well beyond what his informants made explicit, and laid bare meanings that had to do with contradiction and conflict, both social and ideological (1967: 20-5). It is clear that what is unsaid, or unsayable, is far from irrelevant; on the contrary, it enables us to penetrate cultural premises so deeply held or taken for granted that they are never held up to examination.

At this point, the development of symbolic anthropology from within the British tradition converged with the dominant paradigm of the epoch, namely French STRUCTURALISM. It was axiomatic that the structures that interested Claude LÉVI-STRAUSS were unconscious, and this similarity, together with a shared heritage from Durkheim and the *Année Sociologique* school, was enough to make symbolic anthropology attractive to those already inclined toward structuralism. Many anthropologists merged the two, especially in ethnographic accounts drawing on the symbolism of all manner of cultural practices, typically analyzed in dyadic fashion. Issues of classification in particular lent themselves to this treatment, as for example in Mary DOUGLAS's (1966: 55–72) well-known account of Judaic food taboos.

Just how close the convergence was remains debatable. Where Turner valued indigenous explanations as one amongst several sources of data, Lévi-Strauss was uninterested in what participants had to say. He argued that what were bound to be inaccurate conscious models could only obstruct his analysis (1963a: 274). As far as the end product is concerned, if we look at the interpretations that Lévi-Strauss offers of the mythology of South American Indians, for example in *The raw and the cooked* (1969b), we find that they do not much resemble those in, say, Turner's account of the Ndembu curing ritual of *Chihamba* (1962). When the two approaches were merged, they produced a middle-of-the-road structuralism that abandoned Lévi-Strauss's more radical claims to discovering fundamental features of the mind.

A similar merging occurred with various currents in American cultural anthropology originating with Franz BOAS and his students. The American school rejected functionalism and always favored interpretive approaches. In the 1970s its most conspicuous exponent was Clifford GEERTZ, who was explicit about his SEMIOTIC view of culture. When he spoke of anthropology as "not an experimental science in search of law but an interpretive one in search of meaning" (1973: 5), the intersection with Turner's course away from Radcliffe-Brown's science of society was plain. American anthropologists brought to symbolic anthropology a special concern for LANGUAGE, for instance in *The social use of metaphor* (D. Sapir & Crocker 1977).

The merging of national traditions stimulated the growth of symbolic anthropology, but also made it more diffuse. Some elements were incompatible; Geertz, for instance, spoke scathingly of Lévi-Strauss's de-humanized "cerebral savage" (1973: 345–59). Meanwhile, in the 1990s both structuralist and semiotic approaches are under attack. The core issues of symbolism remain relevant, but they are now widely assimilated in the discipline; only in the strictest brands of behaviorism or materialism is it possible to conceive of an anthropology that is nonsymbolic.   PM

See also RELIGION, RITUAL

symbolic capital   is the social credit or prestige that marks and partially constitutes the STATUS of a social actor and can, in principle, be exchanged for goods, services, or social recognition (Bourdieu 1990).

MR

syntax   is the study of the organization of words into phrases and sentences within LINGUISTICS. A degree of consensus has emerged through the 1970s and 1980s that phrase structure is largely neutral over the major lexical categories of noun, adjective, verb, and preposition. Any X ranging over these is taken to combine with its complements/objects to form an X' ("X-bar"), which combines in turn with a constituent referred to as its "Specifier" (Spec), to form a maximal "projection" X" ("X-double bar"), as illustrated in figure 1, where X equals N (noun), N" being a Noun Phrase (NP). The exact category of specifiers and complements will depend on the "head" (X).

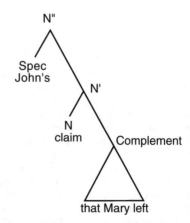

Figure 1   John's claim that Mary left.

While full sentences may appear to be simply verb phrases (with V replacing N in figure 1 for the sentence "John claims that Mary left"), actual analyses are more complex. Since the mid-1980s, one influential line has treated them as projections of an abstract category I ("IPs") – representing verb inflection.

A further major concern in syntax are dependencies across the phrase structure, such as the one in the following sentence, where the underscored is selected as a complement/object of the verb *shred*, and yet appears as the subject of *are likely*:

Those documents are likely to have been shredded.

Such duplicities have been dealt with by postulating a representation called "D(eep)-Structure," in which the underscored is indeed the object of *shred*, and certain syntactic "transformations" derive the "S(urface)" structure.   LB

See also GRAMMAR, TRANSFORMATIONAL GRAMMAR

further reading C. Baker 1995; Haegeman 1994; Radford 1981

systems theory began in ecology, in the study of the processes by which organisms and communities of species exchange matter and energy with each other and their surrounding environments. The mathematical foundations of systems theory were largely the creation of Alfred Lotka, who argued that "evolution proceeds in such direction as to make the total energy flux through the system the maximum compatible with ecosystems" (1925: 357). Lotka's work was the major (if less than fully acknowledged) inspiration for Ludwig von Bertalanffy's (1968) attempt to create a general systems theory, an attempt now widely regarded as having failed. More fruitfully, Lotka's ideas were taken up by systems ecologists to study such questions as species diversity, community structure, and succession in ecosystems. Eugene Odum (1953), for example, argued that homeostasis could be maintained in an ecosystem because of the existence of compensatory pathways for exchanges between species. If one pathway was disrupted, its loss could be compensated for by increased flow through other pathways.

Although Clifford GEERTZ (1963c) first urged anthropologists to adopt an "ecosystem" perspective, his own research on agricultural development in Indonesia did not employ the methodology of systems ecology and its best-known application in anthropology is Roy A. Rappaport's study (1967) of the role of ritual in the management of pigs and gardens among the Tsembaga, a community of horticulturists in highland New Guinea. Using an explicit systems-ecology methodology, Rappaport described the Tsembaga as a population engaged in energetic exchanges with plants and animals in their environment, and in competition with their neighbors. The common currency in these exchanges was energy: Rappaport calculated the energy costs of activities such as clearing swidden gardens and raising pigs, and measured the returns in terms of caloric values. Rappaport extended his analysis well beyond the horizons of systems ecology, as practiced by biologists, to include the role of ritual in timing the interlocking cycles of pig feasts, population growth, and warfare.

Following Rappaport's lead, a number of studies have attempted to apply systems ecology to human groups, particularly in high mountain areas in South America and Europe (R. Thomas 1972; Netting 1981) and among pastoralists in East Africa (Little 1992). However, the widespread application of the method has been handicapped because the amount of variance in experimental controls is often embarrassingly large. By the 1970s ecologists like Robert May (1973, 1976) had concluded that the equations used to describe communities of living organisms were inherently unstable. This discovery became an important chapter in the development of the mathematical theory of deterministic chaos.

Partly in response to chaos theory, a new approach to systems theory has appeared in recent years. Under such rubrics as "complexity theory," "dynamical systems theory," and "nonlinear dynamics," its major focus is on the role of self-organization in complex adaptive systems (CAS). A CAS consists of a network of interacting agents that exhibit a dynamic, aggregate behavior. Nonlinear models (e.g., where the solution to two equations is not equal to the solution of the sum of the equations) of CAS suggest that spontaneous patterns of order can emerge from the activities of the agents (Kauffman 1993). This approach relies so heavily on computer modeling that it has been described by the eminent biologist John Maynard Smith (1995: 29) as "fact-free science"; but nevertheless "should become part of the mental furniture of scientists in the future."

In the social sciences, the study of CAS was initially taken up by economists and game theorists. In anthropology, J. S. Lansing and J. N. Kremer (1993) created a nonlinear simulation of the role of networks of "water temples" in the management of rice-terrace ecology on the Indonesian island of Bali. For over a thousand years, generations of Balinese farmers have gradually transformed the landscape of their island, clearing forests, digging irrigation canals and tunnels, and terracing hillsides to enable themselves and their descendants to grow irrigated rice. Paralleling the physical system of terraces and irrigation works, the farmers also constructed intricate networks of shrines and temples whose priests managed the water flow. Studies of the structure of water temple networks along two Balinese rivers revealed that they provided an optimal pattern of management nearly identical to the actual structure of real water networks (Lansing 1991). In archaeology, with its concern with the development and collapse of human organizations through time, the theory of complex adaptive systems has recently been applied to the rise and fall of complex societies in the prehistoric American Southwest (Gummerman & Gell-Mann 1993; Kohler 1992, 1993).

JSL

further reading Hofbauer & Sigmund 1988; Kremer 1978; Moran 1990

T

taboo is a ritually sanctioned prohibition against contact with a thing, a person, or an activity. The word itself is of Polynesian origin, where taboos played an important cultural role, but the concept is universal. Common taboos include injunctions against eating certain foods, touching kings or outcasts, contact with corpses, and sexual relations with certain people. The subject of the taboo may be regarded either as sacred or as polluted, and violation of the taboo is not merely a crime but also an act of defilement. Breaking a taboo ordinarily brings either a specific supernatural sanction or a sort of general misfortune. Taboo is particularly associated with people in LIMINAL social positions. Persons at the margins of society, such as rulers, untouchables, and hermits, are often taboo to ordinary people; persons in social transition, such as initiates and new parents, are usually required to observe an unusual number of taboos.

Like many early observers, FRAZER (1890) regarded taboo as a symptom of primitive irrationality, a defense against the supernatural dangers that primitive man imagined all around him. Functionalists saw more reason to taboo. DURKHEIM viewed it as a means for maintaining the distinction between sacred and profane (1915); RADCLIFFE-BROWN (1939) argued that it was a mechanism for emphasizing the social importance of certain people and objects. Mary DOUGLAS (1966) took a symbolic approach, suggesting that objects and people become taboo when they fail to fit into the standard symbolic CLASSIFICA-TIONS of their culture. Certain very widespread taboos have also interested psychological and biological anthropologists. Sociobiologists, for example, have argued that the universal taboo against INCEST with parents and siblings is a biological mechanism for avoiding genetic defects (E. Wilson 1978).   AB
See also PURITY/POLLUTION, RITUAL, SYMBOLIC ANTHROPOLOGY, TOTEMISM

technology is the means and agencies by which human societies cope with and transform their material environment. As a process or system, technology includes the materials that are acted upon, tools or other means by which that action is carried out, the application of an operating procedure to effect the desired action, and the knowledge of how to perform it.

To the extent that anthropologists have recognized *Homo faber* as a kind of social archetype and stressed the use of tools as one subset of cultural artifacts, technology has always been present in the anthropological repertory. But in "classical" cultural and social anthropology it has been undertheorized. An early attempt at theorization was Augustus Pitt-Rivers's (1906) evolutionary sequencing of families of technical artifacts, which, according to Spencerian and Darwinian reasoning, developed from simpler to more complex forms by a process of selection: people unconsciously select the tool best suited for a specific task, thus gradually modifying the artifact until the form was perfectly adapted to its function. There have been numerous attempts to categorize historical periods in terms of technology, the most noteworthy being Lewis Henry MORGAN's division of human history into periods of savagery, barbarism, and civilization characterized mainly on the basis of technologies. Thus the bow and arrow characterized the upper-savage period; pottery, lower barbarism; irrigation, maize cultivation, and stone and adobe construction, middle barbarism; and so forth. Although Morgan's technological sequence contained a number of ethnographic and historical errors, it drew attention to technological innovations responsible for revolutionary increments in population size and density and in the agricultural base necessary to sustain them (Harris 1968: 181, 185). A similar kind of design, but much more sophisticated, is Mumford's (1934) schematization of technology over the last two millennia:

1. an eotechnic phase characterized by the "diminished use of human beings as prime movers, and the separation of the production of energy from its application and immediate control" (late antiquity to around 1700)
2. a paleotechnic phase extending from 1700 to 1900, embracing the industrial revolution and the preeminence of the "coal and iron complex"
3. a neotechnic period characterized by the effective fusion of science with technology

The significance of Mumford's scheme lies in its inclusivity, integrating the facts of technology to social, economic, and (quite significantly) aesthetic and stylistic considerations.

A different kind of classification is Lewis Binford's (1962) division of techniques themselves into functional categories: technomic (those techniques that interact with the physical environment), sociotechnic (those that function to articulate social groups); and idiotechnic (those that relate to the symbolic). Thus a pot may be both technomic in respect to its function of containing food and idio- or sociotechnic by virtue of its decoration.

Traditional techniques have been more the province of anthropology than has modern industrial technology. There is an ample literature on the conservative nature of traditional technology, linked both to technical and economic considerations. Artisans are characteristically unwilling to risk abandoning an economically viable technique for an untried innovation. Specific techniques may be confined (in the form of secret knowledge) within a family or small group of craftsmen, a practice which is conducive both to diversification of techniques and to resistance to innovation. This kind of conservatism explains why an artisan might not utilize a technique to its full potential, but only to serve the more limited end required: thus potters' wheels may be used only as turntables without realizing the advantage of centrifugal force (Nicklin 1971–2). The motor-pattern components of technology – that is, the physical movements and operations made by artisans while pursuing their craft – are both highly resistant to change and, if lost in a given population, not easily recoupable (Kroeber 1948).

Anthropologists have also stressed the systemic nature of production to demonstrate the ways in which systemic constraints tend to produce long-term stability. Thus the natural-resource base of local pottery production (clay, fuel) provides the basis for functional adaptations that potters are reluctant to change (P. Rice 1984). Similarly, the systemic requirements of IRRIGATION also conspire to produce sets of institutions for water allocation and the avoidance of conflict that are "ultra-stable" (Ostrom 1990): communal values informing the principles of allocation are both formalized in a structure of water rights and operationalized in physical structures and operating procedures that transform those abstract principles into the delivery of aliquot portions of the total stream flow to farmers. Once in place and working to the community's satisfaction, such arrangements can persist for centuries, even when appropriated by conquering groups (Glick 1995). For such reasons, technology has been viewed anthropologically as an extremely conservative cultural subsystem, dependent on tradition and social institutions for long-term stability. It is not always clear, however, whether different technologies require organizational forms specific to them or whether such organization can be borrowed from other cultural subsystems, such as religion or kinship (Lechtman & Steinberg 1979). To return to irrigation, for example, tribal irrigation systems typically encode kinship, particularly clan or lineage structures, in their water-rights systems, whereas Balinese "water temples" provide an example of the integration of technological and ritual subsystems (Lansing 1991).

The traditional anthropological approach to technical artifacts as specific bundles of traits or cultural elements has come under attack from a number of perspectives. Thus there has been an attempt to integrate the study of preindustrial technologies into explanatory frameworks based on general SYSTEMS THEORY, which has more frequently been applied to contemporary industrial technologies. Thus the notion of a sociotechnical system aims to explain how "people employ artifacts to accomplish social purposes in everyday life" (Pfaffenberger 1992: 492), while a technoeconomic subsystem is introduced to distinguish between the technical and social components of a given production system (Gibbon 1984). Such concepts are little more than rhetorical devices designed to legitimate the integration of technology studies into anthropology. The notions that technology is socially and culturally constructed and is inextricably linked to the organization of work are hardly surprising conclusions. Moreover, the approach is not new. Mumford (1934) observed that "Almost any part of a technological complex will point to and symbolize a whole series of relationships within that complex."

Systems theory is much more successful in a synchronic framework than it is in explicating change over time. Yet technical systems, like other social and cultural subsystems, change recursively, and thus historically sensitive models are ultimately more productive. Therefore understanding the historical development of specific technologies, according to cultural and cognitive processes internal to them (the subject matter of the history of technology proper), would seem a prerequisite to working out broader, systemic linkages. In Basalla's view (1988), artifacts are not simply traits with synchronic linkages to a broader cultural system but are always related to what has been made before. Technological novelty is accounted for not only by necessity but by imaginative, creative, and stylistic concerns as well. Artifacts, once invented, are then subjected to a multivalent range of selective pressures, including "economic and military necessity, social and cultural attitudes" and even "the pursuit of technological fads." Basalla's conclusion that economic necessity is not always the mother of invention is an effective endorsement of a culturological approach to technology, in which the choice of techniques and the evolution of artifacts are sharply dependent on the interaction between specific value systems and families of techniques.

Lemonnier (1989) has shown that even in quintessential modern technologies like aviation it is possible to apply an ethnological approach to variations in design, so long as one recognizes that variability is linked to performance demands: the higher the demands, the less the variability. Thus early airplane design displayed a surprisingly broad range of stylistic features, suggesting that the variation cannot be accounted for purely by engineering or aerodynamic considerations.

Traditional technology is knowledge-intensive; that is, it depends upon the collective experience of rather large constituencies in executing productive tasks. Knowledge intensiveness lends stability to the technological system, and at the same time it accounts for the vulnerability of such technologies once interrupted. This is particularly significant when traditional agroecosystems that have enjoyed long-term success are interrupted by less functional innovations, such as those associated with the GREEN REVOLUTION.   TG

teknonymy is the practice of referring to or addressing a person as the parent of their named offspring rather than by their personal name. Thus Jane, the mother of Charles, would be known as "Mother of Charles."   MR

textual analysis See LITERARY ANTHROPOLOGY, QUALITATIVE METHODS

thick description is ethnographic writing in which, through a careful attention to detail and context, there is an integration of description with interpretation. The term was popularized by Clifford GEERTZ (1973).   MR

time is a metaphysical category. As such it poses difficulties concerning what anthropology can and should say about it. Aware of the pitfalls of relativism, but determined to claim thought as a realm proper for sociological investigation, DURKHEIM (1915) argued that the categories of human understanding were social in origin, *but also* corresponded to reality. They perfectly imitate nature, to which societies must adapt in order to survive.

At least since Durkheim's colleague Henri Hubert (1905) published his classic study of time and ritual, there has been a tendency in anthropology to argue that cultures represent time in different ways, that there are different kinds of time. In an influential study, EVANS-PRITCHARD (1939) said that the Nuer and Europeans have different interests and therefore different time values and that Nuer time concepts are manmade, social notions referring to preponderant communal interests. Points of this order are frequently demonstrated by anthropologists and cause little difficulty. More controversial are his assertions that Nuer perceptions of time are culturally determined, that they have no concept of time, and that they have a different sense of time from our own. Read in a certain way, these statements would appear to deny to the Nuer fundamental capacities generally deemed essential for human reason. Interpreted differently, they might be taken to mean little more than that Nuer CLASSIFICATIONS and expressions of time reflect Nuer concerns, that they lack a developed discourse about time in the abstract, and that in their actions and choices they do not suffer from a sense of the pressure of time. The first reading would suggest that Evans-Pritchard was influenced by Durkheim's generally Kantian position, but in radical disagreement with Kant's view that time is a universal category of understanding. The second reading would allow less distracted access to what is otherwise a sensitive and illuminating ethnographic description of Nuer use and conception of time. In a similarly influential pair of articles, LEACH (1953, 1955) demonstrated that a wide and disparate vocabulary may be employed in another language where in English the word "time" would appear. Following on from Hubert, Leach attempted to argue that primitives have what is essentially a

repetitive, noncumulative concept of time, whereas modern time concepts are linear and emphasize irreversibility. LÉVI-STRAUSS (1953a, 1953b) even suggested that different kinds of time might be found within different lines in a single relationship terminology.

The problem with statements of this kind is that the authors may be confusing an inherent capacity to perceive the passage of time with empirical representations of the ordering of events in time. In some statements time itself, a dimension of the physical world, becomes relativized, misshapen, and distorted. Anthropology cannot effectively engage in debates in scientific cosmology about the direction of time and its possible reversal and generally should avoid appearing to try to do so. The tendency to speak as though time itself were a relative value has been attacked by Maurice Bloch (1977) and Gell (1992a). Bloch asserted that if anthropologists were right that other peoples had different concepts of time (in the most abstract sense), we could not communicate with them. In fact, any position arguing that the categories and laws of reason vary from society to society would undermine the standards by which we judge scholarship to be coherent and valid. Much like Hubert, Bloch nevertheless argued that the people of Bali have two different conceptions of time. In criticism of Leach, R. Barnes (1974) interpreted Kédang time concepts as being unitary and irreversible but as marking the passage of time by reference to recurrent events in nature. Howe (1981) offered similar criticisms of Bloch's interpretations of Balinese time. He in turn influenced Farriss (1983) on Mayan time. Several of the world's great calendrical systems, such as those of the Maya or ancient India, utilize true, mathematical, cycles. Much of the best anthropological work on time has been devoted to the cultural peculiarities of calendar systems, uses of history, and the remembrance of events (see, e.g., Turton & Ruggles 1978; Hughes & Trautmann 1995). It is easier to make sense of these patterns and variations if we do not confuse them with time itself. As Bloch and Gell put it, we should not confuse time with what calibrates and measures it. Gell in turn offered an ingenious metaphysical argument to show that the anthropology of time should emulate time-budget studies and certain developments in geography and economics dealing with time.   RB

totemism is derived from "totem," a word of native North American origin (Ojibwa) meaning "He is my relative" and by implication, a member of one's own EXOGAMOUS clan (B. Morris 1987: 270). Following W. Robertson SMITH (1889), DURKHEIM (1915) argued that the earliest RELIGIONS were based on such clans, each expressing its solidarity through the "emblem" of its respective totems and, together, their distinctive relationships to each other in a wider-level solidarity. Durkheim drew his conclusions from analysis of Australian Aborigine religion, in which heads of clans worshipped at totemic sites regarded as sacred, as were the clan's ritual objects, which only initiated men could handle and which were designed to symbolize the clan's totems. Each clan had its own totems, shared by no one else, which could be any plant, animal, or feature of nature (even rain or forest). These had to be protected and allowed to flourish, since their own well-being was consubstantive with that of the clan. Hence Durkheim argued that the totems symbolized and indeed *were* the social group: religion was therefore society worshipping itself through the tangible and visible totem. Social differentiation and solidarity expressed themselves through the structure of totems, which themselves reflected a universal human belief in a mystical or sacred principle or force.

MAX WEBER (1963) regarded Durkheim's claims for the universal origin of religion and society in totemism as unlikely. RADCLIFFE-BROWN (1930) held broadly to Durkheim's position but he later argued (1951) that totemism was the basis not just of religion and society but of scientific thought, a view that was not absent from Durkheim but was subordinated to his concern with the social determination of human activity. LÉVI-STRAUSS (1963b) grouped Radcliffe-Brown's early interpretation of totemism with that of MALINOWSKI (1948), seeing them both as

utilitarian claims that totems were venerated because the plants and animals they represented were "good to eat." Radcliffe-Brown's later suggestion that there are analogic relations between totems and social relations is the one taken up by Lévi-Strauss: for instance, night owls and the nightjars both live in trees and both eat meat, just as people do. In this respect their similarities are analogic of similarities in the human condition. But they can also represent the differences between humans, in that one bird is a "hunter" and the other a "thief," and so on (Lévi-Strauss 1963b: 160–1). It is this human capacity to think in terms of relational similarities and differences, or correlations and oppositions, across natural and social or cultural domains, that induced Lévi-Strauss to see totemism as not specifically to do with religion but as an aspect of a universal propensity to classify in terms of a kind of associative logic.

Freud's theory of totemism as resting on the Oedipus complex (1918) stands largely outside these preceding theories. Freud argued that in an early primal horde sons killed their father in order to have access to his females. Then, out of guilt, they created the INCEST TABOO and reenacted ceremonially, for purposes of expiation, the original sinful murder in the form of a SACRIFICE of an animal, which is really the substitute father and the first animal totem. The theory thus posits the origin of totemism as well as that of exogamy, the incest taboo, sacrifice, and religion itself.

Much ethnographic work has been carried out on totemism, the complexity of which has been taken into newer concerns with indigenous and outsider CLASSIFICATION systems and taxonomies of nature and with ecology (B. Morris 1976, 1979; Ingold 1988b).   DP
See also SYMBOLIC ANTHROPOLOGY
further reading Leach 1967; R. Needham 1973; R. Nelson 1983; Roe 1982; R. Willis 1990 [esp. the introduction by Willis]

trade is a two-way exchange in which the transactions usually occur close to each other in time. Trade describes two types of exchange: (1) exchanges mediated by some sort of MONEY, where buying and selling are key elements; and (2) BARTER, in which two goods or services are exchanged for each other without any intervention of, or use of, money. It is debatable whether GIFT EXCHANGE should be included under the rubric of trade. Although used often in anthropological writing, trade is not a well-formed technical concept.

The forms of trade that are of particular interest to anthropologists are "long distance" or "down-the-line," because they frequently involve many different societies, often with different cultural values. Long-distance trade moves objects far from where they originated (copper, bronze, obsidian, gem stones, stone axes, cowry shells, etc.). In some cases expeditions travel to the site of the resource, acquire the raw materials (and perhaps manufacture the object), and then return home. This does not constitute trade because it does not involve an exchange. More common are trading expeditions where people travel to the point of origin and "trade" for the objects, then return home. We have plentiful archeological evidence of such expeditions in the ancient Near East, and the history of the last several hundred years of overseas trade in such goods as spices, silk, and tea. Where one of the parties to the exchange has vast superiority of weapons and can arbitrarily impose the terms of trade, the distinction between trade and tribute can be very hard to draw.

Another means of acquiring goods from a distance has been called "down-the-line" trade and is widely found in the ethnographic record. In this type of trade objects are transferred from one local group to a neighboring group. Often a different kind of object is transferred in the opposite direction, and the two objects are involved in the same transaction. Thus, for example, cowry shells and green stone axes were traded for each other on a north–south axis across what is now Papua New Guinea. (The cowry shells originated on the south coast, and the green stone axes on the north coast.) Some of the objects were kept at any given point, and others were sent on. The relative value of each (compared with the other) was a function of distance from point of origin.

Small EGALITARIAN SOCIETIES have systematic exchange systems, and objects may travel a very great distance by this means. Exchange can occur in periodic gatherings or in dyadic exchanges at any point in time. These exchanges are sometimes called "trade," and sometimes "gift exchange." The criteria for differentiating these two concepts are not clear. For example, an important part of the KULA expeditions in the Trobriand Islands of the Pacific was the organized trading between visitors and hosts, quite apart from the delivery of the kula valuables.

Larger societies, particularly those that are STRATIFIED, may and often do have much more organized opportunities for trade. In politically centralized societies the polity itself may engage in trade by setting up "ports of trade" – special trading emporia, cities, or settlements devoted largely to exchange, often located at the borders of different polities. There can be trade within a polity, facilitated by a unicentric organization of laws, judges, and money that makes and enforces local laws of contract; local systems of measurement; and often local commercial languages to create a uniform set of rules. Exchanges between polities are often less uniform and are often talked about in terms of "tribute" or "barter."

Finally, individuals or corporations can trade across polity boundaries. Though extremely important there has been very little systematic study of the social and occupational roles of the long-distance trader and the merchant who crosses political boundaries. The skills demanded of such people are formidable: measurement systems are rarely identical in two different places, and so the long-distance merchant must have facility in two or more measurement systems; currency varies from place to place, its value fluctuates through time, and the customs and contract laws vary from place to place. The successful merchant must learn and operate all these different systems. Furthermore, the safety of the merchant and his assets is a function of the military strength that backs him, peace and justice in the places he does business, or even the strength of his network. All these vary from place to place and from time to time and can be subject to sudden fluctuations, such as a declaration of war, a currency crisis, or change in tax policy. For this reason the more uncertain the conditions, the more likely such trade is to be concentrated in high-value luxury goods, light in weight compared to their value.

Trade has the effect of making foreign objects (and perhaps some services) available locally. Virtually all human societies have been involved in such trade. Among the effects are to increase the range of goods and resources available in a given locality, which presumably increases the ability of the local people to manage their environment. There may in addition be the social advantage of maintaining peaceful social interaction with neighboring societies. Trading partners can be a source of refuge in case of trouble.   RHun

See also CAPITALISM, COLONIALISM, MIDDLEMAN MINORITIES, WORLD-SYSTEM THEORY

further reading Curtin 1984; Earle & Ericson 1977; Plattner 1989; K. Polanyi et al. 1957

tradition Connoting an inherited body of traits, "tradition" is a category that individuals and societies ascribe to expressions, beliefs, and behaviors in the present to add value for the future. Always referring to the past, this categorizing adds weight and momentum to what it names: symbolically designating something a tradition implies meaning and value. By placing its subject in history, such a designation opposes modernity and adds a burden of significance. It offers a rationale for preservation, for special treatment, for care; something termed a tradition is likely to be encouraged to continue, and its momentum grows stronger. Thus, tradition is a territory of the imagination, but its presence has very significant consequences in social life. To say that something is traditional is to use a powerful social strategy to claim that it is valuable, that it speaks eloquently about us, and that we should attend to it.

Although "tradition" has enjoyed a long currency among scholars and is also a powerful term in many discourses outside the academy, Raymond Williams (1976: 269) noted that in its modern usages it is "a particularly difficult word" because its academic and commonsense meanings have changed over time. For scholars interested in the confluence of culture and history, the word once signified both an expanse of time reaching into the past and the processes that allowed aspects of the past to continue into the present. Accordingly, scholars could then talk about whether they could certify something – a practice, a belief, an expression – as traditional. To certify something as traditional was to connect it to another difficult term, "authenticity." For anthropologists and folklorists, particularly between the mid-nineteenth and mid-twentieth centuries, tradition implied appropriate age, and to call something traditional was to assert its cultural authenticity, often set against modernity. Its authenticity gave it authority; it became especially worthy of attention. For Franz BOAS, tradition, FOLKLORE, and CULTURE mingled and overlapped, and tradition was very nearly the same thing as culture. At the very least, tradition was the historical component of culture (Stocking 1968: 195–233). Later, it came even closer to being synonymous with culture, as in formulations positing a tension between "great tradition" – urban and complex ways of life with a strong and formal historical consciousness – and "little traditions," constellations of local knowledge underlying ways of life, often in peasant communities (Redfield 1960; Milton Singer 1972).

Although tradition continues to imply a depth of time as well as continuity, today scholars are coming to see it not as an innate quality, imbued by continuity and stasis, but rather as an imperative in social life, a way in which the present interprets and characterizes the past with an eye to the future. Although some write of "invented" or "selective" traditions, and still others write of "traditionalizing," the common thread of many contemporary discussions is that tradition results from social imperatives (Hobsbawm & Ranger 1983; Handler & Linnekin 1984; R. Williams 1961; Hymes 1975). Societies designate aspects of their culture as traditions to infuse them with meaning and historicity. Sometimes this labeling recognizes the continuity of old practices. At other times it adds the weight of the past to forms and practices that have less continuity than the designation implies. To call something traditional is to institutionalize it by setting it off from less authentic practices, to reduce it to a pared-down essence, to encourage its social performance, and to imply the need for stewardship into the future. At the very least, it comes from a need to make the social familiar by repeated performances. More than that, though, to call something a tradition is an act of interpretation, a way of selecting and naming, a fundamental manner of imposing order on the disarray of social life.   BF

See also MODERNIZATION

further reading Ben-Amos 1984; Eisenstadt 1973; Glassie 1995; Rudolph & Rudolph 1967; Shils 1981

trance is a dissociated psychological state in which individuals are noticeably disconnected from their everyday reality: they may appear to be completely withdrawn, unresponsive, see objects and people that others cannot see, and be impervious to exhaustion or to the normal passage of TIME. In recounting the experience they often report no memory of time or a sense of time that seems much longer or shorter than the actual time elapsed. All such states are "conditions in which sensations, perceptions, cognitions and emotions are altered" (Bourguignon 1979: 236).

These altered states are readily induced by DANCE, hyperventilation, DRUGS, or ALCOHOL. They can also be induced through formal training in concentration techniques such as meditation, visualization, or PRAYER, although these formal techniques often have as their end state the more peculiar and harder-to-achieve state of mystical experience. While trance is only one of many altered states that include dreams, drug-related states, and states of spiritual concentration, trance states are particularly interesting because of their wide range of cultural meanings.

The important anthropological question about these states is how they are interpreted within any particular culture. They are frequently associated with spirituality and healing, and often identified as the cause of an individual's illness. They are also often given two quite different glosses: (1) that the body has been occupied by some alien spirit, and (2) that the person's own spirit has departed the body in order to carry out some task. The former is usually deemed "possession," and the latter "trance," although the combination of both elements is a definitive characteristic of SHAMANISM. When trance is interpreted a journey out of the body, and particularly if it is associated with the attempt to enter an overworld or underworld in order to reclaim a sick soul as part of a healing ritual, it is usually understood in the context of shamanism. Bourguignon (1973) demonstrated that possession trance is highly correlated with more complex agricultural societies rather than simpler societies engaged in hunting, gathering, or fishing.

Possession as a phenomenon is not exclusively limited to trance. Individuals sometimes claim to be possessed in order to have the freedom to express needs and desires that cannot be accepted in an ordinary state. For this reason possession is often associated with women and with men of low status, and the freedom it gives them has been the focus of much anthropological work on the topic. Through possession rituals people can express their resentment at being controlled by others and gain some kind of mystical compensation that I. Lewis (1971) in passing referred to as "ritualized rebellion." Such compensation is one of the themes, for instance, in Crapanzano's (1980) study of Tuhami, an unmarried Moroccan tilemaker who was partnered by a demoness.

One of the best studied possession systems is the *Zar* cult in the northern Sudan in which women use the cult in order to have some imaginative play within a complicated life (Boddy 1989). A woman in Islamic north Sudan lives what appears to be a beleaguered life. Before she is 10 the midwife circumcises her, snipping off her clitoris and stitching together the outer labia. In her late teens, she beautifies herself for marriage by removing all her body hair and the outer layer of her skin. Reliably virginal at marriage, she is soon abandoned by her husband for most of the year while he works in the city and she remains with the children in the village. Her marriage in these circumstances is fragile. Men divorce easily for other women, or take other wives, particularly if the first is barren. Throughout life a woman is legally under the control of her father, her brothers, and her husband, and her behavior is tightly regulated. But they cannot control the SPIRITS who possess the women and force them into rude, wanton behavior. Such spirits attack FERTILITY and cause ILLNESS. To cure herself, a possessed woman must appease the spirit through ceremonies in which the spirit descends into her and states its demands: new sandals, new clothes, a husband's acquiescence in a wife's desires. Many anthropologists would interpret such a cult simply as the means through which subordinate individuals express their needs in public. Although Boddy saw this, she also argued that the cult does more, that it is the major form of symbolic PLAY for these adults. The spirits that possess them are prostitutes, doctors, military men, gypsies, cannibalistic sorcerers, and women of holiness and purity – a range of northern Sudanese cultural characters. This vividly imagined other world, Boddy noted, is in itself aesthetically and creatively rewarding. And through the variety of these self-representations the cult enables its women to reflect upon their actual world, so that the spirit possession becomes almost a satiric commentary upon their experience of the feminine. Through imaginatively playing at being other, Boddy suggested, these women become more adept at imagining themselves.   TL

further reading Besmer 1983; Deikman 1982; Drury 1982; Lambek 1981; Ornstein 1973; Rouget 1985

transactional analysis   is a model of SOCIAL EXCHANGE associated particularly with Fredrik Barth's *Models of social organization* (1966). By focusing on the transactions of individuals, as opposed to groups, it sought to explain how normative systems are generated and maintained by the actors themselves making strategic choices that maximize their interests. The model was particularly attractive to anthropologists dissatisfied with the notions of exchange previously employed both in FUNCTIONALISM and STRUCTURALISM. The former had long been criticized for its inability to deal with SOCIAL CHANGE, while the latter's focus on groups and normative values to characterize systems such as MARRIAGE EXCHANGE implied that individuals were captives of fixed social structures.

Transactional analysis attracted a flurry of interest and debate (Kapferer 1976a). The idea that the "rules of the game" set the parameters in which individual actors made strategic choices, and that these choices had an impact on the overall system, was widely accepted. However, many critics accused the model of going too far in its primary focus on voluntary individual actions. Actions could be compelled and history, the accumulation of past actions, often highly resticted choice (Asad 1972). A more practical problem was that the larger the number of individuals being studied, the more difficult it was to keep track of their individual decisions and the possible outcomes. Indeed, as recently recognized in SYSTEMS THEORY, the outcome of such interactions may be inherently unpredictable: in any complex adaptive system spontaneous patterns of order can emerge from the activities of the agents, often producing new or unexpected outcomes.

Although transactional analysis has fallen out of use as a specific model, its basic components have been incorporated into so many succeeding anthropological theories that its impact is still significant.
                                            TB

further reading F. Bailey 1969; Barth 1981

transformational grammar   is the theory of language structure first proposed in Noam Chomsky's (1957) book *Syntactic structures*. Although the theory has developed in a number of different directions since that time, all of its versions share the same two principal goals: (1) to characterize in formal terms those elements, principles, and rules that are universal, that is, are true of language by biological necessity; and (2) to construct grammars of individual languages. These twin tasks lead to an account of the tacit knowledge (or "competence") that native speakers have about syntactic, phonological, morphological, and semantic patterning in their language.

The theory is often referred to as "transformational generative grammar" or simply as "generative grammar." A GRAMMAR is generative if it specifies formally the sentences of the language. A generative grammar is also "transformational" if it contains a particular type of rule, namely one that transforms one structure into another. Thus in the classic analysis of the passive construction, the sentences *Mary saw John* and *John was seen by Mary* were derived from the same abstract underlying structure, which was then transformed to produce these two sentences. However, in recent years transformational rules have played a much diminished role in the theory and in some versions of generative grammar are nonexistent. Hence, "generative grammar" has come to be used more frequently than "transformational grammar" as a cover term for theoretical models in this tradition.

Transformational grammar sees the theory of competence as forming but one component, albeit a central one, of LANGUAGE as a whole. This component interacts with principles from cognition, sociology, physiology, and so on to give language its overall complex character. As the theory has developed, therefore, an increasing number of investigations have been devoted to the interaction of grammatical competence with conversational and pragmatic principles, to its utilization in language processing, to its representation in the brain, and so on (Newmeyer 1988).

The historical roots of transformational grammar are in the structuralist intellectual tradition. In particular, transformationalists hold to the idea that the grammar of a language is a statement of the systematic structural interrelationships among linguistic elements. Nevertheless, there are enough significant differences between transformational grammar and earlier structuralist theories of language (Bloomfield 1933; Saussure 1959) to have led to a widely held conception that 1957 initiated a "Chomskyan" or "transformationalist" revolution in the field.

Perhaps the most profound departure of *Syntactic structures* from earlier work is Chomsky's reinterpretation of the goals of linguistic theory. In particular, Chomsky proposed a novel conception of what a linguistic theory is a theory *of*. Whereas in most earlier structuralist accounts, linguists set the rather modest goal of constructing inventories of the linguistic elements in particular languages along with statements of their distributions, Chomsky's goal was that of providing a rigorous and formal characterization of a "possible human language," that is, to distinguish as precisely as possible the class of grammatical processes that can occur in language from those that cannot. This characterization, or "universal grammar," specifies the limits within which languages may vary. In Chomsky's view, natural scientists set parallel tasks for themselves: the goal of physics is to characterize the class of possible physical processes, that of biologists to characterize the class of biological processes, and so on.

Furthermore, Chomsky has repeatedly identified universal grammar as part of the innate endowment of the human mind, and has gone so far as to categorize (generativist) linguistic theory as a branch of the field of cognitive psychology. Thus Chomsky sees explanation in linguistics as being tied ultimately to an account of the process of language acquisition by the child. One can be said to have explained a universal grammatical principle by showing that it is brought forth by the child in the acquisition process, just as one might say that the normal human propensity to have two arms and two legs is explained by providing an account of the biological preprogramming that causes this propensity to be realized. In this respect, as well, he has departed from most structuralist thinkers, who in general have shrunk from drawing nativist psychological conclusions from the facts of linguistic structure.

There have been profound changes in transformational theory since 1957. Early work tended to present direct descriptions of particular constructions. In general, the researcher identified a construction, then formulated a transformational rule coming as close as possible to mimicking its surface characteristics: passives were derived by the passive transformation, relative clauses by the relative-clause-formation transformation, and so on. As Riemsdijk and Williams (1986: 175) noted, "From today's perspective most work carried out before the late 1960s appears data-bound, construction bound, and lacking in the appreciation for the existence of highly general principles of linguistic organization."

Chomsky (1973) himself initiated a major conceptual shift in transformational grammar, one that accelerated with the initiation of his "Government–Binding" theory (Chomsky 1981). In this approach, the idea that language is an elaborate rule system is abandoned. Rather, the internal structure of the grammar is modular; syntactic complexity results from the interaction of grammatical subsystems, each characterizable in terms of its own set of general principles. The central goal of syntactic theory thus becomes to identify such systems and to characterize the degree to which they may vary (be "parameterized") from language to language.

Not all generative grammarians hold to the mainstream Chomskyan model, the most recent general exposition of which is *Language and problems of knowledge* (Chomsky 1988). The two alternative generative frameworks with the greatest support are Generalized Phrase Structure Grammar (Gazdar et al. 1985) and Lexical-Functional Grammar (Bresnan 1982). These models are far more surface-structure oriented than the Government–Binding theory. Although they do not spurn universal syntactic principles, their emphasis has been on proposing language-particular formal rules generating enough sentences to produce substantial grammar fragments of individual languages. These models also pay far greater heed than Government–Binding to the notion that syntactic structures require formal semantic interpretation.   FN

See also LINGUISTICS

further   reading Lightfoot   1982; Newmeyer 1983, 1986; Pinker 1994

translation is the creation of a derivative text in a second (target) language based on a primary text in an original language, and has been fundamental in anthropologists' presentation of data. The process often involves the conversion from an oral to a literary text, a complex task even when the base language is the same, given the incommensurability of such paralinguistic features of meaning making as pitch, pause, voice quality, or gesture in speech, and (in writing) punctuation. Until about 1960, a rough dichotomy was made that distinguished between "verbatim" or "close" translations and "literary" or "free" translations. The former was generally offered with a minimum of literary pretensions but with a promise of close approximation of alien concepts (generally achieved at a cost of strained syntax in the target language and abundant footnotes to cope with problems of lexicography and semantic nonequivalence). The latter proposed to approximate aesthetic effects of the original text in its original setting (genre, social contexts of reception, etc.), or else promised to achieve a more autonomous aesthetic effect in the target language that nonetheless made claims for the literary value of the original. Roman Jakobson's (1960) foundational assertion of the significance of poetic effects viewed linguistically has turned attention to the interdependence of poetic effects, rhetorical power, and meaning in texts, and made it less defensible to choose one at the expense of the other. This led to the blossoming of the field of poetics in the 1960s and after (Hymes 1981; Tedlock 1983; see POETRY). Issues of representation and interpretation in ethnographic writing have fueled discussion on the politics of translation, with the understanding that the issue is not just what to represent or how, but who has the authority to do so, and to what ends and effects (Swann 1992; Richic 1993; Behar 1993).   MM

further reading J. Felstiner 1980; M. Mills 1991; Steiner 1993

transvestism or   cross-dressing   is dressing in the clothes of the opposite sex. What constitutes transvestism depends on how a culture defines GENDER roles and whether certain clothes are gender-specific. A male Scot in a skirt is a transvestite; the same Scot in a kilt is not. The study of transvestism cross-culturally encompasses a variety of phenomena that often have very different meanings:

1. temporary gender role reversals during religious rituals (Matory 1994) or periods of license such as carnival (Babcock 1978)
2. gender role reversals as theater, such as female impersonators who cross-dress for performance but maintain their expected dress and gender roles in other contexts (Newton 1972)
3. permanent and publicly accepted gender role reversals by individuals such as *xanith* in Oman (Wikan 1977), the BERDACHE among the Plains Indians (Callendar & Kochems 1987), or women warriors like Joan d'Arc who choose to take on the role of the opposite sex and signal this in part by cross-dressing
4. hermaphroditism, where the definition of gender and dress is often problematic (Herdt 1994)
5. transsexuals who alter not only dress but their bodies as well, such as the Hijras of India, who are eunuchs (Nanda 1990), or transsexuals who have not fully completed their surgical transformation from one sex to the other (Bolin 1992)
6. same-sex couples in which each partner assumes a complementary gender role in dress: by definition one will be cross-dressed

Anthropologists have focused mostly on the social rather than sexual aspects of transvestism because it provides a unique perspective on gender roles in any given culture, particularly where gender boundaries are alleged to be fixed.   TB
See also HOMOSEXUALITY, SEX

tribe, tribal organization The word "tribe" has a long and ignoble history and remains one of the most variably used terms within and outside of anthropology (Helm 1968). Anthropologists often use it as a catch-all substitute for "primitive," avoiding the invidious comparison of "nonstate." But most who use the term analytically narrow it to mean some form of *political unit*, as distinct from "ethnie" or "nation," which suggest a cultural identity.

At least two kinds of political unit are imagined: tribe as an EVOLUTIONARY STAGE, and tribe as a recognized group around a state frontier. These two meanings framed a debate about tribe in the 1960s and 1970s.

Service (1962) followed a long tradition in positing tribe as a stage in political evolution falling between more independent BANDS and more centralized and hierarchical CHIEFDOMS. Sahlins (1968b) also saw tribes as evolutionary predecessors of states but was more concerned with mechanisms of integration than boundaries. Here tribes were seen as unified and bounded by kinship or other ties and constituted the broadest level of cooperation in a segmented hierarchy of functions. By contrast, Fried (1967, 1975) disputed the evolutionary existence of such bounded groups, arguing instead that tribes arose from interactions with existing states. Despite their differences, all three agreed that boundedness of tribes was a result of external conflict, or WAR.

As the debate about tribe faded in cultural anthropology, it grew in ARCHAEOLOGY. Some theorists proposed that tribal networks evolved as cooperative responses to increasing environmental or other risk (Braun & Plog 1982), while others saw tribes as systems of exchange with a structural tendency toward inequality (Friedman & Rowlands 1977; Kristiansen 1982; Bender 1985). Still other approaches stressed boundaries, arguing that cooperative networks among the Anasazi, for example, were chopped into separate and competing groups in response to increasing resource stress (Haas & Creamer 1993). In general, however, approaches stressing the connections and permeability of groups are far more common than those that posit firm borders in both archaeology (Green & Perlman 1985) and ethnohistory (N. Whitehead 1994). Some archaeologists would prefer to drop "tribe" altogether (B. Hayden 1995).

ETHNOLOGY offers various models of tribal integration. In contrast to the agnatically based segmentary lineage emphasized by Sahlins (1961), matrilocal societies unify by dispersing related men (R. Murphy 1957). Institutions such as military societies, AGE SYSTEMS, MARRIAGE SYSTEMS, and RITUAL provide other ligatures. Tribes may be at their most cohesive when faced with external enemies, and a common ideal is the suppression or limitation of collective VIOLENCE within the tribe (Evans-Pritchard 1940). Most tribal leaders are noncoercive consensus managers, often working in formal councils. However, tribes of the Middle East and Central and Southwestern Asia have chiefs and even khans (Barfield 1993).

Tribal identity is often a matter of degree, shaped by a particular combination of unifying structure and circumstance and variably dominant over local autonomy and alternative identities. In the Middle East, unambiguous tribal identities are well known among PASTORAL NOMADS who have mobile bounded groups and a long history of interaction with states (Crone 1986). Even there, however, varying levels of integration dominate in different contexts, and tribal identifications come and go over time (Khazanov 1984; Mattingly 1992). In the New Guinea highlands, tribes were bounded more arbitrarily when colonial administrations assigned tribal status by choosing to recognize only one level in a complex hierarchy of ever-shifting collectivities (Paula Brown 1978; A. Strathern 1992).

Such tribe formation by fiat is particularly common in contact situations. Here agents of expanding states capitalize one identity in an effort to impose manageable polities in areas that are beyond their direct administration but are still influenced by their proximity – the tribal zone (R. Ferguson & Whitehead 1992b). Such policies, and intensifying conflict, serve to harden social divisions and undermine indigenous leadership and existing integrating mechanisms to produce the more-bounded but less-complex colonial tribes that populate ETHNOHISTORY (N. Whitehead 1992). Although ancient states often coexisted symbiotically with tribes – suggesting that tribe and state may be simultaneous rather than successive expressions of one system (Moerman 1968).

The expanding Eurocentric world-system destroyed or incorporated most of the tribes it created, in locally and histori-cally specific ways. In sub-Saharan Africa, for instance, modern "tribalism" does not represent indigenous political systems. It was cultivated in missions, imposed and employed in colonial administration (Vail 1989), brought to life in the mining towns (Hannerz 1980), and skillfully manipulated in post-colonial states by ethnic entrepreneurs seeking control of governments (E. Skinner 1968). In North America, tribes carved out along expanding frontiers were segregated on reservations, then registered and regulated by government policy (Berkhofer 1978). Since being an official tribe may now entail substantial benefits, tribal status can be disputed, and anthropological debates spill over into litigation (Sturtevant 1983). At present, a new wave of tribalization is occurring in Amazonia and elsewhere, as nongovernmental organizations and other agencies encourage the formation of federations and cooperatives (M. Miller 1993). Comparative tribalization suggests itself as a rich and relevant area for future research.

RBF

further reading Richard Adams 1975; Boehm 1983; Eder 1987; Gottwald 1979; Schapera 1956

Turner, Victor (1920–83)

Turner, Victor (1920–83) A prolific writer active in the 1960s and 1970s, Victor Turner played a major part in the revival of interest in comparative RELIGION that took place within anthropology during those years, and also in shaping the approach known as "SYMBOLIC ANTHROPOLOGY."

Turner's first book did not concern religion, however. Like most of his peers trained in England in the 1940s by such people as A. R. RADCLIFFE-BROWN and Meyer FORTES, he began by privileging SOCIAL ORGANIZATION in his research, which was conducted among the Ndembu of northwestern Zambia (then Northern Rhodesia) under the auspices of the Rhodes–Livingstone Institute. But as fieldwork progressed, he soon discovered that villages were extremely unstable owing to the clash between norms of matrilineal descent and virilocal residence. A man wanted both to keep his wife and children with him and also to bring home his sisters and their children, who were his heirs. DIVORCE was frequent, and the constant scheming of ambitious men to expand their own villages at the expense of others ensured that there were no fixed corporate groups. Turner's response, set out in great detail in *Schism and continuity* (1957), the ethnography that first made his name, was to find orderliness not in social structure but in the power struggles themselves, the repeated scenes of domestic strife that he labeled "social dramas." He gives many examples, analyzed in terms of a simple schema: a breach of social norms results in a crisis; this leads to redressive action of some kind, and finally to reintegration. The persistence of a homeostatic model shows the underlying influence of FUNCTIONALISM, since even when schism is the outcome, it only reproduces Ndembu society as Turner found it.

Three things now pointed Turner toward RITUAL: (1) it was the most common "redressive action;" (2) his schema suggested that three phases of a RITE OF PASSAGE as described by Arnold van GENNEP applied more generally to ritual; (3) most profoundly, it emerged that the true stability of Ndembu life lay not in social organization at all but in abstract religious or philosophical ideas that were most clearly expressed in ritual. (Interestingly, it was Max GLUCKMAN, Turner's doctoral supervisor at the University of Manchester, who first suggested that the Ndembu might be worth study because of their complex rites. Gluckman always displayed more interest in ritual than other functionalists.) In a series of articles and monographs (1961, 1962, 1968, 1975), Turner explored an array of Ndembu "cults of affliction," complex rites in which the spiritual resources of the community were brought to bear on the misfortunes of individuals. In so doing, he worked out techniques for the interpretation of the symbolism in ritual, and these are best described in his most successful book, *The forest of symbols* (1967). These techniques were widely adopted and influenced a whole generation of anthropologists.

At the same time, Turner moved beyond his African ethnography in several studies that elaborated van Gennep's notion of the liminal. Where van Gennep had seen dangerous transitions, Turner found something more positive: a release from the constraints of prescribed social roles. The egalitarian and invigorating state that a shared liminality could induce he called "communitas," and his most convincing demonstrations of it concern Christian PILGRIMAGE (1974; esp. Turner & Turner 1978). In *The ritual process* (1969) liminality is found everywhere; in all manner of social and religious phenomena, in the counterculture of the times, and in the arts. In contemporary societies, Turner argued, marginal people assume a permanently liminal, or *liminoid*, condition. Some of this now seems dated, and the very wide extension of the notion of liminality had the unfortunate consequence of undermining its initial power. Nevertheless, Turner was ahead of his time in his willingness to move beyond a narrow ethnographic base. In his later years Turner was drawn toward performance theory, though he always took the keenest delight in the dramatic; perhaps in the end drama and ritual were for him synonymous.

Turner was born in Scotland in 1920. After his period with the Rhodes–Livingstone Institute (1950–4), he held a lectureship at Manchester until 1963. His most productive years were spent in the United States, however, first at Cornell University, then at Chicago University, and finally at the University of Virginia, where he died in 1983.   PM
See also BLOOD, HUMANISTIC ANTHROPOLOGY, POETRY

Tylor, Edward Burnett (1832–1917)

E. B. Tylor was responsible for developing a theory of social EVOLUTION that laid the basis for treating anthropology as a science in the nineteenth century. The theory, outlined in his two-volume *Primitive culture* (1871), laid out an idea of progress in which human societies evolved and improved through time.

Tylor argued that all human beings had similar intellectual potential. He rejected the notion, common at the time, that contemporary primitive societies had degenerated after a common Biblical origin. As a basis for demonstrating his evolutionary sequences, Tylor employed what he called the "doctrine of survivals." Survivals were obsolete or archaic aspects of culture preserved from one stage of social evolution into another. Living cultural fossils, they could provide clues to the past and proved that contemporary stages of culture must have evolved from earlier ones.

Tylor's evolutionism differed from that of SPENCER and MORGAN by concentrating more on such humanist topics as the evolution of RELIGION, particularly ANIMISM, and less on material culture. He defined animism as the belief in spiritual beings and argued it was the basis of all religions, developing an elaborate evolutionary sequence that ran from a multiplicity of spirits to monotheism.

Born in London in 1832 to a Quaker family that owned a successful brass foundry, Tylor did not come to anthropology by way of formal study. He was sent to recover from ill health in Cuba and Mexico in 1856. There in the company of Henry Christy, an active and inspired antiquarian, he first encountered anthropology in the form of very different cultures and archeological evidence of great civilizations. Inspired, he wrote a book about his Mexican trip in 1861 and took a first stab at anthropology with the publication of *Researches into the early history of mankind* (1865), followed by his greatest work, *Primitive culture* (1871). Unlike many other evolutionary theorists, who depended entirely on reading for their evidence, Tylor's experience in Mexico had given him first-hand experience with other cultures. It was undoubtedly this experience that grounded his insistence that the human mind worked in similar ways under similar conditions; so for him the question of whether change came about by DIFFUSION or independent invention and evolution was not particularly important.

Tylor's work was recognized quickly, although he had never attended a university or received a degree. (Until the latter part of the nineteenth century, Quakers were still excluded by religious tests from many institutions in Britain.) He was elected a fellow of the Royal Society in 1871 before the age of 30 and received an honorary degree from Oxford in 1875. He then wrote a popular textbook (Tylor 1881) and was instrumental in establishing the Anthropology Section of the British Association in 1884. Around this time he also joined Oxford as a faculty member, lectured widely, and had a profound influence on the development of anthropology as an academic discipline, although he never wrote another book. He retired as an emeritus professor in 1907 and died ten years later.   TB

U

ultimogeniture is an inheritance rule in which the youngest child receives either the whole or the greater portion of his or her parent's legacy. MR
See also SUCCESSION

underdevelopment *See* DEVELOPMENT

unilineal descent *See* DESCENT

unilocal residence prescribes a single place of residence for a couple after marriage, such as UXORILOCAL or VIRILOCAL systems. MR
See also AMBILOCAL RESIDENCE

universals are those traits that exist in all cultures. Language, for instance, is a universal, whereas writing is not. The existence, or nonexistence, of universals and their specification was important in early anthropological debates on the respective merits of cultural EVOLUTION and DIFFUSIONISM and their various schools. The nature and even reality of universals continue to be significant points of contention in contemporary debates on such questions as, for instance, whether or not male dominance in found in all cultures and if so, why. MR
further reading D. Brown 1991

urban anthropology examines the social organization of the city, looking at the kinds of social relationship and pattern of social life unique to cities and comparing their different cultural and historical contexts. It emerged as a separate subdiscipline of sociocultural anthropology during the 1950s and 1960s. In contrast to earlier studies of URBANISM, urban anthropology applied anthropological concepts and field research methods to urban populations where the city was the context of the research rather than the phenomenon under study.

This focus is most readily apparent in the tendency of urban anthropologists to examine the social organization of small social worlds within the city, analyzing their social life in terms of larger institutional structures of power. Some of these studies are based on territorial units such as neighborhoods; others examine social networks, webs of relationships linking people who may or may not live nearby. Social networks in cities are frequently nonlocalized, stretching from rural areas of origin to larger ethnic settlements in the cities (Boissevain 1974; Gmelch & Zenner 1995).

Urban anthropology also examines social problems characteristic of large cities such as crime, social disorder, poverty, homelessness, and transience. These studies examine the social organization and cultural practices of distinct groups within the city such as gangs (Suttles 1968), ethnic villagers (H. Gans 1962), kinship networks (Stack 1974), homeless alcoholics (Spradley 1970), and criminals and prostitutes (Merry 1981). These studies usually include the systems of bureaucratic regulation, urban politics, welfare administration, urban renewal, and economic conditions that shape local communities. Other research focuses on systems of formal social control such as police, courts, and prisons.

Despite the concentration of research on the United States and Great Britain, urban anthropology is a comparative field. Studies of kinship and neighborhood in British (Michael D. Young & Willmott 1957) and American cities (Liebow 1967; Lamphere

1987) are paralleled by similar studies in India (Lynch 1969), South Africa (Philip Mayer 1961), Japan (Bestor 1989), and many other parts of the world. Some anthropologists explore the changing nature of work and union movements in urban centers in developing countries (Epstein 1958). Others examine the disproportionate growth of primate cities at the expense of regional towns as a result of economic development in Third World countries.

Urban anthropologists have worked extensively on the migration of rural peasants to the cities. This research has challenged the proposition that as rural migrants settle in cities their social order and cultural life disintegrates, an argument fundamental to the theory of urbanism as a way of life. Studies of the squatter settlements that grew up as a result of rural migrants flooding into the cities of developing countries during the 1960s and 1970s revealed not anarchy, but emerging forms of social order, planning, and institutional structure (Peattie 1968; Mangin 1970; B. Roberts 1978).

Urban anthropology has always focused particularly on the plight of the urban poor. In his controversial work, Oscar Lewis (1966) argued that there was a CULTURE OF POVERTY, a uniform way of life that emerged among the poorest groups in a variety of urban environments such as Mexico, Puerto Rico, and New York. Although this concept has been extensively criticized, it was an important effort to theorize the social impacts of living on the economic fringes of a large industrial city (Valentine 1968). More recent research views local communities in large industrial cities as the product of late-capitalist development and the progressive impoverishment of the poor. Susser (1982), for example, explored how the changing political economy of the city shapes the life situations of poor people. D. Harvey (1989b) examined changes in urban life as a result of global capital and labor flows. Anthropologists examine political and economic forces that transform urban neighborhoods such as urban renewal, gentrification, disinvestment in cities, the flight of jobs from the city, racial discrimination in the private housing market, pub-

lic housing policies, and the creation of new towns. Some work explores the way features of architectural design and urban planning shape social life or foster criminal behavior (J. Jacobs 1961; Merry 1981). There has been considerably less published on the way POSTMODERNITY is redefining urban life.

RACE, ETHNIC GROUP, CLASS, and GENDER as forms of differentiation and exclusion are fundamental to the field, and studies frequently examine how categories of race and ethnicity shape migration and settlement patterns, job opportunities, voluntary organizations, community institutions, access to work and leisure, and the maintenance of kinship relationships (Philip Mayer 1961; Mullings 1987). Ethnicity, in particular, persists in urban areas in the form of ethnic neighborhoods or in such voluntary associations as rotating credit associations and burial societies (Hannerz 1980). Thus, urban anthropology, although inspired in its earlier years by theories of urbanism, now examines social life in the city as it exists for the people who live in it, rather than the city itself.

SEM

further reading Eames & Goode 1977; Richard Fox 1977; Halperin 1990; Hannerz 1992; Perin 1977

urbanism or city life as a specific social phenomenon became a focus of detailed social science research in the early twentieth century, initially based on substantial ethnographic research in Chicago. There sociologists and anthropologists at the University of Chicago developed a theory of urbanism as a distinctive type of social life. In a classic essay, Louis Wirth (1938) argued that ecological conditions of size, density, permanency, and social heterogeneity created a social world of impersonal, superficial, transitory, and segmented social relationships. No longer anchored in the primary ties of family or neighborhood, urbanites lived fragmented lives where they played a variety of roles in widely separated and segmented social worlds. Social order was maintained by formal institutions more than informal social sanctions and, in comparison to rural communities, neighborhood and family ties atrophied.

This theory of urbanism painted a dark picture of city life. It contended that urbanites often experienced normlessness – the lack of attachment to any moral code. In the absence of community consensus about a normative order, there was pervasive social disorganization, marked by crime, corruption, personality breakdown, suicide, and mass movements. Wirth labeled this condition anomie – the social void – citing DURKHEIM's use of the concept as a way of understanding social disorganization in technological society. Anomie was produced by the breakdown in the collective conscience resulting from increasing heterogeneity and division of labor (Hannerz 1980). This theory was grounded in Simmel's (1950) theory of the stranger, R. Park's (1928) analysis of the marginal man, and two decades of ethnographic research on Chicago neighborhoods during the tumultuous 1920s and 1930s covering gangs, taxi-dance halls, hoboes, elites, and ethnic neighborhoods. Thus urbanism as a way of life was Chicago writ large.

This theory has been criticized for its tendency to equate urbanism with the conditions of large Western industrial cities. Critics noted that these social patterns are not characteristic of cities in general. In a pioneering study of the preindustrial city, for example, Sjoberg (1960) argued that in these settlements, social order was based on social-class hierarchies and enduring ties of kinship and specialization of work. They lacked the qualities of anonymity and disorder Wirth described. Studies of Timbuctu (Miner 1953) and Yoruba cities (Krapf-Askari 1969; Bascom 1959) described large, dense, permanent settlements organized through kinship and guild relationships that were not characterized by social disorganization and anomie.

Students of URBAN ANTHROPOLOGY have also criticized Wirth's notion of urbanism for its lack of attention to enclaves within cities that are characterized by ongoing, intimate relationships of friendship, kinship, and voluntary associations. In these stable, often ethnically homogenous, settlements relationships are lasting and personal, and social order is produced by kinship and neighborhood ties (H. Gans 1962; Hannerz 1969). Even in multi-ethnic neighborhoods residents often create close-knit communities by uniting with neighbors from the same background. If the world seems full of strangers, it is because it is created that way: the same social boundaries that serve to unite members of one ethnic group also separate neighbors of different ethnicities (Merry 1981).

The reasons for the different perceptions of urban life are based in part on who is being studied and how communities are defined. Studies that document urban disorganization often examine the lives of migrants in marginal economic positions, such as the work of Oscar Lewis (1966) on the CULTURE OF POVERTY in the United States and Latin America – although some studies do reveal forms of ordering even within marginal urban populations such as African-American welfare mothers (Stack 1974). Because of their focus on territorially defined communities, many researchers neglected the importance of nonlocalized social networks through which urbanites are joined into ongoing social ties (Liebow 1967; Jacobson 1973). Studies that emphasize the social order of urban life often examine the shape and content of social networks as a method of mapping out the contours of urban sociality (Boissevain 1974). There has also been considerable study of voluntary associations such as religious groups, political organizations, recreational groups, ethnic associations, and other institutions by which urbanites create social order.

Nevertheless, the question of the sociology of the stranger remains an important problem in the analysis of urban life, even though the extent to which urban life involves interactions between strangers varies greatly among cities (Richard Fox 1977). The idea that a city fosters social interactions with strangers and that the pervasiveness of these interactions challenges the maintenance of social control, undermines the creation of trust and the predictability of social life, and fosters crime and anomie, continues to be a compelling aspect of the theory of urbanism.

More recently, the focus of research on cities has shifted from the ways in which dense settlement patterns shape social life

to the study of social relationships and institutions that happen to occur in cities. At the same time, cities are increasingly seen as part of a global economic and cultural system, so that they have important linkages to hinterlands and to other cities. The city has become the context, rather than the focus, of urban research.   SEM
See also INDUSTRIAL SOCIETIES

further reading J. Abu-Lughod & Hay 1977; Gmelch & Zenner 1995; Portes & Stepick 1993; Suttles 1968

uxorilocal residence requires that a couple resides with the wife's family or kin after marriage. It has largely replaced the synonymous term **"matrilocal residence."**   MR

V

violence is the intentional use of force to inflict bodily harm. It also refers to the totality of such acts within a social collectivity or to a state of affairs in which violent acts are prevalent. By this definition natural events (earthquakes, floods, etc.) and accidents of human technology (fires, automobile collisions, etc.) are excluded because though they entail force and result in injury, there is either no human actor or no intent to harm. More problematically, this definition also excludes social, political, and economic inequities that, even where deliberately created or maintained, do not have bodily harm as their primary motivation or outcome.

Even this narrow construal faces challenges from an anthropological perspective: local notions of force and of bodily harm are quite variable and are not always consonant with those of Western scientific categories. The practices of SORCERY, for example, do not entail the mechanisms of physical force acknowledged by science, yet these techniques are believed by their practitioners (and victims) to be capable of bringing bodily harm to their targets. The foot-binding of girls in traditional China would be characterized as physically harmful by Western medicine, yet it was not so considered by those who participated in the custom, at least not by the men. This qualification regarding GENDER differences implies that notions of violence may not be uniform even within a single culture and that *legitimacy* is a crucial element in what is and isn't recognized as violence; Riches (1986a) suggested that what is constant across all designations of violence is that the act so characterized is considered to be an illegitimate application of physical force. Thus, for a business executive, actions by organized labor that result in injury or property damage are violence whereas equally forceful state suppression of them is not; killings by citizens are violence, executions by the state are not. As male violence against women and severe physical punishment of children have come increasingly (although by no means universally) to be regarded as morally illegitimate, so too the conceptualization of them as violence has become more common.

Most of the work in the ETHNOLOGY of violence is concerned not with teasing out native conceptions of violence but with social, political, and economic relationships that govern the occurrence of violence. The definition of violence in this work, often only implicit, is the infliction, with malevolent intent, of bodily harm of the sort recognized by biomedical science. Violence in the private domain, especially by men against women, tends to be slighted by a preoccupation with violence outside the home, as is true also of research on violence in industrialized societies.

A few generalizations can be gleaned from this literature. In simple societies – those lacking hierarchies of political authority and marked disparities in material well-being – overt AGGRESSION is less common than in more complex ones. However, because formal means of adjudicating conflicts and enforcing judgments are little developed in simple societies, there is a substantial probability that animosity that does break through the constraints of everyday decorum will escalate to HOMICIDE, a pattern yielding homicide rates equivalent to those of the more violent industrialized nations. Most such incidents arise out of sexual jealousy or violations of norms of reciprocity. Armed conflict between groups of this level of political complexity is rare. In politically stratified groups, by contrast, overt aggression of both the intra- and intergroup variety is fairly common, originating in efforts to gain resources, typically land or animals, or in strategies to acquire political power (Knauft 1991).

Otterbein's (1994) research on the causes of group violence indicates that the presence of fraternal interest groups – coresident collections of related males – is as important as the general level of social and political complexity. Among societies without centralized political authority, internal FEUDING and intergroup violence will be likely wherever marriage patterns produce localized aggregations of male relatives. The causal role of such groups is less straightforward in societies with political centralization, that is, where a political authority presides over several communities.

Marc Ross's (1986) analysis of violent group conflict in 90 nonindustrial groups also found the presence of fraternal interest groups to be an important determinant of violence, but he found modes of childrearing, which presumably engender life-long psychological dispositions, to be equally predictive. Harsh, affectionless socialization is strongly linked to violence, with social-structural variables, especially cross-cutting ties, rates of local endogamy, and prominence of fraternal interest groups, determining whether the hostility generally occurs within or between communities.   JW

See also AGGRESSION, LEGAL ANTHROPOL-
   OGY, SOCIALIZATION, WAR

further reading Paula Brown & Schuster
   1986; M. Foster & Rubinstein 1986;
   Heelas 1982; Riches 1986b

viri-avunculocal residence is a postmarital residence pattern in which the couple lives with the husband's mother's brother. **viri-patrilocal residence** would be the same pattern but with the husband's father.   MR

virilocal residence is a post-marital residence pattern in which the couple lives with the husband's family. It has largely replaced the more general term "PATRILOCAL RESIDENCE."   MR
See also VIRI-AVUNCULOCAL RESIDENCE

visual anthropology is the visual and perceptual study of culture, material culture, and forms of human behavior in different communities and environments. As a foundational capability for doing observational fieldwork, the visual and perceptual capacities have been a part of anthropological research since the inception of the field. As a systematized subfield of anthropology, visual anthropology has been undergoing rapid expansion since the 1960s in terms of theory and practice, as well as the availability of resources for teaching and carrying out research. Today, advancing communication technologies are making it possible for anthropological researchers and film- and videomakers to present elements of their visual and intellectual experience to a much wider audience worldwide.

Certain basic elements have been of central concern in visual anthropology since Felix Regnault first shot four short film sequences of a Wolof woman in Paris in 1895. These include purpose, depth of knowledge of the subject, nature of the relationship to the subject, techniques and strategies of expression such as the storyline, themes, editing, intertitles, narration, voice-over, dialogue, subtitles, style, artistic and aesthetics sensibilities, and accuracy and film truth (Hockings 1995; Crawford & Simonsen 1992).

What exactly is an "ethnographic" film has been a source of anguish to many, and the debate has not necessarily helped produce more accurate or telling renditions of social life and behavior. Notwithstanding all the problems of intervention, interpretation, positionality, and subjectivity, today, with the high-level word and image interface, film, video, and television are playing a crucial role in making people better informed cross-culturally. The actual record – as images, films, videos is much in demand by audiences, academic and otherwise, worldwide.

More recently issues of levels and acknowledgment of collaboration, gender, authorship, indigenous media, and power have been of concern. Indeed, the concern with power, politics, and poetics of representation is a serious one for cultural translation, comparison, and identity. To be behind the camera is to possess technology, power, and operational knowledge. The dynamics of power sharing and collaboration in the field and in the sites of production and consumption are complex, and morally and ethically delicate. To have control and influence over the distribution of media into today's global market is to have an overriding power to represent and define the terms of cultural identity and cross-cultural recognition (L. Taylor 1991; Crawford & Turton 1992; Lutkehaus 1995b).

Early ethnographic films were aimed at large popular audiences and included Spencer's footage of Australian aborigines (1901), Curtis's *In the land of the head hunters* (1914), Laherty's *Nanook of the North* (1922), Cooper and Shoedsack's *Grass* (1924), and Wright and Grierson's *Song of Ceylon* (1934). The use of film as part of ethnographic research began with Gregory Bateson and Margaret MEAD's (1942) pioneering work in Bali and New Guinea. With the availability of lighter hand-held cameras, sound and image synchronization, color film, and video technology, filmmakers since the 1950s have endeavored to render their engagement with different peoples, cultures, and places in the world. In the English- and French-speaking world, filmmakers whose works have been milestones in the field include John Marshall. Marshall's nearly 45-year involvement with the !Kung San of southern Africa, particularly his decade-long collaboration with Timothy Asch, produced more than twenty films exploring and vividly portraying specific dimensions of San cultures and society (Ruby 1993). The work of Jean Rouch in West Africa and in Europe, particularly his influential Paris-set *Chronique d'un été* (1960) with Edgar Morin, has been important in introducing a provocative documentary approach to filmmaking and in ushering in the style of *cinéma vérité* (Stoller 1992). The work of Robert Gardner, from *Dead birds* (1963) through *Forest of bliss* (1985), has been central to anthropological and cross-cultural filmmaking (Robert S. Gardner 1992; Oster 1994). Timothy Asch's collaboration with Napoleon Changnon produced thirty-seven films on the life of the Yanomamo,

with *Axe fight* (1975) receiving much attention because it dealt with the issues of filmmaker/researcher subjectivity and reflexivity more poignantly than others (Lutkehaus 1995a; D. Marks 1995).

The work of David and Judith MacDougall in East Africa, Australia, India, and Europe has attempted to take us beyond the omnipresent, omniscient, and omnipotent observer and camera (observational cinema), to engage with and acknowledge the filmmakers' social encounter with their subjects (participatory cinema). David MacDougall has reminded us not mistake the filmic fragment for the larger entities, and that the camera only captures images of events, persons, and fragments of other cultures and places. More recently (1995a,b), he has tried to explore the workings of the subjective voice in ethnographic films and the possibilities for discourses between different subjectivities, or finding intersubjective ways of looking at social and cultural life (intertextual cinema).

From the 1970s onward anthropological filmmakers with greater sensitivity to the ontology of the filmic medium – sensoriness, the complex light, image, sound, and word interplay and interface, artistic and aesthetic possibilities, the fabricated nature of film, time–space manipulation, and storytelling – have attempted to free themselves from restrictive notions of how to make film and ethnography. Some of these films are more fine grained, reach for more detail, and strive for deeper depictions of social life and behavior. Examples include Rundstrom, Rundstrom and Bergum's *The path* (1971), Nairn's *Kwelelka – Onka's big moka* (1974), Leach and Kildea's *Trobriand cricket* (1976), O'Rourke's *Cannibal tours* (1987), Connolly and Anderson's *Black harvest* (1992), and Taylor and Barbash's *In and out of Africa* (1992).

A domain not well explored and undertheorized is the realm of spectatorship in the chain of anthropological filmic and cinematic experience – that is film as a sensory medium – and the added cross-cultural demands of ethnographic situation. Visual anthropology is in need of stronger theories of spectatorship

(Martinez 1992), and as Lucien Taylor (1996: 72) stated, "cinematic production and reception is not some transhistorical, transcultural given. Spectatorship is a 'total social fact' . . . [it] is embedded in a cultural context and historical moment, and thus susceptible to sociological as well as psychological interpretation."

The field of visual anthropology and ethnographic filmmaking, with its strong real-world documentary claim and heritage, has remained largely oblivious to films and filmmakers whose work straddles the line of "real" and "unreal," "fiction" and "nonfiction," in ways that are highly illuminating of human social life – as in some of the films of Abbas Kiarostami, or the narrative fiction films that speak to cultural specificities and ways, such as some of the films of Satyajit Ray, Ousmane Sembene, Yilmaz Guney, Mira Nair, and many other Third World as well as First World filmmakers (Armes 1987; Appadurai 1991). Needless to say, even the most documentary film is an image of the real, and it has to be put together or fabricated. And as a subject of study for visual anthropology, the narrative fiction films of a society are as much a cultural practice, product, or artifact as a society's tools, architecture, music, or religious manuscripts (M. Fischer 1984; Traube 1992). With the globalization of the technologies of transmission and communication, anthropologists have begun to pay attention to the translocal and transnational production and consumption of televisual media. In particular, the context in which such televisual material is produced by government-backed, commercial and advertisement-driven, or independent production groups and consumed in a multitude of localities by people of different age, sex, class, and nationality is important for understanding its objectives, meaning, and impact. This is an area to which visual anthropology can make valuable contributions in the years to come (L. Abu-Lughod 1993).

More than any other medium or art form, film and video depend on real-world experience as form and content, discourse and representation, subject and object. If anthropology is to create a space for the visual it must seek neither to disavow

discontinuities between the written and filmic media nor to transform one into another. It must find innovative ways to take advantage of the already high levels of visual and media literacy among today's students and audiences.   FS

See also PHOTOGRAPHY

further reading Conner et al. 1986; Devereaux & Hillman 1995; Heider 1976; Hockings & Omori 1988; Loizos 1993; Rollwagen 1988; Warren 1996

voice The concept of "voice" arose in response to a critique of anthropological representation, started in the 1970s that complained that the informant is rarely heard because the anthropologist takes the stance of the insider, one who can represent what others think and feel. This has sometimes been called the "violence" of representation. Feminists, for example, charged that women do not "speak" in traditional anthropological descriptions of cultures, and that the absence of their position or point of view raised a problem of difference.

In the 1980s, dialogic anthropology emerged in part as an attempt to redress the problem of difference and voice in traditional ethnography. Anthropologists like Kevin Dwyer (1982) and Dennis Tedlock (1983) envisioned the encounter between anthropologist and informant(s) along the lines of a dialogue where authorship should be viewed as a collaborative effort. In this approach cultural representation is supposed to be a negotiated construction and the ways in which it is a construction should be apparent in the ethnographic work. Perhaps, retrospectively, these anthropologists and others found their inspiration in the work of the great Russian literary critic M. M. Bakhtin (1981), who argued against what he called the "monological" view of language promulgated by formalist literary and structuralist linguistic theories, and in the work of Volosinov (1973), who developed a "dialogic" model of language in more detail.

Doubt has been cast, however, on the possibility of the dominated subject ever having a "voice" in the project of cultural representation, no matter how politically self-critical the ethnographer may be.

Gayatri Chakravorty Spivak (1988), for example, concluded that "The subaltern cannot speak" because the power dynamic between anthropologist and informant is rarely, if ever, equal, and the violence of representation might be inescapable. That leaves open the question of whether ethnography done by "others" might not be more "authentic." This claim too is fraught with epistemological problems, resting on assumptions about experience that were exposed as "logocentric" by Derrida (1976: 98), who spoke of "voice" as a concept of "self-presence" in Western metaphysics and thus indefensibly held to be originary.

SC

See also CRITICAL ANTHROPOLOGY, ETHNOGRAPHY AND ETHNOLOGY, FEMINIST ANTHROPOLOGY, LITERARY ANTHROPOLOGY, POSTMODERNISM, STRUCTURALISM

further reading Joan Scott 1993

W

war, warfare is deadly VIOLENCE between groups. Some investigators specify that war occurs between distinct political or territorial units, and that killing has social legitimacy, although any such definition encounters exceptional cases. War is often contrasted with FEUD, in which socially sanctioned killing occurs within such units, and HOMICIDE, where killing is usually defined as socially illegitimate. Some theorists separate war from raiding, and others restrict "true war" to state-level societies, particularly in models of evolutionary sequences.

War developed rather late in human history. The first evidence of multiple killings is from semisedentary peoples of the Nile Valley from about 14,000 years ago (Wendorf et al. 1986), and around the world, war generally appears long after the shift to settled villages (Haas & Creamer 1993). The walls of Jericho are often taken as the earliest evidence of war, but these may have been for flood control not war (Bar-Yosef 1986). Besides Jericho probable indications of war occur in the seventh millennium B.C.E. Near East, and seem conclusive in the sixth millennium B.C.E. (Roper 1975). In the ethnohistorical and ethnographic record, war is common, although many societies have little or none of it (Knauft 1991).

Since the late nineteenth century, the longest sustained anthropological scrutiny of war has focused on the relationship between war and political evolution, particularly on how war changed with, and promoted greater, centralization and complexity. Although there is considerable argument over details, dissenting voices (C. Ember 1978), and a wide range of empirical variation acknowledged by all, the general conclusion of repeated investigation is that waging war becomes more sophisticated and efficient with political evolution, and that war plays *some* role, primary or secondary, in moving that process along (Otterbein 1970).

A flurry of investigations on the subject of war attracted anthropological attention in the period of World War II. Malinowski (1941) and others attempted to synthesize existing knowledge. Turney-High's *Primitive war* (1949) remains unsurpassed on the actual practice of fighting. Several studies reexamined North American Indian warfare as a strategic response to changing circumstances with an expanding Euro-American presence (G. Hunt 1940) – a line of investigation that is receiving renewed attention today (R. Ferguson & Whitehead 1992a).

After diminished interest in the 1950s (Newcomb 1960), studies of war increased in the 1960s, stimulated by the American war in Vietnam and the wide publicity given to instinct explanations of war (Fried et al. 1968). The latter had a long history in psychology (Freud 1964), and the arguments were made anew by theorists in ethology such as Konrad Lorenz (1966), who argued that war was an outgrowth of an innate aggressive drive. This entered popular culture through a best-selling book by screenwriter Robert Ardrey (1966), who portrayed humans as descendants of "killer apes" with violent territorial instincts. Such simple instinct theories were critcized from many angles – such as the apparent absence of war during most of human evolution. They have few (if any) serious advocates today, in part because they were replaced in late 1970s by SOCIOBIOLOGICAL approaches, which posited that going to war might be a strategy to increase reproductive success, with special reference to the well-known case of the Yanomami (Chagnon 1992). This work continues today, embroiled in controversy over evidence, theory, and even politics.

The role of warfare as an adaptation of people to the natural environment has had a much greater impact in anthropology, particularly ECOLOGICAL ANTHROPOLOGY. These range in scope from war as a way of effectively distributing populations to resources (Vayda 1969a) to a global theory of war as regulating population growth and promoting a male supremacist complex (Divale & Harris 1976). More recent ecological studies (R. Ferguson 1984) see environmental resources and other characteristics as often involved in war but without the FUNCTIONALISM.

Research in POLITICAL ANTHROPOLOGY has examined the relationship between war and politics, from the structural absence of overarching conflict resolution mechanisms (Koch 1974), to the self-interested machinations of a BIGMAN (Sillitoe 1978), to the logic of imperial hegemony (Hassig 1988). These studies argue that political organization provides a necessary base for understanding how and why a people wage war.

CROSS-CULTURAL STUDIES employing statistical comparisons have been prominent in the anthropological understanding of war. Such studies have explored the relationship between war and social structure, where strong evidence links local warfare and "fraternal interest groups" of agnatically related males (Otterbein 1977). A weaker association exists for long-distance warfare and "cross-cutting ties" of uxorilocality (Divale 1984). Other structural characteristics have been linked to aspects or types of war, such as the segmentary lineage as "an organization of predatory expansion" (Sahlins 1961) or exchange and intermarriage as the alternative to war (Lévi-Strauss 1943). Psychological variables and SOCIALIZATION practices and their relationship to war have also been examined, although this work has been less conclusive (M. Ember & Ember 1994).

Since the 1980s new and overlapping lines of investigation have developed. One focuses on PEACE, arguing that peace is more than just the absence of war; it is a positive state with its own supporting institutions, practices, and beliefs. Another seeks to delineate the local cultural logics that shape and give meaning to military action. A third frames war in historical perspective, often stressing long-term exogenous influences on warfare of people once thought to be "isolated" (for examples of each, see Haas 1990). The latter approach calls into question the Hobbesian condition often inferred from bloody reports of tribal warfare, recasting it not as a result of the absence of a STATE system but as a consequence of recent state intrusions.

Another noteworthy trend in recent anthropological works has been the increased attention to the problems of war in the contemporary world. Volumes have focused on a variety of such timely concerns as the culture of international security professionals (Foster & Rubinstein 1986), local variations in the Guatemalan civil war (Carmack 1988), cultures of domination, resistance, and terror (Nordstrom & Martin 1992), and the rise of "ethnic" and other violence in challenges to post–Cold War states.   RBF

further reading R. Ferguson 1988, 1995; Meggitt 1977; Otterbein 1994; Reyna & Downs 1994; Rodman & Cooper 1979; R. Rosaldo 1980; P. Turner & Pitt 1989; K. Warren 1993; N. Whitehead 1988

water   *See* IRRIGATION

Weber, Max (1864–1920)   Max Weber is probably the most prominent figure in the history of sociology. Three-quarters of a century after his death hardly a year goes by that a commentary on his work is not published in the English-speaking world as well as elsewhere. His native Germany was somewhat slow in recognizing his genius but is now treating him as a national monument. His collected works are being published in a scholarly edition of a scope that is usually only given to literary or philosophical giants, like Kant or Goethe.

Both of Weber's parents were long-established members of the upper class. Weber's father was a fairly typical bourgeois German politician who served in the

Prussian legislature and the national parliament. Weber's mother, on the other hand, was an intensely religious person with strong Calvinist beliefs.

Weber grew up in a household whose salon was frequented by the political and intellectual elite of Berlin, but the incompatibility of his parents is likely to have been responsible for the psychic troubles that accompanied him throughout his career.

Weber remained in his father's house for many years while he was a student of law with a major interest in history and economics at the University of Berlin. Quickly recognized as one of the most brilliant scholars of his generation, his Ph.D. thesis on *The history of commercial societies in the Middle Ages* (1889) and his postdoctoral thesis on *Roman agrarian history* (1891) do not read like the work of a beginner but rather as the fruits of a mature scholar's pen. As a result, and despite the rigidities of the German university system, Weber was offered a chair in economics at the renowned University of Freiburg at the age of 30.

After a short stay at Freiburg, Weber moved to the famous university of Heidelberg, where he spent the rest of his academic career. This career seemed to come to an end in 1897 when he suffered a complete breakdowm and did not recover for more than five years. Yet he finally made an almost miraculous recovery and began the most productive period of his life, which lasted to his death in 1920, a victim of the influenza epidemic that ravaged Europe. He died in Munich, where for the first time since his breakdown, he offered regular lectures and delivered his twin papers on *Science as a vocation* (1946) and *Politics as a vocation* (1965), which are among his most impressive essays.

Among Weber's major works, the best known is his *The Protestant ethic and the spirit of capitalism* (1930). His overall thesis is that Calvinist and post-Calvinist religious orientations provided the spiritual climate that decisively influenced the emergence of CAPITALISM after the breakdown of the medieval world. It stimulated scholarly debate and controversy for nearly a century. His companion studies, above all

Ancient Judaism (1952) and *The religion of China* (1951), are much less known but arguably of the same high value. *Economy and society* (1968), on which he worked during the last years of his life and which he considered his masterpiece, remained unfinished but still has been a foundation for a great number of his scholarly heirs. His volumes of collected essays, especially the one devoted to the methodology of the social sciences (Weber 1949a), have decisively influenced subsequent treatment of this subject.

Space does not allow more than bare mention of the other high points of Weber's omnivorous scholarship. Moving in the wake of Dilthey and neo-Kantian philosophers such as Rickert, Weber stressed that historian and social scientist should move in a direction at variance with the methods of the natural sciences. Although trying, like them, to establish causal relationships, they were enabled to approach their subject matter through the *verstehen*, the understanding, of the motives of human actors. Rather than being limited to external knowledge, the human sciences could proceed through reexperiencing the meaning of historical or contemporary actions and actors. All in all, Weber tried to build bridges between the German idealistic tradition and the positivism of much French and English thought by stressing that *verstehen* should only be the first step in a process of causal imputation. When it came to the perennial quarrel between idiocratic and nomothetic approaches to the data of human history he tried to defend a middle position. He argued that these distinctions hinged on the cognitive interests of the investigator rather than on principled differences or subject matter.

In a effort to escape from the individualizing and particularizing tendency of the German idealistic tradition, Weber put forward the notion of the "ideal type" as a construct that serves the investigator as a measuring rod when engaged in comparative studies so as to ascertain similarities as well as differences between phenomena that are to be explained.

Weber's insistence on *value* or *ethical neutrality* has elicited, more than any of his other writings, controversy and misunderstanding. Weber argued in essence that the social scientist necessarily chooses problems in terms of his or her own scale of values. A value element is hence inevitable when it comes to dealing with human affairs rather than natural phenomena; but whether a statement is true or false is logically distinct from its relevance to the values of the scholar. Schemata of proof are independent of these values. In addition, ethical neutrality is meant to free the scholar from any obligation to those who finance or sponsor his work. He who pays the piper should not control the tune. Those parties that sponsor or finance scholarly work necessarily possess a private scale of value, but they should lay it aside when they sponsor scholarly work.

When looking at his contemporary world and its likely development, Weber took a largely pessimistic stance. In contrast to his contemporaries, who for the most part still clung to an evolutionary optimism of progress, Weber felt that the future would most likely be an "iron cage" rather than a land of milk and honey. The trends favoring rationalization and bureaucratization that had marked the postmedieval world were most likely to continue. The breakdown of religious and moral guideposts had led to a "disenchantment" of the moral landscape that would grow and prevail. There was a vague hope that some future charismatic (miraculous) hero could succeed in arresting the descent into a human hell similar to the Egyptian world of antiquity, but this was not very likely. Calculative reasoning, rather than human warmth, was likely to be the predominant aspect of the world to come.   LC

See also SOCIOLOGY, RELIGION
further reading Gerth & Mills 1946

White, Leslie A. (1900–75) Leslie

White was a champion of social EVOLUTION at a time when it had virtually disappeared from anthropology following its rejection by Franz BOAS and his students. He is best known for his strict materialist approach to evolution, particularly his model relating energy use to social complexity (White 1943). At the same time he argued equally strongly for a theory of cultural determinism he labeled "culturology" (White 1940).

White was born in Colorado in 1900. After returning from a stint in the Navy in World War I, he got his B.A. and M.A. at Columbia. Perhaps surprisingly he never took a course with Boas, who dominated anthropology in New York at the time, although he was familiar with his approach from courses he took at the New School of Social Research. In 1925 White went to the University of Chicago to study sociology but quickly found anthropology more to his taste. He completed a dissertation in 1927 based on fieldwork among the Pueblo Indians of the southwest United States. He continued this fieldwork throughout his career, eventually publishing five monographs on different Pueblo groups.

It was not until he took a position at the University of Buffalo (1927–30) that White developed the theoretical passion that became his life's work: the revival of evolutionary theory. The hallmark of nineteenth-century anthropology, social evolution, particularly the work of Louis Henry MORGAN, had been dismissed as speculative and worthless by Boas and his students, who argued that cultures were unique and could not be compared (see HISTORICAL PARTICULARISM). Living on Morgan's home ground of upstate New York, White was inspired to study his work. Impressed by the power of Morgan's model and its logic, White decided that whatever problems evolutionary theory had, it could not be dismissed. He then went on to read the work of TYLOR and SPENCER and visited the Soviet Union in 1929, where he was exposed to the work of Marx and Engels.

White set about reviving the evolutionary tradition in anthropology when he moved to the University of Michigan in 1930, where he taught for the next 40 years. An impressive and popular instructor, he often provoked public controversy by predicting the collapse of capitalism, delivering lectures in support of atheism to undergraduates, and attacking Boasian anthropology whenever possible. However as the Anthropology Department's chairman from 1932 to 1957 he was also instrumental in building what was to become one of the premier anthropology programs in the country (Carniero 1981b).

White's support of evolutionary theory was not well received until near the end of his career, in part because he took aim at Boas and his followers in a polemical style that took no prisoners. His position, stated most completely in *The evolution of culture* (1959a), was strongly materialist and became best known for its assertion that use of energy per capita was the best way to measure social complexity and rank societies in an evolutionary scheme. Although Julian STEWARD (whom White had replaced at Michigan) argued along similar lines, White rejected his model as not general enough and too focused on the environment (Carniero 1973).

The environmental objection may seem strange for a materialist, but White's other passion was promoting what he called "culturology," the idea that CULTURE was defined only by human manipulation of symbols and formed an autonomous class of phenomena that could be studied as a science. Similar to KROEBER's (1917a) "superorganic," culture was something real that existed outside the individual, independent of psychology, biology, or the environment. Expressed at length in *The science of culture* (1949), White's theory suggested that there could be laws of culture. Many found White's position contradictory: how could a materialist give primacy to cultural determinism when his own evolutionary model had focused on such noncultural criteria as energy use? Nor were students of SYMBOLIC ANTHROPOLOGY likely to believe that they were producing a set of scientific laws.

The specifics of White's theories have ultimately proved less influential than his support of the principle of evolution. White insisted on its value over many decades when such models were looked upon with distaste or derision. His writings and his students laid the groundwork for evolution's reemergence into the mainstream of anthropology beginning in the 1960s, although few adopted his specific models. By the end of his career White had received numerous awards, including his election as President of the American Anthropological Association in 1964. After retiring from Michigan in 1970, he moved to the University of California at Santa Barbara, where he died in 1975.   TB

Whorfian (or Sapir–Whorf) hypothesis According to the Whorfian hypothesis highly habituated forms of language structure thought so that the "real world is to a large extent unconsciously built up on language habits of the group" (E. Sapir 1929a). Thus different languages would produce different WORLDVIEWS. Classic examples include grammatical forms such as gendered singular pronouns in English (*he, she*), hierarchical markers such as elder brother/younger brother in Chinese and *tu/vous* in French, and whether a language has generic or specific words to define varieties of things such as snow, plants, cars, etc.

As critics have often pointed out, the writings of neither Benjamin Whorf (1956) nor Edward SAPIR (1949) ever explicitly called this assumption a hypothesis in the formal sense; rather it was presented as a way to understand the relationship between LANGUAGE and CULTURE. Nevertheless, perhaps because of its simplicity, it has permeated popular culture. The oft-cited example of Eskimos having many more categories of snow than other people has taken on the status of anthropological legend: widely believed but seemingly without firm substance. Linguists have long rejected the direct link between language and culture, noting that people borrow or develop new words as they need them and that concepts can be translated from one language to another. Yet in the popular mind you are what you speak, and, conversely, if you can change speech patterns then you can change beliefs. Thus the use of singular pronouns in English has become a minefield for writers of all genders (although the absence of gendered pronouns in Persian, a related Indo-European language, has not markedly improved the status of women in the Islamic Republic of Iran). Similarly attempts to eliminate terms of social hierarchy during the French Revolution and Mao's Cultural Revolution in China also failed to permanently transform those societies.   TB

See also LINGUISTICS

further reading Hill & Mannheim 1992

witchcraft is the supernatural action of witches, a term commonly used to describe people, usually WOMEN, supposed to have dealings with the devil or evil spirits. Witches are commonly said to use their power to attack the fertility of humans, their domestic animals, or crops, to fly through the night, to engage in cannibalistic and incestuous acts, to assume animal form or have animal companions, and to be often quite unconscious of their nighttime activities during daylight. Witchcraft fantasies are most commonly associated with agrarian societies, where conflict cannot be resolved by distance (as is possible in hunter–gatherer bands), and accusations of practicing witchcraft are far more prevalent than the small number of people who claim to practice it.

It is sometimes said that the analysis of witchcraft in Africa was one of the most impressive achievement of FUNCTIONAL-ISM. Most of these analyses, including work by Max Marwick (1965), John Middleton (1960), Esther Goody (1973), Audrey RICHARDS (1932), and Mary DOUGLAS (1963), were based on ethnographic work in Africa and argued that witchcraft accusations were used to verbalize social conflicts inherent in face-to-face societies and possibly to resolve them. All the work on witchcraft suggests that it is in these closed, tight-knit communities, tied to the land and complexly interdependent, that witchcraft accusations are most likely to arise, because conflicts are rarely simple and usually emotionally and historically dense. Here, as John Demos (1982) observed, close living conditions and shared living experiences were as likely to breed conflict as cooperation.

Marwick (1965) coined the term "social strain gauge" to describe his conclusion that witchcraft accusations flowed along the lines of greatest social tension. Among the matrilineal African Cewa, for instance, this was between matrilineal kin and particularly around the emotional knot of relations between a man, his son, and his sister's son – the "matrilineal puzzle." In such a society a man's sister's son has first claim on his property, so if he gives a field to his own son, his nephew may rightfully complain of being cheated. Marwick wrote of one case where a man had given a field to his son and his nephew had demanded a field in compensation but he was given only a piece of the son's field, resulting in a great quarrel. Later, when the man fell ill and died, it was this sister's son who was accused of witchcraft. The witchcraft accusation was accepted as plausible by the community first because it explained a misfortune (the illness) and second because the accused witch had a known grudge against the victim.

Although the community focuses on the individuals involved, anthropologists of witchcraft have argued that the power of witchcraft accusations serves as an enforcer of moral behavior for the whole group. For example a person who is stingy with others may attract a witch's curse and die, and the community may feel he got what he deserved; but at the same time the witch must also be found and punished for murder. By this analysis both the witch's curse and the punishment of a known witch are perceived to serve as sanctions for good behavior: ignoring community standards may be dangerous and lead to supernatural punishments, and holding grudges too openly against others (even legitimate ones) may bring down the wrath of the community in the event of an unexpected death. The one problem of this approach is that it is derived from cases in Africa that occurred after colonial authorities had banned witch killing. So the central claim of the functionalist explanation, which is that the cost of witch beliefs to the society is less than the cost of outright confrontation, could not be demonstrated independently.

Historians have applied this functional analysis to the study of the early modern "witchcraze," when tens of thousands of people, perhaps even more, were killed in Europe as witches, primarily in the sixteenth and seventeenth centuries. The approach fits the English and American data particularly well. In England, for instance, where the death toll was relatively low, both K. Thomas (1971) and Macfarlane (1970) were able to explain the rash of accusations as a consequence of changing standards of neighborly help and the rise of individualism, through which people would refuse help to indigent neighbors but feel guilty for doing so, and then blame their subsequent misfortunes on the witchcraft generated by what they, in their guilt, took to be the legitimate grudge of the rejected poor. However, what in the African contexts was a relatively harmless agrarian fantasy, was in Europe transformed into a demonic pact, given legal standing, and, when mixed with widespread social change, somehow snowballed into hysteria and multiple accusations.

The functionalist-approach-gone-mad works less well to explain outbreaks of witchcraft accusation elsewhere in Britain or on the continent. In the Scottish craze, for example, witch killing took on a political symbolism under the reign of the "Godly King" James VI (Larner 1981). And throughout much of Europe religious tensions following the Reformation seem to have been a dominant force. The enduring fascination of the witchcraze is the difficulty of using any one explanation to make sense of this historical puzzle.

These days, in Europe and America, there are people who describe themselves as practicing witchcraft. Such people emerged first in England sometime in the early decades of the twentieth century, long after the early modern sanctions on the witch had disappeared. They call themselves witches, meet in small groups called "covens" run by "high priestesses" and "high priests," and conceive of themselves as reviving or reenacting a pre-Christian nature religion in which the earth was worshipped as a woman throughout the inhabited world (Luhrmann 1989). They use the symbolism of the early modern period – the stag horns, the cauldron, the cats – combined with the symbolic mythology of Celtic, Nordic, Greek, Egyptian, and Native American traditions, and have created an alternative religion which is syncretic, creative, and ritualistic. Often the practice has political overtones of feminism and deep ecology.   TL

See also CULTS, DIVINATION, MAGIC, SORCERY

further reading M. Douglas 1970b; Marwick 1970; Middleton & Winter 1963

witchdoctor *See* SORCERY

women, women's roles As a social group women are generally defined in opposition to men, an opposition ultimately grounded in the sex-differences between females and males. This definition may appear self-evident, but the analytic concepts "woman" and "women" are complicated by cross-cultural and historical notions of sex, gender, and sexuality (see FEMINIST ANTHROPOLOGY), as well as age, race, and ethnicity. Thus when anthropologists refer to "women" they are more properly referring to a society's "sex/gender system," a neologism defined as the cultural translation of sex-difference into prescriptive rules for, and ascriptive explanations of, gender roles and sexual desires (G. Rubin 1975: 159).

Defined this broadly, "women" is both a sociological fact and a useful analytical tool allowing a researcher, for instance, to focus on the social roles of women in a given society, or how they are culturally understood, in order to contrast women's and men's social roles and values, or their evolving roles and statuses through their life course. Much of the early work in anthropology compared women's lives in different social formations, such as differences between women's lives and social values in BAND SOCIETIES and in COMPLEX SOCIETIES.

However useful the concept, many recent theorists have pointed out some of the problems with assuming a unity to the category "women" without examining the full social, cultural, and historical ways in which it has been defined and without examining how other social identities such as age, sexuality, and ethnicity significantly alter the compositions of this social category. Who is a woman, what that means, and when a person becomes one varies significantly across cultures; and, within any one culture, varies across the life cycle and sexual practices of a female-sexed person. For example, among the Bedouin of the Middle East age and sexuality critically inform the meaning and the composition of the social category "women" over an individual's life cycle. Although they share a common sex with all other Bedouin women, a sex that is locally opposed to the male sex, prepubescent female children are perceived as belonging to a different social class than postpubescent women because their lack of reproductive sexuality exempts them from participating in various cultural activities. Similarly when a Bedouin woman reaches menopause she again ceases to be the same type of "woman" as her reproductive relatives. Because her reproductive capacity has ended, she need no longer abide by many of the social roles and cultural expectations imposed on younger, fertile Bedouin women (L. Abu-Lughod 1986).

Sexual behavior can also disrupt the unity of the analytic term "women" in other ways, by upsetting a woman's claim to properly occupy her gender role. Because many societies do not define "women" simply as a sex category but also as a gender system with a given set of social and sexual roles, women who do not comply with those roles are often culturally excluded from the category of "a proper woman." Where a society defines feminine sexuality as heterosexual and passive, any active role a woman takes in an encounter, or any sexual encounter with another woman, can establish doubt about her essential womanness, either in her own mind or in the eyes of society (Nestle 1992).

Interesting in this regard is the institution of BERDACHE among some native North American groups (Roscoe 1991). If a young girl or boy shows a tendency to socialize with, and engage in the economic practices of, the opposite sex, their kin group organizes a simple ritual to determine if she or he has a berdache spirit. In some native North American groups the ritual consists simply of taking, say, the young boy into a specially prepared hut and presenting him with the option of choosing a bow (a male item) or a burden strap (a female item). If the young boy picks up the bow he is raised as a man and, like his male agemates, made to participate in male initiation, men's economic activities, and men's political life. If, however, he picks the burden strap then he is raised as a woman among women, often having sexual relations with men. Rather than being stigmatized, in many native North American

societies BERDACHE are seen as spiritual leaders because of the sacred nature of berdache SPIRITS. In short, sex categories (anatomical sex) do not absolutely determine gender categories – who is a social woman or man.

Finally, complications of the concept "women" arise when one examines how "women" are culturally articulated to identities based on ETHNIC GROUP and RACE. United States race relations provide us with a compelling example (hooks 1981). In the pre–Civil War period, a variety of racial categories upset the unity of the concept "women." For instance, many white women did not perceive African-American women, enslaved in the South, as the same "kind of" women as they themselves were. Indeed, many biologists of the period attempted to find sex differences not between men and women but between women of different races. Southern and Eastern European women of the lower classes and Jewish women were also regarded as having an essentially different type of sex, gender, and sexuality than white upper-class women.

Women's roles

Women's roles can be defined as either what women (however defined) do; or those roles ascribed as belonging to this particular social group. An example of the first meaning is Nici Nelson's (1979) study of women's economic roles as beer brewers in Kenya, an occupation that provides them with complex social and political networks predicated on, but extending beyond, their immediate kin group. Marilyn Strathern (1988) provided a compelling example of the second meaning in her account of gift giving in Melanesia. She argued that the action of *being exchanged* is what constitutes the female gender. All things that are exchanged become feminized. Shells, pigs, women, *and men* thereby come to have a feminine gender by being situated in a "women's role" as an exchange item.

From the discipline's start in the late nineteenth century anthropologists have recorded women's participation in all aspects of social life, including their economic roles, their ritual and religious roles, their roles as mothers and sexual partners, and their roles in the political life of their community. But since the 1970s, women have been singled out for special focus by feminist anthropologists seeking to demonstrate the wide variation that women's roles can and could take (see FEMINIST ANTHROPOLOGY). They have argued that although the social roles of women have long been noted, the importance of their social practices had been largely ignored. Previous work, they charged, had considered women only as the objects of male action and discussed them in ways similar to cattle, shells, and money: as passive objects of male exchange and as pawns in men's search for greater prestige. By contrast, in feminist anthropology and the anthropology of gender, women are seen and studied as agents of cultural production and reproduction and as negotiators of power in their communities.

Anthropological works studying women's roles are informed by the important analytic distinction between the productive and reproductive aspects of a society. This distinction is often related to the division of social life into public and private (or domestic) spaces where, social scientists once believed, men engaged in the productive roles in the public realm and women filled reproductive roles in the domestic realm. Yet recent research has shown that women play a far more important role in the production of the material and cultural goods of the society than was previously recognized; and that the reproduction of the family is not their exclusive domain, because in some societies men spend a significant amount of their time caring for children. Even in societies in which this is not the case, women often care for their children as they engage in productive activities such as hunting and gathering or agriculture, and in INDUSTRIAL SOCIETIES companies are increasingly adapting the workplace to provide for their workers' reproductive needs. Many companies now provide childcare facilities nearby so that mothers and fathers may interact with their children throughout the day.

Anthropologists have studied women and women's roles throughout the world, including in complex societies and EGALI-TARIAN SOCIETIES. Aihwa Ong (1987), for example, has written on Malay women's roles in Japanese electronics factories in Malaysia. She studied colonial and postcolonial representations of race, gender, and sexuality and their relationship to labor and management practices. Ong showed how Malay women's economic roles were determined by misogynist and racist representations of their bodies and culture.

Anthropologists have also examined the dynamic of gender in simple societies and the wide diversity in what women do and how this work is evaluated. Whereas many complex societies exclude women from leading religious services, such as in the Catholic Church, they may participate equally with men in organizing and leading religious rites in societies such as the Chambri of New Guinea, and they may organize and lead their own ritual practices separate from men, as in central Australia.

Important to the study of complex and simple societies is the way in which a society divides the various labor practices of the community on the basis of perceived sex and gender differences (see DIVISION OF LABOR). Influenced by classical political-economic and marxist accounts of the EVOLUTION of society, anthropologists first argued that simple societies organized their labor and ceremonial practices by age and sex, while complex societies organized labor by caste or class. This overly simple dichotomy has been shown to be false. For instance the Arapesh of New Guinea divide community labor in the following way: "cooking everyday food, bringing fire-wood and water, weeding and carrying – these are women's work; cooking ceremonial food, carrying pigs and heavy logs, house-building, sewing thatch, clearing and fencing, carving, hunting, and growing yams – these are men's work" (M. Mead 1935: 54). But their neighbors, the Chambri, have no significant division of labor by gender (F. Errington & Gewertz 1987). Complex societies show a pronounced division of labor by gender, although this is complicated by intersecting divisions by ethnic, religious, and class identity.   EP

See also MASCULINITY, SEX

further reading Bossen 1984; P. Caplan

& Bujra 1979; Etienne & Leacock 1980; Leacock & Safa 1986; Sacks & Remy 1984; Westwood 1984; K. Young et al. 1981; Zavella 1987

work is the labor done by, or expected of, human beings and includes both mental and physical labor, though we often distinguish between the two. It is the precondition for human life, creating the material culture that both separates and protects human nature from the natural world. Work is the foundation of human culture, since there are no beliefs, values, or behaviors without a material setting, and no material setting without work. The Bible began with God at work, creating the world. In Greek mythology all the Gods, including Zeus, bowed and gave homage to Ananke – the Goddess Necessity – in whose body work lived.

The human dimension of work is central to the anthropological perspective. Time after time, societies and cultures have quickly rebuilt their material environment after the devastation of WAR or NATURAL DISASTERS. Material things are rebuilt because of human culture's knowledge, skills, values, technology, know-how, behavior patterns, and tenacity to rebuild and recreate (Sowell 1981: 288).

Creativity is a human characteristic that finds expression in every type of work, both individually and collectively. Thomas Carlyle (1843) articulated this aspect of work in passionate prose in the nineteenth century, when work was still in the hands of the artisan and the farmer, and when there was still a strong symbiosis between humans and nature in the creation of products with shape and beauty as well as function.

Work is so universal, so taken for granted, so ubiquitous, it is practically invisible (Bromell 1993: 4–5). Among people who live in nonmarket cultures, any activity in any single social field is influenced by that person's position in all of them. Gardening work among the Trobriand Islanders is part of a social system in which there are kinship obligations to turn over 50 percent of the harvest (Malinowski 1922). Cheyenne women built shelters as part of social and kinship obligations (Hoebel 1960). Nuer women milked dairy cows as one of their duties toward their family and community; a woman without a cow to milk had no social standing (Evans-Pritchard 1940). A !Kung Bushman is socialized into his role as a hunter and does not question whether or not this is something he wishes to do (Lee 1979). Work is so embedded in these cultures that there is no separate word for it, and work has no dimension separate from the rest of social structure (Applebaum 1984a: 3–8).

In INDUSTRIAL SOCIETIES, by contrast, humans are occupied and preoccupied with work, hence the term "occupations." When we meet someone for the first time, to break the ice and strike up a conversation, we often ask, "What do you do?," meaning what kind of work do you do.

It is work that creates and erects the system of organization, objectified in material objects, that humans require in order to interact with the physical world. Unlike other living creatures, humans cannot interact physically with nature without the use of tools and systems of work. Tools are the result of work and at the same time, the instruments for performing work. Benjamin Franklin called humans "tool-making animals" (Applebaum 1992a: 400).

Human societies differ greatly in the content of their institutions and in the way they make their living, including the kind of tools and technologies employed, and the meanings they attach to work. Ordering societies on the basis of their organization of work, we find the FORAGING societies with a very ancient history at one extreme and the very recent industrialized societies at the other. Between these two forms there exist a variety of nonmarket and mixed societies, which vary enormously in development, complexity, and unique historical and social characteristics.

Anthropologists are increasingly contributing to the study of work, including how different societies view the nature of work, the universal and particular patterns of work behavior, and attitudes toward work throughout the world.   HA
See also DIVISION OF LABOR, TECHNOLOGY
further reading Applebaum 1984b; Arendt 1958; R. Firth 1972; R. Hall 1994; Neff 1985; Trice 1993

world-system theory As first formulated by the sociologist Immanuel Wallerstein, a world-system is an intersocietal system marked by a self-contained DIVISION OF LABOR, hence the words "world" (as in self-contained) and "system" (having some degree of internal coherence) joined by a hyphen. This whole, the world-system, is the fundamental unit within which all other social structures, including states, are analyzed. Each world-system has a dominant MODE OF PRODUCTION. When the system is unified politically it is called a "world-empire"; otherwise it is a "world-economy." Small, nonstate units (often labeled "TRIBES") are called "minisystems." Wallerstein developed world-system theory to explain the interrelations of the First, Second, and Third Worlds and their origins in the development and spread of modern CAPITALISM and industrialization. Although rooted in SOCIOLOGY, world-system research is found in all the social sciences and is heavily inter- and multidisciplinary in nature. It draws inspiration from the *Annales* school of French historiography and DEPENDENCY THEORY but places stronger emphasis on the holistic and inherently cyclical nature of the entire system. The Fernand Braudel Center at the State University of New York, Binghamton concentrates on world-system studies and publishes its major journal, *Review*.

The "modern world-system," the first capitalist world-economy, developed in Western Europe during the "long sixteenth century," 1450–1650. The need of capitalists for labor, raw materials, and markets drove the expansion of trade networks, sometimes through formal colonization. Expansion of the system did not proceed smoothly but cyclically. These cycles are fundamental to world-system processes. By the middle of the twentieth century the capitalist world-economy had become truly global.

Growth of the world-economy differentiated the system into three components: (1) the core, which specializes in advanced industrial production and distribution and is marked by relatively strong states, a strong bourgeoisie, and a large working class; (2) the periphery, which produces raw materials and is marked by weak states, a small bourgeoisie, and a large peasant class; and (3) the semiperiphery, which shares characteristics of both the core and periphery. The spatial relations of these components is an important topic in geography (Peter Taylor 1993).

Core states, acting on behalf of the capitalist class, extract materials, cheap labor, and new markets from the other regions (see COLONIALISM). Semiperipheral states have a core-like relation to peripheral regions, but a peripheral-like relation to core states. Semiperipheral societies can be either a rising peripheral society, or declining core state. As a whole the semiperiphery blocks polarization between core and periphery, thus stabilizing the system. Since core capitalists pay peripheral producers less than the full value they create, they are able to accumulate capital from the periphery. This unequal exchange fosters DEVELOPMENT in the core and impedes, or even reduces, it in the periphery. Wallerstein claimed that the modern world-system is unique because it is the only capitalist world-system, it is the only world-economy that has not been transformed into a world-empire through conquest by a hegemonic state, and it has become truly global.

A major premise for world-system theory is that the world-system must be studied as a whole. Thus, the study of social, political, economic, or cultural change in any component of the system – nations, states, regions, ethnic groups, classes, gender roles, or "tribes" – must begin by understanding that component's role within the system. This generates a dual research agenda: (1) How do changes in any component affect the entire system? (2) How do the processes of the system affect the internal dynamics and social structures of its components?

Several intertwined polemics permeate world-system literature: (1) if and to what degree underdevelopment in the periphery is necessary to development in the core; (2) whether exogenous factors (primarily MARKETS) or endogenous factors (i.e., social structure, especially CLASS), are the primary agents of change; (3) whether SOCIALISM is possible in a capitalist world-economy (e.g., seeing the former Soviet

Union as state-sponsored capitalism, not socialism); and (4) whether world-system theory is a useful extension or crude distortion of marxist theory. World-system theory has been criticized for being overly economistic, core-centric (Eurocentric), state-centrist, and for paying too little attention to CULTURE and GENDER.

In the last decade world-system theory has begun to address these issues. So much new work has been done (Arrighi 1994; Chase-Dunn & Grimes 1995; W. Martin 1994) that a scholar who consults only the works of Wallerstein, or summary works written through the mid-1980s, would be poorly informed indeed. There have been a tremendous number of quantitative studies of the modern world-system (summarized in Chase-Dunn 1989). Some new or considerably expanded research topics are: cyclical processes in the world-system (Suter 1992); the consequences of the collapse of the Soviet Union (Bergesen 1992); the roles of women, households, and gender in the world-economy (K. Ward 1990, 1993); cities in the world-system (Kasaba 1991); the role of culture in the world-economy (Kiser & Drass 1987); and environmental (Bergesen 1995; Chew 1995) and subsistence (Bradley et al. 1990) issues. Many case studies offer fine-grained analyses of the complex functioning of the world-system with respect to SLAVERY (Tomich 1989), agrarian capitalism (McMichael 1984), and the incorporation of aboriginal populations into the world-economy (Dunaway 1996; T. Hall 1989; Meyer 1994).

A major new area in world-system theory centers on debates about precapitalist world-systems (T. Hall & Chase-Dunn 1993; Frank & Gills 1993). These evolutionary studies transform many assumptions in world-system theory into historically grounded research problems (Chase-Dunn & Hall 1994). They also have begun to call into question the uniqueness of the modern world-system and the entire conception of the "rise of the West," suggesting, rather, that the "East fell," or at least withdrew (J. Abu-Lughod 1989).

Polemical and empirical debates notwithstanding, world-system analysts have focused systematic attention on the roles of historical processes and intersocietal relations in long-term social and cultural change. Among the major contributions of world-system theory are studies of how local actors and world-systems shape each other in virtually every arena of human activity.   TH

See also ECONOMIC ANTHROPOLOGY, SOCIAL EXCHANGE, MARKET, POLITICAL ANTHROPOLOGY

further reading Chase-Dunn & Hall 1997; Peregrine & Feinman 1996; Shannon 1996; Wagar 1992; Wallerstein 1974, 1979, 1980, 1984, 1989, 1991

worldview is the set of cultural and psychological beliefs held by members of a particular culture; the term was borrowed from the German *Weltanschauung*. It is a concept derived in part from the WHORFIAN HYPOTHESIS, which posited that highly habituated forms of language structured thought and thus, as Edward SAPIR (1929a: 210) argued, "The worlds in which different societies live are distinct worlds not merely the same worlds with different labels." The term fell out of use, or was replaced by "ideology," as anthropologists realized that all members of a society did not in fact share the same cultural values and points of view, and that the creation and contestation of cultural belief systems were never static (Hill & Mannheim 1992).   TB

writing systems are clearly a mode of graphic representation but one applied to language. A full writing system can represent the range of speech and adds something of its own by virtue of transforming the oral to a visual form. Some elementary graphic devices can represent bits of language without providing a complete medium for transcribing speech. One of the most notable of these forms of protowriting are the graphic signs of the North American Indians. Called "pictograms" when they consist of isolated signs and "pictographs" when they constitute systems of such signs, grams/graphs may represent natural or arbitrary indices, although the names suggest a natural, pictorial, or figurative form rather than a conventionalized one (Mallery 1893). Figurative does not necessarily mean representing a horse by a horse but metonymically (part for whole) or by association. Both natural and arbitrary signs are equally present in protowriting, as in early writing and indeed in design more generally, and there is little evidence (as BOAS 1927 maintained) of an early progression from one to the other.

The single, isolated signs approach writing when the graphemes are linked together to form a sequence, as in the birch-bark scrolls of the Midewewin society of the Ojibway of North America (Dewdney 1975). However this achievement does not represent a full writing system, as can be seen by the fact that even knowledgeable members provide different translations. In other words the graphemes serve as a mnemonic, suggesting language rather than representing it, just as they might act as a prompt for the words of a song.

The pictograms of North America developed into more complex systems of communication. In immediately precolonial times the Inca of the South made use of color-coded knots (*quipu*) to organize what Murra (1984) called their "pyramidal mode of production." Much earlier in the complex societies of Central America a hieroglyphic form of writing seems to have developed around 600 B.C.E. It took the form of political information placed in a calendrical framework. There are four major systems, the Maya, the Zapotec, the Aztec, and the Mixtec. The first two were the oldest (600 B.C.E. to 900 C.E.), and the other two, more figurative, dated from 900 C.E. Maya had a more extensive lexicon of signs than Zapotec, including verbs, nouns, adjectives, prepositions, and other parts of speech, but the degree to which the body of these signs could be interpreted without verbal commentary remains uncertain (J. Marcus 1976).

Early writing systems differ from the protoliterate use of signs because the graphic system now reduplicates the linguistic one, not only in the semantic correspondence but also phonetically. The first fully fledged system appeared in Mesopotamia at the end of the fourth millennium B.C.E. This does not seem to have arisen from earlier pictograms, for which the area was not noted, but rather from the use of tokens in exchange transactions, possibly of a market kind. From the ninth to the sixth millennium B.C.E. we find clay tokens, sometimes marked, whose shape appears to signify quantity. During the period 3500–3100 B.C.E., which saw the rise of an urban civilization, new modes of notation were needed, and the tokens became more complex. Many were perforated, presumably with a view to stringing them together to represent a single transaction. At the same time clay envelopes or *bullae* appear, with the contents represented by markings on the outside. Eventually in Uruk the three-dimensional tokens inside disappeared in favor of the two-dimensional "writing" on the clay tablets (Schmandt-Besserat 1992).

The system that emerged in Mesopotamia was basically logographic, that is, each character represented a word. However, these systems also possessed signs that stood for syllables and others for phonemes, permitting a certain economy in the numbers of characters. Seven such systems are known:

1. Sumerian-Akkadian of Mesopotamia, 3100 B.C.E. to 75 C.E.
2. Proto-Elamite in Elam, Mesopotamia, 3000–2200 B.C.E.
3. Ancient Egyptian, 3100 B.C.E. to second century C.E.
4. Proto-Indian in the Indus Valley, 2200–1000 B.C.E.
5. Cretan, 2000 to twelfth century B.C.E. (hieroglyphic, Linear A and Linear B)
6. Hittite and Luvian in Anatolia and Syria, 1500–750 B.C.E. (Anatolian hieroglyphics)
7. Chinese, 1500–1400 B.C.E. to today

Of these, the second, the fourth and Cretan Linear A remain undeciphered. Although the languages and the scripts are different, all may have been stimulated by the first Mesopotamian writing (Gelb 1963).

Such a stimulus certainly occurred with the developments toward simplified phonetic systems that followed. Although signs indicating sounds rather than words were found in logosyllabic writing, their elaboration into an entire system that represented sounds rather than meaning (on the rebus principle) first took place on the fringes of the great civilizations. One step was to represent syllables, as has been done recently by missionaries keen to write down Cree, for example, or by the people themselves when, stimulated by European or Near Eastern systems, they have tried to invent their own scripts (as with the Cherokee in North America and the Vai in West Africa in the first quarter of the nineteenth century), or indeed when the Japanese tried to simplify their Chinese script (*kanji*) by inventing *kana*, used largely as a supplement (Diringer 1962).

Regarding the alphabet itself, which seeks to represent individual sounds rather than their combination in syllables, there are two views about its development. Many have seen it as an invention of the Greeks around 750 B.C.E., and it was certainly they who added five signs for vowels. But consonantal alphabets (called "syllabories" by some) originated among the proto-Canaanites, who spoke a Western Semitic language, around 1500 B.C.E. The texts consist of two kinds, the ancient Palestinian (seventeenth to twelfth centuries B.C.E.)

and the proto-Sinaitic, found around the turquoise mines of Sinai. These were followed by Old Phoenician, which was borrowed by the Israelites shortly after the thirteenth century B.C.E. and which also formed the basis of the Greek alphabet (G. Driver 1948).

The proto-Canaanite script was the ancestor of the Phoenician, Hebrew, and Aramaic scripts. The first spread rapidly throughout the Mediterranean as the result of mercantile activity; the Nora stele of Sardinia dates from the eleventh century B.C.E. That and the shape of certain characters has suggested to some scholars on epigraphic grounds that the Greeks may have borrowed the Semitic alphabet as early as the eleventh century B.C.E. However this may be, "Phoenician" in one form or other provided the basis for all the alphabetic scripts in the West, including Etruscan, while Aramaic spread eastwards through the Middle East to India, Tibet and as far as Tagalog in the Philippines, and was even adapted by the Hebrews themselves when they abandoned their own version of proto-Canaanite (Havelock 1976).   JG

See also ORAL CULTURES

further reading J. Goody, 1986, 1987

Bibliography

Aarne, Antti. (1928). *The types of the folktale: a classification and bibliography* [Verzeichnis der Märchentypen, 1910]. Helsinki: Suomalainen Tiedeakatemia, Academia Scientarum Fennica.

Abbott, Andrew. (1988). Transcending general linear reality. *Sociological Theory* 6: 169–186.

——(1992). From causes to events: notes on narrative positivism. *Sociological Methods and Research* 20: 428–455.

Abdalla, Raqiya. (1982). *Sisters in affliction: circumcision and infibulation of women in Africa.* London: Zed.

Abdel-Fadil, Mahmoud. (1989). Colonialism. In John Eatwell, Murray Milgate & Peter Newmans (Eds.), *The New Palgrave: economic development* (pp. 61–67). London: Macmillan.

Abel, Richard. (1979). The rise of capitalism and the transformation of disputing: from confrontation over honor to competition for property. *UCLA Law Review* 27: 223–233.

——(Ed.). (1982). *The politics of informal justice* (2 vols.). New York: Academic.

Abell, Peter. (1987). *The syntax of social life: the theory and method of comparative narratives.* Oxford: Oxford University Press.

Aberle, David et al. (1950). The functional prerequisites of society. *Ethics* 60(2): 100–111.

Abu-Lughod, Janet. (1989). *Before European hegemony: the world system A.D. 1250–1350.* Oxford: Oxford University Press.

Abu-Lughod, Janet & Richard Hay. (Eds.). (1977). *Third world urbanization.* Chicago, IL: Maaroufa Press.

Abu-Lughod, Lila. (1986). *Veiled sentiments: honor and poetry in a Bedouin society.* Berkeley: University of California Press.

——(1990). Shifting politics in Bedouin love poetry. In Catherine Lutz & Lila Abu-Lughod (Eds.), *Language and the politics of emotion* (pp. 24–45). Cambridge: Cambridge University Press.

——(Ed.). (1993). Special section: Screening politics in a world of nations. *Public Culture* 5(2): 465–604.

Acheson, James. (1981). Anthropology of fishing. *Annual Reviews of Anthropology* 10: 275–316.

——(1988). *The lobster gangs of Maine.* Hanover, NH: University Press of New England.

Ackerman, Robert. (1987). *J. G. Frazer: his life and work.* Cambridge: Cambridge University Press.

Adam, Barry D. (1987). *The rise of a lesbian and gay movement.* Boston, MA: Twayne.

Adams, Mark B. (1990). Toward a comparative history of eugenics. In M. Adams (Ed.), *The wellborn science* (pp. 217–226). Oxford: Oxford University Press.

Adams, Richard N. (1975). *Energy and structure: a theory of social power.* Austin: University of Texas Press.

Adams, Robert McC. (1966). *The evolution of urban society: early Mesopotamia and prehispanic Mexico.* New York: Aldine.

Adas, Michael. (1979). *Prophets of rebellion: millenarian protest movements against European colonial order.* Chapel Hill: University of North Carolina Press.

Adorno, Theodor in collaboration with Betty Aron, Maria Hertz Levinson & William Morrow. (1950). *The authoritarian personality.* New York: Harper.

Afshari, Reza. (1994). An essay on Islamic cultural relativism in the discourse on human rights. *Human Rights Quarterly* 16: 235–276.

Agamben, Giorgio. (1993). *Infancy and history: the destruction of experience* [Infanzia e storia, Turin, 1978]. London: Verso.

Agar, Michael H. (1980). *The professional stranger: an informal introduction to ethnography.* New York: Academic.

Agawu, V. Kofi. (1995). *African rhythm: a northern Ewe perspective.* Cambridge: Cambridge University Press.

Agnew, John. (1989). The devaluation of place in social science. In John Agnew & James Duncan (Eds.), *The power of place* (pp. 9–29). Boston: Unwin Hyman.

Agresti, Alan. (1984). *Analysis of ordinal categorical data.* New York: Wiley.

———(1990). *Categorical data analysis.* New York: Wiley.

Ahern, Emily M. (1973). *The cult of the dead in a Chinese village.* Stanford, CA: Stanford University Press.

———(1981). *Chinese ritual and politics.* Cambridge: Cambridge University Press.

Aiello, Leslie & Christopher Dean. (1990). *An introduction to human evolutionary anatomy.* San Diego, CA: Academic.

Alavi, Hamza. (1975). India and the colonial mode of production. In R. Miliband & J. Saville (Eds.), *The Socialist Register* (pp. 167–187). London: Merlin.

Alberoni, Francesco. (1983). *Falling in love* [Innamoramento e amore, Milan, 1981]. New York: Random.

Aldrich, John H. & Forrest D. Nelson. (1984). *Linear probability, logit, and probit models.* Beverly Hills, CA: Sage.

Alexander, Jennifer. (1987). *Trade, traders and trading in rural Java.* Singapore: Oxford University Press.

Alexander, Jennifer & Paul Alexander. (1991). What's a fair price? price setting and trading partnerships in Javanese markets. *Man* 26: 493–512.

Alexander, Richard D. (1974). The evolution of social behavior. *Annual Review of Ecology and Systematics* 5: 325–383.

———(1987). *The biology of moral systems.* Hawthorne, NY: Aldine de Gruyter.

Alland, Alexander. (1971). *Human diversity.* New York: Columbia University Press.

Allen, Nicholas J. (1994). *Primitive classification*: the argument and its validity. In W. S. F. Pickering & H. Martins (Eds.), *Debating Durkheim* (pp. 40–65). London: Routledge.

———(1995). The division of labour and the notion of primitive society: a Maussian approach. *Social Anthropology* 3: 49–59.

Allock, John B. (1989). In praise of chauvinism: rhetorics of nationalism in Yugoslav politics. *Third World Quarterly* 11: 208–222.

Allyn, Eric. (1991). *Trees in the same forest: Thailand's culture and gay subculture.* Bangkok: Bua Luang.

Alonso, Ana M. (1988). The effects of truth: re-presentations of the past and the imagining of community. *Journal of Historical Sociology* 1: 33–57.

———(1994). The politics of space, time and substance: state formation, nationalism and ethnicity. *Annual Review of Anthropology* 23: 379–405.

———(1995). *Thread of blood: colonialism, revolution, and gender on Mexico's northern frontier.* Tucson: University of Arizona Press.

Althusser, Louis. (1971). Ideology and ideological state apparatuses (Notes towards an investigation). In L. Althusser (Ed.), *Lenin and philosophy and other essays* (pp. 121–173). London: New Left.

Althusser, Louis & Etienne Balibar. (1970). *Reading "Capital"* [Lire «Le capital», Paris, 1965]. London: NLB.

Altman, Gerry. (Ed.). (1990). *Cognitive models of speech processing: psycholinguistic and computational perspectives.* Cambridge, MA: MIT Press.

Altman, Irwin & Martin Chemers. (1980). *Culture and environment.* Monterey, CA: Brooks/Cole.

Altman, Irwin & Setha Low. (Eds.). (1992). Special issue: Place attachment. *Human Behavior and Environment: Advances in Theory and Research* 12.

Altoma, Salih. (1969). *The problem of diglossia in Arabic: a comparative study of classical and Iraqi Arabic.* Cambridge, MA: Harvard University Press.

Amadiume, Ifi. (1987). *Male daughters,*

female husbands: gender and sex in an African society. London: Zed Books.

Ames, David W. & Anthony V. King. (1971). *Glossary of Hausa music and its social contexts*. Evanston, IL: Northwestern University Press.

Ames, Michael M. (1992). *Cannibal tours and glass boxes: the anthropology of museums*. Vancouver: University of British Columbia Press.

Amin, Samir. (1972). Under-populated Africa. *Manpower and Unemployment Research in Africa* 5: 5–17.

——(1973). *Neo-colonialism in West Africa* [Afrique de l'Ouest bloquée, Paris, 1971]. Harmondsworth: Penguin.

Ammon, Ulrich & Norbert Dittmar. (Eds.). (1987–88). *Sociolinguistics, an international handbook of the science of language and society* (2 vols.). Berlin: de Gruyter.

Amnesty International. (1992). *Human rights violations against the indigenous peoples of the Americas*. New York: Amnesty International.

Amoss, Pamela T. & Stevan Harrell. (Eds.). (1981). *Other ways of growing old: anthropological perspectives*. Stanford, CA: Stanford University Press.

An-Naim, Abdullahi Ahmed. (1992). Toward a cross-cultural approach to defining international standards of human rights. In A. A. An-Naim (Ed.), *Human rights in cross-cultural perspective* (pp. 19–43). Philadelphia: University of Pennsylvania Press.

Andersen, Raoul. (1972). Hunt and deceive: information management in Newfoundland deep-sea trawler fishing. In Raoul Andersen & Cato Wadel (Eds.), *North Atlantic fishermen* (pp. 120–140). St. John's, Newfoundland: Institute of Social and Economic Research, Memorial University of Newfoundland.

Anderson, Bendict R. (1983, 1991). *Imagined communities: reflections on the origin and spread of nationalism*. London: Verso. [1991 rev. & extended edn.]

Anderson, Edward. (1980). *Peyote, the divine cactus*. Tucson: University of Arizona Press.

Anderson, Eugene N. (1988). *The food of China*. New Haven, CT: Yale University Press.

Anderson, James N. (1973). Ecological anthropology and anthropological ecology. In John J. Honigmann (Ed.), *Handbook of social and cultural anthropology* (pp. 179–239). Chicago: Rand McNally.

——(1986). House gardens: an appropriate technology. In David C. Korten (Ed.), *Community management* (pp. 105–112). West Hartford, CT: Kumarian Press.

Anderson, Stephen R. (1985). *Phonology in the twentieth century: theories of rules and theories of representations*. Chicago, IL: University of Chicago Press.

Andersson, Malte B. (1994). *Sexual selection*. Princeton, NJ: Princeton University Press.

Andreski, Stanislav. (Ed.). (1971). *Herbert Spencer: structure, function and evolution*. London: Nelson.

Anttila, Raimo. (1977). *Analogy*. The Hague: Mouton.

——(1989). *Historical and comparative linguistics* [2nd edn.]. Amsterdam: Benjamins.

Appadurai, Arjun. (Ed.). (1986). *The social life of things: commodities in cultural perspective*. Cambridge: Cambridge University Press.

——(Ed.). (1988a). Special issue: Place and voice in anthropological theory. *Cultural Anthropology* 3.

——(1988b). Putting hierarchy in its place. *Cultural Anthropology* 3(1): 36–49.

——(1991). Marriage, migration and money: Mira Nair's cinema of displacement. *Visual Anthropology* 4: 95–102.

——(1996). *Modernity at large: cultural dimensions of globalization*. Minneapolis: University of Minnesota Press.

Appell, George N. (1978). *Ethical dilemmas in anthropological inquiry: a case book*. Los Angeles, CA: Crossroads Press.

——(1983). Methodological problems with the concepts of corporation, corporate social grouping and cognatic descent group. *American Ethnologist* 10(2): 302–311.

Appell, Laura W. R. (1988). Menstruation among the Rungus of Borneo: an unmarked category. In Thomas Buckley & Alma Gottlieb (Eds.), *Blood magic* (pp. 94–115). Berkeley: University of California Press.

Applebaum, Herbert. (1984a). *Work in non-market and transitional societies.* Albany: State University of New York Press.
——— (1984b). *Work in market and industrial societies.* Albany: State University of New York Press.
——— (1992a). *The concept of work: ancient, medieval, and modern.* Albany: State University of New York Press.
——— (1992b). Work and its future. *Futures* 24: 336–350.
Archer, Dane & Rosemary Gartner. (1984). *Violence and crime in cross-national perspective.* New Haven, CT: Yale University Press.
Archer, John. (1992). *Ethology and human development.* Savage, MD: Barnes & Nobel.
Ardrey, Robert. (1966). *The territorial imperative: a personal inquiry into the animal origins of property and nations.* New York: Atheneum.
——— (1976). *The hunting hypothesis: a personal conclusion concerning the evolutionary nature of man.* New York: Atheneum.
Arendt, Hannah. (1958). *The human condition.* Chicago, IL: University of Chicago Press.
Arens, William. (1979). *The man-eating myth.* Oxford: Oxford University Press.
——— (1986). *The original sin.* Oxford: Oxford University Press.
Arensberg, Conrad. (1964). *Introducing social change: a manual for Americans overseas.* Chicago, IL: Aldine.
Aristotle. (1885 [350 B.C.E.]). *Politics,* transl. by Benjamin Jowett. Oxford: Clarendon.
Armelagos, George & J. R. Dewey. (1970). Evolutionary response to human infectious diseases. *Biosciences* 157: 638–644.
Armes, Roy. (1987). *Third World film making and the West.* Berkeley: University of California Press.
Armstrong, David F., William C. Stokoe & Sherman E. Wilcox. (1995). *Gesture and the nature of language.* Cambridge: Cambridge University Press.
Arnott, Margaret L. (Ed.). (1975). *Gastronomy: the anthropology of food and food habits.* The Hague: Mouton.
Aronoff, Myron J. (1976a). Introduction.

In Myron J. Aronoff (Ed.), *Freedom and constraint* (pp. 1–6). Assen and Amsterdam: Van Gorcum.
——— (Ed.). (1976b). *Freedom and constraint: a memorial tribute to Max Gluckman.* Assen and Amsterdam: Van Gorcum.
Arrighi, Giovanni. (1994). *The long twentieth century.* London: Verso.
Asad, Talal. (1972). Market model, class, structure and consent: a reconsideration of Swat political organization. *Man* 7(1): 74–94.
——— (Ed.). (1973). *Anthropology and the colonial encounter.* London: Ithaca Press.
——— (1990). Ethnography, literature, politics: some readings and uses of Salman Rushdie's *Satanic Verses. Cultural Anthropology* 5(3): 239–269.
Asher, Herbert. (1983). *Causal modeling* [2nd edn.]. Beverly Hills, CA: Sage.
Asher, Robert. (1961). Analogy in archaeological interpretation. *Southwestern Journal of Anthropology* 17: 317–325.
Aston, Trevor H. & C. H. E. Philpin. (Eds.). (1985). *The Brenner debate: agrarian class structure and economic development in pre-industrial Europe.* Cambridge: Cambridge University Press.
Atkinson, James J. (1903). *Primal law.* London: Longmans.
Atran, Scott. (1990). *Cognitive foundations of natural history: towards an anthropology of science.* Cambridge: Cambridge University Press.
Augé, Marc. (1990). Ten questions put to Claude Lévi-Strauss. *Current Anthropology* 31: 85–90.
Aunger, Roger. (1994a). Are food avoidances maladaptive in the Ituri Forest of Zaire? *Journal of Anthropological Research* 50: 277–310.
——— (1994b). Sources of variation in ethnographic interview data: food avoidances in the Ituri Forest, Zaire. *Ethnology* 33: 65–99.
Austin, John. (1962). *How to do things with words.* Cambridge, MA: Harvard University Press.
Axelrod, Robert. (1984). *The evolution of cooperation.* New York: Basic.
Axelrod, Robert & William D. Hamilton. (1981). The evolution of cooperation. *Science* 211: 1390–1396.
Axtell, James. (1981a). Scalping: the

ethnohistory of a moral question. In James Axtell (Ed.), *The European and the Indian* (pp. 201–241). Oxford: Oxford University Press.

——(1981b). *The European and the Indian: essays in the ethnohistory of colonial North America*. Oxford: Oxford University Press.

——(1985). *The invasion within: the contest of cultures in colonial North America*. Oxford: Oxford University Press.

BAAS [British Association for the Advancement of Science]. (1874). *Notes and queries on anthropology*. London: E. Stanford. [6th rev. edn., Routledge, 1951]

Babb, Lawrence A. (1975). *The divine hierarchy: popular Hinduism in central India*. New York: Columbia University Press.

Babcock, Barbara. (Ed.). (1978). *The reversible world: symbolic inversion in art and society*. Ithaca, NY: Cornell University Press.

Bachelard, Gaston. (1964). *The poetics of space* [Poétique de l'espace, Paris, 1957]. New York: Orion Press.

Bachofen, Johann J. (1967). *Myth, religion, and mother right: selected writings of J. J. Bachofen* [Das Mutterrecht, Stuttgart, 1861]. Princeton, NJ: Princeton University Press.

Baerreis, David. (1961). The ethnohistoric approach and archaeology. *Ethnohistory* 8: 49–77.

Bailey, Carol A. (1993). Equality with difference: on androcentrism and menstruation. *Teaching Sociology* 21: 121–129.

Bailey, Frederick G. (1957). *Caste and the economic frontier: a village in highland Orissa*. Manchester: Manchester University Press.

——(1960). *Tribe, caste, and nation: a study of political activity and political change in highland Orissa*. Manchester: Manchester University Press.

——(1969). *Strategems and spoils: a social anthropology of politics*. Oxford: Blackwell.

Bailey, Geoff & John Parkington. (1988). *The archaeology of prehistoric coastlines*. Cambridge: Cambridge University Press.

Bailey, Robert C. & Irven DeVore. (1989). Research on the Efe and Lese populations of the Ituri Forest, Zaire. *American Journal of Physical Anthropology* 78(4): 459–471.

Baker, Carl Lee. (1995). *English syntax* [2nd edn.]. Cambridge, MA: MIT Press.

Baker, Robin R. & Mark A. Bellis. (1995). *Human sperm competition*. London: Chapman Hall.

Bakhtin, Mikhail M. (1981). *The dialogic imagination* [Voprosy literatury i estetiki, Moscow, 1975]. Austin: University of Texas Press.

Balandier, Georges. (1970). *Political anthropology* [Anthropologie politique, Paris, 1967]. New York: Pantheon Books.

Balée, William. (1994). *Footprints of the forest: Ka'apor ethnobotany – the historical ecology of plant utilization by an Amazonian people*. New York: Columbia University Press.

Ball, Michael S. & Gregory W. H. Smith. (1992). *Analyzing visual data*. Newbury Park, CA: Sage.

Balzer, Marjorie. (1981). Rituals of gender identity: markers of Siberian Khanty ethnicity, status, and belief. *American Anthropologist* 83(4): 850–867.

——(Ed.). (1990). *Shamanism: Soviet studies of traditional religion in Siberia and Central Asia*. Armonk, NY: Sharpe.

Bankes, Marcus & Howard Morphy. (Eds.). (1997). *Rethinking visual anthropology*. New Haven, CT: Yale University Press.

Banta, Melissa & Curtis Hinsley. (Eds.). (1986). *From site to sight: anthropology, photography, and the power of imagery*. Cambridge, MA: Peabody Museum Press.

Banton, Michael. (Ed.). (1966). *The social anthropology of complex societies*. London: Tavistock.

——(1983). *Racial and ethnic competition*. Cambridge: Cambridge University Press.

Baran, Paul. (1957). *The political economy of growth*. New York: Monthly Review.

Barbossa de Almeida, Mauro. (1990). Mathematical metaphors in the work of Lévi-Strauss. *Current Anthropology* 31: 367–377.

Baretta, Silvio & J. Markoff. (1978). Civilization and barbarism: cattle frontiers in Latin America. *Comparative Studies in Society and History* 20: 587–620.

Barfield, Thomas J. (1989). *The perilous frontier: nomadic empires and China.* Oxford: Blackwell.

————(1993). *The nomadic alternative.* Englewood Cliffs, NJ: Prentice-Hall.

Barker, Eileen. (1984). *The making of a Moonie: choice or brainwashing?* Oxford: Blackwell.

Barkin, David, Rosemary Blatt & Billie DeWalt. (1990). *Food crops vs. feed crops: the global substitution of grains in production.* Boulder, CO: Rienner.

Barkow, Jerome, Leda Cosmides & John Tooby. (Eds.). (1992). *The adapted mind: evolutionary psychology and the generation of culture.* Oxford: Oxford University Press.

Barlow, George W. (1989). Has sociobiology killed ethology? In P. Bateson & P. Klopfer (Eds.), *Perspectives in ethology* (8: 1–45). New York: Plenum.

————(1990). Nature–nurture and the debates surrounding ethology and sociobiology. *American Zoologist* 31: 286–296.

Barnaby, Frank. (Ed.). (1988). *The Gaia peace atlas.* New York: Doubleday.

Barnes, Barry. (1988). *The nature of power.* Cambridge: Polity.

Barnes, John A. (1954). Class and committees in a Norwegian island parish. *Human Relations* 7: 39–58.

————(1961). Law as politically active: an anthropological view. In G. Sawer (Ed.), *Studies in the sociology of law* (pp. 167–196). Canberra: Australian National University.

————(1971). *Three styles in the study of kinship.* London: Tavistock.

Barnes, Robert H. (1974). *Kédang: a study of the collective thought of an eastern Indonesian people.* Oxford: Clarendon.

Barnouw, Victor. (1985). *Culture and personality* [4th edn.]. Chicago, IL: Dorsey.

Barraclough, Geoffrey. (1991). *Main trends in history.* New York: Holmes & Meier.

Barraclough, Solon. (1991). *An end to hunger? The social origins of food strategies.* London: Zed.

Barratt-Brown, Michael. (1974). *The economics of imperialism.* Harmondsworth: Penguin.

Barrett, Richard A. (1984). *Culture and conduct: an excursion in anthropology.* Belmont, CA: Wadsworth.

Barrett, Stanley R. (1984). *The rebirth of anthropological theory.* Toronto: University of Toronto Press.

Barth, Fredrik. (1959a). *Political leadership among the Swat Pathans.* London: Athlone.

————(1959b). Segmentary opposition and the theory of games: a study of Pathan organization. *Journal of the Royal Anthropological Institute* 89: 5–21.

————(1961). *Nomads of south Persia.* Boston: Little, Brown.

————(1966). *Models of social organization.* London: Royal Anthropological Institute of Great Britain and Ireland, Occasional Paper no. 23.

————(1969a). Introduction. In Fredrik Barth (Ed.), *Ethnic groups and boundaries* (pp. 1–38). Boston, MA: Little Brown.

————(Ed.). (1969b). *Ethnic groups and boundaries: the social organization of culture difference.* Boston, MA: Little Brown.

————(1981). *Process and form in social life.* London: Routledge.

Barthes, Roland. (1977). The rhetoric of the image. In *Image, music, text* (pp. 32–51). London: Fontana.

————(1981). *Camera lucida: reflections on photography* [Chambre claire, Paris, 1980]. New York: Hill & Wang.

Bartholet, Elizabeth. (1993). *Family bonds: adoption and the politics of parenting.* Boston, MA: Houghton Mifflin.

Bartlett, Frederic C. (1932). *Remembering: a study in experimental and social psychology.* Cambridge: Cambridge University Press.

Bartlett, Robert & Angus MacKay. (Eds.). (1989). *Medieval frontier societies.* Oxford: Oxford University Press.

Barton, Roy F. (1919). *Ifugao law.* Berkeley: University of California Press.

Bar-Yosef, Ofer. (1986). The walls of Jericho: an alternative interpretation. *Current Anthropology* 27: 157–162.

Basalla, George. (1988). *The evolution of*

technology. Cambridge: Cambridge University Press.

Basch, Linda, Nina Schiller & Cristina Szanton Blanc. (1994). *Nations unbound: transnational projects, postcolonial predicaments, and deterritorialized nation-states*. New York: Gordon & Breach.

Bascom, William. (1959). Urbanism as a traditional African pattern. *Sociological Review* 7: 29–43.

Bassett, Thomas J. & Donald E. Crummey. (Eds.). (1993). *Land in African agrarian systems*. Madison: University of Wisconsin Press.

Bates, Daniel G. & Susan H. Lees. (1979). The myth of population regulation. In N. A. Chagnon & William Irons (Eds.), *Evolutionary biology and human social behavior* (pp. 273–289). North Scituate, MA: Duxbury.

Bates, Daniel G. & Fred Plog. (Eds.). (1991). *Human adaptive strategies*. New York: McGraw-Hill.

Bates, J. Douglas. (1993). *Gift children: a story of race, family, and adoption in a divided America*. New York: Ticknor & Fields.

Bateson, Gregory. (1936). *Naven: a survey of the problems suggested by a composite picture of the culture of a New Guinea tribe drawn from three points of view*. Cambridge: Cambridge University Press.

———(1972). *Steps to an ecology of mind*. San Francisco, CA: Chandler.

Bateson, Gregory & Margaret Mead. (1942). *The Balinese character: a photographic analysis*. New York: New York Academy of Sciences.

———(1952). *Trance and dance in Bali* [videorecording]. University Park: Pennsylvania State University.

Bateson, Mary Catherine. (1984). *With a daughter's eye: a memoir of Margaret Mead and Gregory Bateson*. New York: Morrow.

Batten, Mary. (1992). *Sexual strategies: how females choose their mates*. New York: Putnam.

Baudrillard, Jean. (1994). *Simulacra and simulation* [Simulacres et simulation, Paris, 1981]. Ann Arbor: University of Michigan Press.

Bauer, Peter T. (1976). *Dissent on devel-*

opment. Cambridge, MA: Harvard University Press.

Bauman, Richard. (1977). *Verbal art as performance*. Prospect Heights, IL: Waveland.

———(Ed.). (1992). *Folklore, cultural performances, and popular entertainments: a communications-centered handbook*. New York: Oxford University Press.

Bauman, Richard & Charles L. Briggs. (1990). Poetics and performance as critical perspectives on language and social life. *Annual Review of Anthropology* 19: 59–88.

Bauman, Richard & Joel Sherzer. (Eds.). (1974). *Explorations in the ethnography of speaking*. London: Cambridge University Press.

Bausinger, Hermann. (1990). *Folk culture in a world of technology* [Volkskultur in der technischen Welt, Stuttgart, 1961]. Bloomington: Indiana University Press.

Baxter, Paul T. W. & Uri Almagor. (1978). Introduction. In P. Baxter & U. Almagor (Eds.), *Age, generation and time* (pp. 1–35). New York: St. Martin's.

Beals, Ralph. (1975). *The peasant marketing system of Oaxaca, Mexico*. Berkeley: University of California Press.

Beattie, J. H. M. (1958). The blood pact in Bunyoro. *African Studies* 17: 198–203.

———(1970). On understanding ritual. In B. R. Wilson (Ed.), *Rationality* (pp. 240–269). Oxford: Blackwell.

Bechtel, William & Adele Abrahamsen. (1991). *Connectionism and the mind: an introduction to parallel processing in networks*. Oxford: Blackwell.

Beck, Ulrich. (1992). *Risk society: towards a new modernity* [Risikogesellschaft, Frankfurt, 1986]. Newbury Park, CA: Sage.

———(1995). *Ecological enlightenment: essays on the politics of the risk society* [Politik in der Risikogesellschaft, Frankfurt, 1991]. Atlantic Highlands, NJ: Humanities.

Becker, Gary. (1981). *A treatise on the family*. Cambridge, MA: Harvard University Press.

Beckerman, Stephen. (1983). Does the swidden ape the jungle? *Human Ecology* 11(1): 1–12.

Beckford, James. (1975). *The trumpet of prophecy: a sociological study of Jehovah's Witnesses.* Oxford: Blackwell.

Beeman, William. (1986). *Language, status and power in Iran.* Bloomington: Indiana University Press.

———(1993). The anthropology of theater and spectacle. *Annual Review of Anthropology* 22: 369–393.

Befu, Harumi. (Ed.). (1993). *Cultural nationalism in East Asia: representation and identity.* Berkeley: University of California Press, Institute of East Asian Studies, University of California.

Behar, Ruth. (1993). *Translated woman.* Boston, MA: Beacon.

Behrens, Clifford. (1990). Qualitative and quantitative approaches to the analysis of anthropological data: a new synthesis. *Journal of Quantitative Anthropology* 2: 305–328.

———(Ed.). (1994). Special issue on recent advances in the regional analysis of indigenous land use and tropical deforestation. *Human Ecology* 22(3).

Beidelman, Thomas O. (1963). The blood covenant and the concept of blood in Ukaguru. *Africa* 33: 321–342.

———(1966). Swazi royal ritual. *Africa* 36: 373–405.

———(1974a). *A bibliography of the writings of E. E. Evans-Pritchard.* London: Tavistock.

———(1974b). *W. Robertson Smith and the sociological study of religion.* Chicago, IL: University of Chicago Press.

———(1981). The Nuer concept of *thek* and the meaning of sin: explanation, translation, and social structure. *History of Religion* 21: 126–155.

Bell, Daniel. (1968). National character revisited: a proposal for renegotiating the concept. In Edward Norbeck, Douglass Price-Williams & William McCord (Eds.), *The study of personality* (pp. 103–120). New York: Holt.

———(1973). *The coming of post-industrial society: a venture in social forecasting.* New York: Basic.

Bell, Diane. (1983). *Daughters of the dreaming.* North Sydney, NSW: Allen & Unwin.

Bell, Diane, Pat Caplan & Wazir Jahan Karim. (Eds.). (1993). *Gendered fields: women, men, and ethnography.* London: Routledge.

Bellomy, Donald C. (1984). Social Darwinism revisited. *Perspectives in American History* (n.s.) 1: 1–129.

Belmont, Nicole. (1979). *Arnold van Gennep: the creator of French ethnography* [Arnold van Gennep, Paris, 1974]. Chicago, IL: University of Chicago Press.

Belmonte, Thomas. (1979). *The broken fountain.* New York: Columbia University Press.

Belshaw, Cyril S. (1965). *Traditional exchange and modern markets.* Englewood Cliffs, NJ: Prentice-Hall.

Ben-Amos, Dan. (Ed.). (1976). *Folklore genres.* Austin: University of Texas Press.

———(1984). The seven strands of *tradition*: varieties in its meaning in American folklore studies. *Journal of Folklore Research* 21: 97–132.

Bender, Barbara. (1985). Emergent tribal formations in the American midcontinent. *American Antiquity* 50: 52–62.

Bendix, Regina. (1988). Folklorism: the challenge of a concept. *International Folklore Review* 6: 5–15.

Bendix, Reinhard. (1960). *Max Weber: an intellectual portrait.* Garden City, NY: Doubleday.

Benedict, Ruth. (1934a). *Patterns of culture.* Boston, MA: Houghton Mifflin.

———(1934b). Anthropology and the abnormal. *Journal of General Psychology* 10: 59–80.

———(1935). *Zuni mythology* (2 vols.). New York: Columbia University Press.

———(1936). Marital property rights in bilateral society. *American Anthropologist* 38: 368–373.

———(1940). *Race: science and politics.* New York: Modern.

———(1946). *The chrysanthemum and the sword: patterns of Japanese culture.* Boston, MA: Houghton-Mifflin.

———(1948). Anthropology and the humanities. *American Anthropologist* 50(4): 585–593.

Benfer, Robert A., Edward E. Brent & Louanna Furbee. (1993). *Expert systems.* Newbury Park, CA: Sage.

Benjamin, Walter. (1968). *Illuminations* [Illuminationen]. New York: Schocken.

———(1994). *The correspondence of Walter Benjamin, 1910–1940* ed. by Gershom Scholem & Theodor W. Adorno. Chicago, IL: University of Chicago Press.

Bennett, John W. (1976). *The ecological transition: cultural anthropology and human adaptation.* New York: Pergamon.

———(1993). *Human ecology as human behavior: essays in environmental and development anthropology.* New Brunswick, NJ: Transaction.

Benson, Paul. (Ed.). (1993). *Anthropology and literature.* Urbana: University of Illinois Press.

Bentley, G. Carter. (1987). Ethnicity and practice. *Comparative Studies in Society and History* 29: 24–55.

Bentley, Jeffrey W. (1987). Economic and ecological approaches to land fragmentation. *Annual Review of Anthropology* 16: 31–67.

Beneviste, Émile. (1956). The nature of pronouns. In Morris Halle (Ed.), *For Roman Jakobson* (pp. 34–37). The Hague: Mouton.

———(1973). *Indo-European language and society* [Vocabulaire des institutions indo-européennes, Paris, 1969]. London: Faber.

Berger, Peter L. (1963). *Invitation to sociology: a humanistic perspective.* Garden City, NY: Doubleday.

Berger, Peter L. & Thomas Luckmann. (1966). *The social construction of reality.* Garden City, NY: Doubleday.

Bergesen, Albert. (1992). Communism's collapse: a world-system explanation. *Journal of Military and Political Sociology* 20: 133–151.

———(1995). Eco-alienation. *Humboldt Journal of Social Relations* 21: 111–126.

Berkes, Fikre. (Ed.). (1989). *Common property resources: ecology and community-based sustainable development.* London: Belhaven.

Berkhofer, Robert. (1978). *The white man's Indian: images of the American Indian from Columbus to the present.* New York: Knopf.

Berkowitz, Leonard. (1989). Frustration–aggression hypothesis: examination and reformulation. *Psychological Bulletin* 106: 59–73.

Berlin, Brent. (1992). *Ethnobiological classification: principles of categorization of plants and animals in traditional societies.* Princeton, NJ: Princeton University Press.

Berlin, Brent & Paul Kay. (1969). *Basic color terms: their universality and evolution.* Berkeley: University of California Press.

Berlin, Brent, D. E. Breedlove & P. H. Raven. (1966). Folk taxonomies and biological classification. *Science* 155(14): 273–275.

———(1968). Covert categories and folk taxonomies. *American Anthropologist* 70: 290–299.

———(1973). General principles of classification and nomenclature in folk biology. *American Anthropologist* 75(1): 214–242.

———(1974). *Principles of Tzeltal plant classification: an introduction to the botanical ethnography of a Mayan-speaking community of highland Chiapas.* New York: Academic.

Berliner, Paul. (1978). *The soul of Mbira.* Berkeley: University of California Press.

Bernard, H. Russell. (1988). *Research methods in cultural anthropology.* Newbury Park, CA: Sage. [2nd edn. 1994].

Bernard, Jessie. (1970). No news, but new ideas. In Paul Bohannan (Ed.), *Divorce and after* (pp. 3–25). Garden City, NY: Doubleday.

Bernardi, Bernardo. (1985). *Age class systems: social institutions and polities based on age.* Cambridge: Cambridge University Press.

Berndt, Ronald. (1974). *Australian aboriginal religion.* Leiden: Brill.

Bernstein, Eugene, Christian Crandall & Shinobu Kitayama. (1994). Some neo-Darwinian decision rules for altruism: weighing cues for inclusive fitness as a function of the biological importance of the decision. *Journal of Personality and Social Psychology* 67: 773–789.

Berreman, Gerald. (1968). Caste as a structural principle. In Anthony de-Reuck & Julie Knight (Eds.), *Caste and race.* London: Churchill.

———(1972). Race, caste, and other invidious distinctions in social stratification. *Race* 4: 385–414.

————(1979). *Caste and other inequities: essays on inequality.* Meerut: Folklore Institute.

Berry, Brian J. L. & Allen Pred. (1961). *Central place studies: a bibliography of theory and applications.* Philadelphia: Regional Science Research Institute.

Berry, William. (1984). *Nonrecursive causal models.* Beverly Hills, CA: Sage.

————(1993). *Understanding regression assumptions.* Newbury Park, CA: Sage.

Bertalanffy, Ludwig von. (1968). *General system theory: foundations, development, applications.* New York: Braziller.

Besmer, Fremont E. (1983). *Horses, musicians and gods: the Hausa cult of possession-trance.* South Hadley, MA: Bergin & Garvey.

Bestor, Theodore C. (1989). *Neighborhood Tokyo.* Stanford, CA: Stanford University Press.

Beteille, André. (1965). *Caste, class, and power: changing patterns of stratification in a Tanjore village.* Berkeley: University of California Press.

————(1986). Individualism and equality. *Current Anthropology* 27: 121–134.

Bettinger, Robert. (1991). *Hunter-gatherers: archaeological and evolutionary theory.* New York: Plenum.

Betzig, Laura. (1989). Causes of conjugal dissolution: a cross-cultural study. *Current Anthropology* 30(5): 654–676.

Betzig, Laura, Monique Borgerhoff Mulder & Paul Turke. (Eds.). (1988). *Human reproductive behaviour: a Darwinian perspective.* Cambridge: Cambridge University Press.

Bhabha, Homi. (1994). *The location of culture.* London: Routledge.

Bhardwaj, S. M., G. Rinschede & A. Sievers. (Eds.). (1994). *Pilgrimage in the old and new world.* Berlin: Dietrich Reimer Verlag.

Bicchieri, Marco. (1972). *Hunters and gatherers today.* New York: Holt.

Biebuyck, Daniel. (1963). *African agrarian systems.* London: Oxford Univesity Press.

Binford, Lewis R. (1962). Archaeology as anthropology. *American Antiquity* 28: 217–235.

————(1965). Archaeological systematics and the study of culture process. *American Antiquity* 31: 203–210.

————(1967a). Smudge pits and hide smoking: the use of analogy in archaeological reasoning. *American Antiquity* 32: 1–12.

————(1967b). Comment on K. C. Chang's major aspects of the interrelationship of archaeology and ethnology. *Current Anthropology* 8: 234–235.

————(1968). Methodological considerations in the archaeological use of ethnographic date. In Richard Lee & Irven Devore (Eds.), *Man the hunter* (pp. 268–273). Chicago, IL: University of Chicago Press.

————(1983a). *In pursuit of the past: decoding the archaeological record.* London: Thames & Hudson.

————(1983b). *Working at archaeology.* New York: Academic.

Binford, Sally & Lewis R. Binford. (Eds.). (1968). *New perspectives in archeology.* Chicago, IL: Aldine.

Binkley, Marion. (1991). Nova Scotian offshore fishermen's awareness of safety. *Marine Policy* 30: 170–182.

Binswanger, Ludwig. (1958). The case of Ellen West. In Rollo May (Ed.), *Existence* (pp. 237–364). New York: Basic.

————(1963). *Being-in-the-world: selected papers.* New York: Basic.

Bion, Wilfred. (1961). *Experiences in groups.* New York: Basic.

Bird-David, Nurit. (1992). Beyond "The original affluent society." *Current Anthropology* 33: 25–47.

Birdwhistell, Ray L. (1952). *Introduction to kinesics: an annotation system for analysis of body motion and gesture.* Louisville, KY: University of Louisville.

————(1970). *Kinesics and context: essays on body motion communication.* Philadelphia: University of Pennsylvania Press.

Birkhead, Tim R. & Anders P. Møller. (1992). *Sperm competition in birds: evolutionary causes and consequences.* London: Academic.

Bishop, Yvonne M., Stephen Fienberg & Paul Holland. (1975). *Discrete multivariate analysis: theory and practice.* Cambridge, MA: MIT Press.

Bjarnason, Thoroddur & Thorolfur Thorlindsson. (1993). In defense of a folk model: the "skipper effect" in the Icelandic cod fishery. *American Anthropologist* 95(2): 371–394.

Black, Donald. (1976). *The behavior of law.* New York: Academic.

Black, Francis L. (1990). Infectious disease and evolution of human populations: the example of south American forest tribes. In Alan Swedlund & George Armelagos (Eds.), *Disease in populations in transition* (pp. 55–75). New York: Bergin & Garvey.

Blacking, John. (1973). *How musical is Man?* Seattle: University of Washington Press.

Black-Michaud, Jacob. (1975). *Cohesive force: feud in the Mediterranean and the Middle East.* Oxford: Blackwell.

Blaikie, Piers & Harold Brookfield. (Eds.). (1987). *Land degradation and society.* London: Methuen.

Blake, Judith & Kingsley Davis. (1964). Norms, values and sanctions. In Robert Faris (Ed.), *The handbook of modern sociology* (pp. 456–484). Chicago, IL: Rand McNally.

Blanchet, Thérèse. (1984). *Meanings and rituals of birth in rural Bangladesh: women, pollution, and marginality.* Dhaka: University Press.

Blanton, Richard. (1994). *Houses and households: a comparative study.* New York: Plenum.

Blier, Suzanne. (1987). *The anatomy of architecture: ontology and metaphor in Batammaliba architectural expression.* Cambridge: Cambridge University Press.

Bloch, Marc. (1967). *Land and work in mediaeval Europe* [Mélanges historiques, Paris, 1963]. Berkeley: University of California Press.

Bloch, Maurice. (Ed.). (1975). *Marxist analyses and social anthropology.* New York: Wiley.

———(1977). The past in the present and the past. *Man* 12(2): 278–292.

Bloch, Maurice & Jonathan Parry. (Eds.). (1982). *Death and the regeneration of life.* Cambridge: Cambridge University Press.

Blok, Anton. (1974). *The Mafia of a Sicilian village, 1860–1960: a study of violent peasant entrepreneurs.* Oxford: Blackwell.

Bloomfield, Leonard. (1933). *Language.* New York: Holt.

Blount, Ben G. (Ed.). (1974). *Language, culture, and society: a book of readings.* Cambridge, MA: Winthrop.

Bluebond-Langner, Myra. (1978). *The private worlds of dying children.* Princeton, NJ: Princeton University Press.

Blumberg, Baruch S. (1982). Hepatitis B infection and human behavior. *Medical Anthropology* 6: 11–20.

Blumenberg, Hans. (1987). *The genesis of the Copernican world* [Genesis der Kopernikanischen Welt, Frankfurt, 1975]. Cambridge, MA: MIT Press.

Bly, Robert. (1990). *Iron John: a book about men.* Reading, MA: Addison-Wesley.

Boas, Franz. (1887). Museums of ethnology and their classification. *Science* 9(29): 587–589, 485–486, 614.

———(1911). *The mind of primitive man.* New York: Macmillan.

———(1914). Mythology and folk-tales of the North American Indians. *Journal of American Folklore* 27: 374–410 [reprinted in Boas 1940].

———(1916). Eugenics. *Scientific Monthly* 3: 471–478.

———(1927). *Primitive art.* Cambridge, MA: Harvard University Press.

———(1928). *Anthropology and modern life.* New York: Norton.

———(1931). Anthropology. In Edwin Seligman (Ed.), *Encyclopaedia of the social sciences* (pp. 73–110). New York: Macmillan.

———(Ed.). (1938). *General anthropology.* Boston, MA: Heath.

———(1940). *Race, language, and culture.* New York: Macmillan.

Boas, Franziska. (1944). *The function of dance in human society.* New York: The Boas School.

Boase, Roger. (1977). *The origin and meaning of courtly love: a critical study of European scholarship.* Manchester: Manchester University Press.

Bock, Philip. (1988). *Rethinking psychological anthropology: continuity and change in the study of human action.* New York: Freeman.

Boddy, Janice. (1989). *Wombs and alien spirits: women, men and the Zar cult in* *northern Sudan*. Madison: University of Wisconsin Press.

Bodley, John H. (1982). *Victims of progress* [2nd edn.]. Menlo Park, CA: Cummings.

——(1994). *Cultural anthropology: tribes, states and the global system*. Mountain View, CA: Mayfield.

Boehm, Christopher. (1983). *Montenegrin social organization and values: political ethnography of a refuge area tribal adaptation*. New York: AMS.

——(1984). *Blood revenge: the anthropology of feuding in Montenegro and other tribal societies*. Lawrence: University Press of Kansas.

——(1989). Ambivalence and compromise in human nature. *American Anthropologist* 91: 921–939.

Bogoras, Waldemar. (1904). *The Chukchee*. Leiden: Brill [reprinted 1975, AMS].

Bohannan, Paul J. (1957). *Justice and judgment among the Tiv*. London: Oxford University Press.

——(Ed.). (1960). *African homicide and suicide*. Princeton, NJ: Princeton University Press.

——(1963). *Social anthropology*. New York: Holt.

Bohannan, Paul & George Dalton. (Eds.). (1962). *Markets in Africa*. Evanston, IL: Northwestern University Press.

Bohle, Hans-Georg, T. E. Downing, J. O. Field & F. N. Ibrahim. (Eds.). (1993). *Coping with vulnerability and criticality: case studies in food-insecure people and places*. Saarbrücken: Breitenback.

Bohrer, Vorsila L. (1986). Guideposts in ethnobotany. *Journal of Ethnobiology* 6(1): 27–43.

Boissevain, Jeremy. (1974). *Friends of friends: networks, manipulators and coalitions*. New York: St. Martin's.

Bolin, Anne. (1992). Coming of age among transsexuals. In Tony Whitehead & Barbara Reid (Eds.), *Gender constructs and social issues* (pp. 13–39). Urbana: University of Illinois Press.

Bolinger, Dwight. (1963). The atomization of meaning. *Language* 39: 170–210.

Bollen, Kenneth. (1989). *Structural equations with latent variables*. New York: Wiley.

Bolton, James L. (1980). *The medieval English economy, 1150–1500*. London: Dent.

Bolton, Ralph. (1992). Mapping terra incognita: sex research for AIDS prevention. In Gilbert Herdt & Shirley Lindenbaum (Eds.), *The time of AIDS* (pp. 124–158). London: Sage.

Bonacich, Edna. (1973). A theory of middleman minorities. *American Sociological Review* 38: 583–594.

Bonacich, Edna & John Modell. (1980). *The economic basis of ethnic solidarity: small business in the Japanese-American community*. Berkeley: University of California Press.

Bonta, Bruce D. (Ed.). (1993). *Peaceful peoples: an annotated bibliography*. Metuchen, NJ: Scarecrow.

Borgatta, Edgar & Marie Borgatta. (Eds.). (1992). *Encyclopedia of sociology* (4 vols.). New York: Macmillan.

Borgatti, Stephen. (1993). ANTHROPAC 4.0. Columbia, SC: Analytic Technologies.

Borgatti, Stephen, Martin Everett & Linton Freeman. (1992). UCINET IV (version 1.0). Columbia, SC: Analytic Technologies.

Borgerhoff Mulder, Monique. (1987). On cultural and reproductive success: Kipsigis evidence. *American Anthropologist* 89: 617–634.

——(1990). Kipsigis women's preferences for wealthy men: evidence for female choice in mammals. *Behavioral Ecology and Sociobiology* 27: 255–264.

——(1991). Human behavioural ecology. In John R. Krebs & N. B. Davies (Eds.), *Behavioural ecology* [3rd edn.] (pp. 69–98). Oxford: Blackwell Scientific.

Borjas, George J. & Marta Tienda. (1987). The economic consequences of immigration. *Science* 235: 645–651.

Boserup, Ester. (1965). *The conditions of agricultural growth: the economics of agrarian change under population pressure*. London: Allen & Unwin.

——(1970). *Woman's role in economic development*. New York: St. Martin's.

——(1981). *Population and technological*

change: a study of long-term trends. Chicago, IL: University of Chicago Press.

Boss, Medard. (1965). *A psychiatrist discovers India* [Indienfahrt eines Psychiaters, Berlin, 1959]. London: Wolff.

Bossen, Laurel. (1984). *The redivision of labor: women and economic choice in four Guatemalan communities.* Albany: State University of New York Press.

Bott, Elizabeth. (1957). *Family and social network: roles, norms, and external relationships in ordinary urban families.* London: Tavistock.

Bougle, Celestin. (1971). *Essays on the caste system* [Essais sur le régime des castes, Paris, 1927]. Cambridge: Cambridge University Press.

Bourdieu, Pierre. (1977). *Outline of a theory of practice* [Esquisse d'une théorie de la pratique, Geneva, 1972]. Cambridge: Cambridge University Press.

——— (1984). *Distinction: a social critique of the judgement of taste* [La Distinction, Paris, 1979]. Cambridge, MA: Harvard University Press.

——— (1990). *The logic of practice* [Sens pratique, Paris, 1980]. Stanford, CA: Stanford University Press.

——— (Ed.). (1993). *La misère du monde.* Paris: Editions du Seuil.

Bourgois, Philippe. (1995). *In search of respect: selling crack in El Barrio.* Cambridge: Cambridge University Press.

Bourguignon, Erika. (1968). World distribution and patterns of possession states. In Raymond Prince (Ed.), *Trance and possession states* (pp. 3–34). Montreal: Burke Memorial Society.

——— (1973). *Religion, altered states of consciousness, and social change.* Columbus: Ohio State University Press.

——— (1979). *Psychological anthropology: an introduction to human nature and cultural differences.* New York: Holt.

Bousfield, John. (1985). Good, evil and spiritual power: reflections on Sufi teachings. In David Parkin (Ed.), *The anthropology of evil* (pp. 194–208). Oxford: Blackwell.

Bowen, Elenore Smith [nom de plume of Laura Bohannan]. (1954). *Return to laughter.* London: Gollancz.

Bowen, John R. (1991). *Sumatran politics*

and poetics: Gayo history, 1900–1989. New Haven, CT: Yale University Press.

Bowker, John W. (1970). *The problems of suffering in the religions of the world.* Cambridge: Cambridge University Press.

Boyd, James W. (1975). *Satan and Mara: Christian and Buddhist symbols of evil.* Leiden: Brill.

Boyer, Pascal. (1994). *The naturalness of religious ideas: a cognitive theory of religious ideas.* Berkeley: University of California Press.

Brace, C. Loring. (1995). *The stages of human evolution* [5th edn.]. Englewood Cliffs, NJ: Prentice Hall.

Bradley, Candice, Carmella Moore, Michael Burton & Douglas White. (1990). A cross-cultural historical study of subsistence change. *American Anthropologist* 92: 447–457.

Brady, Ivan. (Ed.). (1976). *Transactions in kinship: adoption and fosterage in Oceania.* Honolulu: University Press of Hawaii.

——— (Ed.). (1991). *Anthropological poetics.* Savage, MD: Rowman & Littlefield.

Brandes, Stanley H. (1980). *Metaphors of masculinity: sex and status in Andalusian folklore.* Philadelphia: University of Pennsylvania Press.

Braude, Benjamin & Bernard Lewis. (Eds.). (1982). *Christians and Jews in the Ottoman empire: the functioning of a plural society.* New York: Holmes & Meiers.

Braudel, Fernand. (1981). *The structures of everyday life: the limits of the possible* [Structures du quotidien, Paris, 1979]. New York: Harper & Row.

Braun, David & Stephen Plog. (1982). Evolution of "tribal" social networks: theory and prehistoric North American evidence. *American Antiquity* 47: 504–525.

Bremond, Claude. (1973). *Logique du récit.* Paris: Editions du Seuil.

Brenneis, Donald. (1994). Discourse and discipline at the National Research Council: a bureaucratic *Bildungsroman. Cultural Anthropology* 9(1): 23–36.

Brenner, Robert. (1976). Agrarian class structure and economic development in pre-industrial Europe. *Past and Present* 70: 30–75.

Bresnan, Joan W. (Ed.). (1982). *The*

mental representation of grammatical relations. Cambridge, MA: MIT Press.

Brewer, Anthony. (1980). *Marxist theories of imperialism: a critical survey*. London: Routledge.

Briggs, Charles. (1993). Metadiscursive practices and scholarly authority in folklore. *Journal of American Folklore* 106: 387–434.

Briggs, Charles & Amy Shuman. (Eds.). (1993). Special issue: Theorizing folklore: toward new perspectives on the politics of culture. *Western Folklore* 52(2–4).

Briggs, Jean. (1970). *Never in anger: portrait of an Eskimo family*. Cambridge, MA: Harvard University Press.

———(1992). Mazes of meaning: how a child and a culture create each other. In William Corsaro & Peggy J. Miller (Eds.), *Interpretive approaches to children's socialization* (pp. 25–49). San Francisco, CA: Jossey-Bass.

Brokensha, David & Peter Little. (Eds.). (1988). *Anthropology of development and change in East Africa*. Boulder, CO: Westview.

Brokensha, David, D. M. Warren & Oswald Werner. (Eds.). (1980). *Indigenous knowledge systems and development*. Washington, DC: University Press of America.

Bromell, Nicholas K. (1993). *By the sweat of the brow: literature and labor in antebellum America*. Chicago, IL: University of Chicago Press.

Bromley, Daniel W. (Ed.). (1992). *Making the commons work: theory, practice, and policy*. San Francisco, CA: ICS Press.

Bromley, David & Anson Shupe. (1981). *Strange gods: the great American cult scare*. Boston, MA: Beacon.

Brondizio, Eduardo, Emilio F. Moran, Paul Mausel & You Wu. (1994). Land use in the Amazon estuary: patterns of Caboclo settlement and landscape management. *Human Ecology* 22(3): 249–279.

Brooks, Daniel R. & Deborah A. McLennan. (1991). *Phylogeny, ecology, and behavior: a research program in comparative biology*. Chicago, IL: University of Chicago Press.

Broom, Leonard, Bernard J. Siegel,

Evan Z. Vogt & James B. Watson. (1954). Acculturation: an exploratory formulation. *American Anthropologist* 56: 973–1000.

Broude, Gwen. (1975). Norms of premarital sexual behavior: a cross-cultural study. *Ethos* 3: 381–402.

Brow, James & Theodore Swedenberg. (Eds.). (1990). Special Issue: Tendentious revisions of the past in the construction of community. *Anthropological Quarterly* 63(1).

Browman, David L. (1974). Pastoral nomadism in the Andes. *Current Anthropology* 15: 188–196.

Brown, Cecil H. (1984). *Language and living things: uniformities in folk classification and naming*. New Brunswick, NJ: Rutgers University Press.

Brown, Donald E. (1991). *Human universals*. Philadelphia, PA: Temple University Press.

Brown, Karen. (1991). *Mama Lola: a Vodou priestess in Brooklyn*. Berkeley: University of California Press.

Brown, Lester R. (1970). *Seeds of change: the green revolution and development in the 1970's*. New York: Praeger.

Brown, Lester R. & Hal Kane. (1994). *Full house: reassessing the earth's population carrying capacity*. New York: Norton.

Brown, Paula. (1978). *Highland peoples of New Guinea*. Cambridge: Cambridge University Press.

Brown, Paula & Ilsa Schuster. (Eds.). (1986). Special Issue: Culture and aggression. *Anthropological Quarterly* 59(4).

Brown, Peter J., B. Ballard & J. Gregg. (1994). Culture, ethnicity, and the practice of medicine. In Alan Stoudemire (Ed.), *Human behavior* [2nd edn.] (pp. 84–106). New York: Lippincott.

Brown, Peter J., Marcia Inhorn & D. J. Smith. (1996). Disease, ecology, and human behavior. In Carolyn Sargent & Thomas M. Johnson (Eds.), *Medical anthropology* [2nd edn.] (pp. 183–218). Westport, CT: Greenwood.

Brown, Richard H. (1977). *A poetic for sociology: toward a logic of discovery for the human sciences*. Cambridge: Cambridge University Press.

Brown, Roger & Albert Gillman. (1960). The pronouns of power and solidarity. In Thomas A. Sebeok (Ed.), *Style in language* (pp. 253–276). Cambridge, MA: MIT Press.

Browner, Carole & Carolyn Sargent. (1990). Anthropology and studies of human reproduction. In Thomas M. Johnson & Carolyn F. Sargent (Eds.), *Medical anthropology* (pp. 215–229). New York: Praeger.

Brumberg, Joan Jacobs. (1993). "Something happens to girls": menarche and the emergence of the modern American hygienic imperative. *Journal of the History of Sexuality* 4(1): 99–127.

Brumfiel, Elizabeth. (1980). Specialization, exchange and the Aztec market. *Current Anthropology* 21: 459–478.

Brumfiel, Elizabeth & John Fox. (Eds.). (1994). *Factional competition and political development in the New World*. Cambridge: Cambridge University Press.

Bruner, Edward M. (Ed.). (1984). *Text, play and story: the construction and reconstruction of self and society*. Washington, DC: American Ethnological Society.

——— (1986). Ethnography as narrative. In Victor Turner & Edward Bruner (Eds.), *The anthropology of experience* (pp. 135–155). Urbana: University of Illinois Press.

Bruzina, Ronald. (1970). *Logos and eidos: the concept in phenomenology*. The Hague: Mouton.

Bryant, M. Darrol & Donald Dayton. (Eds.). (1983). *The coming kingdom: essays in American millennialism and eschatology*. Barrytown, NY: International Religious Foundation.

Buckley, Thomas. (1988). Menstruation and the power of Yurok women. In Thomas Buckley & Alma Gottlieb (Eds.), *Blood magic* (pp. 94–115). Berkeley: University of California Press.

Buckley, Thomas & Alma Gottlieb. (1988a). A critical appraisal of theories of menstrual symbolism. In Thomas Buckley & Alma Gottlieb (Eds.), *Blood magic* (pp. 1–50). Berkeley: University of California Press.

——— (Eds.). (1988b). *Blood magic: the anthropology of menstruation*. Berkeley: University of California Press.

Bugos, Paul E. & Lorraine M. McCarthy. (1984). Ayoreo infanticide: a case study. In Glenn Hausfater & Sarah B. Hrdy (Eds.), *Infanticide* (pp. 503–520). New York: Aldine.

Bühler, Karl. (1990). *Theory of language: the representational function of language* [Sprachtheorie, Jena, 1934]. Amsterdam: Benjamins.

Bujra, Abdalla. (1971). *The politics of stratification: a study of political change in a south Arabian town*. Oxford: Clarendon.

Bulliet, Richard. (1977). *The camel and the wheel*. Cambridge, MA: Harvard University Press.

Bulmer, Ralph. (1963). Why the cassowary is not a bird. In Mary Douglas (Ed.), *Rules and meanings* (pp. 167–193). Harmondsworth: Penguin.

Burbank, Victoria K. (1988). *Aboriginal adolescence: maidenhood in an Australian community*. New Brunswick, NJ: Rutgers University Press.

——— (1994). *Fighting women: anger and aggression in Aboriginal Australia*. Berkeley: University of California Press.

Burch, Ernest & Linda Ellanna. (Eds.). (1994). *Key issues in hunter–gatherer research*. Oxford: Berg.

Burger, Richard L. (1988). Unity and heterogeneity within the Chavin horizon. In Richard Keating (Ed.), *Peruvian prehistory* (pp. 99–144). Cambridge: Cambridge University Press.

Burghardt, Gordon. (1973). Instinct and innate behavior: toward an ethological psychology. In John A. Nevin (Ed.), *The study of behavior* (pp. 323–400). Glenview, IL: Scott Foresman.

Burke, Kenneth. (1941). *The philosophy of literary form: studies in symbolic action*. Baton Rouge: Louisiana State University Press.

——— (1966). *Language as symbolic action: essays on life, literature, and method*. Berkeley: University of California Press.

Burling, Robbins. (1964). Cognition and componential analysis: God's truth or hocus-pocus? *American Anthropologist* 66: 20–28.

——— (1969). Linguistics and ethnographic description. *American Anthropologist* 71(4): 817–827.

Burridge, Kenelm. (1960). *Mambu: a Melanesian millennium*. New York: Humanities.

———(1969). *New heaven, new earth: a study of millenarian activities*. Oxford: Blackwell.

Burrow, John W. (1966). *Evolution and society: a study in Victorian social theory*. Cambridge: Cambridge University Press.

Burton, John W. (1981). Atuot ethnicity. *Africa* 51(1): 496–507.

———(1992). *An introduction to Evans-Pritchard*. Fribourg: University Press.

Burton, Michael & Karl Reitz. (1981). The plow, female contribution to agricultural subsistence, and polygyny: a loglinear analysis. *Behavior Science Research* 15: 275–305.

Burton, Michael & Douglas R. White. (1987). Cross-cultural surveys today. *Annual Review of Anthropology* 16: 143–160.

Burton, Michael, Lilyan Brudner & Douglas White. (1977). A model of the sexual division of labor. *American Ethnologist* 4: 227–251.

Burton, Richard Francis. (1885–6). Terminal essay. In *A plain and literal translation of the Arabian Nights*. Benares: Kama Shastra Society.

Buss, David M. (1989). Sex differences in human mate preferences: evolutionary hypotheses tested in thirty-seven cultures. *Behavioral and Brain Sciences* 12: 1–14.

———(1994). *The evolution of desire: strategies of human mating*. New York: Basic.

Butler, Judith. (1990). *Gender trouble: feminism and the subversion of identity*. New York: Routledge.

Butterfield, Herbert. (1973). Historiography. In Philip P. Wiener (Ed.), *Dictionary of the history of ideas* (pp. 464–498). New York: Scribner.

Butzer, Karl. (1982). *Archaeology as human ecology: method and theory for a contextual approach*. Cambridge: Cambridge University Press.

Buytendijk, F. J. J. (1968). *Woman: a contemporary view* [De vrouw, haar natuur, verschijning en bestaan, Utrecht, 1951]. Glen Rock, NJ: Newman.

Bynon, Theodora. (1977). *Historical linguistics*. Cambridge: Cambridge University Press.

Caffrey, Margaret M. (1989). *Ruth*

Benedict: stranger in this land. Austin: University of Texas Press.

Caldarola, Victor. (1987). The generation of primary photographic data in ethnographic fieldwork: context and the problem of objectivity. In Martin Taureg & Jay Ruby (Eds.), *Visual explorations of the world* (pp. 217–227). Aachen: Edition Herodot.

Callendar, Charles & Lee M. Kochems. (1987). The North American berdache. *Current Anthropology* 24(4): 443–456.

Camino, Linda A. & Ruth M. Krulfeld. (Eds.). (1994). *Reconstructing lives, recapturing meaning: refugee identity, gender, and culture change*. Langhorne, PA: Gordon & Breach.

Campbell, Bernard. (1985). *Human ecology: the story of our place in nature from prehistory to the present* [3rd edn.]. New York: Aldine.

Campbell, John K. (1964). *Honour, family and patronage: a study of institutions and moral values in a Greek mountain community*. Oxford: Clarendon.

Campbell, Joseph. (1949). *The hero with a thousand faces*. New York: Pantheon.

Campbell, Lyle, Terrence Kaufman & Thomas Smith-Stark. (1986). Meso-America as a linguistic area. *Language* 62: 530–570.

Cancian, Francesca M. (1968). Varieties of functional analysis. In David Sills (Ed.), *International encyclopedia of the social sciences* 6: 29–42. New York: Macmillan.

Cancian, Frank. (1965). *Economics and prestige in a Maya community: the religious cargo system in Zinacantan*. Stanford, CA: Stanford University Press.

Canfield, Robert L. (1973). *Faction and conversion in a plural society: religious alignments in the Hindu Kush*. Ann Arbor: University of Michigan Press.

Caplan, Lionel. (Ed.). (1987). *Studies in religious fundamentalism*. Houndmills: Macmillan.

Caplan, Patricia. (Ed.). (1987). *The cultural construction of sexuality*. London: Tavistock.

Caplan, Patricia & Janet Bujra. (Eds.). (1979). *Women united, women divided: comparative studies of ten contemporary* *cultures*. Bloomington: Indiana University Press.

Carlson, Greg & Michael Tanenhaus. (Eds.). (1989). *Linguistic structure in language processing*. Dordrecht: Kluwer Academic.

Carlyle, Thomas. (1843). *Past and present*. London: Chapman & Hall.

Carmack, Robert M. (Ed.). (1988). *Harvest of violence: the Maya Indians and the Guatemalan crisis*. Norman: University of Oklahoma Press.

Carmichael, David L., Jane Huber, Brian Reevers & Audhild Schanche. (Eds.). (1994). *Sacred sites, sacred places*. London: Routledge.

Carmichael, Peter. (Ed.). (1991). *Nomads*. London: Collier & Brown.

Carneiro, Robert. (1970). A theory of the origin of the state. *Science* 169: 733–738.

———(1973). The four faces of evolution. In John J. Honigmann (Ed.), *Handbook of social and cultural anthropology* (pp. 89–110). Chicago, IL: Rand McNally.

———(1981a). The chiefdom as precursor of the state. In Grant Jones & Robert Kautz (Eds.), *The transformation to statehood in the New World* (pp. 37–97). Cambridge: Cambridge University Press.

———(1981b). Leslie White. In Sydel Silverman (Ed.), *Totems and teachers* (pp. 208–251). New York: Columbia University Press.

———(1990). Chiefdom-level warfare as exemplified in Fiji and the Cauca Valley. In Jonathan Haas (Ed.), *The anthropology of war* (pp. 190–211). Cambridge: Cambridge University Press.

Carrier, Joseph M. (1995). *"Los otros": male homosexual encounters in Mexico*. New York: Columbia University Press.

Carrithers, Michael. (1990). Is anthropology art or science? *Current Anthropology* 31: 263–282.

———(1992). *Why humans have cultures: explaining anthropology and social diversity*. Oxford: Oxford University Press.

Carrithers, Michael, Steven Collins & Steven Lukes. (1985). *The category of the person: anthropology, philosophy, history*. Cambridge: Cambridge University Press.

Carroll, Vern. (1970). Introduction: What does "adoption" mean? In Vern Carroll (Ed.), *Adoption in Eastern Oceania* (pp. 3–17). Honolulu: University of Hawaii Press.

Casagrande, Joseph. (1960). *In the company of man: twenty portraits by anthropologists*. New York: Harper & Row.

Casagrande, Joseph B. & Kenneth Hale. (1967). Semantic relationships in Papago folk-definitions. In Dell Hymes (Ed.), *Studies in Southwestern ethnolinguistics* (pp. 165–193). The Hague: Mouton.

Cassidy, Claire. (1982). Protein-energy malnutrition as a culture-bound syndrome. *Culture, Medicine, and Psychiatry* 6: 625–645.

Castles, Stephen & Mark J. Miller. (1993). *The age of migration: international population movements in the modern world*. New York: Guilford.

Caton, Steven C. (1985). Poetic construction of self. *Anthropological Quarterly* 58(4): 141–151.

———(1990). *"Peaks of Yemen I summon": poetry as cultural practice in a North Yemeni tribe*. Berkeley: University of California Press.

———(1991). Diglossia in North Yemen: a case of competing linguistic communities. *Southwestern Journal of Linguistics* 10: 143–159.

Cavalli-Sforza, Luigi Luca, Paolo Menozzi & Alberto Piazza. (1994). *The history and geography of human genes*. Princeton, NJ: Princeton University Press.

Cavalli-Sforza, Luigi Luca & Francesco Cavalli-Sforza. (1995). *The great human diasporas: the history of diversity and evolution* [Chi siamo, Milan, 1993]. Reading, MA: Addison-Wesley.

Cavell, Stanley. (1994). *A pitch of philosophy: autobiographical exercises*. Cambridge, MA: Harvard University Press.

Caws, Peter. (1974). Operational, representational and explanatory models. *American Anthropologist* 76: 1–11.

Cazeneuve, Jean. (1972). *Lucien Levy-Bruhl* [Lucien Levy-Bruhl, Paris, 1963]. Oxford: Blackwell.

Cernea, Michael. (Ed.). (1991). *Putting people first: sociological variables in rural* *development* [rev. edn.]. Oxford: Oxford University Press.

Cernea, Michael M. & Scott E. Guggenheim. (Eds.). (1993). *Anthropological approaches to resettlement: policy, practice, and theory.* Boulder, CO: Westview.

Cernea, Ruth Fredman. (1981). *The Passover Seder: afikoman in exile.* Philadelphia: University of Pennsylvania Press.

Cesara, Manda. (1982). *Reflections of a woman anthropologist: no hiding place.* London: Academic.

Chagnon, Napoleon. (1988). Life histories, blood revenge, and warfare in a tribal population. *Science* 239: 935–992.

——(1992). *Yanomamo* [4th edn.]. Fort Worth, TX: Harcourt.

Chagnon, Napoleon & William Irons. (Eds.). (1979). *Evolutionary biology and human social behavior: an anthropological perspective.* North Scituate, MA: Duxbury Press.

Chakrabarty, Dipesh. (1992). Postcoloniality and the artifice of history: who speaks for "Indian" pasts? *Representations* 37: 1–26.

Chambers, Erve. (1985). *Applied anthropology: a practical guide.* Englewood Cliffs, NJ: Prentice-Hall.

Chambers, J. K. & Peter Trudgill. (1980). *Dialectology.* Cambridge: Cambridge University Press.

Chang, K. C. (Ed.). (1977). *Food in Chinese culture: anthropological and historical perspectives.* New Haven, CT: Yale University Press.

——(1983). *Art, myth, and ritual: the path to political authority in ancient China.* Cambridge, MA: Harvard University Press.

Chanock, Martin. (1985). *Law, custom and social order: the colonial experience in Malawi and Zambia.* Cambridge: Cambridge University Press.

Charbonnier, Guy. (1969). *Conversations with Claude Lévi-Strauss* [Entretiens avec Claude Lévi-Strauss, Paris, 1961]. London: Cape.

Charnov, Eric L. (1982). *The theory of sex allocation.* Princeton, NJ: Princeton University Press.

Charny, Israel W. (Ed.). (1988–94). *Genocide: a critical bibliographic review* (3 vols.). London: Mansell.

Chase-Dunn, Christopher. (1989). *Global formation: structures of the world-economy.* Oxford: Blackwell.

Chase-Dunn, Christopher & Peter Grimes. (1995). World-systems analysis. *Annual Review of Sociology* 21: 387–417.

Chase-Dunn, Christopher & Thomas D. Hall. (1994). The historical evolution of world-systems. *Sociological Inquiry* 64: 257–280.

——(1997). *Rise and demise: comparing world-systems.* Boulder, CO: Westview Press.

Chavez, Leo R. (1992). *Shadowed lives: undocumented immigrants in American society.* Fort Worth, TX: Harcourt.

Chayanov, A. V. (1966). *The theory of peasant economy* [Organizatsiia krest'ianskogo khoziaistva, Moscow, 1925]. Homewood, IL: Irwin.

Cheater, Angela P. (1989). *Social anthropology: an alternative introduction* [2nd edn.]. London: Unwin Hyman.

Chejne, Anwar G. (1969). *The Arabic language: its role in history.* Minneapolis: University of Minnesota Press.

Cheney, Dorothy L. & Robert M. Seyfarth. (1990). *How monkeys see the world: inside the mind of another species.* Chicago, IL: University of Chicago Press.

Chernoff, John M. (1979). *African rhythm and African sensibility.* Chicago, IL: University of Chicago Press.

Chew, Sing. (1995). On environmental degradation: let the earth live. *Humboldt Journal of Social Relations* 21: 9–13.

Chilcote, Ronald H. (1981). Issues of theory in dependency and marxism. *Latin American Perspective* 8(3–4): 3–16.

——(1984). *Theories of development and underdevelopment.* Boulder, CO: Westview.

Childe, V. Gordon. (1936). *Man makes himself.* London: Watts.

——(1951). *Social evolution.* London: Watts.

Chirot, Daniel & Thomas D. Hall. (1982). World-system theory. *Annual Review of Sociology* 8: 81–106.

Chomsky, Noam. (1957). *Syntactic structures.* The Hague: Mouton.
——(1965). *Aspects of the theory of syntax.* Cambridge, MA: MIT Press.
——(1973). Conditions on transformations. In Stephen Anderson & Paul Kiparsky (Eds.), *A festschrift for Morris Halle* (pp. 232–286). New York: Holt.
——(1981). *Lectures on government and binding.* Dordrecht: Foris.
——(1986). *Knowledge of language: its nature, origin, and use.* New York: Praeger.
——(1988). *Language and problems of knowledge: the Managua lectures.* Cambridge, MA: MIT Press.

Chrisman, N. J. & Thomas Johnson. (1996). Clinically applied anthropology. In Carolyn Sargent & Thomas Johnson (Eds.), *Medical anthropology* [rev. edn.] (pp. 88–109). Westport, CT: Greenwood.

Christensen, Hanne. (1985). *Refugees and pioneers: history and field study of a Burundian settlement in Tanzania.* Geneva: UNRISD.

Claessen, Henri & P. Skalnik. (Eds.). (1978). *The early state.* The Hague: Mouton.

Clanchy, M. T. (1979). *From memory to written record, England, 1066–1307.* Cambridge, MA: Harvard University Press.

Clark, J. Desmond & Steven A. Brandt. (Eds.). (1984). *From hunters to farmers: the causes and consequences of food production in Africa.* Berkeley: University of California Press.

Clarke, David L. (1968). *Analytical archaeology.* London: Methuen.

Clastres, Pierre. (1987). *Society against the state: essays in political anthropology* [Société contre l'état, Paris, 1974]. New York: Zone.

Clay, Jason W. & Bonnie K. Holcomb. (1986). *Politics and the Ethiopian famine, 1984–1985* [rev. edn.]. New Brunswick, NJ: Transaction.

Cleveland, David A. & Daniela Soleri. (1987). Household gardens as a development strategy. *Human Organization* 46: 259–270.

Clifford, James. (1982). *Person and myth: Maurice Leenhardt in the Melanesian world.* Berkeley: University of California Press.
——(1983). On ethnographic authority. *Representations* 1(2): 118–146 [reprinted in Clifford 1988: 21–54].
——(1986). Introduction: Partial truths. In James Clifford & George Marcus (Eds.), *Writing culture* (pp. 1–26). Berkeley: University of California Press.
——(1988). *The predicament of culture: twentieth-century ethnography, literature, and art.* Cambridge, MA: Harvard University Press.

Clifford, James & George Marcus. (Eds.). (1986). *Writing culture: the poetics and politics of ethnography.* Berkeley: University of California Press.

Clifton, Charles & Lyn Frazier. (Eds.). (1994). *Perspectives on sentence processing.* Hillsdale, NJ: Erlbaum.

Clogg, Clifford & Edward Shihadeh. (1994). *Statistical models for ordinal variables.* Thousand Oaks, CA: Sage.

Coalter, Fred. (Ed.). (1989). *Freedom and constraint: the paradoxes of leisure.* New York: Routledge.

Cocchiara, Giuseppe. (1981). *History of folklore in Europe* [Storia del folklore in Europa, 1952]. Philadelphia, PA: ISHI.

Codere, Helen. (1950). *Fighting with property: a study of Kwakiutl potlatching and warfare, 1792–1930.* New York: Augustin.
——(1968). Exchange and display. In David L. Sills (Ed.), *International encyclopedia of the social sciences* 5: 239–244. New York: Macmillan.

Codrington, Robert Henry. (1891). *The Melanesians: studies in their anthropology and folk-lore.* Oxford: Clarendon.

Cohen, Abner. (1969). *Custom and politics in urban Africa: a study of Hausa migrants in Yoruba towns.* Berkeley: University of California Press.
——(1974). Introduction: The lesson of ethnicity. In Abner Cohen (Ed.), *Urban ethnicity* (pp. ix–xxiv). London: Tavistock.

Cohen, David William. (1994). *The combing of history.* Chicago, IL: University of Chicago Press.

Cohen, Donald. (1978). Ethnicity: problem and focus in anthropology. *Annual Reviews of Anthropology* 7: 379–404.

Cohen, Erik. (1992). Pilgrimage and tourism: convergence and divergence. In Alan Morinis (Ed.), *Sacred journeys* (pp. 47–64). Westport, CT: Greenwood.

Cohen, Fay G. (1986). *Treaties on trial: the continuing controversy over Northwest Indian fishing rights*. Seattle: University of Washington Press.

Cohen, Mark N. (1977). *The food crisis in prehistory: overpopulation and the origins of agriculture*. New Haven, CT: Yale University Press.

———(1989). *Health and the rise of civilization*. New Haven, CT: Yale University Press.

Cohen, Mark N. & George J. Armelagos. (Eds.). (1984). *Paleopathology at the origins of agriculture*. Orlando, FL: Academic.

Cohen, Ronald. (1971). *Dominance and defiance: a study of marital instability in an Islamic African society*. Washington, DC: American Anthropological Association.

Cohen, Ronald & Elman Service. (Eds.). (1978). *Origin of the state: the anthropology of political evolution*. Philadelphia, PA: ISHI.

Cohn, Bernard S. (1987). *An anthropologist among the historians and other essays*. Delhi: Oxford University Press.

Cohn, Bernand S. & Nicholas Dirks. (1988). Beyond the fringe: the nation state, colonialism, and the technologies of power. *Journal of Historical Sociology* 12: 224–229.

Cohn, Norman. (1970). *Pursuit of the millennium: revolutionary Messianism in the Middle Ages and its bearing on modern totalitarian movements* [rev. edn.]. Oxford: Oxford University Press.

———(1993). *Cosmos, chaos, and the world to come: the ancient roots of apocalyptic faith*. New Haven, CT: Yale University Press.

Cole, Sally. (1991). *Women of the Praia: work and lives in a Portuguese coastal community*. Princeton, NJ: Princeton University Press.

Collier, Jane F. (1973). *Law and social change in Zinacantan*. Stanford, CA: Stanford University Press.

———(1988). *Marriage and inequality in classless societies*. Stanford, CA: Stanford University Press.

Collier, Jane F. & Michelle Z. Rosaldo. (1981). Politics and gender in simple societies. In Sherry B. Ortner & Harriet Whitehead (Eds.), *Sexual meanings* (pp. 275–329). Cambridge: Cambridge University Press.

Collier, Jane F. & Sylvia Yanagisako. (Eds.). (1987). *Gender and kinship: essays toward a unified analysis*. Stanford, CA: Stanford University Press.

Collier, Jane F., M. Z. Rosaldo & S. J. Yanagisako. (1992). Is there a family? new anthropological views. In Barrie Thorne (Ed.), *Rethinking the family* [2nd edn.] (pp. 31–48). Boston, MA: Northeastern University Press.

Collier, John. (1975). Photography and visual anthropology. In Paul Hockings (Ed.), *Principles of visual anthropology* (pp. 211–230). The Hague: Mouton.

Collier, John & Malcolm Collier. (1986). *Visual anthropology: photography as a research method* [2nd edn.]. Albuquerque: University of New Mexico Press.

Collins, Randall. (1992). *Sociological insight: an introduction to non-obvious sociology* [2nd edn.]. Oxford: Oxford University Press.

Colson, Elizabeth. (1953). Social control and vengeance in Plateau Tonga society. *Africa* 23: 199–212.

———(1971). *The social consequences of resettlement: the impact of the Kariba resettlement upon the Gwembe Tonga*. Manchester: Manchester University Press.

———(1979). In good years and bad: food strategies in self-reliant societies. *Journal of Anthropological Research* 35: 18–29.

Comaroff, Jean. (1985). *Body of power, spirit of resistance: the culture and history of a South African people*. Chicago, IL: University of Chicago Press.

Comaroff, Jean & John Comaroff. (1992). *Ethnography and the historical imagination*. Boulder, CO: Westview.

Comaroff, John. L. (Ed.). (1980). *The meaning of marriage payments*. London: Academic.

Comaroff, John L. & Simon Roberts. (1981). *Rules and processes: the cultural logic of dispute in an African context*. Chicago, IL: University of Chicago Press.

Commons, John R. (1924). *Legal foundations of capitalism.* New York: Macmillan.

Comrie, Bernard. (1989). *Language universals and linguistic typology: syntax and morphology* [2nd edn.]. Chicago, IL: University of Chicago Press.

Conant, F. (1990). 1990 and beyond: satellite remote sensing and ecological anthropology. In E. F. Moran (Ed.), *The ecosystem approach in anthropology* (pp. 357–388). Ann Arbor: University of Michigan Press.

Condominas, Georges. (1977). *We have eaten the forest: the story of a Montagnard village in the central highlands of Vietnam* [Nous avons mangé la forêt de la pierre-génie Goo, Paris 1957]. New York: Hill & Wang.

Condon, Richard G. (1987). *Inuit youth: growth and change in the Canadian Arctic.* New Brunswick, NJ: Rutgers University Press.

Conkey, Margaret & Sarah Williams. (1991). Original narratives: the political economy of gender in archaeology. In Micaela di Leonardo (Ed.), *Gender at the crossroads of knowledge* (pp. 102–139). Berkeley: University of California Press.

Conklin, Harold C. (1954a). An ethnoecological approach to shifting agriculture. *Transactions of the New York Academy of Sciences* (2nd ser.) 17: 133–142.

——— (1954b). Hanunoo color categories. *Southwestern Journal of Anthropology* 11: 339–334.

——— (1957). *Hanunoo agriculture: a report on an integral system of shifting cultivation in the Philippines.* Rome: FAO.

——— (1964). Ethnogenealogical method. In Ward Goodenough (Ed.), *Explorations in cultural anthropology* (pp. 25–55). New York: McGraw-Hill.

——— (1980). *Ethnographic atlas of Ifugao: a study of environment, culture, and society in Northern Luzon.* New Haven, CT: Yale University Press.

Connell, Robert W. (1995). *Masculinities.* Berkeley: University California Press.

Conner, Linda, Patsy Asch & Timothy Asch. (1986). *Jero Tapakan, Balinese healer: an ethnographic film monograph.* Cambridge: Cambridge Univerity Press.

Connor, Walker. (1984). *The national question in Marxist–Leninist theory and strategy.* Princeton, NJ: Princeton University Press.

Constantinides, Pamela. (1985). Women heal women: spirit possession and sexual segregation in a Muslim society. *Social Science and Medicine* 21: 685–692.

Cook, Karen S. & Joseph M. Whitmeyer. (1992). Two approaches to social structure: exchange theory and network analysis. *Annual Review of Sociology* 18: 109–127.

Cook, Scott. (1982). *Zapotec stoneworkers: the dynamics of rural simple commodity production in modern Mexican capitalism.* Washington, DC: University Press of America.

Cook, Scott & Martin Diskin. (Eds.). (1976). *Markets in Oaxaca.* Austin: University of Texas Press.

Cook-Gumperz, Jenny, W. A. Corsaro & J. Streeck. (Eds.). (1986). *Children's worlds and children's language.* Berlin: Mouton de Gruyter.

Cooper, Francis & Ann Stoler. (1989). Tensions of empire: colonial control and visions of rule. *American Ethnologist* 16: 609–621.

Cooper, J. M. (1949). A cross-cultural survey of South American Indian tribes: stimulants and narcotics. In Julian Steward (Ed.), *Handbook of South American Indians* 5: 589–627. Washington, DC: Government Printing Office.

Cooper, Matthew & Margaret Rodman. (1992). *New neighbours: a case study of cooperative housing in Toronto.* Toronto: University of Toronto Press.

Coppinger, R. & P. Rosenblatt. (1968). Romantic love and subsistence dependence of spouses. *Southwestern Journal of Anthropology* 24: 310–318.

CORD (Committee on Research in Dance). (1974). *New directions in dance research: anthropology and the dance.* New York: Committee on Research in Dance.

Coreil, Jeannine & J. Dennis Mull. (Eds.). (1990). *Anthropology and primary health care.* Boulder, CO: Westview.

Coronil, Fernando & Julie Skurski. (1991). Dismembering and remembering the nation: the semantics of political violence in Venezuela. *Comparative Studies in Society and History* 33: 288–337.

Corrigan, Phillip & Derek Sayer. (1985). *The great arch: English state formation as cultural revolution.* Oxford: Blackwell.

Corsaro, William & Peggy J. Miller. (Eds.). (1992). *Interpretive approaches to children's socialization.* San Francisco, CA: Jossey-Bass.

Cosmides, Leda & John Tooby. (1989). Evolutionary psychology and the generation of culture part 2, case study: a computational theory of social exchange. *Ethology and Sociobiology* 10: 51–97.

Counts, Dorothy Ayers & David R. Counts. (Eds.). (1985). *Aging and its transformations: moving toward death in Pacific societies.* Lanham, MD: University Press of America.

Cove, John J. (1973). Hunters, trappers and gatherers of the sea: a comparative study of fishing strategies. *Journal of the Fisheries Research Board of Canada* 30: 249–259.

Cowan, Jane. (1990). *Dance and the body politic in northern Greece.* Princeton, NJ: Princeton University Press.

Coward, E. Walter. (1980). *Irrigation and agricultural development in Asia: perspectives from the social sciences.* Ithaca, NY: Cornell University Press.

Coward, Rosalind & John Ellis. (1977). *Language and materialism: developments in semiology and the theory of the subject.* London: Routledge.

Cowgill, Donald O. & Lowell Holmes. (Eds.). (1972). *Aging and modernization.* New York: Appleton-Century-Crofts.

Crandon-Malamud, Libbet. (1991). *From the fat of our souls: social change, political process, and medical pluralism in Bolivia.* Berkeley: University of California Press.

Crane, Julia G. & Michael V. Angrosino. (1992). *Field projects in anthropology: a student handbook* [3rd edn.]. Morristown, NJ: General Learning Press.

Crapanzano, Vincent. (1973). *The Hamadsha: a study in Moroccan ethnopsychiatry.* Berkeley: University of California Press.

———(1977). The life history in anthropological field work. *Anthropology and Humanism Quarterly* 2: 3–7.

———(1980). *Tuhami: portrait of a Moroccan.* Chicago, IL: University of Chicago Press.

———(1985). *Waiting: the Whites of South Africa.* New York: Random.

———(1992). *Hermes' dilemma and Hamlet's desire.* Cambridge, MA: Harvard University Press.

Crawford, Peter Ian & Jan K. Simonsen. (Eds.). (1992). *Ethnographic film aesthetics and narrative traditions.* Aarhus: Intervention Press.

Crawford, Peter Ian & David Turton. (Eds.). (1992). *Film as ethnography.* Manchester: Manchester University Press.

Crawley, Alfred E. (1902). *The mystic rose: study of primitive marriage.* London: Macmillan.

Croce, Benedetto. (1909). *Aesthetic as science of expression and general linguistic* [Estetica, Milan, 1902]. London: Macmillan [republished Cambridge University Press 1992].

Crocker, William. (1990). *The Canela (Eastern Timbira), I: an ethnographic introduction.* Washington, DC: Smithsonian.

Croll, Elizabeth & David Parkin. (Eds.). (1992). *Bush base, forest farm: culture, environment and development.* London: Routledge.

Crone, Patricia. (1986). The tribe and the state. In John A. Hall (Ed.), *States in history* (pp. 48–77). Oxford: Blackwell.

Cronin, Helena. (1991). *The ant and the peacock: altruism and sexual selection from Darwin to today.* Cambridge: Cambridge University Press.

Cronk, Lee. (1991). Preferential parental investment in daughters over sons. *Human Nature* 2: 387–417.

Cronon, William. (1983). *Changes in the land: Indians, colonists, and the ecology of New England.* New York: Hill & Wang.

Crook, David P. (1994). *Darwinism, war, and history: the debate over the biology of war from the "Origin of species" to the First World War.* Cambridge: Cambridge University Press.

Crosby, Alfred W. (1972). *The Columbian exchange: biological and cul-*

tural consequences of 1492. Westport, CT: Greenwood.

———(1986). *Ecological imperialism: the biological expansion of Europe, 900–1900.* Cambridge: Cambridge University Press.

Crow, Ben & Mary Thorpe. (1986). *Survival and change in the Third World.* Cambridge: Polity.

Cruise O'Brien, Donal B. (1971). *The Mourides of Senegal: the political organization of an Islamic brotherhood.* Oxford: Clarendon.

Crumley, Carole. (1987). Dialectical critique of hierarchy. In T. Patterson & C. W. Gailey (Eds.), *Power relations and state formation* (pp. 155–169). Washington, DC: American Anthropological Association.

———(Ed.). (1994). *Historical ecology: cultural knowledge and changing landscapes.* Santa Fe, NM: School of American Research Press.

Crump, Thomas. (1981). *The phenomenon of money.* London: Routledge.

Crumrine, N. Ross & Alan Morinis. (Eds.). (1991). *Pilgrimage in Latin America.* New York: Greenwood.

Csordas, Thomas. (1994). *The sacred self: a cultural phenomenology of charismatic healing.* Berkeley: University of California Press.

Curtin, Phillip. (1984). *Cross-cultural trade in world history.* Cambridge: Cambridge University Press.

Czaplicka, Marie. (1914). *Aboriginal Siberia: a study in social anthropology.* Oxford: Clarendon.

Dahlberg, Frances. (Ed.). (1981). *Woman the gatherer.* New Haven, CT: Yale University Press.

Dahlberg, Kenneth A. (1979). *Beyond the green revolution: the ecology and politics of global agricultural development.* New York: Plenum.

Dalton, George. (1960). A note of clarification on economic surpluses. *American Anthropologist* 62: 483–490.

———(1961). Economic theory and primitive society. *American Anthropologist* 63: 1–25.

———(1963). Economic surplus, once again. *American Anthropologist* 65: 389–394.

———(1973). Peasant markets. *Journal of Peasant Studies* 1: 240–243.

———(1974). How exactly are peasants "exploited?" *American Anthropologist* 76: 553–561.

———(1977). Further remarks on exploitation. *American Anthropologist* 79: 125–134.

D'Altroy, Terence & Timothy Earle. (1985). Staple finance, wealth finance, and storage in the Inka political economy. *Current Anthropology* 26: 187–206.

Daly, Martin & Margo Wilson. (1978). *Sex, evolution, and behavior.* North Scituate, MA: Duxbury Press.

———(1984). A sociobiological analysis of human infanticide. In G. Hausfater & S. B. Hrdy (Eds.), *Infanticide* (pp. 487–502). New York: Aldine.

———(1988a). Evolutionary social psychology and family homicide. *Science* 242: 519–524.

———(1988b). *Homicide.* Hawthorne, NY: Aldine de Gruyter.

D'Andrade, Roy. (1985). Character terms and cultural models. In Janet Dougherty (Ed.), *Directions in cognitive anthropology* (pp. 321–343). Urbana, IL: University of Chicago Press.

———(1987). A folk model of the mind. In Dorothy Holland & Naomi Quinn (Eds.), *Cultural models in language and thought* (pp. 112–148). Cambridge: Cambridge University Press.

———(1990). Some propositions about the relations between culture and human cognition. In James W. Stigler, Richard A. Schweder & Gilbert Herdt (Eds.), *Cultural psychology* (pp. 65–129). Cambridge: Cambridge University Press.

———(1995). *The development of cognitive anthropology.* Cambridge: Cambridge University Press.

D'Andrade, Roy & Claudia Strauss. (Eds.). (1992). *Human motives and cultural models.* Cambridge: Cambridge University Press.

Daniel, E. Valentine. (1984). *Fluid signs: being a person the Tamil way.* Berkeley: University of California Press.

Daniel, E. Valentine & John Knudsen. (Eds.). (1995). *Mistrusting refugees.* Berkeley: University of California Press.

Daniel, Glyn E. (1950). *A hundred years of archaeology.* London: Duckworth.

——(1962). *The idea of prehistory.* London: Watts.

——(1967). *The origins and growth of archaeology.* New York: Crowell.

Daniel, Yvonne. (1995). *Rumba: dance and social change in contemporary Cuba.* Bloomington: Indiana University Press.

Dant, Tim. (1991). *Knowledge, ideology and discourse: a sociological perspective.* London: Routledge.

D'Aquili, Eugene G., Charles Laughlin & John McManus. (1979). *The spectrum of ritual: a biogenetic structural analysis.* New York: Columbia University Press.

Darnell, Regna. (Ed.). (1974). *Readings in the history of anthropology.* New York: Harper & Row.

——(1990). *Edward Sapir: linguist, anthropologist, humanist.* Berkeley: University of California Press.

Darnton, Robert. (1968). *Mesmerism and the end of the Enlightenment in France.* Cambridge, MA: Harvard University Press.

Darwin, Charles. (1868). *The variation of plants and animals under domestication* (2 vols.). London: Murray.

——(1871). *The descent of man, and selection in relation to sex.* London: Murray.

——(1872). *The expression of emotions in man and animals.* London: Murray.

Das, Veena. (1995). *Critical events: an anthropological perspective on contemporary India.* New Delhi: Oxford.

Das Gupta, Monica. (1995). Life course perspectives on women's autonomy and health outcomes. *American Anthropologist* 97(3): 481–491.

Davenport, William H. (1959). Nonunilineal descent and descent groups. *American Anthropologist* 61: 557–572.

——(1968). Sculpture of the Eastern Solomons. *Expedition* 10: 4–25.

——(1971). Sex in cross-cultural perspective. In Donald Marshall & Robert Suggs (Eds.), *Human sexual behavior* (pp. 115–163). New York: Basic.

Davies, Nicholas B. (1992). *Dunnock behaviour and social evaluation.* Oxford: Oxford University Press.

Davis, Allison. (1960). *Psychology of the child in the middle class.* Pittsburgh, PA: University of Pittsburgh Press.

——(1983). *Leadership, love, and aggression.* San Diego, CA: Harcourt, Brace Jovanovich.

Davis, Allison & J. Dollard. (1940). *Children of bondage: the personality of Negro youth in the urban south.* Washington, DC: American Council on Education.

Davis, Allison & R. J. Havighurst. (1947). *Father of the man: how your child gets his personality.* Boston, MA: Houghton Mifflin.

Davis, Allison, B. B. Gardner & M. R. Gardner. (1941). *Deep South: a social anthropological study of caste and class.* Chicago, IL: University of Chicago Press.

Davis, Dona L. & R. Whitten. (1987). The cross-cultural study of human sexuality. *Annual Review of Anthropology* 16: 69–98.

Davis, John. (1972). Gifts and the UK economy. *Man* 7: 408–429.

——(Ed.). (1982). *Religious organization and religious experience.* London: Academic.

——(1991). An interview with Ernest Gellner. *Current Anthropology* 32(1): 63–72.

——(1992). *Exchange.* Buckingham: Open University Press.

Davis, Susan S. & D. A. Davis. (1989). *Adolescence in a Moroccan town: making social sense.* Brunswick, NJ: Rutgers University Press.

Davis, Wade. (1995). Ethnobotany: an old practice, a new discipline. In Richard Schultes & Siri von Reis (Eds.), *Ethnobotany* (pp. 40–51). Portland, OR: Dioscorides.

Davis-Floyd, Robbie E. (1992). *Birth as an American rite of passage.* Berkeley: University of California Press.

——(1997). Intuition as authoritative knowledge in midwifery and home birth. In Robbie Davis-Floyd & Carolyn Sargent (Eds.), *Childbirth and authoritative knowledge.* Berkeley: University of California Press.

Davis-Floyd, Robbie E. & Carolyn Sargent. (1997). *Childbirth and authoritative knowledge: cross-cultural perspectives.* Berkeley: University of California Press.

Davison, Jean. (1989). *Voices from Mutira: lives of rural Gikuyu women.* Boulder, CO: Lynne Rienner.

Dawkins, Richard. (1979). Twelve misunderstandings of kin selection. *Zeitschrift für Tierpsychologie* 51: 184–200.

———(1986). *The blind watchmaker: why the evidence of evolution reveals a universe without design.* New York: Norton.

d'Azevedo, Warren. (1973). Mask makers and myth in western Liberia. In Anthony Forge (Ed.), *Primitive art and society* (pp. 126–150). London: Oxford University Press.

Deacon, Terrence W. (1990a). Fallacies of progression in theories of brain size evolution. *International Journal of Primatology* 11: 193–236.

———(1990b). Rethinking mammalian brain evolution. *American Zoologist* 30: 629–705.

———(1992). The human brain. In Steve Jones, Robert Martin & David Pilbeam (Eds.), *Cambridge encyclopedia of human evolution* (pp. 115–123). Cambridge: Cambridge University Press.

———(1997). *The symbolic species: the co-evolution of language and the brain.* New York: Norton.

Deane, Phyllis. (1965). *The first industrial revolution.* Cambridge: Cambridge University Press [2nd edn. 1979].

Degler, Carl N. (1990). Darwinians confront gender: or, there is more to it than history. In Deborah L. Rhode (Ed.), *Theoretical perspectives on sexual difference* (pp. 33–46). New Haven, CT: Yale University Press.

De Grazia, Sebastian. (1962). *Of time, work, and leisure.* New York: Twentieth Century Fund.

Deikman, Arthur. (1982). *The observing self: mysticism and psychotherapy.* Boston, MA: Beacon.

Delaney, Janice, Emily Toth & Mary Jane Lupton. (1993). *The curse: a cultural history of menstruation* [2nd edn.]. Urbana: University of Illinois Press.

Deleuze, Gilles. (1987). *A thousand plateaus: capitalism and schizophrenia* [Mille plateaux, Paris, 1980]. Minneapolis: University of Minnesota Press.

Deleuze, Gilles & Felix Guattari. (1977). *Anti-Oedipus: capitalism and schi-*zophrenia [Capitalisme et schizophrénie: l'anti-Oedipe, Paris, 1972]. New York: Viking.

DeMaris, Alfred. (1992). *Logit modeling: practical applications.* Newbury Park, CA: Sage.

DeMarrais, Elizabeth, Luis Jaime Castillo & Timothy Earle. (1996). Ideology, materialization and power strategies. *Current Anthropology* 37(1): 15–31.

Demos, John. (1982). *Entertaining Satan: witchcraft and the culture of early New England.* Oxford: Oxford Univesity Press.

Denich, Bette. (1994). Dismembering Yugoslavia: nationalist ideologies and the symbolic revival of genocide. *American Ethnologist* 21: 367–390.

Dening, Greg. (1988). *History's anthropology: the death of William Gooch.* Lanham, MD: University Press of America.

Densmore, Francis. (1918). *Teton Sioux music.* Washington, DC: Smithsonian.

Dentan, Robert K. (1968). *The Semai: a nonviolent people of Malaya.* New York: Holt.

Denzin, Norman K. & Yvonna S. Lincoln. (Eds.). (1994). *Handbook of qualitative research.* Newbury Park, CA: Sage.

Derman, William & Michael Levin. (1977). Peasants, propaganda, economics, and exploitation: a response to Dalton. *American Anthropologist* 79: 119–125.

Derman, William & Scott Whiteford. (Eds.). (1985). *Social impact analysis and development planning in the Third World.* Boulder, CO: Westview.

Derrida, Jacques. (1976). *Of grammatology* [De la grammatologie, Paris, 1967]. Baltimore: Johns Hopkins University Press.

Desjarlais, Robert. (1992). *Body and emotion: the aesthetics of illness and healing in the Nepal Himalayas.* Philadelphia: University of Pennsylvania Press.

De Soto, Hermine G. (Ed.). (1992). *Culture and contradiction: dialectics of wealth, power, and symbol.* San Francisco, CA: Mellen Research University Press.

Despres, Leo A. (Ed.). (1975). *Ethnicity and resource competition in plural societies.* The Hague: Mouton.

Detienne, Marcel & Jean-Pierre Vernant. (1978). *Cunning intelligence in Greek culture and society.* Atlantic Highlands, NJ: Humanities.

Devereaux, Leslie & Roger Hillman. (Eds.). (1995). *Fields of vision: essays in film studies, visual anthropology and photography.* Berkeley: University of California Press.

Devereux, George. (1955). Charismatic leadership and crisis. *Psychoanalysis and the social sciences* 4: 145–157.

———(1963). Shamans as neurotics. *American Anthropologist* 65: 1088–1093.

———(1978). *Ethnopsychoanalysis: psychoanalysis and anthropology as complementary frames of reference.* Berkeley: University of California Press.

Devine, John. (1995). Can metal detectors replace the panoptican? *Cultural Anthropology* 10(2): 171–195.

DeVoe, Pamela A. (Ed.). (1992). *Selected papers on refugee issues, 1992.* Washington, DC: American Anthropological Association.

Devor, Eric Jeffrey. (Ed.). (1992). *Molecular applications in biological anthropology.* Cambridge: Cambridge University Press.

De Vos, George. (1973). *Socialization for achievement: essays on the cultural psychology of the Japanese.* Berkeley: University of California Press.

———(1975). The dangers of pure theory in anthropology. *Ethos* 3: 77–91.

———(1992). *Social cohesion and alienation: minorities in the United States and Japan.* Boulder, CO: Westview.

De Vos, George & Lola Romanucci-Ross. (Eds.). (1975). *Ethnic identity: cultural continuities and change.* Palo Alto, CA: Mayfield.

De Vos, George & Marcelo M. Suárez-Orozco. (1990). *Status inequality: the self in culture.* Newbury Park, CA: Sage.

de Waal, Alexander. (1988). Refugees and the creation of famine: the case of Dar Masalit, Sudan. *Journal of Refugee Studies* 1(2): 127–140.

———(1989). *Famine that kills: Darfur, Sudan 1984–1985.* Oxford: Clarendon.

———(1990). Conceptions of Famine. In Malcolm Chapman & Helen Macbeth (Eds.), *Food for humanity* (pp. 18–25). Oxford: Centre for the Sciences of Food & Nutrition, Oxford Polytechnic.

De Waal Malefijt, Annemarie. (1963). *The Javanese of Surinam: segment of a plural society.* Assen: Van Gorcum.

DeWalt, Kathleen. (1983). *Nutritional strategies and agricultural change in a Mexican community.* Ann Arbor: University of Michigan Research Press.

Dewdney, Selwyn. (1975). *The sacred scrolls of the Southern Ojibway.* Toronto: University of Toronto Press.

Dewey, Alice. (1962). *Peasant marketing in Java.* Glencoe, IL: Free Press.

Diamond, Alan. (Ed.). (1991). *The Victorian achievement of Sir Henry Maine: a centennial reappraisal.* Cambridge: Cambridge University Press.

Diamond, Stanley. (Ed.). (1986). Special issue on poetry and anthropology. *Dialectical Anthropology* 11(2–4).

Dickemann, Mildred. (1979). Female infanticide, reproductive strategies, and social stratification: a preliminary model. In N. A. Chagnon & W. Irons (Eds.), *Evolutionary biology and human social behavior* (pp. 321–67). Littleton, MA: Duxbury.

di Leonardo, Micaela. (1984). *The varieties of ethnic experience: kinship, class, and gender among California Italian-Americans.* Ithaca, NY: Cornell University Press.

———(1991a). Gender, culture, and political economy: feminist anthropology in historical perspective. In Micaela di Leonardo (Ed.), *Gender at the crossroads of knowledge* (pp. 1–48). Berkeley: University of California Press.

———(Ed.). (1991b). *Gender at the crossroads of knowledge: feminist anthropology in the postmodern era.* Berkeley: University of California Press.

Dilley, Roy. (Ed.). (1992). *Contesting markets: analysis of ideology, discourse and practice.* Edinburgh: Edinburgh University Press.

Dilthey, Wilhelm. (1961). *Pattern and meaning in history: thoughts on history and society.* New York: Harper.

Dioszegi, Vilmos & M. Hoppal. (Eds.). (1978). *Shamanism in Siberia.* Budapest: Academiai Kiado.

Diringer, David. (1962). *Writing.* New York: Praeger.

Dirks, Nicholas. (1987). *The hollow crown: ethnohistory of an Indian kingdom.* Cambridge: Cambridge University Press.

———(1994). Ritual and resistance: subversion as social fact. In Nicholas Dirks, Geoff Eley & Sherry Ortner (Eds.), *Culture/power/history* (pp. 483–503). Princeton, NJ: Princeton University Press.

Dirlik, Arif. (1994). The postcolonial aura: Third World criticism in the age of global capitalism. *Critical inquiry* 20: 328–356.

Divale, William. (1984). *Matrilocal residence in pre-literate society.* Ann Arbor: University of Michigan Research Press.

Divale, William & Marvin Harris. (1976). Population, warfare, and the male supremacist complex. *American Anthropologist* 78: 521–538.

Dixon, Robert M. W. (1971). A method of semantic description. In Danny Steinberg & Leon Jakobovits (Eds.), *Semantics* (pp. 436–471). Cambridge: Cambridge University Press.

Dobb, Maurice H. (1946). *Studies in the development of capitalism.* London: Routledge.

Dobkin de Rios, Marlene. (1976). *The wilderness of mind: sacred plants in cross-cultural perspective.* Beverly Hills, CA: Sage.

Dobson, Andrew. (Ed.). (1991). *The green reader.* London: Deutsch.

Dominguez, Virginia. (1989). *People as subject, people as object: selfhood and peoplehood in contemporary Israel.* Madison: University of Wisconsin Press.

———(1994). A taste for "the Other": intellectual complicity in racializing practices. *Current Anthropology* 35(4): 333–348.

Donham, Donald. (1990). *History, power, ideology: central issues in Marxism and anthropology.* Cambridge: Cambridge University Press.

Donnelly, Jack. (1989). *Universal human rights in theory and practice.* Ithaca, NY: Cornell University Press.

Dore, Ronald. (Ed.). (1967). *Aspects of social change in modern Japan.* Princeton, NJ: Princeton University Press.

Dorjahn, Vernon R. (1989). Where do the old folks live? The residence of the elderly among the Temne of Sierra Leone. *Journal of Cross-Cultural Gerontology* 4: 257–278.

Dorson, Richard M. (1971). Fakelore. In R. M. Dorson (Ed.), *American folklore and the historian* (pp. 3–14). Chicago, IL: University of Chicago Press.

———(Ed.). (1972). *Folklore and folklife.* Chicago, IL: University of Chicago Press.

Dorst, John. (1989). *The written suburb: an American site, an ethnographic dilemma.* Philadelphia: University of Pennsylvania Press.

Doughty, Paul. (1988). Crossroads for anthropology: human rights in Latin America. In Theodore Downing & Gilbert Kushner (Eds.), *Human rights and anthropology* (pp. 43–71). Cambridge, MA: Cultural Survival.

Douglas, Bronwen. (1979). Rank, power, authority: a reassessment of traditional leadership in South Pacific societies. *Journal of Pacific History* 14: 2–27.

Douglas, Mary. (1963). *The Lele of the Kasai.* London: Oxford University Press.

———(1966). *Purity and danger: an analysis of concepts of pollution and taboo.* London: Routledge.

———(1968). Pollution. In David Sills (Ed.), *International encyclopedia of the social sciences* (12: 336–342). New York: Macmillan.

———(1970a). *Natural symbols.* London: Barrie & Rockcliff.

———(Ed.). (1970b). *Witchcraft: confessions and accusations.* London: Tavistock.

———(1970c). The healing rite. *Man* (n.s.) 5: 302–308.

———(1971). Deciphering a meal. *Daedalus* 102: 61–82.

———(1975). *Implicit meanings: essays in anthropology.* London: Routledge.

———(1980). *Evans-Pritchard.* New York: Viking.

———(1982). The effects of modernization on religious change. *Daedalus* 111: 1–19.

———(Ed.). (1984). *Food in the social order: studies of food and festivities in three American communities.* New York: Sage.

——— (1986). *How institutions think.* Syracuse, NY: Syracuse University Press.

——— (1990a). The self as risk taker: a cultural theory of contagion in relation to AIDS. *Sociological Review* 38: 445–464.

——— (1990b). Pangolin revisited: a new approach to animal symbolism. In Roy Willis (Ed.), *Signifying animals* (pp. 25–36). London: Unwin Hyman.

——— (1993a). Emotion and culture in theories of justice. *Economy and Society* 22: 501–516.

——— (1993b). "Hunting the pangolin," Comment (with Luc De Heusch & Ioan M. Lewis). *Man* 28(1): 159–166.

——— (1993). Emotion and culture in theories of culture. *Economy and Society* 22: 501–516.

——— (1996). *Thought styles: critical essays on good taste.* London: Sage.

Douglas, Mary & David Hull. (Eds.). (1992). *How classification works: Nelson Goodman among the social sciences.* Edinburgh: Edinburgh University Press.

Douglas, Mary & Baron Isherwood. (1979). *The world of goods: towards an anthropology of consumption.* New York: Basic.

Douglas, Mary & Phyllis M. Kaberry. (Eds.). (1969). *Man in Africa.* London: Tavistock.

Douglas, Mary & Aaron Wildavsky. (1982). *Risk and culture: an essay on the selection of technological and environmental dangers.* Berkeley: University of California Press.

Dove, Michael R. (1982). The myth of the "communal" longhouse in rural development. In Colin MacAndrews & Lucas S. Chin (Eds.), *Too rapid rural development* (pp. 14–78). Athens: Ohio University Press.

——— (1984). The Chayanov slope in a swidden society: household demography and extensive agriculture in western Kalimantan. In E. Paul Durrenberger (Ed.), *Chayanov, peasants, and economic anthropology* (pp. 97–132). New York: Academic.

——— (1985). *Swidden agriculture in Indonesia: the subsistence strategies of the Kalimantan Kantu'.* Berlin: Mouton.

——— (1990). Review article: socio-political aspects of home gardens in Java. *Journal of Southeast Asian Studies* 21: 155–163.

——— (1993a). Smallholder rubber and swidden agriculture in Borneo: a sustainable adaptation to the ecology and economy of the tropical forest. *Economic Botany* 47(2): 136–147.

——— (1993b). Uncertainty, humility and adaptation to the tropical forest: the agricultural augury of the Kantu'. *Ethnology* 32: 145–167.

Dove, Michael R. & Mahmudel Huq Khan. (1995). Competing constructions of calamity: the April 1991 Bangladesh cyclone. *Population and Environment* 16(5): 445–472.

Dow, Malcolm. (1984). A biparametric approach to network autocorrelation. *Sociological Methods and Research* 13: 201–218.

——— (1985). Agricultural intensification and craft specialization: a non-recursive model. *Ethnology* 24: 137–152.

——— (1989). Categorical analysis of cross-cultural survey data: effects of clustering on chi-square. *Journal of Quantitative Anthropology* 1: 335–352.

Dow, Malcolm & Frans de Waal. (1989). Assignment methods for the analysis of network subgroup interactions. *Social Networks* 11: 237–255.

Downie, R. Angus. (1970). *Frazer and "The golden bough".* London: Gollancz.

Downing, Theodore & Gilbert Kushner. (1988). *Human rights and anthropology.* Cambridge, MA: Cultural Survival.

Downs, Richard E. & S. P. Reyna. (Eds.). (1988). *Land and society in contemporary Africa.* Hanover, NH: University Press of New England.

Downs, Richard E., Donna Kerner & Stephen Reyna. (Eds.). (1991). *The political economy of African famine.* Philadelphia, PA: Gordon & Breach.

Drake, St. Clair. (1955). The colour problem in Britain: a study in social definitions. *The Sociological Review* (n.s.) 3: 197–217.

——— (1960). Traditional authority and social action in former British West Africa. *Human Organization* 19: 150–158.

——— (1974). In the mirror of Black

scholarship: W. Allison Davis and *Deep South*. In Institute of the Black World (Eds.), *Education and black struggle* (pp. 42–54). Cambridge, MA: Harvard Educational Review.

———(1980). Anthropology and the Black experience. *The Black Scholar* 11(7): 2–31.

———(1987, 1990). *Black folk here and there: an essay in history and anthropology*, 2 vols. Los Angeles: Center for Afro-American Studies, University of California.

Drake, St. Clair & H. Cayton. (1945). *Black metropolis: a study of Negro life in a northern city*. New York: Harcourt, Brace.

Draper, Patricia & Harry Harpending. (1982). Father absence and reproductive strategy: an evolutionary perspective. *Journal of Anthropological Research* 38: 255–273.

Drennan, Robert. (1991). Pre-Hispanic chiefdom trajectories in Mesoamerica, Central America, and northern South America. In T. Earle (Ed.), *Chiefdoms* (pp. 263–287). Cambridge: Cambridge University Press.

Drennan, Robert & Carlos Uribe. (Eds.). (1987). *Chiefdoms in the Americas*. Lanham, MD: University Press of America.

Dresch, Paul. (1986). The significance of the course events take in segmentary systems. *American Ethnologist* 13: 309–324.

———(1987). Segmentation: its roots in Arabia and its flowering elsewhere. *Cultural Anthropology* 3(1): 50–67.

Dreyfus, Hubert L. & Paul Rabinow. (1982). *Michel Foucault: beyond structuralism and hermeneutics*. Chicago, IL: University of Chicago Press.

Drèze, Jean & Amartya Sen. (1989). *Hunger and public action*. Oxford: Clarendon.

Driver, Godfrey R. (1948). *Semitic writing: from pictograph to alphabet*. London: Oxford University Press.

Driver, Harold. (1953). Statistics in anthropology. *American Anthropologist* 55: 42–59.

———(1961). *Indians of North America*. Chicago, IL: University of Chicago Press.

Driver, Harold & A. L. Kroeber. (1932). *Quantitative expression of cultural*

relationships. Berkeley: University of California publications in American archaeology and ethnology, 31(4).

Drucker, Philip & Robert F. Heizer. (1967). *To make my name good: a reexamination of the southern Kwakiutl potlatch*. Berkeley: University of California Press.

Drury, Nevill. (1982). *The shaman and the magician: journeys between the worlds*. London: Routledge.

Du Bois, Cora. (Ed.). (1960). *Lowie's selected papers in Anthropology*. Berkeley: University of California Press.

DuBois, W. E. B. (1899). *The Philadelphia Negro: a social study*. Boston, MA: Ginn.

Dumézil, Georges. (1970a). *Archaic Roman religion* [Religion romaine archaique, 1966]. Chicago, IL: University of Chicago Press.

———(1970b). *The destiny of the warrior* [Heur et malheur du guerrier, 1969]. Chicago, IL: University of Chicago Press.

———(1973). *From myth to fiction: the saga of Hadingus* [Du mythe au roman, 1970]. Chicago, IL: University of Chicago Press.

———(1981). *Mythe et épopée* [3rd edn.]. Paris: Gallimard.

———(1986). *The plight of a sorcerer* [Entre les dieux et les demons: un sorcier (Kavya Usanas, Kavi Usan)]. Berkeley: University of California Press.

———(1988). *Mitra-Varuna: an essay on two Indo-European representations of sovereignty* [Mitra-Varuna: essai sur deux représentations indo-européennes de la souveraineté, 1940]. New York: Zone.

Dumond, Don E. (1965). Population growth and cultural change. *Southwestern Journal of Anthropology* 21: 302–324.

———(1975). The limitation of human population. *Science* 187: 713–721.

Dumont, Louis. (1957). *Hierarchy and marriage alliance in South Indian kinship*. London: Royal Anthropological Institute of Great Britain and Ireland.

———(1970). *Homo hierarchicus: an essay on the caste system* [Homo hierarchicus, Paris, 1966]. Chicago, IL: University of Chicago Press.

———(1971a). The marriage alliance. In

Jack Goody (Ed.), *Kinship* (pp. 183–198). Harmondsworth: Penguin.

——— (1971b). *Introduction à deux théories d'anthropologie sociale.* Paris: Mouton.

——— (1977). *From Mandeville to Marx: the genesis and triumph of economic ideology.* Chicago, IL: University of Chicago Press.

——— (1983). *Affinity as a value: marriage alliance in South India.* Chicago, IL: University of Chicago Press.

——— (1986a). Marcel Mauss: a science in process of becoming. In L. Dumont, *Essays on individualism* [Essais sur l'individualisme, Paris, 1972] (pp. 183–201). Chicago, IL: University of Chicago Press.

——— (1986b). *Essays on individualism: modern ideology in anthropological perspective* [Essais sur l'individualisme, Paris, 1983]. Chicago, IL: University of Chicago Press.

Dunaway, Wilma A. (1996). *The first American frontier: transition to capitalism in southern Appalachia, 1700–1860.* Chapel Hill: University of North Carolina Press.

Duncan, Dayton. (1993). *Miles from nowhere: tales from America's contemporary frontier.* New York: Viking.

Duncan, James. (Ed.). (1981). *Housing and identity: cross-cultural perspectives.* London: Croom Helm.

Duncan, James & David Ley. (Eds.). (1993). *Place/culture/representation.* London: Routledge.

Dundes, Alan. (1966a). The American concept of folklore. *Journal of the Folklore Institute* 3: 226–249.

——— (1966b). *The complete bibliography of Robert H. Lowie.* Berkeley: Lowie Museum of Anthropology.

——— (1991). The ritual murder or blood libel legend: a study of anti-Semitic victimization through projective inversion. In Alan Dundes (Ed.), *The blood libel legend* (pp. 236–278). Madison: University of Wisconsin Press.

Dunnell, Robert C. (1978). Archaeological potential of anthropological and scientific models of function. In Robert Dunnell & Edwin Hall, Jr. (Eds.), *Archaeological essays in honor of Irving B. Rouse* (pp. 41–73). The Hague: Mouton.

Dunteman, George H. (1989). *Principal components analysis.* Newbury Park, CA: Sage.

Duranti, Alessandro. (1994). *From grammar to politics: linguistic anthropology in a Western Samoan village.* Berkeley: University of California Press.

Durham, Edith. (1923). Head-hunting in the Balkans. *Man* 11–12: 19–21.

Durkheim, Émile. (1915). *The elementary forms of the religious life* [Les formes élémentaires de la vie religieuse: le système totémique en Australie, Paris, 1912]. New York: Macmillan.

——— (1933). *The division of labor in society* [De la division du travail social, étude sur l'organisation des sociétés supérieures, Paris, 1893]. New York: Free Press.

——— (1938). *The rules of sociological method* [Règles de la méthode sociologique, Paris, 1901]. Glencoe, IL: Free Press.

——— (1951). *Suicide, a study in sociology* [Suicide, étude de sociologie, Paris, 1897]. Glencoe, IL: Free Press.

——— (1963). *Incest: the nature and origin of the taboo.* New York: Lyle Stuart [La Prohibition de l'inceste et ses origines, *l'Année Sociologique*, 1897]

Durkheim, Émile & Marcel Mauss. (1963). *Primitive classification* [De quelques formes primitives de classification, Paris, 1904]. Chicago, IL: University of Chicago Press.

Durrenberger, Paul E. (Ed.). (1984). *Chayanov, peasants, and economic anthropology.* New York: Academic.

Durrenberger, Paul E. & Gísli Pálsson. (1986). Finding fish: the tactics of Icelandic skippers. *American Ethnologist* 13: 213–229.

Duster, Troy. (1990). *Backdoor to eugenics.* London: Routledge.

Dwyer, Daisy & Judith Bruce. (Eds.). (1988). *A home divided: women and income in the Third World.* Stanford, CA: Stanford University Press.

Dwyer, Kevin. (1982). *Moroccan dialogues: anthropology in question.* Baltimore, MD: Johns Hopkins University Press.

——— (1991). *Arab voices: the human rights debate in the Middle East.* Berkeley: University of California Press.

Dyson-Hudson, Rada & Neville Dyson-Hudson. (1981). Nomadic pastoralism. *Annual Review of Anthropology* 9: 15–61.

Eade, John & Michael J. Sallnow. (Eds.). (1991). *Contesting the sacred: the anthropology of Christian pilgrimage.* London: Routledge.

Eades, Jeremy. (Ed.). (1987). *Migrants, workers, and the social order.* London: Tavistock.

Eames, Edwin & Judith Goode. (1977). *Anthropology of the city: an introduction to urban anthropology.* Englewood Cliffs, NJ: Prentice-Hall.

Earle, Timothy. (1977). Exchange systems in archaeological perspective. In T. Earle & J. Ericson (Eds.), *Exchange systems in prehistory* (pp. 3–12). New York: Academic.

——— (1978). *Economic and social organization of a complex chiefdom: the Halelea district, Kauai, Hawaii.* Ann Arbor: Museum of Anthropology, University of Michigan.

——— (1987). Chiefdoms in archaeological and ethnohistorical perspective. *Annual Review of Anthropology* 16: 279–308.

——— (1989). Style and iconography as legitimation in complex chiefdoms. In Margaret Conkey & Christine Hastorf (Eds.), *The uses of style in archaeology* (pp. 73–81). Cambridge: Cambridge University Press.

——— (Ed.). (1991). *Chiefdoms: power, economy, and ideology.* Cambridge: Cambridge University Press.

——— (1994). Political domination and social evolution. In Tim Ingold (Ed.), *Companion encyclopedia of anthropology* (pp. 940–961). London: Routledge.

Earle, Timothy & Terence D'Altroy. (1989). Political economy. In C. C. Lamberg-Karlovsky (Ed.), *Archaeological thought in America* (pp. 183–204). Cambridge: Cambridge University Press.

Earle, Timothy & J. Ericson. (Eds.). (1977). *Exchange systems in prehistory.* New York: Academic.

Eastman, Carol. (1975). *Aspects of language and culture.* San Francisco, CA: Chandler & Sharp.

Eaton, Boyd, Marjorie Shostak & Melvin Konner. (1988). *The Paleolithic prescription: a program of diet and exercise and a design for living.* New York: Harper & Row.

Eco, Umberto. (1976). *A theory of semiotics* [Trattato di semiotica generale, Milan, 1975]. Bloomington: Indiana University Press.

——— (1990). *The limits of interpretation* [I limiti dell'interpretazione, Milan, 1990]. Bloomington: Indiana University Press.

Eder, James. (1987). *On the road to tribal extinction: depopulation, deculturation, and adaptive well-being among the Batak of the Philippines.* Berkeley: University of California Press.

Edgerton, Robert. (1992). *Sick societies: the myth of primitive harmony.* New York: Free Press.

Edwards, Carolyn P. (1987). Culture and the construction of moral values: a comparative ethnography of moral encounters in two cultural settings. In J. Kagan & S. Lamb (Eds.), *The emergence of morality in young children* (pp. 123–149). Chicago, IL: University of Chicago Press.

Edwards, David Busby. (1986). Marginality and migration: cultural dimensions of the Afghan refugee problem. *International Migration Review* 20(2): 313–325.

Edwards, Elizabeth. (Ed.). (1992). *Anthropology and photography, 1860–1920.* New Haven, CT: Yale University Press.

Edwards, Jeannette, Sarah Franklin, Eric Hirsch, Frances Price & Marilyn Strathern. (1993). *Technologies of procreation: kinship in the age of assisted conception.* Manchester: Manchester University Press.

Efron, David. (1941). *Gesture and environment.* New York: King's Crown Press. [republished as *Gesture, race and culture,* Mouton, 1972]

Eggan, Fred. (Ed.). (1937). *The social anthropology of North American tribes.* Chicago, IL: University of Chicago Press.

——— (1968). One hundred years of ethnology and social anthropology. In J. O. Brew (Ed.), *One hundred years of anthropology* (pp. 119–149). Cambridge, MA: Harvard University Press.

Eibl-Eibesfeldt, Irenaus. (1989). *Hu-*

man ethology. New York: Aldine de Gruyter.

Eisenstadt, Shmuel N. (1956). *From generation to generation: age groups and social structure.* Glencoe, IL: Free Press.

———(Ed.). (1968). *Max Weber on charisma and institution building.* Chicago, IL: University of Chicago Press.

———(1973). *Tradition, change, and modernity.* New York: Wiley.

———(1990). Functional analysis in anthropology and sociology: an interpretative essay. *Annual Review of Anthropology* 19: 243–260.

Ekman, Paul. (1984). Expression and the nature of emotion. In Klaus Scherer & Paul Ekman (Eds.), *Approaches to emotion* (pp. 319–340). Hillsdale, NJ: Erlbaum.

Ekman, Paul & Wallace V. Friesen. (1981). The repertoire of nonverbal behavior: categories, origins, usage and coding. In Adam Kendon (Ed.), *Nonverbal communication* (pp. 57–105). The Hague: Mouton.

El Dareer, Asma. (1982). *Woman, why do you weep? Circumcision and its consequences.* London: Zed.

Eliade, Mircea. (1959). *The sacred and the profane: the nature of religion* [Le sacré et le profane, Paris, 1955]. New York: Harcourt, Brace.

———(1964). *Shamanism: archaic techniques of ecstasy* [Chamanisme et les techniques archaiques de l'extase, Paris, 1951]. Princeton, NJ: Princeton University Press.

———(1978). *A history of religious ideas* (3 vols.) [Histoire des croyances et des idées religieuses, Paris, 1976]. Chicago, IL: University of Chicago Press.

Elias, Norbert. (1978). *The civilizing process* [Über den Prozess der Zivilisation, Basel, 1939]. New York: Urizen.

Ellegård, Alvar. (1959). Statistical measurement of linguistic relationship. *Language* 35: 38–55.

Ellen, Roy F. (1982). *Environment, subsistence and system: the ecology of small-scale social formations.* Cambridge: Cambridge University Press.

———(Ed.). (1984). *Ethnographic research: a guide to general conduct.* London: Academic.

Ellen, Roy F. & David Reason. (Eds.). (1979). *Classifications in their social context.* London: Academic.

Ellingson, Ter. (1992). Transcription. In Ter Ellingson (Ed.), *Ethnomusicology* (pp. 110–152). New York: Norton.

Ellis, Alexander J. (1885). On the musical scales of various nations. *Journal of the Royal Society of Arts* 33: 485–527.

Else, Anne. (1991). *A question of adoption: closed stranger adoption in New Zealand 1944–1974.* Wellington: Bridget Williams.

Ember, Carol. (1978). Myths about hunter–gatherers. *Ethnology* 14: 439–448.

———(1983). The relative decline in women's contribution to agriculture with intensification. *American Anthropologist* 85: 285–304.

Ember, Carol & David Levinson. (1991). Substantive contributions of worldwide cross-cultural studies using secondary data. *Behavior Science Research* 25(1–4): 79–140.

Ember, Melvin & Carol Ember. (1971). The conditions favoring matrilocal versus patrilocal residence. *American Anthropologist* 73: 571–594.

———(1994). Cross-cultural studies of war and peace: recent achievements and future possibilities. In S. P. Reyna and R. E. Downs (Eds.), *Studying war* (pp. 185–208). Langhorne, PA: Gordon & Breach.

Embleton, Sheila M. (1986). *Statistics in historical linguistics.* Bochum: Brockmeyer.

Emboden, William. (1972a). *Narcotic plants.* New York: Macmillan.

———(1972b). Ritual use of *Cannabis sativa* L.: a historical-ethnographic survey. In Peter Furst (Ed.), *Flesh of the gods* (pp. 214–236). New York: Praeger.

Embree, John & Hans-Dieter Evers. (Eds.). (1969). *Loosely structured social systems: Thailand in comparative perspective.* New Haven, CT: Yale University Southeast Asia Studies no. 17.

Embree, John & W. L. Thomas. (1950). *Ethnic groups of northern Southeast Asia.* New Haven, CT: Yale University Southeast Asia Studies.

Endelman, Robert. (1989). *Love and sex*

in twelve cultures. New York: Psyche Press.

Endicott, Kirk. (1970). *An analysis of Malay magic*. Oxford: Clarendon.

————(1979). *Batek Negrito religion: the world-view and rituals of a hunting and gathering people of Peninsular Malaysia.* Oxford: Clarendon.

Eng, Robert Y. & Thomas C. Smith. (1976). Peasant families and population control in 18th century Japan. *Journal of Interdisciplinary History* 11: 417–445.

Engelbrecht, William. (1987). Factors maintaining low population density among the prehistoric New York Iroquois. *American Antiquity* 52: 13–27.

Engels, Friedrich. (1902). *The origin of the family, private property, and the state* [Ursprung der Familie, des Privateigentums und des Staats, Zurich, 1884]. Chicago, IL: Kerr.

England, Paula. (Ed.). (1993). *Theory on gender/feminism on theory.* New York: A. de Gruyter.

Epstein, A. L. (1958). *Politics in an urban African community.* Manchester: Manchester University Press.

————(1968). Sanctions. In David Gillis (Ed.), *International encyclopedia of the social sciences* 14: 1–5. New York: Macmillan and Free Press.

————(Ed.). (1974). *Contention and dispute: aspects of law and social control in Melanesia.* Canberra: Australian National University Press.

Erdsman, Carl. (Ed.). (1967). *Studies in shamanism.* Stockholm: Almqvist & Wiksell.

Eribon, Didier. (1991). *Michel Foucault* [Michel Foucault, Paris, 1989]. Cambridge, MA: Harvard University Press.

Ericsson, K. Λ. & H. A. Simon. (1980). Verbal reports as data. *Psychological Review* 87: 215–251.

Erikson, Erik. (1963). *Childhood and society* [2nd edn.]. New York: Norton.

————(1970). On the nature of psychohistorical evidence: in search of Gandhi. In Dankwart Rustow (Ed.), *Philosophers and kings* (pp. 33–68). New York: Braziller.

Erlmann, Veit. (1995). *Nightsong: performance, power, and practice in South Africa.*

Chicago, IL: University of Chicago Press.

Errington, Frederick & Deborah Gewertz. (1987). *Cultural alternatives and a feminist anthropology: an analysis of culturally constructed gender interests in Papua New Guinea.* Cambridge: Cambridge University Press.

Errington, J. Joseph. (1988). *Structure and style in Javanese: a semiotic view of linguistic etiquette.* Philadelphia: University of Pennsylvania Press.

Errington, Shelly & Jabe M. Atkinson. (Eds.). (1990). *Power and difference: gender in island Southeast Asia.* Stanford, CA: Stanford University Press.

Ervin, Susan M. (1964). Language and thought. In Sol Tax (Ed.), *Horizons of anthropology* (pp. 81–91). Chicago, IL: Aldine.

Escobar, Arturo. (1991). Anthropology and the development encounter: the making and marketing of development anthropology. *American Ethnologist* 18(4): 658–682.

————(1994). *Encountering development: the making and unmaking of the Third World.* Princeton, NJ: Princeton University Press.

Essock-Vitale, Susan M. & Michael T. McGuire. (1985). Women's lives viewed from an evolutionary perspective. *Ethology and Sociobiology* 6: 155–173.

Esteva, Gustavo. (1992). Development. In Wolfgang Sachs (Ed.), *The development dictionary* (pp. 6–26). London: Zed.

Etherington, Norman. (1984). *Theories of imperialism: war, conquest, and capital.* London: Croom Helm.

Etienne, Mona & Eleanor Leacock. (Eds.). (1980). *Women and colonization: anthropological perspectives.* New York: Praeger.

Evans, Gillian R. (1982). *Augustine on evil.* Cambridge: Cambridge University Press.

Evans, Peter. (1979). *Dependent development: the alliance of multinational, state, and local capital in Brazil.* Princeton, NJ: Princeton University Press.

Evans-Pritchard, E. E. (1928). The dance. *Africa* 1: 446–452.

————(1933). Zande blood-brotherhood.

Africa 3: 369–401 [reprinted in *Social anthropology and other essays* (pp. 157–187), Free Press, New York, 1962].

——— (1937). *Witchcraft, oracles and magic among the Azande.* Oxford: Clarendon.

——— (1939). Nuer time-reckoning. *Africa* 12(2): 189–216.

——— (1940). *The Nuer.* Oxford: Clarendon.

——— (1949). *The Sanusi of Cyrenaica.* Oxford: Clarendon.

——— (1950). Kinship and local community among the Nuer. In A. R. Radcliffe-Brown & Daryll Forde (Eds.), *African systems of kinship and marriage.* London: Oxford University Press.

——— (1951). *Kinship and marriage among the Nuer.* Oxford: Clarendon.

——— (1956). *Nuer religion.* Oxford: Clarendon.

——— (1962). *Social anthropology and other essays.* New York: Free Press.

——— (1965). *Theories of primitive religion.* Oxford: Clarendon.

——— (1970). Sexual inversion among the Azande. *American Anthropologist* 72: 1428–1434.

——— (1974). *Man and woman among the Azande.* New York: Free Press.

——— (1981). *A history of anthropological thought* ed. by André Singer. London: Faber.

Ewers, John. (1961). Symposium on the concept of ethnohistory: comment. *Ethnohistory* 8: 262–270.

Fabbro, D. (1978). Peaceful societies: an introduction. *Journal of Peace Research* 15(1): 67–83.

Fabian, Johannes. (1983). *Time and the Other: how anthropology makes its object.* New York: Columbia University Press.

——— (1990). *Power and performance: ethnographic explorations through proverbial wisdom and theater in Shaba, Zaire.* Madison: University of Wisconsin Press.

Fabrega, Horacio. (1975). The need for an ethnomedical science. *Science* 189: 969–975.

Fackelmann, Kathy. (1993). Marijuana and the brain. *Science News* 143: 88–94.

Fairclough, Norman. (1989). *Language and power.* London: Longman.

Falk, Dean. (1990). Brain evolution in *Homo*: The "radiator" theory. *Behavioral and Brain Sciences* 13: 333–381.

Fallers, Lloyd A. (1963). Equality, modernity, and democracy in the new states. In Clifford Geertz (Ed.), *Old societies and new states* (pp. 158–219). New York: Free Press.

——— (1973). *Inequality: social stratification reconsidered.* Chicago, IL: University of Chicago Press.

Fanon, Frantz. (1963). *The wretched of the earth* [Damnes de la terre, Paris, 1961]. New York: Grove.

Farb, Peter & George Armelagos. (1980). *Consuming passions: the anthropology of eating.* Boston, MA: Houghton Mifflin.

Fardon, Richard. (1990). *Between God, the dead and the wild.* Washington, DC: Smithsonian.

Faris, James. (1968). *Cat Harbor: a Newfoundland fishing settlement.* St. John's: Memorial University of Newfoundland [rev. edn. 1972]

Farmer, Paul. (1988). Bad blood, spoiled milk: bodily fluids as moral barometers in rural Haiti. *American Ethnologist* 15(1): 62–83.

——— (1990). Sending sickness: sorcery, politics, and changing concepts of AIDS in rural Haiti. *Medical Anthropology Quarterly* 4(1): 6–27.

——— (1992). *AIDS and accusation: Haiti and the geography of blame.* Berkeley: University of California Press.

——— (1994). *The uses of Haiti.* Monroe, ME: Common Courage Press.

Farnell, Brenda. (Ed.). (1995a). *Human action signs in cultural context: the visible and the invisible in movement and dance.* Metuchen, NJ: Scarecrow Press.

——— (1995b). *Do you see what I mean? Plains Indian sign talk and the embodiment of action.* Austin: University of Texas Press.

Farriss, Nancy M. (1983). Remembering the future, anticipating the past: history, time, and cosmology among the Maya of Yucatan. *Comparative Studies in Society and History* 29(3): 566–593.

Faure, Bernard. (1992). Relics and flesh bodies: the creation of Ch'an pilgrimage sites. In Susan Naquin & Chun-fang Yu

(Eds.), *Pilgrims and sacred sites in China* (pp. 150–189). Berkeley: University of California Press.

Fausto-Sterling, Anne. (1993). The five sexes: why male and female are not enough. *The Sciences* 33(2): 20–25.

Favret-Saada, Jeanne. (1980). *Deadly words: witchcraft in the bocage* [Mots, la mort, les sorts, Paris, 1977]. Cambridge: Cambridge University Press.

——(1990). About participation. *Culture, Medicine, and Psychiatry* 14(2): 189–199.

Feaver, George. (1969). *From status to contract: a biography of Sir Henry Maine, 1822–1888.* London: Longman.

Feeley-Harnik, Gillian. (1981). *The Lord's table: Eucharist and Passover in early Christianity.* Philadelphia: University of Pennsylvania Press.

Feinman, Gary & Jill Neitzel. (1984). Too many types: an overview of sedentary prestate societies in the Americas. *Advances in Archaeological Method and Theory* 7: 39–102.

Feld, Steven. (1982). *Sound and sentiment: birds, weeping, poetics, and song in Kaluli expression.* Philadelphia: University of Pennsylvania Press.

Feldman, Allen. (1991). *Formations of violence: the narrative of the body and political terror in Northern Ireland.* Chicago, IL: University of Chicago Press.

Feldman, Douglas A. (Ed.). (1990). *Culture and AIDS.* New York: Praeger.

Felstiner, John. (1980). *Translating Neruda: the way to Macchu Picchu.* Stanford, CA: Stanford University Press.

Felstiner, William. (1974). Influences of social organization on dispute processing. *Law and Society Review* 9: 63–94.

Ferguson, Charles. (1959). Diglossia. *Word* 15: 325–340.

——(1991). Diglossia revisited. *Southwestern Journal of Linguistics* 10(1): 214–234.

Ferguson, James. (1990). *The anti-politics machine: "development," depoliticization and bureaucratic power in Lesotho.* Cambridge: Cambridge University Press.

Ferguson, R. Brian. (Ed.). (1984). *Warfare, culture, and environment.* Orlando, FL: Academic.

——(1988). *The anthropology of war: a bibliography.* New York: Harry Frank Guggenheim Foundation.

——(1995). *Yanomami warfare: a political history.* Santa Fe, NM: School of American Research Press.

Ferguson, R. Brian & Leslie Farragher. (1988). *The anthropology of war: a bibliography.* New York: Harry Frank Harry Guggenheim Foundation.

Ferguson, R. Brian & Neil L. Whitehead. (Eds.). (1992a). *War in the tribal zone: expanding states and indigenous warfare.* Santa Fe, NM: School of American Research Press.

——(1992b). The violent edge of empire. In R. Brian Ferguson & Neil Whitehead (Eds.), *War in the tribal zone* (pp. 1–30). Santa Fe, NM: School of American Research Press.

Fernandez, James W. (1977). *Fang architectonics.* Philadelphia, PA: ISHI.

——(1982). *Bwiti: an ethnography of religious imagination in Africa.* Princeton, NJ: Princeton University Press.

——(1984). Emergence and convergence in some African sacred places. *Geoscience and Man* 24: 31–42.

——(1985). Exploded worlds: text as a metaphor for ethnography (and vice versa). *Dialectical Anthropology* 10: 15–26.

——(1986). *Persuasions and performances: the play of tropes in culture.* Bloomington: Indiana University Press.

——(Ed.). (1991). *Beyond metaphor: the theory of tropes in anthropology.* Stanford, CA: Stanford University Press.

Fernández, Mauro. (1993). *Diglossia: a comprehensive bibliography 1960–1990.* Amsterdam and Philadelphia, PA: Benjamins.

Fernea, Robert A. (1970). *Shaykh and Effendi: changing patterns of authority among the El Shabana of southern Iraq.* Cambridge, MA: Harvard University Press.

Feuchtwang, Stephan. (1992). *The imperial metaphor: popular religion in China.* London: Routledge.

Feyerabend, Paul. (1975). *Against method: outline of an anarchistic theory of knowledge.* Atlantic Highlands, NJ: Humanities.

Fiedler, Deborah. (1997). Issues of birth in contemporary Japan. In Robbie Davis-Floyd & Carolyn Sargent (Eds.), *Childbirth and authoritative knowledge.* Berkeley: University of California Press.

Fieldhouse, David. (1981). *Colonialism 1870–1945: an introduction.* London: Weidenfeld & Nicolson.

Fienberg, Stephen. (1980). *The analysis of cross-classified categorical data.* Cambridge, MA: MIT Press.

Finlay, Barbara L. & Richard B. Darlington. (1995). Linked regularities in the development and evolution of mammalian brains. *Science* 268: 1578–1584.

Finn, Robert. (1996). Biological determination of sexuality heating up as a research field. *The Scientist* 10(1): 13, 16.

Finnegan, Ruth. (1977). *Oral poetry: its nature, significance, and social context.* Cambridge: Cambridge University Press.

———(1988). *Literacy and orality.* London: Oxford University Press.

Firth, John R. (1957). *Papers in linguistics 1934–1951.* London: Oxford University Press.

Firth, Raymond. (1929). *Primitive economics of the New Zealand Maori.* London: Routledge.

———(1936). *We the Tikopia: a sociological study of kinship in primitive Polynesia.* New York: American. [2nd edn. London: Allen & Unwin, 1957].

———(1940). *The work of the gods in Tikopia* (2 vols.). London: Percy Lund.

———(1946). *Malay fishermen: their peasant economy.* London: Kegan Paul [2nd rev. edn. 1966].

———(1951). Contemporary British social anthropology. *American Anthropologist* 53: 474–489.

———(1951). *Elements of social organization.* London: Watts.

———(1956a). Function. In W. L. Thomas (Ed.), *Current anthropology* (pp. 237–258). Chicago, IL: University of Chicago Press.

———(1956b). A. R. Radcliffe-Brown, 1881–1955. *Proceedings of the British Academy* 42: 287–302.

———(1956c). *Two studies of kinship in London.* London: Athlone.

———(Ed.). (1957). *Man and culture: an evaluation of the work of Bronislaw Malinowski.* London: Routledge.

———(1959). *Social change in Tikopia: re-study of a Polynesian community after a generation.* New York: Macmillan.

———(1964). *Essays on social organization and values.* London: Athlone.

———(1967). *Tikopia ritual and belief.* Boston, MA: Beacon.

———(1968). Social anthropology. In David Sills (Ed.), *International encyclopedia of the social sciences* (pp. 320–339). New York: Macmillan.

———(1970). *Rank and religion in Tikopia: a study in Polynesian paganism and conversion to Christianity.* London: Allen & Unwin.

———(1972). Anthropological background to work. In Clifton D. Bryant (Ed.), *The social dimensions of work* (pp. 8–16). Englewood Cliffs, NJ: Prentice-Hall.

Firth, Raymond & Brian Yamey. (Eds.). (1964). *Capital, saving and credit in peasant societies.* London: Allen & Unwin.

Firth, Raymond, Jane Hubert & Anthony Forge. (1970). *Families and their relatives: kinship in a middle-class sector of London – an anthropological study.* New York: Humanities Press.

Fischer, Helen. (1992). *The anatomy of love: the natural history of monogamy, adultery, and divorce.* New York: Norton.

Fischer, Michael M. J. (1977). Interpretive anthropology. *Reviews in Anthropology* 4(4): 391–404.

———(1980a). *Iran: from religious dispute to revolution.* Cambridge, MA: Harvard University Press.

———(1980b). Becoming Mulla: Walter Benjaminite reflections on Iranian clerics in a revolutionary age. *Iranian Studies* 13(1–4): 83–177.

———(1984). Towards Third World poetics: seeing through fiction and film in the Iranian Culture Area. *Knowledge and Society* 5: 171–241.

———(1995). Film as ethnography and as cultural critique: a curriculum. In Diane Carson & Lester Friedman (Eds.), *Shared differences* (pp. 29–56). Urbana: University of Illinois Press.

Fischer, Michael M. J. & Mehdi Abedi. (1990). *Debating Muslims: cultural dialogues in postmodernity and tradition.* Madison: University of Wisconsin Press.

Fishman, Joshua. (1967). Bilingualism with and without diglossia, diglossia with and without bilingualism. *Journal of Social Issues* 23(2): 29–38.

——(1972). *The sociology of language: an interdisciplinary social science approach to language in society.* Rowley, MA: Newbury House.

——(1973). *Language and nationalism: two integrative essays.* Rowley, MA: Newbury House.

Fison, Lorimer. (1880). *Kamilaroi and Kurnai.* Melbourne: Robertson.

Fitzgerald, Thomas K. (Ed.). (1976). *Nutrition and anthropology in action.* Assen: Van Gorcum.

Fjellman, Steven. (1992). *Vinyl leaves: Walt Disney World and America.* Boulder, CO: Westview.

Flanagan, James. (1988). The cultural construction of equality on the New Guinea highlands fringe. In James G. Flanagan & Steve Rayner (Eds.), *Rules, decisions, and inequality in egalitarian societies* (pp. 164–177). Aldershot: Avebury.

——(1989). Hierarchy in simple "egalitarian" societies. *Annual Review of Anthropology* 18: 245–266.

Flanagan, James & Steve Rayner. (Eds). (1988). *Rules, decisions, and inequality in egalitarian societies.* Aldershot: Avebury.

Flannery, Kent. (1972). The cultural evolution of civilization. *Annual Review of Ecology and Systematics* 3: 399–426.

——(1973). The origins of agriculture. *Annual Review of Anthropology* 2: 271–310.

Fleagle, John G. (1988). *Primate adaptation and evolution.* San Diego, CA: Academic.

Flinn, Mark V. & Bobbi S. Low. (1986). Resource distribution, social competition, and mating patterns in human societies. In Daniel Rubenstein & Richard Wrangham (Eds.), *Ecological aspects of social evolution* (pp. 217–243). Princeton, NJ: Princeton University Press.

Fogelson, Raymond D. (1982). Person, self, and identity: some anthropological retrospects, circumspects, and prospects. In Benjamin Lee (Ed.), *Psychosocial theories of the self* (pp. 67–109). New York: Plenum.

——(1989). The ethnohistory of events and nonevents. *Ethnohistory* 36: 133–147.

Foley, John Miles. (Ed.). (1990). *Oral-formulaic theory: a folklore casebook.* New York: Garland.

Foley, Robert. (1987). *Another unique species: patterns in human evolutionary ecology.* New York: Wiley.

Ford, Clellan & Frank Beach. (1951). *Patterns of sexual behavior.* New York: Harper.

Ford, Richard I. (1978). Ethnobotany: historical diversity and synthethis. In Richard Ford (Ed.), *The nature and status of ethnobotany* (pp. 33–49). Ann Arbor: Museum of Anthropology, University of Michigan.

——(Ed.). (1985). *An ethnobiology source book: the uses of plants and animals by American Indians.* New York: Garland.

Forde, Daryll. (1931). *Ethnography of the Yuma Indians.* Berkeley: University of California Press.

——(1934). *Habitat, economy and society: a geographical introduction to ethnology.* New York: Harcourt, Brace.

——(1941). *Marriage and the family among the Yako in south-eastern Nigeria.* London: Lund, Humphries.

——(Ed.). (1954). *African worlds: studies in the cosmological ideas and social values of African peoples.* London: Oxford University Press.

——(1958). *The context of belief: a consideration of fetishism among the Yako.* Liverpool: Liverpool University Press.

——(1964). *Yako studies.* London: Oxford University Press.

Forge, Anthony. (1970). Learning to see in New Guinea. In P. Mayer (Ed.), *Socialization: the approach from social anthropology.* London: A.S.A. monograph no. 8.

——(1972). Tswamung: a failed big-man. In Solon Kimball & James B. Watson (Eds.), *Crossing cultural boundaries* (pp. 257–273). San Francisco, CA: Chandler.

———(1973). Style and meaning in Sepik art. In Anthony Forge (Ed.), *Primitive art and society* (pp. 169–192). London: Oxford University Press.

Fortes, Meyer. (1945). *The dynamics of clanship among the Tallensi.* London: Oxford University Press.

———(1949a). Time and social structure: an Ashanti case study. In Meyer Fortes (Ed.), *Social structure* (pp. 54–84). Oxford: Clarendon.

———(1949b). *The web of kinship among the Tallensi.* London: Oxford University Press.

———(1953). The structure of unilineal descent groups. *American Anthropologist* 55: 17–41.

———(1955). Radcliffe-Brown's contribution to the study of social organization. *British Journal of Sociology* 6: 16–30.

———(1959a). Descent, filiation and affinity. *Man* 59: 193–197, 206–212.

———(1959b). *Oedipus and Job in West African religion.* Cambridge: Cambridge University Press.

———(1969). *Kinship and the social order: the legacy of Lewis Henry Morgan.* Chicago, IL: Aldine.

———(1970). *Time and social structure and other essays.* London: Athlone.

———(1978). An anthropologist's apprenticeship. *Annual Review of Anthropology* 7: 1–30.

———(1983). *Rules and the emergence of society.* London: Anthropological Institute.

———(1987). *Religion, mortality and the person: essays on Tallensi religion.* Cambridge: Cambridge University Press.

Fortes, Meyer & E. E. Evans-Pritchard. (1940a). Introduction. In Meyer Fortes & E. E. Evans-Pritchard (Eds.), *African political systems.* London: Oxford University Press.

——— (Eds.). (1940b). *African political systems.* London: Oxford University Press.

Fortmann, Louise & John W. Bruce. (Eds.). (1988). *Whose trees? Proprietary dimensions of forestry.* Boulder, CO: Westview.

Fortune, Reo. (1932). *The sorcerers of Dobu: the social anthropology of the Dobu Islanders of the western Pacific.* New York: Dutton.

———(1935). *Manus religion: an ethnological study of the Manus natives of the Admiralty Islands.* Philadelphia: Memoirs of the American Philosophical Society, vol. 3.

Foster, George M. (1953). Cofradía and compadrazgo in Spain and Spanish America. *Southwestern Journal of Anthropology* 9: 1–28.

———(1962). *Traditional cultures, and the impact of technological change.* New York: Harper.

———(1976). Disease etiologies in non-Western medical systems. *American Anthropologist* 78: 773–782.

Foster, George M. & Barbara G. Anderson. (1979). *Medical anthropology.* New York: Wiley.

Foster, Mary LeCron & Robert A. Rubinstein. (Eds.). (1986). *Peace and war: cross-cultural perspectives.* New Brunswick, NJ: Transaction.

Foster, Nelson & Linda S. Cordell. (Eds.). (1992). *Chilies to chocolate: food the Americas gave the world.* Tucson: University of Arizona Press.

Foster, Robert J. (1991). Making national cultures in the global ecumene. *Annual Reviews of Anthropology* 20: 235–260.

Foster-Carter, Aidan. (1978). Can we articulate "articulation"? In John Clammer (Ed.), *The new economic anthropology* (pp. 210–249). New York: St. Martin's.

Foucault, Michel. (1965). *Madness and civilization: a history of insanity in the age of reason* [Folie et déraison: histoire de la folie, Paris, 1961]. New York: Pantheon.

———(1970). *The order of things: an archaeology of the human sciences* [Mots et les choses, Paris, 1966]. New York: Pantheon.

———(1972). *The archaeology of knowledge* [Archéologie du savoir, Paris, 1969]. New York: Harper & Row.

———(1973). *The birth of the clinic: an archaeology of medical perception* [Naissance de la clinique, Paris, 1963]. New York: Pantheon.

———(1977a). What is an author? In *Language, counter-memory, practice* (pp. 113–138). Ithaca, NY: Cornell University Press.

——— (1977b). *Discipline and punish* [Surveiller et punir, Paris, 1975]. New York: Pantheon.

——— (1978). *The history of sexuality* [Histoire de la sexualité, Paris, 1976]. New York: Pantheon.

——— (1980). *Power/knowledge: selected interviews and other writings, 1972–1977.* New York: Pantheon.

——— (1982). The subject and power. In Hubert Dreyfus & Paul Rabinow (Eds.), *Michel Foucault* (pp. 208–226). Chicago, IL: University of Chicago Press.

——— (1991). The discourse on power. In Michel Foucault & Duccio Trombadori, *Remarks on Marx* [Colloqui con Foucault, Salerno, 1981] (pp. 147–181). New York: Semiotext(e).

Fourastie, Jean. (1972). From the traditional to the "tertiary" life cycle. In W. Petersen (Ed.), *Readings in population* (pp. 29–38). New York: Macmillan.

Fournier, Marcel. (1994). *Marcel Mauss.* Paris: Fayard.

Fox, Bonnie J. (1988). Conceptualizing "patriarchy". *Canadian Review of Sociology and Anthropology* 25(2): 163–182.

Fox, James J. (Ed.). (1980). *The flow of life: essays on eastern Indonesia.* Cambridge, MA: Harvard University Press.

Fox, Richard. (1977). *Urban anthropology: cities in their cultural settings.* Englewood Cliffs, NJ: Prentice-Hall.

——— (Ed.). (1990). *Nationalist ideologies and the production of national cultures.* Washington, DC: American Anthropological Association.

Fox, Robin. (1967). *Kinship and marriage: an anthropological perspective.* Harmondsworth: Penguin.

——— (1980). *The red lamp of incest.* New York: E. P. Dutton.

Frake, Charles O. (1962a). The ethnographic study of cognitive systems. In *Anthropology and human behavior* (pp. 72–93). Washington, DC: Anthropological Society of Washington.

——— (1962b). Cultural ecology and ethnography. *American Anthropologist* 64: 53–59.

——— (1964). Notes on queries in ethnography. *American Anthropologist* 66(3): 132–145.

——— (1980). *Language and cultural de-* *scription: essays.* Stanford, CA: Stanford University Press.

Francis, Emerich K. (1976). *Interethnic relations: an essay in sociological theory.* New York: Elsevier.

Frank, André G. (1967). *Capitalism and underdevelopment in Latin America: historical studies of Chile and Brazil.* New York: Monthly Review [2nd rev. edn., 1969].

Frank, André G. & Barry Gills. (Eds.). (1993). *The world system: five hundred years or five thousand?* London: Routledge.

Frank, Jerome D. (1961). *Persuasion and healing: a comparative study of psychotherapy.* Baltimore, MD: Johns Hopkins University Press.

Franke, Richard & Barbara Chasin. (1980). *Seeds of famine: ecological destruction and the development dilemma in the West African Sahel.* Montclair, NJ: Allanheld.

Frankenberg, Ruth. (1993). *White women, race matters: the social construction of whiteness.* Minneapolis: University of Minnesota Press.

Frankfort, Henri. (1948). *Kingship and the gods, a study of ancient Near Eastern religion as the integration of society and nature.* Chicago, IL: University of Chicago Press.

Fraser, Robert. (1990a). *The making of "The golden bough": the origins and growth of an argument.* New York: St. Martin's.

——— (Ed.). (1990b). *Sir James Frazer and the literary imagination: essays in affinity and influence.* Houndmills: Macmillan.

Fratto, Toni Flores. (1976). Toward an anthropological humanism. *Anthropology and Humanism Quarterly* 1(1): 1–5.

Frayser, Suzanne. (1985). *Varieties of sexual experience: an anthropological perspective on human sexuality.* New Haven, CT: HRAF Press.

Frazer, James. (1890). *The golden bough* (2 vols.). London: Macmillan. [2nd edn., 3 vols., 1900; 3rd. edn., 12 vols., 1906–15; abridged edn., 1 vol., 1922]

——— (1910). *Totemism and exogamy.* London: Macmillan.

Freedman, Maurice. (1958). *Lineage organization in southeastern China.* London: Athlone.

Freeman, Derek. (1960). Iban augury. In Bertram E. Smythies (Ed.), *The birds of Borneo* (pp. 73–98). Edinburgh: Oliver & Boyd.

———(1970). *Report on the Iban.* New York: Humanities.

———(1983). *Margaret Mead and Samoa: the making and unmaking of an anthropological myth.* Cambridge, MA: Harvard University Press.

Freeman, James M. (1979). *Untouchable: an Indian life history.* Stanford, CA: Stanford University Press.

Freeman, Linton, Douglas R. White, A. Kimball Romney. (Eds.). (1989) *Research methods in social network analysis.* Lanham, MD: University Publishing Associates.

Freeman, Michael. (1977). Sung. In K. C. Chang (Ed.), *Food in Chinese culture* (pp. 141–192). New Haven, CT: Yale University Press.

Freeman, Milton M. R. (1971). A social and ecological analysis of systematic female infanticide among the Netsilik Eskimo. *American Anthropologist* 73: 1011–1018.

Freilich, Morris. (Ed.). (1970). *Marginal natives at work: anthropologists in the field.* Cambridge, MA: Schenkman.

Freud, Sigmund. (1913). *The interpretation of dreams* [Die Traumdeutung, Vienna, 1900]. New York: Macmillan.

———(1918). *Totem and taboo: resemblances between the psychic lives of savages and neurotics* [Totem und Tabu, Leipzig, 1913]. New York: Moffat.

———(1930). *Civilization and its discontents* [Das Unbehagen in der Kultur, Vienna, 1930]. London: Hogarth.

———(1964). Why war? In Leon Bramson & George Goethals (Eds.), *War* (pp. 71–80). New York: Basic.

Freud, Sigmund & D. E. Oppenheim. (1958). *Dreams in folklore* [Träume im Folklore]. New York: International Universities Presss.

Fried, Morton. (1967). *The evolution of political society: an essay in political anthropology.* New York: Random.

———(1975). *The notion of tribe.* Menlo Park, CA: Cummings.

Fried, Morton, Marvin Harris & Robert Murphy. (Eds.). (1968). *War: the anthropology of armed conflict and aggression.* Garden City, NY: Natural History Press.

Friedl, Ernestine. (1975). *Women and men: an anthropologist's view.* New York: Holt.

———(1994). Sex the invisible. *American Anthropologist* 96(4): 833–844.

Friedman, Jonathan. (1975). Tribes, states and transformations. In Maurice Bloch (Ed.), *Marxist analyses and social anthropology* (pp. 161–202). New York: Wiley.

Friedman, Jonathan & Michael Rowlands. (1977). Notes towards an epigenetic model of the evolution of civilisation. In J. Friedman & M. J. Rowlands (Eds.), *The evolution of social systems* (pp. 201–276). London: Duckworth.

Friedrich, Paul. (1978). *The meaning of Aphrodite.* Chicago, IL: University of Chicago Press.

———(1979). *Language, context, and the imagination.* Stanford: Stanford University Press.

———(1986). *The language parallax: linguistic relativism and poetic indeterminacy.* Austin: University of Texas Press.

Friedson, Steven M. (1996). *Dancing prophets: musical experience in Tumbuka healing.* Chicago, IL: University of Chicago Press.

Frisancho, A. Roberto. (1993). *Human adaptation and accommodation.* Ann Arbor: University of Michigan Press.

Frith, Simon. (1983). *Sound effects: youth, leisure, and the politics of rock.* London: Constable.

Fromkin, Victoria & Robert Rodman. (1993). *An introduction to language* [5th edn.]. Fort Worth, TX: Harcourt, Brace Jovanovich.

Fromm, Erich. (1941). *Escape from freedom.* New York: Holt.

Fry, Christine L. & Jennie Keith. (Eds.). (1986). *New methods for old-age research: strategies for studying diversity.* South Hadley, MA: Bergin & Garvey.

Fry, Peter. (1985). Male homosexuality and spirit possession in Brazil. *Journal of Homosexuality* 11(3–4): 137–153.

Fujitani, Takashi. (1993). Inventing, forgetting, remembering: toward a historical ethnography of the nation-state. In Harumi Befu (Ed.), *Cultural nationalism in East Asia* (pp. 77–106). Berkeley: University of California Press.

Fürer-Haimendorf, Christoph von. (1943). *The Chenchus, jungle folk of the Deccan*. London: Macmillan.

——(1945). *The Reddis of the Bison Hills: a study in acculturation*. London: Macmillan.

——(1948). *The Raj Gonds of Adilabad: a peasant culture of the Deccan*. London: Macmillan.

——(1964). *The Sherpas of Nepal: Buddhist highlanders*. Berkeley: University of California Press.

——(1967). *Morals and merit: a study of values and social controls in South Asian societies*. London: Weidenfeld & Nicolson.

——(1969). *The Konyak Nagas: an Indian frontier tribe*. New York: Holt.

——(1979). *The Gonds of Andhra Pradesh: tradition and change in an Indian tribe*. London: George Allen & Unwin.

Fürer-Haimendorf, Christoph von, H. U. E. Thoden van Velzan & Wilhelmina van Wetering. (1960). Residence, power groups, and intrasocietal aggression: an enquiry into the conditions leading to peacefulness within non-stratified societies. *International Archives of Ethnography* 94(1). Leiden: Brill.

Furnivall, John S. (1939). *Netherlands India: a study of plural economy*. Cambridge: Cambridge University Press.

——(1948). *Colonial policy and practice: a comparative study of Burma and Netherlands India*. Cambridge: Cambridge University Press.

Furst, Peter T. (Ed.). (1972). *Flesh of the gods: the ritual use of hallucinogens*. New York: Praeger.

——(1976). *Hallucinogens and culture*. San Francisco, CA: Chandler & Sharp.

Furth, Charlotte & Shu-yueh Ch'en. (1992). Chinese medicine and the anthropology of menstruation in contemporary Taiwan. *Medical Anthropology Quarterly* 6(1): 27–48.

Gadamer, Hans G. (1975). Hermeneutics and social science. *Cultural Hermeneutics* 2: 307–316.

Galaty, John. (1982). Being "Maasai", being "People-of-Cattle": ethnic shifters in East Africa. *American Ethnologist* 9(1): 1–20.

Galaty, John & Pierre Bonte. (Eds.). (1991). *Herders, warriors, and traders: pastoralism in Africa*. Boulder, CO: Westview Press.

Galaty, John & Phillip Salzman. (Eds.). (1981). *Change and development in nomadic and pastoral societies*. Leiden: Brill.

Galbraith, John Kenneth. (1985). *The new industrial state* [4th edn.]. Boston, MA: Houghton, Mifflin.

Galton, Francis. (1883). *Inquiries into human faculty and its development*. New York: Macmillan.

Gann, Lewis H. (1958). *The birth of a plural society: the development of Northern Rhodesia under the British South Africa Company, 1894–1914*. Manchester: Manchester University Press.

Gans, Herbert. (1962). *The urban villagers: group and class in the life of Italian Americans*. New York: Free Press.

Gans, Lydia P. & Corinne Wood. (1985). Discriminant analysis as a method for differentiating potential acceptors of family planning. *Human Organization* 44: 228–233.

Gardiner, Patrick. (Ed.). (1964). *Theories of history*. Glencoe, IL: Free Press.

Gardner, R. Allen & Beatrice T. Gardner. (1969). Teaching sign language to a chimpanzee. *Science* 165: 664–672.

Gardner, Robert S. (1992). The more things change. *Transition* 58: 34–66.

Garfinkel, Harold. (1967). *Studies in ethnomethodology*. Englewood Cliffs, NJ: Prentice-Hall.

Garine, Igor de & Geoffrey A. Harrison. (Eds.). (1988). *Coping with uncertainty in food supply*. Oxford: Clarendon.

Garrett, Laurie. (1994). *The coming plague: newly emerging diseases in a world out of balance*. New York: Farrar.

Garro, Linda. (1988). Explaining high blood pressure: variation in knowledge about illness. *American Ethnologist* 15(1): 98–119.

Gaulin, Steven J. C. & Alice Schlegel. (1980). Paternal confidence and paternal investment: a cross-cultural test of a sociobiological hypothesis. *Ethology and Sociobiology* 1: 301–309.

Gaylin, William & Ellen Person. (Eds.). (1988). *Passionate attachments: thinking about love.* New York: Free Press.

Gazdar, Gerald, E. Klein, G. Pullum & I. Sag. (1985). *Generalized phrase structure grammar.* Cambridge, MA: Harvard University Press.

Geary, Christraud. (1988). *Images from Bamum: German colonial photography at the court of King Njoya, Cameroon, West Africa, 1902–1915.* Washington, DC: Smithsonian.

Geertz, Clifford. (1960). *The religion of Java.* Glencoe, IL: Free Press.

———(Ed.). (1963a). *Old societies and new states: the quest for modernity in Asia and Africa.* New York: Free Press.

———(1963b). The integrative revolution: primordial sentiments and civil politics in the new states. In Clifford Geertz (Ed.), *Old societies and new states* (pp. 105–157). New York: Free Press. [reprinted in Geertz 1973: 255–310]

———(1963c). *Agricultural involution: the process of ecological change in Indonesia.* Berkeley: University of California Press.

———(1963d). *Peddlers and princes: social change and economic modernization in two Indonesian towns.* Chicago, IL: University of Chicago Press.

———(1968). *Islam observed: religious development in Morocco and Indonesia.* New Haven, CT: Yale University Press.

———(1972). Deep play: notes on the Balinese cockfight. *Daedalus* 101(1): 1–37. [reprinted in C. Geertz 1973]

———(1973). *The interpretation of cultures.* New York: Basic.

———(1977). Centers, kings and charisma. In Joseph Ben-David & T. N. Clark (Eds.), *Culture and its creators* (pp. 150–171). Chicago, IL: University of Chicago Press. [reprinted Geertz 1983: 121–147]

———(1979). Suq: the bazaar economy in Sefrou. In Clifford Geertz et al. (Eds.), *Meaning and order in Moroccan society* (pp. 123–313). Cambridge: Cambridge University Press.

———(1980). *Negara: the theater state in nineteenth-century Bali.* Princeton, NJ: Princeton University Press.

———(1983). *Local knowledge: further essays in interpretive anthropology.* New York: Basic.

———(1984a). "From the native's point of view": on the nature of anthropological understanding. In Richard Shweder & Robert LeVine (Eds.), *Culture theory* (pp. 123–126). Cambridge: Cambridge University Press.

———(1984b). Distinguished lecture: anti anti-relativism. *American Anthropologist* 86: 263–278.

———(1988). *Works and lives: the anthropologist as author.* Stanford, CA: Stanford University Press.

———(1995). *After the fact: four decades, two countries, one anthropologist.* Cambridge, MA: Harvard University Press.

Geertz, Clifford, Hildred Geertz & Lawrence Rosen. (Eds.). (1979). *Meaning and order in Moroccan society: three essays in cultural analysis.* Cambridge: Cambridge University Press.

Geertz, Hildred. (1959). The vocabulary of emotion: a study of Javanese socialization processes. *Psychiatry* 22: 225–236.

Gehlen, Arnold. (1980). *Man in the age of technology* [Die Seele im technischen Zeitalter, Hamburg, 1957]. New York: Columbia University Press.

Gelb, Ignace J. (1963). *A study of writing* [2nd rev. edn.]. Chicago, IL: University of Chicago Press.

Gell, Alfred. (1975). *Metamorphosis of the cassowaries.* London: Athlone.

———(1992a). *The anthropology of time: cultural constructions of temporal maps and images.* Oxford: Berg.

———(1992b). Inter-tribal commodity barter and reproductive gift exchange in old Melanesia. In Caroline Humphrey & Stephen Hugh-Jones (Eds.), *Barter, exchange and value* (pp. 142–168). Cambridge: Cambridge University Press.

———(1993). *Wrapping in images: tattooing in Polynesia.* Oxford: Clarendon.

Gellner, Ernest. (1959a). *Words and things: a critical account of linguistic philosophy and a study in ideology.* London: Gollancz.

———(1959b). Holism versus individualism in history and sociology. In Patrick Gardiner (Ed.), *Theories of history* (pp. 489–502). Glencoe, IL: Free Press.

——— (1969). *Saints of the Atlas*. Chicago, IL: University of Chicago Press.

——— (1970). Concepts and society. In Dorothy Emmet & Alasdair MacIntyre (Ed.), *Sociological theory and philosophical analysis* (pp. 115–149). New York: Macmillan.

——— (1975). Ethnomethodology: the re-enchantment industry or Californian way of subjectivity. *Philosophy and the Social Sciences* 5: 431–450.

——— (Ed.). (1980). *Soviet and Western anthropology*. London: Duckworth.

——— (1981). *Muslim society*. Cambridge: Cambridge University Press.

——— (1983). *Nations and nationalism*. Oxford: Blackwell.

——— (1988a). *Plough, sword, and book: the structure of human history*. London: Collins Harvill.

——— (1988b). *State and society in Soviet thought*. Oxford: Blackwell.

——— (1992). *Reason and culture: the historical role of rationality and rationalism*. Oxford: Blackwell.

——— (1994). *Conditions of liberty: civil society and its rivals*. London: Hamish Hamilton.

Gellner, Ernest & Charles Michaud. (1973). *Arabs and Berbers: from tribe to nation in North Africa*. London: Duckworth.

Gellner, Ernest & John Waterbury. (1977). *Patrons and clients in Mediterranean societies*. London: Duckworth.

Genette, Gerard. (1980). *Narrative discourse*. Ithaca, NY: Cornell University Press.

Gennep, Arnold van. (1904). *Tabou et totémisme à Madagascar: étude descriptive et théorique*. Paris: Leroux.

——— (1906). *Mythes et legendes d'Australie: études d'ethnographie et de sociologie*. Paris: Guilmoto.

——— (1920). *L'état actuel du problème totémique*. Paris: Leroux.

——— (1943–58). *Manuel de folklore français contemporain* (9 vols). Paris: Picard.

——— (1960). *The rites of passage* [Rites de passage, Paris, 1909]. Chicago, IL: University of Chicago Press.

Gerber, Eleanor. (1985). Rage and obligation: Samoan emotions in conflict. In Geoffrey White & John Kirkpatrick (Eds.), *Person, self and experience* (pp. 121–167). Berkeley: University of California Press.

Gernsbacher, Morton. (Ed.). (1994). *Handbook of psycholinguistics*. San Diego, CA: Academic.

Gero, Joan M. (1985). Socio-politics and the woman-at-home ideology. *American Antiquity* 50: 342–350.

Gero, Joan M. & Margaret W. Conkey (Eds.). (1991). *Engendering archaeology: women and prehistory*. Oxford: Blackwell.

Gerth, Hans & C. Wright Mills. (Eds.). (1946). *From Max Weber: essays in sociology*. Oxford: Oxford University Press.

Ghosh, Amitav. (1992). *In an antique land*. London: Granta.

Gibbon, Guy. (1984). *Anthropological archaeology*. New York: Columbia University Press.

Giddens, Anthony. (1976). *New rules of sociological method: a positive critique of interpretative sociologies*. London: Hutchinson.

——— (1979a). *Emile Durkheim*. New York: Viking.

——— (1979b). *Central problems of social theory*. New York: Random House.

——— (1984). *The constitution of society: outline of the theory of structuration*. Berkeley: University of California Press.

——— (1990). *The consequences of modernity*. Cambridge: Polity.

——— (1991). *Modernity and self-identity: self and society in the late modern age*. Stanford, CA: Stanford University Press.

Gilman, Benjamin I. (1908). Hopi songs. *Journal of American Ethnology and Archaeology* 5.

Gilmore, David. (1990). *Manhood in the making: cultural concepts of masculinity*. New Haven, CT: Yale University Press.

Gilsenan, Michael. (1973). *Saint and Sufi in modern Egypt*. Oxford: Clarendon.

——— (1996). *Lords of the Lebanese Marches: violence, power and culture in an Arab society*. London: Taurus.

Ginsburg, Faye. (1989). *Contested lives:*

the abortion debate in an American community. Berkeley: University of California Press.

——(1991). Indigenous media: Faustian contract or global village? *Cultural Anthropology* 6(1): 92–112.

Ginsburg, Faye & Rayna Rapp. (1991). The politics of reproduction. *Annual Review of Anthropology* 20: 311–343.

——(Eds.). (1995). *Conceiving the new world order: the global politics of reproduction.* Berkeley: University of California Press.

Ginzberg, Eli & George J. Vojt. (1981). The service sector of the United States economy. *Scientific American* 244(3): 48–49.

Girard, Rene. (1977). *Violence and the sacred* [Violence et le sacré, Paris, 1972]. Baltimore, MD: Johns Hopkins University Press.

Giurchescu, Anca & Lisbet Torp. (1991). Theory and methods in dance research: a European approach to the holistic study of dance. *Yearbook for Traditional Music* 23: 1–10.

Glacken, Clarence. (1967). *Traces on the Rhodian shore: nature and culture in Western thought from ancient times to the end of the eighteenth century.* Berkeley: University of California Press.

Gladwin, Christina H. (1989). *Ethnographic decision tree modeling.* Newbury Park, CA: Sage.

Gladwin, Thomas. (1970). *East is a big bird: navigation and logic on Puluwat Atoll.* Cambridge, MA: Harvard University Press.

Glaser, Barney G. & Anselm L. Strauss. (1964). Awareness contexts and social interaction. *American Sociological Review* 29: 669–679.

——(1971). *Status passage.* Chicago, IL: Aldine.

Glass, James M. (1993). *Shattered selves: multiple personality in a postmodern world.* Ithaca, NY: Cornell University Press.

Glassie, Henry. (1975). *Folk housing in middle Virginia: a structural analysis of historic artifacts.* Knoxville: University of Tennessee Press.

——(1995). Tradition. *Journal of American Folklore* 430: 395–412.

Glassman, Ronald. (1986). *Democracy and despotism in primitive societies: a neo-Weberian approach to political theory.* New York: Associated Faculty Press.

Glassman, Ronald & Wiliam Swatos. (1986). *Charisma, history and social structure.* New York: Greenwood.

Glick, Thomas F. (1970). *Irrigation and society in medieval Valencia.* Cambridge, MA: Harvard University Press.

——(1995). *From Muslim fortress to Christian castle: social and cultural change in medieval Spain.* Manchester: Manchester University Press.

Gluckman, Max. (1940a). The kingdom of the Zulu of South Africa. In Meyer Fortes & E. E. Evans-Pritchard (Eds.), *African political systems* (pp. 25–55). London: Oxford University Press.

——(1940b). Analysis of a social situation in modern Zululand. *Bantu Studies* 14: 1–30, 147–174.

——(1954). *Rituals of rebellion in Southeast Africa.* Manchester: Manchester University Press.

——(1955a). *The judicial process among the Barotse of Northern Rhodesia.* Manchester: Manchester University Press.

——(1955b). *Custom and conflict in Africa.* Oxford: Blackwell.

——(1963). *Order and rebellion in tribal Africa.* London: Cohen & Wests.

——(1964). *Closed systems and open minds: the limits of naivety in social anthropology.* Chicago, IL: Aldine.

——(1965a). *The ideas in Barotse jurisprudence.* New Haven, CT: Yale University Press.

——(1965b). *Politics, law and ritual in tribal society.* Oxford: Blackwell.

Gluckman, Max & Elizabeth Colson. (Eds.). (1951). *Seven tribes of British Central Africa.* Oxford: Oxford University Press.

Gmelch, George & Walter Zenner. (Eds.). (1995). *Urban life: readings in urban anthropology* [3rd rev. edn.]. Prospect Heights, IL: Waveland.

Godelier, Maurice. (1973). *Rationality and irrationality in economics* [Rationalité et irrationalité en économie, Paris, 1965]. New York: Monthly Review.

————(1977). *Perspectives in Marxist anthropology* [Horizon, trajets marxistes en anthropologie, Paris, 1973]. Cambridge: Cambridge University Press.

————(1986). *The making of great men: male domination and power among the New Guinea Baruya* [Production des grands hommes, Paris, 1982]. Cambridge: Cambridge University Press.

————(1995). Is social anthropology indissolubly linked to the West, its birthplace? *International Social Science Journal* 47: 141–158.

Godelier, Maurice & Marilyn Strathern. (Eds.). (1991). *Big men and great men: personifications of power in Melanesia.* Cambridge: Cambridge University Press.

Goer, Henci. (1995). *Obstetric myths versus research realities: a guide to the medical literature.* Westport, CT: Bergin & Garvey.

Goethals, Peter. (1961). *Aspects of local government in a Sumbawan village.* Ithaca, NY: Cornell University Southeast Asia Program.

Goffman, Erving. (1956). *The presentation of self in everyday life.* Edinburgh: University of Edinburgh.

————(1961). *Asylums: essays on the social situation of mental patients and other inmates.* Garden City, NY: Doubleday.

————(1981). *Forms of talk.* Philadelphia: University of Pennsylvania Press.

Goheen, Mitzi & Parker Shipton. (Eds.). (1992). Special issue: Rights over land. *Africa* 62(3).

Gold, Ann Grodzins. (1988). *Fruitful journeys: the ways of Rajasthani pilgrims.* Berkeley: University of California Press.

Golde, Peggy. (Ed.). (1970). *Women in the field: anthropological experiences.* Chicago, IL: Aldine.

Goldschmidt, Walter. (Ed.). (1959). The anthropology of Franz Boas: essays on the centennial of his birth. *American Anthropologist* 61(5).

————(1973). Guilt and pollution in Sebai mortuary rituals. *Ethos* 1(1): 75–105.

Goldstein, Melvyn & Cynthia Beall. (1989). *Nomads of western Tibet: the survival of a way of life.* Berkeley: University of California Press.

Golub, Sharon. (Ed.). (1983). *Lifting the curse of menstruation: a feminist appraisal of the influence of menstruation on women's lives.* New York: Haworth.

Good, Anthony. (1981). Prescription, preference and practice: marriage patterns among the Kondaiyankottai Maravar of South India. *Man* 16: 108–129.

Good, Byron. (1994). *Medicine, rationality, and experience: an anthropological perspective.* Cambridge: Cambridge University Press.

Good, Mary-Jo. (Ed.). (1992). *Pain as human experience: an anthropological perspective.* Berkeley: University of California Press.

Goodale, Jane C. (1971). *Tiwi wives: a study of the women of Melville Island, North Australia.* Seattle: University of Washington Press.

Goodall, Jane. (1986). *The chimpanzees of Gombe: patterns of behavior.* Cambridge, MA: Harvard University Press.

Goode, Judith. (1989). Cultural patterns and group-sharing rules in food systems. In Gretel Pelto et al. (Eds.), *Research methods in nutritional anthropology* (pp. 126–161). Tokyo: United Nations University.

Goode, William. (1956). *After divorce.* Glencoe, IL: Free Press.

————(1959). The theoretical importance of love. *American Sociological Review* 24: 38–47.

Goodenough, Ward H. (1956). Componential analysis and the study of meaning. *Language* 32: 195–216.

————(1957). Cultural anthropology and linguistics. *Georgetown University Monograph Series on Languages and Linguistics* no. 9 (pp. 167–173).

————(1963). *Cooperation in change: an anthropological approach to community development.* New York: Sage.

————(1964). (Ed.). *Explorations in cultural anthropology: essays in honor of George Peter Murdock.* New York: McGraw-Hill.

————(1965a). Yankee kinship terminology: a problem in componential analysis. *American Anthropologist* 67: 259–287.

————(1965b). Rethinking "status" and "role": toward a general model of the cultural organization of social relationships. In Michael Banton (Ed.), *The relevance of models for social anthropology* (pp. 1–24). London: Tavistock.

———(1967). Componential analysis. *Science*, 156 (no. 3779): 1203–1209.

———(1970). *Description and comparison in cultural anthropology*. Chicago, IL: Aldine.

Goodwin, Marjorie H. (1990). *He-said-she-said: talk as social organization among black children*. Bloomington: Indiana University Press.

Goody, Esther N. (1973). *Contexts of kinship: an essay in the family sociology of the Gonja of Northern Ghana*. Cambridge: Cambridge University Press.

Goody, Jack. (1962). *Death, property and the ancestors: a study of the mortuary customs of the LoDagaa of West Africa*. Stanford: Stanford University Press.

———(Ed.). (1966). *Succession to high office*. Cambridge: Cambridge University Press.

———(Ed.). (1968). *Literacy in traditional societies*. Cambridge: Cambridge University Press.

———(1971). *Technology, tradition and the state in Africa*. London: Oxford University Press.

———(1973). Bridewealth and dowry in Africa and Eurasia. In Jack Goody & Stanley J. Tambiah (Eds.), *Bridewealth and dowry* (pp. 1–58). Cambridge: Cambridge University Press.

———(1976). *Production and reproduction: a comparative study of the domestic domain*. Cambridge: Cambridge University Press.

———(1977). *The domestication of the savage mind*. Cambridge: Cambridge University Press.

———(1982). *Cooking, cuisine and class: a study in comparative sociology*. Cambridge: Cambridge University Press.

———(1983a). *The development of the family and marriage in Europe*. Cambridge: Cambridge University Press.

———(Ed.). (1983b). Special issue: In memory of Meyer Fortes. *Cambridge Anthropology* 8.

———(1986). *The logic of writing and the organization of society*. Cambridge: Cambridge University Press.

———(1987). *The interface between the written and the oral*. Cambridge: Cambridge University Press.

———(1990). *The oriental, the ancient and the primitive: systems of marriage and the family in the pre-industrial societies of Eurasia*. Cambridge: Cambridge University Press.

———(1991). Towards a room with a view: a personal account of contributions to local knowledge, theory, and research in fieldwork and comparative studies. *Annual Review of Anthropology* 20: 1–23.

———(1993). *The culture of flowers*. Cambridge: Cambridge University Press.

———(1995). *The expansive moment: the rise of social anthropology in Britain and Africa 1918–1970*. Cambridge: Cambridge University Press.

———(1996). Cognitive contradictions and universals: creation and evolution in oral cultures. *Social Anthropology* 4: 1–16.

Goody, Jack & J. Buckley. (1980). Implications of the sexual division of labor in agriculture. In J. Clyde Mitchell (Ed.), *Numerical techniques in social anthropology* (pp. 33–47). Philadelphia, PA: ISHI.

Goody, Jack & Meyer Fortes. (Eds.). (1958). *The developmental cycle of domestic groups*. Cambridge: Cambridge University Press.

Goody, Jack & Stanley J. Tambiah. (1973). *Bridewealth and dowry*. Cambridge: Cambridge University Press.

Goody, Jack, Joan Thirsk & E. P. Thompson. (Eds.). (1976). *Family and inheritance: rural society in Western Europe 1200–1800*. Cambridge: Cambridge University Press.

Gordan, Jane. (1976). *Margaret Mead: the complete bibliography, 1925–1975*. The Hague: Mouton.

Gordon, A. D. (1981). *Classification: methods for the exploratory analysis of multivariate data*. London: Chapman & Hall.

———(1987). A review of hierarchical classification. *Journal of the Royal Statistical Society* (ser. A) 150: 119–137.

Gordon-Grube, Karen. (1988). Anthropophagy in post-Renaissance Europe. *American Anthropologist* 90: 405–407.

Gorenflo, Larry & Nathan Gale. (1986). Population and productivity in the

Teotihuacan Valley. *Journal of Anthropological Archaeology* 5: 199–228.

Gorz, André. (1985). *Paths to paradise: on the liberation from work* [Chemins du paradis, Paris, 1983]. London: Pluto.

Gossen, Gary H. (1989). Life, death, and apotheosis of a Chamula Protestant leader: biography as social history. In Victoria R. Bricker & Gary H. Gossen (Eds.), *Ethnographic encounters in southern Mesoamerica* (pp. 217–229). Austin: University of Texas Press.

Gottlieb, Alma. (1988a). American premenstrual syndrome: a mute voice. *Anthropology Today* 4(6): 10–13.

———(1988b). Menstrual cosmology among the Beng of Ivory Coast. In Thomas Buckley & Alma Gottlieb (Eds.), *Blood magic* (pp. 55–74). Berkeley: University of California Press.

Gottlieb, Alma & Phillip Graham. (1993). *Parallel worlds: an anthropologist and a writer encounter Africa.* New York: Crown.

Gottwald, Norman. (1979). *The tribes of Yahweh: a sociology of the religion of liberated Israel, 1250–1050 B.C.E.* Maryknoll, NY: Orbis.

Gough, Kathleen. (1959). The Nayars and the definition of marriage. *Journal of the Royal Anthropological Institute* 89: 23–34.

———(1981). *Rural society in southeast India.* Cambridge: Cambridge University Press.

Gould, James & Peter Marler. (1987). Learning by instinct. *Scientific American* 256: 74–85.

Gould, Richard A. & Patty Jo Watson. (1982). A dialogue on the meaning and use of analogy in ethnoarchaelogical reasoning. *Journal of Anthropological Archaeology* 1: 355–381.

Gould, Stephen J. (1996). *The mismeasure of man* [rev. edn.]. New York: Norton.

Gouldner, Alvin W. (1954). *Patterns of industrial bureaucracy.* Glencoe, IL: Free Press.

Gowlett, John A. J. (1992). Early human mental abilities. In Steve Jones, Robert Martin & David Pilbeam (Eds.), *Cambridge encyclopedia of human evolution* (pp. 341–345). Cambridge: Cambridge University Press.

Graburn, Nelson H. H. (Ed.). (1976).

Ethnic and tourist arts: cultural expressions from the fourth world. Berkeley: University of California Press.

Grandguillaume, Gilbert. (1983). *Arabisation et politique linguistique au maghreb.* Paris: Maisonneuve et Larose.

Grant Duff, Sir Mountstuart E. (1892). *Sir Henry Maine: a brief memoir of his life.* London: Murray.

Granzberg, Gary. (1973). Twin infanticide: a cross-cultural test of a materialistic explanation. *Ethos* 1: 405–412.

Gray, Robert F. (1963). *The Sonjo of Tanganyika: an anthropological study of an irrigation-based society.* London: Oxford University Press.

Greaves, Tom. (Ed.). (1994). *Intellectual property rights for indigenous peoples: a sourcebook.* Oklahoma City: Society for Applied Anthropology.

Green, Stanton & Stephen Perlman. (Eds.). (1985). *The archaeology of frontiers and boundaries.* Orlando, FL: Academic.

Greenacre, Michael. (1984). *Theory and applications of correspondence analysis.* London: Academic.

Greenberg, David F. (1988). *Construction of homosexuality.* Chicago, IL: University of Chicago Press.

Greenberg, Joseph H. (1966). *Language universals.* The Hague: Mouton.

———(1971). The Indo-Pacific hypothesis. In Thomas A. Sebeok (Ed.), *Current trends in linguistics,* vol. 8 (pp. 807–871). The Hague: Mouton.

———(1987). *Language in the Americas.* Stanford, CA: Stanford University Press.

Greenberg, Stanley. (1980). *Race and state in capitalist development.* New Haven, CT: Yale University Press.

Greene, Lawrence. (Ed.). (1977). *Malnutrition, behavior, and social organization.* New York: Academic.

Greenfeld, Liah. (1985). Reflections on the two charismas. *British Journal of Sociology* 36: 117–132.

Greenhalgh, Susan. (Ed.). (1995). *Situating fertility: anthropology and demographic inquiry.* Cambridge: Cambridge University Press.

Greenhouse, Carol J. (1986). *Praying for justice: faith, order and community in an American town.* Ithaca, NY: Cornell University Press.

Gregersen, Edgar. (1983). *Sexual practices: the story of human sexuality.* New York: Franklin Watts.

———(1994). *The world of human sexuality: behaviors, customs, and beliefs.* New York: Irvington.

Gregor, Thomas. (1977). *Mehinaku: the drama of daily life in a Brazilian Indian village.* Chicago, IL: University of Chicago Press.

———(1985). *Anxious pleasures.* Chicago, IL: University of Chicago Press.

Gregory, Chris A. (1982). *Gifts and commodities.* London: Academic.

———(1987). Gifts. In John Eatwell, Murray Millgate & Peter Newman (Eds.), *The New Palgrave* (2: 524–528). New York: Stockton Press.

Gregory, Steven & Roger Sanjek. (Eds.). (1994). *Race.* New Brunswick, NJ: Rutgers University Press.

Greimas, Algirdas J. (1983). *Structural semantics: an attempt at a method* [Semantique structurale, Paris, 1966]. Lincoln: University of Nebraska Press.

Greuel, Peter J. (1971). The Leopard-Skin Chief: an examination of political power among the Nuer. *American Anthropologist* 73: 1115–1120.

Griaule, Marcel. (1954). The Dogon. In Daryll Forde (Ed.), *African worlds* (pp. 83–110). London: Oxford University Press.

———(1965). Conversations with Ogotemmeli: an introduction to Dogon religious ideas [Dieu d'eau, Paris, 1948]. London: Oxford University Press.

Grigg, David. (1980). *Population growth and agrarian change: an historical perspective.* Cambridge: Cambridge University Press.

Grillo, Ralph & Alan Rew. (Eds.). (1985). *Social anthropology and development policy.* London: Tavistock.

Grim, John. (1983). *The shaman: patterns of Siberian and Ojibway healing.* Norman: University of Oklahoma Press.

Grimes, Barbara F. (Ed.). (1992a). *Ethnologue index* [12th edn.]. Dallas, TX: Summer Institute of Linguistics.

———(Ed.). (1992b). *Ethnologue: languages of the world* [12th edn.]. Dallas, TX: Summer Institute of Linguistics.

Grimes, Joseph E. (1964). Measures of linguistic divergence. In Horace G. Lunt (Ed.), *Proceedings of the Ninth International Congress of Linguists* (pp. 44–50). The Hague: Mouton.

Grimes, Joseph E. & Barbara F. Grimes. (1993). *Ethnologue language family index.* Dallas, TX: Summer Institute of Linguistics.

Grimes, Ronald. (1976). *Symbol and conquest: public ritual and drama in Santa Fe, New Mexico.* Ithaca, NY: Cornell University Press.

Grimm, Jacob. (1967). Germanic grammar [Deutsche Grammatik, Göttingen, 1822]. In Winfred P. Lehmann (Ed.), *A reader in nineteenth-century historical Indo-European linguistics* (pp. 46–60). Bloomington: Indiana University Press.

Grindal, Bruce T. (1983). Into the heart of Sisala experience: witnessing death divination. *Journal of Anthropological Research* 39: 60–80.

———(1993). The spirit of humanistic anthropology. *Anthropology and Humanism Quarterly* 18(2): 46–47.

Groebel, Jo & Robert A. Hinde. (Eds.). (1989). *Aggression and war: their biological and social bases.* Cambridge: Cambridge University Press.

Gross, Daniel & Barbara Underwood. (1971). Technological change and caloric costs: sisal agriculture in northeast Brazil. *American Anthropologist* 7: 724–740.

Gross, Larry, John Katz & Jay Ruby. (Eds.). (1988). *Image ethics: the moral rights of subjects in photographs, film, and television.* Oxford: Oxford University Press.

Gruenbaum, Ellen. (1991). The Islamic movement, development, and health education: Recent changes in the health of rural women in central Sudan. *Social Science and Medicine* 33: 637–645.

Gudeman, Stephen. (1972). The compadrazgo as a reflection of the natural and spiritual person. *Proceedings of the Royal Anthropological Institute for 1971* 8: 45–71.

———(1986). *Economics as culture: models and metaphors of livelihood.* London: Routledge.

Gudeman, Stephen & Alberto Rivera. (1990). *Conversations in Colombia: the* *domestic economy in life and text.* Cambridge: Cambridge University Press.

Gudschinsky, Sarah C. (1956). The ABCs of lexicostatistics (glottochronology). *Word* 12: 175–210.

Guilbault, Jocelyne. (1993). *Zouk: World Music in the West Indies.* Chicago, IL: University of Chicago Press.

Gulliver, Phillip H. (1955). *The family herds: a study of two pastoral tribes in East Africa, the Jie and the Turkana.* London: Routledge.

———(1958). The Turkana age organization. *American Anthropologist* 60: 900–922.

———(1963). *Social control in an African society: a study of the Arusha, agricultural Masai of Northern Tanganyika.* Boston, MA: Boston Universitry Press.

———(1968). Age differentiation. In David Sills (Ed.), *International encyclopedia of the social sciences* 1: 157–162. New York: Macmillan.

———(1977). On mediation. In Ian Hamnett (Ed.), *Social anthropology and law* (pp. 15–53). London: Academic.

———(1979). *Disputes and negotiations: a cross-cultural perspective.* New York: Academic.

Gummerman, George & Murray Gell-Mann. (1993). *Understanding complexity in the prehistoric southwest.* Reading, MA: Addison-Wesley.

Gumperz, John. (1982). *Discourse strategies.* Cambridge: Cambridge University Press.

Gumperz, John & Dell Hymes. (Eds.). (1972). *Directions in sociolinguistics: the ethnography of communication.* New York: Holt, Rinehart & Winston.

Gumperz, John & J. Wilson. (1971). Convergence and creolization: a case from the Indo-Aryan/Dravidian border. In Dell Hymes (Ed.), *Pidginization and creolization of languages* (pp. 151–167). Cambridge: Cambridge University Press.

Gupta, Akhil. (1995). Blurred boundaries: the discourse of corruption, the culture of politics, and the imagined state. *American Ethnologist* 22(2): 375–402.

Gupta, Akhil & James Ferguson. (1992). Beyond culture: space identity and the politics of difference. *Cultural Anthropology* 7: 6–23.

Gusfield, Joseph. (1963). *Symbolic crusade: status politics and the American temperance movement.* Urbana: University of Illinois Press.

Gutmann, Matthew C. (1996). *The meanings of macho: being a man in Mexico City.* Berkeley: University of California Press.

Guyer, Jane I. (1981). Household and community in African studies. *African Studies Review* 24: 87–137.

———(1988). The multiplication of labor: historical methods in the study of gender and agricultural change in modern Africa. *Current Anthropology* 29: 247–272.

———(Ed.). (1995). *Money matters: instability, values and social payments in the modern history of West African communities.* Portsmouth, NH: Heinemann.

Guyer, Jane I. & Eric F. Lambin. (1993). Land use in an urban hinterland: ethnography and remote sensing in the study of African intensification. *American Anthropologist* 95: 839–859.

Haas, Jonathan. (1982). *The evolution of the prehistoric state.* New York: Columbia University Press.

———(Ed.). (1990). *The anthropology of war.* Cambridge: Cambridge University Press.

Haas, Jonathan & Winifred Creamer. (1993). *Stress and warfare among the Kayenta Anasazi of the thirteenth century A.D.* Chicago, IL: Field Museum of Natural History.

Habbakuk, H. J. (1950). Marriage settlement in the eighteenth century. *Transactions of the Royal Historical Society* 32: 15–30.

———(1955). Family structure and economic change in nineteenth-century Europe. *Journal of Economic History* 14: 1–12.

Habermas, Jurgen. (1971). *Knowledge and human interests* [Erkenntnis und Interesse, Frankfurt, 1968]. Boston, MA: Beacon.

Hadden, Kenneth & Billie DeWalt. (1974). Path analysis: some anthropological examples. *Ethnology* 13: 105–138.

Haddon, Alfred C. (1901-35). *Reports of*

the Cambridge Anthropological Expedition to Torres Straits (6 vols.). Cambridge: Cambridge University Press.

Haegeman, Liliane. (1994). *Introduction to government and binding theory* [2nd edn.]. Oxford: Blackwell.

Haeri, Niloofar. (1995). *The sociolinguistic market of Cairo: gender, class, and education.* London: Kegan Paul International.

Haeri, Shahla. (1989). *Law of desire: temporary marriage in Shi'i Iran.* Syracuse, NY: Syracuse University Press.

Hagestad, Gunhild O. (1990). Social perspectives on the life course. In Robert Binstock & Linda George (Eds.), *Handbook of aging and the social sciences* [3rd edn.] (pp. 151–168). San Diego, CA: Academic.

Hahn, Robert A. (1995). *Sickness and healing: an anthropological perspective.* New Haven, CT: Yale University Press.

Haig, David. (1993). Genetic conflicts in human pregnancy. *Quarterly Review of Biology* 68: 495–532.

Hakansson, Thomas. (1988). *Bridewealth, women and land: social change among the Gusii of Kenya.* Stockholm: Almqvist & Wiksell.

Hall, Edward T. (1959). *The silent language.* Garden City, NY: Doubleday.

———(1966). *The hidden dimension.* Garden City, NY: Doubleday.

Hall, Richard H. (1994). *Sociology of work: perspectives, analyses, and issues.* Thousand Oaks, CA: Pine Forge Press.

Hall, Stuart. (1996). When was "the post-colonial"? Thinking at the limit. In Iain Chambers & Lidia Curti (Eds.), *The post-colonial question* (pp. 242–260). London: Routledge.

Hall, Thomas D. (1989). *Social change in the Southwest, 1350–1880.* Lawrence: University Press of Kansas.

Hall, Thomas D. & Christopher Chase-Dunn. (1993). The world-systems perspective and archaeology: forward into the past. *Journal of Archaeological Research* 1: 121–143.

Hallowell, A. Irving. (1943). The nature and function of property as a social institution. *Journal of Legal and Political Sociology* 1: 115–138.

———(1955). *Culture and experience.*

Philadelphia: University of Pennsylvania Press.

———(1960a). Ojibwa ontology, behavior and world view. In Stanley Diamond (Ed.), *Culture in history* (pp. 19–52). New York: Columbia University Press.

———(1960b). The beginnings of anthropology in America. In Frederica de Laguna (Ed.), *Selected papers from the American Anthropologist, 1888–1920* (pp. 1–90). Evanston, IL: Row, Peterson.

Halperin, Rhoda. (1990). *The livelihood of kin: making ends meet "the Kentucky way".* Austin: University of Texas Press.

———(1994). *Cultural economies past and present.* Austin: University of Texas Press.

Hames, Raymond. (1979). Relatedness and interaction among the Ye'Kwana: a preliminary analysis. In N. A. Chagnon & W. Irons (Eds.), *Evolutionary biology and human social behavior* (pp. 239–249). North Scituate, MA: Duxbury Press.

Hamilton, Annette. (1970). The role of women in Aboriginal marriage arrangements. In Fay Gale (Ed.), *Woman's role in Aboriginal society* (pp. 17–20). Canberra: Australian Institute of Aboriginal Studies.

Hamilton, Lawrence S. (Ed.). (1993). *Ethics, religion and biodiversity: relations between conservation and cultural values.* Cambridge: White Horse Press.

Hamilton, William D. (1964). The genetical evolution of social behavior, I & II. *Journal of Theoretical Biology* 7: 1–52.

Hammel, Eugene A. (Ed.). (1965). Special Issue: Formal semantic analysis. *American Anthropologist* 67(5/2).

———(1993). Demography and the origins of the Yugoslav Civil War. *Anthropology Today* 9: 4–9.

Hammel, Eugene A. & Nancy Howell. (1987). Research in population and culture: an evolutionary framework. *Current Anthropology* 28: 141–160.

Hammersley, Martyn & Paul Atkinson. (1995). *Ethnography: principles in practice* [2nd edn.]. London: Routledge.

Hamnett, Ian. (Ed.). (1977). *Social anthropology and law.* London: Academic.

Handelman, Don. (1976). Some contributions of Max Gluckman to anthropological thought. In Myron J. Aronoff (Ed.), *Freedom and constraint* (pp. 7–14). Assen: Van Gorcum.

Handler, Richard. (1988). *Nationalism and the politics of culture in Quebec.* Madison: University of Wisconsin Press.

———(1990). Boasian anthropology and the critique of American culture. *American Quarterly* 42(2): 252–274.

———(1991). An interview with Clifford Geertz. *Current Anthropology* 32: 603–613.

Handler, Richard & Jocelyn Linnekin. (1984). Tradition, genuine or spurious. *Journal of American Folklore* 97: 273–290.

Handwerker, W. Penn. (1980). Market places, travelling traders, and shops: commercial structural variation in the Liberian interior prior to 1940. *African Economic History* 9: 3–26.

———(1983). The first demographic transition. *American Anthropologist* 85: 5–27.

———(1986a). The modern demographic transition. *American Anthropologist* 88: 400–417.

———(Ed.). (1986b). *Culture and reproduction: an anthropological critique of demographic transition theory.* Boulder, CO: Westview.

———(1989a). Demography. In T. M. Johnson & C. F. Sargent (Eds.), *Medical Anthropology* (pp. 319–347). Westport, CT: Greenwood.

———(1989b). *Women's power and social revolution.* Newbury Park, CA: Sage.

———(Ed.). (1990). *Births and power: social change and the politics of reproduction.* Boulder, CO: Westview.

———(1993). Gender power differences between parents and high-risk sexual behavior among their children. *Journal of Women's Health* 2: 301–315.

Hanks, Lucien M. (1972). *Rice and man: agricultural ecology in southeast Asia.* Chicago, IL: Aldine Atherton.

Hanks, William F. (1990). *Referential practice: language and lived space among the Maya.* Chicago, IL: University of Chicago Press.

Hanna, Judith Lynne. (1979). *To dance is human: a theory of nonverbal communication.* Austin, TX: University of Texas Press.

Hannerz, Ulf. (1969). *Soulside: inquiries into ghetto culture and community.* New York: Columbia University Press.

———(1980). *Exploring the city: inquiries toward an urban anthropology.* New York: Columbia University Press.

———(1987). World in creolisation. *Africa* 57(4): 546–559.

———(1992). *Cultural complexity: studies in the social organization of meaning.* New York: Columbia University Press.

Hanoteau, Aristide & Adolphe Letourneux. (1873). *La Kabylie et les coutumes kabyles,* vol. 2. Paris: Impr. National.

Hansen, Art. (1979). Once the running stops: assimilation of Angolan refugees into Zambian border villages. *Disasters* 3(4): 369–374.

Hansen, Art & Della McMillan. (Eds.). (1986). *Food in sub-Saharan Africa.* Boulder, CO: Lynne Rienner.

Hansen, Art & Anthony Oliver-Smith. (Eds.). (1982). *Involuntary migration and resettlement: the problem and responses of dislocated people.* Boulder, CO: Westview.

Hanson, Jeffery R. (1988). Age-set theory and Plains Indian age-grading: a critical review and revision. *American Ethnologist* 15: 349–364.

Hanushek, Eric & John Jackson. (1977). *Statistical methods for social scientists.* Orlando, FL: Academic.

Haraway, Donna. (1988). Situated knowledges. *Feminist Studies* 14(3): 575–599.

———(1989). *Primate visions: gender, race, and nature in the world of modern science.* New York: Routledge.

———(1991). *Simians, cyborgs, and women: the reinvention of nature.* New York: Routledge.

Hardesty, Donald L. (1977). *Ecological anthropology.* New York: Wiley.

Harding, Robert & Geza Teleki. (Eds.). (1981). *Omnivorous primates: gathering and hunting in human evolution.* New York: Columbia University Press.

Harding, Sandra G. (1991). *Whose science? Whose knowledge? Thinking from women's lives.* Ithaca, NY: Cornell University Press.

———(Ed.). (1993). *The "racial" economy of science.* Bloomington: Indiana University Press.

Harding, Susan F. (1987). Convicted by the holy spirit: the rhetoric of fundamental Baptist conversion. *American Ethnologist* 14(1): 167–181.

Hareven, Tamara K. & Kathleen J. Adams. (Eds.). (1982). *Aging and life course transitions: an interdisciplinary perspective.* New York: Guilford.

Harkness, Sara. (1992). Human development in psychological anthropology. In Theodore Schwartz, G. White & C. A. Lutz (Eds.), *New directions in psychological anthropology* (pp. 102–124). Cambridge: Cambridge University Press.

Harkness, Sara & Charles M. Super. (Eds.). (1996). *Parents' cultural belief systems: their origins, expressions, and consequences.* New York: Guilford.

Harkness, Sara, Charles M. Super & C. H. Keefer. (1992). Learning to be an American parent: how cultural models gain directive force. In Roy D'Andrade & C. Strauss (Eds.), *Human motives and cultural models* (pp. 163–178). Cambridge: Cambridge University Press.

Harner, Michael J. (1972). *The Jívaro, people of the sacred waterfalls.* Garden City, NY: Natural History.

——(Ed.). (1973). *Hallucinogens and shamanism.* Oxford: Oxford University Press.

——(1980). *The way of the shaman.* New York: Harper & Row.

Harper, Douglas. (1989). Visual sociology: expanding sociological vision. In Grant Blank, James McCartney & Edward Brent (Eds.), *New technology in sociology* (pp. 81–93). New Brunswick, NJ: Transaction.

Harrell, Steven & Sara A. Dickey. (1985). Dowry systems in complex societies. *Ethnology* 24: 105–120.

Harrell-Bond, Barbara E. (1986). *Imposing aid: emergency assistance to refugees.* Oxford: Oxford University Press.

Harris, Marvin. (1959). The economy has no surplus? *American Anthropologist* 61: 189–199.

——(1964). *Patterns of race in the Americas.* New York: Walker.

——(1966). The cultural ecology of India's sacred cattle. *Current Anthropology* 7: 51–66.

——(1968). *The rise of anthropological theory.* New York: Crowell.

——(1970). Referential ambiguity in the calculus of Brazilian racial identity. *Southwestern Journal of Anthropology* 26: 1–14.

——(1974). *Cows, pigs, wars, and witches: the riddles of culture.* New York: Random.

——(1977). *Cannibals and kings: the origins of cultures.* New York: Random.

——(1979). *Cultural materialism: the struggle for a science of culture.* New York: Random.

——(1981). *America now: the anthropology of a changing culture.* New York: Simon & Schuster [reissued as *Why nothing works*, 1988].

——(1985). *Good to eat: riddles of food and culture.* New York: Simon & Schuster [reissued as *Sacred cows and abominable pigs*, 1987].

——(1997). *Culture, people, nature: an introduction to general anthropology* [7th edn.]. White Plains, NY: Longman.

Harris, Marvin & Conrad Kottak. (1963). The structural significance of Brazilian racial categories. *Sociologia* 25: 203–208.

Harris, Marvin & Eric Ross. (1987a). *Death, sex and fertility: population regulation in preindustrial and developing societies.* New York: Columbia University Press.

——(Eds.). (1987b). *Food and evolution: toward a theory of human food habits.* Philadelphia, PA: Temple University Press.

Harris, Marvin, Josildeth Gomes Consork, J. Lang & Bryan Byrne. (1993). Who are the whites? Imposed census categories and the racial demography of Brazil. *Social Forces* 72(2): 451–462.

Harrison, Faye V. (1988). Introduction: An African diaspora perspective for urban anthropology. *Urban Anthropology* 17: 111–141.

——(1992). The DuBoisian legacy in anthropology. *Critique of Anthropology* 12(3): 239–260.

Harrison, Geoffrey A. (Ed.). (1988). *Famine.* Oxford: Oxford University Press.

Harriss, John. (Ed.). (1991). *The family: a social history of the twentieth century.* Oxford: Oxford University Press.

Hart, Donn V. (1977). *Compadrinazgo: ritual kinship in the Philippines.* DeKalb: Northern Illinois University Press.

Harvey, David. (1982). *The limits to capital.* Oxford: Blackwell.

——(1989a). *The condition of postmodernity: an enquiry into the origins of cultural change.* Oxford: Blackwell.

——(1989b). *The urban experience.* Oxford: Blackwell.

Harvey, Paul H. & Mark D. Pagel. (1991). *The comparative method in evolutionary biology.* Oxford: Oxford University Press.

Harwood, Jonathan. (1989). Genetics, eugenics and evolution. *British Journal for the History of Science* 22: 257–265.

Hasluck, Margaret. (1954). *The unwritten law in Albania.* Cambridge: Cambridge University Press.

Hassan, Fekri A. (1981). *Demographic archeology.* New York: Academic.

Hassig, Ross. (1985). *Trade, tribute, and transportation: the sixteenth-century political economy of the Valley of Mexico.* Norman: University of Oklahoma Press.

——(1988). *Aztec warfare: imperial expansion and political control.* Norman: University of Oklahoma Press.

Hatch, Elvin. (1973). *Theories of man and culture.* New York: Columbia University Press.

——(1983). *Culture and morality: the relativity of values in anthropology.* New York: Columbia University Press.

——(1989). Theories of social honor. *American Anthropologist* 91: 341–353.

Hauser, Marc D. (1993). The evolution of nonhuman primate vocalizations: effects of phylogeny, body weight, and social context. *The American Naturalist* 142(3): 528–543.

Hausfater, Glenn & Sarah Blaffer Hrdy. (Eds.). (1984). *Infanticide: comparative and evolutionary perspectives.* New York: Aldine.

Havelock, Eric A. (1976). *The origins of Western literacy.* Toronto: Ontario Institute for Studies in Education.

——(1986). *The muse learns to write: reflections on orality and literacy from antiq-*uity to the present. New Haven, CT: Yale University Press.

Hawkes, Christopher, F. C. (1954). Archaeology theory and method: some suggestions from the Old World. *American Anthropologist* 56: 155–168.

Hawkes, Kristen. (1991). Showing off: tests of a hypothesis about men's foraging goals. *Ethology and Sociobiolology* 12(1): 29–54.

Hawkes, Terence. (1977). *Structuralism and semiotics.* Berkeley: University of California Press.

Hawkins, John A. & Murray Gell-Mann. (Eds.). (1992). *The evolution of human languages.* Redwood City, CA: Addison-Wesley.

Hayden, Brian. (1981). Research and development in the Stone Age. *Current Anthropology* 22: 519–548.

——(1995). Pathways to power: principles for creating socioeconomic inequalities. In T. Douglas Price & Gary Feinman (Eds.), *Foundations of social inequality* (pp. 15–86). New York: Plenum.

Hayden, Robert M. (1995). Serbian and Croatian nationalism and the wars in Yugoslavia. *Cultural Survival Quarterly* 19: 25–28.

Hayes, Eugene & Tanya Hayes. (Eds.). (1970). *Claude Lévi-Strauss: the anthropologist as hero.* Cambridge, MA: MIT Press.

Hays, Hoffman R. (1958). *From ape to angel: an informal history of social anthropology.* New York: Knopf.

Headland, Thomas N., Kenneth L. Pike & Marvin Harris. (Eds.). (1990). *Emics and etics: the insider/outsider debate.* Newbury Park, CA: Sage.

Heath, Dwight B. (1987). Anthropology and alcohol studies: current issues. *Annual Review of Anthropology* 16: 99–120.

——(Ed.). (1995). *International handbook on alcohol and culture.* Westport, CT: Greenwood.

Heath, Dwight B. & A. M. Cooper. (1981). *Alcohol use and world cultures.* Toronto: Addiction Research Foundation.

Heath, Shirley Brice. (1983). *Ways with words: language, life, and work in communities and classrooms.* Cambridge: Cambridge University Press.

Hebdige, Dick. (1979). *Subculture: the meaning of style.* London: Methuen.

Heelas, Paul. (1982). Anthropology, violence and catharsis. In Peter Marsh & Anne Campbell (Eds.), *Aggression and violence* (pp. 47–61). Oxford: Blackwell.

Heelas, Paul & Andrew Lock. (Eds.). (1981). *Indigenous psychologies: the anthropology of the self.* London: Academic.

Heesterman, J. C. (1985). Power, priesthood, and authority. In J. C. Heesterman (Ed.), *The inner conflict of tradition* (pp. 141–157). Chicago, IL: University of Chicago Press.

Hegel, Georg Wilhelm Friedrich. (1975). *Lectures on the philosophy of world history: introduction, reason in history* [Vorlesungen über die Philosophie der Geschichte: Einleitung, Jena, 1837]. Cambridge: Cambridge University Press.

Heidegger, Martin. (1962). *Being and time* [Sein und Zeit, Halle, 1929]. London: SCM.

Heider, Karl G. (1976). *Ethnographic film.* Austin: University of Texas Press.

———(1991). *Landscapes of emotion: mapping three cultures in Indonesia.* Cambridge: Cambridge University Press.

Heise, David. (1991). Event structure analysis. In Nigel Fielding & Raymond Lee (Eds.), *Using computers in qualitative research* (pp. 136–163). Newbury Park, CA: Sage.

Heldenbrand, Kathleen. (1996). Unwitting pioneers: Sudanese refugees in the Midwest. In Ann M. Rynearson & James Phillips (Eds.), *Selected papers on refugee issues,* 4 (pp. 106–129). Arlington, VA: American Anthropological Association.

Helm, June. (Ed.). (1968). *Essays on the problem of tribe.* Seattle: University of Washington Press.

Helms, Mary. (1979). *Ancient Panama: chiefs in search of power.* Austin: University of Texas Press.

Hempel, Carl. (1959). The logic of functional analysis. In Llewellyn Gross (Ed.), *Symposium on sociological theory* (pp. 271–307). New York: Row & Peterson.

Hendricks, J. (1992). Dependency theory. In E. Borgatta & M. Borgatta (Eds.), *Encyclopedia of sociology* (1: 458–766). New York: Macmillan.

Henry, Frances & Satish Saberwal. (Eds.). (1969). *Stress and response in fieldwork.* New York: Holt.

Henry, Jules. (1973). *On sham vulnerability and other forms of self-destruction.* New York: Vintage.

Henry, Jules & Zunia Henry. (1944). *Doll play of Pilaga Indian children: an experimental and field analysis of the behavior of the Pilaga Indian children.* New York: American Orthopsychiatric Association.

Herdt, Gilbert H. (1981). *Guardians of the flutes: idioms of masculinity.* New York: McGraw-Hill.

———(Ed.). (1982). *Rituals of manhood.* Berkeley: University of California Press.

———(Ed.). (1984). *Ritualized homosexuality in Melanesia.* Berkeley: University of California Press.

———(Ed.). (1992). *Gay culture in America: essays from the field.* Boston, MA: Beacon.

———(Ed.). (1994). *Third sex, third gender: beyond sexual dimorphism in culture and history.* New York: Zone.

Herdt, Gilbert H. & Robert J. Stoller. (1990). *Intimate communications: erotics and the study of a culture.* New York: Columbia University Press.

Héritier, Françoise. (1982). The symbolics of incest and its prohibition. In Michel Izard & Pierre Smith (Eds.), *Between belief and transgression* [Fonction symbolique, Paris, 1979] (pp. 152–179). Chicago, IL: University of Chicago Press.

Hern, Warren M. (1971). Is pregnancy really normal? *Family Planning Perspectives* 3: 5–10.

———(1975). The illness parameters of pregnancy. *Social Science and Medicine* 9: 365–372.

———(1990). Why are there so many of us? Description and diagnosis of a planetary ecopathological process. *Population and Environment* 12: 9–39.

Herodotus. (1987 [440 B.C.E.]). *The history* transl. by David Grene. Chicago, IL: University of Chicago Press.

Herskovits, Melville J. (1926). The cattle complex in East Africa. *American Anthropologist* 28: 230–72, 361–88, 494–528.

———(1940). *The economic life of primitive peoples.* New York: Knopf.

——— (1941). *The myth of the Negro past.* New York: Harper.

——— (1948). *Man and his works: the science of cultural anthropology.* New York: Knopf.

——— (1965). A genealogy of ethnological theory. In Melford E. Spiro (Ed.), *Context and meaning in cultural anthropology* (pp. 403–15). New York: Free Press.

——— (1972). *Cultural relativism.* New York: Random.

Hertz, Robert. (1960a). A contribution to the study of the collective representation of death [Représentation collective de la mort, Paris, 1907]. In *Death and the right hand.* Glencoe, IL: Free Press.

——— (1960b). The pre-eminence of the right hand [Prééminence de la main droite, Paris, 1909]. In *Death and the right hand.* Glencoe, IL: Free Press.

——— (1970). *Sociologie religieuse et folklore.* Paris: Presses Universitaires de France.

Herzfeld, Michael. (1985). *The poetics of manhood: contest and identity in a Cretan mountain village.* Princeton, NJ: Princeton University Press.

——— (1987). *Anthropology through the looking-glass: critical ethnography in the margins of Europe.* Cambridge: Cambridge University Press.

Herzog, George. (1936). A comparison of Pueblo and Pima musical styles. *Journal of American Folklore* 49: 283–417.

Hesse, Brian. (1982). Slaughter patterns and domestication: the beginnings of pastoralism in western Iran. *Man* 17(3): 403–417.

Heusch, Luc de. (1985). *Sacrifice in Africa: a structuralist approach.* Manchester: Manchester University Press.

Hewitt, Kenneth. (Ed.). (1983). *Interpretations of calamity from the viewpoint of human ecology.* Boston, MA: Allen & Unwin.

Hewitt de Alcantara, Cynthia. (1994). *Economic restructuring and rural subsistence in Mexico: corn and the crisis of the 1980s.* Geneva: UNRISD.

Hewlett, Barry S. (1991). *Intimate fathers: the nature and context of Aka Pygmy paternal infant care.* Ann Arbor: University of Michigan Press.

——— (Ed.). (1992). *Father–child relations: cultural and biosocial contexts.* Hawthorne, NY: Aldine De Gruyter.

Hiatt, Lester R. (1965). *Kinship and conflict: a study of an Aboriginal community in Northern Arnhem Land.* Canberra: Australian National University Press.

——— (1967). Authority and reciprocity in Australian Aboriginal marriage arrangements. *Mankind* 6: 468–475.

——— (1968). Gidjingali marriage arrangements. In Richard B. Lee & Irven DeVore (Eds.), *Man the hunter* (pp. 165–175). Chicago, IL: Aldine.

Hickey, Gerald C. (1982). *Free in the forest: ethnohistory of the Vietnamese central highlands, 1954–1976.* New Haven, CT: Yale University Press.

Hicks, John Richard. (1969). *A theory of economic history.* Oxford: Clarendon.

Higgins, Michael James. (1983). *Somos tocayos: anthropology of urbanism and poverty.* Lanham, MD: University Press of America.

Hildreth, Ellen C. & Shimon Ullman. (1989). The computational study of vision. In Michael I. Posner (Ed.), *Foundations of cognitive science.* (pp. 581–630). Cambridge, MA: MIT Press.

Hill, Jane & Kenneth Hill. (1986). *Speaking Mexicano: dynamics of syncretic language in Central Mexico.* Tucson: University of Arizona Press.

Hill, Jane & Judith Irvine. (Eds.). (1993). *Responsibility and evidence in oral discourse.* Cambridge: Cambridge University Press.

Hill, Jane & Bruce Mannheim. (1992). Language and world view. *Annual Review of Anthropology* 21: 381–406.

Hillier, Bill & Julienne Hanson. (1984). *The social logic of space.* Cambridge: Cambridge University Press.

Hinde, Robert A. (1966). *Animal behavior: a synthesis of ethology and comparative psychology.* New York: McGraw-Hill.

——— (1982). *Ethology: its nature and relations with other sciences.* Oxford: Oxford University Press.

Hinsley, Curtis M. (1994). *The Smithsonian and the American Indian: making a moral anthropology in Victorian America.* Washington, DC: Smithsonian.

Hirschon, Renée. (Ed.). (1984). *Women*

and property: women as property. London: Croom Helm.

Hobart, Mark. (Ed.). (1993). *An anthropological critique of development: the growth of ignorance.* London: Routledge.

Hobbes, Thomas. (1651). *Leviathan: or, The matter, forme, and power of a common wealth, ecclesiasticall and civil.* London: Andrew Crooke.

Hoben, Allan. (1973). *Land tenure among the Amhara of Ethiopia: the dynamics of cognitive descent.* Chicago, IL: University of Chicago Press.

——— (1982). Anthropologists and development. *Annual Review of Anthropology* 11: 349–376.

——— (1995). Paradigms and politics: the cultural construction of environmental policy in Ethiopia. *World Development* 23(6): 1007–1021.

Hobhouse, Leonard T. (1906). *Morals in evolution: a study in comparative ethics* (2 vols.). New York: Holt.

Hobsbawm, Eric. (1987). *Age of empire, 1875–1914.* New York: Pantheon.

Hobsbawm, Eric & Terence Ranger (Eds.). (1983). *The invention of tradition.* Cambridge: Cambridge University Press.

Hocart, Arthur M. (1954). *Social origins.* London: Watts.

Hochschild, Arlie. (1983). *The managed heart: commercialization of human feeling.* Berkeley: University of California Press.

Hock, Hans Henrich. (1986). *Principles of historical linguistics.* Berlin: Mouton de Gruyter.

Hockett, Charles. (1960). The origin of speech. *Scientific American* 203(3): 88–96.

——— (1966). The problem of universals in language. In Joseph H. Greenberg (Ed.), *Universals of language* [2nd edn.] (pp. 1–29). Cambridge, MA: MIT Press.

Hockings, Paul. (Ed.). (1995). *Principles of visual anthropology* [2nd edn.]. Berlin: de Gruyter.

Hockings, Paul & Yaushiro Omori. (Eds.). (1988). *Cinematographic theory and new directions in ethnographic film.* Osaka: National Museum of Ethnology.

Hodder, Ian. (1985). Postprocessual archaeology. In Michael Schiffer (Ed.), *Advances in archaeological method and theory,* vol. 8 (pp. 1–26). New York: Academic.

——— (1991a). *Reading the past: current approaches to interpretation in archaeology* [2nd edn.]. Cambridge: Cambridge University Press.

——— (1991b). Postprocessual archaeology and the current debate. In Robert Preucel (Ed.), *Processual and postprocessual archaeologies* (pp. 30–41). Carbondale, IL: Center for Archaeological Investigations, Southern Illinois University.

Hodder, Ian & Clive Orton. (1976). *Spatial analysis in archaeology.* Cambridge: Cambridge University Press.

Hodges, Richard. (1988). *Primitive and peasant markets.* Oxford: Blackwell.

Hoebel, E. Adamson. (1954). *The law of primitive man: a study in comparative legal dynamics.* Cambridge, MA: Harvard University Press.

——— (1960). *The Cheyennes: Indians of the Great Plains.* New York: Holt.

Hofbauer, Josef & Karl Sigmund. (1988). *The theory of evolution and dynamical systems.* Cambridge: Cambridge University Press.

Hoffman, Stanley. (1981). *Duties beyond borders: on the limits and possibilities of ethical international politics.* Syracuse: Syracuse University Press.

Hofstadter, Richard. (1955). *Social Darwinism in American thought* [rev. edn.]. Boston, MA: Beacon.

Hoijer, Harry. (Ed.). (1954). *Language and culture: conference on the interrelations of language and other aspects of culture.* Chicago, IL: University of Chicago Press.

Holland, Dorothy & Naomi Quinn. (Eds.). (1987). *Cultural models in language and thought.* Cambridge: Cambridge University Press.

Hollis, Martin & Steven Lukes. (Eds.). (1982). *Rationality and relativism.* Oxford: Blackwell.

Hollis, Susan T., Linda Pershing & M. Jane Young. (Eds.). (1993). *Feminist theory and the study of folklore.* Urbana: University of Illinois Press.

Holloway, Ralph. (1992). Culture: a human domain. *Current Anthropology* 33: 47–64.

Holmes, Lowell Don. (1987). *Quest for the real Samoa: the Mead/Freeman controversy and beyond.* South Hadley, MA: Bergin & Garvey.

Holmes, Janet. (1992). *An introduction to sociolinguistics.* London: Longman.

Holquist, Michael. (1990). *Dialogism: Bakhtin and his world.* London: Routledge.

Holston, James. (1989). *The modernist city: an anthropological critique of Brasília.* Chicago, IL: University of Chicago Press.

Holt, Claire. (1939). *Dance quest in Celebes.* Paris: Archives Internationales de la Danse.

Homer-Dixon, Thomas, Jeffery Boutwell & George Rathjens. (1993). Environmental change and violent conflict. *Scientific American* 268: 38–45.

Honigmann, John J. (1976). *The development of anthropological ideas.* Homewood, IL: Dorsey Press.

Hood, Mantle. (1971). *The ethnomusicologist.* New York: McGraw-Hill.

hooks, bell. (1981). *Ain't I a woman? Black women and feminism.* Boston, MA: South End Press.

Hopkins, MaryCarol & Nancy D. Donnelly. (Eds.). (1993). *Selected papers on refugee issues: II.* Arlington, VA: American Anthropological Association.

Hopper, Paul J. & Elizabeth Traugott. (1993). *Grammaticalization.* Cambridge: Cambridge University Press.

Horkheimer, Max & Theodor Adorno. (1972). *The dialectic of enlightenment* [Philosophische Fragmente, Frankfurt, 1969]. New York: Seabury.

Horowitz, Irving. (Ed.). (1967). *The rise and fall of Project Camelot: studies in the relationship between social science and practical politics.* Cambridge, MA: MIT Press.

Horowitz, Michael & Thomas Painter. (Eds.). (1986). *Anthropology and rural development in West Africa.* Boulder, CO: Westview.

Horton, Robin. (1967). African traditional thought and Western science. *Africa.* 37: 50–71, 155–187.

———(1968). Neo-Tylorianism: sound sense or sinister prejudice? *Man* 3: 625–634.

———(1993). *Patterns of thought in Africa and the West: essays on magic, religion, and science.* Cambridge: Cambridge University Press.

Horton, Robin & Ruth Finnegan. (Eds.). (1973). *Modes of thought: essays on thinking in Western and non-Western societies.* London: Faber.

Hosken, Fran. (1993). *The Hosken report: genital and sexual mutilation of females* [4th rev. edn.]. Lexington, MA: Women's International Network News.

Hoskins, Janet. (Ed.). (1996). *Headhunting and the social imagination in Southeast Asia.* Stanford: Stanford University Press.

Hostetler, John. (1993). *Amish society* [4th edn.]. Baltimore, MD: Johns Hopkins University Press.

Howard, Alan. (1985). Ethnopsychology and the prospects for a cultural psychology. In Geoffrey White & John Kirkpatrick (Eds.), *Person, self, and experience* (pp. 401–420). Berkeley: University of California Press.

Howard, Jane. (1984). *Margaret Mead, a life.* New York: Simon & Schuster.

Howard, Michael & Patrick McKim. (1983). *Contemporary cultural anthropology.* Boston, MA: Little, Brown.

Howe, Leopold E. A. (1981). The social determination of knowledge: Maurice Bloch and Balinese time. *Man* 16(2): 220–234.

Howell, Nancy. (1979). *The demography of the Dobe !Kung.* New York: Academic.

———(1986). Demographic anthropology. *Annual Review of Anthropology* 15: 219–246.

Howell, Signe. (1984). *Society and cosmos: Chewong of peninsular Malaysia.* Oxford: Oxford University Press.

Howell, Signe & Roy Willis. (Eds.). (1989). *Societies at peace: anthropological perspectives.* London: Routledge.

Hoy, David C. (Ed.). (1986). *Foucault: a critical reader.* Oxford: Blackwell.

Hrdy, Sarah. (1981). *The woman that never evolved.* Cambridge, MA: Harvard University Press.

Hsu, Francis. (Ed.). (1961). *Psychological anthropology: approaches to culture and personality.* Homewood, IL: Dorsey.

Hubert, Henri. (1905). *Étude sommaire de*

la représentation du temps dans la religion et la magie. Paris: Impr. Nationale.

Hubert, Henri & Marcel Mauss. (1964). *Sacrifice: its nature and function* [Essai sur la nature et le fonction du sacrifice, Paris, 1899]. Chicago, IL: University of Chicago Press.

Hubert, Lawrence J. (1987). *Assignment methods in combinatorial data analysis*. New York: Dekker.

Hudson, Alan. (1992). Diglossia: a bibliographic review. *Language in Society* 21: 611–674.

Hudson, Richard A. (1980). *Sociolinguistics*. Cambridge: Cambridge University Press.

Hugh-Jones, Christine. (1979). *From the milk river: spatial and temporal processes in Northwest Amazonia*. Cambridge: Cambridge University Press.

Hughes, Diane Owen & Thomas R. Trautmann. (Eds.). (1995). *Time: histories and ethnologies*. Ann Arbor: University of Michigan Press.

Hughes, H. Stuart. (1975). *The sea change: the migration of social thought 1930–1965*. New York: Harper & Row.

Hughes, J. Donald. (1983). *American Indian ecology*. El Paso: Texas Western.

Hull, David. (1992). Biological species: an inductivist's nightmare. In Mary Douglas & David Hull (Eds.), *How classification works* (pp. 42–68). Edinburgh: Edinburgh University Press.

Humphrey, Caroline. (1983). *Karl Marx collective*. Cambridge: Cambridge University Press.

Humphrey, Caroline & Stephen Hugh-Jones. (Eds.). (1992a). *Barter, exhange and value: an anthropological approach*. Cambridge: Cambridge University Press.

———(1992b). Introduction: Barter, exchange and value. In Caroline Humphrey & Stephen Hugh-Jones (Eds.), *Barter, exhange and value* (pp. 1–20). Cambridge: Cambridge University Press.

Hunn, Eugene S. (1977). *Tzeltal folk zoology: the classification of discontinuities in nature*. New York: Academic.

Hunt, Eva. (1977). *The transformation of the hummingbird: cultural roots of a Zinacantecan mythical poem*. Ithaca, NY: Cornell University Press.

Hunt, George. (1940). *The wars of the Iroquois: a study of intertribal trade relations*. Madison: University of Wisconsin Press.

Hunt, Robert C. & Eva Hunt. (1976). Canal irrigation and local social control. *Current Anthropology* 17: 389–411.

Huntington, Richard & Peter Metcalf. (1979). *Celebrations of death: the anthropology of mortuary ritual*. Cambridge: Cambridge University Press.

Huss-Ashmore, Rebecca & Solomon H. Katz. (Eds.). (1989–90). *African food systems in crisis* (2 vols.). New York: Gordon & Breach.

Husserl, Edmund. (1964). *The idea of phenomenology* [Idee der Phänomenologie, Hague, 1950]. The Hague: Nijhoff.

———(1970). *The crisis of European sciences and transcendental phenomenology* [Krisis der europäischen Wissenschaften und die transzendentale Phänomenologie, Hague, 1954]. Evanston, IL: Northwestern University Press.

Hutchins, Edwin. (1987). Myth and experience in the Trobriand Islands. In Dorothy Holland & Naomi Quinn (Eds.), *Cultural models in language and thought*. (pp. 269–289). Cambridge: Cambridge University Press.

Hutchinson, Sharon. (1990). Rising divorce among the Nuer, 1936–1983. *Man* 25(3): 393–411.

———(1996). *Nuer dilemmas: coping with money, war, and the state*. Berkeley: University of California Press.

Huxley, Julian S. (1942). *Evolution, the modern synthesis*. London: Allen & Unwin.

Hymes, Dell. (1962). The ethnography of speaking. In Thomas Gladwin & William Sturtevant (Eds.), *Anthropology and human behavior* (pp. 15–53). Washington, DC: Anthropology Society of Washington.

———(1964a). A perspective for linguistic anthropology. In Sol Tax (Ed.), *Horizons of anthropology* (pp. 92–107). Chicago, IL: Aldine.

———(1964b). *Language in culture and society: a reader in linguistics and anthropology*. New York: Harper & Row.

————(1974). *Foundations in sociolinguistics: an ethnographic approach.* Philadelphia: University of Pennsylvania Press.

————(1975). Folklore's nature and the sun's myth. *Journal of American Folklore* 88: 345–369.

————(1981). *"In vain I tried to tell you": essays in Native American ethnopoetics.* Philadelphia: University of Pennsylvania Press.

Ibn Khaldun. (1967). *The Muqaddimah* (abridged). Princeton, NJ: Princeton University Press.

Ibrahim, Muhammad H. (1983). Linguistic distance and literacy in Arabic. *Journal of Pragmatics,* 7: 507–515.

Inden, Ronald. (1990). *Imagining India.* Oxford: Blackwell.

Ingold, Tim. (1980). *Hunters, pastoralists and ranchers.* Cambridge: Cambridge University Press.

————(Ed.). (1988a). *What is an animal?* London: Unwin Hyman.

————(1988b). Introduction. In Tim Ingold (Ed.), *What is an animal?* (pp. 1–16). London: Unwin Hyman.

Ingold, Tim, David Riches & James Woodburn. (Eds.). (1988). *Hunters and gatherers.* Oxford: Berg.

Inhorn, Marcia & Peter J. Brown. (Eds.). (1997). *The anthropology of infectious diseases: international health perspectives.* New York: Gordon & Breach.

Inkeles, Alex & Donald J. Levinson. (1996). *National character: a psycho-social perspective.* New Brunswick, NJ: Transaction.

Insel, T., J. Zohar, C. Benkelfat & D. Murphy. (1990). Serotonin in obsessions, compulsions, and the control of aggressive impulses. *Annals of the New York Academy of Sciences* 600: 574–586.

Isaac, Glynn. (1989). *The archaeology of human origins: papers* ed. by Barbara Issac. Cambridge: Cambridge University Press.

Jackendoff, Ray. (1993). *Patterns in the mind: language and human nature.* New York: Harvester Wheatsheaf.

Jackson, Bruce. (1987). *Fieldwork.* Urbana: University of Illinois Press.

Jackson, Jean E. (1990). "I am a fieldnote": fieldnotes as a symbol of professional identity. In Roger Sanjek (Ed.), *Fieldnotes* (pp. 3–33). Ithaca, NY: Cornell University Press.

Jackson, John A. (Ed.). (1968). *Social stratification.* London: Cambridge University Press.

Jackson, Michael. (1986). *Barawa and the ways birds fly in the sky: an ethnographic novel.* Washington, DC: Smithsonian.

————(1989). *Paths toward a clearing: radical empiricism and ethnographic inquiry.* Bloomington: Indiana University Press.

————(Ed.). (1996). *Things as they are: new directions in phenomenological anthropology.* Bloomington: Indiana University Press.

Jacobs, Jane. (1961). *The death and life of great American cities.* New York: Random.

————(1996). *Edge of empire: postcolonialism and the city.* London: Routledge.

Jacobs, Sue-Ellen. (1983). Response to the North American berdache. *Current Anthropology* 24(4): 459–460.

Jacobson, David. (1973). *Itinerant townsmen: friendship and social order in urban Uganda.* Menlo Park, CA: Cummings.

Jakobson, Roman. (1956). *Fundamentals of language.* The Hague: Mouton.

————(1957). *Shifters, verbal categories and the Russian verb.* Cambridge, MA: Harvard University Russian Language Project.

————(1960). Concluding statement: linguistics and poetics. In Thomas A. Sebeok (Ed.), *Style in language* (pp. 350–385). Cambridge, MA: MIT Press.

————(1978). *Six lectures on sound and meaning.* Cambridge, MA: MIT Press.

————(1987). *Language in literature.* Cambridge, MA: Belknap Press.

James, Wendy. (1979). *Kwanim Pa: the making of the Uduk people.* Oxford: Clarendon.

Jameson, Fredric. (1991). *Postmodernism, or, the cultural logic of late capitalism.* Durham, NC: Duke University Press.

Jankowiak, William. (1993). *Sex, death, and hierarchy in a Chinese city: an anthropological account.* New York: Columbia University Press.

————(Ed.). (1995). *Romantic passion: the universal experience?* New York: Columbia University Press.

Jankowiak, William & Edward Fischer. (1992). A cross-cultural perspective on romantic love. *Ethnology* 31: 149–155.

Jankowiak, William, Elizabeth Hill & James Donovan. (1992). The effects of gender and sexual orientation on attractiveness judgments: an evolutionary interpretation. *Ethnology and Sociobiology* 13: 73–85.

Janzen, John. (1978). *The quest for therapy in Lower Zaire.* Berkeley: University of California Press.

Jay, Martin. (1973). *The dialectical imagination: a history of the Frankfurt School and the Institute for Social Research 1923–1950.* Boston, MA: Little, Brown.

Jeffers, Robert J. & Ilse Lehiste. (1979). *Principles and methods for historical linguistics.* Cambridge, MA: MIT Press.

Jencks, Christopher & Paul E. Peterson. (1991). *The urban underclass.* Washington, DC: Brookings Institution.

Jenkins, Richard. (1982). Pierre Bourdieu and the reproduction of determinism. *Sociology* 16: 270–281.

————(1992). *Pierre Bourdieu.* London: Routledge.

Jerison, Harry J. (1973). *Evolution of the brain and intelligence.* New York: Academic Press.

Jerome, Norge, Randy Kandel & Gretel Pelto. (Eds.). (1980). *Nutritional anthropology.* Pleasantville, NY: Redgrave.

Johannes, Robert E. (1978). Traditional marine conservation methods in oceania and their demise. *Annual Review of Ecology and Systematics* 9: 349–364.

————(1981). *Words of the lagoon: fishing and marine lore in the Palau district of Micronesia.* Berkeley: University of California Press.

John, Mary. (1996). *Discrepant dislocations: feminism, theory and postcolonial histories.* Berkeley: University of California Press.

Johnson, Allen & Clifford Behrens. (1989). Time allocation research and aspects of method in cross-cultural comparisons. *Journal of Quantitative Anthropology* 1: 313–334.

Johnson, Allen & Timothy Earle.

(1987). *The evolution of human societies: from foraging group to agrarian state.* Stanford, CA: Stanford University Press.

Johnson, Douglas. (1982). Evans-Pritchard, the Nuer, and the Sudan Political Service. *African Affairs* 81: 231–246.

Johnson, Gregory A. (1982). Organizational structure and scalar stress. In Colin Renfrew, M. Rowlands & B. Segraves (Eds.), *Theory and explanation in archaeology* (pp. 389–421). New York: Academic.

Johnson, Jeffrey. (1994). Anthropological contributions to the study of social networks. In Stanley Wasserman & Joseph Galaskiewicz (Eds.), *Advances in social network analysis* (pp. 113–151). Thousand Oaks, CA: Sage.

Johnson, Mark. (1987). *The body in the mind: the bodily basis of meaning, imagination, and reason.* Chicago, IL: University of Chicago Press.

Johnson, Patricia L., James W. Wood, Kenneth L. Campbell & Ila Maslar. (1987). Long ovarian cycles in women of highland New Guinea. *Human Biology* 59: 837–845.

Johnston, Barbara R. (Ed.). (1994). *Who pays the price? The sociocultural context of environmental crisis.* Washington, DC: Island Press.

Johnston, Francis E. & Setha Low. (1984). Biomedical anthropology: an emerging synthesis. *Yearbook of Physical Anthropology* 27: 215–227.

Jones, Delmos & Ida Susser. (Eds.). (1993). Special issue: The widening gap between rich and poor. *Critique of Anthropology* 13(3).

Jones, Ernest. (1925). Mother-right and the sexual ignorance of savages. *International Journal of Psycho-Analysis* 6: 109–130.

Jones, Greta. (1980). *Social Darwinism and English thought: the interaction between biological and social theory.* Brighton: Harvester Press.

Jones, Steve, Robert D. Martin & David R. Pilbeam. (Eds.). (1992). *The Cambridge encyclopedia of human evolution.* Cambridge: Cambridge University Press.

Jongmans, D. G. & P. C. W. Gutkind.

(Eds.). (1967). *Anthropologists in the field.* Assen: Van Gorcum.

Jordan, Brigitte. (1978/93). *Birth in four cultures: a cross-cultural investigation of childbirth in Yucatan, Holland, Sweden and the United States.* Montreal: Eden Press [4th rev. edn. by Robbie Davis-Floyd, Waveland, 1993].

Jordan, Glenn. (1991). On ethnography in an intertextual situation: reading narratives or deconstructing discourse? In Faye Harrison (Ed.), *Decolonizing anthropology* (pp. 42–67). Washington, DC: American Anthropological Association.

——— (1997). *Racism and the black subject.* Oxford: Blackwell.

Jordan, Glenn & Chris Weedon. (1995). *Cultural politics: class, gender, race and the modern world.* Oxford: Blackwell.

Josephides, Lisette. (1985). *The production of inequality: gender and exchange among the Kewa.* London: Tavistock.

Judge, George et al. (1985). *The theory and practice of econometrics* [2nd edn.]. New York: Wiley.

Jung, Carl G. et al. (Eds.). (1964). *Man and his symbols.* London: Aldus.

Junker, Laura. (1990). The organization of intra-regional and long-distance trade in prehispanic Philippine complex societies. *Asian Perspectives* 29: 167–209.

Kaeppler, Adrienne. (1972). Method and theory in analyzing dance structure with an analysis of Tongan dance. *Ethnomusicology* 16(2): 173–217.

——— (1978). *Artificial curiosities.* Honolulu, HI: Bishop Museum.

——— (1985). Structured movement systems in Tonga. In Paul Spencer (Ed.), *Society and the dance* (pp. 92–118). Cambridge: Cambridge University Press.

——— (1993). *Hula pahu: Hawaiian drum dances* (2 vols.). Honolulu: Bishop Museum Press.

Kahn, Joel & Josep Llobera. (1981). *The anthropology of pre-capitalist societies.* London: Macmillan.

Kakar, Sudhir. (1981). *The inner world: a psycho-analytic study of childhood and society in India* [2nd edn.]. Delhi: Oxford University Press.

Kan, Sergei. (1989). *Symbolic immortality: the Tlingit potlatch of the nineteenth century.* Washington, DC: Smithsonian.

Kapferer, Bruce. (Ed.). (1976a). *Transaction and meaning: directions in the anthropology of exchange and symbolic behavior.* Philadelphia, PA: ISHI.

——— (1976b). Introduction: Transactional models reconsidered. In Bruce Kapferer (Ed.), *Transaction and meaning* (pp. 1–22). Philadelphia, PA: ISHI.

——— (1983). *A celebration of demons: exorcism and the aesthetics of healing in Sri Lanka.* Bloomington: Indiana University Press [2nd rev. edn., Smithsonian, 1993].

——— (1987). The anthropology of Max Gluckman. *Social Analysis* 22: 3–21.

——— (1988). *Legends of people, myths of state: violence, intolerance, and political culture in Sri Lanka and Australia.* Washington, DC: Smithsonian.

Kaplan, Hillard & Kim Hill. (1985). Hunting ability and reproductive success among Ache foragers: preliminary results. *Current Anthropology* 26(1): 131–133.

Kaplan, Joanna Overing. (1975). *The Piaroa: a people of the Orinoco Basin: a study in kinship and marriage.* Oxford: Clarendon.

Kaplan, Martha. (1995). Panoptican in Poona: an essay on Foucault and colonialism. *Cultural Anthropology* 10(1): 85–98.

Kardiner, Abram. (1939). *The individual and his society: the psychodynamics of primitive social organization.* New York: Columbia University Press.

——— (1945). *The psychological frontiers of society.* New York: Columbia University Press.

Karim, Wazir-Jahan. (1981). *Ma Betisek concepts of living things.* London: Athlone.

Karp, Ivan & Steven D. Lavine. (Eds.). (1991). *The poetics and politics of museum display.* Washington, DC: Smithsonian.

Karp, Ivan & Kent Maynard. (1983). Reading the Nuer. *Current Anthropology* 24: 481–503.

Kasaba, Resat. (Ed.). (1991). *Cities in the world system.* New York: Greenwood.

Katz, Jacob. (1993). *Tradition and crisis: Jewish society at the end of the Middle Ages* [rev. edn.]. New York: New York University Press.

Katz, Jerrold J. & Jerry A. Fodor. (1963). The structure of a semantic theory. *Language* 39: 170–210.

Kauffman, Stuart A. (1993). *The origins of order: self-organization and selection in evolution.* Oxford: Oxford University Press.

Kaufman, Debra R. (1991). *Rachel's daughters: newly Orthodox Jewish women.* New Brunswick, NJ: Rutgers University Press.

Kay, Geoffrey. (1975). *Development and underdevelopment: a marxist analysis.* London: Macmillan.

Kealiinohomoku, Joann. (1976). *Reflections and perspectives on two anthropological studies of dance.* New York: Committee on Research in Dance.

Kearney, Michael. (1986). From the invisible hand to visible feet: anthropological studies of migration and development. *Annual Review of Anthropology* 15: 331–361.

Keesing, Roger. (1972). Paradigms lost: the New Ethnography and the New Linguistics. *Southwestern Journal of Anthropology* 28(4): 299–332.

———(1985). Kwaio women speak: the micropolitics of autobiography in a Solomon Island society. *American Anthropologist* 87(1): 27–39.

———(1987). Models, "folk" and "cultural": paradigms regained? In Dorothy Holland & Naomi Quinn (Eds.), *Cultural models in language and thought* (pp. 369–393). Cambridge: Cambridge University Press.

Keil, Charles. (1979). *Tiv Song: the sociology of art in a classless society.* Chicago, IL: University of Chicago Press.

Keil, Charles & Steven Feld. (1994). *Music grooves: essays and dialogues.* Chicago, IL: University of Chicago Press.

Keith, Jennie & Associates. (1994). *The aging experience: diversity and commonality across cultures.* Thousand Oaks, CA: Sage.

Keller, Evelyn Fox & Elisabeth Anne Lloyd. (1992). *Keywords in evolutionary biology.* Cambridge, MA: Harvard University Press.

Keller, Stephen L. (1975). *Uprooting and social change: the role of refugees in development.* Delhi: Manohar Book Service.

Kelley, Robert. (1995). *The foraging spectrum: diversity in hunter–gatherer lifeways.* Washington, DC: Smithsonian.

Kelly, Raymond. (1993). *Constructing inequality: the fabrication of a hierarchy of virtue among the Etoro.* Ann Arbor: University of Michigan Press.

Kelly-Byrne, Diana. (1989). *A child's play life: an ethnographic study.* New York: Teacher's College Press.

Kendon, Adam. (1977). *Studies in the behavior of social interaction.* Bloomington: Indiana University Press.

———(Ed.). (1981). *Non-verbal communication, interaction and gesture.* The Hague: Mouton.

Kennedy, Elizabeth L. & Madeline D. Davis. (1993). *Boots of leather, slippers of gold: the history of a lesbian community.* New York: Routledge.

Kenstowicz, Michael. (1994). *Phonology in generative grammar.* Oxford: Blackwell.

Kent, Susan. (Ed.). (1990). *Domestic architecture and the use of space: an interdisciplinary, cross-cultural study.* Cambridge: Cambridge University Press.

Kermode, Frank. (1979). *The genesis of secrecy: on the interpretation of narrative.* Cambridge, MA: Harvard University Press.

Kertzer, David. (1978). Theoretical developments in the study of age group systems. *American Ethnologist* 5: 368–374.

———(1988). *Ritual, politics, and power.* New Haven, CT: Yale University Press.

Kertzer, David & Tom Fricke. (Eds.). (1997). *Anthropological demography: towards a new synthesis.* Chicago, IL: University of Chicago Press.

Kertzer, David & Jennie Keith. (Eds.). (1984). *Age and anthropological theory.* Ithaca, NY: Cornell University Press.

Kevles, Daniel K. (1985). *In the name of eugenics: genetics and the uses of human heredity.* Berkeley: University of California Press.

Key, Mary Ritchie. (1975). *Paralanguage and kinesics (non-verbal communication).* Metuchen, NJ: Scarecrow.

Keyes, Charles F. (1976). Towards a new formulation of the concept of ethnic group. *Ethnicity* 3: 202–213.

———(1977). Millennialism, Theravada

Buddhism, and Thai society, *Journal of Asian Studies* 36: 283–302.

———(1981). The dialectics of ethnic change. In Charles F. Keyes (Ed.), *Ethnic change* (pp. 8–30). Seattle: University of Washington Press.

———(1991). The proposed world of the school: Thai villagers' entry into a bureaucratic state system. In Charles F. Keyes (Ed.), *Reshaping local worlds* (pp. 87–138). New Haven, CT: Yale University Southeast Asian Studies.

———(1996). Who are the Tai? Reflections on the invention of local, ethnic and national identities. In George De Vos & Lola Romanucci Ross (Eds.), *Ethnic change* [2nd. rev. edn.] (pp. 136–160). Walnut Creek, CA: Alta Mira.

Keyes, Charles F., Helen Hardacre & Laurel Kendall. (1994). Contested visions of community in East and Southeast Asia. In Charles F. Keyes, Laurel Kendall & Helen Hardacre (Eds.), *Asian visions of authority* (pp. 1–16). Honolulu: University of Hawaii Press.

Khare, Ravindra. (1976). *The Hindu hearth and home.* Durham, NC: Carolina Academic.

Khazanov, Anatoly. (1984). *Nomads and the outside world.* Cambridge: Cambridge University Press [rev. edn., University of Wisconsin Press, 1994].

———(1992). Soviet social thought in the period of stagnation. *Philosophy and the Social Sciences* 22: 231–237.

Kiernan, James P. (1982). "The problem of evil" in the context of ancestral intervention in the affairs of the living in Africa. *Man* 17: 287–301.

Kimball, Solon & James B. Watson. (Eds.). (1972). *Crossing cultural boundaries: the anthropological experience.* San Francisco, CA: Chandler.

Kimura, Doreen. (1996). Sex, sexual orientation and sex hormones influence cognitive function. *Current Opinion in Neurobiology* 6: 259–263.

King, Anthony. (1984). *The bungalow: the production of a global culture.* London: Routledge.

King, J. C. H. (1981). *Artifical curiosities from the Northwest Coast of America.* London: British Museum.

King, Leslie J. (1984). *Central place theory.* Beverly Hills, CA: Sage.

King, Robert D. (1969). *Historical linguistics and generative grammar.* Englewood Cliffs, NJ: Prentice Hall.

Kingsbury, Henry. (1988). *Music, talent and performance: a conservatory cultural system.* Philadelphia, PA: Temple University Press.

Kinzey, Warren G. (Ed.). (1987). *The evolution of human behavior: primate models.* Albany: State University of New York Press.

Kirch, Patrick. (1984). *The evolution of Polynesian chiefdoms.* Cambridge: Cambridge University Press.

Kirk, Geoffrey S. (1970). *Myth: its meaning and functions in ancient and other cultures.* Berkeley: University of California Press.

Kirkpatrick, John & Geoffrey M. White. (1985). Exploring ethnopsychologies. In Geoffrey White & John Kirkpatrick (Eds.), *Person, self, and experience* (pp. 3–34). Berkeley: University of California Press.

Kirshenblatt-Gimblett, Barbara. (1988). Mistaken dichotomies. *Journal of American Folklore.* 101: 140–155.

Kiser, Edagar & Kriss A. Drass. (1987). Changes in the core of the world-system and the production of utopian literature in Great Britain and the United States, 1883–1975. *American Sociological Review* 52: 286–293.

Kitayama, Shinobu & Hazel Markus. (Eds.). (1994). *Emotion and culture: empirical studies of mutual influence.* Washington, DC: American Psychological Association.

Kitzinger, Sheila. (1978). *Women as mothers: how they see themselves in different cultures.* New York: Random.

———(Ed.). (1991). *The midwife challenge.* London: Pandora.

Klass, Morton. (1980). *Caste: the emergence of the South Asian social system.* Philadelphia, PA: Institute for the Study of Social Issues.

Klee, Gary A. (Ed.). (1980). *World systems of traditional resource management.* New York: Wiley.

Klein, Anne. (1994). *Meeting the Great*

Bliss Queen: Buddhists, feminists, and the art of the self. Boston, MA: Beacon.

Kleinman, Arthur. (1980). *Patients and healers in the context of culture: an exploration of the borderland between anthropology, medicine, and psychiatry.* Berkeley: University of California Press.

———(1992). Pain and resistance. In Mary-Jo DelVecchio Good (Ed.), *Pain as human experience* (pp. 169–197). Berkeley: University of California Press.

———(1995). *Writing at the margin: discourse between anthropology and medicine.* Berkeley: University of California Press.

Kleinman, Arthur & Byron Good. (Eds.). (1985). *Culture and depression: studies in the anthropology and cross-cultural psychiatry of affect and disorder.* Berkeley: University of California Press.

Kleinman, Arthur, Veena Das & Margaret Lock. (Eds.). (1995). Special Issue: Social suffering. *Daedalus* 124(3).

Klekamp, Jörg, Agnes Riedel, Clive Harper & Hans Joachim Kretschmann. (1994). Morphometric study on the postnatal growth of the cerebral cortex of Australian Aborigines and Caucasians. *Journal für Hirnforschung* 35: 541–548.

Klima, Edward & Ursula Bellugi. (1979). *The signs of language.* Cambridge, MA: Harvard University Press.

Kluckhohn, Clyde. (1953). Universal categories of culture. In A. L. Kroeber (Ed.), *Anthropology today* (pp. 507–523). Chicago, IL: University of Chicago Press.

Knauft, Bruce M. (1985). *Good company and violence: sorcery and social action in a lowland New Guinea society.* Berkeley: University of California Press.

———(1989). Bodily images in Melanesia: cultural substances and natural metaphors. In Michel Feher (Ed.), *Fragments for a history of the human body,* vol. 3 (pp. 199–279). New York: Urzone.

———(1991). Violence and sociality in human evolution. *Current Anthropology* 32: 391–428.

Knight, Chris. (1985). Menstruation as medicine. *Social Science and Medicine* 21: 671–683.

———(1991). *Blood relations: menstruation*

and the origins of culture. New Haven, CT: Yale University Press.

Koch, Klaus-Friedrich. (1974). *War and peace in Jalemo: the management of conflict in Highland New Guinea.* Cambridge, MA: Harvard University Press.

———(1978). Pigs and politics in the New Guinea highlands: conflict escalation among the Jale. In Laura Nader & Harry Todd (Eds.), *The disputing process* (pp. 41–58). New York: Columbia University Press.

Koerner, Konrad. (1984). *Edward Sapir, appraisals of his life and work.* Amsterdam: Benjamins.

Köhler, Gernot. (1978). Global apartheid. World Order Models Project paper 7. New York: Institute for World Order. [republished in W. A. Haviland & R. J. Gordon (Eds.), *Talking about people,* Mayfield, 1993]

Kohler, Timothy A. (1992). Field houses, villages, and the tragedy of the commons in the early northern Anasazi Southwest. *American Antiquity* 57: 617–635.

———(1993). News from the northern American Southwest: prehistory on the edge of chaos. *Journal of Archaeological Research* 1: 267–321.

Köhler, Wolfgang. (1929). *Gestalt psychology.* New York: Liveright.

Kohn, Alfie. (1990). *The brighter side of human nature: altruism and empathy in everyday life.* New York: Basic.

Kondo, Dorinne. (1990). *Crafting selves: power, gender, and discourses of identity in a Japanese workplace.* Chicago, IL: University of Chicago Press.

Konner, Melvin. (1982). *The tangled wing: biological constraints on the human spirit.* New York: Holt.

Konner, Melvin & Marjorie Shostak. (1987). Timing and management of birth among the !Kung: biocultural interaction in reproductive adaptation. *Cultural Anthropology* 2(1): 11–28.

Konrad, Gyorgy & Ivan Szelenyi. (1979). *Intellectuals on the road to class power* [Ertelmiseg utja az osztalyhatalomboz, Budapest]. New York: Harcourt, Brace, Jovanovich.

Kopytoff, Igor. (1982). Slavery. *Annual Review of Anthropology* 11: 207–230.

Korn, Francis. (1973). *Elementary structures reconsidered: Lévi-Strauss on kinship.* London: Tavistock.

Koso-Thomas, Olayinka. (1987). *The circumcision of women: a strategy for eradication.* London: Zed.

Kottak, Conrad Philip. (Ed.). (1982). *Researching American culture: a guide for student anthropologists.* Ann Arbor: University of Michigan Press.

Kracke, Waud. (1978). *Force and persuasion: leadership in an Amazonian society.* Chicago, IL: University of Chicago Press.

Krapf-Askari, Eva. (1969). *Yoruba towns and cities: an enquiry into the nature of urban social phenomena.* Oxford: Clarendon.

Kratz, Corinne A. (1994). *Affecting performance: meaning, movement, and experience in Okiek women's initiation.* Washington, DC: Smithsonian.

Krebs, Dennis. (1987). The challenge of altruism in biology and psychology. In Charles Crawford, Martin Smith & Dennis Krebs (Eds.), *Sociobiology and psychology* (pp. 81–118). Hillsdale, NJ: Lawrence Erlbaum Associates.

Krebs, John R. & N. B. Davies. (Eds.). (1991). *Behavioural ecology* [3rd edn.]. Oxford: Blackwell.

———(1993). *An introduction to behavioural ecology* [3rd edn.]. Oxford: Blackwell.

Krech, Shepard. (1991). The state of ethnohistory. *Annual Review of Anthropology* 20: 345–375.

Kremer, James N. (1978). *A coastal marine ecosystem: simulation and analysis.* Berlin: Springer-Verlag.

Krieger, Leonard. (1989). *Time's reasons: philosophies of history old and new.* Chicago, IL: University of Chicago Press.

Krige, Eileen J. (1974). Woman-marriage, with special reference to the Lovedu: its significance for the definition of marriage. *Africa* 44: 11–36.

Kristiansen, Kristian. (1982). The formation of tribal systems in later European prehistory. In Colin Renfrew, Michael Rowlands, Barbara Seagraves (Eds.), *Theory and explanation in archaeology* (pp. 241–280). New York: Academic.

———(1984). Ideology and material culture: an archaeological perspective. In Matthew Spriggs (Ed.), *Marxist perspectives in archaeology* (pp. 72–100). Cambridge: Cambridge University Press.

———(1987). From stone to bronze: the evolution of social complexity in northern Europe, 2300–1200 BC. In E. Brumfiel & T. Earle (Eds.), *Specialization, exchange, and complex societies* (pp. 30–51). Cambridge: Cambridge University Press.

———(1991). Chiefdoms, states and systems of social evolution in northern Europe. In Timothy Earle (Ed.), *Chiefs* (pp. 16–43). Cambridge: Cambridge University Press.

Kroeber, Alfred L. (1909). Classificatory systems of relationship. *Journal of the Royal Anthropological Institute* 39: 77–84.

———(1915). The eighteen professions. *American Anthropologist* 17: 283–289.

———(1917a). The superorganic. *American Anthropologist* 19: 207–236.

———(1917b). *California kinship systems.* Berkeley: University of California Press.

———(1923). *Anthropology: race, language, culture, psychology, pre-history.* New York: Harcourt, Brace [rev. edn. 1948].

———(1925). *Handbook of the Indians of California.* Washington, DC: Smithsonian, Bureau of American Ethnology.

———(1935). History and science in anthropology. *American Anthropologist* 37: 539–569.

———(1936). *Area and climax.* Berkeley: University of California Press.

———(1939). *Cultural and natural areas of native North America.* Berkeley: University of California Press.

———(1944). *Configurations of culture growth.* Berkeley: University of California Press.

———(1948). *Anthropology: race, language, culture, psychology, pre-history* [rev. edn.]. New York: Harcourt, Brace.

———(1952). *The nature of culture.* Chicago, IL: University of Chicago Press.

———(1957). *Ethnographic interpretations.* Berkeley: University of California Press.

Kroeber, Alfred L. & Talcott Parsons. (1958). The concept of culture and of social system. *American Sociological Review* 23: 582–583.

Kroeber, Alfred L. & Jane Richardson. (1940). *Three centuries of women's dress fashions, a quantitative analysis.* Berkeley: University of California Press.

Kruskal, Joseph B. & Myron Wish. (1978). *Multidimensional scaling.* Beverly Hills, CA: Sage.

Krzanowski, Wojtek J. & F. H. Marriott. (1994). *Multivariate analysis.* London: Arnold.

Kuhn, Thomas S. (1962). *The structure of scientific revolutions.* Chicago, IL: University of Chicago Press.

Kuklick, Henrika. (1991). *The savage within: the social history of British anthropology, 1885–1945.* Cambridge: Cambridge University Press.

Kummer, Hans. (1971). *Primate societies: group techniques of ecological adaptation.* Chicago, IL: Aldine Atherton.

Kunstadter, Peter, E. C. Chapman & Sanga Sabhasri. (Eds.). (1978). *Farmers in the forest: economic development and marginal agriculture in Northern Thailand.* Honolulu: University of Hawaii Press.

Kuper, Adam. (1973). *Anthropology and anthropologists: the British School, 1922–1972.* Cambridge: Cambridge University Press.

———(Ed.). (1977). *The social anthropology of Radcliffe-Brown.* Boston, MA: Routledge.

———(1982a). *Wives for cattle: bridewealth and marriage in Southern Africa.* London: Routledge.

———(1982b). Lineage theory: a critical retrospective. *Annual Review of Anthropology* 11: 71–95.

———(1983, 1996). *Anthropology and anthropologists: the modern British school* (2nd rev. edn. 1983; 3rd rev. edn. 1996). London: Routledge.

———(1988). *The invention of primitive society: transformations of an illusion.* London: Routledge.

Kuper, Hilda. (1947). *An African aristocracy: rank among the Swazi.* London: Oxford University Press.

Kuper, Leo. (1974). *Race, class, and power: ideology and revolutionary change in plural societies.* Chicago, IL: Aldine.

———(1981). *Genocide: its political use in the twentieth century.* New Haven, CT: Yale University Press.

———(1984a). International protection against genocide in plural societies. In David Maybury-Lewis (Ed.), *The prospects for plural societies* (pp. 207–219). Washington, DC: American Ethnological Society.

———(1984b). *International action against genocide* [rev. edn.]. London: Minority Rights Group.

Kuper, Leo & M. G. Smith. (Eds.). (1969). *Pluralism in Africa.* Berkeley: University of California Press.

Kurath, Gertrude Prokosch. (1960). Panorama of dance ethnology. *Current Anthropology* 1(3): 233–254.

———(1986). *Half a century of dance research: essays.* Flagstaff, AZ: Cross-Cultural Dance Resources.

Kurzweil, Edith. (1980). *The age of structuralism: Lévi-Strauss to Foucault.* New York: Columbia University Press.

Kuznar, Lawrence A. (1991). Mathematical models of pastoral production and herd composition in traditional Andean herds. *Journal of Quantitative Anthropology* 3: 1–17.

Kwong, Peter. (1996). *The new Chinatown* [rev. edn.]. New York: Hill & Wang.

La Barre, Weston. (1938). *The Peyote cult.* New Haven, CT: Yale University Press. [5th rev. edn., University of Oklahoma Press, 1989]

———(1970). *The ghost dance: origins of religion.* Garden City, NY: Doubleday.

———(1977). Anthropological views of Cannabis. *Reviews in Anthropology* 4: 237–250.

———(1980). *Culture in context: selected writings of Weston La Barre.* Durham, NC: Duke University Press.

———(1995). The importance of ethnobotany in American anthropology. In Richard Schultes & Siri von Reis (Eds.), *Ethnobotany* (pp. 226–234). Portland, OR: Dioscorides.

Labov, William. (1972). *Sociolinguistic patterns.* Philadelphia: University of Pennsylvania Press.

———(1994). *Principles of linguistic change.* Oxford: Blackwell.

Laderman, Carol. (1983). *Wives and midwives: childbirth and nutrition in rural Malaysia.* Berkeley: University of California Press.

La Fontaine, Jean S. (Ed.). (1972). *The interpretation of ritual: essays in honour of A. I. Richards.* London: Tavistock.

———(1985). *Initiation.* Middlesex: Penguin.

Lakoff, George. (1971). On generative semantics. In Danny B. Steinberg & Leon A. Jakobovits (Eds.), *Semantics* (pp. 233–296). Cambridge: Cambridge University Press.

———(1987). *Women, fire, and dangerous things: what categories reveal about the mind.* Chicago, IL: University of Chicago Press.

Lakoff, George & Mark Johnson. (1980). *Metaphors we live by.* Chicago, IL: University of Chicago Press.

Lakoff, George & Zoltan Kövecses. (1987). The cognitive model of anger inherent in American English. In Dorothy Holland & Naomi Quinn (Eds.), *Cultural models in language and thought* (pp. 195–211). Cambridge: Cambridge University Press.

Lamar, Howard R. & Leonard Thompson. (Eds.). (1981). *The frontier in history: North America and Southern Africa compared.* New Haven, CT: Yale University Press.

Lambek, Michael. (1981). *Human spirits: a cultural account of trance in Mayotte.* Cambridge: Cambridge University Press.

Lamp, Frederick. (1988). Heavenly bodies: menses, moon, and rituals of license among the Temne of Sierra Leone. In Thomas Buckley & Alma Gottlieb (Eds.), *Blood magic* (pp. 210–231). Berkeley: University of California Press.

Lamphere, Louise. (1987). *From working daughters to working mothers: immigrant women in a New England community.* Ithaca, NY: Cornell University Press.

Lancaster, Roger N. (1992). *Life is hard: machismo, danger, and the intimacy of power in Nicaragua.* Berkeley: University of California Press.

Lancaster, William. (1981). *The Rwala Bedouin today.* Cambridge: Cambridge University Press.

Landau, Misia. (1991). *Narratives of human evolution.* New Haven, CT: Yale University Press.

Landmann, Michael. (1974). *Philosophical anthropology* [Philosophische Anthropologie, Berlin, 1964]. Philadelphia, PA: Westminster.

———(1979). *De homine: man in the mirror of his thought* [De homine, Freiberg, 1962]. Ann Arbor, MI: Applied Literature Press.

———(1982). *Fundamental anthropology* [Fundamental-Anthropologie, Bonn, 1979]. Lanham, MD: University Press of America.

Landsman, Gail & Sara Ciborski. (1992). Representation and politics: contesting histories of the Iroquois. *Cultural Anthropology* 7(4): 425–447.

Landtman, Gunnar. (1938). *The origin of the inequality of the social classes.* Chicago, IL: University of Chicago Press.

Lange, Roderyk. (1980). The development of anthropological dance research. *Dance Studies* 4: 1–36.

Langness, Lewis L. & Gelya Frank. (1981). *Lives: an anthropological approach to biography.* Novato, CA: Chandler & Sharp.

Lansing, J. Stephen. (1991). *Priests and programmers: technologies of power in the engineered landscape of Bali.* Princeton, NJ: Princeton University Press.

Lansing, J. Stephen & James N. Kremer. (1993). Emergent properties of Balinese water temples. *American Anthropologist* 95: 97–114.

Lanternari, Vittorio. (1963). *Religions of the oppressed: a study of modern messianic cults* [Movimenti religiosi di libertà, Milan, 1960]. New York: Knopf.

———(1976). *La grande festa: vita rituale e sistemi di produzione nelle società tradizionali.* Bari: Dedalo.

LaPointe, Françoise & Claire LaPointe. (1977). *Claude Lévi-Strauss and his critics: an international bibliography of criticism (1950–1976) followed by a bibliography of the writings of Claude Lévi-Strauss.* New York: Garland.

Laqueur, Thomas. (1990). *Making sex:*

body and gender from the Greeks to Freud. Cambridge, MA: Harvard University Press.

Larner, Christina. (1981). *Enemies of God: the witch-hunt in Scotland.* London: Chatto & Windus.

Lash, Scott & John Urry. (1994). *Economies of signs and space.* Thousand Oaks, CA: Sage.

Laslett, Peter. (1973). Age at menarche in Europe since the eighteenth century. In Theodore Rabb & Robert Rotberg (Eds.), *The family in history* (pp. 28–47). New York: Harper & Row.

Last, Murray. (1996). The professionalization of indigenous healers. In Carolyn Sargent & Thomas M. Johnson (Eds.), *Medical anthropology* [2nd edn.] (pp. 374–395). Westport, CT: Greenwood.

Laszlo, Ervin & Jong J. Yoo. (Eds.). (1986). *World encyclopedia of peace.* Oxford: Pergamon.

Latour, Bruno. (1979). *Laboratory life: the social construction of scientific facts.* Beverly Hills: Sage.

———(1987). *Science in action.* Cambridge, MA: Harvard University Press.

Lattimore, Owen. (1962). *Studies in frontier history: collected papers, 1928–58.* London: Oxford University Press.

Laughlin, Charles D. & Eugene G. D'Aquili. (1974). *Biogenetic structuralism.* New York: Columbia University Press.

Laughlin, Charles D., John McManus & Eugene G. D'Aquili. (1990). *Brain, symbol and experience: toward a neurophenomenology of human consciousness.* Boston, MA: New Science Library.

Laughlin, William S. (1968). Hunting: an integrated biobehavioral mechanism and its evolutionary importance. In Richard Lee & Irven DeVore (Eds.), *Man the hunter* (pp. 304–320). Chicago, IL: Aldine.

Lave, Jean. (1990). The culture of acquisition and the practice of understanding. In James Stigler, Richard Shweder & Gilbert Herdt (Eds.), *Cultural psychology* (pp. 309–327). Cambridge: Cambridge University Press.

Lave, Jean & Etienne Wenger. (1991). *Situated learning: legitimate peripheral participation.* Cambridge: Cambridge University Press.

Lave, Jean, Paul Duguid, Nadine Fernandez & Erik Axel. (1992). Coming of age in Birmingham: cultural studies and conceptions of subjectivity. *Annual Review of Anthropology* 21: 257–282.

Lavie, Smadar. (1990). *The poetics of military occupation: Mzeina allegories of Bedouin identity under Israeli and Egyptian rule.* Berkeley: University of California Press.

Lavie, Smadar, Kirin Naranyan & Renato Rosaldo. (Eds.). (1993). *Creativity/anthropology.* Ithaca, NY: Cornell University Press.

Lawrence, Denise & Setha Low. (1990). The built environment and spatial form. *Annual Review of Anthropology* 19: 453–505.

Lawrence, Elizabeth. (1982). *Rodeo: an anthropologist looks at the wild and the tame.* Knoxville: University of Tennessee Press.

Lawrence, Roderick. (1989). Structuralist theories in environment–behavior-design research. In Ervin Zube & Gary Moore (Eds.), *Advances in environment behavior and design*, vol. 2 (pp. 37–70). New York: Plenum Press.

Lawson, E. Thomas & Robert McCauley. (1990). *Rethinking religion: connecting cognition and culture.* Cambridge: Cambridge University Press.

Lawson, Edward. (1991). *Encyclopedia of human rights.* New York: Taylor & Francis.

Layoun, Mary. (1990). *Travels of a genre: the modern novel and ideology.* Princeton, NJ: Princeton University Press.

Leach, Edmund. (1953). Cronus and chronos. *Explorations: studies in culture and communication* 1: 15–23. [reprinted in Leach 1961b: 124–136]

———(1954). *Political systems of highland Burma: a study of Kachin social structure.* London: London School of Economics and Political Science.

———(1955). Time and false noses. *Explorations: Studies in Culture and Communication* 5: 30–35. [reprinted in Leach 1961b: 124–136]

———(1957). Aspects of bridewealth and

marriage stability among the Kachin and Lakher. *Man* 57: 50–55.

——(1960a). What should we mean by caste? In Edmund Leach (Ed.), *Aspects of caste in south India, Ceylon, and north-west Pakistan* (pp. 1–10). Cambridge: Cambridge University Press.

——(1960b). Descent, filiation and affinity. *Man* 60: 9–10.

——(1961a). *Pul Eliya, a village in Ceylon: a study of land tenure and kinship.* Cambridge: Cambridge University Press.

——(1961b). *Rethinking anthropology.* London: Athlone.

——(1961c). Golden bough or gilded twig? *Daedalus* 90: 371–399.

——(1964). Anthropological aspects of language: animal categories and verbal abuse. In Eric H. Lenneberg (Ed.), *New directions in the study of language* (pp. 23–63). Cambridge, MA: MIT Press.

——(Ed.). (1967). *The structural study of myth and totemism.* London: Tavistock.

——(1970). *Claude Lévi-Strauss.* New York: Viking.

——(1973). Levels of communication and problems of taboo in appreciation of primitive art. In J. A. Forge (Ed.), *Primitive art and society* (pp. 221–234). London: Oxford University Press.

——(1976). *Culture and communication: the logic by which symbols are connected.* Cambridge: Cambridge University Press.

——(1982). *Social anthropology.* Oxford: Oxford University Press.

——(1983). The gatekeepers of heaven: anthropological aspects of grandiose architecture. *Journal of Anthropological Research* 39: 234–264.

Leach, Jerry W. & Edmund Leach. (Eds.). (1983). *The kula: new perspectives on Massim exchange.* Cambridge: Cambridge University Press.

Leacock, Eleanor. (Ed.). (1971). *The culture of poverty: a critique.* New York: Simon & Schuster.

——(1978). Women's status in egalitarian society: implications for social evolution. *Current Anthropology* 19: 247–276.

Leacock, Eleanor & Richard Lee. (Eds.). (1982). *Politics and history in band societies.* Cambridge: Cambridge University Press.

Leacock, Eleanor & Helen Safa. (Eds.). (1986). *Women's work: development and the division of labor by gender.* South Hadley, MA: Bergin & Garvey.

Leap, William L. & Ellen Lewin. (Eds.). (1996). *Out in the field: reflections of lesbian and gay anthropologists.* Urbana: University of Illinois Press.

Le Bon, Gustave. (1896). *The crowd: a study of the popular mind* [Psychologie de foules, Paris, 1895]. London: Unwin.

Lebot, Vincent, Mark Merlin & Lamont Lindstrom. (1992). *Kava: the Pacific drug.* New Haven, CT: Yale University Press.

Lechtman, Heather & Arthur Steinberg. (1979). The history of technology: an anthropological point of view. In George Bugliarello & Dean B. Doner (Eds.), *The history and philosophy of technology* (pp. 135–160). Urbana: University of Illinois Press).

LeClair, Edward E. & Harold K. Schneider. (Eds.). (1968). *Economic anthropology: readings in theory and analysis.* New York: Holt.

Lederberg, Joshua, Robert E. Shope & Stanley C. Oaks. (1992). *Emerging infections: microbial threats to health in the United States.* Washington, DC: National Academy Press.

Lederman, Rena. (1990). Big men, large and small? Towards a comparative perspective. *Ethnology* 29: 3–15.

——(1991). Interests in exchange: increment, equivalence and the limits of big-manship. In M. Godelier & M. Strathern (Eds.), *Big men and great men* (pp. 215–233). Cambridge: Cambridge University Press.

Lee, Richard B. (1979). *The !Kung San: men, women, and work in a foraging society.* Cambridge: Cambridge University Press.

——(1982). Politics, sexual and non-sexual, in an egalitarian society. In Eleanor Leacock & Richard B. Lee (Eds.), *Politics and history in band societies* (pp. 37–59). Cambridge: Cambridge University Press.

——(1984). *The Dobe !Kung.* New York: Holt.

Lee, Richard B. & Irven DeVore. (Eds.). (1968). *Man the hunter.* Chicago, IL: Aldine.

————(Eds.). (1976). *Kalahari hunter-gatherers: studies of the !Kung San and their neighbors.* Cambridge, MA: Harvard University Press.

Leeds, Anthony. (1994). *Cities, classes, and the social order* ed. by Roger Sanjek. Ithaca, NY: Cornell University Press.

Leeds, Anthony & Andrew P. Vayda. (Eds.). (1965). *Man, culture, and animals: the role of animals in human ecological adjustments.* Washington, DC: American Association for the Advancement of Science.

Leenhardt, Maurice. (1975). Preface to *The notebooks on primitive mentality, Lucien Levy-Bruhl.* Oxford: Blackwell.

————(1979). *Do kamo: person and myth in the Melanesian world* [Do kamo, Paris, 1947]. Chicago, IL: University of Chicago Press.

Leeuw, Gerardus van der. (1938). *Religion in essence and manifestation* [Phänomenologie der Religion, Tübingen, 1933]. London: Allen & Unwin.

Lehmann, David. (Ed.). (1974). *Peasants, landlords, and governments: agrarian reform in the Third World.* New York: Holmes & Meier.

Lehmann, Winfred P. (1967). *A reader in nineteenth-century historical Indo-European linguistics.* Bloomington: Indiana University Press.

Lehrer, Adrienne. (1974). *Semantic fields and lexical structure.* New York: American Elsevier.

Lehrman, Daniel S. (1953). A critique of Konrad Lorenz's theory of instinctive behavior. *Quarterly Review of Biology* 28: 337–363.

————(1970). Semantic and conceptual issues in the nature–nurture problem. In Lester R. Aronson et al. (Eds.), *Development and evolution of behavior* (pp. 17–52). San Francisco, CA: Freeman.

Lemonnier, Pierre. (1989). Bark capes, arrowheads and concorde: on social representations of technology. In Ian Hodder (Ed.), *The meanings of things* (pp. 156–171). London: Unwin Hyman.

Lenin, Vladimir Il'ich. (1926). *Imperialism: the state and revolution* [Gosudarstvo i revoliutsiia, Petrograd, 1918]. New York: Vanguard Press.

Lenski, Gerhard E. (1966). *Power and privilege: a theory of social stratification.* New York: McGraw-Hill.

————(1970). *Human societies: a macro-level introduction to sociology.* New York: McGraw-Hill.

Leone, Mark P. (1982). Some opinions about recovering mind. *American Antiquity* 47: 742–760.

Lepowsky, Maria. (1993). *Fruit of the motherland: gender in an egalitarian society.* New York: Columbia University Press.

L'Équipe écologie et anthropologie des sociétés pastorales. (Eds.). (1979). *Pastoral production and society.* Cambridge: Cambridge University Press.

Leupp, Gary. (1996). *Male colors: the construction of homosexuality in Tokugawa Japan.* Berkeley: University of California Press.

LeVay, Simon. (1993). *The sexual brain.* Cambridge, MA: MIT Press.

Levelt, Willem. (1989). *Speaking: from intention to articulation.* Cambridge, MA: MIT Press.

Lévi-Strauss, Claude. (1943). Guerre et commerce chez les Indiens de l'Amérique du Sud. *Renaissance* 1: 122–139.

————(1953a). Social structure. In A. L. Kroeber (Ed.), *Anthropology today* (pp. 524–553). Chicago, IL: University of Chicago Press.

————(1953b). Results of the conference of anthropology and linguistics. *International Journal of American Linguistics,* Supplement 192: 1–10.

————(1963a). *Structural anthropology* [Anthropologie structurale, Paris, 1958]. New York: Basic.

————(1963b). *Totemism* [Le totémisme aujourd'hui, Paris, 1962]. Boston, MA: Beacon.

————(1963c). *Tristes tropiques* [Paris, 1955]. New York: Atheneum.

————(1965). The culinary triangle [Le triangle culinaire, Paris, 1966]. *Partisan Review* 33: 586–595.

————(1966). *The savage mind* [Pensée sauvage, Paris, 1962]. Chicago, IL: University of Chicago Press.

————(1969–81). *Mythologiques: Introduction to a science of mythology* (4 vols.) [Mythologiques, Paris, 1964–71; see Lévi-Strauss 1969b, 1973, 1978, 1981.]

———(1969a). *The elementary structures of kinship* [Les structures élémentaires de la parenté, Paris, 1949]. Boston, MA: Beacon.

———(1969b). *The raw and the cooked* [Cru et le cuit, Paris, 1964]. New York: Harper & Row.

———(1973). *From honey to ashes* [Du miel aux cendres, Paris, 1966]. New York: Harper & Row.

———(1978). *The origin of table manners* [Origine des manières de table, Paris, 1968]. London: Cape.

———(1981). *The naked man* [Homme nu, Paris, 1971]. New York: Harper & Row.

———(1982). *The way of the masks* [La voie des masques, Geneva, 1975]. Seattle: University of Washington Press.

———(1987). *Introduction to the work of Marcel Mauss* [Introduction à l'oeuvre de Marcel Mauss, Paris, 1950]. London: Routledge.

———(1995). *The story of Lynx* [Histoire de Lynx, Paris, 1991]. Chicago, IL: University of Chicago Press.

Lévi-Strauss, Claude & Didier Eribon. (1991). *Conversations with Claude Lévi-Strauss* [De près et de loin, Paris, 1988]. Chicago, IL: University of Chicago Press.

LeVine, Robert A. (1982). *Culture, behavior and personality: an introduction to the comparative study of psychosocial adaptation* [2nd edn.]. Chicago, IL: Aldine.

———(1988). Human parental care: universal goals, cultural strategies, individual behavior. In Robert LeVine, Patrice Miller & Mary West (Eds.), *Parental behavior in diverse societies* (pp. 3–12). San Francisco, CA: Jossey-Bass.

———(1990). Infant environments in psychoanalysis: a cross-cultural view. In James Stigler, Richard Shweder & Gilbert Herdt (Eds.), *Cultural psychology* (pp. 454–476). Cambridge: Cambridge University Press.

LeVine, Robert A. & Merry I. White. (1986). *Human conditions: the cultural basis of educational development.* London: Routledge.

LeVine, Robert A., P. M. Miller & M. West. (Eds.). (1988). *Parental behavior in diverse societies.* San Francisco, CA: Jossey-Bass.

Levine, Nancy E. (1983). *The dynamics of polyandry: kinship, domesticity, and population on the Tibetan border.* Chicago, IL: University of Chicago Press.

Levinson, David. (1994). *Aggression and conflict: a cross-cultural encyclopedia.* Santa Barbara, CA: ABC-CLIO.

Levinson, David & Martin J. Malone. (1980). *Toward explaining human culture: a critical review of the findings of worldwide cross-cultural research.* New Haven, CT: HRAF Press.

Levinson, Stephen C. (1983). *Pragmatics.* Cambridge: Cambridge University Press.

Levy, Marion J. (1968). Structural-functional analysis. In David Sills (Ed.), *International encyclopedia of the social sciences,* vol. 6 (pp. 21–28). New York: Macmillan.

Levy, Robert I. (1973). *Tahitians: mind and experience in the Society Islands.* Chicago, IL: University of Chicago Press.

———(1976). A conjunctive pattern in middle class informal and informal education. In Theodore Schwartz (Ed.), *Socialization as cultural communication* (pp. 177–187). Berkeley: University of California Press.

———(1978). Tahitian gentleness and redundant controls. In Ashley Montague (Ed.), *Learning non-aggression* (pp. 222–235). Oxford: Oxford University Press.

———(1984). Emotion, knowing, and culture. In Richard A. Shweder & R. A. LeVine (Eds.), *Culture theory* (pp. 214–237). Cambridge: Cambridge University Press.

———(1990). *Mesocosm: Hinduism and the organization of a traditional Newar city in Nepal.* Berkeley: University of California Press.

Levy-Bruhl, Lucien. (1926). *How natives think* [Fonctions mentales dans les sociétés inférieures, Paris, 1912]. London: Allen & Unwin.

Lewellen, Ted. (1992). *Political anthropology: an introduction* [2nd edn.]. Westport, CT: Bergin & Garvey.

Lewin, Roger. (1993). *Human evolution: an illustrated introduction* [3rd edn.]. Boston, MA: Blackwell Scientific.

Lewis, I. M. (1971). *Ecstatic religion: an*

anthropological study of spirit possession and shamanism. Harmondsworth: Penguin.

——(1976). *Social anthropology in perspective: the relevance of social anthropology.* New York: Penguin.

——(1986). *Religion in context: cults and charisma.* Cambridge: Cambridge University Press.

Lewis, J. Lowell. (1992). *Ring of liberation: deceptive discourse in Brazilian capoeira.* Chicago, IL: University of Chicago Press.

Lewis, Michael & Jeannette Haviland. (Eds.). (1993). *Handbook of emotions.* New York: Guilford.

Lewis, Oscar. (1951). *Life in a Mexican village: Tepoztlán restudied.* Urbana: University of Illinois Press.

——(1952). Urbanization without breakdown: a case study. *Science Monthly* 75: 31–41.

——(1961). *The children of Sanchez.* New York: Random.

——(1966). *La vida: a Puerto Rican family in the culture of poverty – San Juan and New York.* New York: Random.

Lewis-Beck, Michael. (1980). *Applied regression: an introduction.* Beverly Hills, CA: Sage.

Liao, Tim Futing. (1994). *Interpreting probability models: logit, probit, and other generalized models.* Thousand Oaks, CA: Sage.

Lieban, Richard W. (1967). *Cebuano sorcery: malign magic in the Philippines.* Berkeley: University of California Press.

Lieberman, Leonard. (1968). The debate over race: a study in the sociology of knowledge. *Phylon* 39: 127–141.

Lieberman, Philip. (1984). *The biology and evolution of language.* Cambridge, MA: Harvard University Press.

——(1991). *Uniquely human: the evolution of speech, thought, and selfless behavior.* Cambridge, MA: Harvard University Press.

Lieberman, Seymour. (1956). The effects of changes in roles on the attitudes of social role occupants. *Human Relations* 9: 385–402.

Liebow, Elliot. (1967). *Tally's corner: a study of Negro streetcorner men.* Boston, MA: Little, Brown.

Liederman, P. Herbert, Steven Tulkin

& Anne Rosenfeld. (1977). *Culture and infancy.* New York: Academic.

Lienhardt, R. Godfrey. (1961). *Divinity and experience: the religion of the Dinka.* Oxford: Clarendon.

——(1964). *Social anthropology.* London: Oxford University Press.

Liep, John. (1991). Great man, big man, chief: a triangulation of the Massim. In M. Godelier & M. Strathern (Eds.), *Big men and great men* (pp. 28–47). Cambridge: Cambridge University Press.

Lightfoot, David. (1979). *Principles of diachronic syntax.* Cambridge: Cambridge University Press.

——(1982). *The language lottery: toward a biology of grammars.* Cambridge, MA: MIT Press.

Limerick, Patricia N., Clyde A. Milner & C. Rankin. (Eds.). (1991). *Trails: toward a new Western history.* Lawrence: University Press of Kansas.

Limón, José & M. Jane Young. (1986). Frontiers, settlements, and developments in folklore studies. *Annual Review of Anthropology* 15: 437–460.

Lindholm, Charles. (1986). Caste in Islam and the problem of deviant systems: a critique of recent theory. *Contributions to Indian Sociology* 20: 61–73.

——(1988). Lovers and leaders: a comparison of social and psychological models of romance and charisma. *Social Science Information* 27: 3–45.

——(1990). *Charisma.* Oxford: Blackwell.

Ling, Trevor O. (1962). *Buddhism and the mythology of evil.* London: Allen & Unwin.

Linton, Adelin & Charles Wagley. (1971). *Ralph Linton.* New York: Columbia University Press.

Linton, Ralph. (1936). *The study of man: an introduction.* New York: Appleton-Century.

——(Ed.). (1940). *Acculturation in seven American Indian tribes.* New York: Appleton-Century.

——(1943). Nativistic movements. *American Anthropologist* 45: 230–240.

——(1945). *The cultural background of personality.* New York: Appleton-Century.

Lipset, Seymour M. (1963). *The first new*

nation: the United States in historical and comparative perspective. New York: Basic.

———(1968). Social stratification: social class. In D. L. Sills (Ed.), *International encyclopedia of the social sciences*, vol. 15 (pp. 296–316). New York: Macmillan.

Lipsitz, George. (1988). *A life in the struggle: Ivory Perry and the culture of opposition*. Philadelphia: Temple University Press.

———(1990). *Time passages: collective memory and American popular culture*. Minneapolis: University of Minnesota Press.

Little, Peter D. (1992). *The elusive granary: herder, farmer, and state in northern Kenya*. Cambridge: Cambridge University Press.

Livingstone, Frank B. (1962). On the non-existence of human races. *Current Anthropology* 33: 279–281.

———(1976). Hemoglobin history in west Africa. *Human Biology* 48: 487–500.

Llewelyn, Karl N. & E. A. Hoebel. (1941). *The Cheyenne way: conflict and case law in primitive jurisprudence*. Norman: University of Oklahoma Press.

Lock, Margaret. (1991). Life-cycle transitions. In Renato Dulbecco (Ed.), *Encyclopedia of human biology* 4: 697–710. San Diego, CA: Academic.

———(1993a). *Encounters with aging: mythologies of menopause in Japan and North America*. Berkeley: University of California Press.

———(1993b). The politics of mid-life and menopause: ideologies for the second sex in North America and Japan. In Shirley Lindenbaum & Margaret Lock (Eds.), *Knowledge, power and practice: the anthropology of medicine in everyday life*. Berkeley: University of California Press.

Lock, Margaret & Nancy Scheper-Hughes. (1996). A critical-interpretive approach in medical anthropology: rituals and routines of discipline and dissent. In Carolyn Sargent & Thomas Johnson (Eds.), *Medical anthropology* [rev. edn.] (pp. 41–70). Westport, CT: Greenwood.

Loeb, Edwin M. & J. O. M. Broek. (1947). Social organization and the longhouse in southeast Asia. *American Anthropologist* 49: 414–425.

Loeber, Rolf & M. Stouthamer-

Loeber. (1987). Prediction. In Hebert C. Quay (Ed.), *Handbook of juvenile delinquency* (pp. 325–382). New York: Wiley.

Lofland, John. (1969). *Deviance and identity*. Englewood Cliffs, NJ: Prentice-Hall.

Lofland, Lyn. (1973). *A world of strangers: order and action in urban public space*. New York: Basic.

Loizos, Peter. (1993). *Innovation in ethnographic film: from innocence to self-consciousness, 1955–85*. Chicago, IL: University of Chicago Press.

Lomax, Alan. (1968). *Folk song style and culture*. Washington, DC: American Association for the Advancement of Science.

———(1976). *Dance and human history* (motion picture). Berkeley: University of California.

Lomax, Alan, Irmgard Bartenieff & Forrestine Pauley. (1968). Dance style and culture, and choreometric profiles. In Alan Lomax (Ed.), *Folk song style and culture* (pp. 222–261). Washington, DC: American Association for the Advancement of Science.

Lomnitz, Larrisa. (1977). *Networks and marginality: life in a Mexican shantytown*. New York: Academic.

Long, Lynellyn. (1993). *Ban Vinai: the refugee camp*. New York: Columbia University Press.

Long, Norman & Ann Long. (Eds.). (1992). *Battlefields of knowledge: the interlocking of theory and practice in social research and development*. London: Routledge.

Lord, Albert J. (1960). *The singer of tales*. Cambridge, MA: Harvard University Press.

Lorenz, Konrad. (1941). Vergleichende Bewegungsstudien an Anatinen. *Journal of Ornithology* Supplement 39: 194–294.

———(1952). *King Solomon's ring: new light on animal ways*. London: Methuen.

———(1966). *On aggression* [Das sogenannte Böse, Vienna, 1963]. New York: Harcourt, Brace & World.

Lotka, Alfred J. (1925). *Elements of physical biology*. Baltimore: Williams & Wilkins.

Lounsbury, Floyd. (1956). A semantic analysis of the Pawnee kinsip usage. *Language* 32: 158–194.

Lovejoy, C. Owen. (1981). Origins of man. *Science* 211: 341–350.

Low, Bobbi S. (1989). Cross-cultural patterns in the training of children: an evolutionary perspective. *Journal of Comparative Psychology* 103: 311–319.

Low, Setha. (1993). Cultural meaning of the plaza: the history of the Spanish-American gridplan-plaza urban design. In Robert Rotenberg & Gary McDonogh (Eds.), *The cultural meaning of urban space* (pp. 75–94). Westport, CT: Bergin & Garvey.

Low, Setha & Erve Chambers. (Eds.). (1989). *Housing, culture and design: a comparative perspective.* Philadelphia: University of Pennsylvania Press.

Lowie, Robert H. (1915). Oral tradition and history. *American Anthropologist* 17: 597–599.

———(1916). Plains Indians age-societies: historical and comparative summary. *American Museum of Natural History Anthropological Papers* 11: 881–1031.

———(1917). *Culture and ethnology.* New York: McMurtrie.

———(1920). *Primitive society.* New York: Boni & Liveright.

———(1924). *Primitive religion.* New York: Boni & Liveright.

———(1927). *The origin of the state.* New York: Harcourt, Brace.

———(1934). *An introduction to cultural anthropology.* New York: Farrar & Rinehart.

———(1935). *The Crow Indians.* New York: Farrar & Rinehart.

———(1937). *The history of ethnological theory.* New York: Farrar & Rinehart.

———(1948). *Social organization.* New York: Rinehart.

———(1954a). *Toward understanding Germany.* Chicago, IL: University of Chicago Press.

———(1954b). *Indians of the Plains.* New York: McGraw-Hill.

———(1959). *Robert H. Lowie, ethnologist: a personal record.* Berkeley: University of California Press.

———(1960). Cultural anthropology: a science. In Cora Du Bois (Ed.), *Lowie's selected papers in anthropology* (pp. 391–410). Berkeley: University of California Press.

Ludmerer, Kenneth M. (1972). *Genetics and American society: a historical appraisal.* Baltimore, MD: Johns Hopkins University Press.

Luhrmann, Tanya M. (1989). *Persuasions of the witch's craft: ritual magic and witchcraft in present-day England.* Cambridge, MA: Harvard University Press.

———(1992). Audrey I. Richards: a bibliography. In Shirley Ardener (Ed.), *Persons and powers of women in diverse cultures* (pp. 51–58). Oxford: Berg.

Lumsden, Charles J. & Edward O. Wilson. (1981). *Genes, mind and culture: the coevolutionary process.* Cambridge, MA: Harvard University Press.

Luong, Hy V. (1990). *Discursive practices and linguistic meanings: the Vietnamese system of person reference.* Amsterdam: Benjamins.

Lupton, Mary Jane. (1993). *Menstruation and psychoanalysis.* Urbana: University of Illinois Press.

Lurie, Nancy O. (1961). Ethnohistory: an ethnological point of view. *Ethnohistory* 8: 78–92.

Lutkehaus, Nancy. (Ed.). (1995a). Special section: tribute to Timothy Asch. *Visual Anthropology Review* 11(1): 2–91.

———(Ed.). (1995b). Special section: Visible evidence I. *Visual Anthropology Review* 11(2): 64–106.

Lutz, Catherine. (1985). Ethnopsychology compared to what? Explaining behavior and consciousness among the Ifaluk. In Geoffrey White & John Kirkpatrick (Eds.), *Person, self, and experience* (pp. 35–79). Berkeley: University of California Press.

———(1988). *Unnatural emotions: everyday sentiments on a Micronesian atoll and their challenge to modern Western theory.* Chicago, IL: University of Chicago Press.

———(1992). Culture and consciousness: a problem in the anthropology of knowledge. In Frank Kessel, Pamela Cole, Dale L. Johnson (Eds.), *Self and consciousness* (pp. 64–87). Hillsdale, NJ: Erlbaum.

Lutz, Catherine & Lila Abu-Lughod. (Eds.). (1990). *Language and the politics of emotion.* Cambridge: Cambridge University Press.

Lutz, Catherine & J. L. Collins. (1993). *Reading National Geographic.* Chicago, IL: University of Chicago Press.

Lutz, Catherine & Geoffrey White. (1986). The anthropology of emotions. *Annual Review of Anthropology* 15: 405–436.

Lynch, Owen. (1969). *The politics of untouchability: social mobility and social change in a city of India.* New York: Columbia University Press.

———(1990). The Mastram: emotion and person among Mathura's Chaubes. In Owen Lynch (Ed.), *Divine passions* (pp. 91–115). Berkeley: University of California Press.

Lyons, John. (1968). *Introduction to theoretical linguistics.* Cambridge: Cambridge University Press.

———(1977). *Semantics* (2 vols.). Cambridge: Cambridge University Press.

Lyotard, Jean-François. (1984). *The postmodern condition: a report on knowledge* [La condition postmoderne, Paris, 1979]. Minneapolis: University of Minnesota Press.

———(1988). *The differend: phrases in dispute* [Le différend, Paris, 1983]. Minneapolis: University of Minnesota Press.

———(1991). *Phenomenology* [Phénoménologie, Paris, 1956]. Albany: State University of New York Press.

Maass, Arthur & Raymond L. Anderson. (1978). *. . . and the desert shall rejoice: conflict, growth, and justice in arid environments.* Cambridge, MA: MIT Press.

McAllester, David P. (1954). *Enemy way music: a study of social and esthetic values as seen in Navaho music.* Cambridge, MA: Harvard University Press.

MacAndrew, Craig & Robert Edgerton. (1969). *Drunken comportment: a social explanation.* Hawthorne, NY: Aldine.

Macaulay, Stewart. (1986). Private government. In Leon Lipson & Stanton Wheeler (Eds.), *Law and the social sciences* (pp. 445–518). New York: Sage.

McCabe, Justin. (1983). FBD Marriage. *American Anthropologist* 85: 50–69.

McCay, Bonnie & James Acheson. (Eds.). (1987). *The question of the commons: the culture and ecology of communal resources.* Tucson: University of Arizona Press.

McClintock, Anne. (1992). The angel of progress: pitfalls of the term "post-colonialism." *Social Text* 31: 84–92.

McClintock, Martha K. (1971). Menstrual synchrony and suppression. *Nature* 229(5285): 244–245.

Maccoby, Eleanor & Carol Jacklin. (1974). *The psychology of sex differences.* Stanford, CA: Stanford University Press.

MacCormack, Carol. (Ed.). (1982). *Ethnography of fertility and birth.* New York: Academic. [2nd edn., Waveland, 1994]

MacCormack, Carol & Marilyn Strathern. (Eds.). (1980). *Nature, culture and gender.* Cambridge: Cambridge University Press.

Macdonell, Dianne. (1986). *Theories of discourse: an introduction.* Oxford: Blackwell.

MacDougall, David. (1995a). Beyond observational cinema. In Paul Hockings (Ed.), *Principles of visual anthropology* [2nd edn.] (pp. 109–124). Berlin: de Gruyter.

———(1995b). The subjective voice in ethnographic film. In Leslie Devereaux & Roger Hillman (Eds.), *Fields of vision* (pp. 217–255). Berkeley: University of California Press.

Macey, David. (1993). *The lives of Michel Foucault: a biography.* London: Hutchinson.

Macfarlane, Alan. (1970). *Witchcraft in Tudor and Stuart England: a regional and comparative study.* New York: Harper & Row.

———(1986). *Marriage and love in England: modes of reproduction, 1300–1840.* Oxford: Blackwell.

MacGaffey, Wyatt. (1983). *Modern Kongo prophets: religion in a plural society.* Bloomington: Indiana University Press.

McGoodwin, James R. (1990). *Crisis in the world's fisheries: people, problems, and policies.* Stanford, CA: Stanford University Press.

McGuire, Randall. (1983). Breaking down cultural complexity: inequality and heterogeneity. *Advances in Archaeological Method and Theory* 6: 91–142.

Macintyre, Martha. (1983). *The kula: a*

bibliography. Cambridge: Cambridge University Press.

McKeever, Patricia. (1984). The perpetuation of menstrual shame: implications and directions. *Women and Health* 9(4): 33–47.

Mackey, William Francis. (1993). Introduction. In Mauro Fernández (Ed.), *Diglossia* (pp. xiii–xx). Philadelphia, PA: Benjamins.

McLennan, John Ferguson. (1896). *Studies in ancient history* [2nd ser.]. New York: Macmillan.

McLuhan, Marshall. (1962). *The Gutenberg galaxy: the making of typographic man.* Toronto: University of Toronto Press.

McMichael, Philip. (1984). *Settlers and the agrarian question: foundations of capitalism in colonial Australia.* Cambridge: Cambridge University Press.

McNeely, Jeffrey A. & David Pitt. (Eds.). (1985). *Culture and conservation: the human dimension in environmental planning.* London: Croom Helm.

McNeill, William H. (1976). *Plagues and peoples.* Garden City, NY: Doubleday.

MacWhinney, Brian. (Ed.). (1987). *Mechanisms of language acquisition.* Hillsdale, NJ: Erlbaum.

Maddala, G. S. (1983). *Limited-dependent and qualitative variables in econometrics.* Cambridge: Cambridge University Press.

Magana, J. R., M. Burton & J. Ferreira-Pinto. (1995). Occupational cognition in three nations. *Journal of Quantitative Anthropology* 5: 149–168.

Maine, Henry S. (1861). *Ancient law, its connection with the early history of society and its relation to modern ideas.* London: Murray.

———(1871). *Village-communities in the East and West.* London: Murray.

———(1875). *Lectures on the early history of institutions.* London: Murray.

———(1883). *Dissertations on early law and custom.* London: Murray.

Mair, Lucy. (1962). *Primitive government: a study of traditional political systems in eastern Africa.* Baltimore: Penguin [rev. edn., Indiana University Press, 1977].

———(1965). *An introduction to social anthropology.* Oxford: Clarendon.

———(1969). *Witchcraft.* New York: McGraw Hill.

Makhlouf Obermeyer, Carla. (1995). A cross-cultural perspective on reproductive rights. *Human Rights Quarterly* 17(2): 366–381.

Makkreel, Rudolf. (1975). *Dilthey, philosopher of the human studies.* Princeton, NJ: Princeton University Press.

Malalgoda, Kitsiri. (1970). Millennialism in relation to Buddhism. *Comparative Studies in Society and History* 12: 424–441.

Malinowski, Bronislaw. (1913). *The family among the Australian Aborigines: a sociological study.* London: University of London Press.

———(1922). *Argonauts of the western Pacific.* London: Routledge.

———(1923). The problem of meaning in primitive languages. In Charles K. Ogden & I. A. Richards (Eds.), *The meaning of meaning* (pp. 296–336). New York: Harcourt, Brace.

———(1926). *Crime and custom in savage society.* New York: Harcourt, Brace.

———(1927). *Sex and repression in savage society.* New York: Harcourt, Brace.

———(1929). *The sexual life of savages in North-Western Melanesia.* London: Routledge.

———(1930). Kinship. *Man* 30: 19–29.

———(1935). *Coral gardens and their magic.* New York: American.

———(1941). An anthropological analysis of war. *American Journal of Sociology* 46: 521–550.

———(1944). *A scientific theory of culture.* Chapel Hill: University of North Carolina Press.

———(1945). *The dynamics of culture change: an inquiry into race relations in Africa.* New Haven, CT: Yale University Press.

———(1948). *Magic, science and religion.* Boston, MA: Beacon.

———(1962). *Sex, culture, and myth.* New York: Harcourt, Brace & World.

———(1967). *A diary in the strict sense of the term.* New York: Harcourt, Brace & World.

Malkki, Liisa. (1992). National geographic: the rooting of peoples and the territorialization of national identity among scholars and refugees. *Cultural Anthropology* 7(1): 24–44.

——(1995a). *Purity and exile: violence, memory, and national cosmology among Hutu refugees in Tanzania.* Chicago, IL: University of Chicago Press.

——(1995b). Refugees and exile: from "refugee studies" to the national order of things. *Annual Review of Anthropology* 24: 495–523.

Mallery, Garrick. (1893). *Picture-writing of the American Indians.* Washington.

Mallory, J. P. (1989). *In search of the Indo-Europeans: language, archaeology and myth.* London: Thames & Hudson.

Malthus, Thomas R. (1789). *An essay on the principle of population, as it affects the future improvement of society.* London: Johnson.

Mandel, Ruth. (1989). Ethnicity and identity among migrant guestworkers in West Berlin. In Nancie Gonzalez & Carolyn McCommon (Eds.), *Conflict, migration, and the expression of ethnicity* (pp. 60–74). Boulder, CO: Westview.

Mandelbaum, David. (1968). Cultural anthropology. In David Sills (Ed.), *International encyclopedia of the social sciences,* vol. 3 (pp. 313–319). New York: Macmillan.

——(1973). The study of life history: Gandhi. *Current Anthropology* 14(3): 177–206.

Manderson, Lenore. (1981). Traditional food classifications and humoral medical theory in Peninsular Malaysia. *Ecology, Food and Nutrition* 11: 11–93.

——(Ed.). (1986). *Shared wealth and symbol: food, culture, and society in Oceania and Southeast Asia.* Cambridge: Cambridge University Press.

Manganaro, Marc. (Ed.). (1990). *Modernist anthropology: from field work to text.* Princeton, NJ: Princeton University Press.

Mangin, William P. (Ed.). (1970). *Peasants in cities: readings in the anthropology of urbanization.* Boston, MA: Houghton Mifflin.

Manly, Bryan F. J. (1986). *Multivariate statistical methods: a primer.* London: Chapman.

Mann, Michael. (1986). *The sources of social power: a history of power from the begin-*
ning to A.D. *1760,* vol. 1. Cambridge: Cambridge University Press.

——(1993). *The sources of social power: a history of power from the beginning to A.D. 1760,* vol. 2. Cambridge: Cambridge University Press.

Manning, Peter K. & Horacio Fabrega. (1976). Fieldwork and the "New Ethnography." *Man,* 11(1): 39–52.

Manuel, Peter. (1993). *Cassette culture: popular music and technology in north India.* Chicago, IL: University of Chicago Press.

Maquet, Jacques. (1961). *The premise of inequality in Ruanda: a study of political relations in a central African kingdom.* London: Oxford University Press.

Maranhao, Tullio. (Ed.). (1990). *The interpretation of dialogue.* Chicago, IL: University of Chicago Press.

Marçais, William. (1930). La Diglossie arabe. *L'Enseignement public* 97: 401–409.

March, Kathryn & Rachelle Taqqu. (1985). *Women's informal associations in developing countries: catalysts for change?* Boulder, CO: Westview.

Marcus, George. (1986). Contemporary problems of ethnography in the modern world system. In James Clifford & George Marcus (Eds.), *Writing culture* (pp. 165–193). Berkeley: University of California Press.

——(1989). Chieftainship. In A. Howard & R. Borofsky (Eds.), *Developments in Polynesian ethnology* (pp. 175–209). Honolulu: University of Hawaii Press.

——(Ed.). (1992). *Rereading cultural anthropology.* Durham, NC: Duke University Press.

——(Ed.). (1993). *Perilous states: conversations on culture, politics, and nation.* Chicago, IL: University of Chicago Press.

——(Ed.). (1995). *Technoscientific imaginaries.* Chicago: University of Chicago Press.

Marcus, George & Dick Cushman. (1982). Ethnographies as texts. *Annual Review of Anthropology* 11: 25–69.

Marcus, George & Michael M. J. Fischer. (1986). *Anthropology as cultural critique: an experimental moment in the hu-*

man sciences. Chicago, IL: University of Chicago Press.

Marcus, George with Peter D. Hall. (1992). *Lives in trust: the fortunes of dynastic families in late twentieth-century America.* Boulder, CO: Westview.

Marcus, Joyce. (1976). The origins of Mesoamerican writing. *Annual Review of Anthropology* 5: 35–67.

Marcuse, Herbert. (1968). *Eros and civilization.* Boston, MA: Beacon.

Marger, Martin. (1985). *Race and ethnic relations: American and global perspectives.* Belmont, CA: Wadsworth.

Marglin, Frédérique. (1985). *Wives of the god-king: rituals of the devadasis of Puri.* Oxford: Oxford University Press.

Marks, Dan. (1995). Ethnography and ethnographic film: from Flaherty to Asch and after. *American Anthropologist* 97(2): 339–347.

Marks, Jonathan. (1995). *Human biodiversity: genes, race, and history.* New York: Aldine de Gruyter.

Marks, Stuart. (1991). *Southern hunting in black and white: nature, history, and ritual in a Carolina community.* Princeton, NJ: Princeton University Press.

Marrett, Robert R. (1909). *The threshold of religion.* London: Methuen.

Marriott, McKim. (1976). Hindu transactions: diversity without dualism. In Bruce Kapferer (Ed.), *Transaction and meaning* (pp. 109–142). Philadelphia, PA: ISHI.

———(Ed.). (1990). *India through Hindu categories.* Newbury Park, CA: Sage.

Marriott, McKim & Ronald Inden. (1974). Caste systems. *Encyclopedia Britannica,* vol. 3 (pp. 982–991).

Marshall, Alfred. (1890). *Principles of economics.* London. [9th edition, republished (2 vols.). Macmillan, New York, 1961]

Marshall, G. A. (1993). Racial classifications. In Sandra Harding (Ed.), *The "racial" economy of science* (pp. 116–127). Bloomington: Indiana University Press.

Marshall, Mac. (1977). The nature of nurture. *American Ethnologist* 4: 643–662.

———(Ed.). (1979). *Beliefs, behaviors and alcoholic beverages: a cross-cultural survey.*

Ann Arbor: University of Michigan Press.

Marslen-Wilson, William. (Ed.). (1989). *Lexical representation and process.* Cambridge, MA: MIT Press.

Martin, Calvin. (1978). *Keepers of the game: Indian–animal relationships and the fur trade.* Berkeley: University of California Press.

Martin, David. (1990). *Tongues of fire: the explosion of Protestantism in Latin America.* Oxford: Blackwell.

Martin, Emily. (1987). *The woman in the body: a cultural analysis of reproduction.* Boston, MA: Beacon.

———(1994). *Flexible bodies: tracking immunity in American culture from the days of polio to the age of AIDS.* Boston, MA: Beacon.

Martin, Gary J. (1995). *Ethnobotany: a methods manual.* London: Chapman & Hall.

Martin, M. Kay & Barbara Voorhies. (1975). *Female of the species.* New York: Columbia University Press.

Martin, Robert D. & Anne-Elise Martin. (1990). *Primate origins and evolution: a phylogenetic reconstruction.* Princeton, NJ: Princeton University Press.

Martin, William G. (1994). The world-systems perspective in perspective: assessing the attempt to move beyond nineteenth-century eurocentric conceptions. *Review* 17: 145–185.

Martinet, André. (1965). *La linguistique synchronique: études et recherches.* Paris: Presses Universitaires de France.

Martinez, Wilton. (1992). Who constructs anthropological knowledge? toward a theory of ethnographic film spectatorship. In Peter Ian Crawford & David Turton (Eds.), *Film as ethnography* (pp. 131–161). Manchester: University of Manchester Press.

Marty, Martin. (1986). *Protestantism in the United States: righteous empire* [2nd edn.]. New York: Scribners.

Marwick, Max. (1965). *Sorcery in its social setting.* Manchester: Manchester University Press.

———(Ed.). (1970). *Witchcraft and sorcery: selected readings.* Harmondsworth: Penguin.

Marx, Karl. (1887). *Capital: a critique of*

political economy [Das Capital, Hamburg, 1867]. London: Sonnenschein.

———(1903). Theses on Feuerbach. In Frederick Engels (Ed.), *Feuerbach, the roots of the socialist philosophy* [Ludwig Feuerbach und der Ausgang der klassischen deutschen Philosophie, Stuttgart, 1845]. Chicago, IL: Kerr.

———(1933). *Critique of the Gotha programme* [Randglossen zum Programm der Deutschen Arbeiterpartei, 1875]. New York: International Publishers.

———(1963). Economic and philosophical manuscripts. In Erich Fromm (Ed.), *Marx's concept of man* (pp. 87–196). New York: Ungar.

———(1964). *Pre-capitalist economic formations* [Formen der kapitalistischen Produktion vorhergehen, Berlin, 1857]. New York: International.

———(1972). *The ethnological notebooks of Karl Marx* ed. by Lawrence Krader. Assen: Van Gorcum.

Marx, Karl & Friedrich Engels. (1888). *The Communist manifesto* [Manifest der Kommunistischen Partei, London, 1848]. Chicago, IL: Kerr.

———(1947). *The German ideology* [Die deutsche Ideologie, 1932]. New York: International.

Maryanski, Alexandra & Jonathan Turner. (1992). *The social cage.* Stanford, CA: Stanford University Press.

Mason, Peter. (1990). *Deconstructing America.* London: Routledge.

Mather, Lynn & Barbara Yngvesson. (1981). Language, audience, and the transformation of disputes. *Law and Society Review* 15: 775–821.

Mathias-Mundy, Evelyn & Constance M. McCorkle. (1989). *Ethnoveterinary medicine: an annotated bibliography.* Ames: Technology and Social Change Program, Iowa State University.

Matory, James. (1994). *Sex and the empire that is no more: gender and the politics of metaphor in Oyo Yoruba religion.* Minneapolis: University of Minnesota Press.

Mattingly, David. (1992). War and peace in Roman North Africa: observations and models of state-tribe interaction. In R. Brian Ferguson & Neil Whitehead (Eds.), *War in the tribal zone* (pp. 31–60).

Santa Fe, NM: School of American Research Press.

Mattingly, Susan & Linda Garro. (1994). Introduction: narratives and illness. *Social Science and Medicine* 38(6): 776–774.

Mauss, Marcel. (1947). *Manuel d'ethnographie.* Paris: Payot.

———(1950). *Sociologie et anthropologie.* Paris: Presses Universitaires de France.

———(1954). *The gift: forms and functions of exchange in archaic societies* [Essai sur le don, Paris, 1925]. Glencoe, IL: Free Press.

———(1968-9). *Oeuvres* (3 vols.). Paris: Minuit.

———(1972). *A general theory of magic* [Paris, 1904]. London: Routledge.

———(1979). *Sociology and psychology: essays* [Paris, 1924, 1926, 1938, 1935]. London: Routledge.

Mauss, Marcel & Henri Beuchat. (1979). *Seasonal variations of the Eskimo: a study in social morphology* [Essai sur les variations saisonnières des sociétés eskimos, Paris, 1906]. London: Routledge.

May, Robert M. (1973). *Stability and complexity in model ecosystems.* Princeton, NJ: Princeton University Press.

———(1976). Simple mathematical models with very complicated dynamics. *Nature* 261: 459–467.

Maybury-Lewis, David. (1965a). *The savage and the innocent.* Boston, MA: Beacon.

———(1965b). Prescriptive marriage systems. *Southwestern Journal of Anthropology* 21: 207–230.

———(1967). *Akwe Shayante society.* Oxford: Clarendon.

———(1971). Prescriptive marriage systems. In Jack Goody (Ed.), *Kinship* (pp. 199–224). Harmondsworth: Penguin.

———(Ed.). (1979). *Dialectical societies: the Ge and Bororo of central Brazil.* Cambridge, MA: Harvard University Press.

Maybury-Lewis, David. (1967). *Akwe-Shavante society.* Oxford: Clarendon.

———(Ed.). (1984). *The prospects for plural societies.* Washington, DC: American Ethnological Society.

Maybury-Lewis,   David   &   Uri

Almagor. (Eds.). (1989). *The attraction of opposites: thought and society in the dualistic mode.* Ann Arbor: University of Michigan Press.

Mayer, Ann E. (1995). *Islam and human rights: tradition and politics* [2nd edn.]. Boulder, CO: Westview.

Mayer, Philip. (1961). *Townsmen or tribesmen: conservatism and the process of urbanization in a South African city.* Cape Town: Oxford University Press.

———(Ed.). (1970). *Socialization: the approach from social anthropology.* London: Tavistock.

Maynard Smith, John. (1978). Optimization theory in evolution. *Annual Review of Ecology and Systematics* 9: 31–56.

Mayr, Ernst. (1983). How to carry out the adaptationist program? *American Naturalist* 121: 324–334.

Mbiti, J. S. (1990). *African religions and philosophy* [2nd rev. edn.]. Oxford: Heinemann.

Mead, George H. (1934). *Mind, self and society: from the standpoint of a social behaviorist.* Chicago, IL: University of Chicago Press.

Mead, Margaret. (1928). *Coming of age in Samoa: a psychological study of primitive youth for Western civilisation.* New York: Morrow.

———(1930). *Growing up in New Guinea.* New York: Morrow.

———(1935). *Sex and temperament in three primitive societies.* London: Routledge.

———(1942). *And keep your powder dry: an anthropologist looks at America.* New York: Morrow.

———(1949). *Male and female: a study of the sexes in a changing world.* New York: Morrow.

———(1953a). National character. In A. L. Kroeber (Ed.), *Anthropology today* (pp. 642–667). Chicago, IL: University of Chicago Press.

———(Ed.). (1953b). *Cultural patterns and technical change.* Paris: UNESCO.

———(1953c). *The study of culture at a distance.* Chicago, IL: University of Chicago Press.

———(1956). *New lives for old: cultural transformation – Manus, 1928–1953.* New York: Morrow.

———(Ed.). (1959). *An anthropologist at work: writings of Ruth Benedict.* Boston, MA: Houghton-Mifflin.

———(1963). Socialization and enculturation. *Current Anthropology* 4: 184–188.

———(1964). *Food habits research: problems of the 1960's.* Washington, DC: National Academy of Sciences.

———(1972). *Blackberry winter: my earlier years.* New York: Morrow.

Mead, Margaret & Ruth Bunzel. (Eds.). (1960). *The golden age of American anthropology.* New York: George Braziller.

Meek, Charles K. (1946). *Land law and custom in the colonies.* London: Oxford University Press.

Meeker, Michael. (1979). *Literature and violence in North Arabia.* Cambridge: Cambridge University Press.

Meggers, Betty J. (1995). *Amazonia: man and culture in a counterfeit paradise* [rev. edn.]. Washington, DC: Smithsonian.

Meggitt, Mervyn. (1977). *Blood is their argument: warfare among Mae Enga tribesmen of the New Guinea highlands.* Palo Alto, CA: Mayfield.

Mehlman, Jeffrey. (1974). *A structural study of autobiography: Proust, Leiris, Sartre, Lévi-Strauss.* Ithaca, NY: Cornell University Press.

Meigs, Anna S. (1984). *Food, sex, and pollution: a New Guinea religion.* New Brunswick, NJ: Rutgers University Press.

Meillassoux, Claude. (Ed.). (1971). *The development of indigenous trade and markets in West Africa.* London: Oxford University Press.

———(1981). *Maidens, meal and money: capitalism and the domestic community* [Femmes, greniers et capitaux, Paris, 1975]. Cambridge: Cambridge University Press.

———(1991). *The anthropology of slavery: the womb of iron and gold* [Anthropologie de l'esclavage: le ventre de fer et d'argent, Paris, 1986]. Chicago, IL: University of Chicago Press.

Meillet, Antoine. (1967). *The comparative method in historical linguistics* [Méthode comparative en linguistique historique, Oslo, 1925]. Paris: Honoré Champion.

Mellen, Sydney. (1981). *The evolution of love.* San Francisco, CA: Freeman.

Menard, Scott W. (1995). *Applied logistic*

regression analysis. Thousand Oaks, CA: Sage.

Mendonsa, Eugene. (1989). Characteristics of Sisala diviners. In Arthur Lehmann & James Myers (Eds.), *Magic, witchcraft, and religion* [2nd edn.] (pp. 278–288). Mountain View, CA: Mayfield.

Menefee, Samuel P. (1981). *Wives for sale: an ethnographic study of British popular divorce.* New York: St Martin's.

Merchant, Carolyn. (1992). *Radical ecology: the search for a livable world.* New York: Routledge.

———(Ed.). (1994). *Ecology.* Atlantic Highlands, NJ: Humanities.

Merleau-Ponty, Maurice. (1962). *Phenomenology of perception* [Phénoménologie de la perception, Paris, 1945]. New York: Humanities.

Merrell, James H. (1989). *The Indians' new world: Catawbas and their neighbors from European contact through the era of removal.* Chapel Hill: University of North Carolina Press.

Merriam, Alan P. (1964). *The anthropology of music.* Evanston, IL: Northwestern University Press.

———(1967). *Ethnomusicology of the Flathead Indians.* Chicago, IL: Aldine.

Merry, Sally Engle. (1979). Going to court: strategies of dispute management in an American urban neighborhood. *Law and Society Review* 13: 891–925.

———(1981). *Urban danger: life in a neighborhood of strangers.* Philadelphia, PA: Temple University Press.

———(1987). Disputing without culture: review of Goldberg, Green & Sander: *Dispute resolution. Harvard Law Review* 100(8): 2057–2073.

———(1988). Legal pluralism. *Law and Society Review* 22: 869–896.

———(1990). *Getting justice and getting even: legal consciousness among working-class Americans.* Chicago, IL: University of Chicago Press.

———(1992). Anthropology, law and transnational processes. *Annual Reviews in Anthropology* 21: 357–379.

Merry, Sally Engle & Neal Milner. (Eds.). (1993). *The possibility of popular justice: a case study of community mediation in America.* Ann Arbor: University of Michigan Press.

Merry, Sally Engle & Susan S. Silbey. (1984). What do plaintiffs want? Reexamining the concept of dispute. *Justice System Journal* 9: 151–179.

Merton, Robert K. (1949). *Social theory and social structure.* Glencoe, IL: Free Press [republished as *On theoretical sociology: five essays, old and new,* 1967].

———(1976). *Sociological ambivalence and other essays.* New York: Free Press.

———(1982). *Social research and the practicing professions.* Cambridge, MA: Abt.

Messer, Ellen. (1981). Hot–cold classification: theoretical and practical implications of a Mexican study. *Social Science and Medicine* 158: 133–145.

———(1984). Anthropological perspectives on diet. *Annual Review of Anthropology* 13: 205–249.

———(1986). Some like it sweet: estimating sweetness preferences and sucrose intakes from ethnographic and experimental data. *American Anthropologist* 88: 637–647.

———(1989a). Small but healthy? Some cultural considerations. *Human Organization* 48(1): 39–52.

———(1989b). Seasonality in food systems. In David E. Sahn (Ed.), *Seasonal variability in Third World agriculture* (pp. 151–175). Baltimore, MD: Johns Hopkins University Press.

———(1993). Anthropology and human rights. *Annual Review of Anthropology* 22: 221–249.

Messick, Brinkley. (1993). *The calligraphic state: textual domination and history in a Muslim society.* Berkeley: University of California.

Metcalf, Peter. (1976). Birds and deities in Borneo. *Bijdragen* 132: 96–123.

———(1982). *A Borneo journey into death: Berawan eschatology from its rituals.* Philadelphia: University of Pennsylvania Press.

———(1989). *Where are you, spirits: style and theme in Berawan prayer.* Washington, DC: Smithsonian.

Metcalf, Peter & Richard Huntington. (1991). *Celebrations of death: the anthropology of mortuary ritual* [2nd edn.]. Cambridge: Cambridge University Press.

Meyer, Melissa L. (1994). *The White Earth tragedy: ethnicity and dispossession at* *a Minnesota Anishinaabe reservation, 1889–1920.* Lincoln: University of Nebraska Press.

Michaelson, Karen. (1988). *Childbirth in America: anthropological perspectives.* South Hadley, MA: Bergin & Garvey.

Middleton, John. (1960). *Lugbara religion: ritual and authority among an East African people.* London: Oxford University Press.

——(Ed.). (1967). *Magic, witchcraft, and curing.* Garden City, NY: Natural History.

——(Ed.). (1970). *From child to adult.* Austin: Texas: University of Texas Press.

Middleton, John & David Tait. (1958). Introduction. In John Middleton & David Tait (Eds.), *Tribes without rulers.* London: Routledge.

Middleton, John & E. H. Winter. (Eds.). (1963). *Witchcraft and sorcery in East Africa.* New York: Praeger.

Miers, Suzanne & Igor Kopytoff. (Eds.). (1977). *Slavery in Africa: historical and anthropological perspectives.* Madison: University of Wisconsin Press.

Mihalic, Francis. (1971). *The Jacaranda dictionary and grammar of Melanesian Pidgin.* Milton, Queensland: Jacaranda Press.

Miles, Douglas. (1964). The Ngadju longhouse. *Oceania* 36: 45–57.

Miles, Matthew B. & A. Michael Huberman. (1994). *Qualitative data analysis: an expanded sourcebook* [2nd edn.]. Thousand Oaks, CA: Sage.

Miller, Barbara. (1987). Female infanticide and child neglect in rural north India. In Nancy Scheper-Hughes (Ed.), *Child survival* (pp. 95–112). Dordrecht: Reidel.

Miller, Daniel. (Ed.). (1995). *Worlds apart: modernity through the prism of the local.* London: Routledge.

Miller, Joseph C. (1993). *Slavery and slaving in world history: a bibliography, 1900–1991.* Millwood, NY: Kraus International.

Miller, Marc S. (Ed.). (1993). *State of the peoples: a global human rights report on societies in danger.* Boston, MA: Beacon.

Miller, Peggy J. & L. Hoogstra. (1992). Language as tool in the socialization and apprehension of cultural meanings. In Theodore Schwartz, Geoffrey White & Catherine Lutz (Eds.), *New directions in psychological anthropology* (pp. 83–101). Cambridge: Cambridge University Press.

Miller, Peggy J. & B. B. Moore. (1989). Narrative conjunctions of caregiver and child: a comparative perspective on socialization through stories. *Ethos* 17: 428–449.

Miller, Peggy J. & L. L. Sperry. (1987). The socialization of anger and aggression. *Merrill-Palmer Quarterly* 33: 1–31.

Miller, Peggy J., Randolph Potts, Heidi Fung, Lisa Hoogstra & Judy Mintz. (1990). Narrative practices and the social construction of self in childhood. *American Ethnologist* 17: 292–311.

Mills, Antonia & Richard Slobodin. (Eds.). (1994). *Amerindian rebirth: reincarnation belief among North American Indians and Inuit.* Toronto: University of Toronto Press.

Mills, Margaret. (1991). *Rhetorics and politics in Afghan traditional storytelling.* Philadelphia: University of Pennsylvania Press.

Milne, Alan J. M. (1986). *Human rights and human diversity: an essay in the philosophy of human rights.* Albany: State University of New York Press.

Milton, Kay. (Ed.). (1993). *Environmentalism: the view from anthropology.* New York: Routledge.

Miner, Horace. (1952). The folk–urban continuum. *American Sociological Review* 17: 529–537.

——(1953). *The primitive city of Timbuctoo.* Princeton, NJ: Princeton University Press.

Mintz, Sidney. (1985). *Sweetness and power: the place of sugar in modern history.* New York: Viking.

Mintz, Sidney & Eric R. Wolf. (1950). An analysis of ritual co-parenthood (compadrazgo). *Southwestern Journal of Anthropology* 6: 341–368.

Mitchell, J. Clyde. (Ed.). (1969). *Social networks in urban situations: analyses of personal relationships in Central African towns.* Manchester: Manchester University Press.

——(1974). Social networks. *Annual Review of Anthropology* 3: 279–299.

Mitchell, W. J. Thomas. (Ed.). (1981). *On narrative.* Chicago, IL: University of Chicago Press.

Mitchell, William P. & David Guillet, with Inge Bolin. (Eds.). (1994). *Irrigation at high altitudes: the social organization of water control systems in the Andes.* Arlington, VA: American Anthropological Association.

Moberg, Carl-Axel. (1970). Comments on *Analytical archaeology, Norwegian Archaeological Review* 34: 3–4, 21–24.

Modell, Judith. (1983). *Ruth Benedict: patterns of a life.* Philadelphia: University of Pennsylvania Press.

——— (1994). *Kinship with strangers: adoption and interpretations of kinship in American culture.* Berkeley: University of California Press.

Moerman, Michael. (1965). Ethnic identity in a complex civilization: who are the Lue? *American Anthropologist* 67: 1215–1230.

——— (1968). Being Lue: uses and abuses of ethnic identification. In June Helm (Ed.), *Essays on the problem of tribe* (pp. 153–169). Seattle: University of Washington Press.

——— (1988). *Talking culture: ethnography and conversation analysis.* Philadelphia: University of Pennsylvania Press.

Moffatt, Michael. (1989). *Coming of age in New Jersey: college and American culture.* New Brunswick: Rutgers University Press.

Møller, Anders P. (1994). *Sexual selection and the barn swallow.* Oxford: Oxford University Press.

Money-Kyrle, Roger E. (1930). *The meaning of sacrifice.* London: Hogarth.

Monod, Theodore. (Ed.). (1975). *Pastoralism in tropical Africa.* London: Oxford University Press.

Montagne, Robert. (1930). *Les Berbères et le Makhzen dans le Sud du Maroc: essai sur la transformation politique des Berbères sédentaires (groupe chleuh).* Paris: Felix Alcan.

Montagu, Ashley. (1942). *Man's most dangerous myth: the fallacy of race.* New York: Columbia University Press.

——— (Ed.). (1978). *Learning non-aggression: the experience of non-literate societies.* Oxford: Oxford University Press.

Montgomery, Douglas & Elizabeth Peck. (1992). *Introduction to linear regression analysis* [2nd edn.]. New York: Wiley.

Mooney, James. (1896). *Ghost-dance religion and the Sioux outbreak of 1890.* Washington, DC: Smithsonian, Bureau of American Ethnology.

Moore, Alexander G. (1973). *Life cycles in Atchalán: the diverse careers of certain Guatemalans.* New York: Teachers College Press.

Moore, Henrietta L. (1988). *Feminism and anthropology.* Cambridge: Polity.

Moore, Omar Khayam. (1957). Divination: a new perspective. *American Anthropologist* 59: 69–74.

Moore, Sally F. (1970). Law and anthropology. *Biennial Review of Anthropology* 6: 232–300.

——— (1973). Law and social change: the semi-autonomous social field as an appropriate subject of study. *Law and Society Review* 7: 719–746.

——— (1978). *Law as process: an anthropological approach.* London: Routledge.

——— (1986a). *Social facts and fabrications: customary law on Kilimanjaro, 1880–1980.* New York: Columbia University Press.

——— (1986b). Legal systems of the world: an introductory guide to classifications, typological interpretations, and bibliographic resources. In Leon Lipson & Stanton Wheeler (Eds.), *Law and the social sciences* (pp. 11–62). New York: Sage.

Moore, Sally F. & Barbara Myerhoff. (Eds.). (1977). *Secular ritual.* Assen: Van Gorcum.

Moore, Wilbert E. (1963). *Man, time, and society.* New York: Wiley.

Moran, Emilio. (1979). *Human adaptability: an introduction to ecological anthropology.* North Scituate, MA: Duxbury Press.

——— (Ed.). (1990). *The ecosystem approach in anthropology: from concept to practice.* Ann Arbor: University of Michigan Press.

Moran, Emilio, Eduardo Brondizio, Paul Mausel & You Wu. (1994). Integrating Amazonian vegetation, land-use and satellite data. *BioScience* 44(5): 329–338.

Morgan, Lewis Henry. (1851). *League of the Ho-dé-no-sau-nee, or Iroquois*. Rochester, NY: Sage.

———(1871). *Systems of consanguinity and affinity of the human family*. Washington, DC: Smithsonian.

———(1877). *Ancient society*. New York: Holt.

———(1881). *Houses and house-life of the American aborigines*. Washington, DC: Government Printing Office. [reprinted, University of Chicago Press, 1965]

Morinis, Alan. (1992). Introduction. In Alan Morinis (Ed.), *Sacred journeys* (pp. 1–28). Westport, CT: Greenwood.

Morris, Brian. (1976). Whither the savage mind? *Man* 11: 452–470.

———(1979). Symbolism and ideology: thoughts around Navaho taxonomy and symbolism. In Roy Ellen & David Reason (Eds.), *Classifications in their social context* (pp. 117–138). New York: Academic.

———(1987). *Anthropological studies of religion*. Cambridge: Cambridge University Press.

Morris, Charles. (1938). *Foundations of the theory of signs*. Chicago, IL: University of Chicago Press.

Mosko, Mark. (1991). Great men and total systems: North Mekeo hereditary authority and social reproduction. In M. Godelier & M. Strathern (Eds.), *Big men and great men* (pp. 97–114). Cambridge: Cambridge University Press.

Much, Nancy & Richard Shweder. (1978). Speaking of rules: the analysis of culture in breach. In William Damon (Ed.), *Moral development* (pp. 19–39). San Francisco, CA: Jossey-Bass.

Muecke, Marjorie. (1987). Resettled refugees' reconstruction of identity: Lao in Seattle. *Urban Anthropology* 6(3–4): 273–289.

Mueller-Hill, Benno. (1988). *Murderous science: elimination by scientific selection of Jews, Gypsies, and others, Germany 1933–1945* [Tödliche Wissenschaft, Hamburg, 1984]. Oxford: Oxford University Press.

Mukhopadhyay, Carol. (1979). The function of romantic love: a re-appraisal of the Coppinger and Rosenblatt study. *Behavior Science Research* 14: 57–63.

Müller-Wille, Christopher F. (1978).

The forgotten heritage: Christaller's antecedents. In Brian J. L. Berry (Ed.), *The nature of change in geographical ideas* (pp. 37–64). DeKalb: Northern Illinois University Press.

Mullings, Leith. (Ed.). (1987). *Cities in the United States*. New York: Columbia University Press.

Mumford, Lewis. (1934). *Technics and civilization*. New York: Harcourt, Brace.

Munroe, Robert, John Whiting & David Hally. (1969). Institutionalized male transvestism and sex distinction. *American Anthropologist* 71: 87–91.

Munson, Henry. (1986). Geertz on religion: the theory and the practice. *Religion* 16: 19–32.

———(1989). On the irrelevance of the segmentary lineage model in the Moroccan Rif. *American Anthropologist* 91: 386–400.

Muratorio, Blanca. (1991). *The life and times of Grandfather Alonso: culture and history in the upper Amazon* [Rucuyaya Alonso y la historia social y economica del Alto Napo, Quito, 1987]. New Brunswick, NJ: Rutgers University Press.

Murdock, George P. (1947). Bifurcate merging. *American Anthropologist* 49: 56–69.

———(1949). *Social structure*. New York: Macmillan.

———(1951). British social anthropology. *American Anthropologist* 53: 465–473.

Murdock, George P. & Caterina Provost. (1973). Factors in the division of labor by sex: a cross-cultural analysis. *Ethnology* 12: 203–225.

Murdock, George P., Clellan Ford, W. M. Whiting, Alfred Hudson & Leo Simmons. (1982). *Outline of cultural materials* [5th rev. edn.]. New Haven, CT: HRAF Press.

Murphy, Robert. (1957). Intergroup hostility and social cohesion. *American Anthropologist* 59: 1018–1035.

———(1967). Tuareg kinship. *American Anthropologist* 69: 163–167.

———(1972). *Robert H. Lowie*. New York: Columbia University Press.

———(1987). *The body silent*. New York: Holt.

———(1991). Julian Steward. In Sydel Silverman (Ed.), *Totems and teachers* (pp.

170–206). New York: Columbia University Press.

Murphy, Robert & Julian Steward. (1955). Tappers and trappers: parallel processes in acculturation. *Economic Development and Culture Change* 4: 335–355.

Murphy, Yolanda & Robert Murphy. (1974). *Women of the forest.* New York: Columbia University Press.

Murra, John V. (1975). *Formaciones economicas y politicas en el mundo andino.* Lima: Instituto de estudios Peruanos.

——(Ed.). (1976). *American anthropology, the early years.* St Paul, MN: West.

——(1980). *The economic organization of the Inca state.* Greenwich, CT: JAI Press.

——(1984). Andean societies. *Annual Review of Anthropology* 13: 119–141.

Murray, Stephen O. (1982). The dissolution of classical ethnoscience. *Journal of the History of Behavioral Sciences* 18(2): 163–175.

——(1992). *Oceanic homosexualities.* New York: Garland.

——(1995). *Latin American male homosexualities.* Albuquerque: University of New Mexico Press.

——(1996). *American Gay.* Chicago, IL: University of Chicago Press.

Murray, Stephen O. & Will Roscoe. (1996). *Islamic homosexualities.* New York: New York University Press.

Myerhoff, Barbara. (1974). *Peyote Hunt: the sacred journey of the Huichol Indians.* Ithaca, NY: Cornell University Press.

——(1978). *Number our days.* New York: Dutton.

Myerhoff, Barbara & Andrei Simic. (Eds.). (1978). *Life's career – aging: cultural variations on growing old.* Beverly Hills, CA: Sage.

Myers, Fred. (1986). *Pintupi country, Pintupi self: sentiment, place, and politics among Western Desert Aborigines.* Washington, DC: Smithsonian.

Nadel-Klein, Jane & Dona Lee Davis. (1988). *To work and to weep: women in fishing economies.* St. John's, Newfoundland: Institute of Social and Economic Research, Memorial University of Newfoundland.

Nader, Laura. (1965). Choices in legal procedure: Shia Moslem and Mexican Zapotec. *American Anthropologist* 67(2): 394–399.

——(1969). Introduction. In Laura Nader (Ed.), *Law in culture and society* (pp. 1–10). Chicago, IL: Aldine.

——(1990). *Harmony ideology: justice and control in a mountain Zapotec village.* Stanford, CA: Stanford University Press.

Nader, Laura & Harry F. Todd. (Eds.). (1978). *The disputing process: law in ten societies.* New York: Columbia University Press.

Nagel, Ernst. (1959). Some issues in the logic of historical analysis. In Patrick Gardiner (Ed.), *Theories of history* (pp. 373–385). Glencoe, IL: Free Press.

Nakao, Keiko & A. Kimball Romney. (1984). A method for testing alternative theories: an example from English kinship. *American Anthropologist* 86: 668–673.

Nanda, Serena. (1990). *Neither man nor woman: the Hijras of India.* Belmont, CA. Wadsworth.

Naquin, Susan & Chun-fang Yu. (Eds.). (1992). *Pilgrims and sacred sites in China.* Berkeley: University of California Press.

Naroll, Raoul. (1964). On ethnic unit classification. *Current Anthropology* 5: 283–291, 306–312.

Nash, June. (1979). *We eat the mines and the mines eat us: dependency and exploitation in Bolivian tin mines.* New York: Columbia University Press.

Nash, June & Maria P. Fernandez-Kelly. (Eds.). (1983). *Women, men and the international division of labor.* Albany: State University of New York Press.

Natanson, Maurice. (Ed.). (1973). *Phenomenology and the social sciences* (2 vols.). Evanston, IL: Northwestern University Press.

Nations, Marilyn & L. Rebhun. (1988). Angels with wet wings can't fly: maternal sentiment in Brazil and the image of neglect. *Culture, Medicine, and Psychiatry* 12: 141–200.

Neale, Walter C. (1976). *Monies in societies.* San Francisco, CA: Chandler & Sharp.

Needham, Joseph. (1956). *Science and civilization in China,* vol. 2. Cambridge: Cambridge University Press.

Needham, Rodney. (1962). *Structure and sentiment: a test case in social anthropology.* Chicago, IL: University of Chicago Press.

———(1963). Explanatory notes on prescriptive alliance and the Purum. *American Anthropologist* 65: 1377–1386.

———(1972). *Belief, language and experience.* Oxford: Blackwell.

———(Ed.). (1973). *Right and left: essays on dual symbolic classification.* Chicago, IL: University of Chicago Press.

———(1975). Polythetic classification. *Man* 10: 349–367.

———(1983). Skulls and causality. In Rodney Needham (Ed.), *Against the tranquility of axioms* (pp. 66–92). Berkeley: University of California Press.

Neel, James V. (1958). The study of natural selection in primitive and civilized human populations. *Human Biology* 30(1): 43–72.

Neff, Walter S. (1985). *Work and human behavior* [3rd edn.]. New York: Aldine.

Neihardt, John G. (Ed.). (1932). *Black Elk speaks.* New York: Morrow.

Nelson, Geoffrey K. (1969). Spiritualist movement and the need for a redefinition of cult. *Journal for the Scientific Study of Religion* 8: 152–160.

Nelson, Nici. (1979). Women must help each other. In Patricia Caplan & Janet Bujra (Eds.), *Women united, women divided* (pp. 77–98). Bloomington: Indiana University Press.

Nelson, Richard. (1983). *Make prayers to the raven: a Koyukon view of the northern forest.* Chicago, IL: University of Chicago Press.

Ness, Sally Ann. (1994). *Body, movement, and culture.* Philadelphia: University of Pennsylvania Press.

Nestle, Joan. (Ed.). (1992). *The persistent desire: a femme–butch reader.* Boston, MA: Alyson.

Netting, Robert McC. (1981). *Balancing on an Alp: ecological change and continuity in a Swiss mountain community.* Cambridge: Cambridge University Press.

———(1982). Territory, property, and tenure. In Robert McC. Adams, Neil J. Smelser & Donald J. Treiman (Eds.), *Behavioral and social science research* (pp. 446–502). Washington, DC: National Academy Press.

———(1986). *Cultural ecology* [2nd edn.]. Prospect Heights, IL: Waveland.

———(1993). *Smallholders, householders: farm families and the ecology of intensive, sustainable agriculture.* Stanford, CA: Stanford University Press.

Nettl, Bruno. (1983). *The study of ethnomusicology: twenty-nine issues and concepts.* Urbana: University of Illinois Press.

———(1989). *Blackfoot musical thought: comparative perspectives.* Kent, OH: Kent State University Press.

———(1995). *Heartland excursions: ethnomusicological reflections on schools of music.* Urbana: University of Illinois Press.

Neuman, Daniel M. (1980). *The life of music in north India.* Detroit, MI: Wayne State University Press.

Newcomb, William W. (1960). Toward an understanding of war. In Gertrude Dole & Robert Carneiro (Eds.), *Essays in the science of culture* (pp. 317–336). New York: Crowell.

Newcomer, Peter J. (1977). Toward a scientific treatment of "exploitation": a critique of Dalton. *American Anthropologist* 79: 115–119.

Newman, Lucile. (Ed.). (1990). *Hunger in history.* Oxford: Blackwell.

Newmeyer, Frederick J. (1983). *Grammatical theory: its limits and its possibilities.* Chicago, IL: University of Chicago Press.

———(1986). *Linguistic theory in America* [2nd edn.]. Orlando, FL: Academic.

———(Ed.). (1988). *Linguistics: the Cambridge survey,* vol. 2: *Linguistic theory: extensions and implications.* Cambridge: Cambridge University Press.

Newton, Esther. (1972). *Mother camp: female impersonators in America.* Englewood Cliffs, NJ: Prentice-Hall.

Nichols, Bill. (1981). *Ideology and the image: social representation in the cinema and other media.* Bloomington: Indiana University Press.

Nichols, Johanna. (1992). *Linguistic diversity in space and time.* Chicago, IL: University of Chicago Press.

Nicholson,   Heather   &   Ralph

Nicholson. (1979). *Distant hunger: agriculture, food, and human values.* West Lafayette, IN: Purdue University.

Nichter, Mark. (Ed.). (1992). *Anthropological approaches to the study of ethnomedicine.* Philadelphia, PA: Gordon & Breach.

Nicklin, Keith. (1971–72). Stability and innovation in pottery manufacture. *World Archaeology* 3: 13–48.

Nieboer, Herman J. (1910). *Slavery as an industrial system: ethnological researches* [2nd rev. edn.]. The Hague: Nijhoff.

Nietzsche, Friedrich. (1917). *Beyond good and evil* [Jenseits von Gut und Böse, Leipzig, 1886]. New York: Modern Library.

Nisbet, Robert A. (1969). *Social change and history: aspects of the Western theory of development.* Oxford: Oxford University Press.

Nisbett, Richard E., G. Polly & S. Lang. (1995). Homicide and the U.S. regional culture. In R. Barry Ruback & N. S. Weiner (Eds.), *Interpersonal violent behaviors* (pp. 135–151). New York: Springer.

Nolan, Mary Lee & Sidney Nolan. (1989). *Christian pilgrimage in modern Western Europe.* Chapel Hill: University of North Carolina Press.

Noll, Richard. (1983). Shamanism and schizophrenia: a state specific approach to the "schizophrenia metaphor" of shamanic states. *American Ethnologist* 10: 443–459.

Nordstrom, Carolyn & JoAnn Martin. (Eds.). (1992). *The paths to domination, resistance, and terror.* Berkeley: University of California Press.

North, Douglass C. (1981). *Structure and change in economic history.* New York: Norton.

North, Douglass C. & Robert P. Thomas. (1977). The first econonomic revolution. *Economic History Review* 30: 229–241.

Novack, Cynthia. (1990). *Sharing the dance: contact improvisation and American culture.* University of Wisconsin Press.

NRC (National Research Council). (1945). *Manual for the study of food habits.* Washington, DC: National Academy of Sciences.

Nuckolls, Charles. (1993). Sibling myths in a south Indian fishing village: a case study in sociological ambivalence. In Charles Nuckolls (Ed.), *Siblings in South Asia* (pp. 191–218). New York: Guilford.

Nuckolls, Janet. (1996). *Sounds like life: sound-symbolic grammar, performance, and cognition in Pastaza Quechua.* Oxford: Oxford University Press.

Nugent, Christopher. (1983). *Masks of Satan: the demonic in history.* London: Sheed & Ward.

Nutini, Hugo G. & Betty Bell. (1980–1984). *Ritual kinship: the structure and historical development of the compadrazgo system in rural Tlaxcala* (2 vols.). Princeton, NJ: Princeton University Press.

Obbo, Christine. (1990). Adventures with fieldnotes. In Roger Sanjek (Ed.), *Fieldnotes* (pp. 290–302). Ithaca, NY: Cornell University Press.

Obeyesekere, Gananath. (1968). Theodicy, sin and salvation in a sociology of Buddhism. In Edmund R. Leach (Ed.), *Dialectic in practical religion* (pp. 7–40). London: Cambridge University Press.

———(1975). Sinhalese-Buddhist identity in Ceylon. In George De Vos & Lola Romanucci-Ross (Eds.), *Ethnic identity* (pp. 231–258). Palo Alto, CA: Mayfield.

———(1981). *Medusa's hair: an essay on personal symbols and religious experience.* Chicago, IL: University of Chicago Press.

———(1983). *The cult of the goddess Pattini.* Chicago, IL: University of Chicago Press.

———(1990). *The work of culture: symbolic transformation in psychoanalysis and anthropology.* Chicago, IL: University of Chicago Press.

———(1992). *The apotheosis of Captain Cook.* Princeton, NJ: Princeton University Press.

Oboler, Regina S. (1980). Is the female husband a man? women/woman marriage among the Nandi of Kenya. *Ethnology* 19: 69–88.

O'Brien, Denise. (1977). Female husbands in Southern Bantu societies. In Alice Schlegel (Ed.), *Sexual stratification* (pp. 109–126). New York: Columbia University Press.

Odum, Eugene. (1953). *Fundamentals of ecology.* Philadelphia, PA: Saunders.

O'Flaherty, Wendy. (1976). *The origins of evil in Hindu mythology.* Berkeley: University of California Press.

O'Grady, William & Michael Dobrovolsky. (1993). *Contemporary linguistics: an introduction* [2nd edn.]. New York: St. Martin's.

O'Hanlon, Michael. (1989). *Reading the skin: adornment, display and society among the Wahgi.* London: British Museum.

Ohnuki-Tierney, Emiko. (1980). Shamans and *imu* among two Ainu groups. *Ethos* 8: 204–228.

O'Keefe, Phil, K. Westgate & Ben Wisner. (1976). Taking the naturalness out of natural disaster. *Nature* 260: 566–567.

O'Laughlin, Brigette. (1974). Mediation of contradiction: why Mbum women do not eat chicken. In Michelle Rosaldo & Louise Lamphere (Eds.), *Woman, culture, and society* (pp. 301–318). Stanford, CA: Stanford University Press.

Oldfield, Margery L. & Janis Alcorn. (Eds.). (1991). *Biodiversity: culture, conservation, and ecodevelopment.* Boulder, CO: Westview.

Oliver, Douglas L. (1955). *A Solomon Island society: kinship and leadership among the Siuai of Bougainville.* Cambridge, MA: Harvard University Press.

Oliver, Paul. (1987). *Dwellings: the house across the world.* Austin: University of Texas Press.

Ollman, Bertell. (1971). *Alienation: Marx's conception of man in capitalist society.* Cambridge: Cambridge University Press.

Olszewska, Anna & K. Roberts. (Eds.). (1989). *Leisure and life-style: a comparative analysis of free time.* London: Sage Publications.

Omi, Michael & Howard Winant. (1986). *Racial formation in the United States: from the 1960s to the 1980s.* London: Routledge.

Omran, Abdel R. (1971). The epidemiological transition. *Milbank Memorial Fund Quarterly* 49: 509–538.

O'Neill, William. (1967). *Divorce in the progressive era.* Berkeley, CA: University of California Press.

O'Nell, Theresa D. (1994). Telling about Whites, talking about Indians: oppression, resistance, and contemporary American Indian identity. *Cultural Anthropology* 9(1): 94–126.

Ong, Aihwa. (1987). *Spirits of resistance and capitalist discipline: factory women in Malaysia.* Albany: State University of New York Press.

———(1993). On the edge of empires: flexible citizenship among Chinese in diaspora. *Positions* 1: 745–778.

Ong, Walter J. (1982). *Orality and literacy: the technologizing of the word.* London: Methuen.

Ongka. (1979). *Ongka: a self-account by a New Guinea big man.* London: Duckworth.

Opie, Iona & Peter Opie. (1959). *The lore and language of schoolchildren.* Oxford: Clarendon.

Opler, Morris. (1965). Anthropological and cross-cultural aspects of homosexuality. In Judd Marmor (Ed.), *Sexual inversion* (pp. 108–123). New York: Basic.

Orans, Martin. (1968). Surplus. In Yehudi Cohen (Ed.), *Man in adaptation* (pp. 204–214). Chicago, IL: Aldine.

———(1996). *Not even wrong: Margaret Mead, Derek Freeman, and the Samoans.* Novato, CA: Chandler & Sharp.

Orbach, Michael. (1977). *Hunters, seamen and entrepreneurs: the tuna seinermen of San Diego.* Berkeley: University of California Press.

Orlove, Benjamen S. (1980). Ecological anthropology. *Annual Review of Anthropology* 9: 235–273.

Orme, Bryony. (1981). *Anthropology for archaeologists: an introduction.* Ithaca, NY: Cornell University Press.

Ornstein, Robert E. (Ed.). (1973). *The nature of human consciousness: a book of readings.* New York: Viking.

Ortega y Gasset, José. (1972). *Meditations on hunting* [La caza y los toros, Madrid, 1962]. New York: Scribner.

Ortiz, Sutti. (Ed.). (1983). *Economic anthropology: topics and theories.* Lanham, MD: University Press of America.

Ortner, Sherry. (1974a). Purification rites and customs. *New Encyclopaedia*

Britannica: micropaedia [15th edn.]. Chicago, IL: Encyclopaedia Britannica.

—— (1974b). Is female to male as nature is to culture? In Michele Z. Rosaldo & Louise Lamphere (Eds.), *Woman, culture and society* (pp. 67–88). Stanford, CA: Stanford University Press.

—— (1984). Theory in anthropology since the sixties. *Comparative Studies in Society and History* 26: 126–166.

Ortner, Sherry & Harriet Whitehead. (Eds.). (1981). *Sexual meanings: the cultural construction of gender and sexuality.* Cambridge: Cambridge University Press.

Oster, Akos. (1994). "Forest of bliss," film and anthropology. *East–West Film Journal* 8(2): 70–104.

Osthoff, Hermann & Karl Brugmann. (1967). Preface to Morphological investigations in the sphere of the Indo-European languages I [Morphologische Untersuchungen auf dem Gebiete der indogermanischen Sprachen, Leipzig, 1878]. In Winfred P. Lehmann (Ed.), *A reader in nineteenth-century historical Indo-European linguistics* (pp. 197–209). Bloomington: Indiana University Press.

Ostrom, Elinor. (1990). *Governing the commons: the evolution of institutions for collective action.* Cambridge: Cambridge University Press.

Ottenberg, Simon. (1968). *Double descent in an African society: the Afikpo village-group.* Seattle: University of Washington Press.

Otterbein, Keith F. (1970). *The evolution of war: a cross-cultural study.* New Haven, CT: HRAF.

—— (1977). Warfare: a hitherto unrecognized critical variable. *American Behavioral Scientist* 20: 693–710.

—— (1994). *Feuding and warfare: selected works of Keith Otterbein.* Langhorne, PA: Gordon & Breach.

Otterbein, Keith F. & Charlotte Otterbein. (1965). An eye for an eye, a tooth for a tooth: a cross-cultural study of feuding. *American Anthropologist* 67: 1470–1482.

Otto, Rudolf. (1923). *The idea of the holy: an inquiry into the non-rational factor in the idea of the divine and its relation to the rational* [Das Heilige, Breslau, 1920]. London: Oxford University Press.

Overing, Joanna. (Ed.). (1985). *Reason and morality.* London: Tavistock.

Owen, Lara. (1993). *Her blood is gold: celebrating the power of menstruation.* San Francisco, CA: Harper.

Oxfeld, Ellen. (1993). *Blood, sweat, and mahjong: family and enterprise in an overseas Chinese community.* Ithaca, NY: Cornell University Press.

Pace, David. (1983). *Claude Lévi-Strauss: the bearer of ashes.* Boston, MA: Routledge.

Pader, Ellen J. (1993). Spatiality and social change: domestic space use in Mexico and the United States. *American Ethnologist* 20: 114–137.

Padoch, Christine. (1982). *Migration and its alternatives among the Iban of Sarawak.* The Hague: Nijhoff.

Pagel, Mark. (1994). The evolution of conspicuous oestrous advertisement in Old World monkeys. *Animal Behaviour* 47(6): 1333–1342.

Paige, Karen E. & Jeffery M. Paige. (1981). *The politics of reproductive ritual.* Berkeley: University of California Press.

Paine, Robert. (Ed.). (1985). *Advocacy and anthropology, first encounters.* St. John's: University of Newfoundland Press.

Palencia-Roth, Michael. (1993). Cannibal Law of 1503. In Jerry M. Williams & Robert E. Lewis (Eds.), *Early images of the Americas: transfer and invention* (pp. 21–63). Tucson: University of Arizona Press.

Pálsson, Gísli. (1991). *Coastal economies, cultural accounts: human ecology and Icelandic discourse.* Manchester: Manchester University Press.

Paluch, Andrzej K. (1981). The Polish background to Malinowski's work. *Man* 16: 276–285.

Pan, Lynn. (1975). *Alcohol in colonial Africa.* Helsinki: Finnish Foundation for Alcohol Studies.

Pandian, Jacob. (1985). *Anthropology and the Western tradition: toward an authentic anthropology.* Prospect Heights, IL: Waveland.

Pappas, Gregory. (1989). *The magic city:*

unemployment in a working-class community. Ithaca, NY: Cornell University Press.

Paredes, Americo & Richard Bauman. (Eds.). (1972). *Toward new perspectives in folklore.* Austin: University of Texas Press.

Paredes, J. Anthony & Marcus J. Hepburn. (1976). The split brain and the culture-and-cognition paradox. *Current Anthropology* 17: 121–127.

Parish, Steven M. (1994). *Moral knowing in a Hindu sacred city: an exploration of mind, emotion, and self.* New York: Columbia University Press.

Park, Robert. (1928). Human migration and the marginal man. *American Journal of Sociology* 33: 881–893.

Park, Willard. (1938). *Shamanism in western North America: a study in cultural relationships.* Evanston, IL: Northwestern University Press.

Parkin, David. (1979). *The cultural definition of political response: lineal destiny among the Luo.* London: Academic.

——(1980). Kind bridewealth and hard cash: eventing a structure. In J. L. Comaroff (Ed.), *The meaning of marriage payments* (pp. 197–220). London: Academic.

——(Ed.). (1985). *The anthropology of evil.* Oxford: Blackwell.

——(1991). *Sacred void: spatial images of work and ritual among the Giriama of Kenya.* Cambridge: University Press.

Parmigiani, Stefano & F. S. vom Saal. (Eds.). (1994). *Infanticide and parental care.* Langhorne, PA: Harwood Academic.

Parrinder, Geoffrey. (1956). Varieties of belief in reincarnation. *Hibbert Journal* 55: 260–267.

Parry, Jonathan. (1982). Sacrificial death and the necrophagous ascetic. In Maurice Bloch & Jonathan Parry (Eds.), *Death and the regeneration of life* (74–110). Cambridge: Cambridge University Press.

——(1986). *The gift,* the Indian gift and the "Indian gift". *Man* 21: 453–473.

——(1994). *Death in Banaras.* Cambridge: Cambridge University Press.

Parry, Jonathan & Maurice Bloch. (Eds.). (1989). *Money and the morality of exchange.* Cambridge: Cambridge University Press.

Parry, Milman. (1971). *The making of Homeric verse: the collected papers of Milman Parry.* Oxford: Clarendon.

Parsons, Elsie C. (1906). *The family: an ethnographical and historical outline.* New York: Putnam.

——(Ed.). (1922). *American Indian life, by several of its students.* New York: Huebsch.

Parsons, Talcott. (1937). *The structure of social action.* New York: McGraw-Hill.

——(1951a). *The social system.* Glencoe, IL: Free Press.

——(1951b). Illness and role of the physician: a sociological perspective. *American Journal of Orthopsychiatry* 21: 452–460.

——(1954). *Essays in sociological theory.* Glencoe, IL: Free Press.

——(1964). Evolutionary universals in society. *American Sociological Review* 29: 339–357.

——(1966). *Societies: evolutionary and comparative perspectives.* Englewood Cliffs, NJ: Prentice-Hall.

——(1971). *The system of modern societies.* Englewood Cliffs, NJ: Prentice-Hall.

Patterson, Orlando. (1982). *Slavery and social death: a comparative study.* Cambridge, MA: Harvard University Press.

Paul, Diane B. (1984). Eugenics and the left. *Journal of the History of Ideas* 45: 567–590.

——(1992). Eugenic anxieties, social realities, and political choices. *Social Research* 59: 663–683.

——(1995). *Controlling human heredity: 1865 to the present.* Atlantic Highlands, NJ: Humanities.

Paul, Hermann. (1888). *Principles of the history of language* [Principien der Sprachgeschichte, Halle, 1886]. London: Swan. [reprint of 2nd rev. edn., McGrath, 1970]

Paul, Robert. (1989). Psychoanalytic anthropology. *Annual Review of Anthropology* 18: 177–202.

Paulme, Denise. (1973). Blood pacts, age classes and castes in black Africa. In Pierre Alexandre (Ed.), *French perspectives in African studies* (pp. 73–95). London: Oxford University Press.

Payer, Lynn. (1988). *Medicine and culture: varieties of treatment in the United States, England, West Germany, and France.* New York: Holt.

Peacock, James. (1968). *Rites of modernization: symbolic and social aspects of Indonesian proletariat drama.* Chicago, IL: University of Chicago Press.

Pearson, Harry. (1957). The economy has no surplus: critique of a theory of development. In Karl Polanyi, Conrad Arensberg & H. W. Pearson (Eds.), *Trade and markets in the early empires* (pp. 320–341). Glencoe, IL: Free Press.

Peattie, Lisa R. (1968). *The view from the barrio.* Ann Arbor: University of Michigan Press.

———(1983). Research, policy and ideas in good currency: the squatter settlement phenomenon. *Studies in Third World Societies* 24: 93–113.

Pedersen, Holger. (1931). *Linguistic science in the nineteenth century: methods and results* [Sprogvidenskaben i det nittende århundrede, metoder og resultater, Copenhagen, 1924]. Cambridge, MA: Harvard University Press.

Peel, John D. Y. (1971). *Herbert Spencer: the evolution of a sociologist.* London: Heinemann.

Peirce, Charles S. (1931–58). *Collected papers of Charles Sanders Peirce.* Cambridge, MA: Harvard University Press.

Peires, Jeffrey B. (1989). *The dead will arise: Nongqawuse and the great Xhosa cattle-killing movement of 1856-7.* Johannesburg: Ravan Press.

Peletz, Michael G. (1988). *A share of the harvest: kinship, property, and social history among the Malays of Rembau.* Berkeley: University of California Press.

———(1995). Kinship studies in late twentieth-century anthropology. *Annual Review of Anthropology* 24: 343–372.

Pellow, Deborah. (1993). Chinese privacy. In Robert Rotenberg & Gary McDonogh (Eds.), *The cultural meaning of urban space* (pp. 17–31). Westport, CT: Bergin & Garvey.

Pelto, Gretel, Pertti Pelto & Ellen Messer. (Eds.). (1989). *Research methods in nutritional anthropology.* Tokyo: United Nations University.

Pelzer, Karl J. (1978). *Planter and peasant: colonial policy and the agrarian struggle in East Sumatra 1863-1947.* The Hague: Nijhoff.

Pendleton, Wade C. (1996). *Katutura: a place where we stay: life in a post-apartheid township in Namibia.* Athens: Ohio University Center for International Studies.

Penniman, Thomas K. (1935). *A hundred years of anthropology.* London: Duckworth.

Peregrine, Peter & Gary M. Feinman. (Eds.). (1996). *Pre-Columbian world systems.* Madison, WI: Prehistory Press.

Perin, Constance. (1977). *Everything in its place: social order and land use in America.* Princeton, NJ: Princeton University Press.

Peristiany, Jean G. (Ed.). (1966). *Honor and shame: the values of Mediterranean society.* Chicago, IL: University of Chicago Press.

———(Ed.). (1976). *Mediterranean family structures.* Cambridge: Cambridge University Press.

Peteet, Julie. (1996). The writing on the walls: the graffiti of the Intifada. *Cultural Anthropology* 11(2): 139–159.

Peters, Emrys L. (1967). Some structural aspects of feuding among the camel-herding Bedouin of Cyrenaica. *Africa* 37: 261–282.

Peters, Francis E. (1986). *Jerusalem and Mecca: the typology of the holy city in the Near East.* New York: New York University Press.

———(1994). *The Hajj: The Muslim pilgrimage to Mecca and the holy places.* Princeton, NJ: Princeton University Press.

Peters, Larry. (1982). Trance, initiation and psychotherapy in Tamang shamanism. *American Ethnologist* 9: 21–46.

Pfaffenberger, Bryan. (1990). The harsh facts of hydraulics: technology and society in Sri Lanka's colonization schemes. *Technology and Culture* 31: 361–397.

———(1992). Social anthropology of technology. *Annual Review of Anthropology* 21: 491–516.

Philips, Susan, Susan Steele & Christine Tanz. (Eds.). (1987). *Language, gender and sex in comparative perspective.* Cambridge: Cambridge University Press.

Phillips, Roderick. (1988). *Putting asunder: a history of divorce in Western society.* Cambridge: Cambridge University Press.

Picone, Mary. (1989). The ghost in the machine: religious healing and representations of the body in Japan. In Michel Feher (Ed.), *Fragments for a history of the human body,* vol. 2 (pp. 466–489). New York: Urzone.

Piddocke, Stuart. (1967). The potlatch system of the southern Kwakiutl: a new perspective. *Southwestern Journal of Anthropology* 21: 244–264.

Piette, Albert. (1993). Epistemology and practical applications of anthropological photography. *Visual Anthropology* 6: 157–170.

Pike, Kenneth L. (1954). Emic and etic standpoints for the description of behavior. In K. L. Pike, *Language in relation to a unified theory of the structure of human behavior,* Part I: preliminary edition (pp. 8–28). Glendale: Summer Institute of Linguistics.

Pilbeam, David. (1983). The naked ape: an idea we could live without. In Morris Freilich (Ed.), *The pleasures of anthropology* (pp. 421–431). New York: New American Library.

Pine, Stephen. (1995). *World fire: the culture of fire on earth.* New York: Holt.

Pinker, Steven. (1991). Rules of language. *Science.* 253: 530–535.

———(1994). *The language instinct: how the mind creates language.* New York: Morrow.

Pinkerton, Evelyn. (1989). *Co-operative management of local fisheries: new directions for improved management and community development.* Vancouver: University of British Columbia Press.

Pinney, Christopher. (1989). The quick and the dead. *Society for Visual Anthropology Review* 6(2): 42–54.

———(1992). The parallel histories of anthropology and photography. In Elizabeth Edwards (Ed.), *Anthropology and photography 1860–1920* (pp. 74–95). New Haven, CT: Yale University Press.

Piore, Michael J. (1979). *Birds of passage: migrant labor and industrial societies.* Cambridge: Cambridge University Press.

Pitt-Rivers, Augustus. (1906). *The evo-lution of culture.* Oxford: Oxford University Press.

Pitt-Rivers, Julian. (1958). Ritual kinship in Spain. *Transactions of the New York Academy of Sciences* 20: 424–431.

Plath, David W. (1980). *Long engagements: maturity in modern Japan.* Stanford, CA: Stanford University Press.

———(1987). Making experience come out right: culture as biography. *Central Issues in Anthropology* 7: 1–8.

Plattner, Stuart. (Ed.). (1985). *Markets and marketing.* Lanham, MD: University Press of America.

———(Ed.). (1989). *Economic anthropology.* Stanford, CA: Stanford University Press.

Plessner, Helmuth. (1970). *Laughing and crying: a study of limits of human behavior* [Lachen und weinen, Munich, 1950]. Evanston, IL: Northwestern University Press.

Plotkin, Mark. (1993). *Tales of a shaman's apprentice: an ethnobotanist searches for new medicines in the Amazon rain forest.* New York: Viking.

Plotnicov, Leonard & Arthur Tuden. (Eds.). (1970). *Essays in comparative social stratification.* Pittsburgh, PA: University of Pittsburgh Press.

Pocock, David. (1973). *Mind, body and wealth: a study of belief and practice in an Indian village.* Oxford: Blackwell.

Poggie, John J. & Richard Pollnac. (1988). Danger and rituals of avoidance among New England fishermen. *Maritime Anthropological Studies* 1(1): 66–78.

Polanyi, Karl. (1944). *The great transformation.* New York: Rinehart.

———(1957). The economy as instituted process. In Karl Polanyi, Conrad Arensberg & Harry Pearson (Eds.), *Trade and markets in the early empires* (pp. 243–270). Glencoe, IL: Free Press.

Polanyi, Karl, Conrad Arensberg & Harry Pearson. (Eds.). (1957). *Trade and markets in the early empires.* Glencoe, IL: Free Press.

Polanyi, Michael. (1969). *Knowing and being.* Chicago, IL: University of Chicago Press.

Polgar, Steven. (1972). Population history and population policies from an anthropological perspective. *Current Anthropology* 13: 203–211.

Pomian, Kryzysztof. (1990). *Collectors and curiosities: Paris and Venice, 1500–1800.* Cambridge: Polity.

Pope, Kenneth. (Ed.). (1980). *On love and loving.* San Francisco, CA: Jossey-Bass.

Porter, Philip W. (1965). Environmental potentials and economic opportunities: a background for cultural adaptation. *American Anthropologist* 67: 409–420.

Portes, Alejandro & Alex Stepick. (1993). *City on the edge: the transformation of Miami.* Berkeley: University of California Press.

Portmann, Adolf. (1990). *A zoologist looks at humankind* [Zoologie und das neue Bild des Menschen, Hamburg, 1956]. New York: Columbia University Press.

Pospisil, Leopold. (1958). *Kapauku Papuans and their law.* New Haven, CT: Yale University Publications in Anthropology, 54.

——— (1971). *Anthropology of law: a comparative theory.* New York: Harper & Row.

Poster, Mark. (1990). *The mode of information: poststructuralism and social context.* Cambridge: Polity.

Powdermaker, Hortense. (1966). *Stranger and friend: the way of an anthropologist.* New York: Norton.

Poyer, Lin. (1993). Egalitarianism in the face of hierarchy. *Journal of Anthropological Research* 49: 111–133.

Prakash, Gyan. (1994). Subaltern studies as postcolonial criticism. *American Historical Review* 99: 1475–1490.

——— (Ed.). (1995). *After colonialism: imperial history and postcolonial displacements.* Princeton, NJ: Princeton University Press.

Prance, Ghillean T. (1991). What is ethnobotany today? *Journal of Ethnopharmacology* 32(1–3): 209–216.

Pred, Allan. (1984). Place as a historically contingent process: structuration and the time-geography of becoming places. *Annals of the Association of American Geographers* 74: 279–297.

Preucel, Robert W. (Ed.). (1991a). *Processual and postprocessual archaeologies:*

multiple ways of knowing the past. Carbondale, IL: Center for Archaeological Investigations, Southern Illinois University.

——— (1991b). The philosophy of archaeology. In Robert Preucel (Ed.), *Processual and postprocessual archaeologies* (pp. 17–29). Carbondale, IL: Center for Archaeological Investigations, Southern Illinois University.

Price, Richard. (1983). *First-time: the historical vision of an Afro-American people.* Baltimore: Johns Hopkins University Press.

Price, Sally. (1989). *Primitive art in civilized places.* Chicago, IL: University of Chicago Press.

Price, T. Douglas & James A. Brown. (Eds.). (1985). *Prehistoric hunter-gatherers: the emergence of cultural complexity.* Orlando, FL: Academic.

Prichard, James. (1813, 1836–47). *Researches into the physical history of mankind* (4 vols.). London: Arch. [3rd rev. edn. (5 vols), 1836–47; reprinted, University of Chicago Press, 1973]

Prince, Gerald. (1987). *A dictionary of narratology.* Omaha: University of Nebraska Press.

Prins, Adriaan H. J. (1965). *Sailing from Lamu a study of maritime culture in Islamic East Africa.* Assen: Van Gorcum.

Propp, Vladimir. (1958). *The morphology of the folktale* [Morfologiia skazki, Leningrad, 1928]. Bloomington: Indiana University Research Center in Anthropology, Folklore and Linguistics.

Prunier, Gerard. (1995). *The Rwanda crisis: history of a genocide.* New York: Columbia University Press.

Pryor, Frederic L. (1973). *Property and industrial organization in communist and capitalist nations.* Bloomington: Indiana University Press.

Putnam, Hilary. (1975). *Mind, language, and reality.* Cambridge: Cambridge University Press.

Quandt, Sara & Cheryl Ritenbaugh. (Eds.). (1986). *Training manual in nutritional anthropology.* Washington, DC: American Anthropological Association.

Quarles van Ufford, Phillip & Matthew Schoffeleers. (Eds.). (1988). *Religion and development: towards an integrated* *approach.* Amsterdam: Free University Press.

Quigley, Colin. (1985). *Close to the floor: folk dance in Newfoundland.* St John's: Memoral University of Newfoundland Folklore Department.

——(1993). International Council for Traditional Music Study Group on Ethnochoreology: 17th symposium. *Dance Research Journal* 25(1): 51–55.

Quinn, Naomi. (1977). Anthropological studies on women's status. *Annual Review of Anthropology* 6: 181–225.

Quinn, Naomi & Dorothy Holland. (1987). Culture and cognition. In D. Holland & N. Quinn (Eds.), *Cultural models in language and thought* (pp. 3–42). Cambridge: Cambridge University Press.

Rabinow, Paul. (1977). *Reflections on fieldwork in Morocco.* Berkeley: University of California Press.

——(1985). Discourse and power: on the limits of ethnographic authority. *Dialectical Anthropology* 10(1–2): 1–13.

——(1986). Representations are social facts: modernity and post-modernity in anthropology. James Clifford & George Marcus (Eds.), *Writing culture* (pp. 234–261). Berkeley: University of California Press.

——(1988). Comment. *Current Anthropology* 29: 429–439.

——(1989). *French modern: norms and forms of the social environment.* Cambridge, MA: MIT Press.

——(Ed.). (1991). *The Foucault reader.* New York: Pantheon.

——(1996). *Making PCR: a story of biotechnology.* Chicago, IL: University Chicago Press.

Radcliffe-Brown, A. R. (1922). *The Andaman Islanders: a study in social anthropology.* Cambridge: Cambridge University Press.

——(1930). The sociological theory of totemism. In *Proceedings of the fourth Pacific Science Congress.* Batavia-Bandoeng: Pacific Science Association. [reprinted in Radcliffe Brown 1952: 117–132]

——(1930–31). The social organization of Australian tribes. *Oceania* 1: 34–63, 206–246, 322–341, 426–456.

——(1933). Law: primitive: social sanctions. In Edwin R. A. Seligman (Ed.), *Encyclopedia of the social sciences,* vol. 9 (pp. 202–206). New York: Macmillan.

——(1934). Sanctions, social. In Edwin R. A. Seligman (Ed.), *Encyclopedia of the social sciences,* vol. 13 (pp. 531–534). New York: Macmillan.

——(1939). Taboo. The Frazer Lecture. [reprinted in Radcliffe Brown 1952: 133–152].

——(1951). The comparative method in social anthropology. *Journal of the Royal Anthropological Institute* 81: 15–22.

——(1952). *Structure and function in primitive society.* London: Cohen & West.

——(1957). *A natural science of society.* Glencoe, IL: Free Press.

——(1958). *Method in social anthropology: selected essays.* Chicago, IL: University of Chicago Press.

Radcliffe-Brown, A. R. & Daryll Forde. (Eds.). (1950). *African systems of kinship and marriage.* London: Oxford University Press.

Radford, Andrew. (1981). *Transformational syntax: a student's guide to Chomsky's extended standard theory.* Cambridge: Cambridge University Press.

Radin, Paul. (Ed.). (1920). *The autobiography of a Winnebago Indian.* Berkeley: University of California.

——(Ed.). (1926). *Crashing Thunder: the autobiography of an American Indian.* New York: Appleton.

——(1932). *Social anthropology.* New York: McGraw-Hill.

Radner, Joan. (Ed.). (1993). *Feminist messages: coding in women's folklore.* Urbana: University of Illinois Press.

Ragin, Charles C. (1987). *The comparative method: moving beyond qualitative and quantitative strategies.* Berkeley: University of California Press.

Ragoné, Helena. (1994). *Surrogate motherhood: conception in the heart.* Boulder, CO: Westview.

Raheja, Gloria G. (1988). *The poison in the gift: ritual, prestation, and the dominant caste in a north Indian village.* Chicago, IL: University of Chicago Press.

Rainwater, Lee. (1967). *The Moynihan report and the politics of controversy: a Trans-action social science and public policy report.* Cambridge, MA: MIT Press.

Randall, Robert. (1976). How tall is a taxonomic tree? Some evidence for dwarfism. *American Ethnologist* 3: 543–553.

Rank, Otto. (1914). *The myth of the birth of the hero: a psychological interpretation of mythology* [Der mythus von der Geburt des Helden, Vienna, 1909]. London: Hogarth.

Rao, Aparna. (1987). *The other nomads: peripatetic minorities in cross-cultural perspective.* Cologne: Bohlau.

Rapoport, Amos. (1969). *House form and culture.* Englewood Cliffs, NJ: Prentice-Hall.

———(1982). *The meaning of the built environment: a nonverbal communication approach.* Beverly Hills, CA: Sage.

Rappaport, Roy A. (1967). *Pigs for the ancestors.* New Haven, CT: Yale University Press. [2nd rev. edn., 1984]

———(1979). *Ecology, meaning and religion.* Richmond, CA: North Atlantic.

Rasmussen, Susan J. (1991). Lack of prayer: ritual restrictions, social experience, and the anthropology of menstruation among the Tuareg. *American Ethnologist* 18(4): 751–769.

Read, Dwight W. (1989). Statistical methods and reasoning in archaeological research: a review of praxis and promise. *Journal of Quantitative Anthropology* 1: 5–78.

Reader, Ian. (1987). From asceticism to the package tour: the pilgrim's progress in Japan. *Religion* 17: 133–148.

———(1988). Miniaturization and proliferation: a study of small-scale pilgrimages in Japan. *Studies in Central and East Asian Religions* 1: 50–66.

Redfield, Robert. (1930). *Tepoztlán, a Mexican village: a study of folk life.* Chicago, IL: University of Chicago Press.

———(1934). *Chan Kom, a Maya village.* Washington, DC: Carnegie Institution.

———(1941). *The folk culture of Yucatan.* Chicago, IL: University of Chicago Press.

———(1947). *Equality of educational opportunity: a radio discussion.* Chicago, IL: University of Chicago Press.

———(1950). *A village that chose progress: Chan Kom revisited.* Chicago, IL: University of Chicago Press.

———(1953). *The primitive world and its transformations.* Ithaca, NY: Cornell University Press.

———(1955). *The little community: view points for the study of a human whole.* Uppsala: Almqvist. [reprinted Redfield 1960]

———(1956). *Peasant society and culture: an anthropological approach to civilization.* Chicago, IL: University of Chicago Press.

———(1960). *The little community, and peasant society and culture.* Chicago, IL: University of Chicago Press.

———(1964). Primitive law. *University of Cincinnati Law Review* 33(1): 1–22 [republished 1967, in Paul Bohannan (Ed.), *Law and warfare*, Austin: University of Texas Press, pp. 3–25].

Redfield, Robert, Ralph Linton & Melville J. Herskovits. (1936). Memorandum for the study of acculturation. *American Anthropologist* 38: 149–152.

Reichard, Gladys. (1944). *Prayer: the compulsive word.* New York: Augustin.

Reichel-Dolmatoff, Gerardo. (1971). *Amazonian cosmos: the sexual and religious symbolism of the Tukano Indians.* Chicago, IL: University of Chicago Press.

Reidhead, Van A. (1979). Linear programming models in archaeology. *Annual Review of Anthropology* 8: 543–578.

Reik, Theodor. (1931). *Ritual: psychoanalytic studies* [Probleme der Religionspsychologie, Leipzig, 1919]. London: Hogarth.

Reilly, Philip. R. (1991). *The surgical solution: a history of involuntary sterilization in the United States.* Baltimore, MD: Johns Hopkins University Press.

Reiter, Rayna R. (Ed.). (1975a). *Toward an anthropology of women.* New York: Monthly Review.

———(1975b). Introduction. In Rayna Reiter (Ed.), *Toward an anthropology of women* (pp. 11–19). New York: Monthly Review Press.

Relph, Edward. (1976). *Place and placelessness.* London: Pion.

Rencher, Alvin. (1995). *Methods of multivariate analysis.* New York: Wiley.

Renfrew, Colin. (1984). *Approaches to social archaeology.* Edinburgh: Edinburgh University Press.

Renteln, Alison D. (1990). *International human rights: universalism versus relativism.* Newbury Park, CA: Sage.

Resek, Carl. (1960). *Lewis Henry Morgan, American scholar.* Chicago, IL: University of Chicago Press.

Rey, Pierre-Philippe. (1973). *Les alliances de classes: sur l'articulation des modes de production.* Paris: Maspero.

Reyna, Stephen P. (1994). Literary anthropology and the case against science. *Man* 29: 555–581.

Reyna, Stephen P. & R. E. Downs. (Eds.). (1994). *Studying war: anthropological perspectives.* Langhorne, PA: Gordon & Breach.

Rhodes, Lorna A. (1996). Studying biomedicine as a cultural system. In Carolyn Sargent & Thomas M. Johnson (Eds.), *Medical anthropology* [2nd edn.] (pp. 165–182). Westport, CT: Greenwood.

Rice, Prudence M. (1984). Change and conservatism in pottery-producing systems. In Sander E. van der Leeuw & Alison Pritchard (Eds.), *The many dimensions of pottery* (pp. 231–278). Amsterdam: Universiteit van Amsterdam.

Rice, Timothy. (1994). *May it fill your soul: experiencing Bulgarian music.* Chicago, IL: University of Chicago Press.

Richard, Alison F. (1985). *Primates in nature.* New York: Freeman.

Richards, Audrey I. (1932). *Hunger and work in a savage tribe: a functional study of nutrition among the southern Bantu.* London: Routledge.

——— (1939). *Land, labour and diet in Northern Rhodesia.* London: Oxford University Press.

——— (1950). Some types of family structure among the Central Bantu. In A. R. Radcliffe-Brown & Daryll Forde (Eds.), *African systems of kinship and marriage* (pp. 207–251). London: Oxford University Press.

——— (1954). *Economic development and tribal change: a study of immigrant labour.* Cambridge: Heffer.

——— (1956). *Chisungu: a girl's initiation among the Bemba.* London: Faber & Faber.

——— (Ed.). (1960). *East African chiefs: a study of political development in some Uganda and Tanganyika tribes.* London: Faber & Faber.

——— (1967). African systems of thought: an Anglo-French dialogue. *Man* 2: 286–298.

Richards, Audrey I. & E. M. Widdowson. (1936). A dietary study in North-eastern Rhodesia. *Africa* 9: 166–196.

Richards, Paul. (1985). *Indigenous agricultural revolution: ecology and food production in West Africa.* London: Hutchinson.

Richardson, Miles. (1982). Being-in-the-market versus being-in-the-plaza: material culture and the construction of social reality in Spanish America. *American Ethnologist* 9: 421–436.

Riches, David. (1986a). The phenomenon of violence. In David Riches (Ed.), *The anthropology of violence* (pp. 1–27). Oxford: Blackwell.

——— (Ed.). (1986b). *The anthropology of violence.* Oxford: Blackwell.

——— (1994). Shamanism: the key to religion. *Man* 29: 381–406.

Richie, Susan. (1993). Ventriloquist folklore: who speaks for representation? *Western Folklore* 52: 365–378.

Rickford, John. (1987). *Dimensions of a Creole continuum: history, texts and linguistic analysis of Guyanese Creole.* Stanford, CA: Stanford University Press.

Ricklefs, Robert. (1973). *Ecology.* Newton, MA: Chiron Press.

Ricoeur, Paul. (1967). *The symbolism of evil* [Symbolique de mal, Paris, 1960]. New York: Harper & Row.

——— (1971). The model of the text: meaningful action considered as a text. *Social Research* 35: 529–536.

——— (1981). *Hermeneutics and the human sciences: essays on language, action, and interpretation.* Cambridge: Cambridge University Press.

Riemsdijk, Henk van & Edwin Williams. (1986). *Introduction to the theory of grammar.* Cambridge, MA: MIT Press.

Riesman, Paul. (1983). On the irrelevance of child rearing practices for the formation of personality: an analysis of childhood, personality, and values in two African communities. *Culture, Medicine, and Psychiatry* 7: 103–129.

———(1992). *First find your child a good mother: the construction of self in two African communities.* New Brunswick, NJ: Rutgers University Press.

Rindos, David. (1984). *The origins of agriculture: an evolutionary perspective.* Orlando, FL: Academic.

Rinschede, Gisbert & S. M. Bhardwaj. (1990). *Pilgrimage in the United States.* Berlin: D. Reimer.

Ritenbaugh, Cheryl. (1978). Human foodways: a window on evolution. In E. E. Bauwens (Ed.), *The anthropology of health* (pp. 111–120). St. Louis: Mosby.

———(1982). Obesity as a culture-bound syndrome. *Culture, Medicine, and Psychiatry* 6: 347–361.

Rivers, W. H. R. (1906). *The Todas.* London: Macmillan.

———(1914a). *Kinship and social organization.* London: Constable. [New York: Humanities, 1968]

———(1914b). *The history of Melanesian society* (2 vols.). Cambridge: Cambridge University Press.

———(1924). *Social organization.* London: Kegan.

———(1926). *Psychology and ethnology.* London: Kegan.

Rivière, Peter G. (1971). Marriage: a reassessment. In Rodney Needham (Ed.), *Rethinking kinship and marriage* (pp. 57–74). London: Tavistock.

Robben, Antonius C. G. M. (1989). *Sons of the sea goddess: economic practice and discursive conflict in Brazil.* New York: Columbia University Press.

Roberts, Bryan. (1978). *Cities of peasants: the political economy of urbanization in the Third World.* Beverly Hills, CA: Sage.

Roberts, Helen. (Ed.). (1981). *Doing feminist research.* London: Routledge.

Roberts, Helen H. (1936). *Musical areas in aboriginal North America.* New Haven, CT: Yale University Press.

Robertson, A. F. (1991). *Beyond the family: the social organization of human reproduction.* Berkeley: University of California Press.

Robson, John R. (Ed.). (1980). *Food, ecology, and culture: readings in the anthropology of dietary practice.* New York: Gordon & Breach.

Rockefeller, Steven & John C. Elder. (Eds.). (1992). *Spirit and nature: why the environment is a religious issue.* Boston, MA: Beacon.

Rodda, Annabel. (1991). *Women and the environment.* London: Zed.

Rodman, Margaret. (1992). Empowering place: multilocality and multivocality. *American Anthropologist* 94: 640–656.

Rodman, Margaret & Matthew Cooper. (Eds.). (1979). *The pacification of Melanesia.* Ann Arbor: University of Michigan Press.

Rodney, Walter. (1972). *How Europe underdeveloped Africa.* London: Bogle.

Roe, Peter. (1982). *The cosmic zygote: cosmology in the Amazon basin.* New Brunswick, NJ: Rutgers University Press.

Rogers, Everett M. (1995). *Diffusion of innovations* [4th edn.]. New York: Free Press.

Rogoff, Barbara. (1990). *Apprenticeship in thinking: cognitive development in social context.* Oxford: Oxford University Press.

Roheim, Geza. (1950). *Psychoanalysis and anthropology: culture, personality and the unconscious.* New York: International Universities Press.

Rohlen, Thomas P. (1974). *For harmony and strength: Japanese white-collar organization in anthropological perspective.* Berkeley: University of California Press.

Rohner, Ronald. (Ed.). (1969). *The ethnography of Franz Boas.* Chicago, IL: University of Chicago Press.

Rollwagen, Jack. (Ed.). (1988). *Anthropological filmmaking: anthropological perspectives on the production of film and video for general public audiences.* New York: Harwood.

Romaine, Suzanne. (1994). *Language in society: an introduction to sociolinguistics.* Oxford: Oxford University Press.

Romney, A. Kimball. (1980). Multidimensional scaling applications in anthropology. In J. Clyde Mitchell (Ed.), *Numerical techniques in social anthropology* (pp. 71–84). Philadelphia, PA: ISHI.

———(1989). Quantitative models, science, and cumulative knowledge. *Journal of Quantitative Anthropology* 1: 153–223.

Romney, A. Kimball, Susan Weller & William Batchelder. (1986). Culture as consensus: a theory of culture and informant accuracy. *American Anthropologist* 99: 313–338.

Romney, A. Kimball, William Batchelder & Susan Weller. (1987). Recent applications of cultural consensus theory. *American Behavioral Scientist* 31: 163–177.

Rooks, Judith P., Norman L. Weatherby, Eunice K. M. Ernst, Susan Stapleton, David Rosen & Allan Rosenfield. (1989). Outcomes of care in birth centers: The National Birth Center Study. *New England Journal of Medicine* 321: 1804–1811.

Roper, Marilyn. (1975). Evidence of warfare in the Near East from 10000–4300 B.C. In Martin Nettleship, R. Dale Givens & Anderson Nettleship (Eds.), *War* (pp. 299–344). The Hague: Mouton.

Rorty, Richard. (1991). *Objectivity, relativism, and truth*. Cambridge: Cambridge University Press.

Rosaldo, Michelle. (1980). *Knowledge and passion: Ilongot notions of self and social life*. Cambridge. Cambridge University Press.

————(1984). Toward an Anthropology of self and feeling. In Richard Shweder & Robert Levine (Eds.), *Culture theory* (pp. 137–157). Cambridge: Cambridge University Press.

Rosaldo, Michelle & Louise Lamphere. (Eds.). (1974). *Women, culture and society*. Stanford, CA: Stanford University Press.

Rosaldo, Renato. (1980). *Ilongot headhunting, 1883–1974: a study in society and history*. Stanford: Stanford University Press.

————(1989). *Culture and truth: the remaking of social analysis*. Boston, MA: Beacon.

————(1993). Notes toward a critique of patriarchy from a male position. *Anthropological Quarterly* 66(2): 81–86.

Rosch, Eleanor & Barbara Lloyd. (Eds.). (1978). *Cognition and categorization*. New York: Halsted.

Roscoe, Will. (1987). Bibliography of berdache and alternative gender roles among North American Indians. *Journal of Homosexuality* 14: 81–171.

————(1991). *The Zuni man–woman*. Al-

buquerque: University of New Mexico Press.

Rose, Frederick G. G. (1960). *Classification of kin, age structure, and marriage amongst the Groote Eylandt Aborigines: a study in method and a theory of Australian kinship*. Berlin: Akademie-Verlag.

Rose, Laurel. (1992). *The politics of harmony: land dispute strategies in Swaziland*. Cambridge: Cambridge University Press.

Roseberry, William. (1989). Anthropology, history, and modes of production. In Benjamin Orlav et al. (Eds.), *State, capital, and rural society* (pp. 9–37). Boulder, CO: Westview.

Roseman, Marina. (1991). *Healing sounds from the Malaysian rainforest: Temiar music and medicine*. Berkeley: University of California Press.

Rosen, Lawrence. (1989). *The anthropology of justice: law as culture in Islamic society*. Cambridge: Cambridge University Press.

Rosenfeld, Richard & Steven F. Messner. (1991). The social sources of homicide in different types of societies. *Sociological Forum* 6(1): 51–70.

Rosman, Abraham & Paula G. Rubel. (1971). *Feasting with mine enemy: rank and exchange among northwest coast societies*. New York: Columbia University Press.

————(1990). Structural patterning in Kwakiutl art and ritual. *Man* 25: 620–640.

Ross, Eric B. (Ed.). (1980). *Beyond the myths of culture: essays in cultural materialism*. New York: Academic.

Ross, Marc. (1981). Socioeconomic complexity, socialization, and political differentiation: a cross-cultural study. *Ethos* 9: 217–247.

————(1986). A cross-cultural theory of political conflict and violence. *Political Psychology* 7: 427–469.

Roth, Julius A. (1963). *Timetables: structuring the passage of time in hospital treatment and other careers*. Indianapolis: Bobbs-Merrill.

Roth, Paul A. (1989). Ethnography without tears. *Current Anthropology* 30: 555–569.

Rothenberg, Jerome & Diane

Rothenberg. (1983). *Symposium of the whole: a range of discourse toward an ethnopoetics.* Berkeley: University of California Press.

Rothenberg, Winifred Barr. (1992). *From market-places to a market economy: the transformation of rural Massachusetts 1750–1850.* Chicago, IL: University of Chicago Press.

Rouget, Gilbert. (1985). *Music and trance: a theory of the relations between music and possession* [Musique et la transe, Paris, 1980]. Chicago, IL: University of Chicago Press.

Rouland, Norbert. (1994). *Legal anthropology* [Anthropologie juridique, Paris, 1988]. Stanford, CA: Stanford University Press.

Rousseau, Jean-Jacques. (1768). *Dictionnaire de musique.* Paris.

———(1791). *An inquiry into the nature of the social contract: or Principles of political right* [Du contrat social, Amsterdam, 1762]. Dublin: Smith.

Roy, Manisha. (1975). *Bengali women.* Chicago, IL: University of Chicago Press.

Royce, Anya Peterson. (1977). *The anthropology of dance.* Bloomington: Indiana University Press.

Rubel, Arthur J. & M. R. Hass. (1996). Ethnomedicine. In Carolyn Sargent & Thomas Johnson (Eds.), *Medical anthropology* [rev. edn.] (pp. 113–130). Westport, CT: Greenwood.

Rubel, Arthur, Carl O'Nell & Rolando Collado. (1984). *Susto, a folk illness.* Berkeley: University of California Press.

Rubin, Gayle. (1975). The traffic in women: notes on the "political economy" of sex. In Rayna Reiter (Ed.), *Toward an anthropology of women* (pp. 157–210). New York: Monthly Review.

Rubin, William. (Ed.). (1984). *Primitivism in twentieth century art.* New York: Museum of Modern Art.

Ruby, Jay. (Ed.). (1993). *The cinema of John Marshall.* Philadelphia, PA: Harwood.

Ruck, Carl A. P. & Danny Staples. (1994). *The world of classical myth: gods and goddesses, heroines and heroes.* Durham, NC: Carolina Academic.

Ruddle, Kenneth & R. E. Johannes.

(1985). *The traditional knowledge and management of coastal systems in Asia and the Pacific.* Jakarta Pusat: UNESCO.

Rudolph, Lloyd I. & Susanne H. Rudolph. (1967). *The modernity of tradition: political development in India.* Chicago, IL: University of Chicago Press.

Ruhlen, Merritt. (1987). *A guide to the world's languages,* vol. 1: *Classification.* Stanford, CA: Stanford University Press.

Rumney, Jay. (1934). *Herbert Spencer's sociology: a study in the history of social theory.* London: Williams & Norgate.

Russell, Jeffrey B. (1977). *The devil: perceptions of evil from antiquity to primitive Christianity.* Ithaca, NY: Cornell University Press.

Russell, John. (1991). Race and reflexivity: the black other in contemporary Japanese mass culture. *Cultural Anthropology* 6(1): 3–25.

Ruthenberg, Hans. (1980). *Farming systems in the tropics* [3rd edn.]. Oxford: Clarendon.

Rynearson, Ann M. & James Phillips. (Eds.). (1996). *Selected papers on refugee issues,* vol. 4. Arlington, VA: American Anthropological Association.

Rynkiewich, Michael A. & James P. Spradley. (1976). *Ethics and anthropology: dilemmas in fieldwork.* New York: Wiley.

Sachs, Curt. (1937). *World history of the dance* [Weltgeschichte des Tanzes, Berlin, 1933] New York: Norton.

Sacks, Karen. (1979). *Sisters and wives: the past and the future of sexual equality.* Westport, CT: Greenwood.

Sacks, Karen & Dorothy Remy. (Eds.). (1984). *My troubles are going to have trouble with me: everyday trials and triumphs of women workers.* New Brunswick, NJ: Rutgers University Press.

Sade, Donald S. & Malcolm Dow. (1994). Primate social networks. In Stanley Wasserman & Joseph Galaskiewicz (Eds.), *Advances in social network analysis* (pp. 153–166). Thousand Oaks: Sage.

Sahlins, Marshall. (1958). *Social stratification in Polynesia.* Seattle: University of Washington Press.

———(1960). Evolution: specific and general. In Marshall D. Sahlins & Elman R.

Service (Eds.), *Evolution and culture* (pp. 298–308). Ann Arbor: University of Michigan Press.

——(1961). The segmentary lineage: an organization of predatory expansion. *American Anthropologist* 63: 322–345.

——(1963). Poor man, rich man, big man, chief: political types in Melanesia and Polynesia. *Comparative Studies in History and Society* 5: 285–303.

——(1968a). Notes on the original affluent society. In Richard Lee & Irven DeVore (Eds.), *Man the hunter* (pp. 85–89). Chicago, IL: Aldine.

——(1968b). *Tribesmen.* Englewood Cliffs, NJ: Prentice-Hall.

——(1971). The intensity of domestic production in primitive societies: social inflections of the Chayanov slope. In George Dalton (Ed.), *Studies in economic anthropology* (pp. 30–51). Washington, DC: American Anthropological Association.

——(1972). *Stone age economics.* Chicago, IL: Aldine-Atherton.

——(1976a). *Culture and practical reason.* Chicago, IL: University of Chicago Press.

——(1976b). *The use and abuse of biology: an anthropological critique of sociobiology.* Ann Arbor: University of Michigan Press.

——(1985). *Islands of history.* Chicago, IL: University of Chicago Press.

——(1995). *How natives think: about Captain Cook, for example.* Chicago, IL: University of Chicago Press.

——(1996). The sadness of sweetness: the native anthropology of Western cosmology. *Current Anthropology* 37(3): 395–429.

Sahlins, Marshall & Elman Service. (Eds.). (1960). *Evolution and culture.* Ann Arbor: University of Michigan Press.

Said, Edward. (1978). *Orientalism.* New York: Pantheon.

Sakata, Hiromi L. (1983). *Music in the mind: the concepts of music and musician in Afghanistan.* Kent, OH: Kent State University Press.

Salem-Murdock, Muneera & Michael M. Horowitz. (Eds.). (1990). *Anthropology and development in North Africa and the Middle East.* Boulder, CO: Westview.

Sallnow, Michael J. (1987). *Pilgrims of the Andes: regional cults in Cusco.* Washington, DC: Smithsonian.

Salzman, Phillip. (1978). Does complementary opposition exist? *American Anthropologist* 80: 53–70.

Samuel, Geoffrey. (1993). *Civilized shamans: Buddhism in Tibetan societies.* Washington, DC: Smithsonian.

Sanday, Peggy. (1981a). *Female power and male dominance: on the origins of inequality.* Cambridge: Cambridge University Press.

——(1981b). The socio-cultural context of rape: a cross-cultural study. *Journal of Social Issues* 37(4): 5–27.

——(1986). *Divine hunger.* Cambridge: Cambridge University Press.

Sanday, Peggy & Ruth Goodenough. (Eds.). (1990). *Beyond the second sex: new directions in the anthropology of gender.* Philadelphia: University of Pennsylvania Press.

Sander, Frank. (1976). Varieties of dispute processing. *Federal Rules Decisions* 70: 111–120.

Sanders, William. (1956). The central Mexican symbiotic region. In Gordon Willey (Ed.), *Prehistoric settlement patterns in the New World* (pp. 115–127). New York: Wenner-Gren.

Sanderson, Stephen K. (1990). *Social evolutionism: a critical history.* Oxford: Blackwell.

——(1995a). *Macrosociology: an introduction to human societies* [3rd edn.]. New York: HarperCollins.

——(1995b). *Social transformations: a general theory of historical development.* Oxford: Blackwell.

Sandin, Benedict. (1980). *Iban adat and augury.* Penang: Universiti Sans Malaysia.

Sangren, P. Steven. (1988). Rhetoric and the authority of ethnography: "postmodernism" and the social reproduction of texts. *Current Anthropology* 29: 405–435.

——(1995). "Power" against ideology: a critique of Foucaultian usage. *Cultural Anthropology* 10(1): 3–40.

Sanjek, Roger. (Ed.). (1990a). *Fieldnotes:*

the makings of anthropology. Ithaca, NY: Cornell University Press.

——(1990b). A vocabulary for fieldnotes. In Roger Sanjek (Ed.), *Fieldnotes* (pp. 92–121). Ithaca, NY: Cornell University Press.

——(1993). Anthropology's hidden colonialism: assistants and their ethnographers. *Anthropology Today* 9(9): 13–18.

Santos, Theotonio dos. (1970). The structure of dependence. *American Economic Review* 60: 231–236.

Sapir, David & J. Christopher Crocker. (Eds.). (1977). *The social use of metaphor: essays on the anthropology of rhetoric*. Philadelphia: University of Pennsylvania Press.

Sapir, Edward. (1916). *Time perspective in aboriginal American culture, a study in method*. Ottawa: Government Printing Bureau.

——(1917). Do we need a "superorganic"? *American Anthropologist* 19: 441–449.

——(1921). *Language: an introduction to the study of speech*. New York: Harcourt, Brace.

——(1924). The grammarian and his language. *American Mercury* 1: 149–155 [reprinted in Sapir 1949: 150–159].

——(1929a). The status of linguistics as a science. *Language* 5: 207–214 [reprinted in Sapir 1949: 160–166].

——(1929b). A study of phonetic symbolism. *Journal of Experimental Psychology* 12: 225–239 [reprinted in Sapir 1949: 61–72].

——(1931). Communication. In Edwin R. A. Seligman (Ed.), *Encyclopedia of the social sciences* 4: 78–81. New York: Macmillan.

——(1933). Le réalité psychologique des phonèmes [The psychological reality of the phoneme]. *Journal de Psychologie Normale et Pathologique* 30: 247–265 [translated and reprinted in Sapir 1949: 46–60].

——(1934). The emergence of the concept of personality in a study of cultures. *Journal of Social Psychology* 5: 408–415 [reprinted in Sapir 1949: 590–597].

——(1938). Why cultural anthropology needs the psychiatrist. *Psychiatry* 1: 7–12 [reprinted in Sapir 1949: 569–577].

——(1949). *Selected writings of Edward Sapir in language, culture and personality*. Berkeley: University of California Press.

——(1990–91). *American Indian languages* (2 vols.). Berlin: Mouton de Gruyter.

——(1994). *The psychology of culture: a course of lectures*. Berlin: Mouton de Gruyter.

Sargent, Carolyn. (1982). *The cultural context for therapeutic choice: obstetrical care decisions among the Bariba of Benin*. Dordrecht: Reidel.

——(1989). *Maternity, medicine, and power: reproductive decisions in urban Benin*. Berkeley: University of California Press.

Sargent, Carolyn & Caroline Brettell. (1996). *Gender and health: an international perspective*. New Jersey: Prentice Hall.

Sarkisyanz, Emanuel. (1965). *Buddhist backgrounds of the Burmese revolution*. The Hague: Martinus Nijhoff.

Sarris, Greg. (1993). *Keeping slug woman alive: a holistic approach to American Indian texts*. Berkeley: University of California Press.

Sartre, Jean Paul. (1956). *Being and nothingness* [Être et le néant, Paris, 1943]. New York: Philosophical Library.

Sarup, Madan. (1988). *An introductory guide to post-structuralism and post-modernism*. New York: Harvester Wheatsheaf.

Sassen, Saskia. (1991). *The global city: New York, London, Tokyo*. Princeton, NJ: Princeton University Press.

Sauer, Carl. O. (1952). *Agricultural origins and dispersals*. New York: American Geographical Society.

Saussure, Ferdinand de. (1959). *Course in general linguistics* [Cours de linguistique générale, Paris, 1916]. New York: Philosophical Library.

Savage-Rumbaugh, E. Sue. (1986). *Ape language: from conditioned response to symbol*. New York: Columbia University Press.

Savage-Rumbaugh, E. Sue & Roger Lewin. (1994). *Kanzi: the ape at the brink of the human mind*. New York: Wiley.

Sax, William S. (1991). *Mountain goddess: gender and politics in a Himalayan* *pilgrimage*. Oxford: Oxford University Press.

Schapera, Isaac. (1956). *Government and politics in tribal societies*. London: Watts.

Schapiro, Meyer. (1953). Style. In A. L. Kroeber (Ed.), *Anthropology today* (pp. 287–312). Chicago, IL: Aldine.

Scharer, Hans. (1963). *Ngaju religion: the conception of God among a South Borneo people* [Die Gottesidee der Ngadju Dajak in Sud-Borneo, Leiden, 1946]. The Hague: Martinus Nijhoff.

Scheffler, Harold W. (1966). *Choiseul Island social structure*. Berkeley: University of California Press.

———(1970). *The elementary structures of kinship*, by Claude Lévi-Strauss: a review article. *American Anthropologist* 72: 251–268.

———(1973). Kinship, descent, and alliance. In John J. Honigmann (Ed.), *Handbook of social and cultural anthropology* (pp. 747–793). Chicago, IL: Rand McNally.

———(1977). Kinship and alliance in South India and Australia. *American Anthropologist* 79: 869–882.

Scheffler, Harold W. & Floyd G. Lounsbury. (1971). *A study in structural semantics: the Siriono kinship system*. Englewood Cliffs, NJ: Prentice-Hall.

Scheper-Hughes, Nancy. (1985). Culture, scarcity, and maternal thinking: maternal detachment and infant survival in a Brazilian shantytown. *Ethos* 13(4): 291–317.

———(Ed.). (1987). *Child survival: anthropological approaches to the treatment and maltreatment of children*. Dordrecht: Reidel.

———(1992). *Death without weeping: the violence of everyday life in Brazil*. Berkeley: University of California Press.

Scherer, Joanna. (Ed.). (1990). Special issue: Picturing cultures. *Visual Anthropology* 3(2–3).

Schieffelin, Bambi B. & E. Ochs. (1986a). Language socialization. *Annual Review of Anthropology* 15: 163–191.

———(1986b). *Language socialization across cultures*. Cambridge: Cambridge University Press.

Schieffelin, Edward L. (1976). *The sorrow of the lonely and the burning of the dancers*. New York: St Martin's.

Schildkrout, Enid. (1978). Roles of children in urban Kano. In J. S. Fontaine (Ed.), *Sex and age as principles of social differentiation* (pp. 109–137). New York: Academic.

Schlegel, Alice. (1972). *Male dominance and female autonomy: domestic authority in matrilineal societies*. New Haven, CT: HRAF.

———(1977). *Sexual stratification: a cross-cultural view*. New York: Columbia University Press.

———(1990). Gender meanings: general and specific. In Peggy Sanday & Ruth Goodenough (Eds.), *Beyond the second sex* (pp. 21–42). Philadelphia: University of Pennsylvania Press.

———(1991). Status, property, and the value on virginity. *American Ethnologist* 18: 719–734.

———(Ed.). (1995). Special Issue: Adolescence. *Ethos* 23(1).

Schlegel, Alice & Herbert Barry. (1991). *Adolescence: an anthropological inquiry*. New York: Free Press.

Schlegel, Alice & Rohn Eloul. (1987). Marriage transactions: a cross-cultural code. *Behavior Science Research* 21: 118–140.

———(1988). Marriage transactions: labor, property, and status. *American Anthropologist* 90: 291–309.

Schleicher, August. (1967). Introduction to a compendium of the comparative grammar of the Indo-European, Sanskrit, Greek and Latin languages [Compendium der vergleichenden Grammatik der indogermanischen Sprachen, Weimar, 1866]. In Winfred P. Lehmann (Ed.), *A reader in nineteenth-century historical Indo-European linguistics* (pp. 87–96). Bloomington: Indiana University Press.

Schmandt-Besserat, Denise. (1992). *Before writing* (2 vols.). Austin: University of Texas Press.

Schmidt, Johannes. (1872). *Die Verwandtschaftsverhältnisse der indogermanischen Sprachen* [The genetic relations among the Indo-European languages]. Weimar: Böhlau.

Schmidt, Wilhelm. (1912). *Der Ursprung der Gottesidee.* Munster: Aschendorff.

———(1939). *The culture historical method of ethnology: the scientific approach to the racial question* [Handbuch der Methode der kulturhistorischen Ethnologie, Munster, 1937]. New York: Fortuny's.

Schneider, David. (1965). Some muddles in the models: or how the system really works. In *The relevance of models in social anthropology,* A.S.A. Monographs. London: Tavistock.

———(1968). *American kinship: a cultural account.* Englewood Cliffs, NJ: Prentice-Hall.

———(1984). *A critique of the study of kinship.* Ann Arbor: University of Michigan Press.

Schneider, David & Calvert B. Cottrell. (1975). *The American kin universe: a genealogical study.* Chicago, IL: University of Chicago Press.

Schneider, David & Kathleen Gough. (Eds.). (1961). *Matrilineal kinship.* Berkeley: Univeristy of California Press.

Schneider, Harold K. (1957). The subsistence role of cattle among the Pokot in East Africa. *American Anthropologist* 59: 278–300.

———(1968). People as wealth in Tutu society. *Southwestern Journal of Anthropology* 24: 375–395.

———(1974). *Economic man: the anthropology of economics.* New York: Free Press.

———(1979). *Livestock and equality in East Africa: the economic basis for social structure.* Bloomington: Indiana University Press.

Schneider, William H. (1990). *Quality and quantity: the quest for biological regeneration in twentieth-century France.* Cambridge: Cambridge University Press.

Schnepel, Burkhard. (1991). Corporations, personhood and ritual in tribal society: three interconnected topics in the anthropology of Meyer Fortes. *Journal of the Anthropological Society of Oxford* 21(1): 1–31.

Scholte, Bob. (1978). Critical anthropology since it's [sic] reinvention. *Anthropology and Humanism Quarterly* 3: 4–17.

Schopenhauer, Arthur. (1889). *Parerga and paralipomena* [Parerga und Paralipomena: kleine philosophische Schriften]. London: Swan Sonnenschein. [reprinted by Penguin, New York, 1970]

Schultes, Richard. (1972). Hallucinogens in the Western hemisphere. In Peter Furst (Ed.), *Flesh of the gods* (pp. 3–45). New York: Praeger.

Schultes, Richard & Albert Hofmann. (1979). *Plants of the gods: origins of hallucinogenic use.* New York: McGraw-Hill.

Schutz, Alfred. (1962–6). *Collected papers* (3 vols.). The Hague: Nijhoff.

———(1967). *The phenomenology of the social world* [Der sinnhafte Aufbau der sozialen Welt, Vienna, 1932]. Evanston, IL: Northwestern University Press.

Schwartz, Benjamin I. (1985). *The world of thought in ancient China.* Cambridge: Belknap Press.

Schwartz, Theodore. (1975). Cultural totemism: ethnic identity primitive and modern. In George De Vos & Lola Romanucci-Ross (Eds.), *Ethnic identity* (pp. 16–31). Palo Alto, CA: Mayfield.

———(1976a). Relations among generations in time-limited cultures. In T. Schwartz (Ed.), *Socialization as cultural communication* (pp. 217–230). Berkeley: University of California.

———(Ed.). (1976b). *Socialization as cultural communication.* Berkeley: University of California Press.

Schwartz, Theodore, Geoffrey White & Catherine Lutz. (Eds.). (1992). *New directions in psychological anthropology.* Cambridge: Cambridge University Press.

Schwartzman, Helen. (1978). *Transformations: the anthropology of children's play.* New York: Plenum.

Scott, David. (1992). Anthropology and colonial discourse: aspects of the demonological construction of Sinhala cultural practice. *Cultural Anthropology* 7(3): 301–326.

———(1995). Colonial governmentality. *Social Text* 45: 191–220.

Scott, James C. (1976). *The moral economy of the peasant: rebellion and subsistence in Southeast Asia.* New Haven, CT: Yale University Press.

Scott, Joan W. (1993). The evidence of experience. In Henry Abelove (Ed.), *The* *lesbian and gay studies reader* (pp. 397–415). New York: Routledge.

Scrimshaw, Susan C. M. (1978). Infant mortality and behavior in the regulation of family size. *Population and Development Review* 4: 383–404.

Seagrave, Sterling. (1995). *Lords of the rim: the invisible empire of the overseas Chinese.* New York: Putnam.

Searle, John. (1969). *Speech acts: an essay in the philosophy of language.* London: Cambridge University Press.

Sebeok, Thomas A. (1965). Animal communication. *Science* 147(3661): 1006–1014.

Sebeok, Thomas A., Alfred Hayes & M. Catherine Bateson. (Eds.). (1964). *Approaches to semiotics: cultural anthropology, educations, linguistics, psychiatry, psychology.* The Hague: Mouton.

Secoy, Frank R. (1953). *Changing military patterns on the Great Plains.* Locust Valley, NY: Augustin. [reprinted, University of Nebraska Press, 1992]

Seeger, Anthony. (1990). *Why Suyá sing: a musical anthropology of an Amazonian people.* Cambridge: Cambridge University Press.

Segalen, Martine. (1986). *Historical anthropology of the family.* Cambridge: Cambridge University Press.

Segall, Marshall, Donald Campbell & Melville Herskovits. (1966). *The influence of culture on visual perception.* Indianapolis, IN: Bobbs-Merrill.

Selby, Henry A. (1971). Social organization. In B. J. Siegel (Ed.), *Biennial review of anthropology.* Stanford, CA: Stanford University Press.

Senft, Gunter. (1996). *Classificatory particles in Kilivila.* Oxford: Oxford University Press.

Sered, Susan. (1994). *Priestess, mother, sacred sister: religions dominated by women.* Oxford: Oxford University Press.

Serres, Michel. (1982). *The parasite* [Le parasite, Paris, 1980]. Baltimore, MD: Johns Hopkins University Press.

Service, Elman. (1962). *Primitive social organization: an evolutionary perspective.* New York: Random. [2nd edn. 1971]

———(1966). *The hunters.* Englewood Cliffs, NJ: Prentice-Hall.

———(1971). *Cultural evolutionism: theory in practice* [2nd edn.] New York: Random House.

———(1975). *Origins of the state and civilization: the process of cultural evolution.* New York: Norton.

Shanin, Teodor. (Ed.). (1987). *Peasants and peasant societies: selected readings* [2nd edn.]. Oxford: Blackwell.

———(1990). *Defining peasants: essays concerning rural societies, expolary economies, and learning from them in the contemporary world.* Oxford: Blackwell.

Shanklin, Eugenia. (1985). Sustenance and symbol: anthropological studies of domesticated animals. *Annual Review of Anthropology* 14: 375–403.

———(1994). *Anthropology and race.* Belmont, CA: Wadsworth.

Shankman, Paul. (1984). The thick and the thin: on the interpretive theoretical program of Clifford Geertz. *Current Anthropology* 25: 261–270.

Shanks, Michael & Christopher Tilley. (1987). *Re-constructing archaeology: theory and practice.* Cambridge: Cambridge University Press. [2nd edn., Routledge, 1992].

Shannon, Claude E. & Warren W. Weaver. (1971). *The mathematical theory of communication.* Urbana: University of Illinois Press.

Shannon, Thomas R. (1996). *An introduction to the world-system perspective* [2nd edn.]. Boulder, CO: Westview.

Shapiro, Judith R. (1984). Marriage rules, marriage exchange, and the definition of marriage in Lowland South American societies. In Kenneth M. Kensinger (Ed.), *Marriage practices in lowland South America* (pp. 1–30). Urbana: University of Illinois Press.

Shapiro, Warren. (1979). *Social organization in Aboriginal Australia.* Canberra: Australian National University Press.

———(1981). *Miwuyt marriage: the cultural anthropology of affinity in Northeast Arnhem Land.* Philadelphia, PA: ISHI.

———(1982). The place of cognitive extensionism in the history of anthropological thought. *The Journal of the Polynesian Society* 91: 257–297.

Sharer, Robert J. & Wendy Ashmore. (1993). *Archaeology: discovering our past*

[2nd edn.]. Mountain View, CA: Mayfield.

Sharer, Robert J. & David C. Grove. (Eds.). (1989). *Regional perspectives on the Olmec.* Cambridge: Cambridge University Press.

Sharman, Anne, Janet Theophano, Karen Curtis & Ellen Messer. (Eds.). (1991). *Diet and domestic life in society.* Philadelphia, PA: Temple University Press.

Shepard, Roger N., A. Kimball Romney & Sara Nerlove. (1972). *Multidimensional scaling: theory and applications.* New York: Seminar.

Shepher, Joseph. (1983). *Incest.* New York: Academic.

Shepperson, George. (1970). The comparative study of millennial movements. In Sylvia Thrupp (Ed.), *Millennial dreams in action* (pp. 44–52). New York: Schocken.

Sheridan, Alan. (1980). *Michel Foucault: the will to truth.* London: Tavistock.

Sherman, Paul W. (1977). Nepotism and the evolution of alarm calls. *Science* 197: 1246–1253.

Sherzer, Joel. (1987). A discourse centered approach to language and culture. *American Anthropologist* 89(3): 295–309.

———(1990). *Verbal art in San Blas: Kuna culture through its discourse.* Cambridge: Cambridge University Press.

Shils, Edward. (1965). Charisma, order, status. *American Sociological Review* 30: 199–213.

———(1981). *Tradition.* Chicago, IL: University of Chicago Press.

———(1985). Sociology. In A. Kuper & J. Kuper (Eds.), *The social science encyclopedia* (pp. 799–811). London: Routledge.

Shimkin, Dimitri B. (1964). Julian H. Steward: a contributor to fact and theory in cultural anthropology. In Robert Manners (Ed.), *Process and pattern in culture* (pp. 1–17). Chicago, IL: Aldine.

Shipman, Pat. (1994). *The evolution of racism: human differences and the use and abuse of science.* New York: Simon & Schuster.

Shipton, Parker. (1989). *Bitter money: cultural economy and some African meanings of forbidden commodities.* Washington,

DC: American Anthropological Association.

———(1990). African famines and food security: anthropological perspectives. *Annual Review of Anthropolology* 19: 353–394.

———(1994). Land and culture in tropical Africa: soils, symbols, and the metaphysics of the mundane. *Annual Review of Anthropology* 23: 347–377.

Shirokogoroff, S. M. (1935). *Psychomental complex of the Tungus.* London: Kegan Paul.

Shiva, Vandana. (1989). *Staying alive: women, ecology, and development.* London: Zed.

———(Ed.). (1991). *Biodiversity: social and ecological perspectives.* London: Zed.

Shostak, Marjorie. (1981). *Nisa: the life and words of a !Kung woman.* Cambridge, MA: Harvard University Press.

Shweder, Richard. (1979, 1980). Rethinking culture and personality theory. *Ethos* 7: 255–311; 8: 60–94.

———(1991). *Thinking through culture: expeditions in cultural psychology.* Cambridge, MA: Harvard University Press.

Shweder, Richard & Nancy Much. (1986). Determinations of meaning: discourse and moral socialization. In W. Kuritines & J. Gewirtz (Eds.). *Moral development through social interaction* (pp. 197–244). New York: Wiley.

Shweder, Richard, M. Mahapatra & J. G. Miller. (1987). Culture and moral development. In Jerome Kagan & Sharon Lamb (Eds.), *The emergence of morality in young children* (pp. 1–83). Chicago, IL: University of Chicago Press.

Siegel, Bernard J. (1945). Some methodological considerations for a comparative study of slavery. *American Anthropologist* 47: 357–392.

Siegel, Lee. (1991). *The net of magic: wonders and deceptions in India.* Chicago, IL: University of Chicago Press.

Sillitoe, Paul. (1978). Big men and war in New Guinea. *Man* 13: 252–271.

Silverman, Philip. (Ed.). (1987). *The elderly as modern pioneers.* Bloomington: Indiana University Press.

Silverstein, Michael. (1976). Shifters, linguistic categories, and cultural description. In Keith A. Basso & Henry A. Selby (Eds.), *Meaning in anthropology* (pp. 11–55). Albuquerque: University of New Mexico Press.

Silverstein, Michael & Greg Urban. (Eds.). (1996). *Natural histories of discourse.* Chicago, IL: University of Chicago Press.

Simmel, Georg. (1950). *The sociology of Georg Simmel.* Glencoe, IL: Free Press.

———(1978). *The philosophy of money* [Philosophie des Geldes, Leipzig, 1900]. London: Routledge.

Simmons, Leo W. (1942). *Sun chief: the autobiography of a Hopi Indian.* New Haven, CT: Yale University Press.

———(1945). *The role of the aged in primitive society.* New Haven, CT: Yale University Press.

Simon, William & John H. Gagnon. (1986). Sexual scripts. *Archives of Sexual Behavior* 15: 97–120.

Simons, Ronald & Charles Hughes. (Eds.). (1985). *Culture-bound syndromes: folk illness of anthropological and psychiatric interest.* Dordrecht: Reidel.

Simpson, George Eaton. (1973). *Melville J. Herskovits.* New York: Columbia University Press.

Singer, Irving. (1984–87). *The nature of love* (3 vols.). Chicago, IL: University of Chicago Press.

Singer, Merrill. (1989). The coming age of critical medical anthropology. *Social Science and Medicine* 28: 1193–1203.

Singer, Milton. (1972). *When a great tradition modernizes: an anthropological approach to Indian civilization.* New York: Praeger.

Siu, Paul C. P. (1952). The sojourner. *American Journal of Sociology* 58: 34–44.

Sivaramakrishnan, K. (1995). Situating the subaltern: history and anthropology in the Subaltern Studies Project. *Journal of Historical Sociology* 8: 395–429.

Sjoberg, Gideon. (1960). *The preindustrial city, past and present.* Glencoe, IL: Free Press.

Skinner, Debra & Dorothy Holland. (1996). Schools and the cultural production of the educated person in a Nepalese hill community. In Bradley A. Levinson, Douglas Foley & Dorothy Holland (Eds.), *The cultural production of the edu-*

cated person (pp. 273–299). Albany, NY: State University of New York Press.

Skinner, Elliot. (1968). Group dynamics in the politics of changing societies: the problem of "tribal" politics in Africa. In June Helm (Ed.), *Essays on the problem of tribe* (pp. 170–185). Seattle: University of Washington Press.

Skinner, William G. (1964–65). Marketing and social structure in rural China (3 parts). *Journal of Asian Studies* 24: 3–43, 195–228, 363–399.

Sklar, Deidre. (1994). Can bodylore be brought to its senses? *Journal of American Folklore* 107(423): 9–22.

Skorupski, John. (1976). *Symbol and theory: a philosophical study of theories of religion in social anthropology.* Cambridge: Cambridge University Press.

Skultans, Vieda. (1988). Menstrual symbolism in south Wales. In Thomas Buckley & Alma Gottlieb (Eds.), *Blood magic* (pp. 137–160). Berkeley: University of California Press.

Slater, Candace. (1986). *Trail of miracles: stories from a pilgrimage in northeast Brazil.* Berkeley: University of California Press.

Slatta, Richard W. (1983). *Gauchos and the vanishing frontier.* Lincoln: University of Nebraska Press.

———(1990). *Cowboys of the Americas.* New Haven, CT: Yale University Press.

Slobin, Dan I. (1979). *Psycholinguistics* [2nd edn.]. Glenview, IL: Scott, Foresman.

Slobodin, Richard. (1978). *W. H. R. Rivers.* New York: Columbia University Press.

Slocum, Sally. (1975). Woman the gatherer: male bias in anthropology. In Rayna R. Reiter (Ed.), *Toward an anthropology of women* (pp. 36–50). New York: Monthly Review Press.

Smedley, Audrey. (1993). *Race in North America: origin and evolution of a worldview.* Boulder, CO: Westview.

Smelser, Neil. (Ed.). (1988). *Handbook of sociology.* Newbury Park, CA: Sage.

Smith, Adam. (1776). *An inquiry into the nature and causes of the wealth of nations* (2 vols.). London: W. Strahan & T. Cadell.

Smith, Anthony D. (1986). *The ethnic origins of nations.* Oxford: Blackwell.

Smith, Carol. (1974). Economics of marketing systems: models from economic geography. *Annual Review of Anthropology* 3: 167–201.

——(Ed.). (1976). *Regional analysis.* New York: Academic.

Smith, Courtland. (1979). *Salmon fishers of the Columbia.* Corvallis: Oregon State University Press.

Smith, Eric A. (1992). Human behavioral ecology: I & II. *Evolutionary Anthropology* 1(1): 20–25; 1(2): 50–55.

Smith, Eric A. & Bruce Winterhalder. (Eds.). (1992). *Evolutionary ecology and human behavior.* New York: Aldine de Gruyter.

Smith, Estellie. (1990). Chaos in fisheries management. *Maritime Anthropological Studies* 3(2), 1–13.

Smith, John Maynard. (1995). Life at the edge of chaos? *New York Review of Books*, March 2, 1995: 28–30.

Smith, Michael G. (1960). Social and cultural pluralism. In Dorothy Keur & Vera Rubin (Eds.), *Social and cultural pluralism in the Caribbean* (pp. 763–777). New York: Annals of the New York Academy of Sciences.

——(1965). *The plural society in the British West Indies.* Berkeley: University of California Press.

——(1974). *Corporations and society: the social anthropology of collective action.* London: Duckworth.

Smith, Philip E. L. (1990). Transhumant Europeans overseas: the Newfoundland case. *Current Anthropology* 28: 241–250.

Smith, Raymond T. (1973). The matrifocal family. In Jack Goody (Ed.), *The character of kinship* (pp. 121–144). Cambridge: Cambridge University Press.

——(1984). The concept of social class in anthropology. *Annual Review of Anthropology* 13: 467–494.

Smith, W. Robertson. (1878). Bible. *Encyclopaedia Britannica* [9th edn.], vol. 3 (pp. 634–648). Edinburgh: Black.

——(1882). *The prophets of Israel and their place in history to the close of the eigth century B.C.* New York: Appleton [rev. edn. reprinted, New York: AMS Press, 1982]

——(1885). *Kinship and marriage in early Arabia.* Cambridge: Cambridge University Press [rev. edn. reprinted, Boston, MA: Beacon, 1967]

——(1889). *Lectures on the religion of the Semites.* Edinburgh: Black.

——(1912). *Lectures and essays of William Robertson Smith.* London: Black.

Smouse, Peter & J. W. Wood. (1987). The genetic demography of the Gainj of Papua New Guinea. In B. D. Chepko-Sade & Z. Halpern (Eds.), *Mammalian dispersal patterns* (pp. 211–224). Chicago, IL: University of Chicago Press.

Smouse, Peter, Jeffery Long & Robert Sokal. (1986). Multiple regression and correlation extensions of the mantel test of matrix correspondence. *Systematic Zoology* 35: 627–632.

Smuts, Barbara B. (1985). *Sex and friendship in baboons.* New York: Aldine.

——(1987). *Primate societies.* Chicago, IL: University of Chicago Press.

So, Alvin. (1990). *Social change and development: modernization, dependency, and world-system theories.* Newbury Park, CA: Sage.

Sobo, Elisa. (1992). "Unclean deeds": menstrual taboos and binding "ties" in rural Jamaica. In Mark Nichter (Ed.), *Anthropological approaches to the study of ethnomedicine* (pp. 101–126). Philadelphia, PA: Gordon & Breach.

——(1993). Bodies, kin, and flow: family planning in rural Jamaica. *Medical Anthropological Quarterly* 7(1): 50–73.

Soja, Edward. (1989). *Postmodern geographies: the reassertion of space in critical social theory.* London: Verso.

Sokolovsky, Jay. (Ed.). (1990). *The cultural context of aging: worldwide perspectives.* New York: Bergin & Garvey.

Sollers, Werner. (1986). *Beyond ethnicity: consent and descent in American culture.* Oxford: Oxford University Press.

Solomon, Robert. (1981). *Love: emotion, myth, and metaphor.* Garden City, NY: Anchor.

Sommers, Marc. (1993). Coping with fear: Burundi refugees and the urban experience in Dar es Salaam, Tanzania. In MaryCarol Hopkins & Nancy D. Donnelly (Eds.), *Selected papers on refugee issues*, vol. 2 (pp. 13–25). Arlington, VA: American Anthropological Association.

————(1995). Representing refugees: assessing the role of elites in Burundi refugee society. *Disasters* 19(1): 19–25.

Sontag, Susan. (1977). *On photography.* New York: Farrar.

————(1990). *Illness as metaphor; and, AIDS and its metaphors.* New York: Doubleday.

Sorenson, John. (1990). Opposition, exile and identity: the Eritrean case. *Journal of Refugee Studies* 3(4): 298–319.

————(1991). Politics of social identity: "Ethiopians" in Canada. *Journal of Ethnic Studies* 19(1): 67–86.

Southwold, Martin. (1978). Buddhism and the definition of religion. *Man* 13: 362–379.

————(1983). *Buddhism in life: the anthropological study of religion and the Sinhalese practice of Buddhism.* Manchester: Manchester University Press.

Sowell, Thomas. (1981). *Ethnic America: a history.* New York: Basic.

Speck, Frank G. (1935). *Naskapi, the savage hunters of the Labrador peninsula.* Norman: University of Oklahoma Press.

Spencer, Andrew. (1991). *Morphological theory: an introduction to word structure in generative grammar.* Oxford: Blackwell.

Spencer, Baldwin & F. J. Gillen. (1899). *The native tribes of central Australia.* London: Macmillan.

Spencer, Charles. (1987). Rethinking the chiefdom. In Robert Drennan & Carlos Uribe (Eds.), *Chiefdoms in the Americas* (pp. 369–390). Lanham, MD: University Press of America.

Spencer, Herbert. (1855). *The principles of psychology.* London: Longman.

————(1858–74). *Essays – scientific, political and speculative* (3 vols.). London: Longman.

————(1862). *First principles.* London: Williams & Norgate.

————(1864–7). *The principles of biology* (2 vols.). London: Williams & Norgate.

————(1873). *Descriptive sociology.* London: Williams & Norgate.

————(1876). *The principles of sociology* (3 vols.). London: Williams & Norgate.

————(1892–3). *The principles of ethics* (2 vols.). New York: Appleton.

Spencer, Jonathan. (1989). Anthropology as a kind of writing. *Man* 24: 145–164.

Spencer, Joseph. (1966). *Shifting cultivation in Southeastern Asia.* Berkeley: University of California Press.

Spencer, Paul. (Ed.). (1985). *Society and the dance: the social anthropology of process and performance.* Cambridge: Cambridge University Press.

Spicer, Edward H. (Ed.). (1952). *Human problems in technological change: a casebook.* New York: Sage.

————(1971). Persistent cultural systems: a comparative study of identity systems that can adapt to contrasting environments. *Science* 174: 795–800.

Spickard, James & Mary Douglas. (1989). A guide to Mary Douglas's three versions of grid/group theory. *Sociological Analysis* 50: 151–170.

Spiegelberg, Herbert. (1960). *The phenomenological movement: a historical introduction* (2 vols.). The Hague: Nijhoff.

Spielmann, Katherine A. (1989). A review: dietary restrictions of hunter–gatherer women and implications for fertility and infant mortality. *Human Ecology* 17(3): 321–345.

Spielmann, Katherine A. & James F. Eder. (1994). Hunters and farmers: then and now. *Annual Review of Anthropology* 23: 303–323.

Spindler, George. (Ed.). (1970). *Being an anthropologist: fieldwork in eleven cultures.* New York: Holt.

Spiro, Melford. (1951). Culture and personality: The natural history of a false dichotomy. *Psychiatry* 13: 19–46.

————(1957). *Kibbutz: venture in Utopia.* Cambridge, MA: Harvard University Press.

————(1958). *Children of the kibbutz: a study in child training and personality.* Cambridge, MA: Harvard University Press.

————(1978). Culture and human nature. In George Spindler (Ed.), *The making of psychological anthropology* (pp. 330–360). Berkeley: University of California Press.

————(1982). *Oedipus in the Trobriands.* Chicago, IL: University of Chicago Press.

————(1984). Some reflections on cultural determinism and relativism with special reference to emotion and reason. In Richard Shweder & Robert Levine (Eds.), *Culture theory* (pp. 323–346). Cambridge: Cambridge University Press.

——(1992a). Oedipus redux. *Ethos* 20(3): 358–376.

——(1992b). *Anthropological other or Burmese brother: studies in cultural analysis*. New Brunswick, NJ: Transaction.

Spivak, Gayatri Chakravorty. (1988). Can the subaltern speak? In Cary Nelson & Lawrence Grossberg (Eds.), *Marxism and the interpretation of culture* (pp. 271–313). Urbana: University of Illinois Press.

Sponsel, Leslie E. (1986). Amazon ecology and adaptation. *Annual Review of Anthropology* 15: 67–97.

——(1987). Cultural ecology and environmental education. *Journal of Environmental Education* 19(1): 31–42.

——(1992). The environmental history of Amazonia: natural and human disturbances, and the ecological transition. In Harold K. Steen & Richard P. Tucker (Eds.), *Changing tropical forests* (pp. 233–251). Durham, NC: Forest History Society.

——(1994). The Yanomami holocaust continues. In Barbara R. Johnston (Ed.), *Who pays the price?* (pp. 37–46). Washington, DC: Island.

——(Ed.). (1995). *Indigenous peoples and the future of Amazonia: an ecological anthropology of an endangered world*. Tucson: University of Arizona Press.

Sponsel, Leslie E. & Thomas Gregor. (Eds.). (1994). *The anthropology of peace and nonviolence*. Boulder, CO: Lynne Rienner.

Sponsel, Leslie, Thomas N. Headland & Robert C. Bailey. (Eds.). (1996). *Tropical deforestation: the human dimension*. New York: Columbia University Press.

Spradley, James P. (1970). *You owe yourself a drunk: an ethnography of urban nomads*. Boston, MA: Little, Brown.

——(Ed.). (1972a). *Culture and cognition: rules, maps, and plans*. San Francisco, CA: Chandler.

——(1972b). Adaptive strategies of urban nomads. In James P. Spradley (Ed.), *Culture and cognition* (pp. 235–262). San Francisco, CA: Chandler.

——(1980). *Participant observation*. New York: Holt.

Spradley, James P. & David W. McCurdy. (1972). *The cultural experience: ethnography in complex society*. Chicago, IL: Science Research Associates.

Spring, Anita. (1979). Women and men as refugees: differential assimilation of Angolan refugees in Zambia. *Disasters* 3(4): 423–428.

Spring, David & Eileen Spring. (Eds.). (1974). *Ecology and religion in history*. New York: Harper & Row.

Springer, Sally P. & Georg Deutsch. (1993). *Left brain, right brain* [4th edn.]. New York: Freeman.

Srinivas, Mysore N. (1962). *Caste in modern India and other essays*. London: Asia Publishing House.

Stacey, Judith. (1990). *Brave new families: stories of domestic upheaval in late twentieth century America*. New York: Basic.

Stacey, Peter W. & Walter D. Koenig. (Eds.). (1990). *Cooperative breeding in birds*. Cambridge: Cambridge University Press.

Stack, Carol. (1974). *All our kin: strategies for survival in a Black community*. New York: Harper & Row.

Starr, June. (1978). Turkish village disputing behavior. In Laura Nader & Harry Todd (Eds.), *The disputing process* (pp. 122–151). New York: Columbia University Press.

Starr, June & Jane F. Collier. (1989). (Eds.). *History and power in the study of law: new directions in legal anthropology*. Ithaca, NY: Cornell University Press.

Starr, June & Barbara Yngvesson. (1975). Scarcity and disputing: zeroing-in on compromise decisions. *American Ethnologist* 2: 553–566.

Stavrianos, Leften S. (1981). *Global rift: the Third World comes of age*. New York: Morrow.

Stein, Howard F. (1987). *Developmental time, cultural space*. Norman: University of Oklahoma Press.

Steiner, George. (1993). *After Babel: aspects of language and translation* [2nd edn.]. Oxford: Oxford University Press.

Steklis, Horst D. & Michael J. Raleigh. (Eds.). (1979). *Neurobiology of social communication in primates: an evolutionary perspective.* New York: Academic Press.

Stepan, Nancy L. (1991). *The hour of eugenics: race, gender and nation in Latin America.* Ithaca, NY: Cornell University Press.

Stephan, Heinz, Georg Baron & Heiko D. Frahm. (1988). Comparative size of brains and brain components. In Horst Steklis & J. Erwin (Eds.), *Comparative primate biology* (4: 1–38). New York: Liss.

Stevenson, Ian. (1975–83). *Cases of the reincarnation type* (4 vols.). Charlottesville: University Press of Virginia.

———(1985). The belief in reincarnation among the Igbo of Nigeria. *Journal of African and Asian Studies.* 20: 13–30.

———(1987). *Children who remember previous lives: a question of reincarnation.* Charlottesville: University Press of Virginia.

Steward, Julian H. (1936). The economic and social basis of primitive bands. In Robert Lowie (Ed.), *Essays in anthropology* (pp. 331–350). Berkeley: University of California Press.

———(1938). *Basin-plateau aboriginal sociopolitical groups.* Washington, DC: Smithsonian, Bureau of American Ethnology Bulletin 120.

———(Ed.). (1946–59). *Handbook of South American Indians* (7 vols.). Washington, DC: Smithsonian, Bureau of American Ethnology Bulletin 143.

———(1950). *Area research: theory and practice.* New York: Social Science Research Council Bulletin 63.

———(1955). *Theory of culture change: the methodology of multilinear evolution.* Urbana: University of Illinois Press.

———(Ed.). (1967). *Contemporary change in traditional societies* (3 vols.). Urbana: University of Illinois Press.

———(1973). *Alfred Kroeber.* New York: Columbia University Press.

———(1977). *Evolution and ecology: essays on social transformation.* Urbana: University of Illinois Press.

Steward, Julian H. & L. C. Faron. (1959). *Native peoples of South America.* New York: McGraw-Hill.

Steward, Julian H., Robert A. Manners, Eric Wolf, Elena Padilla Seda, Sidney Mintz & Raymond Scheele. (1956). *The people of Puerto Rico: a study in social anthropology.* Urbana: University of Illinois Press.

Stewart, Frank Henderson. (1977). *Fundamentals of age-group systems.* New York: Academic.

Stewart, John O. (1989). *Drinkers, drummers, and decent folk: ethnographic narratives of village Trinidad.* Albany: State University of New York Press.

Stigler, James W., Richard Shweder & Gilbert Herdt. (Eds.). (1990). *Cultural psychology: essays on comparative human development.* Cambridge: Cambridge University Press.

Stocking, George W. (1968). *Race, culture, and evolution: essays in the history of anthropology.* New York: Free Press.

———(Ed.). (1974). *The shaping of American anthropology, 1883–1911: a Franz Boas reader.* New York: Basic.

———(Ed.). (1984). *Functionalism historicized: essays on British social anthropology.* Madison: University of Wisconsin Press.

———(Ed.). (1986). *Malinowski, Rivers, Benedict and others: essays on culture and personality.* Madison: University of Wisconsin Press.

———(1987). *Victorian anthropology.* New York: Free Press.

———(1995). *After Tylor: British social anthropology 1888–1951.* Madison: University of Wisconsin Press.

Stoler, Ann. (1978). Garden use and household economy in rural Java. *Bulletin of Indonesian Economic Studies* 14: 85–101.

———(1995). *Race and the education of desire: Foucault's History of sexuality and the colonial order of things.* Durham, NC: Duke University Press.

Stoller, Paul. (1989). *The taste of ethnographic things: the senses in anthropology.* Philadelphia: University of Pennsylvania Press.

———(1992). *The cinematic griot: the ethnography of Jean Rouch.* Chicago, IL: University of Chicago Press.

Stoller, Paul & Cheryl Olkes. (1987). *In sorcery's shadow: a memoir of apprentice-*

ship among the Songhay of Niger. Chicago, IL: University of Chicago Press.

Stone, Lawrence. (1977a). History and the social sciences in the twentieth century. In Charles F. Delzell (Ed.), *The future of history* (pp. 3–42). Nashville: Vanderbilt University Press.

———(1977b). *The family, sex and marriage in England, 1500–1800.* New York: Harper & Row.

———(1993). *Broken lives: separation and divorce in England, 1660–1857.* Oxford: Oxford University Press.

Stonier, Tom. (1989). Technological change and the future. In Fred Coalter (Ed.), *Freedom and constraint* (pp. 23–33). New York: Routledge.

Strathern, Andrew. (1971). *The rope of moka: big-men and ceremonial exchange in Mount Hagen, New Guinea.* Cambridge: Cambridge University Press.

———(1980). The central and the contingent: bridewealth among the Melpa and the Wiru. In John L. Comaroff (Ed.), *The meaning of marriage payments* (pp. 49–66). London: Academic.

———(Ed.). (1982). *Inequality in New Guinea highlands societies.* Cambridge: Cambridge University Press.

———(1992). Let the bow go down. In R. Brian Ferguson & Neil Whitehead (Eds.), *War in the tribal zone* (pp. 229–250). Santa Fe, NM: School of American Research Press.

Strathern, Andrew & Marilyn Strathern. (1971). *Self-decoration in Mount Hagen.* Toronto: University of Toronto Press.

Strathern, Marilyn. (1972). *Women in between: female roles in a male world: Mount Hagen, New Guinea.* London: Seminar.

———(1981). *Kinship at the core.* Cambridge: Cambridge University Press.

———(1984). Marriage exchanges: a Melanesian comment. *Annual Review of Anthropology* 13: 41–73.

———(Ed.). (1987). *Dealing with inequality: analysing gender relations in Melanesia and beyond.* Cambridge: Cambridge University Press.

———(1988). *The gender of the gift: problems with women and problems with society*

in Melanesia. Cambridge: Cambridge University Press.

———(1991). Introduction. In M. Godelier & M. Strathern (Eds.), *Big men and great men* (pp. 1–4). Cambridge: Cambridge University Press.

———(1992). *Reproducing the future: essays in anthropology, kinship, and the new reproductive technologies.* New York: Routledge.

Straus, Erwin. (1966). *Phenomenological psychology: the selected papers of Erwin W. Straus.* New York: Basic.

Strauss, Anselm. (1987). *Qualitative analysis for social scientists.* Cambridge: Cambridge University Press.

Strauss, Anselm & Juliet Corbin. (1990). *Basics of qualitative research: grounded theory procedures and techniques.* Newbury Park, CA: Sage.

Strauss, Claudia. (1992). What makes Tony run? Schemas as motives reconsidered. In Roy D'Andrade & Claudia Strauss (Eds.), *Human motives and cultural models* (pp. 197–224). Cambridge: Cambridge University Press.

Strauss, David J. & A. Kimball Romney. (1982). Log-linear multiplicative models for the analysis of endogamy. *Ethnology* 11: 79–99.

Strauss, Jean. (1994). *Birthright: the guide to search and reunion for adoptees, birthparents, and adoptive parents.* New York: Penguin.

Street, Brian V. (1984). *Literacy in theory and practice.* Cambridge: Cambridge University Press.

Stubbs, Michael. (1983). *Discourse analysis: the sociolinguistic analysis of natural language.* Oxford: Blackwell.

Sturtevant, William. (1964). Studies in ethnoscience. *American Anthropologist* 66(3): 99–131.

———(1966). Anthropology, history, and ethnohistory. *Ethnohistory* 13: 1–51.

———(1983). Tribe and state in the 16th and 20th centuries. In Elizabeth Tooker (Ed.), *The development of political organization in native North America* (pp. 3–16). Washington, DC: American Ethnological Society.

Suárez-Orozco, Marcelo. (1989). *Central American refugees and U.S. high* *schools: a psychosocial study of motivation and achievement*. Stanford, CA: Stanford University Press.

——— (1994). Remaking psychological anthropology. In Marcelo M. Suárez-Orozco, George & Louise Spindler (Eds.), *The making of psychological anthropology*, vol. 2 (pp. 10–59). Fort Worth, TX: Harcourt, Brace.

Sudnow, David. (1967). *Passing on: the social organization of dying*. Englewood Cliffs, NJ: Prentice Hall.

Sullivan, Harry Stack. (1964). *The fusion of psychiatry and social science*. New York: Norton.

Super, Charles & Sara Harkness. (1980). *Anthropological perspectives on child development*. San Francisco, CA: Jossey-Bass.

Susser, Ida. (1982). *Norman Street: poverty and politics in an urban neighborhood*. Oxford: Oxford University Press.

——— (1993). Creating family forms. *Critique of Anthropology* 13(3): 267–283.

Suter, Christian. (1992). *Debt cycles in the world-economy: foreign loans, financial crises, and debt settlements, 1820–1990*. Boulder, CO: Westview.

Suttles, Gerald. (1968). *The social order of the slum: ethnicity and territory in the inner city*. Chicago, IL: University of Chicago Press.

Sutton, Constance & Elsa Chaney. (1992). *Caribbean life in New York City: sociocultural dimensions*. New York: Center for Migration Studies.

Swadesh, Morris. (1959). Linguistics as an instrument of prehistory. *Southwestern Journal of Anthropology* 15: 20–35.

——— (1971). *The origin and diversification of language*. Chicago, IL: Aldine, Atherton.

Swann, Brian. (Ed.). (1992). *On the translation of native American literatures*. Washington, DC: Smithsonian.

Sway, Marlene. (1975). Gypsies as a perpetual minority: a case study. *Humboldt Journal of Social Relations* 3: 48–55.

——— (1988). *Familiar strangers: gypsy life in America*. Urbana: University of Illinois Press.

Swedenburg, Ted. (1995). *Memories of revolt: the 1936–1939 rebellion and the Pal-estinian national past*. Minneapolis: University of Minnesota Press.

Swedlund, Alan C. (Ed.). (1975). *Population studies in archaeology and biological anthropology: a symposium*. Washington, DC: Society for American Archaeology.

Sweetser, Eve E. (1990). *From etymology to pragmatics: metaphorical and cultural aspects of semantic structure*. Cambridge: Cambridge University Press.

Symons, Donald. (1979). *The evolution of human sexuality*. Oxford: Oxford University Press.

Tagg, John. (1988). *The burden of representation: essays on photographies and histories*. Amherst: University of Massachusetts Press.

Talai, Vered Amit. (1989). *Armenians in London: the management of social boundaries*. Manchester: Manchester University Press.

Tambiah, Stanley J. (1969). Animals are good to think and good to prohibit. *Ethnology* 8(4): 424–459.

——— (1970). *Buddhism and spirit cults in north-east Thailand*. Cambridge: Cambridge University Press.

——— (1973). Dowry and bridewealth and the property rights of women in South Asia. In Jack Goody & Stanley J. Tambiah (Eds.), *Bridewealth and dowry* (pp. 59–169). Cambridge: Cambridge University Press.

——— (1976). *World conqueror and world renouncer: a study of Buddhism and polity in Thailand against a historical background*. Cambridge: Cambridge University Press.

——— (1984). *Magic, science, religion, and the scope of rationality*. Cambridge: Cambridge University Press.

——— (1992). *Buddhism betrayed? Religion, politics, and violence in Sri Lanka*. Chicago, IL: University of Chicago Press.

Tannen, Deborah. (1984). *Conversational style: analyzing talk among friends*. Patterson, NJ: Ablex.

——— (1990). *You just don't understand: women and men in conversation*. New York: Morrow.

Tanner, James M. (1990). *Foetus into man: physical growth from conception to* *maturity* [rev. edn.]. Cambridge, MA: Harvard University Press.

Tapp, Nicholas. (1988). The reformation of culture: Hmong refugees from Laos. *Journal of Refugee Studies* 1(1): 20–37.

Tarde, Gabriel de. (1903). *The laws of imitation* [Les Lois de l'imitation, Paris, 1890]. New York: Holt.

Tattersall, Ian. (1995). *The fossil trail: how we know what we think we know about human evolution.* Oxford: Oxford University Press.

Taussig, Michael. (1980). *The devil and commodity fetishism in South America.* Chapel Hill: University of North Carolina Press.

——— (1987). *Shamanism, colonialism, and the wild man: a study in terror and healing.* Chicago, IL: University of Chicago Press.

——— (1992). *The nervous system.* New York: Routledge.

——— (1993). *Mimesis and alterity: a particular history of the senses.* New York: Routledge.

Tax, Sol. (1953). *Penny capitalism: a Guatemalan Indian economy.* Washington, DC: Smithsonian.

Tax, Sol, Loren Eiseley, Irving Rouse & Carl Voegelin. (Eds.). (1953). *An appraisal of anthropology today,* Chicago, IL: University of Chicago Press.

Taylor, Christopher. (1988). The concept of flow in Rwandan popular medicine. *Social Science and Medicine* 27: 1343–1348.

Taylor, George R. (Ed.). (1972). *The Turner thesis concerning the role of the frontier in American history* [3rd edn.]. Lexington, MA: Heath.

Taylor, Lucien. (Ed.). (1991). Special section: Other visions? Problems and prospects of indigenous media. *Visual Anthropology Review* 7(2): 48–106.

——— (Ed.). (1994). *Visualizing theory: selected essays from V.A.R. 1990–1994.* New York: Routledge.

——— (1996). Iconophobia, how anthropology lost it at the movies. *Transition* 6(1): 64–88.

Taylor, Penny. (Ed.). (1988). *After 200 years: photographic essays of Aboriginal and Islander Australia today.* Canberra: Aboriginal Studies Press.

Taylor, Peter J. (1993). *Political geography: world-economy, nation-state, and locality* [3rd edn.]. Harlow, Essex: Longman.

Tedlock, Dennis. (1983). *The spoken word and the work of interpretation.* Philadelphia: University of Pennsylvania Press.

Teeter, Karl V. (1963). Lexicostatistics and genetic relationship. *Language* 39: 638–648.

Tegnaeus, Harry. (1952). *Blood brothers: an ethno-sociological study of the institution of blood-brotherhood with special reference to Africa.* New York: Philosophical Library.

TenHouten, Warren D. (1991). Into the wild blue yonder: on the emergence of the ethnoneurologies. *Journal of Social and Biological Structures* 14: 381–408.

Terray, Emmanuel. (1972). *Marxism and "primitive" societies: two studies.* New York: Monthly Review Press.

——— (1975). Classes and class consciousness in the Abron kingdom of Gyaman. In Maurice Bloch (Ed.), *Marxist analyses and social anthropology* (pp. 85–135). New York: Wiley.

Terrell, John. (1986). *Prehistory in the Pacific Islands: a study of variation in language, customs, and human biology.* Cambridge: Cambridge University Press.

Terrell, John & J. Modell. (1994). Anthropology and adoption. *American Anthropologist* 96: 155–161.

Thomas, David H. (1986). *Refiguring anthropology: first principles of probability and statistics.* Prospect Heights, IL: Waveland.

——— (1989). *Archaeology* [2nd edn.]. Fort Worth, TX: Holt.

Thomas, Keith. (1971). *Religion and the decline of magic.* New York: Scribner.

Thomas, Nicholas. (1994). *Colonialism's culture: anthropology, travel and government.* Cambridge: Polity.

Thomas, R. Brooke. (1973). *Human adaptation to a high Andean energy flow system.* University Park: Pennsylvania State University, Department of Anthropology.

Thomas, William I. & Florian Znaniecki. (1918–20). *The Polish peasant in Europe and America* (5 vols.). Chicago, IL: University of Chicago

Press. [reprinted, 2 vols., Dover Publications, 1958]

Thomason, Sarah Grey & Terrence Kaufman. (1988). *Language contact, creolization, and genetic linguistics.* Berkeley: University of California Press.

Thompson, Catherine. (1985). The power to pollute and the power to preserve: perceptions of female power in a Hindu village. *Social Science and Medicine* 21: 701–711.

Thompson, E. P. (1963). *The making of the English working class.* London: Gollancz.

———(1967). Time, work discipline and industrial capitalism. *Past and Present* 38: 56–97.

———(1978). *The poverty of theory and other essays,* New York: Monthly Review Press.

Thompson, Stith. (1932–36). *Motif-index of folk-literature* (6 vols.). Bloomington: Indiana University Press. [reprocessed as laser optical disk, InteLex, 1993]

Thornhill, Nancy W. (1991). An evolutionary analysis of rules regulating human inbreeding and marriage. *Behavioral and Brain Sciences* 14: 249–264.

Thornton, Russell. (1981). Demographic antecedents of a revitalization movement: population change, population size, and the 1890 Ghost Dance. *American Sociological Review* 46: 88–96.

Thorpe, William H. (1956). *Learning and instinct in animals.* London: Methuen.

———(1979). *The origins and rise of ethology: the science of the natural behaviour of animals.* New York: Praeger.

Tibi, Bassam. (1994). Islamic law/shari'a, human rights, universal morality and international relations. *Human Rights Quarterly* 16: 277–299.

Tierney, Patrick. (1995). *Last tribes of El Dorado: the gold wars in the Amazon rain forest.* New York: Viking.

Tinbergen, Niko. (1951). *The study of instinct.* Oxford: Clarendon.

———(1963). On aims and methods of ethology. *Zeitschrift für Tierpsychologie* 20: 410–433.

Tobin, Joseph, David Y. H. Wu & Dana H. Davidson. (1989). *Preschool in three cultures: Japan, China, and the United States.* New Haven, CT: Yale University Press.

Toelken, J. Barre. (1979). *The dynamics of folklore.* Boston, MA: Houghton-Mifflin.

Toledo, Victor M. (1995). New paradigms for a new ethnobotany. In Richard Schultes & Siri von Reis (Eds.), *Ethnobotany* (pp. 75–92). Portland, OR: Dioscorides.

Tomich, Dale W. (1990). *Slavery in the circuit of sugar: Martinique and the world economy, 1830–1848.* Baltimore, MD: Johns Hopkins University Press.

Tonkinson, Robert. (1988a). "Ideology and domination" in Aboriginal Australia: a Western Desert test case. In Tim Ingold, David Riches & James Woodburn (Eds.), *Hunters and gatherers* (pp. 170–184). Oxford: Berg.

———(1988b). Egalitarianism and inequality in a Western Desert culture. *Anthropological Forum* 5: 545–558.

Tönnies, Ferdinand. (1957). *Community and society* [Gemeinschaft und Gesellschaft, Leipzig, 1887]. East Lansing: Michigan State University Press.

Tooker, Elisabeth. (1983). The structure of the Iroquois League: Lewis H. Morgan's research and observations. *Ethnohistory* 30: 141–154.

———(1992). Lewis H. Morgan and his contemporaries. *American Anthropologist* 94: 357–375.

Torry, William I. (1988). Famine warning systems: the need for an anthropological dimension. *Human Organization* 47(3): 273–281.

Toubia, Nahid. (1993). *Female genital mutilation: a call for global action.* New York: Women, Ink.

Traube, Elizabeth. (1992). *Dreaming identities: class, gender, and generation in 1980s Hollywood movies.* Boulder, CO: Westview.

Trautmann, Thomas R. (1981). *Dravidian kinship.* Cambridge: Cambridge University Press.

———(1984). Decoding Dravidian kinship: Morgan and McIlvaine. *Man* 19: 421–431.

———(1987). *Lewis Henry Morgan and the invention of kinship.* Berkeley: University of California Press.

————(1992). The revolution in ethnological time. *Man* 27: 379–397.

Trautmann, Thomas R. & Karl Sanford Kabelac. (1994). *The library of Lewis Henry Morgan.* Philadelphia, PA: American Philosophical Society.

Traweek, Sharon. (1988). *Beamtimes and lifetimes: the world of high energy physicists.* Cambridge, MA: Harvard University Press.

————(1992). Border crossings: narrative strategies in science studies and among physicists in Tsukuba Science City, Japan. In Andrew Pickering (Ed.), *Science as practice and culture* (pp. 429–465). Chicago, IL: University of Chicago Press.

Trevathan, Wenda. (1987). *Human birth: an evolutionary perspective.* New York: Aldine de Gruyter.

Trice, Harrison M. (1993). *Occupational subcultures in the workplace.* Ithaca, NY: ILR.

Trigger, Bruce G. (1989). *A history of archaeological thought.* Cambridge: Cambridge University Press.

Trillin, Calvin. (1984). *Killings.* New York: Ticknor & Fields.

Trinkaus, Erik & Pat Shipman. (1993). *The Neandertals: changing the image of mankind.* New York: Knopf.

Trivers, Robert. (1971). The evolution of reciprocal altruism. *Quarterly Review of Biology* 46: 35–57.

————(1985). *Social evolution.* Menlo Park, CA: Benjamin-Cummings.

Trudgill, Peter. (1983). *Sociolinguistics: an introduction to language and society* [rev. edn.]. Harmondsworth: Penguin.

Tsing, Anna L. (1993). *In the realm of the diamond queen: marginality in an out-of-the-way place.* Princeton, NJ: Princeton University Press.

Tucker, Mary E. & John Grim. (Eds.). (1994). *Worldviews and ecology: religion, philosophy, and the environment.* Maryknoll, NY: Orbis.

Tunstall, Jeremy. (1962). *The Fishermen: the sociology of an extreme occupation.* London: MacGibbon & Kee.

Turino, Thomas. (1992). *Moving away from silence: Andean music of the Peruvian Altiplano and the experience of urban migration.* Chicago, IL: University of Chicago Press.

Turkle, Sherry. (1984). *The second self: computers and the human spirit.* New York: Simon & Schuster.

————(1995). *Life on the screen: identity in the age of the Internet.* New York: Simon & Schuster.

Turnbull, Colin. (1965). *Wayward servants: the two worlds of the African pygmies.* Garden City, NY: Natural History.

Turnbull, Colin & Francis S. Chapman. (Eds.). (1992). *Mbuti pygmies of the Ituri rainforest* [sound recording]. Washington, DC: Smithsonian Folkways.

Turner, Billie L., William A. Clark, Robert Kates, John F. Richards, Jessica T. Mathews & William Meyers. (Eds.). (1990). *The Earth as transformed by human action: global and regional changes in the biosphere over the past 300 years.* Cambridge: Cambridge University Press.

Turner, Billie L., Goran Hyden & Robert Kates. (Eds.). (1993). *Population growth and agricultural change in Africa.* Gainesville: University Press of Florida.

Turner, David H. (1974). *Tradition and transformation: a study of the Groote Eylandt area Aborigines of northern Australia.* Canberra: Australian Institute of Aboriginal Studies.

Turner, Jonathan H. (1985). *Herbert Spencer: a renewed appreciation.* Beverley Hills, CA: Sage.

Turner, Nancy J. & Alison Davis. (1993). "When everything was scarce": the role of plants as famine foods in northwestern North America. *Journal of Ethnobiology* 13(2): 171–201.

Turner, Paul R. & David Pitt. (Eds.). (1989). *The anthropology of war and peace: perspectives on the nuclear age.* South Hadley, MA: Bergin & Garvey.

Turner, Terence. (1991). Representing, resisting, rethinking: historical transformations of Kayapo culture and anthropological consciousness. In George Stocking (Ed.), *Colonial situations* (pp. 285–313). Madison: University of Wisconsin Press.

————(1995). Social body and embodied subject: bodiliness, subjectivity, and sociality among the Kayapo. *Cultural Anthropology* 10(2): 143–170.

Turner, Victor. (1957). *Schism and continuity in an African society: a study of Ndembu village life.* Manchester: Manchester University Press.

——(1961). *Ndembu divination: its symbolism and techniques.* Manchester: Manchester University Press [reprinted in Turner 1975].

——(1962). *Chihamba, the white spirit: a ritual drama of the Ndembu.* Manchester: Manchester University Press [reprinted in Turner 1975].

——(1967). *The forest of symbols: aspects of Ndembu ritual.* Ithaca, NY: Cornell University Press.

——(1968). *The drums of affliction: a study of religious processes among the Ndembu of Zambia.* Oxford: Clarendon.

——(1969). *The ritual process: structure and anti-structure.* Chicago, IL: Aldine.

——(1974). *Dramas, fields, and metaphors: symbolic action in human society.* Ithaca, NY: Cornell University Press.

——(1975). *Revelation and divination in Ndembu ritual.* Ithaca, NY: Cornell University Press.

——(1979). *Process, performance and pilgrimage: a study in comparative symbology.* New Delhi: Concept.

——(1982). *From ritual to theatre: the human seriousness of play.* New York: Performing Arts Journal Publications.

Turner, Victor & Edward Bruner. (Eds.). (1986). *The anthropology of experience.* Urbana: University of Illinois Press.

Turner, Victor & Edith Turner. (1978). *Image and pilgrimage in Christian culture: anthropological perspectives.* New York: Columbia University Press.

Turney-High, Harry H. (1949). *Primitive war: its practice and concepts.* Columbia: University of South Carolina Press.

Turton, David & Clive Ruggles. (1978). Agreeing to disagree: the measurement of duration in a southwestern Ethiopian community. *Current Anthropology* 19(3): 585–593.

Tyler, Stephen. (Ed.). (1969). *Cognitive anthropology.* New York: Holt.

——(1978). *The said and the unsaid: mind, meaning, and culture.* New York: Academic.

——(1987). *The unspeakable: discourse, dialogue, and rhetoric in the postmodern world.* Madison: University of Wisconsin Press.

Tylor, Edward Burnett. (1865). *Researches into the early history of mankind.* London: Murray.

——(1871). *Primitive culture: researches into the development of mythology, philosophy, religion, art, and custom* (2 vols.). London: Murray.

——(1881). *Anthropology: introduction to the study of man and civilization.* New York: Appleton.

——(1889). On a method of investigating the development of institutions. *Journal of the Royal Anthropological Institute* 18: 245–269.

——(1958). *Religion in primitive culture* [reprint of vol. 2 of Tylor 1871]. New York: Harper & Row.

Udry, Christopher. (1990). Credit markets in northern Nigeria: credit as insurance in a rural economy. *World Bank Economic Review* 4: 251–269.

Ullmann, Stephen. (1951). *The principles of semantics.* Oxford: Blackwell.

——(1962). *Semantics: an introduction to the science of meaning.* New York: Barnes & Noble.

United Nations. (1987). *1985 Demographic Yearbook.* New York: United Nations.

Urban, Greg. (1991). *A discourse-centered approach to culture: native South American myths and rituals.* Austin: University of Texas Press.

Vail, Leroy. (Ed.). (1989). *The creation of tribalism in Southern Africa.* Berkeley: University of California Press.

Valdman, Albert. (1986). Applied linguistics and language planning: a case study. In Joshua Fishman et al. (Eds.), *The Fergusonian impact,* vol. 1 (pp. 517–536). New York: Mouton de Gruyter.

Valentine, Charles. (1968). *Culture and poverty: critique and counter-proposals.* Chicago, IL: University of Chicago Press.

Valeri, Valerio. (1991). Afterword. In Stephen Lansing, *Priests and programmers* (pp. 134–143). Princeton, NJ: Princeton University Press.

Van Arsdale, Peter W. (Ed.). (1993). *Refugee empowerment and organiza-*

tional change: a systems perspective. Arlington, VA: American Anthropological Association.

Vance, Carol (1991). Anthropology rediscovers sexuality: a theoretical comment. *Social Science and Medicine* 33(8): 875–884.

Van de Geer, John P. (1993). *Multivariate analysis of categorical data* (2 vols.). Newbury Park, CA: Sage.

Van Den Berge, Pierre L. (1969). Pluralism and the polity: a theoretical exploration in pluralism in Africa. In Leo Kuper & M. G. Smith (Eds.), *Pluralism in Africa.* Berkeley: University of California Press.

——(1973). In John J. Honigmann (Ed.), *Handbook of social and cultural anthropology* (pp. 959–977). Chicago, IL: Rand McNally.

——(1978). Race and ethnicity: a sociobiological perspective. *Ethnic and Racial Studies* 1: 401–411.

——(1981). *The ethnic phenomenon.* New York: Elsevier.

Van Esterik, Penny. (1989). *Beyond the breast-bottle controversy.* New Brunswick, NJ: Rutgers University Press.

Van Maanen, John. (1988). *Tales of the field: on writing ethnography.* Chicago, IL: University of Chicago Press.

van Willigen, John (1991). *Anthropology in use: a source book on anthropological practice.* Boulder, CO: Westview.

——(1993). *Applied anthropology: an introduction* [rev. edn.]. Westport, CT: Bergin & Garvey.

van Willigen, John & Timothy L. Finan. (Eds.). (1990). *Soundings: rapid and reliable research methods for practicing anthropologists.* Washington, DC: American Anthropological Association.

Vayda, Andrew P. (1969a). A study of the causes of war, with special reference to head-hunting raids in Borneo. *Ethnohistory* 16: 211–224.

——(Ed.). (1969b). *Environment and cultural behavior: ecological studies in cultural anthropology.* Garden City, NY: Natural History.

Vayda, Andrew P. & Roy A. Rappaport. (1968). Ecology: cultural and non-cultural. In James A. Clifton (Ed.), *Introduction to cultural anthropology*

(pp. 477–497). Boston, MA: Houghton Mifflin.

Veblen, Thorstein. (1898). Why is economics not an evolutionary science? *Quarterly Journal of Economics* 12.

——(1899). *The theory of the leisure class.* New York: Macmillan.

Veer, Peter van der. (1988). *Gods on earth: the management of religious experience and identity in a North Indian pilgrimage centre.* London: Athlone.

Velsen, J. van. (1967). The extended-case method and situational analysis. In Arnold Epstein (Ed.), *The craft of social anthropology* (pp. 129–149). London: Tavistock.

Verdery, Katherine. (1991). Theorizing socialism: a prologue to the transition. *American Ethnologist* 18: 419–439.

——(1996). *What was socialism, and what comes next?* Princeton, NJ: Princeton University Press.

Vermeulen, Hans F. (1995). Origins and institutionalization of ethnography and ethnology in Europe and the USA, 1771–1845. In Hans F. Vermeulen & Arturo Alverez Roldán (Eds.), *Fieldwork and footnotes* (pp. 39–59). London: Routledge.

Vernant, Jean-Pierre. (1980). *Myth and society in ancient Greece.* Atlantic Highlands, NJ: Humanities.

——(1982). *The origins of Greek thought.* Ithaca, NY: Cornell University Press.

——(1983). *Myth and thought among the Greeks.* London: Routledge.

Vesperi, Maria D. (1985). *City of green benches: growing old in a new downtown.* Ithaca, NY: Cornell University Press.

Vidal-Naquet, Pierre. (1986). *The black hunter: forms of thought and forms of society in the Greek world.* Baltimore, MD: Johns Hopkins University Press.

Vigil, James Diego. (1988). *Barrio gangs: street life and identity in Southern California.* Austin: University of Texas Press.

Vincent, Joan. (1982). *Teso in transformation: the political economy of peasant and class in eastern Africa.* Berkeley: University of California Press.

——(1990). *Anthropology and politics: visions, traditions, and trends.* Tucson: University of Arizona Press.

Visweswaran, Kamala. (1994). *Fictions*

of feminist ethnography. Minneapolis: University of Minnesota Press.

Voegelin, Carl & Florence Voegelin. (Eds.). (1966). Special issue: Ethnoscience. *Anthropological Linguistics* 8(8).

Voget, Fred. (1973). The history of cultural anthropology. In John Honigmann (Ed.), *Handbook of social and cultural anthropology* (pp. 1–88). Chicago, IL: Rand McNally.

——— (1975). *A history of ethnology.* New York: Holt, Rinehart & Winston.

Volosinov, Valentin N. (1973). *Marxism and the philosophy of language* [Marksizm i filosofiia iazyka, Leningrad, 1930]. New York: Seminar.

Vygotsky, Lev S. (1978). *Mind in society: the development of higher psychological processes.* Cambridge, MA: Harvard University Press.

Waal, Frans B. M. de. (1989). *Peacemaking among primates.* Cambridge, MA: Harvard University Press.

Wacquant, Loic. (1993). Urban outcasts: stigma and division in the black American ghetto and the French urban periphery. *International Journal of Urban and Regional Research* 17(3): 366–384.

Wagar, W. Warren. (1992). *A short history of the future* [2nd edn.]. Chicago, IL: University of Chicago Press.

Wagner, Marsden. (1994). *Pursuing the birth machine: the search for appropriate birth technology.* Campersdown, Australia: ACE Graphics.

Wagner, Roy. (1972). *Habu: the innovation of meaning in Daribi religion.* Chicago, IL: University of Chicago Press.

Waite, Robert. (1977). *The psychopathic god: Adolf Hitler.* New York: Basic.

Wakin, Eric. (1992). *Anthropology goes to war: professional ethics and counterinsurgency in Thailand.* Madison: University of Wisconsin, Center for Southeast Asian Studies.

Wallace, Alfred Russel. (1853). *A narrative of travels on the Amazon and Rio Negro, with an account of the native tribes.* London: Reeve.

Wallace, Anthony. (1956). Revitalization movements. *American Anthropologist* 58: 264–281.

——— (1961). *Culture and personality.* New York: Random.

——— (1970). *The death and rebirth of Seneca.* New York: Knopf.

Wallerstein, Immanuel. (1974). *Capitalist agriculture and the origins of European world-economy in the sixteenth century.* New York: Academic.

——— (1979). *The capitalist world-economy: essays.* Cambridge: Cambridge University Press.

——— (1980). *Mercantilism and the consolidation of the European world-economy, 1600–1750.* New York: Academic.

——— (1984). *The politics of the world-economy: the states, the movements, and the civilizations.* Cambridge: Cambridge University Press.

——— (1989). *The second era of great expansion of the capitalist world-economy, 1730–1840s.* New York: Academic.

——— (1991). *Geopolitics and geoculture: essays on the changing world-system.* Cambridge: Cambridge University Press.

Wallman, Joel. (1992). *Aping language.* Cambridge: Cambridge University Press.

Walser, Robert. (1993). *Running with the devil: power, gender, and madness in heavy metal music.* Hanover, NH: University Press of New England.

Wang, William S.-Y. (1977). *The lexicon in phonological change.* The Hague: Mouton.

Wanner, Eric & Lila Gleitman. (Eds.). (1982). *Language acquisition: the state of the art.* Cambridge: Cambridge University Press.

Ward, Kathryn B. (Ed.). (1990). *Women workers and global restructuring.* Ithaca, NY: ILR Press.

——— (1993). Reconceptualizing world-system theory to include women. In Paula England (Ed.), *Theory on gender/ feminism on theory* (pp. 43–68). New York: Aldine de Gruyter.

Ward, Martha C. (1986). *Poor women, powerful men: America's great experiment in family planning.* Boulder, CO: Westview.

——— (1989). *Nest in the wind: adventures in anthropology on a tropical island.* Prospect Hights, IL: Waveland.

Wardhaugh, Ronald. (1992). *An introduction to sociolinguistics* [2nd edn.]. Oxford: Blackwell.

Warner, W. Lloyd. (1937). *A black civili-*

zation: a social study of an Australian tribe. London: Harper.

———(1941–59). *Yankee City series* (5 vols.). New Haven, CT: Yale University Press.

Warner, William. (1983). *Distant water: the fate of the North Atlantic fisherman.* Boston, MA: Little-Brown.

Warren, Bill. (1980). *Imperialism, pioneer of capitalism.* London: NLB.

Warren, Charles. (Ed.). (1996). *Beyond document: essays on nonfiction film.* Hanover, NH: University Press of New England.

Warren, Dennis Michael. (Ed.). (1990). *Akan arts and aesthetics: elements of change in a Ghanaian indigenous knowledge system.* Studies in Technology and Social Change no. 16. Ames: Iowa State University, Technology and Social Change Program.

———(1991). *Using indigenous knowledge in agricultural development.* Washington, DC: The World Bank.

Warren, Dennis Michael, L. Jan Slikkerveer & S. Oguntunji Titilola. (Eds.). (1989). *Indigenous knowledge systems: implications for agriculture and international development.* Ames: Iowa State University, Technology and Social Change Program.

Warren, Dennis Michael, L. Jan Slikkerveer & David Brokensha. (Eds.). (1995). *The cultural dimension of development: indigenous knowledge systems.* London: Intermediate Technology Publications.

Warren, Kay. (Ed.). (1993). *The violence within: cultural and political opposition in divided nations.* Boulder, CO: Westview.

Washburn, Sherwood L. (1978). Human behavior and the behavior of other animals. *American Psychologist* 33: 405–418.

Washburn, Sherwood L. & C. Lancaster. (1968). The evolution of hunting. In Richard Lee & Irven DeVore (Eds.), *Man the hunter* (pp. 293–303). Chicago, IL: Aldine.

Washburn, Wilcomb E. (1961). Ethnohistory: history "in the round." *Ethnohistory* 8: 31–48.

———(1987). Cultural relativism, human rights, and the A.A.A. *American Anthropologist* 89: 939–943.

Wasserman, Stanley & Katherine Faust. (1994). *Social network analysis: methods and applications.* Cambridge: Cambridge University Press.

Wasson, R. Gordon. (1968). *Soma: divine mushroom of immortality.* New York: Harcourt.

———(1980). *The wondrous mushroom: mycolatry in Mesoamerica.* New York: McGraw-Hill.

Waterman, Christopher A. (1990). *Jùjú: a social history and ethnography of an African popular music.* Chicago, IL: University of Chicago Press.

Watson, James L. (Ed.). (1980). *Asian and African systems of slavery.* Oxford: Blackwell.

Watson, Lawrence C. & Maria-Barbara Watson-Franke. (1985). *Interpreting life histories: an anthropological inquiry.* New Brunswick, NJ: Rutgers University Press.

Watson-Gegeo, Karen. (1992). Thick explanation in the ethnographic study of child socialization. In William Corsaro & Peggy J. Miller (Eds.), *Interpretive approaches to children's socialization* (pp. 51–66). San Francisco, CA: Jossey-Bass.

Watts, Michael. (1996). Mapping identities: place, space and community in an African city. In Patricia Yeager (Ed.), *The geography of identity* (pp. 59–97). Ann Arbor: University of Michigan Press.

Wax, Rosalie H. (1971). *Doing fieldwork: warnings and advice.* Chicago, IL: University of Chicago Press.

Webb, Michael. (1975). The flag follows trade: an essay on the necessary interaction of military and commercial factors in state formation. In J. Sabloff & C. C. Lamberg-Karlovsky (Eds.), *Ancient civilization and trade* (pp. 155–209). Albuquerque: University of New Mexico Press.

Weber, Max. (1889). *Zur Geschichte der Handelsgesellschaften im Mittelalter.* Stuttgart: Enke.

———(1891). *Die römische Agrargeschichte in ihrer Bedeutung für das Staats und Privatrecht* (2 vols.). Stuttgart: Enke.

————(1927). *General economic history* [Wirtschaftsgeschichte, Munich, 1924]. New York: Greenberg.

————(1930). *The Protestant ethic and the spirit of capitalism* [Die Protestantische Ethik und der Geist des Kapitalismus, Tübingen, 1920]. New York: Scribner.

————(1946). Science as a vocation [Wissenschaft als Beruf, Tübingen, 1917/1919]. In H. H. Gerth & C. Wright Mills (Eds.), *From Max Weber* (pp. 129–156). Oxford: Oxford University Press.

————(1949a). *Max Weber on the methodology of the social sciences* ed. by Edward Shils & Henry Finch. Glencoe, IL: Free Press.

————(1949b). "Objectivity" in social science [Die "Objektivität" in dem Sozialwissenschaften, Frankfurt, 1904]. In *Max Weber on the methodology of the social sciences* ed. by Edward Shils & Henry Finch (pp. 50–112). Glencoe, IL: Free Press.

————(1951). *The religion of China: Confucianism and Taoism* [Konfuzianismus und Taoismus, Tübingen, 1920]. New York: Free Press.

————(1952). *Ancient Judaism* [Antike Judentum, Tübingen, 1920]. Glencoe, IL: Free Press.

————(1958). *The religion of India* [Hinduismus und Buddhismus, Tübingen, 1920]. Glencoe, IL: Free Press.

————(1963). *The sociology of religion* [Religionssoziologie, Tübingen, 1920]. Boston, MA: Beacon.

————(1965). *Politics as a vocation* [Politik als Beruf, Tübingen, 1919]. Philadelphia: Fortress Press.

————(1968). *Economy and society: an outline of interpretive sociology* [Wirtschaft und Gesellschaft, Tübingen, 1921]. New York: Bedminster.

Weber, Robert P. (1990). *Basic content analysis* [2nd edn.]. Beverly Hills, CA: Sage.

Webster, Paula. (1975). Matriarchy: a vision of power. In Rayna Reiter (Ed.), *Toward an anthropology of women* (pp. 141–156). New York: Monthly Review Press.

Weedon, Chris. (1996). *Feminist practice and poststructuralist theory* [2nd edn.]. Oxford: Blackwell.

Weiner, Annette B. (1976). *Women of value, men of renown: new perspectives in Trobriand exchange.* Austin: University of Texas Press.

Weiner, James F. (1991). *The empty place: poetry, space, and being among the Foi of Papua New Guinea.* Bloomington: Indiana University Press.

Weinreich, Uriel. (1972). *Explorations in semantic theory.* The Hague: Mouton.

Weinreich, Uriel, William Labov & Marvin Herzog. (1968). Empirical foundations for a theory of language change. In W. P. Lehmann & Yakov Malkiel (Eds.), *Directions for historical linguistics* (pp. 95–188). Austin: University of Texas Press.

Weisberg, Sanford. (1985). *Applied linear regression* [2nd edn.]. New York: Wiley.

Weisner, Thomas. (1982). Sibling interdependence and child caretaking: a cross-cultural view. In Michael Lamb & Brian Sutton-Smith (Eds.), *Sibling relationships* (pp. 305–327). Hillsdale, NJ: Erlbaum.

————(1989). Social support for children among the Abaluyia of Kenya. In Deborah Belle (Ed.), *Children's social networks and social supports* (pp. 70–90). New York: Wiley.

————(1996). Why ethnography should be the most important method in the study of human development. In Richard Jessor, Anne Colby & Richard Shweder (Eds.), *Ethnography and human development* (pp. 436–531). Chicago, IL: University of Chicago Press.

Weisner, Thomas & Ronald Gallimore. (1977). My brother's keeper: child and sibling caretaking. *Current Anthropology* 18: 169–190.

Weisner, Thomas & Helen Garnier. (1992). Nonconventional family lifestyles and school achievement: a 12-year longitudinal study. *American Educational Research Journal* 29(3): 605–632.

Weisner, Thomas, Ronald Gallimore & Cathie Jordan. (1988). Unpacking cultural effects on classroom learning: Hawaiian peer assistance and child-generated activity. *Anthropology and Educational Quarterly* 19: 327–353.

Weisner, Thomas, Catherine C. Mathoson & Lucinda P. Bernheimer. (1996). American cultural models of early influence and parent recognition of development delays. In Sara Harkness & Charles M. Super (Eds.), *Parents' cultural belief systems* (pp. 436–531). New York: Guilford.

Weiss, Kenneth M. (1989). A survey of human biodemography. *Journal of Quantitative Anthropology* 1: 79–152.

——(1993). *Genetic variation and human disease: principles and evolutionary approaches.* Cambridge: Cambridge University Press.

Weiss, Wendy A. (1990). Challenge to authority: Bakhtin and ethnographic description. *Cultural Anthropology* 5(4): 414–430.

Weller, Susan & Charles H. Buchholtz. (1986). When a single clustering method creates more than one tree: a reanalysis of the Salish languages. *American Anthropologist* 88: 667–674.

Weller, Susan & A. Kimball Romney. (1988). *Systematic data collection.* Newbury Park, CA: Sage.

——(1990). *Metric scaling: correspondence analysis.* Newbury Park, CA: Sage.

Wendorf, Fred, Romuald Schild & Angela E. Close. (1986). *The prehistory of Wadi Kubbaniya* (3 vols.). Dallas, TX: Southern Methodist University Press.

Werbner, Richard P. (1984). The Manchester school in south-central Africa. *Annual Review of Anthropology* 13: 157–185.

——(1991). *Tears of the dead: the social biography of an African family.* Edinburgh: Edinburgh University Press.

Werner, Oswald. (1972). Ethnoscience. *Annual Review of Anthropology* 1: 271–308.

Werner, Oswald & G. Mark Schoepfle. (1987). *Systematic fieldwork: foundations of ethnography and interviewing* (2 vols.). Newbury Park, CA: Sage.

Westen, Drew. (1992). The cognitive self and the psychoanalytic self: can we put ourselves together? *Psychological Inquiry* 3(1): 1–13.

Westermarck, Edward. (1891). *The history of human marriage.* London: Macmillan.

Westermeyer, Joseph. (1982). *Poppies, pipes, and people: opium and its use in Laos.* Berkeley: University of California Press.

Weston, Kath. (1991). *Families we choose: lesbians, gays, kinship.* New York: Columbia University Press.

——(1994). Forever is a long time: romancing the real in gay kinship ideologies. In Sylvia Yanagisako & Carol Delaney (Eds.), *Naturalizing power* (pp. 87–110). New York: Routledge.

Westwood, Sallie. (1984). *All day, every day: factory and family in the making of women's lives.* London: Pluto.

Wetherell, Margaret & Jonathan Potter. (1993). *Mapping the language of racism: discourse and the legitimation of exploitation.* New York: Columbia University Press.

Whitam, Frederick. (1987). A cross-cultural perspective on homosexuality, transvestism and trans-sexualism. In Glen Wilson (Ed.), *Variant sexuality* (pp. 176–201). Baltimore, MD: Johns Hopkins University Press.

White, Douglas, Michael Burton & Lilyan Brudner. (1977). Entailment theory and method: a cross-cultural analysis of the sexual division of labor. *Behavior Science Research* 12: 1–24.

White, Geoffrey. (1987). Proverbs and cultural models: an American psychology of problem solving. In Dorothy Holland & Naomi Quinn (Eds.), *Cultural models in language and thought* (pp. 151–172). Cambridge: Cambridge University Press.

White, Hayden. (1973). *Metahistory: the historical imagination in nineteenth-century Europe.* Baltimore, MD: Johns Hopkins University Press.

——(1978). The historical text as cultural artefact. In *Tropics of discourse: essays in cultural criticism* (pp. 81–100). Baltimore, MD: Johns Hopkins University Press.

White, Leslie A. (1940). The symbol: the origin and basis of human behavior. *Philosophy of Science* 7: 451–463.

——(1943). Energy and the evolution of culture. *American Anthropologist* 45: 335–356.

———(1949). *The science of culture, a study of man and civilization.* New York: Farrar, Strauss.

———(1959a). *The evolution of culture.* New York: Grove Press.

———(1959b). *Lewis Henry Morgan: the Indian journals 1859–62.* Ann Arbor: University of Michigan Press.

———(1959c). Culture concept. *American Anthropologist* 61: 22–252.

White, Luise. (1993). Vampire priests of central Africa: African debates about labor and religion in colonial northern Zambia. *Comparative Studies in Society and History.* 35(4): 746–772.

———(1994). Blood, brotherhood revisited: kinship, relationship, and the body in East and Central Africa. *Africa* 64(3): 359–372.

White, Richard. (1983). *The roots of dependency: subsistence, environment, and social change among the Choctaws, Pawnees, and Navajos.* Lincoln: University of Nebraska Press.

White, Tim. (1992). *Prehistoric cannibalism at Mancos.* Princeton, NJ: Princeton University Press.

Whiteford, Linda M. & Marilyn L. Poland. (Eds.). (1989). *New approaches to human reproduction: social and ethical dimensions.* Boulder CO: Westview.

Whiteford, Scott & Anne Ferguson. (Eds.). (1991). *Harvest of want: hunger and food security in Central America and Mexico.* Boulder, CO: Westview.

Whitehead, Harriet. (1981). The bow and the burden strap: a new look at institutionalized homosexuality in native North America. In Sherry Ortner & Harriet Whitehead (Eds.), *Sexual meanings* (pp. 80–115). Cambridge: Cambridge University Press.

———(1986). The varieties of fertility cultism in New Guinea. *American Ethnologist* 13: 80–99, 271–289.

———(1987). *Renunciation and reformulation: a study of conversion in an American sect.* Ithaca, NY: Cornell University Press.

Whitehead, Neil. (1988). *Lords of the tiger spirit: a history of the Caribs in colonial Venezuela and Guyana, 1498–1820.* Dordrecht: Forbis Publications.

———(1992). Tribes make states and states make tribes: warfare and the creation of colonial tribes and states in northeastern South America. In R. Brian Ferguson & Neil Whitehead (Eds.), *War in the tribal zone* (pp. 127–150). Santa Fe, NM: School of American Research Press.

———(1994). The ancient Amerindian polities of the Lower Orinoco, Amazon, and Guyana coast: a preliminary analysis of their passage from antiquity to extinction. In Anna Roosevelt (Ed.), *Amazonian Indians* (pp. 33–54). Tucson: University of Arizona Press.

Whitehead, Tony L. & Mary E. Conaway. (Eds.). (1986). *Self, sex, and gender in cross-cultural fieldwork.* Urbana: University of Illinois Press.

Whiting, Beatrice. (Ed.). (1963). *Six cultures: studies of child rearing.* New York: Wiley.

Whiting, Beatrice & C. P. Edwards. (1988). *Children of different worlds: the formation of social behavior.* Cambridge, MA: Harvard University Press.

Whiting, Beatrice & John Whiting. (1975). *Children of six cultures.* Cambridge, MA: Harvard University Press.

Whiting, John. (1941). *Becoming a Kwoma: teaching and learning in a New Guinea tribe.* New Haven, CT: Yale University Press.

Whiting, John & Irvin L. Child. (1953). *Child training and personality: a cross-cultural study.* New Haven, CT: Yale University Press.

Whorf, Benjamin. (1956). *Language, thought, and reality: selected writings of Benjamin Lee Whorf.* Cambridge, MA: MIT Press.

Whyte, Martin. (1978). *The status of women in preindustrial societies.* Princeton, NJ: Princeton University Press.

Whyte, Robert O. (1968). *Grasslands of the monsoon.* New York: Praeger.

Wiberg, Hakan. (1981). JPR 1964–1980: what have we learnt about peace? *Journal of Peace Research* 18(2): 111–148.

Wierzbicka, Anna. (1986). Human emotions: universal or culture-specific? *American Anthropologist* 88: 584–594.

Wiggershaus, Rolf. (1994). *The Frankfurt School: its history, theories, and political sig-*

nificance [Frankfurter Schule, Munich, 1986]. Cambridge: Polity.

Wikan, Unni. (1977). Man becomes woman: transsexualism in Oman as key to gender roles. *Man* 12: 304–319.

———(1993). *Managing turbulent hearts: a Balinese formula for living.* Chicago, IL: University of Chicago Press.

Wilbert, Johannes. (1987). *Tobacco and shamanism in South America.* New Haven, CT: Yale University Press.

Wilkie, David S. (1987). Cultural and ecological survival in the Ituri forest. *Cultural Survival Quarterly* 11: 72–74.

———(1994). Remote sensing imagery for resource inventory in central Africa: the importance of detailed field data. *Human Ecology* 22(3): 379–404.

Wilkinson, Gary S. (1984). Reciprocal food sharing in the vampire bat. *Nature* 308: 181–184.

Willey, Gordon R. (1953a). Comments on cultural and social anthropology. In Sol Tax, Loren Eiseley, Irving Rouse & Carl Voegelin (Eds.), *An appraisal of anthropology today* (pp. 229–230). Chicago, IL: University of Chicago Press.

———(1953b). *Prehistoric settlement patterns in the Viru Valley, Peru.* Washington, DC: Bureau of American Ethnology, Bulletin 155.

———(1977). A consideration of archaeology. *Daedalus* 106(3): 81–96.

Willey, Gordon R. & Philip Phillips. (1958). *Method and theory in American archaeology.* Chicago, IL: University of Chicago Press.

Willey, Gordon R. & Jeremy A. Sabloff. (1993). *A history of American archaeology* [3rd edn.]. New York: Freeman.

Williams, Brackette. (1989). A class act: anthropology and the race to nation across ethnic terrain. *Annual Review of Anthropology* 18: 401–444.

Williams, Drid. (1991). *Ten lectures on theories of the dance.* Metuchen, NJ: Scarecrow Press.

Williams, Francis Edgar. (1976). *"The Vailala madness," and other essays.* London: Hurst.

Williams, George C. (1966). *Adaptation and natural selection: a critique of some current evolutionary thought.* Princeton, NJ: Princeton University Press.

Williams, John E. & Deborah Best.

(1982). *Measuring sex stereotypes: a thirty-nation study.* Beverly Hills, CA: Sage.

Williams, Patrick & Laura Chrisman. (Eds.). (1994). *Colonial discourse and post-colonial theory: a reader.* New York: Columbia University Press.

Williams, Raymond. (1958). *Culture and society, 1780–1950.* New York: Columbia University Press.

———(1961). *The long revolution.* New York: Columbia University Press.

———(1975). *Television: technology and cultural form.* New York: Schocken.

———(1976). *Keywords: a vocabulary of culture and society.* Oxford: Oxford University Press.

———(1977). *Marxism and literature.* Oxford: Oxford University Press.

Williams, Thomas R. (1972). The socialization process: a theoretical perspective. In Frank Poirier (Ed.), *Primate socialization* (pp. 207–260). New York: Random.

Williams, Walter. (1986). *The spirit and the flesh: sexual diversity in American Indian culture.* Boston, MA: Beacon.

Willis, Paul. (1977). *Learning to labour: how working class kids get working class jobs.* Farnborough: Saxon House.

Willis, Roy. (Ed.). (1990). *Signifying animals: human meaning in the natural world.* London: Unwin Hyman.

Willner, Ann Ruth. (1984). *The spellbinders: charismatic political leadership.* New Haven, CT: Yale University Press.

Wilmsen, Edwin. (1989a). *Land filled with flies: a political economy of the Kalahari.* Chicago, IL: University of Chicago Press.

———(Ed.). (1989b). *We are here: the politics of aboriginal land tenure.* Berkeley: University of California Press.

Wilson, Christine. (1973). Food habits: a selected annotated bibliography. *Journal of Nutrition Education* 5, Supplement 1.

———(1980). Food taboos of childbirth: the Malay experience. In J. R. Robson (Ed.), *Food, ecology, and culture* (pp. 67–74). New York: Gordon & Breach.

Wilson, David J. (1988). *Prehispanic settlement patterns in the lower Santa Valley, Peru.* Washington, DC: Smithsonian.

Wilson, Edward O. (1975). *Sociobiology: the new synthesis.* Cambridge MA: Harvard University Press.

————(1978). *On human nature*. Cambridge, MA: Harvard University Press.

Wilson, James, James Acheson, Mark Metcalfe & Paul Kleban. (1994). Chaos, complexity and community management of fisheries. *Marine Policy*, 18(4): 291–305.

Wilson, Margo, Martin Daly & Joanna Scheib. (1997). Femicide: an evolutionary psychological perspective. In Patricia A. Gowaty (Ed.), *Feminism and evolutionary biology* (pp. 431–465). New York: Chapman Hall.

Wilson, Monica. (1951). *Good company: a study of Nyakyusa age-villages*. London: Oxford University Press.

Wilson, William J. (1987). *The truly disadvantaged: the inner city, the underclass, and public policy*. Chicago, IL: University of Chicago Press.

Winkelman, Michael. (1986). Trance states: a theoretical model and cross-cultural analysis. *Ethos* 14: 174–203.

Winkler, John J. (1990). *The constraints of desire: the anthropology of sex and gender in ancient Greece*. New York: Routledge.

Winks, Robin W. (Ed.). (1972). *Slavery: a comparative perspective*. New York: New York University Press.

Wirth, Louis. (1938). Urbanism as a way of life. *American Journal of Sociology* 44: 1–24.

Wisner, Ben. (1993). Disaster vulnerability: scale, power, and daily life. *GeoJournal* 30(2): 127–140.

Wissler, Clark. (Ed.). (1909). *The Indians of Greater New York and the Lower Hudson*. New York: American Museum of Natural History.

————(1917). *The American Indian: an introduction to the anthropology of the New World*. New York: McMurtrie.

————(1923). *Man and culture*. New York: Crowell.

————(1926). *The relation of nature to man in aboriginal America*. London: Oxford University Press.

————(1929). *Introduction to social anthropology*. New York: Holt.

Wittfogel, Karl. (1957). *Oriental despotism: a comparative study of total power*. New Haven, CT: Yale University Press.

Wolcott, Harry F. (1994). *Transforming qualitative data: description, analysis, and interpretation*. Thousand Oaks, CA: Sage.

Wolf, Arthur. (1993). Westermarck redivivus. *Annual Review of Anthropology* 22: 157–175.

Wolf, Arthur & C. S. Huang. (1980). *Marriage and adoption in China, 1845–1945*. Stanford, CA: Stanford University Press.

Wolf, Deborah. (1979). *The lesbian community*. Berkeley: University of California Press.

Wolf, Eric. (1966). *Peasants*. Englewood Cliffs, NJ: Prentice-Hall.

————(1969). *Peasant wars of the twentieth century*. New York: Harper & Row.

————(1982). *Europe and the people without history*. Berkeley: University of California Press.

————(1994). Perilous ideas: race, culture, people. *Current Anthropology* 35(1): 1–7, 10–12.

Woodburn, James. (1982). Egalitarian societies. *Man* 17: 431–451.

Worsley, Peter. (1968). *The trumpet shall sound: a study of "cargo" cults in Melanesia* [2nd rev. edn.]. New York: Schocken.

Worth, Sol. (Ed.). (1981). *Studying visual communication*. Philadelphia: University of Pennsylvania Press.

Wouden, F. A. E. van. (1968). *Types of social structure in eastern Indonesia* [Sociale structuurtypen in de groote Oost, Leiden, 1935]. The Hague: Martinus Nijhoff.

Wright, Erik O. (1985). *Classes*. London: Verso.

Wright, Henry. (1978). Toward an explanation of the origin of the state. In Ronald Cohen & Elman Service (Eds.), *Origins of the state* (pp. 49–68). Philadelphia: ISHI.

————(1984). Prestate political formations. In Timothy Earle (Ed.), *On the evolution of complex societies* (pp. 41–77). Malibu, CA: Undena.

Wright, Robin. (1988). Anthropological presuppositions of indigenous advocacy. *Annual Review of Anthropology* 17: 365–390.

Wright, Susan. (Ed.). (1994). *The anthropology of organizations*. London: Routledge.

Wuthnow, Robert. (Ed.). (1984). *Cultural analysis: the work of Peter L. Berger, Mary Douglas, Michel Foucault, and Jurgen Habermas*. London: Routledge.

————(Ed.). (1991). *Between states and markets: the voluntary sector in comparative perspective*. Princeton, NJ: Princeton University Press.

Wylie, Alison. (1985). The reaction against analogy. *Advances in Archaeological Method and Theory* 8: 63–111.

————(1991). Gender theory and the archaeological record. In Joan Gero & Margaret Conkey (Eds.), *Engendering archaeology* (pp. 31–56). Oxford: Blackwell.

Xiaomingxiong. (1984). *History of homosexuality in China*. Hong Kong: Pink Triangle.

Yalman, Nur. (1967). *Under the Bo tree*. Berkeley: University of California Press.

Yanagisako, Sylvia. (1979). Family and household: the analysis of domestic groups. *Annual Review of Anthropology* 8: 161–205.

Yanagisako, Sylvia & Jane F. Collier. (Eds.). (1987). *Gender and kinship: essays toward an unified analysis*. Stanford, CA: Stanford University Press.

Yeager, Patricia. (Ed.). (1996). *The geography of identity*. Ann Arbor: University of Michigan Press.

Yesner, David R. (1980). Maritime hunter–gatherers: ecology and prehistory. *Current Anthropology* 21(6), 727–750.

Yngvesson, Barbara. (1993). *Virtuous citizens, disruptive subjects: order and complaint in a New England court*. New York: Routledge.

Young, Allan. (1983). The relevance of traditional medical cultures to modern primary health care. *Social Science and Medicine* 17(16): 1205–1211.

Young, Kate, Carol Wolkowitz & Roslyn McCullah. (Eds.). (1981). *Of marriage and the market: women's subordination internationally and its lessons*. London: CSE.

Young, Michael Dunlop & P. Willmott. (1957). *Family and kinship in East London*. London: Routledge.

Young, Michael W. (1971). *Fighting with food: leadership, values and social control in a Massim society*. Cambridge: Cambridge University Press.

————(1979). *The ethnography of Malinowski: the Trobriand Islands, 1951–18*. London: Routledge.

Young, Robert. (1990). *White mythologies: writing history and the West*. London: Routledge.

————(1995). *Colonial desire: hybridity in theory, culture, and race*. London: Routledge.

————(1996). *Post-colonial theory*. Oxford: Blackwell.

Zablocki, Benjamin. (1980). *Alienation and charisma: a study of contemporary American communes*. New York: Free Press.

Zahan, Dominique. (1979). *The religion, spirituality and thought of traditional Africa* [Religion, spiritualité, et pensée africaines, Paris, 1970]. Chicago, IL: University of Chicago Press.

Zaharlick, Amy & Jeffery L. MacDonald. (Eds.). (1994). *Selected papers on refugee issues*, vol. 3. Arlington, VA: American Anthropological Association.

Zaner, Richard M. (1977). *Interdisciplinary phenomenology*. The Hague: Martinus Nijhoff.

Zavella, Patricia. (1987). *Women's work and Chicano families: cannery workers of the Santa Clara Valley*. Ithaca, NY: Cornell University Press.

Zelizer, Viviana. (1994). *The social meaning of money*. New York: Basic Books.

Zenner, Walter P. (1988). *Persistence and flexibility: anthropological perspectives on the American Jewish experience*. Albany: State University of New York Press.

————(1991). *Minorities in the middle: a cross-cultural analysis*. Albany: State University of New York Press.

Zillmann, Dolf. (1983). Transfer of excitation in emotional behavior. In John T. Cacioppo & R. E. Petty (Eds.), *Social psychophysiology* (pp. 215–240). New York: Guilford.

Zuidema, Tom. (1989). The moieties of Cuzco. In David Maybury-Lewis & Uri Almagor (Eds.), *The attraction of opposites* (pp. 255–276). Ann Arbor: University of Michigan Press.

Zukin, Sharon. (1991). *Landscapes of power: from Detroit to Disney World*. Berkeley: University of California Press.